CANADIAN EDITION

DEBORAH C. **BEIDEL**
University of Central Florida

CYNTHIA M. **BULIK**
University of North Carolina at Chapel Hill

MELINDA A. **STANLEY**
Baylor College of Medicine

STEVEN **TAYLOR**
University of British Columbia

ABNORMAL**PSYCHOLOGY**

To our parents (DCB, CMB, MAS):
Anthony and Jean Casamassa
Frank and Marie Bulik
Pat and Bob Stanley
Thank you for teaching us the value of education and for providing the love and encouragement that allowed us to achieve our dreams.

To my children (ST):
Alex and Anna Taylor

Editorial Director: Claudine O'Donnell
Acquisitions Editor: Darcey Pepper
Marketing Manager: Lisa Gillis
Program Manager: Madhu Ranadive
Project Manager: Kimberley Blakey
Developmental Editor: Daniella Balabuk
Media developer: Tiffany Palmer
Production Services: iEnergizer Aptara®, Ltd.
Permissions Project Manager: Kathryn O'Handley
Photo Permissions Research: Integra Software Services Pvt. Ltd.
Text Permissions Research: Integra Software Services Pvt. Ltd.
Interior Designer: Anthony Leung
Cover Designer: Anthony Leung
Cover Image: Vizerskaya/E+/Getty Images
Vice-President, Cross Media and Publishing Services: Gary Bennett

Pearson Canada Inc., 26 Prince Andrew Place, Don Mills, Ontario M3C 2T8.

Library and Archives Canada Cataloguing in Publication

Beidel, Deborah C., author
Abnormal psychology / Deborah C. Beidel, Cynthia M. Bulik, Melinda A. Stanley.—First edition.
Includes bibliographical references and index.
ISBN 978-0-13-273534-6 (paperback)
1. Psychology, Pathological—Textbooks. I. Stanley, M. A. (Melinda Anne), author II. Bulik, Cynthia M., author III. Title.
RC454.B429 2016 616.89 C2016-905458-6

1 16

ISBN-10: 0-132-73534-2
ISBN-13: 978-0-132-73534-6

brief contents

contents

preface

When the first U.S. edition was introduced, we wondered whether instructors and students would perceive the need for a new textbook. We were pleased to find so many people who resonated with the scientist–practitioner approach. Abnormal psychology remains one of the most popular courses among undergraduate students as local and world events drive us to try to understand human behaviour and the forces that shape and act on it. For example, why would a celebrity, who seemingly has everything—wealth, family, fame—shoplift a $50 item of jewellery? The answer to such a question does not come easily, as we see with simplistic answers such as "the measles vaccine causes autism," a theory first accepted and now completely discredited.

The first Canadian edition of this textbook is another opportunity for students to see science in action. Prompted, in part, by the revision of the *Diagnostic and Statistical Manual of Mental Disorders*, Fifth Edition (DSM-5), students will be exposed to the ever-changing nature of our understanding of human behaviour, as research sheds new light on disorders, forcing scientists and clinicians to grapple with disparate data sets and to work together to produce what is hopefully a scientific and clinically meaningful system for understanding and communicating about abnormal behaviour. Because the DSM-5 has been recently introduced, in some areas of abnormal behaviour the science has not yet caught up to the new criteria, and in some cases, the new diagnoses. This is particularly relevant in those chapters where revisions to the diagnostic criteria were extensive. The new criteria are there, but epidemiological data for the new disorders are not available—researchers simply have not had time to conduct new studies using the new criteria. In those instances, we rely on the published data based on the DSM-IV categories, while giving appropriate caveats about the need for more research.

Despite the changing criteria, understanding human behaviour requires integration of brain and behaviour, data from scientists, *and* insights from clinicians and patients. A scientist–practitioner approach integrates biological data with research from social and behavioural sciences to foster the perspective that abnormal behaviour is complex and subject to many different forces. Furthermore, these variables often interact in a reciprocal fashion. Psychotherapy was built in part on the assumption that behaviour could be changed by changing the environment, but science has now shown us that environmental factors can also change the brain. Scientific advances in molecular genetics have expanded our understanding of how genes influence behaviour. As this new edition illustrates, we remain firm in our conviction that the integration of leading-edge biological and behavioural research, known as the *translational approach*, or *from bench to bedside*, is needed to advance the study of abnormal psychology. As we did in previous editions, we reach beyond the old clichés of nature or nurture, clinician or scientist, genes or environment, and challenge the next generation of psychologists and students to embrace the complexity inherent in replacing these historical "ors" with contemporary "ands."

The Scientist–Practitioner Model

Understanding abnormal psychology rests on knowledge generated through scientific studies and clinical practice. Many psychologists are trained in the scientist–practitioner model and adhere to it to some degree in their professional work. We live and breathe this model. In addition to our roles as teachers at the undergraduate, graduate, and postdoctoral levels, we are all active clinical researchers and clinical practitioners. However, the scientist–practitioner model means more than just having multiple roles; it is a philosophy that guides all of the psychologist's activities. Those who are familiar with the model know this quote well: "Scientist-practitioners embody a research orientation in their practice and a practice relevance in their research" (Belar & Perry, 1992). This philosophy reflects our guiding principles, and we wrote this text to emphasize this rich blend of science and practice. We have endeavoured to "bring to life" the nature of psychological disorders by providing vivid clinical descriptions. In addition to the clinical material that opens each chapter and the short clinical descriptions that are used liberally throughout each chapter, a fully integrated case study drawn from one of our practices is presented at the end of each chapter, again illustrating the interplay of biological, psychosocial, and emotional factors. Of course, details have been changed and some cases may represent composites in order to protect the privacy of those who have shared their life stories with us throughout our careers.

The goal of our text is to avoid a dense review of the scientific literature while maintaining a strong scientific focus. Similarly, we wanted to avoid "pop" psychology, an overly popularized approach that we believe presents easy answers that do not truly reflect the essence of psychological disorders. Having used the text with our own undergraduate classes, we find that students respond positively to material and features that make these conditions more understandable and vivid. Our goal is to "put a face" on these sometimes perplexing and unfamiliar conditions by using rich clinical material such as vignettes, case histories, personal accounts, and the feature "Real People, Real Disorders." We hope that these illustrations will entice students to learn more about abnormal psychology while acquiring the important concepts. Thus, although the book represents leading-edge science, our ultimate goal is to portray the human face of these conditions.

A Developmental Trajectory

It has become increasingly clear that many types of abnormal behaviours either begin in childhood or have childhood precursors. Similarly, without treatment, most disorders do not merely disappear with advancing age and, in fact, new disorders may emerge. Quite simply, as we grow, mature, and age, our physical and cognitive capacities affect how symptoms are expressed. Without this developmental perspective, it is easy to overlook important clues that indicate the presence of a specific disorder at a particular phase of life. We embraced this concept before its introduction in the DSM-5. Failure to understand the various manifestations of a disorder means that theories of etiology may be incorrect or incomplete, and that interventions may be inappropriately applied. Now that DSM-5 has shifted to a developmental focus, students and instructors will find that certain disorders are not in the same chapters in which they were in previous editions. In each chapter where we discuss psychological disorders, we also include a section called "Developmental Considerations," which highlights what is known about the developmental trajectory of each condition. In the margins of those pages, you will find the developmental trajectory icons, which indicate that important developmental features are discussed in that paragraph.

Ethics and Responsibility

In this edition, we continue our newest feature titled "Ethics and Responsibility." The discussion of ethics and responsibility varies with respect to the individual chapter. However, in each case, we have attempted to select a topic that is timely and illustrates how psychologists consider the impact of their behaviour on those with whom they work and on society in general. We hope that this feature will generate class discussion and impress on students the impact of one's behaviour upon others.

Clinical Features

Consistent with our belief that the clinical richness of this text will bring the subject matter to life, each chapter begins with a clinical description that introduces and illustrates the topic of the chapter. These descriptions are not necessarily extensive case studies, but rather provide the reader with a global "feel" for each disorder. Additionally, small case vignettes are used liberally throughout the text to illustrate specific clinical elements. Another important clinical element is the "Side by Side Case Studies," in which we illustrate the differences between typical human emotions (such as elation) and abnormal behaviour (such as mania). We included these descriptions in each chapter devoted to an area of abnormal behaviour to emphasize that the difference between normal emotions and what we call *psychological disorders* is not simply the presence of emotion or specific behaviour, but whether the behaviour creates distress or impairs daily functioning.

Each chapter discussion concludes with a case study "Real Science, Real Life," which provides a clinical presentation, assessment, and treatment of a patient with a particular disorder, again drawn from our own clinical files. Each concluding case study illustrates much of the material covered in the chapter and uses the scientist–practitioner approach to understanding, assessing, and treating the disorder. Furthermore, this concluding case study demonstrates how the clinician considers biological, psychological, environmental, and cultural factors to understand the patient's clinical presentation. Finally, we describe the treatment program and outcome, highlighting how all of the factors are addressed in treatment. Through this process, the case study allows the student to view "firsthand" the scientist–practitioner approach to abnormal behaviour, dispelling myths often propagated through the media about how psychologists think, work, and act.

Canadian Perspectives

There were many reasons for writing a text on abnormal psychology from a Canadian perspective. There are many excellent American texts on abnormal psychology, but they discuss clinical and cultural issues, and mental health systems and laws, that do not necessarily apply to Canada. Our aim in writing this text was to present the current state of knowledge based on the best research from throughout the world, while also highlighting important findings and issues that are pertinent to Canada. This includes Canada's health care system as it applies to mental health, historical perspectives on mental health from a Canadian perspective, Canadian laws as they apply to mental health, and cultural issues relevant to Canada. We also present Canadian statistics on the prevalence of mental disorders, and, when relevant, we discuss how they compare to statistics from other countries. This is important because the prevalence of mental disorders varies, to some extent, across countries. For example, addiction to crack cocaine is more common in the United States than in Canada, while addiction disorders in Canada more commonly involve other substances. We also highlight important research from Canada. Many key findings have come from Canadian universities. Chances are that some of this work is being conducted on your own campus. Canadian clinical examples are also presented throughout the text. These are significant because they highlight the important fact that mental health issues are, in some way, relevant to all of us. By presenting Canadian case examples, we hope to show that mental illness can afflict any of us.

Special Features

We draw the reader's attention to four specific features that appear in each chapter. The first, "Examining the Evidence," presents a current controversy related to the disorder under study in the chapter. However, we do not simply present the material; rather, to be consistent with the scientist–practitioner focus, we present both sides of the controversy and lead students through the data, allowing them to draw their own conclusions. Thus, "Examining the Evidence" features do not just present material, but also foster critical thinking skills about issues in abnormal psychology. By considering both sides of the issues, students will become savvy consumers of scientific literature.

The second feature is "Research Hot Topic," which presents topical, leading-edge research at the time of publication. Consistent with the focus of this text, these features illustrate how science informs our understanding of human behaviour in a manner that is engaging to students (e.g., "Virtual Reality Therapy for the Treatment of Anxiety Disorders"). As teachers and researchers who open our clinical research centres to undergraduate students, we know that many students think research is "dull." What they discover by participating in our research programs, and what students reading this text will discover, is that research is exciting.

The third feature, "Real People, Real Disorders," presents a popular figure who has suffered from the disorder discussed in the chapter. As we indicated in Chapter 1, although many people, including undergraduate students, suffer from these disorders, they often feel that they are alone or "weird." We wanted to break down the stereotypes that many undergraduate students have about people with psychological disorders. Using well-known figures to humanize these conditions allows students to connect with the material on an emotional, as well as an intellectual, level.

The fourth feature, "Canadian Focus," appearing in each chapter, highlights important Canadian research and other issues pertinent to understanding mental health from a Canadian perspective. Many Canadian investigators are internationally recognized leaders in various fields of mental health research. The "Canadian Focus" boxes provide a showcase for some of this important work.

Intermediate and End-of-Chapter Reviews

Finally, we would like to draw the reader's attention to the "Concept Checks" that are found throughout the chapter, as well as the "Test Yourself" sections at the end of each chapter. The "Concept Checks" provide quick reviews at the end of chapter sections, allowing students to be sure that they have mastered the material before proceeding to the next section. Instructors can use the "Concept Checks" and "Critical Thinking Questions" to challenge students to think "outside the box" and critically examine the material presented within that section. "Test Yourself" provides another opportunity for students to review and master the material using the format that they will most likely find on their class examinations.

Supplemental Teaching Materials

Revel™

Designed for the way today's students read, think, and learn, REVEL is a groundbreaking immersive learning experience. It is based on a simple premise: When students are engaged deeply, they learn more and get better results.

Built in collaboration with educators and students, REVEL brings course content to life with rich media and assessments—integrated directly within the authors' narrative—that provide opportunities for students to read, learn, and practise in one environment.

Learn more about REVEL: www.pearsonhighered.com/revel.

These instructor supplements are available for download from a password-protected section of Pearson Canada's online catalogue (www.pearsoncanada.ca/highered). Navigate to your book's catalogue page to view a list of available supplements. Speak to your local Pearson sales representative for details and access.

Instructor's Manual

A comprehensive tool for class preparation and management, each chapter includes a chapter-at-a-glance overview; key terms; teaching objectives; a detailed chapter outline including lecture starters, demonstrations and activities, and handouts; a list of references, films and videos, and web resources; and a sample syllabus.

Test Bank

The Test Bank has been rigorously developed, reviewed, and checked for accuracy to ensure the quality of both the questions and the answers. It includes fully referenced multiple-choice and true/false questions, as well as concise essay questions. Each question is accompanied by a page reference, difficulty level, skill type (factual, conceptual, or applied), topic, and a correct answer.

Computerized Test Bank

Pearson's computerized test banks allow instructors to filter and select questions to create quizzes, tests or homework. Instructors can revise questions or add their own, and may be able to choose print or online options. These questions are also available in Microsoft Word format.

Learning Solutions Managers

Pearson's Learning Solutions Managers work with faculty and campus course designers to ensure that Pearson technology products, assessment tools, and online course materials are tailored to meet your specific needs. This highly qualified team is dedicated to helping schools take full advantage of a wide range of educational resources, by assisting in the integration of a variety of instructional materials and media formats. Your local Pearson Canada sales representative can provide you with more details on this service program.

Lecture PowerPoint Slides

The PowerPoint slides provide an active format for presenting concepts from each chapter and feature relevant figures and tables from the text.

Acknowledgments

As the first three authors wrote in the first U.S. edition, this book began with the vision of our mentor and friend Samuel M. Turner, Ph.D. He was the one who believed that the book could be written, convinced us to write it with him, and contributed substantially to the initial book prospectus. The success of the first edition surprised us, but we often felt that Sam would have just looked at us and said, "I told you so." We hope this edition continues to honour him and his lasting influence on us.

The first three authors met Sam and each other more than 20 years ago when three of us were in various stages of graduate training under his tutelage at Western Psychiatric Institute and Clinic (WPIC), University of Pittsburgh School of Medicine. We want to thank David Kupfer, M.D., who was Director of Research at WPIC at that time, for creating the cross-disciplinary and fertile research environment that allowed us to learn and grow. We are also grateful to the other scientist–practitioners who mentored us at various stages of our undergraduate and graduate careers: Alan Bellack, Michel Hersen, Stephen Hinshaw, Alan Kazdin, and Sheldon Korchin.

Second, a big thank you goes to our students, colleagues, and friends who listened endlessly, smiled supportively, and waited patiently as we said, once again, "Next month will be easier."

Third, we thank our patients and their families, whose life journeys or bumps along life's road we have shared. Good psychologists never stop learning. Each new clinical experience adds to our knowledge and understanding of the illnesses we seek to treat. We thank our patients and families for sharing their struggles and their successes with us, and for the unique opportunity to learn from their experience. It is an honour and a privilege to have worked with each of you.

Fourth, our thanks go to our partners, Ed Beidel, Patrick Sullivan, and Bill Ehrenstrom, children (Brendan, Emily, Natalie, Brendan, Jacob, Anna, and Alex), and families who celebrate the publication of each edition with us and smile understandingly when we tell them we have to start on the next edition.

As authors, each of us feels enormous gratitude to our coauthors for their tireless work, unending support and friendship, and dedication to this project. Abnormal psychology is a broad topic, requiring ever-increasing specialization. Having colleagues who share an orientation but possess distinct areas of expertise represents a rare and joyful collaborative experience.

Finally, we hope the students and instructors who used the first and second editions and who will use this new text experience the joy and wonder that comes with learning about the challenging and intriguing topic of abnormal psychology. We are passionate about our science and compassionate with our patients. We are also dedicated educators. As such, we encourage you to contact us with comments, questions, or suggestions on how to improve this book. No textbook is perfect, but with your help, we will continue to strive for that goal.

Text and Content Reviewers

We would like to thank the following colleagues who reviewed this text at various stages and gave us a great many helpful suggestions:

Christopher Bowie, Queen's University; Peter Hoaken, Western University; Melanie Macnab, Seneca College; Leonard George, Capilano University; Kristi D. Wright, University of Regina; R. Nicholas Carleton, University of Regina; Amanda Maranzan, Lakehead University; Linda Williams, Algoma University; David Vollick, Western University; Jo Anne Nugent, Humber College; Katrina Craig, Fanshawe College; Simon Sherry, Dalhousie University; Danielle DeSorcy, University of Saskatchewan; Dean Tripp, Queen's University.

about the authors

DEBORAH C. BEIDEL

received her B.A. from the Pennsylvania State University and her M.S. and Ph.D. from the University of Pittsburgh, completing her pre-doctoral internship and postdoctoral fellowship at Western Psychiatric Institute and Clinic. Before joining the faculty at the University of Central Florida, where she is Pegasus Professor of Psychology and Medical Education and the Director of the Center for Trauma, Anxiety, Resilience and Prevention (C-TARP), she was on the faculty at the University of Pittsburgh, Medical University of South Carolina, University of Maryland—College Park, and Penn State College of Medicine-Hershey Medical Center. Currently, she holds American Board of Professional Psychology (ABPP) Diplomates in Clinical Psychology and Behavioral Psychology and is a Fellow of the American Psychological Association, the American Psychopathological Association, and the Association for Psychological Science. She is Chair-elect of the Council for University Directors in Clinical Psychology (CUDCP), a past Chair of the American Psychological Association's Committee on Accreditation, the 1990 recipient of the Association for Advancement of Behavior Therapy's New Researcher Award, and the 2007 recipient of the Samuel M. Turner Clinical Researcher Award from the American Psychological Association. While at the University of Pittsburgh, Dr. Beidel was twice awarded the "Apple for the Teacher Citation" by her students for outstanding classroom teaching. In 1995, she was the recipient of the Distinguished Educator Award from the Association of Medical School Psychologists. She is a former Editor-in-Chief of the *Journal of Anxiety Disorders*, author of over 230 scientific publications, including journal articles, book chapters, and books, including *Childhood Anxiety Disorders: A Guide to Research and Treatment* and *Shy Children, Phobic Adults: The Nature and Treatment of Social Anxiety Disorder*. Her academic, research, and clinical interests focus on child, adolescent, and adult anxiety disorders, including their etiology, psychopathology, and behavioural interventions. Her research is characterized by a developmental focus, and includes high-risk and longitudinal designs, psychophysiological assessment, treatment development, and treatment outcome. She is the recipient of numerous grants from the Department of Defense, the National Institute of Mental Health, and the Autism Speaks Foundation. At the University of Central Florida, she teaches abnormal psychology at both the undergraduate and graduate level.

CYNTHIA M. BULIK

is the Distinguished Professor of Eating Disorders in the Department of Psychiatry in the School of Medicine at the University of North Carolina at Chapel Hill, where she is also Professor of Nutrition in the Gillings School of Global Public Health, Director of the UNC Center of Excellence for Eating Disorders, and Co-Director of the UNC Center for Psychiatric Genomics. A clinical psychologist by training, Dr. Bulik has been conducting research and treating individuals with eating disorders since 1982. She received her B.A. from the University of Notre Dame and her M.A. and Ph.D. from the University of California, Berkeley. She completed internships and postdoctoral fellowships at the Western Psychiatric Institute and Clinic in Pittsburgh, Pennsylvania. She developed outpatient, partial hospitalization, and inpatient services for eating disorders both in New Zealand and the United States. Her research has included treatment, laboratory, epidemiological, twin, and molecular genetic studies of eating disorders and body weight regulation. She integrates technology into treatment for eating disorders and obesity in order to broaden the public health reach of interventions. She is the Director of the first NIMH-sponsored Post-Doctoral Training Program in Eating Disorders. She has active research collaborations in 21 countries around the world. Dr. Bulik has written over 450 scientific papers and chapters on eating disorders and is author of the books *Eating Disorders: Detection and Treatment* (Dunmore), *Runaway Eating: The 8 Point Plan to Conquer Adult Food and Weight Obsessions* (Rodale), and *Crave: Why You Binge Eat and How to Stop,The Woman in the Mirror: How to Stop Confusing What You Look Like with Who You Are*, and *Midlife Eating Disorders: Your Journey to Recovery* (Walker). She is a recipient of the Eating Disorders Coalition Research Award, the Hulka Innovators Award, the Academy for Eating Disorders Leadership Award for Research, the Price Family National Eating Disorders Association Research Award, the Carolina Women's Center Women's Advocacy Award, the Women's Leadership Council Faculty-to-Faculty Mentorship Award, and the Academy for Eating Disorders Meehan-Hartley Advocacy Award. She is a past President of the Academy for Eating Disorders, past Vice-President of the Eating Disorders Coalition, and past Associate Editor of the *International Journal of Eating Disorders*. Dr. Bulik holds the first endowed professorship in eating disorders in the United States. She balances her academic life by being happily married with three children and a competitive ice dancer.

MELINDA A. STANLEY

is Professor and Head of the Division of Psychology in the Menninger Department of Psychiatry and Behavioral Sciences at Baylor College of Medicine. She holds The McIngvale Family Chair in Obsessive Compulsive Disorder Research and a secondary appointment as Professor in the Department of Medicine. Dr. Stanley is a clinical psychologist and senior mental health services researcher within the Health Services Research and Development Center of Excellence, Michael E. DeBakey Veterans Affairs Medical Center, Houston, and an affiliate investigator for the South Central Mental Illness Research, Education, and Clinical Center (MIRECC). Before joining the faculty at Baylor, she was Professor of Psychiatry at the University of Texas Health Science Center at Houston, where she served as Director of the Psychology Internship program. Dr. Stanley completed an internship and postdoctoral fellowship at Western Psychiatric Institute and Clinic, University of Pittsburgh School of Medicine. She received a Ph.D. from Texas Tech University, an M.A. from Princeton University, and a B.A. from Gettysburg College, where she was a Phi Beta Kappa and summa cum laude graduate. Dr. Stanley's research interests involve the identification and treatment of anxiety and depressive disorders in older adults. Her current focus is on expanding the reach of services for older people into primary care and underserved communities where mental health needs of the older people often remain unrecognized and undertreated. In these settings, the content and delivery of care require modifications to meet cultural, cognitive, sensory, and logistic barriers. Some of Dr. Stanley's work in this domain includes the integration of religion and spirituality into therapy to enhance engagement in care for traditionally underserved groups. Dr. Stanley and her colleagues have been awarded continuous funding from the National Institute of Mental Health (NIMH) for 14 years to support her research in late-life anxiety. In 2008, Dr. Stanley received the Excellence in Research Award from the South Central MIRECC. In 2009, she received the MIRECC Excellence in Research Education Award. She has received numerous teaching awards and has served as mentor for five junior faculty career development awards. Dr. Stanley is a Fellow of the American Psychological Association, and she has served as a regular reviewer of NIMH grants. She is the author of over 150 scientific publications, including journal articles, book chapters, and books.

STEVEN TAYLOR

received his B.Sc. (Hons) and M.Sc. from the University of Melbourne and completed his Ph.D. in clinical psychology at the University of British Columbia. After completing his doctorate, he joined the faculty of the Department of Psychiatry at the University of British Columbia, where he is currently a professor. He is also Associate Editor of the *Journal of Obsessive-Compulsive and Related Disorders*. Previously, he was Associate Editor of *Behaviour Research and Therapy* and Editor-in-Chief of the *Journal of Cognitive Psychotherapy*. Dr. Taylor is a Fellow of several scholarly organizations, including the Canadian Psychological Association, the American Psychological Association, and the Association for Psychological Science. He is the author of over 300 scientific publications, including journal articles, book chapters, and books. His books include *Understanding and Treating Panic Disorder* (Wiley), *Treating Health Anxiety: A Cognitive-behavioral Approach* (Guilford), and *Clinician's Guide to PTSD* (Guilford). His research focuses on anxiety and related disorders, conceptualized from a biopsychosocial perspective. Specific research interests include cognitive-behavioral etiology and treatment of anxiety disorders and related conditions, as well as the genetics of these disorders. His research has been funded by various organizations including the Canadian Institutes for Health Research. He has been the recipient of numerous awards for his research, including investigator awards from the Canadian Psychological Association, the Association for Advancement of Behavior Therapy, the Anxiety Disorders Association of America, and the British Columbia Psychological Association. When not engaged in academic activities, Dr. Taylor enjoys spending time with his children, Alex and Anna, and also enjoys scuba diving and underwater photography, both in the tropics and off the coast of beautiful British Columbia.

chapter 1

abnormal psychology

digitalskillet/Getty Images

historical and modern perspectives

abnormal psychology

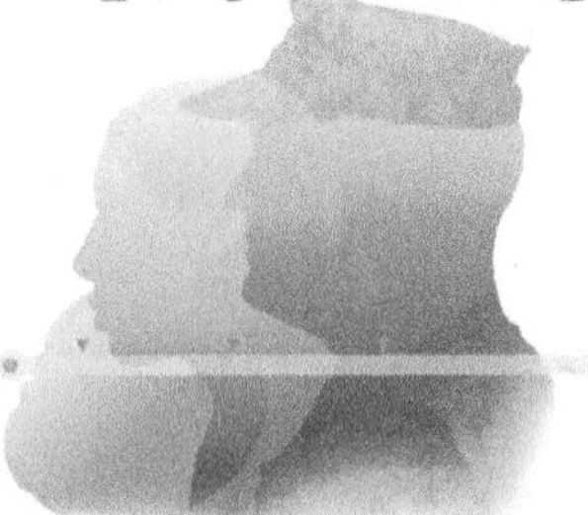

historical and modern perspectives

learning objectives

After reading this chapter, you should be able to:

1.1
Explain the difference between behaviours that are different, deviant, dangerous, and dysfunctional.

1.2
Identify at least two factors that need to be considered when determining whether a behaviour is abnormal.

1.3
Discuss spiritual/religious, biological, psychological, and sociocultural theories of the origins of abnormal behaviour in their historical context.

1.4
Discuss the scientist–practitioner model of abnormal psychology.

1.5
Describe the modern biological, psychological, sociocultural, and biopsychosocial perspectives on the origins of abnormal behaviour.

Tyler offers a shy smile as he talks about the social anxiety disorder that took over his life. "I feel like I lost three years of my life," he says. Three years is a long time when you're only 18, an age when most teens are hanging out with friends, developing social skills, and deciding on their future. Instead, Tyler was trapped inside his house, paralyzed by anxiety that was slowly taking over his life. It began in Grade 5 when he was transferred to a gifted program in another school. The pressure was overwhelming, and he immediately asked to be moved back. Once back, however, he became "the kid from gifted" who couldn't cut it. That made him the perfect target for bullies, says Tyler, who remembers being viciously bullied and beaten on a regular basis. "I needed help but I didn't know how to ask for it," he says. The bullying continued on and off into Grade 8. He finally stopped going to school. "I would pretend to go then I'd take the bus back home," says Tyler. In addition to school pressures, he was worried about whether his mother, a single mom, could pay the bills. He began spending his days playing video games while his mother was at work, dropping into school once or twice a month so they didn't call home. "A lot of the days I just crawled into bed and stayed there," he says.

(Source: Kids, Poverty and Mental Health: Anxiety a growing problem. Retrieved from http://www.cbc.ca/news/canada/hamilton/kids-poverty-and-mental-health-anxiety-a-growing-problem-1.2542001. © CBC Learning. Used with permission.)

Mariette couldn't wait to become a student at McMaster University in Hamilton, Ontario. But toward the end of her second year she began to feel overwhelmed. "I was trying to do too much simultaneously, to be the perfect student," says Mariette, age 22. She began skipping class, and she wasn't eating right; she became increasingly withdrawn, gripped by sadness or anxiety for reasons she couldn't understand. "I remember sitting in class, and a whole hour would go by without me realizing it." It wasn't until a friend reached out to her—one who said he himself had psychological problems—that Mariette understood she needed to talk to someone. She got help, first at the campus health clinic, and then at St. Joseph's Healthcare in Hamilton. Mariette was diagnosed with depression. At first, she was shy about sharing her diagnosis, but once Mariette saw others were supportive, she opened up. "If people don't talk about it, they won't recognize the signs," she says.

(Source: www.macleans.ca/education/uniandcollege/the-mental-health-crisis-on-campus. Accessed March 4, 2015.)

Psychologists and other mental health professionals often encounter psychological problems like Tyler's and Mariette's. Although often unrecognized, psychological disorders exist in substantial numbers of people across all ages, races, ethnic groups, and cultures, and in both sexes. Furthermore, they cause great suffering and impair academic, occupational, and social functioning.

Defining abnormality is challenging because behaviours must be considered in context. For example,

Donna and Matthew were very much in love. They had been married for 25 years and often remarked that they were not just husband and wife but also best friends. Then Matthew died suddenly, and Donna felt overwhelming sadness. She was unable to eat, cried uncontrollably at times, and started to isolate herself from others. Her usually vivacious personality disappeared.

When a loved one dies, feelings of grief and sadness are common, even expected. Donna's reaction to her husband's death would not be considered abnormal; rather, its *absence* at such a time might be considered abnormal. A theme throughout this book is that *abnormal behaviour must always be considered in context.*

Normal vs. Abnormal Behaviour

Sometimes it's fairly easy to identify behaviour as abnormal, such as when someone is still deeply troubled by events that happened 45 years ago or is feeling so hopeless that he or she cannot get out of bed. But sometimes identifying behaviour as abnormal is not clear-cut. Put simply, *abnormal* means "away from normal," but that is a circular definition. By this standard, normal becomes the statistical average and any deviation becomes "abnormal." For example, if the average weight for a woman living in Canada is about 70 kg, then women who weigh less than 45 kg or more than 110 kg deviate significantly from the average. Their weight would be considered abnormally low or high. For abnormal psychology, defining abnormal behaviour as merely being away from normal assumes that deviations on both sides of average are negative and in need of alteration or intervention. This assumption is often incorrect. Specifically, we must first ask whether simply being different is abnormal.

Is Being Different Abnormal?

Many people deviate from the average in some way. Jerry Sokoloski is the tallest man in Canada, measuring 226 cm (7 feet 4 inches)—far above average height. However, his deviant stature does not affect him negatively. Indeed, he has a career in film and television. Basketball star Steve Nash has unusual athletic abilities, which have led him to become a top basketball player. Celine Dion has an abnormal vocal range—she is one of a few singers whose voice spans possibly as many as five octaves. Because of her different ability, she has sold millions of songs. Professor Stephen Hawking, one of the world's most brilliant scientists, has an intellectual capacity that exceeds that of virtually everyone else, yet he writes best-selling and popular works about theoretical physics and the universe and appears on popular television shows like *The Big Bang Theory*. He does this despite suffering from amyotrophic lateral sclerosis (ALS, also known as Lou Gehrig's disease), a debilitating neurological disease. Each of these individuals has abilities that distinguish him or her from the general public; that is, they are away from normal. However, their "abnormalities" (unusual abilities) are not negative; rather, they result in positive contributions to society. Furthermore, their unusual abilities do not cause distress or appear to impair their daily functioning (as appears to be the case for Tyler and Mariette). In summary, being different is not the same as being psychologically abnormal.

Steve Nash, Celine Dion, and Stephen Hawking differ from most people (in athletic ability, vocal range, and intelligence, respectively). However, these differences are not abnormalities and have resulted in positive contributions to society.

(left): Cal Sport Media/Alamy Stock Photo; **(centre):** Oliver Berg/dpa picture alliance archive/Alamy Stock Photo; **(right):** Douglas Kirkland/Corbis

Is Behaving Deviantly (Differently) Abnormal?

When the definition of abnormal behaviour broadens from simply *being* different to *behaving* differently, we often use the term *deviance*. Deviant behaviours differ from prevailing societal standards.

On February 9, 1964, four young men from Liverpool, England, appeared on *The Ed Sullivan Show* and created quite a stir. Their hair was "long," their boots had "high (Cuban) heels," and their "music" was loud. Young people loved them, but their parents were appalled.

The Beatles looked, behaved, and sounded deviant in the context of the prevailing cultural norms. In 1964, they were considered outrageous. Today their music, dress, and behaviour appear rather tame. Was their behaviour abnormal? They looked different and acted differently, but their looks and behaviour did no harm to themselves or others. The same behaviour, outrageous and different in 1964 but tame by today's standards, illustrates an important point: *deviant behaviour* violates societal and cultural norms, but those norms are always changing.

Derek is 7 years old. From the time he was an infant, he has always been "on the go." He has a hard time paying attention and has boundless energy. His parents compensate for his high level of energy by involving him in lots of physical activities (soccer, Cub Scouts, karate). Derek had an understanding Grade 1 teacher. Because he could not sit still, the teacher accommodated him with "workstations" so that he could move around the classroom. But now Derek is in Grade 2, and the new teacher does not allow workstations. She believes that he must learn to sit like all the other children. He visits the principal's office often for "out-of-seat behaviour."

Understanding behaviour within a specific context is known as **goodness of fit** (Chess & Thomas, 1991). Simply put, a behaviour can be problematic or not problematic depending on the environment in which it occurs. Some people change an environment to accommodate a behaviour in the same way that buildings are modified to assure accessibility by everyone. Derek's situation illustrates the goodness-of-fit concept. At home and in Grade 1, his parents and teacher changed the environment to meet his high activity level. They did not see his activity as a problem, but simply as behaviour that needed to be accommodated. In contrast, his Grade 2 teacher expects Derek to fit into a nonadaptable environment. In Grade 1, Derek was considered "lively," but in Grade 2, his behaviour is considered abnormal. When we attempt to understand behaviour, it is critical to consider the context in which the behaviour occurs.

GROUP EXPECTATIONS The expectations of family, friends, neighbourhood, and culture are consistent and pervasive influences on why people act the way they do. Sometimes the standards of one group are at odds with those of another group. Adolescents, for example, often deliberately behave very differently than their parents do (they violate expected standards or norms) as a result of their need to *individuate* (separate) from their parents and be part of their peer group. In this instance, deviation from the norms of one group involves conformity to those of another. Like family norms, cultural traditions and practices also affect behaviour in many ways. For example, holiday celebrations usually include family and cultural traditions. As young people mature and leave their family of origin, new traditions from extended family, marriage, or friendships often blend into former customs and traditions, creating a new context for holiday celebrations.

Often, these different cultural traditions are unremarkable, but sometimes they can cause misunderstanding:

> Maleah is 12 years old. Her family recently moved to Vancouver from the Philippines. Her teacher insisted that Maleah's mother take her to see a psychologist because of "separation anxiety." The teacher was concerned because Maleah told the teacher that she had always slept in a bed with her grandmother. However, a psychological evaluation revealed that Maleah did not have any separation fears. Rather, children sleeping with parents or grandparents is what people normally do (what psychologists call normative) in Philippine culture.

Culture refers to shared behavioural patterns and lifestyles that differentiate one group of people from another. Culture affects an individual's behaviour but also is reciprocally changed by the behaviours of its members (Tseng, 2003). We often behave in ways that reflect the values of the culture in which we were raised. For example, in some cultures, children are expected to be "seen and not heard," whereas in other cultures, children are encouraged to freely express themselves. **Culture-bound syndrome** is a term that originally described abnormal behaviours that were specific to a particular location or group (Yap, 1967); however, we now know that some of these behavioural patterns extend across ethnic groups and geographic areas. How culture influences behaviour will be a recurring theme throughout this text. Maleah's behaviour is just one example of how a single behaviour can be viewed differently in two different cultures.

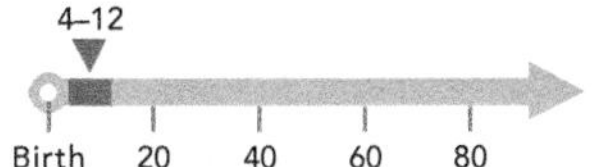

Childhood is a period of rapid development. As children mature, behaviours once considered typical can became deviant.

DEVELOPMENT AND MATURITY Another important context that must be taken into account when considering behavioural abnormality is age. As a child matures (physically, mentally, and emotionally), behaviours previously considered developmentally appropriate and therefore normal can become abnormal.

> Nick is 4 years old and insists on using a night light to keep the monsters away.

At age 4, children do not have the *cognitive*, or mental, capacity to understand fully that monsters are not real. However, at age 12, a child should understand the difference between imagination and reality. Therefore, if at age 12 Nick still needs a night light to keep the monsters away, his behaviour would be considered abnormal and perhaps in need of treatment. Similarly, very young children do not have the ability to control their bladder; bedwetting is common in toddlerhood. However, after the child achieves a certain level of physical and cognitive maturity, bedwetting becomes an abnormal behaviour and is given the diagnostic label of *enuresis* (see Chapter 12).

ECCENTRICITY What about the millionaire who wills his entire estate to his dog? This behaviour violates cultural norms, but it is often labelled eccentric rather than abnormal. Eccentric behaviour may violate societal norms, but it is not always negative or harmful to others. However, sometimes behaviours that initially appear eccentric cross the line into dangerousness (see "Real People, Real Disorders: Vincent Li").

REAL people REAL disorders

Vincent Li

Vincent Li started having problems in 2001. His wife reported that he was acting "weird" and was not sleeping or eating regularly. He cried a lot and said that he saw God. Although trained as a software engineer, Li held various menial jobs in Winnipeg, Edmonton, and elsewhere. In early July, 2008, he was fired from Walmart following an argument with co-workers.

On the night of July 30, 2008, Li was having auditory hallucinations in which God told him to move from Edmonton to Winnipeg. He travelled by Greyhound bus. At a stop in Erickson, Manitoba, he left the bus for a while, during which he obeyed auditory hallucinations that commanded him to dispose of some personal possessions. He boarded another bus and worried that God might be angry with him for not strictly following instructions. He sat at the back of the bus next to a perfect stranger, Tim McLean, a 22-year-old carnival worker. Thirty-seven passengers were aboard. As they travelled on an isolated stretch of the TransCanada Highway bound for Winnipeg, McLean turned and smiled at Li and asked him how he was doing. Then McLean resumed listening to music on his headphones. While McLean had his eyes closed, dozing, Li suddenly stood up, pulled out a large knife, and began stabbing McLean dozens of times. Li stated that he attacked because God's voice told him that McLean was an alien force of evil and was about to execute Li. The bus pulled over near Portage la Prairie, Manitoba, and passengers fled the bus in horror as Li continued stabbing and mutilating McLean's body. Li carved up McLean's body, ate part of the flesh, cut off McLean's head, and displayed it to passengers outside the bus. Passengers huddled by the roadside, some of them crying and vomiting at the sight of the carnage.

Li attempted to escape from the bus by breaking a window. Police shot him twice with a Taser and arrested him. Parts of McLean's body were retrieved from the bus, while his nose, tongue, and an ear were found in Li's pocket. McLean's eyes and a part of his heart were never recovered, presumably eaten by Li. According to eyewitness reports, Li appeared to be totally calm during the attack and oblivious to others. According to witness Garnet Caton, "There was no rage or anything; he was like a robot, stabbing the guy."

During the court hearing, Li was found to be not criminally responsible for his acts on account of a mental disorder. That is, he did not understand at the time that his actions were wrong. He was suffering from schizophrenia. When Li was placed on medication and his psychotic symptoms abated, he realized the full horror of what he had done, and expressed great remorse for his actions. He was confined to the Selkirk Mental Health Centre in Manitoba, but has since been granted more freedom, such as supervised excursions, because his mental state has improved, he has continued to take his medication, and he was judged to be at low risk for reoffending.

The case of Vincent Li illustrates how abnormal experiences—auditory hallucinations—can have tragic consequences, especially if the person believes that the hallucinations are real voices that must be obeyed. It is important to point out, however, that most people who have psychological disorders are not dangerous and do not commit crimes or attempt to harm other people.

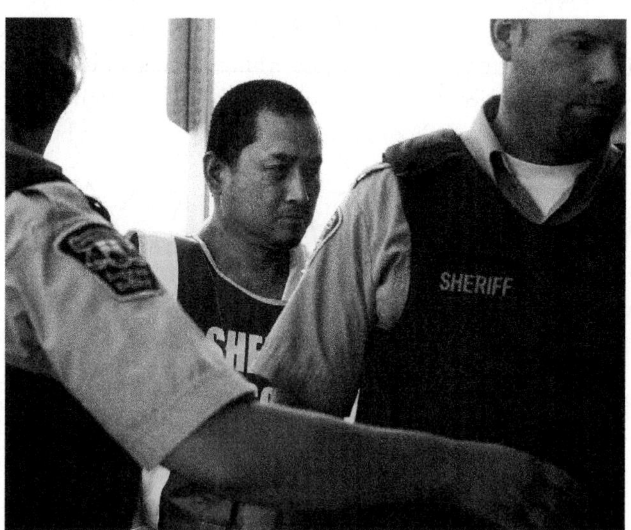

Sources: Review Board dispensation letter, Province of Manitoba, June 11, 2010; www.ctvnews.ca/canada/vince-li-who-beheaded-bus-passenger-granted-move-to-group-home-1.2366319; www.ctvnews.ca/police-don-t-know-what-prompted-vicious-bus-attack-1.312559; www.thestar.com/news/canada/2009/03/03/man_pleads_not_guilty_in_bus_beheading.html. Accessed January 14, 2016.

John Woods/The Canadian Press

Is Behaving Dangerously Abnormal?

The police arrive at the emergency room of a university hospital with a man and a woman in handcuffs. Jon is 23 years old. He identifies himself as the chauffeur for Melissa, who is age 35 and also in handcuffs. They are both dressed in tight leather pants and shirts, have unusual "spiked" haircuts, and wear leather "dog collars" with many silver spikes. Jon and Melissa live in the Toronto suburbs, but spent a day in the city buying clothes and getting their hair cut. As they were leaving the parking garage to return home, Melissa began to criticize Jon's hair. Jon became angry and ran the car, which belonged to Melissa, into the wall of the parking garage—several times. When a clinician asked the police officer why they were brought to the emergency room, the officer replied, "Well, would a sane person keep ramming a car into the wall of a parking garage?" Neither Jon nor Melissa had any previous history of psychological disorders. An interview revealed that Jon's behaviour was the result of a lover's quarrel, and although their relationship was often volatile, they denied any incidents of physical aggression toward each other or anyone else.

Certainly, repeatedly ramming a car into the wall of a parking garage is dangerous, is outside of societal norms, and could be labelled abnormal. Dangerous behaviour can result from intense emotional states, and in Jon's case, the behaviour was directed outwardly (toward another person or an inanimate object). In other cases, dangerous behaviour, such as suicidal thoughts, may be directed toward oneself. However, it is important to understand that most people with psychological disorders do not engage in dangerous behaviour (Pulay et al., 2008). Individuals with seriously disordered thinking rarely present any danger to society even though their behaviours may appear dangerous to others. Therefore, behaviour that is dangerous may signal the presence of a psychological disorder, but dangerous behaviour alone is not necessary or sufficient for the label of abnormality to be assigned.

Is Behaving Dysfunctionally Abnormal?

1.1 Explain the difference between behaviours that are different, deviant, dangerous, and dysfunctional.

Thus far, simply being different, behaving differently, or behaving dangerously clearly does not constitute abnormal behaviour. A final consideration when attempting to define abnormal behaviour is whether that behaviour causes *distress* or *dysfunction* for the individual or others. Consider the examples of Robert and Stan (see "Side-by-Side Case Studies").

SIDE by SIDE case studies — Dimensions of Behaviour: From Normal to Abnormal

Normal Behaviour Case Study

A Cautious Person—No Disorder

→ Robert is a very cautious person. He does not like to make mistakes and believes that the behaviour standards that he sets for himself are high but fair. He is concerned about safety and worries that other people might take advantage of him if he makes a mistake. Before leaving his house or going to sleep, he walks through the house, checking to make sure that every door and window is locked and the oven and stove are turned off. This usually takes about five minutes.

Abnormal Behaviour Case Study

Obsessive-Compulsive Disorder

→ Stan also is cautious and very concerned. When away from home, he worries that he forgot to lock a door and that his house has been robbed. Often he returns home to check that the house is locked. But even after he checks, he remains doubtful and spends hours each day checking and rechecking. He has an elaborate system of checking the locks, the doors, the garage door, and the burglar alarm system. He checks the stove seven times to make sure that the oven and the burners are off. Thoughts of a burglar in his house or his house burning down cause him great distress, sometimes interfering with his sleep. He is often late for work or for social engagements because he needs to go back to the house to check and recheck.

Both Robert and Stan engage in checking behaviours, but Robert's behaviour falls into the category of what is called "normal checking" (Antony et al., 2007). Stan's routine of checking the house before he leaves for work or goes to bed is *different* from the way in which most people lock up their house before going to work, so his behaviour *deviates* from the norm. Even though simple deviance is not abnormal, Stan's behaviour differs from Robert's in another way: Stan's checking occurs more frequently. Frequency alone does not mean a behaviour is maladaptive, but frequency can lead to two other conditions: distress and dysfunction. Specifically, Stan's worries are so frequent and pervasive that they cause him to feel anxious and lose sleep at night. In this case, maladaptive behaviour results in *distress*; Stan's worries result in a negative mood (anxiety) and cause him to lose sleep. Frequently, they also cause him to arrive late for work or for social engagements. Thus, his behaviours create occupational and social *dysfunction*. When one of these conditions is evident, the presence of a psychological disorder must be considered.

A Definition of Abnormal Behaviour

1.2 Identify at least two factors that need to be considered when determining whether a behaviour is abnormal.

To summarize, to define abnormal behaviour, we need to consider several factors. Merely being different or behaving differently is not enough, although the latter certainly might be a signal that something is wrong. Some abnormal behaviours are dangerous, but dangerousness is not necessary for a definition of abnormality. In this text, we define **abnormal behaviour** as behaviour that is inconsistent with the individual's developmental, cultural, and societal norms, and creates emotional distress or interferes with daily functioning.

The following chapters will examine many different types of abnormal behaviour. As a guide, the behaviours are considered using the *Diagnostic and Statistical Manual of Mental Disorders*, fifth edition (American Psychiatric Association [APA], 2013), commonly known as the DSM-5. This diagnostic system uses an approach that focuses on symptoms and the scientific basis for the disorders, including their *clinical presentation* (what specific symptoms cluster together?), *etiology* (what causes the disorder?), *developmental stage* (does the disorder look different in children than it does in adults?), and *functional impairment* (what are the immediate and long-term consequences of having the disorder?). The DSM system uses a *categorical approach* to defining abnormal behaviour. Although this method is somewhat controversial (see "Research Hot Topic: Categorical vs. Dimensional Approaches to Abnormal Behaviour"), it remains the most widely accepted diagnostic system in Canada and throughout many parts of the world.

ABNORMAL BEHAVIOUR IN THE GENERAL POPULATION Psychological disorders are common in the general population. In a 2012 survey by Statistics Canada (Pearson et al., 2013), it was estimated that about one in three Canadians (9.1 million people) meet the criteria for at least one of the six disorders assessed in the survey at some point in their lives (see Figure 1.1). The survey results revealed that about 6 million Canadians (20%) meet the criteria for a substance use disorder, and 3.5 million (13%) meet the criteria for a mood disorder. Figure 1.1 shows that alcohol abuse and dependence are the most common substance use disorders. Mood disorders and generalized anxiety disorder are more common among women, whereas substance use disorders are more common for men. The prevalence of disorders (i.e., the percentage of people with the disorder at the time of the study) was highest in people aged 15–24 years. An earlier Canadian survey found that many other kinds of disorders are also common in Canada (Statistics Canada, 2004). Similar rates have been reported in surveys conducted in the United States and elsewhere in the world (e.g., Kessler et al., 2005a). Clearly, many people suffer from serious psychological disorders. This emphasizes the need for more understanding of these conditions and the development of effective treatments.

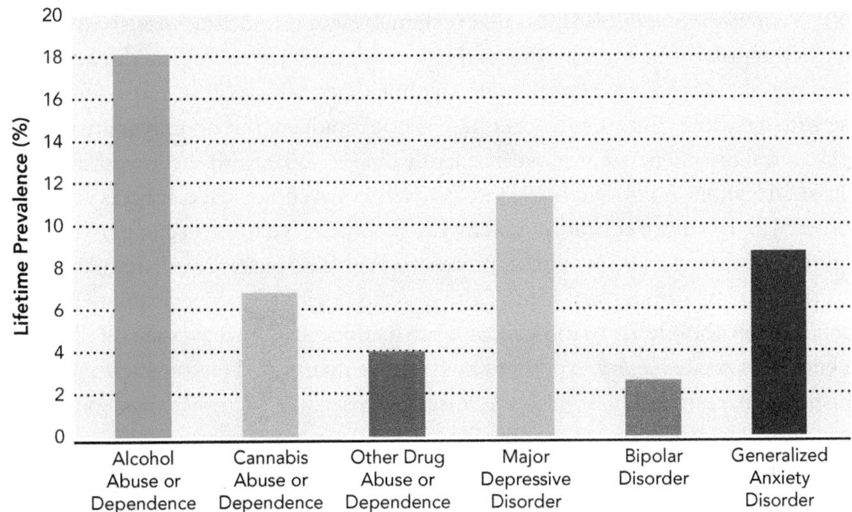

FIGURE 1.1

Lifetime Prevalence of Various Psychiatric Disorders Among Canadians.

Source: Data from Statistics Canada, Canadian Community Health Survey – Mental Health, 2012. © Deborah Beidel.

FACTORS INFLUENCING THE EXPRESSION OF ABNORMAL BEHAVIOURS Contextual factors play an important role when considering if and when abnormal behaviours may develop. Some factors include personal characteristics such as sex and race or ethnicity. For example, women are more likely to suffer from anxiety disorders (see Chapter 4) and mood disorders (see Chapter 6), and men are more likely to suffer from alcohol and drug abuse (see Chapter 9). In addition, as we shall see throughout this text, culture may influence how symptoms are expressed.

research HOT topic

Categorical vs. Dimensional Approaches to Abnormal Behaviour

The current diagnostic system, the *Diagnostic and Statistical Manual of Mental Disorders* (DSM), presents a primarily *categorical* approach to understanding psychological disorders. The DSM assumes that a person either has a disorder or does not, just as one is pregnant or not pregnant. The current DSM is superior to previous diagnostic systems, which were tied to theory but not necessarily to data. However, two issues continue to present problems for a categorical approach: (a) Symptoms rarely fall neatly into just one category, and (b) symptoms often are not of sufficient severity to determine that they represent a psychological disorder despite distress and impairment.

In fact, people in psychological distress rarely have only one psychological disorder (Carragher et al., 2015). A woman struggling with an eating disorder often feels depressed as well. Does she have two distinct disorders, or is her depression merely part of her abnormal eating pattern? Making these distinctions is more than just an academic exercise—it affects whether someone receives treatment. It may, for example, determine whether a psychologist decides to refer a depressed patient for medication treatment or just monitors her sadness to see whether it disappears when the eating disorder is successfully treated.

The following example illustrates the second issue—deciding when a person has "enough" of a symptom to have a diagnosis. Shyness and sadness are two behaviours that may be personality dimensions rather than a distinct category. When is a person "sad enough" or "shy enough" to be diagnosed with a psychological disorder? Is shyness a personality feature or a psychological disorder? Currently, a person is considered to have a psychological disorder when the distress is severe enough or when functional impairment results. However, in many instances, this is an artificial distinction and may deny people with moderate distress the opportunity to seek services. Scientifically, a **dimensional approach** would allow an understanding of how abnormal behaviour varies in severity over time, perhaps increasing and decreasing, or how behaviours change from one disorder to another.

Researchers continue to investigate the most accurate way to describe abnormal behaviour. The DSM-5 emphasizes the need to consider not just the presence of symptoms, but also whether those symptoms affect functioning when attempting to understand abnormal behaviour.

Socioeconomic status (SES), defined by family income and educational achievement, is another important factor that affects the prevalence of psychological disorders in the general population. Except for drug and alcohol abuse, which occur more often among those with a middle education level (a high school graduate but no university degree), psychological disorders occur most frequently among those with the lowest incomes and the least education. A continuing debate is whether psychological disorders are the result of lower SES. Do more education and higher income serve to protect a person against psychological disorders by providing more supportive resources? An alternative hypothesis is that the impairment that *results* from a psychological disorder (inability to sleep, addiction to alcohol) leads to job loss or limited educational achievement, a phenomenon known as *downward drift*. Another alternative is that a third factor, such as genetic predisposition, contributes both to the onset of a psychiatric disorder and to the inability to achieve academically or occupationally.

Few studies specifically address the relationship of SES to psychological disorders, but one study of the development of psychological disorders in children does help us understand this relationship. In this study, children were interviewed at yearly intervals, in some cases for nine consecutive years. During that time, children from all SES groups *developed* psychological disorders at the same rate (Wadsworth & Achenbach, 2005). However, once the disorder was present, children from the lower SES category were less likely to *overcome* or recover from their disorder. Lower income usually means fewer economic resources and less access to treatment. Over time, reduced recovery resulted in more children from the lower SES group having more psychological disorders.

As the preceding example illustrates, children as well as adults suffer from psychological disorders, and we know that age and developmental stage are important factors affecting abnormal behaviours. In another study, Costello and colleagues (2003) examined the presence of psychological disorders in children who were assessed yearly, in some cases for up to seven consecutive years. Figure 1.2 illustrates the prevalence of psychological disorders in children and adolescents.

It may be quite surprising to learn that by age 16, one out of three children and adolescents (36%) has suffered from a psychological disorder. As illustrated in Figure 1.3, the prevalence of disorders was highest among 9- to 10-year-old children, lower at age 12, and higher again in adolescence. Developmental maturity affects when

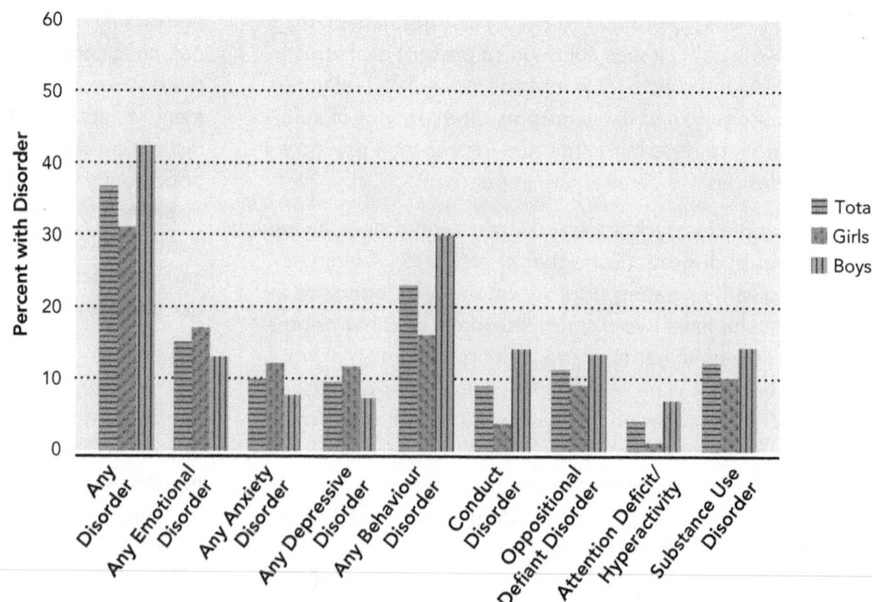

FIGURE 1.2

Prevalence of DSM-IV Psychiatric Disorders by Age 16.

Source: Data from Costello, E. J., Mustillo, A., Erkanli, A., Keeler, G., & Angold, A. (2003). Prevalence and development of psychiatric disorders in childhood and adolescence. *Archives of General Psychiatry, 60*, 837–844. © Deborah Beidel

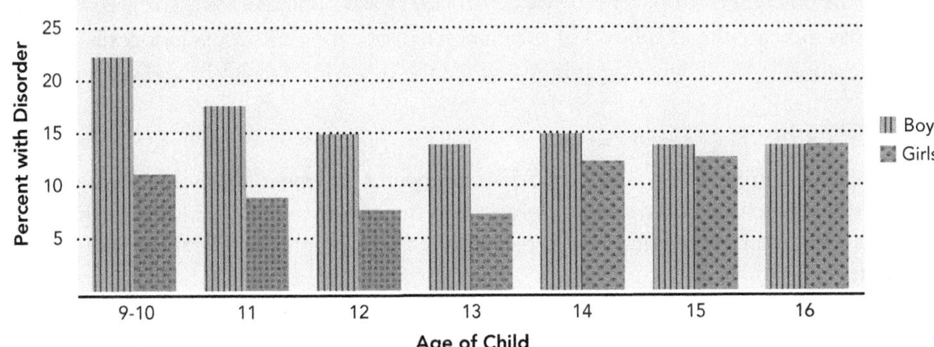

FIGURE 1.3

Prevalence of DSM-IV Psychological Disorders in Children by Age and Sex. For boys, the prevalence of disorders peaks around age 9 or 10; for girls, prevalence peaks around age 16.

Source: Data from Costello, E. J., Mustillo, A., Erkanli, A., Keeler, G., & Angold, A. (2003). Prevalence and development of psychiatric disorders in childhood and adolescence. *Archives of General Psychiatry, 60*, 837–844.
© Deborah Beidel

and how symptoms develop, what types of symptoms develop, and even what kinds of disorders occur. The idea that the common symptoms of a disorder vary according to a person's age is known as the **developmental trajectory** (a *trajectory* is a path or progression). For example, compared with children who are diagnosed with depression, adolescents with depression are more likely to feel hopelessness or helplessness, to lack energy or feel tired, to sleep too much, and to commit serious suicidal acts (Yorbik et al., 2004). Therefore, the symptoms of depression may change as a child matures. Even among adults, age also plays a role in the frequency of specific depressive symptoms. As adults mature, they are less likely to report feelings of sadness or negative thoughts about themselves or others (Goldberg et al., 2003). Therefore, even an emotion as common as sadness can appear differently at different ages.

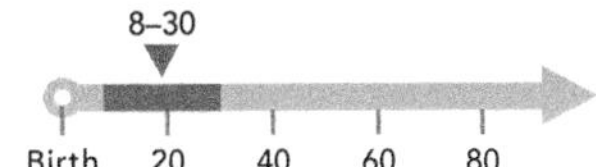

Social anxiety disorder affects both children and adults, but the situations that create fear vary by age.

Inattention to developmental differences may result in inaccurate detection of psychological disorders. For example, social anxiety disorder is characterized by a behavioural pattern of pervasive social timidity (see Chapter 4). Adults with social anxiety disorder report extreme fear when asked to give a speech. Young children rarely have to give a speech, and because they have no experience in the situation, they deny fear of giving speeches. However, a similar childhood activity would be reading aloud in front of the class. Children with social anxiety disorder often report great fear when asked to read aloud. Therefore, accurately diagnosing social anxiety disorder depends on understanding not only the disorder, but also how the disorder appears at different ages. Similarly, older adults with depression are less likely to report feelings of sadness and negative thoughts, but all adults (regardless of age) report physical symptoms of depression (inability to sleep or eat or being easily tired). Therefore, a clinician who assesses depression only by asking about sadness may overlook depression in older adults. Throughout this text, we often will return to this issue of developmental psychopathology and how the same disorder may appear differently across the lifespan.

This developmental perspective also illustrates why the prevalence of psychological disorders varies by age (see Figure 1.3). Certain disorders that are common in childhood (separation anxiety disorder, attention deficit/hyperactivity disorder; see Chapters 4 and 12) become less common as children mature physically, cognitively, and emotionally. During adolescence, other disorders begin to emerge (depression, alcohol and drug use, eating disorders, panic disorder, and generalized anxiety disorder; see Chapters 4, 6, 7, and 9). The emergence of some disorders has practical and societal components (e.g., older adolescents are more likely to have access to alcohol, which is a prerequisite to developing substance abuse). The emergence of other disorders coincides with cognitive maturity. Generalized anxiety disorder is defined, in part, by worry about future events (APA, 2013). This requires the ability to understand the concept of "future," a cognitive skill that usually emerges around age 12 (Alfano et al., 2002). Therefore, although it is possible for younger children to suffer from generalized anxiety disorder, many more cases occur later as cognitive maturity is achieved. Finally, biological changes also influence the emergence of psychological disorders. Hormonal changes associated with puberty may increase the likelihood of the emergence of eating disorders (anorexia and bulimia nervosa) in those who are at high risk for the development of these disorders.

CONCEPT check

- Being different, or behaving differently, does not necessarily mean that someone is suffering from a psychological disorder. Determining the presence of abnormal behaviour requires evaluation of the behaviour in terms of its developmental, cultural, and societal contexts.
- In addition to determining context, the definition of abnormal behaviour requires that the behaviour create emotional distress or functional impairment.
- The current diagnostic system uses a primarily categorical approach to classification of abnormal behaviour. However, psychological symptoms rarely fall into one neat category. Furthermore, it is often difficult to determine the boundary between normal feelings such as sadness and psychological disorders such as depression. In these instances, a dimensional approach may be more useful.

critical thinking question At different ages, the same disorder may appear with very different symptoms. Young children are still developing in many ways. How might immature physical and cognitive development affect the emotional expression of psychological disorders?

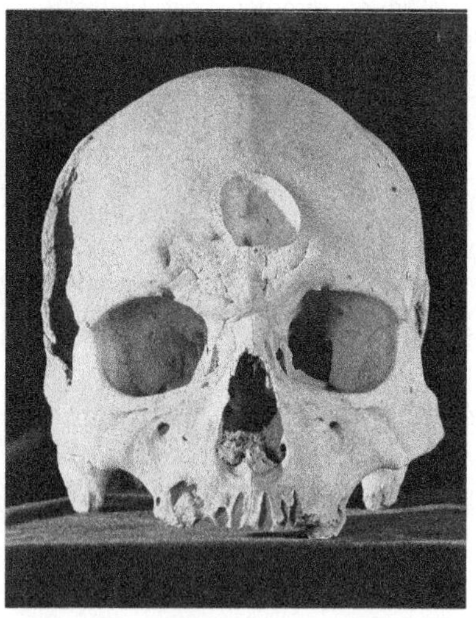

Trephination involved making a hole in the skull. It may have been a way that ancient peoples used to try to release evil spirits from the body of an afflicted person.

Bierwert/American Museum of Natural History

The History of Abnormal Behaviour and Its Treatment

Throughout history, certain behaviours have been recognized as abnormal—often the same ones we recognize today. However, the explanations for these abnormal behaviours have evolved, ranging from an imbalance of bodily fluids to possession by demons, genetic abnormalities, and traumatic learning experiences. Today, new technologies allow us to watch the brain as it processes sights, smells, and sounds; solves problems; and experiences emotions. As this knowledge has increased, some of the earlier ideas about abnormal behaviour seem outlandish or quaint. Here, we review those theories and show how scientific advances have changed our understanding of abnormal behaviour.

Ancient Theories

1.3 Discuss spiritual/religious, biological, psychological, and sociocultural theories of the origins of abnormal behaviour in their historical context.

Much of what we know about ancient theories of abnormal behaviour is based on available archeological evidence and ancient texts. Ancient Egyptians believed that spirits controlled much of the environment as well as aspects of a person's behaviour. Even before the Egyptians, some cultures engaged in a practice called **trephination**, which involved using a circular instrument to cut away sections of the skull. One interpretation of trephination is that it was a treatment for abnormal behaviours. Opening up the skull, it may have been thought, released the evil spirits that had assumed control of the person (Arnott et al., 2003). This is only an assumption. Trephination might simply have been used to treat head wounds received in battles (Maher & Maher, 1985). Even today, we are not sure why ancient peoples practised it.

Classical Greek and Roman Periods

The ancient Greeks believed that the gods controlled abnormal behaviour and that defiance of the deities could result in mental illness. Around the thirteenth century BCE, the physician Melampus of Pilus introduced an organic model of illness to explain psychological symptoms and provided treatment using plants and other natural sub stances. He prescribed root extract for "agitated uterine melancholia" and iron powder for "traumatic impotence" (Roccatagliata, 1997). Asclepius, best known as a Greek god, is now believed to have been a historical figure whose healing abilities were so widely respected that he was elevated to the status of a god (www.nlm.nih.gov/hmd/greek/greek_asclepius.html). Many temples were established throughout Greece to honour Asclepius, one of which was the first known sanctuary for mental disorders. It offered biological (mandrake root and opium), physical (music, massage, drama), and psychological treatments (dream interpretation); (Roccatagliata, 1997). During this period, mental illnesses were considered to result from either traumatic experiences or an imbalance in fluids (such as blood) found within the body. These fluids were called *humors*.

Often considered the father of medicine, Hippocrates (460–377 BCE) was the most famous Greek physician. He produced both a diagnostic classification system and a model by which to explain abnormal behaviour. Hippocrates identified common psychological symptoms such as *hallucinations* (hearing or seeing things not evident to others), *delusions* (beliefs with no basis in reality), *melancholia* (severe sadness), and *mania* (heightened states of arousal that can result in frenzied activity). All of these symptoms are still recognized today. He also introduced the term *hysteria*, now called *conversion disorder* (see Chapter 5). The term *hysteria* was used to describe patients who appeared to have blindness or paralysis for which there was no organic cause. Hippocrates, assuming incorrectly that the condition occurred only in women, attributed it to an empty uterus wandering throughout the body searching for conception. The external symptoms indicated where the uterus was lodged internally. He believed that the cure for hysteria was an environmental one: marriage or pregnancy. Of course, with advanced understanding of human anatomy and physiology, the "wandering uterus" theory was discarded. But even in very recent times, the term *hysteria* continued to describe an intense, dramatic pattern of behaviour once associated with women.

Hippocrates, the ancient Greek physician, believed that abnormal behaviours were caused by an imbalance in four bodily humors.

akg-images/Newscom

Hippocrates believed that other abnormal behaviours resulted when environmental factors (changes of seasons) or physical factors (fever, epilepsy, and shock) created an imbalance in four bodily humors. In his model, the four humors were yellow bile, black bile, blood, and phlegm. Blood was associated with a courageous and hopeful outlook on life, and phlegm was associated with a calm and unemotional attitude. Excessive yellow bile caused mania, and excessive black bile caused melancholia, which was treated with a vegetable diet, a tranquil existence, celibacy, exercise, and sometimes bleeding (controlled removal of some of the patient's blood). Hippocrates advocated the removal of patients from their families as an element of treatment, foreshadowing the practice of humane treatment and institutionalization.

Another very influential Greek physician was Galen, the personal physician of the Roman emperor Marcus Aurelius. Although the terms we use today differ from those used in ancient times, Galen's writings (which still survive) indicate that his areas of expertise included many fields of medicine: neurophysiology and neuroanatomy, neurology, pharmacology, psychiatry, and philosophy (Roccatagliata, 1997; www.nlm.nih.gov/hmd/greek/greek_galen.html). An important distinction can be made between Hippocrates's and Galen's description of hysteria. Because Galen had studied human anatomy, he discounted the "wandering uterus" theory. Galen attributed hysteria to a psychological cause, believing it to be a symptom of unhappiness in women who had lost interest in and enjoyment of sexual activity.

The Islamic philosopher and physician Avicenna wrote an influential medical text that recognized the interconnections between emotional distress and physical illness.

Portrait of Avicenna (c.992-1037), lithography by F Perez (litho), Spanish School, (19th century)/Museo Real Academia de Medicina, Madrid, Spain/Index/Bridgeman Images

After the fall of the Roman Empire, demonology again dominated theories of mental illness in Europe, but the enlightened thinking of Hippocrates and Galen remained influential in Islamic countries. There, Avicenna (980–1037 CE); (Namanzi, 2001), known as the "prince and chief of physicians" and "the second teacher after Aristotle," wrote approximately 450 works, including the *Canon of Medicine*, considered the most influential textbook ever written. Avicenna believed depression resulted from a mix of humors, and that certain physical diseases were caused by emotional distress. He stressed the beneficial effects of music on emotional disturbance. His approach to mental illness foreshadowed what would take an additional 600 years to appear in Europe—humane treatment of the mentally ill.

The Middle Ages Through the Renaissance

In medieval Europe, demons were considered to be the source of all evil, preying on the "captive and outwitted minds of men" (Sagan, 1996). There were many challenges (wars, plagues, social oppression, famine) to survival during the Middle Ages, and people often sought reasons for these events. Church officials interpreted negative behaviour as the work of the devil or as witchcraft, even when other, less dramatic, explanations existed. As a result of the church's powerful influence, witchcraft became a prominent theory to explain abnormal behaviour. Over a 300-year period (1400s to 1700s), at least 200 000 people in Europe were accused of witchcraft and 100 000 were put to death, approximately 80% to 85% of whom were women (Clark, 1997). In fact, many of those accused probably suffered from psychological disorders (Clark, 1997). Once accused of being a witch, the person was tried and always found guilty. Thankfully, the Renaissance period brought new attitudes toward science and the church that challenged the reality of witches. Accusations of witchcraft were not limited to European countries. "Witches" were also executed in the seventeenth century. However, beliefs in the supernatural and paranormal still exist in our modern world.

During the Middle Ages, episodes of **mass hysteria** would sweep through large groups of people. People affected were convinced that they were afflicted or possessed by a demonic spirit (again, similar to beliefs regarding alien abduction). One of the first recorded cases (originating in Italy in the early thirteenth century) is known as *tarantism*, caused by the belief that the bite of a wolf spider (also known as a tarantula) would cause death unless a person engaged in joyous, frenetic dancing. Another form of the legend was that the spider's bite would cause frenetic dancing, jumping, or convulsing (Sigerist, 1943). In fact, the spider's bite was harmless, and people's responses were fuelled by mass hysteria. Another form of mass madness was *lycanthropy*, in which individuals believed that they were possessed by wolves. The belief was so strong that those affected would act like a wolf, even to the point of believing that their bodies were covered in fur.

There is a scientific basis for mass hysteria. **Emotional contagion** is defined as the automatic mimicry and synchronization of expressions, vocalizations, postures, and movements of one person by another (Hatfield et al., 1993). When these overt behaviours converge, emotions come together as well. These mimicking behaviours are not under voluntary control, but nevertheless serve to influence behaviour. Although many people may no longer believe that wolves or spider bites are responsible for abnormal behaviours, the process of emotional contagion remains a powerful influence on behaviour (see "Examining the Evidence: Modern-Day Mass Hysteria").

The Renaissance period (fourteenth to seventeenth century) marked a second time of enlightenment in the treatment of mental illnesses in Europe. Much of this transformation can be traced back to the Dutch physician Johann Weyer (1515–1588) and the Swiss physician Paracelsus (1493–1541). Weyer was the first physician to specialize in the treatment of mental illness, and Paracelsus refuted the idea that abnormal behaviours were linked to demonic possession. Paracelsus believed that mental disorders could be hereditary and that some physical illnesses had a psychological origin (Tan & Yeow, 2003).

These changing views toward mental illness altered treatment approaches as well. A movement arose that was genuinely concerned with providing help, and its goal was to separate those with mental illness from those who engaged in criminal behaviour (Sussman, 1998). Beginning in the sixteenth century, people with mental illness were housed in asylums—separate facilities designed to isolate them from the general public.

Although the concept of asylums was based on good intentions, the asylums quickly filled to capacity (and overcapacity). The lack of effective treatments turned the facilities into warehouses, often called *madhouses*. One of the most famous was St. Mary of Bethlehem in London. Treatment consisted of confinement (chains, shackles, and isolation in dark cells), torturous practices (ice-cold baths, spinning in chairs, and severely restricted diets), and "medical" treatments (emetics, purgatives, and bloodletting). For a small price, people in London could visit the asylum to view the inmates (Tan & Yeow, 2004). They called the place *Bedlam* (a contraction of "Bethlehem"), a word that came to describe chaotic and uncontrollable situations. Similar conditions existed in other parts of Europe as well as eventually in North America.

The Nineteenth Century and the Beginning of Modern Thought

A turning point for the medical treatment of mental illness occurred during the late eighteenth century when French physician Philippe Pinel (1745–1826), English Quaker William Tuke (1732–1822), and Italian physician Vincenzo Chiarugi (1759–1820) radically changed the approach. In 1793, Pinel was the director of Bicêtre, an asylum for men. In his *Memoir on Madness*, he proposed that mental illness was often curable and that to apply appropriate treatment, the physician must listen to the patient and observe his behaviour. Both would help the physician to understand the natural history of the disease and the events that led to its development. Pinel advocated calm and order within the asylum (Tan & Yeow, 2004). He removed the chains from patients, both at Bicêtre and at the women's asylum known as Salpêtrière. Instead of using restraints, Pinel advocated daytime activities, such as work or occupational therapy, to allow for restful sleep at night.

At the same time, across the English Channel, William Tuke established the York Retreat (Edginton, 1997), a small country house deliberately designed to allow people with mental illnesses to live, work, and relax in a compassionate and religious environment. Instead of bars on the windows, Tuke used iron dividers to separate the glass window panes, and even had the dividers painted to look like wood. The Retreat was built on a hill, and although it contained a hidden ditch and a wall to ensure confinement, the barriers could not be seen from the buildings; this gave the illusion of a home rather than an institution (Scull, 2004).

In Italy, Vincenzo Chiarugi was director of the Santa Maria Nuova hospital in Florence from 1785 to 1788. He outlawed chains as a means of restraining psychiatric patients. He was appointed as director of the Bonifacio hospital in 1788, where he played a major role in drafting new humanitarian regulations for the care of patients (Gerard, 1998).

The work of Pinel, Tuke, and Chiarugi heralded *moral treatment*, "summed up in two words, kindness and occupation" (W. A. F. Browne, 1837, cited in Geller & Morrissey, 2004). Moral treatment (in which "moral" was a mistranslation of morale or well-being); (Lightner, 1999) was quite comprehensive. It included removal of the patient from the home and former associates, as well as respectful and kind treatment that included "manual labour, religious services on Sunday, the establishment of regular habits and of self-control, and diversion of the mind from morbid trains of thought" (Brigham, 1847, p. 1, cited in Luchins, 2001).

Philippe Pinel, a French physician, released mental patients from their chains and advocated a more humane form of treatment.

Charles Ciccione/Science Source/Photo Researchers, Inc.

examining the EVIDENCE

Modern-Day Mass Hysteria

- **The Facts** We tend to think of mass hysteria as occurring in an unenlightened era. However, episodes of mass contagion still occur today. The 9/11 attacks and the subsequent global "War on Terror" have led to a wave of terror scares involving mass psychogenic illness, as illustrated by the case of the toxic bus (Bartholomew & Wessely, 2007).
- **The Evidence** In the afternoon of May 25, 2004, a passenger exiting the front of bus in downtown Vancouver said to the bus driver, "How's your day going?" The driver replied, "Good." The passenger, a Middle Eastern–looking man in his twenties, said, "It won't be for long." As the driver continued on his route, he began to feel nauseated and then vomited. The driver asked the passengers if any of them felt ill. One said yes, so the driver parked the bus and radioed for medics, fearing a chemical or biological attack. As the two responding paramedics listened to the driver's account of events, they too felt ill. Others arriving on the scene also reported feeling sick. A total of 19 people, including the driver, passengers, emergency personnel, and journalists, were briefly quarantined. Air quality tests and a forensic examination of the bus were unremarkable, although a later test of the bus identified minute traces of methyl chloride, which is toxic in large concentrations. The incident became the subject of a public dispute between Vancouver's Chief Medical Health Officer Dr. John Blatherwick, who believed the cause was mass psychogenic illness, and the police and ambulance agencies, who disagreed.
- **Let's Examine the Evidence** Evidence that emotional contagion may have been the basis for the symptom reports includes the following:
  1. There was no evidence of a chemical attack. Methyl chloride could have come from the air and built up over time.
  2. The tests failed to include a control condition; that is, there was no attempt to determine whether traces of methyl chloride were evident in other buses in which people did not feel ill.
  3. Both paramedics reported feeling ill, yet only one of them entered the bus. The other did not enter, so it seems unlikely that he was exposed to any toxic chemical.
  4. Other first responders entered the bus prior to the paramedic, without protective equipment, and none of them felt ill.
  5. Some of the symptoms were inconsistent with methyl chloride poisoning and more consistent with anxiety.
  6. Not a single medical complaint could be confirmed by an objective measure, including physical signs or laboratory tests.
- **Conclusion** It is important to note that the individuals experienced the symptoms they reported; it is incorrect to deny that the symptoms occurred. What is at issue, however, is the cause of the symptoms. In the case of the toxic bus, as in many others, after exhausting all possible environmental alternatives, the most likely explanation for the large outbreak of illness was emotional contagion, producing mass psychogenic illness (Bartholomew & Wessely, 2007).

Dorothea Dix was a tireless reformer who brought the poor treatment of the mentally ill to public attention.

The Granger Collection

Moral treatment in North America is most commonly associated with Benjamin Rush (1745–1813) and Dorothea Dix (1802–1887). Rush limited his practice to mental illness, which he believed had its causes in the blood vessels of the brain (Farr, 1994). Although this theory was later disproved, Rush believed that the human mind was a most important area of study (Haas, 1993).

In North America, perhaps no name is more closely associated with humane care than that of Dorothea Dix, a schoolteacher who devoted her life to the plight of the mentally ill in Canada and the United States, and who was a strong advocate for treatment reform. Through her efforts, 32 institutions were established that included programs in psychiatric treatment, research, and education (Gold, 2005). Dix believed that asylums, correctly designed and operated, would allow for treatment and perhaps even cure. Although Dix brought the plight of the mentally ill to public attention, moral treatment alone did not cure most forms of mental illness. In fact, mental hospitals tended to be associated with permanent institutionalization, custodial care, isolation, and very little hope.

CANADIAN Focus:

Historical Perspectives on the Treatment of Abnormal Behaviour

The first asylum in what is now North America was the Hôtel Dieu of Quebec. It was founded in 1639 by the Duchess d'Aiguillon to care for people with psychiatric disorders and intellectual disabilities, as well as the poor and destitute and the physically disabled. The Catholic community took responsibility for the care the patients and oversaw the development of other asylums throughout Quebec (Hurd et al., 1916). A number of facilities for the mentally ill were built in Quebec around that time. However, people with psychological disorders more typically received little or no treatment and were commonly shut away in jails, poorhouses, or charity shelters. No means of addressing their needs were provided until well into the 1800s (Sussman, 1998). Many of the mental institutions in Canada and elsewhere were built in the nineteenth century as a result of the philosophy of moral treatment. Rather than simply confining mental patients, moral treatment offered support, care, and a degree of freedom.

Mental health facilities in Canada were developed on an *ad hoc* basis, with little planning and little coordination among provinces. Often jails or military barracks were converted into asylums (Sussman, 1998). The first privately run asylum in Canada, the Homewood Retreat, was established in 1883 in Guelph (Warsh, 1989). Similar to the private institutions that later developed in the United States and elsewhere, the Homewood Retreat catered to the wealthy, with treatment paid for by patients or their relatives. When the retreat opened, it had a capacity for 50 patients and consisted of an estate mansion, with offices, reception rooms, and a music hall on the ground floor, as well as staff quarters.

During the early decades of its operation, patients at the Homewood Retreat received moral treatment; that is, a regimen based on routine, occupation, healthy diet, and mild exercise. The patients and their families, by virtue of the fact that they were paying for treatment, had a great deal of control over the type of interventions that were administered. People with a variety of clinical problems were admitted to the Homewood Retreat (Warsh, 1989). In terms of today's diagnostic nomenclature, such cases included mood and anxiety disorders, schizophrenia, bipolar disorder, and alcohol dependence.

The first privately run asylum in Canada, the Homewood Retreat, was established in 1883 in Guelph, Ontario.

Photograph appears courtesy of the Guelph Public Library Archives, Main building of Homewood Sanitarium, 1903, (F45-0-14-0-0-479).

During the late 1700s in Europe, the treatment of mental disorders went beyond providing rest and humane care. The German physician Franz Anton Mesmer (1734–1815) hardly followed the conventional medical establishment. His academic thesis explored the clinical implications of astrology (McNally, 1999). Mesmer proposed that the body was a magnet, and that using the physician's body as a second magnet could achieve a cure for mental illness (Crabtree, 2000). Mesmer believed that a substance called **animal magnetism** existed within the body. When it flowed freely, the body was in a healthy state; however, when the flow of this energy force was impeded, disease resulted. The cure involved "magnetic passes" of the physician's hands over the body (McNally, 1999). Mesmerism was roundly criticized by the scientific community at the time.

Nonetheless, Mesmer's experiments constituted an important chapter in psychology. His theory of animal magnetism and his flamboyant cures (including a cape, music, magic poles used to touch various parts of the body, and magnetized water) were ultimately debunked. However, they illustrate the power of the **placebo effect** in which symptoms are diminished or eliminated not because of any specific treatment, but because the patient believes that a treatment is effective. A placebo can be in the form of pills with inert ingredients, such as cornstarch. It can also be in the form of a therapist or physician who displays an attitude of caring about the patient. It is important to add that although placebos may change how patients feel, the effect is usually temporary. Placebos are not the same as actual treatment, although all treatments contain an element of placebo. That is, all effective treatments consist of a combination of specific treatment factors (such as chemical compounds that directly influence neurotransmitter systems) and nonspecific factors (such as the caring and optimistic attitude of the therapist or physician, which leads the patient to expect that therapy will be effective).

A significant event for establishing a biological basis for some psychological disorders occurred in the latter part of the nineteenth century. Scientists discovered that syphilis (a sexually transmitted disease caused by a bacterium) led to the chronic condition called *general paresis*, which manifests as physical paralysis and mental illness and eventually death. The discovery that a physical disease could cause a psychological disorder was a significant advance in understanding abnormal behaviour. However, we now know that bacteria are not the cause of most psychological disorders, even though psychological symptoms may have a medical basis in some cases.

The work of German psychiatrist Emil Kraepelin (1856–1926) was another important chapter in the history of abnormal behaviour. During medical school, Kraepelin attended lectures in the laboratory of Wilhelm Wundt, the founder of modern scientific psychology (Decker, 2004). He applied Wundt's scientific methods to measure behavioural deviations, hoping to provide the theoretical foundations that he considered to be lacking in psychiatry (compared with general medicine and psychology). On Wundt's advice, Kraepelin began to study "the abnormal" (Boyle, 2000). In 1899, after observing hundreds of patients, he introduced two diagnostic categories based not just on symptom differentiation, but also on the *etiology* (cause) and *prognosis* (progression and outcome) of the disease. **Dementia praecox**, now called **schizophrenia** (see Chapter 10), was a term used by Kraepelin to describe a type of mental illness characterized by mental deterioration. *Manic-depressive insanity* was defined as a separate disorder with a more favourable outcome. Kraepelin was best known for his studies of dementia praecox, which he believed resulted from *autointoxication*, the self-poisoning of brain cells as a result of abnormal body metabolism. With new studies documenting the contribution of genetic and biological factors to the onset of schizophrenia, Kraepelin's contributions, in terms of both a classification system and a description of schizophrenia, cannot be overstated.

Another physician interested in the brain was Jean-Martin Charcot (1825–1893), who established a school of neurology at La Salpêtrière in Paris (Haas, 2001). Charcot was interested in hysteria, which he believed was caused by degenerative brain changes. However, at the same time, other researchers, Ambrose August Liébeault (1823–1904) and Hippolyte Bernheim (1840–1919) in Nancy, France, were conducting experiments to determine whether hysteria was a form of self-hypnosis. Debate raged between Charcot and the physicians collectively called the *Nancy School*. Eventually, most scientific data supported the views of the Nancy School. To his credit as a scientist, once the data were established, Charcot became a strong proponent of this view.

At about the same time, Viennese physician Josef Breuer (1842–1925) was studying the effect of hypnotism. Breuer used hypnosis to treat patients with hysteria, including a young woman named Anna O., who had cared for her ailing father until his death. Shortly thereafter, she developed blurry vision, trouble speaking, and difficulty moving her right arm and both her legs. Breuer discovered that when under hypnosis, Anna O. would discuss events and experiences that she was unable to recall otherwise. Furthermore, after discussing these distressing events, her symptoms disappeared. Breuer called his treatment the **talking cure**, laying the foundation for a new approach to mental disorders.

The Twentieth Century

Although biological theories were still influential, two psychological models of abnormal behaviour dominated the early part of the twentieth century: psychoanalytic theory and behaviourism. In this section, we examine the roots of these theories and how they set the stage for modern-day approaches to understanding abnormal behaviour.

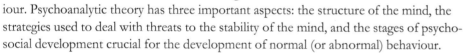

Sigmund Freud introduced psychoanalysis, a theory that attempts to explain abnormal behaviour as driven by unconscious biological and sexual urges.

Mary Evans/The Image Works

PSYCHOANALYSIS Sigmund Freud (1856–1939) was trained as a neurologist. His career in psychiatry began in France, where he worked with Charcot. After settling in Vienna, Freud published *Studies in Hysteria* in 1895 with Josef Breuer. He introduced **psychoanalysis**, a comprehensive theory that attempts to explain both normal and abnormal behaviour. Freud believed that the roots of abnormal behaviour were established in the first five years of life. Because they happened so early, he believed that the person would retain no conscious memory of them—yet the unconscious memories would exert a lifelong influence on behaviour. Psychoanalytic theory has three important aspects: the structure of the mind, the strategies used to deal with threats to the stability of the mind, and the stages of psychosocial development crucial for the development of normal (or abnormal) behaviour.

In psychoanalytic theory, the mind consists of three regions: the id, ego, and superego. Basic instinctual drives and the source of psychic energy, called *libido*, are found in the *id*. Always seeking pleasure, the id is totally unconscious, so its urges and activities are outside our awareness. Think of the id as a professional athlete—"I want a big salary; I want a signing bonus." The *ego* develops when the id comes in contact with reality. Think of the ego as a sports agent who mediates between the id's impulses (the athlete's desires) and the demands and restrictions of reality (the owner's contract offer). Rather than always seeking pleasure, the ego copes with reality, or as Freud put it, the ego obeys the reality principle. The ego has both conscious and unconscious components, so we are often aware of its actions. The third region of the mind is the *superego*. Similar to a conscience, the superego imposes moral restraint on the id's impulses (particularly those of a sexual or an aggressive nature). Think of the superego as the team owner or the league commissioner who doles out monetary fines for breaking team or league rules. When moral rules are violated, the superego punishes with guilt feelings. Like the ego, the superego is partly conscious and partly unconscious and tries to manage or inhibit the id's impulses. Because these three intrapsychic forces are constantly competing, there is ever-changing conflict, creating a dynamic, in this case, a *psychodynamic* system.

Freud proposed that through the use of *defence mechanisms*, the mind's negative or distressing thoughts and feelings are disguised to emerge to consciousness in a more acceptable form. Some defence mechanisms prevent the onset of abnormal behaviour. Other defence mechanisms (such as regression) may result in abnormal or age-inappropriate behaviours. Table 1.1 presents some of the defence mechanisms identified by Freud.

Almost as well known as the id, ego, and superego are Freud's stages of psychosexual development. According to the theory, each person passes through these stages between infancy and 5 years of age. How a child copes with each stage has important effects on psychological development. The *oral phase* occurs during the first one and a half years of life. Sucking and chewing are pleasurable experiences; aggressive impulses emerge after the development of teeth. The *anal phase* (from age 1½ to 3 years) coincides with toilet training. During this time, parents emphasize discipline and control issues, and

TABLE 1.1
Defence Mechanisms and Their Function

Defence	Function	Example
Denial	Dealing with an anxiety-provoking stimulus by acting as if it doesn't exist	Rejecting a physician's cancer diagnosis
Displacement	Taking out impulses on a less-threatening target	Slamming a door instead of hitting someone
Intellectualization	Avoiding unacceptable emotions by focusing on the intellectual aspects of an event	Focusing on a funeral's details rather than the sadness of the situation
Projection	Attributing your own unacceptable impulses to someone else	Making a mistake at work but instead of admitting it, blaming it on a co-worker whom you call "incompetent"
Rationalization	Supplying a plausible but incorrect explanation for a behaviour rather than the real reason	Saying you drink three martinis every night because it lowers your blood pressure
Reaction formation	Taking the opposite belief because the true belief causes anxiety	Overtly embracing a particular race to the extreme by someone who is racially prejudiced
Regression	Under threat, returning to a previous stage of development	Not getting a desired outcome results in a temper tantrum
Repression	Burying unwanted thoughts out of conscious thought	Forgetting aspects of a traumatic event (such as sexual assault)
Sublimation	Acting out unacceptable impulses in a socially acceptable way	Acting out aggressive tendencies by becoming a boxer
Suppression	Pushing unwanted thoughts into the unconscious	Actively trying to forget something that causes anxiety
Undoing	Attempting to take back unacceptable behaviour or thoughts	Insulting someone and then excessively praising the person

Source: Based on *Psychology 101, Freud's Ego Defense Mechanism.* http://allpsych.com/psychology101/defenses.html. Copyright © 1999–2003, AllPsych and Heffner Media Group, Inc.

power struggles develop. Aggressive impulses on the part of the child could lead to personality traits of negativism and stubbornness, as well as the emergence of hostile, destructive, or sadistic behaviours. During the *phallic phase* (ages 3 to 5), psychosexual energy centres on the genital area, and children derive pleasure from touching or rubbing the genitals. During this phase, children may develop romantic fantasies or attachments toward their opposite-sex parent. The two additional stages, the latency phase (the formant stage of psychosexual development when children are disinterested in the opposite sex) and the genital phase (the mature stage of psychosexual development), are considered to play a more limited role in abnormal behaviour.

In psychoanalytic theory, anxiety and depression are caused by negative experiences. Depending on the age at which the experience occurs, individuals become *fixated* (stalled) at a stage of psychosexual development. This leaves a psychological mark on the unconscious. For example, harsh parenting during toilet training results in a toddler who withholds his feces as a reaction. As an adult, this person will be stingy with money or gifts. In psychoanalytic theory, even though the individual is unaware of the early experience, it still influences daily functioning. In short, the individual behaves psychologically at the stage of development when the fixation occurred.

The goals of psychoanalysis, the treatment Freud developed, include *insight*, bringing the troubling material to consciousness, and *catharsis*, releasing psychic energy. Several techniques are used to achieve these goals. In *free association*, the person minimizes conscious control and, without selection or censorship, tells the analyst everything that comes to mind, allowing the analyst to draw out information regarding unconscious conflicts. In *dream analysis*, individuals are encouraged to recall and recount their dreams, which are discussed in the analytic sessions. Freud called dreams the *royal road to the unconscious*. He believed that dream content includes many symbolic images that reveal the meaning of unconscious conflict. Another technique is *interpretation*. In psychoanalytic treatment, the analyst's silence encourages the patient's free association. The analyst offers interpretations about these associations to uncover the patient's resistance to treatment, to discuss the patient's transference feelings, or to confront the patient with inconsistencies. Interpretations may focus on present issues or draw connections between the patient's past and the present. The patient's dreams and fantasies are also sources of material for interpretation.

Freud's ideas were very controversial. His belief that much of human behaviour is controlled by unconscious, innate biological and sexual urges that exist from infancy outraged Viennese society. Freud believed that the first five years of life are very important, and events that occur during that time could even influence adult behaviour. He was one of the first theoreticians to highlight the role of environmental factors in abnormal behaviour, but he considered the early environment to consist almost exclusively of the person's mother and father. This belief sometimes led to detrimental and undeserved blaming of parents as the cause of abnormal behaviour. For Freud, the key therapeutic ingredient was the achievement of *insight*. Overcoming psychological difficulties meant understanding their causes and meaning. Unlike Breuer, Freud did not view hypnosis as necessary to achieve insight, but he did believe in the talking cure, a lengthy relationship between therapist and patient.

BEHAVIOURISM In 1904, Ivan Pavlov (1849–1936) received the Nobel Prize for his research on the physiology of dog digestion, which in turn led to his discovery of conditioned responses. A landmark moment for psychology was Pavlov's discovery of **classical conditioning**, in which an *unconditioned stimulus* (UCS) produces an *unconditioned response* (UCR). For example, you touch a hot stove (UCS) and immediately withdraw your hand (UCR). A *conditioned stimulus* (CS) is something neutral that does not naturally produce the UCR. In the classical conditioning paradigm, the UCS is repeatedly paired with a CS, resulting in the UCR. After sufficient pairings, the CS, presented alone, becomes capable of eliciting a *conditioned response* (CR), which is similar in form and content to the UCR. In Pavlov's paradigm, food powder was the UCS that produced salivation (UCR) in his dogs. Pavlov paired a neutral stimulus, a ringing bell (CS), with the food powder. After a sufficient number of pairings, the CS (the bell alone) produced salivation (CR). This paradigm seems simple, but it is both powerful and more complex than it first appears. We will return to the conditioning theory of emotional disorders later in the chapter.

Ivan Pavlov's pioneering experiments with dogs led him to discover classical conditioning, a process that underlies much normal and abnormal behaviour.

Bettmann/Corbis

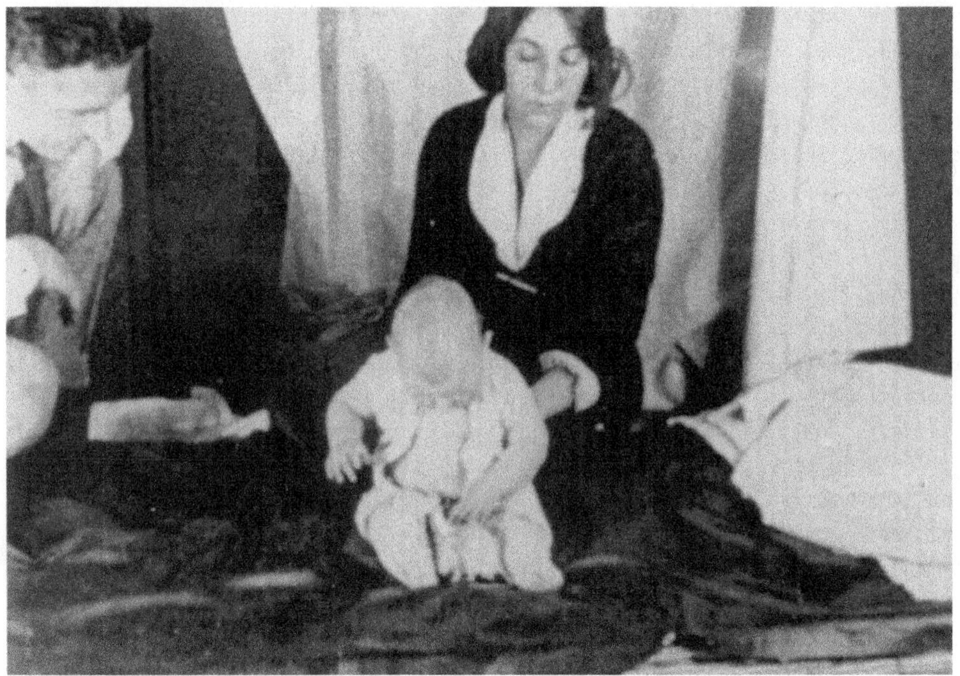

John Watson introduced behaviourism, which in its strictest form asserts that all behaviour is learned. With his student Rosalie Rayner, he studied infants' emotional responses, showing that emotions could be acquired by classical conditioning.

Archives of the History of American Psychology, The Center for the History of Psychology, The University of Akron

John B. Watson (1878–1958) believed that the only appropriate objects of scientific study were observable *behaviours*, not inner thoughts or feelings. This view, known as **behaviourism**, is based on principles that consider all behaviour (normal or abnormal) to be *learned* as a result of experiences or interactions with the environment. Watson and Rayner (1920) published the case of Little Albert, which demonstrated that emotional responses such as fear could be acquired through classical conditioning. In this case, Little Albert's fear of a white rat was established by pairing the white rat with a loud, aversive noise. In addition, not only was an extreme emotional response established, but it generalized to other objects that, like the rat, were white and furry (e.g., a rabbit, a Santa Claus beard).

Today, the case of Little Albert is only of historical interest because of the various methodological and other problems with the study (Digdon et al., 2014; Powell et al., 2014). Nevertheless, the case of Little Albert was a powerful impetus for behaviourism, leading to subsequent case studies and other, more rigorous, forms of research.

One of Watson's students, Mary Cover Jones, later used conditioning procedures to *extinguish* (eliminate) a fear of furry objects in a 2-year-old, Little Peter, who had been conditioned to fear these objects. Jones brought a rabbit into the room where Peter was playing. However, instead of trying to associate a neutral object with fear, she brought in other children who were not afraid of rabbits. When other children were in the room, Peter's fear of the rabbit seemed to decrease. Every time that Peter's fear lessened, she would bring the rabbit a little closer and wait for his fear to diminish again. Eventually, Peter was able to touch and play with the rabbit, which would suggest that he was no longer fearful. The findings of Pavlov, Watson, Rayner, and Jones were powerful demonstrations that behaviours (even abnormal behaviours) could be learned and unlearned using conditioning principles. This view of abnormal behaviour is very different from psychoanalytic theory. Yet, as we shall see, both theories continue to exert significant influence on our current views of abnormal behaviour.

Ethics and Responsibility

Watson and Rayner's (1920) study of Little Albert is considered a landmark study, for it changed the understanding of how abnormal behaviour could be acquired. However, this type of research could not be conducted today. Before beginning research with human participants, particularly children, scientists must submit their proposed research to a committee usually known as a Human Subjects Committee or Institutional Review Board (see Chapter 15). This committee reviews the research plan to make sure that the research will not harm the potential participants. Research studies designed to demonstrate that a scientist can create a psychological disorder in someone, particularly a child, would not be permitted today. Scientists must now be more creative in their research designs, and in many instances use less direct methods to examine how disorders might develop. Although less direct methods sometimes cannot produce the same data as Watson and Rayner produced, protecting research participants from harm is the most important consideration.

CONCEPT check

- Ancient theories held that spirits controlled aspects of human behaviour and that the biological seat of abnormal behaviour was the brain.
- We know from writings from the classical Greek and Roman period that many psychological disorders that exist today were also present then. Hippocrates proposed that abnormal behaviour resulted from an imbalance of bodily humors, indicating a biological cause. Other physicians, such as Galen and Avicenna, proposed that psychological factors also played a role.
- During medieval times, there was a return to theories of spirit possession, and charges of witchcraft were common. This was also the time when people with psychological disorders were locked up in institutional settings with little or no access to care.
- The nineteenth century marked the beginning of humane treatment advanced by leaders such as Pinel, Tuke, Rush, and Dix. During this time, Kraepelin also introduced a system for the classification of mental disorders, and Charcot introduced psychological treatments.

critical thinking question Central figures in abnormal psychology during the twentieth century were Freud, Pavlov, and Watson. How does Freud's theory of the development of abnormal behaviour differ from those of Pavlov and Watson?

Current Views of Abnormal Behaviour and Treatment

1.4 Discuss the scientist–practitioner model of abnormal psychology.

This journey through the history of theories and treatments of abnormal behaviour leads us to several conclusions. First, scientific advances lead to new and more sophisticated approaches to understanding human behaviour. Research findings allow unsupported theories to be discarded and provide new hypotheses to be tested and evaluated. This is the core of a scientific approach to abnormal behaviour. Scientists form hypotheses and conduct controlled experiments to determine whether their hypotheses are supported. If empirical evidence supports the hypotheses, then those theories continue. If the evidence does not provide support, the theory is discarded or changed, and the process begins again.

Second, scientific discoveries in areas other than psychology may later provide insight into abnormal behaviour. For example, the Human Genome Project, officially completed in 2003, sequenced the entire human genome, although analyses will continue for many years. As our understanding of this map develops, new techniques (see Chapter 2) allow us to examine genetic abnormalities that may be associated with specific psychological disorders, such as schizophrenia and autism spectrum disorder. Similarly, new technologies such as magnetic resonance imaging (see Chapter 2) lead us to examine the brain in ways never before possible. Although not developed to study abnormal behaviour, these technologies help us to identify brain areas that we now know are involved in specific emotions such as sadness or fear. These examples illustrate how, as science advances, newer insights replace older theories such as demonology. Furthermore, as scientifically advanced as our current theories appear, they too will be replaced as new discoveries emerge.

For the past 50 years, psychologists who study abnormal behaviour have been trained in the **scientist–practitioner model**, meaning that when providing treatment, psychologists rely on the findings of research. In turn, when conducting research, the psychologist investigates topics that help to guide and improve psychological care. Psychologists who use this perspective have a unique advantage because their scientific training allows them to differentiate fact from opinion when evaluating new theories, new treatments, and new research findings. This perspective also allows psychologists to apply research findings in many different areas to develop more comprehensive models of abnormal behaviour. Critically applying a scientific perspective to theories of etiology and examining the evidence behind proposed theories prevent us from adopting explanations that are without a firm scientific basis (such as witchcraft and demonology). "Treatments" based on such nonscientific ideas could have quite negative results and in some cases might even be deadly. As you read through this text, keep the scientist–practitioner model in mind.

For undergraduates, one of the most frustrating aspects of studying abnormal behaviour is that psychologists often cannot provide a simple explanation for why a behaviour occurs. What causes people to become so depressed that they commit suicide? Society often wants answers to these questions, but the answers are not simple. Unlike medical illness, abnormal behaviour cannot be explained by bacteria or viruses that infect the body. Clinical descriptions and research findings have identified many different, and sometimes conflicting, factors. The different findings have given rise to perspectives, known as *models*, which try to weave coherent explanations from the available clinical observations and research findings. These models consist of basic assumptions that provide a framework for organizing information and a set of procedures and tools that can be used to test aspects of that framework (Kuhn, 1962).

In this chapter, we introduce some of the different models that try to explain abnormal behaviour. You might wonder why so many different models exist. The answer is that abnormal behaviour is very complex, and no one model appears capable of providing a comprehensive explanation. Using a scientific approach, researchers develop, examine, and discard models as new facts emerge. Next we examine some of the currently accepted models of abnormal behaviour.

1.5 Describe the modern biological, psychological, sociocultural, and biopsychosocial perspectives on the origins of abnormal behaviour.

Biological Models

The biological model assumes that abnormal behaviour results from biological processes of the body, particularly the brain. Although long suspected to be the seat of abnormal behaviour, only in the last 20 or 30 years have scientific advances allowed us to observe brain mechanisms directly. One area of scientific breakthrough has been in our understanding of genetics. As already noted, genetic mapping is allowing us to begin to understand whether psychological disorders such as schizophrenia or manic-depressive disorder have a genetic basis, and if so, how that understanding might lead to better intervention and prevention efforts. Technology breakthroughs such as computerized axial tomography (CT) scans and magnetic resonance imaging (MRI) allow direct examination of brain structure and activity. With this direct observation, we now have a much greater understanding of the role of the brain in abnormal behaviour.

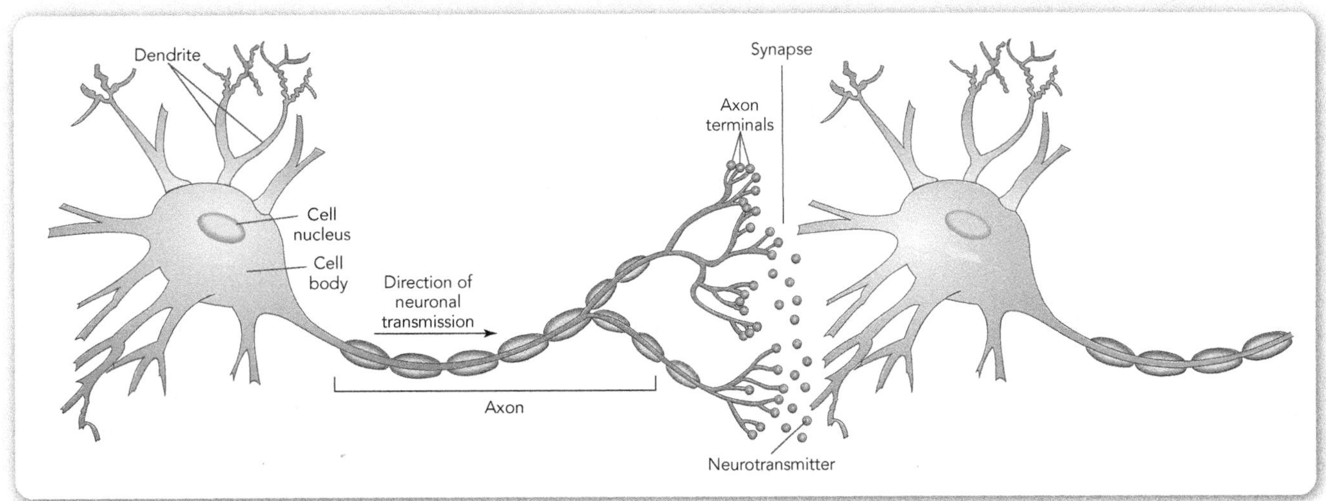

FIGURE 1.4

The Neuron Fires, Sending an Impulse to the Next Neuron. Each individual neuron transmits information that is vital for virtually every aspect of our functioning.

Although we often refer to the brain as if it were a single entity, it is a very complex organ. In fact, about 86 billion **neurons** (brain cells) make up the brain (Azevedo et al., 2009). Between the neurons are spaces known as **synapses**. Neurons (see Figure 1.4) communicate when **neurotransmitters** (chemical substances) are released into the synapse (i.e., the neuron fires) and land on a receptor site of the next neuron. That neuron then fires, sending an electrical impulse down the axon, releasing neurotransmitters into the next synapse, and so the process begins again. Neurotransmitter activity is the basis for brain activity (thinking, feeling, and motor activity) and is related to many physical and mental disorders. Until recently, the activity of neurotransmitters in the brain had to be assessed indirectly from their presence in other parts of the body (blood or spinal fluid). However, it was always unclear how accurately chemicals in blood or spinal fluid really reflected neurotransmitter activity in the brain. Through advances in **neuroscience**, we now rely less on assumptions and indirect measures to understand the structure and function of the nervous system and its interaction with behaviour. We can now directly observe many aspects of the brain's functioning, just as we do external behaviour.

Imaging tests such as the CT scan and MRI examine the *morphology* (structure) of the brain and are used to determine whether parts of the brain are structurally different in those with and without psychological disorders. For example, the brains of patients with Alzheimer's disease have two structural abnormalities, *plaques* and *tangles*, which exist in greater number than among older people without Alzheimer's disease (see Chapter 13). For other psychological disorders, the evidence is less definitive. In some disorders, such as posttraumatic stress disorder (PTSD, an anxiety disorder that occurs after a traumatic event), changes in the brain may be the result of, not the cause of, the disorder (Bellis, 2004). In other words, years of living with the disorder cause changes in the brain, a process sometimes known as **biological scarring**. In other instances, when compared to people with no disorder, the brains of people with schizophrenia show structural brain abnormalities that could have occurred before birth (see Chapter 10). Although we do not know for certain how these structural abnormalities may influence behaviour, they illustrate how our understanding of the brain and abnormal behaviour has changed as a result of new technologies.

Although some abnormal behaviours may be related to structural abnormalities, studies of brain *functioning* appear to be a more promising avenue of research. Advanced neuroimaging techniques such as positron emission tomography (PET) and functional magnetic resonance imaging (fMRI); (see Chapter 2) allow for mapping various areas of the brain and identifying brain areas that might be associated with various disorders.

Differences in brain functioning between patients and controls have been reported for adults with schizophrenia and depression (A. J. Holmes et al., 2005; Milak et al., 2005), adults and children with anxiety disorders (Baxter et al., 1992; Bellis, 2004), eating disorders (van Kuyck et al., 2009), and many other psychiatric disorders. These studies are numerous and will be reviewed throughout this text.

Although neuroscience data provide exciting new avenues for further research, it is still too soon to conclude that brain abnormalities cause psychological disorders. First, not all studies that compare people with and without a disorder find differences in brain structure or function. Furthermore, even when differences are detected, the abnormalities are not always found in a second trial, meaning that the abnormalities are not consistent. Second, to date, when differences exist, they are sometimes found in several different disorders. This means that whatever difference exists probably does not *cause* a specific disorder. Just like a fever that may be associated with many different physical illnesses, abnormal brain functioning may indicate that *something* is wrong, but not specifically what is wrong. Third, in most instances, few data indicate that these structural or functional abnormalities existed *before* the disorder occurred (schizophrenia and autism may be exceptions). It is just as likely that some disorders, such as PTSD, may cause changes in brain functioning, if not necessarily brain structure. Over the next decade, continued research in these areas, coupled with the development of even more sophisticated assessment devices and strategies, may help clarify some of these issues.

The inheritance of physical traits, such as hair colour, eye colour, height, and even predispositions to some diseases (e.g., breast cancer, type I diabetes), is well established. It is perhaps less well known that some behavioural traits, both healthy ones and those that deviate from normal, are heritable. The field of **behavioural genetics** emerged with works by Sir Francis Galton (1822–1911) and his 1869 publication, *Hereditary Genius*. Since that time, behavioural genetics has explored the role of both genes and environment in the transmission of behavioural traits. Models of genetics research are presented in Chapter 2, and specific genetic findings for the various psychological disorders will be presented in other chapters.

Severe behavioural disorders, such as autism in children and schizophrenia in adults, have continued to defy simple explanations of biological or environmental etiology. Based on animal models that have found links between early viral infections and later behavioural changes, some researchers have proposed a **viral infection theory**. Specifically, during the prenatal period or shortly after birth, viral infections might cause brain abnormalities that later lead to behavioural abnormalities (see Chapters 10 and 12). However, we cannot yet say that this is a definitive cause, for the results of one study sometimes directly contradict those of another. Such contradictory findings are not unusual for psychology or any other science. As research continues, disparate findings are either reconciled or the theory is revised or discarded.

Even if future research confirms a relationship between viral infection and the onset of psychological disorders, several different pathways may produce this relationship. First, the virus may act *directly* by infecting the central nervous system (CNS). Similarly, infection elsewhere in the body could trigger the onset of a CNS disease. Second, viruses may act *indirectly* by changing the immune system of the mother or the fetus, thereby making one or both more susceptible to other biological or environmental factors. Third, both mechanisms may be involved (Libbey et al., 2005). Although some animal models suggest a possible relation between certain viruses and changes in the brain, evidence that the virus *triggers* the onset of a disorder has proved elusive. The etiology of most psychological disorders is likely to be complex—not traceable to a single genetic, biological, or environmental factor. Other variables, yet to be discovered, may be responsible for triggering or modifying the course of illness.

Psychological Models

The biological model seeks the causes of abnormal behaviour in the workings of the brain or body. In contrast, psychological approaches emphasize how environmental factors, such as family and cultural factors, may influence the development and maintenance of abnormal behaviour. In actuality, parental influence may be biological or psychological. Parents pass on their genes, but their influence is much broader. Parents can affect their children's behaviour in at least four ways: through direct interaction, their responses to a child's behaviour, modelling certain behaviours, or merely giving instructions. Of course, a child's environment extends far beyond parents or even immediate family. The impact of other environmental factors, such as SES, was illustrated earlier in the chapter. To provide another example, environmental events such as separation from biological parents increase the likelihood of depression in adolescents (Cuffe et al., 2005). Furthermore, in some cases, environmental and cultural influences may produce behaviour that is considered abnormal in one culture but not in another, as in the earlier case of Maleah, in which intergenerational bed sharing was a commonly accepted practice in the Philippines. Cultural influences such as these are addressed subsequently (see "Sociocultural Models").

MODERN PSYCHOANALYTIC MODELS Modern psychoanalysts no longer discuss the id or fixation at the phallic stage. They do, however, still agree that much of mental life is unconscious and that personality patterns begin to form in childhood. They propose that mental representations (views) of the self and others guide our interactions and may lead to psychological symptoms. Finally, they believe that personality development involves not only learning to regulate sexual and aggressive feelings, but also having mature interpersonal relationships with others (Westen, 1998).

Freud's ideas have influenced a number of other theorists. Initially, he named Carl Gustav Jung (1875–1961) as his successor. However, they disagreed over several key theoretical components, and Jung broke away to develop *analytic therapy*. Unlike Freud, Jung believed that behavioural motivators are psychological and spiritual (not sexual), and that future goals rather than past events motivate behaviour. Another former colleague, Alfred Adler (1870–1937), also broke with Freud to develop his own psychoanalytic school called *individual psychology*. Less comprehensive than Freud, Adler introduced several concepts that are part of everyday language and are associated with abnormal behaviour: *sibling rivalry*, the importance of *birth order*, and the *inferiority complex*, by which real or perceived inferiority leads to efforts to compensate for the deficiency.

More contemporary models of psychoanalysis, such as **ego psychology**, deviate from Freud by their increased focus on conscious motivations and healthy forms of human functioning. *Object relations theory*, for example, addresses people's emotional relations with important *objects* (in this sense, people or things to which the person is attached). This theory emphasizes that people have a basic drive for social interactions and that motivations for social contact are more than simply to satisfy sexual and aggressive instincts. Therapy uses the patient's relationship with the therapist to examine and build other relationships in their lives.

BEHAVIOURAL MODELS Unlike the psychodynamic perspective, where internal mental elements exert an influence on behaviour, learning theory stresses the importance of external events in the onset of abnormal behaviours. According to learning theory, *behaviour* is the product of an individual's learning history. Abnormal behaviour is therefore the result of maladaptive learning experiences. Behavioural theories do not ignore biological factors; instead, they acknowledge that biology interacts with the environment to influence behaviour. Strict behaviourists focus on observable and measurable behaviour and do not examine inner psychic causes. They believe that abnormal behaviour results from environmental events that shape future behaviour, such as the conditioning events that led to Little Albert's fear. In contrast to psychoanalytic theory's emphasis on the first five years of life, according to behavioural theory, significant experiences can occur at any point in life.

Despite the pioneering work of Pavlov, Watson, Rayner, and Jones, behaviour therapy remained in its infancy until the 1950s. Then a South African psychiatrist, Joseph Wolpe (1915–1997), dissatisfied with psychoanalysis, began to study experimental *neurosis* (anxiety) in animals. Using a classical conditioning paradigm, a dog learned that food followed the presentation of a circle but not an ellipse. Then Wolpe altered the shape of the circle and the ellipse so that *discrimination* (and therefore, the signal for food) became increasingly difficult (is it a circle? is it an ellipse?). The dog struggled, became agitated, barked violently, and attacked the equipment, behaviours that would indicate the presence of negative emotions. Once Wolpe demonstrated how classical conditioning principles could account for the development of anxiety, he applied the same principles to eliminate fear. In his landmark book *Psychotherapy by Reciprocal Inhibition* (Wolpe, 1958), he proposed that a stimulus will not elicit anxiety if an *incompatible behaviour* (such as feeling relaxed) occurs at the same time. In other words, it is not possible to feel anxious and relaxed (or anxious and happy) at the same time; they are incompatible emotions. As mentioned earlier, Mary Cover Jones treated Peter by selecting a situation that she thought would promote relaxation (other children playing in the room). In contrast, Wolpe specifically taught his patient how to relax. Then he deliberately paired relaxation (the incompatible response) with the fear-producing event. With repeated pairings, he eliminated anxiety.

Just as Jones began treatment of Little Peter by placing the rabbit at the opposite corner of the room and then moving it progressively closer, Wolpe used a *hierarchy*, in which elements of the anxiety-producing object are presented in a gradual fashion. For someone who fears flying, the hierarchy might include going to the airport, sitting in the boarding area, getting on the plane, taking off, and so on. Relaxation is paired with each step in the hierarchy. This therapy, called *systematic desensitization*, is very effective for a range of anxiety problems. Although used less frequently today than 30 to 40 years ago, systematic desensitization still forms the foundation for many current behaviour therapy procedures.

"The more often I tell him to sit down, the more he stands up." This line, which could have been spoken by Derek's Grade 2 teacher, illustrates the powerful effect of attention. Sometimes yelling at a child for bad behaviour actually increases it. To understand why, it is necessary to first understand the work of B. F. Skinner (1904–1990). He observed that many behaviours occur without *first* being elicited by a UCS. Using animal models, Skinner demonstrated that behaviour could be acquired or changed by the events that happened *afterward*. Known as **operant conditioning**, these principles are relevant to the behaviours of individuals, groups, and entire societies.

B. F. Skinner explained how behaviours could be acquired or changed by reinforcement, a process called *operant conditioning*.

Joe Wrinn/The LIFE Images Collection/Getty Images

The basic principle behind operant theory is **reinforcement**, which is defined as a contingent event that strengthens the behaviour that precedes it. In its simplest form, a reinforcer may be considered to be a reward—a child does household chores and the reward is a weekly allowance. If the allowance is contingent upon (occurs only after) the completion of the chores, it is likely that the child will do chores again. The allowance is a *reinforcer* because it functions to increase behaviour. Skinner identified several principles of reinforcement. First, reinforcers are always individual: What is a reinforcer for one person is not necessarily a reinforcer for another person (e.g., chocolate is not a reinforcer for everyone). Second, there are primary and secondary reinforcers. *Primary reinforcers* are objects such as food, water, or even attention. They have their own intrinsic value (i.e., they satisfy basic needs of life or make one feel good). *Secondary reinforcers* are objects that have acquired value because they become associated with primary reinforcers. Money is a secondary reinforcer because it symbolizes the ability to acquire other reinforcers (e.g., heat in cold weather, a cold drink when thirsty). Much of Skinner's work was devoted to *schedules of reinforcement*, which establish the "when" and "how" of reinforcement and set forth conditions under which behaviour is more likely to be acquired or less likely to be extinguished. Skinner's work has applications for parenting, education, psychology, and many other aspects of behaviour. How does this work apply to Derek? For children, adult attention is a powerful reinforcer. If every time Derek stands up, the teacher calls out his name (gives him attention) and asks him to sit down (or even worse, calls him aside and spends time asking him why he keeps standing up), this positive attention could be reinforcing, increasing the likelihood that when Derek wants attention, he will stand up again.

Whereas reinforcement serves to increase the frequency of a behaviour, **punishment** has the opposite effect: It decreases or eliminates a behaviour. Punishment can be the application of something painful (spanking) or the removal of something positive (no television). Sometimes punishment is necessary to quickly eliminate a very dangerous behaviour, for example, a child with severe intellectual disabilities engages in self-mutilating behaviours. The withdrawal of something positive, such as in a *time-out* (having a child sit in a corner for a few minutes), is often effective for behaviours such as tantrums. Skinner advocated the use of reinforcement rather than punishment. Punishment suppresses a behaviour, but if an alternative, substitute behaviour is not acquired, the punished behaviour re-emerges. Therefore, when punishment is used to suppress a behaviour, reinforcement of an alternative, positive behaviour must also occur.

How do dolphins in captivity learn to leap into the air, spin around three times, and then slide on a ramp to receive the applause of a human audience? The trainers use a procedure called *shaping*, a process whereby closer steps, or successive approximations, to a final goal are rewarded. Dolphin trainers begin by reinforcing (with food) any initial attempt or slight movement that resembles a turn. Gradually, the trainer requires a larger turn before providing reinforcement, until finally the dolphin must completely spin around before receiving reinforcement. Shaping is an effective procedure for the acquisition of new behaviours in children and adults and will be discussed in several other chapters in this text.

A third type of learning was described by Albert Bandura (1925–) in the early 1960s. **Vicarious conditioning** is characterized by *no trial learning*—the person need not actually do the behaviour in order to learn it. Learning occurs when the person watches a model; that is, someone who demonstrates a behaviour. Observation of another person can have a disinhibiting or inhibiting effect on current behaviours or can teach new behaviours. This kind of *social learning* can explain the acquisition of abnormal behaviours such as aggression.

Behaviour therapists focus therapy on the elimination of abnormal behaviours and on the acquisition of new behaviours and skills. Treatment targets the patient's current symptoms. Although the past is considered important in understanding the present and the patient's current psychological distress, behaviour therapy does not focus specifically

Children often learn behaviours by watching a model perform them, a process called *vicarious conditioning.*

The Asahi Shimbun/Getty Images

on the early years of life. Furthermore, achieving insight is not considered sufficient to produce behaviour change. Rather, behaviour therapists focus directly on helping patients change their behaviour in order to alleviate their psychological problems.

THE COGNITIVE MODEL The cognitive model proposes that abnormal behaviour is a result of distorted cognitive (mental) processes, not internal forces or external events. According to cognitive theory, situations and events do not affect our emotions and behaviour; rather, the way we perceive or think about those events does. Imagine that you fail the first test in your Abnormal Psychology class. If you think to yourself, "Well, that was a hard test, but now I know what the instructor wants and I'll do better the next time," you are likely to feel okay about yourself and study harder for the next test. However, if instead you think, "I'm an idiot—why did I ever think I could be a psychologist?" you may feel sad and lose your enthusiasm for the class. You may even decide that you should drop out. In each case, the situation was the same. It was what you thought about the situation, and yourself, that affected your mood and your future behaviour. That is the core of cognitive theory. According to Aaron Beck (1921–), one of the primary originators of cognitive therapy, people with depression have three types of negative thoughts: a negative view of the self, the world, and the future. Beck called this the negative cognitive triad. These negative assumptions are often called *cognitive distortions*. People may have many different types of distorted cognitive processes that affect their mood and behaviour (see Table 1.2).

TABLE 1.2
Common Cognitive Distortions

Type	Example
All-or-nothing thinking	If I don't go to a leading university, I'll be a bum.
Overgeneralizing	Everything I do is wrong.
Mental filtering	The instructor said the paper was good, but he criticized my example on page 6. He really hated the paper.
Disqualifying the positive	Sure, I got an A but that was pure luck. I'm not that smart.
Jumping to conclusions	The bank teller barely looked at me. She really hates me.
Magnifying	I mispronounced that word in my speech. I really screwed up.
Minimizing	I can dance well but that's not really important—being smart is what's important, and I'm not smart.
Catastrophizing	I failed this quiz. I'll never graduate from university.
Reasoning emotionally	I feel hopeless, so this situation must be hopeless.
Making "should" statements	I should get an A in this class even though it is really hard.
Mislabelling	I failed this quiz. I'm a complete and total idiot.
Personalizing	We didn't get that big account at work. It's all my fault.

Source: Based on Burns, D. D. (1989). *The feeling good handbook.* New York, NY: William Morrow and Company.

To change abnormal behaviours, cognitive therapy is directed at modifying the distorted thought processes. Therapists assign behavioural experiments in which the patient engages in a certain activity and then examines the thoughts that accompany the activity. With therapist assistance, the patient learns to challenge negative thoughts, to assess the situation more realistically, and to generate alternative, more positive, thoughts. Cognitive therapy and behaviour therapy share many similarities, but there are some differences. First, cognitive therapy is based on the assumption that internal cognitive processes must be the target of therapy, whereas behaviour therapy assumes that changing behaviour will lead to a change in cognitions. Second, cognitive therapy relies more on the use of traditional talk psychotherapy and insight than does traditional behaviour therapy. Despite some theoretical differences, comparisons of behaviour therapy and cognitive therapy suggest that they are equally effective treatments for most psychological disorders. In many cases, treatment procedures originally developed under one model or the other are now used together, thus the term *cognitive–behaviour therapy*.

THE HUMANISTIC MODEL Based on **phenomenology**, a school of thought that holds that a person's subjective perception of the world is more important than the actual world, humanists believe that people are basically good and are motivated to *self-actualize* (develop their full potential). Abnormal behaviours occur when there is a failure in the process of self-actualization, usually as a result of people's failure to recognize their weaknesses and establish processes and strategies to fulfill their potential for positive growth.

The psychologist most closely associated with humanistic psychology is Carl Rogers (1902–1987). His theory of abnormal behaviour begins with the assumption that psychopathology is associated with psychological incongruence, or a discrepancy between one's self-image and one's actual self. The greater the discrepancy, the more emotional and real-world problems the person experiences. Incongruence results from the experience of *conditional* positive regard—a person is treated with respect and caring only when meeting the standards set by others (i.e., conditionally). The person comes to believe that he or she is worthy only when meeting those standards. Because this is an inaccurate, overly-demanding image, emotional or behavioural problems result.

The goal of Rogers's psychotherapy, called *client-centred therapy*, is to release the individual's existing capacity to self-actualize (reach full potential) through interactions with the therapist. Therapy is based on three components. *Genuineness* means that the therapist relates to the person in an open, honest way and does not hide behind a professional mask. *Empathic understanding* means that the therapist understands the client's world as the client sees it. Finally, the therapist expresses *unconditional positive regard* by genuinely accepting the client with full understanding, trusting the client's resources for self-understanding and positive change. Whereas psychoanalytic therapy focuses on understanding the patient's past experiences, client-centred therapy focuses on present experiences, believing that the reestablishment of awareness and trust in that experience will lead to positive change.

Sociocultural Models

All of the models of abnormal behaviour discussed so far begin with the assumption that abnormality lies within the individual. Instead, **sociocultural models** propose that abnormal behaviour must be understood within the context of social and cultural forces, such as gender roles, social class, interpersonal resources, and ethnicity. From this perspective, abnormal behaviour does not simply result from biological or psychological factors, but also reflects the social and cultural environment in which a person lives. Many social and cultural forces may influence behaviour; we discuss only a few here.

One well-studied social factor is *gender role*, defined as the cultural expectations regarding accepted behaviours for men and women, boys and girls. These differing role

Gender role expectations affect behaviour. In Western cultures, showing emotion openly is more acceptable among females than among males.

Allan Tannenbaum/The Image Works

expectancies often exert a powerful influence on the expression of abnormal behaviour. Consider the fact that girls (and women) are much more likely than boys (or men) to admit to having a phobia. Could gender role expectations, rather than biology, explain this difference? In Western cultures, girls are allowed to express emotions openly, whereas society discourages such behaviour among boys—consider the phrases "boys don't cry" or "take it like a man." The implication is that showing emotion is not appropriate behaviour for males and therefore not accepted in Western society. So boys learn to hide or deny emotions, such as fear. Other disorders possibly influenced by gender role are eating disorders, which are more common in girls and may be triggered in some cases by pervasive sociocultural pressures on females to be thin (see Chapter 7).

In addition to gender role, other social factors such as hunger, work, and domestic violence may make women more vulnerable to psychological distress (Lopez & Guarnaccia, 2000). More than 60% of women in developing countries do not have adequate food. In both developed and developing countries, women do not receive equal pay even when they are performing dangerous, labour-intensive jobs, and they are more likely to be victims of domestic violence. These factors, perhaps in combination with others, are perceived to play a significant role in the development of psychological disorders, perhaps placing women at higher risk—not because of their biology, but because of the social context in which they live.

SES is another social factor that may affect the development of psychological disorders. People with low income, compared to those with high income, have fewer resources to cope with stressful life events such as natural disasters. If the home of a lower income family is washed away by a flood, then they may become homeless and thereby experience great psychological distress. In comparison, a higher income family will have greater financial resources to cope with the loss of a home.

Interpersonal support is an important social factor that helps people during times of emotional distress. The lack of such support can be highly stressful. To illustrate, a 2011 spring flood in Manitoba caused about 2000 First Nations people to be displaced from their homes and community. The evacuees had to move to hotel and rental accommodations around urban Winnipeg. As a result, children missed school (and school friends), and residents became disconnected from each other and their traditional ways (www.ctvnews.ca/canada/manitoba-flood-evacuees-adjusting-poorly-to-urban-life-red-cross-study-1.1591379, accessed March 6, 2015).

Cultural factors may affect symptom expression and diagnosis. With respect to symptom expression, several different variables are important. First, behaviours that are considered abnormal in one culture may be considered normal in other cultures. In Puerto Rico, *dissociation* (a feeling of being detached from one's body—sometimes called an *out-of-body experience*) is considered a normal part of spiritual and religious experiences, but it would be regarded as abnormal in other Western cultures (Lewis-Fernandez, 1998; Tsai et al., 2001). Similarly, behaviours that suggest extreme suspiciousness and mistrust of others may justifiably be labelled paranoia in some patients. Among other cultures and groups, however, suspiciousness may simply be an adaptive response from people who have been marginalized because of sociodemographic factors or who have been the victims of stereotype or racial discrimination (Whaley, 1998).

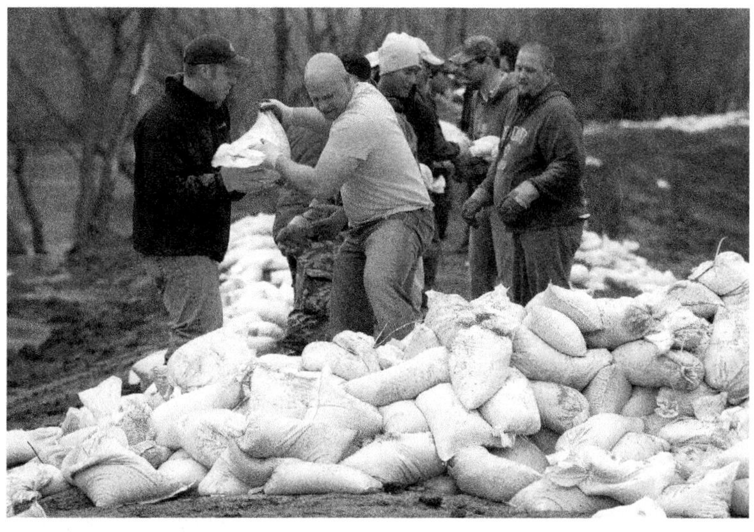

Although natural disasters such as floods and hurricanes may affect many people, the impact can be lessened when people pull together to help one another, thereby creating a social network.

John Woods/The Canadian Press

Researchers with a sociocultural perspective examine how psychological disorders may express themselves differently in different cultures. Certain conditions that are specific to a culture are known as *culture-bound syndromes* (Lopez & Guarnaccia, 2007; Miranda & Fraser, 2002). One such disorder, *koro*, occurs among people of South and East Asia and consists of intense anxiety that the penis (or vulva and nipples in women) will disappear or cause one's death (APA, 2013).

As researchers gain a better understanding of the important roles that social and cultural factors play in the onset, expression, and treatment of psychological disorders, they are developing culturally sensitive treatments for many different disorders. These treatment approaches incorporate cultural values and expressions that may enhance the therapeutic process by increasing the number of people who seek, and benefit from, these enhanced interventions.

The Biopsychosocial Model

In this chapter, we examined biological, psychological, social, and cultural factors that affect the development and expression of abnormal behaviours. One reason there are so many different models is that no one perspective is able to explain all aspects of behaviour, and certainly not all cases of abnormal behaviour.

Current approaches to physical medicine assume that all illnesses are based on biological processes that can be reduced to a biological cause, even if the specific physical process has not yet been determined. For example, we know that cancer occurs when abnormal cells develop and attack the body's systems, even though we do not know yet what physical processes caused these cells to develop. In contrast, in the case of mental disorders, there is no single model of abnormal behaviour, although scientists have searched for such single explanations since the days of Hippocrates (Lake, 2007). Instead, there are many different models, and often the training backgrounds of mental health professionals result in different perspectives being emphasized.

Modern scientists now recognize that (a) abnormal behaviour is complex, (b) abnormal behaviour cannot be understood using a single theoretical explanation, and (c) understanding abnormal behaviour will advance only if we embrace and integrate the various conceptual models (Kendler, 2005). A significant challenge to understanding abnormal behaviour is to understand how the mind and the brain interact and how to combine these very different perspectives to create a coherent theory of psychological disorders. In fact, modern scientists have moved past trying to reduce all behaviour to one singular explanation. It is clear that causality can begin in the brain *or* the mind and can set off a chain of events that ultimately also affects the other component, leading to the onset of abnormal behaviour (Kendler, 2005). Other researchers (Lake, 2007) have argued that

FIGURE 1.5

The Diathesis-Stress Model. In this model, a diathesis, or vulnerability, interacts with individual stressors to produce a psychological disorder. The biopsychosocial model uses the concept of diathesis-stress to acknowledge that many different factors (biological, psychological, and social) may contribute to the development of a disorder.

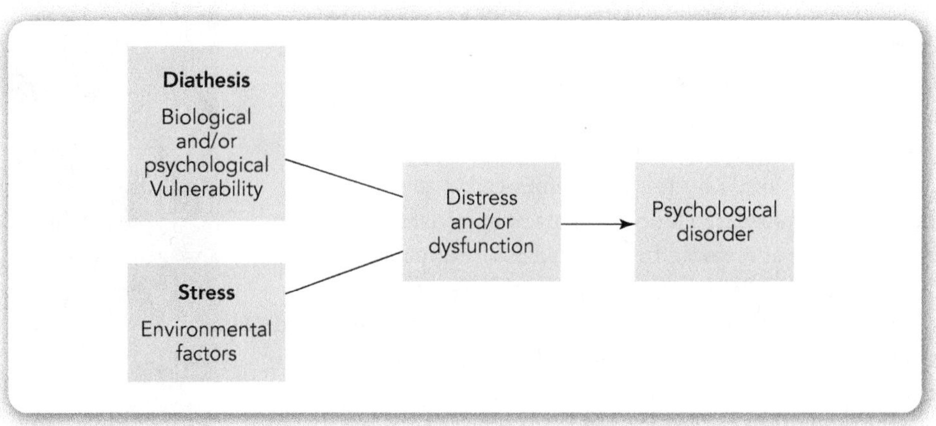

integrating the perspectives of biomedicine, human consciousness, and neuroscience will lead to significant advances in understanding and treating psychological disorders.

Currently, most mental health clinicians subscribe to a **biopsychosocial perspective**, which acknowledges that many different factors probably contribute to the development of abnormal behaviour and that different factors may be important for different people. This perspective uses a **diathesis-stress model of abnormal behaviour**, which begins with the assumption that psychological disorders may have a biological basis (see Figure 1.5). The presence of a biological or psychological predisposition to a disease or disorder is called a *diathesis*. However, just having a *predisposition* for a disorder does not mean that a person will actually *develop* it. Rather, the predisposition is assumed to lie dormant (as if it does not exist) until stressful environmental factors create significant distress for the individual. People react differently to stressful events. The combination of a biological or psychological predisposition and the presence of environmental stress create psychological disorders. The diathesis-stress model integrates biological, psychological, and sociocultural systems to provide explanations that are consistent with what we know are complex human behaviours. We will return to this biopsychosocial model and the diathesis-stress model many times throughout this text.

CONCEPT check

- The biological model of abnormal behaviour assumes that abnormal behaviour is rooted in a person's biology. The basis may be a genetic abnormality, abnormal brain structures, or abnormal brain functioning.
- Within the psychological model are several distinctive approaches, including modern psychoanalytic, behavioural, and cognitive models. Rather than looking to biology as the basis for psychological disorders, these models assume that environmental events and the way we interpret and react to them play a causal role in the onset of abnormal behaviour.
- Sociocultural models are based on a broader perspective, proposing that broad social and cultural forces (not individual or unique environmental events) contribute to the onset of psychological disorders.
- The biopsychosocial perspective incorporates a diathesis-stress model, in which biology is thought to lay the foundation for the onset of the disorder through the presence of biological abnormalities. However, biology alone is insufficient; environmental, social, and cultural factors are always part of the equation that leads to the onset of psychological disorders.

critical thinking question Using a biopsychosocial perspective, what factors might influence the development of a psychological disorder in a member of the Canadian armed forces who served in Operation IMPACT in Iraq?

real **SCIENCE** real **LIFE**

Marcie—How One Disorder Might Have Been Understood and Treated Throughout the Ages

Feelings of depression have been documented since the beginning of recorded history, and depression is a common psychological disorder.

THE PATIENT

Marcie just started university. She grew up in a small town but enrolled in a major university far from home. Her family has few financial resources, and the university scholarship was her only opportunity for a university education. She was reluctant to leave home, but her family and teachers encouraged her because it was a tremendous opportunity. When Marcie was a child, she went to camp one summer and was very homesick for an entire week. Now Marcie is having those same feelings again as she tries to adjust to university life in a new town. She is very sad, cries for no reason, and has stopped attending classes. She believes that she is a failure for being unable to adjust and is afraid to tell her parents how she feels. She barely talks to her roommate, who is very concerned about the change in her behaviour. Marcie no longer takes a shower, sometimes does not get out of bed, and will go for several days without eating. She talks about being "better off dead."

Depression can be conceptualized from various perspectives, each of which would provide a unique approach toward treatment. If we were to convene a panel of experts to discuss various approaches to Marcie's treatment, we might hear the following perspectives:

THE TREATMENT

Hippocrates (380 BCE)

"It is obvious that the patient is suffering from an excess of black bile, which causes feelings of melancholia. To restore the humors to a balanced state, she needs to eat a vegetable diet and engage in physical activity. She also needs a tranquil existence."

Roman Catholic Priest (1596)

"Her symptoms are a direct result of possession by a demon with whom she has engaged in illicit relations. Her failure to follow the rules of authority (i.e., go to class) and her wish to die are sinful acts and clearly indicate that she is in league with the devil. She may even be a witch."

Philippe Pinel, M.D. (1800)

"Mental illness is curable if we take the time to understand it. Marcie must be taken away from the environment that caused this problem and placed in the hospital, where she will be assigned to work in the garden. This physical activity will allow her to rest in the evening, and her spirit will be restored."

Sigmund Freud, M.D. (1920)

"Although on one level, Marcie is grateful for the opportunity to study at the university, on a deeper, more unconscious level, she may feel anger and resentment toward her parents for not having the resources to allow her to study at a more prestigious school that was closer to home. This anger is particularly scary because her mother is suffering from breast cancer. Her superego, whose job it is to keep these unacceptable emotions in check, turned the anger she felt toward her parents back onto herself, resulting in depression, which, especially because of her mother's condition, is a more socially acceptable emotion."

B. F. Skinner, Ph.D. (1965)

"Marcie has learned depressive behaviours through a series of reinforcing experiences. She probably receives significant attention from her family every time that she calls home and tells them she is homesick. She may feel sad, but the way to change emotion is to change behaviour and the contingencies that control it. I suggest that all those who interact with her provide positive reinforcement for 'nondepressive' behaviours (e.g., engaging in social activities, completing assignments) and extinguish, or ignore, depressive behaviours (e.g., not going to class, staying in her dorm room)."

Cognitive Psychologist, Ph.D. (2005)

"Marcie's depression is the result of her negative perspective regarding herself and the world. Many university students have trouble adjusting to new environments. However, Marcie's cognitive schema has falsely interpreted this adjustment difficulty as a sign of personal weakness and failure. In therapy, we will examine these dysfunctional beliefs and help Marcie develop a more positive, functional perspective."

Biological Psychiatrist, M.D. (2006)

"This patient meets diagnostic criteria for major depressive disorder, single episode. She has no history of mania. Her family history is positive for depression (mother, maternal aunt, possibly grandmother), and her paternal grandfather committed suicide. Because her mother had a positive response to a selective serotonin reuptake inhibitor, I recommend a course of fluoxetine (Prozac) 20 mg/day as an initial dose."

(continued)

Biopsychosocial Psychologist (2016)

"Marcie's depression clearly shows how numerous factors combine to create her distress. Her family history indicates the presence of a genetic predisposition, leaving her vulnerable to the development of depression. However, she did not have any difficulties until she went to university, and the stress from (a) moving far away from home for the first time and (b) needing to keep her grades high so that she could maintain her scholarship are most likely environmental and social factors that triggered the actual onset of the negative mood. Medication may be useful in the short term, but Marcie needs to learn how to cope with stress so that she has the tools to counteract her biological predisposition and prevent future episodes because she will face stressors throughout her lifetime."

Summary

abnormal psychology

historical and modern perspectives

1.1 Explain the difference between behaviours that are different, deviant, dangerous, and dysfunctional.

Abnormal behaviour is sometimes difficult to define. It is not just behaviour that is different, because certain differences can sometimes be positive for the individual and perhaps for society. Behaviour that is deviant may be different but not necessarily abnormal. New trends often start as deviant but then become accepted by mainstream society. Dangerous behaviour may be abnormal, but many individuals who have psychological disorders do not engage in dangerous behaviour. Dangerous behaviour is not necessary or sufficient to meet the definition of abnormal behaviour. Two primary considerations for determining whether a behaviour is abnormal is whether it creates dysfunction (interferes with daily activities) or emotional distress.

1.2 Identify two factors that need to be considered when determining whether a behaviour is abnormal.

Abnormal behaviour is defined as behaviour that is inconsistent with the individual's developmental, cultural, and societal norms, and creates significant emotional distress or interferes with daily functioning. Behaviour must always be considered in context. Context includes culture as defined by both individual and social spheres of influence, as well as cultural traditions. It also includes consideration of developmental age, physical and emotional maturity, and SES.

1.3 Discuss spiritual/religious, biological, psychological, and sociocultural theories of the origins of abnormal behaviour in their historical context.

Historically, spirit possession was among the first proposed causes of abnormal behaviour. However, as early as the classical Greek and Roman periods, biological and environmental explanations were given for some of the major psychiatric disorders (depression, schizophrenia). Such theories fell out of favour in Western Europe shortly afterward, although they continued to flourish in the Middle East. It was not until the Renaissance period that theories based on biology and environmental factors re-emerged in Europe.

1.4 Discuss the scientist–practitioner model of abnormal psychology.

To understand abnormal behaviour, adopting a scientist–practitioner approach is a distinct advantage. Critically applying a scientific perspective to theories of etiology and examining the evidence behind proposed theories prevent adhering to explanations that are without a firm scientific basis (such as witchcraft). "Treatments" based on such ideas could have quite negative results and, in some cases, might even be deadly.

1.5 Describe the modern biological, psychological, sociocultural, and biopsychosocial perspectives on the origins of abnormal behaviour.

Today, biological, psychological, sociocultural, and biopsychosocial explanations dominate the explanations for the development of abnormal behaviour. Each of the etiological theories has strengths and weaknesses, and each alone is inadequate to fully explain the presence of abnormal behaviour. Determining abnormal behaviour is complex, and it is likely that a combination of factors is responsible for any specific psychological disorder. There are many competing theories, and as science progresses, new theories will be developed and others will be discarded.

Key Terms

abnormal behaviour 8
animal magnetism 17
behavioural genetics 26
behaviourism 22
biological scarring 25
biopsychosocial perspective 34
classical conditioning 21
culture 5
culture-bound syndrome 5
dementia praecox 18
developmental trajectory 11
diathesis-stress model of abnormal behaviour 34
dimensional approach 9
ego psychology 27
emotional contagion 14
goodness of fit 4
mass hysteria 14
neuron 25
neuroscience 25
neurotransmitter 25
operant conditioning 28
phenomenology 31
placebo effect 17
psychoanalysis 19
punishment 29
reinforcement 28
schizophrenia 18
scientist–practitioner model 24
sociocultural model 31
synapse 25
talking cure 18
trephination 12
vicarious conditioning 29
viral infection theory 26

TEST yourself

1. Abnormal behaviour must always be considered in context because
a. normal feelings, such as grief, can be mistaken for illness
b. a person's cultural background may affect behaviour
c. a person's age may affect his or her symptoms
d. all of the above

2. To be considered abnormal, a person's behaviour must be "away from normal" and
a. a violation of the individual's culture
b. a cause of emotional distress and/or functional impairment
c. a source of conflict with a person's peer group
d. an embarrassment to the person's family

3. Contextual factors that should be considered in evaluating abnormal behaviour include sex, race/ethnicity, and
a. cognitive skills
b. dimensional approaches
c. personality problems
d. socioeconomic status

4. It is important to consider a person's age and developmental stage when evaluating behaviour because
a. children have more serious disorders than adults do
b. adults may not report all their symptoms
c. developmental maturity affects what disorders occur and what symptoms are present
d. disorders not treated during childhood will always persist throughout life

5. Our knowledge of early theories of abnormal behaviour is limited because
a. historical evidence is scanty
b. modern technology cannot study demons and spirits
c. only organic models were used before the modern era
d. until recently, no records of patients' symptoms were kept

6. Hippocrates was an ancient Greek physician who
a. produced a diagnostic classification system and a model by which to explain abnormal behaviour
b. identified common psychological symptoms such as hallucinations, melancholia, and mania
c. introduced the term *hysteria*
d. all of the above

7. In the Middle Ages, groups of people believed that demons possessed them. Such episodes of mass hysteria are now explained by the concept of
a. mimicry behaviour
b. emotional contagion
c. alien abduction
d. lycanthropy

8. Moral treatment, the eighteenth-century innovation of Philippe Pinel and William Tuke, was characterized by
a. daily compulsory church attendance
b. imposition of a work schedule to teach patients duty and productivity
c. separation of patients from evil influences outside their homes
d. kind treatment of patients and work to occupy their minds

9. When symptoms are diminished or eliminated not because of any specific treatment but because the patient believes that a treatment is effective, we see the power of the
a. therapeutic relationship
b. placebo effect
c. humane care movement
d. animal magnetism effect

10. German psychiatrist Emil Kraepelin contributed to the study of abnormal psychology by
a. observing hundreds of living patients
b. introducing two diagnostic categories
c. laying the groundwork for a classification system
d. all of the above

11. The scientist–practitioner approach is important in the treatment of patients because patients are
a. treated by clinicians who have developed models of human behaviour
b. taught how to evaluate research and choose treatments

c. treated by clinicians who use empirical research to guide the treatment process
d. able to help advance psychological research by being research participants

12. The biological model seeks knowledge of abnormal behaviour by studying
a. the biology of the body, particularly the brain
b. biological scarring and structural abnormalities
c. brain morphology as it affects bodily processes
d. neuroimaging techniques

13. Biological scarring, or the process whereby years of living with a disorder causes changes in the brain, demonstrates the
a. interaction among biopsychosocial factors
b. importance of the psychoanalytic model
c. interaction between psychological and social factors
d. significance of downward drift

14. Compared with Freud, contemporary psychoanalytic theorists place less emphasis on psychosexual development and more importance on
a. phenomenology
b. sibling rivalry
c. conscious motivation
d. dream analysis

15. Pioneer behaviourist Joseph Wolpe discovered that a stimulus will not elicit fear or anxiety if
a. conditioning prevents negative emotions
b. operant conditioning reinforces relaxation
c. discrimination becomes increasingly difficult
d. incompatible behaviour occurs at the same time

16. Behaviourist B. F. Skinner demonstrated that behaviour could be changed by events that happened afterward, a phenomenon known as
a. operant conditioning
b. systematic desensitization
c. fear hierarchy
d. contingent reinforcement

17. Vicarious conditioning is different from other types of conditioning in that it involves
a. shaping rather than punishment
b. learning without punitive consequences
c. learning without actually doing a behaviour
d. acquiring new behaviours through practice

18. The cognitive model is based on the idea that our
a. perceptions and interpretations of events are more important than the events themselves
b. cognitive abilities differ depending on our developmental stage
c. brains are permanently affected by external events
d. intelligence level determines which disorders we are prone to

19. A clinician who notes the role of a patient's sex, income level, and race in his or her problems is illustrating the influence of
a. class differences
b. sociocultural models
c. symptom expression
d. feminist psychology

20. When a clinician finds that several members of a patient's family have similar symptoms, he or she may suspect that the patient has a predisposition to illness known as a
a. stressor
b. biological model
c. genetic abnormality
d. diathesis

Answers:
1 d, 2 b, 3 d, 4 c, 5 a, 6 d, 7 b, 8 d, 9 b, 10 d, 11 c, 12 a, 13 a, 14 c, 15 d, 16 a, 17 c, 18 a, 19 b, 20 d.

chapter 2

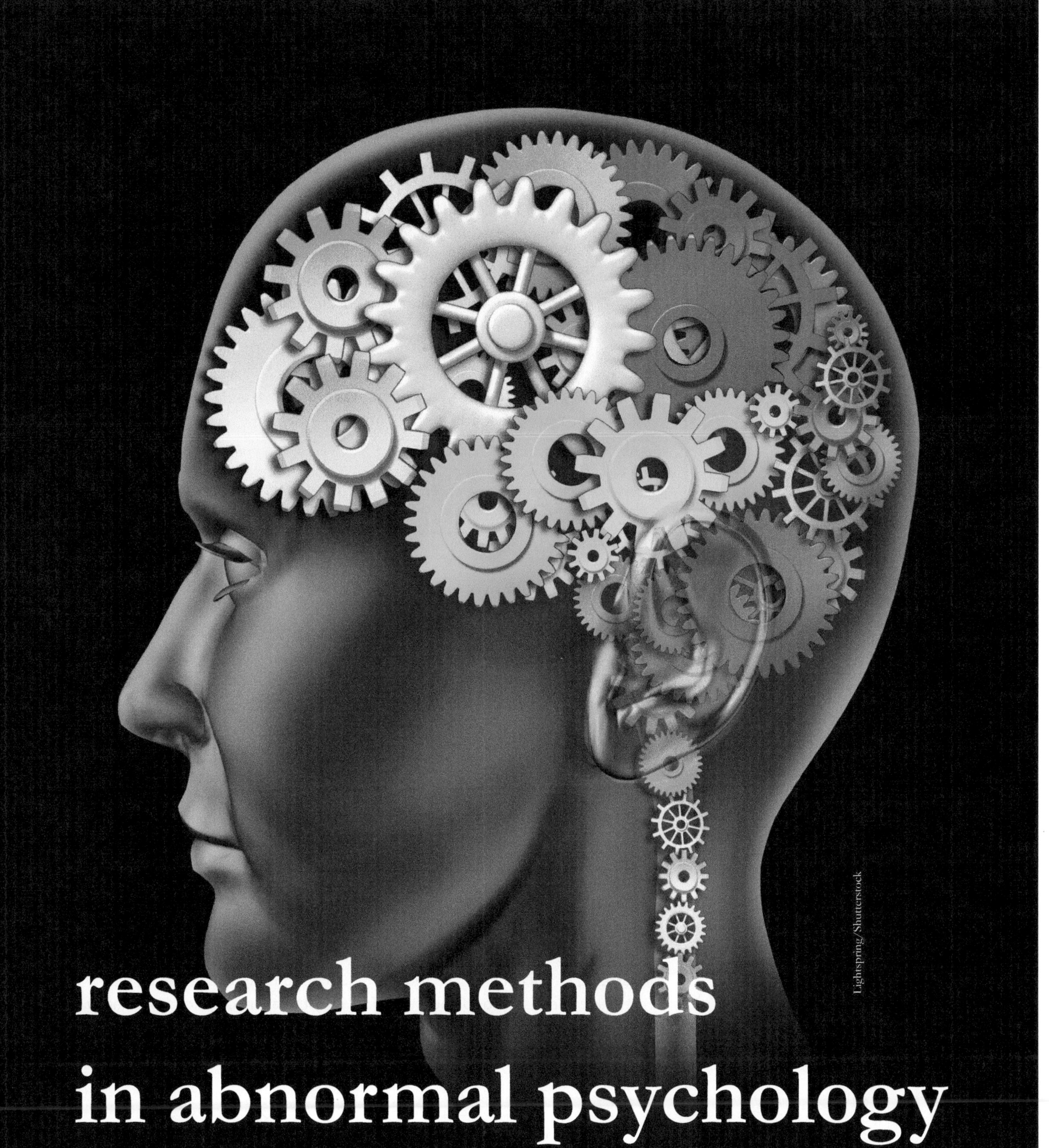

research methods in abnormal psychology

Lightspring/Shutterstock

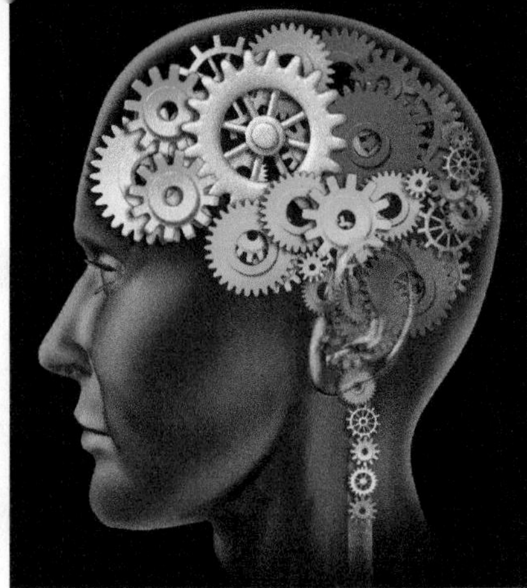

Learning Objectives

After reading this chapter, you should be able to:

2.1
Understand how research in psychology ranges from the cellular to the population level.

2.2
Recognize new techniques used to study abnormal psychology at the cellular or neuroanatomical level.

2.3
Understand the differences between family, twin, and adoption studies (which do not study genes directly) and molecular genetics research (which does directly study genes) and the strengths and limitations of both approaches.

2.4
Describe the strengths and limitations of case studies and single-case designs.

2.5
Understand the principles and applications of correlational research.

2.6
Describe the factors that influence outcomes of randomized controlled trials.

2.7
Recognize the principles and applications of epidemiological research as they relate to the understanding of abnormal behaviour.

I was taking introductory psychology, and we had the option of participating in research to get extra credit. There was an information board in the department where we could read about studies and sign up. There were lots of studies we could choose from. I saw one that caught my interest and signed up.

The first thing I did was read the information sheet and fill in the consent form. On the first day, the researcher asked me all sorts of questions about my family history of alcohol use as well as how much I drink. I also had to fill out several questionnaires—mostly about alcohol and drug use.

She then scheduled me to come back the next day, and I was told not to eat for 1.5 hours before I came in and also not to smoke or brush my teeth!

The researcher then had me taste 10 different sweet solutions. She told me to sip the solution, swish it around in my mouth, and spit it out. Then I had to rate the solution, rinse my mouth with distilled water, and proceed to the next solution. For each solution, she asked me to rate how sweet and how pleasurable the taste was.

That was pretty much it. Afterward, the researcher told me that she was studying the association between a family history of alcoholism and sweet taste preference.

A few years later, I was checking around on the Internet to see if anything ever came of the study, and I typed in the researcher's name. To my surprise, she published a paper on the study and concluded that people with a family history of alcoholism actually do prefer sweeter tastes! It was pretty incredible to have been a participant in a study that actually got published.

(Source: Republished with permission of John Wiley & Sons, Inc., from Kampov-Polevoy, A., Garbutt, J., & Khalitov, E. Family history of alcoholism and response to sweets. *Alcoholism, Clinical and Experimental Research, 11*, 1743–1749. Copyright © 2003. Permission conveyed through Copyright Clearance Center, Inc.)

In introductory psychology classes, psychology is often described as the scientific study of behaviour and mental processes. To understand human behaviour, psychologists require research volunteers such as the participant described above. Much of what we know about abnormal behaviour is based on studies conducted using university students. Without such research, our understanding would be limited. In much of psychological research, investigators are looking at one individual's observable behaviours. However, for abnormal psychology, a scientific approach requires research of human behaviour at all levels (biological variables such as heart rate, internal events such as thoughts and feelings, and observable behaviours such as interacting with another person). The National Institutes of Health (NIH) (2005) emphasize that to fully understand health and disease, it is important to conduct research at every level—from a single cell to society. **Translational research** is a scientific approach that focuses on communication between basic science and applied clinical research. The NIH states:

To improve human health, scientific discoveries must be translated into practical applications. Such discoveries typically begin at "the bench" with basic research—in which scientists study disease at a molecular or cellular level—then progress to the clinical level, or the patient's "bedside." The translational approach is really a two-way street. Basic scientists provide new tools for use with patients, and clinical researchers make novel observations about the nature and progression of disease that often stimulate basic investigations. Translational research has proven to be a powerful process that drives the clinical research engine.

Our introductory case illustrates one type of basic research—understanding how taste mechanisms may be related to alcoholism. This case illustrates another important point as well. The goal of most research is to publish the results so that other investigators can use the data to create new hypotheses and further our understanding of abnormal behaviour. Members of the public—those who do not do research—also need to be aware of research findings that have implications for their lives.

Consistent with a translational approach, this chapter begins with research strategies that focus on factors at the cellular and neuroanatomical levels and that affect behaviour in the entire organism. We then examine research at the individual and group levels, where most scientific inquiry in the area of abnormal psychology occurs. Finally, we turn to studies examining behaviour at the population level. Each approach provides a unique perspective on mental illness. Combined, they allow us to understand broadly the biological, psychological, and societal aspects of mental illness.

Ethics and Responsibility

Our research participant read an information sheet before deciding to participate in the study and signing a consent form. One of the core principles in the scientific study of abnormal behaviour is that the research must be conducted in an ethical manner in accord with the principles described in Chapter 15. This includes three fundamental ethical principles. First is *respect for persons*. That means that individuals participating in a study must be capable of making decisions about themselves. Anyone lacking that ability is entitled to protection: A parent or guardian must give consent for that person to participate. Second is the principle of **beneficence**. This means that researchers not only must respect participants' decisions and protect them from harm, but also must attempt to secure their well-being. This obligates the researcher to do no harm and to maximize possible benefits and minimize possible harms. The third ethical principle, *justice*, emphasizes "fairness in distribution" or "what is deserved." An injustice occurs when a benefit to which a person is entitled is denied without good reason or when an unnecessary burden is imposed. It would be unjust, for example, for a person who is qualified and willing to participate in a study to be excluded.

A researcher who designs a study and the consent form makes sure that all potential participants can easily understand the informed consent document and clarifies that participation in the research project is voluntary. The researcher also takes time to consider all foreseeable risks and benefits of participating in the project. Risks may include side effects of medication or the possibility that agreeing to participate in the study may exclude the opportunity to participate in a different study. The individual must choose one study, risking the possibility that the other one might have been the better choice. Finally, the researcher must ensure that subjects are selected through a fair process. A *research ethics board*, also known as an *institutional review board*, must review and approve all research conducted on humans. In Canada, these boards are guided by the principles of the Tri-Council Policy Statement (2014), which sets the standard for research ethics boards in Canada. These bodies both approve and oversee all research to ensure that researchers adhere to all mandated ethical principles.

Research in Abnormal Psychology at the Cellular Level

2.1 Understand how research in psychology ranges from the cellular to the population level.

Research at the cellular level is one of the newest and most exciting areas of study for abnormal psychology. Although the idea that the brain is the site of abnormal behaviour dates back to ancient times, only recently have we had the tools to accurately study the brain and the nervous system. Before discussing these new research findings, we will review the workings of the nervous system and the other parts of the body that influence behaviour.

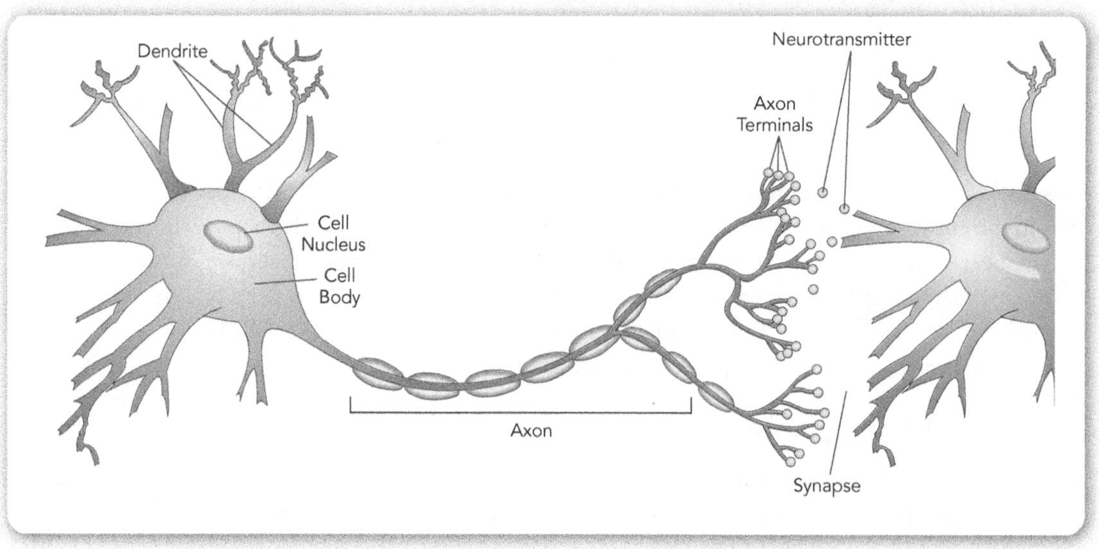

FIGURE 2.1

The Neuron. The cell body contains the nucleus and has projections called *dendrites*, which branch out and receive information from other neurons. Nerve impulses pass down the neuron. The gap between the axon terminals and the dendrites of the next neuron is called the *synapse*. Chemicals called *neurotransmitters* enable the nerve impulse to cross the gap to the receptors of the next neuron.

Neuroanatomy

The two main parts of the human nervous system are the **central nervous system** (CNS) and the **peripheral nervous system** (PNS).

The CNS consists of the brain and the spinal cord. The brain contains approximately 86 billion nerve cells, or neurons. Each neuron extends along distinct and specific pathways, creating a complex but ordered web of neural circuitry. Typical neurons are composed of the *soma*, or the cell body, which contains the nucleus. The *dendrites* are fingerlike projections that extend from the soma. Dendrites branch out and receive information from other neurons. The fibre through which a cell transports information to another cell is called the *axon*. *Axon terminals* are the branched features at the end of the axon that form *synapses*, or points of communication with dendrites or cell bodies of other neurons (see Figure 2.1).

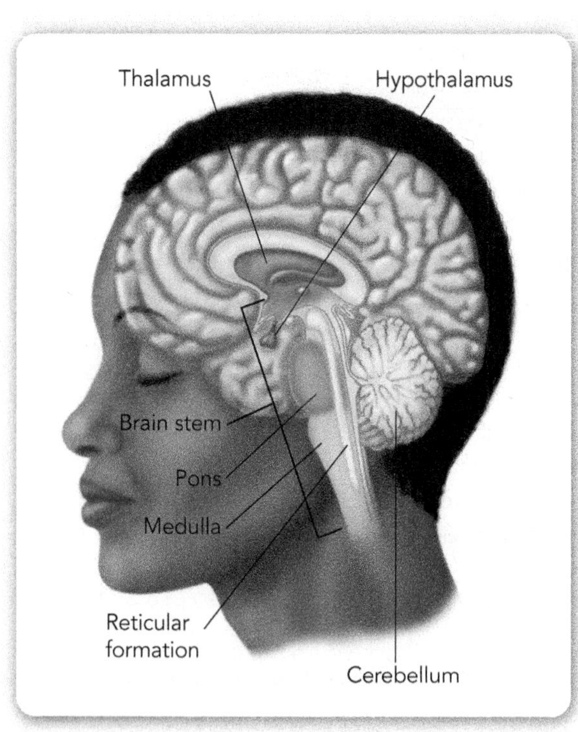

FIGURE 2.2

The Brain Stem. The oldest part of the brain, located at its base, controls most basic biological functions, such as breathing.

Source: Zimbardo, Philip G.; Johnson, Robert L.; Hamilton, Vivian McCann, Psychology: Core Concepts, 6th Ed., © 2009, pp. 74, 69, 75. Reprinted and Electronically reproduced by permission of Pearson Education, Inc., Upper Saddle River, New Jersey.

Having a general understanding of the structure of the brain is important because as we discuss the various psychological disorders, you will see that we are starting to understand the relationship between specific parts of the brain and specific disorders. An evolutionary perspective helps us to understand which parts of the brain appeared earliest in the course of human evolution and govern the most basic aspects of our functioning.

Starting with the oldest parts of the brain, at its base is the **brain stem**, which controls most of the fundamental biological functions associated with living, such as breathing. The brain stem has several sections with separate functions (see Figure 2.2). At its base is the *hindbrain*, consisting of the *medulla*, *pons*, and *cerebellum*. These structures regulate breathing, heartbeat, and motor control: activities required for life that occur automatically. You do not need to think about breathing or making your heart beat in order for those processes to occur. The term *lesion* refers to an area of damage or abnormality. We can tell a lot about the function of a particular brain structure by observing what happens to people when a specific structure is lesioned. For example, the cerebellum is critical for motor coordination. When lesions occur in the cerebellum, they result in disorders of fine movement, balance, and motor learning.

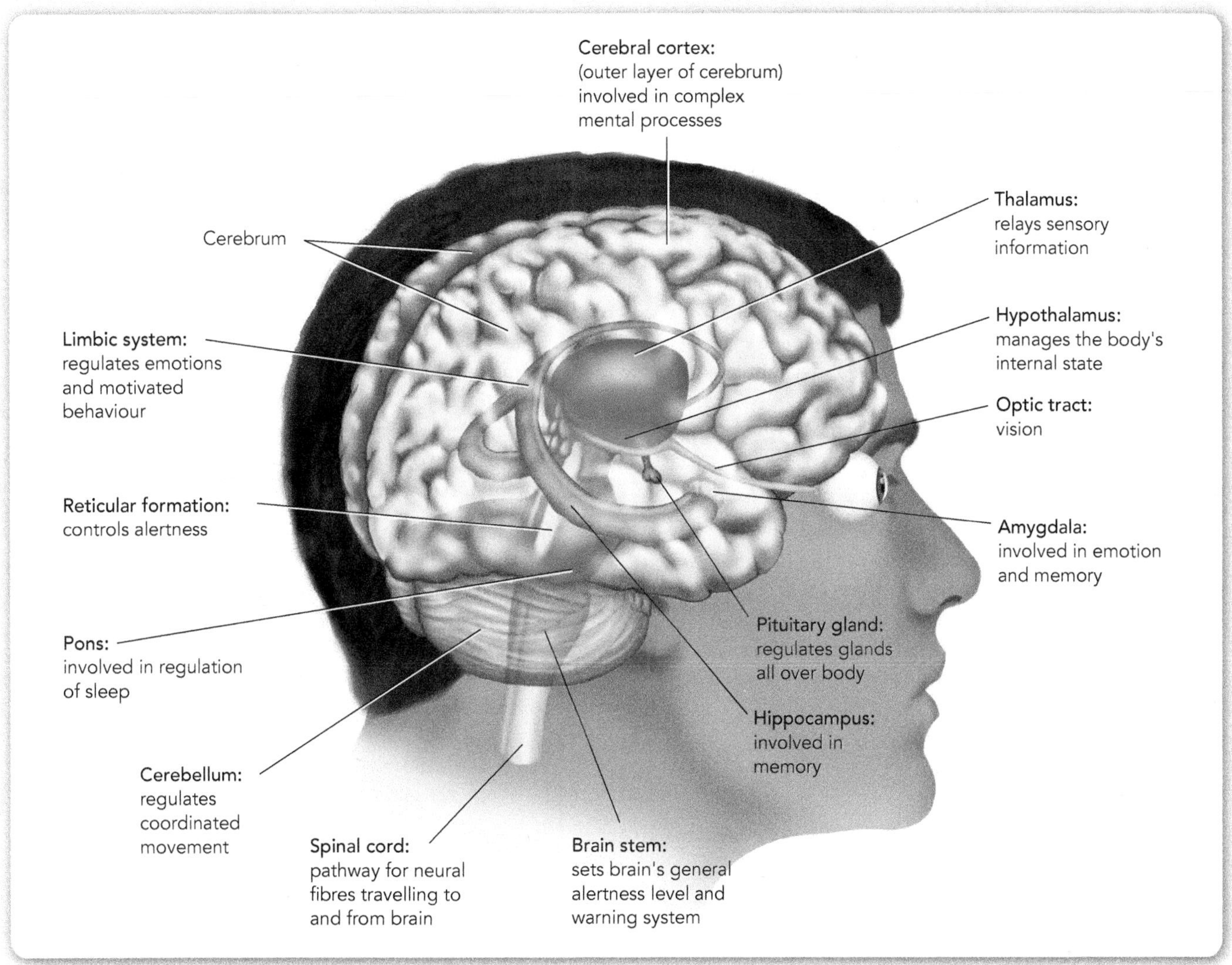

FIGURE **2.3**

The Thalamus, Hypothalamus, and the Limbic System. The thalamus is the brain's relay system, directing sensory information to the cortex; the hypothalamus regulates bodily functions; and the limbic system is a major centre for human emotion.

Source: Zimbardo, Philip G.; Johnson, Robert L.; Hamilton, Vivian McCann, Psychology: Core Concepts, 6th Ed., © 2009, pp. 74, 69, 75. Reprinted and Electronically reproduced by permission of Pearson Education, Inc., Upper Saddle River, New Jersey.

The **midbrain** portion of the brain stem has two important functions. First, it is a coordinating centre that brings together sensory information with movement. It also houses the *reticular activating system*, which regulates our sleep and arousal systems.

Moving upward structurally and evolutionarily from the brain stem are the *thalamus* and the *hypothalamus* (see Figure 2.3). Think of the thalamus as the brain's relay station because it directs nerve signals that carry sensory information to the cortex. A primary function of the hypothalamus is *homeostasis*, which is the regulation of bodily functions such as blood pressure, body temperature, fluid and electrolyte balance, and body weight.

Moving further up the evolutionary ladder from the midbrain to the **forebrain**, we find the *limbic system*, an umbrella term for several brain structures that are very important for the study of abnormal psychology. The **limbic system** includes the *amygdala*, the *cingulate gyrus*, and the **hippocampus**. The limbic system deals primarily with emotions and impulses. It is involved with the experience of emotion, the regulation of emotional expression, and the basic biological drives such as aggression, sex, and appetite. The hippocampus also has a role in memory formation and has been linked with the memory deficits that are characteristic of Alzheimer's disease (see "Real People, Real Disorders: Henry Gustav Molaison [H.M.]").

The *basal ganglia* are also at the base of the human forebrain. Structures within the basal ganglia include the *caudate*, *putamen*, *nucleus accumbens*, *globus pallidus*, *substantia nigra*,

REAL people REAL disorders

Henry Gustav Molaison (H.M.)

The brain of Henry Gustav Molaison (H.M.) is believed to have been studied more than that of any person in history. For reasons of confidentiality, he was known to psychologists only as "H.M." until his death. Born in 1926, H.M. banged his head hard at age 7 after being hit by a bicycle rider in his neighbourhood. At about age 16, he developed epilepsy and experienced many *grand mal* (severe) seizures. In 1953, at age 27, he underwent major surgery in which parts of his medial temporal lobe were removed on both sides of his brain, which was where the seizures originated.

Two thirds of H.M.'s hippocampus was removed. After the surgery, H.M. suffered from a form of amnesia in which he could not save new experiences as long-term memories. However, H.M. was able to complete tasks that required recall from his short-term memory. He was also able to recall long-term memories of events that occurred before his operation. But he could not recall events that occurred after the operation.

The case of H.M. was first reported in a paper published jointly by his neurosurgeon, William Scoville, and McGill University neuropsychologist Brenda Milner (Scoville & Milner, 1957). Milner was one of the key founders of neuropsychology. Henry Molaison died on December 2, 2008, of respiratory failure in a nursing home. Although he was unsure of exactly how old he was, had to be reintroduced to his doctors every day, and repeatedly grieved when he heard about the death of his mother, he had a positive outlook on life. He was quoted as saying that he hoped his medical condition would help others and allow researchers to learn more about memory.

Scientific research has benefited greatly from H.M.'s experience. It has resulted in two key findings: Short-term memories do not depend on a functioning hippocampus, but long-term memories must go through the hippocampus in order to be permanently stored (Kolb & Whishaw, 2008). These findings have forever changed the way scientists view the formation, retention, and recall of short- and long-term memory.

and *subthalamic nucleus*. In general, these structures are thought to regulate movement. Diseases that affect the basal ganglia are marked by abnormal movements; these include Parkinson's disease (rigidity and tremor), bradykinesia (slow movements), and Huntington's disease (uncontrollable dancelike movements of the face and limbs).

Moving even further up the evolutionary ladder, we encounter the largest part of the forebrain, the **cerebral cortex**. Here we find the structures that contribute to the abilities that make us uniquely human, such as reasoning, abstract thought, perception of time, and creativity. The cerebral cortex is divided into two hemispheres, known as the left and right. Popular psychology commonly refers to people as "left brained" or "right brained," but brain functioning is more complicated than that simple distinction. Although the two hemispheres look structurally similar, they appear to oversee different processes. Indeed, some people tend to favour one type of processing over the other.

The **left hemisphere** is primarily responsible for language and cognitive functions and tends to process information in a more linear and logical manner. The left hemisphere processes information in parts, sequentially, and uses both language and symbols (including numbers). The **right hemisphere** processes the world in a more holistic manner, a spatial context (i.e., the relationship of an object to other objects around it), and is more associated with creativity, imagery, and intuition. Considerable communication occurs between the hemispheres, and, in some cases, they can also compensate for each other by taking over some of the functions of the damaged area.

Each hemisphere consists of four lobes: temporal, parietal, occipital, and frontal (see Figure 2.4). The **temporal lobe** is associated with processing and therefore understanding auditory and visual information, and it plays a role in the naming or labelling of objects and verbal memory. The **parietal lobe** integrates sensory information from various sources and may also be involved with visuospatial processing (e.g., when you imagine rotating a three-dimensional object in space). The **occipital lobe**, located at the back of the skull, is the centre of visual processing. The **frontal lobe** is the seat of reasoning

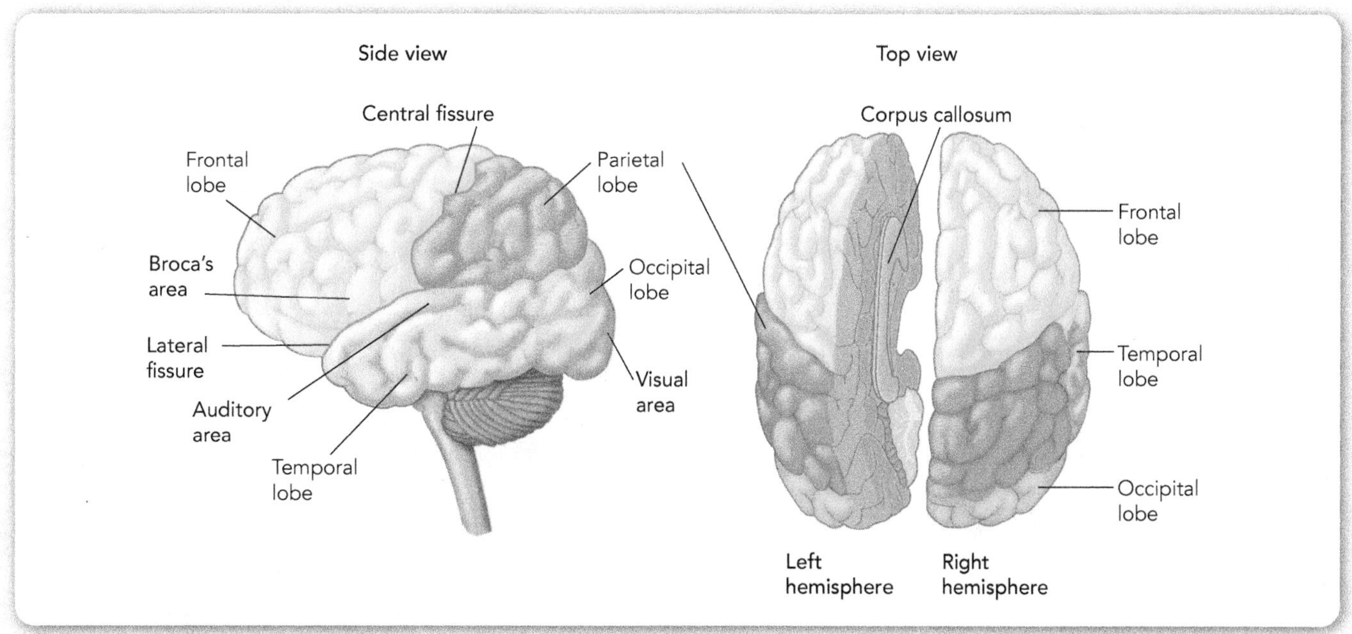

FIGURE 2.4

The Cerebrum. The four lobes of the cerebrum (temporal, parietal, occipital, and frontal) control sensory, motor, speech, and reasoning functions. The outer ("grey matter") layer of the cerebrum is known as the cerebral cortex.

Source: Zimbardo, Philip G.; Johnson, Robert L.; Hamilton, Vivian McCann, Psychology: Core Concepts, 6th Ed., © 2009, pp. 74, 69, 75. Reprinted and Electronically reproduced by permission of Pearson Education, Inc., Upper Saddle River, New Jersey.

and plays a critical role in impulse control, judgment, language, memory, motor function, problem solving, and sexual and social behaviour. Frontal lobes are instrumental in planning, coordinating, inhibiting, and executing behaviour. The *corpus callosum* connects the two sides of the brain, allowing them to communicate. A severed corpus callosum is not entirely incapacitating, but it can lead to an inability to integrate certain brain functions. For example, if an image of a key is flashed in the right field of vision, a person whose corpus callosum has been severed might *recognize* the image but not be able to correctly *name* it. A flash in the opposite field of vision could yield the correct *label*, but the person would not be able to discuss its *function*.

Beyond the brain and the spinal cord, the other major division of the human nervous system is the PNS. It is subdivided into the sensory-somatic nervous system and the autonomic nervous system. The *sensory-somatic nervous system* consists of the cranial nerves, which control sensation and muscle movement. The *autonomic nervous system* includes the sympathetic and parasympathetic nervous systems. The *sympathetic nervous system* (SNS) primarily controls involuntary movements. It serves to activate the body, creating a state of physical readiness. The SNS stimulates heartbeat; raises blood pressure; dilates the pupils; diverts blood away from the skin and inner organs to the skeletal muscles, brain, and heart; and inhibits digestion and peristalsis in the gastrointestinal tract, creating a bodily state of arousal that could indicate the presence of stress or anxiety (see Chapter 4). In contrast, the *parasympathetic nervous system* returns the body functions to resting levels after the SNS has activated them.

Finally, the body's **endocrine system** regulates bodily functions but uses hormones rather than nerve impulses to do so (see Figure 2.5). Endocrine glands produce **hormones**, which are chemical messengers released directly into the bloodstream that act on target organs. The pituitary gland, located at the base of the brain, is known as the "master gland." It controls many endocrine functions, including those central to the female menstrual cycle, pregnancy, birth, and lactation. Another gland, the hypothalamus, regulates the pituitary gland. The adrenal glands (located on top of the kidneys) release epinephrine (adrenaline) in response to external and internal stressors such as fright, anger, caffeine, or low blood sugar. Thyroid hormones regulate metabolism, including body temperature and weight. The pancreas includes a gland (islets of Langerhans) that secretes insulin and glucagon to regulate blood sugar level. A number

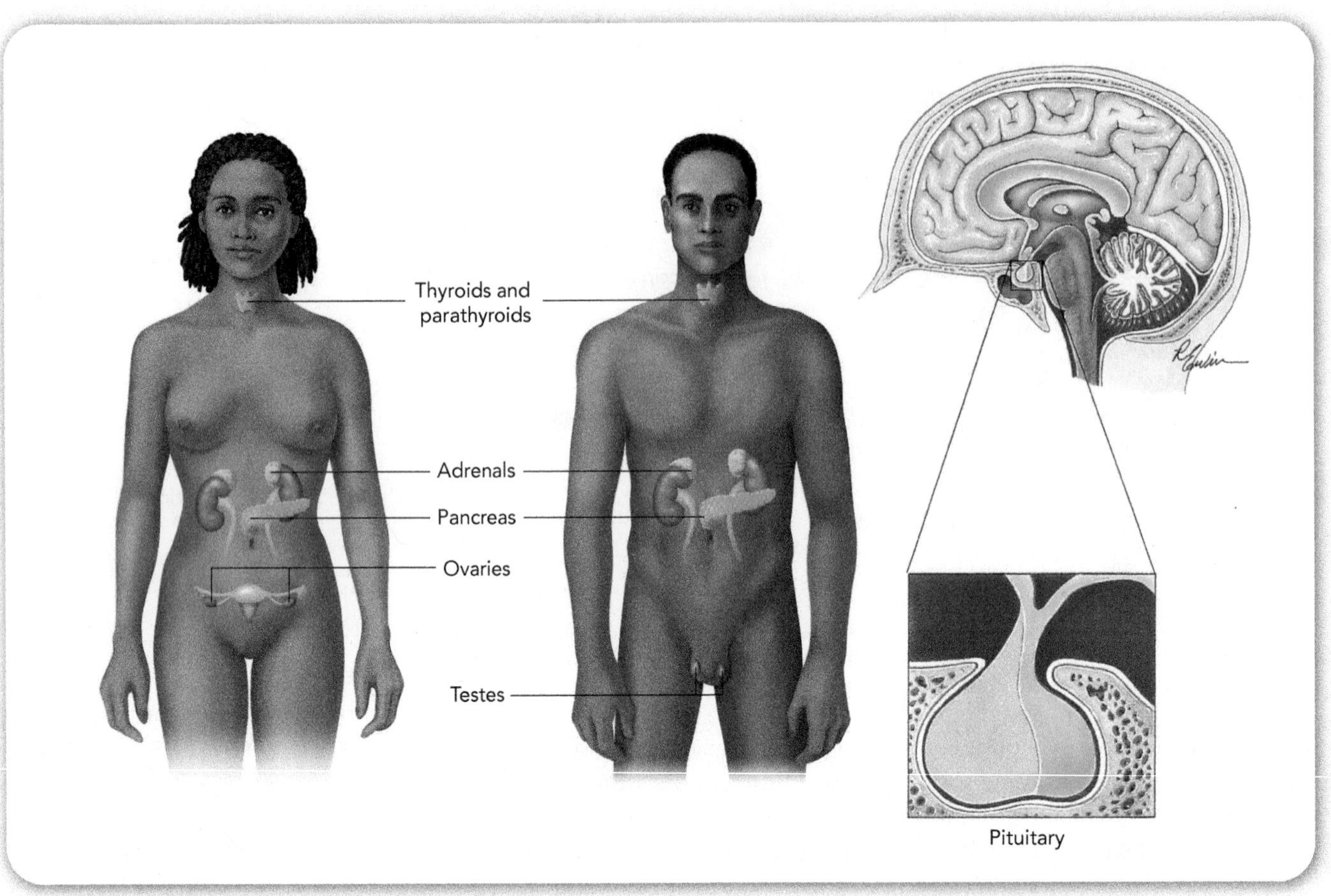

FIGURE 2.5 The Endocrine System. This system includes glands, such as the thyroid, gonads, adrenal, and pituitary, and the hormones they produce, such as thyroxin, estrogen, testosterone, and adrenaline. Hormones are chemical messengers that transmit information and instructions throughout the bloodstream, targeting cells that are genetically programmed to receive and respond to specific messages.

Source: Zimbardo, Philip G.; Johnson, Robert L.; Hamilton, Vivian McCann, Psychology: Core Concepts, 6th Ed., © 2009, p. 63. Reprinted and Electronically reproduced by permission of Pearson Education, Inc., Upper Saddle River, New Jersey.

Canadian FOCUS:

Neural Networks

In order to better understand the complexities of brain function, neuroscientists and computer scientists working in the field of artificial intelligence develop and test neural network models of normal and abnormal brain function. In these models, layers of neurons are connected to one another by axons and dentrites. The connections can be modified so that neurons can vary in their excitatory or inhibitory effects on one another. The connections change as a function of experience, according to various rules or algorithms. In other words, the networks can demonstrate learning.

One of the pioneers in this approach was Donald O. Hebb (1904–1985) at McGill University. Hebb (1949) realized that human behaviour and mental functioning could not be adequately explained by focusing only on the workings of the brain. Instead, Hebb emphasized a systems approach, whereby environmental events and psychological experiences (e.g., emotions) interact with the nervous system in a way that each modifies the other. So, for example, specific environmental events could produce particular changes in brain function, and in turn changes in brain function could lead the organism to influence the environment in particular ways. Hebb developed models of how networks of neurons can be modified to recognize incoming stimuli ("inputs") and to produce specific responses ("outputs"). Thus, networks of neurons could be modified to perform various tasks.

Neural network models have developed considerably since Hebb's early work. Scientists have developed neural network models to simulate many disorders, such as schizophrenia. These models propose that symptoms of mental disorders arise from aberrations in the way the networks process information. These models help guide neuroscientists in their search for the biological correlates of mental disorders.

of studies have demonstrated that certain hormones (e.g., cortisol, prolactin) are elevated in people with depression, anxiety, and other psychological symptoms.

Neurohormones and Neurotransmitters

Clearly, many different mini-systems exist within the overall nervous system. To understand human emotions, we need to know how these various systems operate and cooperate. Communication in the nervous system is both electrical and chemical. Neurons do not actually touch each other, but chemicals called **neurotransmitters** relay the electrical signals from one neuron to the next (see Figure 2.6). When the electrical signal reaches the axon terminal, the neurotransmitters are released. They travel across the space between the neurons (called the *synapse*) and land on the surface of the neighbouring neuron, at which point they trigger the second neuron to "fire," releasing the electrical impulse. Research on neurotransmitters has revolutionized psychiatry because most drug treatments affect one or more of the core neurotransmitters by influencing their availability or their action in the brain. This highly active field of research is constantly identifying new substances that function as neurotransmitters. Specific neurotransmitter systems have been widely studied and will be discussed in the chapters on specific disorders.

Understanding the basics of the nervous system, we are ready to begin the journey from the individual cell to the level of society. Throughout this journey, we will examine the many different procedures that psychologists use to study human behaviour at each of these levels. The brief case description that follows provides a context for those strategies.

Monica is 26 years old. She has been feeling sad, helpless, and hopeless, and crying for no reason. She has thought about taking her life. She has trouble falling asleep at night, and when she finally does, she wakes up several times. She has lost 10 kg in two months because she does not feel like eating. Her primary care physician sent her to a psychologist, who diagnosed her with depression.

We will look closely at depressive disorders in Chapter 6, but here we will explore the methodologies that researchers typically use to study this disorder.

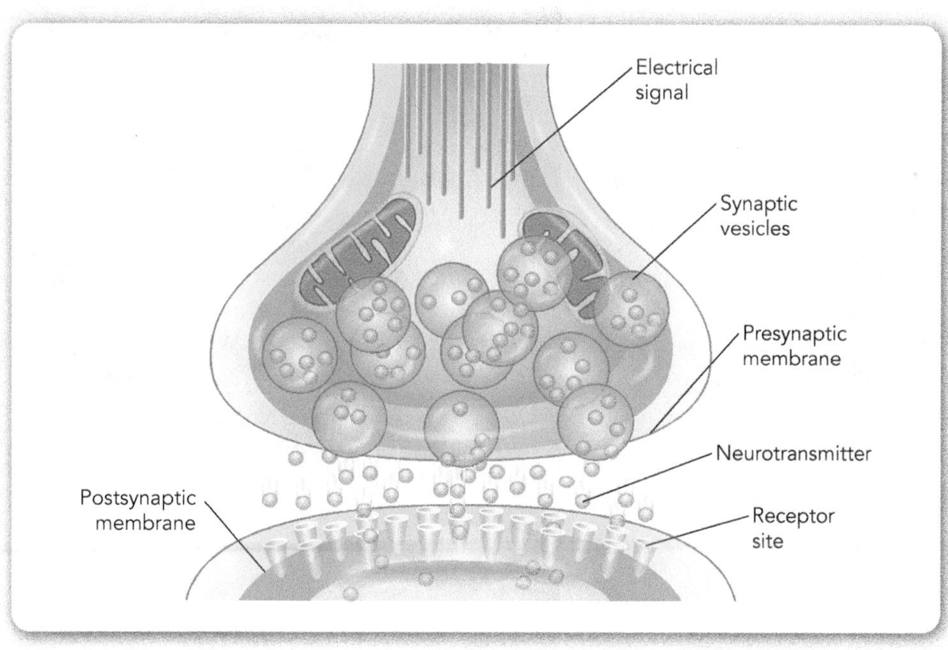

FIGURE 2.6

How Neurotransmitters Work. The electrical signal reaches the end of the first neuron, causing it to fire and release the neurotransmitters from their vesicles at the presynaptic membrane. The neurotransmitters travel across the synapse and land on receptors on the postsynaptic membrane. This initiates a signal in the second neuron, relaying the message.

Neuroimaging

2.2 Recognize new techniques used to study abnormal psychology at the cellular or neuroanatomical level.

You may wonder how scientists know how the brain functions and which of its structures are responsible for human abilities and activities. Much of our early information came from unique cases such as accident victims or survivors of surgery (like H.M.) that allowed us to understand what functions were lost if a certain part of the brain was damaged or removed. More recently, understanding the structure and the function of the brain has been facilitated by advances in **neuroimaging** technology, which takes pictures of the brain. Tests such as CT (computerized tomography) and MRI (magnetic resonance imaging) scans provide static images like snapshots. With such images, clinicians can detect lesions or damaged areas in the brain. For a CT scan, the patient is injected with a radioactive dye, and specialized X-ray equipment photographs the brain from different angles. The computerized images create a cross-sectional picture of the brain. MRI scans use radiofrequency waves and a strong magnetic field to provide highly detailed pictures of the brain. MRI has an advantage over CT technology in that it does not require the use of radiation. Instead, radiofrequency waves are directed at protons in a strong magnetic field. The protons are first "excited" and then "relaxed," emitting radio signals that can be computer processed to form an image.

CT and MRI technology explore **neuroanatomy** (brain structure). Other tests are used to detect brain function. *Positron emission tomography* (PET) creates images based on the detection of radiation from the emission of positrons. Before the scan occurs, the patient is given a radioactive biochemical substance. As the radioactive isotope in the substance decays, it emits tiny particles that can be measured. PET brain imaging enables scientists to trace neurotransmitter pathways in the brain and from these data to determine which brain structures and pathways are involved in specific aspects of human behaviour. Functional MRI (fMRI) identifies increases in blood flow that are associated with increases in neural activity in various parts of the brain. This technique allows not only a map of brain anatomy, but also a map of brain function. fMRI allows the researcher to isolate specific brain activity in response to an event or stimulus (e.g., flashing

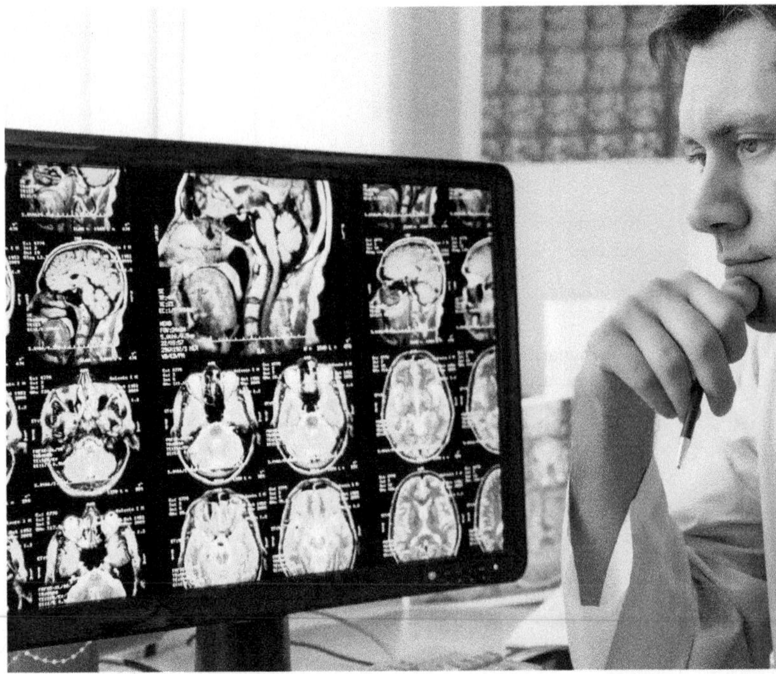

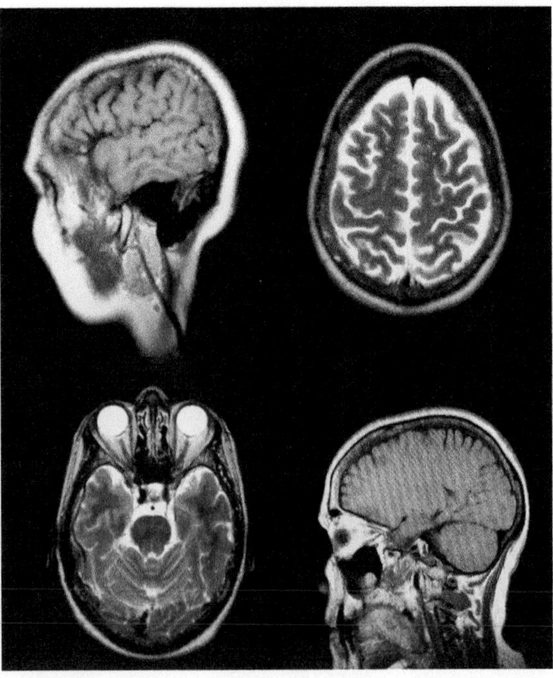

CT and MRI scans, in which X-ray or radio waves scan the brain, produce images that reveal brain anatomy.

(left): Beerkoff/Fotolia; **(right):** Tobkatrina/Shutterstock

an image of a spider to someone with a fear of spiders or examining the brain activity of someone experiencing auditory hallucinations, or "hearing voices").

Neuroimaging is an elegant, sophisticated, and expensive research tool. In typical clinical practice, neuroimaging is not needed to diagnose depression.

However, Monica and all those with psychological disorders are benefiting greatly from neuroimaging studies that help mental health professionals understand what brain structures and functions appear to be affected when someone is depressed. In turn, understanding altered brain functioning has helped with the development of interventions that target specific brain areas and functions.

Genetics

2.3 Understand the differences between family, twin, and adoption studies (which do not study genes directly) and molecular genetics research (which does directly study genes) and the strengths and limitations of both approaches.

Studies of brain structure and function provide many insights about the brain and its relationship to psychological disorders. However, knowing that brain activity is altered does not fully explain why abnormal behaviour occurs. Scientists must still explain how and why brain abnormalities exist. Applying genetics to the study of behaviour has revolutionized abnormal psychology, and research on genetic factors now reaches from the cell to the population level. *Behavioural genetics* approaches include family, twin, and adoption studies. These studies allow critical glimpses into whether certain behavioural traits or mental disorders run in families and the extent to which these familial patterns are due to genetics (are heritable) or environment. Modern molecular approaches to genetics and new methods of examining genetic associations have allowed scientists to discover genetic *loci* (specific places on specific chromosomes) that are associated with many complex traits. We now know that single genes rarely cause behavioural traits and mental disorders. Instead, research suggests that many genes and environmental factors that exert small to moderate effects influence most behavioural traits (known as *complex traits*) and disorders.

GENETICS BASICS Recall from your high school biology class that the "building block of life" is *deoxyribonucleic acid* (DNA). The collection of DNA that exists in humans is called the human *genome*. Thanks to the *Human Genome Project*, we know that approximately 20 000 to 25 000 genes make up each person. Each gene is a section of DNA, and together, genes make an organism unique. In humans, the genes are contained on 23 pairs of chromosomes—22 somatic (bodily) chromosome pairs and 1 sex chromosome pair, either XX (female) or XY (male) (see Figure 2.7). The mother always contributes an X chromosome to the sex chromosome pair. If the father's contribution is also an X chromosome, then the baby is a girl. If he contributes a Y chromosome, then the baby is a boy. Genes can exist in several different forms, called *alleles*, and specific alleles create variation in species (e.g., height, hair colour, eye colour, personality, disease risk).

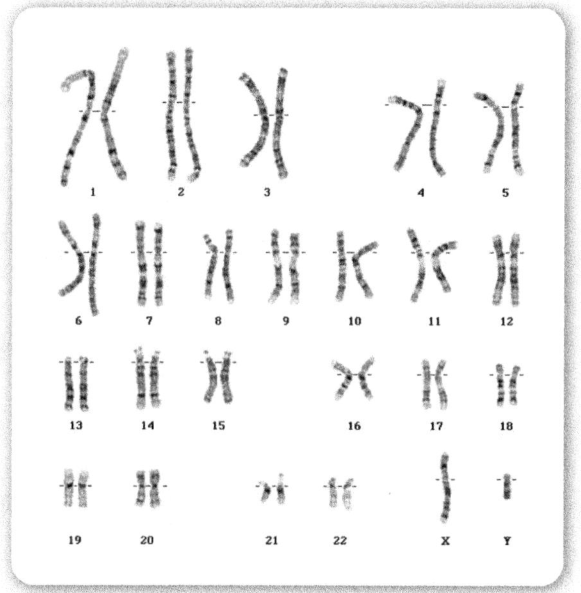

FIGURE 2.7

Human Chromosomes. A normal human being has 46 chromosomes—23 derived from each parent. Sex is determined by X and Y chromosomes; males are XY and females are XX. Is this the DNA of a male or female?

Genes follow several laws. Gregor Mendel (1822–1884), a Czech monk, discovered two genetic laws of heredity while working with the common garden pea. The *law of segregation* states that an individual receives one of two elements from each parent. One of the elements could be *dominant* (in which case the trait would be expressed in offspring), or the element could be *recessive* (genetically present but usually not expressed in offspring). If a child receives two recessive elements—one from each parent—then the recessive element or trait is expressed. In the case of eye colour, brown is a dominant trait and blue is a recessive trait. So, a person with blue eyes must have inherited two recessive elements, one from each parent.

Mendel's second law, the *law of independent assortment*, states that the alleles (variations) of one gene assort independently from the alleles of other genes. For example, the alleles for height and eye colour do not always travel together. Not every short person has blue eyes; short people may have brown eyes or hazel eyes. Similarly, people with blue eyes can be short, average, or tall. In short, genes for eye colour and height assort independently.

Although Mendel laid the foundation for our understanding of genetics, his work was criticized by later scientists (Fisher, 1936) who suggested that Mendel's results were too good to be true. Others scientists supported Fisher's observations. Nevertheless, Mendel's laws provided an important first step toward understanding the basic principles of genetics.

The influence of genes on characteristics such as height, eye colour, and various diseases has been known for generations. However, more recently, behaviour geneticists have studied genetic effects on personality, attitudes, and abnormal behaviour such as depression, extraversion, and schizophrenia.

With so many genes in the human genome, how do we even begin the search for genes that may increase the risk for developing certain psychological conditions? This is the province of scientists in the field of behavioural genetics.

Family, Twin, and Adoption Studies

The term *behavioural genetics* refers to the study of the relationship between genetics and environment in determining individual differences in behaviour. Approaches in this category include family, twin, and adoption studies. Basically, these studies focus on whether traits and disorders run in families and, if so, why.

FAMILY STUDIES Do psychological disorders "run in families"? **Familial aggregation** studies examine whether the family members of someone with a particular disorder (called the **proband**) are more likely to have that disorder than are family members of people without the disorder. If the disorder is more commonly found among the proband's family, the disorder is considered to be familial or to "aggregate in families." Family studies can take two forms. The *family history* method uses information from one or a few family members to provide information about other family members. You are probably familiar with this method if you have completed a checklist in your physician's office about your family's medical history. The *family study* method involves direct interviews with each consenting family member. This method is considered to be more reliable because it involves direct interviews.

In Monica's case, a clinician conducting a diagnostic interview might use the family history method to ask her about the presence of depressive symptoms in any members of her family. If Monica were participating in a family study about the causes of depression, the researchers might invite her relatives to participate in individual interviews to determine whether any of them ever suffered from depression.

From a scientific perspective, determining whether symptoms run in families is an important first step in understanding whether genes might influence a disorder. However, family members also share environmental experiences and cultural contexts, which can influence behaviour. Therefore, any observed familial aggregation could be due to either genetic *or* environmental factors, or most likely some combination of these influences.

Large family studies can be used to explore the extent to which genes or environment contribute to liability to a disorder or trait; however, the relative contributions of genetic and environmental factors can be best determined by adoption and twin study designs.

ADOPTION STUDIES Adoption creates a unique situation in which genetically related individuals live in separate families, and therefore do not share a common family environment. In such cases, similarities between biological parents and their adopted-away offspring are assumed to represent the *genetic* contribution to a given trait or behaviour. By contrast, similarities between the adopted child and his or her adoptive parents measure the *environmental* contribution to parent–child similarity. This approximation holds only when the placement of the adopted child is not selective (e.g., when biological parents request that the adoptive family have similar cultural and religious traditions).

Adoption studies represent a middle ground when it comes to examining behavioural genetic models: They are more able to separate genetic from environmental effects than family studies, but they have their pitfalls and biases as well. One bias is that adoption placement is not always random. Often babies are placed with adoptive families who resemble their own biological parents on a number of dimensions, such as race, religion, and socioeconomic status. As international adoptions become increasingly popular, additional issues are arising, including what conditions the adoptee faced before placement. Many of these conditions, such as placement in orphanages and lack of early attachment experiences, can lead to serious developmental consequences that can confound the interpretation of adoption studies.

TWIN STUDIES The scientific study of twins was another important step in understanding the contribution of genes and environment to abnormal behaviour (Cederlöf et al., 1982; Martin et al., 1997). These studies revolutionized our understanding of several major psychiatric conditions and modernized approaches to treatment. For example, three decades ago, it was widely believed that autism and schizophrenia resulted solely from environmental trauma or parental deficits. However, based on a body of scientific evidence (Folstein & Rosen-Sheidley, 2001; Sullivan, 2008), we now know that these disorders have critically important genetic components.

Twin studies examine the similarities and differences between *monozygotic* (MZ, or identical) and *dizygotic* (DZ, or fraternal) twin pairs to identify genetic and environmental contributions to psychological disorders. MZ twins start out as a single embryo (fertilized egg). At some stage in the first two weeks after conception, the zygote (fertilized egg) separates and yields two embryos that are, for most intents and purposes, genetically identical. Therefore, behavioural differences between MZ twins, who essentially share all of their genes, allow examination of the role of *environmental influences* (Plomin et al., 1994). By contrast, DZ twinning results from the fertilization of two eggs by different spermatozoa. DZ twins are no more similar genetically than other siblings and share, on average, one half of their genes. Thus, behavioural differences between DZ twins can result from genetic or environmental effects.

Identical (MZ) twins separated at birth and raised apart have been found to show strong similarities in adulthood.

Angel Franco/Redux Pictures

One rigorous twin research design uses MZ twins who were separated in infancy and reared apart (i.e., in different environments). In this case, genes and familial environment are distinctly separated. Two large studies of MZ twins reared apart in (Bouchard et al., 1990; Pedersen et al., 1985) were critical in demonstrating the strength of genetic factors in determining IQ. In addition, reunited MZ twins have discovered similarities on dimensions not usually considered to be under genetic control, including where they have moles on their body, the age they started balding, their occupation, their choice of cars and motorcycles, and even their favourite beer.

A problem with a design based on MZ twins reared apart is that such samples are rare and may not be representative of twins in general, or representative of the population at large. Twin studies are more commonly based on samples of MZ and DZ twins in which the twins of a given pair are not separated at birth. Instead, each pair of twins is raised together in the same household. In such studies the researchers need to test the *equal environments assumption*; that is, the assumption that pairs of MZ twins are treated in the same way as DZ twins by family members and friends (Jang, 2005). To illustrate, some parents dress their twin children in identical outfits. The equal environments assumption holds that MZ and DZ twins are equally likely to be dressed in matching outfits. If this assumption is met, then researchers can use statistical methods to analyze data for a given variable (e.g., interview-based diagnoses of obsessive-compulsive disorder) from pairs of MZ and DZ twins to determine the extent to which the variable under investigation is shaped by genetic and environmental factors. Such a design even allows researchers to identify the type of genetic factors (additive vs. nonadditive) and the type of environmental influences, and to identify gene–environment interactions. To date, the largest, longest running twin study in Canada is the UBC Twin Project (Jang et al., 2006), in which investigators have assessed thousands of twins from across Canada. Researchers are investigating the roles of genes and the environment in many different forms of psychopathology, including features of personality disorders and symptoms of anxiety disorders, mood disorders, and substance use disorders (e.g., Jang et al., 2004; Taylor & Jang, 2011; Taylor et al., 2011).

MOLECULAR GENETICS Whereas twin and adoption studies can tell us whether genes are involved in a particular trait or disorder, they do not tell us which of the 20 000 to 25 000 identified genes might be related to the presence of the disorder. To actually identify risk genes, researchers need to drill down to the molecular level. **Molecular genetics** uses three primary methods: genomewide linkage analyses, candidate gene association studies, and genomewide association studies (Slagboom & Meulenbelt, 2002; Wang et al., 2005). **Genomewide linkage analysis** allows researchers to narrow the search for genes from the entire genome to specific areas on specific chromosomes. To conduct a linkage analysis, researchers need large families in which many individuals have a particular disorder *or* large samples of "affected relative pairs" (pairs of relatives who both have the illness under study). Researchers then look for regions of the genome that the affected relatives share. Then they can narrow their search for genes on these areas of increased sharing.

In a **candidate gene association study**, scientists compare specific genes in a large group of individuals who have a specific trait or disorder with a well-matched group of individuals who do not have that trait or disorder. In this approach, the researcher chooses one or several genes in advance based on some knowledge of the biology of the trait or the function of the gene. For example, we know that serotonin may be involved in depression, so a candidate gene study might compare one or a few serotonergic genes in a large sample of people with the disorder (called *cases*) vs. people who do not have the disorder but are similar to the cases in other ways (called *controls*). If scientists find that one variation of the gene is more common in the ill group, there is evidence that this gene might be associated with the illness.

A **genomewide association study (GWAS)** also uses large samples of cases and well-matched controls. Unlike the candidate gene studies in which only one or a few genes are studied at one time, in GWAS, hundreds of thousands of possible genetic variants scattered across the genome are tested for association in the same study. This is a key advantage of GWAS. In the candidate gene studies, a researcher must choose a gene or genes based on some prior knowledge of biology. GWAS does not require any such choice and yields a relatively unbiased search of the genome that can discover new genetic associations. For many diseases, GWAS has unlocked new biological pathways that had not been considered in the past.

Studying Monica's genes would not be part of the usual clinical assessment to determine the diagnosis of depression. However, certain researchers (usually working in medical school settings) may be conducting a study on genetics and depression, and individuals with symptoms like Monica's might be asked to participate by giving a sample of their blood or a scraping of skin from the inside of their cheek—both of which contain DNA.

Epigenetics focuses on heritable changes in the expression of genes, which are not caused by changes in actual DNA sequence but rather by environmental exposures (Petronis, 2010). Unlike your actual genetic sequence, the epigenome has the ability to react and adapt to a rapidly changing environment. What this means is that the environment has the ability to influence which genes are activated and which are silenced. Intriguingly, these changes may actually be passed down to succeeding generations.

CONCEPT check

- Research that teaches us about abnormal psychology can be conducted at the cellular or neuroanatomical level, with individual people or groups of people, or at the population level.
- When researchers study the brain from an evolutionary perspective, moving from the brain stem (which controls fundamental biological functions) to the forebrain (where higher cognitive functions occur) is a helpful way to understand mental disorders.
- New techniques in abnormal psychology research at the cellular level include neuroimaging (taking pictures of the brain), studying the function and interrelation of neurotransmitters (chemicals that relay electrical signals between the cells), and using molecular genetics (identifying genes that are associated with clinical syndromes).
- Family, twin, and adoption studies are behavioural genetic methods that provide insight into how behavioural traits and mental disorders run in families and the extent to which familial patterns are due to genetics or environment.
- Candidate gene, genomewide linkage, and genomewide association studies are more direct techniques than others, and they allow for the actual identification of genetic regions or actual genes associated with a trait or a disorder.

critical thinking question If you conducted a family study and found that relatives of individuals with a disorder were three times more likely to have a particular psychiatric disorder than relatives of similar individuals without that disorder, why would it be incorrect to conclude that genetic factors were completely responsible for the development of that disorder?

Research in Abnormal Psychology at the Individual Level

Studies of brain structure and function and genetics are sophisticated research tools, but they are time consuming and not always cost effective. Most research in abnormal psychology has been based on comparing groups of people who have different characteristics, are tested in different ways, or receive different treatments. Conclusions are drawn based on the average responses for the group. Research at the individual level also helps identify general principles about abnormal behaviour and its treatment. In fact, the practice of clinical psychology is generally directed toward the individual. Valuable information can be learned from intensive study of individual people, families, or small groups of people who can be considered a single unit. This research complements large group-based studies by allowing for richer examination of details and the development of hypotheses and theories that can later be tested in group designs. At the individual level, the two main methods of study are case studies and single-case designs.

Case studies are detailed descriptions of a single person that may help us understand a particularly rare or unusual behaviour. A case study of the serial killer Robert "Willie" Pickton, for example, could shed light on the reasons that a person might engage in multiple murders. Pickton lured women to his pig farm in Port Coquitlam, B.C., where he killed and dismembered them. He is currently serving life in prison.

Getty Images

The Case Study

2.4 Describe the strengths and limitations of case studies and single-case designs.

The brief description of H.M. presented earlier in the chapter is drawn from a **case study**, a comprehensive description of an individual (or group of individuals) using clinical data typically drawn from a clinician's practical experience. The case study provides a detailed narrative of abnormal behaviour and its treatment. It is sometimes accompanied by a quantitative measurement (such as measuring the frequency of a problematic behaviour), but it does not allow us to draw conclusions about causes of behaviour. In the case study, nothing is manipulated by the observer; it is simply the recounting of the individual's story. Nevertheless, case studies are useful for the study of abnormal behaviour.

BENEFITS OF CASE STUDIES Case studies can focus on the assessment and description of abnormal behaviour or its treatment. In both instances, significant background material and detailed clinical information illustrate the complexity of the case. Gathering this detailed clinical material is not possible in group-based research in which the focus is on group data.

As the example of H.M. illustrates, case studies allow the examination of rare phenomena, when group-based research would be nearly impossible simply because an adequate number of cases could not be found (Kazdin, 2003). In his memoir, *Holiday of Darkness*, York University professor Norman S. Endler described his personal struggles with depression. This provides another instance of a case study approach. Endler's frank account of the development of his depression and its successful treatment was an important contribution in raising awareness and lessening the stigma associated with mental disorders. Despite his depression, Professor Endler had a highly successful career and is acclaimed for his research on stress and coping.

Case studies can also generate hypotheses for group studies. In the true spirit of the scientist–practitioner model, clinical observations can lead to the development of testable theories and treatment using group designs. For example, John B. Watson's detailed study of Little Albert and Mary Cover Jones's report of Little Peter (see Chapter 1) served as the basis for the development of treatments for anxiety disorders that have been tested scientifically and are still used today.

In addition, intensive case studies allow practitioners to be involved in research. Clinicians in full-time practice usually do not have the time or resources to develop and carry out research using large group designs. For the full-time clinician, detailed case notes can provide a scholarly report that informs others, illustrating how the scientist–practitioner model operates in the practice and study of abnormal behaviour.

Finally, case studies illustrate important clinical issues that are not readily apparent in a group-based report. An example is a case report of five patients who had both anxiety/depression and chronic obstructive pulmonary disease, a lung disorder

(Stanley et al., 2005), and who participated in a large treatment trial. The case report provided more details about their specific clinical symptoms and their specific responses to treatment than was possible in the full clinical report (Kunik et al., 2008). This increased detail can be useful for clinicians who seek to use empirically supported treatments.

VARIATIONS AND LIMITATIONS OF CASE STUDIES The amount and type of data included in case studies vary considerably. Some of them simply provide case descriptions. Others illustrate clinical points using standardized measures of behaviours or symptoms, allowing comparisons with other larger studies.

Monica's symptoms of depression are more severe than those of patients included in large studies of depression treatments.

Scientifically rigorous case reports also attempt to standardize (keep consistent) the types of assessment and treatment procedures reported. Such reports enable other researchers or clinicians to attempt to replicate the same findings with another patient. Standardizing procedures for assessment or treatment also makes it possible to combine results from a small group of patients into a single report. In addition, standardized procedures make comparing symptoms or the amount of change over time easier than what might be observed in studies of large groups of patients.

Through the course of Monica's interview, her therapist discovered that she had eight brothers and sisters and that all of them suffered from major depression. This was highly unusual, and with her permission, the therapist decided to write a case study of Monica and her extensive family history of depression.

With all their advantages, however, the ability of case studies to help us understand abnormal behaviour is limited. Most importantly, although case studies allow us to develop hypotheses about what might have caused certain symptoms or what type of treatment might be helpful, they do not allow us to make any firm conclusions about the cause(s) of symptoms or change following treatment. For example, improvement in a patient's symptoms could result from the specific treatment or from other factors that are unrelated to that treatment. These factors could include the simple passage of time, attention from a therapist, or subjective biases on the part of the patient or clinician.

To draw conclusions about the causes of symptoms or change, an *experimental control* condition is needed. *Controlled* scientific experiments compare at least two groups that differ only with regard to the variable being tested (often called the **experimental variable**). In the experimental group, the variable being tested is present; in the **control group**, this variable is absent. For example, a treatment for depression might be tested by giving the treatment to half of the depressed patients (experimental group) but not to the other half of patients (control group) who are similar to the experimental group in all other respects. If the experimental group then shows improvement while the control group does not, we can infer that the treatment caused the improvement. Case studies, however, do not include control groups and thus cannot help us draw conclusions about causality.

Single-Case Designs

Single-case designs are experimental studies conducted at the individual level (i.e., with a single person). This approach uses quantitative measurement and incorporates control conditions that allow clearer demonstration of causal relationships in a single individual.

Traditional research compares groups of similar patients before and after they receive different treatments. However, group-based research can make it difficult to observe individual behaviour patterns. Also, group studies are expensive and time consuming (Morgan & Morgan, 2001). Single-case designs are essentially controlled experiments conducted with a single person. They control for alternative hypotheses (i.e., that something other than the treatment caused the change), and unlike case histories, they can lead to causal inferences. They require fewer resources and allow more detailed attention to individual patterns of change. In the single-case design, each person is a complete experiment at various times participating in both the treatment and the comparison (or control) condition. The goal of the experiment is to examine whether behaviour changes systematically, depending on whether the participant is in the treatment or the comparison phase.

Single-case design research begins with a baseline assessment that simply measures the behaviour targeted for change (e.g., how often a child has a tantrum, how frequently panic attacks occur) before implementing any experimental or control condition. An interesting challenge for this type of research is that sometimes merely asking a person to *monitor* a behaviour may change how often or how long the behaviour occurs. For example, asking a cigarette smoker to count the number of cigarettes smoked per day often results in a decrease in smoking. Why? Smokers are sometimes dismayed by the number of cigarettes they record and begin to decrease their smoking. Usually, however, behavioural change as a result of self-monitoring is only temporary. Therefore, baseline monitoring (i.e., assessment that occurs before beginning treatment) continues until the behavioural pattern is stable. Next a treatment is applied and withdrawn with *continuous assessment* of the target behaviour. If the target behaviour decreases with treatment and then returns to baseline when the treatment is withdrawn, the researcher can conclude that the treatment may have been effective (provided alternative explanations can be ruled out). If other researchers do similar research with the same results, the finding is *replicated* and confidence in it increases. Providing sufficient details about the patient, therapist, setting, and nature of the intervention aids in the replication of findings, which reinforces the study's conclusions. Regardless of the number of replications, however, the focus remains on describing individual patterns of behaviour for one person, not aggregate data from multiple patients.

DESIGN STRATEGIES A common single-case design is known as the *ABAB*, or *reversal*, design in which A represents a baseline phase and B represents a treatment phase. In this model, the two phases are alternated to examine their impact on behaviour. Behaviour is first evaluated at baseline until stability is demonstrated (A). The treatment is then applied (B), and assessment continues until behavioural stability is achieved. Next the treatment is withdrawn (A). Behaviour that returns to baseline during the second A phase is evidence that the treatment was the cause of the behaviour change. Even more evidence for the power of the treatment is obtained when the intervention is applied again (another phase B) and another behaviour change takes place. Each AB sequence is considered a replication, and each time the B phase has the same effect provides additional evidence that the treatment is the agent of change (Kazdin, 2003). The ABAB design can be used with patients of all ages, but it often is a particularly useful strategy to test the effects of behavioural treatments for children.

Caitlin is 3 years old. Since she was 15 months old, she has pulled out the hair on her head. Her pediatrician diagnosed her with trichotillomania, a disorder characterized by repetitive hair pulling that results in noticeable hair loss (see Chapter 4). He prescribed several medications, but none of them worked. A psychologist thought that Caitlin's hair pulling was reinforced by the substantial attention her parents gave her when they begged her to stop it. He instructed Caitlin's parents to stop paying attention to her hair pulling, but that had no effect. The psychologist then developed a behavioural treatment plan using a single-case design to try to stop this behaviour.

Because most of Caitlin's hair pulling occurred at night, the psychologist directed her mother to collect the hair from her pillow each morning and put it in a plastic bag and label it by the day of the week. The number of hairs pulled each night would be used to determine whether treatment was effective. The treatment plan was as follows:

Caitlin had a pair of pink mittens that she liked to wear, and her favourite food was cherry jam. If Caitlin wore her mittens all night (which would prevent her from pulling her hair) and they were still on her hands in the morning, she could have cherry jam for breakfast.

Using an ABAB design, the effectiveness of the treatment was evaluated (see Figure 2.8). The A phase was the baseline phase (no pink mittens or cherry jam). The B phase was the actual treatment (cherry jam for breakfast if Caitlin was wearing her mittens in the morning). Her mother continued to collect the hair each morning and recorded the average number of hairs pulled per night. Figure 2.8 shows for the number of hairs on Caitlin's pillow each morning (averaged over the week) during the treatment program. Each phase was three weeks in length. As Caitlin's hair began to grow in, the treatment program was gradually withdrawn. Six months later, she had a full head of hair.

Some interventions also produce learning that cannot easily be reversed. For example, relaxation training may produce changes in physical state (lower blood pressure) that do not quickly revert to baseline levels. When a behaviour cannot be reversed, a *multiple baseline design* may be used (Morgan & Morgan, 2001). This design applies only one AB sequence, but the sequence is repeated across individuals, settings, or behaviours. When the multiple baseline design is conducted *across individuals*, the treatment is introduced at a different time. This is often done by varying the length of the baseline assessment for each person so that the cause of any improvement cannot be attributed to the duration of any standard baseline period. As in the ABAB design, repeating the AB sequence across people increases confidence in the conclusions.

Multiple baseline studies can also be conducted *with a single individual* as the intervention is applied independently *across behaviours* (e.g., first smoking, then overeating) or *settings* (e.g., first home, then school, then on the playground). If the B phase consistently produces the same behaviour change (or is replicated), this is evidence that the intervention is effective.

LIMITATIONS OF SINGLE-CASE DESIGNS Single-case designs allow clinicians working in full-time practice to use experimental strategies to determine whether a treatment is efficacious (reduces psychological symptoms) for a particular patient. These strategies are also useful for situations in which it is unethical to withhold treatment completely, but testing the causal relationship between the treatment and a person's behaviour is needed. Single-case designs do not allow researchers to generalize the results to heterogeneous groups of people, however. Furthermore, they do not address the impact of

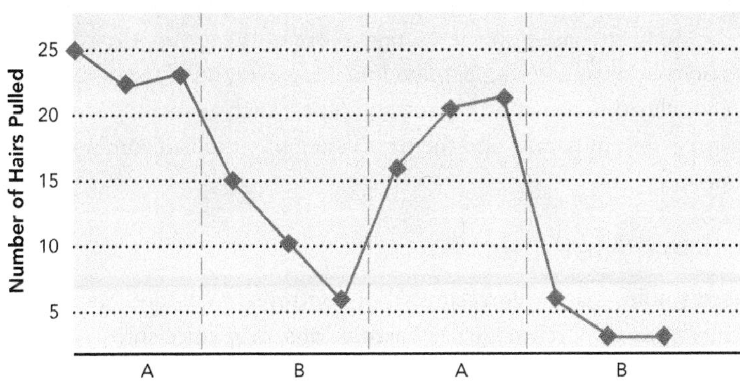

FIGURE 2.8

ABAB Research Design. Number of hairs pulled by Caitlin during baseline (A) and intervention (B) phases of behavioural treatment for hair pulling.

individual differences (related to age, sex, ethnicity), which may be very important in determining treatment response. Group-based research, discussed in the next section, is best suited to address these types of questions.

Ethics and Responsibility

In some cases, reversing a treatment is unethical or impractical. For example, it would be unethical to remove a treatment that reduces self-injurious behaviour, such as head banging in children with developmental disabilities.

In Monica's case, it would be unethical to remove a medication that eliminated her depressive symptoms, including her suicidal thoughts.

CONCEPT check

- Case studies, which provide significant details about abnormal behaviour or its treatment, allow us to study relatively rare psychological conditions and develop hypotheses for larger studies. Case studies do not, however, allow us to draw conclusions about causality.
- To draw causal conclusions, a research study needs to include an experimental control condition (in which the variable to be tested is absent).
- Single-case designs (e.g., the ABAB design, multiple baseline design) are studies of individual people that lead to conclusions about causality. They do not, however, allow us to generalize the results to heterogeneous groups of people, and they do not address the impact of individual differences.

critical thinking question Paul does not like school and throws a temper tantrum every day when it is time to walk to the school bus. If you were a therapist in private practice, how would you set up an experimental test to determine whether a treatment program you designed for Paul's parents was working to decrease the tantrums?

Research in Abnormal Psychology at the Group Level

2.5 Understand the principles and applications of correlational research.

Studies based on groups of people are the most common types of research used in abnormal psychology. Using groups allows researchers to draw conclusions based on the average performance across all participants. For example, an investigator recruits a large number of patients with depression for a study of a new treatment. The investigator measures depressive symptoms before and after treatment. After the experiment, depression decreases by 50%, suggesting that on average, patients who participated improved to that degree. The results do not mean, however, that each patient improved by 50%. Some patients benefited less from the treatment and others more. Because the results of the study are based on the average score of the group, they do not allow us to predict the behaviour of any single individual. However, this type of research allows us to develop conclusions about important outcomes, such as the impact of different treatments on different people and the prevalence of various disorders in different groups of people.

Correlational Methods

Group-based studies may be correlational or controlled in nature. Many important questions in abnormal psychology use **correlations**, or relationships, between different variables or conditions to understand aspects of behaviour. Perhaps an investigator

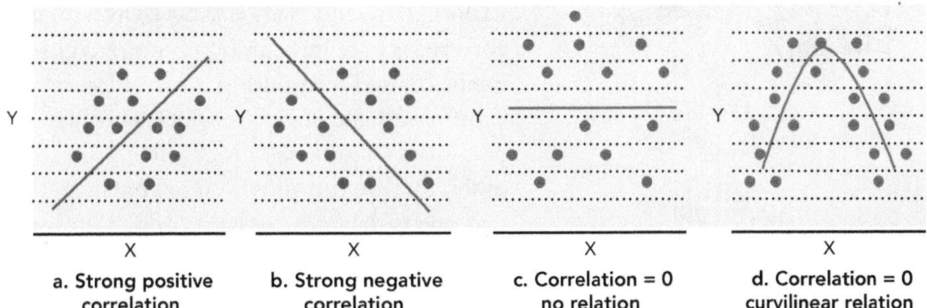

FIGURE 2.9

Examples of Correlational Relations. When data are graphed as points, the shape of the distribution reveals the correlation (or lack of correlation).

wants to know whether the severity of depressive symptoms increases with age. To examine this relationship, the investigator can graphically plot subjects' ages and scores on a depression symptom inventory with age on one axis (perhaps the *X* axis) and depression scores on the other (*Y*) axis. Then, using mathematical calculations, the investigator fits a line to the points to determine the degree of association (see Figure 2.9). A statistical concept known as a **correlation coefficient** indicates the *direction* and *strength* of the relationship. The direction of the relationship is considered positive or negative. When a *positive correlation* exists, an increase in one variable is associated with an increase in another variable (e.g., increased rates of smoking are associated with increased rates of heart disease; Neaton & Wentworth, 1992). In contrast, a *negative correlation* means that an increase in one variable is associated with a decrease in another variable (e.g., increased levels of cognitive engagement such as reading, playing card games, and doing crossword puzzles are associated with decreased risk for Alzheimer's disease; Morris, 2005). The strength of a relationship is determined by the value of the correlation coefficient, which ranges from –1.0 to 1.0. Values close to those end points at 1.0 and –1.0 indicate a stronger relationship. A correlation of 0.0 indicates no linear relationship (see Figure 2.9). It is important to note that a strong relationship can be *either* positive or negative.

Interpreting the significance of a correlation depends on different factors. The first factor involves the size and heterogeneity of the study sample. If the sample of people studied is not sufficiently diverse with regard to the variables of scientific interest, the data may lead to inaccurate conclusions. For example, the relationship between age and memory would appear very different if data were collected from a sample of people between the ages of 18 and 85 compared to a sample of people between the ages of 60 and 70. In the latter group, the restricted age range would lead to correlations that did not represent the true relation between these two variables for the population as a whole.

Another factor important in interpreting correlational data is the way participants are selected. If study participants are chosen because they have a certain psychiatric disorder or because they come from a particular ethnic group, results will generalize only to that subset of people. The study findings may not be relevant for other diagnostic groups or other ethnicities.

Sometimes the relationship between two variables does not appear as a straight line; that is, it is not linear in nature. For example, a popular theory about the association between stress and performance proposes an *inverted-U* relationship. For testing situations or athletic performances, moderate levels of stress are associated with optimal performance. Much higher and lower levels of stress create poor performance (Muse et al., 2003). This is known as a *curvilinear* relationship. Plotting a straight line through an inverted-U shape would yield a linear correlation coefficient near 0 (see Figure 2.9d). This would lead to a false conclusion that no relation exists between the two variables.

Correlation is not causation. Looking at these pictures, you might conclude that larger fires are caused by the presence of more fire trucks. Why would this be an incorrect assumption?

(top): Dariush M/Shutterstock; **(bottom):** Stockbyte/Getty Images

CORRELATION IS NOT CAUSATION Often correlations are inaccurately interpreted to imply a causal relationship. Correlations explain only the degree to which a change in one variable is *associated* with a change in the other; they do not allow you to conclude that one variable *causes* the second. A strong positive correlation between variables *X* and *Y*, for example, may be the result of *X* causing *Y*, *Y* causing *X*, or a third variable (*Z*) that influences both. In this example, the variable *Z* would be referred to as a *moderator* variable. For example, a significant correlation exists between moderate alcohol use (up to three drinks a day) and reduced risk of dementia in people age 55 and over (Ruitenberg et al., 2002). Often inaccurately reported in the media as causal (e.g., drinking moderately can prevent dementia), the data merely suggest that these two phenomena are related. In fact, moderate alcohol use may have a *direct* impact on cognitive functioning through the release of a neurotransmitter (acetylcholine, or ACTH) in the hippocampus (a centre for learning and memory). Alcohol use might also influence cognitive status *indirectly* through its effects on cardiovascular risk factors, decreasing the possibility of high blood pressure or stroke, both of which in turn could affect cognitive functioning. Other explanations might implicate different variables that could influence both alcohol use and the development of dementia (e.g., exercise level, education, genetic predispositions, type of dementia). Any of these alternatives could be the moderator variable (*Z*) that affects the relationship between alcohol and dementia.

It is even more tempting to assume a causal relationship when a significant correlation occurs between two variables that are measured at different points in time (e.g., grades in high school vs. those in college or university). In these cases, terms such as *risk factor* or *predictor* are used to describe this temporal relationship. For example, it is generally well known that cigarette smoking and lack of exercise are *risk factors* for elevated cholesterol and heart disease. However, other intervening factors may affect the relationship (e.g., nutrition). Because it would be unethical to conduct an experiment in which people were assigned to smoke a certain number of cigarettes per day, we can understand these relationships only through the use of correlational data.

Similarly, the severity of a disorder before treatment is often interpreted to *predict* treatment response. In most cases, more severe symptoms are associated with less positive treatment response, but it is not always clear that more severe symptoms *cause* the less positive response. This is an important point to understand because although "predict" may imply causality in everyday language, in psychology it simply indicates that certain levels of Variable X, assessed at Time 1, are significantly associated with certain levels of Variable Y, assessed at Time 2. *Predict* in this sense does not mean *cause*.

In treatment-focused research, correlational analyses can be very useful. By investigating the relationship between patient characteristics (e.g., demographics, clinical severity, social support resources) and improvement as a result of treatment, investigators find correlational analyses useful both theoretically and practically. For example, identifying groups of patients who do not respond to a treatment may lead to the development of alternative treatments. Although correlational designs may yield important information, these studies can measure only covariation between predictors and outcomes. Controlled group designs must be used to draw conclusions about *causality*.

Controlled Group Designs

2.6 Describe the factors that influence outcomes of randomized controlled trials.

Most research in psychology uses **controlled group designs** that expose groups of participants to different conditions that the investigator manipulates and controls. In these designs, participants in at least one *experimental group* are typically compared with at least one *control group*. These groups are usually designed to be highly similar with regard to as many variables as possible (e.g., age, sex, education) and to vary only on the **independent variable (IV)** that the experimenter controls. For example, one group of depressed patients (the experimental group) receives a treatment and the other group (the control group) does not, but in all other ways the groups are similar. The impact of the IV on some **dependent variable (DV)**, or outcome measure, is then assessed. Statistical analyses examine whether group differences on the DV occur more often than chance. If so, and if the groups differed only on the IV, researchers can conclude that the IV is likely to have caused the differences. The strongest inferences about causality come from randomized controlled designs.

RANDOMIZED CONTROLLED DESIGNS The most critical feature of this design is the **random assignment** of participants to groups. When assignment is truly random, each participant has an equal probability of being assigned to either group. In addition to random assignment, other features of randomized controlled designs can affect the study's conclusions. These include *participant selection procedures*, *internal and external validity*, and *assessment strategies*. When deciding how to select participants, an important consideration is whether to recruit an *analogue* or a *clinical* sample. *Analogue samples* (just like an analogy) are people who have the characteristics of interest and resemble treatment-seeking populations but are not seeking clinical services. Researchers interested in obsessive-compulsive disorder, for example, may recruit an analogue sample by seeking people with high scores on questionnaire measures of obsessions and compulsions. Analogue samples are most often recruited from university campuses or community groups. In contrast, *clinical samples* are people who are seeking services for a specific problem. A researcher in an anxiety disorders clinic may approach patients in the clinic to ask them to participate in a treatment study.

The decision to recruit an analogue or clinical sample is based on both theoretical and practical issues (e.g., what question will be addressed and what resources are available), but the decision has significant implications for the study's conclusions. Consider, for example, an investigator who wishes to examine the efficacy of a treatment for depression in young adults. Conclusions may be dramatically different if the sample is recruited from a general university population (who may have a wide range of feelings of sadness) or from the student counselling centre, where higher levels of depression may be more common (because the students are motivated to seek treatment). Results based on one sample simply may not *generalize* (be relevant) to the other. Researchers who use analogue samples are paying increasingly more attention to the question of whether their results generalize to clinical samples. For example, a group of investigators from Canada and the United States

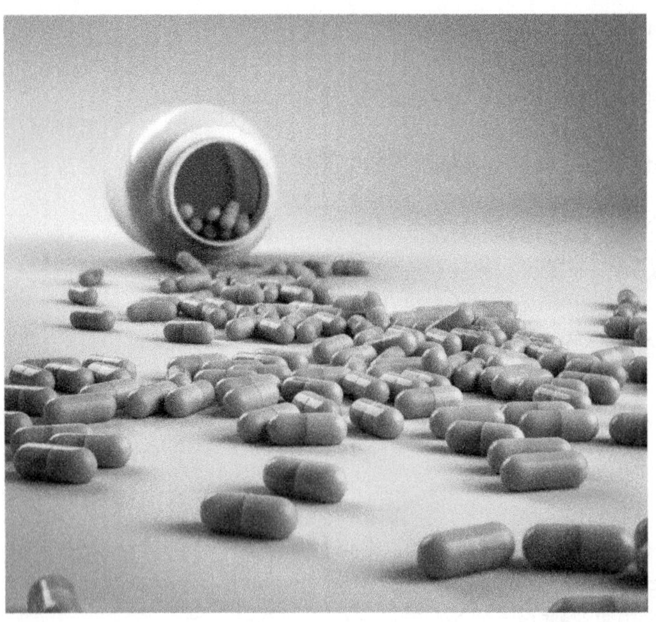

A research study is examining whether therapy is better than no therapy for the treatment of depression. Why would the internal validity of the study be threatened if some participants in the no therapy group started taking an antidepressant drug?

James Steidl/Shutterstock

recently investigated whether findings from studies of obsessive-compulsive (OC) symptoms in university students who did not have obsessive-compulsive disorder (OCD) could be generalized to patients meeting diagnostic criteria for OCD. Results suggest that the findings did generalize for studies concerning the causes of OC symptoms (Abramowitz et al., 2014).

The diversity and representativeness of the recruited sample also affect whether study findings can be generalized. For instance, many studies fail to include a sufficient number of participants representing ethnic minority groups; findings therefore may not be relevant for large segments of the population. In fact, guidelines from the Canadian Institutes of Health Research, which is Canada's leading funding agency for health research, emphasize the importance of including diverse groups of participants in clinical research to represent the population adequately in terms of age, sex, and ethnicity.

Another issue of critical importance when examining the data from any study is the concept of validity. *Internal validity* is the extent to which the study design allows conclusions that the IV (intervention) caused changes in the DV (outcome). To increase internal validity, the researcher tries to control (keep constant) all variables except the one being tested (the IV). Limiting a study sample to women only, for example, increases internal validity and our ability to draw causal conclusions because potential differences in response based on sex need not be considered. To increase internal validity in a treatment study, a researcher would want to make sure that both subgroups of participants (those getting treatment and those not getting treatment) have exactly the same experiences over the course of the study with the exception of the actual treatment being tested. For example, to increase internal validity in a study of depression treatment, it would be important to ensure that participants in both groups receive no additional services or experiences that might reduce depression (e.g., support groups at church, medication from a primary care doctor) during the study period.

When internal validity increases, however, *external validity*, or the ability to generalize study findings to situations and people outside the experimental setting, often decreases. This occurs because study conditions that are well controlled often fail to represent the "real world." For example, results of a study based only on women participants may be relevant only to women but not to men, and studies of depression treatment that restrict participants' activities outside of the experimental treatment may not represent what happens in real life.

A major challenge for researchers is to strike an adequate balance between internal and external validity. Researchers want to be able to draw adequate conclusions about causal relationships, yet they also want results that are relevant to real-life phenomena. In treatment outcome research, internal and external validity are differentially emphasized in *efficacy* versus *effectiveness* research (Roy-Byrne et al., 2003). Efficacy research attempts to maximize internal validity, allowing the researcher to feel confident in identifying causal relationships. Patients are carefully selected to represent a *homogeneous group* (i.e., to have only the disorder the investigators want to study and no other conditions); specialized providers use a highly structured intervention; and comparison groups are chosen carefully to control for key elements of the treatment approach. These well-controlled studies allow the researcher to draw solid conclusions about the impact of the specific treatment, but sometimes the research procedures do not reflect real-world patients and clinics. In effectiveness research, which focuses more on external validity than efficacy research, patients are more heterogeneous and more similar to the types of patients treated in routine care. Treatment is often provided in typical health care settings (e.g., primary care) by clinicians who work in those settings; control conditions more often consist of the type of care typically offered in that clinic; and more emphasis is given to the cost–benefit ratio of treatment. These studies are sometimes less well controlled with respect to research design, but the results are more representative of what might happen when treatments are used in the real world. Efficacy and effectiveness designs are best viewed as complementary approaches to treatment research.

Conclusions from randomized controlled designs also depend on the assessment strategies researchers use. First and foremost, assessment instruments must be *reliable* (measure a particular variable consistently over time and across patients) and *valid* (measure a variable accurately) (see Chapter 3 for more detailed information about reliability and validity) . Using more than one assessment method is also important. For example, some measures of depression emphasize physical symptoms, such as sleep, whereas others emphasize difficulties in thinking, such as concentration and memory problems. Depression can be evaluated using self-report (typically through standardized questionnaires or surveys), global ratings by expert evaluators, direct observations of behaviour, and psychobiological measures. Choosing measures that represent different methods of assessment also increases the confidence and generalizability of study findings.

Two other important issues related to our ability to draw conclusions from controlled research studies include the use of **placebo control** conditions and the consideration of *blinded* assessment. Even in controlled research, the expectations or biases of the researcher and the participants can affect study findings (e.g., participants who think they are getting a good treatment may get better just because they expect to do so). A placebo control group is one in which an inactive treatment is provided; all aspects of this treatment are like those of the experimental condition, but without the active ingredients of the treatment. For example, in medication studies, the placebo control group receives a pill that looks exactly like the real medication, but that in fact has no real medication (i.e., like a "sugar pill"). Because a significant proportion of patients get better with a placebo treatment (called *placebo response*), this type of control condition allows the researcher to estimate what percent of improvement is actually due to expectation alone. Only if the experimental treatment produces greater response than the placebo can we say that the active ingredients of the treatment are important. In placebo-controlled studies, it is important for patients and any people who rate the degree of improvement to remain blinded to (unaware of) the condition to which the patient has been assigned.

For example, what if Monica agreed to participate in a research treatment study for depression, but she and the researchers knew that she had been assigned to the "placebo group"? How would Monica evaluate her improvement if she knew that she was not receiving active treatment?

To reduce bias that may influence study findings, it is important to keep research participants and evaluators blinded, or uninformed, about study goals and hypotheses as well as their assigned treatment condition (active treatment, placebo, or no treatment control). Completely blind assessment is not always feasible, but this assessment strategy is helpful for enhancing study validity because it reduces bias regarding treatment outcome.

CLINICAL VS. STATISTICAL SIGNIFICANCE Another important consideration when evaluating clinical research is clinical versus statistical significance.

Suppose that after treatment, people in the treatment condition report that it now takes only 2 hours to fall asleep compared with 2.2 hours for people in the control group.

Statistical significance refers to the mathematical probability that after treatment, changes that occurred in the treatment group did not occur by chance but were actually due to the treatment. Statistically significant findings show that the treatment changed the target behaviour. But an equally important question is whether the significant findings have any practical or clinical value. Sometimes statistical significance indicates the presence of important clinical changes, but not always. In some studies, particularly those with large samples, statistically significant differences may actually be quite small (as in the sleep example just mentioned) and have no real implications for patient care.

By contrast, *clinical significance* examines whether significant findings have practical or clinical value. For example, do treatments that reduce symptom severity have a meaningful impact on patients' lives?

Does a patient such as Monica, who was so depressed that she could not get out of bed before treatment, now not only feel less depressed but also feel well enough to be able to return to work?

The population sample used in research—whether similar or diverse—greatly influences the conclusions that can be drawn from the study.

(top): Yuri Arcurs/Fotolia; **(bottom):** altrendo images/Stockbyte/Getty Images

Clinical significance addresses whether the patient's functioning is improved as a result of treatment and the patient no longer has symptoms of a disorder. When statistically significant change occurs without major impact on patients' functioning, its clinical value is questionable. From a statistical perspective, various measures of the magnitude of the treatment effect are known as *effect sizes*. The larger the effect size, the greater the difference between the active treatment and the control group.

Improvement of Diversity in Group-Based Research

As noted earlier, one major limitation of group-based research in abnormal psychology is the failure to include sufficiently diverse samples with regard to race, ethnicity, and culture. For many years, samples were also restricted with regard to sex and age. Much medical and clinical research conducted well into the 1980s, for example, excluded women. There are several reasons for this exclusion. One was the difficulty inherent in controlling for biological differences between the sexes, increasing the complexity and costs of any research design. Another concern, especially with medication trials, is the unknown effect of many new medications on the developing fetus and the difficulties inherent in ensuring that women participating in a clinical trial do not become pregnant during the course of the trial. Third, phase of the menstrual cycle can influence response to many interventions and is another variable that needs to be either incorporated into the study design or controlled. Although many of these reasons for exclusion are practical and defensible from a legal and ethical perspective, they have resulted in our knowing less about the efficacy of some medications in women. Older adults were often excluded from research as well because of the complex medical, psychological, and social changes that accompany aging. Such exclusion criteria made it impossible to draw conclusions relevant to diverse groups of people. Similarly, the overabundance of research in abnormal psychology that has been conducted with white individuals (often those attending university) may have little relevance for understanding abnormal behaviour in people of other races, ethnicities, and cultures.

A growing body of research has begun to document differences in the expression, prevalence, and treatment response of mental health symptoms across different racial and ethnic groups, but recruiting adequate samples is still a challenge. As a result of a series of unethical practices that occurred during the first half of the twentieth century (see Chapter 15), lack of trust and fear of stigmatization make some participants from ethnically diverse backgrounds reluctant to participate in research (Shavers et al., 2002). In addition, recruitment strategies often are inadequate for engaging minority participants (Sheikh, 2006). To encourage sex, age, racial, and ethnic diversity in research samples, many grant funding agencies now encourage the recruitment of traditionally underrepresented groups. Increasing diversity in research samples will enhance our ability to generalize study findings to more people. Furthermore, using a diverse sample provides a context for evaluating cultural differences that may affect assessment and treatment. Including diverse participants in research may require increased recruitment resources to target underrepresented groups. It also requires cultural sensitivity to explain the purpose of the research and ensure that assessment instruments are available for persons who speak different languages and come from different educational backgrounds.

Cross-Sectional and Longitudinal Cohorts

One question that has long fascinated researchers who conduct group-based research is how mental illness has changed in the population over time. It appears that some disorders are more common today than they once were, but how do we know this for sure? A related question is whether disorders occur only in one phase of life, such as childhood, or continue to be present once they appear. Specific types of group-based studies, often called **cohort studies**, can be used to answer such questions.

WHAT IS A COHORT? A **cohort** is a group of people who share a common characteristic and move forward in time as a unit. Examples include a *birth cohort* (e.g., all individuals born in a certain geographic area in a given year), an *inception cohort* (e.g., all individuals enrolled in a study at a given point in time based on a unifying factor such as place of work or school of attendance), and an *exposure cohort* (e.g., individuals sampled based on a common exposure such as witnessing the events of 9/11 or exposure to lead paint in childhood). Cohort designs are used to study incidence (onset of new cases), causes, and prognosis (outcome). Because they measure events in chronological order, they can help us to distinguish more clearly between cause and effect. For example, if we observe that experience of a traumatic event precedes the onset of posttraumatic stress disorder (PTSD), we can be more confident that the traumatic events might play a causal role in the development of the disorder than if we had no information on which came first—the trauma or the symptoms. Cohort designs can include longitudinal studies to measure outcomes over time. Longitudinal designs measure the same cohort of individuals on several occasions (see "Longitudinal Design").

CROSS-SECTIONAL DESIGN A **cross-sectional design** provides a snapshot in time. In its most basic form, participants in a cross-sectional design are assessed once for the specific variable under investigation. This design is efficient and can sample large numbers of individuals; however, cause and effect can rarely be determined. Expanding the design to include several cohorts of different ages who are assessed at the same point in

FIGURE 2.10

Percentage of Individuals Who Smoke, by Age and Sex. The data show that males are more likely to smoke in all age groups except the youngest.

Source: www.statcan.gc.ca/pub/82-625-x/2013001/article/11844-eng.htm. Accessed March 4, 2015.

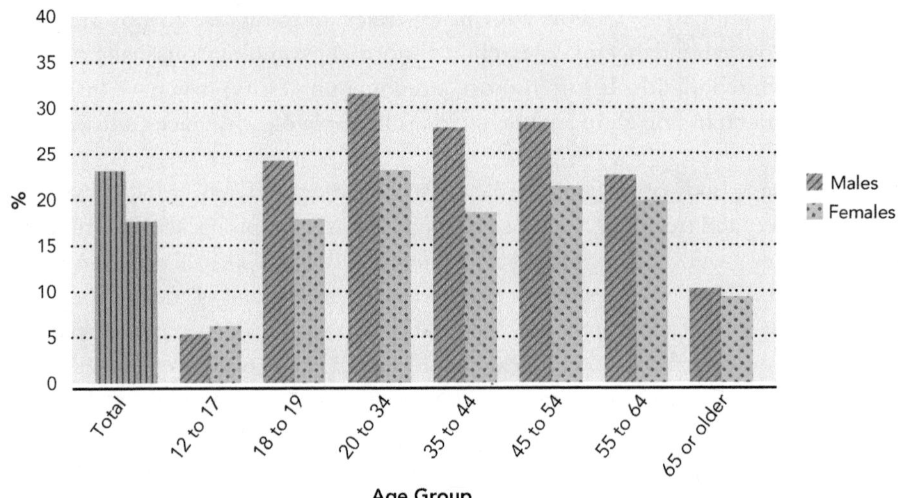

time (e.g., all children enrolled in classes in a specific school district) provides a more complex picture of the variable of interest. To illustrate, the 2012 Canadian Community Health Survey, conducted by Statistics Canada, assessed, among other things, cigarette use in the general population. Figure 2.10 shows the percentage of individuals across age cohorts who reported cigarette use. This research design provides a cross-sectional landscape of people in one year, but it does not follow the same individuals throughout the lifespan.

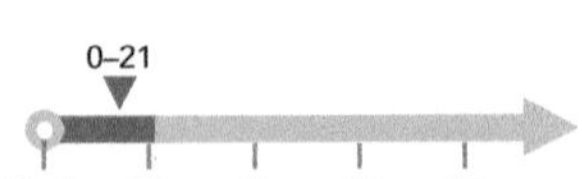

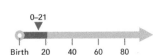

Babies born at the same time represent a birth cohort. If such a cohort is followed over the years, the result is a longitudinal study.

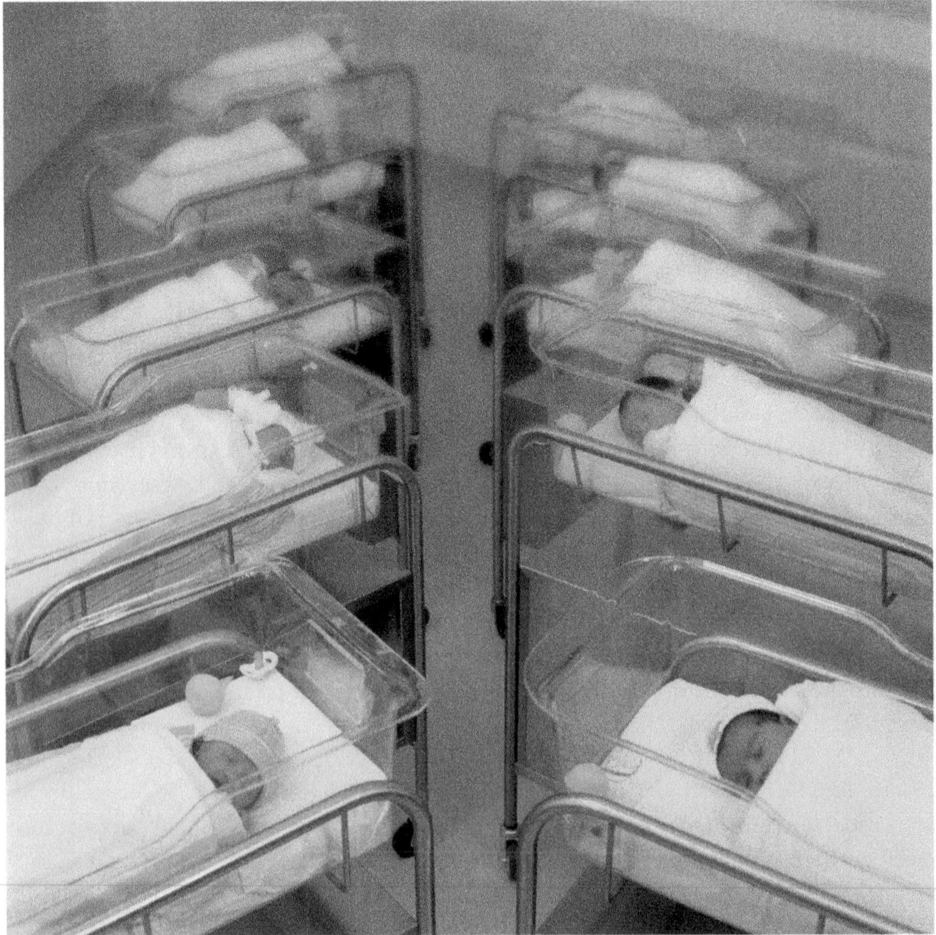

Many longitudinal studies use a birth cohort and follow the members until they reach adulthood.

Ben Edwards/Stockbyte/Getty Images

LONGITUDINAL DESIGN A **longitudinal design** is a study that takes place over time. This design includes at least two and often more measurement periods with the same individuals at different times. Many longitudinal studies have provided valuable data about the development of mental illness across the lifespan. Longitudinal cohorts can be assessed over the years by using age-appropriate measures at each measurement interval. A longitudinal birth cohort might sample all babies born during a certain month in a given area and follow those babies well into adulthood. Early assessments will be based on parental observations of the child, and later assessments will include age-appropriate assessments that the children complete themselves—as well as reports from parents and teachers. Outcomes measured in a longitudinal study may include incidence rates of disease, descriptions of the natural course of a variable of interest, and observations of risk factors. For example, in the birth cohort just mentioned, we could observe the incidence of autism spectrum disorder (or the number of newly diagnosed cases during the observation period), the natural course of autism spectrum disorder (how symptoms develop over the course of the 20-year observation period), and factors that were measured before the onset of the illness that are associated with those individuals who develop autism spectrum disorder (e.g., older parents).

Another example of longitudinal research concerns smoking behaviours. Smoking among young Canadians is a major public health concern, especially because the younger a person starts smoking, the more difficult it will be to quit later in life (Lovato et al., 2013). On average, Canadian smokers report that they started smoking regularly by age 18 (Janz, 2012). School-based programs and policies have been developed to address this addictive behaviour. Researchers at the University of British Columbia implemented the Project Impact Study in which students at 51 Canadian high schools from 5 provinces were followed from 2004 to 2007 to investigate the effects of school-based tobacco control policies, programs, the areas surrounding the schools (neighbourhoods), and regional environments (municipalities) on school smoking prevalence. From 2004 to 2007, smoking prevalence dropped from 13.3% to 10.7%. A lower prevalence of smoking was predicted by the use of school prevention programs as well as particular community characteristics (e.g., higher cigarette prices for cigarettes sold near schools). The findings suggest that many factors influence adolescent smoking behaviour, including various social factors that can be modified to reduce smoking. Although there are biological and psychological factors that influence smoking, the Project Impact Study reminds us of the importance of taking a broader, biopsychosocial approach to understanding and treating harmful behaviours such as smoking. Although longitudinal studies are slow and expensive to complete, their findings are valuable because they show us what happens to the same people over a long period of time.

CONCEPT check

- Correlational research tells us about the relationships between variables, but variables that are highly correlated (related) do not necessarily have a causal relationship (one of the variables does not necessarily cause the other).
- The way participants are selected, the internal and external validity of the study design, and the types of measures used influence the outcomes of a randomized clinical trial.
- Efficacy research attempts to maximize internal validity and the ability to draw causal conclusions, whereas effectiveness research emphasizes external validity and increased applicability to real-world patients and settings.
- Statistical significance refers to the mathematical probability that changes after treatment are due to the treatment itself. Clinical significance examines whether significant findings have practical or clinical value.

research HOT topic

Comorbidity

Comorbidity is the term used to describe the presence of at least two mental disorders affecting an individual. *Current comorbidity* refers to the occurrence of two more disorders at the same time, whereas *lifetime comorbidity* refers to the occurrence of two more disorders at some point in the person's life, even though the disorders need not occur at the same time. Both types of comorbidity are important for several reasons. First, comorbidity is common. According to some community surveys, a third to two thirds of people with a lifetime history of one mental disorder also have a history of at least one other disorder (Gadalla & Piran, 2008; Kessler et al., 2005). Survey data from Statistics Canada further show that mental disorders are often comorbid with migraine headaches and with general medical conditions such as diabetes, hypertension, and cardiovascular disease (Johansen et al., 2011).

The second reason for the importance of comorbidity concerns treatment. People with two or more disorders, compared to people with a single disorder, are more likely to present for treatment (Findlay & Sunderland, 2014). In addition, people with multiple disorders may be sometimes more difficult to treat, or may require longer periods of treatment (Johansen et al., 2011).

The third reason for the importance of comorbidity has to do with the causes of mental disorders. Why do some types of disorders commonly co-occur, such as depressive disorders and substance use disorders? There are several possible explanations. One possibility is that the two might be caused by some common genetic or environmental factor. Another possibility is that one disorder might be a *consequence* of another disorder. A person with substance use disorder might experience many stressors and losses as a result of the disorder, such as financial difficulties, job loss, the breakup of a marital relationship, or even homelessness. Such events may cause a person to become demoralized and even clinically depressed. A person with agoraphobia (see Chapter 4) might be too frightened to leave the house and thereby fail to get sufficient physical exercise, which could lead to general medical conditions associated with a sedentary lifestyle, such as cardiovascular disease. Thus, there are many reasons why comorbidity is an important research topic for understanding and treating mental disorders.

- Increasing the diversity of research participants with regard to race, ethnicity, and culture is essential for increasing our ability to generalize research findings.
- Cohort studies can be used to study the frequency, causes, and prognosis (likely outcome) of mental disorders.

critical thinking question In a new study, the investigators examine the impact of cognitive behaviour therapy (CBT) for depression in a group of children aged 7 to 17. Half of the children will receive CBT, and the other half will get "supportive treatment" (i.e., they will spend time talking to the therapist about whatever they want). The investigators are interested in how well the treatment affects depressive symptoms and quality of life. What are the independent and dependent variables in this investigation?

Research in Abnormal Psychology at the Population Level

2.7 Recognize the principles and applications of epidemiological research as they relate to the understanding of abnormal behaviour.

When a researcher's goal is to understand abnormal psychology at the broadest possible level, the "group" of interest can become the general population. To achieve this bird's-eye view, we use the research tools associated with epidemiological research, which examines abnormal behaviour at its most global level, that of entire populations.

Epidemiology

Epidemiology focuses on disease patterns in human populations and factors that influence those patterns (Gordis, 2013). As applied to abnormal psychology, epidemiology focuses on the occurrence of psychological disorders by time, place, and persons. Several concepts are key to understanding epidemiological research. The first is **prevalence**, which is the total number of cases of a disorder in a given population at a designated time. *Point prevalence* refers to the number of individuals with a disorder at a specified point in time. *Lifetime prevalence* refers to the total number of individuals in a population known to have had a particular disorder at any time during their lifetimes. For example, the lifetime prevalence for major depression is the number of people in Canada who have had an episode of major depressive disorder at any point in their lives.

In contrast, **incidence** refers to the number of new cases that emerge in a given population during a specified period of time. An example of incidence could be the number of new cases of anorexia nervosa reported by pediatricians in Canada over the period of one year. Both incidence and prevalence are valuable in understanding patterns of occurrence of psychological disorders across time and across populations, and we will refer to these concepts throughout this text.

Epidemiological Research Designs

Researchers studying the epidemiology of a disorder typically ask questions such as these: How often do certain disorders occur in the population? Are certain characteristics of people or places more likely to be associated with certain kinds of disorders? Can we do anything to change certain patterns of prevalence and incidence? These research designs can be observational (the researcher simply observes what is happening) or experimental (the researcher tries to change something and examine the effects).

OBSERVATIONAL EPIDEMIOLOGY The most basic form of epidemiological research is *observational epidemiology*, which documents the presence of physical or psychological disorders in human populations. For psychological disorders, the most common method of documentation is to conduct diagnostic interviews using a structured interview format in which all people interviewed are asked the same questions. Using randomly selected segments of the population, this design allows researchers to determine the point or lifetime prevalence of various psychological disorders. Quite simply, it answers these questions: How many people suffer from a disorder (e.g., depression)? Are certain subsets of the population (e.g., women) more likely than others to suffer from the disorder? Data from epidemiological studies were presented in Chapter 1, in the discussion of rates of psychological disorders in Canada.

examining the EVIDENCE

Can Obesity Be Prevented in Children?

- **The Facts** The aim of the Girls, health Enrichment Multi-site Studies (GEMS) was to prevent the onset of obesity (Ebbeling & Ludwig, 2010; Klesges et al., 2010; Robinson et al., 2010).
- **The Evidence** At one site (Site 1), girls aged 8 to 10 were randomly assigned to either a group that used group behavioural counselling to promote healthy eating and increased physical activity (obesity prevention program) or to a self-esteem and social efficacy group (control group). At the second site (Site 2), girls aged 8 to 10 and their families were randomly assigned to either after-school dance classes and programs to reduce screen media use (obesity prevention program) or to information-based health education (control group). Girls participated in the programs for two years. Despite the carefully controlled investigations, culturally appropriate

(continued)

interventions, inclusion of families, and many community and government resources, changes in body mass index (the primary outcome variable that is calculated as weight in kilograms divided by height in metres squared [kg/m2]) was the same for the prevention and control groups, indicating that treatment had no effect. What went wrong?

- **Examining the Evidence** First, this was a trial to prevent obesity, but a number of the girls were already obese (40.6% in Site 1; 33.0% in Site 2). The results may have been different if obese children had not been included in the sample. Second, although the study focused on healthy eating and exercise, many of the girls lived in low-income communities where fresh foods were not available, school lunches were not always nutritious, fast food was common, and neighbourhoods were not necessarily safe places for children to play outdoors. These negative environmental factors may have been more powerful than the positive effects of the intervention. Third, the diet and exercise programs may have been too complicated for 8- to 10-year-old girls to understand.
- **Conclusion** It would be easy to conclude from this study that obesity cannot be prevented, but that would be incorrect. Although it did not produce the expected results, the research provided a number of important clues that researchers can use to develop potentially more effective prevention trials.

EXPERIMENTAL EPIDEMIOLOGY In **experimental epidemiology**, the scientist manipulates exposure to either causal or preventive factors. A scientist might want to assess whether various environmental manipulations would be effective in producing weight loss (see "Examining the Evidence: Can Obesity Be Prevented in Children?"). The focus in this instance is on weight loss for a community as a whole, not for any one individual person. Ten geographically separated communities could be randomly assigned to a community-based weight control program focusing on increasing walking to school, decreasing fast-food consumption, and decreasing video game and TV time. The active intervention communities could be saturated with billboards, ads, local television commercials, and direct mailings, all promoting healthy approaches to weight control. The control communities would receive no intervention. Population-level outcomes would include the extent to which people were reached by the intervention and the extent to which the intervention was effective in producing both behaviour and weight change.

real SCIENCE real LIFE

Susan—A Participant in a Randomized Controlled Trial

Susan had been having episodes of depression and finally went to see her primary care doctor for advice. She gave Susan brochures about a therapy trial for depression at a nearby university and suggested that Susan call for more information. The following describes Susan's experience as a participant in the clinical psychotherapy trial.

SCREENING CALL

Today I called the research coordinator for information. She told me that the study was for women between the ages of 20 and 40 and was designed to compare two different psychotherapies for depression. She described the two treatments to me—one was based on something called cognitive-behaviour therapy, and the other one was based on interpersonal psychotherapy. She explained that I would not be able to choose which treatment I received, but it would be decided by a procedure that was like a flip of a coin [randomization]. She asked me a bunch of questions on the phone about my mood; how long I had been feeling this way; my sleep, appetite, and energy levels; whether I was suicidal; and whether I was on any medications. Then, based on my answers to those questions, she said we could set up an appointment for an initial evaluation.

INITIAL EVALUATION

I got to the clinic and was greeted by the research coordinator. She spent a lot of time explaining the study to me and gave me an information sheet. I read it, and she asked if I had any questions. Then came all of the forms! First I filled out a **consent form** agreeing to the terms of the study and indicating that I understand my rights as a participant. I was assured that I could withdraw from the study at any time. Just when I thought I was finished filling out forms, she gave me a packet of questionnaires that asked all sorts of questions—not only about my mood, but also about anxiety, eating, my family, and all sorts of questions about what sort of person I am. Some of them were really hard to answer, but I had to choose yes or no. That took about an hour and a half.

Then I had a little break, and the coordinator explained that the next step would be a comprehensive evaluation by a psychiatrist. She explained that the psychiatrist would not be the person who would be seeing me for therapy, but would conduct interviews with me throughout the study to see how I was progressing. The psychiatrist would not know which treatment I was receiving. In the evaluation, the psychiatrist asked a lot of the same questions that were on the questionnaire. This was a little irritating, but I guess the psychiatrist went into more depth than the questionnaires. She even asked about the first time I ever felt depressed when I was very young. She also asked questions about whether I heard voices or saw things that other people did not see, asked about my drug and alcohol use (I was honest with her about almost everything—I just couldn't bring myself to tell her about that one experience with Ecstasy, though—I barely know the woman and it was kind of embarrassing). She also asked all sorts of questions about my health and medications.

I met with the research coordinator again, she invited me into the study, and then she got an envelope that had my participant number on it, opened it, and told me I was randomized to cognitive-behaviour therapy.

BASELINE WEEK

At the end of the evaluation day, the research coordinator instructed me on how to "self-monitor" my mood for the baseline week. She gave me a special personal digital assistant (PDA) into which I was supposed to type in how depressed I felt every time it prompted me. I thought that was kind of cool—but worried about whether it would wake me up at night. She explained that the PDA was programmed for 8 a.m. to 10 p.m. and that I would not be bothered by prompts any other time. So off I went with my PDA for a week of recording before my first appointment. I also left with the card of my therapist, Dr. McIntosh, whom I would see the following Thursday. For a week I dutifully responded every time the PDA pinged me. It was kind of interesting. I noticed that my mood ratings always seemed to be worse in the afternoon.

COURSE OF THERAPY

I went to the clinic, and Dr. McIntosh greeted me. The first session went well. I liked her. She had a positive attitude and seemed like she really believed that the therapy had the potential to help. She took her time and explained everything clearly. She also told me that I needed to continue responding to the PDA throughout the study. For the first two weeks we met twice a week. She gave me a workbook and we worked through it step by step. Every session she started off reviewing how things had gone since the last session and whether I had done all of my self-monitoring and homework. It felt a little bit like school, but she really seemed to care about how I was feeling. She helped me start to recognize how negative my thinking was, and she challenged me to start doing some of those fun things that I had lost interest in recently. I never realized how much I catastrophized from the smallest of things, or as Dr. McIntosh said, really made mountains out of molehills. I also had not realized how much my mood improved when I did some of the things on my fun list (even if I had to really push myself to do them in the first place).

After the eighth session, I met with the psychiatrist again for another assessment. She went over many of the same questions as in the beginning, and I had to fill out *more* questionnaires. After eight sessions, I felt as if my mood was getting better. I still had some bad days, but it did not feel like the same oppressive cloud that had been there before. I had eight more sessions—first once a week and then once every two weeks. Dr. McIntosh and I spent a lot of time working on strategies for what to do if I feel like my mood slips again—like identifying early warning signs and taking immediate action. By the end I really felt like I understood how much my own thinking patterns contributed to my staying depressed.

FOLLOW-UP

At the end of treatment I met with the psychiatrist again for an interview and I filled out more questionnaires. The research coordinator also asked me lots of questions about how I liked the treatment and whether I would have it again or recommend it to others. I came back at six months and one year for follow-up appointments and met with the psychiatrist again and filled out more papers. Each time, the research coordinator checked in with me to see how things were going and to update my contact information. The second time, I ran into Dr. McIntosh. It was great to see her and to report that I was still feeling really well. When I look back on the whole experience of being in the study, honestly, I had been a little worried about being a "guinea pig." But truth be told, I felt really taken care of. So many people seemed to care about my well-being, and they were all involved with my treatment. It was an amazing experience.

CONCEPT check

- Epidemiology in abnormal psychology research addresses the occurrence of psychological disorders and the factors that influence them.
- Prevalence refers to the total number of cases of a disorder that appear in a given population at a designated time. Incidence describes the number of new cases that emerge during a given period of time.
- Longitudinal studies can provide key information about the prevalence and correlates of mental disorders in adults and youth.

critical thinking question A researcher wants to design a study to determine how frequently anxiety occurs in adults and whether the frequencies change as people get older. What type of study would be best to conduct, and how might you design it?

summary

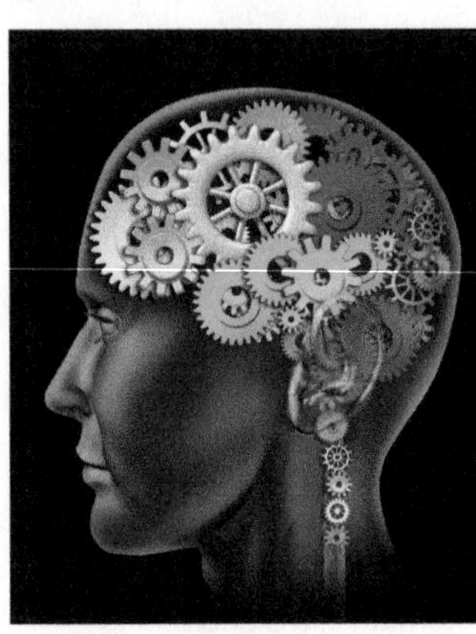

2.1 Understand how research in psychology ranges from the cellular to the population level.

Research on psychological disorders occurs on many levels, from the cellular or neuroanatomical to the individual or group levels, and to the population level. Applying all of these approaches to the study of a single disorder helps us form a comprehensive picture of the nature and course of a particular illness.

2.2 Recognize new techniques used to study abnormal psychology at the cellular or neuroanatomical level.

At the cellular level, we can understand mental disorders as we study the brain from an evolutionary perspective, which involves moving from the brain stem (which controls fundamental biological functions) to the forebrain (where higher cognitive functions occur). New techniques at the cellular level include neuroimaging (taking pictures of the brain), studying the function and interrelation of neurotransmitters (chemicals that relay electrical signals between the cells), and molecular genetics (identifying genes that influence risk for psychological disorders).

2.3 Understand the differences between family, twin, and adoption studies (which do not study genes directly) and molecular genetics research (which does directly study genes) and the strengths and limitations of both approaches.

Researchers have learned much about the genetics of psychological disorders over the past decade. Scientists use the family, twin, and adoption studies to study the role of genes in the development of psychological disorders indirectly. Candidate gene, genomewide linkage, and genomewide association studies are more direct techniques that allow for the actual identification of genetic regions or actual genes associated with a trait or a disorder.

2.4 Describe the strengths and limitations of case studies and single-case designs.

Case studies, which provide significant details about abnormal behaviour or its treatment, allow us to study relatively rare psychological conditions and develop hypotheses for larger studies. Case studies do not, however, allow us to draw conclusions about causality. Single-case designs (e.g., the ABAB design and the multiple baseline design) are studies of individual people that lead to conclusions about causality. These studies do not, however, allow us to generalize the results to heterogeneous groups of people, and they do not address the impact of individual differences.

2.5 Understand the principles and applications of correlational research.

Correlational research tells us about the relationships between different variables, but it does not tell us about causality because variables that are highly correlated (related) do not necessarily have a causal relationship with each other: One of the variables does not necessarily cause the other.

2.6 Describe the factors that influence outcomes of randomized controlled trials.

The outcomes of a randomized clinical trial are influenced by how participants are selected, the study design's internal and external validity, and the types of measures used. Different types of clinical trials are designed to answer different questions. Efficacy research, for example, attempts to maximize internal validity and the ability to draw causal conclusions. Effectiveness research emphasizes external validity and increased applicability to real-world patients and settings.

2.7 Recognize the principles and applications of epidemiological research as they relate to the understanding of abnormal behaviour. Epidemiology, the study of populations, permits a bird's-eye view of the study of causes, course, and outcome of psychological disorders. This type of research can tell us about the prevalence of disorders (the number of times the disorder appears in a population) and their incidence (the number of new cases that emerge during a given period of time), as well as whether certain subsets of the population are more likely to suffer from the disorder.

key terms

beneficence 41
brain stem 42
candidate gene association study 52
case study 54
central nervous system (CNS) 42
cerebral cortex 44
cohort 65
cohort studies 65
comorbidity 68
consent form 71
control group 55
controlled group design 61
correlation 58
correlation coefficient 59
cross-sectional design 65
dependent variable (DV) 61
endocrine system 45
epidemiology 69
epigenetics 53
experimental epidemiology 70
experimental variable 55
familial aggregation 50
forebrain 43
frontal lobe 44
genomewide association study 52
genomewide linkage analysis 52
hippocampus 43
hormones 45
incidence 69
independent variable 61
left hemisphere 44
limbic system 43
longitudinal design 67
midbrain 43
molecular genetics 52
neuroanatomy 48
neuroimaging 48
neurotransmitters 47
occipital lobe 44
parietal lobe 44
peripheral nervous system (PNS) 42
placebo control 63
prevalence 69
proband 50
random assignment 61
right hemisphere 44
single-case design 55
temporal lobe 44
translational research 40

TEST yourself

1. Researchers find that a chemical in a recently discovered rainforest plant significantly reduces appetite in laboratory mice. Other researchers then make the chemical into a drug and test it to see whether it helps obese people lose weight. This type of research is called
   a. bedside
   b. bench
   c. translational
   d. communication
2. Which of the following represents all of the different levels of research in abnormal psychology?
   a. cellular, individual, group, and population
   b. neuroanatomy, neurohormones, neurotransmitters, and genetics
   c. correlational, group, cross-cultural, and multiethnic
   d. cross-sectional, longitudinal, cohort, and epidemiological
3. The human nervous system has two main parts:
   a. the left and right cerebral hemispheres
   b. the central nervous system and the peripheral nervous system
   c. the upper and lower brain
   d. the cortex and the brain stem
4. A primary function of the hypothalamus is homeostasis and the regulation of
   a. thoughts and cognitions
   b. sleep/wake states and consciousness
   c. balance and many motor activities
   d. blood pressure, temperature, and weight
5. The autonomic nervous system includes the
   a. neurotransmitter and neurohormone systems
   b. somatic and hormonal nervous systems
   c. sympathetic and parasympathetic nervous systems
   d. midbrain and brain stem
6. Communication in the nervous system relies on signals transmitted by
   a. electrical impulses called *action potentials*
   b. chemicals called *neurotransmitters*
   c. an electrochemical process
   d. all of the above
7. Neuroscientists who want to see brain activity in people with a snake phobia would use which of the following imaging tests?
   a. CT
   b. MRI
   c. fMRI
   d. PET

8. The study of whether certain behavioural traits or mental disorders are heritable, or influenced by genes, is called
   a. epidemiology
   b. behavioural ecology
   c. behavioural genetics
   d. homogeneous group design

9. Which of the following statements best describes what we know about how genes affect behavioural traits?
   a. a few genetic loci control all complex traits
   b. family studies show that genes are less important than environment
   c. behavioural traits are rarely caused by single genes
   d. complex traits exert only small effects

10. Twin studies have been of particular importance in the study of abnormal behaviour because they have
   a. identified genetic vs. environmental contributions to psychological disorders
   b. examined similarities between twins from many different families
   c. shown that MZ twins in different environments develop different disorders
   d. shown that identical twins are never truly identical

11. We cannot infer the causes of behaviour from case studies, but they do let us
   a. rule out subjective biases of the therapist
   b. rule out subjective biases of the patient
   c. control for the attention of the therapist
   d. objectively describe rare phenomena

12. When a treatment cannot be reversed, or if it would be unethical to withdraw a treatment, the single-case design strategy that should be used is called a(n)
   a. case study design
   b. AB design
   c. multiple baseline design
   d. ABAB design

13. A strong positive correlation between the number of cigarettes smoked and the amount of alcohol consumed per day can be interpreted to mean that
   a. smoking leads to drinking
   b. drinking leads to smoking
   c. a third variable such as stress increases both behaviours
   d. any of the above

14. The most common type of research in abnormal psychology is
   a. single-subject design
   b. controlled group design
   c. longitudinal design
   d. epidemiological design

15. A researcher interested in social anxiety placed an ad seeking people with public speaking anxiety. People who volunteer for this type of study are part of a(n)
   a. analogue sample
   b. proband sample
   c. aggregate sample
   d. clinical sample

16. Research on an exciting new treatment that takes place with carefully selected patients at a world-renowned laboratory is less likely to have
   a. external validity
   b. external reliability
   c. internal validity
   d. internal reliability

17. In placebo-controlled studies, experts who rate the degree of patient improvement following treatment must be kept unaware of
   a. the funding source of the study
   b. which subjects are in the treatment group and which are in the control group
   c. who the authors of the study are and whether they implemented the treatment exactly as originally described
   d. whether enough subjects were recruited so that the study will have generalizable results

18. The meaningfulness of experimental results can be evaluated in several ways. The statistical significance of the results indicates the
   a. mathematical probability that the findings occurred by chance
   b. practical value of the findings
   c. clinical value of the findings
   d. all of the above

19. A criticism of early group-based research in abnormal psychology is that it
   a. regularly used samples that were too small
   b. failed to control for biological differences between the sexes
   c. stigmatized many of its subjects
   d. failed to include diverse samples

20. Children accidentally exposed to mercury when vaccinated are evaluated at one point in time. They are followed for 10 years and evaluated again. These children are part of a study called a
   a. group design
   b. longitudinal design
   c. comorbidity study
   d. randomized clinical trial

Answers:
1 c, 2 a, 3 b, 4 d, 5 c, 6 d, 7 c, 8 c, 9 c, 10 a, 11 d, 12 c, 13 d, 14 b, 15 a, 16 a, 17 b, 18 a, 19 d, 20 b.

chapter 3

assessment and diagnosis

(middle left): Zentilia/Shutterstock; **(middle left):** Zentilia/Shutterstock; **(middle center):** gmnicholas/E+/Getty Images; **(middle center):** Christopher Robbins/DigitalVision/Getty Image; **(middle right):** Elena Schweitzer/Shutterstock

learning objectives

After reading this chapter, you should be able to:

3.1
Understand the goals and uses of clinical assessment.

3.2
Name three important properties of psychological assessment instruments.

3.3
List and explain the function of different types of assessment instruments.

3.4
Explain why classification systems for abnormal behaviour are valuable.

3.5
Recognize the importance of developmental and cultural variables that affect the experience and classification of abnormal behaviour.

3.6
Discuss the pros and cons of dimensional models for understanding abnormal behaviour that serve as alternatives to more traditional classification systems.

Pauline was 82 years old and functioned well for her age. She saw Dr. McGuire, a psychologist, every couple of weeks to help her manage anxiety and depression. Pauline had experienced anxiety and depression much of her life, and the coping skills she had learned in treatment were helping. She was active at church and with volunteer groups, travelled, and had many friends. Dr. McGuire, however, had recently started talking with her about the possibility of memory problems. He had noticed that she was starting to repeat herself during their meetings and that she sometimes forgot major topics of their conversations from one session to the next. Pauline's daughter had also mentioned to her the possibility of memory problems, but Pauline didn't think her memory was that bad. Sure, she misplaced things—and people told her that she repeated herself—but at her age, who didn't? As long as she could stay active and involved, it didn't bother her that she might be having some minor memory problems.

One day before a scheduled appointment, Pauline called Dr. McGuire to say that she was in the hospital. She had suffered a bad fall the day before while walking in a shopping mall, and the doctors were running a series of tests. Dr. McGuire requested Pauline's permission to speak to her doctor and learned that there was some concern that Pauline might have had a minor stroke. The doctor would conduct additional tests before she could be discharged.

When Pauline was released from the hospital, she went home with her daughter and followed up with her internist. She had not suffered a stroke, but the doctor was monitoring her symptoms because her blood pressure was high. She was more unstable on her feet and was using a cane. She was not allowed to drive. When Pauline came to her next therapy appointment with Dr. McGuire, her daughter came along. At this session, Pauline was quite confused. She could not recall many details about her hospitalization, and she repeated herself many times. She reported that she was taking pain medication as prescribed and that she would be seeing her internist the following day.

In the weeks that followed, Pauline began to regain some of her prior abilities, but her memory problems got worse, and she was more depressed and anxious. She was more lethargic than usual and worried more about the future and what might happen to her. Dr. McGuire became increasingly concerned about Pauline's ability to live independently and talked with Pauline and her daughter about the need for a more formal clinical assessment. There was a need to differentiate any medical, cognitive, and emotional reasons for Pauline's overall decline in functioning.

At this point, many questions arose for Pauline and Dr. McGuire. Did the fall result from some undiscovered medical problem? Was her pain medication creating more memory problems and depression? Might Pauline's fall and its consequences, such as losing independence, have produced increased worry and depression? Could Pauline's decreased functioning be the result of a progressive, deteriorating cognitive disease such as a neurocognitive disorder (see Chapter 13)? These questions, posed by Pauline, her therapist, and her family members, suggested the need for a clinical assessment to determine the nature and cause of her increasing difficulties as well as to help guide future treatment. They also illustrate the complexity of the biological, psychological, and social factors that can affect psychological functioning.

Clinical Assessment

The **clinical assessment** of any psychological problem involves a series of steps designed to gather information (or *data*) about a person and his or her environment in order to make decisions about the nature, status, and treatment of psychological problems. Typically, clinical assessment begins with a set of *referral questions* developed in response to a request for help. Usually, the request comes from the patient or someone closely connected to that person, such as a family member, teacher, or other health care professional. These initial questions help determine the goals of the assessment and the selection of appropriate psychological tests or measurements. As in Pauline's case, referral questions sometimes suggest the need for a thorough medical evaluation in addition to a psychological assessment.

Goals of Assessment

3.1 Understand the goals and uses of clinical assessment.

As part of the assessment process, the psychologist decides which procedures to follow and instruments to administer. These include measures of biological function, cognition, emotion, behaviour, and personality style. The patient's age, medical condition, and description of his or her symptoms strongly influence the tools selected for assessment, but the psychologist's theoretical perspective also affects the scope of the assessment (see Chapter 1). When evaluating a patient who is significantly depressed and anxious, for example, a behavioural psychologist focuses on measuring the environmental cues that produce the low moods and the thoughts, behaviours, and consequences associated with them. In contrast, a psychoanalytic psychologist would direct more effort toward assessing the patient's early childhood experiences and typical patterns of interpersonal functioning.

Once an assessment has been completed and all data have been collected, the psychologist integrates the findings to develop preliminary answers to the initial questions. Typically, the psychologist shares those findings with the patient and family members involved in the assessment. Other health care providers who were part of the referral or assessment process also may receive the results of the assessment, but only with the patient's permission. Although it is not the purpose of patient evaluation, the process of assessment sometimes has a therapeutic effect (Maruish, 2004). As people begin to understand their emotions, behaviours, and the links between them, their symptoms tend to improve, at least temporarily. If you start to carefully monitor the number of calories that you consume each day, you might discover that the number is far more than originally estimated. In some cases, this assessment serves as feedback, and you decrease the number of calories that you eat as a result of the feedback.

Assessment can be useful even before a referral is provided through the process of *screening*. Screenings can help identify people who have problems but who may not be aware of them or may be reluctant to mention them or those who may need further evaluation. And, at the end of treatment, clinical assessment can measure a patient's progress or the outcomes of intervention (see "Outcome Evaluation").

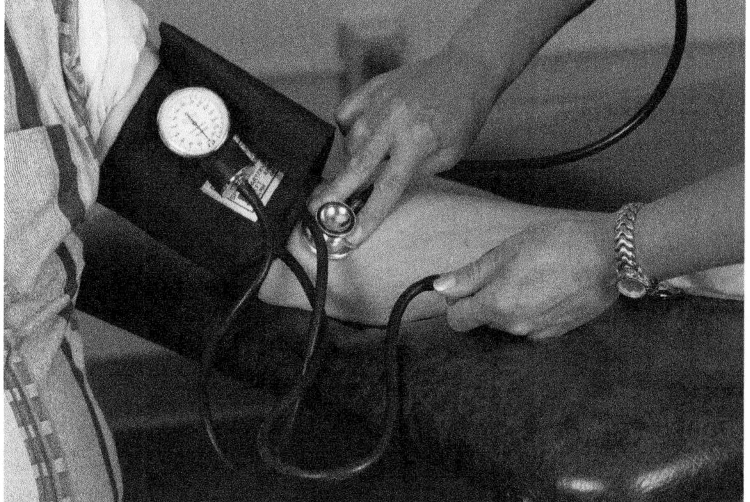

A quick blood pressure screening may be the first step in identifying serious medical problems. Similarly, mental health screenings may be key in the identification of psychological disorders.

PH College/Pearson Education

SCREENING **Screening** assessments identify potential psychological problems or predict the risk of future problems if someone is not referred for further assessment or treatment. In a screening assessment, all members of a group (e.g., a community group, patients in a medical practice) are given a brief measure for which some identified cut-off score indicates the possibility of significant problems. For example, the Center for Epidemiologic Studies—Depression Scale (CES-D; Radloff, 1977) is a 20-item scale used in many community studies to screen people for depression and to estimate its prevalence. A score of 16 or higher on the CES-D indicates the possibility of significant depression and suggests that further evaluation is necessary (Derogatis & Lynn, 1999). Other screening instruments are more broadly based, covering many different psychological symptoms, including depression, anxiety, and social problems (e.g., the General

Health Questionnaire; Goldberg & Hillier, 1979). In most cases, when individuals score above a certain cut-off number on a screening instrument, a more thorough evaluation can determine the nature and extent of their difficulties.

Another set of screening questionnaires has been developed specifically for DSM-5, and they are presented in Section III of that manual (APA, 2013). These measures are the focus of ongoing research evaluation. Many people with psychological problems are more likely to see their physician than a mental health professional. Accordingly, brief methods for screening patients in medical settings have been developed. In fact, very simple two-item screening instruments have been used to identify medical patients with depression (Unützer et al., 2002) or anxiety (Roy-Byrne et al., 2005) who might benefit from psychological or psychiatric treatment. For example, the following questions are used to screen for depression (Spitzer et al., 1994):

- During the past month, have you often been bothered by feeling down, depressed, or hopeless?
- During the past month, have you often been bothered by little interest or pleasure in doing things you normally enjoy?

Asking questions such as these takes just a few minutes in a busy medical practice. Similarly, a 10-item screen can quickly identify substance abuse problems (e.g., Alcohol Use Disorders Identification Test; Barbor et al., 2001). Sample questions include:

- How often do you have a drink containing alcohol?
- How often do you have six or more drinks on one occasion?
- How often during the last year have you been unable to remember what happened the night before because you had been drinking?

Screening measures for use in primary care are also available on the Internet. For example, McMaster University in Ontario offers the MACSCREEN, which is a screening tool for anxiety and is available to the general public (www.macanxiety.com/online-anxiety-screening-test).

To evaluate the usefulness of any particular screening measure, psychologists look for instruments that have strong sensitivity and specificity. *Sensitivity* describes the ability of the screener (or the instrument) to identify a problem that actually exists (e.g., the screener identifies depression and the person is actually depressed). *Specificity* indicates the percent of the time that the screener accurately identifies the absence of a problem (e.g., the cut-off score suggests no depression, and the patient truly is not depressed). *False positives* occur when the screening instrument indicates a problem when no problem exists (e.g., the patient's score exceeds the cut-off, but subsequent evaluation confirms the absence of depression). *False negatives* refer to instances in which the screening tool suggests that there is no depression when the patient actually is depressed. Good screening tools have high specificity and sensitivity, but low false positive and false negative rates (see Figure 3.1).

DIAGNOSIS AND TREATMENT PLANNING One of the major functions of assessment is to determine an individual's diagnosis. **Diagnosis** refers to the identification of an illness. In some branches of medicine, diagnosis can be made on the basis of laboratory tests. In psychology, making a diagnosis is more complicated; it requires the presence of a cluster of symptoms. Typically, a diagnosis is made after a clinical interview with the patient. Clinicians use the term **differential diagnosis** when they attempt to determine which diagnosis most clearly describes the patient's symptoms. Patients often have sets of symptoms that require more than one diagnosis. Using different assessment instruments, the clinician gathers data from the patient and often other sources (partner, parents, and teachers) to make the diagnosis or diagnoses that fit the patient best. Diagnosis also facilitates communication across clinicians and researchers. Diagnostic

		Screening Results (Does the score on a depression measure indicate depression is present?)	
		Positive (Score suggests depression is present.)	Negative (Score suggests depression is absent.)
Actual Problem (Does the person have depression?)	Depression is present.	Sensitivity (Test accurately identifies depression.)	False Negative (Test suggests there is no depression, but patient is depressed.)
	Depression is absent.	False Positive (Test suggests patient is depressed, but patient is not depressed.)	Specificity (Test accurately suggests depression is absent.)

FIGURE 3.1

Evaluating a Screening Tool for Depression. A good screening tool is sensitive and specific: It identifies problems that do exist and does not indicate problems when none exist. The quality of the screening instrument is determined by the numbers in these cells.

REAL people REAL disorders

Cases of Misdiagnosis

In some cases, insufficient assessment and inaccurate diagnosis can lead to inadequate or inappropriate treatment and disastrous consequences. The importance of careful assessment and diagnosis is illustrated in these real cases.

- **Deafness, not Intellectual Disability** Kathy Buckley, comedienne and inspirational speaker (pictured at right), has received numerous awards and accolades for her comic abilities and advocacy for persons with disabilities. Her own poor academic performance in Grade 2 led to a diagnosis of intellectual disability and placement in a school for mentally and physically impaired children. It took professionals a year to determine that Kathy's academic difficulties were due to hearing loss, not mental incapacitation (http://kathybuckley.com).
- **Epilepsy, not Schizophrenia** A 46-year-old woman was hospitalized in a university-affiliated facility with depressive symptoms and hallucinations that had urged her to commit suicide (Swartz, 2001). Laboratory tests (e.g., electroencephalogram, or EEG) revealed that she was having seizures characteristic of complex partial epilepsy, which can also have symptoms such as depression and hallucinations. A review of the patient's clinic records revealed that she had been treated for schizophrenia and schizoaffective disorder (see Chapter 10) for 10 years without an alleviation of her symptoms. Subsequently, she was put on an antiseizure medication, and her symptoms disappeared.

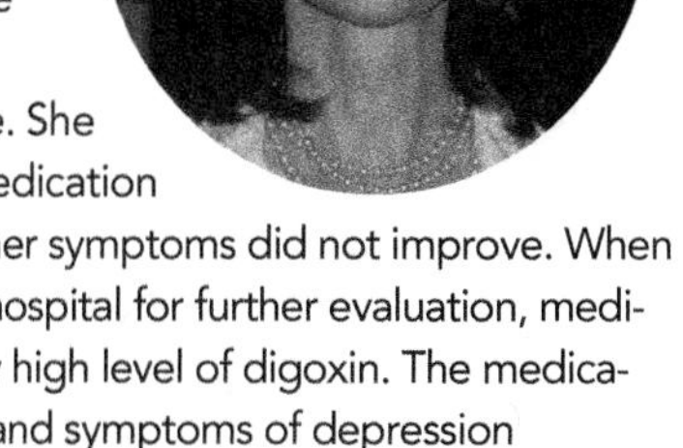

Milan Ryba/ZUMA Press/Newscom

- **Medication Reaction, not Depression** A 77-year-old woman developed symptoms of depression (e.g., fatigue, weight loss, motor slowing, social withdrawal) one month after starting the medication digoxin for congestive heart failure. She took antidepressant medication for seven months, but her symptoms did not improve. When she was admitted to a hospital for further evaluation, medical tests revealed a very high level of digoxin. The medication was discontinued, and symptoms of depression decreased rapidly (Song et al., 2001).
- **Brain Tumour, not Anorexia Nervosa** A 19-year-old girl was admitted to the hospital with symptoms of anorexia nervosa (e.g., rapid weight loss of 7.5 kg (16.5 pounds), dissatisfaction with her body, and occasional binge eating). Doctors started her on nasogastric feeding to increase her caloric intake, and she was given antidepressant medication to help control her anxiety. After the patient was discovered unconscious on the bathroom floor with symptoms consistent with a seizure, a brain scan revealed a brain tumour. Following its surgical removal, the patient's fear of weight gain and her distorted views of her body decreased, and two years later, she no longer showed any residual signs of an eating disorder (Houy et al., 2007).

assessments are more extensive than screens and are designed to provide a more thorough understanding of a person's psychological status.

Accurate diagnoses are critical for planning appropriate treatment (see "Real People, Real Disorders: Cases of Misdiagnosis"). Finally, a diagnosis is often needed for insurance companies to reimburse a psychologist or other health care provider.

A clinical assessment that leads to a diagnosis usually includes the evaluation of symptom and disorder severity, patterns of symptoms over time (e.g., number, frequency, and duration of episodes), and the patient's strengths and weaknesses (Maruish, 2004). The assessment may also include the results from personality tests, neuropsychological tests, and a behavioural assessment. Behavioural psychologists also conduct a *functional analysis* of symptoms, which identifies the relations between situations and behaviours (e.g., what happens before, during, and after certain problem behaviours, moods, or thoughts) to aid in devising a treatment strategy.

OUTCOME EVALUATION Clinical assessments can be repeated at regular intervals during treatment to evaluate a patient's progress. Evaluating outcomes has always been part of clinical psychology as practised from a scientist–practitioner perspective. Outcome evaluations help us know whether patients are getting better, when treatment is "finished," or when a modification to an approach that is not achieving its aims is necessary. Outcome assessment may include evaluating patient satisfaction and providing data to support the marketing of treatment programs.

For outcome assessments to be useful, the same measures must be administered consistently over the course of treatment. The individual measures included in the assessment should represent a range of outcomes (e.g., symptom severity, treatment satisfaction, ability to function, quality of life). When possible, assessment of treatment outcome should go beyond the patient's viewpoint to include the therapist's perspective and perhaps that of family members or others close to the patient (Maruish, 2004). To be useful, the assessment measures must also be reliable and valid. To evaluate whether treatments have the desired effect, both the amount of change and the patient's actual level of functioning after treatment must be assessed. For example, imagine that you are very sick and have a fever of 40 °C. You take some medicine, your fever goes down to 38 °C, and you feel better. The drop in your fever from 40 to 38 °C is the amount of change from the medicine. But you still have a fever of 38 °C, and so you are still sick—this is your actual level of functioning. In evaluating the outcome of psychological disorders, the goal may be to reduce symptoms or to eliminate the disorder.

The amount of change (how much a patient's symptoms have been reduced) is generally considered in terms of **clinical significance** (see Chapter 2). This means that the observed change actually is a meaningful improvement (e.g., social anxiety improves to the extent that the university student can now take courses that require oral presentations). A measure known as the Reliable Change Index (Jacobson & Truax, 1991) is now frequently used to determine whether the degree of change from beginning to end of treatment is meaningful. For example, was the change more than we would expect based on normal changes that occur over time (see "Reliability")? Patients' scores on various measures after treatment are sometimes compared with scores of people without the disorder who have also completed the assessment to evaluate whether symptoms and functioning have moved into the normal range.

Properties of Assessment Instruments

3.2 Name three important properties of psychological assessment instruments.

The potential value of an assessment instrument rests in part on its various *psychometric properties*, which affect how confident we can be in the testing results. We need to know, for example, how well the instrument measures the features or concepts it is intended to measure. How well does a test for depression actually measure depressive symptoms? An instrument's psychometric properties include standardization, reliability, and validity.

STANDARDIZATION To understand the results of clinical assessments, the score must be put in context. Think back to the concept of a fever. A temperature of 40 °C creates concern because it is so much higher than the body's normal temperature of 37 °C. In the same way, to understand the results of a psychological assessment, we must put test results in context. Does a particular score indicate the existence of a problem, its severity, or its improvement over time? Standard ways of evaluating scores can involve normative or self-referent comparisons (or both). **Normative** comparisons require comparing a person's score with the scores of a sample of people who are representative of the entire population (with regard to characteristics such as age, sex, ethnicity, education, and geographic region), or with the scores of a subgroup who are similar to the patient being assessed. If we took the temperature of 100 adults, the average (mean) temperature would be 37 °C. This is the normative body temperature for humans. If a person's score falls too far outside the range of the normative group, we can assume that a problem exists. To decide whether a score is too far outside the range of the normal group, we use a statistic called the *standard deviation* (SD) (see Figure 3.2). SD is a measure that tells us how far away from the mean (average) a particular score is. According to statistical principles, a score that is more than 2 SDs away from the mean is found in only 5% of the population and is considered meaningfully different from what is normal. In comparing scores with normative groups, however, we must always consider the characteristics of both the patient and the group.

If Pauline's scores on the memory tests are low relative to those of the average middle-aged adult but are the same as the scores of other people who are her age and education level, we would not be concerned about the presence of cognitive impairment. If, however, her scores are very low relative to people who are the same as Pauline in terms of age and education, we can conclude that she is experiencing significant cognitive difficulties.

Self-referent comparisons are those that equate responses on various instruments with the patient's own prior performance. They are used most often to examine

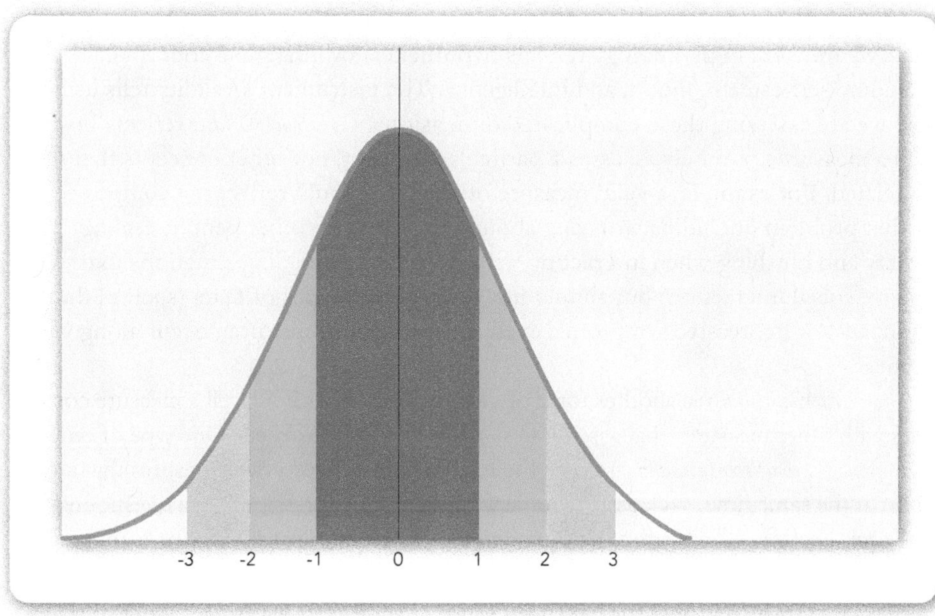

FIGURE 3.2

The Normal Curve. Numbers indicate standard deviations (SDs). A score more than 2 standard deviations away from the mean (the centre point, 0) is considered meaningfully different from normal.

the course of symptoms over time. In the example of the fever, not everyone has a standard body temperature of 37 °C. Some people may have a usual body temperature of 37.3 °C. In a self-referent comparison, we would compare the temperature of 40 °C to the person's usual body temperature of 37.3 °C.

If Pauline's scores on measures of cognitive impairment turn out to be very low compared with how she performed six months ago, we would be concerned about a potentially deteriorating course of symptoms.

Self-referent comparisons are also used to evaluate treatment outcome. Over the course of treatment, we would hope to see self-referent comparisons that indicate improvement of symptoms and quality of life.

RELIABILITY The **reliability** of an instrument is its consistency, or how well the measure produces the same result each time it is used (Groth-Marnat, 2009). Thermometers that measure your body temperature are generally quite reliable: They produce similar readings if you take your temperature now and again in 10 minutes. Psychological measures must also be reliable. If they do not produce consistent results, they are of no use. Reliability is assessed in many ways. **Test-retest reliability** addresses the consistency of scores across time. To estimate test-retest reliability, we administer the same instrument twice to the same people over some consistent interval, such as two weeks or one month. We then calculate a *correlation coefficient* (see Chapter 2) to estimate the similarity between the scores. Correlations of .80 or higher indicate that a measure is highly reliable over time.

Another measure of reliability, **interrater agreement**, is important for measures that depend on clinician judgment. When clinicians interview someone, they must decide whether the person's symptoms are severe enough to warrant a diagnosis and treatment, but not every clinician judges a behaviour in exactly the same way. Before making a diagnosis or recommending treatment, we want to know that the patient's symptoms reflected his or her actual clinical status, not the bias of a specific clinician (i.e., ratings should reflect more about the person being interviewed than about the person doing the interviewing). To estimate interrater agreement, we ask two different clinicians to administer the same interview to the same patients.

VALIDITY A measure must not only be reliable but also valid. **Validity** refers to the degree to which a test measures what it was intended to measure. Much of what we measure in psychology reflects hypothetical or intangible concepts, including self-esteem, mood, and intelligence. The instrument's validity tells us how well we are assessing these complicated dimensions. *Construct validity* reflects how well a measure accurately assesses a particular concept, not other concepts that may be related. For example, a valid measure of shyness should reflect the components of that problem (including worrying about being liked by other people, feeling sweaty and blushing when interacting with others, and avoiding situations that require social interaction) but should not reflect other types of fears (such as the fear of snakes) or depressive symptoms, even if those symptoms often occur along with shyness.

Criterion validity is another form of validity. It assesses how well a measure correlates with other measures that assess the same or similar constructs. One type of criterion validity, *concurrent validity*, assesses the relationship between two measures that are given at the same time, such as an interview measure of depression and a questionnaire measure. *Predictive validity* refers to the ability of a measure to predict performance at a future date. A good measure of depressive symptoms, for example, should correlate well (have good concurrent validity) with a clinician's diagnosis of depression made at the same time. A good measure of intelligence also should correlate well with a person's subsequent academic performance (predictive validity).

Another issue related to validity is the accuracy of a psychologist's predictions or conclusions at the end of the assessment process. After all the assessment data have been collected, a clinician is often asked to make a judgment: Does this person have panic disorder? Will a sex offender re-offend? What type of treatment might be best for this person at this time? Is this student a good match for this academic program? To reach their answers, clinicians can make predictions based on statistical data or clinical observations. *Clinical prediction* relies on a clinician's judgment. Many people believe that psychologists are able to predict dangerous behaviour in people with psychological disorders. An example of a clinical prediction would be a psychologist's interview of a patient and, on the basis of that interview, prediction that the person would commit a violent act in the near future (see Chapter 15 for a discussion on the accuracy of clinical predictions of dangerousness).

Statistical prediction results when a clinician uses data from large groups of people to make a judgment about a specific individual. Insurance companies, for example, decide how to price their policies using data from large studies that determine the probability of death or accidents based on certain identified risk factors, such as age, smoking history, and alcohol use (Compas & Gotlib, 2002). People with more risk factors pay more for their insurance. In general, results of predictions based on the same patient data can be very different when clinical and statistical strategies are used (Grove, 2005), but data from more than 136 studies support the conclusion that statistical predictions are more accurate than clinically based predictions (Grove et al., 2000). Statistical prediction is used in the practice of evidence-based medicine when data are available to predict who will benefit from which treatments. Clinical judgment, however, is useful when relevant statistical data do not exist and when new hypotheses need to be developed. Clinician judgment also plays a role in the use of the structured interview procedures discussed in "Clinical Interviews."

Evidence-Based Assessment

Selecting good assessment instruments can be a time consuming process, given the large number of instruments available. An excellent source of information is *A Guide to Assessments that Work* (2008), edited by John Hunsley (University of Ottawa) and Eric Mash (University of Calgary). This book helps clinicians to select the best assessment instruments for a given clinical problem (e.g., depression) for a given population (e.g., adolescents). The book reviews major assessment instruments, discusses how they are best used, and provides evidence on their reliability and validity, as well as information about norms and scoring.

Hunsley and Mash are strong advocates of evidence-based assessment (EBA), which "emphasizes the use of research and theory to inform the selection of assessment targets, the methods and measures used in the assessment, and the assessment process itself" (Hunsley & Mash, 2007, p. 29). EBA requires more than simply the use of reliable and valid test instruments:

> It involves the recognition that, even with data from psychometrically strong measures, the assessment process is inherently a decision-making task in which the clinician must iteratively formulate and test hypotheses by integrating data that are often incomplete or inconsistent. A truly evidence-based approach to assessment, therefore, would involve an evaluation of the accuracy and usefulness of this complex decision-making task in light of potential errors in data synthesis and interpretation, the costs associated with the assessment process and, ultimately, the impact the assessment had on clinical outcomes for the person(s) being assessed. (Hunsley & Mash, 2007, p. 30)

Developmental and Cultural Considerations

Many factors affect a clinician's choice of assessment techniques and instruments, but probably one of the most important factors is the patient's age and developmental status. The nature of the tests chosen, the normative values against which patient scores are compared, the people involved in the testing process, and the testing environment can vary significantly depending on whether the person to be assessed is a child, an adolescent, an adult, or an older person. The assessment of cognitive abilities in children who are too young to read, for example, requires different tests than those used with educated adults (Kaplan & Saccuzzo, 2012). The abilities of older adults with significant cognitive impairment must also be assessed with unique instruments that capture more specific symptoms of problems such as dementia (e.g., Dementia Rating Scale-2; Mattis, 2001). Measures of psychological symptoms vary across age as well. Tests of psychological distress designed specifically for children, such as the Social Phobia and Anxiety Inventory for Children (Beidel et al., 1995) and the Children's Depression Inventory-2 (Kovacs, 2011), typically have different questions, fewer response choices, and simpler wording than adult measures because of children's limited (still developing) cognitive abilities. Unique measures of psychological symptoms, such as the Geriatric Depression Scale, also exist for older adults (Sheikh & Yesavage, 1986); they have content and response choices that better match the experience and cognitive skill of older people than tests not specific for them.

The assessment process itself may also vary depending on the patient's age. For example, different people may be involved in the assessment process if the patient is a child, an adult, or an older person with major neurocognitive disorder. When assessing children, input from parents and teachers is essential. For older adults with cognitive limitations, obtaining input from another adult who spends time with the patient is helpful. Children who are unable to read and older people with limited vision may need help completing self-report measures. Young children with limited attention capacity and older adults with cognitive or physical limitations may also need short testing sessions with additional breaks.

The assessment process should also consider cultural factors. Many measures used routinely in psychological evaluations were originally developed within the majority culture (i.e., Caucasians). Administering these measures to people with more diverse cultural backgrounds may produce biased results due to differences in educational backgrounds, language use, and cultural beliefs and values (Kaplan & Saccuzzo, 2012). To address these issues, researchers have worked to develop "culture fair" assessments that take into account variables that may affect test performance. Many measures of psychological variables have been translated into other languages, and data from different minority groups have been collected (Novy et al., 2001). Simply translating measures into new languages, however, may not be sufficient to reflect other cultural influences. Thus, some measures of psychological performance have been developed that rely more on nonverbal skills. For example, the Leiter International Performance Scale (Roid & Miller, 2013) is a nonverbal test of intelligence that requires no speaking or writing by either the examiner or the test taker. Some of the tasks on the test include categorizing objects or geometric designs, matching response cards to easel pictures, and remembering and repeating sequences of objects in the correct order. Measures like this help to increase the cross-cultural utility of psychological assessments.

Ethics and Responsibility

The Canadian Psychological Association (CPA) does not have specific guidelines for the use of psychological tests. The CPA recommends the use of the Standards for Educational and Psychological Testing approved by the American Educational Research Association, the American Psychological Association, and the National Council on

Measurement in Education. In conducting psychological assessments, Canadian psychologists should also adhere to the guidelines of the CPA code of ethics, along with ethical codes specific to a given territory or province (see Chapter 15).

Psychologists should only use tests on which they have received training. Psychologists must only use instruments that have good reliability and validity and are appropriate for the purpose of the examination. For example, it would be unethical for a psychologist to give a test if (a) he or she had not been trained to give the test, (b) the test had poor reliability and validity, or (c) the test was designed for adults but the psychologist used it to test a child. Furthermore, psychologists should not use outdated instruments, and they must obtain informed consent from the person whom they want to test (or in the case of a child, the parent). *Informed consent* indicates that the person to be tested understands the test's purpose, its related fees, and who will see the results. In some cases, test results will be shared with employers or other health care professionals, so people need to be aware of confidentiality limits before the assessment begins. Testing data should remain confidential and be stored in a secure location, even for assessments that occur via the Internet.

CONCEPT check

- Clinical assessments are designed to gather information about a person's symptoms and to help clinicians make decisions about the nature, status, and treatment of psychological problems.
- Assessments can be used to screen people for psychological problems, to diagnose problems, to develop treatment plans, and to evaluate outcomes.
- Assessment instruments must be standardized with normative or self-referent data to allow useful interpretation of scores.
- To be useful, assessment measures must produce reliable (consistent) scores across time and across assessors.
- Assessment materials and procedures must consider the age and developmental level of the person being assessed as well as cultural factors that may affect performance or scores.

critical thinking question What are some of the ways that psychological tests might produce biased or inaccurate results? What are some ways this could be avoided?

Assessment Instruments

3.3 List and explain the function of different types of assessment instruments.

Psychologists can select from a wide range of assessment instruments when planning an evaluation. The variety of available tests allows a psychologist to assess a patient's difficulties thoroughly and from many different perspectives. Failing to conduct a thorough assessment can have disastrous consequences (see "Real People, Real Disorders: Cases of Misdiagnosis"). Choosing the best set of instruments depends on the goals of the assessment, the properties of the instruments, and the nature of the patient's difficulties. Some instruments ask patients to evaluate their own symptoms (*self-report measures*); others require a clinician to rate the symptoms (*clinician-rated measures*). Some instruments assess *subjective responses* (what the patient perceives), and others assess *objective responses* (what can be observed). Some measures are *structured* (each patient receives the same set of questions), and others are *unstructured* (the questions vary across patients). When a number of tests are given together, the group of tests is referred to as a *test battery*. We turn now to the major categories of assessment instruments, including clinical interviews, psychological tests, behavioural assessment, and psychophysiological assessment.

Clinical Interviews

Clinical interviews consist of a conversation between an interviewer and a patient, the purpose of which is to gather information and make judgments related to the assessment goals. Interviews can serve any of the major purposes of assessment, including screening, diagnosis, treatment planning, or outcome evaluation. They also can be conducted in either an unstructured or structured fashion.

UNSTRUCTURED INTERVIEWS In an **unstructured interview**, the clinician decides what questions to ask and how to ask them. Typically, the *initial interview* is unstructured, which allows the clinician to get to know the patient and help the clinician determine what other types of assessments might be useful. Another purpose of the initial interview is for the clinician and patient to begin getting to know each other and develop a working relationship.

At the start of an initial interview, the clinician usually provides some information about the assessment process and then asks a series of questions about the patient's difficulties. These questions can be *open ended*, allowing the patient flexibility to decide what information to provide (e.g., "Tell me about what brings you here today"), or *close ended*, allowing the clinician to ask for specific information about a topic (e.g., "Have you been having crying spells?"). Both the *presenting problem* (the identified reason for the evaluation) and the clinician's theoretical perspective guide the content and style of the questions. A psychodynamic clinician, for example, might spend more time in an initial interview asking about the patient's early history, whereas a behavioural clinician might ask more questions about the sequence of events surrounding current symptoms. At the end of an initial interview, the clinician typically summarizes what has been learned and offers some guidelines about what will happen next.

The primary benefit of an unstructured interview is its flexibility: It allows the clinician to move in whatever directions seem most appropriate, following up on the patient's comments. The major limitation is its potential unreliability. It is quite possible, for example, that two different interviewers could come to very different conclusions about the same patient if their interviews did not include the same topics or ask the same questions. For instance, if the interviewer does not ask questions about alcohol use and a patient is reluctant to bring up this topic, the interviewer may erroneously conclude that some other difficulty (e.g., depression) is the major cause of the presenting problem when in fact the patient is drinking heavily, missing work, and feeling depressed because of the likelihood of losing her or his job. Structured interviews help to minimize such problems.

STRUCTURED INTERVIEWS In a **structured interview**, the clinician asks each patient the same standard set of questions, usually with the goal of establishing a diagnosis. In the case of *semistructured interviews*, after the standard question, the clinician uses less structured supplemental questions to gather additional information as needed. Structured or semistructured interviews are used frequently in scientifically based clinical practice and in clinical research (Antony & Barlow, 2010), and they increase the reliability of the interview process. Although a patient's scores still rely on clinician judgment, the consistency in content and the order of questions increase the likelihood of agreement across interviewers.

Many structured and semistructured interviews are available to help clinicians make diagnoses. Choosing one depends on the goal of the assessment, the clinician's knowledge of and training with the particular interview, and the properties of the interview itself (length, content focus, reliability, etc.). Some structured interviews are designed to be used with adults; others are intended for use with children. In some cases, structured interviews provide a broad overview of many diagnostic categories, while others are more focused on particular sets of diagnoses (e.g., anxiety, depression). Frequently, a more focused interview is used after an unstructured screening interview to indicate that certain diagnoses may be appropriate. Focused interviews can be useful in research settings in which it is often important to make sure that all patients in a study have similar diagnoses. These interviews are also important in clinical practice so that a provider has sufficient details about a diagnosis to design an appropriate treatment plan. The drawback of structured interviews is that the interviewer has less flexibility with regard to questioning.

Psychological Tests

Psychological tests measure hundreds of dimensions, ranging from personality to intelligence and specific symptoms. The following sections provide an overview of different types of psychological tests that measure dimensions such as personality characteristics, general levels of psychological functioning, intelligence, and behaviour.

PERSONALITY TESTS The choice of a **personality test**, which measures personality characteristics, depends on its purpose and on whether one is assessing a healthy population or a clinical sample, although many personality tests measure overlapping concepts. Perhaps the best-known personality test is the *Minnesota Multiphasic Personality Inventory* (MMPI), developed in 1943 (Graham, 2000). To develop the pencil-and-paper test, they used a then-innovative technique that overcame some of the subjectivity of earlier scoring approaches. Using a method known as *empirical keying*, they developed statistical analyses to identify items and patterns of scores that differentiated various groups (e.g., patients with and without depression). Only items that differentiated the groups were retained. The MMPI also includes statistical scales to evaluate a number of test-taking behaviours. For example, a *Lie scale* identifies people who may not wish to describe themselves accurately. Other scales determine whether someone is "faking good" (describing oneself as more psychologically healthy than one is) or "faking bad" (presenting oneself as more psychologically distressed than is actually true); many clinical scales assess specific psychological characteristics.

A revised version of the MMPI, the MMPI-2-RF, includes 11 validity scales and 10 clinical subscales: hypochondriasis, depression, hysteria, psychopathic deviance, masculinity-femininity, paranoia, psychasthenia (anxiety), schizophrenia, hypomania, and social introversion (Ben-Porath, 2012). Also included are other restructured clinical subscales that were designed to improve validity and relate more directly to newer theories of personality: demoralization, somatic complaints, low positive emotions, cynicism, antisocial behaviour, ideas of persecution, dysfunctional negative emotions, aberrant experiences, and hypomanic activation. The MMPI-2-RF is scored by a computer program that creates a profile that the testing psychologist can then interpret (see Figure 3.3). Serious concerns exist regarding the use of the MMPI-2-RF with ethnic minority samples, however, because the test was originally standardized on white samples (Nichols et al., 2000).

The Millon Clinical Multiaxial Inventory-3 (MCMI-3; Millon et al., 2006) is a 175-item true–false inventory that corresponds to eight basic personality styles (schizoid, avoidant, dependent, histrionic, narcissistic, antisocial, compulsive, passive-aggressive; see Chapter 11), three pathological personality syndromes (schizotypal, borderline, paranoid), and nine symptom disorders scales (anxiety, somatoform, hypomanic, dysthymia, alcohol abuse, drug abuse, psychotic thinking, psychotic depression, psychotic delusions). The MCMI-3 has adequate reliability and validity, and clinicians sometimes prefer it to the MMPI-2-RF because it requires less time to complete. There also are concerns, however, that the MCMI-3 does not map onto the categories of disorders as they are described in the DSM system. An inventory that does show a closer relationship to the DSM-5 system, in

FIGURE 3.3

Sample MMPI Profile. The MMPI yields scores on several clinical subscales. It is scored by a computer that produces a personality profile.

	VRIN	TRIN	F	FB	Fp	FBS	L	K	S	Hs	D	Hy	Pd	Mf	Pa	Pt	Sc	Ma	Si
Raw Score:	6	8	9	9	0	19	5	14	22	10	41	24	29	32	16	32	23	8	47
K Correction:										7			6			14	14	3	
T Score (Plotted):	54	57F	64	79	41	69	56	47	47	62	95	57	79	62	72	92	68	33	75
Non-Gendered T Score:	54	57F	66	79	42	65	57	47	46	60	94	55	81		71	87	68	33	73
Response %:	100	100	100	98	96	100	100	100	100	100	100	100	100	100	100	100	100	100	100

Cannot Say (Raw): 1
F-K (Raw): -5
Welsh Code: 27*"406'8+15-3/:9# F-L/K:

Percent True: 41
Percent False: 59
Profile Elevation: 69.8

particular the personality disorders, is the *Dimensional Assessment of Personality Pathology* (DAPP), developed by researchers at the University of British Columbia and Western University (Livesley & Jackson, 2009). Another inventory that is widely used to measure personality and psychopathology is the *Personality Assessment Inventory* (PAI: Morey, 2007).

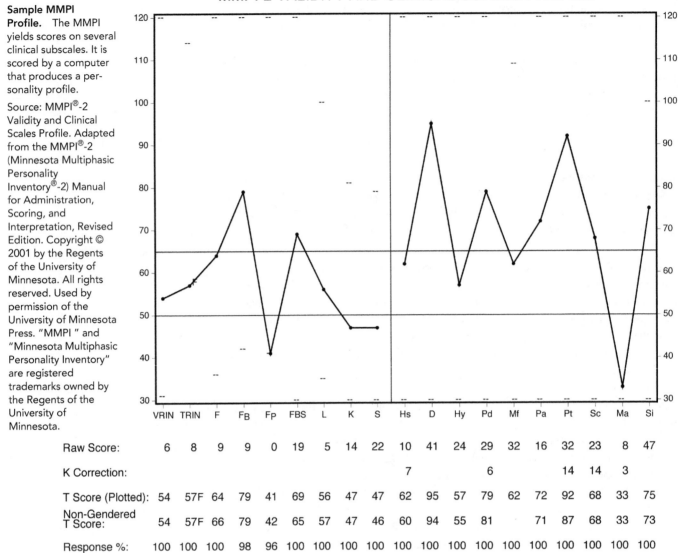

Unlike the inventories such as the DAPP, PAI, and MMPI-2-RF, which are considered objective personality tests, projective testing is a type of personality testing that emerged from psychoanalytic theory. Two widely used **projective tests** are the *Rorschach Inkblot Test* and the *Thematic Apperception Test*. The Rorschach, first published in 1921, was developed by a Swiss psychiatrist, Hermann Rorschach. The patient taking this test is presented increasingly complex and ambiguous inkblots (see Figure 3.4). The first blots are rather simple black-and-white images, and the later blots are more complex and colourful. The test's rationale is that when given such ambiguous stimuli, the patient "projects" a unique interpretation onto them that reflects underlying unconscious processes and conflicts.

Holding the Rorschach to our standards of reliability and validity would be a considerable task. Although Rorschach died before he could develop a reliable scoring system, clinical psychologist John Exner constructed a rigorous system for standardized administration and scoring of the test known as the *Comprehensive System* (CS). The CS is a multivolume work that breaks the inkblot test into a complex matrix of variables. These variables are interpreted and scored to form a Structural Summary, which the clinician can use to understand the person's personality traits and psychological functioning (Exner, 2005). Despite these valiant attempts to impose structure on the Rorschach, many criticisms remain, and its usefulness is highly questionable (see "Examining the Evidence: The Rorschach Inkblot Test").

Researchers at the Harvard Psychological Clinic developed another popular projective test, the *Thematic Apperception Test* (TAT), in 1935. There are a total of 31 cards, but 20 cards are used for the test for each individual, depending upon the person's age and sex. The test taker is asked to make up a story about the black-and-white images on the cards. The examiner interprets each story without a formalized scoring system and is free to evaluate the response from within his or her own theoretical orientation. As with the Rorschach, many clinicians believe that the test taker's descriptions of the images provide insight into the person's psychological and unconscious processes. Given the qualitative nature of the test data and the absence of rigorous scoring and interpretation methods, the TAT remains a subjective test.

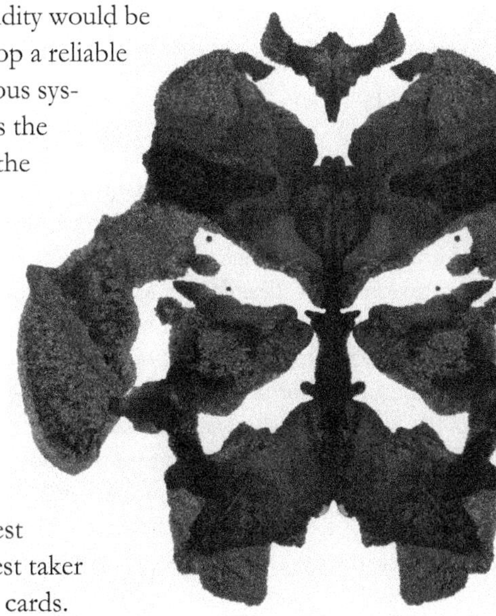

FIGURE 3.4

An Inkblot Similar to Those in the Rorschach Inkblot Test. What does this look like to you?

Despite their weaknesses, projective tests remain popular in some circles. Even when the tests are not used as part of an actual diagnostic battery, many clinicians use them at the start of therapy to "get the patient talking." For patients who have difficulty discussing their emotions, such tests may help them get in touch with what they are feeling.

GENERAL TESTS OF PSYCHOLOGICAL FUNCTIONING These assessments gather general information about the mental functioning of people who participate as healthy controls in a research study. The tests can also be used to compare behaviour across groups or populations or to test people before and after a specific event or intervention. They do not focus on one specific symptom area, such as depression or anxiety, but give a broad overview of how well a person is doing psychologically.

A commonly used brief questionnaire is the 12-item *General Health Questionnaire* (GHQ) (Goldberg & Hillier, 1979). The GHQ gives a snapshot of mental health status over the previous weeks and can provide a meaningful change score. Each item is rated on a four-point scale indicating degree of deviation from the individual's usual experience. These are some example questions: Have you recently: ... Been able to concentrate on what you're doing? Lost much sleep over worry? Been able to enjoy your normal day-to-day activities? Been feeling reasonably happy, all things considered?

Another widely used psychological test, especially for career counselling and professional development, is the Myers-Briggs Type Indicator (MBTI) (Briggs & Myers, 1987). Intended for use in normal (non-clinical) populations, the test purportedly measures various personality "types" (e.g., a "type" characterized by introversion, intuition, a tendency to make decisions on the basis of feeling rather than thinking, and a tendency to use perception rather than judgment to appraise the external world). Despite its popularity, the MBTI is lacking in empirical support, including a lack of evidence for the various supposed psychological types (Hunsley et al., 2015; Pittenger, 2005). The MBTI is not recommended for evidence-based psychological assessment.

examining the EVIDENCE

The Rorschach Inkblot Test

- **The Facts** Despite some declining popularity in recent years, the Rorschach remains a frequently used psychological test that graduate students in clinical psychology are often trained to administer (Lilienfeld et al., 2000). Exner's Comprehensive System (CS) is the most commonly taught administrative and scoring procedure. It results in more than 180 scores usually referred to as *CS scores.* However, the utility of the measure is a hotly contested issue in the psychological community, with many scientific articles either praising or criticizing the test. Its proponents contend that it elicits a type of information from patients that other psychological measures do not obtain, and that is important for clinical decision making. Its critics point to three major limitations: the test's reliability, the adequacy of normative data, and the validity of scores. Is the Rorschach Inkblot Test useful? Let's examine the evidence.

THE EVIDENCE

1. As evidence of reliability, proponents note that 75% of CS scores have adequate interrater agreement (Wood et al., 2006), and the reliability of summary CS scores (based on sums of individual scores) is higher than the reliability of individual items (Hibbard, 2003).
2. As evidence for the adequacy of normative data, proponents note that data have been collected on approximately 600 people (including nonpatient adults, children, and various patient groups) and are adequate for interpretation in psychological assessment. The overdiagnosis of mental health problems in other groups when they are compared with the normative sample (a significant problem for the Rorschach) may be explained by the healthier nature of the normative samples, changes in scoring procedures since the original normative data were collected, increased psychopathology in society over time, and inadequate scoring in subsequent studies (Hibbard, 2003).
3. With respect to validity, proponents note that validity coefficients from research studies may underestimate the test's utility because the Rorschach is most useful when responses are integrated into an individualized assessment. In other words, validity increases when clinicians use their clinical judgment to integrate Rorschach results with other assessment scores. This process may be too complex to be validated (Meyer et al., 2001).

LET'S EXAMINE THE EVIDENCE

1. What does it mean if 25% of CS scores do not meet traditional standards of interrater reliability (Wood et al., 2006)? In a test of this type, is the fact that only 75% of the scores are reliable "good enough"? Furthermore, test-retest reliability for most scores has not been adequately examined (Lilienfeld et al., 2000).
2. Normative data published by Exner and his colleagues are outdated. They were collected during the 1970s and 1980s and not consistently scored according to the most recently established procedures. This leads to overdiagnosis of individuals as having significant mental health problems when, in fact, they do not (Garb et al., 2005).
3. Adequate validity data exist for only 20 of more than 180 CS scores, including those that detect psychotic disorders, dependency, and treatment outcome. Another 160 CS scores have not yet been demonstrated to be valid, yet they continue to be used to make important judgments about people's psychological status (Wood et al., 2006).

- **Conclusions** Critics and advocates of the Rorschach agree that empirical data support the utility of some CS scores used for certain purposes. They also agree that many CS scores have not yet been studied adequately enough to evaluate their usefulness. Differences of opinion beyond these areas of agreement largely reflect the degree to which psychologists rely on empirical data vs. clinician judgment in the assessment process (Wood et al., 2006). Scientifically based psychologists oppose the use of assessment tools that are not empirically validated, and therefore they do not support using unvalidated CS scores in the context of psychological decision making. People in this camp also point to the lack of evidence that clinical judgment improves predictions (see the discussion of clinical vs. statistical prediction in this chapter). Yet proponents of the Rorschach, many of whom define themselves as scientist–practitioners, continue to argue for the clinical utility of patient responses even when relevant empirical data are not available. Still others hang inkblots on their walls as artistic mementos of psychology's past.

NEUROPSYCHOLOGICAL TESTING Neuropsychological tests detect impairment in cognitive functioning using both simple and complex tasks to measure language, memory, attention and concentration, motor skills, perception, abstraction, and learning abilities. Performance on these tasks provides insight into the functioning of the brain.

The *Halstead-Reitan Neuropsychological Battery* (Reitan & Davidson, 1974) is widely used to evaluate the presence of brain damage. The battery differentiates healthy individuals

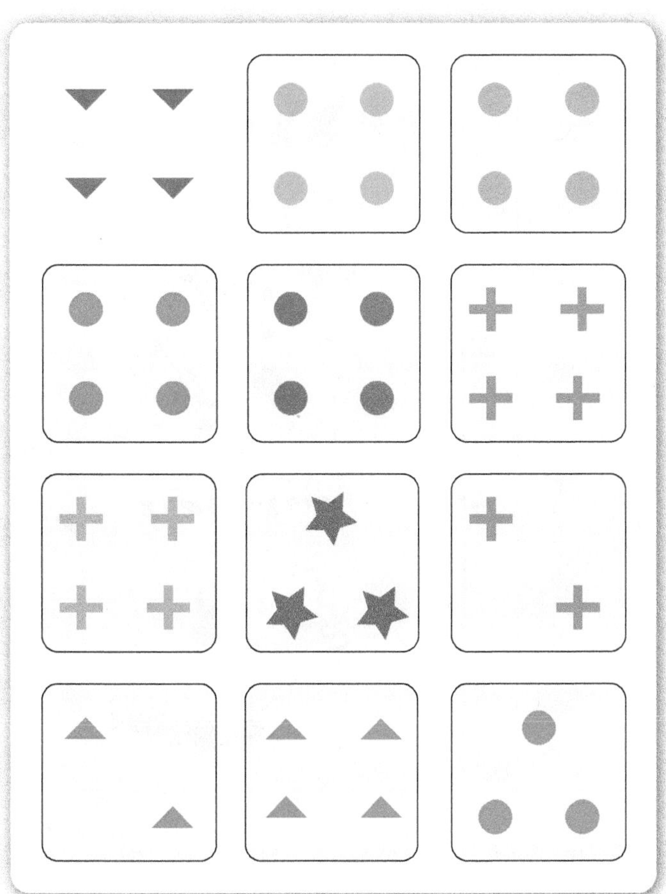

FIGURE 3.5

The Wisconsin Card Sorting Test. This test measures set shifting, the ability to display flexibility in thinking. It is used to test patients with brain disorders.

from those with cortical damage and includes 10 measures of memory, abstract thought, language, sensory-motor integration, perceptions, and motor dexterity.

Another commonly used neuropsychological assessment is the *Wisconsin Card Sorting Test* (WCST), which measures *set shifting*, or the ability to think flexibly as the goal of the task changes (see Figure 3.5). The test taker looks at four stimulus cards, each respectively displaying a red triangle, two green stars, three yellow crosses, and four blue circles. Then, the test taker is given additional cards and asked to match each to the original four stimulus cards. The examiner does not explain *how* to match the cards, but states whether the match is correct based on a specific rule known only to the examiner. The rule is then changed based on the success of the test taker, and the test continues for 128 trials or until all rule changes, or "achieved categories," have been completed (Psychological Assessment Resources, 2003). Completion of the card test requires attention, working memory, and visual processing. The WCST is considered a frontal lobe test because individuals with frontal lobe lesions do poorly on it. Because it discriminates between frontal and nonfrontal lesions, it is useful for testing patients with schizophrenia, brain injuries, and neurodegenerative diseases such as dementia or Parkinson's disease, who often have brain damage in these areas.

Other commonly used neuropsychological assessments include the *Bender Visual Motor Gestalt Test* (see Figure 3.6), a simple screening tool often used to detect problems in visual-motor development in children and general brain damage and neurological impairment (Piotrowski, 1995), and the *Luria-Nebraska Neuropsychological Battery* (Golden et al., 1980). The Luria-Nebraska is similar to the Halstead-Reitan test but is a more precise measure of organic brain damage. In contrast to many batteries, the Luria-Nebraska uses an unstructured qualitative method, generating 14 scores including motor, rhythm, tactile, expressive speech, writing, reading, arithmetic, memory, intellectual processes,

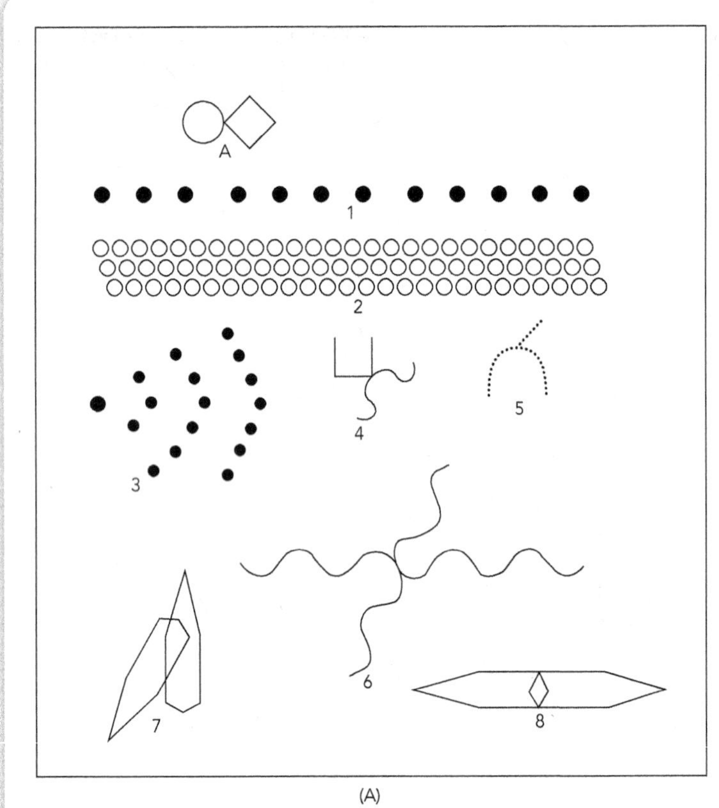

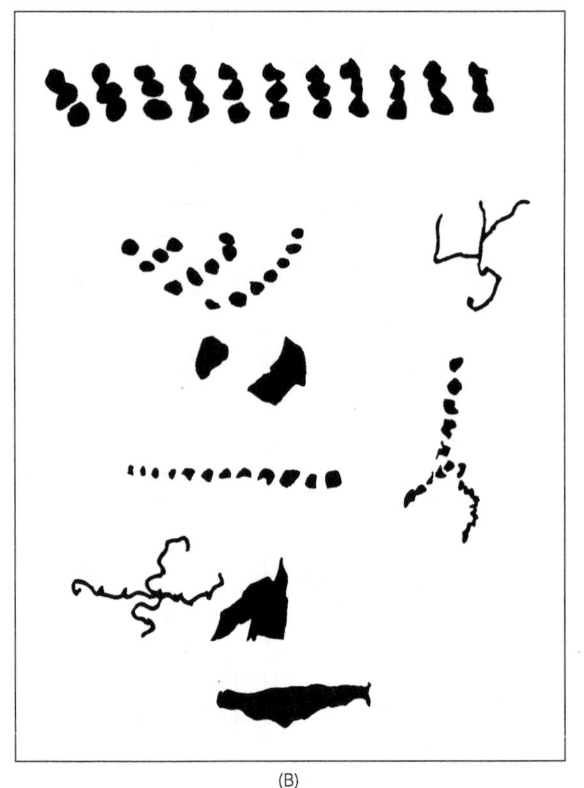

FIGURE 3.6 **The Bender Visual Motor Gestalt Test.** This neuropsychological test is often used to detect brain damage or neurological impairment. The patient's attempts to copy the figures (A) show whether damage or impairment is present (B).

Source: Nevid, Jeffrey S.; Rathus, Spencer A.; Greene, Beverly, Abnormal Psychology in a Changing World, 7th Ed., © 2008, p. 91. Reprinted and Electronically reproduced by permission of Pearson Education, Inc., Upper Saddle River, New Jersey.

and left and right hemispheric function. Clinicians are trained to administer neuropsychological batteries to ensure a standardized approach to administering the tests. In this way, we know that scores are comparable across testers.

INTELLIGENCE TESTS Although their results are often misinterpreted, **intelligence tests** are some of the most frequently used tests among psychologists. Created to predict success in school, these tests were designed to produce an **intelligence quotient**, or IQ, score. Children were tested on a series of questions that reflected cognitive abilities at different ages. Performance on the test yielded a score known as the child's *mental age*. This number was then divided by his or her chronological age, and the resulting number was the child's IQ. Today, scoring focuses on an individual's performance relative to his or her age-matched peers. IQ scores are standardized so that the mean is 100 and the standard deviation is 15. This means that a person with an IQ of 130 is 2 standard deviations above the mean and has performed quite well on the test relative to the rest of the population. IQ scores generally predict academic performance in traditional learning environments, but there is always individual variation. IQ scores do not represent the broader concept of intelligence, which is considered by some theorists to include creativity, artistic and athletic abilities, and other behaviours.

The origin of the IQ test began in France at the turn of the twentieth century with psychologist Alfred Binet and his colleague Theodore Simon, who were commissioned by the French government to create a test to predict academic success. In 1916, Lewis Terman at Stanford University translated a revised edition of Binet's instrument for use in English, which was subsequently named the *Stanford–Binet Intelligence Scale.*

Since its conception, the Stanford–Binet has gone through many revisions and is currently in its fifth edition. Subtests within the Stanford–Binet assess both verbal and nonverbal skills. The most recent version was standardized on 4800 people, and the test items were evaluated for any kind of bias based on the demographic characteristics of the test takers (whether responses to any items would be biased for anyone based on sex, ethnicity, age, etc.). The test's validity was evaluated against other well-validated intelligence tests, including the previous editions of the Stanford–Binet Intelligence Scale and the Weschler Adult Intelligence Scale, another widely used intelligence test. Extensive research suggests that the Stanford–Binet is appropriate for measuring intelligence among people with low intellectual functioning as well as among those at the highly gifted end of the continuum.

First published by David Wechsler in 1955 and currently in its fourth edition, the *Wechsler Adult Intelligence Scale* (WAIS-IV) comes in both American and Canadian versions (and other versions) (Wechsler, 2008). The versions differ in their general knowledge questions and their standardize samples. The Canadian edition asks respondents general knowledge questions relevant to Canada, and the standardization sample was based on a representative sample of Canadians. The WAIS-IV is one of the most commonly used general tests of intelligence to evaluate patients, students, employees, criminals, and other population subgroups. Initially adapted from the intelligence tests used by the military, the test was based on Wechsler's definition of intelligence as "the aggregate or global capacity of the individual to act purposefully, to think rationally, and to deal effectively with his [sic] environment" (Wechsler, 1939, p. 229).

The WAIS-IV produces four index scores: Verbal Comprehension Index (VCI), Working Memory Index (WMI), Perceptual Reasoning Index (PRI), and Processing Speed Index (PSI). The combination of these four index scores creates a composite Full Scale IQ (FSIQ) score. Each of the four index scores reflects a person's performance on a group of subtests that measure similar intellectual skills. The VCI subtests measure verbal reasoning (e.g., the ability to describe how two objects are alike), general fund of knowledge, ability to define words, and understanding of social expressions (e.g., "killing two birds with one stone"). The WMI subtests assess attention, concentration, and memory by asking people to recall sequences of digits forward and backward, perform mental math problems, and remember sequences of letters and numbers. The PRI and PSI subtests all require the test taker to perform certain tasks as quickly as possible. The PRI subtests measure skills such as attention to detail (e.g., what is missing from a certain picture), nonverbal reasoning (putting puzzles together), and spatial perception (arranging blocks to match a printed design). The PSI subtests assess visual-motor coordination and visual perception by asking test takers to determine whether a target symbol is in an array of symbols and to copy numbers that correspond with symbols into a grid. These tasks consider both speed and accuracy.

Taking a little more than 60 minutes to administer, the WAIS-IV (Wechsler, 2008) assesses cognitive functioning in people ages 16 to 90 years. For children under age 16, the Wechsler Intelligence Scale for Children (WISC-IV, 6–16 years) and the Wechsler Preschool and Primary Scale of Intelligence (WPPS-III, 2–7 years) are used.

The measurement of intelligence has always been controversial. This is one area in which the roles of nature and nurture have been hotly debated. In addition to questions about how these factors influence intelligence, our conceptualization of intelligence has changed over time. In contrast to Wechsler's early approach to measuring

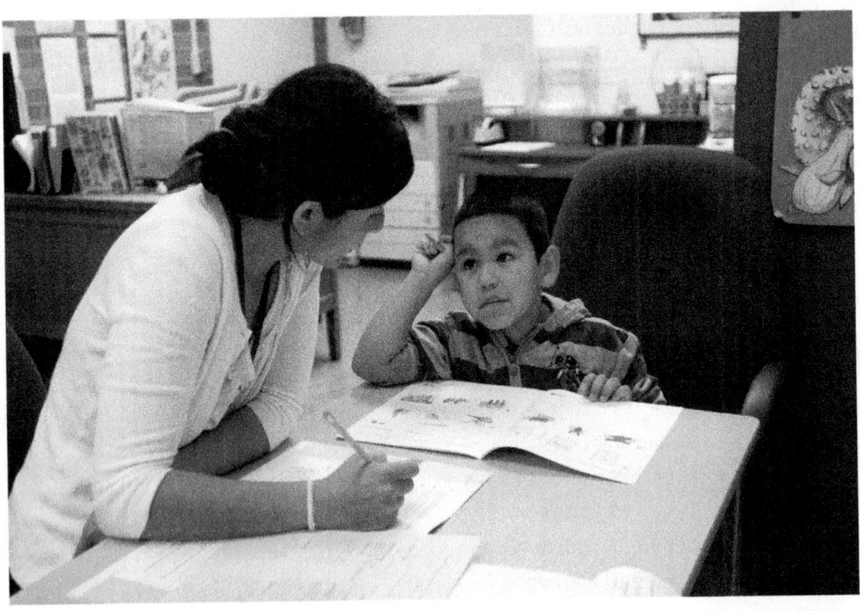

Assessment must consider a person's developmental age. Tests for children have simple wording and few response choices.

Stefanie Felix /The Image Works

cognitive function, current tests of intelligence recognize and assess various subtleties and components of intelligence. Even more intriguing are advances in neuroscience that give us glimpses into the brain and the nature of brain activity associated with various tasks that reflect different aspects of intelligence.

Another controversy involves the bias of intelligence measures along the dimensions of sex, socioeconomic status, and racial, ethnic, and cultural background (Shuttleworth-Edwards et al., 2004). Many argue that because intelligence tests are standardized primarily on white male populations, they are inappropriate for women, ethnic minorities, non-English speakers, and people who are physically challenged (Suzuki et al., 2001). Research is ongoing to develop tests that are free of such potential biases.

Intelligence tests have additional pitfalls. Most importantly, they do not and cannot reflect all types of intelligence. Intelligence is a multifaceted and complex concept, and many believe that its measurement should not be limited to testing attention, perception, memory, reasoning, and verbal comprehension (Gottfredson, 1997). However, provided that an IQ score is not used as a measure of the broad concept of intelligence, it has useful applications, most notably the prediction of academic success and the assessment of performance deficits and inequalities, cognitive impairment, and intellectual disability.

TESTS FOR SPECIFIC SYMPTOMS In addition to tests of general psychological functioning, we also need assessment tools that provide reliable and valid measures of specific types of symptoms, such as depression and anxiety. When testing treatments, we want to know how well certain treatments reduce symptoms of a particular disorder (e.g., which of two treatments better reduces the specific symptoms of depression). A therapist treating someone for a particular problem, such as test anxiety, may administer a questionnaire that measures severity of test anxiety over the course of treatment to see how well the intervention is working. Many scales have been developed for just this purpose. Some are clinician-administered assessments and others are self-report.

The *Brief Psychiatric Rating Scale* (BPRS) (Overall & Gorham, 1988) is a clinician-administered scale that assesses many different psychological symptoms, including bodily concerns, anxiety, emotional withdrawal, guilt feelings, tension, mannerisms and posturing, depressed mood, hostility, suspiciousness, hallucinations, motor retardation, uncooperativeness, unusual thought content, reduced emotional response, excitement, and disorientation. Other tests are more limited in scope, assessing the symptoms of one particular disorder. These disorder-specific scales exist for virtually every psychiatric disorder. Depressive symptoms, for example, are commonly assessed by the *Beck Depression Inventory–II* (BDI–II) (Beck et al., 1996a), a 21-item self-report questionnaire. The *Beck Anxiety Inventory* (BAI) (Beck & Steer, 1993) is a 21-item self-report measure of anxiety that focuses on the severity of anxiety symptoms. The use of such specific scales by different researchers has the added advantage of allowing comparisons of treatment effects across different studies and patient groups. Clinicians who use these measures are also better able to evaluate their patients' progress during treatment.

Canadian FOCUS

Psychological Assessment of Job Applicants

Psychological assessment is not limited to the clinic; it plays an important role in the selection of applicants for many different kinds of occupations. In Canada, psychological evaluations are increasingly being used for job recruitment in general. The goal is to assess candidates' suitability for the job for which they are applying. More Canadian companies in the mainstream business sector are using psychological tests to select job candidates, such as candidates for leadership roles (Wilkinson, 2013). Such assessments may include measures of psychopathology, but they also include measures of personal strengths, such as the extent to which a person is sociable, or the extent to which an individual has good analytical skills.

Psychological assessment is an especially important part of the recruiting process for occupations in which the safety of people is a consideration. For example, potential candidates for law enforcement agencies, such as the Canadian Border Services Agency, are required to complete psychological tests (e.g., the MMPI-2) and complete a clinical interview with a psychologist. This is to ensure that potential new officers are emotionally and psychologically suited to carry out, and use, nonlethal and lethal force equipment such as firearms (see, for example, www.hamiltonpolice.on.ca; www.cbsa-asfc.gc.ca/job-emploi/bso-asf/req-exig-eng.html). The assessments are used to identify a current or past history of psychological problems and to identify possible judgment or behavioural problems that might impair a person's ability to exercise sound decision-making in enforcement situations, particularly in situations in which the use of force may be required.

Psychological assessment for applicants to the Canadian Forces is similarly rigorous, but with a greater emphasis on assessing an applicant's aptitude for particular military occupations. Assessment includes tests of general cognitive ability (e.g., verbal skills, spatial ability, problem-solving), personality testing, and measures of the goodness-of-fit between an applicant and a given job (www.forces.gc.ca/en/about-policies-standards-defence-admin-orders-directives-5000/5002-5.page).

Psychological assessment is also required for a person to become a pilot in Canada. According to Transport Canada, in order to obtain a commercial pilot's licence the applicant should have no current or past mental disorder that would render the person unsafe to fly an aircraft (www.tc.gc.ca/eng/civilaviation/regserv/cars/part4-standards-t42402-1412.htm). This is determined by means of clinical interview. Pilots then undergo regular re-evaluations, at least annually, to ensure that they are safe to fly.

Psychological tests such as the MMPI-2 are not used in the process of hiring and monitoring pilots. Concerns were raised about the adequacy of the psychological assessment of pilots after Andreas Lubitz, a depressed German co-pilot, committed suicide by slamming his plane into a mountain, killing all 150 people on board (Quan, 2015). According to Suzanne Kearns, a professor at Western University, Ontario, evaluation of air crew focuses mainly on physical factors, such as whether the pilot could have a heart attack while flying, and there isn't much ongoing evaluation of mental health (CBC News, March 28, 2015). Suicide by plane crash is statistically rare and therefore difficult to predict. It is unclear whether psychological tests such as the MMPI-2 would improve the selection and performance of airline pilots in general.

Psychological assessments can play an important role in matching the best person to the job, and for screening out candidates who would be unsuitable or unhappy in a given job (Blackwell, 2012). But such assessment needs to be conducted in an ethically responsible manner, in a way that does not discriminate against people with psychological problems, while at the same time ensuring that the person is safe and competent to perform a given task.

Behavioural Assessment

Carla had no idea when she first visited a behaviour therapist to talk about her panic attacks that she would have "homework." Actually, the therapist assigned some at the end of the very first session! When their session was close to ending, he handed her some forms that he called practice records. He asked Carla to use these forms to record every panic attack she had during the next week and every time she avoided doing something that she thought might lead to a panic attack (e.g., going to grocery stores or movie theatres, driving on the highway). The therapist also told Carla that he would be going with her to some of the frightening places that seemed to produce the panic so that he could learn more about her symptoms. That was a little scary, but she was glad that someone was finally going to help her figure out what was going on.

Many of the assessment instruments discussed so far measure internal, enduring states, such as intelligence and personality, that may underlie psychological problems. Behavioural assessment is different. This approach relies instead on applying the principles of learning to understand behaviour, and its ultimate goal is a functional analysis (Haynes et al., 2006). When conducting a **functional analysis** (also known as *behavioural analysis* or *functional assessment*), the clinician attempts to identify causal (or functional) links between problem behaviours and contextual variables (e.g., environmental and internal variables that affect the problem behaviour). Recalling the principles of classical and operant conditioning (see Chapter 1), we know that events that precede or follow certain symptoms or behaviours can have powerful effects in causing or maintaining those symptoms. Thus, to identify causal links, we need to look at both *antecedents* and *consequences* of the behaviour.

To identify antecedents and consequences of behaviour, a behavioural assessment often starts with a behavioural interview. The interviewer asks very specific questions to discover the full sequence of events and behaviours surrounding the patient's primary problems. In Carla's case, the therapist might ask her to describe in detail her most recent panic attack—where she was, whom she was with, and what she was doing or thinking when she noticed the first symptoms. After those first symptoms, what did she think, feel, and do? What happened to the panic as a result of what she was thinking, feeling, and doing? What did other people do and when? All of these details might reveal that Carla was alone in the grocery store, worrying about having a panic attack and monitoring her body, when she noticed her heart rate increasing. She then might have pushed the cart to the side of the aisle and raced to the front door. After leaving the store so suddenly, she felt embarrassed but also completely relieved that the symptoms of panic were subsiding. When she got home and told her husband, he felt sorry for her and gave her a big hug.

Learning about the specific sequence of events can help a clinician identify important functional relationships. In Carla's case, thoughts and expectations about panic may lead her to monitor her body for signs, perhaps noticing symptoms that are normal but that nonetheless frighten her because they have become a cue for panic. Noticing potential panic symptoms leads her to escape from the situation (leave the store), which reduces the panic symptoms and reinforces her need to escape in order to control the symptoms. Her husband's comforting hug further reinforces her fear of panic. A good behavioural interview can uncover many different potential relationships. Other assessment tools that behaviour therapists use include self-monitoring and behavioural observation.

SELF-MONITORING Carla's homework assignment to record her episodes of panic is an example of **self-monitoring**, a process in which a patient observes and records his or her own behaviour as it happens (Compas & Gotlib, 2002). Psychological questionnaires are *retrospective*; that is, they ask about symptoms the patient may have had over the past week or past month. In contrast, self-monitoring requires patients to record their symptoms when they occur, allowing real-time information about the frequency, duration, and nature of the symptoms. Self-monitoring can contribute to a functional analysis if patients record contextual variables (aspects of the environment in which the behaviour takes place) and sequences of events and behaviours (see Figure 3.7). Self-monitoring now incorporates technology such that people are asked to record mood and behaviours using mobile phones and Web-based applications (Agarwal & Lau, 2010; Mouton-Odum et al., 2006; Sinadinovic et al., 2010).

Self-monitoring can also create a record of how often problem behaviours are occurring before treatment begins and how symptoms change over time. For example, before treatment begins, a woman who is monitoring her weight might record every food or drink item that she consumes that day and be surprised to find that she has six "snacks" per day. As treatment progresses, the number of snacks she eats may decline to four, then to two, and finally to one snack per day. Self-monitoring is an important

What situation created stress today? ______________________________

How did you feel?

[ ] anxious
[ ] worried, nervous
[ ] embarrassed
[ ] other: ________
[ ] fearful
[ ] angry
[ ] sad

What physical signs did you have?

[ ] muscle tension
[ ] rapid pulse
[ ] shortness of breath
[ ] butterflies in stomach
[ ] shaking
[ ] sweating
[ ] other: ________

What thoughts/worries did you have? ______________________________

What actions did you take to reduce anxiety? ______________________________

FIGURE 3.7

Awareness Practice Form. Patients use such forms to monitor and record their own behaviour.

component of treatment because the act of recording symptoms by itself may increase patients' awareness of a problem behaviour and reduce its frequency.

BEHAVIOURAL OBSERVATION **Behavioural observation** also involves measuring behaviour as it occurs, but in this approach someone other than the patient monitors the frequency, duration, and nature of behaviour. The first step is to define the behaviour in a way that allows it to be clearly observed and reliably monitored. For a child with attention problems, particular problem behaviours must be specified, such as leaving one's seat, speaking out of turn, and fidgeting (Compas & Gotlib, 2002). Simply asking raters to measure a global concept such as "inattentiveness" would lead to poor reliability across time and across raters.

Next, it is important to decide how to observe the behaviours of interest. *Event recording* involves monitoring each episode of the identified behaviour, such as counting the number of times a child gets out of his or her seat, speaks out of turn, or fidgets during the school day (Compas & Gotlib, 2002; Tyron, 1998). Using *interval recording,* the behavioural assessor measures the number of times the identified behaviour occurs during a particular interval of time (e.g., counting the number of times a child gets out of the seat during each 15-minute interval of a class period). Sometimes behaviour can be observed in a *natural environment.* An assessor could go to a child's classroom to observe behaviour, or a therapist could accompany a patient to the scene of a problem behaviour. In other cases, behaviour must be observed in an *analogue* fashion. In these instances, the assessor creates a situation similar to those in which the problem occurs to allow direct observation. For example, a patient with speech anxiety may be asked to stand up behind a desk or podium and give a speech. The therapist can count the number of times the patient stutters, the duration of silences in the speech, the amount of eye contact the patient makes, and the like.

Actigraphy is a noninvasive way to measure activity level. The actigraph unit looks like a wristwatch and is typically on the wrist of the nondominant arm (a right-handed person wears the actigraph on the left wrist). The unit records vibrations associated with movement, allowing the researcher to detect different patterns of activity (sitting, running, sleeping). Actigraphy has been used often to assess sleep patterns and circadian rhythms, daytime sleepiness, insomnia, and effects of sleep interventions (Belanger et al., 2014; Troxel et al., 2010; Westermeyer et al., 2010), as well as movement in children with attention deficit hyperactivity disorder (Uebel et al., 2010).

Behavioural avoidance tests are often used to assess phobias and avoidance behaviour by asking a patient to approach a feared situation as closely as possible (Compas & Gotlib, 2002). For example, a patient with a height phobia might be asked to climb an outdoor set of stairs as high as possible. The observer measures how close the person can approach the feared situation. As with self-monitoring, behavioural observation strategies can be used to evaluate the severity of symptoms at baseline (before treatment begins) and to assess the degree of change after treatment.

Psychophysiological Assessment

Psychophysiological assessment measures brain structure, brain function, and nervous system activity. This type of assessment measures physiological changes in the nervous system that reflect emotional or psychological events. Different types of measurements assess a range of biochemical alterations in the brain or physiological changes in other parts of the body.

One of the oldest, most common, and least invasive types of psychophysiological measurements is *electroencephalography* (EEG). Researchers first measured and recorded brain waves in dogs in 1912 (Niedermeyer, 1999). Electrodes are placed on the scalp, or in unusual circumstances, in the cerebral cortex, to measure differences in electric voltage between various parts of the brain (Eisen, 1999). Electrode locations and names are standardized to ensure consistency across laboratories and clinical facilities.

The EEG is a useful research tool because it is noninvasive and requires little effort from the participant. In some instances, the brain activity is recorded when the participant is engaged in cognitive processing related to the presentation of a simple, evoked stimulus, called an *event-related potential* (ERP). Changes in brain activity are recorded together with a time-stamped presentation of the stimulus, which can take many forms, including auditory (sounds), visual (flashes of light or images), olfactory (smells), and more cognitive stimuli that can engage memory, pattern recognition, or emotional responses, for example.

EEG patterns include both rhythmic activity and nonrhythmic patterns, and different wave frequencies signal relaxation, sleep, or comatose states. Nonrhythmic patterns may represent seizure activity. EEGs are useful tools for monitoring and diagnosing certain clinical conditions, such as a coma state and brain death, and for monitoring brain function while under anesthesia (Tatum, 2014).

Most people have heard about rapid eye movement (REM) sleep, but the second broad sleep stage is non-REM sleep when the eyes are at rest. Stages of sleep and wakefulness are divided into the following categories: Stage W (wakefulness), Stage N1 (NREM 1 sleep), Stage N2 (NREM 2 sleep), Stage N3 (NREM 3 sleep), and Stage R (REM sleep) (Silber et al., 2007). During Stage W, beta waves dominate our brain activity. As we relax or begin to fall asleep, alpha waves dominate. The sleeper next moves through stage N1, which is marked by even slower theta waves and is experienced as drowsy sleep, then N2 when muscular activity decreases and the sleeper becomes consciously unaware of the external environment, and then N3 when slower *delta waves* predominate. This is the deepest sleep stage. When awakened from the N3 stage, we are likely to feel disoriented and groggy. Also during this stage, sleepwalking (*somnambulism*) and sleeptalking (*somniloquy*) occur, as well as night terrors and nocturnal enuresis.

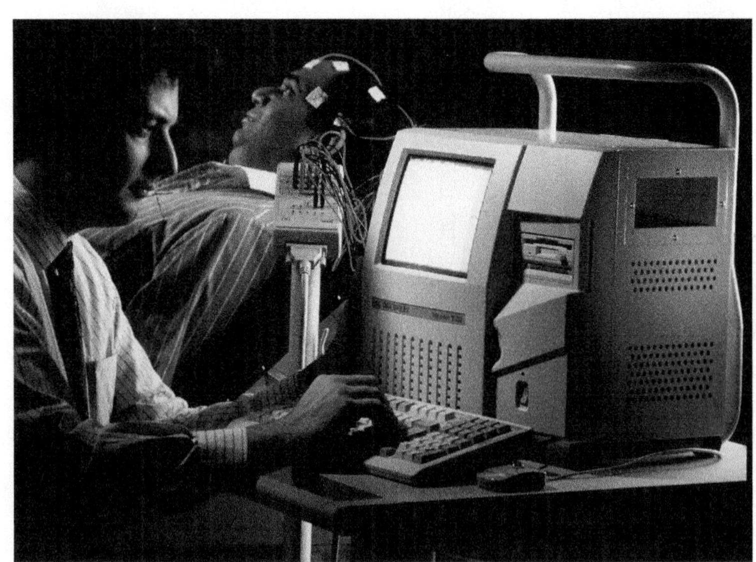

The EEG is one of the oldest psychophysiological assessments, often used in research because it is noninvasive. It records changes in brain activity.

Photo Researchers, Inc./Science Source

The EEG has several advantages as a tool for exploring brain activity. It allows the assessment of very fast responses—measured at the level of a millisecond rather than the second and minute levels of other techniques. Moreover, EEG is the only measure that directly assesses electrical activity in the brain. However, an EEG cannot determine functioning in a specific brain region (Ebersole, 2002). Accordingly, recent research has combined EEG with functional brain imaging techniques (Koessler et al., 2007).

Another type of psychophysiological assessment measure is *electrodermal activity* (EDA), formerly called *galvanic skin response* (GSR). This measurement capitalizes on the fact that the sweat glands on the palms of the hands are controlled by the peripheral nervous system and thus react to emotional states. If you have ever experienced sweaty palms, you know this feeling. EDA measures the changes in electrical conductance produced by increased or decreased sweat gland activity. EDA is a window into the presence of stress or anxiety.

A common type of psychophysical assessment incorporating EEG or EDA strategies is *biofeedback* (see Chapter 14). The term *biofeedback* was first coined in the late 1960s. *Biofeedback* refers to the use of electronic devices to help people learn to control body functions that are typically outside of conscious awareness, such as heart rate or respiratory rate. Biofeedback can be used to promote relaxation and to relieve pain. The goal of this assessment is to train patients to recognize and modify physiological signals by bringing them under conscious control. You probably use a form of biofeedback in your daily life. If you feel yourself getting anxious and your heart rate is increasing, you might start taking some deep breaths to calm yourself. You recognized that your heart is beating fast, and you did something to try to reduce your arousal.

Clinical biofeedback uses the same process but more sophisticated equipment to detect and record physiological reactions and responses with great sensitivity. For example, a patient's biosignals, such as heart rate, blood pressure, or muscle tension, can be recorded and converted into a detectable signal, such as a lightbulb that flashes every time heart rate exceeds 90 beats per minute. The patient responds to this visual signal by trying to relax tense muscles or slow heart rate. Then the light flashes less often, signaling the patient's success. Clinical biofeedback is used to treat various psychological conditions, including anxiety, panic, and attention deficit hyperactivity disorder. In addition to pain, other medical conditions for which biofeedback can be helpful include migraine headaches (Nestoriuc & Martin, 2007), Raynaud's disease (a circulatory disorder; Karavidas et al., 2006), temporomandibular joint (TMJ) dysfunction (Crider et al., 2005), fibromyalgia (Kayiran et al., 2010) epilepsy, incontinence, digestive system disorders, high and low blood pressure, cardiac arrhythmias, and paralysis (Association for Applied Psychophysiology and Biofeedback). Biofeedback is a vivid illustration of how feelings and emotions affect bodily functions and how changing emotional states can directly affect physical functioning.

In an exciting new area of research, scientists are studying how biological compounds (such as oxytocin) may enhance perceptual abilities, such as being better able to understand the emotions of others (see "Research Hot Topic: Oxytocin and 'Mind Reading'").

CONCEPT check

- Clinical interviews usually occur early in the assessment process so that the clinician can begin to gather information and set assessment goals. These interviews can be administered in either an unstructured or a structured format.
- Psychological tests are used to measure personality, general and cognitive functioning, intelligence, and specific clinical symptoms.
- Behavioural assessment, including self-monitoring and behavioural observation, is used to measure behaviour and contextual (environmental) variables that cause and maintain the behaviour.
- Psychophysiological assessment measures changes in the nervous system as they relate to psychological or emotional events. The most common form of psychophysiological assessment is the EEG, a measure of electrical signals in the brain.

critical thinking question What tests might you choose to conduct a psychological assessment for a patient who is having severe headaches, anxiety, trouble concentrating, and marriage difficulties?

research **HOT** topic

Oxytocin and "Mind Reading"

Assessment can take many forms. One fascinating advance is our ability to understand the association between underlying biology and observed social behaviours. Is it possible that the release of a hormone in the brain can affect our ability to form close relationships, to trust other people, and even to read minds? Researchers studying oxytocin, a naturally occurring substance in our bodies, have found that such a link may exist. For years, oxytocin was known only as a hormone involved in labour contractions and lactation. Now it appears that oxytocin can act as a neurotransmitter in the brain, where it is associated with many complex social behaviours. Animal studies have shown that oxytocin increases both maternal behaviour and pair bonding (Carter, 1998; Young & Wang, 2004). A preliminary and intriguing study in humans found that after people took oxytocin, they were more likely to trust another person with their money (Kosfeld et al., 2005). This initial glimpse into the possible role of oxytocin led researchers to wonder whether an increased ability to "read" people was part of the mechanism responsible for the reduction in social stress and apprehension and increased attachment behaviour associated with oxytocin.

The ability to detect another's thoughts and emotions purely through external observation, such as noticing facial expression, is integral to human social interaction. Referred to as *mind reading,* this practice of analyzing another's emotional state based on external cues alone is critical not only in conversation, but also in the establishment and maintenance of trust.

Researchers (Domes et al., 2007) examined the effect of oxytocin on people's ability to "read minds." When asked to describe someone's thoughts or feelings based on a picture of their eyes alone, participants who had been given oxytocin performed better than those not given any hormone. This ability to sense another's emotional state may facilitate social attachment and trusting behaviour. Although the results must be viewed as preliminary, they provide an intriguing window into how our biology may influence our social functioning.

This information may also be useful in the future to researchers studying and treating patients with severe social impairments, especially autism (see Chapter 12). People with autism spectrum disorders have been shown to have a significant impairment in "mind reading" as well as low plasma oxytocin levels.

Diagnosis and Classification

The use of a common language to describe observed clinical phenomena is critical to both clinical practice and research. The following discharge summary illustrates the use of such a common language as one clinician communicates to another clinician in a distant city as the patient is about to be transferred to that location.

3.4 Explain why classification systems for abnormal behaviour are valuable.

Between 2007 and 2010, I treated Susan intermittently for recurrent major depression together with her primary care physician, who managed medication. In that interval, Susan experienced three episodes of major depression lasting between four weeks and four months. Each time, she experienced marked low mood, anhedonia, agitation, early morning awakening, and problems with concentration. She reported frequent passive suicidal ideation but no active suicidal intent or plan. She was prescribed 40 mg fluoxetine/day and remained on the medication throughout this interval. After her initial course of cognitive-behavioural therapy, we contracted that she would contact me for booster sessions each time she identified a lowering of her mood.

These common terms for symptoms and categories allow the new clinician to develop a relatively accurate picture of the patient. Using diagnostic labels to describe sets of symptoms helps clinicians and researchers communicate about their patients.

Deciding which diagnosis best fits a patient's pattern of symptoms also helps the clinician develop an appropriate treatment plan. The way clinicians refer to mental disorders has changed over the years as our understanding of these disorders continues to evolve.

History of Classification of Abnormal Behaviours

Contemporary diagnostic classification in Canada and in many other places in the world is based on the ***Diagnostic and Statistical Manual of Mental Disorders* (DSM)**. This manual is a work in progress, having been through many editions since DSM-I was published in 1952 (American Psychiatric Association [APA], 1952). DSM-I contained 106 categories of mental disorders (Grob, 1994). From that point forward, the DSM has expanded. Published in 1968, the DSM-II (APA, 1968) listed 182 disorders in 134 pages and reflected the dominant psychodynamic perspective of the time. Symptoms were described as reflections of broad underlying conflicts or maladaptive reactions to life problems rather than in observable behavioural terms (Wilson, 1993). In 1974, the task force working to revise the DSM emphasized the importance of establishing more specific diagnostic criteria. The intention was to facilitate mental health research and to establish classifications that would reflect current scientific knowledge.

In the DSM-III (APA, 1980), categorization was based on description rather than assumptions about the causes of the disorder, and a more biomedical approach replaced the psychodynamic perspective (Wilson, 1993). The DSM-III, published in 1980, was more than three times the size of the earlier DSM and described twice as many diagnostic categories (265). The controversial expansion included many new diagnostic categories. For example, the former category of anxiety neurosis was divided into several different and distinct categories, including generalized anxiety disorder, panic disorder, and social phobia. All subsequent revisions have maintained the structure of the DSM-III and have attempted to refine or improve this version rather than to overhaul the diagnostic system entirely. The next version, the DSM-III-R (APA, 1987), included not only revisions but also renaming, reorganization, and replacement of several disorders, which yielded 292 diagnoses (Mayes & Horwitz, 2005). In 1994, DSM-IV listed 297 disorders. This revision emerged from the work of a steering committee, consisting of work groups of experts who (a) conducted an extensive literature review of the diagnoses, (b) obtained data from researchers to determine which criteria to change, and (c) conducted multicentre clinical trials (Shaffer, 1996). DSM-IV-TR (APA, 2000a), a "text" revision, was published in 2000 with most diagnostic criteria unaltered. DSM-5 includes 237 diagnoses and uses a developmental approach to abnormal behaviour. DSM-5 emphasizes the role of culture and gender in the expression of psychiatric disorders and, in comparison to previous editions, uses more dimensional ratings to classify symptom severity.

Although many valid criticisms have arisen as a reaction to the DSM system, it is useful in that it provides a framework and common language for clinicians and researchers. The DSM system helps clinicians examine presenting problems and associated features and to identify appropriate assessments and treatments. Moreover, accurate classification of mental disorders is a critical element of rigorous research. Ideally, as research in neuroscience and genetics progresses, we will see an increased reflection of underlying biology in the classification of mental disorders.

Most of the information presented in subsequent chapters of this text will cover the major clinical syndromes—what are known in everyday language as *mental disorders*. The material will be organized mostly around disorders as they are defined in DSM-5. Beyond listing diagnoses, however, the authors of the DSM wanted to devise a system that would offer more information about patients than a simple clinical diagnosis (e.g., depression). After determining if a person is suffering from a psychiatric disorder and if so, which one, clinicians will also make several ratings that help explain to the patient and other health care workers characteristics of the disorder that might be unique to that person. For example, the clinician will note the presence of any psychosocial or environmental factors that might play a role in the onset or maintenance of the disorder. Additionally the clinician will rate how the disorder affects the person's academic, social, or occupational functioning.

An alternative to the DSM classification system is the **International Classification of Diseases and Related Health Problems (ICD)**, published by the World Health Organization (WHO). The current version is ICD-10. The next revision, ICD-11, is scheduled to be published in 2017. The ICD system uses a code-based classification system for physical diseases and a broad array of psychological symptoms and syndromes. The ICD system for diagnosing mental disorders was developed in Europe at approximately the same time that the original DSM was being developed in the United States, shortly after World War II. The first set of mental disorders was included in the ICD in 1948. The APA and WHO have worked to coordinate the DSM and the relevant sections of ICD, although some differences remain.

The ICD has become the international standard diagnostic classification system for epidemiology and many health management purposes. Beyond its use in classifying diseases and other health problems, the ICD is used for morbidity and mortality statistics for the WHO and for third-party payers and insurance companies (WHO, 2007).

Comorbidity

Comorbidity refers to the presence of more than one disorder (see Chapter 2). Often a patient's symptoms cannot be fully characterized or diagnosed using a single category. For example, a patient with depression may also experience anxiety (panic) attacks and an eating disorder. When more than one disorder is diagnosed, the disorders are said to be *comorbid.* Almost half of people who have one mental disorder have symptoms that meet the criteria for at least one other disorder (Kessler et al., 2005a).

The term *comorbidity* may be misleading because it is unclear whether the co-occurring diagnoses truly reflect the presence of distinct clinical disorders or whether they may actually be different manifestations of a single clinical disorder (Maj, 2005). However, the frequent co-occurrence of multiple psychiatric diagnoses cannot be ignored. Rates of comorbidity are high, and multiple theories exist to explain how the current diagnostic system may contribute to the common observation of comorbidity. For example, it may result from "the rule laid down in the construction of DSM–III that the same symptom could not appear in more than one disorder" (Maj, 2005). Given this rule, anxiety cannot appear in the criteria for depression, although the DSM acknowledges that patients with major depression are frequently anxious. Thus, the assessor is forced to turn to another diagnostic family in order to describe and record this prominent symptom. Another reason for increased comorbidity is the addition of new diagnostic categories with new editions of the DSM. The DSM has significantly increased in

FIGURE 3.8

Comparison of the Number of Psychiatric Diagnoses Included in the *Diagnostic and Statistical Manual of Mental Disorders.*

DSM revision	Year Published	Number of disorders
DSM-I	1952	106
DSM-II	1968	182
DSM-III	1980	265
DSM-IV	1994	297
DSM-5	2013	237

size since its first publication, encompassing more and more categories. If divisions between disorders are made with finer and finer distinctions (which may not actually reflect nature), it is logical that the likelihood of concurrent diagnoses will increase.

3.5 Recognize the importance of developmental and cultural variables that affect the experience and classification of abnormal behaviour.

How Do Developmental and Cultural Factors Affect Diagnosis?

Understanding developmental and cultural variables is important when diagnosing disorders. A major departure for the DSM-5 is the use of a developmental perspective by which to understand psychological disorders. As we noted in Chapter 1, children and adults differ on basic aspects of physical, cognitive, and emotional development, and for any specific disorder, the manner in which the symptoms are expressed also may differ by age. Therefore, when evaluating the presence of a specific disorder, such as depression, it is necessary to understand how specific symptoms may vary by age. Young children for example, do not really understand the concept of "the future." Therefore, it would be unlikely for a young child with depression to endorse "feeling helpless about the future." DSM-5 acknowledges the existence of developmentally appropriate symptoms for a number of diagnoses.

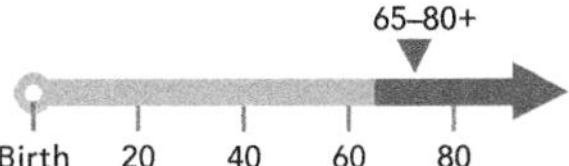

Cognitive difficulties of aging may affect the expression and type of symptoms experienced by older adults.

Clinicians have also found that the prevalence of psychological disorders varies by sex. Women, for example, are more often diagnosed with depression and anxiety, whereas men are more often diagnosed with substance abuse. Men and women may actually develop different disorders at different rates, perhaps with different genetic risk factors for certain syndromes. It is also possible that in some cases, a similar underlying difficulty, such as stress, may be expressed differently for men and women.

Symptoms and disorders may also be influenced by race and ethnicity. *Culture-bound syndromes* are defined as sets of symptoms that occur together uniquely in certain ethnic or racial groups. *Ataque de nervios*, for example, is an anxiety syndrome that occurs uniquely among Latinos. In general, classification systems should consider the developmental, demographic, and cultural variables that affect the experience and description of abnormal behaviour. Some symptoms are universally applicable, but others are not.

When Is a Diagnostic System Harmful?

Despite their benefits for diagnosing and treating mental disorders, a diagnostic system has significant limitations. First, because many diagnostic categories require that a person have a specified number of symptoms from a longer list (e.g., four of six symptoms listed might be required for a diagnosis), not all people with the same diagnosis experience the same symptoms. In addition, most diagnostic classifications do not require that the symptoms be connected to a particular etiology (cause); therefore, different patients with the same disorder may have developed the symptoms in different ways. Finally, two people who have the same diagnosis do not necessarily respond to the same treatments.

Diagnostic categories also can encourage stereotyped conceptions of specific disorders. For example, imagine that a young woman has a grandfather who was diagnosed with bipolar disorder (see Chapter 6). He had a flagrant case marked by excessive spending, sexual indiscretions, and grandiosity (an inflated sense of one's own importance), leading to several hospitalizations and therapy. Although his granddaughter is beginning to experience less extreme signs and symptoms, she might hesitate to believe that she has the same disorder. In her mind, her symptoms don't fit the stereotype associated with the label of bipolar disorder or the behaviour that she saw in her grandfather. Stereotyping by diagnosis can also lead a clinician to premature or inaccurate assumptions about a patient that prevent a thorough evaluation and comprehensive treatment plan. For example, a patient diagnosed with depression may be prescribed an antidepressant without sufficient evaluation of the need for treatments to manage life problems without the use of medication. Similarly, labelling a patient with a diagnosis can lead to *self-fulfilling prophecies* (e.g., I have bulimia so I will never be able to eat normally again) and create *stigmas* that impact the person's ability to function well at work or in social relationships (e.g., who wants to date a woman with an eating disorder?).

Another criticism of the DSM system is that its categories can reflect the beliefs or limited knowledge of an era. A good example was the inclusion of homosexuality as a mental illness before 1974. Because it was classified as a mental disorder, homosexuality was intrinsically defined as something that caused distress and impairment and that should be treated. The classification contributed substantially to the stigmatization of homosexuality, to homosexual persons' beliefs that there was something wrong with them psychiatrically, and to many ill-conceived attempts to change their sexual orientation. Once research began to address homosexuality openly, empirical evidence did not support the claim that homosexuality was a form of mental illness or was inherently associated with psychopathology. After a majority vote, the APA replaced the diagnosis of *Homosexuality* with *Ego-Dystonic Homosexuality* in the DSM-III (APA, 1980), referring to sexual orientation inconsistent with one's fundamental beliefs and personality. However, mental health professionals criticized this new diagnostic category as a political compromise designed to appease psychiatrists who still considered homosexuality pathological (APA, 2006). In 1986, the diagnosis was removed entirely from the DSM. In the DSM-5 (APA, 2013), the only mention of homosexuality is found in the category *Sexual Disorders Not Otherwise Specified.* This category includes homosexuality that is marked by persistent and marked distress about one's sexual orientation, a category that may still reflect continued stigma.

A final criticism of the DSM is that it simply includes too many disorders and that normal variations in human behaviour have been overmedicalized by giving them

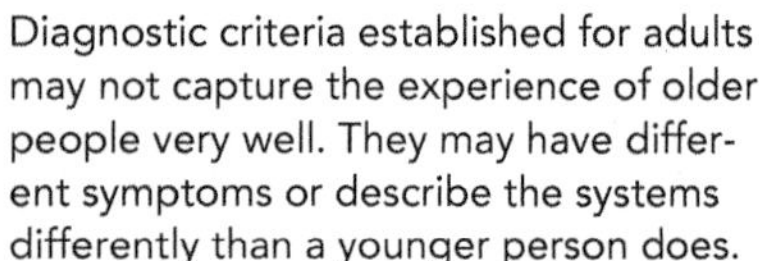

Diagnostic criteria established for adults may not capture the experience of older people very well. They may have different symptoms or describe the systems differently than a younger person does.

Pearson Education

diagnostic labels (see "Research Hot Topic: Too Many Disorders?"). Overall, although diagnostic systems that rely on classifying symptoms into disorders provide substantial benefits for patients, clinicians, and researchers, the limitations of these systems need to be considered. Alternative systems for discussing psychological problems that rely on dimensional models rather than categorical classification have been developed.

3.6 Discuss the pros and cons of dimensional models for understanding abnormal behaviour that serve as alternatives to more traditional classification systems.

Dimensional Systems as an Alternative to DSM Classification

The DSM and ICD are both primarily based on categorical systems that classify sets of symptoms into disorders. One alternative to such categorical diagnostic systems is a dimensional classification of abnormal behaviour, which suggests that people with disorders are not qualitatively distinct from people without disorders. Rather, a dimensional model for understanding abnormal behaviour suggests that symptoms of what are now called *disorders* are simply extreme variations of normal experience. Proponents of this model suggest that psychiatric illness is best conceptualized along dimensions of functioning rather than as discrete clinical conditions (Widiger & Samuel, 2005). Two features of mental illness that support the value of dimensional approaches are the high frequency of comorbidity (two or more disorders occurring together, such as an anxiety disorder and depression) and within-category variability (e.g., multiple people with the same diagnosis can have very different sets of symptoms and experiences). The DSM-5 approach allows for the diagnosis of comorbid conditions, an important feature because 45% of those with any mental disorder meet the criteria for two or more disorders (Kessler et al., 2005a).

Proponents of a dimensional model suggest that this alternative approach would allow for a richer description of patient difficulties across multiple areas of dysfunction. In a dimensional model, for example, a patient's functioning would be rated on a range of dimensions or traits (e.g., introversion, neuroticism, openness, conscientiousness) rather than simply on the presence or absence of a set of symptoms. This type of system also would lead to better categorization and understanding of a patient whose symptoms did not fall squarely into any existing category. In many cases, patients report many symptoms of a particular disorder but not enough of them to actually meet diagnostic criteria. In a categorical system, these people are often considered to have *subthreshold* syndromes. A dimensional approach would allow us to describe all symptoms regardless of whether or not they actually met specified cut-offs or criteria.

research HOT topic

Too Many Disorders?

Ray Moynihan (2006), in a provocative editorial published in the *British Medical Journal*, proposed that "extreme laziness may have a medical basis." The author called the new condition *motivational deficiency disorder* (MoDeD) and described its effects on daily life as being potentially fatal. In its most severe form, it could reduce the motivation to breathe. The article also discussed possible pharmaceutical treatments, as well as criticism that "ordinary laziness" might be improperly diagnosed as MoDeD. Shortly thereafter, online blogs appeared to discuss MoDeD. People speculated about whether their symptoms "qualified them" for the disorder and where to go for treatment. News outlets quickly picked up the study as well, highlighting its results in their daily health columns.

(continued)

Although this cleverly placed article was just an April Fool's joke, MoDeD's initial acceptance from the public highlights a larger issue that pervades society's concept of the human condition. *Are there too many disorders? Do we sometimes turn normal variations in human functioning into medical or psychiatric conditions?*

From 1952 to the present, the number of diagnostic categories in the DSM expanded significantly. Could we really have discovered so many new psychological disorders in the last 60 years? In many cases, empirical data have been used to modify, add, or delete categories. In other cases, categories have been modified based largely on the consensus of clinicians who were part of the DSM Task Forces. Social, political, and economic variables may also play a role (e.g., there may be potential monetary gain from new drugs developed to treat new conditions). Nevertheless, research is needed to determine the validity of various "potential" diagnostic categories (e.g., premenstrual dysphoric disorder, depressive personality disorder). What is necessary for psychological distress to become a psychological disorder?

All health care professionals agree that it is essential to study the reliability and validity of a diagnostic category before establishing it as an official disorder. Much more controversial is the argument by some critics (Chodoff, 2002) that we need clear biological markers that would differentiate psychological disorders from normal variations in human responses. Although some research is under way, the multitude of disorders listed in the DSM must still rely on "subjective checklists of a patient's history." An important research goal is to conduct carefully controlled studies to identify clusters or categories of symptoms that meaningfully describe true psychological disorders such as major depression, but that do not pathologize normal human emotions such as grief following the death of a loved one. Until objective markers (biological or otherwise) are determined, we must carefully guard against MoDeD in all its variations.

The dimensional approach would also allow clinicians to deal somewhat differently with the issue of multiple symptoms within diagnostic categories, known as *heterogeneity*. Despite the DSM's goal of creating relatively homogeneous diagnostic categories that would allow a "common language" of classification, individuals diagnosed with the same disorder actually may share few common features. For example, two people diagnosed with depression may have very different clinical presentations. While one may have depressed mood, crying, difficulty sleeping, fatigue, and difficulty concentrating, another may have loss of interest in things that used to bring pleasure, decreased appetite and weight loss, slowed motor behaviours, feelings of worthlessness, and recurrent thoughts of death. Both sets of symptoms would meet DSM criteria for major depression, but the primary complaints and targets for treatment would be quite different. Overall, this type of heterogeneity within diagnostic categories can adversely affect both clinical practice and research (Krueger et al., 2005).

Dimensional proponents believe that their approach lends itself to an increased amount of relevant clinical information, which can have both clinical and research advantages (Watson, 2005). Arguments against the dimensional model often focus on clinical utility. The categorical system offers a simple approach with a clear diagnostic label that provides an efficient way to share information. Dimensional models are innately more complex. For example, it is much simpler to explain to a patient that she has depression than to discuss with her where her symptoms lie along many dimensions of traits experienced by all people. A simple, easily communicated categorical system also facilitates the nature of clinical decision making (e.g., whether to hospitalize, which medication to use, whether to provide insurance coverage). The complexity of sharing information that is organized along multiple dimensions would make communication with patients extremely difficult; communication across researchers and clinicians trying to share information about common clinical syndromes would also become more difficult. Furthermore, because no single, accepted dimensional theory of psychopathology exists, achieving consensus on the type and number of dimensions required to capture the entire spectrum of mental illness could be quite difficult. Proponents of categorical approaches do concede that boundaries between most diagnoses remain imprecise, and they also acknowledge that psychiatric classification needs further precision (APA, 2013).

CONCEPT check

- The diagnosis and classification of psychological disorders are important for creating a common language for clinicians and researchers to facilitate communication about patients and psychological symptoms and syndromes. Diagnoses also help clinicians to develop appropriate treatment plans.
- The DSM system of classification is most often used in Canada, the United States, and many other countries. An alternative classification system, the *International Classification of Diseases* (ICD), is used in Europe and in other parts of the world.
- Developmental, demographic, and cultural variables affect the nature and experience of abnormal behaviour. These variables must be considered when evaluating the utility of diagnostic classification systems.
- A dimensional model for conceptualizing abnormal behaviour has been suggested and debated as an alternative to traditional categorical classification systems such as the DSM.

critical thinking question What are some of the pros and cons for categorical versus dimensional models of classifying abnormal behaviour?

real SCIENCE real LIFE

Libby—Assessment in a Clinical Research Study

In this case study, we present the experience of Libby, a young woman with bulimia nervosa, an eating disorder that involves binge eating and purging (usually vomiting) (see Chapter 7). Libby is participating in a clinical trial that compares treatment based on medication (Luvox) to cognitive-behavioural therapy. The case is presented from the perspective of the participant with commentary from the investigator about the purpose of each assessment.

I saw an advertisement in the newspaper offering free treatment for bulimia nervosa. I had been suffering for years so I called the number for the study coordinator. She was a very nice woman, and she described the study to me. The first thing she did was ask me some questions on the phone—what was my age, current weight, lowest and highest past weight, and how often did I binge and purge.

Researcher: This was the telephone screening. These questions were to determine preliminary eligibility for the study. We were looking for people with current bulimia nervosa who had been binge eating and purging at least twice per week for the past three months.

The study coordinator set me up with an appointment for the following week and said she would send me a packet of information, a consent form, and some questionnaires in the mail. Three days later I received all of the information. The information sheet pretty much repeated what she had told me about the study—that there would be a randomization procedure (a flip of the coin) and I would receive either medication or group psychotherapy for bulimia. I didn't really care what treatment condition I was in. I just wanted to get some proper treatment for this illness. I read through the consent form and signed on to participate in the study. Then I opened up the packet of questionnaires. I must have answered hundreds of questions. It took me over two hours. They asked about things ranging from eating behaviour, to how I felt about my body shape and size, to how depressed and anxious I was, to how much I drank alcohol, smoked cigarettes, and used drugs. There was also a bunch of questions about what kind of a person I was and another questionnaire that asked about the events that had happened in my life in the last year.

Researcher: The questionnaire battery included the Eating Disorders Examination Questionnaire to measure current eating symptoms, the Beck Depression and Anxiety Inventories to measure negative mood states that often accompany bulimia, the Fagerstrom Nicotine Tolerance Questionnaire to assess smoking and nicotine dependence, and measures of alcohol and drug use. The Life Events Schedule asks about significant environmental events that may have happened to the person in the last year. For an accurate diagnosis, it is important to understand whether any significant stressors (such as financial difficulties) or important events (such as the death of a loved one) could be influencing the person's thoughts or feelings. These were our baseline measures, many of which would be repeated at various times throughout the study.

When I arrived for my appointment, the researcher checked my consent form and checked through to make sure I had answered all of the questions. I then had a rather extensive interview in which the psychiatrist went into real depth about the history of the problems I have had with eating,

(continued)

depression, and anxiety. He also asked a lot about alcohol and drugs, but eventually he seemed to catch on that I was never into those things.

Researcher: We administered the baseline Structured Clinical Interview for DSM-5 to Libby to establish her baseline diagnosis and the Eating Disorders Examination Interview to get in-depth information about the nature of her eating disorder. According to our scoring, she met the diagnostic criteria for bulimia nervosa, major depression, and panic disorder. She was appropriate for inclusion into the study and was invited to participate.

The researchers welcomed me into the study. They then taught me how to self-monitor how often I binged and purged, which I had to do for a full week before starting therapy. I got randomized into the group cognitive-behaviour therapy condition.

Researcher: For the next 12 weeks, Libby took part in cognitive-behavioural group treatment for bulimia nervosa. She continued to self-monitor her symptoms throughout the treatment. We could see from the text messages of her self-monitoring that her binge eating and purging behaviour was improving by Week 4.

I kept going to group and found the homework they gave me to be really helpful in starting to get a handle on my binge eating. It was also reassuring to share my experience with the other patients in the group. I had no idea that so many people faced the same hurdles that I did in keeping my bulimia under control. After 12 weeks of therapy, I was finally starting to feel like there was a light at the end of the tunnel.

Researcher: At the end of the 12 weeks, we asked Libby to fill out the same questionnaires she had at baseline to see how things had changed. We also re-administered the Eating Disorders Examination Interview to get specific information about progress with her eating disorder. The psychiatrist who did the interview was unaware of her treatment group assignment. The interview revealed that she had been abstinent from binge eating for the past four weeks and had purged only once. This corresponded nicely with her self-monitoring data.

After the last interview, I set up my follow-up appointments. I was expected to return three months and six months after treatment. We had learned that relapse is common in bulimia and the best way to tell whether a treatment works is to make sure that the changes we make actually stick. I was happy to return for the evaluations—especially because they assured me they would pay for parking and give me $50 for each session I attended!

Researcher: It is very important for us to make sure that the positive changes that we see persist. The only way to do this is by having scheduled follow-up assessments. Because many people do not return for their follow-ups, we have found that an excellent incentive to bring them back is to reimburse them for parking and provide a reasonable monetary incentive for their time. This is also an excellent opportunity for us to refer them for additional treatment if they are not doing well.

When I returned for my follow-up visits, the psychiatrist (who still didn't know which treatment I was in) asked me many of the same questions that he had at the start of the study. Thinking back to my first assessment, I could even tell how different my answers were. At this point, I had been basically binge and purge free for the past six months with one exception. I went through a bad patch when I broke up with my boyfriend and I purged a couple of times, but I used the skills I had learned in therapy to get that behaviour right back under control. Overall, I think being involved in a clinical trial was an interesting experience. I got great treatment, and the close follow-up helped me keep my symptoms under control.

Summary

3.1 Understand the goals and uses of clinical assessment.

Clinical assessments can be used to gather information about a person's symptoms and to make decisions about the nature, status, and treatment of psychological problems. Assessments can be used for screening, diagnosis, treatment development, or outcome evaluation.

3.2 Name three important properties of psychological assessment instruments.

To determine the meaning of a score from a clinical assessment, it is important to compare the score with scores from other groups of people (called a normative comparison) or to a prior score by the same patient (self-referent comparison). The reliability of assessment measures refers to their ability to produce consistent scores across time and assessors. The validity of a test refers to the ability of scores to measure concepts accurately.

3.3 List and explain the function of different types of assessment instruments.

Clinical interviews usually occur early in the assessment process so that the clinician can begin to gather information and set assessment goals. These interviews can be structured or unstructured. Psychological tests measure personality, general and cognitive functioning, intelligence, and specific clinical symptoms. Behavioural assessment, including self-monitoring and behavioural observation, measures behaviour and environmental variables that cause and maintain the behaviour. Psychophysiological assessment measures changes in the nervous system as they relate to psychological or emotional events. The most common form of psychophysiological assessment is electroencephalography (EEG), which measures electrical signals in the brain.

3.4 Explain why classification systems for abnormal behaviour are valuable.

Diagnosing and classifying psychological disorders are important for creating a common language for clinicians and researchers to facilitate communication about patients and psychological symptoms and syndromes. Diagnoses also help clinicians develop appropriate treatment plans. The DSM system of classification is most often used in North America, but alternative models exist.

3.5 Recognize the importance of developmental and cultural variables that affect the experience and classification of abnormal behaviour.

Assessment materials and procedures need to consider the age and developmental level of the test taker as well as cultural variables.

3.6 Discuss the pros and cons of dimensional models for understanding abnormal behaviour that serve as alternatives to more traditional classification systems.

A dimensional model for classifying abnormal behaviour has been suggested as an alternative to more traditional categorical classification systems. This model suggests that abnormal behaviour is better conceptualized along dimensions of functioning rather than in categories. Proponents of this system suggest that a dimensional model allows better attention to individual differences in symptoms that can occur for different patients with the same disorder. However, others argue that categorical systems are simpler and more efficient ways to share information.

Key Terms

behavioural avoidance test 97
behavioural observation 97
clinical assessment 76
clinical interviews 86
clinical significance 80
comorbidity 102
diagnosis 78
***Diagnostic and Statistical Manual of Mental Disorders* (DSM)** 101
differential diagnosis 78
functional analysis 96
intelligence quotient 92
intelligence test 92
International Classification of Diseases and Related Health Problems (ICD) 102
interrater agreement 82
normative 81
personality test 87
projective test 88
psychophysiological assessment 98
reliability 82
screening 77
self-monitoring 96
self-referent comparisons 81
structured interview 86
test-retest reliability 82
unstructured interview 86
validity 82

TEST yourself

1. Selection of assessment tools is largely determined by the patient's symptoms, age, and medical status. One other factor may be the
   a. early childhood experiences of the patient
   b. referral process
   c. environmental cues perceived by the therapist
   d. therapist's theoretical perspective

2. Physicians and other practitioners may choose to give new patients a screening assessment, which is
   a. a brief measure in which a cut-off score indicates the possibility of significant problems
   b. a test to determine whether the patient has a medical rather than a psychological condition
   c. a test to see whether the patient will benefit from psychotherapy
   d. a questionnaire that determines whether a patient needs to see a physician

3. With psychological disorders, the diagnosis given is primarily based on
   a. the therapist's theoretical perspective
   b. communication across clinicians
   c. a cluster of symptoms
   d. findings of laboratory tests

4. Diagnosis is important to physicians and psychologists because it facilitates
   a. treatment planning
   b. communication across clinicians and researchers
   c. understanding of a person's psychological status
   d. all of the above

5. A measure of clinical significance tells us that
   a. the patient is or is not satisfied with the treatment
   b. a patient's treatment is "finished"
   c. two clinical assessments are in agreement
   d. an observed change in a patient is a meaningful improvement

6. Comparing a person's score on a psychological test to the average scores obtained on that test from a large representative sample of people is a
   a. self-referent comparison
   b. psychometric comparison
   c. normative comparison
   d. clinical comparison

7. After an interview, a psychiatrist rates Jim's depression as severe. The next day a clinical psychologist also conducts an interview and rates Jim's depression as severe. The two clinicians are demonstrating
   a. interrater validity
   b. test-retest reliability
   c. interrater agreement
   d. test-retest validity

8. Dr. Smith develops the Smith Depression Inventory and gives it to hundreds of patients with depression. He also gives those patients the widely used Beck Depression Inventory. He finds that the average scores on the two questionnaires are highly correlated. Dr. Smith has demonstrated that the Smith Depression Inventory has
   a. concurrent validity
   b. predictive validity
   c. statistical prediction
   d. clinical prediction

9. A test publisher describes a psychological test as having extremely high predictive validity. This means the test
   a. has the ability to forecast particular outcomes
   b. has a high correlation with similar measures
   c. discriminates well between related concepts
   d. all of the above

10. Administering psychological tests to someone from another country may produce biased results if which of the following is *not* considered?
   a. the language in which the test was written
   b. the education of the person taking the test
   c. cultural beliefs and values of the person taking the test
   d. all of the above

11. Compared with unstructured interviews, structured interviews have several advantages, including
   a. avoidance of irrelevant questions
   b. shorter time frame
   c. identification of the best course of therapy
   d. increased reliability

12. Susan was sent to a neuropsychologist after a car accident left her having trouble concentrating and remembering things. The neuropsychologist gave her a battery of 10 measures assessing memory, abstract thought, language, sensory-motor integration, perceptions, and motor dexterity. This test battery is called the
   a. MCMI
   b. WAIS
   c. Halstead-Reitan
   d. WCST

13. Although intelligence tests are controversial, they are useful in assessing
   a. genetics and its relative importance
   b. influences from a person's cultural background
   c. prediction of academic success
   d. nonverbal memory

14. Sally suffers from an eating disorder. The psychologist asked her to keep a diary and record what she eats, when she eats something, where she is when she eats, and what she is feeling right before, during, and after she eats. This is called
   a. behavioural application
   b. testing for specific symptoms
   c. self-monitoring
   d. self-report measuring

15. A patient has an extreme spider phobia. He is taken to a room with a cage of spiders against the opposite wall. He is asked to walk as close to the cage as he can. He takes two steps toward the cage and says he cannot go any closer. The psychologist measures the distance on the floor from the patient's feet to the cage. This is a
   a. continuous recording
   b. self-report measure
   c. natural environmental assessment
   d. behavioural avoidance test

16. The great advantage of the electroencephalogram (EEG) is that it
   a. can determine which neurotransmitters are active
   b. is the only measure that directly assesses electrical activity in the brain
   c. can identify functioning in a specific brain region
   d. is able to show specific neurons in the act of firing

17. The primary classification system used in Canada and the United States is the
   a. ICD
   b. DSM
   c. Merck Manual
   d. Psychiatric Census

18. DSM-5 encourages clinicians to do all of the following except:
   a. choose the most accurate diagnosis
   b. indicate likely biological bases for the disorder
   c. describe how the person's disorder influences occupational functioning
   d. describe how environmental factors may have contributed to the disorder

19. More so than its predecessors, DSM-5:

a. considers how the expression of disorders may differ by age

b. considers how cultural factors may influence the expression of disorders

c. considers how sex may influence the expression of disorders

d. all of the above

20. Dimensional classification is an alternative to categorical systems such as the DSM. One advantage of a dimensional system is

a. better description of patients whose problems do not fit into a single category

b. better use of a "common language" to classify patients

c. simpler, clearer diagnostic labels for all conditions

d. exclusion of all patients' comorbidity issues

Answers:
1 d, 2 a, 3 c, 4 d, 5 d, 6 c, 7 c, 8 a, 9 a, 10 d, 11 d, 12 c, 13 c, 14 c, 15 d, 16 b, 17 b, 18 d, 19 d, 20 a.

chapter 4

anxiety, obsessive-compulsive, and trauma- and stressor-related disorders

(bottom left): Andresr/Shutterstock; **(bottom right):** Africa Studio/Shutterstock

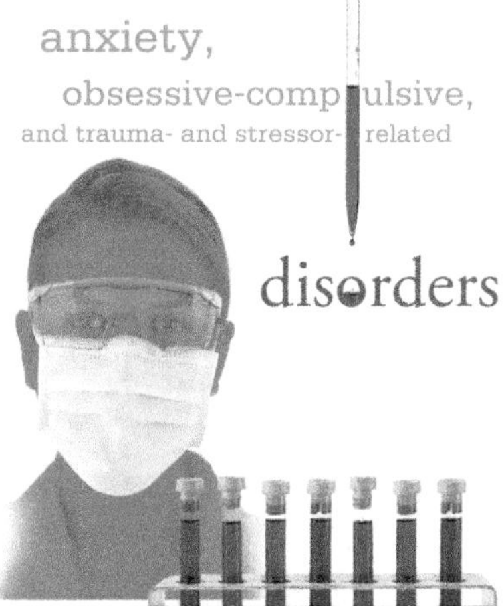

learning objectives

After reading this chapter, you should be able to:

4.1
Identify the three components of anxiety.

4.2
Distinguish between a normal fear response and these anxiety-based disorders.

4.3
Understand how developmental and sociocultural factors affect the expression of anxiety.

4.4
Describe the critical elements that comprise each of the different disorders.

4.5
Identify biological and psychological factors related to the development of these disorders.

4.6
Identify pharmacological and psychological interventions used to treat these disorders.

This chapter covers a collection of disorders that were regarded as anxiety disorders in DSM-IV. In DSM-5 these disorders are split into three chapters: anxiety disorders (e.g., panic disorder, generalized anxiety disorder, specific phobia), obsessive-compulsive and related disorders, and stressor-related disorders. The chapters are grouped next to each other in DSM-5. What this means is that all three groups of disorders are considered to have similarities to one another (i.e., anxiety is a common theme), but the three groups of disorders also differ from one another in some ways, in terms of clinical features, presumed etiology, and treatment. There are many different anxiety-related disorders. We will discuss the major ones. Readers interested in the other disorders are encouraged to consult DSM-5.

Delores is 22 years old, lives with her parents, and has a bachelor's degree in medical technology. She is extremely fearful when in enclosed spaces and when she has to be in front of an audience. Her fear of enclosed spaces began at age 10 when her older brother locked her in a closet and would not let her out. Her fears worsened four years ago when she entered university and began living in a tiny dorm room. Delores feels trapped and confined in many different places, such as driving through a car wash, having a dental examination, riding on a roller coaster or in certain elevators, or having her blood drawn. She is also fearful in situations in which her head and neck are partly or completely covered, such as wearing a motorcycle helmet, a plastic face shield used by dental hygienists, or even a life jacket. When in these circumstances, her heart races, she feels short of breath and dizzy, and she worries that she might die. Delores also has fears in public situations, such as public speaking, being asked to speak at a meeting, and interviewing for a job. She worries that other people can see her anxiety, that she might make a mistake, or that others will think that she is a failure.

Her fears affect her life in many ways. She cannot work as a medical technologist because she has to wear a face shield in the laboratory, and when she puts it on, she panics and feels like she cannot breathe. She accepted jobs at several different hospitals, but each one required her to wear a face shield when working with highly contagious blood specimens. So now her job history is a series of short-term positions, making it appear as if she has a problem keeping a job. She cannot work in her chosen field, and the only job she can find is cleaning houses.

Delores took out loans to pay for university, and now her income is so low that she cannot make her loan payments. Worrying about her financial situation is keeping her up at night: She lies awake for two hours before falling asleep. Her boyfriend is often angry at her because she will not ride roller coasters or on the back of his motorcycle. Once she took a vacation with her parents, but they had to return home immediately after arriving at the hotel. The hotel was spectacular but all of the elevators were made of glass. Delores could not ride up to her room. They lost their hotel deposit and did not have enough money to find another hotel with a room on the ground floor.

Her social fears are also interfering with her life. She dropped out of several different universities until she found one that did not require any oral presentations for graduation. Delores has a beautiful voice, and she would love to sing in church, but she is too anxious to join the choir. Although Delores's boyfriend does not understand her fears, her mother and grandmother do. They both have significant fears: Her mother will not put her head under water, and her grandmother eloped rather than walk down the aisle as a bride with all eyes looking at her.

You can probably relate to aspects of Delores's distress. You may have had similar feelings on your first date, when you had to speak in public, or when you interviewed for a job. You worried about whether you would do well. Your heart raced, you felt tense, or perhaps your palms sweated. Maybe you had trouble sleeping the night before the event.

All of these behaviours are typical of **anxiety**, a common emotion that is characterized by physical symptoms (faster heartbeat, feelings of tension) and thoughts or worries that something bad will happen.

What Is Anxiety?

Anxiety is a future-oriented response ("What if I mess up this speech? What if she does not like me?") and often occurs when people encounter a new situation or anticipate a life-changing event (starting university, getting married). In most instances, the anxiety that occurs in these situations is time limited and goes away when the event is over. In some cases, however, anxiety spirals out of proportion to the actual situation; the anxiety can lead to anxiety, obsessive-compulsive, trauma, or stressor-related disorders. Before examining each of these disorders, it is first necessary to understand the nature of anxiety and a closely related emotion, fear.

The Fight-or-Flight Response

Suppose that you are walking in the park enjoying the solitude. You come upon two vicious-looking dogs that are fighting. You start to back away, but the dogs stop and come toward you. You know that you need to get out of there *fast*. Luckily, evolution has prepared you for this moment. Your *hypothalamus* (the part of your brain that is involved in anxiety responses, among other things) sends a message to your *adrenal glands* to release the hormone *adrenaline*. You suddenly find yourself running faster and jumping higher than you ever thought possible. You did not even know that you could climb a tree, but you are doing it! Fortunately, the dogs soon get bored waiting for you to come down and they leave. Your body's response, called **fight or flight**, was a general discharge of your **sympathetic nervous system (SNS)** (Cannon, 1929). The fight-or-flight response has been part of human behaviour since prehistoric times (see Figure 4.1).

Your body's nervous system consists of two parts: the *central nervous system*, which includes your brain and spinal cord, and the *peripheral nervous system*, which consists of all other nerves in your body. The peripheral nervous system is further broken down into two parts: the *somatic sensory system*, which contains sensory and voluntary motor functions, and the *autonomic nervous system*, which controls involuntary movements. Finally, the autonomic nervous system also has two elements, the *sympathetic nervous system* and the *parasympathetic nervous system*. When activated by stress or fear, the SNS goes into overdrive. Your heart beats faster than normal, supplying more blood to power the muscles. Your respiration rate increases, allowing more oxygen to get to your blood and brain. Whether it was prehistoric man trying to outrun a woolly mammoth or modern-day woman doing some fancy driving on an icy road to avoid careening off a bridge, this fight-or-flight response allows an optimal level of physical functioning in the face of threat.

Of course, such superhuman abilities are time limited. After the SNS has been activated, the **parasympathetic nervous system (PNS)** returns your body to its normal resting state by decreasing your heart rate, blood pressure, and respiration. The fight-or-flight response is usually associated with the emotion that we call *fear*, a reaction to an existing or threatening event. The motivating power of fight or flight allows you to use all available resources to escape from a threatening situation. Some researchers have described this fight-or-flight reaction as an *alarm* to a present danger (Barlow, 2002).

In contrast, anxiety, as we have already noted, is a future-oriented response and sometimes consists of decreased levels of physical reactivity rather than the fight-or-flight response. Anxiety is also characterized by a thought pattern that is sometimes described as imagining the worst possible outcome. Anxiety is often present even when there is no real danger. In the next section, we examine the various components of anxiety.

Nervous System

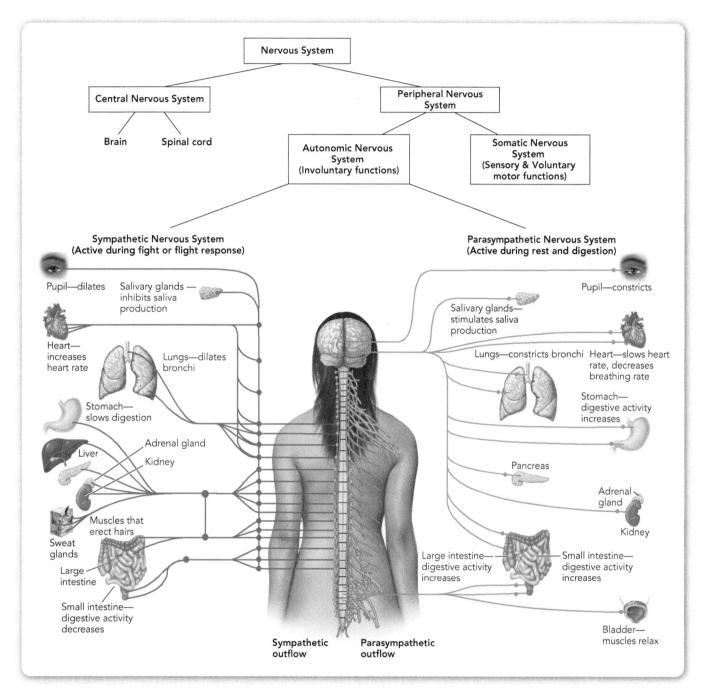

Central Nervous System

Brain

Spinal cord

Peripheral Nervous System

Autonomic Nervous System (Involuntary functions)

Somatic Nervous System (Sensory & Voluntary motor functions)

Sympathetic Nervous System (Active during fight or flight response)

Pupil—dilates

Salivary glands — inhibits saliva production

Heart— increases heart rate

Lungs—dilates bronchi

Stomach— slows digestion

Adrenal gland

Liver

Kidney

Muscles that erect hairs

Sweat glands

Large intestine

Small intestine— digestive activity decreases

Parasympathetic Nervous System (Active during rest and digestion)

Pupil—constricts

Salivary glands— stimulates saliva production

Lungs—constricts bronchi

Heart—slows heart rate, decreases breathing rate

Stomach— digestive activity increases

Pancreas

Adrenal gland

Kidney

Large intestine— digestive activity increases

Small intestine— digestive activity increases

Bladder— muscles relax

Sympathetic outflow

Parasympathetic outflow

FIGURE 4.1

The Sympathetic and the Parasympathetic Nervous Systems. The sympathetic nervous system works to produce the fight-or-flight response, after which the parasympathetic nervous system returns the body to a normal resting state.

Source: Lilienfeld, Scott O.; Lynn, Steven J.; Namy, Laura L.; Woolf, Nancy J., *Psychology: From Inquiry to Understanding*, 1st Ed., © 2009, p. 121. Reprinted and Electronically reproduced by permission of Pearson Education, Inc., Upper Saddle River, New Jersey.

The Elements of Anxiety

4.1 Identify the three components of anxiety.

On their way to a long-anticipated skiing vacation at the Whistler ski resort, Matthew and Eden started driving across Vancouver's Lion's Gate Bridge. Matthew's heart suddenly started thumping in his chest, and he felt like he couldn't breathe. He began sweating profusely and felt dizzy. Fearing a heart attack, he stopped the car in the middle of the bridge and insisted that Eden call an ambulance. Even though the paramedics found no medical reason for Matthew's symptoms, he insisted that they take him to Vancouver General Hospital, leaving Eden to drive the car home.

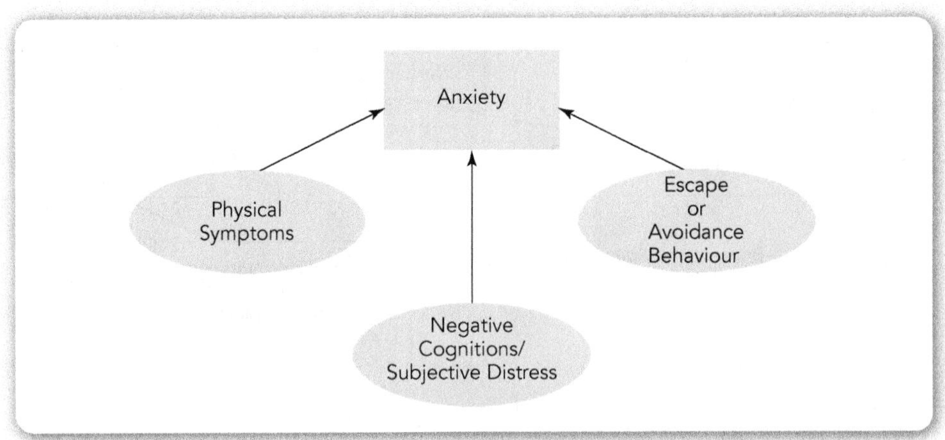

FIGURE 4.2

The Three Components of Anxiety. Anxiety is considered to have three elements: physical symptoms, negative cognitions or subjective distress, and behaviours such as escape or avoidance.

Although Matthew faced no obvious threat, such as a vicious dog, he experienced physical symptoms—but in this case, they occurred unexpectedly or *out of the blue*. Matthew's body, mind, and behaviour were affected by this experience. His *body* was sending out signals that he needed to leave (flee) the situation. His *mind* was worried that something was medically wrong, so he called for help. Even though the paramedics said he was fine, he did not believe them. Because he felt so uncomfortable, he escaped the situation and went to the hospital (*behaviour*), a place where he felt safe. The physical (body), cognitive (mind), and behavioural symptoms that Matthew experienced are elements of the emotion that we call *anxiety*. In Matthew's case, the intense "burst" of anxiety-related physical symptoms is called a **panic attack**, defined as an abrupt surge of intense fear or intense discomfort that reaches a peak within minutes and is accompanied by four or more physical symptoms (APA, 2013). We will return to panic attacks later in this chapter.

Emotions such as anxiety and fear have three distinct components (see Figure 4.2): physiological response, cognitive symptoms or subjective distress, and avoidance or escape. A panic attack such as Matthew's is a dramatic physical manifestation of anxiety, but it is not the only one. Other physical symptoms include blushing, buzzing or ringing in the ears, muscle tension, irritability, fatigue, gastrointestinal distress (indigestion, nausea, constipation, diarrhea), or urinary urgency and frequency. Among children, headaches and stomachaches (or butterflies in the stomach) are common complaints, although older children are more likely than younger children to report physical distress.

In addition to physical responses, anxiety includes subjective distress (also called *cognitive symptoms*). One type of cognitive symptom includes specific thoughts, ideas, images, or impulses. In some instances, the thoughts occur when the person affected sees a feared object or event, such as when someone who is afraid of spiders suddenly sees a spider ("What if that big hairy spider bites me?"). In other instances, the thoughts occur spontaneously ("What if I run over a child when I am driving my car?"). A different type of cognitive symptom is **worry**, which may be defined as apprehensive (negative) expectations about the future that are considered to be unreasonable in light of the actual situation. Worry exists among adults, adolescents, and some children. However, preadolescent children do not always report the thoughts and worries that are common in anxious adults (Alfano et al., 2006), perhaps reflecting their overall cognitive immaturity. Developmentally, young children do not yet have the ability to "think about thinking" (Flavell et al., 2001), a skill known as *metacognition*. Because of this difference, the cognitive symptom of worry is often absent in very young children. It appears later, when children mature sufficiently to allow them to recognize and report their own thoughts.

The most common behavioural symptom of anxiety is escape from or avoidance of the feared object, event, or situation. A person who is afraid of elevators walks up the

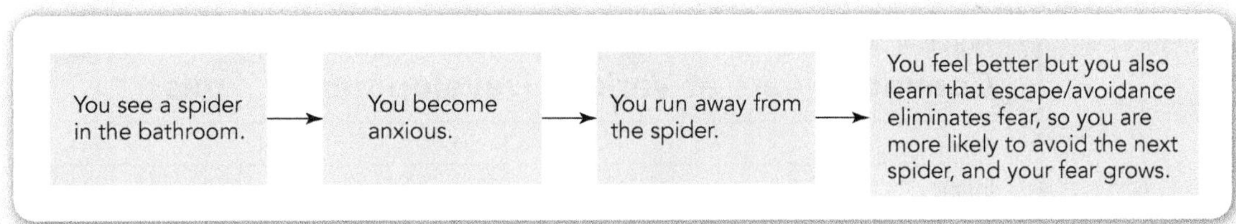

FIGURE 4.3

Negative Reinforcement Increases Avoidance Behaviour and Anxiety. How feeling better can make your anxiety worse.

stairs. After the incident on the bridge, Matthew avoided driving. Avoidance can also take the form of overdoing certain behaviours. For example, fears of contamination may result in excessive behaviours such as washing or cleaning, designed to eliminate the feeling of contamination. Among children, unusual behaviours may be the first sign that a child is fearful. When it is time to go to school, children may play sick, cry, cling to a parent, or throw a tantrum. Some children are disobedient, refusing to follow instructions that involve contact with a feared event or object, even to the point of refusing to go to school.

Escape or avoidance behaviours bring temporary relief from distress, but they also reinforce behavioural avoidance through the process of negative reinforcement. Imagine that you are afraid of spiders. You see one in your bathroom, and you run outside. You feel relieved because you are no longer in the same room as the spider. By running away, you removed a negative feeling of fear, and you feel better. The feeling of relief that follows the removal of something negative is reinforcing; that is, this feeling increases the likelihood that the next time you see a spider, you will run away again. Therefore, eliminating distress by avoiding or escaping the situation can actually make the anxiety worse (see Figure 4.3). A primary goal of psychological treatment for anxiety is to reverse this pattern of negative reinforcement and eliminate avoidance of the feared situations.

How "Normal" Anxiety Differs from Abnormal Anxiety

4.2 Distinguish between a normal fear response and these anxiety-based disorders.

4.3 Understand how developmental and sociocultural factors affect the expression of anxiety.

As we noted, it is normal to feel anxious from time to time, but when does *anxiety* become a *disorder*? The first factor to consider in making this decision is *functional impairment*. Remember Robert and Stan from Chapter 1? Before leaving home, both men walk through the house, checking to make sure that every door and window is locked and the oven is turned off. Robert does a quick five-minute check, but Stan needs several hours to finish checking and as a result is sometimes late for work. Because his checking impairs his ability to get to work on time, Stan's behaviour would meet the criteria for an anxiety disorder.

A second factor that differentiates normal from abnormal anxiety is developmental age. Among children, fears are common, and they follow a developmental trajectory (Antony & Barlow, 2002). Two important aspects of the developmental model include the number and types of fears. The total number of fears declines as age increases. For infants and toddlers, so much of the world is new and initially scary that they are likely to have more fears than when they are older. As illustrated in Table 4.1, different fears are also common at different ages. As children mature

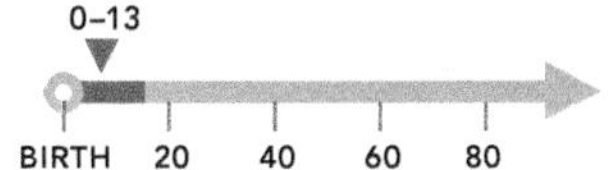

Fears are common in young children. The objects or situations that children fear often reflect the typical developmental challenges for that age.

CONCEPT check

- The fight-or-flight response is an activation of the sympathetic nervous system designed to allow the organism to fight off or flee from a perceived threat. In the case of anxiety disorders, this response may occur even when there is no real threat.
- Anxiety is usually considered to have three components: physiological reactivity (body), subjective distress/negative thoughts (mind), and escape or avoidance (behaviour).
- In children, fears exist along a developmental hierarchy. At certain ages, fears are considered common and a normal part of development. At other ages, they are considered abnormal and in need of treatment.

critical thinking question Girls and women report more fears and anxiety disorders than do men and boys. However, when placed in anxiety-producing situations, both sexes show equal physiological reactions. What societal factors might explain this difference?

What Are the Anxiety Disorders?

4.4 Describe the critical elements that comprise each of the different disorders.

The **anxiety disorders** have in common the physical, cognitive, and behavioural symptoms described earlier. For each disorder, the anxiety is expressed in a different way or is the result of a different object or situation. Some people are anxious about public speaking, others do not like to travel on airplanes, and still others fear separation from certain people. Of course, some people are anxious in more than one type of situation, and in some cases they may have more than one anxiety disorder. The co-occurrence of two or more disorders existing in the same person (either at the same time or at some point in the lifetime) is called *comorbidity*. About 57% of people who are diagnosed with an anxiety disorder are comorbid for another anxiety disorder or depression (Brown et al., 2001). Therefore, although in the following sections we discuss these disorders as distinct conditions, remember that often people who have one disorder may have additional disorders as well.

Prior to DSM-5, the two other groups of disorders included in this chapter (obsessive-compulsive disorders [OCDs] and trauma disorders) also were considered to be anxiety disorders. Therefore, when we discuss below how many people have these disorders, we are describing disorders from all of the diagnostic categories included in this chapter. In this paragraph, we use the term *anxiety disorders* to cover all of the DSM-5 anxiety disorders as well as the DSM-IV disorders of OCD and posttraumatic stress disorder (PTSD). In Canada and the United States, 31% of adults in the general population suffer from one of these disorders at some time in their lives (Katzman et al., 2014), making them one of the most common types of psychological disorders among adults. Anxiety disorders are also common among children and adolescents. The prevalence of anxiety disorders among youth ranges from 8.6% to 15.7% (Costello et al., 2003; Essau et al, 2000). Most anxiety disorders develop early in life. The average age of onset is 11 years, one of the earliest for any psychiatric disorder (Kessler et al., 2005a). In addition to personal suffering, anxiety disorders compromise quality of life and social functioning (Mendlowicz & Stein, 2000), affect educational attainment (Kessler et al., 1995), and increase professional help seeking and medication use (Acarturk et al., 2009; Wittchen et al., 1994). In addition to their serious and pervasive effect on the individual, anxiety disorders exert a substantial financial cost on society, both in terms of health care costs and lost productivity (Acarturk et al., 2009).

Panic Attacks

Remember when Matthew was driving across the bridge? He had a *panic attack*—a discrete period of intense fear and physical arousal. Panic attacks develop abruptly, and symptoms reach peak intensity within minutes (APA, 2013). Somatic and cognitive symptoms of a panic attack may include heart palpitations (pounding heart or accelerated heart rate), sweating, trembling, shortness of breath, choking, chest pain, nausea or abdominal distress, dizziness, derealization or depersonalization (feeling of being detached from one's body or surroundings), fear of losing control or going crazy, fear of dying, paresthesias (tingling in the hands or feet), and chills or heat sensations. Heart palpitations and dizziness are the most commonly reported symptoms, whereas paresthesias and choking sensations are the least common (Craske et al., 2010). As many as 28.3% of adults have had a panic attack during their lifetime (Kessler et al., 2006), but just having a panic attack does not mean that the person has a panic disorder or any other anxiety disorder. Although 28.3% of adults report having had a panic attack, only about 4.7% have panic disorder. Remember that in an anxiety disorder, the anxiety symptoms must cause distress or some form of functional impairment. Many people who have had a panic attack have had only one or a few and are not distressed or impaired by their rare occurrences.

When panic attacks are not isolated events, they may be a symptom of any of the anxiety disorders. Even though only one of the anxiety disorders actually has the word *panic* in the title, panic attacks may be a symptom of other anxiety disorders and occur when a person is facing a frightening situation that is not a real threat to his or her physical well-being. People who are afraid of snakes, for example, might have a panic attack if they see a snake in a glass container at the zoo. In other cases, the anxiety reaction may be out of proportion to the object or situation, such as when you are flying and the airplane encounters mild turbulence, but you become very anxious and believe that you are going to die.

Panic attacks may be one of two types. *Expected panic attacks* are attacks that occur in response to a situational cue or trigger, such as when your friend who fears heights is suddenly confronted with the need to use a glass elevator. Expected attacks may also occur in anticipation of a feared situation, such as when someone with fears of public speaking has a panic attack a week before the speech. In other cases (such as Matthew's), the attack occurs unexpectedly, for no particular reason. People often say the attack came *out of the blue*. This represents the second type of panic attack, called *unexpected attacks*. These unexpected attacks are considered a *false alarm* (Barlow, 2002) because no object, event, or situation appears to precipitate the attack. Many times people misinterpret a panic attack as a heart attack and go to the hospital, which suggests just how frightening these symptoms can be. Yet it is clear that panic attacks are common, occurring in people with various anxiety disorders and sometimes even in people who do not have an anxiety disorder.

Panic Disorder

Lena is 24 years old. Her family has a history of cardiac disease, and several relatives died when they were in their early 40s. Lena is very worried that she will develop high blood pressure, which she considers the first sign of cardiac disease. Her physician referred her to an anxiety disorders clinic because L checks her blood pressure at least 20 times per day (but it is always normal). In the course of the diagnostic interview, Lena reveals that a physician told her she has "hypertensive crises" when for no reason, her heart races, she gets dizzy, she feels very hot, and her hands tingle. These "hypertensive crises" happen several times per month. When the therapist explains to Lena that these are panic attacks, she begins to cry with relief—she is not suffering from cardiac disease after all.

Panic attacks are the defining feature of panic disorder (see "DSM-5: Panic Disorder"). In **panic disorder**, a person has had at least one panic attack and worries about having more

criteria for Panic Disorder DSM-5

A. Recurrent unexpected panic attacks. A panic attack is an abrupt surge of intense fear or intense discomfort that reaches a peak within minutes, and during which time four (or more) of the following symptoms occur:

Note: The abrupt surge can occur from a calm state or an anxious state.

1. Palpitations, pounding heart, or accelerated heart rate.
2. Sweating.
3. Trembling or shaking.
4. Sensations of shortness of breath or smothering.
5. Feelings of choking.
6. Chest pain or discomfort.
7. Nausea or abdominal distress.
8. Feeling dizzy, unsteady, light-headed, or faint.
9. Chills or heat sensations.
10. Paresthesias (numbness or tingling sensations).
11. Derealization (feelings of unreality) or depersonalization (being detached from oneself).
12. Fear of losing control or "going crazy."
13. Fear of dying.

Note: Culture-specific symptoms (e.g., tinnitus, neck soreness, headache, uncontrollable screaming or crying) may be seen. Such symptoms should not count as one of the four required symptoms.

B. At least one of the attacks has been followed by 1 month (or more) of one or both of the following:

1. Persistent concern or worry about additional panic attacks or their consequences (e.g., losing control, having a heart attack, "going crazy").
2. A significant maladaptive change in behaviour related to the attacks (e.g., behaviours designed to avoid having panic attacks, such as avoidance of exercise or unfamiliar situations).

C. The disturbance is not attributable to the physiological effects of a substance (e.g., a drug of abuse, a medication) or another medical condition (e.g., hyperthyroidism, cardiopulmonary disorders).

D. The disturbance is not better explained by another mental disorder (e.g., the panic attacks do not occur only in response to feared social situations, as in social anxiety disorder; in response to circumscribed phobic objects or situations, as in specific phobia; in response to obsessions, as in obsessive-compulsive disorder; in response to reminders of traumatic events, as in posttraumatic stress disorder; or in response to separation from attachment figures, as in separation anxiety disorder).

attacks. The person also might worry about what a panic attack *means* ("Am I developing a heart condition?" "Am I losing my mind?") and may behave differently in response to the attacks, such as calling the doctor after every attack. Not everyone who is diagnosed with panic disorder changes their behaviour or avoids situations (driving, shopping, getting on a bus) because of the fear that a panic attack might occur, but some people do.

Agoraphobia

Agoraphobia (literally meaning "fear of the marketplace") is a marked or intense fear or anxiety that occurs upon exposure to, or in anticipation of, a broad range of situations (see "DSM-5: Agoraphobia"). The fear or anxiety must occur in at least two out of five situations, including public transportation, open spaces, enclosed places, standing in line or being in a crowd, or being outside the home alone. Sometimes people with agoraphobia are able to enter these situations but only with a trusted companion or by carrying certain items (such as a bottle of water) in case a panic attack occurs. In addition to panic symptoms, people with agoraphobia may fear the occurrence of extremely embarrassing physical symptoms such as dizziness or falling, losing control of the bowels or bladder, or, in children, a sense of disorientation or getting lost (APA, 2013). Many people develop agoraphobia after they have developed panic disorder. The fear that a panic attack may occur and they may be in a situation or place where they might not be able to get help often leads to a pattern of behavioural avoidance. Not all individuals with agoraphobia, however, have panic attacks.

Panic disorder is rare in young children and only slightly more common among adolescents. The disorder usually begins in early adulthood (McNally, 2001). In the general adult population, panic disorder (3.7%) is the most common of the three disorders. About 1% have panic disorder and agoraphobia, and 1.4% have agoraphobia without any history of panic disorder (Kessler et al., 2005a). Among adults age 55 and older, 1.2% suffer from panic disorder at any specific time (Chou, 2009). Another age-related difference is that whereas younger adults use the word *fear* when describing the emotion accompanying their physical symptoms, older adults use the word *discomfort* (Craske et al., 2010). It is important for clinicians to remember this distinction when interviewing older adults. If clinicians ask only whether the person feels fearful, they may fail to diagnose panic disorder in an older adult, preventing the person from receiving appropriate treatment. More than 94% of people with panic disorder with or without agoraphobia seek treatment (Kessler et al., 2006); without treatment, symptom-free periods are rare (Batelaan et al., 2010). When a symptom-free period occurs, many people relapse within the year. Even with medication treatment, panic attacks often decrease in frequency but are not eliminated. Five years after receiving medication treatment, 85% of people no longer had *panic disorder*, although 62% still had occasional *panic attacks* (Andersch et al., 1997).

criteria for Agoraphobia — DSM-5

A. Marked fear or anxiety about two (or more) of the following five situations:

1. Using public transportation (e.g., automobiles, buses, trains, ships, planes).
2. Being in open spaces (e.g., parking lots, marketplaces, bridges).
3. Being in enclosed places (e.g., shops, theatres, cinemas).
4. Standing in line or being in a crowd.
5. Being outside of the home alone.

B. The individual fears or avoids these situations because of thoughts that escape might be difficult or help might not be available in the event of developing panic-like symptoms or other incapacitating or embarrassing symptoms (e.g., fear of falling in the elderly; fear of incontinence).

C. The agoraphobic situations almost always provoke fear or anxiety.

D. The agoraphobic situations are actively avoided, require the presence of a companion, or are endured with intense fear or anxiety.

E. The fear or anxiety is out of proportion to the actual danger posed by the agoraphobic situations and to the sociocultural context.

F. The fear, anxiety, or avoidance is persistent, typically lasting for 6 months or more.

G. The fear, anxiety, or avoidance causes clinically significant distress or impairment in social, occupational, or other important areas of functioning.

H. If another medical condition (e.g., inflammatory bowel disease, Parkinson's disease) is present, the fear, anxiety, or avoidance is clearly excessive.

I. The fear, anxiety, or avoidance is not better explained by the symptoms of another mental disorder—for example, the symptoms are not confined to specific phobia, situational type; do not involve only social situations (as in social anxiety disorder); and are not related exclusively to obsessions (as in obsessive-compulsive disorder), perceived defects or flaws in physical appearance (as in body dysmorphic disorder), reminders of traumatic events (as in posttraumatic stress disorder), or fear of separation (as in separation anxiety disorder).

Note: Agoraphobia is diagnosed irrespective of the presence of panic disorder. If an individual's presentation meets criteria for panic disorder and agoraphobia, both diagnoses should be assigned.

Women are more likely to experience panic attacks and panic disorder than men, and symptom variation exists across cultural groups. *Ataque de nervios*, found primarily among Latino people from the Caribbean, is one example of a disorder that might be a cultural variant of panic disorder. Some symptoms of *ataque* (heart palpitations, trembling) are similar to typical panic symptoms, whereas other symptoms (screaming uncontrollably, becoming physically aggressive) are specific to *ataque*. Whereas panic attacks typically occur out of the blue, *ataque de nervios* commonly occurs after social disruptions such as a change in family status (Guarnaccia et al., 1989). Among the Cambodian people, the cultural syndrome of *Khyâl* (wind attacks) is characterized by typical panic attack symptoms such as dizziness and culture-specific symptoms such as ringing in the ears and neck soreness (Craske et al., 2010). In Vietnam, these wind attacks are called *trung gio*. Thus, panic attacks exist across many different populations even though the specific symptom pattern may differ based on an individual's specific cultural background.

In addition to anxiety, people with panic disorder or agoraphobia often feel sad and depressed in part because their anxiety limits their daily functioning (Stein et al., 2005), including the ability to work and socialize. About 50% of people with panic disorder rely on financial assistance through either unemployment, disability, or welfare payments (Goisman et al., 1994). People with panic disorder and secondary (additional) disorders such as depression, eating disorders, and personality disorders may have suicidal thoughts or attempt suicide (Khan et al., 2002; Warshaw et al., 2000). The presence of the additional disorder appears to increase the likelihood of suicidal behaviour.

Generalized Anxiety Disorder

Shelly provided the following account of her problems: Mrs. B. (a pseudonym to protect patient privacy) was a lifelong worrier. Often she would wake up in the middle of the night and start worrying about something, such as worrying about her mother dying. For her, worry seemed to run in the family; she noted that both her parents and her brother and sister were excessive worriers. Mrs. B. described worry as being like a constant background noise in her life. In addition to chronic worry, she suffered from anxiety-related physical symptoms such as insomnia, stomach upset, and muscle tension. Eventually, when she was in her late 40s, Mrs. B. decided to seek treatment for her chronic worry. Her doctor, in Burnaby, BC, prescribed Paxil, which is a medication used for anxiety disorders and other clinical problems such as depression. Mrs. B. was also referred to the Anxiety Disorders Clinic at UBC Hospital in Vancouver. She was assessed by a psychologist, who diagnosed her as having generalized anxiety disorder. At the anxiety clinic Mrs. B. completed a 15-week course of cognitive behavioral group therapy, which among other things worked at helping Mrs. B. change her negative thoughts. She was surprised that the other patients in the group had the same problems as her. Over the course of treatment Mrs. B. successfully learned to control her worry. She began to feel calmer and no long had anxiety-related physical symptoms. (Based on: HYPERLINK https://www.mail.ubc.ca/owa/redir.aspx?C=8lluejqmmyAelcC1MbcOPt9JgmLJMYoaB0-sdVKtbnugNO4U7N-zTCA..&URL=http%3a%2f%2fwww.canadianliving.com%2f"www.canadianliving.com, accessed April 29, 2015)

The key feature of **generalized anxiety disorder (GAD)** is excessive anxiety and worry occurring more days than not and lasting at least six months. People with GAD worry about future events, past transgressions, financial matters, and their own health and that

People who face more real problems in living tend to have more reality-based anxiety than do people who live in more comfortable circumstances.

Arto/Fotolia

of loved ones (APA, 2013). Children may worry about their abilities or the quality of their performance. In addition to being out of proportion to the actual situation, the worry is described as uncontrollable and is accompanied by physical symptoms that include muscle tension, restlessness or feeling keyed up or on edge, being easily fatigued, difficulty concentrating, sleep disturbance, and irritability (see "DSM-5: Generalized Anxiety Disorder"). Cognitive symptoms include an inability to tolerate uncertainty (Ladouceur et al., 2000) and a belief that worrying may allow the person to avoid or prevent negative consequences (Borkovec et al., 2004). People with GAD often say, "I always find something to worry about," and they often have at least one other psychological disorder (Andrews et al., 2010; Bruce et al., 2001), usually another anxiety disorder or major depression. However, the worries of people with GAD are more severe; they complain more frequently of muscle tension, feeling restless, and feeling keyed up or on edge (Andrews et al., 2010).

criteria for Generalized Anxiety Disorder (GAD) — DSM-5

A. Excessive anxiety and worry (apprehensive expectation), occurring more days than not for at least 6 months, about a number of events or activities (such as work or school performance).

B. The individual finds it difficult to control the worry.

C. The anxiety and worry are associated with three (or more) of the following six symptoms (with at least some symptoms having been present for more days than not for the past 6 months):

Note: Only one item is required in children.

1. Restlessness or feeling keyed up or on edge.
2. Being easily fatigued.
3. Difficulty concentrating or mind going blank.
4. Irritability.
5. Muscle tension.
6. Sleep disturbance (difficulty falling or staying asleep, or restless, unsatisfying sleep).

D. The anxiety, worry, or physical symptoms cause clinically significant distress or impairment in social, occupational, or other important areas of functioning.

E. The disturbance is not attributable to the physiological effects of a substance (e.g., a drug of abuse, a medication) or another medical condition (e.g., hyperthyroidism).

F. The disturbance is not better explained by another mental disorder (e.g., anxiety or worry about having panic attacks in panic disorder, negative evaluation in social anxiety disorder [social phobia], contamination or other obsessions in obsessive-compulsive disorder, separation from attachment figures in separation anxiety disorder, reminders of traumatic events in posttraumatic stress disorder, gaining weight in anorexia nervosa, physical complaints in somatic symptom disorder, perceived appearance flaws in body dysmorphic disorder, having a serious illness in illness anxiety disorder, or the content of delusional beliefs in schizophrenia or delusional disorder).

More adults than children have GAD (Wittchen & Hoyer, 2001), and the disorder most commonly starts in the late teens through the late 20s (Kessler et al., 2004). GAD begins gradually and is usually a chronic condition. Even after pharmacological or psychosocial treatment, many people continue to have symptoms (Borkovec, 2002). Five years after it begins, 72% of people with GAD still suffer from the disorder (Woodman et al., 1999). Many people with GAD seek treatment from primary care physicians. In fact, up to 12% of people who seek treatment from their primary care physicians do so because of GAD symptoms (Wittchen & Hoyer, 2001).

Many people suffer from GAD; prevalence estimates range from 5% to 10% of community and clinic samples (Maier et al., 2000; Wittchen & Hoyer, 2001). According to a general population survey by Statistics Canada of people ages 15 years and older, GAD has a lifetime prevalence of 9% (Pearson et al., 2013).

Melissa's mother brought her to the clinic because of her constant worry that she is going to die. Although she is 9 years old and in good health, she worries that she might die from getting sick or that she will "choke on phlegm and die." Melissa told the interviewer that she worries that when she gets older she might have a heart attack and die. She also worries that her parents or her brother might die and she will be all alone. She is afraid that her parents might leave home one day, get lost, and "never, ever find their way back and I'll be all alone." She also worries that she might vomit or that burglars will break into her house and she will "lose everything." Melissa also has sleep problems because she is worried that if she falls asleep, she might die.

Among children, the prevalence of GAD may be as high as 15% of the general population (Costello et al., 2003). Among children with GAD, feelings of tension and apprehension are common, as are a negative self-image and the need for reassurance (Masi et al., 2004). Children with GAD also have physical symptoms such as restlessness, irritability, concentration difficulties, sleep disturbance, fatigue, headaches, muscle tension, and stomachaches (Tracey et al., 1997). Adolescents report more physical symptoms than children, and headaches are more common among adolescents than young children (Tracey et al., 1997). GAD is more common in women than in men (APA, 2013). To illustrate, a Statistics Canada survey found that the 12-month prevalence of GAD is higher in women (3.2%) than in men (2.0%) (Pearson et al., 2013).

Unexpected, negative, or very important life events are associated with the onset of GAD for both men and women (Kendler et al., 2003). When sociocultural factors are considered, GAD is more common among racial/ethnic minorities and people of low socioeconomic status (Kessler et al., 2004). It is important to remember that people with lower socioeconomic status may legitimately have more things to worry about (unsafe living conditions, lower income, poor health care, and therefore more medical conditions) than other groups; thus, their worries may have a more realistic basis. Less certainty regarding the availability of basic necessities may play a role in the onset of GAD.

Another common psychiatric disorder is **social anxiety disorder** (also known as *social phobia*), which has a 12-month prevalence of about 7% (APA, 2013; Health Canada, 2002). The disorder is characterized by a marked fear of social situations that may involve scrutiny by others (APA, 2013). Social situations that create distress include speaking, eating, drinking, or writing in the presence of others; engaging in social interactions such as parties or meetings; and simply initiating or maintaining conversations (see "DSM-5: Social Anxiety Disorder"). When in these situations, people with social anxiety disorder fear that others will detect their anxiety and that they will be evaluated negatively, or that they will be rejected by or will offend other people. Most people with social anxiety disorder have fear in most social interactions (including public speaking, parties, and one-on-one conversations). Diagnostically, there is a specifier called *performance*

criteria for
Social Anxiety Disorder (Social Phobia) DSM-5

A. Marked fear or anxiety about one or more social situations in which the individual is exposed to possible scrutiny by others. Examples include social interactions (e.g., having a conversation, meeting unfamiliar people), being observed (e.g., eating or drinking), and performing in front of others (e.g., giving a speech).

Note: In children, the anxiety must occur in peer settings and not just during interactions with adults.

B. The individual fears that he or she will act in a way or show anxiety symptoms that will be negatively evaluated (i.e., will be humiliating or embarrassing; will lead to rejection or offend others).

C. The social situations almost always provoke fear or anxiety.

Note: In children, the fear or anxiety may be expressed by crying, tantrums, freezing, clinging, shrinking, or failing to speak in social situations.

D. The social situations are avoided or endured with intense fear or anxiety.

E. The fear or anxiety is out of proportion to the actual threat posed by the social situation and to the sociocultural context.

F. The fear, anxiety, or avoidance is persistent, typically lasting for 6 months or more.

G. The fear, anxiety, or avoidance causes clinically significant distress or impairment in social, occupational, or other important areas of functioning.

H. The fear, anxiety, or avoidance is not attributable to the physiological effects of a substance (e.g., a drug of abuse, a medication) or another medical condition.

I. The fear, anxiety, or avoidance is not better explained by the symptoms of another mental disorder, such as panic disorder, body dysmorphic disorder, or autism spectrum disorder.

J. If another medical condition (e.g., Parkinson's disease, obesity, disfigurement from burns or injury) is present, the fear, anxiety, or avoidance is clearly unrelated or is excessive.

only, for people with social anxiety disorder whose fears are limited to just a few situations (usually public speaking or performance situations). Using the DSM-IV-TR descriptions, people with what is now known as the performance specifier typically have less severe anxiety and depressive symptoms (Beidel et al., 2010; Turner et al., 1992; Wittchen et al., 1999), minimal or no social skills deficits (Beidel et al., 2010), a later age of onset (Wittchen et al., 1999), and a less frequent history of childhood shyness (Stemberger et al., 1995).

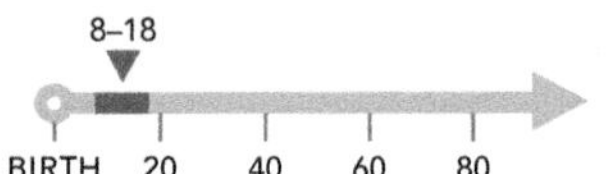

Social anxiety disorder typically develops in childhood or adolescence. The developmental challenge of fitting into a peer group or the increasing demands of school often are difficult for children who are anxious in social settings.

In the introduction to this section, we noted that many people have more than one anxiety disorder. More than 50% of people with social anxiety disorder have additional disorders, such as GAD, agoraphobia, panic disorder, specific phobia, or PTSD (Magee et al., 1996), as well as depression. Social anxiety disorder may substantially impair a person's ability to complete educational plans, advance in a career, work productively, and socialize with others (Zhang et al., 2004). People with social anxiety disorder often use alcohol to lessen their social distress, such as having a drink before a party, although there is little evidence that alcohol actually reduces anxiety (Carrigan & Randall, 2003). Even so, many people with both social anxiety disorder and alcohol dependence report that their substance abuse or dependence developed as a result of their attempts to reduce distress in social settings (Kushner, 1990).

With an average age of onset between 11 and 13 years, social anxiety disorder is one of the earliest appearing anxiety disorders (Kessler, 2003). It can be detected as early as age 8, and 8% of adults with social anxiety disorder report that their disorder began in childhood (Otto et al., 2001). When the disorder begins in childhood, it is not likely to remit without treatment. In fact, there is very little probability of spontaneous recovery when social anxiety disorder begins before age 11 (Davidson, 1993). Although social anxiety disorder rarely resolves without treatment, the symptoms may become better or

TABLE 4.2
Developmental Differences in Distressful Social Situations

Social Situations	Children (%)	Adolescents (%)	Adults (%)
Giving oral presentations	83	88	97
Attending parties/social events	58	61	80
Working in a group	45	62	79
Initiating/maintaining conversations	82	91	77
Dating	8	47	54
Using public bathrooms	17	30	18
Eating in the presence of others	16	34	25
Writing in the presence of others	50	67	12

Source: Based on Rao, P. A., Beidel, D. C., Turner, S. M., Ammerman, R. T., Crosby, L. E., & Sallee, F. R. (2007). Social anxiety disorder in childhood and adolescence: Descriptive psychopathology. *Behaviour Research and Therapy, 45,* 1181–1191.

worse depending on particular life circumstances (Beard et al., 2010). An episode of social anxiety disorder averages 18 years in length, compared with 6 years for panic disorder and 1 year for major depression (Keller, 2003). However, more than 85% of those with social anxiety disorder recover with psychological treatment and remain symptom free 10 years later (Fava et al., 2001).

Approximately 3% to 5% of children and adolescents have social anxiety disorder (Beidel & Turner, 2005; Essau et al., 1999; Gren-Landell et al., 2009; Ranta et al., 2009), as do 12% to 13% of adults (Kessler et al., 2005a; Lecrubier et al., 2000). Even people who spend their lives in the public limelight can suffer from this disorder (see "Real People, Real Disorders: A Story of Social Anxiety Disorder").

The situations that people with social anxiety disorder fear are similar regardless of age. Because social anxiety disorder is a chronic condition, its impact becomes more pervasive and creates significantly more dysfunction with age (see Table 4.2). This *negative developmental trajectory* begins in early childhood. If young children avoid social encounters with others, they are unlikely to learn appropriate social behaviours such as asking others to play, making friends, and interacting in a socially appropriate manner. Because they are anxious and socially unskilled, they begin to avoid others and often are overlooked or invisible to their classmates (Beidel & Turner, 2005; Ranta et al., 2009; Sumter et al., 2009). Avoidance leads to a vicious cycle in which limited social abilities increase the likelihood of negative social interactions, which in turn increase avoidance, resulting in few opportunities to achieve important developmental milestones (e.g., dating, attending university).

Social anxiety disorder affects both sexes equally (Kessler et al., 2005a), and is found across different racial/ethnic groups (Bassiony, 2005; Gökalp et al., 2001). A condition known as *taijin kyofusho,* found in Asian cultures, is sometimes considered a form of social anxiety disorder; it occurs most frequently among young men. Those with taijin kyofusho fear social interactions, but the underlying nature of the fear is different from that of social anxiety disorder (Kirmayer, 2001; Kirmayer et al., 1995). Whereas people with social anxiety disorder fear doing something that will embarrass themselves, people with taijin kyofusho fear offending or making others feel uncomfortable due to their inappropriate social behaviour or perceived physical blemish/deformity. The focus on offending others may be based on Japanese culture, which emphasizes the importance of presenting oneself positively, and collectivism rather than individualism

criteria for
Selective Mutism DSM-5

A. Consistent failure to speak in specific social situations in which there is an expectation for speaking (e.g., at school) despite speaking in other situations.

B. The disturbance interferes with educational or occupational achievement or with social communication.

C. The duration of the disturbance is at least 1 month (not limited to the first month of school).

D. The failure to speak is not attributable to a lack of knowledge of, or comfort with, the spoken language required in the social situation.

E. The disturbance is not better explained by a communication disorder (e.g., childhood onset fluency disorder) and does not occur exclusively during the course of autism spectrum disorder, schizophrenia, or another psychotic disorder.

(Hofmann et al., 2010). Although found most frequently in Japan, the syndrome occurs in Korea and possibly other Asian countries (Chapman et al., 1995).

Selective Mutism

Selective mutism is a disorder most commonly found in children that is defined as a consistent failure to speak in specific social situations despite the ability to speak and despite speaking in other settings (see "DSM-5: Selective Mutism"). Typically children with selective mutism speak in their home with their immediate family. In contrast, they do not speak outside the home or in the presence of other individuals, and sometimes they do not speak to their grandparents. Although this disorder stands alone in DSM-5, behavioural descriptions of the disorder suggests significant overlap with social anxiety disorder, including the reason for the fear, the situations in which the fear occurs, and the treatments that are efficacious for the disorder.

Specific Phobia

Raymond had always been frightened of enclosed spaces, but his fears escalated dramatically when he was briefly trapped inside a stalled elevator in one of Toronto's tall office buildings. Since then, Raymond always insists on taking the stairs rather than riding an elevator, even though he might have to climb dozens of flights of stairs to reach his destination. He is also afraid of being in small rooms. In fact, he has turned down jobs because the offices he was offered were small rooms or cubicles. This has hampered his ability to find employment as a junior accountant. Whenever Raymond is in an enclosed space, he feels like he is might be unable to escape if something bad was to happen. His breathing increases, and he worries that he might suffocate. During the incident in which he was trapped inside the stalled elevator, Raymond was sure he would run out of air and die, despite the assurances of two other people in the elevator. On that occasion, Raymond experienced an intense panic attack.

As Raymond's case illustrates, **specific phobia** (see "DSM-5: Specific Phobia") is a marked fear or anxiety about a specific object or situation that leads to significant disruption in daily functioning. A significant proportion of the general population admits to being fearful of something. You or someone close to you may be afraid of

criteria for
Specific Phobia DSM-5

A. Marked fear or anxiety about a specific object or situation (e.g., flying, heights, animals, receiving an injection, seeing blood).

Note: In children, the fear or anxiety may be expressed by crying, tantrums, freezing, or clinging.

B. The phobic object or situation almost always provokes immediate fear or anxiety.

C. The phobic object or situation is actively avoided or endured with intense fear or anxiety.

D. The fear or anxiety is out of proportion to the actual danger posed by the specific object or situation and to the sociocultural context.

E. The fear, anxiety, or avoidance is persistent, typically lasting for 6 months or more.

F. The fear, anxiety, or avoidance causes clinically significant distress or impairment in social, occupational, or other important areas of functioning.

G. The disturbance is not better explained by the symptoms of another mental disorder, including fear, anxiety, and avoidance of situations associated with panic-like symptoms or other incapacitating symptoms (as in agoraphobia); objects or situations related to obsessions (as in obsessive-compulsive disorder); reminders of traumatic events (as in posttraumatic stress disorder); separation from home or attachment figures (as in separation anxiety disorder); or social situations (as in social anxiety disorder).

heights or snakes or flying or elevators. So when does a fear become a phobia? Two criteria determine when the word *phobia* should be applied to a specific fear. First, the symptoms cause significant emotional distress (even if one is able to engage in the behaviour).

John has to give a presentation at a conference in a distant city, but he is afraid to fly. Since finding out about the presentation, he has not slept, worrying that the plane might crash. On the day that he is to leave for his trip, he is unable to eat. When he arrives at the airport, he is sweating profusely and his mouth is dry. He is exhausted by the time he arrives at the gate.

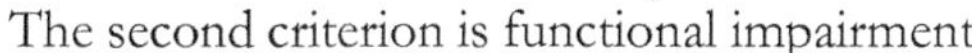

The second criterion is functional impairment.

John was not able to board the plane. His boss is very disappointed, and John is never asked to represent the company again. Soon John notices that he is being "passed over" for promotions, which are being given to younger, less experienced workers.

Therefore, the answer to the question, "When does fear become a phobia?" is when it creates marked distress or impairs an aspect of life functioning.

The diagnostic criteria include one of five specifiers: *animal phobias* (fear of animals or insects); *natural environment phobias* (fear of objects or events such as storms, heights, or water); *blood/injection/injury phobias* (fear of blood, injuries, or needles); *situational phobias* (fear of situations such as using public transportation, driving through tunnels or on bridges, riding elevators, flying, driving, or being in enclosed places), or *other* (used for fears unrelated to the other groups; APA, 2013). See Figure 4.4 for some common specific phobias among adults (Stinson et al., 2007).

People often have more than one specific phobia, and they often have other anxiety disorders (Ollendick et al., 2010). Even though these disorders are severe and disabling, few people who suffer from them ever seek treatment unless the situation becomes extreme, as in the case of Raymond or John.

FIGURE 4.4

Percentage of Adults with a Specific Phobia.

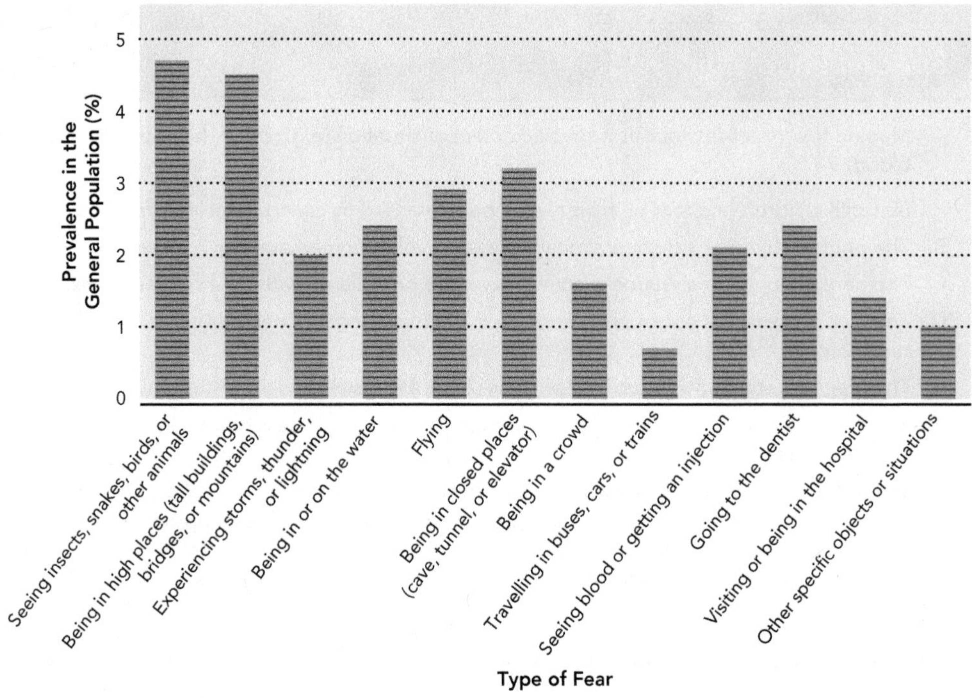

Animal phobias include fears of animals or insects. Maura's case illustrates a phobia of dogs.

Six-year-old Maura had always been a timid child but had never been afraid of dogs until a small energetic dog got away from its owner, entered the schoolyard, and started chasing the children around. Maura was terrified and ran to escape. The little dog apparently thought that Maura was playing a game. The dog ran barking after Maura and repeatedly jumped up on her. Although Maura and none of the other children where physically harmed, the experience left Maura terrified of dogs, especially small barking dogs who might jump up on her. Since then she avoids walking near dog parks and insists on crossing the street if she sees someone coming toward her, walking their dog. After her phobia showed no sign of abating, her parents decided to take her to a psychologist for treatment.

Natural environment phobias include fears of objects or situations that are part of the environment. Situations such as fear of heights or deep water are common, as are fear of events such as electrical storms, hurricanes, or tornadoes.

Blood/injection/injury (BII) *phobia* is a common phobia but is different from other phobias in a significant way. Unlike other phobias in which associated physical responses reflect increased sympathetic nervous system activity, parasympathetic activation dominates the characteristic response of BII. People with fears of needles, blood, or physical injury show **vasovagal syncope**, defined as *bradycardia* (slow heart rate) and *hypotension* (low blood pressure) (Ost, 1996) that can lead to fainting (see Figure 4.5). The reason for this unusual physical response is unclear. It may be biologically determined, perhaps the remnant of an evolutionary response to a serious physical injury. When someone is injured, decreases in heart rate and blood pressure lead to decreased blood flow, which in turn enhances the person's chances of physical survival. This normal biological response is triggered inappropriately in those who fear blood or needles. This phobia can have serious consequences when it leads someone to avoid medical treatment. Martha's case illustrates a BII phobia.

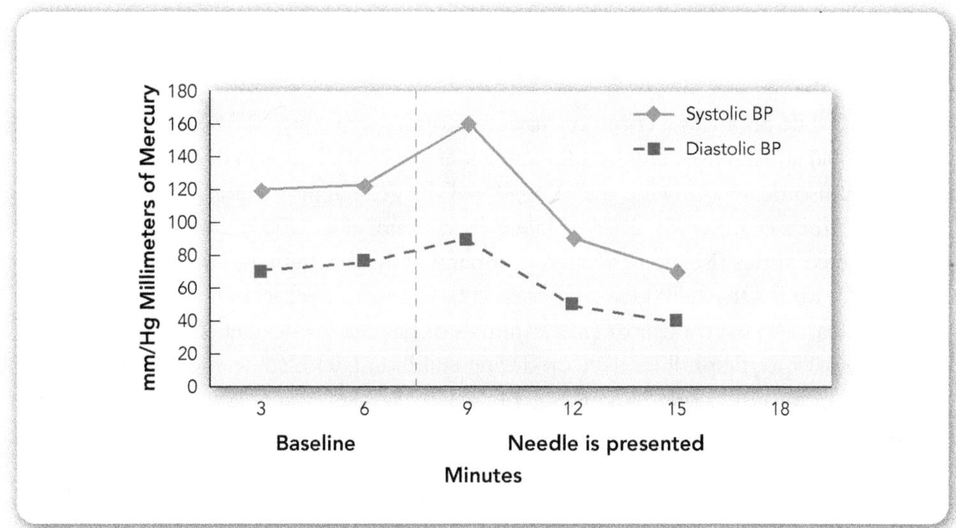

FIGURE 4.5

Vasovagal Response in Blood/Injection/Injury Phobias. When in contact with blood, an injury, or the possibility of an injection, people with BII phobias may experience a physiological response known as *vasovagal syncope*. This sudden drop in blood pressure results in the person "feeling faint" or actually fainting.

Martha has a degenerative eye disease that if untreated by surgery will result in blindness. However, her fear of needles and injections is so intense that she refuses surgery; she even refuses Novocain for dental procedures. She gets dizzy and sweaty when she sees a needle and fainted on the only two occasions when she tried to give blood at the office blood drive. When she came to the anxiety clinic, she had already lost the vision in her left eye. She is seeking treatment for her phobia so she can save the vision in her right eye.

Another type of specific phobia is *situational phobia*. Fears of flying or enclosed places (sometimes called *claustrophobia*) are common situational phobias. John's fear of flying is an example of this phobia. Because people with agoraphobia also report fears and avoidance of certain situations, it is important to differentiate this disorder from specific phobias. People with a specific phobia are afraid of some aspect of the situation itself (e.g., having an accident while driving), whereas people with agoraphobia are

People who have phobias of the natural environment fear such things as storms, hurricanes, and tornadoes.

inhauscreative/Getty Images

afraid of having a panic attack while driving. Thus, although the physical and cognitive symptoms may be the same, the object or situation that precipitates the symptoms differs.

Specific phobia is a common anxiety disorder, affecting 12.5% of adults (Kessler et al., 2005a) and 3.5% of children (Ollendick et al., 2004). It is also one of the most common disorders worldwide, affecting 4% of the general population in Mexico (Medina-Moira et al., 2005), 2.7% in Japan (Kawakami et al., 2005), and 7.7% across six European countries (Belgium, France, Germany, Italy, the Netherlands, and Spain; ESEMeD/MHEDEA 2000 Investigators, 2004). Among people with a diagnosis of specific phobia, 50% have a fear of either animals or heights (LeBeau et al., 2010).

Most specific phobias develop during childhood, with an average age of onset of 7 years (Antony & Barlow, 2002; Kessler et al., 2005a). Specific phobias are more common among girls than boys and are more common among young children than adolescents (Muris et al., 1999). Women are more likely than men to have situational, animal, and natural environment phobias. However, men and women are equally likely to fear heights and BII situations (LeBeau et al., 2010).

Separation Anxiety Disorder

Primarily affecting preadolescent children, **separation anxiety disorder** is a developmentally inappropriate and excessive anxiety concerning separation from someone to whom the child is emotionally attached. The child worries about being harmed or about a caregiver being harmed. Children may worry that they will be kidnapped or that a major attachment figure will be in an automobile accident or a plane crash. When the disorder is severe, the child may refuse to go to school or may not want to be physically separated from the parent, even at home. The child may insist on sleeping with the caregiver or may be unable to sleep overnight elsewhere. Children with this disorder have nightmares with themes of separation. Physical symptoms often accompany the worry and most commonly include headaches or stomachaches (see "DSM-5: Separation Anxiety Disorder").

About 3% to 5% of children may suffer from separation anxiety disorder (Silverman & Dick-Niederhauser, 2004), but many children recover within a short period of time (Foley et al., 2004). Girls are more likely than boys to report separation fears (March et al., 1997), and the disorder is more common among children than adolescents (Breton et al., 1999). In addition to refusing to attend school, children may refuse to attend social activities such as birthday parties or to participate in sports unless their parents accompany them and stay at the event. An emerging area of research interest is the existence of separation anxiety disorder among adults.

There has been speculation that childhood separation anxiety disorder and adult panic disorder may be developmentally different forms of the same disorder. Some adults with panic disorder report experiencing severe separation anxiety disorder when they were children. For some people, panic attacks begin after a major personal loss that results in separation (Klein, 1995). However, despite attempts to understand this relationship from different perspectives, the relationship between separation anxiety disorder and panic disorder is not clear. For example, although one longitudinal (4-year) study did not show a relation between separation anxiety disorder and the development of panic disorder in adolescents (Hayward et al., 2000), another longitudinal (4.5-year) study found that separation anxiety disorder in children predicted the later development of specific phobia, agoraphobia, panic disorder, and major depression (Biederman et al., 2007). When we use a developmental trajectory to understand these two different outcomes, separation anxiety disorder may precede the onset of many different types of anxiety disorders and depression, not just panic disorder.

criteria for Separation Anxiety Disorder

DSM-5

A. Developmentally inappropriate and excessive fear or anxiety concerning separation from those to whom the individual is attached, as evidenced by at least three of the following:
   1. Recurrent excessive distress when anticipating or experiencing separation from home or from major attachment figures.
   2. Persistent and excessive worry about losing major attachment figures or about possible harm to them, such as illness, injury, disasters, or death.
   3. Persistent and excessive worry about experiencing an untoward event (e.g., getting lost, being kidnapped, having an accident, becoming ill) that causes separation from a major attachment figure.
   4. Persistent reluctance or refusal to go out, away from home, to school, to work, or elsewhere because of fear of separation.
   5. Persistent and excessive fear of or reluctance about being alone or without major attachment figures at home or in other settings.
   6. Persistent reluctance or refusal to sleep away from home or to go to sleep without being near a major attachment figure.
   7. Repeated nightmares involving the theme of separation.
   8. Repeated complaints of physical symptoms (e.g., headaches, stomachaches, nausea, vomiting) when separation from major attachment figures occurs or is anticipated.

B. The fear, anxiety, or avoidance is persistent, lasting at least 4 weeks in children and adolescents and typically 6 months or more in adults.

C. The disturbance causes clinically significant distress or impairment in social, academic, occupational, or other important areas of functioning.

D. The disturbance is not better explained by another mental disorder, such as refusing to leave home because of excessive resistance to change in autism spectrum disorder; delusions or hallucinations concerning separation in psychotic disorders; refusal to go outside without a trusted companion in agoraphobia; worries about ill health or other harm befalling significant others in generalized anxiety disorder; or concerns about having an illness in illness anxiety disorder.

What Are the Obsessive-Compulsive and Related Disorders?

Obsessive-Compulsive Disorder

Obsessive-compulsive disorder (OCD) consists of *obsessions* (recurrent, persistent, intrusive thoughts) often combined with *compulsions* (repetitive behaviours) that are extensive, time consuming, and distressful (see "DSM-5: Obsessive-Compulsive Disorder"). Obsessions are usually specific thoughts (e.g., "I might contract HIV if I touch a chair where a sickly-looking person sat"), but they may also be urges (e.g., to jump off a high place) or images (e.g., stabbing a loved one). Defined as recurrent and persistent, obsessions are also intrusive, inappropriate, and often abhorrent, and they create substantial anxiety or distress (see "Real Science, Real Life: Jack—The Psychopathology and Treatment of Obsessive-Compulsive Disorder"). People with OCD recognize that their obsessions are the product of their own minds and not imposed upon them by someone else (as may occur in schizophrenia; see Chapter 10). Common obsessions include thoughts about dirt and germs (e.g., contracting cancer or another disease); aggression (a mother smothering her newborn baby with a blanket); failure to engage locks, bolts, and other safety devices (thereby putting an individual at risk for harm); sex (inappropriate sexual relationships such as molesting a child); and religion (thinking blasphemous thoughts).

Gideon was a normal university student and avid baseball player who developed a peanut allergy—a legitimate health problem. But his worries about the condition snowballed into an obsession and then into severe OCD. It started innocently enough. In 2009, he ate an egg tofu wrap before heading out to a baseball game. The snack contained traces of peanut and triggered an allergic reaction and a panic attack. Gideon recovered physically, but mentally, he was not the same. Gideon feared everything he ate or touched or even inhaled might have traces of peanut. "I was in prison in my mind because everything was contaminated and I had to be very safe and clean everything," he said. He started washing his hands until they were raw. He wouldn't touch doors, opening them with his feet, obsessively washing even food packages. Eventually, he was eating only apple juice, Kraft Dinner, and bread alone in his bedroom. It took him four hours to eat, fearing every bite would kill him. His friends and family thought he could simply stop these odd behaviours. "They said I was crazy and stupid and 'Snap out of it, it's all in your head. It's not the truth and logical, you can tough it out.' Well, no, I can't," he said. By July 2010, Gideon was near starvation, down to just 44.5 kg (98 pounds). His father, Howard, feared for his son's life, yet was unable to find doctors and therapists who could pull his son out of his OCD spiral. Eventually, after scouring the Internet, he found the Obsessive Compulsive Disorder Clinic at McGill University Health Centre, one of the few clinics specializing in OCD, and its director, clinical psychologist Debbie Sookman. Gideon says that Dr. Sookman immediately recognized that his son's case was life threatening. Gideon was admitted to Royal Victoria Hospital in Montreal. (Source: www.ctvnews.ca. Accessed April 30, 2015.)

Compulsions are the second part of OCD. They consist of repetitive behaviours that the person feels driven to do in response to obsessions or according to rigid rules (APA, 2013). Compulsions can be observable behaviours, such as repeatedly washing one's hands. They can also be unobservable, mental activities, such as silent counting. By completing the ritual, people with OCD feel that they can prevent their obsessions from becoming reality: "If I wash my hands for an hour, I won't get cancer." Compulsions are maintained by negative reinforcement. If you are afraid of contamination by "cancer germs," sanitizing your hands temporarily decreases the fear of contamination. Of course, that relief (removal of discomfort) temporarily feels good and increases the likelihood that the next time you feel contaminated, you will sanitize your hands again. In addition to hand washing, common compulsions include excessive bathing, cleaning, checking, counting, and ordering possessions. Sometimes people with OCD are reluctant to discuss their obsessions and compulsions, even with members of their family. They perform their rituals in secret, often in the middle of the night. When the disorder is severe, the compulsions can dictate all of the person's activities.

When Donny came home from school, he had to take a shower immediately. It would take him about an hour in the shower before he felt clean. If someone or something interrupted his routine, it would take a lot longer—he would have to start again from the beginning. Donny washed his clothes in the washing machine constantly. In the past, year, he had used the machine so extensively that his parents had to twice replace it with a new one.

More than half of people with OCD also have comorbid disorders such as depression, social anxiety disorder, specific phobia, GAD, and panic disorder (Stein et al., 2010). Substance abuse may also coexist with OCD. Even when a comorbid disorder is present, the symptoms of OCD usually are most prominent and troubling. OCD is also often accompanied by a personality disorder (see Chapter 11), and in these cases, positive treatment outcome is less likely (Steketee & Barlow, 2002).

OCD is a chronic and severe condition that rarely remits without treatment. It usually begins between late adolescence and early adulthood (Stein et al., 2010). Sometimes significant life events accompany the onset of OCD, including early adversity and trauma (Didie et al., 2006; Lochner et al., 2002), and pregnancy and childbirth (Wisner et al., 1999). Even when OCD begins in early adulthood, the person can often look back and see that elements of the disorder were present at an earlier age. When symptoms are present during childhood, OCD is more severe and results in greater impairment in daily functioning (Rosario-Campos et al., 2001; Sobin et al., 2000).

The lifetime prevalence of OCD is 1.6% (Kessler et al., 2005a), an estimate that is remarkably consistent across different countries (Weissman et al., 1994). Among children, prevalence estimates range from 1.9% to 4% (Geller et al., 1998; Valleni-Basile et al., 1994) and are consistent across world populations. It is important to understand that repetitive behaviours occur among people with psychological disorders other than OCD. For example, children with autism (see Chapter 12) often display repetitive behaviours such as spinning in a circle or flapping their hands. People with body dysmorphic disorder (see Chapter 5) have intrusive thoughts that centre around their dissatisfaction with a body part, such as believing that their nose is very big and ugly. Because repetitive behaviours and intrusive thoughts exist in a number of different disorders, OCD is now separated from the anxiety disorders in DSM-5 and is in a diagnostic category called Obsessive-Compulsive and Related Disorders (see "Examining the Evidence: Is Trichotillomania a Variant of OCD?").

criteria for Obsessive-Compulsive Disorder — DSM-5

A. Presence of obsessions, compulsions, or both.

Obsessions are defined by (1) and (2):

1. Recurrent and persistent thoughts, urges, or images that are experienced, at some time during the disturbance, as intrusive and unwanted, and that in most individuals cause marked anxiety or distress.
2. The individual attempts to ignore or suppress such thoughts, urges, or images, or to neutralize them with some other thought or action (i.e., by performing a compulsion).

Compulsions are defined by (1) and (2):

1. Repetitive behaviours (e.g., hand washing, ordering, checking) or mental acts (e.g., praying, counting, repeating words silently) that the individual feels driven to perform in response to an obsession or according to rules that must be applied rigidly.
2. The behaviours or mental acts are aimed at preventing or reducing anxiety or distress, or preventing some dreaded event or situation; however, these behaviours or mental acts are not connected in a realistic way with what they are designed to neutralize or prevent, or are clearly excessive.

Note: Young children may not be able to articulate the aims of these behaviours or mental acts.

B. The obsessions or compulsions are time consuming (e.g., take more than 1 hour per day) or cause clinically significant distress or impairment in social, occupational, or other important areas of functioning.

C. The obsessive-compulsive symptoms are not attributable to the physiological effects of a substance (e.g., a drug of abuse, a medication) or another medical condition.

D. The disturbance is not better explained by the symptoms of another mental disorder (e.g., excessive worries, as in generalized anxiety disorder; preoccupation with appearance, as in body dysmorphic disorder; difficulty discarding or parting with possessions, as in hoarding disorder; hair pulling, as in trichotillomania [hair-pulling disorder]; skin picking, as in excoriation [skin-picking] disorder; stereotypies, as in stereotypic movement disorder; ritualized eating behaviour, as in eating disorders; preoccupation with substances or gambling, as in substance-related and addictive disorders; preoccupation with having an illness, as in illness anxiety disorder; sexual urges or fantasies, as in paraphilic disorders; impulses, as in disruptive, impulse-control, and conduct disorders; guilty ruminations, as in major depressive disorder; thought insertion or delusional preoccupations, as in schizophrenia spectrum and other psychotic disorders; or repetitive patterns of behaviour, as in autism spectrum disorder).

REAL people REAL disorders

A Story of Obsessive-Compulsive Disorder

Many people know Howie Mandel as the Canadian comedian, actor, and game show host. Fewer people know that he suffers from obsessive-compulsive disorder (OCD). In his case, the disorder is characterized primarily by obsessions about being contaminated with germs, washing compulsions, and efforts to avoid perceived sources of contamination. Born and raised in Toronto, he had a fear of germs ever since he was a child. Kids teased him because he refused to tie his shoes, for fear of being contaminated. Even as an adult, he won't wear shoes with laces. "I'm always on the verge of death in my head," he said. On the set of his game show, *Deal or No Deal*, instead of shaking hands he does a fist bump to prevent his hands from becoming contaminated with germs. Otherwise he would be in the washroom scrubbing his hands. Off stage he requires that his makeup artists use new sponges every day, and he won't touch money unless it has been washed. Howie also avoids touching handrails. Although his main concern has to do with germs, he also has suffered from doubting obsessions ("Did I lock the front door?") and checking compulsions (checking door locks). He recently described his struggle with OCD in an autobiography titled *Here's the Deal: Don't Touch Me* (Mandel & Young, 2010).

Evan Agostini/Invision/AP Images

A small percentage of people with OCD have only obsessions or compulsions, but most adults have both. Among young children, rituals alone are common. Although adults clearly see that their rituals are responses to their obsessions, younger children usually do not know why they perform the rituals and sometimes do not view the rituals as senseless (APA, 2013).

When the interviewer asked Donny about whether he viewed his use of the washing machine as excessive, he said "No, I don't see what the problem is. My parents can always buy a new washer."

For children, it is important to view behaviour through a developmental lens. Ritualistic behaviours alone do not automatically indicate that a child has OCD. As with fears in general, repetitive behaviours appear to have a developmental trajectory. Toddlers have many ritualistic behaviours (e.g., preparing for bedtime using a certain routine, eating food and arranging stuffed animals in a particular way, collecting or storing objects; Zohar & Felz, 2001). Over time, most children stop these behaviours because they lose interest in them. Only in certain instances do ritualistic and repetitive behaviours remain. As noted in Chapter 1, distress and functional impairment are important explanatory concepts for differentiating compulsions from "normal rituals." In comparison to children's typical ritualistic behaviours, compulsions develop at a later age, frequently persist into adulthood, are incapacitating and distressing, and interfere with normal development (Garcia et al., 2009; Storch et al., 2008).

Men and women are equally likely to suffer from OCD, whereas among children, more boys than girls have the disorder (Masi et al., 2004). In addition, boys develop

examining the EVIDENCE

Is Trichotillomania (Hair Pulling Disorder) a Variant of OCD?

- **The Facts** TTM is sometimes considered to be a variant of obsessive-compulsive behaviours (Stein et al., 2010; Wetterneck et al., 2010), but are TTM and OCD the same?
- **Let's Examine the Evidence** TTM and OCD have a number of common features:
  1. Both are characterized by repetitive behaviour over which people feel a lack of control.
  2. Hair pulling in TTM and compulsions in OCD can both decrease anxiety.
  3. Some people with TTM have obsessive thoughts about hair pulling, wanting hair to be symmetrical or free of aberrant hairs (that are too coarse, too short, or too wiry).
  4. Both TTM and OCD are associated with high rates of coexisting anxiety and depressive disorders.
  5. Higher rates of OCD occur in families of people with TTM.
  6. One antidepressant (clomipramine) and a form of behaviour therapy are efficacious for both TTM and OCD.
- TTM and OCD are different in many ways:
  1. People with OCD are usually very focused on trying to reduce fears associated with obsessive thoughts. In TTM, hair pulling is not associated with fears.
  2. Family members of people with OCD are more likely to have OCD than are family members of people with TTM.
  3. TTM is associated with lower rates of OCD symptoms and less severe anxiety and depression than OCD.
  4. Serotonergic medications effective for the treatment of OCD do not work well for TTM.
  5. Methods of behavioural treatment are somewhat different for TTM and OCD.
- **Conclusion** TTM and OCD have some important common features and may share etiological influences. There may be a subtype of TTM that is very much like OCD, with hair pulling occurring in response to obsessive thoughts about hair. However, most studies suggest important differences in the clinical symptoms, associated features, and treatment procedures and responses for people with these two disorders. What factors do you think are most important in determining whether TTM is a form of OCD?

OCD at a younger age and more often have another family member who suffers from the disorder (Taylor, 2011a). The symptoms of OCD are similar across cultures, despite the fact that specific obsessions are sometimes culture specific (e.g., fear of leprosy among those who live in Africa; Steketee & Barlow, 2002).

Body Dysmorphic Disorder

Body dysmorphic disorder (BDD) is a preoccupation with perceived defects or flaws in physical appearance, which individuals believe make them look unattractive, ugly, or deformed (see "DSM-5: Body Dysmorphic Disorder"). Usually, if the concern is even minimally based in reality, it is an extreme exaggeration of a very minor flaw (e.g., a very small acne scar is described as a "huge crater on my face").

Amy is a 26-year-old woman who is convinced that her chin juts out terribly from the rest of her face. Actually an attractive young woman, Amy sees nothing but her chin when she looks in the mirror. She obsesses about how awful she looks—and what she believes others are saying behind her back. She is so distressed about her appearance that she refuses to go outside except to go to the store or see a doctor. When she goes out, she covers her chin with her hand and a tissue, actually making herself more noticeable to others. When at home, she checks herself in the mirror constantly. Each time, she hopes to see a different image staring back at her. But every time, all she sees is a huge chin, making her the ugliest person on earth.

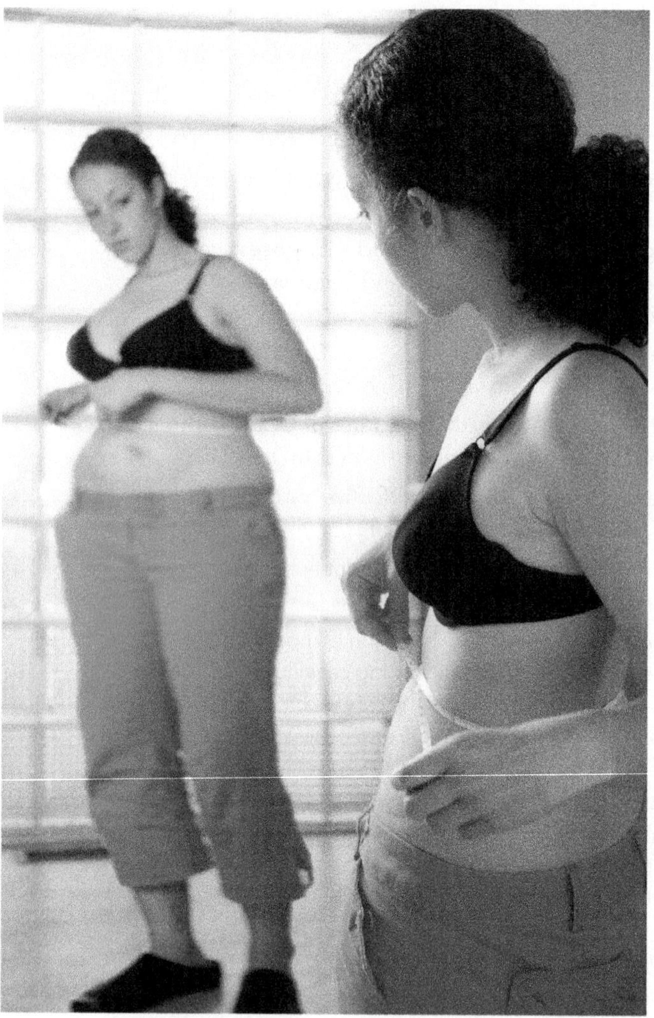

A person with body dysmorphic disorder is convinced that some part of the body is ugly or misshapen. Worry about the "ugly" body part may become so intense that it approaches the point of a delusion.

Palmer Kane LLC/Shutterstock

Although any area of the body may cause concern, patients with BDD most commonly worry about their skin, hair, nose, and face (e.g., size or symmetry of facial features, presence of wrinkles). Women with BDD are more likely to be preoccupied with their hips and weight. They may pick at perceived skin blemishes and try to camouflage any perceived flaws with makeup. Men are more likely to worry about thinning hair, be preoccupied with their genitals, and have *muscle* dysmorphia, which is a preoccupation that the body is not muscular, even when others view them as being of normal weight or muscular (Phillips et al., 2006b).

People with BDD, especially those with delusional beliefs, are at high risk for suicide. In one sample, 78% considered suicide at some point during their illness, and 27.5% had a history of suicide attempts (Phillips et al., 2005). These rates are at least six times higher than those in the general population, and they are higher than rates reported for people with schizophrenia or major depression. When followed prospectively for one year, 2.6% of people with BDD attempted suicide and 0.3% committed suicide (Phillips & Menard, 2006). A strong relationship exists between severity of suicidal ideation, severity of BDD symptoms, and functional impairment. People with the most severe symptoms and the most severe impairment are most likely to attempt suicide.

People with BDD are familiar patients in primary care, dermatology, and plastic surgery clinics. Up to 12% of dermatology patients and 16% of cosmetic surgery patients meet diagnostic criteria for BDD (Bellino et al., 2006; Thompson & Durrani, 2007). Even after undergoing dermatological and surgical treatment, they are rarely satisfied with the outcome (Phillips & Dufresne, 2002). In some instances, they focus on another "ugly" body part and begin the process all over again.

The concern about appearance leads to repetitive behaviours or mental acts. Like Amy, people with BDD frequently check their appearance to monitor changes. They often groom excessively or try to hide the offending feature. They may pick at their skin for hours each day, using their fingers, needles, pins, staple removers, razor blades, or knives to eliminate a blemish or scar (Phillips & Taub, 1995). Men with muscle dysmorphia may follow a rigorous diet and exercise schedule, which can physically damage the body (Phillips et al., 2010). The person's belief that he or she is ugly or has a physical deformity leads to occupational, social, and academic impairment.

criteria for Body Dysmorphic Disorder — DSM-5

A. Preoccupation with one or more perceived defects or flaws in physical appearance that are not observable or appear slight to others.

B. At some point during the course of the disorder, the individual has performed repetitive behaviours (e.g., mirror checking, excessive grooming, skin picking, reassurance seeking) or mental acts (e.g., comparing his or her appearance with that of others) in response to the appearance concerns.

C. The preoccupation causes clinically significant distress or impairment in social, occupational, or other important areas of functioning.

D. The appearance preoccupation is not better explained by concerns with body fat or weight in an individual whose symptoms meet diagnostic criteria for an eating disorder.

Body dysmorphic disorder appears to be particularly impairing for adolescents. They suffer significant distress, are highly likely to experience suicidal ideation (80.6%) and attempt suicide (44.5%), and have impaired academic, social, and occupational functioning (Phillips et al., 2006a). Like adults, adolescents with BDD are more likely to be female, and the most common areas of concern are skin (acne/scarring), hair (excessive body hair or balding), stomach, weight, and teeth. Both males and females worry equally about these areas. A higher proportion of adolescents than adults have worries about their appearance that reached the level of delusional thought.

Among one sample of people with BDD, only 41% revealed their symptoms to their prescribing physician; instead, many were being treated for a secondary disorder such as anxiety or depression. Because many patients with BDD see their problem as solely physical, they often seek and receive treatment from dermatological or surgical clinics. Often they are displeased with the surgical outcome and may become angry and threatening toward the physician (Honigman et al., 2004).

13–18

BIRTH 20 40 60 80

Body dysmorphic disorder occurs in adolescence and can be particularly impairing at this stage of development.

Hoarding Disorder

In previous editions of the DSM, hoarding was considered as either a symptom of OCD or a feature of obsessive-compulsive personality disorder (OCPD). However, it has become increasingly clear that hoarding, as a primary presenting problem, is different in many ways from OCD and OCPD. The prevalence of hoarding is estimated to be between 2% and 6% of the general population (APA, 2013). Thus, in DSM-5, there is the new category of **hoarding disorder**, characterized by the persistent difficulty discarding or parting with obsessions, regardless of their actual value (see "DSM-5: Hoarding Disorder"). This is more than simply collecting coins, stamps, or similar hobbies. Hoarding has harmful effects for the person and the family. Large amounts of clutter can create physical danger as individuals attempt to move through the collected objects, and may create a fire hazard.

Trichotillomania (Hair Pulling Disorder)

Trichotillomania (TTM) is defined as repetitive hair pulling that results in noticeable hair loss. People affected with this repetitive behaviour pull hair from their scalp, eyelashes, eyebrows, and even the pubic area. Sometimes people with TTM wear wigs, scarves, or false eyelashes to cover the damage. They want to stop pulling but feel powerless to do so. Hair pulling can occur without focused awareness (i.e., people who pull can do so

criteria for Hoarding Disorder — DSM-5

A. Persistent difficulty discarding or parting with possessions, regardless of their actual value.

B. This difficulty is due to a perceived need to save the items and to distress associated with discarding them.

C. The difficulty discarding possessions results in the accumulation of possessions that congest and clutter active living areas and substantially compromises their intended use. If living areas are uncluttered, it is only because of the interventions of third parties (e.g., family members, cleaners, authorities).

D. The hoarding causes clinically significant distress or impairment in social, occupational, or other important areas of functioning (including maintaining a safe environment for self and others).

E. The hoarding is not attributable to another medical condition (e.g., brain injury, cerebrovascular disease, Prader-Willi syndrome).

F. The hoarding is not better explained by the symptoms of another mental disorder (e.g., obsessions in obsessive-compulsive disorder, decreased energy in major depressive disorder, delusions in schizophrenia or another psychotic disorder, cognitive deficits in major neurocognitive disorder, restricted interests in autism spectrum disorder).

criteria for
Trichotillomania DSM-5

A. Recurrent pulling out of one's hair, resulting in hair loss.
B. Repeated attempts to decrease or stop hair pulling.
C. The hair pulling causes clinically significant distress or impairment in social, occupational, or other important areas of functioning.
D. The hair pulling or hair loss is not attributable to another medical condition (e.g., a dermatological condition).
E. The hair pulling is not better explained by the symptoms of another mental disorder (e.g., attempts to improve a perceived defect or flaw in appearance in body dysmorphic disorder).

without paying attention to what they are doing). Hair pulling often produces feelings of pleasure. Sensory stimulation (e.g., touching, feeling the hair, or running the hair follicle over one's lips) is a common feature of TTM.

Excoriation (Skin-Picking) Disorder

Excoriation (skin picking) disorder is defined by recurrent skin picking resulting in skin lesions (APA, 2013). This is another new disorder introduced in DSM-5 as a result of research suggesting that its prevalence and treatment outcome are different from OCD, where it was previously included as a type of compulsive behaviour. The prevalence of excoriation disorder is approximately 1.4% of the general population. The diagnosis is assigned when the individual has attempted to stop the skin picking and cannot do so, and there must be some form of social or occupational impairment. Problems as a result of skin picking include physical disfigurement, scarring, infections, and skin lesions (APA, 2013).

What Are the Trauma- and Stressor-Related Disorders?

This diagnostic grouping includes disorders that are related to either a traumatic or stressful event. Reactions to these events can range from mild to dramatic depending upon the event, the person, and the environment. Included in this category are the following disorders: acute stress disorder, adjustment disorder, posttraumatic stress disorder (PTSD),

criteria for
Excoriation (Skin-Picking) Disorder DSM-5

A. Recurrent skin picking resulting in skin lesions.
B. Repeated attempts to decrease or stop skin picking.
C. The skin picking causes clinically significant distress or impairment in social, occupational, or other important areas of functioning.
D. The skin picking is not attributable to the physiological effects of a substance (e.g., cocaine) or another medical condition (e.g., scabies).
E. The skin picking is not better explained by symptoms of another mental disorder (e.g., delusions or tactile hallucinations in a psychotic disorder, attempts to improve a perceived defect or flaw in appearance in body dysmorphic disorder, stereotypies in stereotypic movement disorder, or intention to harm oneself in nonsuicidal self-injury).

TABLE 4.1
Common Fears at Various Developmental Ages

Age	Fears
Infancy	Loss of physical support/falling over
	Sudden, intense, and unexpected noises
	Heights
1–2 years of age	Strangers
	Toilet
	Getting injured
3–5 years of age	Animals (usually dogs)
	Monsters/ghosts/etc.
	Dark
	Being alone
6–9 years of age	Animals
	Lightning and thunder
	Being safe
	School
9–12 years of age	Tests
	Health
13 years and older	Getting injured
	Social interaction/peers
	World events

Source: Ollendick, T. H., Matson, J. L., & Helsel, W. I. (1985). Fears in children and adolescents: Normative data. *Behaviour Research and Therapy, 23*, 465–467.

physically and cognitively, they stop fearing loud noises (such as vacuum cleaners). They begin to understand that noisy things are not necessarily harmful. This *developmental hierarchy of fear* is not simply a matter of chronological age, but also involves cognitive development. When children are cognitively challenged (i.e., they may be 7 to 9 years old but have the cognitive ability of children ages 4 to 6), their fears usually reflect their *cognitive development*, not their chronological (actual) age (Vandenberg, 1993).

Sociodemographic factors (sex, race/ethnicity, and socioeconomic status) are a third consideration when differentiating normal from abnormal fears. In the general population, anxiety disorders are more common among females than males, sometimes at a ratio of three females to one male for any particular anxiety disorder. Why females report more fear than males is unclear, but it may reflect cultural or gender role expectations. Social acceptability may allow girls and women to *report* more fears, but they may not necessarily *have* more fears. For example, girls report more test anxiety than boys, but when physical symptoms (blood pressure and heart rate) are measured during an actual test, test-anxious boys and girls show equal increases (Beidel & Turner, 1998). Even though in the general population more women than men report fears, the sex distribution is more equal among people who seek treatment. Therefore, when fears are severe, men and women are equally represented.

Normal Behaviour Case Study

A Scary Event—No Disorder

→ Last month, Jamal was driving in a snowstorm. The road was icy, and he regretted his decision to drive in the storm, but he wanted to get home to his wife and young son. As he was driving down the highway, his car hit a patch of ice and he began to skid off the road—sideways at first and then in a circle. It was a terrifying few moments, and images of his son and wife flashed before Jamal's eyes. The car landed in a ditch. Jamal was banged up but otherwise safe. That night, after he got home, he was unable to sleep—he kept going in to see his son sleeping in his crib. The next morning, his heart was pounding when he started his car, and for a few weeks afterward, he felt tense every time he drove past that ditch.

Abnormal Behaviour Case Study

Posttraumatic Stress Disorder

→ Brad was injured during his second tour of duty to Afghanistan. His injuries were severe, and although he does not remember much of what happened after the bullet shattered his thigh bone, he does remember feeling extremely cold when he received a blood transfusion. Upon returning home, he was in the grocery store and walked down the frozen food aisle. The cold from the freezers precipitated a flashback, and Brad thought that he was in combat again. Now Brad avoids the grocery store at all costs. Every time he hears a loud noise, such as a banging door, he "hits the ground." Brad has not been able to work since he came home from Afghanistan.

reactive attachment disorder, and disinhibited social engagement disorder. Because the bulk of the scientific literature is focused on PTSD, we review that disorder in depth. For a discussion of the other trauma-related disorders, you may wish to consult DSM-5.

Posttraumatic stress disorder

Posttraumatic stress disorder (PTSD) begins with a traumatic event such as military combat, assault, rape, or observation of the serious injury or violent death of another person. Later, when confronting events or situations that symbolize or resemble part of the trauma, such as a dark alley similar to the one where an assault occurred, the person may suffer an intense psychological and physiological reaction.

Although not necessary for the diagnostic criteria, people with PTSD report the presence of emotions such as fear, helplessness, or horror, and other emotions such as guilt and shame are also commonly reported by people with this disorder. A classic symptom of PTSD is *intrusion (re-experiencing)*, through recurrent and intrusive memories, thoughts, or dreams about the trauma that occur repeatedly despite attempts to suppress them.

Other symptoms of PTSD are *negative alterations in cognitions and mood*, consisting of the inability to feel emotions such as joy, surprise, or even sadness. People report a loss of interest in formerly enjoyable activities and a feeling of detachment from other people and the environment. Another common symptom is an overactive sympathetic nervous system, which creates a state of general and persistent arousal known as *hyperarousal*. This overarousal results in difficulty sleeping and concentrating and creates emotional responses such as irritability or anger. In addition, people with PTSD exhibit *hypervigilance* (a sense of being "on watch") and an *exaggerated startle response* (being easily startled), as well as avoidance of activities, situations, or events that remind them of the traumatic event. Finally, the fourth group of symptoms is the persistent avoidance of situations or objects associated with the trauma.

After a life-threatening or traumatic event, some people develop posttraumatic stress disorder.

Landov LLC

criteria for
Posttraumatic Stress Disorder
DSM-5

Note: The following criteria apply to adults, adolescents, and children older than 6 years. For children 6 years and younger, see corresponding criteria below.

A. Exposure to actual or threatened death, serious injury, or sexual violence in one (or more) of the following ways:
1. Directly experiencing the traumatic event(s).
2. Witnessing, in person, the event(s) as it occurred to others.
3. Learning that the traumatic event(s) occurred to a close family member or close friend. In cases of actual or threatened death of a family member or friend, the event(s) must have been violent or accidental.
4. Experiencing repeated or extreme exposure to aversive details of the traumatic event(s) (e.g., first responders collecting human remains; police officers repeatedly exposed to details of child abuse).

   Note: Criterion A4 does not apply to exposure through electronic media, television, movies, or pictures, unless this exposure is work related.

B. Presence of one (or more) of the following intrusion symptoms associated with the traumatic event(s), beginning after the traumatic event(s) occurred:
1. Recurrent, involuntary, and intrusive distressing memories of the traumatic event(s).

   Note: In children older than 6 years, repetitive play may occur in which themes or aspects of the traumatic event(s) are expressed.
2. Recurrent distressing dreams in which the content and/or affect of the dream are related to the traumatic event(s).

   Note: In children, there may be frightening dreams without recognizable content.
3. Dissociative reactions (e.g., flashbacks) in which the individual feels or acts as if the traumatic event(s) were recurring. (Such reactions may occur on a continuum, with the most extreme expression being a complete loss of awareness of present surroundings.)

   Note: In children, trauma-specific reenactment may occur in play.
4. Intense or prolonged psychological distress at exposure to internal or external cues that symbolize or resemble an aspect of the traumatic event(s).
5. Marked physiological reactions to internal or external cues that symbolize or resemble an aspect of the traumatic event(s).

C. Persistent avoidance of stimuli associated with the traumatic event(s), beginning after the traumatic event(s) occurred, as evidenced by one or both of the following:
1. Avoidance of or efforts to avoid distressing memories, thoughts, or feelings about or closely associated with the traumatic event(s).
2. Avoidance of or efforts to avoid external reminders (people, places, conversations, activities, objects, situations) that arouse distressing memories, thoughts, or feelings about or closely associated with the traumatic event(s).

D. Negative alterations in cognitions and mood associated with the traumatic event(s), beginning or worsening after the traumatic event(s) occurred, as evidenced by two (or more) of the following:
1. Inability to remember an important aspect of the traumatic event(s) (typically due to dissociative amnesia and not to other factors such as head injury, alcohol, or drugs).
2. Persistent and exaggerated negative beliefs or expectations about oneself, others, or the world (e.g., "I am bad," "No one can be trusted," "The world is completely dangerous," "My whole nervous system is permanently ruined").
3. Persistent, distorted cognitions about the cause or consequences of the traumatic event(s) that lead the individual to blame himself/herself or others.
4. Persistent negative emotional state (e.g., fear, horror, anger, guilt, or shame).
5. Markedly diminished interest or participation in significant activities.
6. Feelings of detachment or estrangement from others.
7. Persistent inability to experience positive emotions (e.g., inability to experience happiness, satisfaction, or loving feelings).

E. Marked alterations in arousal and reactivity associated with the traumatic event(s), beginning or worsening after the traumatic event(s) occurred, as evidenced by two (or more) of the following:
1. Irritable behaviour and angry outbursts (with little or no provocation) typically expressed as verbal or physical aggression toward people or objects.
2. Reckless or self-destructive behaviour.
3. Hypervigilance.
4. Exaggerated startle response.
5. Problems with concentration.
6. Sleep disturbance (e.g., difficulty falling or staying asleep or restless sleep).

F. Duration of the disturbance (Criteria B, C, D, and E) is more than 1 month.

G. The disturbance causes clinically significant distress or impairment in social, occupational, or other important areas of functioning.

H. The disturbance is not attributable to the physiological effects of a substance (e.g., medication, alcohol) or another medical condition.

(continued)

Posttraumatic Stress Disorder for Children 6 Years and Younger

A. In children 6 years and younger, exposure to actual or threatened death, serious injury, or sexual violence in one (or more) of the following ways:

1. Directly experiencing the traumatic event(s).
2. Witnessing, in person, the event(s) as it occurred to others, especially primary caregivers.

   Note: Witnessing does not include events that are witnessed only in electronic media, television, movies, or pictures.
3. Learning that the traumatic event(s) occurred to a parent or caregiving figure.

B. Presence of one (or more) of the following intrusion symptoms associated with the traumatic event(s), beginning after the traumatic event(s) occurred:

1. Recurrent, involuntary, and intrusive distressing memories of the traumatic event(s).

   Note: Spontaneous and intrusive memories may not necessarily appear distressing and may be expressed as play reenactment.
2. Recurrent distressing dreams in which the content and/or affect of the dream are related to the traumatic event(s).

   Note: It may not be possible to ascertain that the frightening content is related to the traumatic event.
3. Dissociative reactions (e.g., flashbacks) in which the child feels or acts as if the traumatic event(s) were recurring. (Such reactions may occur on a continuum, with the most extreme expression being a complete loss of awareness of present surroundings.) Such trauma-specific reenactment may occur in play.
4. Intense or prolonged psychological distress at exposure to internal or external cues that symbolize or resemble an aspect of the traumatic event(s).
5. Marked physiological reactions to reminders of the traumatic event(s).

C. One (or more) of the following symptoms, representing either persistent avoidance of stimuli associated with the traumatic event(s) or negative alterations in cognitions and mood associated with the traumatic event(s), must be present, beginning after the event(s) or worsening after the event(s):

Persistent Avoidance of Stimuli

1. Avoidance of or efforts to avoid activities, places, or physical reminders that arouse recollections of the traumatic event(s).
2. Avoidance of or efforts to avoid people, conversations, or interpersonal situations that arouse recollections of the traumatic event(s).

Negative Alterations in Cognitions

3. Substantially increased frequency of negative emotional states (e.g., fear, guilt, sadness, shame, confusion).
4. Markedly diminished interest or participation in significant activities, including constriction of play.
5. Socially withdrawn behaviour.
6. Persistent reduction in expression of positive emotions.

D. Alterations in arousal and reactivity associated with the traumatic event(s), beginning or worsening after the traumatic event(s) occurred, as evidenced by two (or more) of the following:

1. Irritable behaviour and angry outbursts (with little or no provocation) typically expressed as verbal or physical aggression toward people or objects (including extreme temper tantrums).
2. Hypervigilance.
3. Exaggerated startle response.
4. Problems with concentration.
5. Sleep disturbance (e.g., difficulty falling or staying asleep or restless sleep).

E. The duration of the disturbance is more than 1 month.

F. The disturbance causes clinically significant distress or impairment in relationships with parents, siblings, peers, or other caregivers or with school behaviour.

G. The disturbance is not attributable to the physiological effects of a substance (e.g., medication or alcohol) or another medical condition.

Up to 92% of people with PTSD may have a comorbid psychological disorder, most commonly depression, other anxiety disorders, or substance abuse (Brunello et al., 2001; Perkonigg et al., 2000). Because PTSD is such a complex disorder with so many different symptoms, determining whether the sad mood or generalized anxiety is just part of the overall disorder or whether it represents a separate diagnosis is sometimes difficult.

PTSD begins with the occurrence of a traumatic event and can occur at any age (Taylor, 2006). Among adults, the disorder is usually categorized as either civilian PTSD

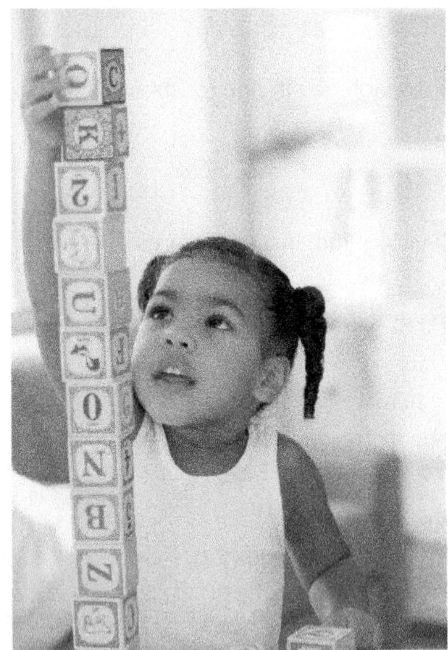

After a trauma, children may engage in traumatic play, such as building a tower and knocking it down. However, engaging in this type of activity does not mean that a child was the victim of a trauma.

Blend Images/Alamy Stock Photo

or combat-related PTSD, depending on the event. General population surveys from Canada and the United States suggest that the lifetime prevalence of PTSD is 7% to 12% (Kessler, 2005a; van Ameringen et al., 2008). Compared to the general population, the prevalence of PTSD is higher in children who were abused (Sochting, 2004). PTSD also may be more prevalent for people working in hazardous occupations. Sex-trade workers, for example, also appear to be at elevated risk of PTSD. According to a Vancouver study of 100 female sex-trade workers, 90% had been physically assaulted, often when they refused to perform particular sex acts, and most (72%) were classified as having PTSD (Farley et al., 2005).

Historically, the onset of PTSD followed a life event defined as "out of the range of normal human experience" (combat, concentration camp imprisonment, natural disasters, assault, or rape). More recent diagnostic criteria have expanded the list of "eligible" events to include many more human experiences, some of which are common (unexpected death of a loved one, serious illness such as cancer in oneself). The person may have experienced the traumatic event directly (such as being in a combat situation), watched the event occur to someone else (being a bystander as a crime was committed), or simply heard about or seen the event via television or the Internet. This expansion in the manner of contact with the traumatic event, known as *conceptual bracket creep* (McNally, 2009), has been at least partly responsible for the increased prevalence in the number of people who are considered to have experienced a traumatic event. Using these expanded criteria, one epidemiological survey reported that 89.6% of adults (92.2% of males and 87.1% of females) have experienced a potentially traumatic event (Breslau & Kessler, 2001). However, despite almost universal exposure to a traumatic event, only 11.1% of the sample had PTSD. These different percentages illustrate a very important point: Exposure to trauma alone does not automatically lead to PTSD. Events such as automobile accidents or the death of a loved one may result in temporary stress reactions (Keppel-Benson et al., 2002; Yehuda, 2002), but the typical response to a traumatic event is resilience, not PTSD (see "Research Hot Topic: Trauma, Grief, PTSD, and Resilience").

Among children exposed to a single traumatic event (e.g., school shootings, earthquakes, boating accidents), estimates of PTSD range from 5.2% to 100% of those exposed (Beidel & Turner, 2005). Prevalence estimates may vary because different investigators use different procedures (direct interviews of children vs. parent report, for example) to make the diagnoses. In addition, the emergence of PTSD depends on proximity to the event. The closer you are to the event, the more likely you are to develop PTSD. After an earthquake in Armenia, for example, more children living at the earthquake's epicentre developed PTSD than did children living 80 km away. One hopeful fact is that for many civilian traumas, PTSD symptoms decline with time (Yule et al., 2000).

Like the other anxiety disorders, symptoms of PTSD are different in children than in adults (see "DSM-5: Posttraumatic Stress Disorder"). Among children, intrusion may take the form of *traumatic play* in which the child re-enacts relevant aspects of the traumatic event. However, it is important to avoid misinterpreting any behaviour as indicating the presence of trauma or PTSD. Consider the following example. After the Oklahoma City bombing (1995), some children in the city were observed building and destroying buildings made of blocks (Gurwitch et al., 2002). Were all of these children suffering from PTSD? Developmentally, many children who have never been victims of bombings build block buildings or sandcastles and then delight in knocking them down. Without knowledge of typical children's play, developmentally appropriate behaviours could be misinterpreted as indicating the presence of PTSD.

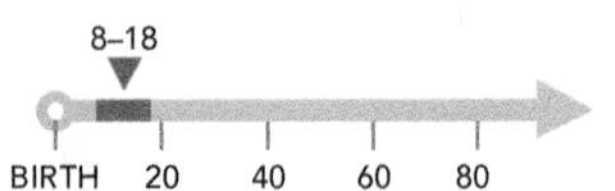

PTSD symptoms in children are often very different than in adults.

In addition to developmental differences in re-experiencing, other aspects of PTSD may differ by developmental age. Under age 6 years, bedwetting, thumb

research **HOT** topic

Trauma, Grief, PTSD, and Resilience

On October 2, 2006, Charles Carl Roberts entered a one-room schoolhouse in a rural Amish community. He lined up 10 young girls and shot them each at point-blank range. Then he killed himself. Five girls died and five were seriously wounded. That night, women from the Amish community went to the house of his widow bringing food and comfort. That weekend, more that half of those at Mr. Roberts's funeral were from the Amish community he had wounded. When asked how they managed to forgive, they replied, "With God's help."

As currently defined, many stressors qualify as traumatic events and could result in a diagnosis of PTSD. Stabbings, shootings, and murder are common occurrences for inner-city adolescents (e.g., Jenkins & Bell, 1994). Natural disasters such as hurricanes, floods, and tornadoes also occur frequently and increase stress. However, merely experiencing a potentially stressful event does not mean that you will develop PTSD.

As research on loss and trauma illustrates, up to 90% of people in North America report exposure to a traumatic event during their lifetime, but as noted above, only 7% to 12% develop PTSD. Although witnessing a traumatic event may result in brief PTSD symptoms or significant stress, for most individuals, these reactions disappear after a few months. Only a relatively small percentage of people exposed to a trauma actually develop PTSD. In the face of traumatic events, *recovery* (threshold or subthreshold psychopathology for a few months followed by a return to pretrauma levels) or *resilience* (maintaining a stable equilibrium in the face of the traumatic event) rather than PTSD is the predominant response (Bonanno, 2004). Researchers are now examining factors that predict (1) who will not recover, (2) what treatments are most likely to promote recovery, and (3) when those treatments should be applied.

What factors would you identify as important in the development of PTSD?

sucking, fear of the dark, and increased difficulties separating from parents may be symptoms of PTSD, but they also occur in many children who have not been exposed to trauma (Fremont, 2004). Attentional problems, impaired school performance, school avoidance, health complaints, irrational fears, sleep problems, nightmares, irritability, and anger outbursts are common in children with PTSD, but they also occur in children with other disorders and sometimes in children with no disorder. Adolescents report symptoms more commonly found among adults: intrusive thoughts, hypervigilance, emotional numbing (a DSM-IV criterion replaced by negative alterations of cognition and mood in DSM-5), nightmares, sleep disturbances, and avoidance. When a diagnosis of PTSD is a possibility, developmental factors must be considered.

Until very recently, PTSD among female military veterans was primarily the result of sexual assault or sexual harassment (Butterfield et al., 2000). However, the changing role of women in the military is likely changing the sex distribution of combat-related PTSD. Among civilian populations, some samples find that more females than males suffer from PTSD (Brunello et al., 2001), whereas others do not. Among women, about 50% of the cases of PTSD are associated with sexual assault (Brunello et al., 2001; Perkonigg et al., 2000).

Sociocultural factors such as socioeconomic status are also important to consider when examining the prevalence of PTSD. In many instances, it may not be the event itself but the ability to recover from the event that creates distress and precipitates the onset of PTSD. After a major hurricane, people with limited incomes have less ability to pay for needed repairs to homes and fewer personal resources to be able to start over. They are also more likely to work in minimum-wage jobs in businesses less likely to rebuild quickly after the storm. Therefore, group differences that appear to be based on racial or ethnic minority status may really reflect socioeconomic status.

canadian FOCUS

Deployment to Afghanistan

Thirty-two year-old Jonathan Woolvett, a Master Corporal in the Canadian Forces, had served two tours of duty to Afghanistan. He returned to Canada suffering from posttraumatic stress disorder (PTSD) arising from his wartime experiences. The first traumatic event arose early in his first tour of duty, near the village of Nalgham, which is about 30 km east of Kandahar. Woolvett was sitting in his vehicle while his fellow soldier and friend, Matthew McCully, was out nearby on foot patrol. The two soldiers were speaking on the radio when suddenly Woolvett heard an explosion. His friend had stepped on an improvised explosive device (IED) and was killed. During his time in Afghanistan, Woolvett lost two other friends in military operations. Woolvett was exposed to other traumatic events, including one in which he and his unit were called to an American convoy that had struck an IED. Woolvett recalls that there were bodies everywhere. Woolvett had the gruesome task of filling body bags with the remains of the soldiers killed in the explosion. His PTSD symptoms began before he left Kandahar and continued to worsen when he returned to Canada. He started drinking heavily and eventually sought out professional help. Woolvett is not alone in his experiences. Many other soldiers in the Canadian Forces similarly developed PTSD during Canada's mission to Afghanistan.

Military deployment, whether it be for combat or peacekeeping missions, is stressful, even for highly trained military personnel. Stressors include combat exposure, separation from friends and family, frequent moves, and stressful living conditions (Pearson et al., 2014). There are many reasons why stress-related and other mental disorders are important to the military (Boulos & Zamorski, 2013). Such disorders are leading causes of impaired functioning, absenteeism, and turnover. Impairments in functioning can jeopardize the safety and success of military operations.

Canada conducted military operations in Afghanistan for about a decade, officially terminating its combat military operations in 2011 but with personnel remaining there to provide training and support for Afghan security forces (Pare, 2011). Approximately 40 000 Canadian Armed Forces personnel were deployed to Afghanistan (Boulos & Zamorski, 2013). This was the largest Canadian military operation since World War II (Pare, 2011).

According to a large scale survey, involving clinical interviews conducted by mental health professionals, about 13.5% of Canadian Armed Forces personnel were diagnosed with a mental disorder that was attributable to involvement in the Afghanistan mission (Boulos & Zamorski, 2013). The most common disorder was PTSD (8%), followed by depressive disorders (6%), which were often comorbid with PTSD (Boulos & Zamorski, 2013). The rate of PTSD was twice as high for military personnel deployed to Afghanistan, compared to those who had not been deployed (Pearson et al., 2014). These findings are similar to past research showing that participation in combat and peacekeeping missions is associated with mental disorders among military personnel (Pearson et al., 2014). Deployment to higher-threat locations in Afghanistan (e.g., those in Kandahar), heavy combat exposure, and lower rank were risk factors for an Afghanistan-related mental disorder in Canadian military personnel (Boulos & Zamorski, 2013; Zamorski et al., 2014).

The population of the Canadian Armed Forces tends to be younger than in the general Canadian population, and there are more males. Compared with the general Canadian population, adjusted for age and sex, the rates of mental disorders are higher among Regular Force members, particularly for major depression, generalized anxiety disorder, and panic disorder (PTSD data were not available for this comparison) (Pearson et al., 2014).

Mental health services represent a large and growing amount of the health care provided by military organizations (Zamorski et al., 2014). Programs have been developed to improve the psychological adjustment of military personnel when they return from deployment, and to lessen the odds that they will develop psychological problems. The Canadian Armed Forces conducts mental health screening, particularly after deployment, and provides treatment for service-related mental health problems (Boulos & Zamorski, 2013). Recently, a five-day Third-Location Decompression (TLD) program has been implemented to improve post-deployment well-being and to help personnel re-adapt to their home environment (Zamorski et al., 2012). This educational program is implemented after personnel leave Afghanistan but before they return to Canada. For various logistical reasons, Cyprus chosen as the venue for the TLD program. In addition to receiving rest and recreation, TLD participants complete a series of educational sessions. Among other things, they have the opportunity to: (a) learn about the effects of stress, (b) identify common challenges and coping strategies to help them re-adjust to returning home, (c) learn to recognize signs that they may need to receive mental health services, (d) identify self-defeating coping strategies (e.g., excessive use of alcohol or drugs), and (e) identify mental health resources (Zamorski et al., 2012). The program also includes elective sessions focusing on

(continued)

specific topics (e.g., Coping with Stress and Anger; Garber & Zamorski, 2012). Mental health consultation is also available.

Preliminary research showed that TLD is favourably regarded by personnel completing the program (Zamorski et al., 2012), although further research is needed to determine whether it reduces the risk of post-deployment psychological problems. Most personnel (75%) completing TLD reported that the program helped them realize that there is nothing wrong with getting help for mental health problems. This is an important message of the program.

Source: Information in first paragraph based on http://globalnews.ca/invisible-wounds/1203097/invisible-wounds-master-corporal-jonathan-woolvett/.

Case Study: Lt. General Roméo Dallaire: *Shake Hands with the Devil*

One of the most prominent advocates for the recognition and treatment of PTSD in the Canadian Forces is retired Lt. General Roméo Dallaire. He experienced PTSD as a result of traumatic events that occurred when he headed a UN peacekeeping mission to Rwanda in 1993–1994. During that time there was a civil war between the Hutus, who controlled the country, and the Tutsis. In 100 days of genocide, about 800 000 Tutsis and politically moderate Hutus were massacred by the ruling Hutus. By the time the killing ended, the Hutu-dominated genocidal government had been driven from power, and three-quarters of the Tutsi population were dead.

General Dallaire's peacekeeping mission was unable to halt the slaughter due a variety of factors, including inadequate troops and supplies, along with orders that peacekeepers should not to actively intervene. Dallaire and his peacekeepers were caught in a bind; their mandate was to help the Rwandan people, but too often they had to stand by helplessly as the slaughter took place. Dallaire was also fired upon and had death threats issued against him, and several of his peacekeepers were butchered (Dallaire, 2003). His experiences, and those of his soldiers, provide a chilling account of what it is like to experience traumatic events.

General Dallaire recalls that Hutu militia readily butchered Tutsis or people without identity cards. Bodies piled up in ditches, and bloated corpses clogged the streams and rivers. Hutu patrols roamed the streets, breaking into houses and killing entire families. Children were hacked to pieces with machetes, often in front of their parents. Girls and women were raped, genitally mutilated, and murdered.

> The [Hutu] Gendarmerie had gone door to door checking identity cards. All Tutsi men, women and children were rounded up and moved to the church . . . Methodically, and with much bravado and laughter, the militia moved from bench to bench, hacking with machetes. Some people died immediately, while others with terrible wounds begged for their lives or the lives of their children. No one was spared. . . . Genitalia were a favourite target, the victim left to bleed to death. There was no mercy, no hesitation, no compassion. . . Those innocent men, women and children were simply Tutsi. That was their crime. (Dallaire, 2003, pp. 279–281)

Dallaire and his peacekeepers saw Rwanda's rustic landscape and mist-capped hills turn into a stinking nightmare of rotting corpses: "the putrid smell of decaying bodies in the huts along the route not only entered your nose and mouth but made you feel slimy and greasy" (p. 325). Dallaire, like many of his peacekeepers, vomited at the putrid horrors they witnessed. Tears, horror, disgust, rage, and stunned numbness were among the many immediate reactions of the peacekeepers to what they had witnessed.

> You cannot put these things behind you . . . And the more people say that [you can], the more you get mad because you know these things will not disappear . . . I can't sleep. I can't stand the loudness of silence . . . Time does not help. (Dallaire, quoted in Growe, 2000)

General Dallaire suffered from daily unwanted recollections of the horrors he experienced in Rwanda. The smell of fresh fruit could trigger traumatic memories, and bushes or piles of wood could trigger memories of corpses piled on top of one another. He became distressed when in crowds or in movie theatres, because they reminded him of being surrounded by massive crowds in Rwanda. Other reminders similarly affected him.

> Villages had been burnt to the ground, and bodies formed a carpet of rags in all directions. We took turns walking in front of my vehicle to make sure that we did not run over any of them. Even to this day, if I encounter an article of clothing dropped on the street, I go around it and must control the urge to check if it is a body. (Dallaire, 2003, p. 325)

One of Dallaire's peacekeepers, Corporal Chris Cassavoy, described similar experiences. He could not eat grilled chicken because it reminded him of dead bodies, and even back in Canada the sight of children reminded him of how the Hutu militia liked to murder children (Growe, 2000).

How does a person make sense of traumatic events, especially those that shatter one's spiritual beliefs and assumptions about humanity and the world? Developing an understanding of such horrors can be an important part of recovering from PTSD (Janoff-Bulman, 1992), and therefore an exploration of the meaning of the traumatic experience is part of cognitive-behavioural treatments for this disorder (Taylor, 2006). It took time for General Dallaire to make sense of the horrors he had experienced:

> The odour of death in the hot sun; the flies, maggots, rats and dogs that swarmed to feast on the dead. At times it seemed the smell had entered the pores of my skin. My Christian beliefs had been the moral framework that had guided me throughout my adult life. Where was God in all this horror? Where was God in the world's response? (Dallaire, 2003, p. 289)
>
> After one of my many presentations following my return from Rwanda, a Canadian Forces padre asked me how, after all I had seen and experienced, I could still believe in God. I answered that I know there is a God because in Rwanda I shook hands with the devil. I have seen him, I have smelled him and I have touched him. I know the devil exists, and therefore I know there is a God. (Dallaire, 2003, p. xviii)

CONCEPT check

- Panic attacks are defined as the presence of physical and cognitive symptoms of anxiety that occur suddenly. At least four symptoms must occur at the same time. Although the length of the attack may vary, it usually does not exceed an hour and is often much briefer. Panic attacks may be part of the clinical picture of any of the anxiety disorders.
- Panic disorder consists of sudden unexpected panic attacks accompanied by worry about when another attack will occur.
- Agoraphobia is marked fear or anxiety about two or more situations, including public transportation, open spaces, enclosed spaces, lines or crowds, and being outside of the home alone.
- Specific phobias are the most common form of anxiety disorder. Although they may begin at any age, most specific phobias emerge during childhood. Specific phobias can create substantial functional impairment, but they respond well to psychological treatment.
- People with social anxiety disorder fear doing or saying something embarrassing in front of others. The most common age of onset for social anxiety disorder is mid-adolescence,

although children also suffer from this disorder. Social anxiety disorder is one of the most chronic anxiety disorders, particularly when it occurs at an early age.

- The primary complaint among people who suffer from GAD is excessive worry about many different everyday events and activities, including finances, personal safety, health, future events, and past events. A range of physical symptoms is common; muscle tension is the most unique physical symptom of GAD relative to other anxiety disorders. GAD is a chronic anxiety disorder.
- OCD affects people at any age and consists of obsessions (intrusive thoughts) and compulsions (ritualistic behaviours). OCD is a chronic disorder and is difficult to treat.
- When a traumatic event occurs, such as the September 11, 2001, attacks, stress reactions are common. For most people, this response is temporary, but a small number of people develop PTSD characterized by repeated intrusion of the event, negative alterations in cognition or mood, and persistent autonomic arousal.

critical thinking question Separation anxiety disorder primarily affects preadolescent children. Although the disorder may result in significant impairment, in many cases the condition is temporary in nature. What environmental factors or events might lead to the development of separation fears in young children?

The Etiology of Anxiety, OCD, and Trauma- and Stressor-Related Disorders

4.5 Identify biological and psychological factors related to the development of these disorders.

It is important to note that because the DSM-5 criteria are so new, studies of etiology and treatment outcome have not been conducted on individuals who meet the new diagnostic criteria. Therefore, in this section, we discuss the literature based on study samples diagnosed using DSM-IV-TR.

How do these disorders develop? As discussed in Chapter 1, Little Albert acquired the fear of a white rat after a series of conditioning trials in which the rat was paired with loud noises. This psychological model is very useful for understanding PTSD, which always develops after a conditioning experience. However, not every anxiety disorder can be traced back to a traumatic event, and not everyone who experiences a negative event develops an anxiety disorder. Just as people may fear many different objects or situations, anxiety disorders may develop in a number of different ways. In some instances, the cause is unknown. Biological and psychological causes have been identified, and the same disorder can develop in very different ways in different people. As will be evident at the end of this section, the biopsychosocial model may be the most comprehensive model of the etiology of the anxiety disorders.

Biological Perspective

As noted in Chapter 1, biological perspectives on abnormal behaviour include investigations in genetics, family history, neuroanatomy, and neurobiology. Even when biological factors cannot fully explain the development of these disorders, they may produce the vulnerability that "sets the stage" for other biological or psychological influences that can lead to the disorder's onset.

FAMILY AND GENETIC STUDIES Are these disorders inherited? The disorders do seem to run in families. Compared with relatives of people without a disorder, relatives (parents, brothers, sisters, aunts, and uncles) of someone with an anxiety disorder are also more likely to have an anxiety disorder (e.g., Hanna, 2000; Pauls et al., 1995). The same relationship exists between parents and children. When a parent has an anxiety disorder, the child is more likely to have one, too (Beidel & Turner, 1997; Lieb et al., 2000). However, not every child in the family will develop anxiety; this means that although genetics may play a role, they do not provide the complete answer.

Twin studies also illustrate the role of genetics in the development of anxiety disorders. The concordance rate (see Chapter 2) for anxiety disorders among monozygotic (MZ) twins is twice as high as that of dizygotic (DZ) twins (34% vs. 17%, respectively; Andrews et al., 1990; Torgersen, 1983), but again, no specific gene or combination of genes has been identified.

Another way to examine genetic contribution is through the concept of **heritability**, which is the proportion of variance in liability to the disorder accounted for by genetic factors. Heritability estimates have been reported for GAD (32%; Hettema et al., 2001), panic disorder (43%; Hettema et al., 2001), social anxiety disorder (20% to 28%; Nelson et al., 2000), specific phobia (25% to 35%; Kendler et al., 2001), and obsessive-compulsive symptoms (38% to 41%; Taylor, 2011b). One study of more than 5000 twins (Hettema et al., 2005) revealed that one common genetic factor appears to influence GAD, panic disorder, and agoraphobia. A second genetic factor influences animal phobias and situational phobias. Social anxiety disorder appeared to be influenced by both genetic factors. However, all available genetic data indicate that genes do not tell the whole story. Because none of the heritability estimates was 100%, environmental factors clearly also are important in the development of anxiety disorders.

The search for specific genes that influence vulnerability to anxiety disorders requires moving from twin studies to the newer area of molecular genetics. In mice, genetic influences for fear and anxiety have been found on 15 different chromosomes (e.g., Einat et al., 2005; Flint, 2004). In humans, studies have identified chromosomal *regions* that may be important, but few specific *genes* have been identified (Kim et al., 2005; Martinez-Barrondo et al., 2005; Oleseon et al., 2005; Politi et al., 2006; Taylor, 2013). Further research is required to determine how genes and environmental factors interact to influence these disorders.

Based on the currently available data, what appears to be inherited is a *general vulnerability factor*, known as **trait anxiety** or *anxiety proneness* (Hettema et al., 2001). Because these types of personality traits exist along a dimension, people can have different degrees of anxiety proneness. Those high on this dimension are more "reactive" to stressful events and therefore more likely in the right circumstances to develop a disorder.

Carolyn and five of her friends were flying home from spring break. The plane flew through a thunderstorm, and wind shear caused the plane to drop suddenly and tilt at a 90-degree angle for approximately 10 seconds until the pilot regained control. The plane landed safely. Several months later, Carolyn's friends wanted to fly to the Caribbean but she declined. She was terrified to get on a plane. Despite their pleadings, Carolyn refused to go. Based on that one experience, she had developed a specific phobia of flying.

Carolyn's case illustrates how anxiety proneness might foster the development of fear. Even though all six women experienced the same environmental event, only Carolyn acquired a phobia. Perhaps Carolyn had an increased genetic vulnerability for the development of anxiety disorders.

NEUROANATOMY Anxiety proneness is a theoretical construct that is very useful in understanding the development of anxiety disorders. A *construct* is not something tangible; it provides only a frame of reference, such as the construct known as *free will*. Saying that someone is anxiety prone does not explain what the abnormality is or where it is located. However, newly emerging CT, MRI, fMRI, and PET imaging data indicate that several areas of the midbrain are involved in anxious emotion.

When someone is stressed, certain areas of the brain—including the amygdala and the hippocampus (Uhde & Singareddy, 2002), as well as the limbic and paralimbic systems (Stein & Hugo, 2004)—become more active. Because these neuroanatomical structures are important in processing emotion, they may also be involved in the development of fear and anxiety. Different areas of the brain may be associated with different disorders. For example, the amygdala and the insula, areas that are associated with anxiety, become activated when adults with social anxiety disorder viewed faces depicting negative emotion (Shah et al., 2009). These same areas were not activated when people without social anxiety disorder viewed the same faces. For OCD, the orbital prefrontal cortex and the caudate nucleus are potentially important (Baxter, 1992). Using OCD as an example, we illustrate how these brain regions may play a role in the onset of these disorders.

Some OCD symptoms consist of impulses to blurt out words or the inability to control thoughts or behaviours. Neuroanatomical studies have shown that two regions, the prefrontal cortex and the caudate nucleus, make up a brain circuit that converts sensations into thoughts and actions (Stein, 2002; Trivedi, 1996). In fact, violent or sexual thoughts or impulses (often reported by people with OCD) appear to originate in the orbital prefrontal cortex. One theory proposes that from there, the neuronal signals travel to the caudate nucleus, where normally they are filtered out. If they are not filtered out, the signals for these thoughts and impulses arrive at the thalamus, causing the person to experience a drive to focus on the thoughts and perhaps to act on them.

From a scientist–practitioner perspective, this is a very interesting theory. Before we can accept it, however, we need a demonstration that brain activity in people with OCD is different from that in people with no disorder. One way to do this is to use *psychological challenge studies.* In such procedures, people confront objects or situations while PET methodology scans suspected areas of the brain for enhanced activity. In one study, when people with OCD and healthy controls were challenged (e.g., they were asked to touch "contaminated" objects), only people with OCD had enhanced brain activity in the orbitofrontal cortex, anterior cingulate, striatum, and thalamus areas (Trivedi, 1996). In other words, people with OCD responded differently when they touched these objects than did people without OCD. However, because the people already had OCD, we cannot know whether this enhanced brain activity originally caused the disorder. Perhaps this activation exists only if the disorder is already present.

Fully answering the question of etiology would require a longitudinal design. In one such study, we could define people at risk for OCD (perhaps a group that reacted with brain activation when touching contaminated objects but had no other OCD symptoms). We would assess this group on a regular basis for a few years to determine whether they later developed OCD. Another study might attempt to determine whether activation in these brain regions occurs only in people with OCD. Higher activation may be common among people with many different anxiety disorders or even other types of psychological disorders. If the same brain activity occurs in people with many different disorders, then we could not conclude that it is a specific cause of OCD. Perhaps it is a general vulnerability factor for many different disorders.

Overall, there do appear to be differences in brain *functioning* between individuals with some types of anxiety disorders and those with no disorder. However, comparative studies examining brain *structures*, such as the size of the amygdala, do not reveal differences between people with anxiety disorders and healthy controls. Therefore, anatomical differences would not appear to be a factor in the development of anxiety disorders. In some cases, PTSD may cause changes in brain function that then affect brain anatomy. Smaller hippocampal volumes have been consistently found in combat veterans with PTSD and in children who were sexually abused (Bremner et al., 1995, 1997; Gurvits et al., 1996; Stein et al., 1997). Although the full meaning of this important difference is not yet clear, this finding suggests that chronic environmental stress may result in neurochemical changes (brain functioning) that over time may change neuroanatomy (brain structure).

In Chapter 2, you learned that neurons in the brain use neurotransmitters—chemicals that exist throughout the nervous system—to carry messages from one neuron to another. Different neurotransmitters are primarily responsible for regulating different brain functions, such as movement, learning, memory, and emotion. The most consistently studied neurotransmitter is serotonin: It regulates mood, thoughts, and behaviour and is considered to play a key role in anxiety disorders. Low serotonin levels in the cerebral cortex will prevent the transmission of signals from one neuron to the next, inhibiting the ability of the brain to effectively regulate mood, thoughts, and behaviour.

What data support the hypothesis that serotonin is important? First, compared with individuals with no psychological disorder, the cerebrospinal fluid (CSF) of people with GAD, panic disorder, PTSD, and OCD shows reduced levels of serotonin and its by-products. Although neurotransmitter levels in the spinal cord and the brain are not perfectly correlated, lower levels in the CSF suggest that these deficiencies may also exist in brain synapses (Stein & Hugo, 2004). Second, using a *biochemical challenge*, researchers gave study participants a substance that alters their level of serotonin and analyzed how the biochemical change is related to increases or decreases in feelings of anxiety. Challenge studies help us understand how decreased serotonin levels may increase feelings of anxiety, but the results are not always consistent (Uhde & Singareddy, 2002). Third, medications known as *selective serotonin reuptake inhibitors* (SSRIs) *increase* serotonin in the neural synapses; people who are prescribed these medications report that their feelings of anxiety *decrease*. Working backward, you might then conclude that less serotonin is related to increased anxiety. Together, all of these studies suggest that decreased serotonin at certain neural synapses is related to feelings of anxiety. However, many of the participants in these studies already had anxiety disorders, and that limits the conclusions that we can make. To conclude that low serotonin levels are a definitive cause of, rather than the result of, anxiety disorders, the studies would need to begin with people who did not have anxiety disorders and would have to manipulate the levels of serotonin in their bodies. Of course, it would not be ethical to conduct this type of study, which could deliberately create anxiety disorders in people.

Another neurotransmitter, gamma aminobutyric acid (GABA), inhibits *postsynaptic activity*, the reaction of the "receiver neuron" when a message is sent from one neuron to another. Reducing this postsynaptic activity inhibits anxious emotion. Thus, medications that allow GABA to inhibit postsynaptic activity effectively are useful for the treatment of anxiety disorders (see "The Treatment of Anxiety Disorders").

A substance called *corticotrophin-releasing factor* (CRF) also may be important for the development of anxiety disorders. CRF neurons are present in areas of the brain that regulate stress and process emotions (Heim & Nemeroff, 1999). These brain areas release CRF, which stimulates production of chemical substances called *adrenocorticotropic hormone* (ACTH) and *beta-endorphins*. We know that when these chemicals are injected into the brains of mice, the animals behave in ways that suggest the presence of depression and anxiety. Similarly, when animals are placed in stressful conditions such as separation and loss, abuse or neglect, and social deprivation, they respond with heightened and persistent CRF activity in the hypothalamus and the amygdala (Heim & Nemeroff, 1999; Sanchez et al., 2001). These data suggest that early life experiences such as loss, separation, or abuse (environmental events) may change brain activity, making an individual biologically vulnerable in the same way that genes produce vulnerability. In turn, when this chemical persists, overactivity (a biological contribution) persists, and the person is at risk for later developing emotional disorders such as anxiety and perhaps depression, depending on other biological or environmental contributors (see Figure 4.6).

Neuroscience offers exciting new ways to understand anxiety disorders. However, many challenges remain. Different technologies (CT, fMRI, SPECT, and

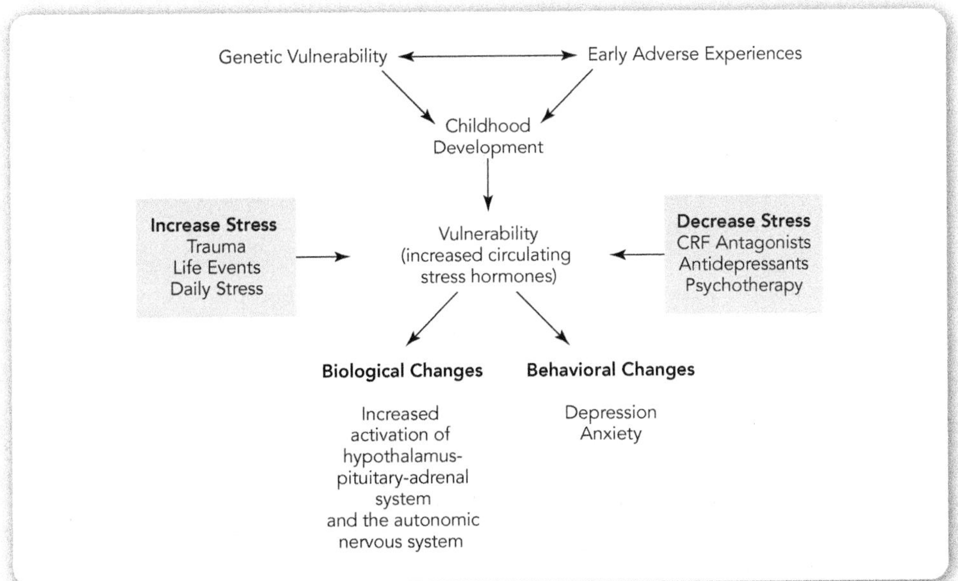

FIGURE 4.6

Stress May Affect Brain Functioning. Early adverse experiences can alter brain functioning, which may in turn increase the likelihood of developing an anxiety disorder.

Source: Adapted from Heim, C., & Nemeroff, C. The impact of early adverse experiences on brain systems involved in the pathophysiology of anxiety and affective disorders. *Biological Psychiatry, 46*, 1509–1522. Copyright © 1999 by the Society of Biological Psychiatry with permission from Elsevier Science Inc.

PET) produce different images in the same brain region (Insel & Winslow, 1992; Trivedi, 1996). In addition, many studies compare people with anxiety disorders only to people with no disorder. This means that we can conclude only that healthy controls differ from those of people with an anxiety disorder; we cannot conclude that a particular brain abnormality is found only in people with anxiety disorders. To draw that conclusion, we would have to examine the brain activity of people with other types of disorders and determine whether people with other disorders (such as depression or eating disorders) did or did not have the same abnormality.

TEMPERAMENT AND BEHAVIOURAL INHIBITION *Temperament* describes individual behavioural differences that are present at a very early age, perhaps even at birth. **Behavioural inhibition**, a concept first proposed by Jerome Kagan (1982), is a temperamental feature that exists in approximately 20% of children. Children with behavioural inhibition withdraw from (or fail to approach) novel people, objects, or situations. They do not speak spontaneously in the presence of strangers, and they cry and cling to their mothers rather than approach other children to play. Children with behavioural inhibition are more likely to show anxiety reactions and to have childhood anxiety disorders, in particular phobias (Gladstone et al., 2005; Hayward et al., 1998). Behavioural inhibition, identifiable at 4 months of age, may be a unique risk factor for the later development of social anxiety disorder (Hirshfeld et al., 1992). However, this relationship is not absolute; not every infant with behavioural inhibition develops social anxiety disorder. Furthermore, not every person with social anxiety disorder was a behaviourally inhibited infant. Therefore, although behavioural inhibition may increase the likelihood of developing social anxiety disorder, it does not account for every single case of the disorder.

Psychological Perspective

Psychological theories of the etiology of anxiety are among the best known and the most researched. Most people understand fears and phobias by explanations that involve having previously been frightened by the object. A traumatic event is only one of many different etiological explanations for the development of anxiety disorders. Other perspectives include the role of individual experiences and broader influences such as family environment and social context. In the following section, we examine explanations for the development of fear based on established psychological theories such as psychoanalysis, behaviourism, and cognitive psychology.

PSYCHODYNAMIC THEORIES OF FEAR ACQUISITION Sigmund Freud believed that free-floating (generalized) anxiety resulted from a conflict between the id and the ego (see Chapter 1). He thought that these conflicts resulted from sexual or aggressive impulses that overwhelmed the person's available defense mechanisms. Freud believed that the defense mechanisms of repression and displacement were operative in the development of phobias. A classic example of the psychoanalytic approach to the development of anxiety disorders is the case of Little Hans.

Hans was a 5-year-old boy born in nineteenth-century Europe. After watching a carriage horse fall down and after playing horses with a friend who fell down, Hans developed a fear that a horse might fall down or bite him. This fear later extended to any horse-drawn vehicle, which he avoided at all cost. Hans refused to leave home when these vehicles might be present. He also was very concerned about his genitalia, fearing that his penis was not sufficiently large. His mother once told him not to touch his "widdler" or she would call a doctor to cut it off. Hans's father asked Freud for assistance. Using detailed information from conversations between Hans and his father (provided mostly by the father), Freud decided that Hans's fear and fixation on his genitalia represented his sexual feelings toward his mother, feelings that Freud called the Oedipus complex. Freud also noted that Hans was particularly afraid of horses with a black bit in their mouths, which Freud interpreted as a symbolic representation of his father's mustache. The horse, like Hans's father, was an object both admired and feared and was obviously a rival for the affection of Hans's mother. Because he could not deal with them directly, Hans displaced all of these feelings onto horses, resulting in fear and avoidance.

Although many alternative theories explain Hans's fears (e.g., classical conditioning, social learning theory; see Chapter 1), this case was extremely influential in the development of psychoanalytic theory in the early part of the twentieth century. Today, its overall influence has decreased markedly.

BEHAVIOURAL THEORIES OF FEAR ACQUISITION Conditioning theory has a prominent role in explaining fear acquisition even though no single behavioural theory adequately accounts for the etiology of all anxiety disorders. Current behavioural theories are much more complicated than the story of Little Albert, the boy who learned to fear a white rat when it was paired with an aversive stimulus (see Chapter 1). The acquisition of fears through classical conditioning remains a primary explanation for the onset of anxiety disorders. However, classical conditioning theories cannot provide an explanation for all anxiety disorders, and thus there are other behavioural explanations.

In addition to direct conditioning theory, people sometimes acquire fears through other forms of learning known as *vicarious learning theory* (see Chapter 1) and *information transmission* (Barlow, 2002). Consider the following example.

Lindsay and Lisa are twins. Lindsay was selected to sing a solo ("Jingle Bell Rock") at the annual Winter Holiday Pageant. She was nervous about the solo but also excited about the opportunity to perform in public. When she went on stage, she opened her mouth but she was nervous and the words would not come out. The audience thought it was part of the act, and they laughed out loud. Lindsay was very embarrassed and ran off stage crying. Lisa, who was in the audience, saw everyone laughing at her sister. Now Lisa refuses to perform in front of an audience, and this week, she failed her English class because she refused to get up and give a speech.

Although in the past Lisa would get a little nervous when she had to speak in front of the class, after watching Lindsay's traumatic event, Lisa acquired a fear of performing in front of others, indicating that she had developed social anxiety disorder. This process is known as *observational learning* or *vicarious conditioning*. Encouragingly, not everyone who experiences a traumatic event develops a disorder via direct conditioning. Remember Carolyn? She developed a fear of flying but her friends did not, although they had the same experience on the plane. How does conditioning theory account for this difference? One explanation is that previous positive experiences with the same situation may protect against the later effects of a traumatic event. Positive experiences may provide immunity against the development of anxiety or traumatic disorders in the same way that a vaccination prevents children from acquiring the measles. Rhesus monkeys, for example, can be "immunized" against a fear of toy snakes (Mineka & Cook, 1986) by first observing other monkeys who are not afraid of a toy snake. When they later see monkeys who behave fearfully in the presence of snakes, these "immunized" monkeys do not acquire the fear.

A third method by which anxiety disorders can develop is through information transfer, which means that a person instructs someone that a situation or object should be feared. Parents must instruct children about the dangers of crossing a busy street or the need to refrain from inserting objects (such as a knife) into an electrical outlet. When asked to report how their fears developed, a subset of children (39%) identified information transfer as the mechanism as compared to direct conditioning (37%) and modelling (56%) (Ollendick & King, 1991).

Current theories about the etiology of anxiety acknowledge that biological and psychological-environmental factors are both important elements. Contemporary models of learning theory acknowledge biological factors (genetics and temperament), environmental vulnerabilities (conditioning and social/cultural learning history), and stress factors (controllability and predictability of stressful events; conditioning experiences). All of these elements affect the quality and intensity of the conditioning event, and therefore the anxiety and fear that develop as a result of the conditioning experience (Mineka & Zinbarg, 2006; see Figure 4.7).

COGNITIVE THEORIES OF FEAR ACQUISITION As is the case with behavioural theories, there is no one cognitive approach to anxiety. However, all approaches assume that anxiety disorders result from inaccurate interpretations of internal events ("My heart is racing, so I must be having a heart attack") or external events ("Here I am giving a speech and my boss is yawning—I must be really boring"). Cognitive theories propose

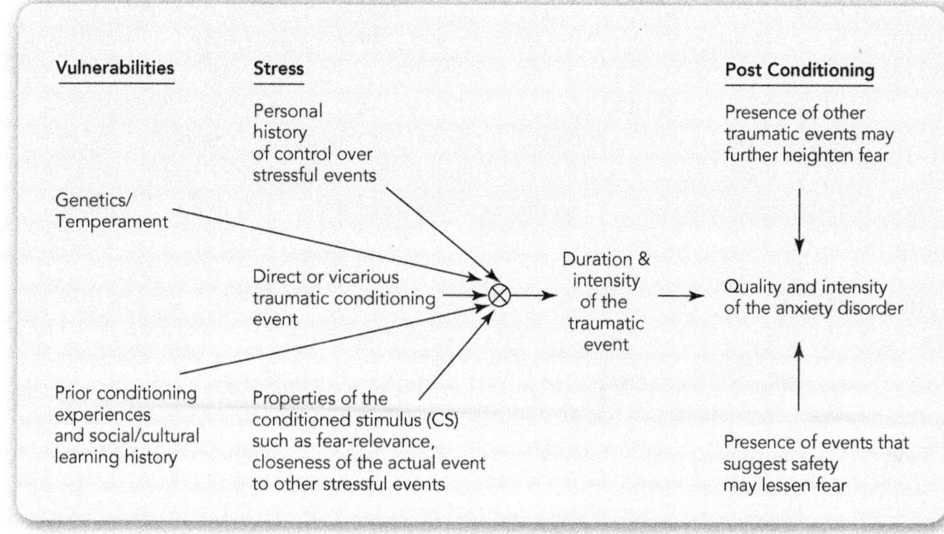

FIGURE 4.7

A Contemporary Theory of Fear Acquisition. Although early theories of learning did not adequately account for fear acquisition, revised models take into account the presence of biological and psychological vulnerabilities as well as environmental stressors that may be present before, during, or after the traumatic (conditioning) event.

Source: Adapted from Mineka, S., & Zinbarg, R. A contemporary learning theory perspective on the etiology of anxiety disorders: It's not what you thought it was. *American Psychologist, 61*, pp. 10–26. Copyright © 2006 by the American Psychological Association.

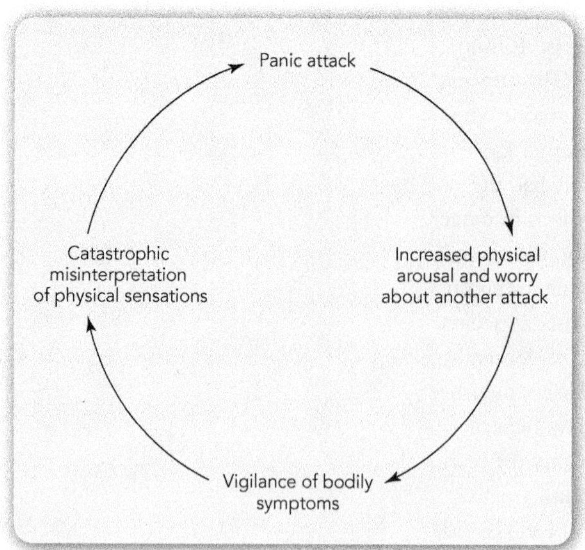

FIGURE 4.8

The Fear of Fear Model. After a panic attack, a person often worries about having another. This worry can create both physical and emotional arousal, which can result in overattention to normal physical symptoms. When these occur, they are overinterpreted as a signal of another panic attack.

that people with anxiety disorders process information differently and this leads to the development of anxiety (McNally, 1995). Aaron Beck, a leading cognitive theorist, suggests that anxiety results from maladaptive thoughts that automatically interpret an ambiguous situation (e.g., "I am short of breath") in a negative fashion (e.g., "I must be having a heart attack"; Clark & Beck, 2011). From a cognitive perspective, anxiety disorders develop because people misinterpret ambiguous situations as dangerous, resulting in physiological and cognitive distress. Because they never attempt to determine whether their beliefs are true, these negative thoughts maintain the presence of the disorder.

A second cognitive theory, and one relevant for panic disorder, is the *fear of fear* model (Goldstein & Chambless, 1978). This theory proposes that after the first panic attack, the person becomes sensitive to any bodily symptom and interprets any change in physiological state (e.g., a sudden heart flutter) as the signal of an impending panic attack (see Figure 4.8). This leads to a vicious cycle of worry, which then increases the likelihood of a panic attack and further increases worry. A third cognitive model is *anxiety sensitivity*, which is a belief that anxiety symptoms will result in negative consequences such as illness, embarrassment, or more anxiety (Taylor, 1995). Anxiety sensitivity is hypothesized to result from several factors, including previous panic attacks, biological vulnerability to panic, and personality needs (to avoid embarrassment or illness, or to maintain control). In this model, we see again how biology and learning interact to produce thoughts that lead to the inaccurate interpretation of future events.

Cognitive theories have evolved since their introduction 20 years ago, and most researchers now postulate that negative or distorted cognitions are important in the *maintenance* of anxiety disorders. There is less evidence that cognitions are the primary mechanism by which disorders initially develop. Models of panic disorder (fear of fear and anxiety sensitivity), for example, propose that an anxiety disorder develops when a person misinterprets the physical symptoms of a panic attack. However, these theories often do not adequately explain how those cognitive biases first came to exist. The specific contribution of cognitions to etiology is actually difficult to identify without longitudinal studies that follow people before they develop the disorder. Studies of people at high risk for developing an anxiety disorder (e.g., children of parents with anxiety disorders) may be necessary in order to understand the role of cognition in the etiology of anxiety.

To summarize, both biological and psychological/environmental factors appear to be important for the development of anxiety, OCD, and trauma- and stressor-related disorders. Biological influences include genetic contributions as well as potential neurotransmitter and hormonal abnormalities. On the psychological/environmental side, conditioning experiences explain the acquisition of some, but not all, anxiety disorders. Family factors may be important in modelling or reinforcing anxiety responses, and environmental stressors may affect not only emotional functioning, but also neuroanatomy. Although much remains to be learned, it is clear that the etiology of anxiety disorders defies a simple explanation.

CONCEPT check

- Biochemical theories regarding the etiology of anxiety disorders have investigated the role of many different neurotransmitters, but the strongest evidence exists for the neurotransmitter serotonin, which has an important role in the regulation of emotion.
- Twin and family studies support the role of genetics in the etiology of anxiety, OCD, and trauma- and stressor-related disorders, although at the current time, the evidence suggests that an anxious temperament, not a specific anxiety disorder, is most likely inherited.

- Strict psychoanalytic interpretations regarding the etiology of anxiety disorders have fallen out of favour.
- From a behavioural perspective, anxiety disorders may develop as a result of direct conditioning, observational learning, or information transfer.

critical thinking question How do cognitive theories of the etiology of anxiety disorder differ from traditional behavioural theories?

The Treatment of Anxiety, OCD, and Trauma- and Stressor-Related Disorders

4.6 Identify pharmacological and psychological interventions used to treat these disorders.

It is important to note that because the DSM-5 criteria are so new, studies of etiology and treatment outcome have not been conducted on individuals who meet the new diagnostic criteria. Therefore, in this section, we discuss the literature based on study samples diagnosed using DSM-IV-TR.

The treatment of these disorders uses several different approaches, including biological, behavioural and cognitive-behavioural, and psychodynamic interventions. Psychodynamic theory is commonly applied in clinical settings but has not been the subject of much empirical research. In contrast, biological and behavioural or cognitive-behavioural approaches have substantial empirical support. All appear to be efficacious, resulting in remission rates of about 70% among those who are treated. In some instances, participants in research studies have a less complicated symptom pattern and do not have the comorbid disorders that are commonly seen in patients in nonresearch outpatient clinics. Because researchers are now only beginning to study how to implement the empirically supported treatments in traditional outpatient clinics, we do not know whether these treatments are as successful when administered to people who have anxiety disorders together with other disorders, such as substance abuse.

Biological Treatments

Today's biological treatments usually come in the form of medication, but, as we shall see, other treatments for anxiety disorders, including neurosurgery, exist. You might recall from Chapter 1 that historically, somatic treatments consisted of bed rest, exercise, and work at simple tasks. Today, somatic treatments are based on modern knowledge of neuroanatomy and neurochemistry, allowing these interventions to target the brain directly.

MEDICATION As we noted in the section on etiology, several disorders (panic disorder, GAD, PTSD, and OCD) are associated with the depletion of serotonin in the neural synapses, which in turn prevents the neurons from functioning properly. At the end of the presynaptic neuron are terminals that release serotonin into the synapse and other terminals that take the serotonin back up into the presynaptic neuron in a process called *reuptake* (see Figure 4.9). When the postsynaptic neuron receives enough serotonin, the neuron fires, and the process continues. Without enough serotonin in the synapse, the signal does not pass to the next neuron as it should. One way to increase brain serotonin is to stimulate the neuron to release more of the neurotransmitter. An alternative is to block its reuptake, allowing the serotonin to remain in the synapse longer. Medications known as **selective serotonin reuptake inhibitors (SSRIs)** are thought to correct serotonin imbalances in this manner by increasing the time that serotonin remains in the synapse.

Medications that influence the serotonin system, such as SSRIs like Prozac, Luvox, and Zoloft, are now the biological treatment of choice for the anxiety disorders

FIGURE 4.9

How SSRIs Work. SSRIs block the neuron's normal reuptake mechanism, allowing serotonin to remain in the synapse and increasing the likelihood that it will land on the next neuron's receptor.

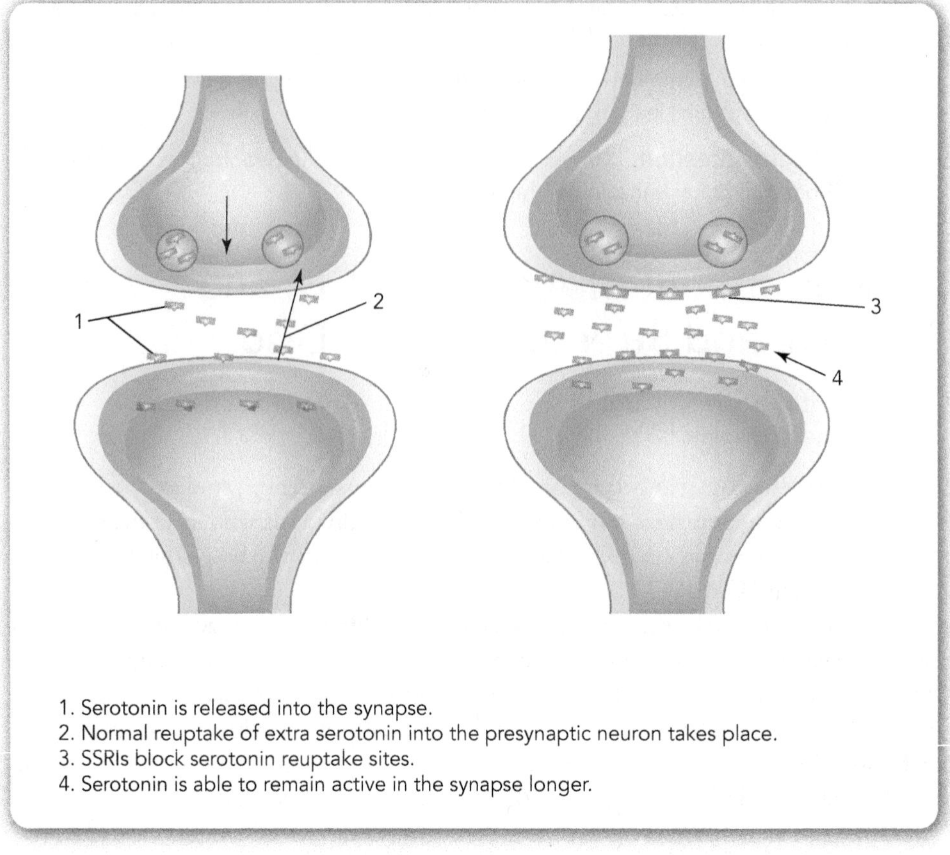

1
2
3
4
1. Serotonin is released into the synapse.
2. Normal reuptake of extra serotonin into the presynaptic neuron takes place.
3. SSRIs block serotonin reuptake sites.
4. Serotonin is able to remain active in the synapse longer.

(Katzman et al., 2014). At least 40 studies demonstrate their efficacy compared with pill placebo. Positive treatment outcome has been demonstrated for panic disorder with or without agoraphobia (e.g., Pollack & Marzol, 2000), social anxiety disorder (e.g., Stein et al., 2003), OCD (e.g., Marazzati, 1999), GAD (Rickels et al., 2000), and PTSD (Steckler & Risbrough, 2012). Although the medications work better than placebos for these disorders, they are not efficacious for everyone. Many people need to remain on these medications for an extended period of time, and perhaps indefinitely, because relapse is common when the medication is withdrawn. Medications play a minimal role in the treatment of specific phobias, mainly because of the lack of research on medications for these disorders and because of the success of behavioural therapies (Katzman et al., 2014).

Using these medications with children and adolescents requires extra caution (Katzman et al., 2014). Both Health Canada and the U.S. Food and Drug Administration issued warnings regarding the possibility that SSRIs may increase the risk of suicidal thinking in children, adolescents, and young adults with depression. Although no such increase has been reported in patients with anxiety disorders, children and adolescents should be monitored closely for the presence of any suicidal thoughts or plans.

GABA is another neurotransmitter that may be associated with anxiety disorders (Stein & Hugo, 2004), although the evidence is weaker for GABA than for serotonin. Drugs known as *benzodiazepines* (tranquilizers such as Valium and Xanax) allow GABA to transmit nerve signals more effectively, which in turn reduces anxiety. Benzodiazepines have efficacy for panic disorder with or without agoraphobia (Cross National Collaborative Panic Study Second Phase Investigation, 1992), GAD (Rickels et al., 1993), and social anxiety disorder (Davidson, 1993). In the 1970s and 1980s, benzodiazepines were the treatment of choice for anxiety disorders, and they were prescribed quite freely.

However, the drugs may cause physical and psychological dependence if they are used for a long period of time. These medications must always be withdrawn under a doctor's supervision because seizures may occur if the withdrawal is not done properly. Therefore, though efficacious, these medications are not considered the first choice for the treatment of anxiety disorders.

PSYCHOSURGERY Before SSRIs and behaviour therapy, OCD was considered to be resistant to treatment. As a last resort, surgery provided some relief of symptoms. In the past, surgery was imprecise, and the side effects included unresponsiveness, decreased attention, restricted or inappropriate affect, and disinhibition (inability to control emotion or behaviour) (Mashour et al., 2005). Today, with the use of MRIs and the ability to destroy tissue with radiation (rather than needing to rely on surgery), many fewer side effects occur (although certainly no surgical procedure is without risk).

Cingulotomy and *capsulotomy* are types of neurosurgery currently used to treat OCD. *Cingulotomy* is more common and involves inserting thin probes through the top of the skull into a portion of the brain called the *cingulate bundle*. The probes burn selective portions of the brain tissue (Clinical Research News, 2004). In *capsulotomy*, *gamma knife surgery* (a form of radiation treatment) makes precise lesions in brain tissue without the need for opening the skull. These surgeries are guided by the use of neuroimaging procedures such as MRI, allowing for surgical precision. Among people with OCD who were treated with cingulotomy, 45% of those unresponsive to pharmacological and behavioural interventions had at least a partial treatment response after neurosurgery (Dougherty et al., 2002). However, neurosurgery is considered only if the person with OCD has failed to benefit from medication and behaviour therapy. Candidates for this surgery are always carefully screened because there are risks, such as memory problems and personality changes. These negative outcomes occur less often than they did in the past because we now have more sophisticated neuroimaging and neurosurgery procedures (Dougherty et al., 2002).

OTHER SOMATIC THERAPIES In addition to psychosurgery, new and potentially exciting interventions have been developed to treat anxiety disorders that are nonresponsive to traditional pharmacological and psychological treatments. These experimental procedures include transcranial magnetic stimulation (see Chapter 10) and deep brain stimulation (see Chapter 6). Although these treatments have shown promise (Mashour et al., 2005), many more research trials are needed before we can draw conclusions regarding their efficacy.

Psychological Treatments

Psychological interventions are among the first treatments for anxiety, OCD, trauma- and stressor-related disorders (Katzman et al., 2014). Interventions are usually developed for adults and then adapted for children. However, in the case of anxiety disorders, some of the earliest case studies described successful treatment of children with phobias. Even so, today much more scientific evidence exists regarding the treatment of adults with anxiety disorders than for children. We next describe psychodynamic and behavioural and cognitive-behavioural treatment for people of all ages.

PSYCHODYNAMIC TREATMENT Psychodynamic treatment uses free association and dream interpretation (see Chapter 1) as a reflection of the patient's experience in the outside world. As in the case of Little Hans, fears and phobias are considered merely signs of internal conflict. Treatment involves discovering and "working through" these conflicts. Some therapists still use psychoanalysis and psychodynamically-oriented treatments to treat anxiety disorders. However, long-term psychodynamically-oriented psychotherapy does not lend itself well to randomized controlled trial design. It is difficult both scientifically and ethically to assign someone to a placebo (i.e., no active treatment) or a wait-list condition that would need to last a number of years. Therefore, we have little knowledge about the efficacy of psychodynamic therapy for the treatment of anxiety disorders.

A review of controlled research examining psychodynamic psychotherapy (Leichsenring, 2005) revealed just two randomized controlled trials for anxiety disorders, only one of which reported a positive outcome. Modern adaptations of psychodynamically-oriented treatments are now available, and because they are briefer in length, they are more suitable for clinical trials. One form of psychodynamically-oriented treatment is interpersonal psychotherapy (IPT) (Klerman et al., 1984), which targets interpersonal disputes and conflicts, interpersonal role transitions, and complicated grief reactions (see Chapter 6 for an extensive description of this form of treatment). IPT has been tested in social anxiety disorder (Lipsitz et al., 1999) and PTSD (Bleiberg & Markowitz, 2005) with encouraging results. Larger controlled clinical trials are required before IPT can be recommended as a primary treatment for anxiety disorders.

BEHAVIOURAL AND COGNITIVE-BEHAVIOURAL TREATMENT After 30 years of study, compelling empirical data indicate that behavioural therapy (BT) and cognitive-behavioural therapy (CBT) interventions are the psychosocial treatments of choice for adults, adolescents, and children with anxiety, OCD, and trauma- and stressor-related disorders. The many different forms of BT and CBT all incorporate a procedure known as **exposure** (i.e., facing your fears to get over them). For example, a person who fears dogs must have contact with a dog. Therapists use many different methods to provide exposure opportunities. For some fears, such as those of dogs or heights, exposure can occur through real-life experiences (called *in vivo exposure*). For other fears, such as being in a plane crash or becoming seriously ill from touching germs, providing exposure involves instructing the person to imagine the feared event (*imaginal exposure*). To treat panic disorder, exposure therapy uses various exercises (e.g., running up and down the stairs) to create the physical symptoms of panic, such as shortness of breath and racing heart in the patient. In this way, the person is exposed to what he or she fears—physical symptoms associated with panic.

Despite the seemingly simple nature of this treatment, determining exactly what the exposure situation should be, how long and how often it should occur, and who should conduct the sessions are all-important factors that contribute to its success. When done correctly, 70% of people with anxiety disorders show improvement (80% for specific phobia; Barlow, 2002; Compton et al., 2004). The only exception is combat-related PTSD, for which the rate is somewhat lower (Turner et al., 2005). Excluding combat-related PTSD, remission rates of 93% after two years and 62% after 10 years are common (Fava et al., 2001). Developing appropriate exposure situations has always been a challenge for therapists. New technologies such as virtual reality now allow therapists to expose people to commonly feared situations without having to leave their office (see "Research Hot Topic: Virtual Reality Therapy").

Sometimes the combination of exposure and other treatments enhances the efficacy of treatment. Because people with social anxiety disorder avoid social interactions, they often do not have the basic skills needed for social communication (when it is a good time to talk to someone, how to be assertive without being aggressive). In this instance, social skills training (SST) is combined with exposure. SST teaches skills, usually conducted in a group setting, allowing for members to observe the therapist, who models the skill. People then practise with the group, which provides opportunities to rehearse skills in a safe, supportive setting.

research HOT topic

Virtual Reality Therapy

The most efficacious treatment for specific phobias is behaviour therapy whose key component is exposure to the feared object, situation, or event. A person afraid of heights can be taken to a high place and can learn to lose this fear by using operant conditioning strategies (see Chapter 1). However, when the specific feared event is a plane crash, this event cannot be re-created. Therefore, therapists need an alternative means of exposure. Virtual reality is becoming a common tool for the treatment of certain specific phobias (heights, flying). The patient is fitted with a head-mounted display that has screens for each eye, earphones, and a device that tracks head, hand, and foot movements. When used to treat fear of flying (Rothbaum et al., 2002), scenarios consist of sitting in a passenger airline compartment during takeoff, flying in both calm and stormy weather, and landing. Noise such as voices of flight attendants and engine noises and vibrations such as the sensations caused by weather effects are added. Virtual reality therapy appears to be as effective as standard exposure treatments for phobias of heights and flying (see Rothbaum et al., 2002), and emerging evidence suggests its usefulness for treating social anxiety disorder and PTSD. With respect to the treatment of PTSD, virtual reality therapy is now being used to treat veterans returning from the conflicts in Iraq and Afghanistan.

Other treatments, such as relaxation training and CBT, can be combined with exposure to enhance treatment effects. *Relaxation training*, described in Chapter 1, may decrease general physical arousal and sometimes is the first step for the treatment of GAD. However, it is rarely used alone. A related intervention, *biofeedback*, combines the monitoring of physical behaviours such as blood pressure, pulse rate, or muscle tension with relaxation training. The goal is to lower these levels of physical arousal by using relaxation. Feedback from the machines in the form of signals that physical arousal is decreasing provides cues that the person is being successful. It is believed that this feedback mechanism helps a person quickly learn what to do to lower his or her physical distress.

CBT combines exposure with cognitive restructuring in an attempt to change negative cognitions. In cognitive restructuring, a therapist asks the person to face an anxiety-producing event (e.g., making a formal speech) and to reflect on any negative thoughts that occur. For example, the thought might be "I'm going to mispronounce a word, make a fool of myself, and everyone will think I'm an idiot." The therapist then asks the person to enter the situation and see whether this "worst thing" actually happens. Of course, it does not happen. The therapist may also ask the patient to generate alternative positive or "coping" cognitions to counteract the negative thoughts; for example, "The audience knows that anyone can make a mistake—they will not see me as a complete fool." Over a series of exposure assignments, the patient's anxiety decreases and negative thoughts become less frequent.

Across all disorders, improvement rates for CBT, whether provided individually or in groups, average about 70% (e.g., Barlow, 2002). Despite what common sense would seem to suggest, more is not better. That is, combining behavioural and cognitive strategies does not seem to enhance their efficacy (Davidson et al., 2004; Hegel et al., 1994). Improvement rates remain in the 70% to 80% range. Reviews of studies (Fairbrother, 2002; Rodebaugh et al., 2004; Zaider & Heimberg, 2003) that compare the impact of different treatment components (Hope et al., 1995; Salaberria & Echeburua, 1998), as well as statistical comparisons of different treatment outcome studies (Gould et al., 1997; Taylor, 1996; Wentzel et al., 1998), clearly indicate that exposure is the key ingredient. Other interventions may be used but do not necessarily increase response rates.

Combining BT or CBT with medication does not produce an enhanced effect in most instances. However, adding CBT to medication improves treatment outcome for patients with panic disorder who are treated in the primary care setting (Craske et al., 2005). BT and CBT have been used successfully to aid in benzodiazepine withdrawal for people with panic disorder (Otto et al., 1993).

Ethics and Responsibility

Critical Incident Stress Debriefing (CISD) is designed to prevent the development of PTSD by intervening very quickly after a traumatic event has occurred. Lasting three to four hours, CISD is typically a one-session treatment that is provided in a group session within 24 to 48 hours of the event (Lohr et al., 2003). During the session, group members are (1) encouraged to discuss and process the event, (2) told the PTSD symptoms that they are likely to experience, and (3) discouraged from leaving the meeting once the session has begun (Lilienfeld, 2007). Despite the goals of this rapid intervention technique, empirical data suggest that CISD may actually do more harm than good. Randomized controlled trials indicate that CISD not only is ineffective (Litz et al., 2002), but also in several instances has actually been harmful, with patients assigned to CISD exhibiting more PTSD or other anxiety symptoms at follow-up than the control groups do (Bisson et al., 1997; Mayou et al., 2000; Sijbrandij et al., 2006).

Interestingly, people who participate in CISD report that subjectively they feel better, even when objective measurement indicates the opposite. This contradiction can be explained by the concept of *resilience* (Lilienfeld, 2007) (see "Research Hot Topic: Trauma Grief, PTSD, and Resilience"). Most people exposed to a trauma do *not* develop PTSD. Therefore, most people assigned to CISD would not have developed PTSD even without any intervention. Furthermore, the fact that they did worse than the control group suggests that CISD may be interfering with the natural resilience process. Another intervention that was used in the past to treat children with PTSD was "rebirthing" therapy (see Chapter 15). No empirical evidence supports the use of this procedure, and its use has led to severe injury or death. As a result, rebirthing is not endorsed by mental health professionals who work with children (American Academy of Child and Adolescent Psychiatry, 2010). When therapists develop or provide interventions, it is crucial that the treatments work or at least not harm (or have the potential to harm) their patients. If the choice is between providing a potentially harmful treatment or doing nothing, psychologists should follow the words of the Hippocratic oath and "First, do no harm."

CONCEPT check

- Several different classes of medications are used for the treatment of anxiety, OCD, and traumatic disorders, but the first choice is the class known as the selective serotonin reuptake inhibitors (SSRIs).
- In addition to pharmacological treatments, other biological treatments for anxiety disorders exist. In severe cases of OCD when behaviour therapy and pharmacotherapy were not efficacious, neurosurgical treatments such as cingulotomy and capsulotomy may provide some symptom relief.
- The combination of psychological and pharmacological treatments for anxiety disorders does not produce an outcome that is superior to either intervention when used alone.

critical thinking question What is the common, and crucial, ingredient for behavioural and cognitive-behavioural therapy for anxiety disorders?

REAL science REAL life

Jack—The Psychopathology and Treatment of OCD

THE PATIENT

Jack, age 20, was living in his parents' garage apartment. He was unemployed but occasionally worked odd jobs in his father's business.

THE PROBLEM

Jack washed his hands at least 30 times a day and had rigid behavioural rituals for showering, dressing, shaving, and brushing his teeth. If interrupted during a ritual, he had to start all over again. His morning ritual lasted more than three hours each day. Jack was concerned that if he did not take care of his personal hygiene in exactly the right way, others would evaluate him negatively. To reduce his anxiety, Jack frequently checked his appearance in the mirror, glancing at his hands, clothing, and shoes to make sure everything was clean and neat. In total, he spent at least five hours a day doing cleaning and related checking rituals.

These symptoms took up so much time that Jack was unable to work. Furthermore, he was awkward in his social interactions. He had trouble carrying on a conversation, he fidgeted when he was talking to someone, and he was not able to look at people when interacting with them. When Jack came to the Anxiety Disorders Clinic, he spent most of his time alone.

Jack recalled that his parents also had problems with anxiety. As a child, he was shy, worried a great deal, and had some rigid behaviours, such as keeping all of his stuffed animals in a very specific order. His obsessive-compulsive (OC) symptoms became a serious problem when he moved away from home to attend university. He sought treatment at the university counselling centre, but weekly "talk therapy" just wasn't helping him. His grades continued to decline over three semesters, and he then moved back home.

TREATMENT

Jack's treatment involved three major components: (1) a trial of medication, (2) behaviour therapy to target OC symptoms, and (3) social skills training to improve his interpersonal functioning. He began treatment with a three-month trial of an SSRI, which improved his mood. He was able to reduce the time spent doing daily rituals to three hours a day. He then began exposure and response prevention. His therapist created situations in which he felt "exposed" to negative evaluation while at the same time preventing the compulsions that he used. During exposure sessions, Jack dressed in a way that he believed would produce negative evaluation from others (e.g., by choosing a shirt that wasn't a perfect match to his pants, "mussing" his hair slightly, pulling his tucked-in shirt up somewhat so that there was "extra" material showing) but would not make him look truly unusual. Jack was then asked to visit a public place (e.g., a bookstore, fast-food restaurant) where others would see him and to avoid "fixing" his appearance. At the start of each session, Jack's anxiety increased significantly. However, over the course of the session, his anxiety decreased even when his appearance was not "perfect." Jack also was asked to begin reducing the time he spent at home with daily grooming. He and his therapist prepared a schedule with time limits. At the end of the time limit, Jack had to stop, regardless of whether he was pleased with the result. Initially, this was extremely difficult. But with time, he further reduced the amount of time consumed with obsessions and compulsions. After another three months of treatment, Jack was able to get a part-time job working in a bookstore.

THE TREATMENT OUTCOME

The third phase of treatment sought to improve Jack's social functioning. Using social skills training, Jack practised making eye contact, conversing with strangers, and assuming a more relaxed body posture that put others more at ease.

As Jack's social skills improved, so did his mood. He made some acquaintances at work, and he even began to enjoy snack and lunch breaks with co-workers. Over time, Jack was able to increase his work hours, and he eventually obtained a full-time position as a manager in the bookstore.

summary

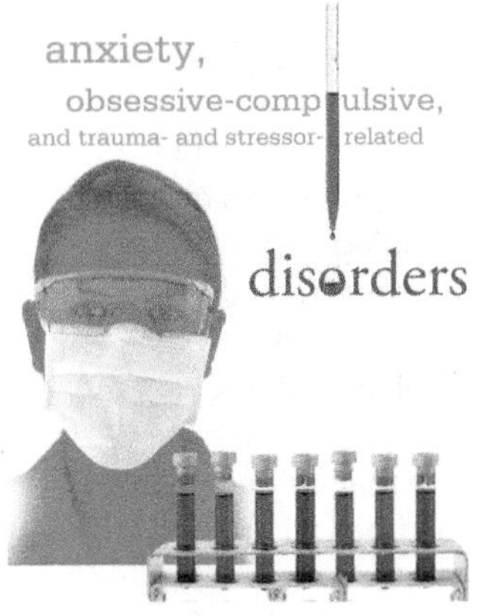

4.1 **Identify the three components of anxiety.** Anxiety consists of three components. The physiological components include sympathetic nervous system activation (e.g., cardiovascular and respiratory activation, gastrointestinal distress). The cognitive or subjective component consists of negative thoughts, impulses, or images and a subjective feeling of anxious distress. The behavioural component is defined by escape from or avoidance of objects, situations, or events that create anxious distress.

4.2 **Distinguish between a normal fear response and these anxiety-based disorders.** Anxiety is a common experience, and certain fears are common at various ages. However, to be considered an anxiety disorder, the fear or anxiety must cause significant distress or create functional impairment by interfering with common life activities.

4.3 **Understand how developmental and sociocultural factors affect the expression of anxiety.** A developmental hierarchy of anxious situations exists. This hierarchy is influenced by the child's cognitive maturity. Demographic factors such as gender, race/ethnicity, age, and socioeconomic status also influence the expression of anxiety. Women and girls seem to report fears at a rate much higher than men and boys, but sociocultural factors may also play a role.

4.4 **Describe the critical elements that comprise each of the different disorders.** Different types of anxiety disorders exist. Some, such as panic disorder with or without agoraphobia, consist of a fear of situations or places from which escape may be impossible if a panic attack occurs. People who have agoraphobia fear situations such as public transportation, open spaces, enclosed spaces, lines or crowds, or being outside of the home alone. In the case of social or specific phobias, the anxiety is restricted to specific situations. Generalized anxiety disorder is characterized by pervasive worry about many different situations. People with OCD suffer from intrusive thoughts and ritualistic behaviours that are distressing and difficult to control. After the occurrence of certain events such as a hurricane, rape, or other traumatic events, some people develop PTSD, which consists of intrusive thoughts of the event and physiological distress. Finally, separation anxiety is most commonly found in children and consists of anxiety surrounding separation from a caregiver.

4.5 **Identify biological and psychological factors related to the development of these disorders.** These disorders develop in many different ways. Results of studies in molecular genetics, neurochemistry, and neuroanatomy are now allowing researchers and clinicians to make advances in basic neuroscience and are providing unique insights into brain functioning. It is becoming clearer that anxiety and stress can alter brain chemistry and perhaps even some brain structures. In turn, these neuroanatomical and neurochemical alterations lead to the expression of anxiety disorders. With respect to psychological etiologies, sometimes a conditioning experience takes place that clearly indicates the etiology of the disorder. In most instances, however, the evidence is less clear, and a model that combines the influences of both biological and psychological/environmental factors may be the most appropriate.

4.6 **Identify pharmacological and psychological interventions used to treat these disorders.** The disorders discussed in this chapter are treatable. Pharmacological and behavioural/cognitive-behavioural interventions are both efficacious, but at this time, combining them does not appear to provide any increased benefit. It is unclear whether other interventions also may be efficacious because they have not been subjected to empirical scrutiny.

key terms

agoraphobia 121
anxiety 114
anxiety disorders 119
behavioural inhibition 153
body dysmorphic disorder 137
excoriation (skin picking) disorder 140
exposure 160
fight or flight 114
generalized anxiety disorder 123
heritability 150
hoarding disorder 139
obsessive-compulsive disorder 133
panic attack 116
panic disorder 120
parasympathetic nervous system 114
post-traumatic stress disorder 141
selective serotonin reuptake inhibitors (SSRIs) 157
separation anxiety disorder 132
social anxiety disorder 125
specific phobias 128
sympathetic nervous system 114
trait anxiety 150
trichotillomania 139
vasovagal syncope 130
worry 116

TEST yourself

1. The three elements of anxiety and fear are
   a. physiology, cognition, and behaviour
   b. self-report, arousal, and worry
   c. worry, anticipation, and subjective distress
   d. escape, avoidance, and subjective distress

2. Sally is extremely apprehensive about her meeting next week with her boss to discuss her annual performance review although she has been doing well at work. She is experiencing excessive
   a. panic reactions
   b. compulsions
   c. worry
   d. phobic discharge

3. Sam has a spider phobia, and he has not gone to the woodshed since his wife complained of all the cobwebs in there. He has responded behaviourally with
   a. arousal
   b. worry
   c. distress
   d. avoidance

4. A normal source of anxiety for a 1- to 2-year-old child is
   a. loss of physical support
   b. strangers
   c. heights
   d. being alone

5. Which of the following is a major factor in distinguishing between normal anxiety and an anxiety disorder?
   a. developmental age
   b. functional impairment
   c. sociodemographics
   d. all of the above

6. Which of the following statements about anxiety disorders is *not* true?
   a. Most anxiety disorders develop in early adulthood.
   b. Comorbidity with depression and other anxiety disorders is common.
   c. CBT is an efficacious treatment.
   d. Panic attacks may be a symptom of any anxiety disorder.

7. Heart palpitations (pounding heart or accelerated heart rate), sweating, trembling, shortness of breath, choking, chest pain, nausea, and dizziness are
   a. cognitive symptoms of panic attack
   b. behavioural symptoms of panic attack
   c. physiological symptoms of panic attack
   d. all of the above

8. Derealization or depersonalization (feelings of being detached from one's body or one's surroundings), fear of losing control or going crazy, and fear of dying are
   a. cognitive symptoms of panic attack
   b. behavioural symptoms of panic attack
   c. physiological symptoms of panic attack
   d. all of the above

9. Todd is afraid of flying. He is invited for a job interview that requires air travel. He has a panic attack while preparing for his interview a week before his flight. His panic attack is
   a. situationally bound
   b. situationally cued
   c. out of the blue
   d. uncued

10. Fear of situations such as public transportation, enclosed spaces, lines or crowds, and being outside of the home alone is termed
    a. panic disorder
    b. social anxiety disorder
    c. generalized anxiety disorder
    d. agoraphobia

11. For the past year, Maya has been experiencing uncontrollable worry about the future of her business, crime in the neighbourhood, whether her husband truly cares for her, and her children's health. All of these concerns are out of proportion to the actual situation. She may be experiencing
    a. panic disorder
    b. agoraphobia
    c. generalized anxiety disorder
    d. social anxiety disorder

12. Stuart has never had a romantic partner. When he talks with his therapist, he says that he is afraid to ask anyone out because he becomes extremely anxious about initiating and maintaining conversations. He likely has
    a. panic disorder
    b. agoraphobia
    c. generalized anxiety disorder
    d. social anxiety disorder

13. Which of the following is *not* one of the four groups of specific phobias?
    a. agoraphobia
    b. natural environment phobia
    c. blood/injection/injury phobia
    d. animal phobia

14. Jack can't leave home without checking the doors and windows repeatedly to see that they are locked. When he finds that everything is locked, a sense of relief comes over him. Which of the following learning principles is likely to be maintaining his compulsive checking behaviour?
    a. self-reinforcement
    b. negative reinforcement
    c. punishment
    d. positive reinforcement

15. Sergio served in Iraq and fought in several difficult battles. Now whenever he hears a car backfire, he jumps out of his chair thinking that he is under attack. Sergio is showing a classic symptom of PTSD called
    a. lethargy
    b. reoccurring and intrusive memories

c. re-experiencing
d. behavioural disinhibition

16. Although PTSD affects people of all ages, sexes, and ethnic backgrounds, it is slightly different in children because
    a. symptoms such as bedwetting may be prominent
    b. the trauma may not be experienced firsthand but through a significant other
    c. children experience fewer traumatic events than adults do
    d. children engage in traumatic play

17. Parents go to a clinical psychologist asking about their child who seems to worry all the time about being hurt. He refuses to go to school and won't sleep alone. On the way to school, he often develops stomachaches or headaches. The clinical psychologist is most likely to suggest that the child be evaluated for
    a. OCD
    b. PTSD
    c. separation anxiety disorder
    d. agoraphobia

18. The currently available data on the heritability of anxiety disorders suggest that
    a. a general vulnerability factor or anxiety proneness is what is inherited
    b. vulnerability to anxiety is likely to be controlled by a single gene
    c. genetic factors are only rarely involved in anxiety disorders
    d. four genetic factors are associated with GAD, panic disorder, and agoraphobia

19. Why do biological theories of anxiety disorders consider serotonin to be important?
    a. Serotonin is lower in the CSF of people with anxiety disorders.
    b. Biochemical challenges that alter serotonin levels are related to increases or decreases in feelings of anxiety.
    c. People who are prescribed SSRIs, which increase serotonin, report that their feelings of anxiety decrease.
    d. all of the above

20. The common ingredient in the most effective forms of behavioural and cognitive-behavioural treatments of anxiety is
    a. exposure
    b. restructuring
    c. relaxation
    d. imagery

Answers:
1 a, 2 c, 3 d, 4 b, 5 d, 6 a, 7 c, 8 a, 9 b, 10 d, 11 c, 12 d, 13 a,
14 b, 15 c, 16 d, 17 c, 18 a, 19 d, 20 a.

chapter 5

somatic symptom, dissociative, and factitious disorders

(top right): Andrzej Tokarski/Fotolia; (center): Roman Sigaev/zoom-zoom/Getty Images; (bottom): Caspar Benson/Getty Images; (bottom): krechet/Shutterstock

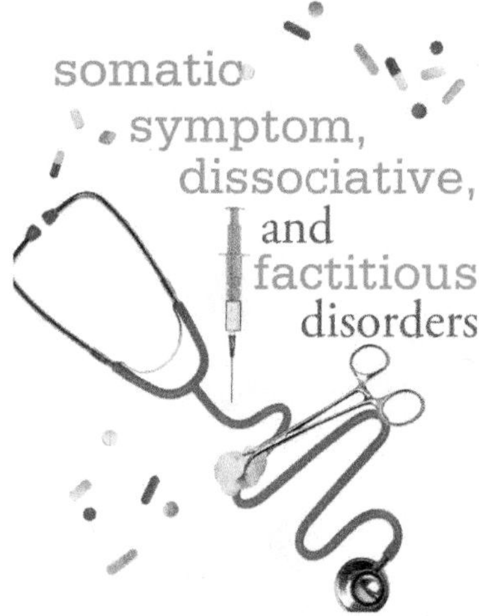

learning objectives

After reading this chapter, you should be able to:

5.1
Understand how normal physical sensations can create abnormal concerns about somatic functioning.

5.2
Differentiate somatic symptom, dissociative, and factitious disorders from malingering.

5.3
Identify the contributions of biological, psychological, and environmental factors to somatic symptom and related disorders.

5.4
Understand the elements of dissociative experiences and the role of sociocultural factors in dissociative disorders.

5.5
Differentiate between the posttraumatic and iatrogenic models of dissociative identity disorder.

5.6
Understand the controversy surrounding repressed/recovered memories.

Lucy, who is married and aged 40, feels awful. None of her doctors has helped her. About 12 years ago, she hurt her back while cleaning her house, and everything has gone downhill since then. She has constant lower back pain and periodic neck pain despite operations to fuse together parts of her spine. Her left arm aches, but her doctors can't find a cause. She has numerous prescriptions for pain, including the powerful drug oxycontin. She complains of blood in her urine and pain during sexual intercourse.

Although her physician did not think it necessary, Lucy had a hysterectomy to reduce excessive menstrual bleeding. Despite this surgery, she recently called her gynecologist, worried that she has uterine cancer (even though her uterus had been removed). Now she believes that she has severe asthma and allergies. She has been taken by ambulance to the hospital emergency room for breathing treatments and regularly uses two inhalers and three asthma medications. Yet allergy testing has revealed only moderate allergic reactions to pollen and dust mites. Several years ago, Lucy had extreme gastrointestinal pain. She complained of nausea, particularly after eating, and diarrhea. She sought out several physicians, but none could find anything wrong. After hearing that a friend had similar symptoms and had gall bladder surgery, Lucy convinced a physician that she too needed the surgery.

At the time of the psychological evaluation, Lucy had numbness in both legs. Her balance was affected, and she had difficulty walking. Last year, a niece was diagnosed with amyotrophic lateral sclerosis. Three physicians have told Lucy that she does not have amyotrophic lateral sclerosis, but she insisted on an MRI. Upon questioning by the psychologist, Lucy revealed contentious relationships with all of her family—her symptoms are always worse when she is fighting with her husband or her children.

Lucy's case is extreme, but we all have occasional aches and pains. In fact, 85% to 95% of the general population has at least one physical symptom every two to four weeks, and some people have unexplained symptoms as often as every five to seven days (Katon & Walker, 1998). According to a survey by Statistics Canada, as many as 5% of Canadians aged 12 years or old (i.e., over 1.2 million Canadians) suffer from chronic medically unexplained physical symptoms, which are associated with impaired daily functioning (Park & Knudson, 2007). Common physical complaints include chest pain, abdominal pain, dizziness, headache, back pain, and fatigue, yet an organic cause is identified only 10% to 15% of the time. Clearly, many people have physical complaints for which there is no identified medical basis. Usually, physician reassurance that "nothing is wrong" allows people to resume their normal activities.

A few people like Lucy resist physician reassurance. Her case poses a challenge for health care professionals. How does one determine when physical symptoms result from psychological distress rather than organic illness? According to researchers from McGill University (Kirmayer & Looper, 2007), this issue requires consideration of three interrelated questions. First, when are physical symptoms medically unexplained? Second, when is worry or distress about physical symptoms excessive? Third, when is physical distress considered to be caused primarily by psychological factors?

To answer the first question, physical complaints are considered to be medically unexplained when physical examination and diagnostic testing cannot determine any biological or physical cause. In Lucy's case, three different physicians could not diagnose her balance problems even when using the most sophisticated medical tests. Therefore, her symptoms were medically unexplained. To answer the second question, worry about physical health is excessive when it results in functional impairment or leads to medically unnecessary procedures (such as Lucy's gall bladder surgery). The answer to the third question—When does physical distress result from psychological factors rather than physical illness?—is much more complicated. Its answer is the focus of this chapter. In fact, the interplay of physical symptoms, environmental stress, and emotional distress can create different types of psychological impairments known as *somatic symptom and related disorders,* and *dissociative disorders.* We begin with the category of somatic symptom and related disorders.

Somatic Symptom and Related Disorders

5.1 Understand how normal physical sensations can create abnormal concerns about somatic functioning.

Somatic symptom and related disorders are characterized by excessive thoughts, feelings, and behaviours related to somatic symptoms. People who suffer from these disorders experience real physical symptoms, but their physical pain cannot be fully explained by an established medical condition. The somatic symptom category is a confusing diagnostic category because the individual disorders do not share an underlying emotion or a common etiology. Instead, people with somatic symptom and related disorders express thoughts, feelings, or behaviours in relation to the physical symptoms that seem out of proportion to the symptoms themselves. The specific disorders include somatic symptom disorder, illness anxiety disorder, conversion disorder, and factitious disorder. Each is described in this section.

Somatic Symptom Disorder

In 1859, the French physician Pierre Briquet (1796–1881) wrote an influential paper describing psychiatric patients with many somatic complaints that seemed to lack a physical cause. These patients were also likely to be depressed, and he noted that stressful life events could be particularly important in the onset and maintenance of their distress. This constellation of symptoms was once called *hysteria* or *Briquet's syndrome*, but these terms are no longer used because they carry negative connotations. Now known as **somatic symptom disorder**, the condition is defined as the presence of one or more somatic symptoms plus abnormal/excessive thoughts, feelings, and behaviours regarding the symptoms. It is important to note that the thoughts, feelings, and behaviours must be considered excessive or disproportionate to the symptoms. As Lucy illustrates, these physical complaints result in excessive health concerns and persistently high anxiety about one's health (see "DSM-5: Somatic Symptom Disorder"). Although any one symptom does not need to be consistently present, the presence of a symptomatic state is necessary.

There are no specific physical symptoms that are needed for the diagnosis of somatic symptom disorder, but some of the more common complaints include pain and gastrointestinal distress. Common pain complaints include back pain, chest pain, and headaches. Much less common but more dramatic are the *pseudoneurological* symptoms such as **psychogenic seizures**, which are sudden changes in behaviour that mimic epileptic seizures but have no apparent organic basis.

The French physician Pierre Briquet was first to identify a condition in which patients had many physical complaints without an obvious medical cause. This problem, once called Briquet's syndrome, is now called somatization disorder.

Rue des Archives / The Granger Collection

Conversion Disorder (Functional Neurological Symptom Disorder)

Somatic symptom disorder is defined by the presence of different physical symptoms, including pseudoneurological complaints. A different disorder, **conversion disorder**, consists of symptoms of altered motor or sensory function (See "DSM-5: Conversion Disorder"). Symptoms of conversion disorder can be quite dramatic, such as sudden paralysis or blindness. These symptoms are not intentionally produced and cannot be fully explained by the presence of any medical condition (see "Real Science, Real Life: Nancy—A Case of Conversion Disorder"). Before assigning this diagnosis, a careful medical evaluation is necessary because about 10% to 15% of people originally diagnosed with conversion disorder will later be found to have a diagnosable medical condition (Binzer & Kullgren, 1998; Hurwitz & Prichard, 2006). However, there is no way to determine which symptoms indicate

criteria for Somatic Symptom Disorder DSM-5

A. One or more somatic symptoms that are distressing or result in significant disruption of daily life.

B. Excessive thoughts, feelings, or behaviours related to the somatic symptoms or associated health concerns as manifested by at least one of the following:

1. Disproportionate and persistent thoughts about the seriousness of one's symptoms.
2. Persistently high level of anxiety about health or symptoms.
3. Excessive time and energy devoted to these symptoms or health concerns.

C. Although any one somatic symptom may not be continuously present, the state of being symptomatic is persistent (typically more than 6 months).

real SCIENCE real LIFE

Nancy—A Case of Conversion Disorder

THE PATIENT

Nancy, 55 years old, came to the psychiatric emergency room accompanied by her husband, George.

THE PROBLEM

Her complaint is as follows: "I have these fits and no one can find the cause." Nancy described the sudden onset of seizures during which she falls down and shakes uncontrollably. She does not lose consciousness, and the seizures do not result in any injury. As a matter of fact, when she "falls," she usually falls slowly into a chair or onto the couch, suggesting some degree of control over her body movements. The last physician who she saw gave her husband some syringes with "antiseizure" medication, which he uses to stop her seizures once they begin.

THE DIAGNOSTIC ASSESSMENT

After detailing the physical symptoms, the psychologist began to interview Nancy about her personal history. As a child, Nancy recalled her mother often taking her to the pediatrician. "My mother was very health conscious. She always worried about us when we were ill. If we had a fever or a headache, she would make us stay in bed, but she would stay in the room with us, playing games to keep us occupied. Once I was in the hospital to have my tonsils removed. This was before the time that parents were encouraged to stay in the hospital with their children. But my mother made such a fuss, the nurses let her stay. She showed me how much she loved me by refusing to leave me, even in the care of health professionals."

Nancy and George have been married for 35 years. She described her marriage as mediocre—she married George because she was pregnant. Her parents were both alcoholic, and as a child she was subjected to a great deal of emotional abuse. Marriage was her way of getting out. George and Nancy have six children. Nancy never worked; her life revolved around her children. As a matter of fact, Nancy and George had nothing in common but their children. Recently, the youngest child moved out of the house. Now there was no one but Nancy and George, a marriage without communication or affection.

When asked how George was responding to her seizures, Nancy's face brightened. "It's the funniest thing," she said. "Ever since my seizures developed, George has become really attentive. He hasn't been this nice since I was pregnant. And I've been really lucky—George has been there every time that I've had a seizure to give me my medication. As soon as I get the injection, my tremors disappear." George had brought one of the syringes to the meeting. When he gave it to the psychologist, she could clearly see the words "saline injection" on the side. In fact, Nancy's antiseizure medication was simply a placebo.

THE TREATMENT

The therapist determined that Nancy was suffering from conversion disorder and that a number of environmental and social factors were maintaining her condition. However, because Nancy was convinced that her symptoms had a physical cause, the psychologist did not attempt to convince her otherwise. First, she had Nancy keep a log of what was happening every time that she had a "seizure." It became clear that her seizures occurred after conflict with her husband, children, or sister. In most instances, the conflict centred on Nancy's inability to assert herself. Therefore, treatment focused on assertiveness training and general social skills training to increase her ability to express her wants and desires to her family. In addition, the therapist instructed George that when a seizure occurred, he should give Nancy her medicine but should not focus on or discuss the seizure in any way. This decreased family attention on this behaviour. The therapist also gave George and Nancy homework assignments to do one pleasant thing per week—having dinner out with friends, going to a movie, taking a French cooking class.

THE TREATMENT OUTCOME

After six months, Nancy's attacks had decreased from three times per week during the first month to only one in the past eight weeks. She reported some increased marital satisfaction and was getting along better with her adult children. Her sister remained the only source of distress, but Nancy vowed to continue to work on that relationship.

a true neurological disorder. Therefore, therapists must strike a balance between excluding possible medical conditions and overdiagnosing and thereby reinforcing the behaviour.

There are various types of symptoms of conversion disorder. The most common group includes *motor symptoms or deficits*, such as impaired coordination or balance, paralysis or weakness, tremor, gait abnormality, and abnormal limb posturing (APA, 2013). Within this group, muscle weaknesses, particularly in the leg, are most frequent (Krem, 2004). An unusual symptom is *globus*, which may include aphonia, sensations of choking, difficulty swallowing, shortness of breath, or feelings of suffocation (Finkenbine & Miele, 2004).

Hannah is a 28-year-old clerk at a car dealership. She has always been the "nervous" type and was very shy as a young girl. Sometimes when customers come in angry, complaining about their service, she starts to feel a lump in her throat. She puts her hand up to her throat like she is choking, and when people ask if she is okay, she gasps and says she can't get her breath. She gets more and more upset and is afraid she will suffocate. Sometimes the sensations go away. At other times, Hannah panics and calls her doctor.

In many instances, globus lasts only for a short period of time. However, if left untreated, it can lead to abnormal eating patterns or food avoidance.

Gina is 6 years old and has a history of fearful and inhibited behaviour. She was referred by her pediatrician because she developed a fear of choking on food. Several weeks ago she was in a crowd of people and told her mother that she was choking. She was not, but her mother could only calm her down by taking her out of the crowd. Since that time, Gina has complained of a sore throat and an inability to eat solid foods. Gina's pediatrician ruled out any medical cause. This past week, her entire food intake consisted of milk, milkshakes, mashed potatoes, and yogurt.

Sensory abnormalities, a less common symptom group, include loss of touch or pain sensations, double vision or blindness, deafness, and hallucinations (APA, 2013). Movies sometimes portray people as having "hysterical blindness," but this condition rarely occurs in real life. Also rare are *psychogenic seizures.*

Symptoms of conversion disorder do not follow known neurological patterns of the human body, a factor that is often important in differentiating between a psychological and a physical disorder. For example, a patient may complain of loss of sensitivity in the hand and wrist, a condition sometimes called *glove anesthesia* (see Figure 5.1). However, the nerves in the hand (median, ulnar, and radial nerves) do not suddenly end at the wrist. These nerves continue, uninterrupted, throughout the arm. Therefore, if one (or all) of the nerves were damaged, the loss of sensation would not stop at the wrist, but the numbness would continue up through the arm. In other words, physical anatomy

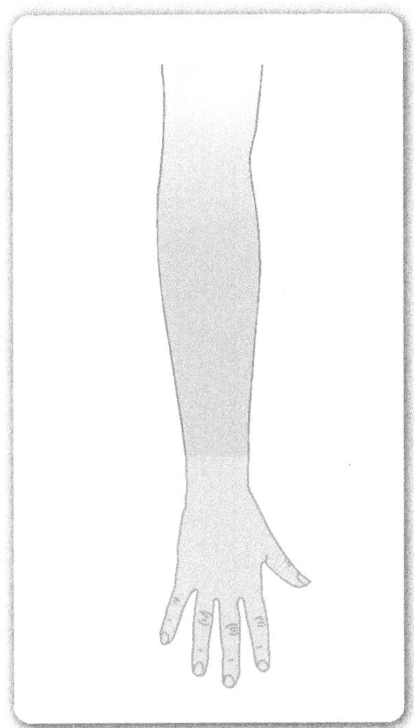

FIGURE 5.1

Glove Anesthesia. A person with conversion disorder might describe numbness in the entire hand or wrist, as shown here. However, the nerves that transmit pain signals do not stop at the wrist—they continue up the arm. Numbness that stops at the wrist is not anatomically possible.

Normal Behaviour Case Study

Major Illness Reaction: No Disorder

→ Sharlene was diagnosed with breast cancer. She had surgery, radiation, and chemotherapy. About six months after she finished treatment, she felt a nagging pain in her upper back. It was not a sharp pain, but rather a dull ache that would not go away. No matter what she did, the ache was there. Sharlene remembered that her mother, who had died from breast cancer, had pain in her back too. It turned out that her mother's cancer had metastasized to her bones. Sharlene was worried, and the doctor ordered a bone scan. The results indicated that she did not have bone cancer. The doctor thought that the pain was the result of a muscle strain or injury. Sharlene felt better after she heard the results. Although the pain was still there and at times kept her from sleeping, she no longer worried about it. After a few months, the pain disappeared.

Abnormal Behaviour Case Study

Somatic Symptom Disorder

→ Margaret married right out of high school and does not have any special vocational skills. She recently divorced and had to take a job in a hospital cafeteria, and she hates it. On some days, she works on the serving line—it is hot and her feet hurt from standing. On other days, she delivers food trays to patients—it is hard work, and the patients do not seem appreciative. At work one day, she slipped and fell. Although the physician cleared her to return to work, Margaret reported severe and chronic pain in her lower back and sometimes pain in her abdomen. An extensive diagnostic battery did not reveal any medical reason for her pain; yet it was so persistent that Margaret applied for disability. Her financial status was so negatively affected that she had to move in with her children.

cannot explain the symptom pattern of glove anesthesia. The lack of a medical reason for this phenomenon suggests that the symptoms could have a psychological basis.

The classic description of conversion disorder includes a symptom called *la belle indifference* (beautiful indifference), defined as substantial emotional indifference to the presence of these dramatic physical symptoms. Even when unable to walk or move their arms, some people appear undisturbed by their paralysis. They deny emotional distress from their unusual symptoms and behave as if nothing is wrong. However, some people with conversion disorder are distressed by their symptoms (Kirmayer & Looper, 2007); thus la belle indifference, though often present, is not a necessary symptom of conversion disorder.

The label *conversion disorder* may seem to be an unusual term for a psychological disorder. If you recall the case of Anna O (see Chapter 1), you will remember that she had many symptoms of this disorder. Psychodynamic theorists, such as Freud and Breuer, theorized that Anna O was not directly expressing her psychological distress (the stress of taking care of her invalid father and his subsequent death). Instead, it was expressed indirectly

criteria for Conversion Disorder DSM-5

A. One or more symptoms of altered voluntary motor or sensory function.

B. Clinical findings provide evidence of incompatibility between the symptom and recognized neurological or medical conditions.

C. The symptom or deficit is not better explained by another medical or mental disorder.

D. The symptom or deficit causes clinically significant distress or impairment in social, occupational, or other important areas of functioning or warrants medical evaluation.

through physical complaints. Simply stated, they thought that her psychological distress was *converted* into physical symptoms. Although there is no strong empirical support for this theory, the term *conversion disorder* is still used to describe the presence of these symptoms.

Illness Anxiety Disorder

Have you ever read about an illness and then worried that you might have it? You may have mentioned your worry to someone who reassured you that you were fine, and so your worry disappeared. However, when fears or concerns about having an illness persist despite medical reassurance, the problem may be **illness anxiety disorder** (APA, 2013). People with this disorder have a high level of worry about health and easily become alarmed about the possibility of having an illness (see "DSM-5: Illness Anxiety Disorder"). They are preoccupied with the possibility of having or developing a physical illness, and often elicit negative reactions from physicians because they cannot be reassured that they are well. Their behaviours are similar to the rituals found in obsessive-compulsive disorder (see Chapter 4). Some people with illness anxiety disorder constantly seek reassurance from physicians and monitor their own physical status (e.g., take their blood pressure). Other people with this disorder avoid situations associated with their fear (Taylor & Asmundson, 2004), such as refusing to go to a hospital for fear of catching an illness. In the past, people with these behaviours were said to have "hypochondriasis," and sometimes the person was called a "hypochondriac." However, because of the presence of these phobia-like behaviours, the disorder has been renamed *illness anxiety disorder.*

Not all worries about illness warrant a diagnosis of illness anxiety disorder. Some people suffer from *transient hypochondriasis*, which may result from contracting an actual acute illness or a life-threatening illness, or even from caring for someone with a medical condition (Barsky et al., 1990; Robbins & Kirmayer, 1996). Someone recovering from a heart attack may be reluctant to engage in physical activities, even though a physician has approved the activity. In contrast, people with traditional hypochondriasis (the previous term for illness anxiety disorder) have persistent fears of contracting an illness and are much more likely to have additional psychological diagnoses such as major depressive disorder or an anxiety disorder. The high rate of comorbid anxiety and depressive disorders (perhaps as high as 78%) led some clinicians and researchers to question whether

criteria for Illness Anxiety Disorder — DSM-5

A. Preoccupation with having or acquiring a serious illness.

B. Somatic symptoms are not present or, if present, are only mild in intensity. If another medical condition is present or there is a high risk for developing a medical condition (e.g., strong family history is present), the preoccupation is clearly excessive or disproportionate.

C. There is a high level of anxiety about health, and the individual is easily alarmed about personal health status.

D. The individual performs excessive health-related behaviours (e.g., repeatedly checks his or her body for signs of illness) or exhibits maladaptive avoidance (e.g., avoids doctor appointments and hospitals).

E. Illness preoccupation has been present for at least 6 months, but the specific illness that is feared may change over that period of time.

F. The illness-related preoccupation is not better explained by another mental disorder, such as somatic symptom disorder, panic disorder, generalized anxiety disorder, body dysmorphic disorder, obsessive-compulsive disorder, or delusional disorder, somatic type.

hypochondriasis (or illness anxiety disorder) exists as a separate disorder (Robbins & Kirmayer, 1996). If the disorder does exist alone, it does so in only approximately 23% of people with hypochondriasis.

Factitious Disorder

5.2 Differentiate somatic symptom, dissociative, and factitious disorders from malingering behaviour.

Factitious disorder differs from other somatic symptom disorders in one very important way: Physical or psychological signs or symptoms of illness are intentionally produced in what appears to be a desire to assume a sick role. Unlike **malingering**, in which a person intentionally produces physical symptoms to avoid military service, criminal prosecution, or work or to obtain financial compensation or drugs, for example, symptom production in factitious disorders is not associated with any external incentives. People are aware that they are producing the symptoms and making themselves ill, but appear to be unaware of *why* they do it. People with factitious disorder (see "DSM-5: Factitious Disorder") may produce primarily physical symptoms, primarily psychological symptoms, or both.

First described in 1951, factitious disorder was originally called *Munchausen syndrome*, named after Baron Karl Friedrich Hieronymus von Munchausen, an eighteenth-century German nobleman known for telling tall (and mostly false) tales. There are two types of factitious disorder. The first is **factitious disorder imposed on self**. People with factitious disorder imposed on self engage in deceptive practices to produce signs of illness. These behaviours include faking elevated body temperature, putting blood in urine to simulate kidney/urinary tract infections, or taking blood-thinning medications to produce symptoms of hemophilia. In addition, people with factitious disorder imposed on self deliberately and convincingly fake chest pain or abdominal pain. They will go through numerous invasive and dangerous diagnostic and therapeutic procedures. To convince physicians that they are physically ill, they manipulate laboratory results to substantiate their illness claims. Many of these manipulations are quite sophisticated, but Table 5.1 lists some of the simple things that patients do to convince health personnel that they are truly ill. Although they seek and often beg for medical intervention, they never reveal the fact that they are creating their own physical distress.

People with factitious disorder imposed on self (see "DSM-5: Factitious Disorder") often go to emergency rooms during evenings and weekends when they are more likely to be evaluated by junior clinical staff (Ford, 2005). Furthermore, they sometimes invent false demographic information, including aliases and false information

TABLE 5.1
Laboratory Results for Patients with Factitious Disorder

Presenting Complaint	Laboratory Evidence
Hematuria (blood in urine)	Red candy in urine sample
Nonhealing wound	Mouthwash found in wound
Diarrhea	Excessive ingestion of castor oil or laxatives
Pain from "kidney stones"	Glass fragments in urine
Anemia	"Self-induced" blood draws with substantial blood loss
Vomiting	Ipecac abuse

Source: From Krahn, L. E., Li, H., & O'Connor, M. K. (2003). Patients who strive to be ill: Factitious disorder with physical symptoms. *American Journal of Psychiatry, 160*, 1163–1168; and Wallach, J. (1994). Laboratory diagnosis of factitious disorders. *Archives of Internal Medicine, 154*, 1690–1696.

criteria for
Factitious Disorder **DSM-5**

Factitious Disorder Imposed on Self

A. Falsification of physical or psychological signs or symptoms, or induction of injury or disease, associated with identified deception.

B. The individual presents himself or herself to others as ill, impaired, or injured.

C. The deceptive behaviour is evident even in the absence of obvious external rewards.

D. The behaviour is not better explained by another mental disorder, such as delusional disorder or another psychotic disorder.

Factitious Disorder Imposed on Another (Previously Factitious Disorder by Proxy)

A. Falsification of physical or psychological signs or symptoms, or induction of injury or disease, in another, associated with identified deception.

B. The individual presents another individual (victim) to others as ill, impaired, or injured.

C. The deceptive behaviour is evident even in the absence of obvious external rewards.

D. The behaviour is not better explained by another mental disorder, such as delusional disorder or another psychotic disorder.

Note: The perpetrator, not the victim, receives the diagnosis.

about their past (such as claiming to be a former professional hockey player or having won some prestigious award). If hospital staff become suspicious, people with factitious disorder might get angry, threaten to sue the hospital, and leave.

Although most people with this disorder fabricate physical symptoms, some patients may fabricate psychological symptoms. Common psychological symptoms include grief and depression over the recent death of a relative, such as a spouse or a child. Later, the "dead" person turns out to be alive or has been dead for a very long time (Ford, 2005). People may also fake other psychological disorders, including multiple personality disorder (see "Real People, Real Disorders: Kenneth Bianchi, Patty Hearst, and Dr. Martin Orne" in Chapter 15), substance dependence, dissociative and conversion disorders, memory loss, and posttraumatic stress disorder.

The physicians were puzzled by 6-year-old Jenny's illnesses. The pieces just did not seem to fit together. Her mother had brought her to the emergency room at least once a month for the past year. Jenny complained of constant nausea, but there did not seem to be a medical reason. She had a multitude of gastrointestinal procedures—upper GI series, lower GI series, CT scans, and endoscopy. Her mother had taken her to seven different hospitals, and insisted on the same tests at each hospital. Jenny saw numerous specialists, and on many occasions, her mother insisted that Jenny be hospitalized. The medical staff became suspicious when Jenny's nausea disappeared upon hospitalization. Their first thought was that there was conflict between Jenny and her mother, and Jenny was experiencing severe anxiety. In children, stomachaches are a common symptom of anxiety. Jenny's mother became angry at the suggestion. She would not consider the possibility that Jenny's distress was psychological. On the latest visit to the emergency room, her mother brought in Jenny's bloody stool sample. The medical staff was informed by the lab that there was definitely blood in the stool—but it was not Jenny's blood type.

When one person induces illness symptoms in someone else, the disorder is known as **factitious disorder imposed on another**. In most instances, a mother produces physical symptoms in the child, as in Jenny's case. After inducing the symptoms, the mother brings the child to the hospital and gives permission, or sometimes insists that the child undergo invasive and dangerous diagnostic procedures. There are few data describing the child victims of this disorder, but what exist indicate that children range in age from infancy through the teenage years and can have many different symptoms, including apnea (the child stops breathing), anorexia/feeding problems, diarrhea, seizures, cyanosis (turning blue from lack of oxygen), behaviour problems, asthma, allergy, fevers, and pain (Sheridan, 2003). Child victims average 3.25 medical problems, ranging as high as 19 illnesses in a single child. Factitious disorder imposed on another, when proved, is considered a form of child abuse, and the parent can be prosecuted. Occasionally, this disorder also occurs in nursing homes, where health care personnel inflict these physical symptoms on adult residents.

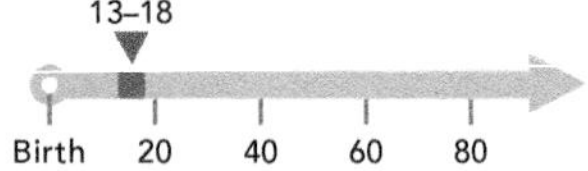

In factitious disorder imposed on another, which occurs more commonly in children than adults, someone else produces the physical symptoms.

A NOTE ABOUT SOMATIC SYMPTOM DISORDERS AND THE DSM-5 Because the DSM-5 is so new, there has not been an opportunity for researchers to collect data on many aspects of these conditions. Therefore, we do not yet know how to answer, for this particular group of disorders, the important questions that we ask throughout this text, including questions about epidemiology, functional impairment, developmental issues, etiology, or treatment. Throughout the rest of this chapter, we will rely on data that were collected using the prior diagnostic system (DSM-IV-TR). Because the names of the disorders were different in DSM-IV and we do not want to confuse the reader, we will not discuss the research by specific diagnostic categories. Rather, we will apply the old term, *somatoform disorders*, to refer to this entire diagnostic grouping, using data that were collected under the old diagnostic labels. As the new DSM-5 system begins to be used, these important questions will be addressed using the new diagnostic categories.

Patients with unexplained physical complaints are often seen in doctors' offices. They may even "doctor-shop" if they are told that their complaints have no medical cause.

Monkey Business Images/Shutterstock

Functional Impairment

Tje disorders in this group produce significant functional impairment. To illustrate, among patients with conversion disorder, only 33% maintained full-time employment (Crimlisk et al., 1998). Similarly, people with somatoform disorders worked fewer days per month (an average of 7.8 days) than people with no disorder (Gureje et al., 1997). These disorders also increase the likelihood of physical disability, occupational impairment, and overuse of health services (Aigner et al., 2003; Gureje et al., 1997.). Figure 5.2 illustrates some of the economic costs associated with these disorders.

In addition to causing functional impairment, these disorders have a complex and chronic course (Creed & Barsky, 2004; olde Hartman et al., 2009). Remission rates are likewise controversial. Early studies reported that less than 10% of people recover (Swartz et al., 1991), but more recent investigations report that between 30% and 50% of individuals recover one year later (Arnold et al., 2006; Creed & Barsky, 2004; olde Hartman et al., 2009). Conversion disorder may be a more acute condition with between

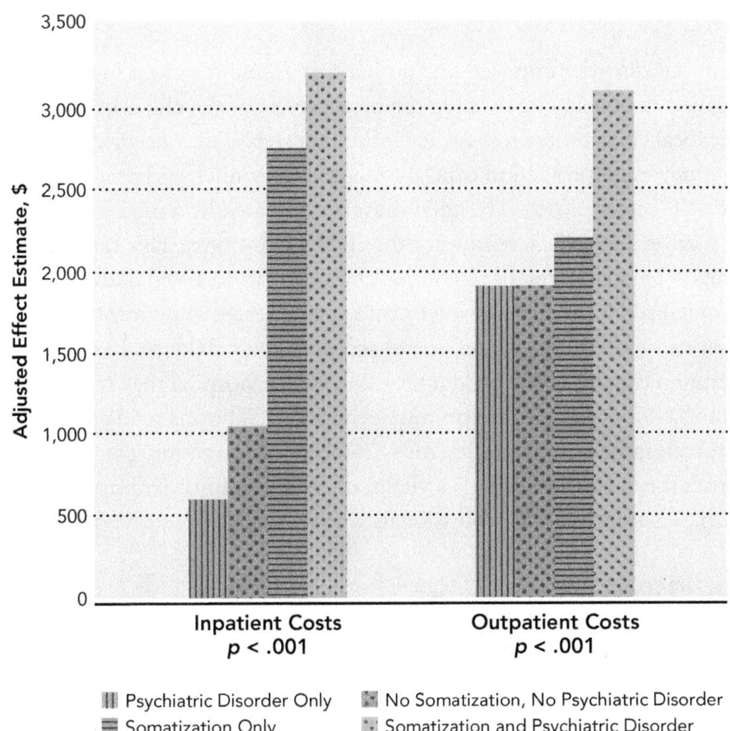

FIGURE 5.2

Somatization Increases Medical Use. As shown here, people with somatization disorder (DSM-IV) use more medical resources, and therefore have higher medical costs, than people with no disorders or people with psychiatric disorders (in this case, depression) alone. People with both mood disorders and somatization disorder have slightly higher costs than people with somatization alone.

Source: Based on Barsky et al. (2005), *Archives of General Psychiatry, 62*(8), pp. 903–910.

33% and 90% of patients remitted or significantly improved two to five years later (Binzer & Kullgren, 1998; Crimlisk et al., 1998; Kent et al., 1995). Of course, the more chronic cases are associated with increased functional impairment (Krem, 2004).

Although many physical complaints lack an organic basis, they still have an enormous impact on our medical system. Canadian research shows that patients with medically unexplained physical symptoms constitute 15% to 30% of all primary care visits (Kirmayer et al., 2004), and sometimes several different physicians evaluate the same patient complaint. People with physical symptoms often "doctor-shop" to find a physician who will provide a medical explanation, and in many instances, they receive different diagnoses from different medical specialists (Kirmayer & Looper, 2007). Some people remain unwilling to accept a psychological diagnosis; this leads to physician frustration, patient demoralization, and a continuing search for a physical explanation.

Doctor-shopping is just one example of how these disorders increase medical use and costs. Over a one-year period, people with somatoform disorders average significantly more primary care visits, more specialty care visits, more emergency room visits, and more hospital admissions, as well as higher inpatient and outpatient care costs, than the general population (Barsky et al., 2005; Robbins & Kirmayer, 1996). Determining a physical basis for these symptoms can be costly to the medical system, sometimes requiring extensive medical evaluation.

People with factitious disorder often have numerous hospitalizations and can develop medical conditions as a result of their self-administered injuries. For example, scar tissue may develop as a result of numerous surgical operations or self-injections. In addition, a phenomenon known as *peregrination* may occur, in which the patient seeks treatment at different hospitals and sometimes travels from place to place using false names. Factitious disorders are considered chronic, and although data from controlled trials are not available, it would appear that this disorder would affect social and occupational functioning.

Among child victims of factitious disorder imposed on another, 6% to 22% die as a result of the medical illnesses inflicted upon them, as do 25% of their siblings. The most common cause of death is suffocation or apnea (Ayoub et al., 2002; Sheridan, 2003). In one investigation (Sheridan, 2003), 7.3% of the child victims had long-term or permanent injuries.

Ethics and Responsibility

Because factitious disorder imposed on another may result in serious injury or death, psychologists have a responsibility to act in the best interest of the child. In these cases, a report to the local child protection agency is the first step. The investigation requires collaboration among child protection officials, medical personnel, and psychological professionals (Day & Moseley, 2010). The child must be evaluated by a medical specialist to ensure that there is no medical reason for the child's symptoms. This can often be difficult as parents often use different physicians and hospitals to avoid detection. Sometimes a child is hospitalized in order to observe symptom patterns, as symptoms often disappear when parents can no longer have unfettered access to their children. In other instances, video observation of parent and child interactions in the hospital may reveal the parent engaging in behaviours designed to produce symptoms. Whereas medical professionals and child protection personnel may be most involved in determining whether the child has a legitimate medical disorder or is a victim of factitious disorder imposed on another, mental health personnel are the professionals who attempt to treat the offending parent.

Epidemiology

In Canada and the United States, about 15% to 20% of the general population reports worrisome physical symptoms that have no apparent organic basis (Faravelli et al., 1997; Grabe et al., 2003; Park & Knudson, 2007). There are no known epidemiological data on the prevalence of factitious disorders in the general population. Among patients referred to one psychiatric consultation liaison service, 0.8% of referrals over a 20-year period had factitious disorder (Sutherland & Rodin, 1990). At children's hospitals, the annual incidence was 2/100 000 or 0.002% (McClure et al., 1996, in Ford, 2005).

research HOT topic

The Challenge of Chronic Fatigue Syndrome

Chronic fatigue syndrome (CFS) is a seriously disabling disorder that has puzzled the medical community for many years. The original medical diagnosis published in 1988 lacked validity because it did not differentiate CFS from other types of unexplained fatigue, leading health professionals to call it a somatoform disorder. Revisions to the diagnostic criteria now yield a more reliable and valid diagnostic condition, requiring (1) severe chronic fatigue for at least six months with no known medical condition, and (2) four or more of the following symptoms: substantial impairment in short-term memory or concentration; sore throat; tender lymph nodes, muscle pain, multi-joint pain without swelling or redness; headaches of a new type, pattern, or severity; unrefreshing sleep; and postexercise tiredness lasting more than 24 hours.

Despite the increasing recognition of the disorder, some people with CFS cannot convince others that they suffer from a real medical condition; many people still consider it a psychosomatic illness. The cause of CFS remains unknown despite intensive research efforts. Many potential causes, including viruses, immunological dysfunction, cortisol dysregulation, autonomic nervous system dysfunction, and nutritional deficiencies, have been investigated and ruled out.

Researchers continue to focus on a viral etiology because typical findings on blood tests suggest the presence of a viral infection. Recently, one investigative group reported that about 10% of people who contract the Ross River virus will develop CFS. Of course, this means that 90% of those with the virus will not. Other researchers have found similar results with Epstein-Barr virus, GB virus, human retroviruses, human herpes virus 6, enteroviruses, rubella, and *Candida albicans*. In each case, a few individuals with CFS may have the virus, but the relationship is small and not statistically significant, as was recently demonstrated for xenotropic murine leukemia virus (Switzer et al., 2010).

Researchers are continuing to pursue possible etiological factors, and they now believe that CFS may not have a single cause, but may instead represent the final outcome of multiple precipitating somatic or psychological factors that act in combination, including viral infections, psychological stress, and toxins.

Sex, Race, and Ethnicity

Because these disorders are rare, we have very limited data on their interplay with variables such as sex, race, and ethnicity. We do know that more women endorse the presence of somatoform disorders more frequently than men (Creed & Barsky, 2004; Kroenke & Spitzer, 1998). The disorders appear to occur equally across racial and ethnic groups (Swartz et al., 1991).

Although few data are available, factitious disorder is more likely to occur in women. Compared with men with the disorder, women in one sample were younger and more likely to have had health care training or health care jobs (Krahn et al., 2003). By contrast, those with the most severe forms of the disorder, including symptoms of peregrination and the adoption of aliases, are more likely to be male. Among people with factitious disorder imposed on another, 77% to 98% are women, typically the child's biological mother, although fathers and foster mothers are also occasional perpetrators (Ayoub, 2006). There are no data available on race or ethnicity.

As we noted earlier, people with these disorders often reject psychological explanations for their symptoms. They believe that professionals are denying their real pain. Such patients may be more likely to accept a sociocultural rather than a psychological explanation. When physicians discuss patients' physical distress in terms of family and community problems, patients are more likely to acknowledge that stress, social conditions, and emotions can affect their physical status (Kirmayer et al., 2004).

Developmental Factors

Diagnostic criteria for these disorders are the same in children and adolescents as in adults, but the data that do exist indicate that somatoform disorders are rare before adulthood (Finkenbine & Miele, 2004; Kozlowska et al., 2007). As in adults, voluntary motor dysfunction is most common, followed by sensory dysfunction and psychogenic seizures (Kozlowska et al., 2007). Factitious disorder imposed on self is most common in adults, but it does exist among children and adolescents as well. In one sample (Libow, 2000), children with the disorder ranged in age from 8 to 18, and 70% were female. Children most commonly produce symptoms such as fever (heating the thermometer to fake a fever), diabetic insulin insufficiency (deliberately manipulating their insulin levels), bruises, and infections.

Etiology

5.3 Identify the contributions of biological, psychological, and environmental factors to somatic symptom and related disorders.

How these disorders develop is poorly understood. Biological factors would seem to play a role, particularly when distorted perceptual processes exist. Yet few controlled trials have examined biological causes. Twin research at the University of British Columbia suggests that illness anxiety, assessed on a continuum from mild to severe, is caused by a combination of genetic and environmental factors (Taylor et al., 2008). However, little is specifically known about the etiology of the DSM-5 diagnostic categories of somatoform disorders.

PSYCHOSOCIAL FACTORS Psychodynamic explanations propose that these disorders result from intrapsychic conflict, personality, and defence mechanisms. From a psychodynamic perspective, Anna O (Chapter 1) most likely had conversion disorder. She was probably emotionally stressed and possibly resentful because of the need to care for her father and because of his subsequent death. Anna O's psychological distress was unacceptable to her superego, and therefore her negative feelings were repressed and converted into physical symptoms—hence, use of the term *conversion disorder* to describe this condition.

Modern-day researchers do not invoke psychodynamic constructs, but empirical data do support the hypothesis that children and adults who complain of physical aches and pains have more negative emotions. More importantly, these children and adults are also more likely to have poor self-awareness of the presence of these emotions and are less able to regulate (change) their emotional state (Gilleland et al., 2009). Perhaps these children and adults are less psychologically minded and do not understand the relation between emotional stress and its effects on physical functioning (for more on this relation, see Chapter 14). Not recognizing the impact of stress, they worry that their somatic symptoms have a medical cause.

Behavioural principles of modelling and reinforcement may also contribute to the development of illness behaviour. Compared with healthy mothers, mothers with a somatoform disorder paid more attention to their children when they played with a medical kit than when they played with a tea set or ate a snack (Craig et al., 2004). This increased attention may lead to an increase in medical concerns, medical tests, or medical procedures in their children. Similarly, the more often adolescent girls were reinforced for expressing complaints about menstrual illness, the more often they had menstrual symptoms and disability days as adults. Also, childhood reinforcement of cold illness

examining the EVIDENCE

Is Childhood Sexual Abuse Associated with DSM-IV Somatoform Disorders?

- **The Evidence** Somatoform disorders (DSM-IV) have been linked to physical and sexual abuse early in life (e.g., Bowman & Markand, 1996; Brown et al., 2005). Some theorists have used these observations to propose a causal relationship between abuse and these disorders. What is the validity of this relationship?
- **Let's Examine the Evidence.**
- **What Types of Research Designs Were Used in These Investigations?** The idea that physical and sexual trauma might lead to the development of somatic symptom and related disorders is based on studies of patients who already have the disorder. Only rarely is a control group of people with no disorder or another disorder included in the research design. Another consideration is that these studies use correlational designs, and the data derived from them cannot support causality. In fact, two large prospective (longitudinal) studies challenge the association between these disorders and sexual/physical abuse (Linton, 2002; Raphael et al., 2001). First, among adults with no history of back pain, self-reported history of *physical* abuse (not *sexual* abuse) predicted the development of back pain one year later. However, no relationship existed between physical or sexual abuse and the emergence of *new* pain when the person had back pain at baseline (Linton, 2002). In a second study, children who had documented histories of early childhood abuse or neglect (n = 676) were compared with controls with no history of abuse (n = 520; Raphael et al., 2001). When assessed as adults, physically and sexually abused and neglected individuals were *not* at risk for increased pain symptoms compared with controls. These prospective studies suggest that the previous correlational relationship between sexual and/or physical abuse and somatoform disorders may be simply a result of biased self-report based on retrospective data.
- **What Other Factors Might Explain the Correlational Relationship?** In many instances, abusive acts occur in family environments that have high levels of conflict, hostility, and aggression, as well as parent–child interactions that are cold, rejecting, or neglectful of children (Repetti et al., 2002). We know that these chronic stressors are related to abnormal neuroendocrine responses in the hypothalamic-pituitary-adrenal (HPA) axis (see Chapter 4), and this dysregulation may result in multiple somatic complaints (Heim et al., 2000).
- **What Evidence for This Relationship Exists?** A carefully designed study not only examined the presence of physical and sexual abuse among people with these disorders, but also measured hostile and rejecting family environments. The study did not find a relationship between abuse and somatic symptoms, but did document an association between hostility/rejection by fathers and somatoform disorders in the children (Lackner et al., 2004).
- **Conclusion** Family environments characterized by high conflict, hostility, and rejection may lead to a dysregulation of the neuroendocrine system that mediates stressful responses in the body. How could a chronic negative environment (in which abusive acts are more likely to occur) lay the foundation for the potential development of somatization symptoms and somatoform disorders?

behaviour significantly predicted cold symptoms and disability days for adults (Whitehead et al., 1994). In summary, there is evidence for the theory that reinforcing somatizing behaviours may increase the future likelihood of somatic complaints.

Other environmental factors also are associated with physical symptoms, distress, and somatoform disorders. Among adults, stress was temporally associated with 72% of these disorders. In contrast, a history of sexual abuse was present in 28% of the cases (Singh & Lee, 1997). Among children (Kozlowska et al., 2007), family separation/loss was associated with the onset of the disorder in 34% of the cases. Family conflict/violence was associated in 20% of the cases, and sexual assault correlated in only 4%. The relationship between these disorders and childhood sexual abuse is controversial (Alper et al., 1993; Coryell & Norten, 1981; see "Examining the Evidence: Is Childhood Sexual Abuse Associated With DSM-IV Somatoform Disorders?").

Despite much speculation about the etiology of factitious disorders, few empirical data exist. Nonspecific neuroanatomical abnormalities have been reported in isolated cases, but in addition to the absence of studies that include experimental controls, the findings are not consistent (Eisendrath & Young, 2005). Among the psychological theories, psychodynamic models explain factitious disorder as (1) an attempt to gain mastery or control that was formerly elusive; (2) a form of masochism (where pleasure occurs as a result of physical or psychological pain inflicted by oneself or another person); (3) the result of a deprived childhood, in which a child did not receive attention or care; or (4) an attempt to master trauma that was experienced as a result of physical or sexual abuse, with the physician unknowingly assuming the symbolic role of the abuser (Eisendrath & Young, 2005).

From a behavioural perspective, factitious behaviours are maintained because other people positively reinforce the person's illness behaviours or expressions. The attention garnered from these illnesses is a powerful reinforcer. From a cognitive perspective, people with factitious disorders, through biased cognitive processes, misinterpret normal physical processes as indicators of physical illness; this cognitive perspective is similar to the hypotheses put forth to explain the etiology of somatoform disorders.

Distorted cognitions may also play a role in the development of these disorders, perhaps from a cognitive process called *somatic amplification* (Barsky & Klerman, 1983), a tendency to perceive bodily sensations as intense, noxious, and disturbing. How this amplification occurs is unclear. This theory suggests that some people have heightened sensory, perceptual, or cognitive-evaluative processes that make them more sensitive to the presence of physical symptoms. This is an interesting theory, but few studies have assessed exactly how these perceptual processes contribute to the onset of somatoform disorders.

Other cognitive theories propose that somatoform disorders develop from inaccurate beliefs about the (1) prevalence and contagiousness of illnesses, (2) meaning of bodily symptoms, and (3) course and treatment of illnesses (Salkovskis, 1989). For example, someone with hypochondriacal fears about contracting breast cancer may hold inaccurate beliefs about the illness, such as

- so many women get breast cancer, it must be some type of unidentified virus,
- a pain in my chest is a signal that I may have breast cancer, and
- I have had this pain for some time.

The cancer is probably throughout my body and no treatment will help me.

These beliefs may be activated by hearing or reading about breast cancer or after perceiving vague bodily sensations. As a result, the person becomes hypervigilant and worried about having, and perhaps dying from, the illness (Rode et al., 2001). Cognitive theories propose that it is not the symptoms but how the symptoms are interpreted that leads to the development of somatoform disorders. Although it is not clear how a person acquires these beliefs, they may result from the reinforcement and modelling theories discussed previously.

AN INTEGRATIVE MODEL Understanding the interplay between psychological and somatic factors can be quite complicated. As we noted at the beginning of this chapter, transient aches and pains and bodily disturbances occur every day: You get a headache, a fleeting pain, or an upset stomach. The reason is not necessarily clear—perhaps you are unknowingly allergic to a certain food. Whatever the reason, your symptoms exist. Whether or not you pay attention to your symptoms depends on their intensity and your learning history, including learning to interpret bodily symptoms as signs of a serious illness. The smallest sensation or change in your physical state may cause you to focus more intently on your body, looking for confirmation that something is wrong. Perhaps sensations such as ringing in your ears cause you to worry. If the ringing continues for some time, you may begin to worry intensely that something is wrong ("What if I have a brain tumour?"). This is normal illness behaviour, and you may decide to see a physician.

A crucial factor is whether the physician's response reassured you ("There is no brain tumour") or whether you continue to worry, even though medical tests and physicians cannot find a reason for your distress. If you do continue to worry, your distress may become so severe that you change your lifestyle. Depending on your own cognitive schemas and learning history, your friends and family may support your "sick role" behaviour, or they may suggest that you are a hypochondriac. The medical profession may also influence whether or how much you worry. If the physician conducts excessive or invasive testing, this may reinforce your belief that something is seriously wrong with you. When treating people with somatoform disorders, health care professionals must carefully convey their understanding of the physical distress, yet help the patient understand the role of psychological stress in creating physical symptoms. Doing this successfully is the first step in the treatment of these disorders.

Treatment

The first challenge in obtaining treatment is the reluctance of people with somatic symptom disorders to reveal their worries to a professional. As noted earlier, a major challenge to successful treatment is the belief of many sufferers that they do not have a psychological disorder. They emphasize their physical symptoms and often resist a psychological intervention (Arnold et al., 2006).

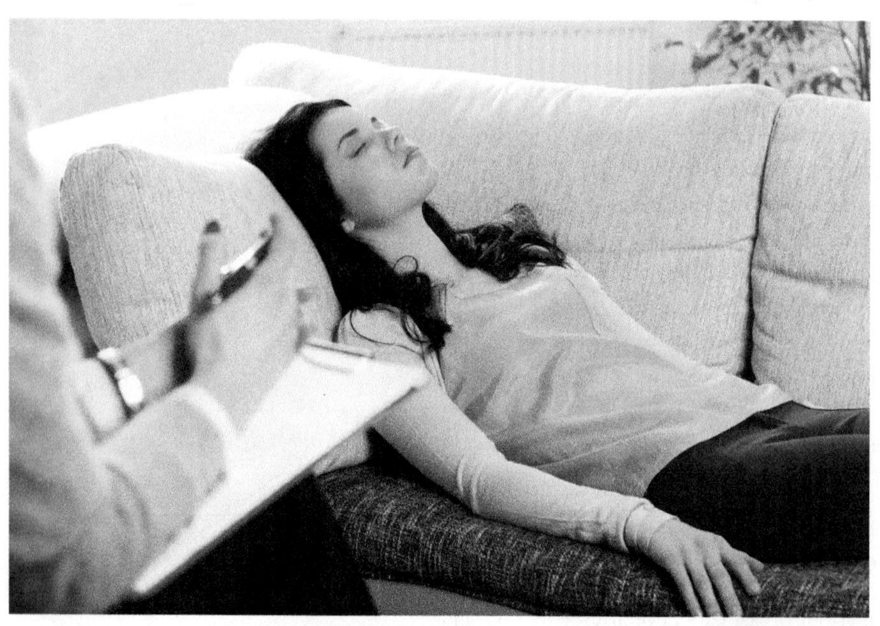

A patient undergoes relaxation training as part of cognitive-behaviour therapy. Relaxation helps the patient cope with troubling thoughts about the body and its symptoms.

alexsokolov/Fotolia

In some cases, basic education about the interplay of physical and emotional factors may reduce the symptoms and distress associated with these disorders. Symptom-focused cognitive-behaviour therapy (CBT) also may be helpful. As we noted earlier, people resist the notion that psychological factors play an important role in symptom onset or maintenance. Therefore, treatment focuses on teaching patients to cope with their symptoms by emphasizing how current psychological and social factors affect their symptoms without forcing people to accept a psychological basis for their disorder.

CBT includes engaging in relaxation training, diverting attention away from the physical symptoms, and correction of automatic thoughts. Similarly, because these disorders are considered to result, at least in part, from environmental and personal stressors, teaching patients strategies to reduce stress may lessen their distress and lower the costs associated with their health care. To date, no controlled trials of CBT for conversion disorder have been undertaken, but a three-pronged approach is recommended: withdrawal of medical and social attention directed at the abnormality, physical and occupational therapy to retrain normal gait and movements, and psychotherapy to help the patient cope with stress (Krem, 2004). Similar behavioural approaches have been used to treat globus hystericus (Donohue et al., 1997).

CONCEPT check

- Physical complaints are common and in many instances do not indicate the presence of a medical disorder.
- In some people, physical complaints that are severe, persistent, and without an organic basis may indicate the presence of a somatic symptom or related disorder. These can involve many different bodily systems (somatic symptom disorder), one particular symptom (conversion disorder), worry that one might have contracted a certain disease (illness anxiety disorder), or the production of physical symptoms in order to assume the sick role (factitious disorder).
- Although isolated physical symptoms without an organic basis are common among the general population, few people (either adults or children) will probably meet strict diagnostic criteria for somatic symptom and related disorders. This limits our ability to understand the etiology of these disorders or to have large enough samples to conduct randomized, controlled trials to examine efficacious treatments.
- Despite our limited knowledge, we do know that the development of these disorders is quite complex and includes physical, psychological, and environmental factors.

critical thinking question How could paying more attention to a toddler playing with a medical kit and ignoring play at other times contribute to the development of a somatic symptom disorder?

Dissociative Disorders

5.4 Understand the elements of dissociative experiences and the role of sociocultural factors in dissociative disorders.

Perhaps no more controversial diagnostic group exitss than the dissociative disorders. In fact, many health care professionals question the validity of the diagnostic category. To illustrate, only 14% of Canadian psychiatrists and 25% of American psychiatrists believe that strong scientific evidence supports the diagnosis (Lalonde et al., 2001; Pope et al., 1999). These different percentages may reflect where mental health professionals work or the specific way in which the question is asked. However, as you will see, the issues run much deeper and have generated many interesting and heated debates.

In general, **dissociative disorders** involve a disruption in the usually integrated functions of consciousness, memory, identity, emotion, perception, body representation, motor control, and behaviour (APA, 2013). But what does this mean? Have you ever been so engrossed in reading something that you suddenly looked up and were startled to see your friend standing right in front of you? You were concentrating so hard that you were briefly unaware of your surroundings, a situation similar to a dissociative experience.

Actually, five types of dissociative experiences exist (Gleaves et al., 2001; Steinberg et al., 1993). *Depersonalization* is a feeling of detachment from one's body—experiencing the self as strange or unreal. Some people describe this feeling as if they were floating above their own body, watching themselves behave. *Derealization* is a feeling of unfamiliarity or unreality about one's physical or interpersonal environment. People describe feeling as if they were in a dream. *Amnesia* is the inability to remember personal information or significant periods of time. It is more than simply forgetting a name, where you put your keys, or what you had for dinner last Thursday night. *Identity confusion* describes being unclear or conflicted about one's personal identity. Finally, *identity alteration* describes overt behaviours indicating that one has assumed an alternate identity (Steinberg et al., 1993).

Isolated episodes of dissociation do not always indicate the presence of a dissociative disorder (e.g., Holmes et al., 2005b). Your engrossment in your work is known as *absorption*, defined as fully engaging all your perceptual resources on one item so that you are no longer attending to other aspects of the environment. Experiences such as absorption are common, and 46% to 74% of people without psychological disorders experience occasional episodes of derealization and depersonalization (Hunter et al., 2005). Furthermore, dissociative symptoms may occur in people with panic disorder, obsessive-compulsive disorder, agoraphobia, posttraumatic stress disorder, depressive disorder, bipolar disorder, and eating disorders (Holmes et al., 2005b). When dissociative experiences are temporary, such as your momentary period of absorption, they create minimal, if any, distress. However, when they develop into chronic conditions, they are called *dissociative disorders* (see "DSM-5: Dissociative Disorders").

Dissociative Amnesia

Have you ever awakened in the morning and for a moment been unable to recognize your surroundings? Or have you ever found yourself driving and for a moment could not remember passing familiar landmarks? Your momentary forgetting/distraction may help you understand the concept of **amnesia**. This condition has many causes, including head injuries, epilepsy, alcoholic "blackouts," and low blood sugar. A temporary state of amnesia may also occur after a stroke or seizure, after electroconvulsive therapy (ECT) for depression, or as a result of drug toxicity or global dementia. Therefore, a medical evaluation must always be the first step in the diagnostic process.

Dissociative amnesia is an inability to recall important information, usually of a personal nature (see "DSM-5: Dissociative Disorders"). When it occurs following a stressful or traumatic event, its cause is considered psychological, not biological. Several types of dissociative amnesia can occur. Failure to recall events that occur during a certain period of time is known as *localized amnesia*, whereas *generalized amnesia* is a total inability to recall any aspect of one's life. A third type of amnesia is *selective amnesia*, in which the person forgets some elements of a traumatic experience. Dissociative amnesia is considered a reversible condition, and in many instances, people can later recall events, or parts of events, that they could not previously describe.

In some instances, dissociative amnesia is accompanied by **dissociative fugue**, which is defined as apparently purposeful travel or bewildered wandering that is associated with identity amnesia (APA, 2013). People with this disorder are found in a physical location away from their usual residence. *Fugue* means *flight*. Fugue states may be associated with physical or mental traumas, depression, or legal problems (Kihlstrom, 2001). Patients in a fugue state may seek treatment if they become aware of their loss of personal identity and memory or if they come to the attention of the police.

Christine Costner-Sizemore, the real "Eve" portrayed in the famous film *The Three Faces of Eve*.

Newscom

Dissociative Identity Disorder

In 1957, Hollywood released the film *The Three Faces of Eve* based on a nonfiction book of the same name. In the book and movie, Eve White is a housewife and mother, but when she is hypnotized as part of her psychotherapy, her psychiatrist discovers an alternate personality, Eve Black, who is outgoing and socially engaging, exactly the opposite of Eve White. Later, a third personality, Jane, emerges. Although the book and movie contain a number of factual inaccuracies, the real Eve, Christine Costner-Sizemore, was able to integrate her personalities. *The Three Faces of Eve* introduced the term *multiple personality disorder*, now called **dissociative identity disorder (DID)**.

Another example of DID is found in the book *Sybil*, which was published in 1976. The book and the movie based on it chronicled the treatment of a young woman who seeks therapy for blackouts and nervous breakdowns. In therapy, the psychiatrist "discovers" that Sybil has 16 different personalities (also known as *alternative personalities*,

criteria for Dissociative Disorders — DSM-5

Dissociative Amnesia

A. An inability to recall important autobiographical information, usually of a traumatic or stressful nature, that is inconsistent with ordinary forgetting.

Note: Dissociative amnesia most often consists of localized or selective amnesia for a specific event or events; or generalized amnesia for identity and life history.

B. The symptoms cause clinically significant distress or impairment in social, occupational, or other important areas of functioning.

C. The disturbance is not attributable to the physiological effects of a substance (e.g., alcohol or other drug of abuse, a medication) or a neurological or other medical condition (e.g., partial complex seizures, transient global amnesia, sequelae of a closed head injury/traumatic brain injury, other neurological condition).

D. The disturbance is not better explained by dissociative identity disorder, posttraumatic stress disorder, acute stress disorder, somatic symptom disorder, or major or mild neurocognitive disorder.

Dissociative Identity Disorder

A. Disruption of identity characterized by two or more distinct personality states, which may be described in some cultures as an experience of possession. The disruption in identity involves marked discontinuity in sense of self and sense of agency, accompanied by related alterations in affect, behaviour, consciousness, memory, perception, cognition, and/or sensory-motor functioning. These signs and symptoms may be observed by others or reported by the individual.

B. Recurrent gaps in the recall of everyday events, important personal information, and/or traumatic events that are inconsistent with ordinary forgetting.

C. The symptoms cause clinically significant distress or impairment in social, occupational, or other important areas of functioning.

D. The disturbance is not a normal part of a broadly accepted cultural or religious practice.

Note: In children, the symptoms are not better explained by imaginary playmates or other fantasy play.

E. The symptoms are not attributable to the physiological effects of a substance (e.g., blackouts or chaotic behaviour during alcohol intoxication) or another medical condition (e.g., complex partial seizures).

Depersonalization/Derealization Disorder

A. The presence of persistent or recurrent experiences of depersonalization, derealization, or both:

1. *Depersonalization:* Experiences of unreality, detachment, or being an outside observer with respect to one's thoughts, feelings, sensations, body, or actions (e.g., perceptual alterations, distorted sense of time, unreal or absent self, emotional and/or physical numbing).
2. *Derealization:* Experiences of unreality or detachment with respect to surroundings (e.g., individuals or objects are experienced as unreal, dreamlike, foggy, lifeless, or visually distorted).

B. During the depersonalization or derealization experiences, reality testing remains intact.

C. The symptoms cause clinically significant distress or impairment in social, occupational, or other important areas of functioning.

D. The disturbance is not attributable to the physiological effects of a substance (e.g., a drug of abuse, medication) or another medical condition (e.g., seizures).

E. The disturbance is not better explained by another mental disorder, such as schizophrenia, panic disorder, major depressive disorder, acute stress disorder, posttraumatic stress disorder, or another dissociative disorder.

or *alters*). The psychiatrist hypothesizes that these alters are the result of extreme physical and sexual abuse, what most people would describe as torture, by her mother, who suffered from schizophrenia.

The case of Sybil proved highly controversial. Sybil, whose real name was Shirley Mason, was treated by a psychoanalyst named Cornelia Wilbur. Mason's subsequent therapist, Herbert Spiegel, came to the opinion that Mason was highly suggestable and that Wilbur had, in a sense, created Mason's multiple personalities by suggesting them to her. For example, Wilbur had apparently taught Mason to refer to a particular feeling as representing the personality "Helen" (Borch-Jacobsen & Spiegel, 1997). In other words,

Spiegel believed that Wilbur was teaching Mason to label different aspects of herself (memories, emotions, etc.) as different personalities. An independent analysis of audiotapes of conversations between Wilbur and Mason led to a similar conclusion, that Wilbur was suggesting multiple personalities to her patient (Rieber, 1999). Critics argued that important aspects of the case, such as the alleged sexual sadist mother, were fictionalized in the book, and there was also the question of whether Mason made up her multiple personalities in order to gain attention and excitement (Nathan, 2011). Cases such as those depicted in *Sybil* and *The Three Faces of Eve* led to the development of the DSM-5 diagnostic category of dissociative identity disorder. Given its dubious provenance, DID has become one of the most controversial psychiatric classifications.

A graduate student in clinical psychology was conducting a study on bulimia nervosa (an eating disorder; see Chapter 7). Participant number 006 was a 32-year-old female with a 10-year history of bulimia nervosa. She had a tumultuous family history, including sexual abuse, physical abuse, and neglect. She binged multiple times per day and purged up to 10 times per day. She also abused laxatives and had comorbid alcohol and drug abuse. She felt that her disorder resulted from trauma inflicted by her parents, and she saw her eating disorder as a result of living in such an abusive family. She was angry, bitter, and deeply pessimistic about her future.

Later, another volunteer, number 026, contacted the graduate student. The telephone number was the same as that of another participant, but the graduate student assumed that they were roommates. When participant 026 arrived, the graduate student was astonished to see participant 006 enter her office! Oddly, the participant did not seem to recognize her surroundings. She got lost on her way to the office and showed no recognition when she met the researcher. Although the student was sure that this was participant 006, the woman's personal and family history was completely different. The patient claimed that she had been bulimic for four years and before that had been overweight since childhood. She recalled her childhood as relatively happy and her parents as nurturing. Their only fault was that they frequently used food as a reward. Her first binge episode occurred after a breakup with a boyfriend, and she denied any history of anorexia nervosa, substance abuse, alcohol abuse, drug abuse, or physical or sexual abuse by her parents.

Curious about these two presentations, the researcher asked subject number 026 if she had ever been involved in research on bulimia nervosa. Astonishingly, she claimed that not only had she never been in a study, but that this was the first time she had ever told anyone that she had bulimia. To cover all her bases, the researcher asked subject 026 whether she had any siblings or if she had a twin. Subject 026 responded that she was an only child. Further inquiry into the patient's medical records and medical history revealed that this patient was known in the community to have DID and possessed several alters. Needless to say, the researcher did not include this/these participant(s) in her final research sample.

DID is a fascinating topic that intrigues most abnormal psychology students. During the 1980s and early 1990s, some mental health therapists began to discuss DID with their patients and the media. An interesting phenomenon occurred. As the media attention increased, so did the number of people reported to be suffering from DID. However, even as therapists seemed to find case after case, the very existence of the disorder was called into question. Why? One of the primary criticisms surrounding DID is that, despite many published descriptions of the disorder, few quantitative studies exist, and even fewer that constitute experimental research (Kihlstrom, 2001). In other words, the scientific status of DID as a diagnostic category is not well established. For example, whether DID can be reliably diagnosed is unclear. According to its proponents, its signs are intermittent, and most DID patients do not recognize the existence of their alters before they begin therapy (Piper & Mersky, 2004b). Therefore, unlike other disorders for which people seek treatment because they are sad or anxious, the existence of alternate personalities is discovered only after the person is in therapy.

Another challenge for DID is that the terms used to describe the symptoms are difficult to define in a way that can be studied. Neither *alter* nor *distinct personality state* has a clear definition. Furthermore, the number of alters seems to be increasing exponentially since the publication of the studies of Eve and Sybil. One descriptive study (Putnam et al., 1986) indicated that among 100 adults with DID, the average number of alternate personalities was 13.3, ranging from 1 to 60. Some therapists reported that their patients had too many alters to count. The most common alter was a child aged 12 years or less. About half of the alters were of the sex opposite of the person seeking treatment, and most reported that the alter first made an appearance before age 12 although the patient was unaware of its presence.

Similarly, no agreement exists on what defines "taking control of the person's behaviour." As a result, each therapist can use *idiosyncratic* definitions. How does an alter take control? Does the alter simply have to speak to the therapist to be legitimate, or must the behaviour be more complicated? Proponents of DID describe alters who engage in "doing schoolwork, selling illicit drugs, dancing in strip clubs, cleaning bathtubs" (Piper & Mersky, 2004a, p. 679). It is obvious that these questions have no clear answers. In the sections that follow, we examine further the validity of DID. However, from the perspective of psychological science, one must question the reliability and validity of a disorder whose symptoms are not consistently present or cannot be independently verified.

Depersonalization/Derealization Disorder

During times of heightened emotionality or stress (e.g., panic disorder, posttraumatic stress disorder, depression, or near-death experiences) or altered physical states such as substance abuse or head injury, many people report feelings of being detached from the body or feeling as if the world around them were unreal (Baker et al., 2003; Kihlstrom, 2001). In one group of people who reported these experiences, 62% had a documented medical condition, and 50% had a previous psychiatric diagnosis; most had depression or panic disorder (Baker et al., 2003). In some people, these experiences occur with great frequency and not necessarily in the context of emotional stress or physical illness.

Lucinda describes multiple periods of time when the world suddenly felt unreal. Once, when she was with her friends, she felt as if they were in a movie and she was sitting in the audience, watching the others perform on the screen in front of her. Another time, she was walking and suddenly felt as if she were floating above the surface of the sidewalk.

When periods of dissociation are frequent and severe, the person may be suffering from **depersonalization/derealization disorder**, described as feelings of being detached from one's body or mind or unreality or detachment with respect to one's surroundings. It is described as a state of feeling as if one is an external observer of one's own behaviour. The changes occur suddenly and are perceived as unreal and inconsistent with a person's prior experiences. People can experience symptoms of either depersonalization (being detached from one's body) or derealization (a feeling of unfamiliarity or unreality about one's physical or interpersonal environment). Most people with this disorder have symptoms of both types of dissociation (Baker et al., 2003).

In depersonalization/derealization disorder, a person feels detached from body or mind, as if observing his or her behaviour from the outside. Or the person may feel that the external environment is unreal.

sarra22/Fotolia

Functional Impairment

There are few data examining the impact of dissociative disorders on social and occupational functioning (Johnson et al., 2006c). In many cases, the presence of other, comorbid disorders does not allow a determination of whether the impairment is the result of another disorder, such as depression, or the result of dissociative disorders.

Epidemiology

The reported prevalence of dissociative disorders varies greatly depending on the characteristics of the sample (community sample or clinic sample) or the degree to which the interviewer believes in the diagnosis. In one epidemiological sample, 0.8% had depersonalization disorder, 1.8% had dissociative amnesia, and 1.5% had DID (Johnson et al., 2006c). Among inpatient samples, dissociative disorders affect from 4% to 21% of all psychiatric inpatients (Foote et al., 2006), and settings specifically established to treat these disorders report higher rates. Data from outpatient samples are very limited. Among one clinic sample of inner-city outpatients, 29% had a dissociative disorder. However, they also had many other disorders, including depression, posttraumatic stress disorder, and anxiety disorders, and it is possible that depersonalization experiences were the result of one of those disorders. The issue of whether dissociative symptoms represent a primary disorder or are secondary to another disorder may seem to be simply an intellectual exercise. However, it is important for determining mental health policy, reimbursement for services, and approaches to treatment.

Sex, Race, and Ethnicity

5.5 Differentiate between the posttraumatic and iatrogenic models of dissociative identity disorder.

Both men and women suffer from dissociative disorders (e.g., Simeon et al., 2003). It is unclear whether there are reliable differences in the prevalence of dissociative disorders across different races and ethnic groups. This is partly because different methods have been used in different countries to assess these disorders, and because of the controversy of the validity of disorders such as dissociative identity disorder.

Developmental Factors

The average age of onset for depersonalization disorder (as defined in DSM-IV-TR) ranges from 15.9 to 22.8 years (Baker et al., 2003; Simeon et al., 2003), although children as young as age 8 have been diagnosed with DID (Hornstein & Putnam, 1992). However, the children who were given this diagnosis also had many other psychological disorders as well as unusual beliefs (i.e., delusions), unusual perceptual experiences (hallucinations, such as hearing voices when no one is present), and histories of suicidal ideation and attempts. This means that as with adults, DID, if it exists at all, rarely occurs alone, even in children (Putnam, 1993; Vincent & Pickering, 1988).

Etiology

5.6 Understand the controversy surrounding repressed/recovered memories.

Because dissociative disorders are very rare, there are few empirical data to help us understand how the disorders develop. Therefore, much of what has been written about the onset of dissociative disorders is based on clinical experience and impressions, not empirical data. In some instances, this theorizing has negatively impacted individuals, often the parents of affected children, by falsely accusing them of committing child abuse. As you read the examples in this section, consider whether some of these behaviours remind you of the concept of *emotional contagion*, which we discussed in Chapter 1.

BIOLOGICAL FACTORS Neurological disorders, such as temporal lobe epilepsy, head injury, tumour, cerebral vascular accident (stroke), migraine, and dementia, may produce symptoms such as blackouts, fugues, depersonalization, amnesia, anxiety and panic symptoms, and auditory, visual, and olfactory hallucinations (Lambert et al., 2002). Several empirical trials suggest that between 10% and 21% of patients with DID have abnormal brain activity (Sivec & Lynn, 1995). Therefore, although abnormal neurological function cannot account for the onset of all cases of dissociative disorders, some dissociative symptoms may result from neurological conditions.

Neuroanatomical and neurochemical studies of dissociative disorders are few (Şar et al., 2001; Vermetten et al., 2006), and those that exist are limited by small sample sizes, lack of adequate control groups, or failure to exclude the presence of other disorders such as posttraumatic stress disorder. In fact, a comparison of people with DID and people with PTSD indicated few differences in brain anatomy and brain function (Loewenstein, 2005). The common denominator in both of these conditions may be chronic stress. As discussed in Chapter 4, the chronic stress associated with PTSD can produce neuroanatomical changes in the hippocampus and amygdala, brain regions known to be involved in memory functions. Neurochemical changes may also occur. During periods of stress, the availability of neuropeptides and neurotransmitters (known collectively as *neuromodulators*) in these regions is altered, which affects establishing memory traces for specific events (Bremner et al., 1996). These neuromodulators may have both strengthening and diminishing effects on memory based on the level of stress and the type of neuromodulator.

PSYCHOSOCIAL FACTORS According to its proponents, DID is a failure of the normal developmental process of "personality integration." The failure is hypothesized to result from traumatic experiences and disordered caregiver–child relationships during critical developmental periods. This leads to the development and elaboration of distinct personality states (International Society for the Study of Dissociation, 2005). The traumas are most commonly incidents of physical or sexual abuse that occur during childhood.

Consistent with the suggested association between abuse and somatoform disorders, data supporting the proposal that DID results from childhood trauma are correlational and based on samples of patients who are seeking treatment. Some proponents of this relationship assert that many or virtually all patients with DID were severely abused as children, but no controlled investigations support these assertions. The available longitudinal studies of the adult effects of childhood sexual abuse do not include DID as one of the negative outcomes (e.g., Bulik et al., 2001; Piper & Merskey, 2004a). Of course, large epidemiological studies are sometimes conducted using telephone interviews, and researchers make decisions about how best to use the interview time. Sometimes rarely-occurring disorders such as DID are not included in epidemiological surveys because they occur so infrequently. This means that the disorder may be present but undetected. However, even if some people who are sexually abused develop DID, this does not mean that all abuse victims develop DID or that DID is the only result of sexual abuse. In one large twin study, a history of childhood sexual abuse was related to increased risk for many different outcomes, such as depression, suicide attempts, conduct disorder, substance abuse, social anxiety, adult rape, and divorce (Nelson et al., 2002a). Therefore, childhood sexual abuse appears to increase the risk for adult psychopathology in general, but it does not appear to predict the development of any one particular disorder (Bulik et al., 2001).

Despite the lack of strong empirical data, clinicians who specialize in DID still propose that dissociation is used to cope with traumatic experiences, blocking painful events from awareness and allowing the person to function as if nothing traumatic had happened (Sivec & Lynn, 1995). Although blocking painful events might help someone cope in the short term, its repeated use results in functional impairments. However, this is where some theorists jump from a behavioural explanation to an etiological theory without the corroborating evidence. They conclude that anyone who experiences dissociative symptoms *must have been abused.* Significant gaps in childhood memories are considered evidence of repeated trauma (Bass & Davis, 1988). Patients are often encouraged to "remember" the trauma as a way of overcoming their symptoms. There is a fallacy in this reasoning, however, because these theories ignore the evidence that memory gaps before the age of 6 years are common in the general population (Holmes et al., 2005b). But what if people only "remember" abuse after a therapist explains that their symptoms are the result of unrecalled child abuse? Are these recovered memories or *false* memories?

The issue of *repressed memories* and *recovered memories* is an emotional and controversial one for psychology and mental health professionals. Consider the following example:

In 1990, George Franklin, Sr., age 51, was found guilty of the murder of 8-year-old Susan Kay Nason. What made the case unusual was that the murder occurred more than 20 years earlier, and the primary evidence was the recovered memory of Franklin's daughter, Eileen, who was also 8 years old at the time. Eileen's memory of the murder did not return at once but in bits and pieces. By the time it had all returned, Eileen described witnessing her father sexually assaulting Susan in the back of a van and then killing her by smashing her head with a rock. Many people believed Eileen's account even though many of the details could have been obtained from newspaper accounts. More disconcerting was the fact that many of the details she provided changed over time. For example, she initially stated that the event occurred in the morning. When later confronted with the fact that Susan had attended school that day, Eileen changed her testimony to state that the event occurred after school (from Loftus, 1993). Because of the inconsistency of Eileen's testimony, George Franklin's conviction was later overturned.

There is no way to determine whether Eileen's memories were fact or fiction, yet throughout the 1980s and 1990s, many people reported "recovered" memories, most often having to do with incidents of child abuse. Many therapists believed that these memories were absolute fact without considering that memory is fallible; in other words, memory can be inaccurate or, even in some cases, completely made up.

This is further illustrated in the Canadian legal case of R. v. Francois (1994). Francois was convicted of repeatedly raping a 13-year-old girl in 1985. The only evidence was the girl's testimony, in which it was claimed that she had repressed memories the assaults. Recollections of the assaults emerged in 1990 when police suggested that if she thought long enough about her past, she might recall something. The conviction was later overturned by the Supreme Court of Canada.

To understand the recovered memory controversy, it is necessary to understand that memory is an active process. First, to remember something, you must have paid attention to it.

Tom was walking down the street when he was physically assaulted. When describing the event to the police, he was unable to recall the face of his assailant.

Some theorists propose that such selective amnesia indicates that the person's mind has actively blocked this aspect of the traumatic event. However, experimental data suggest that under conditions of high arousal, people pay attention to the central feature of an event at the expense of less important details (McNally, 2005). Tom may not have remembered the face of his attacker because his attention was focused on the perpetrator's gun.

Second, most people do not understand that "memory does not operate like a videotape recorder" (McNally, 2005, p. 818). Remembering is an active process and always involves reconstruction. Even very strong memories may change over time. For example, the morning after the space shuttle *Challenger* exploded, undergraduate students were asked to write down where they were and what they were doing when they heard the news (Neisser & Harsch, 1992). Nearly three years later, they were interviewed again. The students were highly confident about the truthfulness of their memory, but the researchers detected many inaccuracies in their recall of the events, including very basic facts such as where they were and what they were doing. In short, memory changes as time progresses.

Just by asking a misleading question, memory researchers have demonstrated that eye witnesses can construct memories for events that did not occur. Ten months after a horrible plane crash that had widespread news coverage, people were asked, "Did you see the television clip of the moment that the plane hit the apartment building?" Actually, no such film was available, but when asked this question, more than 60% of the people responded that they had seen the clip and were able to describe details of television coverage *that did not exist* (Cronbag et al., 1996). Other studies also illustrate that memories of entirely fictionalized events can be constructed. As part of a study of "childhood memories," adult subjects were given three true stories about their childhood as well as a fourth, false story (i.e., that at age 5, they were lost in a mall; Loftus & Pickrell, 1995). During follow-up interviews, when adults described everything they could remember about the four situations, 25% of the participants provided elaborate details about the event that had never occurred.

Even if we leave aside the issue of repressed/recovered memories, controlled clinical trials still provide only limited evidence for the relationship between abuse and DID. There are two reasons for this controversial relationship. First, the descriptions of abuse often are not objectively documented. Second, the definition of abuse can be quite variable. In some studies, it is limited to acts of physical or sexual abuse. In other studies, abuse is defined broadly to include emotional abuse and emotional/physical neglect, situations that are much more difficult to objectively define and quantify. In still other studies, the samples consist solely of individuals already diagnosed with dissociative disorders with no adequate comparison groups, yet the results are described as "definitive" (Lewis et al., 1997).

With these limitations in mind, the data from controlled trials suggest that trauma exposure plays only a limited role. In one sample, trauma exposure accounted for only 4.4% of the dissociative symptoms (Briere et al., 2005). Emotional abuse plays an equally important, if not larger, role than sexual abuse (Simeon et al., 2001b). More general environmental factors, such as a generally poor relationship between parent and child (even without specific acts of abuse), contribute more to the onset of these disorders than does emotional abuse (e.g., Nelson et al., 2002a).

Therapists who adhere to a *posttraumatic model* of DID believe that a person "compartmentalizes" responses to trauma in the form of alternate personalities. They believe that different patient behaviours indicate the possible presence of alters even if the person is unaware of their existence (Piper & Mersky, 2004b). Some therapists report that alters emerge only after repeated requests from the therapist. Could these actions actually cause DID? When the therapist or the therapy itself contributes to the onset of a disorder, the cause is said to be *iatrogenic.* An **iatrogenic** disease is one that is inadvertently caused by a physician, by a medical or surgical treatment, or by a diagnostic procedure. The *sociocultural model* postulates that DID is an iatrogenic disorder that develops using cues from the media and therapists, as well as from personal experiences and observations of others who have enacted multiple identities (see "Canadian Focus: Sociocognitive Theory of DID").

canadian FOCUS

Sociocognitive Theory of DID

Carleton University psychologist Nicholas Spanos (1942–1994) proposed a *sociocognitive theory* of DID, which is a major alternative to the posttraumatic theory of the disorder. Spanos (1994) argued that multiple personalities are caused by role playing. That is, DID develops when a highly suggestible (fantasy-prone) person learns to adopt and enact the roles of multiple identities, mostly because clinicians inadvertently suggest, legitimize, and reinforce them, and because these different identities are geared to the individual's own personal goals. Such role playing is not done intentionally or consciously, but rather occurs with little or no awareness. Consistent with the sociocognitive theory, Spanos, Weekes, and Bertrand (1985) demonstrated that normal college students can be induced by suggestion under hypnosis to exhibit some of the phenomena seen in DID, including the adoption of a second identity with a different name and a different profile on a personality inventory. Thus people can enact a second identity when situational forces encourage it. Related situational forces that may affect the individual outside the therapist's office include memories of one's past behaviour (e.g., as a child), observations of other people's behaviour (e.g., others being assertive and independent, or sexy and flirtatious), and media portrayals of DID (Spanos, 1994).

Although Spanos's demonstration of role playing in hypnotized college students is interesting, it does not prove that this is the way DID develops in patients. Hypnotized participants in experiments by Spanos and others exhibited only a few of the most obvious symptoms of DID, such as more than one identity, and showed them only under short-lived, contrived laboratory conditions. Other sources of evidence are required to investigate whether therapy can cause DID (see "Examining the Evidence: Can Therapy Cause Dissociative Identify Disorder?").

examining the EVIDENCE

Can Therapy Cause Dissociative Identity Disorder?

- **The Facts** The number of cases of DID worldwide rose from 79 in 1970 to approximately 6000 in 1986 (Elzinga et al., 1998), a period of time corresponding to the appearance of the book and movie *Sybil*. By 2000, the number of cases was estimated to be in the tens of thousands (Acocella, 1998). The *sociocultural model* proposes that therapists (and the media) can influence people to develop alternate identities. Might these influences explain the dramatically increased prevalence of DID?
- **The Evidence** Among DID patients, 80% to 100% have no knowledge of their alters before they begin therapy (Dell & Eisenhower, 1990; Lewis et al., 1997; Putnam, 1989). As they continue in therapy, the number of alters reported by a person continues to increase (e.g., North et al., 1993). *Posttraumatic* model theorists address this phenomenon, explaining that patients with DID tend to hide their symptoms before treatment. Perhaps this is so, but are there alternative hypotheses?
- **Let's Examine the Evidence** Several lines of evidence suggest that therapists may shape people to produce alternative personalities (Lilienfeld et al., 1999).

  First, when people with no psychological disorders are given appropriate cues, they can successfully produce DID symptoms, including reports of physical, sexual, and satanic abuse rituals (Stafford & Lynn, 2002).

  Second, both the increase in the number of patients with DID and the number of alters that appear during the course of treatment coincide with increased therapist awareness of the diagnostic features. In other words, the more the therapist believes in the diagnosis, the more likely the patients will be given the diagnosis.

  Third, one DID expert recommends to novice therapists that when an alter does not emerge spontaneously, "Asking to meet an alter directly is an increasingly accepted intervention" (Kluft, 1993, p. 29). Other advice includes giving the person the hypnotic suggestion that "everybody (meaning all the personalities) listen." Would such suggestions lead the patient to believe (i.e., shape the patient to believe) that other personalities must exist?
- Such shaping did occur in the case of children's testimony during a preschool molestation trial in the 1980s, in which a number of daycare workers were falsely accused and convicted of sexually molesting the children in their care (Zirpolo, 2005). Later testimony refuted the original claims. Children who initially denied being molested by daycare workers were repeatedly interviewed until, as one child later reported, "Anytime I

would give them an answer they didn't like, they would ask me again and encourage me to give them the answer they were looking for" (Zirpolo, 2005). In effect, the children were encouraged to provide answers consistent with the therapist's preexisting beliefs.

- **Conclusion** The posttraumatic model asserts that most therapists do not diagnose DID because they neglect to sufficiently probe for its features (Ross, 1997). However, both basic laboratory and behavioural observation data suggest that university students and patients may be vulnerable to therapists' expectations and may produce alters because of suggestions (or probing) by a therapist. This evidence indicates that iatrogenesis and the sociocultural model explanation for the existence of DID cannot be discounted.

Ethics and Responsibility

What conclusions can we draw about the research on recovered/false memories? Even though a person provides a detailed memory and is confident that it is accurate, that does not always mean that the person remembers how an event really happened (Laney & Loftus, 2005). The issue of recovered/false memories is not simply an intellectual curiosity, but is also an important element in the controversy surrounding child abuse and, by extension, DID. It is important to remember that (1) some children do suffer abuse and (2) although some abused children may suffer from psychological disorders as adults, no clear link exists between abuse and DID. Furthermore, despite the disagreement regarding recovered memories, all mental health professionals agree on one key point: Memories of childhood abuse that were always present are almost always authentic, as are those that are spontaneously remembered outside of a therapeutic setting (Holmes et al., 2005b).

Treatment

As noted, dissociative amnesia usually resolves without treatment. No controlled pharmacological trials for derealization disorder or DID have been conducted, but clinical reports suggest that antidepressant medications may be helpful. It is unclear, however, whether these medications work on core dissociative symptoms or treat the associated anxiety and depression. The same conclusion may apply to CBT approaches, which hypothesize that people with dissociative disorders misinterpret normal symptoms of fatigue, stress, or even substance intoxication as abnormal. CBT therapists challenge these misinterpretations by teaching the person to generate alternative explanations for their symptoms (a process known as cognitive restructuring). In some instances, people may avoid situations that elicit their symptoms, in which case exposure therapy (see Chapter 4) may help people enter these feared situations. CBT has been reported to be efficacious for depersonalization disorder, although controlled trials are not available (Holmes et al., 2005b; Hunter et al., 2005).

CONCEPT check

- Dissociative experiences occur in people with dissociative disorders, people with no psychological disorder, and people with many different types of psychological disorders.
- The existence of dissociative disorders as distinct psychological disorders is controversial, and among the entire group of disorders, DID is the most controversial.
- Despite its proponents, few data support the hypothesis that those who experience dissociative disorders are suffering from repressed memories or that when these memories are recovered through the therapeutic process, they are accurate in content.
- Similarly, few data indicate that childhood sexual or physical abuse is a frequent cause of dissociative disorder or that it is a unique etiological component.

critical thinking question Most psychological disorders show a steady rise in prevalence from the mid-1980s through 2003. By contrast, the number of publications regarding dissociative amnesia and DID rose from low levels in the mid-1980s to a sharp peak in the 1990s, followed by an equally sharp decline by 2003 (Pope et al., 2006c). Worldwide, in 2003, the literature reported only 13 explicit cases of dissociative amnesia reported in the literature. How would you explain this phenomenon?

Malingering

You may have engaged in malingering if you ever feigned illness (played sick) in order to avoid going to school, taking a test, or engaging in some other activity. For most of us, these are isolated events. Some individuals, however, may feign psychological disorders in order to avoid criminal prosecution (see Chapter 15). It is extremely important for psychologists to be able to detect malingering. Yet, because diagnosing psychological disorders often depends upon a person's self-report (yes, I feel sad, or no, I do not hear voices), how does a psychologist determine whether a person might be feigning a psychological disorder?

A growing concern on university campuses are students who do not have a history of attention deficit/hyperactivity disorder (ADHD) but who would like to get stimulant medication or increased testing time in order to enhance their academic performance. The challenge for psychologists is to identify students who are really suffering from ADHD (and may not have been diagnosed as a child) and who are in need of psychiatric medication. In some cases, cognitive measures, known as symptom validity tests (SVTs), which measure cognitive abilities and not reports of symptomatology, are useful parts of the diagnostic evaluation. For example, among university students seeking evaluation for ADHD, 31% failed a word memory test. In fact, even though these students were functioning at a cognitive level that allowed them to be admitted to university, they failed a test usually passed by people with severe traumatic brain injury (Suhr et al., 2008), indicating that they were faking memory problems. In another investigation, university students were asked to "fake ADHD" and were given information about the disorder from the Internet. When evaluated by diagnosticians blinded to whether the student really had ADHD or was faking, the two groups had equal scores on ADHD symptom profiles, indicating that they had adequately learned the symptoms of this disorder (Sollman et al., 2010). However, on tests of memory and concentration, the group pretending to have ADHD actually did *much worse* than students who had a legitimate diagnosis, indicating that these cognitive tests were much less susceptible to feigning a psychological disorder. The issue of malingering is an important and understudied area of psychology. Most people seeking psychological help do indeed have legitimate psychological symptoms. Detecting malingering is important not only in forensic (criminal) evaluations and university student campuses, but also in any diagnostic interview. The treatment of psychological disorders involves significant financial and professional resources, and it is important that these limited resources are not used inappropriately.

REAL people REAL disorders

Dorothy Joudrie

Canada's most famous case of dissociative disorder involves Calgary socialite Dorothy Joudrie. She suffered years of physical abuse from her husband, Earl Joudrie, who subsequently left her for another woman. Earl was a highly successful businessman, and for a time was Chair of Canadian Tire and Algoma Steel. On January 21, 1995, Earl went to Dorothy's condominium to exchange some papers about their pending divorce. They had coffee, and Dorothy, age 61, showed Earl an album of their wedding photos and some family Christmas letters she had written. As he rose to leave, she asked him if he still wanted a divorce. When he said yes, she began crying and said, "It's easier for you, I'm alone and you have someone." Earl went to leave through the front door, but Dorothy redirected him to the garage, where she pulled out a .25 calibre Beretta and shot Earl six times. The first three shots hit him in the shoulder, thigh, and lower back. She paused and then shot him again in the midsection, right arm, and chest. The last shot just missed his heart. He survived the attack with a broken arm, collapsed lung, and cardiac injury. (He later died in 2006, at age 72, of non-Hodgkin's lymphoma).

During Dorothy's trial for attempted murder, Earl testified that Dorothy behaved strangely and was not her usual self; she appeared unusually calm and detached. He described her as being "very controlled, very cold" as he lay bleeding on the floor of the garage. She mused about stuffing his body into the trunk of her car. At one point she asked him, "How long is it going to take you to die?" Then, Earl claimed, she appeared to return to her old self and said, "Oh, my God, what have I done?" She reportedly "came to" to discover her husband shot, lying on the garage floor, at which time she phoned for an ambulance. When police arrived on the scene they found Dorothy distraught and disoriented. She said had no recollection of the shooting, but conceded that "I had to have shot him, because I was the only person there."

During the trial, three psychiatrists, including the Crown's own witness, told the jury that Dorothy was in a brief dissociative ("robotic") state during the time of the shooting. This claim was based on the fact that she couldn't remember the shooting (i.e., she supposedly had psychogenic amnesia) and on the fact that Earl testified that his wife was acting unlike the person he had known for more than 40 years. When she returned to her old self, she seemed frightened and agreed to call an ambulance, which saved his life.

The marriage of Dorothy and Earl was troubled and turbulent. Dorothy recalled many happy times, but she also was physically abused and she drank heavily. Dorothy's defence lawyer argued that Dorothy's long years of denial about her marital problems were finally shattered when Earl came to finalize the divorce, causing her to go into a brief dissociative state during which she shot Earl. Dorothy was found to be not criminally responsible by reason of mental disorder (see Chapter 15). She spent five months in a psychiatric hospital and then was released. Dorothy died in 2002 of liver and kidney failure.

Calgary Herald/The Canadian Press

There is a curious ending to this case. After Earl's death, it was claimed that he had told a friend a very different story about the shooting (Martin, 2006). In contrast to his earlier testimony, he later claimed that as he lay bleeding on the garage floor, Dorothy ignored his pleas to call 911 until he promised not to press charges against her for trying to kill him, and that he would do everything in his power not to cause her grief. So, was Dorothy in a dissociative state at the time of the shooting, or was she malingering, with the help of Earl's court testimony? We may never know.

Sources: Andrews (1999); Martin (2006); McSherry (1998); Walton (2010).

CONCEPT check

- People with factitious disorders deliberately create physical symptoms in themselves or others.
- While people who malinger do so for the purpose of compensation or to avoid a negative event, these factors are not apparent in people with factitious disorders.
- People can create symptoms of illness in themselves, as in factitious disorder imposed on self, or can create illness in another person, as in factitious disorder imposed on another.

critical thinking question What factors do you think would cause someone to decide to create illness symptoms in another person (as in a mother making her child/children ill) rather than creating those symptoms in herself?

summary

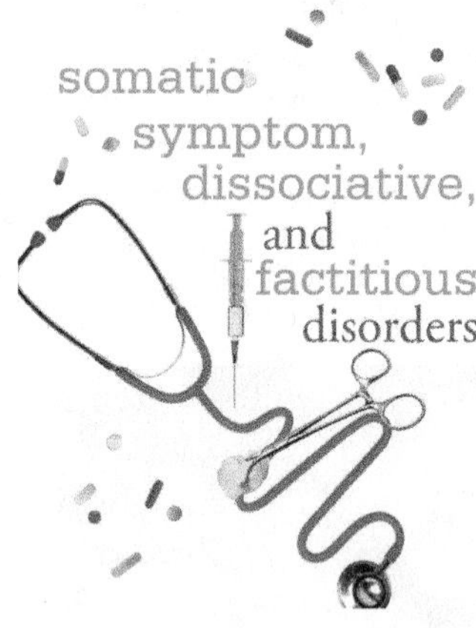

5.1 Understand how normal physical sensations can create abnormal concerns about somatic functioning.

Vague physical sensations, without any apparent organic cause, are common in the general population. These types of complaints are among the most common reasons for visits to primary care physicians. Among people who suffer from somatic symptom and related disorders, these symptoms create significant distress and cannot be reasoned away. It is important to understand that even if the cause of the physical symptoms is not organic, the pain and distress are very real.

5.2 Differentiate somatic symptom, dissociative, and factitious disorders from malingering behaviour.

Malingering involves the creation of physical symptoms and illnesses for the purpose of gaining money or drugs, or avoiding negative events such as work, criminal prosecution, or military service. Factitious disorders involve the deliberate creation of physical symptoms or illness, but there is no apparent observable goal. In contrast, people with dissociative or somatoform disorders do not deliberately produce their physical symptoms and do not understand why the symptoms occur.

5.3 Identify the contributions of biological, psychological, and environmental factors to somatic symptom and related disorders.

Somatic symptom and related disorders are defined by the presence of physical symptoms or concerns about an illness that cannot be explained by an established medical or psychological disorder. Biological, psychological, and environmental factors may play a role in the onset of somatoform disorders. Environmental events, such as chronic stress, may create alterations in neurochemical response systems that automatically respond in times of stress. These altered responses may produce physical symptoms that cause psychological concern. Furthermore, reinforcement of the expression of physical complaints by parents or significant others may create physician-seeking or doctor-shopping as well as social and occupational impairment.

5.4 Understand the elements of dissociative experiences and the role of sociocultural factors in dissociative disorders.

Dissociative disorders involve disruption in the integrated functions of consciousness, memory, identity, or perception, as in depersonalization, derealization, amnesia, or confusion or alteration of identity. Dissociative disorders are a controversial category of psychological dysfunction. Dissociative symptoms and disorders may represent culture-bound syndromes. Some researchers have suggested that DID is a culture-bound disorder that is limited to Western cultures.

5.5 Differentiate between the posttraumatic and iatrogenic models of dissociative identity disorder.

Despite retrospective accounts of patients identified with these disorders, few empirical data support the posttraumatic hypothesis that childhood abuse is a major cause of dissociative disorders. By contrast, there are empirical data to support an iatrogenic model of DID. It is very important to remember that an iatrogenic or sociocultural model does not mean that the disorder does not exist. Rather, it reflects an understanding of how these disorders are acquired.

5.6 Understand the controversy surrounding repressed/recovered memories.

The concept of repressed/recovered memories is inconsistent with current scientific knowledge regarding normal memory processes. Despite the existence of posttraumatic models, amnesia regarding activities before age 6 is common, and creating false memories, even of events as horrific as sexual abuse, is possible. This does not mean that childhood sexual abuse does not exist or is not a problem. However, most people who were abused as children remember it without prompting.

key terms

TEST yourself

1. Julie has been diagnosed with a somatic symptom disorder. This means she is suffering from a condition in which her physical symptoms
   a. are faked in order to receive some type of external compensation
   b. can be explained by a psychological disorder
   c. cannot be explained by a medical or psychological disorder
   d. are confined to a part of her body that is particularly stressed
2. A patient with somatic symptom disorder would, over the course of a lifetime, have which of the following categories of physical complaints?
   a. pain in the head, abdomen, back, joints, and extremities
   b. pain, gastrointestinal distress, sexual dysfunction, and pseudoneurological symptoms
   c. nausea, bloating, vomiting, diarrhea, and food intolerance
   d. sexual disinterest, irregular menstruation, vomiting, and enuresis
3. Patients suffering from conversion disorder have symptoms that consist primarily of
   a. pseudoneurological complaints
   b. severe headaches
   c. unexplained pain
   d. gastrointestinal distress
4. Glove anesthesia is considered a classic conversion disorder. This is because glove anesthesia
   a. occurs in only one hand
   b. does not follow known neurological patterns
   c. follows known pain patterns
   d. occurs when the hand is in one position for a long time
5. Susan is always going to her doctor, asking to be examined for cancer or heart disease even though she doesn't have any symptoms. Her physician says she has illness anxiety disorder. People with this disorder
   a. have anxiety about their health that leads them to deny their physical symptoms
   b. have a dysfunctional mind-set that leads them to worry excessively about their health
   c. avoid medical care because their symptoms aren't real
   d. are typically in poor health and should monitor their symptoms carefully
6. A patient who is successfully recovering from gall bladder surgery and is reluctant to engage in any physical activities even when approved by a physician may be suffering from
   a. illness anxiety disorder
   b. pain disorder
   c. la belle indifference
   d. transient hypochondriasis
7. Which of the following is not a causal or maintenance factor of factitious disorder?
   a. an attempt to master past trauma
   b. an intense need to evoke strong reactions in others
   c. reinforcement via the attention the behaviours garner
   d. misinterpretation of amplication of normal physical processes
8. One of the difficulties in making a diagnosis of somatic symptom disorder is that it is difficult to distinguish it from comorbid or coexisting conditions such as
   a. posttraumatic stress disorder
   b. malingering or factitious disorders
   c. anxiety or depressive disorders
   d. illness anxiety disorder
9. Somatic symptom disorder is most common in
   a. adults
   b. children
   c. adolescents
   d. older adults
10. Environmental factors often associated with somatic symptom and related disorders include
    a. country of origin
    b. time of year
    c. family conflict/violence
    d. presence of toxins in the soil
11. Which of the following cognitive factors have been associated with somatic symptom and related disorders?
    a. somatic amplification
    b. heightened sensory and perceptual sensitivity
    c. inaccurate beliefs
    d. all of the above
12. The first challenge in treating people with somatic symptom and related disorders is that they are often
    a. suffering from several serious medical conditions
    b. unwilling to consult only one doctor
    c. reluctant to consult a professional, especially a psychologist
    d. too depressed or anxious to seek treatment
13. One form of treatment that has been found to be very helpful for people with somatic complaints is
    a. electroconvulsive therapy (ECT)
    b. symptom-focused cognitive-behaviour therapy (CBT)
    c. MAO inhibitors
    d. recovered memory therapy (RMT)
14. A client goes to see a therapist with the following complaints: She feels detachment from her body and is experiencing herself as strange or unreal. In some situations she feels as if she were watching herself. The therapist says she is experiencing
    a. depersonalization
    b. amnesia
    c. multiple personalities
    d. posttraumatic stress disorder

15. A patient is referred to a neurologist for isolated memory loss; the diagnosis of dissociative amnesia is made. The most likely etiology in this patient is
   a. head injury
   b. repeated drug overdose
   c. extreme emotional trauma
   d. stroke

16. A man who owns a hardware store in Halifax mysteriously disappears. Years later the man is discovered in Yukon. His name is changed, he has remarried, and he now works in a different occupation. He claims that he has no memory of his past life. The man may be suffering from
   a. psychogenic fugue
   b. depersonalization/derealization
   c. dissociative identity disorder
   d. posttraumatic stress disorder

17. Some experts argue that DID is an iatrogenic disease, which means that it is caused by
   a. the interaction of biological, social, and environmental factors
   b. the experience of therapy itself
   c. repeated exposure to risk factors
   d. lifestyle factors that are difficult to change

18. The sociocultural model postulates that DID develops when individuals use cues from
   a. the media
   b. therapists
   c. other people who display multiple identities
   d. all of the above

19. Patients with factitious disorders have which of the following characteristics?
   a. brief medical histories
   b. self-administered injuries
   c. symptoms that consist primarily of pseudoneurological complaints
   d. extreme fear and avoidance of medical professionals

20. An 18-month-old infant in the pediatric ICU has been experiencing episodes of difficulty breathing and rapid heart rate with no apparent cause. All tests are negative. These symptoms only occur when the mother is with the child. The most likely cause of the infant's symptoms is
   a. congenital heart disease
   b. asthma
   c. factitious disorder imposed on another
   d. seizure disorder

Answers:
1 c, 2 b, 3 a, 4 b, 5 b, 6 d, 7 b, 8 c, 9 a, 10 c, 11 d, 12 c, 13 b, 14 a, 15 c, 16 a, 17 b, 18 d, 19 b, 20 c.

chapter 6

bipolar and depressive disorders

(top): Vectoria/Shutterstock; (center): ICHIRO/Getty Images

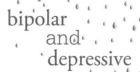

bipolar and depressive disorders

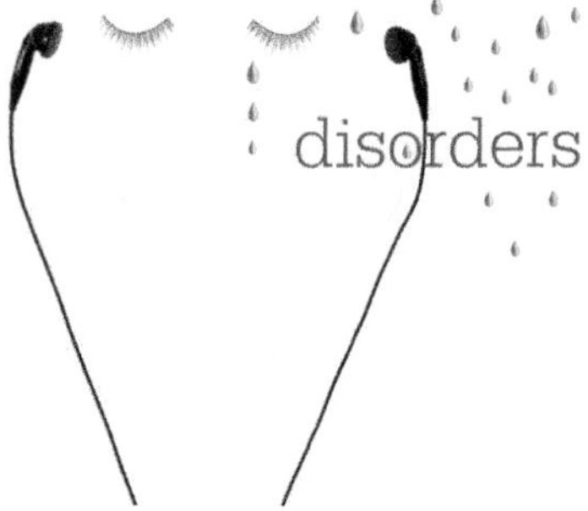

learning objectives

After reading this chapter, you should be able to:

6.1
Distinguish between normal sad mood and depression and between euphoria and mania.

6.2
Understand the differences between bipolar I and bipolar II disorders and between major depressive disorder and persistent depressive disorder.

6.3
Discuss sex differences in the risk for major depressive disorder.

6.4
Discuss factors associated with suicide and the relationship between depression and suicidal ideation and behaviour.

6.5
Understand psychodynamic, behavioural, cognitive, and biological theories of the causes of bipolar and depressive disorders.

6.6
Identify efficacious treatments for major depressive disorder and bipolar disorder.

Erin was a senior in high school and had applied to 10 universities, including four leading ones that were among her top choices. She was pretty confident that she was going to get into her top schools. Her grades were excellent and she was on the debate and tennis teams. After she sent her applications in, she went to visit her top choices. She absolutely fell in love with one of them. She could see herself walking across the campus, she loved the people she met there when she toured, and she started dreaming about the future she would have if she got in. It was the frontrunner by far.

Notification week came. Her top choice was the first to notify. On that day at 5 p.m., she was waiting at her computer. At first, she couldn't get logged on, and her heart was pounding faster and faster. When she finally got on and read the dreaded words, "I regret to inform you . . ." her heart sunk. She felt as if her dreams were dashed—none of the other schools came close to her number one. Her parents tried to placate her, but she was inconsolable. The next day, she was rejected by the rest of her top choices. She spent the night in her bedroom crying and fearful that she wasn't going to get in anywhere. She stayed off Facebook because it seemed like all of her friends were bragging about where they got in, and she might end up at her backup. She would not take calls, moped around the house, hardly ate anything, slept poorly, and cried for days. Finally, she received an acceptance from a university near the bottom of her list. Even getting in there was no consolation. Her mother kept saying that at least she was accepted somewhere, but she felt like her world had crumbled. She remained disappointed with the outcome, but she has resolved to make the best of it and get the absolutely best education she can. Maybe she will be able to go to her first choice school for grad school!

Linda was a senior in high school. She had good grades (As and Bs), was involved in extracurricular activities, and played various sports. Although she was a worrier by temperament, she had friends and a busy high school schedule. In her senior year, she started losing interest in her activities. She quit the student newspaper and found it difficult to drag herself to sports practice. All she wanted to do was stay at home in her room; she stopped seeing her friends and avoided their phone calls. She went to bed at a decent hour but woke up first at 5 a.m., and then gradually earlier and earlier. Soon she was wide awake at 3 a.m. and unable to fall back to sleep. She had no appetite and lost 5 kg, leaving her looking gaunt. She was restless and irritable, lashing out at her brother and parents, which she had never done before. She stared at her homework for hours, reading the same paragraph again and again. Her grades plummeted, and she became ineligible for athletics. One of her teachers recommended that she see the school counsellor, which she did begrudgingly. Her thoughts became very dark, and she often felt there was no reason to live. She considered killing herself and had begun to explore how she might do it.

Linda had never felt this way before. She told the counsellor that her maternal grandmother had been in a psychiatric hospital and that she had seen Prozac in her mother's medicine cabinet. The counsellor contacted Linda's mother and helped her set up an appointment with a psychiatrist immediately. As it turned out, Linda's mother also had had several depressive episodes (often in the autumn months) and had been on medication for years. Linda started antidepressant medication and saw a psychologist for cognitive-behavioural therapy to help her develop skills to combat the negative thought patterns that often accompany depression.

Both Erin and Linda had loss of energy and appetite, trouble sleeping, and sad mood, but their stories illustrate vastly different sources of pain. Erin was dealing with acute disappointment about her university rejections, but she bounced back, whereas Linda could not identify a cause for her depressed mood.

Linda's symptoms are a clear example of a disorder characterized most prominently by a pervasive and unshakable low mood. Linda's problems distressed her and bewildered those around her. Once a high-functioning and active young woman both socially and athletically, she had become a social recluse. The cluster of signs and symptoms that Linda experienced, including social withdrawal, lack of energy and interest, loss of appetite, insomnia, irritability, and restlessness, constitute a disorder known as *major depressive disorder.*

Major depressive disorder is just one type of mood disorder. Actually, the bipolar and depressive disorders consist of several different conditions characterized by various degrees of depressed (low) or manic (high) moods. People with these syndromes have physical, emotional, and cognitive symptoms that may interfere with their ability to work, study, sleep, eat, interact with others, have sexual relations, and enjoy daily life. Although all of us have mood fluctuations from time to time, major depressive disorder is *not* the same as a transient "blue" mood or sad feelings, and mania is *not* the same as being elated. This chapter examines how and why the bipolar and depressive disorders involve more than just bad (or good) moods.

What Are Bipolar and Depressive Disorders?

6.1 Distinguish between normal sad mood and depression and between euphoria and mania.

Bipolar and depressive disorders are syndromes whose predominant feature is a disturbance in mood. The disturbance can take the form of mood that is abnormally low—**depression**—or abnormally high—**mania**. There are two categories: bipolar and related disorders, and depressive disorders. The primary bipolar and related disorders include bipolar I, bipolar II, and cyclothymic disorders, each of which is characterized by both highs and lows in mood. The primary depressive disorders include disruptive mood dysregulation disorder, major depressive disorder, persistent depressive disorder (dysthymia), and premenstrual dysphoric disorder. These presentations are marked by low mood only. The disorders are distinguished from each other by the presence of depressed or elated mood (or both), and by the length of time or the specific times that the mood abnormalities persist.

Bipolar and Related Disorders

Bipolar Disorder

Mood disturbance can include mood that is too low or too high, with the latter known as *mania*. Mania is different from elated mood in which excitement and good feelings naturally match a happy or an enjoyable experience. Rather, mania is high mood that is clearly excessive and is often accompanied by inappropriate and potentially dangerous behaviour, irritability, pressured or rapid speech, and a false sense of well-being (see "DSM-5: Bipolar I Disorder"). The side by side case studies later in this chapter illustrate the contrast between normal elation and mania. Because recurrent mania in the absence of any depressive episodes is extremely rare, the DSM does not recognize it as a separate disorder. Manic episodes almost always occur in tandem with episodes of depression, and a person who has only a single manic episode will very likely have depression as well. Generally, a person is said to suffer from **bipolar disorder** (formerly known as *manic-depressive disorder*) when both episodic depressed mood and episodic mania are present.

Bipolar disorder consists of dramatic shifts in mood, energy, and ability to function. It is a long-term episodic illness in which mood shifts between the two emotional "poles" of mania and depression. In a depressed period, a person may be all but immobile, feeling unable to get out of bed. In a manic period, the same person may be so full of energy as to try to start a new business, buy a house, and plan a trip around the world on the same day. At either extreme, the person cannot cope with the demands of everyday life. Periods of normal feelings and energy commonly occur between these mood changes.

Bipolar disorder is commonly categorized as either **bipolar I** or **bipolar II** (see "DSM-5: Bipolar I Disorder"). The main difference is the degree of mania. In bipolar I, full-blown mania alternates with episodes of major depression; it also includes a single manic episode with or without periods of depression. In bipolar II disorder, *hypomania* alternates with episodes of major depression. **Hypomania** is a mood elevation that is clearly abnormal but not as extremely elevated as frank mania. Behaviourally, a person in a hypomanic state may be overly talkative, excitable, or irritable, but there are no impulsive acts or gross lapses of judgment that are common during mania (such as telephoning the offices of prime ministers and presidents to tell them how the world should be run). Hypomania is "mild mania" and lasts at least four days (APA, 2013). More common than bipolar I, bipolar II disorder is defined by having at least one episode of major depression and at least one hypomanic event. Bipolar II can be especially difficult to diagnose because a person experiencing hypomania may associate these episodes with periods of high productivity or creativity and be less likely to report their symptoms as distressing or problematic.

criteria for Bipolar I Disorder — DSM-5

For a diagnosis of bipolar I disorder, it is necessary to meet the following criteria for a manic episode. The manic episode may have been preceded by and may be followed by hypomanic or major depressive episodes.

Manic Episode

A. A distinct period of abnormally and persistently elevated, expansive, or irritable mood and abnormally and persistently increased goal-directed activity or energy, lasting at least 1 week and present most of the day, nearly every day (or any duration if hospitalization is necessary).

B. During the period of mood disturbance and increased energy or activity, three (or more) of the following symptoms (four if the mood is only irritable) are present to a significant degree and represent a noticeable change from usual behaviour:

1. Inflated self-esteem or grandiosity.
2. Decreased need for sleep (e.g., feels rested after only 3 hours of sleep).
3. More talkative than usual or pressure to keep talking.
4. Flight of ideas or subjective experience that thoughts are racing.
5. Distractibility (i.e., attention too easily drawn to unimportant or irrelevant external stimuli), as reported or observed.
6. Increase in goal-directed activity (either socially, at work or school, or sexually) or psychomotor agitation (i.e., purposeless non-goal-directed activity).
7. Excessive involvement in activities that have a high potential for painful consequences (e.g., engaging in unrestrained buying sprees, sexual indiscretions, or foolish business investments).

C. The mood disturbance is sufficiently severe to cause marked impairment in social or occupational functioning or to necessitate hospitalization to prevent harm to self or others, or there are psychotic features.

D. The episode is not attributable to the physiological effects of a substance (e.g., a drug of abuse, a medication, other treatment) or to another medical condition.

Note: A full manic episode that emerges during antidepressant treatment (e.g., medication, electroconvulsive therapy) but persists at a fully syndromal level beyond the physiological effect of that treatment is sufficient evidence for a manic episode and, therefore, a bipolar I diagnosis.

Hypomanic Episode

A. A distinct period of abnormally and persistently elevated, expansive, or irritable mood and abnormally and persistently increased activity or energy, lasting at least 4 consecutive days and present most of the day, nearly every day.

B. During the period of mood disturbance and increased energy and activity, three (or more) of the following symptoms (four if the mood is only irritable) have persisted, represent a noticeable change from usual behaviour, and have been present to a significant degree:

1. Inflated self-esteem or grandiosity.
2. Decreased need for sleep (e.g., feels rested after only 3 hours of sleep).
3. More talkative than usual or pressure to keep talking.
4. Flight of ideas or subjective experience that thoughts are racing.
5. Distractibility (i.e., attention too easily drawn to unimportant or irrelevant external stimuli), as reported or observed.
6. Increase in goal-directed activity (either socially, at work or school, or sexually) or psychomotor agitation.
7. Excessive involvement in activities that have a high potential for painful consequences (e.g., engaging in unrestrained buying sprees, sexual indiscretions, or foolish business investments).

C. The episode is associated with an unequivocal change in functioning that is uncharacteristic of the individual when not symptomatic.

D. The disturbance in mood and the change in functioning are observable by others.

E. The episode is not severe enough to cause marked impairment in social or occupational functioning or to necessitate hospitalization. If there are psychotic features, the episode is, by definition, manic.

F. The episode is not attributable to the physiological effects of a substance (e.g., a drug of abuse, a medication, other treatment).

Note: A full hypomanic episode that emerges during antidepressant treatment (e.g., medication, electroconvulsive therapy) but persists at a fully syndromal level beyond the physiological effect of that treatment is sufficient evidence for a hypomanic episode diagnosis. However, caution is indicated so that one or two symptoms (particularly increased irritability, edginess, or agitation following antidepressant use) are not taken as sufficient for diagnosis of a hypomanic episode, nor necessarily indicative of a bipolar diathesis.

Note: Criteria A–F constitute a hypomanic episode. Hypomanic episodes are common in bipolar I disorder but are not required for the diagnosis of bipolar I disorder.

Major Depressive Episode

A. Five (or more) of the following symptoms have been present during the same 2-week period and represent a change from previous functioning; at least one of the symptoms is either (1) depressed mood or (2) loss of interest or pleasure.

Note: Do not include symptoms that are clearly attributable to another medical condition.

1. Depressed mood most of the day, nearly every day, as indicated by either subjective report (e.g., feels sad, empty, or hopeless) or observation made by others (e.g., appears tearful). (**Note:** In children and adolescents, can be irritable mood.)
2. Markedly diminished interest or pleasure in all, or almost all, activities most of the day, nearly every day (as indicated by either subjective account or observation).
3. Significant weight loss when not dieting or weight gain (e.g., a change of more than 5% of body weight in a month), or decrease or increase in appetite nearly every day. (**Note:** In children, consider failure to make expected weight gain.)
4. Insomnia or hypersomnia nearly every day.
5. Psychomotor agitation or retardation nearly every day (observable by others; not merely subjective feelings of restlessness or being slowed down).
6. Fatigue or loss of energy nearly every day.
7. Feelings of worthlessness or excessive or inappropriate guilt (which may be delusional) nearly every day (not merely self-reproach or guilt about being sick).
8. Diminished ability to think or concentrate, or indecisiveness, nearly every day (either by subjective account or as observed by others).
9. Recurrent thoughts of death (not just fear of dying), recurrent suicidal ideation without a specific plan, or a suicide attempt or a specific plan for committing suicide.

B. The symptoms cause clinically significant distress or impairment in social, occupational, or other important areas of functioning.

C. The episode is not attributable to the physiological effects of a substance or another medical condition.

Note: Criteria A–C constitute a major depressive episode. Major depressive episodes are common in bipolar I disorder but are not required for the diagnosis of bipolar I disorder.

Note: Responses to a significant loss (e.g., bereavement, financial ruin, losses from a natural disaster, a serious medical illness or disability) may include the feelings of intense sadness, rumination about the loss, insomnia, poor appetite, and weight loss noted in Criterion A, which may resemble a depressive episode. Although such symptoms may be understandable or considered appropriate to the loss, the presence of a major depressive episode in addition to the normal response to a significant loss should also be carefully considered. This decision inevitably requires the exercise of clinical judgment based on the individual's history and the cultural norms for the expression of distress in the context of loss.1

Bipolar I Disorder

A. Criteria have been met for at least one manic episode (Criteria A–D under "Manic Episode" above).

B. The occurrence of the manic and major depressive episode(s) is not better explained by schizoaffective disorder, schizophrenia, schizophreniform disorder, delusional disorder, or other specified or unspecified schizophrenia spectrum and other psychotic disorder.

FIGURE 6.1

The Different Types of Bipolar Disorders. Each type of bipolar disorder (bipolar I disorder, bipolar II disorder, and rapid cycling bipolar disorder) has a different course of illness.

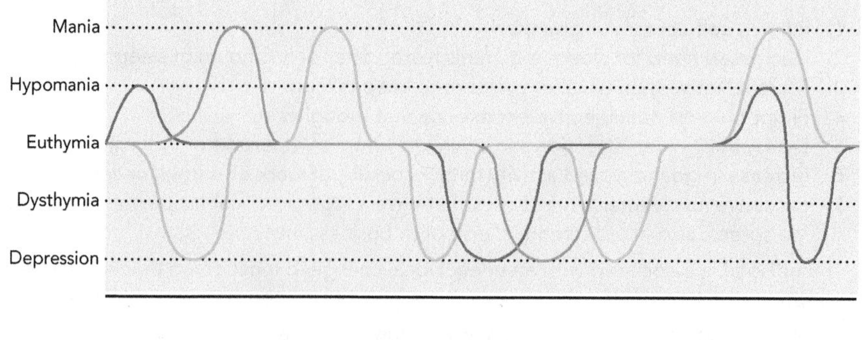

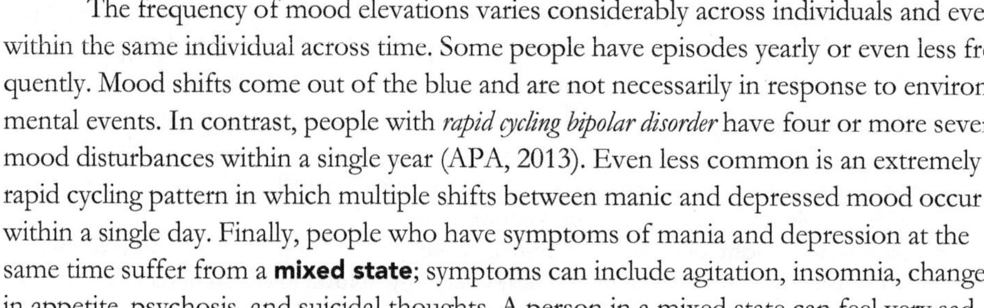
Jack felt on top of the world. He had never had his ideas flow so fast and furious. All week he needed only two hours of sleep per night, and he woke up totally refreshed and ready to go. He felt like a people magnet. He was funny, engaging, and full of energy. He was texting people at all hours of the night and couldn't figure out why other people were signing off when he was in such good form. He wished this feeling could last forever.

The frequency of mood elevations varies considerably across individuals and even within the same individual across time. Some people have episodes yearly or even less frequently. Mood shifts come out of the blue and are not necessarily in response to environmental events. In contrast, people with *rapid cycling bipolar disorder* have four or more severe mood disturbances within a single year (APA, 2013). Even less common is an extremely rapid cycling pattern in which multiple shifts between manic and depressed mood occur within a single day. Finally, people who have symptoms of mania and depression at the same time suffer from a **mixed state**; symptoms can include agitation, insomnia, changes in appetite, psychosis, and suicidal thoughts. A person in a mixed state can feel very sad and very energized at the same time. See Figure 6.1 for an illustration of the episodic nature of bipolar I disorder, bipolar II disorder, and rapid cycling bipolar disorder.

As noted in a consensus statement by Canadian and international experts on bipolar disorder, the disorder typically requires long-term maintenance treatment

Margaret Trudeau, who was formerly married to the late Prime Minister Pierre Trudeau, revealed in 2006 that she had been suffering from bipolar disorder. Since then she has been an active advocate for reducing stigma associated with mental illness.

Colin Mcconnell/ZUMA Press/Newscom

(Yatham et al., 2013). Although some people with bipolar disorder are symptom-free between episodes, many have some continuing symptoms. Even when controlled by medication, many patients report mild to moderate residual symptoms between episodes—typically symptoms of depression rather than mania (Judd et al., 2002; Post et al., 2003). Others, despite treatment, have chronic unremitting symptoms. Bipolar disorder is frequently depicted in literature as the mental illness that rests between the boundaries of creativity and madness, although this is not accurate (see "Examining the Evidence: Is There a Link Between Art and Madness?").

Another disorder, **cyclothymic disorder**, is characterized by fluctuations that alternate between hypomanic and depressive symptoms. In cyclothymia, the episodes are not as severe as with mania or major depression, but they persist for at least two years and, as a result of the cyclical and often unpredictable mood changes, cause impairment (APA, 2013).

Epidemiology

Bipolar disorder affects approximately 1% to 3% of people in North America over their lifetimes (Merikangas et al., 2007; Pearson et al., 2013). The average age of onset of the

SIDE by SIDE case studies Dimensions of Behaviour: From Normal to Abnormal

Normal Behaviour Case Study

Elation Due to Academic Success

→ Ahmed was the first person in his family to go to university. His parents had immigrated to Canada from Bosnia and had given him every possible advantage. He was valedictorian of his high school class and worked hard for the honour. He was never one to party or waste time—for him, school was all about academics and sports. He excelled in basketball and led his school to the local championships. He got a full scholarship to a top university. He was grateful for his athletic skills, but political science was his first love.

Ahmed's teachers recognized that he had a keen sense of international relations, and they felt he had the potential to go far. Given his academic record and athletic success, they encouraged him to apply for a Rhodes scholarship. Ahmed thought that the son of immigrants would never have a chance at getting a Rhodes. He was so convinced of this that after he sent in his application, he put it out of his mind, forgetting about the decision date.

When the letter arrived in the mail, his heart jumped into his throat. He talked himself down, reminding himself of the competition and his background. Then he opened the letter and found he had been selected. He started jumping up and down, knocking on everyone's dorm room, yelling, "You're not going to believe this!" He jumped into the shower with his clothes on, shouting, "Omigod, omigod!" When he called his parents, he was talking so fast in a combination of Bosnian and English that they could hardly understand him. He was positively over the moon! But after the news sank in, he came down to earth, thrilled and honoured by the possibilities his future held.

Abnormal Behaviour Case Study

First Manic Episode

→ Nineteen-year-old Alexis was walking the street in a very short red dress, fashion gloves, high heels, and gaudy jewellery. She was made up with gaudy makeup and bright red lipstick. Alexis approached men she didn't know, asking for a light and coming on to them sexually. An older man, concerned for her well-being, called the police.

In the psychiatric emergency room, Alexis was fawning over the police officer, showing off her legs. She kept walking across the room to strike up conversations with other patients—the topics were inappropriate and flirtatious. Her energy had an edge. She kept asking when she was going to be seen.

Given her disruptive behaviour, the attending psychiatrist and the resident evaluated her immediately. During the interview, she told the resident he was a hunk and asked him what he was doing later that night. Her speech was rapid and pressured, the doctors couldn't get a question in edgewise, and whatever answers she gave were not to the questions they asked. The attending physician gave her a medication to calm her down until her parents could arrive. As it turned out, she had just maxed out her credit card buying all of the clothes, makeup, and jewellery she was wearing. Her parents had called in a missing persons report the previous evening and provided more information.

Her drug screen was negative, and there were no other medical reasons for her bizarre behaviour. Her family history was positive for bipolar disorder, and this was her first manic episode. Alexis was admitted to the hospital and started a course of lithium medication.

first manic or depressive episode is 18 years (Merikangas et al., 2007). With regard to subtypes of the disorder, research from Canada indicates that the lifetime prevalence of bipolar I is higher than that of bipolar II (0.9% vs. 0.6%; McDonald et al., 2015). Canadian research further shows that the prevalence of bipolar disorder is highest in adolescents and young adults, with 3% of 15–24-year-olds receiving a diagnosis (Kozloff et al., 2010).

Sex, Age, Race, and Ethnicity

Canadian epidemiologic research, as with research conducted elsewhere in the world, suggests that bipolar disorder is equally prevalent in women and men (McDonald et al., 2015). However, there are large cross-national differences in the prevalence of bipolar disorder (Yatham et al., 2013). It is currently unclear whether the differences are due to racial or ethnic differences, or due to other factors such as differences in assessment methods and culturally-determined differences in the tendency to present for mental health treatment.

examining the EVIDENCE

Is There a Link Between Art and Madness?

- **The Facts** Throughout history, many remarkably talented artists have struggled through the tumultuous peaks and troughs associated with mood disturbances. In many cases, their personal experiences became the substance of their artistic expression. As Byron observed, "We of the craft are all crazy. Some are affected by gaiety, others by melancholy, but all are more or less touched." But is there really a relationship between art and madness?
- **The Evidence** In *Touched with Fire*, psychiatrist Kay Redfield Jamison examined the lives, works, and familial pedigrees of writers, poets, artists, and musicians and described a common thread among them: volatile cycles of compelling imagination, exuberance, and intelligence countered by periods of grim isolation and melancholy. Emily Dickinson, T. S. Eliot, Ernest Hemingway, Victor Hugo, Michelangelo, Charles Mingus, Georgia O'Keeffe, Sylvia Plath, Peter Tchaikovsky, Vincent van Gogh, and Virginia Woolf are just a few on Jamison's list with probable cyclothymia (cycling between dysthymia and hypomania), major depression, or manic-depressive illness. But without sound psychological and biological data to corroborate the diagnosis, these historical observations are not hard evidence that these individuals actually suffered from psychiatric illness. The question remains: What empirical evidence supports this link?
- **Let's Examine the Evidence** In his research, Professor Arnold Ludwig found that writers had much higher rates of depression and mania than matched controls. In his work *The Price of Greatness*, he writes that members of the artistic professions or creative arts are more likely than others to suffer from a lifetime mental illness. Similarly, in *The Hypomanic Edge*, psychologist John Gartner notes that hypomania may be a common (and potentially positive) trait among those who thrive in Western, bigger-better-faster culture. Yet not all individuals who have mood disorders are creative, and not all artists have mood disorders. So is there another variable that may influence the relationship between mood disorders and creativity?
- **What Are Alternative Explanations for This Relationship?** Perhaps mood disorders foster imaginative thought. Combined with the breadth of deep emotions present in some mood disorders, such intellectual inspiration might lend itself to artistic creativity. Ludwig speculates that those with mood disorders might be naturally drawn to artistic professions, given the potential normalization of the artistic temperament in such fields.
- **Conclusion** The link between creativity and mood disorders is still not well understood but potentially has many implications for artists, medicine, and society. When creativity is a necessary aspect of an individual's work, what are the potential implications of dampening this temperament with pharmacology? What if the person refuses to take medication because of the potential loss of creative ability? What are the implications of untreated depression? How would you feel if you were an artist and your best work occurred during what clinicians referred to as hypomanic episodes, which were often followed by depression? Would you give up your creativity (and perhaps your livelihood) for an opportunity to be free of severe mood swings?

Developmental Factors in Bipolar Disorder

Inability to fall asleep or stay asleep is one of the symptoms of depression.

Dan Race/Fotolia

Children suffer from bipolar disorder, but the symptoms may be very different from those seen in adults. Symptoms of mania are also somewhat different. In children, mania may be chronic rather than episodic, may cycle rapidly, or may appear as a mixed state (Geller & Luby, 1997). During a manic episode, they are more likely to display irritability and temper tantrums rather than a euphoric "high." These different symptoms make it difficult for mental health professionals to distinguish this disorder from other conditions such as attention deficit hyperactivity disorder, conduct disorder, oppositional defiant disorder, or even schizophrenia (Weller et al., 1995) (see Chapters 10 and 12). Accurate diagnosis is critical because the onset of bipolar disorder in childhood or early adolescence may represent a different and possibly more severe condition than the condition that develops in adulthood (Carlson & Kashani, 1988; Geller & Luby, 1997).

At the other end of the age spectrum, for people over the age of 60, manic and depressive symptoms often develop in association with medical illness, especially stroke (Van Gerpen et al., 1999). In addition, older patients who may have had some elements of mania in younger years can experience manic symptoms later in life.

Comorbidity

Bipolar disorder carries considerable medical and psychological comorbidity risk, and often the effects are bidirectional. The comorbid conditions may increase risk for developing bipolar disorder, and bipolar disorder (or its pharmacologic treatments) might increase the risk of some of the comorbid conditions. People with bipolar disorder are at increased risk for thyroid disease, migraine headaches, heart disease, diabetes, and obesity (Krishnan, 2005; Kupfer, 2005). Another common comorbid condition is substance abuse (Bizzarri et al., 2007). Once again, individuals with bipolar disorder might try to self-medicate with drugs or alcohol, drugs or alcohol might trigger or exacerbate manic or depressive episodes, or a third underlying trait (e.g., impulsivity) may contribute to both conditions. Other common comorbid psychological conditions are anxiety disorders, eating disorders, and attention deficit hyperactivity disorder (Krishnan, 2005; Merikangas et al., 2007).

Depressive Disorders

Major Depressive Disorder

6.2 Understand the differences between bipolar I and bipolar II disorders and between major depressive disorder and persistent depressive disorder.

The core symptom of **major depressive disorder** is a persistent sad or low mood that is severe enough to impair a person's interest in or ability to engage in normally enjoyable activities. In adults, depressed mood is central to major depressive disorder, but in children, the persistent mood disturbance may take the form of irritability or hostility. Major depressive disorder can be extremely debilitating in part because of other psychological, emotional, social, and physical problems that often accompany the persistent depressed mood. People with this disorder may feel completely worthless or extremely guilty, and

FIGURE 6.2

The Different Forms of Depressive Disorders. Contrast each of these patterns to normal mood fluctuations.

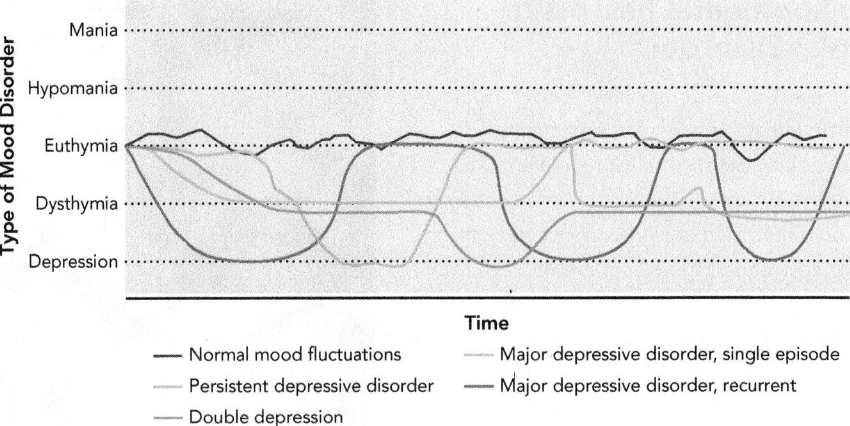

they may be at risk for harming themselves. Major depressive disorder can affect a person physically by disrupting sleep, appetite, and sexual drive (see "DSM-5: Major Depressive Episode"). Often, this means problems falling or staying asleep, feeling tired all the time, and having decreased appetite. However, about 40% of people diagnosed with major depressive disorder actually sleep and eat *more* than usual (referred to as "atypical depression"). Either way, the changes in sleep and appetite can lead to major problems with attention and concentration and can increase an already overwhelming sense of inadequacy and inclination to withdraw from the world.

Major depressive disorder is an episodic illness. Some people have only one episode (*single episode*) during their lifetime, but others suffer from multiple episodes separated by periods of normal mood (*recurrent*). A single episode, according to DSM-5, lasts at least two weeks, but often episodes can persist for several months. Refer to Figure 6.2 for an illustration of the course of the different forms of depression.

In addition to symptoms that last for two weeks, another factor that distinguishes major depressive disorder from sad mood is that the symptoms must affect the person's ability to function in social or work settings. Symptoms of major depressive disorder may sometimes result from physical disorders such as Cushing's syndrome (hypercortisolism, or too much of the hormone cortisol) and hypothyroidism (lack of sufficient thyroid hormone). However, depression is not diagnosed if the symptoms are caused by medical conditions such as these, nor is the diagnosis made if the depressed feelings result from a life event such as the death of a loved one (APA, 2013). Finally, depression can occur even after events that are not typically associated with sadness, such as after having a baby.

The "baby blues" are common among new mothers, but major depressive disorder with peripartum onset is a serious psychological disorder.

Pearson Education

Persistent Depressive Disorder (Dysthymia)

Persistent depressive disorder, or *dysthymia*, can best be conceptualized as a chronic state of depression (see "DSM-5: Persistent Depressive Disorder"). The symptoms are the same as those of major depression, but they are less severe. Whereas major depressive disorder is an episodic disorder with patients often achieving euthymia, or normal mood, between episodes, dysthymia is the consistent persistence of depressed mood. By definition, persistent depressive disorder lasts two or more years, and the individual is never without symptoms for more than two months (APA, 2013). On a day-to-day basis, the symptoms are typically milder than those of major depressive disorder. However, because they are so persistent, they may lead to severe outcomes (e.g., social isolation, high suicide risk) that affect not only the sufferer, but also extended family and friends. Because symptoms are generally less severe than those seen in major depressive disorder, people can suffer

criteria for
Major Depressive Episode DSM-5

A. Five (or more) of the following symptoms have been present during the same 2-week period and represent a change from previous functioning; at least one of the symptoms is either (1) depressed mood or (2) loss of interest or pleasure.

Note: Do not include symptoms that are clearly attributable to another medical condition.

1. Depressed mood most of the day, nearly every day, as indicated by either subjective report (e.g., feels sad, empty, hopeless) or observation made by others (e.g., appears tearful). (Note: In children and adolescents, can be irritable mood.)
2. Markedly diminished interest or pleasure in all, or almost all, activities most of the day, nearly every day (as indicated by either subjective account or observation).
3. Significant weight loss when not dieting or weight gain (e.g., a change of more than 5% of body weight in a month), or decrease or increase in appetite nearly every day. (Note: In children, consider failure to make expected weight gain.)
4. Insomnia or hypersomnia nearly every day.
5. Psychomotor agitation or retardation nearly every day (observable by others; not merely subjective feelings of restlessness or being slowed down).
6. Fatigue or loss of energy nearly every day.
7. Feelings of worthlessness or excessive or inappropriate guilt (which may be delusional) nearly every day (not merely self-reproach or guilt about being sick).
8. Diminished ability to think or concentrate, or indecisiveness, nearly every day (either by subjective account or as observed by others).
9. Recurrent thoughts of death (not just fear of dying), recurrent suicidal ideation without a specific plan, or a suicide attempt or a specific plan for committing suicide.

B. The symptoms cause clinically significant distress or impairment in social, occupational, or other important areas of functioning.

C. The episode is not attributable to the physiological effects of a substance or another medical condition.

Note: Criteria A–C represent a major depressive episode.

Note: Responses to a significant loss (e.g., bereavement, financial ruin, losses from a natural disaster, a serious medical illness or disability) may include the feelings of intense sadness, rumination about the loss, insomnia, poor appetite, and weight loss noted in Criterion A, which may resemble a depressive episode. Although such symptoms may be understandable or considered appropriate to the loss, the presence of a major depressive episode in addition to the normal response to a significant loss should also be carefully considered. This decision inevitably requires the exercise of clinical judgment based on the individual's history and the cultural norms for the expression of distress in the context of loss.[1]

D. The occurrence of the major depressive episode is not better explained by schizoaffective disorder, schizophrenia, schizophreniform disorder, delusional disorder, or other specified and unspecified schizophrenia spectrum and other psychotic disorders.

E. There has never been a manic episode or a hypomanic episode.

Note: This exclusion does not apply if all of the manic-like or hypomanic-like episodes are substance-induced or are attributable to the physiological effects of another medical condition.

from persistent depressive disorder for years before seeking treatment. Meanwhile, friends and family may turn away, often mislabelling the person as too moody and difficult.

Louise was under a constant grey cloud. She felt as if she had lived through the marriage of her daughter and the birth of her first two grandchildren like a zombie. She felt no joy, no wonder, and would rather stay home and cry than visit and play with her grandchildren. When all of the other women at church beamed about the accomplishments of their families, she could only feel guilty for not being part of her own children's lives.

People with persistent depressive disorder may also have major depressive episodes. This is known as **double depression**. In many instances, persistent depressive

criteria for
Persistent Depressive Disorder (Dysthymia) DSM-5

This disorder represents a consolidation of DSM-IV-defined chronic major depressive disorder and dysthymic disorder.

A. Depressed mood for most of the day, for more days than not, as indicated by either subjective account or observation by others, for at least 2 years.

Note: In children and adolescents, mood can be irritable and duration must be at least 1 year.

B. Presence, while depressed, of two (or more) of the following:

1. Poor appetite or overeating.
2. Insomnia or hypersomnia.
3. Low energy or fatigue.
4. Low self-esteem.
5. Poor concentration or difficulty making decisions.
6. Feelings of hopelessness.

C. During the 2-year period (1 year for children or adolescents) of the disturbance, the individual has never been without the symptoms in Criteria A and B for more than 2 months at a time.

D. Criteria for a major depressive disorder may be continuously present for 2 years.

E. There has never been a manic episode or a hypomanic episode, and criteria have never been met for cyclothymic disorder.

F. The disturbance is not better explained by a persistent schizoaffective disorder, schizophrenia, delusional disorder, or other specified or unspecified schizophrenia spectrum and other psychotic disorder.

G. The symptoms are not attributable to the physiological effects of a substance (e.g., a drug of abuse, a medication) or another medical condition (e.g., hypothyroidism).

H. The symptoms cause clinically significant distress or impairment in social, occupational, or other important areas of functioning.

Note: Because the criteria for a major depressive episode include four symptoms that are absent from the symptom list for persistent depressive disorder (dysthymia), a very limited number of individuals will have depressive symptoms that have persisted longer than 2 years but will not meet criteria for persistent depressive disorder. If full criteria for a major depressive episode have been met at some point during the current episode of illness, they should be given a diagnosis of major depressive disorder. Otherwise, a diagnosis of other specified depressive disorder or unspecified depressive disorder is warranted.

disorder is undiagnosed until the person has a major depressive episode. When the person seeks help for the more severe depressive symptoms, the longer history of dysthymia is identified. See Figure 6.2 for the time course of persistent depressive disorder and double depression.

Disruptive Mood Dysregulation Disorder

Disruptive mood dysregulation disorder (DMDD) is a new disorder making its first appearance in the DSM-5, and it is controversial. This category is reserved for children age 6 to 18 years old who have "severe recurrent temper outbursts that are grossly out of proportion in intensity or duration to the situation" (see "DSM-5: Disruptive Mood Dysregulation Disorder"). Arguments for inclusion of the disorder are to slow the rate of diagnoses of childhood bipolar disorder, which was being overdiagnosed in children with disruptive tendencies. Arguments against the disorder are that most children who receive this diagnosis already fit diagnostic criteria for other childhood disorders (e.g., oppositional defiant disorder and conduct disorder), and there is poor reliability in the diagnosis across clinicians (Dobbs, 2012). The harshest critics fear that this category is simply turning temper tantrums into a mental illness (Frances, 2012). Only time and experience will tell how well this diagnostic category differentiates a true mood syndrome from other non-mood disorder syndromes of childhood, and whether its existence reduces the number of children diagnosed with bipolar disorder of childhood.

criteria for Disruptive Mood Dysregulation Disorder — DSM-5

A. Severe recurrent temper outbursts manifested verbally (e.g., verbal rages) and/or behaviourally (e.g., physical aggression toward people or property) that are grossly out of proportion in intensity or duration to the situation or provocation.

B. The temper outbursts are inconsistent with developmental level.

C. The temper outbursts occur, on average, three or more times per week.

D. The mood between temper outbursts is persistently irritable or angry most of the day, nearly every day, and is observable by others (e.g., parents, teachers, peers).

E. Criteria A–D have been present for 12 or more months. Throughout that time, the individual has not had a period lasting 3 or more consecutive months without all of the symptoms in Criteria A–D.

F. Criteria A and D are present in at least two of three settings (i.e., at home, at school, with peers) and are severe in at least one of these.

G. The diagnosis should not be made for the first time before age 6 years or after age 18 years.

H. By history or observation, the age at onset of Criteria A–E is before 10 years.

I. There has never been a distinct period lasting more than 1 day during which the full symptom criteria, except duration, for a manic or hypomanic episode have been met.

Note: Developmentally appropriate mood elevation, such as occurs in the context of a highly positive event or its anticipation, should not be considered as a symptom of mania or hypomania.

J. The behaviours do not occur exclusively during an episode of major depressive disorder and are not better explained by another mental disorder (e.g., autism spectrum disorder, posttraumatic stress disorder, separation anxiety disorder, persistent depressive disorder [dysthymia]).

Note: This diagnosis cannot coexist with oppositional defiant disorder, intermittent explosive disorder, or bipolar disorder, though it can coexist with others, including major depressive disorder, attention-deficit/hyperactivity disorder, conduct disorder, and substance use disorders. Individuals whose symptoms meet criteria for both disruptive mood dysregulation disorder and oppositional defiant disorder should only be given the diagnosis of disruptive mood dysregulation disorder. If an individual has ever experienced a manic or hypomanic episode, the diagnosis of disruptive mood dysregulation disorder should not be assigned.

K. The symptoms are not attributable to the physiological effects of a substance or to another medical or neurological condition.

criteria for Premenstrual Dysphoric Disorder — DSM-5

A. In the majority of menstrual cycles, at least five symptoms must be present in the final week before the onset of menses, start to *improve* within a few days after the onset of menses, and become *minimal* or absent in the week postmenses.

B. One (or more) of the following symptoms must be present:

1. Marked affective lability (e.g., mood swings; feeling suddenly sad or tearful, or increased sensitivity to rejection).
2. Marked irritability or anger or increased interpersonal conflicts.
3. Marked depressed mood, feelings of hopelessness, or self-deprecating thoughts.
4. Marked anxiety, tension, and/or feelings of being keyed up or on edge.

C. One (or more) of the following symptoms must additionally be present, to reach a total of *five* symptoms when combined with symptoms from Criterion B above.

1. Decreased interest in usual activities (e.g., work, school, friends, hobbies).
2. Subjective difficulty in concentration.
3. Lethargy, easy fatigability, or marked lack of energy.
4. Marked change in appetite; overeating; or specific food cravings.
5. Hypersomnia or insomnia.
6. A sense of being overwhelmed or out of control.
7. Physical symptoms such as breast tenderness or swelling, joint or muscle pain, a sensation of "bloating," or weight gain.

Note: The symptoms in Criteria A–C must have been met for most menstrual cycles that occurred in the preceding year.

(continued)

D. The symptoms are associated with clinically significant distress or interference with work, school, usual social activities, or relationships with others (e.g., avoidance of social activities; decreased productivity and efficiency at work, school, or home).

E. The disturbance is not merely an exacerbation of the symptoms of another disorder, such as major depressive disorder, panic disorder, persistent depressive disorder (dysthymia), or a personality disorder (although it may co-occur with any of these disorders).

F. Criterion A should be confirmed by prospective daily ratings during at least two symptomatic cycles. (**Note:** The diagnosis may be made provisionally prior to this confirmation.)

G. The symptoms are not attributable to the physiological effects of a substance (e.g., a drug of abuse, a medication, other treatment) or another medical condition (e.g., hyperthyroidism).

Premenstrual Dysphoric Disorder

Many women will verify that there can be mood changes in the days preceding menstruation. However, **premenstrual dysphoric disorder (PMDD)** is a more severe form of these premenstrual changes that afflict 3% to 8% of women of reproductive age (Halbreich et al., 2003). PMDD follows a cyclic pattern and typically begins in the late luteal phase of the menstrual cycle (see "DSM-5: Premenstrual Dysphoric Disorder"). Mood symptoms can vary and include deep sadness or despair, anxiety and tension, anger or irritability, or panic. Changes in sleep, appetite, and libido can also emerge. PMDD not only affects the sufferers, but can also have significant effects on interpersonal relationships, which can be vulnerable to the extremes of emotionality often associated with the disorder.

Major Depressive Disorder with Peripartum Onset

All of the books painted such a rosy picture—the happy mothers breastfeeding, talking with other moms, developing that special bond with their new babies. What is wrong with me? Why do I just want this child to stop crying and go away? I can't bear to have my husband touch me. What kind of a mother am I? All the baby does is scream. Help me! Where's the joy? Why can't I feel what they're feeling?—*Susan, new mother*

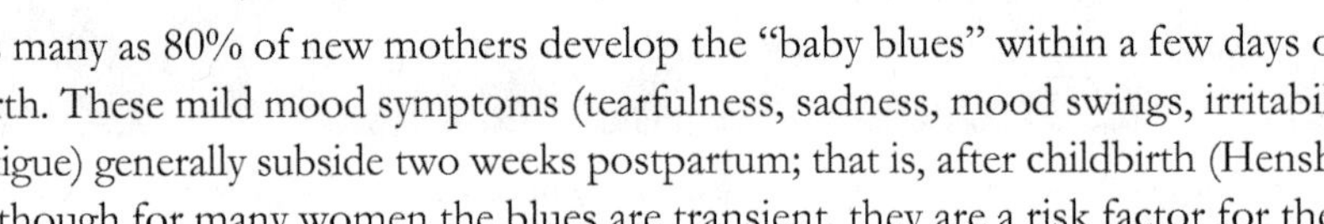

As many as 80% of new mothers develop the "baby blues" within a few days of childbirth. These mild mood symptoms (tearfulness, sadness, mood swings, irritability, fatigue) generally subside two weeks postpartum; that is, after childbirth (Henshaw, 2003). Although for many women the blues are transient, they are a risk factor for the development of postpartum depression (Reck et al., 2009). The prevalence of depression with onset in the first six months postpartum ranges from 6.5% to 12.9% across studies, peaking at two and six months after delivery (Gavin et al., 2005).

This disorder not only negatively affects mothers' functioning, but also is associated with temperamental, social, emotional, cognitive, and behavioural difficulties in the children (Pearlstein et al., 2009). In very rare cases, women may suffer a condition known as postpartum mood episodes with psychotic features (see Chapter 10).

Epidemiology

Major depressive disorder is a common psychiatric disorder, both in Canada and the rest of the world. In a 2012 survey by Statistics Canada, an estimated 3.2 million people (11.3% of the population) had major depressive disorder (Pearson et al., 2013). The median age of onset of major depressive disorder is 30 years (Kessler et al., 2005a). Dysthymia is less common, affecting approximately 2.5% of people (Kessler et al., 2005a).

Depression ranks fourth in terms of the global burden of disease (WHO, 2011). Disease burden uses an indicator called *disability adjusted life years (DALY)*, which measures the total amount of healthy life lost to all causes, whether from premature death or disability. People with depression reported a fivefold increase in the time away from work than people without depression (Kessler & Frank, 1997). Clearly, major depression is a burden to both the individual and society.

In a manic state, people with bipolar disorder may act impulsively, such as spending excessive amounts of money.

jordanfotografi/Shutterstock

Sex, Race, and Ethnicity

6.3 Discuss sex differences in the risk for major depressive disorder.

Despite their commonality, depressive disorders do not occur with equal frequency across all sex, racial, and ethnic groups. Although the precise reasons are unknown, some differences—especially the disproportionate number of women affected by depression—have consistently been observed and remain a topic of considerable scientific debate.

DEPRESSION IN WOMEN Across cultures and countries, almost twice as many women as men suffer from major depressive disorder (Pearson et al., 2013; Weissman et al., 1993), but the exact ratio changes with age (Angold et al., 1991). Depressive symptoms are more common among women who have few financial resources, are less educated, and are unemployed (McGrath et al., 1990). Even among women, rates of depression vary by age. Reproductive events such as puberty, the premenstrual period, pregnancy, the postpartum period, and menopause all are risks for mood disturbances (Angold & Costello, 2006; Bennett et al., 2004; Driscoll, 2006; Harsh et al., 2009), suggesting that the ebb and flow of female hormones may have some role. Yet the precise manner in which hormonal fluctuations influence risk for major depressive disorders is unclear.

DEPRESSION IN RACIAL AND ETHNIC MINORITIES AND ACROSS CULTURES The National Comorbidity Study-Replication reported a higher prevalence of major depression in whites (17.9%) than non-Hispanic blacks (10.8%) or Hispanics (13.5%) (Breslau et al., 2005). Understanding racial, ethnic, and cultural differences requires an appreciation of culture and context. Breslau et al. (2005) underscore the importance of exploring racial and ethnic factors that may be protective against the emergence of depression. Two factors, ethnic identity (Herd & Grube, 1996; Mossakowski, 2003) and religious participation (Lee & Newberg, 2005; Varon & Riley, 1999; Wallace & Forman, 1998), seem to function as protective factors, lowering risk for depression.

A more fundamental question is whether the concept of depression is based primarily on a European (Western) understanding of mental illness. Many languages and cultures do not have words for depression, so simple translations of Western interview questions can complicate the diagnostic process, yielding inaccurate diagnoses and incorrect prevalence data. Overall, individuals from various cultures tend to report both psychological and physical symptoms of depression (Simon et al., 1999). Nonetheless, culturally appropriate terminology would ensure recognition of depression across cultures, races, and ethnic groups, in addition to enhanced treatment delivery and adherence (Patel, 2001).

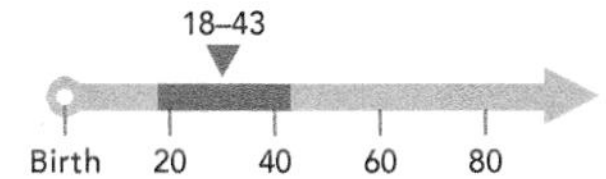

The peak age of onset for major depression is between 18 and 43, but onset can occur at any time.

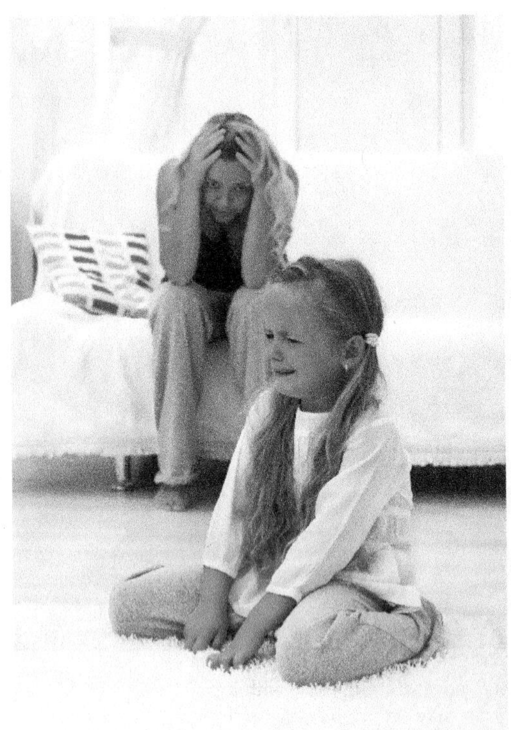

Children as well as adolescents and adults may suffer from depression, but the signs and symptoms of the disorder may be different in children.

Ilike/Fotolia

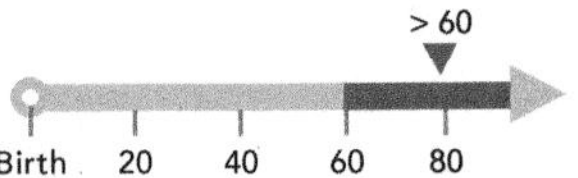

Depression in older people can be associated with declining health or use of certain medications. The language that older adults use to describe depression also can be different from younger adults.

Developmental Factors

The primary age-band of risk for depression is between 18 and 43, with the median age of onset around 30 years (Kessler et al., 2005a). However, depression exists across all ages. An estimated 3% to 8% of children and adolescents report suffering from depression (National Institute of Mental Health, 2005; Public Health Agency of Canada, 2011). Although the diagnostic criteria are the same, the observable signs of depression may differ, and young people may lack the necessary vocabulary and insight to describe depressed mood. Warning signs can include nonspecific physical complaints such as headaches, muscle aches, stomachaches, or tiredness; school absence or poor performance; unexplained irritability; crying spells; boredom; social withdrawal; alcohol or substance abuse; anger or hostility; relationship difficulties; and recklessness. If untreated, depression in adolescence can lead to school failure, alcohol or other drug use, and suicide.

Developmental factors also influence the sex ratio of depression. Throughout childhood, girls and boys are equally likely to have depression. However, around age 13, rates begin to climb for girls but remain constant or even decrease for boys (Cyranowski et al., 2000; Nolen-Hoeksema, 2001; Parker & Brotchie, 2004). By late adolescence, the 2:1 ratio (girls to boys) is established and remains fairly constant thereafter. As yet there is no clear explanation for this developmental sex difference, but biological, psychological, and environmental factors may be involved. These factors may include hormones, self-consciousness about bodily changes during puberty, poor sense of competence, socioeconomic disadvantage, victimization, chronic life stressors, low self-esteem, and higher reactivity to stress. Any or all of these factors may converge to both increase risk and perpetuate mood disturbances in women (Nolen-Hoeksema, 2001; Parker & Brotchie, 2004; Angold & Costello, 2006). Depression often goes unrecognized and untreated in children and adolescents. This is unfortunate because early onset depression often persists, recurs, and continues into adulthood (Weissman et al., 1999).

The prevalence of depression is particularly high in people over 60, especially those with major medical problems. To illustrate, in a sample of 50 000 Canadian seniors living in residential care facilities (e.g., nursing homes), nearly half (44%) had depressive symptoms and 26% had a diagnosis of depression (Canadian Institute for Health Information, 2010). Older adults are also more likely to suffer from medical illnesses. Both the illnesses and the medications used to treat them can complicate the detection and diagnosis of depression (Árean & Reynolds, 2005).

Comorbidity

Depression may co-occur with many different kinds of medical conditions, including cardiovascular disease, central nervous system diseases, cancer, and migraines (Fleischhacker et al., 2008). Coronary heart disease often coexists with depression, and depression can influence outcome from coronary illness (van Melle et al., 2004). Major depressive disorder also commonly coexists with other psychiatric conditions. Nearly three quarters (72.1%) of people with lifetime major depressive disorder have at least one additional mental disorder, including anxiety disorders (59.2%), substance use disorder (24%), and impulse control disorders (30%) (Kessler et al., 2005a). Depression is also the most common comorbid disorder in eating disorders (Fernandez-Aranda et al., 2007) and often persists even after recovery from the eating disorder (Sullivan et al., 1998). In most cases, depression occurs before the other conditions.

Much research has been directed at understanding the relationship between anxiety and depression. Twin studies examine how the same genetic and environmental factors can contribute to two different disorders. In fact, the genetic correlation between major depressive disorder and generalized anxiety disorder is 100% (Kendler, 1996; Kendler et al., 2007a; Kendler et al., 1992), suggesting that the same genetic factors influence the risk for both disorders. Genetically vulnerable individuals may develop major depressive disorder, generalized anxiety disorder, or both, depending on their environmental experiences. In other words, genes provide the vulnerability to a negative mood state, and the environment shapes which negative mood state emerges. This conclusion—that depression and anxiety represent the same gene(s) but different environments—is one compelling explanation for why these two disorders co-occur so commonly. As yet, we have not unravelled the second part of the equation—namely, which environmental experiences result in depression, anxiety, or both?

CONCEPT check

- Bipolar I disorder is marked by the presence of manic episodes either with or without depressive episodes. Bipolar II is characterized by hypomanic episodes coupled with depressive episodes.
- Major depressive disorder is an episodic disorder and is marked by persistent low mood lasting at least two weeks. Persistent depressive disorder has a more chronic profile and consists of persistent low mood lasting a period of two years or more.
- Across the lifespan and across sexes, the prevalence of major depressive disorder varies. Overall, depression is almost twice as common in women as in men.
- Bipolar disorder in children is often marked by irritability rather than euphoria.
- Depression may look different in children and adolescents in part because of their level of cognitive development, insight, and available vocabulary to describe their feelings.
- Ethnic, racial, and cultural issues must be considered when determining the prevalence of depression across various groups.

critical thinking question Depression in women is associated with both reproductive events and socioeconomic disadvantage. How would you go about determining the relative contribution of biology and environment?

Suicide

Although not all suicides are associated with depression, thoughts of suicide or of death are a frightening component of depression both for the sufferer and for family and friends. Suicide is one of the most perplexing of human behaviours and the most devastating outcome of depression. Its effects reach far beyond the person who dies and can have a deep and long-lasting impact on family, friends, the community, the nation, and sometimes even the world. Family members and friends may never understand what drove a person to suicide.

Suicide is a leading cause of death for people of all ages. In 2009, it ranked as the ninth leading cause of death in Canada (Navaneelan, 2012). In Canada, the most common methods of suicide are hanging (44%), poisoning, which includes drug overdose (25%), and firearm use (16%) (Navaneelan, 2012). The World Health Organization (WHO) estimates that every year, nearly 1 million people die from suicide, yielding a "global" mortality rate of 16 per 100 000. Globally, suicide rates have increased by 60% in the past 45 years. Suicide is among the three leading causes of death among those aged 15 to 44 years in some countries, and the second leading cause of death in the 10 to 24 years age group (WHO, 2011). It is commonly believed that suicide rates are underreported due to the misclassification of cause of death in situations such as single-vehicle car accidents.

Suicidal Ideation, Suicide Attempts, and Completed Suicide

Suicidal ideation and behaviour range from mere thoughts about suicide or death, to plans about how to commit suicide, to the completed act. Although varying in intensity,

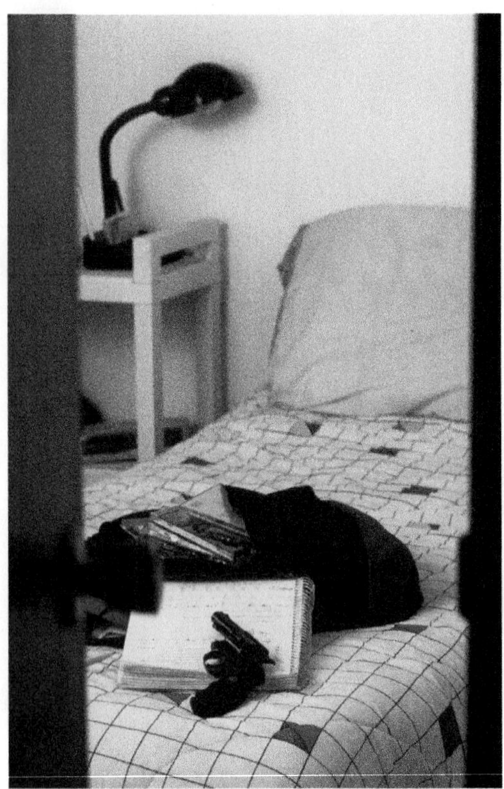

Firearms in the home increase the risk of suicide.

Jim CorwinMore/Getty Images

at each level, these thoughts and behaviours should be taken seriously and should raise concern about the person's psychological well-being.

Thoughts of death, also known as **suicidal ideation**, may take different forms. *Passive suicidal ideation* is a wish to be dead but does not include active planning about how to commit suicide. *Active suicidal ideation* includes thoughts about how to commit the act, including details such as where, when, and how. Although some suicidal acts are impulsive, detailed suicidal plans are of considerable clinical concern because they indicate premeditation and determination to complete the act.

Suicidal acts are evaluated based on lethality and intent. Some acts, sometimes called *parasuicides*, are behaviours such as superficial cutting of the wrists or overdoses of nonlethal amounts of medications. These acts are unlikely to result in death. However, intent cannot necessarily be inferred from lethality. For example, a woman who takes some pills to end her life may be unaware that the dose was not lethal; she may have fully intended to die. In contrast, violent attempts such as hanging, self-inflicted gunshot wounds, and jumping from a building are almost always associated with serious intent. Previous attempts at suicide increase the risk of suicide 30 to 40 times (Harris & Barraclough, 1997). A history of deliberate self-harm is the strongest predictor of future suicidal behaviour (Zahl & Hawton, 2004). All attempts should be taken seriously and require immediate treatment.

Who Commits Suicide?

6.4 Discuss factors associated with suicide and the relationship between depression and suicidal ideation and behaviour.

Suicide remains the second leading cause of death for young Canadians, second only to motor vehicle accidents (Cheung & Dewa, 2007). Suicide accounts for 24% of all deaths among 15- to 24-year-olds, and 16% among 25- to 44-year-olds (Health Canada, 2002). Males are more likely to commit suicide than females, although females are more likely to report suicidal ideation (Borges et al., 2006; Navaneelan, 2012) (see Figure 6.3). This difference exists across the age spectrum and may reflect the fact that males choose more lethal methods such as hanging or using firearms. Among adolescent males, the highest risk factors are major depressive and bipolar disorders, previous suicidal attempts, substance abuse, conduct disorder, and presence of a gun in the home. In females, depressive and bipolar disorders, previous suicidal attempts, and presence of a handgun in the home increase risk (Shaffer et al., 1996).

Youth from socially disadvantaged backgrounds (less education and lower socioeconomic status) are at a higher risk of serious suicide attempts (Beautrais et al., 1997, 1998). Other contributors are parental psychiatric illness, parental suicide attempt—a phenomenon called *drifting* (being generally disconnected from school, work, and family)—sociodemographic disadvantage, and adverse family circumstances (Beautrais et al., 1997;

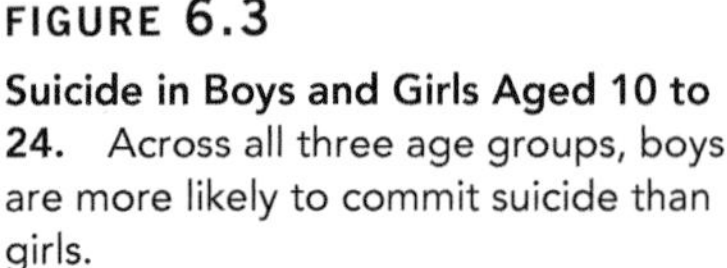

FIGURE 6.3

Suicide in Boys and Girls Aged 10 to 24. Across all three age groups, boys are more likely to commit suicide than girls.

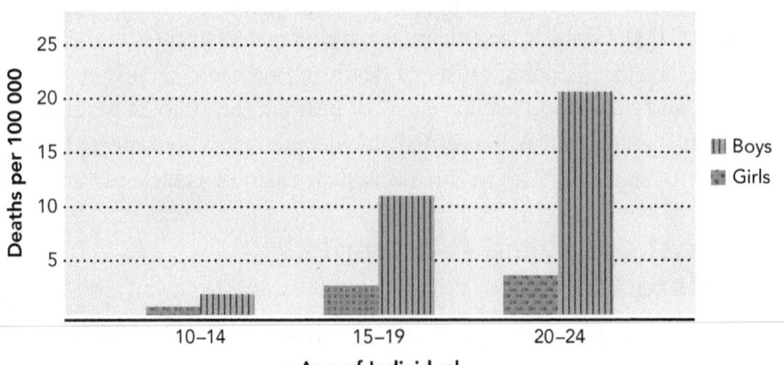

Gould, 1990). In terms of immediate events likely to precipitate a suicide attempt, relationship breakdowns, interpersonal problems, and financial difficulties are most commonly reported in youth. Research from Canada and elsewhere shows that exposure to suicide (e.g., the suicide of a classmate) predicts suicidal ideation and attempts in others (Swanson & Colman, 2013).

The likelihood of committing suicide also varies with race and ethnicity. In Canada, the Inuit (indigenous people of the Arctic) suffer from one of the highest rates of suicide in the world. Inuit youth are at especially high risk of suicide, with suicide rates 30 times higher than those of youth in the Canadian general population (Fraser et al., 2015). The high rates of suicide in the Inuit are a relatively recent phenomenon; rates of suicide were low in the 1950s, but steadily rose thereafter. Possible reasons for the increase are factors such as rapid cultural change, including political marginalization and forced assimilation through residential schools, along with geographic isolation and lack of personal and career opportunities (Fraser et al., 2015).

Ethics and Responsibility

Developmental issues can help in understanding suicide in children. First, because their brains are still developing, they might not realize the finality of suicide. Moreover, they are more impulsive than adults and may not be able to understand that the troubles they face are not necessarily permanent. Teachers and authorities must also work to prevent copycat suicide attempts. They need to avoid glamorizing suicide or presenting an overly positive image of the suicide victim as someone children should try to model. Because suicides in children do occur, psychologists must assist parents and teachers in taking threats seriously and developing effective, developmentally tailored interventions for children at risk.

Risk Factors for Suicide

Many factors may affect the risk of acting on suicidal thoughts or impulses, but one of the strongest predictors is a history of prior attempts (Borges et al., 2006).

FAMILY HISTORY Suicidal behaviours run in families. This is demonstrated by both family studies and highly visible cases in which multiple family members across generations have committed suicide (see "Real People, Real Disorders: The Heritability of Suicide—The Hemingway and van Gogh Families"). However, family studies cannot disentangle the extent to which this familial factor is genetic or environmental. Twin studies of suicidal ideation and suicide attempts clearly implicate genetic influences, even when accounting for the effects of psychopathology (Pedersen & Fiske, 2010).

PSYCHIATRIC ILLNESS Although suicide does not always occur within the context of mental illness, approximately 90% of attempted or completed suicides are committed by individuals who suffer from psychological disorders (Kessler et al., 2005b). Clinicians are seriously concerned about the relation between major depression and suicide. According to epidemiological research, 89% of individuals who attempted suicide had major depression in the last 12 months (Kessler et al., 2005b). Suicide is also associated with postpartum depression, as illustrated in the following case:

> Dr. Suzanne Killinger-Johnson, a successful psychotherapist and well-to-do daughter of a psychologist and endocrinologist, killed herself and her six-month-old baby, Cuyler, by jumping in front of an oncoming subway train. The night before, Suzanne was seen clutching her baby in a Toronto subway station. She had been standing by the platform for quite some time. Transit officials became concerned, so they called the police. Officers spoke with Suzanne, and she left. About 90 minutes later, a similar thing happened at another subway station.

This time the police drove her home, leaving her in the care of her husband and relatives. During rush hour the next morning, Suzanne slipped out of the house with her baby and drove her silver Mercedes sports utility vehicle to yet another subway station. Commuters watched in horror as Suzanne dived in front of an oncoming train, clutching her baby to her chest. The infant was killed instantly. Suzanne died several days later. What caused the murder/suicide? Suzanne and her husband lived in a fashionable Toronto neighbourhood and appeared to live a life of affluence. It is thought that she suffered from extreme postpartum depression after Cuyler's birth, perhaps leading to an urge to remove the baby and herself from what seemed to be an intolerable world. (Sources: Robertson & Cairns, 2000; Saunders & Procuta, 2009).

Suicide is also associated with bipolar disorder. Here, suicide attempts tend to occur during severe depressive or mixed states and are often deadly (Baldessarini et al., 2006). Approximately 50% of patients with bipolar disorder attempt suicide during their lifetime, and between 15% and 20% die by suicide (Harris & Barraclough, 1997; Jamison & Baldessarini, 1999).

Other disorders associated with suicide attempts include substance use disorder, anxiety disorders, antisocial disorders, anorexia nervosa, and schizophrenia. Patients with schizophrenia may act on auditory hallucinations ("hearing voices") commanding them to kill themselves.

BIOLOGICAL FACTORS In addition to genetics, neuroimaging and brain autopsy studies reveal very low levels of serotonin in the brains of people who have committed suicide (Mann et al., 2001). The biology and genetics of suicide appear to be at least partially independent of the biology of depression and other mental illnesses (Brent & Mann, 2005). In other words, depression alone does not lead to suicide, although it increases the risk. For example, behaviours such as impulsivity and pathological aggression, both of which are associated with low levels of serotonin, also may contribute to risk for suicidal behaviours.

Understanding Suicide

It is impossible to completely re-create the thoughts, circumstances, and triggers that lead to suicide. Although different approaches exist, they remain at best crude approximations of what actually occurs when the decision is made to end one's own life.

THE PSYCHOLOGICAL AUTOPSY Piecing together the events leading to suicide is complicated. Between one fifth and one third of those who commit suicide leave suicide notes, but these notes are not typically detailed accounts of what led to the act (Kuwabara et al., 2006). Putting together the information often involves a process known as a **psychological autopsy**. Clinicians interview family, friends, co-workers, and health care providers to identify psychological causes in much the same way that a coroner searches for physical causes of death. A structured interview is sometimes used to reconstruct motives and circumstances. The interview addresses potential precipitants and stressors, motivation, lethality, and intentionality. For example, the interviewer may try to determine whether the person had distributed personal objects or written a will or other letters that would suggest deliberate suicidal intent.

Although this approach can help survivors understand factors that contributed to a suicide, it does little to diminish their anguish. Commonly, those left behind search for clues and blame themselves for not noticing them in time. For this reason, comments about suicide or passive death wishes should always be taken seriously. Dismissing such comments as passing moods or cries for attention can be a devastating error. If a person is troubled enough to mention suicide, then something is wrong, and getting professional help is critical.

REAL people REAL disorders

The Heritability of Suicide—The Hemingway and van Gogh Families

In the mid-nineteenth century, the poet Alfred Lord Tennyson described multiple melancholic relatives as "taint[s] of blood" (Jamison, 1993). Perhaps a more striking reality is that suicide may also be heritable, as in the families of Ernest Hemingway and Vincent van Gogh.

Hemingway's family tree is tragically replete with suicide. Over two generations, four members committed suicide—the writer, his father, his brother, and his sister—and in 1996, the daughter of Ernest's oldest son, model Margaux Hemingway, died from a barbiturate overdose. Ernest was diagnosed with bipolar disorder, and a clear pattern of depression, rages, and mania exists in his family (Jamison, 1993; Lynn, 1987). Before the writer took his own life in 1961, he had been hospitalized and received electroconvulsive therapy for psychotic depression. The author's writing reflected the experience of his father's suicide: Many of his characters come face to face with death and are admired for confronting death bravely and without emotional expression (Magill, 1983).

Suicide also runs strongly in the van Gogh family. Both Vincent van Gogh and his brother Cornelius took their own lives. Although Vincent van Gogh's condition has been debated for nearly a century, much evidence taken from letters and medical records suggests that the painter suffered from depression, possibly bipolar disorder (Jamison, 1993). His brother Theo also had psychotic and manic-depressive symptoms, and his sister Wilhelmina suffered from chronic psychosis, spending most of her life in a mental institution. Before shooting himself in 1890, van Gogh wrote of his illness in a letter to his brother Theo as "a fatal inheritance, since in civilization the weakness increases from generation to generation."

Newscom

Rene Burri/Magnum Photos

Research corroborates the existence of these suicidal clusters. Researchers in Denmark compared 4262 people who had committed suicide with control subjects and evaluated their family histories of suicide and psychiatric illness (Qin et al., 2002). People with a family history of suicide were 2.5 times more likely to commit suicide than those without a family history. Other studies have found that the familiality of suicide might be genetically transmitted.

The heritability of suicide complicates the already difficult matter of coping with a family member's suicide—a process that can leave survivors with complex emotions as well as a feeling of stigma surrounding the act of suicide. Various local organizations throughout North America provide support and treatment resources to survivors. Joining these efforts, Mariel Hemingway, granddaughter of the writer, has become an outspoken advocate for suicide prevention.

Prevention of Suicide

Because suicide is a final act, interventions must focus on prevention. Remarkably, 50% of suicidal Canadian adolescents and young adults do *not* use mental health services such as counselling (Cheung & Dewa, 2007). Similar findings have been reported in other countries (Cheung & Dewa, 2007). This suggests that in order to address the problem of suicide in youth and young adults, we need to understand the barriers that prevent them from obtaining appropriate mental health services. If the primary reason is the shame or stigma associated with having a mental illness, then there needs to be community-based programs to tackle this issue. For example, programs can be created that educate people that depression and suicidality are common, important problems and that it is a sigh of courage, not weakness, to seek appropriate help. Unfortunately, such programs will not be sufficient to address the problem of youth suicide in Canada because there are not enough mental health services for suicidal youth, including a lack of school psychologists and child psychiatrists (Goar, 2005). Improving the availability of clinical services is therefore another vital way of addressing the problem. Accordingly, an independent report commissioned by the Canadian government recommended that a national suicide prevention program should be developed (Kirby & Keon, 2006).

CRISIS INTERVENTION Suicide hotlines exist across North America and are generally staffed by people with crisis intervention training. People with suicidal thoughts are urged to call these hotlines to receive support in the hope of preventing a suicide attempt. A counsellor who determines that the caller is in immediate danger attempts to locate the person and sends help immediately. Because hotlines are anonymous, it is virtually impossible to assess their specific effectiveness on a population level. However, even if the hotline provides only a referral for further psychiatric care, it represents a meaningful component of suicide prevention.

FOCUS ON HIGH-RISK GROUPS One approach to suicide prevention targets people with several known risk factors (Brent & Mann, 2005). The children of parents with mood disorders who have attempted suicide themselves are clearly an at-risk group. For those children, early detection and treatment of mood disturbances, substance abuse, and other comorbid symptoms could create an early connection with mental health professionals and provide parents and children with tools to deal with emerging symptoms before they become severe.

SOCIETAL LEVEL PREVENTION Using teacher and peer support, societal approaches try to "reconnect" youth who are drifting with social and emotional supports, thereby improving both their school and family functioning (Eggert et al., 1995; Thompson & Eggert, 1999; Thompson et al., 2000). Other interventions try to eliminate access to methods of committing suicide, such as detoxifying domestic gas and decreasing access to firearms (Brent & Mann, 2005). Effective strategies involve working directly with the gun owner to secure rather than remove the gun and providing psychoeducation regarding the increased risk of suicide when a gun is in the home. However, some evidence suggests that people who are determined to commit suicide will simply find alternative methods (Marzuk et al., 1992). It is not possible to eliminate every hazard (e.g., bridges and tall buildings), but limiting access to lethal means at least introduces a delay that creates an opening for intervention. To illustrate, Toronto's Bloor Street Viaduct is the bridge with the world's second highest annual rate of suicide by jumping, second only to the Golden Gate Bridge in San Francisco. The erection of a simple barrier at the Bloor Viaduct reduced the number of suicides by jumping, although similar barriers at other bridges and tall buildings are needed to reduce the rate of suicide by jumping (Sinyor & Levitt, 2010).

PREVENTING SUICIDAL CONTAGION The media's portrayal of suicides of famous people has been associated with copycat suicides (Gould, 1990). The careless inclusion of details about suicide attempts and the portrayal of those who commit suicide as tragic or flawed heroes or martyrs can lead to a pathological obsession with suicide as a solution to life's problems—especially in youth. In addition, suicide clusters, suicide pacts, and Internet sites that function as how-to or support groups that encourage suicide are frightening and dark portrayals of youth whose thinking is detached from reality.

When a youth commits suicide, schools often act immediately, intervening with *critical incident debriefing* (CID), a strategy that brings together people who witnessed a trauma to talk about the event and their reaction to it. CID is a controversial intervention that, when used incorrectly, may do more harm than good (Bootzin & Bailey, 2005). However, when trained professionals join with school officials to administer CID appropriately, it may provide an outlet for those affected to express their fears and grief by talking about the event. They can also seek support and learn concrete ways to "say goodbye" to the suicide victim. CID can also help to identify fellow students at risk for suicide, allow students to process the death of a peer, and provide an accurate and balanced (rather than glorified) account of the pain and futility of suicide (Macy et al., 2004; Meilman & Hall, 2006).

Treatment After Suicide Attempts

Serious suicide attempts require immediate medical care; however, prolonged psychological care beyond the effects of the attempt is sometimes necessary.

Jackie was seriously depressed and felt that life was hopeless. She attempted suicide by jumping out of a fifth-story window. Although she shattered almost every bone in her body, she did not die. Now she faces a life with severe facial disfigurement, impaired ability to speak, and confinement to a wheelchair. All she thinks about is how to "finish the job." Jackie desperately needs help, now more than ever, to cope with and find some relief from her depressed mood and her physical ailments. But as long as she remains focused on ending her life, her mood is bound to stay depressed, making it very difficult for her to seek out and receive the help she deserves.

Deliberate self-harm is a major risk factor for suicide. Various psychological and psychosocial interventions reduce self-harm behaviour and improve mood in people who previously attempted suicide. However, more studies are needed to determine the impact of these interventions in reducing subsequent suicide attempts or completed suicides (Hepp et al., 2004). All individuals should receive follow-up psychiatric care after an attempt, but data suggest that many people who attempt suicide do not receive proper psychotherapeutic attention afterward (Beautrais et al., 1997).

Canadian FOCUS

Cyberbullying, Depression, and Suicide

In 2012, Amanda Todd, age 15, committed suicide in her home in Port Coquitlam, B.C. Prior to her death she posted a YouTube video in which she used a series of flash cards to describe how she was blackmailed into exposing her breasts via webcam and the subsequent bullying she endured. The video went viral after her death, attracting over 17 million views. In grade 7 she was using video chat to meet new people. A stranger persistently complimented Amanda on her looks and eventually persuaded her to bare her breasts on camera. The person then threatened to send the topless photo to her friends unless she gave him a "show." The police became involved, but then, to Amanda's horror, she discovered that the topless photo was being circulated on the Internet. Her family moved to a new home, where she started a new school. A year later, the bully reappeared, creating a Facebook profile using Amanda's topless photo as the profile image and contacting classmates at her new school. Amanda was teased at school and changed schools for a second time. Other complications occurred. She had sex with an old friend while the friend's girlfriend was out of town. The girlfriend and her friends confronted and assaulted Amanda. After that humiliating episode, Amanda attempted suicide by drinking bleach, but survived after being rushed to hospital to have her stomach pumped. Upon returning home there were abusive messages on Facebook about her failed suicide attempt. Her family moved to another city, but every time she moved schools the bully would become her Facebook friend, pretending to be a new student, and then post embarrassing images of Amanda. After six months of this abuse, Amanda began cutting herself. She overdosed on antidepressant medication and was hospitalized. After leaving hospital she was taunted by the other students for being in a "mental hospital." Not long afterward, Amanda was found dead. A coroner's investigation deemed her death a suicide. In April 2014, police arrested 35-year-old suspect Aydin Coban in the Netherlands and charged him with extortion, luring and criminal harassment, and possession of child pornography for the purpose of distribution.

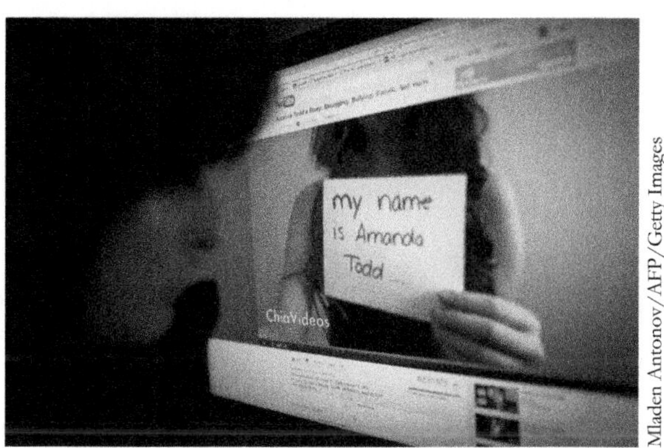

Mladen Antonov/AFP/Getty Images

Source: https://en.wikipedia.org/wiki/Suicide_of_Amanda_Todd. Accessed June 29, 2015.

(continued)

Amanda's tragic death highlights the seriousness of cyberbulling. Bullying in general is aggressive behaviour that is intentional, repetitive in nature, and involves an imbalance of power between the aggressor and victim (Haltigan & Vaillancourt, 2014). In some ways, cyberbullying is worse than ordinary (face-to-face) bullying. Cyberbullying involves the sending or posting of harmful or cruel text or images using the Internet or other digital communication devices. This might include name-calling, spreading rumours, or circulating embarrassing texts or images. Abusive messages can be sent privately, such as by email or cellphone, or by widely disseminated means, such as by Facebook or Twitter. Cyberbullying is worse than ordinary bullying because (a) the bullying can happen 24/7, (b) it intrudes into the victim's home, (c) it is widely disseminated, even worldwide in a viral manner, and (e) it may potentially never end, as in the case of embarrassing photos circulated on the Internet.

According to a 2009 survey by Statistics Canada, 17% of young adult Internet users (age 18–24 years) reported that they had been cyberbullied, often anonymously (Perreault, 2011). A survey of British Columbian junior high students (grades 7–9) found that about a quarter had been cyberbullied (Li, 2010). Similar findings were reported for grade 6–11 students in Alberta (Wade & Beran, 2011) and in studies conducted in other countries (Hamm et al., 2015; Li, 2015; Wade & Beran, 2011). Girls are more likely to be cyberbullied than boys (Hamm et al., 2015).

Research conducted in Canada and other countries suggests that cyberbullying can lead to anxiety, depression, school avoidance and poor school grades, suicidal ideation, and, in some cases, suicide attempts (Bonanno & Hymel, 2013;Hamm et al., 2014; van Geel et al., 2014). Cyberbullying is more strongly related to suicidal ideation compared with traditional (face-to-face) bullying (van Geel et al., 2015).

The question is how to best address the problem of cyberbullying. Raising public awareness is important; for example, schoolchildren should be educated about the seriousness of cyberbullying and given information about what to do if it happens to them. Children who are cyberbullied are often reluctant to disclose the problem to their parents (Hamm et al., 2015; Li, 2010), sometimes for fear that they will lose computer privileges (Hamm et al., 2015). Parents need to be alert to the possibility that their child might someday become the victim of cyberbullying. Parents can discuss this with their child and work together on a plan to avoid cyberbullying (e.g., by being careful of what they post online) and on a plan of how to deal with cyberbullying if it arises (e.g., block the sender; notify parents, teachers, or website administrators; or, if a crime has been committed, contact the police) (Moreno, 2014).

CONCEPT check

- The best predictors of a future suicide attempt include a family history of completed suicide, the presence of a psychological disorder, and past self-harm behaviour (including a previous suicide attempt).
- Women are more likely to report suicidal ideation, but men are more likely to complete suicide.
- Few individuals leave notes explaining why they committed suicide.
- Although not all those who commit suicide are seriously depressed, approximately 90% of individuals who commit suicide have a mental illness.

critical thinking question Suicide is a uniquely human behaviour. What features of humans as a species influence our desire to commit suicide?

The Etiology of Bipolar and Depressive Disorders

6.5 Understand psychodynamic, behavioural, cognitive, and biological theories of the causes of bipolar and depressive disorders.

An occasional feeling of low mood is a universal human experience, and we usually can identify the reason. For example, if you missed going home for a holiday or if you did not do well on an important exam, it would be reasonable to feel down for a day or two. Other events—such as losing a job or ending an important relationship—are more stressful and could lead to the onset of a major depressive episode. However, sometimes depressive and bipolar disorders can seem mysterious, and symptoms can turn into full-blown episodes with no obvious cause. Research provides valuable clues into the causes of depressive and bipolar disorders, although no one perspective adequately explains its onset.

Biological Perspective

With the adoption of new technologies and methods, studies of genetics and biological determinants have provided exciting new insights about depression's underlying causes and risk factors. Twin and adoption studies provide evidence of heritability. Neuroimaging studies map out brain circuitry and function that are altered in the context of mood disorders. These studies, in turn, help shape our understanding of how environmental and sociocultural factors influence the course of depressive and bipolar disorders. All this information is being synthesized to develop new interventions and strategies for treating and managing bipolar and depressive disorders.

GENETICS AND FAMILY STUDIES Evidence converging from family, twin, and genetic studies indicates that genes influence the risk for major depressive disorder (Sullivan et al., 2000). This is not to say that genes alone cause depression. By definition, depression is a complex trait that is influenced by both genetic and environmental factors and their interaction. Research from the University of British Columbia suggests individual depressive symptoms vary widely in their heritability. Symptoms such as depressed mood or tearfulness do not appear to be heritable, whereas other symptoms (e.g., loss of libido and appetite) have a heritable basis (Jang et al., 2004).

Bipolar disorder Multiple factors are implicated in the etiology of bipolar disorder (Perlis et al., 2006). Family, twin, and adoption studies all support a strong familial and genetic component (Barnett & Smoller, 2009). Estimates of the heritability of bipolar disorder range from 59% to 87% (McGuffin et al., 2003).

Linkage studies have identified several areas of the genome that may harbour genes that influence susceptibility to bipolar disorder (Hayden & Nurnberger, 2006). As part of the Psychiatric Genomics Consortium, a large scale genomewide association study (GWAS) was conducted of 7481 individuals with bipolar disorder and 9250 controls, together with a replication study of 4496 cases and 42 422 controls. This major study confirmed genomewide significant evidence of association with the *CACNA1C* gene, identified a new genetic target, *ODZ4*, and suggested that calcium channels may be involved in the etiology of both bipolar disorder and schizophrenia (Psychiatric GWAS Consortium Bipolar Disorder Working Group, 2011), although we do not know how these channels may exert their influence. Very large sample size GWASs are beginning to open new doors to understanding the biology of mental illness.

Major depressive disorder Major depressive disorder runs in families. First-degree relatives of people with depression are two to three times more likely to suffer from depression than are first-degree relatives of people without depression (Sullivan et al., 2000). In particular, the genetic predisposition appears stronger in those individuals who suffer from recurrent depression and when there is an early age at onset. In addition to the family studies, twin studies estimate that the heritability of major depressive disorder is around 37% (Sullivan et al., 2000). That means that about 37% of the liability to major depressive disorder is due to genetic factors, with the remaining risk due to environmental factors.

Family and twin studies suggest a genetic component. The next critical step in research on causes of depression is to identify the specific genes involved and determine their function. One approach, called a *linkage study*, narrows the search to particular areas on a chromosome or several chromosomes that have a high likelihood of harbouring risk genes. Linkage studies are valuable because this approach narrows the search of the more than 20 000 genes in the human genome. Based on linkage studies, risk genes for depression may lie on chromosomes 1, 3, 4, 6, 8, 11, 12, 15, and 18 (Levinson, 2005).

A second genetic approach, called an *association study*, starts by identifying a gene that is believed to be associated with a disorder and then examines whether genetic variations are more common among persons with a disorder (such as depression) than in controls without the disorder. For depression, association studies have focused on genes that regulate the *serotonergic system*, a network of neurons and neurotransmitters in the brain, one function of which is to regulate emotion (Levinson, 2005). Although several significant associations have been found, the available data do not yet solve the genetic puzzle.

As we noted in Chapter 2, GWAS association studies do not focus on a single gene but scan the entire genome to identify genetic variants. A large GWAS mega-analysis that combined data from several studies compared single nucleotide polymorphisms (SNPs) from 9240 individuals with major depressive disorder and 9519 controls. The analysis did not reveal any SNPs that met the stringent genomewide significance criterion. Although this sample size might seem like a very large number of research participants, the researchers estimated that much larger sample sizes will be needed to understand the role of genes in the onset of depression.

Ultimately, understanding depression involves understanding both genetic and environmental factors. Exploring this interaction may help determine why some people are more vulnerable to environmental stressors (see "Research Hot Topic: The Interaction Between Genes and Environment"). New technologies and approaches will make it more likely that specific genes will be identified. Future research may identify genetic variants that influence response to medication and perhaps to psychotherapy (Malhotra et al., 2004). This would allow mental health professionals to target treatment to an individual, enhancing its likelihood of success.

NEUROIMAGING STUDIES Neuroimaging studies have begun to elucidate brain regions and pathways that may be implicated in bipolar and depressive disorders. In depression, functional neuroimaging studies have focused on four main brain regions: the amygdala, which is associated with memory and emotional responses to stimuli; the orbitofrontal cortex, which is responsible for cognitive processing and decision making; the dorsolateral prefrontal cortex, which is involved with emotion regulation, planning, and decision making; and the anterior cingulate cortex, which is involved with error detection, motivation, and modulation of emotional responses (Koenigs & Grafman, 2009).

In bipolar disorder, many of the brain regions implicated are involved with emotional reactivity and regulation and parallel findings for major depression. The amygdala, prefrontal cortex, anterior cingulate cortex, and hippocampus show differences in individuals with bipolar disorder compared with controls (Davidson et al., 2002; Mayberg et al., 2004).

fMRI studies of people with bipolar disorder engaging in emotional and cognitive tasks have identified abnormal brain

Experiences of loss and grief can contribute to the onset of depression.

DreamPictures/Blend Images/Getty Images

activity in frontal, subcortical, and limbic regions (Yurgelun-Todd & Ross, 2006). An example of an emotional task would be looking at happy versus angry faces. The sheer number of identified abnormalities makes it difficult to conclude that any one brain area is responsible for bipolar disorder. In fact, the symptoms of bipolar disorder may emerge from the dysfunction of interconnected brain networks (Adler et al., 2006).

Although intriguing, these studies were conducted with people who had the disorder, so we cannot use the data to draw conclusions regarding causality. An alternative hypothesis is that differences in brain function may be the *result* of the disorder (i.e., *biological scarring*) rather than its cause. To ultimately determine the role of neurobiology, we will need to conduct neuroimaging studies of individuals who are at risk for bipolar disorder but who do not yet show any symptoms (e.g., children of parents with bipolar disorder) and follow them over time. This research design could help determine whether any premorbid abnormalities exist and are associated with the development of bipolar and depressive disorders.

ENVIRONMENTAL FACTORS AND LIFE EVENTS Genetic studies suggest that biological factors play an important role in the etiology of bipolar and depressive disorders, but the environment is involved as well. Environmental factors that contribute to the onset of major depressive disorder include stress, loss, grief, threats to relationships, occupational problems, health challenges, and the burdens of caregiving (Brown et al., 1996; Kendler et al., 1998; Monroe et al., 2001). Canadian epidemiological research indicates that low social support and high-stress jobs are associated with an elevated risk of developing major depression (Patten et al., 2010; Szeto & Dobson, 2013). Stressors such as abuse, maternal deprivation, neglect, or loss that occur early in life may have enduring effects on brain regions that influence stress and emotion (see Chapter 4). These permanent brain changes, such as heightened stress responsiveness throughout life, may increase the risk for depression (Kaufman & Charney, 2001).

Teasing apart the relationship between a stressful life event and the onset of a bipolar and depressive disorder is a challenge for clinicians. Was the stressful event truly independent of the disorder (e.g., a parent suddenly dies from a heart attack), or did the person's depression contribute to the emergence of the stressful life event (a romantic relationship ends)—a dependent life event?

Right out of law school, John landed a prime job with a prominent law firm in his home city. The hours were gruelling. At first he was energized by the challenge, but after months of getting by on four hours of sleep per night, he started to have pervasive self-doubt about his abilities, forget important facts about cases, and have altercations with his colleagues. He was late for work, and when he arrived, he looked dishevelled and often disoriented. He was fired from his job and blamed his depression on this loss. In reality, the job stress precipitated the depression, and his job loss was a dependent life event.

Although stressful life events are commonly reported in first episodes of major depressive disorder, over time, recurrent episodes seem to be more independent of life events (Kendler et al., 2000a).

An important question is why stressful life events seem to lead to depression in some people but not in others. For example, women who are at high genetic risk for major depressive disorder not only report more stressful life events (Kendler & Karkowski-Shuman, 1997; Kendler & Prescott, 1999), but also are more sensitive to their effects (Kendler et al., 1995). This phenomenon is called *genetic control of sensitivity to the environment* (Kendler & Karkowski-Shuman, 1997). This basically means that two people can encounter the same stressful life event, but because of their genetic makeup, one person experiences that event as more stressful (see "Research Hot Topic: The Interaction Between Genes and Environment").

Psychological Perspective

Long before we understood the role of biology, clinicians and researchers sought psychological explanations for depressive disorders. Older psychological theories have evolved over time, and some factors, such as loss, have been consistently identified. Research has produced a complex picture that questions some early psychological theories and supports others. Nevertheless, these theories reflect our changing ideas of depression and provide a foundation for formulating new research questions and for designing new interventions.

PSYCHODYNAMIC THEORY Freud conceptualized depression as "anger turned inward" (Freud, 1917). The anger, he proposed, arises after the loss of an object—either real or imagined. In Freudian terms, an "object" is anything to which someone is emotionally attached (e.g., another person, an aspect of the self, an animal). The loss may be real, such as the death of a friend or of a romantic partner, or it may be a process that is completely contained in the unconscious, below the person's level of awareness. An unconscious loss might be the loss of some aspect of youth about

research HOT topic

The Interaction Between Genes and Environment

We know that both genes and environmental factors are involved in the onset of depression. One controversial study by Avshalom Caspi, Terrie Moffitt, and colleagues (Caspi et al., 2003) reported intriguing findings on a gene–environment interaction.

The Caspi study inspired headlines from newspapers worldwide, such as "Gene more than doubles risk of depression following life stresses." Specifically, the study showed that among people who suffered multiple stressful life events over five years, 43% with one version of a gene (the "short" version) developed depression compared with only 17% with another version of the gene (the "long" version). Regardless of the number of stressful life events, people with the "long" or protective version had no more depression than people who were more stress free. The gene studied in this investigation is responsible for programming the actions of a particular protein. That protein, in turn, is responsible for recycling the neurotransmitter serotonin after it enters the neural synapse. The most widely prescribed class of antidepressants acts by blocking this transporter protein. This allows more serotonin to stay in the synapse and to be available in pathways involved in regulation of the emotions. For this reason, the gene has been a prime suspect in mood and anxiety disorders.

The authors believed the key to understanding these findings was studying both genes and environment. Dr. Moffit stated, "We found the connection only because we looked at the study members' stress history." The study followed 847 Caucasian New Zealanders born in the early 1970s from birth into adulthood; 17% carried two copies of the stress-sensitive short version, 31% carried two copies of the protective long version, and 51% carried one copy of each version. Drawing on research with animals, the researchers hypothesized that the interaction of genes and environment would be evident, and they therefore tallied life stresses on participants in the study. Although those with the short variant and at least four life events represented only 10% of the study sample, they accounted for nearly 25% of the cases of depression. Among those with four or more stressful life events, 43% of those with two copies of the short variant developed depression compared with 17% of those with two copies of the long variant. After publication of this study, several groups attempted to replicate the findings. In 2009, a meta-analysis of more than 14 studies that examined the association between the serotonin transporter gene, life events, and risk for depression showed no interaction of genotype and stressful life events on risk for depression. These results clearly illustrate the importance of replication in science and suggest caution when interpreting unreplicated findings.

which the person was not actively aware. In *Mourning and Melancholia*, Freud distinguished between these two terms. According to Freud, *melancholia* (a condition akin to major depression) is a "profoundly painful dejection, cessation of interest in the outside world, loss of the capacity to love, inhibition of all activity, and a lowering of the self-regarding feelings to a degree that finds utterance in self-reproache and self-reviling, and culminates in a delusional expectation of punishment." To illustrate anger turned inward, Freud noted that melancholics were often highly self-accusatory—usually in ways that were not realistic or justified. These accusations were misdirected against the self; Freud believed that they were actually directed against someone whom the patient loved. Freud focused on internal representations of our relationships in the external world. He emphasized that the loss of a person in the real world leads to an internal loss, which is experienced as a psychic wound or a lesion in one's self-esteem.

Psychodynamic theorists consider depression and mania as intricately interlinked. They view hypomania and mania as defenses against the unwanted and intolerable experience of depression. Exaggerated self-esteem and grandiosity protect the person against confronting the underlying distressing thoughts associated with low self-esteem or self-loathing.

Both clinical experience and research support the hypothesis that loss (as well as other stressful life events) can precipitate depression. Advances in psychodynamic theory focus on the role of real-world relationships and loss in the emergence of depression rather than on unverifiable unconscious processes (Horner, 1974). Moreover, psychodynamic underpinnings contributed to the development of a successful intervention for depression called Interpersonal Psychotherapy (see "The Treatment of Bipolar and Depressive Disorders") (Klerman et al., 1984).

ATTACHMENT THEORY Guided by data from animal studies, John Bowlby examined how disruptions in mother–infant attachment could lead to depression and anxiety. According to Bowlby, attachment has evolutionary significance for survival and is related to maternal protection of offspring from predators. Bowlby proposed that a child's response to maternal separation consists of three stages: (1) protest; (2) despair, pain, and loss; and (3) detachment or denial of affection for the mother. Others have expanded Bowlby's ideas to highlight how early attachment affects later life functioning and how disruptions in attachment lead to vulnerability to depression, anxiety, and problems with attachment in adulthood (Ainsworth, 1982).

BEHAVIOURAL THEORIES

Charles is a widower. After his wife died, he decided to fill his time by volunteering at the hospital two blocks from his home. His volunteer work was fulfilling, and he won several hospital awards for his dedication to his work and the people whom he served. Financial pressures forced the hospital to close. Charles no longer felt comfortable driving, and there was no public transportation in his neighbourhood. Now Charles had no way to occupy his time, no opportunity to feel needed, and no one to praise him for his work. Soon, Charles stopped getting dressed and told his children, who lived in another city, that there really was no reason to leave his house any more.

Behavioural theory (e.g., Skinner, 1953) proposes that depression results from the withdrawal of reinforcement (aspects of the social environment) for healthy behaviours. Changes in reinforcement may result from decreases in the number and types of reinforcing stimuli or the inability to obtain reinforcement due to a lack of social skills (Lewinsohn, 1974).

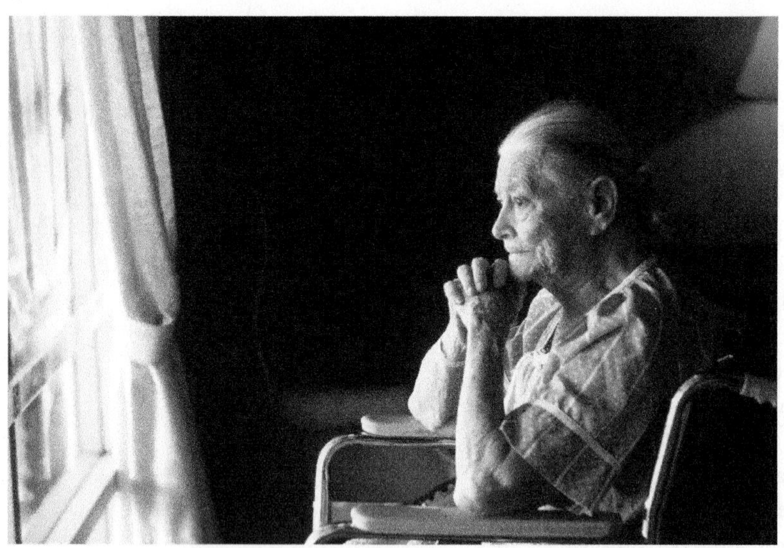

Environmental factors, such as the loss of social support or social reinforcement, are significant in the onset and maintenance of depressive episodes.

Mark Richard/PhotoEdit

Jana was always shy but had a close circle of friends whom she had to leave behind when she moved cross-country to a new city for what she thought would be a fabulous new job. Suddenly, there was no one with whom she felt close enough to go out to dinner or share her thoughts (there was a decrease in available social reinforcers). Her severe shyness prevented her from meeting new people (she was unable to obtain reinforcement because of a lack of social skills). Although she called her friends when she could, they could no longer drop by for a glass of wine or call her to go shopping. The longer she was in her new environment, the sadder she became. Her new colleagues saw a quiet person who did not smile, and they were not inclined to approach her.

LEARNING AND MODELLING Many researchers have been interested in discovering how learning theory might play a role in the in etiology of depression. Among them is Martin Seligman, who developed his theory of **learned helplessness** while exploring the effects of inescapable shock on avoidance learning (Seligman, 1975). In his experimental avoidance learning paradigm, dogs were restrained in a harness while several shocks (an unconditioned stimulus—UCS) were paired with a conditioned stimulus (CS), in this case a light. After the conditioning trials, the dogs were placed in a box where they could easily avoid a shock by jumping over a low barrier (see Figure 6.4). Surprisingly, most of the dogs failed to learn to avoid the shock. They remained sitting when the light came on, receiving shocks that they could easily have escaped. Seligman theorized that their earlier experience with inescapable shocks interfered with the dogs' ability to learn that escape was possible in a new situation. Seligman called this "learned helplessness." About a third of the dogs did learn to escape, suggesting that there are fundamental underlying differences in the likelihood of developing learned helplessness. Although we do not know the nature of these underlying differences, they may be either biologically or environmentally based.

FIGURE 6.4

Learned Helplessness. After being in an inescapable situation, the dog is put in a situation from which escape from painful shock is possible. However, because of prior learning, most of the dogs did not try to escape the shock by jumping over the very small barrier.

Source: Lilienfeld, Scott O.; Lynn, Steven J.; Namy, Laura L.; Woolf, Nancy J., *Psychology: From Inquiry to Understanding,* 1st Ed., © 2009. Reprinted and Electronically reproduced by permission of Pearson Education, Inc., Upper Saddle River, New Jersey.

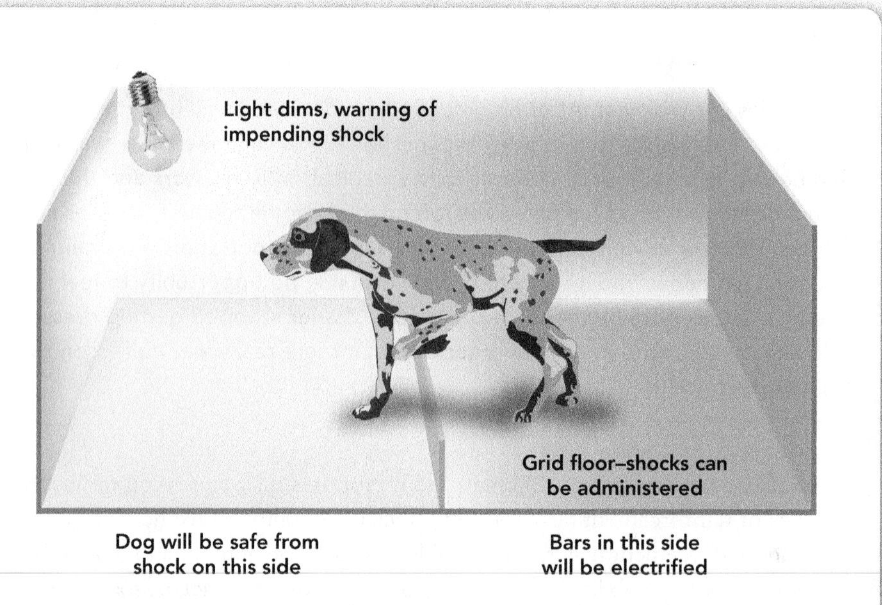

Learned helplessness proposes that externally uncontrollable environments (e.g., repeated abuse, failure at school or work, relationship failures) and presumably internally uncontrollable environments (e.g., pervasive low mood, thoughts of death) are inescapable stimuli that can lead to *dysphoria* (sadness or low mood) and major depressive disorder. Why some people develop learned helplessness and others do not may depend on whether the individual thinks the situation is inescapable (Abramson et al., 2002). If the situation is attributed to an internal cause that is personal, pervasive, and permanent (e.g., I lost my job because I'm a jerk, and I will always be a jerk), then helplessness, hopelessness, and depression may result. In contrast, if negative events are seen as external and impermanent (e.g., I lost my job because my boss is a jerk, and in my next job I will work for someone better), helplessness and depression are averted.

Three aspects of learning theory are relevant to understanding the development of depression. The first concerns individuals' appraisal of themselves, their lives, and others (Alloy et al., 2000; Beck, 1979). The second focuses on problem solving, whether an individual has a proactive (positive) or an avoidant approach to solving problems (D'Zurilla & Nezu, 1999). The third aspect focuses on the success of previous attempts to deal with stress (Folkman & Lazarus, 1986). Each of these factors appears to contribute to a person's vulnerability to depression and its chronicity.

COGNITIVE THEORY Aaron Beck, the father of cognitive therapy, proposed that thoughts cause feelings and behaviours, and that *negative* thoughts can cause depressive feelings and behaviours. The theory proposes that *negative cognitive schemas* (patterns of negativistic thinking) can develop early in life and become part of an individual's self-concept (Beck, 1961, 1967). Negative thinking is characterized by persistently pessimistic and critical thoughts. Individuals with negativistic thinking are also more prone to low self-esteem (Verplanken et al., 2007). This thinking style contributes to the inability to find pleasure from previously pleasant experiences and to the social isolation commonly seen in depression (Cacioppo et al., 2010). Negative schemas can be identified by the presence of *automatic thoughts*, which are dysfunctional thoughts that represent beliefs about the self that become a habitual pattern of thinking: I'm a failure, I have no willpower, and I have no luck in love. Automatic thoughts tend to be extreme and counterproductive and produce negative feelings. They go untested, become fixed, and lead to *self-fulfilling prophecies* (e.g., you expect to fail and so you do). Beck proposed that individuals with depression experience a *negative cognitive triad*—negative thoughts about the self, the world, and the future. He described a variety of thinking errors that sustain the negative thoughts in the triad (see Figure 6.5).

Dichotomous or "all or nothing" thinking: Thinking in "all-or-nothing" terms. "If I can't do something perfectly, I may as well quit."

Overgeneralizing: Condemning yourself as a total person on the basis of a single event. "I got a C on a psychology test—I will never be a psychologist."

Selective thinking: Concentrating on your weaknesses and forgetting your strengths. "It does not matter that I am a good singer. I cannot dance or act."

Catastrophizing: Only paying attention to the dark side of things, or overestimating the chances of disaster. "I didn't get into the best university. I'll never have a decent career."

Personalizing: Taking things personally that have little or nothing to do with you. "Jenny is so quiet. She must really be angry with me."

Personal Ineffectiveness: Assuming you can do nothing to change your situation. "Jack always criticizes me. I wish he would quit."

FIGURE 6.5
Common Thinking Errors.

CONCEPT check

- Psychodynamic theories focus on the concept of "anger turned inward" and the role of loss in the etiology of depression.
- Behavioural theory focuses on the loss of reinforcement; depression results from the withdrawal of reinforcement (usually pleasant aspects of the social environment) that supports our participation in healthy behaviours.
- Learned helplessness theory focuses on perceiving uncontrollable environments as inescapable stimuli that lead to feelings of dysphoria and major depression.
- Cognitive theory focuses on the negative cognitive triad—negative thoughts about the self, the world, and the future.

critical thinking question Ming started feeling depressed at the end of her first year of university. Earlier that year, she had injured her knee, which kept her sidelined from the varsity women's soccer team. After she got a C on an important exam in biology, she began to question her ability to enter medical school, her longtime goal. In the spring, her father died suddenly of a heart attack. How do you think each of these events might have contributed to her depression?

The Treatment of Bipolar and Depressive Disorders

6.6 Identify efficacious treatments for major depressive disorder and bipolar disorder.

Several treatments are available for people who suffer from mood disorders, ranging from "talk" therapies to antidepressant medication and other biologically-based treatments. Just as mood disorders may involve symptoms of the mind and body, treatment in some cases involves both psychotherapy and medication.

Bipolar Disorder

Medications are the primary treatment for bipolar disorder; psychotherapy alone is insufficient (Yatham et al., 2013). However, psychotherapy may provide emotional support to both the patient and family members and help the patient develop behavioural strategies to cope with symptoms and stabilize his or her mood. Psychotherapy reduces hospitalizations and improves daily functioning (Yatham et al., 2013). Different forms of psychotherapy are available to people with bipolar disorder, including cognitive-behavioural therapy, psychoeducation, family therapy, and interpersonal and social rhythm therapy.

PSYCHOLOGICAL TREATMENTS Various types of psychotherapy benefit individuals with bipolar disorder when used adjunctively to effective pharmacotherapy.

Cognitive-behavioural therapy (CBT) Cognitive-behavioural therapy (CBT) for bipolar disorder develops skills to change inappropriate or negative thought patterns and behaviours. CBT appears to decrease depressive symptoms, improve outcome, and increase adherence to treatment recommendations (Miklowitz & Scott, 2009). Psychoeducation teaches the patient about bipolar disorder, its treatment, and how to recognize warning signs or precursors of mood shifts. Early recognition can prompt patients to seek treatment, reduce the risk of relapse, and improve social and occupational functioning (Miklowitz & Scott, 2009). Education can also be informative for family and friends. Family-based treatment, sometimes initiated while an individual is still receiving inpatient care, focuses on developing strategies to reduce personal and familial stress and engage families in early recognition and treatment of impending mood shifts (Glick et al., 1993; Miklowitz & Scott, 2009).

Interpersonal and social rhythm therapy (IPSRT) Interpersonal and social rhythm therapy (IPSRT) (Frank et al., 1997) promotes adherence to regular daily routines (including regular sleep patterns). This treatment is based on interpersonal psychotherapy (Klerman et al., 1984) coupled with a social zeitgeber hypothesis (Grandin et al., 2006). (In German, social zeitgebers are "time givers." The word refers to persons, social demands, or tasks that set the biological clock.) The hypothesis states that the loss of social zeitgebers may result in unstable biological rhythms. In vulnerable individuals, this leads to manic or depressive episodes (Ehlers et al., 1988; Frank et al., 2005). Not getting enough sleep or getting too much sleep and not enough physical activity in one's day can both contribute to negative mood. Thus, patients treated under this therapeutic approach are coached to go to bed and get out of bed at the same time of day, every day. They are also advised to eat meals on a regular schedule during the day and to take breaks during long workdays whenever possible. They are encouraged to keep a reasonable and consistent schedule of social events. IPSRT increases the regularity of social rhythms in individuals with bipolar disorder, which in turn is associated with decreased likelihood of new affective episodes (Frank et al., 2005).

A large multi-site trial, the Systematic Treatment Enhancement Program for Bipolar Disorder (STEP-BD), compared the effects of three specialized psychosocial interventions for bipolar disorder—family-focused treatment, IPSRT, and CBT relative to a collaborative care condition (six sessions of relapse prevention) when delivered in conjunction with pharmacotherapy. Although the outcome did not differ significantly among the three specialist therapies, patients who received the specialty interventions fared better than those in the collaborative care condition, suggesting a role for psychotherapy in the management of bipolar disorder (Miklowitz et al., 2007).

BIOLOGICAL TREATMENTS Bipolar disorder requires care by a psychiatrist and treatment with medication. A patient in a manic or depressive episode may need hospitalization to be safe and to receive needed treatment. The most commonly used medication is lithium (Yatham et al., 2013), which moderates mood swings from manic to depressive episodes.

Lithium is a naturally occurring metallic element. Its therapeutic effects in treating bipolar disorder were discovered by accident in the 1940s by John Cade, an Australian doctor. However, it was not widely used until the 1970s. For many years, lithium was used to treat bipolar disorder with no clear understanding of why it worked. Then, in 1998, researchers at the University of Wisconsin discovered that a neurotransmitter called *glutamate* was the key to its efficacy. Too much glutamate in the synapse causes mania, whereas too little causes depression. Lithium moderates glutamate levels in the brain, and therefore it is an efficacious treatment for people with bipolar disorder.

Lithium is intended as a long-term therapy and must be taken consistently. Often when patients are *euthymic* (in a period of normal mood between depressive and manic episodes) or manic, they stop taking their medication either because they believe they are well or because they would like to keep experiencing some aspects of mania (e.g., increased energy, decreased need for sleep). Discontinuing the medication often leads to a clinical relapse. Patients must be monitored carefully because if the dose is not exactly right, toxic levels of lithium may build up in the bloodstream.

Anticonvulsant medications (normally used to treat epilepsy) are also used to manage bipolar disorder, sometimes in combination with lithium (Yatham et al., 2013). Other medications (such as atypical antipsychotics) may be added during depressive episodes (Yatham et al., 2013). Even though episodes of mania and depression can be controlled, bipolar disorder is a long-term illness that currently has no cure. It is important for patients to stay on their medications, even when well, to keep the disease under control and reduce the chance of recurrent, worsening episodes.

Electroconvulsive therapy (ECT) can also be used in the treatment of bipolar disorder, particularly for severe depressive episodes, extreme or prolonged mania, or catatonia. It is used primarily when medications and psychotherapy are not effective, when a person is at high risk for suicide, or when use of medications is contraindicated, such as during pregnancy (Yatham et al., 2013).

Depressive Disorders

Because many medical illnesses can masquerade as depression, an important first step in treatment is a comprehensive physical exam. In addition to ruling out a medical cause (such as cancer, malnutrition, mild stroke, certain metabolic disorders), a complete review of current medications is important because certain drugs can have side effects (such as fatigue or hyperactivity that disrupts sleep) that mimic depression. Once these possibilities are ruled out, the next step is selecting an appropriate treatment strategy. Surprisingly, only about half of those with major depression obtain professional treatment, and of these, only about 22% receive clinically adequate care (Kessler et al., 2003).

Many efficacious treatments for major depression are available. Psychotherapy helps people express distressing emotions and learn more effective ways to deal with factors that may have contributed to or resulted from depression. Medications and other physical treatments (e.g., electroconvulsive therapy and deep brain stimulation) can help individuals who are too depressed to benefit from psychotherapy alone. Many choices exist, and often more than one approach is needed until an efficacious treatment is found (Ebmeier et al., 2006; Moore & McLaughlin, 2003).

PSYCHOLOGICAL TREATMENTS Psychological treatments focus on understanding how thoughts, perceptions, and behaviours influence depressed mood and vice versa. Generally, these treatments are delivered by a trained clinician (in most cases a clinical psychologist or licensed clinical social worker) in individual or group settings and are an essential component of a comprehensive treatment plan for depression.

Cognitive-Behavioural Therapy (CBT) Cognitive-behavioural therapy (CBT) (Beck, 1979) is based on the premise that an individual can learn to think and behave differently, which can lead to improved mood. A key ingredient involves having patients record their thoughts, feelings, and behaviours (see Figure 6.6). Through this monitoring, patients identify situations or triggers for low mood, as well as situations associated with improved mood. Once triggers are identified, the patient learns to recognize and modify automatic or distorted thoughts and change behaviours to improve mood and functioning.

FIGURE 6.6

Thought Restructuring Record. After identifying a negative, automatic thought, a cognitive-behavioural therapist encourages the person with depression to replace that thought with a more positive idea. Reframing the situation in more positive terms often helps the person feel less negative about the self, the world, and the future.

Situation: Got a C on a test for which I studied really hard

Automatic Thought: I'm so stupid. I'll never get my degree.

Emotion: Sad and discouraged

New Thought: This was the first test—next time, I'll be better prepared.

Outcome: Concerned but motivated to continue in class

After keeping her mood and thought records, Bonita noticed that her moods were consistently worse as the weekends approached. Earlier in the week she was focused on work-related tasks, but then she noticed that around Wednesday, she started having thoughts like "everyone else is making plans for the weekend, and I'm going to be all alone as usual." By Friday morning she was consistently negative, and the thoughts would get worse: "I am a complete loser." "No one wants to be around me." Working with her therapist, Bonita challenged her negative thoughts with other thoughts that were more balanced, less "all or nothing." For example, she replaced "No one wants to be around me" with "I haven't given people the chance to see who I am; I have to take initiative." Once she recognized the weekly pattern, she used the negative thoughts as calls to action rather than as signs of an inevitable slide into a weekend of misery and loneliness.

Interpersonal psychotherapy (IPT) IPT is a focused time-limited therapy (Klerman et al., 1984). It has its roots in the work of Harry Stack Sullivan, who emphasized the importance of current interpersonal relationships for mental health. Its core principle is that interpersonal problems can trigger depression, and depression itself can influence interpersonal functioning.

Sam had grown increasingly frustrated with his job since his new boss took over; they always disagreed about his effort, and his boss was constantly on his case. In addition, all of his co-workers avoided him in the break room in large part because Sam always complained about the boss's heavy-handed tactics. He found himself having trouble getting up in the morning to go to work, and showing up late just led to more criticism. He withdrew from his co-workers and eventually from his wife, who was having trouble understanding Sam's sullen and angry mood. Losing his job was the last straw. He stopped coaching his son's baseball team because he was too ashamed to face the other dads, and he started staying out late at night to avoid the inevitably tough conversations with his wife about bills that were piling up.

IPT uses 12 to 16 sessions and focuses on an interpersonal problem area (grief, role transition, disputes, interpersonal deficits) that guides treatment. Therapeutic techniques include expression of mood, clarification of feelings, communication analysis, and behaviour change. IPT is efficacious for mild to moderate depression and is also used to treat dysthymia, adolescent and late-life depression, anxiety, and eating disorders (Fairburn, 1993; Frank et al., 1991; Lipsitz et al., 2006; Mufson et al., 1994; Stuart, 1995).

Behavioural activation Based on the theory that depression is maintained by a lack of positive reinforcement, early behavioural interventions focused on increasing access to pleasant, and therefore reinforcing, events through daily scheduling of pleasurable activities, social skills training, and time management strategies (e.g., Lewinsohn & Graf, 1973). *Behavioural activation treatment for depression* (BATD) (Lejuez et al., 2001) modifies this approach, emphasizing increased contact with positive reinforcement for healthy behaviours, thereby increasing positive mood. For example, for someone who is stuck in a "dead-end" job, therapy may include scheduling weekly trips to the library to read about career development. With BATD, the therapist and patient develop a comprehensive list of goals in major life areas. Each week, they develop more specific goals and activities to be completed by the patient (Hopko et al., 2003). As the patient completes the goals, increased positive reinforcement helps reduce depressive symptoms (e.g., Lejuez et al., 2001).

BIOLOGICAL TREATMENTS Biological treatments are most often medications designed to alter mood-regulating chemicals in the brain (and body). These treatments are generally prescribed by a psychiatrist, but may also be given by family practitioners (in part because of the stigma attached to seeking psychiatric care and the long waiting lists for referrals to see a psychiatrist). These treatments are moderately efficacious in reducing symptoms of moderate to severe depression, especially when combined with psychological treatment (NICE, 2004).

First-generation antidepressants—Tricyclic antidepressants and monoamine oxidase inhibitors The first drugs marketed to treat depression were the monoamine oxidase inhibitors (MAOIs) and the tricyclic **antidepressants** (TCA), sometimes called *traditional* or *first-generation antidepressants*. MAOIs treat depression by inhibiting (preventing) the action of the enzyme monoamine oxidase. Normally, this enzyme breaks down the neurotransmitters norepinephrine, serotonin, and dopamine in the brain. By preventing the enzyme from doing its work, the availability of these neurotransmitters in the neural synapses is increased, which is believed to cause the antidepressant effect.

MAOIs are efficacious, especially in people who have depressive symptoms such as hypersomnia (sleeping too much) and weight gain (Thase & Kupfer, 1996). People who take MAOIs must not eat foods containing the substance tyramine because the interaction of the drug and these foods can cause extremely high blood pressure and possibly death. Foods containing tyramine include smoked, aged, or pickled meat or fish; sauerkraut; aged cheeses; yeast extracts; fava beans; beef or chicken liver; aged sausages; game meats; red and white wines; beer; hard liquor; avocados; meat extracts; caffeine-containing beverages; chocolate; soy sauce; cottage cheese; cream cheese; yogurt; and sour cream. Owing to their potentially dangerous side effects, MAOIs are usually prescribed only for people who have not responded to other medications.

Tricyclic antidepressants work by preventing the reuptake of various neurotransmitters in the brain—primarily norepinephrine and serotonin. By blocking the reuptake of the neurotransmitter back into the neuron, they remain in the synapse longer, thereby increasing their availability for activation of the next neuron. The name of these drugs comes from the fact that they share a three-ring molecular structure. Countless randomized clinical trials document their efficacy compared to placebo controls. Typically, patients take the medication for six to eight weeks. If the response is positive, the medication may need to be continued for many months to prevent a relapse (Ebmeier et al., 2006). These medications must not be stopped abruptly. First-generation antidepressants are often accompanied by multiple side effects, including dry mouth, constipation, bladder problems, sexual problems, blurred vision, dizziness, daytime drowsiness, and increased heart rate. Thus, they are no longer the first choice for pharmacological treatment of depression (Gartlehner et al., 2005).

Second-generation antidepressants The second-generation antidepressants include **selective serotonin reuptake inhibitors (SSRIs)** and serotonin and norepinephrine reuptake inhibitors (SNRIs) (Lam et al., 2009). Perhaps the best known antidepressant is fluoxetine (Prozac). We do not fully understand how most second-generation antidepressants work, but in general, they act by selectively inhibiting the reuptake of serotonin at the presynaptic neuronal membrane, restoring the normal chemical balance. The SNRIs inhibit both serotonin and norepinephrine reuptake, as well as that of dopamine to a lesser extent.

The SSRIs and other second-generation antidepressants appear to be as efficacious as the TCAs and MAOIs (Gartlehner et al., 2005). They have fewer and milder side effects than the TCAs, and patients generally tolerate them well (Anderson, 2001; Taylor et al., 2006). (Side effects may include sexual problems, headache, nausea, nervousness, trouble falling asleep or waking often during the night, and jitteriness.)

In the early 2000s, concerns grew about a potentially lethal adverse effect of SSRIs. Several highly publicized cases led to "black box" warning labels, stating that antidepressants increased the risk of suicidal thinking in children and adolescents with major depressive disorder. Youth treated with SSRIs need to be monitored very closely, especially during the first four weeks, for intensification of depression, emergence of suicidal thoughts or behaviour, or behavioural changes such as sleeplessness, agitation, or social withdrawal. These substances have not been prohibited despite their potentially dangerous side effects because they provide substantial benefits for adolescents with moderate and severe depression, including many with suicidal ideation (National Institute of Mental Health, 2005).

We do not fully understand the increase in suicidal thoughts and suicidal behaviour that sometimes appear to be associated with SSRI medication. It could be that SSRIs improve physical symptoms before mood actually lifts. So, in the early stages of treatment, young people may feel more energy, and this increased energy and ongoing depressed mood increases the probability of acting on suicidal thoughts (Hall, 2006). A review of several studies ultimately concluded that the benefits of SSRI treatment far outweigh the risks, but caution and careful monitoring are necessary (Bridge et al., 2007).

Electroconvulsive therapy Drug therapies are not the only biological treatment for major depressive disorder. **Electroconvulsive therapy (ECT)** is one of the most efficacious treatments for major depression, especially for people who are severely depressed, have not responded to medication or psychotherapy, are unable to take antidepressants, are at serious risk of suicide, or present with psychotic symptoms (Kennedy et al., 2009). ECT can also be useful in the treatment of mania (Gitlin, 2006).

ECT has a history that concerns many people decades after it was first used to treat psychotic disorders (Cerletti & Bini, 1938). When ECT was new, patients were not given muscle relaxants, and the resulting violent seizures often caused injuries. In addition, the electrodes were placed on both sides of the head, often resulting in substantial and permanent memory loss.

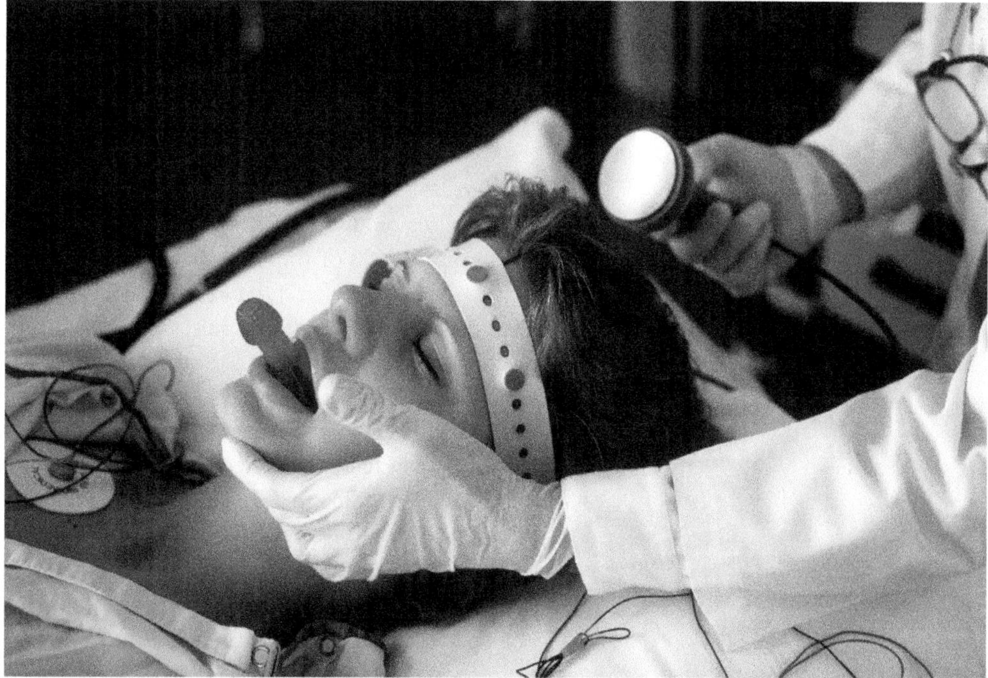

A clinician prepares a patient to undergo electroconvulsive therapy. Many precautions are taken to be sure that the patient is not injured and does not feel pain during the procedure.

Will McIntyre/Photo Researchers, Inc./Science Source

Today a muscle relaxant is administered along with a brief period of general anesthesia before ECT. Electrodes, placed at precise locations on the scalp, deliver electrical impulses, which cause brief seizures in the brain. The seizures induced are not specific to one particular brain area and appear to influence the production of a number of neurotransmitters (Post et al., 2000). Exactly how ECT works remains a mystery, but it often leads to speedier improvement in severely depressed patients than either medication or psychotherapy (Husain et al., 2004).

Modern one-side (unilateral) approaches are equally efficacious and result in less memory loss. The most common side effects of the therapy as presently administered are confusion after the procedure and temporary amnesia (Ebmeier et al.., 2006). ECT is usually administered several times a week for a number of weeks.

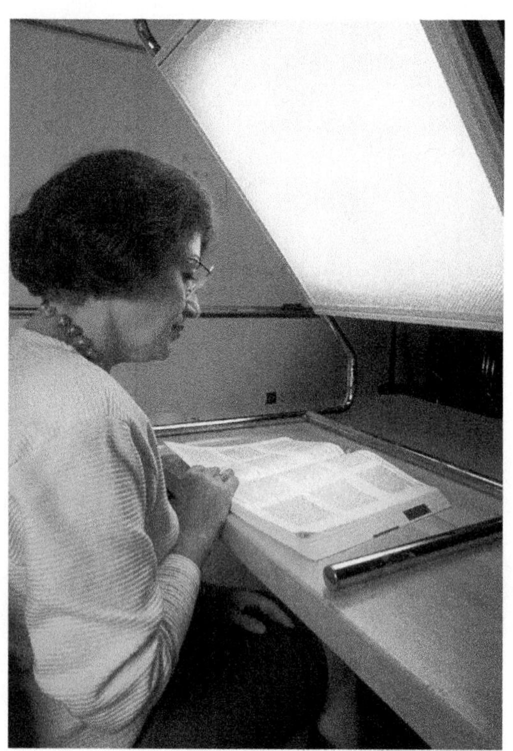

Light box therapy is sometimes used as a treatment for SAD.

John Griffin/The Image Works

Light therapy for major depressive disorder with a seasonal pattern Psychiatrist Norman Rosenthal first described **seasonal affective disorder (SAD)** in 1984. Now a specifier in DSM-5 labelled "depressive disorder with a seasonal pattern," this variant of major depressive disorder afflicts millions of people worldwide and is characterized by depressive episodes that vary by season. Although some patients experience summer depression, most are affected during December, January, and February. Symptoms of the winter pattern include increased appetite, increased sleep, weight gain, interpersonal difficulties, and a heavy, leaden feeling in one's limbs.

Patients with this variant are sometimes treated with *light therapy*. This involves exposure to an artificial source of bright light, usually a light box, a light visor, or a dawn simulator. These devices produce light that is approximately 10 times brighter than regular household lightbulbs. Light therapy sessions take place at the same time each day (usually in the morning) and generally last between 30 and 90 minutes. The patient sits by the light source, eyes open, so that light reaches the retina. Treatment usually begins with the onset of symptoms each winter and continues until spring.

Because full-spectrum light is not necessary to reap the benefits of light therapy, UV rays are filtered out to avoid damage to the eyes and skin. Nonetheless, there are occasional side effects, including photophobia (eye sensitivity to light), headache, fatigue, irritability, hypomania, and insomnia. In addition, light boxes are expensive and often are not covered by insurance. Despite these potential drawbacks, light therapy appears to be effective in a substantial proportion of cases of depression with a seasonal pattern (Lam & Levitt, 1999; Rohan et al., 2004).

Transcranial magnetic stimulation *Transcranial magnetic stimulation* (TMS) uses a magnetic coil placed over the patient's head to deliver a painless, localized electromagnetic pulse to a part of the brain. We do not know why the treatment works, but several clinical trials comparing it with a sham procedure have supported its use as a potentially effective alternative to ECT or medication (Ebmeier et al., 2006; Janicak et al., 2002). (See Chapter 10 in this text for a detailed description of TMS.)

Deep brain stimulation *Deep brain stimulation* (DBS) is a therapy targeting an area of the brain important for regulating negative mood changes, the subgenual cingulate region. DBS works by surgically implanting electrodes into specific, improperly functioning areas of the brain. These electrodes are attached by wire to a pulse generator (or "brain pacemaker") that is implanted into the chest wall. The electrodes continuously release tiny electrical impulses that deactivate (but do not kill) immediately surrounding brain cells. In this way, DBS inhibits abnormal activity in targeted parts of the brain and treats disorders characterized by overactivity. The FDA has approved DBS for use in treating Parkinson's disease and some types of bodily tremors. It has also been used to treat psychiatric disorders. In 2001, DBS was used to treat obsessive-compulsive disorder (OCD), leading to significant improvement in anxiety, compulsions, and comorbid depression (Greenberg et al., 2006).

A study of DBS for depression treated 20 patients with six months of DBS to the subcallosal cingulate gyrus (Brodmann's area 25) (Lozano et al., 2008). To participate, all patients had to have failed to respond to at least four other treatments (including antidepressant, psychotherapy, and ECT). In the first six months, 60% of patients responded to DBS and the remission rate was 30%. In a 3.5-year follow-up, the average response rate was 64% and the remission rate was 35% (Kennedy et al., 2011). Patients reported improvements in psychosocial functioning and physical health as well. Although more research is needed, DBS may prove to be a promising intervention for people with refractory depression.

June had suffered from recurrent depression for more than 20 years. She had been prescribed what seemed like every antidepressant on the planet and had two courses of electroconvulsive therapy. Occasionally she would find some relief, but she never seemed to be able to climb out of the pit of depression. When offered the opportunity for DBS, although frightened at first, she realized she had nothing to lose. Her experience was transformative. June reported experiencing an almost physical removal of weight from her shoulders. She said she could "see the light" for the first time in 20 years. Her description of a visceral and physical removal of weight underscored the extent to which depression had literally weighed her down both mentally and physically over the previous two decades.

Selecting a Treatment

With so many available options, clinicians and patients often feel challenged to determine the best treatment. The initial decision depends on several factors, including the nature and severity of symptoms, unipolar or bipolar features, psychotic features or suicidal intent, patient's age, preferences, tolerance of side effects, and treatments available in the patient's community.

Decades of placebo-controlled, randomized clinical trials indicate that major depressive disorder responds to both psychotherapy and pharmacotherapy. Interpersonal psychotherapy and CBT have the strongest empirical support (Parikh et al., 2009). Psychodynamic approaches have not proved to be very useful. Combining medication and psychotherapy provides only moderate additional benefit over either treatment alone (Hollon et al., 1992; Parikh et al., 2009). Although approximately 60% of patients respond to psychotherapeutic or drug treatments, relapse may occur—especially if treatment is not maintained and if symptoms are not entirely remitted at the end of treatment (Prien & Kupfer, 1986). For both pharmacological and psychological interventions, continuation and maintenance treatment reduces relapse after the initial acute treatment phase ends. ECT is a viable option for individuals who are severely depressed or suicidal or who cannot tolerate antidepressants.

For bipolar disorder, medication with lithium or anticonvulsants is the treatment of choice. Although drug treatment is effective, many patients continue to experience occasional manic episodes or lingering symptoms (Gitlin, 2006). Psychotherapy alone is not effective for bipolar disorder. Family therapy, interpersonal and social rhythm therapy, and CBT in combination with medication can help the patient adjust to having a chronic illness, adhere to a treatment plan, and avoid relapses (Craighead & Miklowitz, 2000; Frank et al., 1999).

CONCEPT check

- Many efficacious treatments are available for major depressive disorder, including psychotherapy, CBT, medication, electroconvulsive therapy, and light therapy.
- Psychotherapy helps patients become more effective in dealing with factors that contribute to or result from depression.
- Medications help regulate brain chemicals involved in emotion regulation.
- Psychotherapy alone may not be sufficient for more severe cases of depression; medication can be efficacious in more severe cases, but it may cause side effects that can interfere with long-term use.
- Behaviour therapy seeks to restore patients' daily activity schedules (eating, sleeping, working, socializing) as a means of increasing the positive reinforcement of healthy behaviours.
- Electroconvulsive therapy (ECT) is particularly useful in cases of major depressive disorder and bipolar disorder that do not respond to other treatments.

- Similar to ECT, transcranial magnetic stimulation (TMS) and deep brain stimulation (DBS) manipulate electrical activity in the brain, presumably counteracting existing abnormal patterns in key emotion-regulating brain regions.
- Light therapy is useful in the treatment of major depressive disorder with a seasonal pattern.

critical thinking question With only half of depressed individuals receiving health care and less than one quarter of them receiving adequate care, how could we improve health service delivery to individuals suffering from major depressive disorder?

real SCIENCE real LIFE

Latisha—Treatment of Major Depressive Disorder

THE PATIENT

Latisha was a 22-year-old student attending a university in eastern Canada. She appeared at Student Health complaining of sadness and tearfulness, a drop in her grades, and a sense of being lost about her future. She awakened too early in the morning, had lost her appetite, and had lost interest in the things that she normally enjoyed. She sometimes thought it would be better if she were dead. Because of her religion, she stated that she would never commit suicide, but she wished that the Lord would take her life. There was no evidence of mania or psychosis.

THE PROBLEM

Latisha had been in a stable relationship for three years. She and Ted had been inseparable, and everyone thought they would graduate from university, get married, and live happily ever after. It felt like a slap in the face when Ted announced a month ago that he no longer wanted to be in a serious relationship. Soon she saw him walking arm in arm with another woman. Latisha was devastated. Even more important, she watched as her friends got jobs and chose their life paths after university, while after three changes of her major she felt lost and directionless.

Latisha came from a healthy and happy family. Her maternal grandmother, to whom she was quite close, had died a year ago. Latisha was not terribly independent, latching on to other people and following the crowd. Of note, her mother, two aunts, and her brother had all been treated for depression. Latisha had never used drugs, drank alcohol occasionally, and had been drunk only a few times. She was physically healthy. Her only medications were vitamins and the birth control pill.

THE TREATMENT

The clinician diagnosed Latisha with major depressive disorder and recommended interpersonal psychotherapy (IPT). The therapist and Latisha together identified her main problem as role transitions; grief over Ted was secondary. Therapy focused on helping Latisha make the transition to independent life. She saw that she relied on others and that it was critical for her to make her own choices. With support from her therapist, she started to emerge from her depression after about three weeks and sought career counselling. After eight weeks, her mood lifted. She started sleeping better, spent more time with her friends, and improved her grades.

Latisha completed graduate school and landed an excellent job as a media relations manager in a hospital associated with the university medical school. She married a supportive man, and all seemed well. Two months after the birth of her first child, at age 27, Latisha was unable to shake a pervasive sense of feeling overwhelmed and was nearly incapacitated with depression. She cried all day, could barely muster the energy to shower, and was unable to care for her baby. When the baby cried at night, she would just bury her head under the pillow and lament what a horrible mother she was.

After a thorough evaluation, a psychiatrist diagnosed Latisha with depression with peripartum onset. After two weeks on an SSRI, she was able to play with her daughter. Her sense of humour came back, and her husband felt comfortable leaving Latisha with the baby. After five weeks, she felt much better—although she still was not back to her normal self. She saw a psychologist who specialized in peripartum depression and began a course of CBT. After a few weeks, Latisha could recognize the cycle of automatic thoughts that perpetuated her low mood. Whenever she perceived herself as failing at a task of motherhood, she would think "I'm a terrible mother." She worked to replace the thought with less self-deprecating thoughts. She eventually climbed back to her normal level of functioning and engaged in all aspects of mothering. After 12 weeks, she went back to work part-time. She felt some pangs of regret about leaving the baby in day care, but she was glad to be back at work and continued to enjoy time with her daughter.

THE TREATMENT OUTCOME

Latisha continued to take SSRIs for another year before the medication was gradually withdrawn. Her psychiatrist helped her to identify warning signs of depression because Latisha now had had two episodes in her lifetime. For her, changes in sleep and appetite signalled a need to seek treatment immediately. Therapy gave her new tools for life. She began using them in other aspects of her life as well when she recognized dysfunctional cognitions.

summary

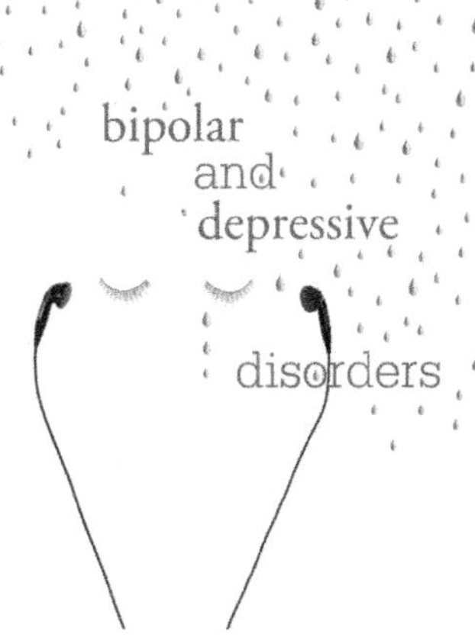

6.1 Distinguish between normal sad mood and depression and between euphoria and mania.

Distinctions must be made between transient changes in mood (either low or high) and more persistent and pervasive mood disturbances. Duration of the mood change and degree of impairment that results from the mood change are critical to making this distinction.

6.2 Understand the differences between bipolar I and bipolar II disorders and between major depressive disorder and persistent depressive disorder.

Depression is the most common psychiatric illness worldwide, although its expression may differ across cultures. Bipolar I disorder is diagnosed in individuals who have experienced at least one episode of mania—regardless of whether a depressive episode has occurred. Bipolar II disorder includes depression and hypomania. Major depressive disorder is marked by either a single episode or recurrent episodes. The symptoms are persistent, lasting two weeks or more. Persistent depressive disorder refers to a more protracted, less severe course of low mood lasting two years or more.

6.3 Discuss sex differences in the risk for major depressive disorder.

After puberty, depression is more common in females than in males. In addition, mood disturbances increase during the premenstrual period, and mood disorders are common during pregnancy, the postpartum period, and menopause.

6.4 Discuss factors associated with suicide and the relationship between depression and suicidal ideation and behaviour.

Suicide risk is elevated in both major depression and bipolar disorder, and behaviours that suggest suicidal intent should always be evaluated and not dismissed.

6.5 Understand psychodynamic, behavioural, cognitive, and biological theories of the causes of bipolar and depressive disorders.

Both biology (genetic factors) and environment (e.g., stressful life events) contribute to the risk for mood disorders.

6.6 Identify efficacious treatments for major depressive disorder and bipolar disorder.

For major depressive disorder, both psychotherapeutic and pharmacological options for treatment exist—either alone or in combination. Although the contribution of biology and genetics is clear, both CBT and IPT are highly effective treatments for major depressive disorder. Bipolar disorder generally requires medical management; however, psychotherapy can help the patient manage symptoms over time.

key terms

antidepressants 234
bipolar disorder 201
bipolar I 202
bipolar II 202
bipolar and depressive disorders 201
cyclothymic disorder 205
depression 201
disruptive mood dysregulation disorder 210
double depression 209
electroconvulsive therapy (ECT) 235
hypomania 202
learned helplessness 228
lithium 231
major depressive disorder 207
mania 201
mixed state 204
persistent depressive disorder 208
premenstrual dysphoric disorder 212
psychological autopsy 218
seasonal affective disorder (SAD) 236
selective serotonin reuptake inhibitors (SSRIs) 234
suicidal ideation 216

TEST yourself

1. To be diagnosed with major depressive disorder, a person must have abnormally low mood that
   a. causes thoughts of suicide
   b. alternates with episodes of elevated mood
   c. affects the ability to function in social or work settings
   d. results from misfortune in life, such as a death in the family

2. People with persistent depressive disorder may also have major depressive episodes, a condition known as
   a. episodic depression
   b. double depression
   c. bipolar disorder
   d. chronic depression

3. Mania is not recognized in the DSM as a separate disorder because it
   a. is normal in conjunction with positive life events
   b. is an exciting and enjoyable experience
   c. is a less serious condition than hypomania
   d. almost never occurs without depressive episodes
4. The main difference between bipolar I and bipolar II disorders is the
   a. severity of the periods of mania
   b. interval between episodes of mania and depression
   c. severity of periods of depression
   d. level of medication necessary to treat the disorder
5. A person experiencing hypomanic episodes might not consider them problematic because they
   a. end very quickly
   b. are associated with a rapid cycling pattern
   c. are rare and part of a mixed state
   d. may be times of high productivity or creativity
6. Which of the following statements best describes the epidemiology of major depressive disorder?
   a. It is much more common among older people than among any other group.
   b. It is less common worldwide than dysthymia.
   c. It is the most common psychiatric disorder worldwide and affects far more women than men.
   d. It is more common among blacks than among whites.
7. Before age 13, girls and boys are equally likely to have depression. During adolescence, rates of depression climb for girls, possibly because of
   a. hormones
   b. self-consciousness about bodily changes during puberty
   c. victimization
   d. all of the above
8. Passive suicidal ideation includes
   a. impulsive suicidal acts
   b. nonlethal attempts
   c. a wish to be dead
   d. all of the above
9. Compared with completed suicides, suicide attempts are
   a. always preceded by a specific precipitating factor
   b. more likely in females than in males
   c. uncommon in adolescents
   d. less common in youth from a disadvantaged background
10. Which of the following is a *myth* about suicide?
   a. People who talk about committing suicide are never serious about it.
   b. Suicidal behaviour runs in families.
   c. Most suicides are associated with psychological disorders.
   d. Most people who commit suicide do not leave notes.
11. Which of the following is *not* considered a suicide prevention technique?
   a. portraying famous people who have committed suicide in the media
   b. targeting people with several known risk factors
   c. reconnecting youth who are drifting with social and emotional supports
   d. providing suicide hotlines
12. Neuroimaging studies of individuals with bipolar and depressive disorders have shown that
   a. dysfunction is linked to a single area of the brain
   b. no significant brain dysfunction is involved
   c. bipolar disorder cannot be linked to brain dysfunction
   d. mood disorders involve a number of brain abnormalities
13. Stressful life events seem to lead to depression in some people but not in others. A likely reason is that
   a. stressful events in childhood do not lead to depression
   b. some people have more genetic sensitivity to life stress
   c. some people erroneously report more stress than they actually experience
   d. stress affects men far more seriously than women
14. In an interview with a clinician, a woman says, "I fail at everything I try." Such a statement is an example of
   a. learned helplessness
   b. major depressive disorder
   c. lack of positive reinforcement
   d. an automatic thought
15. One technique used in cognitive-behavioural therapy for depression asks patients to
   a. record their thoughts, feelings, and behaviours
   b. recall any early childhood traumas
   c. examine role transitions in their life
   d. focus on communication analysis
16. In behavioural activation treatment for depression, the therapist and patient
   a. talk about a single behaviour to be modified
   b. focus on uncontrollable activities that lead to helplessness
   c. participate in activating group therapy
   d. develop a comprehensive list of specific goals and activities in major life areas
17. Second-generation antidepressants are often preferred over first-generation drugs because
   a. their mechanism of action is better understood
   b. they have fewer troublesome side effects
   c. they are not associated with suicidal thinking
   d. they can be used without careful monitoring
18. Electroconvulsive therapy is most appropriate for patients who
   a. need to take large doses of antidepressants
   b. have depression with a known biological cause
   c. have a specific abnormality on one side of the brain
   d. are severely depressed and who have not responded to other treatments
19. Which of the following is *not* a biological treatment for depressive disorders?
   a. electroconvulsive therapy
   b. transcranial magnetic stimulation
   c. deep brain stimulation
   d. neuroimaging
20. Major depressive disorder with a seasonal pattern is often treated by means of
   a. first-generation antidepressants
   b. transcranial magnetic stimulation
   c. exposure to bright light
   d. electroconvulsive therapy

Answers:
1 c, 2 b, 3 d, 4 a, 5 d, 6 c, 7 d, 8 c, 9 b, 10 a, 11 a, 12 d, 13 b, 14 d, 15 a, 16 d, 17 b, 18 d, 19 d, 20 c.

chapter 7

feeding and eating disorders

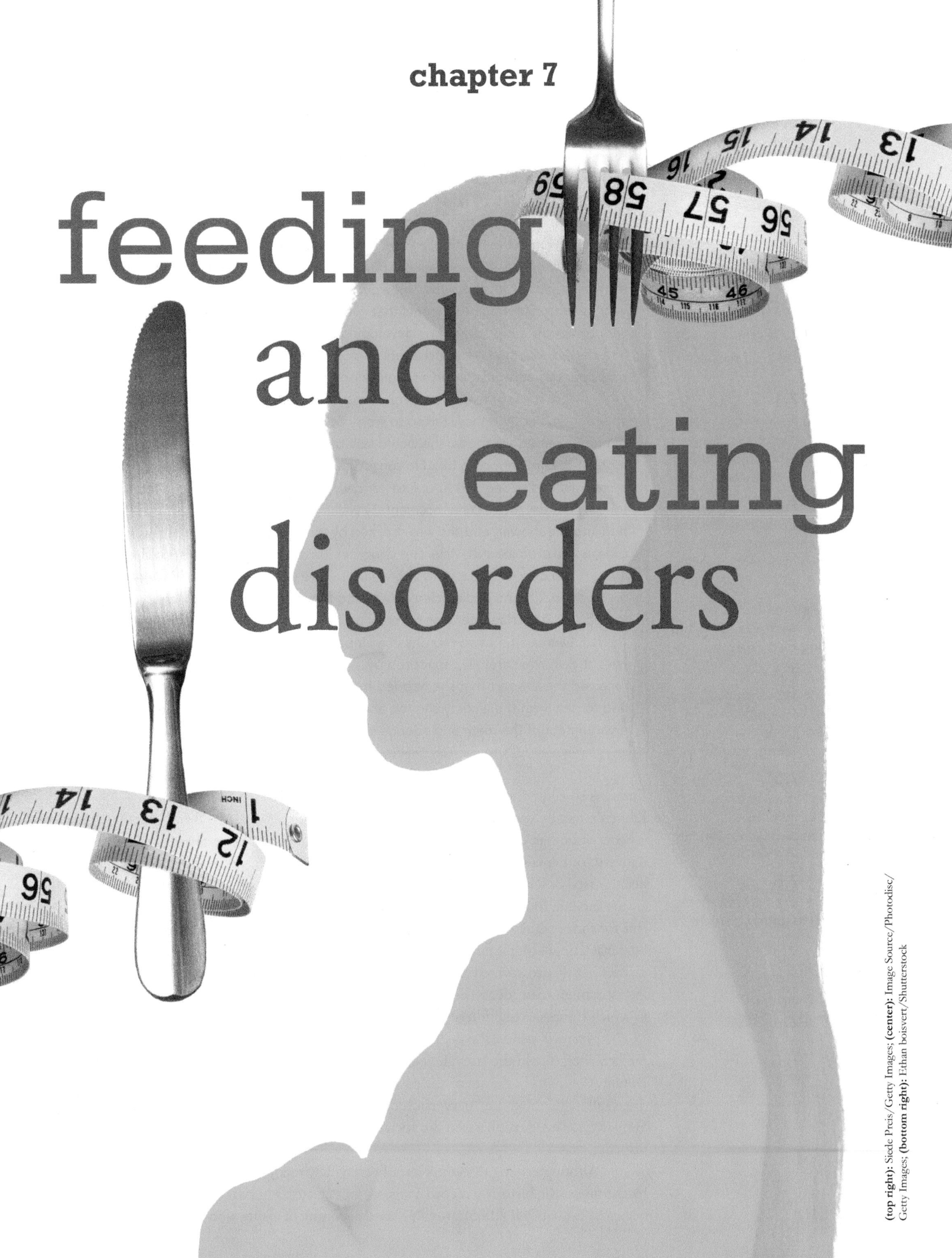

(top right): Siede Preis/Getty Images; **(center):** Image Source/Photodisc/Getty Images; **(bottom right):** Ethan boisvert/Shutterstock

learning objectives

After reading this chapter, you should be able to:

7.1
Understand the features of anorexia nervosa, bulimia nervosa, binge eating disorder, and other feeding and eating disorders.

7.2
Discuss sex differences in the risk for feeding and eating disorders and why these differences exist.

7.3
Discuss developmental life course changes in the risk for feeding and eating disorders.

7.4
Explore psychodynamic, behavioural, cognitive, and biological theories on the causes of feeding and eating disorders.

7.5
Discuss personality features and comorbid conditions that are commonly associated with feeding and eating disorders.

7.6
Compare and contrast treatments for feeding and eating disorders.

Having excelled in middle school, Lauren was accepted into a prestigious boarding high school that focused on science and mathematics. Before school started, she had a physical exam. At the visit in early summer, her pediatrician weighed her and said, "My, you are filling out nicely." Embarrassed by this comment, Lauren went home and examined her body in the mirror. She saw her budding breasts and her expanding hips and did not like it one bit. She turned sideways and looked at the protrusion where her flat stomach used to be and was determined to make it go away. Using all of her persistence and determination, she developed a strict regimen of running (3 km in the morning, 8 km in the evening) and a "healthy balanced diet" in terms of nutrients but that contained only 400 calories per day. She rationalized that if she got something from all the major food groups, she would be fine. Even so, any fats or oils made her very nervous. She told her parents that over the summer she would be preparing for a very competitive high school by developing the discipline she would need to excel. She started wearing layers and layers of clothes, checking her weight on the scale four times per day at regular intervals, and skipping regular family meals.

At first her parents were proud that she was taking her educational opportunity so seriously, but then they started to worry as her temper began to flare. If they ran out of one of her regular foods, she would lash out at her mother for not having bought more at the last shopping trip. No substitutions were allowed. She became more and more rigid and added 300 sit-ups to her daily exercise regimen to keep her abdomen toned. One day, her mother accidentally walked into the bathroom as Lauren was getting into the shower, and she was shocked by the emaciated body she saw: ribs, vertebrae, and a prominent clavicle. Her daughter looked like a concentration camp victim.

This discovery occurred two weeks before school was to start. Lauren's parents took her back to the pediatrician only to find that she had lost 15 kg, dropping to 39 kg at 165 cm. Their daughter was severely underweight. Rather than starting school in the fall, Lauren spent two months in an inpatient eating disorders unit where her weight gain was carefully monitored by a dietitian and physicians, and where she received the support that she needed from a psychologist to regain a healthy weight and to deal with the anxiety she felt about her ability to succeed in the high-pressure environment of the math and science school.

Eating is so central to human nature that disturbances in normal eating behaviour, like Lauren's, can be very difficult to understand. For most people, food and eating are rich aspects of human existence. Our ethnic legacies are marked by certain dishes that are native to our ancestors; our family legacies are marked by traditional dishes that have been passed down for generations; holidays are celebrated with friends and family and always include food; and few social occasions occur without the involvement of food. But for those who are vulnerable to eating disorders, such seemingly harmless events can be devastatingly frightening. What would lead a healthy young woman like Lauren to restrict her diet so severely, resulting in a body weight far below what even the fashion industry might consider to be thin? In this chapter, we examine psychological disorders in which the basic function of eating is disturbed.

Anorexia nervosa, the disorder from which Lauren suffered, was recognized in the medical literature in the late nineteenth century in both France (Lasègue, 1873) and Britain (Gull, 1874). Aware of the psychological or "nervous" components of the disorder, Gull highlighted the "perversion of the will" and focused on the role of starvation. Similarly, Lasègue emphasized the social and psychological factors associated with the disorder.

Although eating disorders have been widely recognized only in comparatively recent times, the historical record suggests that anorexia nervosa and other disorders occurred earlier. Bell (1985) provides vivid accounts of saints who starved themselves pursuing purity or devotion to God. This is a classic example of how social context may alter the clinical expression of a disorder. The self-starvation mirrored the symptoms that we see today in anorexia nervosa, yet the cultural context embedded the disorder in religion. Today, as in Lauren's case, we see the symptoms in a very different sociocultural context—one that is interpreted as a young woman's internalization of the ideal of extreme thinness. Although anorexia occurs most often in adolescents, it occurs across the lifespan in both sexes.

Another eating disorder with a long history is *bulimia nervosa*, characterized by binge eating followed by vomiting or other compensatory behaviour. Even historical accounts reveal that eating disorders are not confined to females. History is peppered with case reports of individuals who engaged in the perplexing behaviours associated with bulimia nervosa (e.g., binge eating or self-induced vomiting). Some Roman emperors, for example, appear to have engaged in these behaviours (Keel et al., 2005). But despite its long history, bulimia nervosa was not recognized as a psychological disorder until 1979 (Russell, 1979).

A more recent addition to the psychiatric nomenclature is **binge eating disorder** (BED). This condition shares the symptom of binge eating with bulimia nervosa, but in the absence of purging behaviours. Only having made its official debut in DSM-5, we know less about the course and outcome of BED than the other eating disorders.

St. Catherine of Siena was born in 1347, the 24th of 25 children. Her fasting, self-denial, and suffering bear close resemblance to modern-day anorexia nervosa.

Giovanni di Paolo di Grazia/Fogg Art Museum, Harvard Art Museums, USA/Gift of Sir Joseph Duveen/Bridgeman Images

Anorexia Nervosa

7.1 Understand the features of anorexia nervosa, bulimia nervosa, binge eating disorder, and other feeding and eating disorders.

Anorexia nervosa is a serious condition marked by a restriction of energy intake relative to needed energy requirements, resulting in significantly low body weight in the context of age, sex, developmental trajectory, and physical health. Younger patients fail to achieve the weight (and often height) increases expected as part of normal growth. Psychologists measure just how thin their patients are by calculating **body mass index** (BMI). Weight, in kilograms, is divided by height, in metres squared (kg/m^2). See Table 7.1 for the cutoffs for underweight, normal weight, overweight, and obese. Table 7.2 gives examples of just what these measures mean in terms of a typical woman (168 cm) and a typical man (180 cm). When measuring BMI in children, both sex and age are considered, and the appropriate metric is BMI percentile.

Anorexia nervosa is a visible eating disorder—patients are noticeably thin—although they may conceal their *emaciation* by wearing layers of clothes or otherwise hiding their bodies. Anorexia nervosa has two subtypes, initially proposed by Canadian

TABLE 7.1
BMI Categories

BMI	Weight Status
Below 18.5	Underweight
18.5–24.9	Normal
25.0–29.9	Overweight
30.0 and above	Obese

TABLE 7.2
BMI to Weight Examples for Typical Woman and Man

BMI	Woman 168 cm Age 20 Weight (kg)	Man 180 cm Age 20 Weight (kg)
13.0	36	42
18.5	52	60
21.0	59	68
25.0	70	81
30.0	84	98
40.0	112	130

criteria for
Anorexia Nervosa
DSM-5

A. Restriction of energy intake relative to requirements, leading to a significantly low body weight in the context of age, sex, developmental trajectory, and physical health. *Significantly low weight* is defined as a weight that is less than minimally normal or, for children and adolescents, less than that minimally expected.

B. Intense fear of gaining weight or of becoming fat, or persistent behaviour that interferes with weight gain, even though at a significantly low weight.

C. Disturbance in the way in which one's body weight or shape is experienced, undue influence of body weight or shape on self-evaluation, or persistent lack of recognition of the seriousness of the current low body weight.

(F50.01) Restricting type: During the last 3 months, the individual has not engaged in recurrent episodes of binge eating or purging behaviour (i.e., self-induced vomiting or the misuse of laxatives, diuretics, or enemas). This subtype describes presentations in which weight loss is accomplished primarily through dieting, fasting, and/or excessive exercise.

(F50.02) Binge-eating/purging type: During the last 3 months, the individual has engaged in recurrent episodes of binge eating or purging (i.e., self-induced vomiting or the misuse of laxatives, diuretics, or enemas).

Many individuals with anorexia nervosa see their bodies as larger than they actually are. The mechanism for this distortion remains unknown.

Getty Images

eating disorders researchers (Garfinkel et al., 1980): restricting and binge eating/purging (see "DSM-5: Anorexia Nervosa"). In the restricting subtype, patients maintain their low weight only by reducing their caloric intake and increasing their physical activity. In the binge eating/purging subtype, individuals may engage in **binge eating** (eating an unusually large amount of food in a short period of time and feeling out of control), **purging** (self-inducing vomiting or using laxatives, diuretics [water pills], or enemas), or both.

The second clinical feature of anorexia nervosa is an intense fear of gaining weight or becoming fat, even though the person is already seriously underweight. Individuals with anorexia nervosa, even in the most extreme phases of emaciation, fear weight gain. They are not merely afraid of becoming fat; they are terrified by even the smallest amount of weight gain. This is commonly expressed as "feeling fat," although the precise meaning of that phrase differs by individual, as "fat" is not truly a feeling.

The third feature includes three possible problems. Patients may have one, two, or all three of these features. The first problem is experiential and possibly perceptual, in which patients *experience their weight or shape as large even when they are emaciated.* The mechanism of this perceptual distortion remains unknown, but it may work in the same way that some people who have been overweight and lose weight still perceive themselves as overweight. Betsy recalls,

> I remember during treatment when Anne, the dietitian, was working with me to include a muffin for breakfast. I put the muffin on my plate and just stared at it. It may as well have been a tarantula or a python. I took a bite and I could literally see my thighs getting fatter. The muffin was going straight to my thighs. After four bites, I just panicked and threw the muffin away. I had to go running to get rid of it.

The second problem is *placing undue importance on body weight and shape as a measure of self-evaluation.* People with anorexia nervosa are totally preoccupied by weight. In fact, their self-worth and self-esteem can be almost entirely determined by their weight or shape. Slight weight increases can lead to a downward spiral of mood and self-worth.

The third problem is *lack of recognition of the seriousness of the low body weight.* Even when facing severe medical complications, individuals with anorexia nervosa insist that everything is fine. This creates considerable problems in reaching and accepting treatment and, on occasion, can result in patients being hospitalized involuntarily (see Chapter 15) because they are a clear danger to themselves.

Even at 32 kg (BMI = 12 kg/m^2), Betsy maintained her rigorous exercise schedule of running 8 km per day, doing 400 sit-ups, and spending one hour on the exercise bike.

In previous versions of the diagnostic criteria for anorexia, **amenorrhea**, or the absence of menstruation for at least three consecutive months, was a requirement. Amenorrhea is a common response to starvation and weight loss as the body shuts down reproductive functioning in the face of famine. In recognition that there are no meaningful differences between individuals with anorexia nervosa who do and do not menstruate (Gendall et al., 2006), this criterion was removed in DSM-5. Nonetheless, menstrual functioning should always be assessed in individuals with eating disorders as it can be an important indicator of severity.

Anorexia nervosa is commonly associated with a long list of other psychological and medical features. Depression and anxiety are commonly present, and patients often have slow heart rates, low blood pressure, and lowered body temperature (which might explain their tendency to wear layers of clothes, even in warm temperatures). Table 7.3 presents additional clinical features associated with anorexia nervosa.

Epidemiology and Course of Anorexia Nervosa

It is estimated that between 0.5% and 4% of women in Canada will develop anorexia nervosa (Health Canada, 2002; LeBlanc, 2014). For males, the rate is lower (0.2% to 0.3%), but possibly rising (Hoek & van Hoeken, 2003; Hudson et al., 2007; LeBlanc, 2014; Woodside et al., 2001).

Anorexia nervosa tends to cluster in certain segments of the population. These segments include the entertainment industry and sports, in which undue emphasis is placed on body shape and weight as part of performance. Actors, dancers, models, and athletes are at greater risk of developing the disorder than other groups. To illustrate, a survey of students from Canada's National Ballet School found that 26% had anorexia nervosa and 14% had either bulimia nervosa or other eating problems (Garner et al., 1987).

TABLE 7.3

Features Associated with Anorexia Nervosa

Physical Features	Psychological/Behavioural Features
Dehydration	Cognitive impairment
Electrolyte imbalances (sodium, potassium levels)	Body checking (touching and pinching to measure fatness)
Osteoporosis (decreased bone density)	Depression
Lanugo hair (fine downy hair on body)	Anxiety
Dry brittle hair	Low self-esteem
Low body temperature	Self-absorption
Hypotension (low blood pressure)	Ritualistic behaviours
Bradycardia (slow heart rate)	Extreme perfectionism
Growth retardation	Self-consciousness
Bloating	
Constipation	
Fidgeting	
Loss of tooth enamel and dentin	

Even after recovery, people who have suffered from anorexia nervosa tend to continue to have low BMIs (Sullivan et al., 1998). The course of anorexia nervosa can be protracted and often includes periods of relapse, remission, and crossover to bulimia nervosa. Between 8% and 62% of people who start with anorexia nervosa develop bulimic symptoms at some point during the course of the disorder—usually during the first five years (Bulik et al., 1997b; Tozzi et al., 2005).

As in other Western countries, in Canada anorexia nervosa has the highest mortality rate of any mental disorder, with about 10% to 15% of people with anorexia dying from the disorder (LeBlanc, 2014). The principal causes of death include both direct effects of starvation and suicide (Birmingham et al., 2005).

Personality and Anorexia Nervosa

When we look back at Lauren's case, we have to ask whether there were any hints in her personality that might hold clues to why she developed this devastating disorder. Some personality traits do seem to come before the eating disorder, get worse during the eating disorder, and often persist after recovery. The most important is *perfectionism.* Studies by several investigators, including Paul Hewitt at the University of British Columbia and Gordon Flett at York University, have demonstrated that young women with eating problems (including features of anorexia and bulimia) are perfectionists both about eating and weight, and about general expectations for themselves (Cockell et al., 2002; McGee et al., 2005; Sherry et al., 2014). People who develop anorexia nervosa are often described as model children and model students who set extremely high standards for themselves. They also apply that perfectionism to their pursuit of thinness and hold themselves to dieting standards above what others could possibly attain.

REAL people REAL disorders

Kathleen Rea: Ballet, Anorexia, and Bulimia

From a young age I loved to dance. On Saturday mornings before my parents woke up, I danced in my living room like a wild swan in a magical kingdom. At age 10, I was accepted into the National Ballet School of Canada training program. I attended school nine hours a day, working toward transcending the limitations of the body through discipline and control. My attraction to ballet did not just evolve out of my love of dance, but from a desire to gain control over my life. When my parents divorced, life was chaotic. The strict rules of ballet instantly resonated with me because they provided a set of ideals to reach for—a magical recipe that promised to make everything right. But my world of perfect pliés and pretty pirouettes left little room for the wild swan girl. In puberty I developed curves that were considered too fat for the ballet world. The message that "thin was better" did not just come from my ballet teachers, but from female role models, billboards, magazines, and movies.

I decided to diet my curves away, as the accolades in ballet went to girls who looked deathly thin. But my calculated "career move" soon became my nightmare. I became borderline anorexic and then bulimic. After dieting intensely for days, a famished "creature" would seize control, and an intense desire to eat would overcome my willpower. In a trance-like state, I would binge on cakes, ice cream, and greasy foods. Emerging from my daze, I would try to erase the calories by making myself throw up. By the time I joined the National Ballet Company of Canada, I was binging and purging up to eight times a day. My required performance weight was 105 pounds (about 47 kg), and at 5′6″ (167 cm) that was bone thin. My ballet mistress told me that I needed to be thinner than the other girls because of my "larger" breasts (my cup size was B!). Life under such pressure was hard, but being part of an elite dance community with extravagant productions and performances throughout the world was enthralling.

The rewards seemed worth the hardships—until I hit rock bottom. After being told I might lose a role unless I dropped more weight, I successfully starved myself for a week. And then my willpower failed. I spent most of the night eating loaves of bread with butter and quarts of ice cream, and then forcing myself to throw up. But I knew that it wouldn't matter how hard I tried to purge the calories; they had already made their way to my thighs.

I lay on the bathroom floor holding a sharp knife against my thigh, fighting the urge to cut off the fat. I lay like that on the cold tiles until morning. Preparing for work, I curled my hair into a tight bun and paused, looking into my sunken eyes. I could see in them that I was dying—a soul death that would eventually result in a physical death if I stayed on the path I was on.

I found an eating disorder therapist and began the recovery process. He suggested I work on softening my steady stream of self-critique. This critique was not really my voice, but a repetition of messages I received as a dancer. If I was going to recover, I had to find my own voice.

I spoke with the National Ballet Company, telling them I was in recovery from an eating disorder and might gain weight, but I would try to get back to my performance weight as soon as possible. Shortly after this, the company went on tour to Washington DC. After we returned, the artistic director told me I had been far too fat to appear onstage, but due to so many dancers being injured, they were forced to keep me in the performance lineup. As a result, he informed me, I had embarrassed the nation of Canada on the international stage! Five weeks later, they fired me. I felt shame that my body size was an embarrassment and grief at the loss of my dream, but there was also a sense of relief. I was free.

The first thing I did with my newly acquired freedom was to stop dieting. Yet my obsessive thoughts about food still ran though my head continuously. There was a safety in these thoughts; they protected me from the inherent risks of truly engaging in life. I decided that every time my presence slipped away into diet la-la land, I would wipe the obsessive thought away and think of something more productive.

Gradually, there was more and more of myself available to focus on life. A few months after leaving the ballet, I choreographed a solo dance inspired by my recovery from bulimia. To do so, I had to overcome the disease's tendency for secretive behaviour. I designed an empty mirror frame that I danced on, through, and around wearing pointe shoes glued to clunky bathroom scales. During the creative process, I discovered a new internal strength: a creative drive that superseded the "perfect me." The plan for the ending involved me stripping down naked in near darkness and running off stage. On opening night, I took off my clothes as planned, but the lights got brighter, revealing my naked body to everyone watching.

Angry, I asked my lighting designer what had happened. He explained it wasn't right for the piece to end with me in hiding, so he changed the lights. My ballet friends came to see the show and broke down crying as they watched. It was not just my story; it was also their story. I forgave my lighting designer when I read the following review: "In the final hymn of freedom … Rea revealed her beautiful naked body, more lush than the world of ballet would allow, and made her run to a new life."

And what is my new life? I have come to appreciate my body and to follow its cues. I eat when hungry and stop when full. I have made it my life's work to help others express their life stories through the arts, and in so doing be healed by the connection to self and to others this brings. And most importantly I have returned to my "wild swan" dances.

Source: Rea, K. (2013). How my national ballet career led to bulimia. *Huffington Post*, www.huffingtonpost.ca/kathleen-rea/eating-disorder-ballet_b_2235176.html. Accessed July 12, 2015.

Other common personality factors are *obsessionality* (going over and over things in their mind) and *neuroticism* (being a worrier and having difficulty shaking things off) (Bardone-Cone et al., 2007; Bulik et al., 2006; Wonderlich et al., 2005). This cluster of personality traits may help explain why adolescence and young adulthood are typical periods of risk for the development of eating disorders. Many of the developmental tasks of this life period involve substantial change and encounters with unfamiliar stimuli (e.g., leaving home for university, dating). Such transitions can be challenging even for healthy youth. People who are worriers, who tend toward unwavering perfectionism, and who find change difficult may experience this period of life as a trigger for an underlying predisposition to eating disorders. Addressing these fundamental underlying personality traits is often an important aspect of treatment.

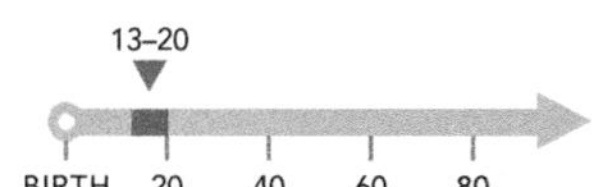

Anorexia nervosa most commonly begins during adolescence.

Comorbidity and Anorexia Nervosa

People with anorexia often suffer from anxiety, depression, and other problems. Up to 80% will experience major depression at some time during their lives (Fernandez-Aranda et al., 2007), and up to 75% will suffer from anxiety disorders, especially obsessive-compulsive disorder (Bulik et al., 1997; Kaye et al., 2004). Even after recovery, depression and anxiety commonly persist (Sullivan et al., 1998). Effective treatment for anorexia nervosa must also address these disorders to completely restore healthy functioning.

REAL people REAL disorders

Kate's Anorexia

Nineteen-year-old Kate knows firsthand what it's like to struggle with an eating disorder. By the time she was 13, the North Vancouver high-school graduate had developed a case of anorexia so serious that she found herself being monitored in a cardiac unit because of a dangerously low heart rate. "I would reward myself at my lowest weight," Kate recalled. "I kept thinking, 'If I made it this far, I can make it even further.' I remember the feeling of my bones protruding. It hurt to lie on the bed because my bones against the flat mat were so uncomfortable."

Kate may look like a typical teen, cellphone in hand, multiple silver earrings, and cherry-red lipstick to match her top, but her level-headedness belies her age. She says a number of factors led up to her anorexia. She wasn't immune to the proliferation of media images of sticklike women. She had lost two grandparents within a short period of time. A relative was dealing with schizophrenia. And she wanted to be in control. She may not have had much say over the world around her, but she *could* control what she ate and how much she weighed. By age 12, she cut out meat. The next year, she became obsessed with exercise.

"Food became an enemy," Kate says. "I remember one morning at home. My mom made me breakfast, and I ran out of the room, yelling and screaming up to my room. I remember thinking about calories. I couldn't drink water because I thought it was bad for me. I thought it had too many calories in it."

Kate spent most of the summer of grade 8 in B.C.'s Children's Hospital. "I was pissed off," she says. "I didn't want to be there. I didn't think I had a problem. It was a complete refusal. ... I would storm out of the room and tell people to F off. That was my thing, telling people to fuck off constantly. I couldn't handle it. I was scared."

"I looked like a junkie," she adds. "I looked so sick. I didn't have any nourishment. But that's part of recovery; you have to acknowledge you have anorexia before you're able to do something about it."

Now, Kate is doing whatever she can to maintain healthy eating habits. And she tries not to pay much attention to media images of "perfect" women. "I see these things every day. I'm not, 'I've got to look like that.' Now I think, '*whatever.*'" She has also spoken at one of the parents' support groups at Children's Hospital. "It was neat to hear from their perspective," she says, "They felt they were helpless and wanted to know what they could do to help. One parent started crying, they were so upset their child was going through this. Another said I could give people hope, that this isn't the end."

Source: Adapted from Gail Johnson, "Fear of fat," *Georgia Straight*, June 13-20, 2002, pp. 19–22.

CONCEPT check

- Anorexia nervosa is a visible eating disorder marked by low body weight and fear of weight gain.
- BMI is a way of expressing both weight and height as one measurement.
- Girls and women are more likely to develop anorexia nervosa than boys and men.
- The typical age of onset for anorexia nervosa is adolescence, although more and more cases are being reported in childhood and older adulthood.

critical thinking question How might the personality trait of perfectionism increase the risk for development of anorexia nervosa?

Bulimia Nervosa

Elisa was 21 years old, 178 cm, and 65 kg (BMI = 20.7 kg/m^2) when she first came to the eating disorders service. She reported four years of untreated binge eating and self-induced vomiting. Her high-risk binge times were in the evening when she would close the blinds in her kitchen and, in her words, "go hog wild." A typical binge included a gallon of ice cream, dry cereal straight from the box, and, sometimes, a whole package of cookies. Then she would switch from sweet to salty and start with chips and anything else she could find. In the last year, desperate to control her weight, she began taking laxatives. Her use started with some herbs from the health food store, but she soon progressed to stronger laxatives. First she took the recommended dose, but then she needed more to get the desired effect. In the months before she sought treatment, Elisa lost her job and was basically housebound in her parents' home. She was binge eating and purging over 20 times per day and taking more than 70 laxatives each night. She had developed large ulcers and scrapes in her esophagus because she was pushing objects down her throat to induce vomiting. She had had two emergency room visits for dehydration. On one visit, a blood test showed her potassium level to be dangerously low. After she was stabilized medically, she was admitted to a partial hospitalization program for eating disorders. She had difficulty adhering to the hospital's nonsmoking rules, and she frequently disappeared from the treatment facility during the day. When faced with the ultimatum of adhering to the program rules or being discharged against medical advice, she opted to leave. Two days later, Elisa was again in the emergency room with dehydration, an irregular heartbeat, and a low potassium level. This time she was admitted to a medical floor for monitoring, later to be transferred to an inpatient eating disorders program.

Unlike anorexia nervosa, **bulimia nervosa** (see "DSM-5: Bulimia Nervosa") is an invisible eating disorder because patients are of normal weight or overweight. It is characterized by recurrent episodes of binge eating in combination with recurrent inappropriate *compensatory behaviours* in order to prevent weight gain. Binge eating is the consumption of an amount of food in a discrete period of time that is definitely larger than most people would consume. Unlike simple overeating, the hallmark feature of a binge is a sense of lack of control over eating. The person cannot stop the urge to binge once it has begun or has difficulty ending the eating episode even when long past being full. Some patients talk about a trance or a "binge mode" in which everything else melts away during this time. Running out of food, being interrupted by other people, or experiencing an extreme urge to purge usually stops the binge.

Canadian author Evelyn Lau (2001), who suffered from bulimia nervosa, provided the following description of one of her binges:

> I think of how many people would like to have more than one cookie out of the bag they bring home from the supermarket. Some of them do have several cookies, savouring them, then place the rest of the bag in the cupboard. Others have a harder time doing that; they eat too many cookies, half the package perhaps, then feel repentant and disgusted with themselves. But imagine ratcheting that urge up further. Imagine that you are unable to sleep because of the cookies in your cupboard, that you can't work or read or leave the house knowing the uneaten cookies are there. That feeling of anxiety begins to build in you, a desperation and a kind of anger, until you break down and cram the cookies into your mouth several at a time, devouring them until you throw up. If, after you throw up, there are still some cookies left in the bag, you have to keep eating them, even though by then you are sick of their taste and texture. If there are ten bags of cookies and no way that you can eat them all, you will have to bury the rest of them immediately at the bottom of the garbage pail—first crushing them and soaking them in water, say, to prevent your retrieving them later—in order to be rid of them. (Adapted from Lau, 2001, pp. 81–82.)

Placing an actual caloric level on what constitutes a binge is difficult. Most agree that around 1000 calories is the minimum amount to be considered a binge—but in

criteria for
Bulimia Nervosa DSM-5

A. Recurrent episodes of binge eating. An episode of binge eating is characterized by both of the following:

1. Eating, in a discrete period of time (e.g., within any 2-hour period), an amount of food that is definitely larger than what most individuals would eat in a similar period of time under similar circumstances.
2. A sense of lack of control over eating during the episode (e.g., a feeling that one cannot stop eating or control what or how much one is eating).

B. Recurrent inappropriate compensatory behaviours in order to prevent weight gain, such as self-induced vomiting; misuse of laxatives, diuretics, or other medications; fasting; or excessive exercise.

C. The binge eating and inappropriate compensatory behaviours both occur, on average, at least once a week for 3 months.

D. Self-evaluation is unduly influenced by body shape and weight.

E. The disturbance does not occur exclusively during episodes of anorexia nervosa.

some cases, as many as 20 000 calories may be consumed. The way to judge is to ask whether the amount of food is more than a typical person would eat under similar circumstances. What is most important is whether overeating is coupled with a sense of loss of control. Indeed, some people (especially those with anorexia nervosa) might feel out of control even when they eat relatively small amounts of food. So someone with anorexia nervosa might say she binged after eating two cookies. The term *subjective binge* defines eating a typical or even small amount of food (e.g., a cookie) coupled with the feeling that the eating is out of control. This is in contrast to an *objective binge*, which is defined as eating a comparatively large amount of food plus feeling out of control.

The pattern of binge eating also varies. The frequency can range from occasionally to a few times per week to 20 or 30 times per day. Once per week for three months is the required frequency for a threshold diagnosis of bulimia nervosa. Some people become locked in an entrenched binge–purge cycle, which comes to dominate their lives. For Elisa, evenings were clearly her high-risk times for binge eating, and she became locked into a vicious cycle of binge eating and purging that could not be interrupted.

Inappropriate compensatory behaviours are any actions that a person uses to counteract a binge or to prevent weight gain. These behaviours include self-induced vomiting; misuse of laxatives, diuretics, enemas, or other agents; fasting; and excessive exercise. It is important to note that some people purge without binge eating (see "Other Specified Feeding and Eating Disorders"). People with bulimia nervosa tend to be either of normal weight or overweight. Many calories associated with the binge are absorbed, and those calories lead to weight gain. Laxatives, which work in the colon (after all of the nutrients have been absorbed in the stomach and the small intestine), are ineffective but dangerous purge agents. Only 5% of calories consumed are lost, but losing water and necessary electrolytes (such as potassium) make abusing laxatives very dangerous.

In addition to the core symptoms of bulimia nervosa, many other physical and psychological features exist. Some are similar to those of individuals with anorexia nervosa, but others are quite distinct. Table 7.4 presents additional clinical features of bulimia nervosa.

TABLE 7.4
Features Associated with Bulimia Nervosa

Physical Features	Psychological/Behavioural Features
Dehydration	Depression
Electrolyte imbalances (sodium and potassium levels)	Low self-esteem
	Self-absorption
Acid reflux	Ritualistic behaviours
Ruptures of esophagus	Extreme perfectionism
Loss of tooth enamel and dentin	Self-consciousness
Swollen parotid glands	Anxiety
Gastrointestinal complications	Alcohol and drug abuse
Irregular menstruation	Irritability
Constipation	Impulsive spending
Bloating	Shoplifting

Epidemiology and Course of Bulimia Nervosa

Many people with bulimia nervosa keep their behaviour secret because of the stigma and shame attached to it. Bulimia typically starts somewhat later than anorexia nervosa—in middle to late adolescence or early adulthood—although even later onset is not uncommon. It is estimated that 1% to 4% of Canadian women will develop bulimia nervosa (Health Canada, 2002a; LeBlanc, 2014). For males, the rates are lower (0.1% to 0.5%) (Hoek & van Hoeken, 2003; Hudson et al., 2007; Woodside et al., 2001).

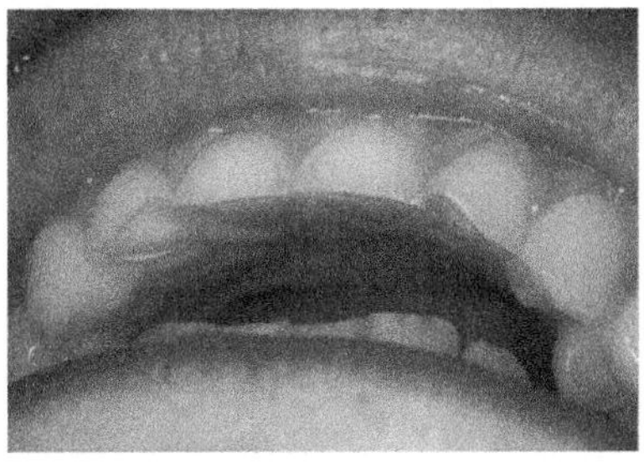

Erosion of dental enamel as a result of frequent vomiting.

K.L. Boyd/Custom Medical Stock Photo

Is the incidence of bulimia nervosa rising? Few data exist to address this question, but individuals born after 1960 are at greater risk for the disorder (Kendler et al., 1991), suggesting that bulimia nervosa is a more "modern" phenomenon than anorexia. What is clear is that eating disorder behaviours such as binge eating, purging, and restricting do appear to have risen in the decade between 1995 and 2005 (Hay et al., 2008). Some believe that bulimia nervosa is more of a culture-bound syndrome than anorexia nervosa (Keel & Klump, 2003), reflecting the trend that began in the 1960s toward thinner cultural ideals of beauty. Bulimia nervosa also tends to be more common in urban than in rural areas (Hoek et al., 1995). This suggests that environmental exposure, social learning, or information transfer may play a role in the development of this disorder. Many patients state that they first got the idea to purge from something they read. However, virtually all young girls are exposed to this information at some time or another, so why do only 5% or so develop the disorder? This question is considered in the section on genetics later in this chapter.

Bulimia nervosa is also associated with serious physical complications, including fatigue, lethargy, bloating, and gastrointestinal problems. The disorder is hard on the body. Frequent vomiting leads to erosion of dental enamel, swelling of the parotid (salivary) glands, and calluses on the backs of the hands (Mitchell et al., 1991). Those who frequently misuse laxatives can have *edema* (bodily swelling), fluid loss and subsequent dehydration, electrolyte abnormalities, serious metabolic problems, and permanent loss of normal bowel function (Mitchell et al., 1991).

The mortality rate for bulimia nervosa is around 3.9% (Crow et al., 2009). In one 10-year outcome study, 11% of individuals continued to meet full diagnostic criteria for bulimia nervosa and 18.5% met criteria for the DSM-IV-TR residual diagnosis of **eating**

disorder not otherwise specified (EDNOS); that is, their eating patterns were abnormal but did not actually fit the diagnostic criteria for any other eating disorder as defined in the DSM at the time. Approximately one-half to two-thirds of patients eventually achieve full or partial remission (Berkman et al., 2007).

Personality and Bulimia Nervosa

People with bulimia nervosa share some personality features with those who have anorexia nervosa, primarily perfectionism and low self-esteem, but differences also exist. Unlike the classic restricting subtype of anorexia nervosa, people with bulimia tend to be more impulsive (acting before thinking) and have higher *novelty-seeking* (stimulus or sensation-seeking) behaviour (Bulik et al., 1995; Fassino et al., 2004; Steiger et al., 2004). These different personality factors are intriguing and reflect the symptom profiles of the disorders. Individuals with the restricting subtype of anorexia nervosa display more rigid and obsessional personalities—congruent with their rigid eating patterns. In contrast, people with bulimia nervosa exhibit more erratic and impulsive traits—consistent with the impulsive and fluctuating nature of alternating starving, binge eating, and compensatory behaviours.

Comorbidity and Bulimia Nervosa

Approximately 80% of patients with bulimia nervosa have another psychiatric disorder at some time in their lives (Fichter & Quadflieg, 1997); this is a very high rate. Some individuals have several disorders at the same time, and some continue to suffer from other disorders even after they recover from bulimia nervosa. The most common comorbid psychiatric conditions include anxiety disorders, major depression, substance use, and personality disorders (Braun et al., 1994; Brewerton et al., 1995; Bushnell et al., 1994).

CONCEPT check

- Bulimia nervosa is an eating disorder marked by binge eating and compensatory behaviours. Most patients are of normal weight or are overweight.
- Bulimia occurs more often in females than males and tends to begin in late adolescence or early adulthood.
- The incidence of bulimia has increased since 1960 and is more common in urban than rural populations.
- Comorbid depression, anxiety, and substance abuse are common in individuals with bulimia nervosa.
- Individuals with bulimia nervosa are perfectionistic and have low self-esteem, but they also tend to be more impulsive and have higher novelty-seeking behaviour than people with anorexia nervosa.

critical thinking question How might cultural factors have led to an increase in bulimia nervosa since the 1960s?

Binge Eating Disorder

Olexa was a 42-year-old emergency room nurse. She had been overweight since childhood and was currently 165 cm and 88 kg (BMI = 32.4 kg/m^2). Her typical day started out late; she shunned both the scale and breakfast in the morning. She had to get the kids off to school and always prepared their breakfast, but she said her stomach didn't wake up until about 11 a.m. But then it woke up with a vengeance. On her 11 a.m. break, the vending machines "started calling her name." She started craving the prepackaged sandwiches she could get from the machines, loaded with packets of mayonnaise and relish. Once she got the salt cravings out of the way, she stopped by the candy machine. The best way to satisfy the deep need inside her was something with both chocolate and nuts—hit the sweet and salt cravings in one fell swoop. She had to get back to work in the afternoon, but she still had cravings. All she could think of was being alone in her kitchen after the kids were in bed and finally satisfying her needs. She would make it through the day with half of her mind on food the whole time. She fed the kids dinner, only eating a small salad herself. Once they were safely tucked in bed, she could have her "date with her pantry." Olexa said that food was her best friend. It was always there when she needed it. It was the only one that listened to her sadness, her loneliness, and her pain. For those few hours, surrounded by chocolate cupcakes, chips, chocolates, and ice cream, she felt comfort. She would be infuriated if one of the kids woke up and interrupted her binge. Most nights, she would retire to her bedroom in tears. Her "friend" had an edge. She would lie in bed with thoughts of failure running through her head, thinking she would never get her eating and her life under control. The next morning she would wake up with what she called a "food hangover" and start the process all over again.

Binge eating was first recognized in a subset of obese individuals by Stunkard in 1959. In 2013, with the publication of DSM-5, BED became an official diagnostic category (see "DSM-5: Binge Eating Disorder"). The disorder is characterized by recurrent binge eating behaviour but without the recurrent inappropriate compensatory behaviours that are part of bulimia nervosa. "Real People, Real Disorders" presents the true story of tennis sensation Monica Seles's struggle with BED.

Epidemiology and Course of BED

BED is estimated to affect about 2% of the population (Health Canada, 2002a). BED is correlated with obesity (Klatzkin et al., 2015). However, not all people with BED are obese (Flament et al., 2015), possibly because some people with BED are able to compensate by reducing their caloric intake in between binges.

Because BED is a recent addition to the DSM, little is known about its morbidity and mortality. One study followed a clinical sample for six years after treatment to determine

REAL people REAL disorders

Monica Seles: Tennis and Binge Eating Disorder Don't Mix

Monica Seles was ranked number one for 178 weeks and won nine Grand Slam singles titles, 53 career titles, and a bronze medal at the Sydney Olympics in 2000. Before 1993, she was unstoppable. During a quarterfinal match in Hamburg, Germany, in which Seles, then age 19, was leading 6–4, 4–3. Günter Parche, a fan who was obsessed with rival tennis star Steffi Graf, stabbed Seles between her shoulder blades with a 23 cm (9 inch) knife. Parche was sentenced to only two years' probation and psychological treatment. In her book *Getting a Grip*, Seles describes that incident as the point when her "reality was ripped away." She claims the emotional scars took much longer to heal than the physical ones, and food became her "comfort and her poison." For nine years, while the press constantly commented on her size and the physical shape she was in, she vacillated between periods of strict dieting and gut-wrenching workouts and periods of depression and all-out binges (Seles, 2009). Her mood, self-esteem, and athletic self-confidence all became dependent on the number on the scale. She worked her way out of the trap by abandoning diets, restoring her love for food, and journalling. She describes the first step of her recovery as abandoning the search for answers outside herself and instead "listening to the quiet voice inside."

Landov

criteria for Binge Eating Disorder — DSM-5

A. Recurrent episodes of binge eating. An episode of binge eating is characterized by both of the following:

1. Eating, in a discrete period of time (e.g., within any 2-hour period), an amount of food that is definitely larger than what most people would eat in a similar period of time under similar circumstances.
2. A sense of lack of control over eating during the episode (e.g., a feeling that one cannot stop eating or control what or how much one is eating).

B. The binge-eating episodes are associated with three (or more) of the following:

1. Eating much more rapidly than normal.
2. Eating until feeling uncomfortably full.
3. Eating large amounts of food when not feeling physically hungry.
4. Eating alone because of feeling embarrassed by how much one is eating.
5. Feeling disgusted with oneself, depressed, or very guilty afterward.

C. Marked distress regarding binge eating is present.

D. The binge eating occurs, on average, at least once a week for 3 months.

E. The binge eating is not associated with the recurrent use of inappropriate compensatory behaviour as in bulimia nervosa and does not occur exclusively during the course of bulimia nervosa or anorexia nervosa.

their long-term outcome; 57.4% of women had a good outcome, 35.7% an intermediate outcome, and 5.9% a poor outcome (Fichter et al., 1998). Only one patient had died. Six years later, 6% still had BED, 7.4% had developed bulimia nervosa, and 7.4% continued to have some form of EDNOS. BED can be a chronic condition—the average length of time a person is ill is 14.4 years—suggesting that BED is not just a passing phase (Pope et al., 2006c). "Side-by-Side Case Studies" highlights the critical differences between binge eating and overeating.

Personality and BED

Less is known about the personality precursors to BED than about those to anorexia and bulimia nervosa. Although many investigations have explored the personality variables and the symptoms of binge eating, few have looked specifically at individuals with BED. What little we do know suggests that they score higher on measures of harm avoidance than healthy control individuals (Peterson et al., 2010). Another study, which compared obese individuals with BED to both obese individuals without BED and normal weight controls on a number of personality variables, found no distinct differences between the obese individuals with and without binge eating. However, those two groups scored higher than normal weight controls on sensitivity to reward and to punishment, harm avoidance, impulsivity, and addictive personality traits (Davis et al., 2008).

Comorbidity and BED

Individuals with BED experience many of the same forms of comorbidity as those with anorexia and bulimia nervosa. In a treatment-seeking sample, nearly 74% reported at least one additional psychological disorder, with the most common being mood disorders, anxiety disorders, and substance use disorders (Grilo et al., 2009). BED is also associated with risk for development of components of metabolic syndrome, such as hypertension, dyslipidemia, and type 2 diabetes. This increased risk appears to be independent of the effects of obesity.

Other Specified Feeding and Eating Disorders

As we have noted, the DSM criteria for anorexia nervosa, bulimia nervosa, and BED are very specific. In fact, many people who have eating disorders do *not* meet these criteria. Instead, they are given the diagnosis of other specified feeding and eating disorder (OSFED). DSM-5 lists five categories of OSFED. The first is atypical anorexia nervosa, in which a person has all the features of anorexia nervosa, except the person's weight is within or above the normal range. Next is bulimia nervosa (of low frequency or limited duration), in which a person meets all the criteria for bulimia nervosa, but the binge eating and purging happen less than once a week or for less than three months. Third is binge-eating disorder (of low frequency or limited duration), in which a person has all the criteria of binge eating disorder, but binge eating happens less than once a week or for less than three months. Fourth is purging disorder in which a person uses purging behaviour to control their weight or shape, but they are not binge eating. Fifth is night

SIDE by SIDE case studies Dimensions of Behaviour: From Normal to Abnormal

Normal Behaviour Case Study

Overeating

Josh liked to eat. His mother loved having him come home from university because she could cook all of his favourite dishes. She knew that nothing would spoil in the refrigerator as it did when Josh was at university. Over spring break, he went home to freshly baked cookies, his favourite dinners, red velvet cupcakes, and gallons and gallons of milk! His mom went all out, making sure the refrigerator and pantry were stocked with his favourite foods. At dinner, she offered seconds, and even though he was full, he did not want to hurt her feelings, so he ate second helpings. He felt really overstuffed but decided to take a run the next day and cut down a little. But he woke up to her famous apple coffee cake, and he just couldn't say no! That afternoon, he went to the gym because he was feeling stuffed. In addition, he knew his mom had invited his grandparents over for a special meal that night. Josh ate a healthy portion and took seconds, but he had no room for dessert. After dinner, he plopped down on the couch and watched football with his dad. He almost couldn't wait to get back to cafeteria food at school. Josh was overeating, but he was not out of control. He did not have an eating disorder.

Abnormal Behaviour Case Study

Binge Eating Disorder

Vince had always had a healthy appetite. His grandmother always referred to him as "her best eater." Even when his schoolmates started teasing him about being overweight, his loving Italian grandmother still showered him with his favourite foods. Not one to turn down something tasty and not wanting to hurt his grandmother's feelings, he always obliged. He managed to keep his weight under control throughout high school by joining the swim team. But even with all of that training, he still always seemed to have an extra layer of fat compared with the other guys. Once he hit university, he stopped swimming, but he did not stop eating. His weight started creeping up, and with a full course load and copyediting for a newspaper until the wee hours of the morning, he just didn't have time for exercise. He started to wonder what he was doing with his life, and his nights at the newspaper became more and more depressing. At first he ordered in a pizza and would eat and edit all night, but stop at one pie. But then he found that a whole pizza simply was not satisfying some need he felt inside. He added garlic bread, then doughnuts to top it off with something sweet, and sometimes he would go home and eat even more in the dorm. He was disgusted with himself but he couldn't stop. This was happening two or three times a week. One night, one of the section editors came back to the office late at night and found Vince surrounded by pizza boxes, doughnut boxes, chocolate wrappers, and gallons of soft drinks. The editor asked if they had been partying. Vince lied and said the other folks had just left. His eating was out of control. Vince had binge eating disorder.

eating syndrome, in which a person eats after waking up during the night, or eats excessively after the evening meal (and they can recall the eating); these behaviours cause distress or impairment of normal functioning.

Many changes were made to the previous diagnostic and classification system of eating disorders, in which the residual category used to be called eating disorder not otherwise specified (EDNOS) (APA, 2004). Changes were made to that classification system because most people who sought treatment for an eating disorder received a diagnosis of EDNOS (Fairburn & Walsh, 2002; Turner & Bryant-Waugh, 2003). The DSM-IV classification system did not adequately capture eating-related pathology as it existed in the real world. Only time, clinical observation, and research will tell whether the revisions in DSM-5 more accurately capture the true landscape of eating disorders.

Feeding and Eating Disorders of Childhood

Before DSM-5, feeding-related conditions commonly seen in children were included in a category entitled other disorders of childhood and adolescence. With the publication of DSM-5, these disorders were merged with the eating disorders category, thereby acknowledging some continuity of dysregulated eating patterns across developmental stages. This new arrangement could encourage additional research addressing how feeding disorders in childhood might be related to the eating disorders that typically emerge in adolescence and adulthood.

Many children, particularly infants and toddlers, are "picky eaters."

Sarah was five years old. Although she had no medical problems, her height and weight were at the second percentile for her age. Sarah refused to eat any foods except peanut butter sandwiches and candy. When offered other foods, she would cry and hold her breath until her mother gave her a peanut butter sandwich.

Sarah had no need to eat other foods—when she held her breath, she got her way. Treatment consisted of offering Sarah other foods and teaching her mother to ignore her tantrums. In Sarah's case, abnormal eating was the result of environmental factors and was not really dangerous. But other disordered eating behaviours, *pica* and *rumination*, are conceptually more perplexing and difficult to treat.

Pica is the persistent eating of nonnutritive, nonfood substances. The term comes from the Latin word for "magpie," a bird that voraciously consumes food and nonfood substances (Stiegler, 2005). According to one parent, "Over the last couple years we have pulled out of [our son's] throat: a set of keys, large bulldog clips, sticks, rocks, wads of paper, open safety pins, wire (from the screen, etc.). Plus all the stuff that he gets down before we can get it out: magnets from the fridge, Barbie parts, paper, money, paper clips, etc." (Menard, cited in Stiegler, 2005). Although children with developmental disabilities constitute the largest group of people with pica, the disorder also occurs in people with intellectual disability, people with schizophrenia, and sometimes people with no psychological disorder.

Pica occurs in various socioeconomic groups, both sexes, and all ages (Stiegler, 2005), but may be more common among women, children, and people of lower socioeconomic status (Rose et al., 2000). Pica can result in serious health consequences, including lead poisoning, parasitic infections, malnutrition, dental trauma, oral lacerations, gum disease, and erosion of tooth enamel. Consuming safety pins, glass, or nails can obstruct or perforate the esophagus, stomach, or intestines. Finally, the ingestion of certain items may repulse caregivers or peers, leading to social isolation or rejection (Stiegler, 2005).

Cultural pica occurs in many countries. Some women in India consume soil and its by-products (mud, clay, ash, lime, charcoal, and brick) in response to pregnancy cravings

(Nay, 1994). Some East African women consume soil for purposes of fertility (Abrahams & Parsons, 1996). Certain cultures in South America eat clay for its purported medicinal value (Rose et al., 2000).

Pica has many different causes. Iron and zinc deficiencies may result in the urge to ingest certain foods or substances, but many people without these conditions also engage in pica. Environmental factors (stress and impoverished living environments) or developmental disorders are important causal factors (Stiegler, 2005). Among people without psychological disorders, pica sometimes begins after stressful events such as surgery or the loss of a family member (Soykan et al., 1997). Overcorrection and other behavioural interventions are effective for pica (Foxx & Martin, 1975; Matson et al., 2013).

Nina was 14 years old and had moderate intellectual disability. When not closely monitored, she would eat any foreign object that she found on the floor. The psychologist developed an overcorrection program that consisted of Nina's spitting out the object and throwing it away. Then she would be led to the bathroom to brush her teeth for 10 minutes using an antiseptic toothpaste. After one week of consistent overcorrection, Nina's pica was reduced by 60%.

In a rare eating disorder, **rumination disorder**, recently eaten food is effortlessly regurgitated into the mouth, followed by rechewing, reswallowing, or spitting it out. Rumination disorder occurs in both sexes and may begin in infancy, childhood, or adolescence. Episodes may occur several times per day and may last for over an hour (Chial et al., 2003). Because rumination resembles vomiting, some people are initially diagnosed with bulimia nervosa or gastroesophageal reflux disease. They sometimes undergo gastrointestinal surgical procedures and consult several physicians before getting a correct diagnosis (O'Brien et al., 1995b).

Medications are not efficacious for the treatment of feeding disorders. Behavioural interventions such as habit reversal, relaxation training, and cognitive-behavioural therapy are efficacious for rumination disorder (Chial et al., 2003). *Habit reversal* is a behavioural treatment in which a problem behaviour is eliminated by consistently using a competing (i.e., alternative) behaviour. In the case of rumination, the patient is taught *diaphragmatic* (deep) breathing, a competing response that eliminates rumination in most patients (Chial et al., 2003).

Avoidant–restrictive food intake disorder (ARFID) was introduced into the DSM-5 given the frequency with which children with certain types of presentations were given diagnoses of EDNOS (the DSM-IV residual category). ARFID captures the behaviour of those children who exhibit restricted or otherwise inadequate eating (see "DSM-5: Avoidant/Restrictive Food Intake Disorder"). Although this is most common in children and adolescents, it can persist into adulthood.

Examples of ARFID include individuals who eat only a very narrow range of foods, and individuals who restrict their food intake to regulate emotions, an emotional crisis, or an unpleasant experience. Although often misunderstood as "picky eating," these presentations can be associated with clinically significant levels of impairment in development or functioning, and potentially severe medical complications.

CONCEPT check

- BED is characterized by recurrent binge eating in the absence of inappropriate compensatory behaviours.
- Individuals with BED are often but not always overweight or obese.
- OSFED is a residual category for those who do not meet strict criteria for anorexia nervosa, bulimia nervosa, or BED.

criteria for
Avoidant/Restrictive Food Intake Disorder DSM-5

A. An eating or feeding disturbance (e.g., apparent lack of interest in eating or food; avoidance based on the sensory characteristics of food; concern about aversive consequences of eating) as manifested by persistent failure to meet appropriate nutritional and/or energy needs associated with one (or more) of the following:
1. Significant weight loss (or failure to achieve expected weight gain or faltering growth in children).
2. Significant nutritional deficiency.
3. Dependence on enteral feeding or oral nutritional supplements.
4. Marked interference with psychosocial functioning.

B. The disturbance is not better explained by lack of available food or by an associated culturally sanctioned practice.

C. The eating disturbance does not occur exclusively during the course of anorexia nervosa or bulimia nervosa, and there is no evidence of a disturbance in the way in which one's body weight or shape is experienced.

D. The eating disturbance is not attributable to a concurrent medical condition or not better explained by another mental disorder. When the eating disturbance occurs in the context of another condition or disorder, the severity of the eating disturbance exceeds that routinely associated with the condition or disorder and warrants additional clinical attention.

- Three categories of childhood feeding disorders exist—pica, rumination disorder, and ARFID. The nature of the relation between these childhood disorders and anorexia nervosa, bulimia nervosa, and BED remains incompletely understood.

critical thinking question How could BED contribute to the growing obesity epidemic, and how could treatment for BED be one approach to obesity prevention?

Sex, Race, Ethnicity, and Developmental Factors

Unlike some psychological disorders, eating disorders do not affect everyone equally, nor do they occur with equal frequency across the lifespan. Understanding eating disorders requires a careful understanding of who develops them and when.

Eating Disorders in Females and Males

7.2 Discuss sex differences in the risk for feeding and eating disorders and why these differences exist.

As we mentioned earlier, anorexia nervosa is more common in females than males. Many theories have been suggested, including increased pressures on girls and women to attain a thin ideal, objectification of the female body, and the influences of female hormones on appetite and weight regulation (Klump et al., 2006; Striegel-Moore & Bulik, 2007).

Although the sex ratio for bulimia nervosa is imbalanced, the diagnostic criteria are somewhat sex biased. This is because men tend to rely on nonpurging forms of compensatory behaviour after binge eating, such as excessive exercise (Anderson &

Bulik, 2003; Lewinsohn et al., 2002). Changing our definition of bulimia nervosa may alter the sex ratio in this disorder (Anderson & Bulik, 2003; Woodside et al., 2001). Male athletes are among those who feel strong pressure to remain slim and who may focus excessive attention on their weight and body shape.

Unlike anorexia and bulimia nervosa, the sex distribution of BED is fairly equal (Hay, 1998; Hudson et al., 2007).

Race, Ethnicity, and Eating Disorders

It was once believed that eating disorders were restricted to white upper-middle-class girls. However, the picture is clearly not so simple. These early stereotypes more likely reflected who was able to access and afford treatment rather than who was actually suffering from the disorders (Smolak et al., 2001). Unfortunately, we do not have enough epidemiologic data to give us a clear picture of the racial and ethnic distribution of eating disorders and behaviours. A study using nationally representative data from the U.S. population found no racial/ethnic differences in lifetime prevalence of anorexia nervosa (Marques et al., 2011). Other U.S. studies have found no racial or ethnic differences in the prevalence of recurrent binge eating or BED (Reagan & Hersch, 2005; Smith et al., 1998; Striegel-Moore et al., 2001). Little is known about the prevalence of eating disorders among Canadian minorities (LeBlanc, 2014). Preliminary data suggest that there may be increased risk for BED in lower socioeconomic classes (Langer et al., 1992; Warheit et al., 1993).

Developmental Factors in Eating Disorders

7.3 Discuss developmental life course changes in the risk for feeding and eating disorders.

Despite the typical age of onset and the highly imbalanced sex ratio, principles of developmental psychology have not yet been adequately applied to examine the causes of eating disorders. Few studies have examined the relation between the feeding disorders of childhood, childhood weight problems, and the emergence of eating disorders in adolescence. Given the new placement of the childhood feeding disorders with the eating disorders, this section focuses on what we know about developmental factors in anorexia nervosa, bulimia nervosa, and BED.

Anorexia nervosa in childhood is uncommon, although the incidence may be increasing (Lask & Bryant-Waugh, 2000). Bulimia nervosa before puberty is rarely reported (Stein et al., 1998). Clinical reports suggest that disordered eating behaviours and attitudes are clearly present in some preadolescent girls (Killen et al., 1994; Leon et al., 1993). In one study, childhood predictors of disordered eating behaviours included the mother's own body dissatisfaction, internalization of the thin body ideal (or how much the person accepted society's pressure to be thin), bulimic symptoms, and maternal and paternal BMI, which predicted the emergence of childhood eating disturbance (Stice et al., 1999). The extent to which this familial relationship reflects environmental or genetic factors is unknown.

When anorexia nervosa begins in early adolescence, social and emotional development are clearly interrupted by its medical and psychological consequences (Bulik, 2002). The disorder itself, and associated symptoms such as depression, anxiety, social withdrawal, difficulty eating in social situations, self-consciousness, fatigue, and medical complications, can lead to isolation from peers and family. Often recovery requires facing challenges that normally would have been faced years before, such as establishing independence from family, developing trust in friendships, and dating and establishing romantic relationships. Although the physical toll of eating disorders is often emphasized, the social and psychological effects are equally disruptive. In addition, anorexia nervosa has dramatic effects on the family both emotionally and financially. Family

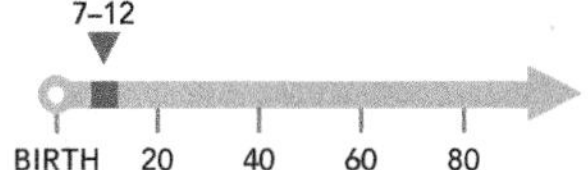

Earlier onset of menstruation may increase the risk of bulimia nervosa.

meals often become battlegrounds marked by refusal to eat, power struggles about food, and frustration and tears. Parents struggle to understand as their child becomes increasingly unreachable and unable to think rationally about a function, eating, that to them seems a simple fact of life. The needs of siblings and other family members commonly become secondary to the demands of the eating disorder. This, coupled with the enormous expense of treatment, can wreak havoc on the most functional of families.

Addressing the issue of who develops bulimia nervosa, population-based studies of older children indicate that early menarche (onset of menstruation) may increase the risk for bulimia nervosa (Fairburn et al., 1997). Girls whose body fat percentage increases more rapidly, and who develop mature figures earlier than their peers, may develop greater body dissatisfaction. This may lead to early experimentation with behaviours designed to control eating and weight (Attie & Brooks-Gunn, 1989), which, in turn, increases the risk of developing eating disorders. For example, among middle school girls, higher body fat (an indication of maturational status) was associated with the development of eating problems two years later (Attie & Brooks-Gunn, 1989). Similarly, among 971 middle school girls (Killen et al., 1992), those who were more developmentally mature for their age were more likely to meet diagnostic criteria for bulimia nervosa. There may be important differences in family background as well. Compared to people with anorexia nervosa, the family background of individuals with bulimia nervosa also includes the same high achievement orientation. However, these families also have more problems with drug and alcohol dependence and higher frequency of sexual abuse than in anorexia nervosa. It is important to note, however, that sexual abuse is no more common in families of individuals with eating disorders than in families of individuals with other psychological disorders.

We know even less about developmental factors associated with BED. Retrospective reports from obese women with BED indicate that binge eating before age 18 was associated with an earlier onset of obesity, dieting, and psychopathology (Marcus et al., 1995). Most studies indicate that BED generally begins in late adolescence or early adulthood (Hudson et al., 2006). Some people report that they began binge eating earlier in life (11 to 13 years old)—often before they even went on their first diet (Grilo & Masheb, 2000). Among children ages 6 to 12, those who reported binge eating gained an additional 15% of fat mass compared with children who said they did not binge (Tanofsky-Kraff et al., 2006). Researchers also focus on children who report a loss of control over their eating without consuming an unambiguously large amount of food (i.e., loss of control [LOC] eating). Studies of overweight youth report that LOC eating is associated with elevated eating-related distress, anxiety, depressive symptomatology, and lower self-esteem (Tanofsky-Kraff et al., 2007) and may be related to the rise in childhood obesity.

CONCEPT check

- Sufficient data do not exist to make definitive statements about racial and ethnic patterns in anorexia and bulimia nervosa. BED seems to be evenly distributed across racial and ethnic groups.
- Anorexia and bulimia nervosa are both more common in females than males. Although the exact reason for this is unclear, several theories exist, ranging from sociocultural (increased emphasis on thinness for women) to hormonal (related to hormonal changes secondary to reproductive events). BED seems to be more equally distributed across sexes.
- Anorexia nervosa typically begins in early adolescence and bulimia somewhat later. Childhood and later adult onsets also occur. Less is known about the developmental course of BED, although LOC eating in children is reported.

critical thinking question How could early puberty influence body image and body dissatisfaction in young girls and thereby contribute to the development of eating disorders?

The Etiology of Eating Disorders

Although researchers have been studying eating disorders for decades, the causes are still elusive. Many theories have been proposed, ranging from purely sociocultural to purely biological. A complete understanding of the causes of eating disorders will no doubt require a reasonable synthesis of the different contributions of biology and environment.

Biological Perspectives

7.4 Explore psychodynamic, behavioural, cognitive, and biological theories on the causes of feeding and eating disorders.

Observing animals in the lab is one way to understand the underlying biology of the core symptoms of eating disorders. This research focuses on those aspects of the disorder for which animal analogues exist. Although we cannot develop animal models of some of the psychological components of eating disorders, such as body dissatisfaction or body image distortion, we can develop models of more behavioural components, such as food restriction and binge eating (see "Research Hot Topic: Do Animals Binge?").

research HOT topic

Do Animals Binge?

What circumstances can lead a rodent to engage in what surely looks like binge eating? Answering this question can help us understand some of the underlying biology of what may happen in people who binge.

Three major factors can lead to what appears to be binge eating in rodents: exposure to stress, periods of food deprivation, and repeated intermittent exposure to appetizing food and fluids (Boggiano & Chandler, 2006; Boggiano et al., 2005, 2007). These three factors sound curiously like human stress, dieting, and walking through the food court in the mall.

The concept of *binge priming* has been coined in the animal literature. This refers to putting animals through repeated cycles of food deprivation followed by exposure to food that they consider to be delicious. This laboratory paradigm leads them to overeat—not only right after the food deprivation period, but even after their weight is restored, indicating that binge priming has long-term effects on their eating behaviour. This animal model mimics what we see in humans who go on a strict diet and then break the diet with a delicious food (it is unusual to break a diet with a low-calorie food such as celery). This repeated pattern of food deprivation followed by a delicious falling off the wagon may, in fact, be priming the brain for binge eating.

Animals that go through these cycles of deprivation and exposure to delicious foods are also more likely to misuse drugs such as alcohol and cocaine. Apparently, this binge priming paradigm leads to changes in the reward circuits in the brain and affects many of the neurotransmitters in the brain that are associated with the experience of pleasure and reward—for example, dopamine, acetylcholine, endogenous opiates, and cannabinoids.

Experts are especially worried about adolescents who undergo these repeated cycles of dieting and eating palatable foods because their brains are still developing and are more susceptible to reward (that, in addition to availability, is why adolescence is such a prime time for trying cigarettes, alcohol, drugs, and sex). The concern is that binge priming during this time might set up adolescents for a lifetime vulnerability to not only binge eating, but also substance abuse.

Mary M. Boggiano

Stress and repeated food deprivation can lead to increased Oreo consumption.

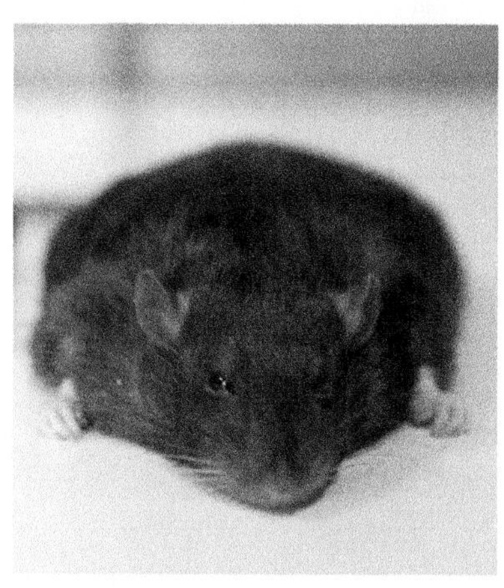

The hypothalamus is central to weight and appetite regulation, and when a rat's hypothalamus is lesioned ventromedially, great weight gain results. When a rat's hypothalamus is lesioned laterally, it becomes extremely thin.

Voisin/Phanie/SuperStock

ROLE OF THE HYPOTHALAMUS We know from animal studies that the hypothalamus (a region of the brain that regulates certain metabolic processes and other autonomic activities) is influential in appetite and weight control. When researchers make surgical lesions in the *ventromedial hypothalamus* in mice, the mice overeat and become obese. In contrast, when lesions are made in the lateral hypothalamus, the mice reduce their food intake and lose weight. Therefore, the hypothalamus appears central to appetite and weight regulation in mice, but its function constitutes only one aspect of eating disorders. Furthermore, no evidence of consistent hypothalamic abnormalities has been observed in humans with eating disorders.

ACTIVITY-BASED ANOREXIA Another animal model for anorexia nervosa focuses on the excessive hyperactivity seen in patients with anorexia nervosa, which persists even in the underweight state. In this rodent model, unlimited access to a running wheel, together with scheduled feeding, leads to increased running wheel activity and decreased feeding. Under these conditions, rodents can lose over 20% of their body weight and can die from emaciation (Hillebrand et al., 2005). This model is intriguing because it captures one perplexing symptom of anorexia nervosa (hyperactivity) and uses that symptom to further understand its biological underpinnings and as a basis to understand pharmacological action (Kas et al., 2003). Breaking down complex psychological disorders into component parts, and developing animal models for these component behaviours, constitute a valuable scientific approach to understanding etiology.

ADDICTION MODEL OF BINGE EATING To what extent are the same brain systems that are involved with alcohol and drug abuse also involved with binge eating? Some neuropsychological systems that are associated with addiction-related processes, including systems related to impulsivity and the executive (decision-making) system, may play a role in the development of BED (Tanofsky-Kraff et al., 2013). These systems may involve the reinforcing value of food for individuals and whether they experience loss of control over eating. Using PET scans, it was observed that the caudate and putamen areas of the brains of obese individuals with BED release more dopamine after exposure to a food stimulus than do the brains of obese individuals without BED (Wang et al., 2011). This is an important finding because dopamine regulates our motivation to eat, suggesting that obese individuals with BED are getting stronger signals to eat when they are exposed to food stimuli. In addition, based on functional MRI data, overweight individuals with BED show more activity in the orbitofrontal cortex when viewing pictures of food than either overweight or normal weight individuals without BED (Schienle et al., 2009). The orbitofrontal cortex is involved in decision making, but it also houses structures related to taste reward and olfaction.

Much like work on drugs and alcohol, stress reactivity also increases the reinforcing value of food for individuals with BED. Individuals without BED tend to find food less reinforcing under conditions of stress (Goldfield et al., 2008). However, further research is needed to better understand how the full range of impulsive and executive system processes relate to BED, as well as how these brain circuit abnormalities compare with other addictive disorders.

NEUROENDOCRINE AND NEUROHORMONAL FACTORS Several neurotransmitter systems reviewed in Chapter 2 have been implicated in regulating feeding behaviour. We focus here on the role of serotonin and dopamine, although several other neurotransmitters may also have an influence on *feeding initiation* (starting eating), *satiety* (fullness), craving, and appetite (Badman & Flier, 2005; O'Connor & Roth, 2005; Scammell & Saper, 2005). Serotonin and dopamine have been linked to changes in the psychological and behavioural features of eating disorders, such as impulsivity and obsessionality (Roth & Shapiro, 2001; Simansky, 2005; Swerdlow, 2001). Indeed, serotonin has been directly related to the development of eating disorders (Jimerson et al., 1997; Kaye, 1997). In patients who have been free from anorexia or bulimia nervosa for more than a year, levels of serotonin remain high (Kaye et al., 1991, 1998). However, it is not clear whether this increased brain serotonin activity is the *result* of the disorder or if it was present earlier and could predispose someone to develop an eating disorder. In addition, abnormalities in serotonin might also contribute to some of the personality features of eating disorders, such as perfectionism, rigidity, and obsessionality in anorexia nervosa (Kaye et al., 2000). Moreover, the profile of individuals with anorexia suggests that they are able to maintain a state of denial and, with the exception of weight loss, find little pleasure in life. This led some researchers to suggest that dopamine, the primary neurotransmitter for pleasure, might be involved. Data from PET studies indicate that individuals with anorexia might have a dopamine-related disturbance of reward mechanisms that contributes to their behavioural style of self-denial (Frank et al., 2005).

BRAIN STRUCTURE AND FUNCTIONING STUDIES Structural brain abnormalities exist in patients with anorexia nervosa. Several measures suggest that, when ill, these patients have reduced brain mass, including loss of grey matter (Muhlau et al., 2007) and brain ventricles that are increased in size (Dolan et al., 1988) (see Chapter 2). Structural brain changes have also been observed in individuals with bulimia nervosa, although these changes are less prominent in bulimia nervosa than in anorexia nervosa (Hoffman et al., 1989; Krieg et al., 1989). One long-term follow-up study has suggested that many of the structural brain differences seen in anorexia and bulimia nervosa normalize over time and with recovery (Wagner et al., 2006).

It is not known whether these differences existed before the disorder developed or are the result of it. Demonstrating that these changes persist after weight recovery does not provide evidence that these changes are causal. Indeed, starvation (or alternating starvation and binge eating) could cause lasting biological "scars," indicating that these changes were a result of the disorders, not the reason that they developed.

In terms of functional brain differences (see Chapter 2 on functional MRI), individuals with anorexia and bulimia nervosa have globally decreased brain glucose metabolism at rest (Delvenne et al., 1999) and increased serotonin activity in certain regions of the brain (Bailer & Kaye, 2011). These abnormalities are consistent with the rigid, inflexible, overcontrolled behaviour seen in individuals with anorexia nervosa and in some forms of bulimia nervosa.

FAMILY AND GENETIC STUDIES Family studies show that anorexia nervosa, bulimia nervosa, and BED clearly run in families (see "Examining the Evidence: Genes or Environment in Anorexia Nervosa?"). Relatives of individuals with anorexia and bulimia nervosa have approximately 10 times the lifetime risk of having an eating disorder as do relatives of people without eating disorders (Hudson et al., 1987; Strober et al., 2000). However, family members do not necessarily share the same eating disorder; rather, families often include members with anorexia nervosa, bulimia nervosa, and various types of EDNOS (the DSM-IV-TR residual category) (Strober et al., 2000). BED also runs in families independently of obesity (Hudson et al., 2006). Moreover, relatives of individuals with BED are 2.5 times more likely to be severely obese than are relatives of individuals without BED.

To what extent is this familial pattern due to genes, and to what extent can it be attributed to the environment or modelling of unhealthy behaviours? Twin studies consistently show that eating disorders and related traits are moderately heritable (Bulik et al., 2000). The heritability of anorexia nervosa is estimated to be around 60%, and the heritability of bulimia nervosa between 28% and 83% (Bulik et al., 2000, 2006). The remaining variance (in both disorders) is attributable to individual specific environmental factors (see Chapter 2). For BED, the best current estimate of heritability is approximately

examining the EVIDENCE

Genes or Environment in Anorexia Nervosa?

Is this just an example of the "fat phobic" environment terrorizing two young girls into anorexia nervosa, or could it be the manifestation of an underlying genetic predisposition?

LET'S EXAMINE THE EVIDENCE

- **The Role of Environment** The environment is a major contributor to eating disorders. Issues such as weight intolerance, teasing, fat phobia, and the societal pressure to be thin all contribute to young girls developing eating disorders. Teasing or bullying because of being overweight is also another powerful environmental influence. If such environmental factors influence eating disorders, then one approach to preventing such disorders would include a focus on decreasing bullying and teasing in school, as well as putting pressure on the media and the modelling industry to stop flaunting unrealistic ideals of thinness.
- **The Facts** Twin sisters Michaela and Samantha Kendall considered themselves to be overweight at age 14 and started dieting to lose weight. The notion that they were overweight was not their own idea. The girls were taunted and ridiculed by classmates (their mother estimated that they each weighed over 90 kg before they started dieting). Although the dieting began innocently, it ended up being devastating. The girls had no idea how controlling eating disorders could be. Samantha abused laxatives and eventually became unable to control her bowels. She soiled her bed sheets almost nightly. Both twins became pregnant at age 22 but had abortions for fear of getting fat. The twins attracted international media attention in the 1990s when they appeared on the Maury Povich Show and shared their heartbreaking struggles with eating disorders. Both sisters eventually died from complications of anorexia nervosa. Michaela died first, lying next to her twin sister in bed. After Michaela died in 1994, Samantha tried desperately to turn her life around and recover. Unfortunately, the damage to her body had already been done, and although Samantha managed a short recovery period, she died in 1997.
- **The Role of Genetics** The fact that the Kendall twins already weighed over 90 kg by age 14 suggests that they were indeed biologically predisposed to eating and weight dysregulation. Although they were teased in school, countless overweight kids get teased in school but never develop an eating disorder. The twins decided to go on their first diet together, and they never came off it. Even though that first diet was a choice, once they were in negative energy balance (expended more calories than they took in), the anorexia took on a life of its own—because they were genetically predisposed. They were different from other teens because of their bodies' response to starvation. Indeed, most teens who are overweight and go on a diet have a hard time losing weight and often become obese adults. In the Kendall twins' situation, their weight dropped dramatically, and they were able to maintain that frightening low weight until their deaths. In this case, their biology trapped them in the prison of anorexia nervosa. A rational approach to preventing eating disorders would be to identify the genes that predispose to anorexia nervosa and develop medications to counteract the biological factors that inhibit eating and enable maintenance of low body weight.
- **Conclusion** A combination of nature *and* nurture likely caused the Kendall twins' anorexia nervosa. Whereas countless adolescents are teased about their weight, only a small fraction ever goes on to develop anorexia nervosa. What made them more vulnerable? What made their bodies respond to dieting differently than the majority of their peers? It is very likely that their genetic predisposition rendered them more sensitive to negative energy balance than others. Their ability to maintain such low intake and low weight is testimony to the fact that they were biologically different from their peers. A rational approach to preventing eating disorders would be to identify high-risk individuals based on their genotype. These individuals could then be provided strategies and tools to develop environments that would allow them to avoid situations of negative energy balance that could trigger an eating disorder.

Source: Adapted from Bateman, M. (1997, November 16). These are not just desserts. *The London Independent.*

41% (Reichborn-Kjennerud et al., 2004). As a result of the consistent replication across samples and across countries, it appears that eating disorders are indeed influenced by genetic factors.

Little is known about the molecular genetics of BED. For anorexia nervosa, one area of interest is chromosome 1 (Devlin et al., 2002; Grice et al., 2002). Two genes have been isolated in that area—one related to serotonergic function and one to opioidergic function. Both are under study for their potential role in the development of anorexia nervosa (Bergen et al., 2003). Using the association approach (see Chapter 2), many other studies have explored genes that are known to influence appetite, weight regulation, and mood. This research is focused on genes that influence the function of serotonin and dopamine, along with several other genes involved in functions central to the etiology of eating disorders.

For bulimia nervosa, a specific area of chromosome 10 has been identified as a "hot spot" (Bulik et al., 2003). This area was also identified as a hot spot in a genetic study of obesity (Froguel, 1998). Montreal researchers reported that a genetic variation associated with the serotonin system is linked with eating disorders that include binge eating and purging (Steiger et al., 2005).

Three studies have used genome-wide association approaches to compare people with anorexia nervosa to people with no psychological disorder; however, no results have yet met the stringent criteria for genome-wide significance (Boraska et al., 2014; Nakabayshi et al., 2009; Wang et al., 2011). Based on results from genetic studies for other psychiatric disorders, larger sample sizes are required in order for this approach to yield significant findings.

The most likely causal explanations will involve an interaction between genes and the environment, just having risk genes does not mean that someone will develop an eating disorder. In fact, someone with several risk genes may never develop a disorder if she or he is not exposed to environmental factors that trigger the genetic predisposition. Although our genes establish our baseline risk, our environment can be protective (buffering) or triggering (risk enhancing). As with so many psychological disorders, the complex interplay between genes and the environment will be the key to understanding the emergence of these syndromes.

Psychological Perspectives

7.5 Discuss personality features and comorbid conditions that are commonly associated with feeding and eating disorders.

Several psychological theories attempt to explain eating disorders. Some of these theories still contribute to our understanding of aspects of the disorders, but they are best considered together with what we know about biological risk factors.

PSYCHODYNAMIC PERSPECTIVES As you may recall from Chapter 1, psychodynamic thinking focuses on the influence of early experience. Early psychoanalytic theory viewed anorexia nervosa as an attempt to defend against anxiety associated with emerging adult sexuality (Waller et al., 1940). Anorexia nervosa was considered an unconscious attempt to reverse or reject adult female sexuality via starvation to a prepubertal state (Dare et al., 1994). As psychoanalytic theory moved away from a narrow focus on sexuality, the explanation shifted to interpersonal relationships and the interpersonal context in which these disorders arose (Kaufman & Heiman, 1964). One of the key clinicians and writers in the field, Hilde Bruch (1973, 1978), introduced rich clinical descriptions of patients with anorexia nervosa in her book *The Golden Cage*. Through her careful insights and keen ability to understand what motivated her patients to maintain such rigid control on food intake, she identified features such as body image distortion and a pervasive sense of ineffectiveness as core aspects of anorexic pathology.

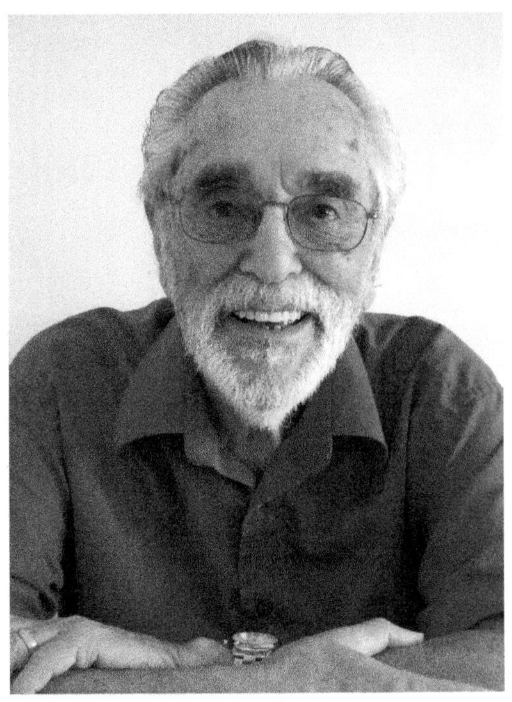

Argentinean psychiatrist Salvador Minuchin championed the concept of the "psychosomatic family" and worked with families around the dinner table.

Salvador Minuchin

FAMILY MODELS OF EATING DISORDERS Early family models of eating disorders, especially anorexia nervosa, focused on patterns of family dysfunction among patients who sought treatment. Perhaps best known is the work of Argentinean psychiatrist Salvador Minuchin (Minuchin et al., 1978), who identified four dysfunctional patterns. He noted enmeshment, rigidity, overprotectiveness, and poor conflict resolution as characteristic of what he referred to as *psychosomatic families*. The word **enmeshment** described

The fashion industry's emphasis on thinness has often been identified as a sociocultural factor contributing to the rising prevalence of eating disorders.

Gruber/Newscom

the overinvolvement of all family members in the affairs of any one member. *Rigidity* described the difficulty families faced in adapting to the changing developmental needs of their children; for example, children's increasing need for autonomy. Rigid families have great difficulty maturing along with their children. *Overprotectiveness* meant that parents shielded children from age-appropriate experiences. Finally, *poor conflict resolution* reflected the difficulties these families had in dealing with problematic, negative situations.

According to Minuchin's theory, family pathology was expressed as a psychosomatic disorder in one child (in this case anorexia nervosa). He used the family mealtime to assess family functioning and as a therapeutic tool. His vivid examples of family meals provided insights into how families functioned at a high-risk time (namely, around food). Although his work brought the study of anorexia nervosa into the realm of scientific inquiry, his sample was biased toward families who could afford treatment at an academic centre. Later studies suggested that his descriptions were oversimplified and that families of patients with anorexia nervosa were not so homogeneous. Many of the patterns he observed may have been the results of the family living with anorexia nervosa rather than the effects of anorexia on the family.

COGNITIVE-BEHAVIOURAL THEORIES The cognitive-behavioural model focuses on distorted cognitions about body shape, weight, eating, and personal control that lead to and maintain unhealthy eating and weight-related behaviours. Consider the following classic example of a cognitive distortion. After eating one doughnut, someone with bulimia nervosa might think, "I've already blown it. I may as well go ahead and eat the whole dozen!" Proponents of a cognitive-behavioural model emphasize the power of thoughts to influence feelings and behaviours. In bulimia nervosa, distorted thoughts about food, shape, and weight lead to particular feelings and behaviours that then perpetuate the binge–purge cycle. Several cognitive-behavioural models of bulimia nervosa have been developed (Fairburn, 1981; Mitchell, 1990).

SOCIOCULTURAL THEORIES Sociocultural models emphasize the Western cultural preoccupation with thinness as beauty. The sociocultural model follows the path from being exposed to the ideal of thinness, to internalizing this ideal, and then to observing a discrepancy between actual and ideal body to dissatisfaction with one's body, to dietary restraint, and finally to restriction (Striegel-Moore et al., 1986). Because girls and women are often valued primarily for their appearance (Moradi et al., 2005), they are more likely to internalize the thin ideal. Subtle and overt messages to achieve the thin ideal can significantly impact a woman's self-esteem and body esteem. In general, exposure to media images of the thin ideal is associated with adverse consequences among university-age women (Irving, 1990; Stice & Shaw, 2002). Even brief exposure to a cosmetic surgery reality show can lead to decreased self-esteem—especially in individuals who have significantly internalized the thin ideal (Mazzeo et al., 2007).

Although the thin ideal primarily targets girls and women, sociocultural forces also operate on boys and men. Increasing emphasis on leanness and muscularity can contribute to males turning to unhealthy weight control behaviours, including using anabolic steroids to achieve the prized "six-pack" or "ripped" physical ideal (Kanayama et al., 2006). Just as for women, even brief exposure to media images of the thin body ideal can negatively affect men's views of their own bodies (Leit et al., 2002). Support for the role of sociocultural factors in eating disorders comes from a landmark study conducted by Becker and her colleagues in Fiji. In 1995, before television was available on the island, Becker and her team surveyed 63 Fijian secondary school girls who were on average 17 years old. Three years later, after television had saturated the island, the researchers surveyed 65 girls from the same schools, who were matched in age, weight, and other characteristics with the girls in the earlier group. Remarkably, whereas only 3% of the original girls had reported self-induced vomiting for weight control in the initial study, a full 15%

reported such vomiting three years later (Becker et al., 2002). Additionally, new data indicate that the amount of television watching by someone's friends can influence a girl's body image even if the girl does not own or watch television herself (Becker et al., 2011). Thus, social network can strongly affect a person's risk for developing an eating disorder.

Four lines of evidence provide partial support for the sociocultural model (Striegel-Moore & Bulik, 2007). This evidence includes the imbalanced sex ratio in anorexia and bulimia nervosa; the increasing incidence of anorexia and bulimia nervosa in parallel with the decreasing body size ideal for women; cross-cultural differences in the incidence or prevalence of eating disorders (with higher rates in cultures that value extreme female thinness); and the significant prospective relationship between internalization of the thin ideal and disordered eating.

Sociocultural theory cannot account for the development of all eating disorders. Virtually all young girls are exposed to the thin ideal, and many internalize it, yet only a few go on to develop full eating disorder syndromes (Striegel-Moore et al., 1986). The most plausible explanation is that environment affects individuals to different degrees and in different ways. The reason for this could rest in genetic factors and suggest gene X environment interactions, as we discussed in Chapter 2. A genetic predisposition may make an individual more vulnerable to behaviours such as dieting, which are triggered by exposure to sociocultural pressures toward thinness. Although the first diet may be nothing more than an unpleasant hunger-inducing experience for someone with low genetic vulnerability, for someone with high genetic vulnerability, the first diet may trigger the descent into full-blown anorexia nervosa. Another factor requiring further research is the role of increased average weight (which is increasing in children and young adults) and more frequent dieting (which is starting earlier and affecting many more people).

CONCEPT check

- Early psychodynamic models focused on anorexia nervosa as an escape from adult sexuality; later models focused on the interpersonal aspects of the disorder.
- Recent research highlights the role of neuroendocrine and neurohormonal systems in eating disorders.
- Eating disorders run in families and are moderately heritable; studies have identified areas on specific chromosomes for both anorexia and bulimia nervosa.
- Early family models focused on enmeshment, rigidity, overprotectiveness, and lack of conflict resolution as characteristic of families of individuals with anorexia; later models acknowledge that there is no "typical" family from which anorexia nervosa arises.
- Cognitive-behavioural models highlight the role of dysfunctional thoughts on the emergence and perpetuation of unhealthy eating and dieting behaviours.
- Sociocultural models focus on the ubiquitous pressure on girls and women to be thin and the internalization of the thin ideal.

critical thinking question What are some of the ways in which biology and culture may interact to influence risk for the development of eating disorders?

The Treatment for Eating Disorders

7.6 Compare and contrast treatments for feeding and eating disorders.

Treatment goals for patients with anorexia nervosa, bulimia nervosa, and BED differ somewhat, although they have commonalities. The normalization and stabilization of eating behaviour and weight is the central treatment goal for all eating disorders; however, the precise nature of the desired change differs. In anorexia nervosa, the initial goals are to increase caloric intake and weight gain so that later stages of treatment can deal more effectively with the psychological aspects of the disorder. For bulimia nervosa, for which weight is usually within the healthy range, the focus of treatment is to normalize eating, eliminate binge eating and purging episodes, and improve the psychological aspects of the disorder. In BED, controversy exists over whether weight loss should be a therapeutic outcome for patients who are overweight or obese, as many people argue that repeated attempts to lose weight often cause BED. The best way to achieve the therapeutic goals is different for each disorder.

Inpatient Treatment for Anorexia Nervosa

Treatment for anorexia nervosa can be difficult and is best accomplished by a multidisciplinary team. The first and most critical step is restoring weight. Psychotherapy is difficult to conduct when the patients are acutely ill because starvation impairs their ability to think. Psychotherapeutic approaches include individual psychotherapy (cognitive-behavioural, interpersonal, behavioural, supportive, and psychodynamic), family therapy (especially for younger patients), and group therapy. Individuals who are below 75% of their ideal body weight should be hospitalized (APA Work Group on Eating Disorders, 2000).

Besides weight, other factors that influence the decision to hospitalize individuals suffering from anorexia nervosa include medical complications; suicide attempts or plans; failure to improve with outpatient treatment; comorbid psychiatric disorders; interference with school, work, or family; poor social support; pregnancy; and the unavailability of other treatment options (APA Work Group on Eating Disorders, 2000). Inpatient treatment involves highly specialized multidisciplinary teams, including psychologists, psychiatrists, internists or pediatricians, dietitians, social workers, and nurse specialists. At severely low weights, patients may be prescribed bed rest or have their activity limited for safety reasons and as a way to give their bodies a chance to start gaining weight. Typically, as patients eat and gain weight, they are given increasing privileges on the treatment unit. Often, a dietitian initially chooses menus for the patients. As patients get better and are able to make healthy choices, they take on responsibility for food selections in order to continue the weight gain.

Inpatient treatment for anorexia nervosa can be very difficult for both the patients and their families. Treatment presents an unusual situation: Patients are deeply afraid of giving up the symptoms (starvation and low weight), and the medicine the doctor offers is something the patients avoid (food). Developing a collaborative relationship is critical to decreasing patients' anxiety about weight gain and to making the hospitalization a success.

Ethics and Responsibility

Involuntary treatment for anorexia nervosa by means of legal commitment occurs for a minority of patients with eating disorders, and this is sometimes a controversial action. Legal commitment is less controversial when the patient is suicidal, clearly intending to harm herself or himself. Yet part of the diagnostic criteria for anorexia nervosa is an inability to recognize the seriousness of the low weight, and patients with this disorder will not express an intent to harm themselves, although their behaviours may result in severe harm or death. Self-starvation is generally considered a behaviour that endangers life and constitutes a grave disability, thereby allowing civil commitment of patients with severe anorexia who refuse treatment (Bell, 2010).

Patients with anorexia nervosa show equivalent rates of weight gain during hospitalization whether they enter the hospital voluntarily or involuntarily as a result of a legal commitment process (Bell, 2010). Moreover, when asked later, patients who were committed involuntarily commonly report that their involuntary treatment was justified and view their treatment teams with good will (Watson et al., 2000). In principle, involuntary commitment should be viewed as an approach of last resort only after patients decline voluntary hospitalization, their physical safety is at risk, and there is likely to be therapeutic gain from hospitalization (Applebaum & Rumpf, 1998).

Biological Treatments for Eating Disorders

Although medications are commonly prescribed for the treatment of anorexia nervosa, none has yet been identified as effective (Watson & Bulik, 2013). There is a critical need to develop medications that target the core symptoms of anorexia nervosa (Bulik et al., 2007). For bulimia nervosa, the antidepressant fluoxetine (Prozac) appears to reduce the core symptoms of binge eating and purging, and associated psychological features such as depression and anxiety, at least in the short term (Shapiro et al., 2007). Although fluoxetine reduces the core symptoms, it is still unclear whether its effects are long lasting or associated with permanent remission. The optimal duration of treatment and the best strategy for maintaining treatment gains also remain unknown. For BED, several medications that target the core symptoms of binge eating or weight loss, or both, have been tried, but further evaluation is needed.

Nutritional Counselling

For all eating disorders, nutritional rehabilitation is a necessary but not sufficient intervention. Although patients with anorexia nervosa often spend inordinate amounts of time pondering nutrition labels and counting calories, they are unable to apply this information to their own eating. Dietitians trained in the treatment of eating disorders can assess nutritional deficiencies in patients with anorexia nervosa, set appropriate goal weights, develop strategies for renormalization of eating, and calculate caloric requirements for weight gain. For bulimia nervosa and BED, dietitians can help the patient relearn appropriate portion sizes, eat meals in a normal way, and develop strategies for decreasing urges to binge. In addition, in BED, the dietitian can help determine appropriate caloric intake for either body weight maintenance or weight loss. Although an important adjunct, nutritional therapy is ineffective as a sole intervention and is unacceptable to patients, as reflected in high dropout rates when delivered as the only intervention (Hsu et al., 2001).

Cognitive-Behavioural Therapy

As discussed in earlier chapters, cognitive-behavioural therapy (CBT) helps patients change patterns in thinking that contribute to their problems. The application of CBT to the treatment of eating disorders focuses on faulty cognitions about body shape, weight, eating, and personal control that lead to and perpetuate the dysfunction in eating and weight. The therapist addresses both relatively easily accessible thoughts, called *automatic thoughts*, which are often evaluative in nature, and deeper *core beliefs*, which are the guiding principles or self-truths of the individual. CBT involves identifying and challenging distorted cognitions about food, eating, and body shape and weight and replacing them with health-promoting alternatives. Studies that have dismantled the cognitive and behavioural components of CBT have shown that the cognitive component appears to be most critical in effecting behaviour change.

Recovery rates with CBT for eating disorders vary from 35% to 75% at five or more years of follow-up (Fairburn et al., 2000; Fichter & Quadflieg, 1997; Herzog et al., 1999). The rates differ in part because of varying definitions of recovery. However, approximately 33% of individuals with bulimia nervosa relapse, and the risk is highest during the year following treatment (Shapiro et al., 2007).

For anorexia nervosa, preliminary evidence suggests that CBT may reduce relapse in adults after weight has been restored (Pike et al., 1996). CBT may be less effective when patients are extremely underweight. This therapy requires active cognitive effort, so patients whose cognitive processing is impaired by self-starvation may not be able to benefit from CBT during the acute stage of their disorder (McIntosh et al., 2005). What we know about the efficacy of CBT for anorexia nervosa is limited to adults, as no studies

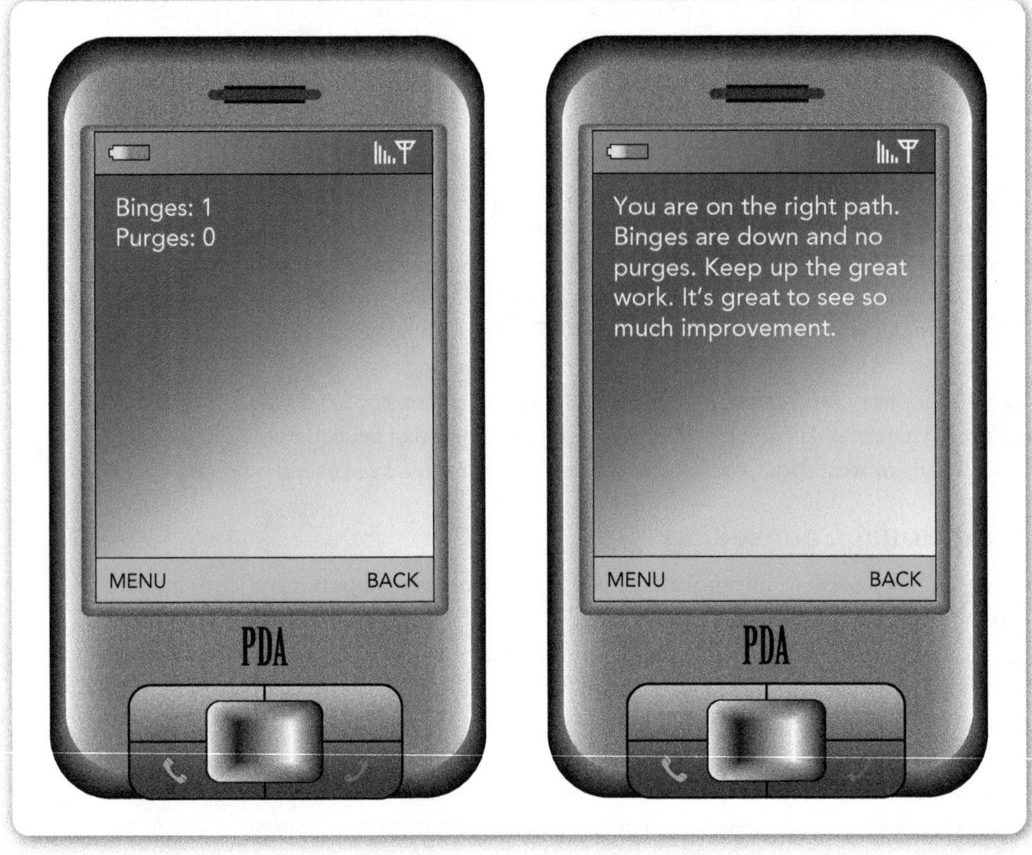

FIGURE 7.1

Self-Monitoring via Text Message. Patients type in their status and receive a return message from their therapist.

have adequately evaluated developmentally tailored cognitive-behavioural treatments for adolescents.

The cornerstone of CBT for bulimia nervosa is self-monitoring. Patients keep track of what they ate, whether it was a binge or purge episode, the situation they were in, who else was present, and their thoughts and feelings (see Figure 7.1). By analyzing the data, the patient and therapist can identify patterns of unhealthy behaviour, including high-risk times and situations for binge eating and purging, which serves as a first step in establishing healthier behaviour patterns. More recently, modern information technology has been adapted for self-monitoring, including the use of smartphone apps and cellphone–based text messaging.

The next steps involve mastering the language and concepts of CBT, including recognizing thoughts, feelings, and behaviours that are associated with unhealthy eating behaviour; learning to recognize cues for, and consequences of, disordered eating; learning to control automatic thoughts; and learning to restructure distorted cognitions that perpetuate unhealthy eating behaviours. The final goal of CBT is preventing relapse, and clinicians provide tools to patients for maintaining healthy behaviours (see Figure 7.2).

CBT is also effective in the treatment of BED (Brownley et al., 2007). Self-help, often incorporating CBT principles, is useful as a first step in treating the disorder (National Institute of Clinical and Health Excellence, 2004). Patients with BED might first be offered a self-help book or an online cognitive-behavioural program to use at their own pace. For some, this approach might be enough to put them on the path to recovery. At the next check-in, if doing well, they might be encouraged to continue. If they have made no progress or if their condition has deteriorated, they are referred for specialist treatment as a second step in care.

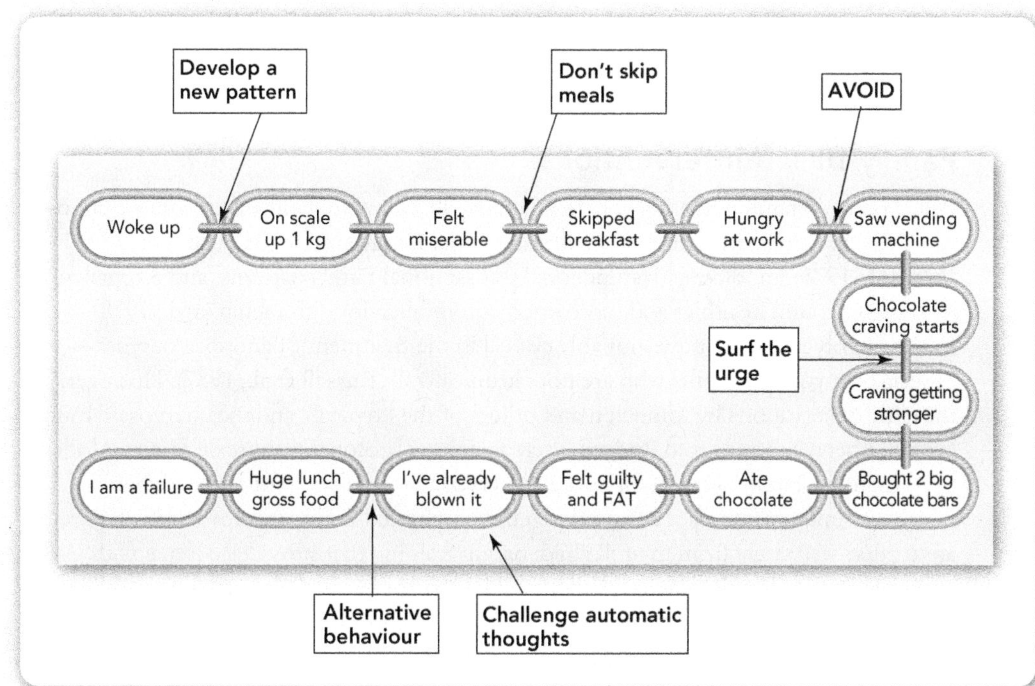

FIGURE 7.2

A Behavioural Chain. *Chaining* allows the patient to map out how thoughts, feelings, and behaviours cascade to unhealthy consequences. The object of the technique is to help the patient learn strategies to break the chain at every link.

By extension, dialectical behavioural therapy (DBT) focuses on emotional dysregulation as the core problem in eating disorders, and views symptoms as attempts to manage unpleasant emotional states. A small but growing body of research suggests that DBT may be useful in treating eating disorders (Chen et al., 2015; Fischer & Peterson, 2015; Lenz et al., 2014).

Interpersonal Psychotherapy

Initially developed for the treatment of depression, interpersonal psychotherapy (IPT) is a brief, time-limited psychotherapy (Klerman et al., 1984). IPT is based on the theory that, regardless of their cause, the current depressive symptoms are "inextricably intertwined" with the patient's interpersonal relationships. The goals of IPT for depression are to decrease depressive symptoms and to improve interpersonal functioning by enhancing communication skills in significant relationships. The adaptation of IPT for the treatment of bulimia nervosa (Fairburn, 1993), anorexia nervosa (McIntosh et al., 2000), and BED (Wilfley et al., 1993) applies the same principles of focusing on reducing symptoms related to eating disorders. IPT for eating disorders intervenes at the symptom and social functioning levels by addressing one of four problem areas: interpersonal disputes, role transitions, abnormal grief, or interpersonal deficits.

For anorexia nervosa, IPT has been found to be less effective than a therapy based on supportive psychotherapy and sound clinical management or CBT (McIntosh et al., 2005). For bulimia nervosa, IPT has been found to be as effective as CBT, but CBT shows more rapid decreases in bulimic symptoms (Fairburn et al., 1991, 1993). IPT, delivered both individually and in group therapy, has also shown preliminary efficacy in BED (Wilfley et al., 1993). It is interesting that a treatment that does not directly address the core symptoms of the eating disorder (especially bulimia and BED), but focuses solely on current interpersonal relationships, produces results equivalent to CBT, which focuses specifically on the disordered eating and body image issues. How IPT helps to decrease the symptoms of bulimia nervosa and BED is unknown. Clearly, eating disorders often have profound effects on interpersonal relationships, and IPT highlights the many ways in which the eating disorder disrupts social functioning.

Family-Based Interventions

Based on early family theories of anorexia nervosa, Minuchin and Palazzoli have advocated therapy aimed at changing the dysfunctional family system (Minuchin et al., 1978; Palazzoli, 1978), modifying dysfunctional transactional family patterns, and reorganizing the family around healthier and more open communication (Minuchin et al., 1978). Family involvement is unquestionably critical in the treatment of anorexia nervosa—especially in young patients who are not chronically ill (Russell et al., 1987). However, the early observations by Minuchin and others of the "typical" anorexia nervosa family have not been substantiated. Indeed, there is no one prototypic anorexic family. Modern approaches to family therapy for anorexia nervosa include conjoint family therapy in which all family members are treated together; separated family therapy in which parents are treated separately from their ill child; parent training that provides parents with psychoeducation and tools to manage their child's eating disorder (Zucker et al., 2005); and a popular approach, the Maudsley method, which focuses on parental control of the initial stages of renutrition (Lock et al., 2002, 2010). The Maudsley approach hinges on seven principles:

1. Work with experts who know how to help you.
2. Work together as a family.
3. Don't blame your child or yourself for the problems you are having. Blame the disorder.
4. Focus on the problem before you.
5. Don't debate with your child about eating—or weight-related concerns.
6. Know when to back off.
7. Take care of yourself. You are the child's best hope.

The Maudsley approach empowers parents to take an active role in achieving successful treatment. This approach also includes therapist-assisted family meals.

Although family therapy is effective with adolescents, as currently conceptualized, it is less developmentally appropriate for adults with anorexia nervosa (Bulik et al., 2007), although couple-based interventions that join partners in recovery from anorexia nervosa are being evaluated (Bulik et al., 2011). One clinical trial has shown initial promise for family-based treatment of bulimia nervosa (le Grange et al., 2007). There have been no clinical trials of family or couple therapy for BED.

CONCEPT check

- Renutrition is a critical first step in the treatment of anorexia nervosa. Inpatient treatment may be necessary to help the patient gain adequate weight.
- Fluoxetine (Prozac) is efficacious for bulimia nervosa.
- CBT is effective in the treatment of bulimia nervosa and may be beneficial for adults with anorexia nervosa after they have gained weight.
- IPT is also effective in the treatment of bulimia nervosa, although symptom change comes about more slowly than with CBT.
- Family therapy is effective in the treatment of adolescents with anorexia nervosa but has not yet been shown to be effective with adults.

critical thinking question How could family therapy be adapted for use for older patients?

Canadian FOCUS

Challenges in the Treatment of Eating Disorders

Canada enjoys one of the best health-care systems in the world, but as in other countries, when it comes to treating eating disorders, there is much room for improvement. Given the seriousness of eating disorders in terms of prevalence and mortality, the Canadian government struck a committee to investigate the nature and treatment of eating disorders across the country (LeBlanc, 2014). A series of experts and people suffering from eating disorders presented to the committee. The report from the committee identified several important concerns:

- Unintended adverse effects of educational programs on eating behaviour
- Harmful stigma and stereotypes concerning eating disorders
- Bias among health-care professionals concerning these disorders
- Lack of suitably qualified clinicians for treating eating disorders
- Shortage of treatment programs and lengthy waiting times for treatment
- Lack of treatment programs for people who have eating disorders comorbid with other disorders
- Difficulties faced by marginalized populations

Specifically, according to the report, some perfectionistic, anxious children take dietary guidelines to extremes. Some children become hospitalized due of nutritional deficiencies because they only eat vegetables and avoid "bad" foods such as those containing fat, sodium, or sugar. Accordingly, it is important to teach children how to take a balanced approach to dietary guidelines, so that we can reduce childhood obesity via healthy diets without leading children to develop overly restrictive diets and eating disorders. The committee recommended that the Government of Canada review the information it provides on nutrition to encompass greater sensitivity in its guidelines on "good" and "bad" foods. The goal is to help prevent unintended consequences, such as children as young as five years old developing eating disorders, which have been alleged to arise from the current guidance.

Among prevention campaigns geared to adolescents, the population at greatest risk of developing an eating disorder, the report stated that organizations should be cautious when designing campaigns to teach youth about eating disorders. Research indicates that poorly-designed campaigns can glorify eating disorders and provide "how-to" information (e.g., laxative abuse), which can trigger eating disorders in people with a predisposition for developing the disorder.

The committee identified several treatment-related obstacles. Some patients perceived themselves to be disrespected and blamed by health-care professionals when they sought assistance for themselves or for someone else who had an eating disorder. This may reflect a lack of understanding of eating disorders among many health-care professionals. The committee noted that some general practitioners or doctors in hospital emergency departments appear to have little knowledge of eating disorders and provide misguided advice to patients, such as "gain some pounds." Accordingly, it is important that health-care professionals be better educated about the nature and treatment of eating disorders.

The committee also reported that individuals with eating disorders who have comorbid disorders (e.g., bulimia combined with alcohol abuse) are passed between service providers who do not treat both conditions. Most eating disorder treatment programs do not address concurrent disorders, despite the connection between the two health issues. Similary, many mental health programs refuse to accept, or are not equipped for, patients who also have an eating disorder comorbid with another disorder. Current treatment programs also face other limitations. For example, young men with eating disorders face challenges as they must often seek treatment through programs designed for young women.

The committee proposed a series of recommendations to address these concerns. The full report is available at: www.parl.gc.ca/content/hoc/Committee/412/FEWO/Reports/RP6772133/feworp04/feworp04-e.pdf

real SCIENCE real LIFE

Lisa—Detection and Treatment of Anorexia Nervosa in a Student Athlete

THE PATIENT

Lisa loved to run. In elementary school, she outran the boys. In middle school, she joined the cross-country team, was team captain, and won the regional championships. Running was her life, and she was good at it. She ran cross-country throughout high school, winning many competitive races. But that was just like Lisa—she was always driven to do her best, whether it was in academics or athletics. Even in grade 1,

(continued)

she often cried and would tell her mother that she was worried that she did not do her best—and she had to be the best. So she was thrilled when she was awarded full athletic scholarships to two excellent universities. She chose a university that excelled in women's track and field.

THE PROBLEM

The cross-country season started off well her first year of university, but Lisa developed tendonitis. The trainers had her sit out the season so that she would be ready for the next season. Not competing caused her great distress. She watched her teammates at home meets, listened to their tales of victory at away meets, and longed to be out there with them. She found it difficult to concentrate on her schoolwork. Previously an A student, she started to get Cs in chemistry and calculus. Not only that, but she also started to gain weight. Even though she was swimming and cross training to try to stay in shape, it wasn't the same as being on the team. Carrying around an extra 5 kg made her feel like she didn't belong. She felt fat and disgusting.

With only one month to go before outdoor season, she felt desperate to get back into shape. She was limiting herself to 300 calories per day and was exercising about six hours a day—swimming, using an elliptical machine, running, doing hundreds of crunches on her dorm room floor—she never sat still. Her tendonitis improved a little, and she was able to start training with the team again—but she didn't stop her extra exercising. She was quickly back to her training weight, but the coach noticed that her running wasn't quite back to her previous outstanding level. He assumed that it was just from the time off and worked with her to increase the distance of her training runs and to improve her overall conditioning. The attention paid off; her running improved, she took second at the relays, and she was contributing to the team's success. But she started looking really thin. Her teammates noticed her in the locker room and were shocked that they could count every rib and vertebra. They went to the coach with their concerns. The coach listened but had a dilemma. An important competition was coming up and they were well positioned to win—but not without Lisa. Could he wait until after the finals to talk to Student Health? He decided to sit on it for a couple of days and then decide.

THE TREATMENT

Two days later, he got a call from EMS. One of his athletes had collapsed during a 24 km training run and was being transported to the emergency room. He rushed to the ER and found Lisa hooked up to an IV, exhausted and dehydrated. She was tearful and determined to go to the finals, saying she was letting everyone down.

The coach told Lisa about the conversation he had had with her teammates. Avoiding talking about the finals, he told her that he would do whatever he could to work with her to get healthy and that was the only goal right now. The coach agonized over not having approached her immediately. Waiting two days could have meant her life.

At first, Lisa's treatment focused on support while she was being renourished. Her weight had dropped to 35 kg and she was 165 cm (BMI = 13 kg/m^2). Her therapist noted that her thinking was very negative. It was unclear whether she was also suffering from depression or if her low mood and negative thoughts were simply secondary to starvation. Lisa continued to believe that she had let down the team, the school, her family, and herself. She also believed that she could run well only if she were the thinnest girl on the team.

Initially, Lisa was afraid that the therapist's only goals were to make her fat and to keep her from running. However, she began to see that the therapist would indeed work with her to get her back to her sport, but only after she was fully recovered. As her thinking cleared, her therapist had her begin self-monitoring—not only of her food intake, but also of her urges to exercise and her thoughts. They worked together to ensure that she was eating properly and not engaging in unhealthy exercise that would make weight gain nearly impossible. Lisa began to recognize patterns in her urges to exercise, as well as some of the automatic thoughts that had maintained the eating-disordered behaviours. She realized that every time she saw a female athlete in revealing clothing, she started to feel as if she needed to get back to her waiflike weight. She would develop an overwhelming urge to go running or punish herself in the gym. Her therapist helped her to unpack the distorted thinking that fuelled that urge ("I will be a successful runner only if I am back to my previous low weight") and helped her integrate the realization that her low weight actually interfered with her running rather than helping it. Gradually, Lisa became more and more confident in her ability to resist the urge to exercise, although she still felt waves of envy as she saw the thinner girls. As she gained weight, her mood improved, so her physician saw no immediate need for medication but did continue to monitor Lisa's mood over time to see whether the depression would return and medication might be required.

THE TREATMENT OUTCOME

The following year before cross-country season, and with Lisa's permission, a meeting was set up with Lisa, her parents, her coach, her athletic trainer, and her therapist. Together they developed a plan for Lisa's competitive season, including reasonable training schedules and procedures for action if warning signs emerged. Lisa also talked openly about her struggle with her teammates, who were supportive of her efforts toward recovery.

In many ways Lisa was a highly successful young woman—academically and athletically. The transition from high school to university, though exciting, posed significant challenges for her. Her university was far from home, so she was on her own in a highly competitive school. Precisely those traits (competitiveness and determination) that made her a great success were her undoing after her injury. Lisa didn't have the personal tools to deal with this setback in a healthy way; instead, she went overboard with exercise as a means of feeling a sense of control over her situation. Once she was able to engage in a supportive relationship with her therapist, she was able to change her behaviour, although many cues in the environment clearly led to urges to exercise. With the support of her family, therapist, trainer, coach, and teammates, Lisa was able to successfully finish her competitive university career.

summary

7.1 Understand the features of anorexia nervosa, bulimia nervosa, binge eating disorder, and other feeding and eating disorders.
Anorexia nervosa is marked by extreme low weight, fear of gaining weight, and undue emphasis on shape and weight as part of self-evaluation. Binge eating and inappropriate compensatory behaviours, such as self-induced vomiting or laxative abuse, mark bulimia nervosa, which is seen in individuals who are of normal weight or overweight. BED also includes binge eating behaviour but without recurrent inappropriate compensatory behaviours.

7.2 Discuss sex differences in the risk for feeding and eating disorders and why these differences exist.
Anorexia nervosa and bulimia nervosa are more common in females than in males. BED has a more even sex distribution.

7.3 Discuss developmental life course changes in the risk for feeding and eating disorders.
Anorexia nervosa typically begins in early adolescence; bulimia typically begins somewhat later. Child and later adult onsets also occur. Less is known about the developmental course of BED.

7.4 Explore psychodynamic, behavioural, cognitive, and biological theories on the causes of feeding and eating disorders.
Many theories of the causes of eating disorders exist, including psychodynamic, biological/genetic, cognitive-behavioural, and sociocultural. A complete appreciation of the factors that cause and maintain eating disorders will probably involve a combination of genetic and environmental factors.

7.5 Discuss personality features and comorbid conditions that are commonly associated with feeding and eating disorders.
Depression and anxiety are commonly comorbid with anorexia and bulimia nervosa. Personality styles characteristic of both disorders include perfectionism; however, bulimia also tends to be associated with more impulsive features.

7.6 Compare and contrast treatments for feeding and eating disorders.
The initial and critical step in the treatment of anorexia nervosa is renutrition and weight gain in a supportive environment. Family involvement is critical for younger patients. CBT may be helpful after weight restoration. For bulimia nervosa, both CBT and fluoxetine (Prozac) have been shown to be effective in reducing binge eating and purging behaviour, although the long-term efficacy of medication treatment is unknown. For BED, CBT is a viable option.

key terms

amenorrhea 245
anorexia nervosa 243
avoidant–restrictive food intake disorder (AFRID) 257
binge eating 244
binge eating disorder 243
body mass index (BMI) 243
bulimia nervosa 249
eating disorder not otherwise specified 251
enmeshment 265
inappropriate compensatory behaviour 250
pica 256
purging 244
rumination disorder 257

TEST yourself

1. Which of the following criteria is necessary for a diagnosis of anorexia nervosa?
   a. significantly low body weight
   b. a BMI of 20–22
   c. a history of purging behaviours
   d. recent weight loss

2. Even at a very low body weight, a person with anorexia nervosa may experience
   a. lack of concern about physical appearance
   b. complete absence of appetite
   c. intense fear of gaining weight
   d. unusually high self-esteem

3. The attitude most difficult to overcome in patients with anorexia nervosa is their
   a. rationalization of any weight gain
   b. acceptance of obese family members
   c. inability to recognize the seriousness of the low weight
   d. preoccupation with the societal thin ideal

4. The two subtypes of anorexia nervosa are
   a. OSFED and BED
   b. restricting and binge eating/purging
   c. typical and atypical
   d. objective and subjective

5. The physical effects of anorexia nervosa after recovery may include
   a. osteoporosis
   b. decreased intellectual ability
   c. poor integration into society
   d. occupational disability

6. Anorexia nervosa is considered a very serious psychological problem primarily because
   a. it often includes periods of relapse
   b. it has the highest mortality rate of any psychological disorder
   c. it is routinely ignored by patients' families
   d. patients deny their condition and are reluctant to get help

7. The diagnosis of bulimia nervosa requires the presence of
   a. strict eating patterns
   b. alternating purging and nonpurging behaviours
   c. binge eating and inappropriate compensatory behaviours
   d. behaviours designed to ensure weight loss

8. The hallmark feature of a binge is the
   a. perceived number of calories
   b. type of food
   c. length of time
   d. sense of lack of control

9. A patient with bulimia nervosa who sometimes eats a typical or even small amount of food but still feels that the eating is out of control is experiencing
   a. excessive guilt
   b. subjective binge eating
   c. compensatory behaviour
   d. objective binge eating

10. Which of these is not a form of childhood feeding disorder?
    a. pica
    b. rumination disorder
    c. OSFED
    d. ARFID

11. David has become morbidly obese. He regularly eats at restaurants that serve meals buffet style. He prefers to eat alone, however, and he often eats until he is uncomfortable. He does not purge. He may be suffering from
    a. binge eating disorder
    b. bulimia nervosa
    c. compensatory behaviour disorder
    d. anorexia nervosa—binge eating/purging type

12. The prevalence of bulimia nervosa in men may be underestimated because
    a. it is socially unacceptable for men to admit to having emotional difficulties
    b. men tend to use other compensatory behaviours besides purging, such as exercise
    c. few studies have been conducted with men
    d. it is associated with illegal steroid use

13. Lian is going through puberty before most of her middle school classmates. She may be at
    a. greater risk for developing an eating disorder
    b. lower risk for developing body dissatisfaction
    c. greater risk for being sexually abused
    d. less risk for being underweight

14. In animal studies, surgical lesions in the brain indicate that the neuroanatomical centre for appetite and weight control is the
    a. pituitary gland
    b. occipital lobe
    c. hypothalamus
    d. frontal lobe

15. The obsessionality and rigidity associated with some eating disorders have been associated with what aspect of brain functioning?
    a. serotonin and dopamine levels
    b. glucose absorption
    c. plaque formation
    d. synaptic efficiency

16. What structural brain abnormalities are seen in patients with anorexia nervosa?
    a. frontal lobe distortion
    b. decrease in ventricle size
    c. loss of grey matter and reduced brain mass
    d. all of the above

17. According to an early family model, patients who seek treatment for anorexia nervosa are members of families who are experiencing enmeshment. This means that the family is
   a. having difficulty dealing with problematic, negative situations
   b. overinvolved in the affairs of the patient
   c. not adapting to the changing developmental needs of the child
   d. excessively shielding the child from age-appropriate experiences

18. The multidisciplinary team's critical first step in the treatment of anorexia nervosa is
   a. prescribing medication
   b. encouraging a realistic body image
   c. ensuring renutrition
   d. promoting healthy family communication

19. Which component of CBT appears to be the most effective in promoting behavioural change?
   a. forming a therapeutic alliance
   b. changing thinking patterns
   c. increasing personal control
   d. increasing self-esteem

20. The most effective way to approach the treatment of anorexia nervosa is with
   a. nutritional counselling
   b. conjoint family therapy
   c. interpersonal psychotherapy
   d. a multidisciplinary team

Answers:
1 a, 2 c, 3 c, 4 b, 5 a, 6 b, 7 c, 8 d, 9 b, 10 c, 11 a, 12 b, 13 a,
14 c, 15 a, 16 c, 17 b, 18 c, 19 b, 20 d.

chapter 8

gender dysphoria, sexual dysfunctions, and paraphilic disorders

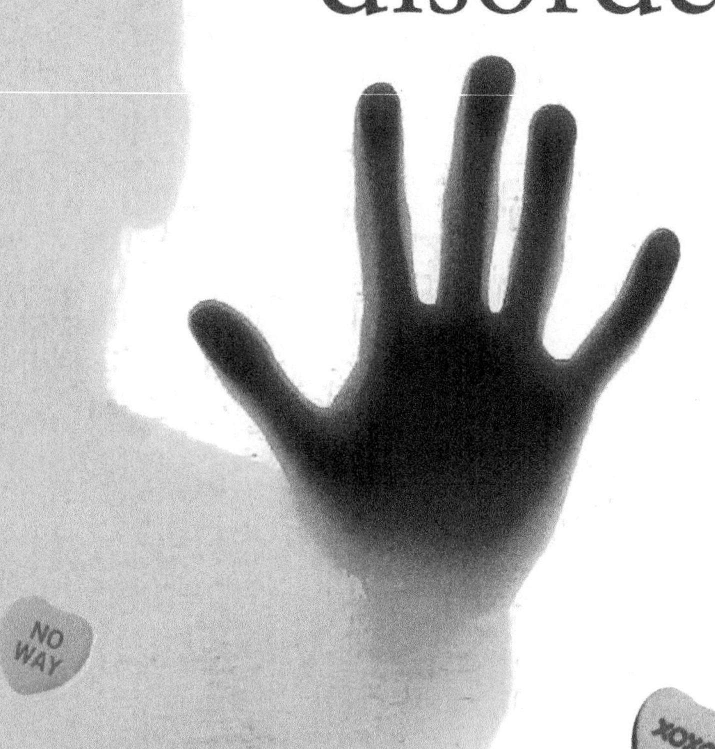

(top): Perry van Munster/Alamy Stock Photo; **(center):** Mode Images Limited/Alamy Stock Photo; **(center):** Zee/Alamy Stock Photo; **(bottom):** D. Hurst/Alamy Stock Photo

gender dysphoria, sexual dysfunctions, and paraphilic disorders

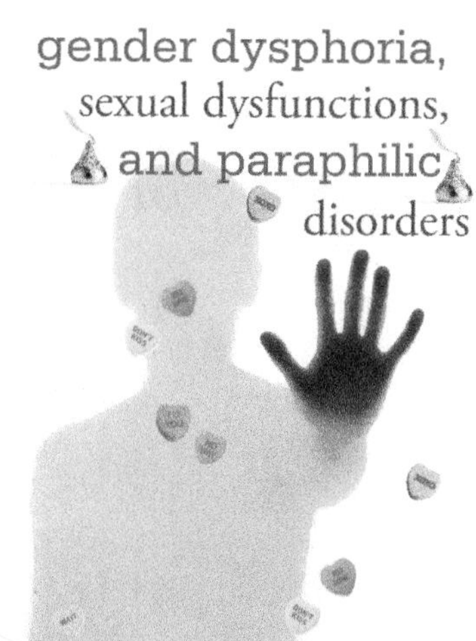

learning objectives

After reading this chapter, you should be able to:

8.1 Understand that "normal sexual behaviour" is difficult to define and depends on biological and cultural factors.

8.2 Identify the characteristics of gender dysphoria, and understand how it relates to transsexualism and transvestic fetishism.

8.3 Recognize that men and women exhibit different patterns of sexual behaviour, and identify the role of gender in the definition and development of sexual dysfunction.

8.4 Understand the biological and psychological complexities involved in the etiology and treatment of sexual dysfunction.

8.5 Identify the types of paraphilic disorders, and give examples of each type.

8.6 Identify the most promising biological and psychosocial treatments for the paraphilic disorders and the ethical issues that affect the conduct of clinical research.

At 30 years old, Margaret was referred to the clinic by her gynecologist. All of her friends were married, and she thought that she should be too. But unlike her friends, she had no desire to engage in sexual acts and never had sexual desires, fantasies, and urges regarding men or women. This lack of desire included all forms of sexual intimacy. Margaret felt very uncomfortable with any physical contact, including hugging her family and her best friend. Although she dated in high school and university, the relationships always ended when the boy tried to kiss her or touch her breasts. Margaret was never sexually abused or the victim of sexual assault, but in middle school she had a serious problem with her spine and she walked with a limp. The other children called her "gimpy." After several surgeries and a year in a body cast, she returned to school. She had matured physically and the boys thought that she was attractive, but she remained very self-conscious of her body. Someone started a rumour that she had a sexual relationship with a recently-fired science teacher. The rumour was not true, and the science teacher was fired for having child pornography on his computer, but no one knew the truth and the rumour spread. She had some female friends in the high school band and some positive interactions with her church group. Although shy, she enjoyed social interactions with people and longed for the type of intimate relationships she saw among her friends.

Now, for the first time since high school, Margaret had a boyfriend. A friend had arranged for a blind date with Amery, a man who was even shyer than Margaret. He was respectful and a real gentleman, and Margaret enjoyed his company as they dated for a few months. They went to movies, concerts, and dinners with friends, and Amery never asked for anything other than a quick good-night kiss on her cheek, which Margaret endured. After three months, Amery desired more intimacy. Margaret had been hoping that her feelings about sex would change because he was such a great guy. But now they seemed to fight a lot because her extreme discomfort with all physical contact was still there. She described feelings of panic and disgust when Amery tried to hug her. In fact, she was so anxious that she rejected all of his romantic advances, even including holding hands. She volunteered to seek help, but Amery was angry and frustrated and broke off the relationship. Margaret was crushed—she was sure she would never find another guy as great as Amery.

Margaret suffered from a sexual dysfunction, and her situation highlights many of the issues that we address in this chapter. First, even people who long for a committed, loving relationship can have difficulty with sexual intimacy. Second, difficulties in sexual performance never occur in isolation. Biological, psychological, interpersonal, and environmental factors often contribute to the development and persistence of sexual dysfunction. Margaret was different in one respect. Unlike many other people, she decided to seek treatment for her intimacy issues.

Sexual dysfunctions are one of the three types of disorders discussed in this chapter. They are defined as a clinically significant disturbance in the person's ability to respond sexually or experience sexual pleasure (APA, 2013). Another category, *gender dysphoria*, describes individuals who feel a marked incongruence between their assigned gender and their experienced/expressed gender (APA, 2013). It is not dissatisfaction with a sexual behaviour or attitude but dissatisfaction with and distress over one's identity as male or female. *Paraphilic disorders* are yet a different category and consist of intense and persistent sexual interest that is not directed toward phenotypically normal, physically mature, consenting human partners (APA, 2013). As these disorders illustrate, sexual behaviour is complex and multifaceted. It is also the subject of frequent misunderstandings and misconceptions. To understand these behaviours and their impact, we first review our historic understanding of sexual function and dysfunction.

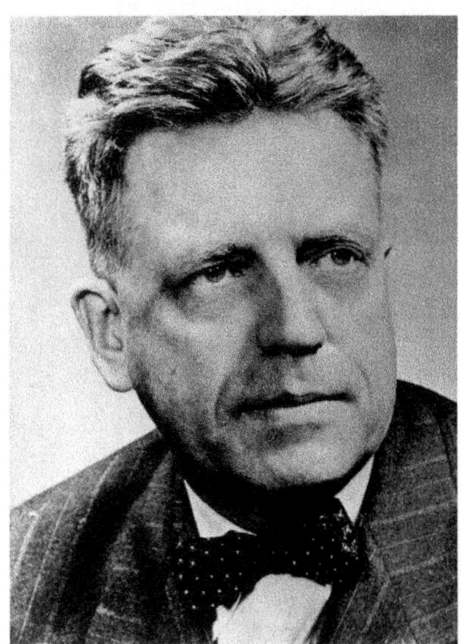

Alfred Kinsey was one of the first scientists to investigate the sexual behaviours of men and women.

Alamy Stock Photo

Human Sexuality

Perhaps because the subject is highly personal and often considered taboo, people find it difficult to discuss sexual attitudes and behaviours. This leads to many misconceptions about normal sexual functioning. One of the first formal attempts to understand sexual behaviour occurred in 1938 when Alfred Kinsey, a professor of biology at Indiana University, interviewed people about their sexual practices. Kinsey published his findings in *Sexual Behavior in the Human Male* in 1948 and *Sexual Behavior in the Human Female* in 1953. The books created public and scientific controversies. The most serious scientific criticism was that Kinsey's samples were not representative of the general population. Nevertheless, Kinsey's groundbreaking work was a significant force in the scientific study of sexuality.

Shortly after Kinsey's publications, William Masters, a gynecologist, and his wife, Virginia Johnson, a psychologist, began their own research program in human sexuality. In addition to interviews, Masters and Johnson actually recorded the physical responses of more than 700 adults as they engaged in sexual activity. They published their research in their books, *Human Sexual Response* (1966) and *Human Sexual Inadequacy* (1970). In these books, they described the physical and psychological bases of sexual response, measured the body's sexual responses, examined deviations from normal sexual functioning, and developed treatments to address dysfunction. Much of what we know about the physical responses leading to orgasm stems from the work of Masters and Johnson.

Sexual Functioning

The basis of sexual functioning is the human sexual response cycle. Originally, Masters and Johnson described four stages of sexual functioning: arousal, plateau, orgasm, and resolution (Masters & Johnson, 1966). Helen Singer Kaplan, a psychotherapist who specialized in sex therapy, described sexual response as consisting of desire, excitement, and orgasm (Kaplan, 1979). Most contemporary explanations incorporate some combination of these terms, conceptualizing four phases of sexual response (see Figure 8.1). First is the *desire phase*, which begins in response to external or internal cues. This is followed by the *arousal phase*, characterized by physical and psychological signs of sexual arousal. In men, the most overt response is *penile tumescence*, which occurs as blood flow to the penis increases. In women, arousal is marked by *vasocongestion* (swelling of the blood vessels) in the genital area and vaginal lubrication. Psychologically, there is a positive emotional response. Next is the *orgasm phase*. Men have a feeling of the inevitability of ejaculation followed by actual ejaculation of seminal fluid. Women experience contractions in the outer third of the vagina. Both men and women also experience a strong subjective feeling of pleasure that is based in the brain rather than the genitalia. The *resolution phase* is more common in men than

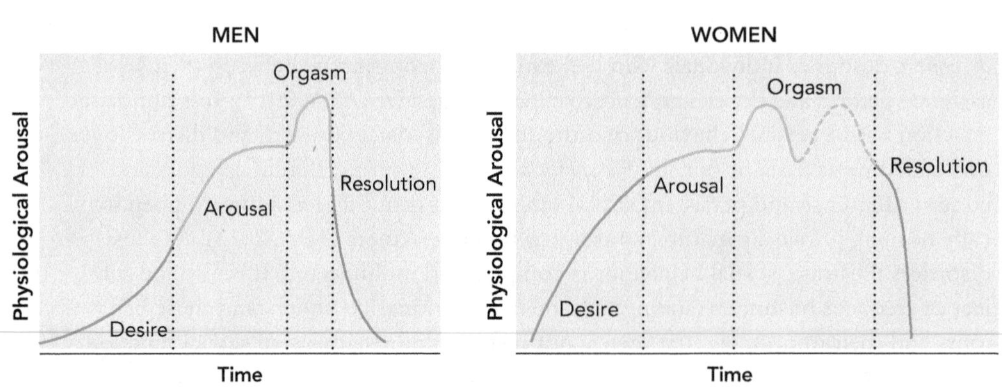

FIGURE 8.1 The Human Sexual Response Cycle. The sexual response cycle typically consists of four phases. In contrast to men, women may have more than one orgasm prior to the resolution phase.

women. Physical arousal decreases followed by a refractory (resting) period during which penile erection cannot occur. Women may experience two or more orgasms before experiencing a resolution phase. Health and mental health professionals use this model of sexual response to understand sexual dysfunctions. However, this sexual model response may not be the best "fit" for understanding sexual behaviour in men and women.

William Masters and Virginia Johnson observed sexual interactions of men and women, recording their physiological responses during different phases of sexual activity.

Bettmann/Corbis

Sex Differences in Sexual Response

All surveys of sexual practices indicate that men engage in more frequent sexual activity than do women. Does this mean that males have a stronger biological **sex drive**, defined as craving for sexual activity and pleasure? Most people assume that the answer is "yes," but that is not necessarily true. Men do think about sex more often than women do, are more frequently sexually aroused, have more frequent and different fantasies, desire sex more often, desire more partners, masturbate more often, are less able or willing to go without sex, initiate sex more often, refuse sex less often, use more resources to get sex, make more sacrifices for sex, have a more favourable attitude toward and enjoy a wider variety of sexual practices, and rate themselves as having stronger sex drives than women. However, women have a higher capacity for sex, are biologically capable of engaging in sexual behaviour for a longer period of time, are capable of more orgasms than men, and do not have a refractory period (Baumeister et al., 2001).

The way each sex defines sexual drive also differs. For many men, sexual desire is defined primarily by physical pleasure and sexual intercourse. Women appear to define sexual desire more broadly and include in their definition the need for emotional intimacy (Basson, 2002; Peplau, 2003). Female sexual responses may be more complicated than a biological-affective drive marked by sexual thoughts, fantasies, and a conscious urge to engage in sexual activity (Tiefer, 2001). Thus sexual desire may exist equally in both sexes when different definitions are applied. Understanding these differences is important because the current diagnostic system has evolved from a model of male sexual functioning and may not appropriately identify sexual dysfunction in women.

Biological sex also interacts with age to affect sexual behaviour. In men, the effects of age are most apparent in genital response (inability to achieve an erection), whereas in women, the effects of age are most apparent in declining sexual interest (Bancroft et al., 2003). A psychological difference exists too. Unlike men, many women do not consider normal age-related changes in their sexuality or sexual practices to be problematic.

Understanding Sexual Behaviour

8.1 Understand that "normal sexual behaviour" is difficult to define and depends on biological and cultural factors.

Since the time of Kinsey and Masters and Johnson, research aimed at understanding sexual behaviour has increased. Over the past 20 years, several large well-controlled surveys have been conducted: One targeted men aged 20 to 39 (Billy et al., 1993), a second targeted university-age women (DeBuono et al., 1990), and a third targeted adults aged 40 to 80 (Nicolosi et al., 2006). Surveys of typical sexual practices provide a context for understanding the deviations that are the topics of this chapter.

Over a 12-month period (see Figure 8.2), 95% of males between the ages of 18 and 30 and 87% of females between the ages of 18 and 22 years had vaginal intercourse (Billy et al., 1993; DeBuono et al., 1990). In addition, 74% of men and 86% of women

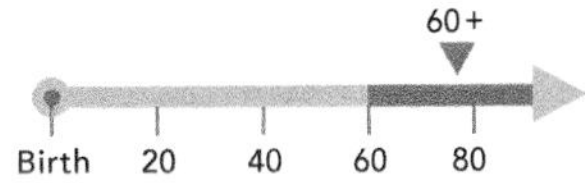

Older adults remain sexually active even though the frequency of sexual behaviour decreases as one matures.

FIGURE 8.2

Sexual Activity of Males Between Ages 18 and 30 and Females Between 18 and 22. As this graph shows, both young men and women engage in a variety of different sexual behaviours, although the percentages differ by sex and by type of behaviour.

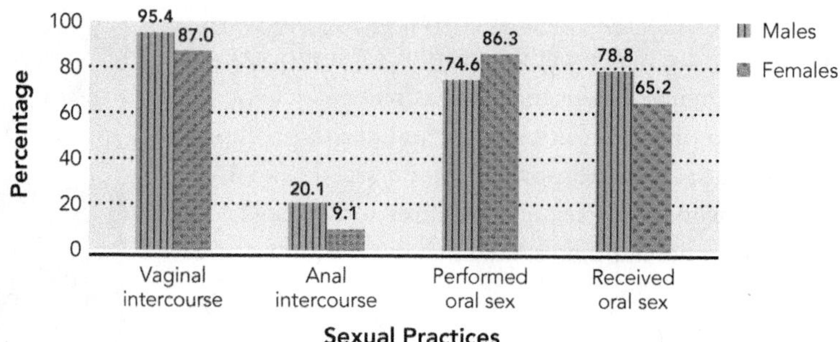

orally stimulated the genitalia of their partner, and 79% and 65% were the recipients of oral stimulation by a partner, respectively. In contrast, only a minority (20% of males and 9% of females) engaged in anal intercourse during a 12-month period.

One of the largest surveys assessed 27 900 people aged 40 to 80 in 29 countries. This study found that in this large group, 82% of men and 76% of women believed that "satisfactory sex is essential to maintain a relationship" (Nicolosi et al., 2006). Although there is a decline with age, 48% of men and 25% of women aged 70 to 79 think about sexual activity at least several times per month (see Figure 8.3) (Nicolosi et al., 2006). In fact, 22% of men aged 70 to 79 reported still thinking about sex every day. Clearly, satisfactory sexual functioning is important to many middle-aged and older adults. Consistent with their belief in its importance, 93% of men aged 40 to 49 are sexually active, as are 53% of men aged 70 to 80 years (Nicolosi et al., 2004). For women aged 40 to 49, 88% were sexually active, as were 21% of women aged 70 to 80. As with younger adults, middle-aged and older men were more likely to think about and engage in sexual activity than were women.

What constitutes sexuality and sexual behaviour varies a great deal across cultures (Nieto, 2004). Some researchers have suggested that sexual attraction is not simply biological or sociocultural—it is an integrated response (Tolman & Diamond, 2001). We have already noted one biological factor, age, which may affect sexual functioning. Within a sociocultural context, sexual relationships exist within societies that in turn exist within a larger culture and also within a historical context (recall from Chapter 1 how Freud shocked Victorian society by suggesting that young children had sexual feelings and desires). Yet among the Khumbo of Nepal, children are considered sexual beings at age 5, when they must begin to cover their genitalia with clothing, behaviour that is expected of adults but not the younger children (Nieto, 2004). Therefore, there is no universal standard of "normal" sexuality or sexual behaviour. In fact, one type of sexual behaviour, called *cybersex*, is becoming more common as more people have access to the Internet (see "Research Hot Topic: The Internet and Cybersex").

FIGURE 8.3

Frequency with Which Men and Women of Various Ages Think About Sexual Activity. Across English-speaking populations, there is a decline in the frequency with which men and women think about sexual activity on a daily basis, but even at advanced ages, interest in sex does not disappear.

Source: Nicolosi, A., Laumann, E. O., Glasser, D. B., Brock, G., King, R., & Gingell, C. (2006). Sexual activity, sexual disorders, and associated help-seeking behavior among mature adults in five Anglophone countries from the Global Survey of Sexual Attitudes and Behaviors (GSSAB). *Journal of Sex & Marital Therapy, 32*, 331–342. Copyright © 2006, Taylor & Francis Group (www.informaworld.com). Reprinted by permission of the publisher.

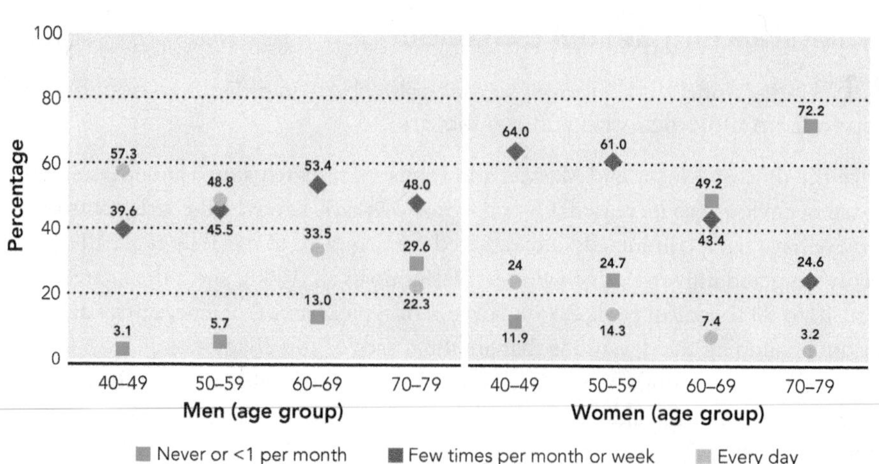

People may engage in sexual behaviour with someone of the opposite sex (heterosexuality), someone of the same sex (homosexuality), or partners of either sex (bisexuality). Until about 25 years ago, many people considered a homosexual orientation to be a mental disorder, but for a long time it was not clear how many people engaged in sexual behaviours with someone of the same sex. One reason was that, given how difficult it is to get people to discuss sexuality, questions about same-sex practices were rarely included in surveys of adult sexual behaviours.

Overall, it appears that 2% to 5% of men and 1% to 2% of women are exclusively same-sex attracted (Diamond, 1993; Laumann et al., 1994; Wellings et al., 1994). These rates appear to be consistent worldwide, although cultural customs and sanctions often dictate the frequency of same-sex *behaviour*, as opposed to a gay/lesbian or bisexual *identity*. In other words, people may feel sexual attraction toward someone of the same sex but may not act on that emotion because of religious or cultural practices. As with heterosexual attraction, there are sex differences in the strength of same-sex attraction; men are more likely to be exclusively attracted to the same sex, and women are more likely to describe themselves as attracted to both sexes (Bailey et al., 2000). This sex difference may reflect more erotic plasticity among women (Rahman & Wilson, 2003); their sex drive is more likely to be influenced by cultural and social factors.

Developmentally, same-sex attraction or bisexual attraction is often seen as "experimentation" in adolescents and young adults. The results of a 10-year longitudinal study of women from age 19 to 29 years indicated that 67% of the women changed their sexual orientation self-label over that period of time and 33% changed their self-label two times or more. However, in contrast to an "experimental" or "transitional" hypothesis, over this critical period of time, more women adopted a bisexual label than gave it up (Diamond, 2008). Thus there does appear to be fluidity in sexual orientation among women, but it is not clear whether these changes in labelling or behaviour continue to change as women continue to mature. Scientists are now beginning to understand that sexual desire and romantic love emerge from different social behavioural systems that have different goals (Diamond, 2003). Sexual desire is controlled by the sexual mating system that has the goal of reproduction of the species (Fisher et al., 2002b). Romantic attraction is controlled by the attachment or pair-bonding system that has the goal of an enduring relationship with another individual. Even though these systems often work together, it is possible that an individual, regardless of his or her sexual orientation, can be romantically attracted to people of either sex (Diamond, 2003).

Appropriate dress for girls and women is dictated by culture. (top) Typical dress for teenagers from Western countries. (bottom) Typical dress for women in Esfahan, Iran.

(top): Blend Images/Alamy Stock Photo; **(bottom):** Kazuyoshi Nomachi/Corbis

The development of sexual orientation appears to be based primarily on one's biology. In fact, over half a century of research has not provided any support for etiology based on psychological theories (Rahman & Wilson, 2003). Homosexual or same-sex orientation appears to be at least in part genetically determined (Kendler et al., 2000b; Kirk et al., 2000). In one study, the heritability estimates for homosexuality were between 50% and 60% for females and 30% for males (Kirk et al., 2000). However, further efforts are needed to understand the basis of the genetic contribution in determining sexual orientation.

Other attempts to understand the biology of sexual orientation have focused on the role of sex hormones called *androgens*. Atypical levels or timing of androgens during fetal development (high or low, early or late) do not always create differences in secondary sexual characteristics, genital anatomy, or gonadal function, but they may affect sexual orientation. Some researchers have examined the relationship between homosexuality and (1) non-righthandedness, (2) differences in the ratio of the second (index) finger to the fourth (ring) finger, and (3) symmetry in patterns of fingerprint ridges. In the latter two cases, gay men show fingerprint patterns more like heterosexual women than they do heterosexual men. Although these three differences may be related to abnormal levels of androgens during prenatal development (Rahman & Wilson, 2003), the data so far are not conclusive because the sample sizes in these studies are small. Also, the methods of

research **HOT** topic

The Internet and Cybersex

Internet sex sites are the third largest industry on the World Wide Web (Carnes et al., 2001). A Google search of "cybersex" yielded over more than 5 million hits. In contrast, there were only 143 hits using a scientific search engine (PubMed), and only 22 studies were controlled research trials. Clearly, public interest in cybersex far outstrips scientific knowledge. But cybersex can result in personal distress and negatively affect areas of functioning. Researchers are beginning to study this increasingly common behaviour.

- **How do we define cybersex?** Currently, there is no accepted definition. Some researchers include all Internet sex activity as cybersex. Others distinguish between *online sexual activity*, which may include searching for information about sexual dysfunctions or sex therapy, and cybersex, defined as interchanges with a partner for the purpose of sexual pleasure (Southern, 2008). Still others break down cybersex participants into three subgroups: recreational users, sexually compulsive users, and at-risk users (Cooper et al., 2004).
- **How many people engage in cybersex?** A Swedish study indicated that 30% of men and 34% of women had engaged in at least one cybersex experience (Daneback et al., 2005); 38% were between the ages of 18 and 24, and 13% were over age 50. When questioned about their ability to control their online sexual activity, 19% of respondents to an online survey admitted being unable to stop their behaviour (Cooper et al., 2004). Still another study determined that perhaps as many as 11.8 million people have problems controlling online sexual behaviour (Goldberg et al., 2008).
- **What are the negative implications?** Cybersex use can result in changes in personality or sleep patterns, disregard for responsibility, and loss of sexual interest in real-life partner sex, real-life infidelity, sexual exploitation, and divorce (Goldberg et al., 2008; Schneider, 2003; Southern, 2008). If sites charge a fee, users may incur substantial debts. Employee productivity is at risk; 70% of Internet sexual activity occurs on weekdays between 9 a.m. and 5 p.m. Downloading sexual material from certain sites may lead to charges of trafficking in child pornography (Cooper et al., 2004).
- **Who is at risk for overuse of cybersex?** One of the most pressing research issues is identifying who might be at risk for these behaviours. However, no empirical data addressing this issue are available.

In summary, cybersex is clearly an emerging problem, but as yet our knowledge is based on clinical reports and survey research. However, its increasing prevalence and potentially harmful effects are motivating mental health professionals to initiate research in order to better understand and therefore be able to treat this behaviour if it rises to the level of an addiction.

determining a relationship are indirect. Specifically, this research uses physical features of adults to hypothesize about the presence of *prenatal hormones* that were present when the fetus was in the uterus (i.e., in utero). More direct, and perhaps more conclusive, evidence would come from directly measuring these hormones in utero.

More conclusive data have been reported for fraternal birth order in males. Across numerous and diverse samples (Gooren, 2006), gay men had a greater number of older brothers than did heterosexual men. One explanation for this phenomenon is that there is an incompatibility between the mother's immune system and the androgens that are in the male fetus. The mother's body responds to the presence of male androgens with an immune response in the form of antibodies (to fight off the androgens). These antibodies cross the placental barrier and affect fetal hormonal level. As the number of male-offspring pregnancies increases, this immunological response becomes stronger and may affect fetal brain masculinization, although it is unclear whether the entire brain is affected or only certain specific areas (Blanchard & Bogaert, 2004; Blanchard et al., 2006; Kauth, 2005). Estimates of risk indicate that each older brother increases a younger brother's risk by 33% to 48%, but overall, this accounts for only a small increase in overall prevalence. Furthermore, not all gay men have older brothers, and, of course, the theory cannot account for homosexuality or bisexuality among women (Gooren, 2006). Therefore, although this androgen theory may explain the origin of sexual orientation for some gay men, it will most likely remain only one of many potential etiologies.

CONCEPT check

- The work of Kinsey and Masters and Johnson provided the impetus for scientifically studying sexual behaviour.
- The human sexual response consists of four phases: desire, arousal, orgasm, and resolution.
- Although sexual behaviours decline in frequency with age, satisfactory sexual functioning is considered important by people at any age.
- Sexual orientation appears to be biologically based with both genetic and prenatal hormonal influences. However, this research is still in its infancy, and emerging theories appear to account for only a small percentage of people who experience an exclusive same-sex attraction, highlighting the need for further research.

critical thinking question If sexual desire is defined in terms of a craving for sexual activity or pleasure, men have a stronger sex drive than women. However, women have a greater capacity for sexual activity than do men, and for women, the concept of sexual drive includes emotional intimacy in addition to sexual activity and pleasure. How might such different concepts of "sex" affect our interpretations of emotional states such as "love" and "commitment"?

Gender Dysphoria

8.2 Identify the characteristics of gender dysphoria, and understand how it relates to transsexualism and transvestic fetishism.

William is 23 years old. He came to the psychology clinic after hearing one of the psychologists talking about depression on TV. He thought that the psychologist seemed very understanding, leading him to seek treatment. William felt sad, but his real reason for coming to the clinic was that he "no longer wanted to be a man." Ever since he was a young child, William had felt like a girl. His happiest time was sneaking into his sister's room and putting on her pink dancing costume. In fact, he coveted any of his sister's clothing. His father was horrified and forced William to play with guns, a football, and anything that would help him "be a man." William tried, but he always felt as if he were pretending. He felt that he was a woman trapped in a man's body.

How does a child know if he or she is a boy or a girl? The answer seems obvious but it is not. Traditionally, *sex* was considered to be determined by genes, hormones, and physical genitalia, whereas *gender* could be defined as categories of male or female defined by cultural role expectations. Some researchers consider these definitions to be very simplistic (Lyons & Lyons, 2006), and the complex issue of defining these terms is outside the scope of abnormal psychology. But what if you have male genitalia yet you feel like a girl? To understand William's behaviour and feelings, we need to explore the concept of *gender identity*, the personal understanding of oneself as male or female. According to Toronto experts on gender dysphoria Kenneth Zucker and Susan Bradley, gender identity typically develops by age 3 or 4 (Bradley & Zucker, 1997). Usually, biological sex and gender identity match—boys who are genetically male describe themselves as boys, and girls who are genetically female describe themselves as girls. However, in cases of **gender dysphoria**, biological sex and gender identity do not match, as with William, leading to distress and impairment.

Gender dysphoria (see "DSM-5: Gender Dysphoria") is not simply a momentary wish to be the opposite sex because of cultural or social advantages (e.g., "men have all the power"). It is a marked incongruence between the gender to which a person was assigned (usually at birth) and the person's experienced/expressed gender (APA, 2013). Among children, gender dysphoria is apparent in repeated statements that the child *wants* to be the opposite sex or *is* the opposite sex; cross-dressing in clothing stereotypical of the other sex (as with William); persistent fantasies of being the opposite sex or persistent preference for cross-gender roles in pretend play; a strong desire to participate in games and activities usually associated with the opposite sex; and a strong preference for playmates of the opposite sex.

In addition to identifying with the opposite sex, people with gender dysphoria have persistent discomfort with their own sex. Boys express disgust about their penis or testes, state that the penis will disappear, or state that it would be better not to have one. They avoid rough-and-tumble play or stereotypically male activities. Girls express persistent discomfort by refusing to sit on the toilet to urinate, stating that they have a penis or will grow one and that they do not want to grow breasts or begin menstruation. They also dislike female clothing, refusing to wear dresses. Among adolescents and adults, this is called **transgender behaviour**. Some people with this disorder may attempt to pass as the opposite sex through cross-dressing, disguising their sexual genitalia, or changing other sexual characteristics.

It is important to differentiate between the terms **transsexualism** and *transvestic disorder*. The latter is the desire and perhaps even the need among heterosexual men to dress in women's clothes (Bradley & Zucker, 1997), but not the desire to *be* the opposite sex (Lawrence & Zucker, 2012; Sharma, 2007). We discuss transvestic disorder later in this chapter in the section on paraphilic disorders.

criteria for Gender Dysphoria — DSM-5

Gender Dysphoria in Children

A. A marked incongruence between one's experienced/expressed gender and assigned gender, of at least 6 months' duration, as manifested by at least six of the following (one of which must be Criterion A1):

1. A strong desire to be of the other gender or an insistence that one is the other gender (or some alternative gender different from one's assigned gender).
2. In boys (assigned gender), a strong preference for cross-dressing or simulating female attire; or in girls (assigned gender), a strong preference for wearing only typical masculine clothing and a strong resistance to the wearing of typical feminine clothing.
3. A strong preference for cross-gender roles in make-believe play or fantasy play.
4. A strong preference for the toys, games, or activities stereotypically used or engaged in by the other gender.
5. A strong preference for playmates of the other gender.
6. In boys (assigned gender), a strong rejection of typically masculine toys, games, and activities and a strong avoidance of rough-and-tumble play; or in girls (assigned gender), a strong rejection of typically feminine toys, games, and activities.
7. A strong dislike of one's sexual anatomy.
8. A strong desire for the primary and/or secondary sex characteristics that match one's experienced gender.

B. The condition is associated with clinically significant distress or impairment in social, school, or other important areas of functioning.

Gender Dysphoria in Adolescents and Adults

A. A marked incongruence between one's experienced/expressed gender and assigned gender, of at least 6 months' duration, as manifested by at least two of the following:

1. A marked incongruence between one's experienced/expressed gender and primary and/or secondary sex characteristics (or in young adolescents, the anticipated secondary sex characteristics).
2. A strong desire to be rid of one's primary and/or secondary sex characteristics because of a marked incongruence with one's experienced/expressed gender (or in young adolescents, a desire to prevent the development of the anticipated secondary sex characteristics).
3. A strong desire for the primary and/or secondary sex characteristics of the other gender.
4. A strong desire to be of the other gender (or some alternative gender different from one's assigned gender).
5. A strong desire to be treated as the other gender (or some alternative gender different from one's assigned gender).
6. A strong conviction that one has the typical feelings and reactions of the other gender (or some alternative gender different from one's assigned gender).

B. The condition is associated with clinically significant distress or impairment in social, occupational, or other important areas of functioning.

Because it is so rare, gender dysphoria is not a disorder that is included in epidemiological investigations, making its prevalence difficult to determine. The most commonly reported prevalence estimates are 1 in 7400 to 12 800 for men and 1 in 30 000 to 1 in 52 100 for women (Lawrence & Zucker, 2012). As in William's case, feeling trapped in one's body can lead to feelings of depression. In fact, people with gender dysphoria often have other psychiatric disorders, most commonly anxiety, depression, and personality disorders (Cohen-Kettenis et al., 2003; Hepp et al., 2005; Meyer, 2004; Taher, 2007; Zucker, 2004). Anxiety and depressive symptoms are a response to gender dysphoria and to the ridicule that people with gender dysphoria often face as a result of their behaviour. Cross-gender identification sometimes becomes so strong that people seek **sex reassignment surgery**, a series of procedures that matches their physical anatomy and their gender identity (see "Real People, Real Disorders: Chaz Bono: Transition in the Spotlight").

Cross-dressing may provide sexual gratification for some men; male entertainers sometimes dress as females to entertain the public.

Ryan McVay/Photodisc/Getty

Functional Impairment

Among young children, cross-gender behaviours are common, and their presence alone does not seem to create significant distress. However, these behaviours may result in peer rejection or social isolation, which can in turn lead to negative mood states (Bartlett et al., 2000). Sometimes the distress associated with gender dysphoria is not found in the child but in his or her parents. As one mother reported,

> He was very excited about [putting on a blouse of mine] and leaped and danced around the room. I didn't like it and I just told him to take it off and I put it away. He kept asking for it. He wanted to wear that blouse again (Green, 1987, p. 2).

REAL people REAL disorders

Chaz Bono: Transition in the Spotlight

In the 1970s, the singing team of Sony and Cher Bono closed each episode of their popular TV show by bringing out their precocious little blond-haired daughter, Chastity. The audience delighted in seeing the little girl dressed in an outfit similar to the costume of her famous mother, who appeared to fully embrace her female sexuality and her often jaw-dropping designer evening gowns. Little did the audience know that even as a little child, Chastity preferred to dress like her father, noting that "as a kid, I thought I was a little boy." Despite pressure from his mother to be a "girlie girl," Chaz preferred male clothing. He came out as a lesbian to his parents in 1987 at the age of 18, doing so publicly in 1995. His parents did not always understand, but Cher always supported Chaz's decisions. Six years later, Chaz began questioning his gender identity when he was fighting addictions to alcohol and drugs. After conquering those addictions and remaining clean since that time, Chaz decided to make the transition to live his life consistent with his identity as a man.

In June 2009, just after his 40th birthday, Chaz announced that he was in the process of becoming a man—going through the steps of counselling, living as a man, and having hormone therapy and surgery. He will not disclose the extent of his surgery, preferring to keep some things private. Going through this transition in the public eye was difficult, but with a supportive family, as well as notes from other people that his public transition had inspired them to take similar steps, Chaz is now living as a man. In addition to his busy life as an LGBT rights advocate, author, and speaker, Chaz works with transgender children and their families. As he sums up this journey, "It's hard for me to articulate how this feels—when you've lived your whole life in a body and having everyone related to you as something you don't feel. When that finally gets righted, it's just amazing. I finally get to live my life the way I've always wanted to."

RE/Westcom/starmaxinc.com/Newscom

Sources: Bartolomeo, J. (2009). Becoming Chaz. Retrieved April 20, 2013, from www.chazbono.net/press/printarticles/peoplejune262009.html; and Zuckerman, B. (2009). Chaz Bono: I'm a Happy Guy. Retrieved April 20, 2013, from www.chazbono.net/press/printarticles/peopledec212009.html.

Among children with gender dysphoria, distress does not result from cross-gender behaviours, but rather from being *prevented* from engaging in the desired behaviours. Among adults with gender dysphoria, lifetime prevalence of comorbid disorders range from 14% for current disorders to 71% for lifetime disorders (Hepp et al., 2005; Hoshiai et al., 2010). However, even when the existence of a second disorder is low, lifetime prevalence of suicidal ideation (74%) and self-mutilation (33%) are significant (Hoshiai et al., 2010), indicating the severity of distress that can accompany this disorder.

Sex, Race, and Ethnicity

Occasional cross-gender behaviour is common among elementary school children (Sandberg et al., 1993) and does not necessarily indicate the presence of gender dysphoria. When present, gender dysphoria is usually first detected between ages 2 and 4. The earliest signs include persistent cross-gender dressing and play. Verbal wishes to be a member of the other sex do not usually occur before age 6 or 7 (Bartlett et al., 2000). Before puberty, there are five to seven preadolescent boys for every one preadolescent girl evaluated and treated for gender dysphoria. By contrast, in adolescence, the ratio of boys to girls with gender dysphoria is virtually equal (Bradley & Zucker, 1997; Zucker, 2004). Among adults, and based mostly on studies from European countries, gender dysphoria is more common in males than females (Lawrence & Zucker, 2012).

In some Arab countries, gender dysphoria exists even when contradicted by religious, moral, and social values (Taher, 2007). Sometimes, transsexual individuals do not self-identify unless they know that sympathetic health professionals and treatment are available. For example, once sex reassignment surgery was available in Singapore, transsexuals of Chinese, Malaysian, and Indian ethnicity began to seek treatment (Tsoi & Kok, 1995). The appearance of these patients contradicted previously held beliefs that transsexualism was rare among the Chinese (Tseng, 2003).

Although Western cultures recognize two gender categories, other cultures have a greater number of classifications. For example, in India, a third gender is known as the *hijra* (Nanda, 1985). Although most are biologically male, hijra are not considered to be male or female but to possess elements of both sexes. They usually dress as women and refer to themselves as female.

Hijra are found in different cultures and are considered a third gender, neither masculine nor feminine.

Maciej Dakowicz/Alamy Stock Photo

Similarly, in independent Samoa, males who are sexually attracted to men are referred to as *fa'afafine*, literally meaning "in the manner of a woman" (Vasey & Bartlett, 2007). Fa'afafine adults recall engaging as children in significantly more female-typical behaviour and significantly fewer male-typical behaviours (Bartlett & Vasey, 2006). Although some individuals report that parents attempted to force them to behave in culturally prescribed ways, others report that individuals were very tolerant of atypical gender choices. Overall, these results suggest that gender identity issues exist across cultures and that in some cases, a great deal of social tolerance exists for those who behave in a gender atypical fashion (Vasey & Bartlett, 2007).

Etiology

A number of theories explain the etiology of gender dysphoria, but virtually no empirical data support many of them. On the biological side, some hormonal data provide intriguing but nonspecific evidence for a biological contribution to the development of this disorder.

Psychosocial theories have examined the role of family, particularly parent–child relationships.

BIOLOGICAL THEORIES To date, little evidence suggests a genetic contribution to gender dysphoria. Neuroanatomical research has identified differences in the brains of men and women (Michel et al., 2001). One study found that the brains of male transsexuals were similar in size and shape to those of heterosexual women and unlike the brains of heterosexual men (Zhou et al., 1995). However, these findings have not been replicated and data from neuroanatomical and neurobiological studies remain contradictory and inconclusive.

A hormonal condition that may contribute to the development of gender dysphoria is *congenital adrenal hyperplasia* (CAH). Boys and girls with CAH are missing an enzyme necessary to make the hormones cortisol and aldosterone. As a result, the body produces too much of the male hormone androgen, causing early and inappropriate male sexual development in both sexes. At birth, girls with CAH have ambiguous genitalia, often appearing more male than female. As they grow, these girls develop male secondary sexual features such as a deep voice and facial hair. Boys begin puberty as early as 2 to 3 years of age.

In addition to physical differences, girls with CAH display more cross-gender role behaviours than girls without this condition (Berenbaum et al., 2000; Cohen-Bendahan et al., 2005; Zucker, 2004). They do become more feminine with age, but some adult women with CAH (particularly those with the most severe form) have less heterosexual interest and are less feminine than those with no hormonal disorder (Hines et al., 2004; Long et al., 2004). We still do not know whether CAH, or any other hormonal imbalance, leads to the development of gender dysphoria. We do know that this condition affects prenatal hormonal levels, the development of physical sex characteristics, and gender behaviours. Understanding CAH may help us understand the development of gender dysphoria in girls, but not in boys.

Ethics and Responsibility

For the past 20 years, efforts have been made to treat CAH before birth in an attempt to prevent the development of ambiguous sexual genitalia in females (Nimkarm & New, 2010). Because this disorder is a genetic condition, pregnant women whose fetus is at risk for CAH may be offered treatment with dexamethasone. When given prior to the ninth week of pregnancy and continued for a number of weeks, this steroid decreases the amount of androgen to which the fetus is exposed and may prevent genital ambiguity in affected females. Short-term follow-up data suggest that children exposed to dexamethasone before birth have normal growth and development (Hughes, 2006), but the data are few and long-term follow-up is not available. However, the amount of prenatal exposure to androgen also appears to have some effect on sexual orientation: Higher levels are associated with more masculine behaviours (Meyer-Bahlburg et al., 2008).

The practice of prenatal dexamethasone administration has led some *bioethicists* (researchers who study the ethical and moral implications of new medical discoveries) to question whether this drug might be used by parents or promoted by physicians to prevent homosexual or bisexual orientations in girls (Dreger et al., 2010). The implication of this controversy is that something is inherently wrong with people who do not have a heterosexual orientation (Dreger et al., 2010). These ethical issues will likely occupy researchers for many years to come. At this time, almost all involved agree that, for now, administration of dexamethasone for CAH should occur only in closely-monitored clinical trials with substantial long-term follow-up.

PSYCHOSOCIAL THEORIES Psychoanalysts postulate that parental rejection may play a role in the onset of gender dysphoria. For example, if parents really wanted a girl but

canadian FOCUS

Nature and Nurture in Gender Identity

Gender identity and gender identity disorders are multifaceted phenomena, which likely arise from complex interactions among genes and environmental events. The latter include things that take place in the womb, such as the exposure to intrauterine sex hormones by the developing fetus. The fact that learning experiences are insufficient to determine gender identity is underscored by the tragic case of a Winnipeg boy, originally named Bruce, who was raised as a girl. Bruce had an identical twin brother. When the twins were 8 months old, a doctor badly botched Bruce's circumcision, leaving Bruce with a charred stump of a penis. The distraught parents were persuaded by a leading sexologist, John Money, to raise Bruce as a girl. Money reasoned, erroneously as it turned out, that Bruce's gender identity could be changed from male to female simply as a result of raising Bruce in the female gender role, supplemented with female hormones and, during adolescence, by sexual reassignment surgery (e.g., surgically creating a vagina). The fact that Bruce had an identical twin brother provided a scientifically important case control; if gender identity was largely due to environmental influences such as being raised in a female gender role, then it should be possible to take two people with identical genes (i.e., Bruce and his twin) and to successfully raise one as a girl and one as a boy.

Accordingly, Bruce was renamed Brenda and for the next 13 years the family struggled to raise him as a girl. The results were disastrous. Even though he was named Brenda and wore dresses, he was clearly masculine in his appearance, interests, and behaviour, and he always felt that he was really a boy. His masculinity was clearly evident from an early age. Even in kindergarten there was a "rough-and-tumble rowdiness, an assertive, pressing dominance, and a complete lack of any demonstrable feminine interests" (Colapinto, 2000, p. 61). A female classmate came up to the kindergarten teacher and complained, "How come Brenda stands *up* when she goes to the bathroom?" No amount of coaxing from her mother could persuade Brenda to consistently sit down to urinate.

At age 11, Brenda continued to have clearly masculine interests; she had "marvelous plans for building tree houses, go-carts with CB radios, model gas airplanes . . . [and] appears to be more competitive and aggressive than her brother" (Colapinto, 2000, p. 112). Brenda had a very masculine gait, looked quite masculine, and was teased by the other children, who call her "cavewoman." Life for Brenda was miserable. She fought with boys who teased her. Brenda was ostracized, and had few friends apart from her twin brother.

Brenda steadfastly refused to have surgery to create a vagina, but complied with great reluctance to take the feminizing hormones. At age 14, Brenda was told of the botched operation, and shortly thereafter changed her name to David and began living in the male role. Later, David had reconstructive surgery to remove the breasts that had grown as a result of estrogen therapy, and had multiple operations to create an artificial penis and testicles. David also received testosterone injections to make his physique more masculine. David married and helped raise three adopted children, and worked for many years in a Winnipeg abattoir. The work was tough and physically demanding, but he enjoyed it. It is clear that years of socialization into the female gender role were unsuccessful in altering his gender identity.

David had survived many hardships throughout his troubled life, and had had thoughts of killing himself during his years as Brenda. Life as David seemed to be an improvement, but he remained prone to bouts of depression, and quite likely brooded about what had been done to him. And then a series of stressful events unfolded that proved too much for him; his twin brother died from an overdose of antidepressant medication, then his marriage fell apart and he was laid off from his job. David committed suicide in May 2004, at the age of 38.

Sources: CBC News Online (2004), Colapinto (2000, 2004), Diamond (1982), Diamond & Sigmundson (1997).

had a boy instead (Sharma, 2007), they may reject their son. That rejection may cause the boy to try to please the parent by behaving like a girl. Although parents who reinforce masculine or feminine behaviours increase the frequency of those behaviours, simple reinforcement alone does not appear to affect gender identity. One well-known case suggests that biology is stronger than environmental forces (see "Canadian Focus: Nature and Nurture in Gender Identity.")

Treatment

Few longitudinal studies of children with gender dysphoria have been conducted, but available evidence suggests that only a minority of children who originally receive this diagnosis continue to be distressed about their gender into adulthood (Zucker, 2008). In two follow-up studies conducted 10 to 15 years after the original diagnosis, between 12% and 27% of individuals were still classified as gender dysphoric (Drummond et al., 2008; Wallien & Cohen-Kettenis, 2008). In those studies, children who had the most severe symptoms of gender dysphoria were the ones still likely to have the disorder and most likely to have a homosexual or bisexual orientation. Among the adults who no longer had gender dysphoria, half of the boys and all of the girls had a heterosexual orientation (Wallien & Cohen-Kettenis, 2008).

Perhaps because the disorder is quite rare, no controlled trials for treatments of gender dysphoria have been conducted. Clinically, several different treatment approaches exist, some of which are available only in specialized clinics. The most common procedure for adults is surgical reassignment.

SEX REASSIGNMENT SURGERY Historically, treatment for adults with gender dysphoria attempted to change the person's social and sexual behaviours to match his or her biological sex. Currently, treatment focuses on helping adults live as their chosen gender identity, maximizing their psychological and social adjustment. The change to live as their chosen gender identity involves three phases: living as the desired gender, using hormone therapy, and undergoing sex reassignment surgery (Meyer et al., 2001b). Not every person who begins treatment completes the sex reassignment surgery phase.

In the first stage, the person lives in the new gender role for at least two years (Meyer et al., 2001b). The person dresses and socializes in a manner consistent with the desired gender role, allowing the person to examine how this change affects every aspect of life. This step is considered absolutely necessary for the treatment program. The second step is hormone therapy. Testosterone is given to biological females and estrogen to biological males, reducing unwanted secondary sex characteristics and leading to the secondary sexual characteristics of the preferred sex. The third and final phase is the actual surgery. For males transitioning to females, this includes surgical removal of the penis and the creation of a clitoris, labia, and artificial vagina. For females transitioning to males, it includes removal of the breasts, vagina, and uterus, the formation of a scrotum and testicular prostheses, and the creation of a neophallus (an artificial penis). The goal is to try to preserve sexual functioning in order to achieve optimal quality of life (Lawrence, 2003).

Compared with treatments for other psychological disorders, sex reassignment surgery is an extensive and radical procedure (Smith et al., 2005). Although early studies suggested that a percentage of those who had surgery were not satisfied with the results, more recent and long-term follow-up data indicate that the outcome has become more positive (Landén et al., 1999). Sex reassignment surgery can (but will not always) eliminate gender dysphoria (Lawrence, 2003; Smith et al., 2005), improve body satisfaction and interpersonal relationships, and reduce anxiety and depression (Smith et al., 2001, 2005; Weyers et al., 2008). In one long-term follow-up study (Weyers et al., 2008), participants described some difficulties with sexual arousal, lubrication, and pain. Across different studies, more than 95% of patients reported satisfaction with sex reassignment surgery (Lawrence, 2003; Smith et al., 2005). A few patients were dissatisfied; most commonly, those individuals lacked family support or had additional psychological disorders affecting overall functioning (Eldh et al., 1997; Landén et al., 1998).

Some adolescents with gender dysphoria seek sex reassignment surgery, and it is reasonable to question whether adolescents can make such an irreversible decision. Early sex reassignment surgery may prevent gender dysphoria during adolescence (Delemarre-van de Waal & Cohen-Kettenis, 2006), and the physical outcome is more satisfactory when secondary sex characteristics have not yet developed. However, such surgery requires absolute certainty because the intervention is nonreversible. Only a small number of adolescents receive sex reassignment therapy, and many questions remain about the procedure, including at what age the surgery should occur and whether those who have surgery continue to feel positively about the procedure as adults.

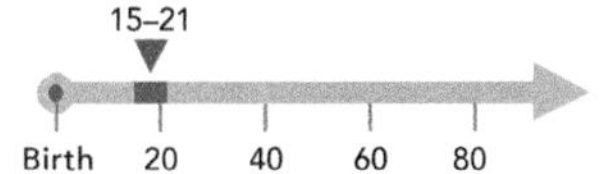

Adolescents with gender dysphoria sometimes seek sex reassignment surgery, but it is important to consider if this type of decision can be made at this stage of cognitive development.

PSYCHOLOGICAL TREATMENT No randomized controlled trials of psychosocial interventions have been conducted. In the past, behavioural, psychoanalytic, and eclectic approaches attempted to alter the child's perception of her or his gender with her or his biological sex by focusing attention and reinforcement on same-sex activities and friendships, spending time with the same-sex parent, and having play dates with same-sex peers (Bradley & Zucker, 1997). Same-gender behaviours were rewarded (prizes given), and cross-gender behaviours were punished (prizes removed) (Rekers & Lovaas, 1974; Rekers & Mead, 1979; Rekers et al., 1974). The interventions were reported to be efficacious for some children, but these approaches have been criticized for forcing specific gender stereotypes (i.e., stereotypical masculine behaviours) (Bryant, 2006) onto young children, and they have fallen out of use.

CONCEPT check

- Gender dysphoria, sometimes called *transsexualism* in adults, is the sense that one's biological sex does not match one's gender identity.
- The disorder appears to be more common in males than females among adults and can have a pervasive effect on all aspects of functioning.
- The cause of gender dysphoria is unknown, but it may be related to hormonal imbalances that begin prenatally.
- Sex reassignment surgery matches the person's physical anatomy with his or her gender identity.

critical thinking question Children with the most severe symptoms of gender dysphoria may continue to have gender dysphoria as an adult, but this outcome occurs in a minority of people with this disorder. Furthermore, the distress associated with gender dysphoria is often that of the parent, not the child. Applying what you know about diagnosis and treatment, would you recommend treatment of a child who has gender dysphoria symptoms to a parent?

Sexual Dysfunctions

As we discussed in the opening section of this chapter, many factors contribute to sexual performance, including age, sex, and culture. Therefore, the diagnostic criteria for all **sexual dysfunctions** consist of an absence or an impairment of some aspect of sexual response *that causes significant distress or functional impairment and includes consideration of age, sex, and culture.* In some instances, the prevalence of a disorder changes when these factors are considered. In addition, a person's life circumstances, such as physical illness or physical separation from the sexual partner, must be considered when determining the presence or absence of a sexual dysfunction. With these issues in mind, we turn our attention to disorders of sexual functioning, which are classified as disorders of sexual desire, sexual arousal, orgasm, and pain.

Sexual Interest/Desire Disorders

8.3 Recognize that men and women exhibit different patterns of sexual behaviour, and identify the role of gender in the definition and development of sexual dysfunction.

Sexual desire is an interest in sexual activity or objects, or wishes to engage in sexual activity. Disorders of sexual desire/arousal are indicated by a diminished or absent interest in sexual activity and may include *male hypoactive sexual desire disorder*, *female sexual interest/arousal disorder*, and *erectile disorder*.

Male hypoactive sexual desire disorder is defined as persistently or recurrently deficient or absent sexual/erotic thoughts or fantasies and desire for sexual activity

criteria for
Sexual Interest/Desire Disorders
DSM-5

Male Hypoactive Sexual Desire Disorder

A. Persistently or recurrently deficient (or absent) sexual/erotic thoughts or fantasies and desire for sexual activity. The judgment of deficiency is made by the clinician, taking into account factors that affect sexual functioning, such as age and general and sociocultural contexts of the individual's life.

B. The symptoms in Criterion A have persisted for a minimum duration of approximately 6 months.

C. The symptoms in Criterion A cause clinically significant distress in the individual.

D. The sexual dysfunction is not better explained by a nonsexual mental disorder or as a consequence of severe relationship distress or other significant stressors and is not attributable to these effects of a substance/medication or another medical condition.

Female Sexual Interest/Arousal Disorder

A. Lack of, or significantly reduced, sexual interest/arousal, as manifested by at least three of the following:
1. Absent/reduced interest in sexual activity.
2. Absent/reduced sexual/erotic thoughts or fantasies.
3. No/reduced initiation of sexual activity, and typically unreceptive to a partner's attempts to initiate.
4. Absent/reduced sexual excitement/pleasure during sexual activity in almost all or all (approximately 75%–100%) sexual encounters (in identified situational contexts or, if generalized, in all contexts).
5. Absent/reduced sexual interest/arousal in response to any internal or external sexual/erotic cues (e.g., written, verbal, visual).
6. Absent/reduced genital or nongenital sensations during sexual activity in almost all or all (approximately 75%–100%) sexual encounters (in identified situational contexts or, if generalized, in all contexts).

B. The symptoms in Criterion A have persisted for a minimum duration of approximately 6 months.

C. The symptoms in Criterion A cause clinically significant distress in the individual.

D. The sexual dysfunction is not better explained by a nonsexual mental disorder or as a consequence of severe relationship distress (e.g., partner violence) or other significant stressors and is not attributable to the effects of a substance/medication or another medical condition.

Erectile Disorder

A. At least one of the three following symptoms must be experienced on almost all or all (approximately 75%–100%) occasions of sexual activity (in identified situational contexts or, if generalized, in all contexts):
1. Marked difficulty in obtaining an erection during sexual activity.
2. Marked difficulty in maintaining an erection until the completion of sexual activity.
3. Marked decrease in erectile rigidity.

B. The symptoms in Criterion A have persisted for a minimum duration of approximately 6 months.

C. The symptoms in Criterion A cause clinically significant distress in the individual.

D. The sexual dysfunction is not better explained by a nonsexual mental disorder or as a consequence of severe relationship distress or other significant stressors and is not attributable to the effects of a substance/medication or another medical condition.

(APA, 2013) (see "DSM-5: Sexual Desire Disorders"). Factors often associated with decreased sexual desire include low sexual satisfaction, the presence of another sexual dysfunction (such as pain), negative thoughts about sexuality, and other forms of psychological distress such as depression, anxiety, and couple distress (Trudel et al., 2001).

Alice is just not interested in sex anymore. She loves her husband; they have been married for 25 years and have three children, ages 20, 18, and 15. Alice denies feeling depressed and has no history of sexual abuse. She is still menstruating regularly, so hormonal changes are not likely. Alice loves her husband, Rob, but she no longer wants an intimate relationship with him. Rob is frustrated and, at times, angry.

Female sexual interest/arousal disorder is defined as significantly reduced, or absent, sexual interest/arousal as indicated by reduced interest in sexual activity or lack of sexual excitement/pleasure/response during sexual activity. As noted by University of British Columbia sexologist Rosemary Basson, symptoms can be primarily psychological or primarily physiological (Basson et al., 2003). When primarily psychological, the condition is sometimes called *subjective sexual arousal disorder.* In these cases, a physical response to sexual stimulation (e.g., vaginal lubrication) but no subjective feeling of sexual excitement or sexual pleasure may occur. In contrast, when primarily physiological (also called *genital sexual arousal disorder*), subjective feelings of sexual desire but no physiological response may occur. The third subgroup, *combined sexual arousal disorder*, includes lack of both subjective and physiological response. Female sexual interest/arousal disorder is a controversial diagnosis, and as defined in DSM-5, the prevalence is unknown. Some data suggest that low sexual interest is commonly reported in gynecological settings—up to 75% of women seeking routine care in one sample (Nusbaum et al., 2000).

Approximately 15% of men and 30% of women ages 19 to 59 experience dissatisfaction with their sexual desire (Laumann et al., 1999). Across cultures, this disorder is more frequent in women than men. However, because men and women may have different sexual goals and define sexual desire differently, we must be careful not to overinterpret these data. Patterns of male sexuality, for example, are not necessarily the best standard by which to compare the behaviours of females. Also, the media often reports that inappropriate behaviour on the part of well-known celebrities is the result of sexual addiction or hypersexuality (see "Research Hot Topic—Sexual Addiction and Hypersexual Disorder").

Erectile disorder is a common male sexual dysfunction known also as *erectile dysfunction* (formerly *impotence*). It is the repeated failure to obtain or maintain erections during partnered sexual activities (APA, 2013). An important element of this definition is the word *repeated.* Most men experience an occasional episode of erectile

research HOT topic

Sexual Addiction and Hypersexual Disorder

Jesse James and David Duchovny are only two among a number of recent celebrities who have announced that they have been treated for sexual addiction. This term is now widely used to explain sexual behaviour associated with progressive risk taking, loss of control, and significant psychosocial consequences such as discovery of infidelity by one's spouse. Although widely criticized in the media, some empirical support for sex as an addictive or dependency syndrome exists (Kafka, 2010). Self-identified sexual addicts describe withdrawal symptoms, unsuccessful attempts to control or reduce their behaviour, and engaging in the behaviour longer than they intended (Wines, 1997). However, the topic remains confusing because it is unclear whether this behaviour (1) meets criteria for an addiction, (2) is a symptom of an underlying problem, or (3) merely represents a bad decisions that often lead to significant distress for the marital partner (Levine, 2010; Steffens & Rennie, 2006).

Hypersexual disorder is a proposed sexual dysfunction characterized by increasing frequency and intensity of sexually-motivated fantasies, arousal, urges, and behaviours along with an impulsivity component (Kafka, 2010). Behaviours that are consistently associated with hypersexual disorder include excessive behaviours concerning masturbation, seeking out and viewing pornography, sexual behaviour with consenting adults, and cybersex, all of which can have significant adverse effects. Negative outcomes can include unplanned pregnancies, relationship breakups, marital separation and divorce, and the risk of sexually transmitted diseases including HIV. Attempting to empirically define hypersexual behaviour remains a challenge for researchers, and much more research is needed to understand its clinical presentation, etiology, and course and prognosis. As researchers address these questions, the scientific validity of this proposed disorder will be confirmed or disproved, leading to improved understanding of another aspect of sexual behaviour.

Normal Behaviour Case Study

Stress and Alcohol Induced Diminished Performance

→ Barry had had a really stressful week at school. He was in graduate school, and it was time for his dissertation proposal—a very important oral examination. He found that preparing the oral proposal took longer than he had expected. He stayed up all night preparing just to be sure he would be ready, and after the presentation, he was pretty confident that things had gone well. He wanted only to sleep, but it was Friday night and his wife's birthday. He had promised her dinner at a romantic restaurant, and he did not want to disappoint. Sarah looked beautiful, and he felt so lucky to be in love with such a beautiful woman. They drank a bottle of champagne to celebrate, and after dinner, they walked home. Sarah was giving him all the signals that she wanted a night of romance and cognitively; so did Barry. But his body wasn't responding. No matter how hard he concentrated, he just could not achieve an erection. Sarah knew he was stressed and that he had had quite a bit of alcohol. When she realized what was happening, she pulled him close and told him they should just get some sleep. Although Barry was worried that something was wrong with him, the next time they had the chance to be together, he was rested and sober and did not have any problem achieving an erection.

Abnormal Behaviour Case Study

Erectile Dysfunction

→ Jack was always anxious around girls. He dated a little in high school but was always nervous, stumbling over his words, acting clumsy, and seeming to always make the wrong move. He had hoped the anxiety would go away as he grew older, but it did not. Instead, it seemed to get worse. The stakes got higher. In high school, the pressure to have sex was not so great, but in university it seemed to be everywhere. The girls dressed differently, the guys were always talking about their latest conquest, and Jack felt totally alone. He could barely talk to a woman, let alone think about engaging in sex. His first attempt at sexual intercourse was a failure—he was so nervous, he was unable to achieve a full erection. The girl pretended it did not matter, but she no longer answered his telephone calls. Then he decided to try a prostitute. He thought if he did not know the woman, he might not be so nervous. But he was wrong—he was nervous and the prostitute was impatient. She kept telling him to "hurry up" and "you only paid for an hour, honey, don't you want to use it?" His anxiety was so overwhelming, he just walked out. He tried with a different prostitute and the same thing happened—despite his cognitive desire, he was unable to achieve an erection. Then he got drunk—alcohol always seemed to make him less nervous in social situations, so maybe it would help with sex. But that did not help either; the alcohol made things worse. Now, every time he finds a woman who is sexually attractive, he avoids any interaction with her. He feels that depression and loneliness are better than the humiliation of not being able to perform sexually.

dysfunction, usually caused by fatigue, stress, or anxiety. The diagnosis is not given unless there is consistent inability to achieve or maintain an erection or there is marked decrease in erectile rigidity. Significant distress or interpersonal difficulty must also occur.

Orgasmic Disorders

Another group of sexual dysfunctions include the orgasmic disorders: female orgasmic disorder, delayed ejaculation, and premature ejaculation (see "DSM-5: Orgasmic Disorders"). **Delayed ejaculation**, sometimes called *retarded ejaculation*, is a marked delay in or inability to achieve ejaculation despite adequate sexual stimulation. This disorder is not as common as premature ejaculation. Some men might consider delayed ejaculation to be an advantage as it could increase the sexual pleasure of a partner. In these cases, a diagnosis may not be warranted because there would not be any distress or functional impairment. However, some men who suffer from delayed ejaculation report frustration, distress, and sometimes pain (Brotto & Klein, 2007).

criteria for
Orgasmic Disorders DSM-5

Delayed Ejaculation

A. Either of the following symptoms must be experienced on almost all or all occasions (approximately 75%–100%) of partnered sexual activity (in identified situational contexts or, if generalized, in all contexts), and without the individual desiring delay:
 1. Marked delay in ejaculation
 2. Marked infrequency or absence of ejaculation.

B. The symptoms in Criterion A have persisted for a minimum duration of approximately 6 months.

C. The symptoms in Criterion A cause clinically significant distress in the individual.

D. The sexual dysfunction is not better explained by a nonsexual mental disorder or as a consequence of severe relationship distress or other significant stressors and is not attributable to the effects of a substance/medication or another medical condition.

Female Orgasmic Disorder

A. Presence of either of the following symptoms and experienced on almost all or all (approximately 75%–100%) occasions of sexual activity (in identified situational contexts or, if generalized, in all contexts):
 1. Marked delay in, marked infrequency of, or absence of orgasm.
 2. Markedly reduced intensity of orgasmic sensations.

B. The symptoms in Criterion A have persisted for a minimum duration of approximately 6 months.

C. The symptoms in Criterion A cause clinically significant distress in the individual.

D. The sexual dysfunction is not better explained by a nonsexual mental disorder or as a consequence of severe relationship distress (e.g., partner violence) or other significant stressors and is not attributable to the effects of a substance/medication or another medical condition.

Female orgasmic disorder is defined as difficulty experiencing orgasm or markedly reduced intensity of orgasmic sensations. Sometimes called *anorgasmia*, the symptoms must occur on all or almost all sexual activity experiences. Before making a diagnosis, it is necessary to consider age, adequacy of sexual stimulation, and sexual experience. Unlike most other sexual disorders, female orgasmic disorder is most common among younger women (Laumann et al., 1999).

Alice's husband, Brian, is a senior stockbroker in a major brokerage house, and he is working 16 hours a day. He is stressed and anxious much of the time. Brian loves Alice but is frustrated that their sex life has not been good for some time. About six months ago, Brian had a heart attack and afterward had difficulty with sexual performance. Although he still has sufficient sexual desire, once he initiates sexual activity, he worries that he is straining his heart. Added to this, Alice is not responsive when they do have intercourse, so he feels pressure to "get it over with." Now he has developed a pattern of premature ejaculation.

Sometimes known as *rapid ejaculation* (see "Real Science, Real Life: Michael—Treatment of Sexual Dysfunction"), **premature (early) ejaculation** is a common male dysfunction and, depending on the definition, may affect approximately 30% of men

criteria for
Premature (Early) Ejaculation DSM-5

A. A persistent or recurrent pattern of ejaculation occurring during partnered sexual activity within approximately 1 minute following vaginal penetration and before the individual wishes it.

Note: Although the diagnosis of premature (early) ejaculation may be applied to individuals engaged in nonvaginal sexual activities, specific duration criteria have not been established for these activities.

B. The symptom in Criterion A must have been present for at least 6 months and must be experienced on almost all or all (approximately 75%–100%) occasions of sexual activity (in identified situational contexts or, if generalized, in all contexts).

C. The symptom in Criterion A causes clinically significant distress in the individual.

D. The sexual dysfunction is not better explained by a nonsexual mental disorder or as a consequence of severe relationship distress or other significant stressors and is not attributable to the effects of a substance/medication or another medical condition.

(Laumann et al., 1999). The process of ejaculation consists of four phases. *Erection*, or penile tumescence, is the first phase and is controlled by the parasympathetic nervous system. The second phase is *emission*, in which semen is collected and transported in preparation for the third stage, *ejaculation*, which is the release of seminal fluids from the penis. This occurs when signals from nerves in the urethra reach the spinal cord and cause a reflex response. The sympathetic and somatic branches of the nervous system (see Chapter 2) are responsible for Stages 2 and 3. The final stage, *orgasm*, is the subjective feeling of pleasure associated with ejaculation and is believed to be a cortical (brain) experience (Metz et al., 1997).

Premature ejaculation is defined as ejaculation during sexual activity with a partner that occurs within about one minute after vaginal penetration and before the individual wishes it (APA, 2013). Among self-identified premature ejaculators, 90% ejaculated within one minute of vaginal insertion and 80% ejaculated within 30 seconds (Waldinger, 2002). In contrast, other samples of men who described themselves as premature ejaculators reported ejaculation that occurred before vaginal insertion or as long as 10 minutes after insertion, although most (79%) reported ejaculation ranging from before insertion to two minutes after penetration (Symonds et al., 2003).

A different definition involves an inability to inhibit ejaculation long enough for a partner to reach orgasm 50% of the time (Masters & Johnson, 1970). The advantage of this definition is that it is not tied to a specific number of minutes, but the disadvantage is that it depends on the partner's sexual response (Metz et al., 1997). This definition acknowledges that often sexual dysfunction may be a dysfunction of the couple, not of a single person, such as we saw earlier in the case of Brian and Alice.

Still other researchers (e.g., Kaplan, 1974) define premature ejaculation as simply a lack of control over ejaculation. To come to some consensus, the International Society for Sexual Medicine held a meeting of experts in the field. They agreed on the following definition of premature ejaculation for heterosexual males: "always or nearly always occurring before or within one minute of vaginal penetration, and the inability to delay ejaculation on all or nearly all vaginal penetrations, and negative personal consequences such as distress, bother, frustration and/or the avoidance of sexual intimacy" (McMahon et al., 2008, p. 347). As can be seen, the majority of research in this area has been conducted with heterosexual couples. More work is required to determine the extent to which patterns of dysfunction are similar in homosexual or bisexual individuals.

real SCIENCE real LIFE

Michael—Treatment of Sexual Dysfunction

THE PATIENT

Michael is 21 years old. His first real girlfriend just broke up with him, and he is sure it is because of his inadequate sexual performance. Michael is very shy around girls, and he admits that he does not even know how to talk to them. Furthermore, he has had few sexual experiences. He lost his virginity in the backseat of a car, and he said, "It was over before I knew it."

THE PROBLEM

Until now, Michael's sexual experience consisted of visits to local prostitutes during which he always felt rushed both by the woman and by the thought that he might get caught in a police raid. With his first real girlfriend, he often ejaculated before intromission. His girlfriend kept saying that it did not matter, but he knew that it did. His friends told him to think about baseball when having sex in an effort to delay ejaculation, but that did not work. Michael is desperate to get help.

THE TREATMENT

The psychologist knows that premature ejaculation can be treated by the stop-squeeze technique, but Michael does not have a partner. The therapist begins by explaining the rationale to Michael and educates him about the normal male sexual response cycle and the four-step process of ejaculation. This is important because Michael needs to learn to recognize the plateau phase in order to implement the procedure correctly. Once Michael understands these biological processes, the therapist teaches him to use the procedure himself through masturbation. In session, the therapist discusses the procedure and uses drawings to show Michael where and when to squeeze. The therapist develops a self-monitoring sheet so that Michael can track his progress. Michael is instructed to practise the procedure each day, trying to lengthen the time between his initial erection and ejaculation.

At each treatment session, Michael reports on his progress. In session, the therapist focuses on social skills training, particularly heterosocial interactions and dating skills. As Michael's confidence grows, he is able to invite a girl to a movie. He does not attempt to engage in a sexual relationship at once, but waits until he feels very comfortable. He continues to practise the stop-squeeze technique and does not visit any prostitutes in order to not impede his progress.

THE TREATMENT OUTCOME

After three months of dating, Michael and his girlfriend become sexually intimate. Michael reports that the first time was "not very long"—only about three minutes after intromission. His girlfriend attributed it to the fact that they had had a lot of wine that evening and told him not to worry. Because he did not feel rejected, Michael was able to try again. At the end of treatment, Michael is engaging in vaginal intercourse for about five minutes before ejaculation. He also has increased confidence in his ability to interact socially, not just sexually, with women.

Premature ejaculation is considered *primary* when a man has suffered from this condition since his first sexual encounter. The preceding definition of premature ejaculation was limited to primary (or lifelong) premature ejaculation. *Secondary* premature ejaculation is the term used when a man initially had no difficulty controlling ejaculation but now ejaculates prematurely (such as Brian). Among men with secondary premature ejaculation, 75% have a physical disease that might account for it, while the other 25% do not have a physical disorder but do report relationship problems (Metz et al., 1997).

Genito-pelvic pain/penetration disorder

This disorder consists of persistent or recurrent difficulties with (a) vaginal penetration during intercourse, (b) vulvovaginal or pelvic pain during intercourse, (c) fear or anxiety about pain during vaginal penetration, or (d) tension/tightening of the pelvic floor muscles (see "DSM-5: Genito-Pelvic Pain/Penetration Disorder").

Among women seeking routine gynecological care, 72% report pain from sexual activity (Nusbaum et al., 2000). Even minimal attempts at sexual intercourse can result in dyspareunia, leading to severe distress and avoidance of sexual behaviour. Although the diagnostic criteria for **genito-pelvic pain/penetration disorder** refer to pain in the

criteria for
Genito-Pelvic Pain/Penetration Disorder DSM-5

A. Persistent or recurrent difficulties with one (or more) of the following:
  1. Vaginal penetration during intercourse.
  2. Marked vulvovaginal or pelvic pain during vaginal intercourse or penetration attempts.
  3. Marked fear or anxiety about vulvovaginal or pelvic pain in anticipation of, during, or as a result of vaginal penetration.
  4. Marked tensing or tightening of the pelvic floor muscles during attempted vaginal penetration.

B. The symptoms in Criterion A have persisted for a minimum duration of approximately 6 months.

C. The symptoms in Criterion A cause clinically significant distress in the individual.

D. The sexual dysfunction is not better explained by a nonsexual mental disorder or as a consequence of a severe relationship distress (e.g., partner violence) or other significant stressors and is not attributable to the effects of a substance/medication or another medical condition.

vaginal or pelvic region, some men also report pain during sexual intercourse. Among men in Western countries, 3% to 5% report the presence of dysparenia, which is pain during intercourse (Laumann et al., 2005). Among gay men, 14% suffer frequent and severe pain during receptive anal sex, a condition sometimes known as *anodyspareunia* (Damon & Simon Rosser, 2005).

Marianne is in love with Mateo. After several months of dating, they want to become sexually intimate. They have tried on several occasions, but every time, Marianne feels her vaginal muscles contract and she cries out in pain. It is not just being physically intimate with Mateo that causes pain. She has never been able to insert a tampon into her vagina. The physician wants to perform an internal exam to rule out the presence of infection, which could cause pain. Although he tried to insert a speculum, Marianne cried out and asked to discontinue the examination.

Marianne's pain is sometimes called **vaginismus**, unwanted involuntary spasms of the vaginal muscles that interfere with intercourse or vaginal insertion. As with other categories of sexual pain disorder, few empirical studies have addressed the validity of this diagnosis. Subjective experience of a vaginal spasm does not always correlate with actual spasms measured during gynecological examination (Reissing et al., 2004), indicating the importance of psychological factors in this diagnosis. Furthermore, most women who report vaginismus also report the presence of dyspareunia (de Kruiff et al., 2000).

Subtypes

Any of the sexual dysfunctions may be classified according to the following dimensions: lifelong (always existed) vs. acquired (develops only after a period of normal functioning), generalized (sexual difficulties that are not limited to certain types of stimulation, situations, or partners) vs. situational (only in certain situations, partners or types of stimulation), and due to psychological factors vs. due to combined factors (psychological plus medical).

Functional Impairment

Any sexual dysfunction can lead to dissatisfaction. Depending on the particular complaint, between 65% and 87% of people with a sexual dysfunction report dissatisfaction (Fugl-Meyer & Sjögren Fugl-Meyer, 1999). Furthermore, sexual difficulties between partners are common. Among men with erectile disorder, lower sexual desire affected 60% and lack of sexual arousal affected 44% of their partners (Sjögren Fugl-Meyer & Fugl-Meyer, 2002). In addition, the existence of a sexual dysfunction, whether in one's partner or oneself, affects both individuals' sexual well-being. However, sexual disorders may sometimes affect sexual functioning without impacting overall functioning. Men who report premature ejaculation indicate that fulfilling a partner's need is an important part of their own sexual satisfaction (Rowland et al., 2004). While their disorder may affect their own self-esteem and ongoing sexual relationship, it does not always impact their overall relationship (Byers & Grenier, 2003). In one study, only 6% of men with premature ejaculation reported that they declined an opportunity for sexual intercourse because of their problem, and even this occurred only rarely (Grenier & Byers, 2001).

Reflecting society's reluctance to talk about sex is the fact that less than 19% of adults with sexual dysfunctions have ever sought professional help (Moreira et al., 2005). Even when the problem was frequent, 36% did not seek any advice. Among those who did, 55% sought support from family or friends, 19% went to media sources, and 32% sought medical advice (Nicolosi et al., 2006). When asked why they did not consult a professional, 72% said that they did not consider the behaviour to be a problem, 54% did not think it was a medical problem, 23% were embarrassed to talk about it, and 12% did not have access to medical care. These data, once again, illustrate two important points. First, what one person considers a problem is not necessarily a problem for someone else. Second, even people who are frequently bothered by sexual dysfunctions may not realize that the problem can be treated or are reluctant to discuss it with a professional.

Epidemiology

Tables 8.1 and 8.2 illustrate the prevalence of common sexual difficulties in men and women. According to data in Tables 8.1 and 8.2, the presence of some sexual dysfunctions

TABLE 8.1
Prevalence (%) of Sexual Difficulties in Men Aged 18 to 59

	Age			
Sexual Difficulty	18–29	30–39	40–49	50–59
Lacks interest in sex	14	13	15	17
Is unable to achieve orgasm	7	7	9	9
Climaxes too early	30	32	28	31
Finds sex not pleasurable	10	8	9	6
Is anxious about performance	19	17	19	14
Has trouble maintaining or achieving an erection	7	9	11	18

Sources: Brotto, L. A., & Klein, C. (2007). Sexual and gender identity disorders. In M. Hersen, S. M. Turner, & D. C. Beidel (Eds.). *Adult psychopathology and diagnosis* (6th ed.) (pp. 504–570). New York: John Wiley and Sons; Laumann, E. O., Paik, A., & Rosen, R. C. (1999). Sexual dysfunction in the United States. *The Journal of the American Medical Association, 281*, 537–544.

TABLE 8.2

Prevalence (%) of Sexual Difficulties in Women Aged 18 to 59

	Age			
Sexual Difficulty	**18–29**	**30–39**	**40–49**	**50–59**
Lacks interest in sex	32	32	30	27
Is unable to achieve orgasm	26	28	22	23
Experiences pain during sex	21	15	13	8
Finds sex not pleasurable	27	24	17	17
Is anxious about performance	16	11	11	6
Has trouble lubricating	19	18	21	27

Sources: Brotto, L. A., & Klein, C. (2007). Sexual and gender identity disorders. In M. Hersen, S. M. Turner, & D. C. Beidel (Eds.). *Adult psychopathology and diagnosis* (6th ed.) (pp. 504–570). New York: John Wiley and Sons; Laumann, E. O., Paik, A., & Rosen, R. C. (1999). Sexual dysfunction in the United States. *The Journal of the American Medical Association, 281*, 537–544.

increases with age. Problems with erectile dysfunction in men and difficulty with vaginal lubrication in women appear to become more prevalent with increasing age (Fugl-Meyer & Sjögren Fugl-Meyer, 1999; Laumann et al., 1999).

Sex, Race, and Ethnicity

Sexual dysfunctions occur across race and ethnicity. In the Global Study of Sexual Attitudes and Behaviours, which assessed 27 500 adults between the ages of 40 and 80 in 29 countries, 28% of the men and 39% of the women reported ever having a sexual dysfunction (Nicolosi et al., 2004). Among men, 28% had at least one sexual dysfunction; premature ejaculation was most common (14%), followed by erectile difficulties (10%) (Nicolosi et al., 2004). Among women, 39% had at least one sexual problem; lack of sexual interest was most common (21%), with 16% reporting inability to achieve orgasm and 16% reporting vaginal lubrication difficulties. Across cultures, prevalence of erectile dysfunction is higher in Eastern Asia and Southeastern Asia (27.1% and 28.1%) than in Western countries. Men in Southeastern Asia also had higher prevalence of retarded ejaculation. Similarly, women from Southeast Asia had the highest prevalence of female orgasmic disorder (41.2%) (Laumann et al., 2005).

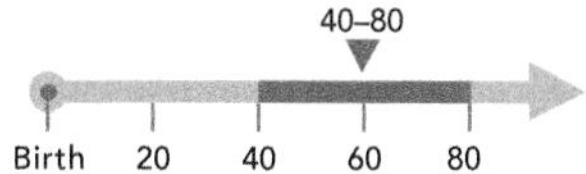

Sexual dysfunctions are common at all ages, although the specific disorder varies by age.

Developmental Factors

Few epidemiological data on the prevalence of sexual dysfunctions among young adults are available; most studies have focused on various sexual practices and risky sexual behaviours such as those that might lead to HIV infection. The few available data indicate that premature ejaculation is the most common complaint among adolescent and young adult men. This problem is usually the result of limited sexual experience or feelings of fear, guilt, or anxiety accompanying sexual activity (Seftel & Althof, 2000). In another sample, problems with low sexual desire were reported by 7% and 16% of 30-year-old men and women, respectively (Ernst et al., 1993).

Etiology

8.4 Understand the biological and psychological complexities involved in the etiology and treatment of sexual dysfunction.

Some sexual dysfunctions are related to medical conditions, and a physical examination is necessary to rule out physical causes. In addition, medications for physical disorders such as hypertension and for psychological disorders such as depression may lead to sexual dysfunction, as can the use of illicit drugs.

BIOLOGICAL FACTORS Biological conditions may affect sexual desire. Hormonal imbalances, such as hypothyroidism and hypogonadism (Maurice, 2005), can occur at any age and may decrease sexual interest directly by lowering the amount of sex hormones in the body. These conditions may also function indirectly by causing negative mood states, which in turn decrease sexual desire. Other hormonal imbalances are age related. Menopausal changes in women reduce estrogen, which affects vaginal lubrication and vaginal tissue elasticity, which in turn results in discomfort and possibly dyspareunia. In men, testosterone levels decrease with age (beginning in the 30s and 40s). How this decline decreases sexual desire and performance is unclear (Isidori et al., 2005), but decreases in testosterone can lower sexual desire and produce erectile dysfunction.

Physical disorders, such as cardiovascular disease, hypertension, diabetes, kidney failure, and cancer, can decrease sexual desire or performance. Among men treated for diabetes, 28% had erectile dysfunction (Feldman et al., 1994). Men who have had surgery for prostate cancer may subsequently suffer from erectile dysfunction (Stanford et al., 2000). Alternatively, physical illness may impair sexual arousal indirectly by causing psychological distress, which may in turn decrease desire.

Androgens contribute to feelings of sexual desire in women as well as in men, although their specific effect on female sexual functioning is not yet known (Brotto & Klein, 2007). Women who have had their ovaries removed have lower levels of androgens, and this can decrease sexual desire. In addition, pelvic surgery, chemotherapy, and radiation treatment have been associated with dyspareunia, vaginal dryness, and hypoactive sexual desire (Amsterdam et al., 2006).

Alcohol and drugs can create temporary sexual dysfunction, including premature ejaculation and delayed ejaculation in men and orgasmic disorders in men and women. Drugs that block dopamine receptors or serotonin reuptake in the brain can also delay ejaculation (Metz et al., 1997; Waldinger, 2002). Antidepressant medications, such as the selective serotonin reuptake inhibitors (SSRIs), improve mood but produce significant sexual side effects (Ferguson, 2001). They decrease physical response, inhibit the ability to achieve orgasm, and retard ejaculation in males, although they may improve psychological desire or arousal (see "Biological Treatments" later in this chapter).

PSYCHOSOCIAL FACTORS Negative emotional states such as depression may be associated with sexual dysfunction. University women who were depressed were more likely than nondepressed women to report difficulties with sexual arousal, inability to achieve orgasm, and painful intercourse (e.g., Cyranowski et al., 2004; Frohlich & Meston, 2002). In addition, they reported less satisfaction with their sexual relationship and less pleasure during sexual activity. Among normally aging men (ages 40 to 70), depression and erectile dysfunction were strongly correlated, and this effect was independent of aging, health status, medication use, and hormones (Araujo et al., 1998). It is unclear whether low sexual desire is a cause or a result of depression—and the relationship may be different for different people.

Behaviour theorists and sex therapists (Masters & Johnson, 1970) propose that anxiety and stress play a role in sexual dysfunction because both anxiety and premature ejaculation are associated with the sympathetic nervous system. Performance anxiety appears to be a major cause of erectile dysfunction and can cause other sexual dysfunctions as well. If a man experiences temporary dysfunction as a result of alcohol, stress, or anxiety, the temporary problem may become a concern, and erectile dysfunction may become a self-fulfilling prophecy. Sex theorists also suggest that premature ejaculation results from conditioning experiences involving the need to ejaculate quickly, such as hurried sexual contacts in parked cars (see "Real Science, Real Life: Michael—Treatment of Sexual Dysfunction" earlier in this chapter), sex with prostitutes, and engagement with sexual partners with whom there is a lack of intimacy (Metz et al., 1997). Although such patterns are sometimes present in the history of men with premature ejaculation, few empirical data address this issue (Grenier & Byers, 2001).

Factors such as couple distress or negative life events may result in temporary changes in sexual functioning in both sexes (Bancroft et al., 2003). Environmental events such as sexual assault may result in cases of genito-pelvic pain/penetration disorder (Weijmar Schultz & Van de Wiel, 2005). Such dysfunctions do not indicate permanent changes in biological functioning, in contrast to those caused by aging.

Treatment

It is unfortunate that some people who are distressed by their sexual functioning never seek treatment because of ignorance or embarrassment. Many treatments are available with documented efficacy for improving sexual functioning.

BIOLOGICAL TREATMENTS Because low levels of certain hormones, particularly testosterone, may affect sexual functioning, physicians may prescribe testosterone replacement therapy. Available as an injection, patch, or gel, replacement therapy is efficacious for men with low testosterone and sexual desire (Isidori et al., 2005). Testosterone patches may also improve sexual desire and satisfaction among women who have undergone *hysterectomy* (removal of the uterus) or *oophorectomy* (removal of the ovaries) (Braunstein et al., 2005; Buster et al., 2005; Kingsberg, 2007; Shiren et al., 2000).

The relationship between depression and sexual functioning is complicated. Depression can decrease sexual desire. As noted earlier, some antidepressants that improve depressed mood (e.g., SSRIs) increase sexual *desire* but impair sexual *performance* by delaying ejaculation and inhibiting orgasm. The side effect of delayed ejaculation means that some men may be reluctant to take the medication to treat their depression. However, this side effect means that SSRIs may be a useful treatment for premature ejaculation by delaying ejaculation for several minutes (Kara et al., 1996; Strassberg et al., 1999). This illustrates how a medication's negative effect in one context may be a positive therapeutic effect when used differently.

We noted at the beginning of this section that people with sexual dysfunctions often fail to seek treatment because they do not know that help is available. However, this cannot be said about pharmacological treatments for erectile dysfunction. In fact, it is difficult to watch television or read a newspaper without seeing an advertisement for Viagra, Levitra, or Cialis. The drug Viagra (generic name sildenafil) was introduced in early 1998 for the treatment of erectile dysfunction. Tadalafil (Cialis) and vardenafil (Levitra) soon followed. These drugs are known as *phosphodiesterase type-5* (PDE5) inhibitors. PDE5 is a molecule found in the *corpus cavernosum*, the spongy erectile tissue in the penis and the clitoris. PDE5 is involved in *detumescence* (loss of erection), so PDE5 inhibitors allow penile erection to occur. Since the introduction of these drugs, thousands of studies have examined the efficacy of PDE5 inhibitors for erectile dysfunction. All three drugs are more efficacious than placebo, with 43% to 80% efficacy depending on the reason for the dysfunction (Lewis et al., 2005; Osterloh & Riley, 2002; Porst et al., 2001). The success of the PDE5 inhibitors for male erectile dysfunction has encouraged clinical trials of Viagra as a treatment for female sexual arousal disorder (see "Examining the Evidence: Viagra for Female Sexual Arousal Disorder").

Before the introduction of PDE5 inhibitors, erectile dysfunction was treated with a substance known as *prostaglandin E1*, which was either injected into the penis or inserted into the urethra. Positive effects ranged from 70% to 87% (Linet & Ogrinc, 1996; Padma-Nathan et al., 1997). However, the discomfort associated with the drug's administration makes many men unwilling to use it. A cream version of prostaglandin E1 applied externally to treat female sexual arousal disorder does not appear to be better than placebo (Padma-Nathan et al., 2003).

Finally, physical treatments can address erectile dysfunction. Penile implants are prosthetic devices that consist of a pump placed in the penis or scrotum that forces fluid into an inflatable cylinder, producing an erection. Similarly, vacuum devices consist of a plastic cylinder and a constriction ring that is placed around the penis. A vacuum is created using a pump, which produces an erection. The cylinder is then removed. Physical treatments are common when there is a physical reason for erectile dysfunction, such as diabetes or prostate surgery. Though efficacious and without side effects, they are awkward to use and do not always produce satisfactory results.

PSYCHOSOCIAL TREATMENTS First developed in the 1970s and 1980s, psychosocial treatments for sexual dysfunctions are efficacious (Hawton, 1995; Heiman, 2002), but many have been studied only in randomized controlled trials conducted more than 20 years ago (Brotto & Klein, 2007). Although further and more sophisticated research is necessary, we now review the available and empirically supported treatments.

Sex therapy (Masters & Johnson, 1970) consists of teaching couples about sexual functioning, enhancing communication skills, and eliminating performance anxiety through specific couples' exercises. Using *sensate focus and nondemand pleasuring*, treatment focuses on decreasing performance anxiety and increasing communication. Sensate focus has three steps. Both partners must become comfortable at each level of intimacy before proceeding to the next step. The first step focuses simply on pleasurable, nonsexual touching. Partners take turns touching the other's body, but they are prohibited from touching the genitals and breasts. During the second step, partners touch any part of the other's body including the genitals and breasts. The focus remains on the sensation of touching. Intercourse is not allowed. The third step involves mutual touching, eventually leading to sexual intercourse. Sex therapy is most effective for genito-pelvic pain/penetration disorder and erectile dysfunction that are psychological in origin (Hawton, 1995) and for female disorders of sexual interest or sexual arousal (what used to be known as female hypoactive sexual desire disorder) (Trudel et al., 2001). The long-term outcome is variable. In some instances, initial treatment effects were not maintained when patients were followed up several years later (Brotto & Klein, 2007).

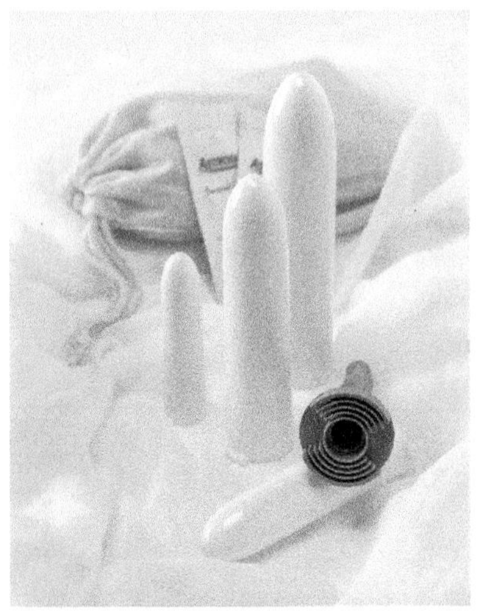

Vaginal dilators, of increasing sizes, are used to treat genito-pelvic pain/penetration disorder.

vaginismus.com

Used by Masters and Johnson (1970) and Kaplan (1979), the *stop-squeeze technique* (Semans, 1956) is highly efficacious for premature (early) ejaculation. In this treatment, the sexual partner stimulates the penis until an ejaculatory urge occurs. At that point, sexual stimulation stops and the partner squeezes the glans of the penis (the tip) until the urge disappears. This sequence is repeated until the interval between initial sexual stimulation and ejaculatory urge lengthens. Then the couple practices briefly inserting the penis into the vagina without thrusting, and the practice continues until the man is able to control the timing of ejaculation and the couple reports sexual enjoyment. This treatment can be adapted for a man to use alone (see "Real Science, Real Life: Michael—Treatment of Sexual Dysfunction" earlier in this chapter). The stop-squeeze technique has a success rate of about 60% (Althof, 2006; Metz et al., 1997),

examining the EVIDENCE

Viagra for Female Sexual Arousal Disorder

The success of Viagra in treating erectile dysfunction invariably led to questions about whether this medication might help other sexual dysfunctions. For example, given the high prevalence of sexual dysfunctions among women, would Viagra be a useful treatment for female hypoactive sexual desire disorder or female sexual arousal disorder?

- **The Evidence** PDE5 inhibitors block a molecule in the corpus cavernosum (spongy tissue) that creates detumescence in the penis. Corpus cavernosum tissue is also present in the clitoris of females. Six placebo-controlled trials, primarily conducted in Canada, have studied the efficacy of Viagra for women. Two studies (Berman et al., 2003; Caruso et al., 2001) reported positive effects (enhanced orgasm, improved sexual satisfaction). However, four other studies (Basson & Brotto, 2003; Basson et al., 2002; Berman et al., 2003; Kaplan et al., 1999) did not find any positive effects, including a very large multicentre trial that had a sample of 788 women (Basson et al., 2002).
- **Let's Examine the Evidence** The studies that found positive outcomes for Viagra versus those that found no effects had methodological differences.

  First, positive effects occurred when the sample consisted of women with female sexual arousal disorder. No effects were found for samples of women with more heterogeneous sexual dysfunctions (such as hypoactive sexual desire disorder or both hypoactive sexual desire disorder and female sexual arousal disorder).

  Second, in one of the two positive trials (Caruso et al., 2001), women received both the active drug and the placebo (though at separate times), and each condition was compared with the baseline condition (no pill). When someone takes an active drug and later a placebo (or vice versa), the side effects of the medication may "unblind" the patients. Side effects, more likely to accompany active medication, allow participants to correctly guess which substance they are taking. When the dependent variable is a subjective report, such as "feel more aroused," knowing when you are taking the active medication could influence your judgment of how well the pill worked.
- Third, in one of the positive studies, changes were found on two specific questions on a self-report measure of sexual satisfaction but not on the overall score. Although an entire self-report inventory may be reliable and valid, the same psychometric properties cannot be said to apply to a single question. Therefore, conclusions based on a positive response to a single item must be regarded cautiously.
- **Conclusion** In contrast to the thousands of studies examining the efficacy of Viagra for erectile dysfunction, the few studies examining its effect on women present a mixed picture. Although the same biological tissue exists in both sexes, it appears that Viagra works for only a few women. What hypothesis might you suggest to account for these differences?

although positive long-term outcome is achieved in only a minority of cases (Metz et al., 1997).

For female orgasmic disorder, therapists commonly prescribe *directed masturbation* (Heiman & LoPiccolo, 1987; Masters & Johnson, 1970). Women focus on sexually erotic cues and use graduated stimulation to the genital area, particularly the clitoris. Allowing the woman to focus on sexual stimulation that is effective for her without worrying about a partner's behaviour enables her to more effectively communicate her wishes to a partner. Approximately 90% of women treated with directed masturbation become orgasmic after this treatment (Heiman & LoPiccolo, 1987).

Treatment for genito-pelvic pain/penetration disorder is based on standard systematic desensitization (see Chapter 4) and uses different sizes of vaginal dilators. Using a hierarchical approach, the dilators are inserted into the vagina, by either the woman or her partner, while she practises relaxation. Over time, a woman becomes comfortable engaging in sexual activity. This procedure, sometimes coupled with cognitive-behaviour therapy to challenge irrational beliefs such as "intercourse will always be painful," is a highly successful treatment (Kabakçi & Batur, 2003; Leiblum, 2000; ter Kuile et al., 2007).

CONCEPT check

- Sexual dysfunctions encompass a broad range of sexual behaviours and include disorders of sexual desire, arousal, orgasm, and pain.
- Sexual dysfunctions may affect as many as 31% of men and 43% of women.
- Diagnoses of sexual dysfunctions must include consideration of distress and impairment, as well as age, sex, and prior sexual experience.
- Sexual dysfunction may result from physical diseases, psychological disorders, or environmental events. Sexual dysfunction may also be a contributing factor to psychological disorders.

critical thinking question Efficacious pharmacological and psychosocial treatments for men with sexual dysfunctions and efficacious psychosocial treatments for women are available. Because talking about sex has become more common among young adults in Western cultures, how might this affect our understanding of the prevalence and treatment of sexual dysfunctions? Do you think that this new "openness" would affect males and females in the same way?

Paraphilic Disorders

8.5 Identify the types of paraphilic disorders, and give examples of each type.

The term *paraphilia* is defined as "intense and persistent sexual interests other than sexual interest in genital stimulation or preparatory fondling with phenotypically normal, physically mature, consenting human partners" (APA, 2013, p. 685). Paraphilic disorders are paraphilias that cause distress or impairment to the person or when the satisfaction of a paraphilia has caused harm, or risk of harm, to another person. Paraphilias sometimes concern the person's erotic activities, whereas others concern the person's erotic targets. The public sometimes associates paraphilic disorders with criminal activity, but the relationship is not so simple. Some paraphilic disorders, such as *transvestic disorder*, are unusual but do not involve criminal activity. Other paraphilic disorders, however, such as *exhibitionistic disorder* or *pedophilic disorder*, may result in criminal charges. In addition, some sexual offenders, such as rapists, do not commit that act because of a paraphilia (McElroy et al., 1999). Therefore, not every paraphilic activity is criminal, but some may lead a person to engage in criminal acts.

Paraphilic disorders are sometimes classified into two groups: disorders based on anomalous (deviating from expected) target preferences or disorders based on anomalous activity preferences. Defining the limits of a paraphilia is difficult because some behaviours (such as physical restraint during sexual activity) do not necessarily cause distress or functional impairment for some adults (Krueger & Kaplan, 2001). Therefore, before any behaviour is labelled a paraphilia, its impact in terms of distress and functional impairment must be considered.

Paraphilic Disorders Based on Anomalous Target Preferences

In some instances, sexual urges, fantasies, or behaviours are associated with targets that deviate from what is considered normal or expected (see "DSM-5: Paraphilic Disorders Based on Anomalous Target Preferences"). Many different objects may be associated with sexual arousal, although certain categories, such as women's lingerie, occur more frequently. However, it is important to remember that not everything that a person identifies as "sexy" indicates the presence of deviant sexual arousal. A young man may find that seeing his girlfriend wearing lacy underwear enhances his sexual desire for her, but a person with a paraphilia would find the underwear alone arousing.

criteria for
Paraphilic Disorders Based on Anomalous Target Preferences DSM-5

Fetishistic Disorder

A. Over a period of at least 6 months, recurrent and intense sexual arousal from either the use of nonliving objects or a highly specific focus on nongenital body part(s), as manifested by fantasies, urges, or behaviours.

B. The fantasies, sexual urges, or behaviours cause clinically significant distress or impairment in social, occupational, or other important areas of functioning.

C. The fetish objects are not limited to articles of clothing used in cross-dressing (as in transvestic disorder) or devices specifically designed for the purpose of tactile genital stimulation (e.g., vibrator).

Transvestic Disorder

A. Over a period of at least 6 months, recurrent and intense sexual arousal from cross-dressing, as manifested by fantasies, urges, or behaviours.

B. The fantasies, sexual urges, or behaviours cause clinically significant distress or impairment in social, occupational, or other important areas of functioning.

Pedophilic Disorder

A. Over a period of at least 6 months, recurrent, intense sexually arousing fantasies, sexual urges, or behaviours involving sexual activity with a prepubescent child or children (generally age 13 years or younger).

B. The individual has acted on these sexual urges, or the sexual urges or fantasies cause marked distress or interpersonal difficulty.

C. The individual is at least age 16 years and at least 5 years older than the child or children in Criterion A.

Note: Do not include an individual in late adolescence involved in an ongoing sexual relationship with a 12- or 13-year-old.

FETISHISTIC DISORDER

Micky was referred to the clinic after his second arrest for shoplifting. A high school senior who was a loner for most of his school career, Micky was overweight and clumsy, and had bad acne. He had mediocre grades and was the classic "last kid to get picked for the team." He never had a girlfriend. Micky loved to cook. He spent hours in the kitchen baking because his goal was to become a pastry chef. In the first shoplifting offense, he was caught stealing a pair of red underpants from the women's lingerie department. He avoided charges by telling the security guard that he wanted to buy his girlfriend a birthday present but didn't have enough money. The guard felt sorry for him and let him go. The second time, he wasn't so lucky. He had taken a bag of women's panties and was caught on the security camera masturbating with them in one of the men's changing rooms. When the store security guard called his mother, she was horrified. She searched his room and found stashes of women's underwear in the back of his drawers and under his bed. At the court-ordered assessment, Micky was reluctant to discuss his sexuality at all. He seemed indifferent to his fetishism and only hoped that this arrest would not interfere with his ability to get into a culinary academy.

Recurrent and intense sexual arousal (fantasies, urges, or behaviours) that involves nonliving objects or a highly specific focus on nongenital body parts is known as **fetishistic disorder**. It would be impossible to provide a complete list of fetish objects, but the most common are female underwear, stockings, footwear, or other apparel (APA, 2013). It is important to add that the sexual arousal or behaviour must be accompanied by clinically significant distress or impairment in order to be considered a disorder. Sexual arousal may occur after looking at or fondling, rubbing, licking, or smelling the object; seeing someone else wearing the object; or manipulating the object by cutting or burning it (Chalkley & Powell, 1983). We have virtually no empirical data on this disorder, although those who engage in fetishism are primarily men, and once established, the disorder is chronic (Brotto & Klein, 2007).

TRANSVESTIC DISORDER

Berk is a successful physician with a big secret. It started when he was a teenager. His sister had hung her bra over the shower rod. He was curious—how did girls wear them? What did it feel like? He found himself getting excited at the thought of the lacy bra against his skin. One day he took the bra and matching panties out of the fresh laundry. His sister never noticed. Whenever he wore them, he felt sexually aroused. Berk was shy and awkward around girls. He rationalized that he did not have time for girls—he had to study if he wanted to become a doctor. All through high school, university, medical school, and residency, he satisfied his sexual urges by wearing women's underwear underneath his shirt and pants. Now he is a physician and he is interested in marrying and settling down. He is seeking treatment because he is quite distressed; he wants to date an attractive nurse who seems interested in him. But he does not feel the same sexual excitement thinking about her that he does when he thinks about wearing the lacy underwear.

Also known as *cross-dressing*, **transvestic disorder** is recurrent and intense sexual arousal that results from cross-dressing and is accompanied by significant distress or impairment. Not every man who cross-dresses suffers from functional transvestic fetishism. Female impersonators, for example, wear women's clothing to impersonate female singers or actresses on stage; these performers are not necessarily sexually aroused when wearing the clothing or performing. Transvestic disorder occurs almost exclusively in men. Among one sample of cross-dressers, 60% were married and 83% of the wives were aware of their husband's activities (Docter & Prince, 1997). Among the wives, 28% completely accepted their husband's behaviour, whereas 19% were described as completely antagonistic. The rest were reported to have less clear feelings.

PEDOPHILIC DISORDER **Pedophilic disorder** is defined as recurrent and intense sexual urges, sexually arousing fantasies, or behaviours involving sexual activity directed toward a prepubescent child or children (see "DSM-5: Paraphilic Disorders Based on Anomalous Target Preferences"). The sexual arousal may be toward girls, boys, or girls and boys. The diagnosis for this disorder is appropriate if the person has acted on the urges or fantasies but denies distress or functional impairment (APA, 2013). Although the terms *pedophile* and *child molester* are sometimes used interchangeably, they are not synonymous. Someone with pedophilia could have urges or fantasies involving sexual activity with a child but never act on them. That person would not be a child molester. Yet much of what we know about pedophila comes from samples of convicted child molesters and does not describe all of those who suffer from the disorder.

The most common pedophilic acts are fondling and genital exposure. Intercourse (oral, vaginal, or anal) is less common, and rape and abduction are the least common (Fagan et al., 2002). Perpetrators can be familial or nonfamilial. Among one offending group, 29% of offenders were natural parents, 29% other parents, and 40% other caretakers (Sedlak & Broadhurst, 1996). When the offender and the child are related, pedophilia is called *incest.* Although incest perpetrators share many similarities to perpetrators who abuse biologically unrelated children, incest victims are usually at the age of puberty. Younger children are most often the victims of nonbiologically related males with pedophilic disorder (Rice & Harris, 2002).

Girls are more often the victims of pedophilic disorder than are boys, although a perpetrator who prefers boys will often have a much higher number of victims (Abel &

TABLE 8.3
Men's Pedophilic Acts with Boys and Girls

Male Perpetrator/Female Victim	Male Perpetrator/Male Victim
Has few victims	Has many victims (up to hundreds)
Offends repeatedly with same victim	Offends only once with a victim
Offends in victim's home	Offends away from victim's home
Offends with victim of mean age of 8 years	Offends with victim of mean age of 10 years
Is also attracted to older women	Is not attracted to adults of either sex
Is commonly married	Is single
Has had behaviour since adulthood	Has had behaviour since adolescence
Has characteristics of low income, unemployed, alcoholic, lower IQ, psychopathic	Is stable/employed, average IQ, "immature," prefers company of children to adults

Source: McConaghy, N. (1993). *Sexual behavior: Problems and management.* New York: Plenum.

Oxborn, 1992). Table 8.3 illustrates the difference between those who have heterosexual pedophilic disorder and homosexual pedophilic disorder. These differences include the number of victims involved, where the offenses occur, the sex and age of the victims, and whether the perpetrator is also sexually attracted to adults. Initially considered to be a disorder of men, evidence now indicates that some women suffer from pedophilia (Brotto & Klein, 2007; Fagan et al., 2002). Clearly, those who qualify for a diagnosis of pedophilic disorder are not a homogeneous group.

Pedophilic disorder involving fantasies or impulses about engaging in sexual behaviour with children is not considered criminal unless the person acts on the sexual urges. In that case, the behaviours do constitute a crime and may bring the individual to the attention of the criminal justice system. Criminal behaviours are not simply limited to sexual acts with a minor child. Possessing sexual images of children (child pornography, even when obtained over the Internet) is a criminal offense. Because epidemiological studies do not include questions about pedophilic fantasies and behaviours, the prevalence of pedophilia in the general population is not known (Fagan et al., 2002). Furthermore, the percentage of child abusers who suffer from pedophilic disorder is also unknown.

Paraphilic Dysfunctions Based on Anomalous Activity Preferences

The common factor that groups these paraphilias together is that they are based on sexual activities that are considered anomalous (deviating from what is considered normal or expected) (see "DSM-5: Paraphilic Dysfunctions Based on Anomalous Activity Preferences"). These urges or fantasies must cause clinically significant distress or functional impairment in order to consider that the person has a disorder. Some behaviours in this category, such as exhibitionism, may elicit temporary startle reactions or annoyance from the victims. In addition, some of the behaviours in this category are not only deviant sexual behaviours but also criminal offenses, although the extent of the legal implications varies with the particular activity.

EXHIBITIONISTIC DISORDER

Max is not sure why he does it, but wow, it sure feels good. He experiences a tremendous urge that cannot otherwise be satisfied—nothing else feels the same. When he feels the urge, he dresses in only a dark raincoat and ski mask. Right before dusk,

criteria for
Paraphilic Dysfunctions Based on Anomalous Activity Preferences DSM-5

Exhibitionistic Disorder

A. Over a period of at least 6 months, recurrent and intense sexual arousal from the exposure of one's genitals to an unsuspecting person, as manifested by fantasies, urges, or behaviours.

B. The individual has acted on these sexual urges with a nonconsenting person, or the sexual urges or fantasies cause clinically significant distress or impairment in social, occupational, or other important areas of functioning.

Frotteuristic Disorder

A. Over a period of at least 6 months, recurrent and intense sexual arousal from touching or rubbing against a nonconsenting person, as manifested by fantasies, urges, or behaviours.

B. The individual has acted on these sexual urges with a nonconsenting person, or the sexual urges or fantasies cause clinically significant distress or impairment in social, occupational, or other important areas of functioning.

Voyeuristic Disorder

A. Over a period of at least 6 months, recurrent and intense sexual arousal from observing an unsuspecting person who is naked, in the process of disrobing, or engaging in sexual activity, as manifested by fantasies, urges, or behaviours.

B. The individual has acted on these sexual urges with a nonconsenting person, or the sexual urges or fantasies cause clinically significant distress or impairment in social, occupational, or other important areas of functioning.

C. The individual experiencing the arousal and/or acting on the urges is at least 18 years of age.

Sexual Masochism Disorder

A. Over a period of at least 6 months, recurrent and intense sexual arousal from the act of being humiliated, beaten, bound, or otherwise made to suffer, as manifested by fantasies, urges, or behaviours.

B. The fantasies, sexual urges, or behaviours cause clinically significant distress or impairment in social, occupational, or other important areas of functioning.

Sexual Sadism Disorder

A. Over a period of at least 6 months, recurrent and intense sexual arousal from the physical or psychological suffering of another person, as manifested by fantasies, urges, or behaviours.

B. The individual has acted on these sexual urges with a nonconsenting person, or the sexual urges or fantasies cause clinically significant distress or impairment in social, occupational, or other important areas of functioning.

he drives to a part of town where he is not known. He hides in the bushes until a woman walkes by—he jumps out and opens his raincoat, exposing his genitals. Usually the woman screams. For Max, the possibility of being caught naked and the surprise of the victim are important elements of his sexual satisfaction.

Defined as recurrent and intense sexual arousal involving exposing one's genitals to an unsuspecting person, **exhibitionistic disorder** may also include the act of masturbation in front of a stranger. The shock of the victim is sometimes the sexually arousing component. Most often the perpetrator is male (Federoff et al., 1999), and most victims are female. Exhibitionistic disorder is a "high victim" crime. Among 142 people with a history of exhibitionistic disorder, there were a total of 72 074 victims (Tempelman & Stinnett, 1991). People who engage in this behaviour are not different from the general population in terms of academic achievement, intelligence, socioeconomic status, or emotional adjustment (Brotto & Klein, 2007). They are more likely than people with other types of paraphilic disorders to be in committed relationships. They also are less likely than others to see their behaviour as harmful to the victim (Cox & Maletzky, 1980).

FROTTEURISTIC DISORDER

Kwan is a 20-year-old university student. Socially introverted since middle school, he has a few male friends and has had a few dates with girls. Around age 13, he realized that he became sexually aroused by fantasies about women he saw in the mall, at sports games, or at the movie theatre. He had no interest in meeting them, but he was sexually aroused by the idea of rubbing his body against them. When Kwan was 17, he began to act on this urge. On a crowded morning subway ride, Kwan would brush his body up against women. He would say, "Excuse me," as if he intended to pass them, but he would linger for a few seconds to press his penis up against the woman's derriere or hip. Soon he was not satisfied just doing it once; by age 18, he was spending hours on the subway each day. He began to have fantasies of exclusive, caring relationships with his female victims. Once at university in a rural area, he worried that he would not be able to fulfill his sexual urge. He tried to stop and began dating a woman. However, his sexual compulsion was so powerful that actual romantic interactions with a partner left him unfulfilled. Kwan is very distressed. Then, in an abnormal psychology class, he heard the word frotteurism. He is astonished, ashamed, but also somewhat relieved—he is not the only one with this secret behaviour.

Recurrent and intense sexual arousal (in the form of urges, fantasies, or behaviours) that involve touching or rubbing against a nonconsenting person is known as **frotteuristic disorder**. The word comes from the French word *frotter*, meaning "to rub." As in Kwan's case, the behaviour occurs in public places such as crowded buses or subways. Areas of contact are primarily thighs, buttocks, genitals, or breasts. Usually the person fantasizes about a positive emotional relationship with the victim (APA, 2013). What few data exist suggest that the disorder occurs almost exclusively in adolescent or young adult men who have many victims, are rarely arrested, and when arrested, serve minimal sentences (Krueger & Kaplan, 1997).

VOYEURISTIC DISORDER **Voyeuristic disorder** involves sexually arousing urges, fantasies, and behaviours that are associated with seeing an unsuspecting person naked, undressing, or engaging in sexual activity (APA, 2013). To be considered a disorder, the person must experience significant distress or perform actual voyeuristic acts. Although we have few empirical data, people with voyeurism are thought to have limited social skills, limited sexual knowledge, and problems with sexual dysfunction and intimacy (Marshall & Eccles, 1991).

SEXUAL MASOCHISM DISORDER AND SEXUAL SADISM DISORDER The terms *masochist* and *sadist* are commonly used in our society and do not always refer to sexual behaviours. However, sexual masochism and sexual sadism are diagnostic categories that involve pain and humiliation during sexual activity (see "DSM-5: Paraphilic Dysfunctions Based on Anomalous Activity Preferences"). It is important to understand that what defines these disorders is not a specific behaviour, but rather the resultant pain, humiliation, or suffering that creates sexual arousal.

Jack had a secret. He experienced intense sexual arousal and orgasm when his supply of oxygen was cut off during sexual activity. When he could not find a partner willing to choke him while they engaged in intercourse, Jack would "do it himself"—using a chair and a rope to briefly hang himself while he masturbated. He was always extremely careful to have an escape route. One day he did not show up at a meeting. It was not like Jack to miss meetings, and his concerned colleagues went to his office. They found Jack, naked and dead, hanging from a ceiling beam, an overturned step ladder nearby.

Sexual masochism disorder is recurrent and intense sexual arousal that occurs as a result of being humiliated, beaten, bound, or otherwise made to suffer. The events actually occur and are not simulated. Pain may result from being slapped, spanked, or whipped. Humiliation may result from acts such as wearing diapers, licking shoes, or displaying one's naked body. Other acts might include being urinated or defecated on, self-mutilation, or, as in Jack's case, being deprived of oxygen (Brotto & Klein, 2007). Males and females who engage in sexual masochism may do so by mutual agreement and use a safety signal when they want to stop. Yet in some cases these activities lead to injury or death, as happened to Jack.

Sexual sadism disorder also involves the infliction of pain or humiliation, but in this case, the physical or psychological suffering is inflicted on another person. The disorder is found primarily in males. In some instances, the sadistic acts may be nonconsensual, resulting in the crime of sexual assault.

Many of those who engage in sexual sadism had formerly engaged in sexual masochism (Baumeister, 1989). In some individuals, sexual fantasies and behaviours alternate between sadism and masochism (Abel et al., 1988).

Functional Impairment

People who have paraphilic disorders often have more than one. Among one group of sex offenders with a paraphilic disorder, 29% had two paraphilic disorders and 14% had three paraphilic disorders. Specifically, 81% met criteria for pedophilic disorder, 43% for frotteuristic disorder, 19% for sexual sadism disorder, 14% for voyeuristic disorder, and 14% for paraphilic disorder not otherwise specified (McElroy et al., 1999).

Despite their unusual sexual practices, people with paraphilic disorders are often indistinguishable from other people in nonsexual areas of functioning. They do not seek out pain or humiliation in other types of activities. They are described as well adjusted, successful, and above the norm on assessments of mental health (Brotto & Klein, 2007). Men with transvestic disorder are happy with their biological sex and gender identity. Their behaviours, occupations, and hobbies are typical of those found in other heterosexual males (Buhrich & McConaghy, 1985; Chung & Harmon, 1994). However, accidental deaths, such as Jack's, sometimes occur from oxygen deprivation.

Sex, Race, and Ethnicity

As noted, most epidemiological surveys of psychological disorders do not ask questions about paraphilic disorders. Most people find these behaviours difficult to discuss, and it is highly unlikely that they would admit them to a stranger. Furthermore, in some instances, these behaviours could lead to criminal charges, making it even more unlikely that people would admit to them. Therefore, most of what we know about paraphilic disorders comes from those who seek or are referred for treatment or who have been apprehended as a result of their sexual behaviour. This results in confusing and conflicting prevalence estimates. At this time, the most accurate statement is that paraphilic disorders are probably rare, but their actual prevalence remains unknown.

Almost all people with paraphilic disorders are men, but females with paraphilic disorder have been reported (Krueger & Kaplan, 2001). Sexual masochism disorder is also found among women, although the ratio is still approximately 20 males to 1 female (APA, 2000a). Another sex difference is that women prefer less pain than men during sexually masochistic activities (Baumeister, 1989).

Cultural factors are particularly important to consider in the case of paraphilic disorders. For example, exhibitionistic disorder is considered a paraphilic disorder when cultural norms require wearing clothing that covers the genitalia. When exposure of the genitals is the norm, as in some tropical areas where clothing is not traditionally worn, the diagnosis of exhibitionistic disorder may not be appropriate (Tseng, 2003).

Developmental Factors

The most common age of onset for all paraphilic disorders is adolescence to young adulthood (APA, 2013), although the disorders may begin at any age. Particularly in the case of pedophilic disorder, we usually think about children as the victims. However, young boys (some as young as age 4) have been known to sexually molest even younger children. In one sample, boys who abused younger children were an average of 8 years old at the time that they committed their first offense, and the victims averaged 6 years of age (Cavanagh-Johnson, 1988). The perpetrators used coercion to commit the offenses and knew the children they victimized.

Across one sample of sex offenders, the average age of onset for a paraphilic disorder was 16 years, but ranged from 7 to 38 years (McElroy et al., 1999). Compared with sexual offenders without paraphilic disorders, sexual offenders with a paraphilia were significantly younger when they committed their first sexual offense; had offended for a longer period of time before being arrested; had had more victims; and were significantly more likely to suffer from anxiety, depression, substance abuse, and impulse-control disorders (Krueger & Kaplan, 2001).

Boys as young as age 8 may sexually abuse even younger children. The average age of onset for a paraphilia is age 16.

Etiology

The etiology of paraphilic disorders is unknown (Krueger & Kaplan, 2001), although various theories have been proposed. With respect to biology, several studies have examined the role of endocrine abnormalities in paraphilic disorders, but data have failed to document differences in those with paraphilic disorders (Krueger & Kaplan, 2001). Neuroanatomical and neurochemical studies have not detected specific brain abnormalities (Hucker et al., 1988; O'Carroll, 1989; Tarter et al., 1983), and few data support a role for genetics in the onset of paraphilic disorders (Krueger & Kaplan, 2001).

With respect to psychosocial theories, a commonly held belief is that people who abuse children were abused themselves. However, the available data do not support this contention. If estimates of abuse are correct, as many as 1 in 10 children may be sexually abused before the age of 18, but the vast majority of these children do not develop pedophilia (Murphy & Peters, 1992). Research tells us that a history of child abuse is not necessary or sufficient for the development of pedophilic disorder. In one sample, 28% of sex offenders reported a history of sexual abuse as children compared with 10% among a nonoffending community sample (Hanson & Slater, 1988). Although the rate among offenders is higher, it still means that almost three of four offenders did not have a history of childhood sexual abuse.

Behavioural conditioning theories have been proposed to explain the development of paraphilic disorders, but we have few empirical data. For example, if a person engages in a paraphilic disorder and achieves sexual release, engaging in that behaviour is reinforced and likely to be repeated. In a similar vein, negative family environments and disrupted family structures have been hypothesized to play an etiological role, but these hypotheses are based primarily on isolated case reports with few supporting data (Brotto & Klein, 2007).

Treatment

8.6 Identify the most promising biological and psychosocial treatments for the paraphilic disorders and the ethical issues that affect the conduct of clinical research.

Again, it is important to note that a diagnosis requires significant distress or functional impairment. People with paraphilic disorders often are not motivated to change because the sexual behaviour is very reinforcing. It creates a pleasurable state and therefore is likely to be repeated. Individuals who seek treatment usually do so because the legal system mandates it, and individuals often discontinue treatment once legal oversight is terminated. Some investigators consider pedophilic disorder to be a chronic disorder with treatment directed toward stopping abuse and helping the perpetrator learn to control the deviant behaviour (Fagan et al., 2002). Sometimes treatments are combined to achieve optimum results. Positive outcomes have been reported for these treatments, but the available data are few, and the sample sizes are small and far from conclusive.

Determining the efficacy of interventions requires accurate assessment of the problem before and after treatment. This is particularly difficult in the case of paraphilic disorders because most people are reluctant to discuss these behaviours. Furthermore, admitting to certain sexual behaviours may have legal consequences. Therefore, many researchers and some clinicians depend on objective measures of sexual arousal known as **plethysmography**: penile plethysmography for males and vaginal photoplethysmography for females. Most research has been directed at the *penile plethysmograph*, considered a reliable and valid form of assessing sexual arousal including deviant sexual arousal. The penile plethysmograph measures changes in penile tumescence when the man is shown sexually arousing or nonarousing stimuli. The stimuli usually consist of photographs of males and females, of all ages, against a plain background. The man is instructed to look at the slide, and his erectile response is recorded.

As noted by Canadian researchers Barbaree and Marshall (1989), by identifying patterns of sexual arousal, penile plethysmography can distinguish between sexual and nonsexual offenders (although it is more accurate in detecting those who did not commit a sexual offense than those who did commit one) and between rapists or child molesters and nonoffenders. Penile plethysmography also predicts violent recidivism among sexual offenders, and informs clinicians and researchers about the efficacy of treatment (Lalumière & Quinsey, 1994; Seto, 2001). In the psychosocial treatment section we also show how penile plethysmography can assess treatment outcome.

Despite the advances in understanding sexual deviations made possible by plethysmography, a number of ethical, social, and medical concerns surround its use (Abel et al., 1998). Because the assessment uses nude photographs, one concern is the potential exploitation of children. Even when the photos are used solely for purposes of assessment and treatment, transporting them can result in arrest for trafficking in child pornography. Second, researchers must be concerned about the transmission of HIV/AIDS when the plethysmograph is used. Third, the device is very intrusive because it must be placed on the penis, and sometimes a technician's assistance is required. This raises questions about its use with adolescents, who later could accuse the technician of abuse. Finally, although it is difficult, some men can "beat the machine" and control their physiological response to appear less aroused than they actually are.

In response to these concerns, a new assessment strategy, the *visual reaction time task*, has been developed. This procedure measures the length of time that people look at slides of males and females (of all ages) who are wearing bathing suits. The theory is that people will look longer at the pictures that they find sexually arousing (e.g., heterosexual women should look longer at slides of adult males rather than children of either sex or adult females). The visual reaction time task appears to be as reliable and valid as penile plethysmography (Abel et al., 1988, 2004) and is more acceptable for use with adolescents (Abel et al., 2004).

BIOLOGICAL TREATMENT Surgical castration, though efficacious for some people, is no longer used to treat paraphilic disorders due to obvious legal and ethical constraints (Rösler & Witztum, 2000). Pharmacological interventions include SSRIs and antiandrogens. Because some forms of paraphilic disorder are considered to be compulsive in nature, the SSRIs were initially considered to have some promise due to their efficacy in treating obsessive-compulsive disorder (see Chapter 4). However, to date, their efficacy for paraphilic disorders is not established (Gijs & Gooren, 1996; Rösler & Witztum, 2000).

The primary goal of *antiandrogen medications* is to reduce the sexual drive. Medroxyprogetertone acetate (Depo-Provera) and leuprolide acetate (Depo-Lupron) are testosterone-lowering medications used to inhibit *luteinizing hormone secretion*, which in turn is responsible for decreasing testosterone levels (Rösler & Witztum, 2000). Depending on the dosage used, there often is still enough testosterone for erectile function to allow sexual intercourse with an appropriate partner (Fagan et al., 2002). The drug controls behaviours such as pedophilic disorder, exhibitionistic disorder, and voyeuristic disorder as long as the patient continues to take the medication, but there are significant side effects and a high recidivism rate (an average of 27%) that limit its usefulness (Rösler & Witztum, 2000).

PSYCHOSOCIAL TREATMENT Among psychological interventions, behavioural and cognitive-behavioural treatments for paraphilic disorders are the most common psychosocial intervention and at this time are considered the most efficacious (Krueger & Kaplan, 2002; Marshall et al., 2006). The current empirical database has two limitations. First, the majority of research is based on sexual offenders who have been incarcerated. Second, randomized controlled trials are usually not possible because having no treatment control conditions for sexual offenders is unethical. Despite these limitations, behavioural and cognitive-behavioural treatments result in reduced recidivism rates compared to programs that use other approaches or compared to offenders who do not receive treatment due to lack of financial and therapeutic resources. Treatments based on learning theory have been applied to the treatment of paraphilic disorders since the 1970s and usually involve two parts: decreasing sexual arousal to inappropriate sexual stimuli and enhancing appropriate sexual behaviour.

Eliminating or decreasing inappropriate sexual arousal Treatments based on classical and operant conditioning (see Chapter 1) have been successfully developed for various paraphilic disorders. **Satiation** involves exposing the person to the arousing stimuli and continuing that exposure for an extended period until the stimuli no longer produce positive, erotic feelings. For example, a man who fantasizes about exposing his genitals to adolescent females would be asked to imagine that fantasy and masturbate for an extended period of time (perhaps for two hours) until he reports an absence of sexual arousal or perhaps even aversion to the idea. A number of sessions must be conducted until even any initial sexual arousal is eliminated. **Covert sensitization** is a similar procedure in which the individual is asked to imagine doing the deviant act but also visualize the negative consequences that result from it. The scene is presented to the patient for a period of time and over repeated sessions until the patient reports that urges to engage in the deviant behaviour have been eliminated.

For example, a patient who is troubled by urges to expose himself might be presented the following:

> You hear the teenage babysitter next door playing outside with the children. You feel the urge to stand in front of a window that faces that house and expose yourself. If you stand on a chair, you can expose your genitals and no one will see your face. You know it is wrong, but the urge keeps getting stronger. You climb into the window and pull down your pants. You hear the babysitter gasp—her voice trembles as she tells the children to get into the house. You feel so good. But before you can pull up your pants, the door opens and your mother screams, "Ben, what are you doing? How could you do this?" She is crying and you struggle to pull up your pants. Soon there is a pounding at your door—and when your mother opens it, still crying and screaming, "What's wrong with you," the babysitter is at the door with a police officer. You stand there embarrassed and humiliated as the girl watches you, standing in your underwear, being arrested for exposing your genitals. As you are taken away, the entire neighbourhood sees you, wearing just your underwear, being

handcuffed and led out to a police car. You are humiliated, your mother is humiliated, and tomorrow everyone will know what a pervert you are. As the police officer shoves you into the police car, you are terrified about what will happen to you when you are taken off to jail.

Olfactory aversion is the pairing of noxious but harmless odours (such as ammonia) with either sexual fantasies or sexual behaviours. It is an application of classical conditioning theory. Typically, the person is presented deviant sexual stimuli and then inhales the ammonia fumes, which cause burning and watering eyes, runny nose, and coughing. With repeated pairings, the deviant sexual behaviour is suppressed, usually within a few weeks (Laws, 2001).

Cognitive-behavioural group therapy is the treatment of choice for those who suffer from pedophilic disorder. The intervention includes psychoeducational groups, anger management, assertiveness training, human sexuality education, communication training, control of deviant sexual arousal, and relapse prevention in which participants are educated about identifying high-risk relapse situations (Studer & Aylwin, 2006). Cognitive-behavioural treatments include *cognitive restructuring* in which distorted or faulty cognitions ("I'll never be normal") are identified and more adaptive positive thoughts are substituted ("I can change"). A second cognitive-behavioural treatment is *empathy training* that teaches offenders to recognize the harmful aspects of their behaviour and put themselves in the place of the victim to build empathy toward him or her. As noted, behavioural and cognitive-behavioural treatments are efficacious, but it is not clear that they produce permanent behavioural change for paraphilic disorders (Laws, 2001). Booster sessions are probably needed. In addition, these interventions are only one aspect of an overall treatment plan (Krueger & Kaplan, 2002).

Enhancing appropriate sexual interest and arousal Sex is a biological drive, and eliminating deviant sexual urges, fantasies, or behaviour will be ineffective unless the person finds a more appropriate sexual outlet. To address this dimension of functioning, clinicians use interventions such as *social skills training*. This strategy teaches the person basic social conversation skills including initiating and maintaining conversations, using assertive behaviour, and developing dating skills to establish relationships with appropriate adults. When a person with paraphilic disorder is in an established adult relationship, the aberrant sexual behaviour may severely strain the relationship, particularly if there are legal complications. Therefore, *couples therapy* may be necessary. Finally, people with paraphilic disorders often lack a basic understanding of sexual behaviour, particularly appropriate adult sexual behaviours, and treatment may therefore need to include *sex education* (Krueger & Kaplan, 2001).

CONCEPT check

- Paraphilic disorders are defined as intense and persistent sexual interest other than sexual interest in genital stimulation or preparatory fondling with phenotypically normal, physically mature, consenting human partners.
- Pedophilic disorder is a paraphilic disorder. *Sexual offender* and *child molester* are terms applied to people whose behaviours involve criminal sexual activities.
- Paraphilic disorders, compared with other forms of psychological disorders, are an under-researched area.
- Behaviour therapy is the most empirically supported treatment for paraphilic disorders.

critical thinking question Do you think that culture might influence the expression or labelling of a certain behaviour as paraphilic disorder?

summary

gender dysphoria, sexual dysfunctions, and paraphilic disorders

8.1 Understand that "normal sexual behaviour" is difficult to define and depends on biological and cultural factors.
The term *normal sexual behaviour* is hard to define. The human sexual response cycle consists of four phases: desire, arousal, orgasm, and resolution. Vaginal intercourse is the most frequently practised sexual activity. Yet biological (age, sex) and cultural factors play a role in how frequently sexual activity occurs and what type of sexual behaviours are practised.

8.2 Identify the characteristics of gender dysphoria, and understand how it relates to transsexualism and transvestic fetishism.
Gender dysphoria, also known as *transsexualism* in adults, is a strong and persistent cross-gender identification and persistent discomfort with one's own sex. Transsexualism differs from transvestic disorder, which consists of sexual arousal that occurs when dressing in female clothing.

8.3 Recognize that men and women exhibit different patterns of sexual behaviour, and identify the role of gender in the definition and development of sexual dysfunction.
Sexual dysfunction occurs in both men and women, but the nature of the dysfunction differs by sex. Whereas deficits in sexual performance are most common in men, lack of sexual desire is often the most common complaint among females. There are also differences between the sexes in the degree to which males and females perceive their sexual behaviour to be problematic.

8.4 Understand the biological and psychological complexities involved in the etiology and treatment of sexual dysfunction.
Sexual dysfunctions may have a biological basis, including hormonal imbalances, physical illnesses, and surgical complications. Psychological factors may also lead to sexual dysfunction and in turn, sexual dysfunction can lead to psychological distress. Treatment is also complex and can include biological or psychological interventions, both of which have established efficacy. However, treatments that work with one sex are not always efficacious for the other sex.

8.5 Identify the types of paraphilic disorders, and give examples of each type.
Paraphilic disorders are paraphilias that cause distress or impairment or whose satisfaction results in personal harm, or risk to harm, to another person. A person who has a paraphilic disorder is not necessarily a sexual offender, which is a term restricted to those who are arrested and convicted of a sexual offense. In some cases, a paraphilic disorder such as pedophilic disorder can result in conviction of a crime. However, individuals with sexual urges or fantasies to commit acts, such as those with exhibitionistic disorder or voyeuristic disorder, who do not act on those urges, have not committed a sexual offense.

8.6 Identify the most promising biological and psychosocial treatments for the paraphilic disorders and the ethical issues that affect the conduct of clinical research.
Psychological interventions are the most efficacious treatment for paraphilic disorders, but many who suffer from these disorders either are reluctant to seek treatment or do not see the need for it. Often they participate in treatment only when required by court order and quit when they are no longer compelled to do so. Furthermore, because paraphilic disorders are unusual and often misunderstood, those who suffer from these disorders rarely seek treatment. This makes it difficult to conduct the clinical trials necessary to fully determine the efficacy of these treatments.

key terms

covert sensitization 315
delayed ejaculation 295
erectile disorder 294
exhibitionistic disorder 310
female orgasmic disorder 296
female sexual interest/arousal disorder 294
fetishistic disorder 307
frotteuristic disorder 311
gender dysphoria 285
genito-pelvic pain/penetration disorder 298
male hypoactive sexual desire disorder 292
olfactory aversion 316
pedophilic disorder 308
plethysmography 314
premature (early) ejaculation 296
satiation 315
sex drive 281
sex reassignment surgery 287
sexual dysfunctions 292
sexual masochism disorder 312
sexual sadism disorder 312
transgender behaviour 286
transsexualism 286
transvestic disorder 308
voyeuristic disorder 311

TEST yourself

1. One of the first formal attempts to study human sexuality using extensive surveys of thousands of people was conducted by
   a. B. F. Skinner
   b. Masters and Johnson
   c. Alfred Kinsey
   d. Helen Singer Kaplan

2. Masters and Johnson's studies of human sexuality differed from those of other researchers because they
   a. interviewed adults instead of conducting survey-based research
   b. interviewed couples together instead of separately
   c. observed and recorded psychosexual development and social attitudes
   d. observed and recorded the physical responses of their subjects while they engaged in sexual activity

3. According to contemporary theories, which of the following is *not* considered one of the four phases of the sexual response cycle?
   a. refractory
   b. desire
   c. resolution
   d. orgasm

4. Surveys of sex practices show differences in males and females. Women have a greater
   a. capacity for sex
   b. need for a resolution phase
   c. variety of sex practices
   d. number of fantasies

5. Which of the following statements accurately reflects our understanding of sexual functioning in middle-aged and older adults?
   a. Most men and women between the ages of 40 and 49 are no longer sexually active.
   b. Satisfactory sexual functioning is important to most adults over age 40.
   c. Middle-aged and older women generally do not regard satisfactory sex as essential to maintaining a relationship.
   d. Men's sexual interest declines sharply after middle age.

6. Which of the following statements best characterizes what we know about the development of sexual orientation?
   a. In cultures that frown on same-sex behaviour, homosexual orientation is rare.
   b. Worldwide, about 5% of men and women develop same-sex orientation.
   c. Sexual orientation appears to be biologically based.
   d. There is greater erotic plasticity among men than among women.

7. Congenital adrenal hyperplasia is a hormonal condition in which too much of the hormone androgen is produced during the prenatal period and the first few years of life. This condition causes
   a. transvestic disorder in boys as early as 4 to 6 years of age
   b. extremely feminine behaviour in young boys
   c. hyperfeminine behaviour in young girls
   d. early and exaggerated male sex characteristics in both sexes

8. Louis called his co-workers together for a meeting at the end of the week and explained that beginning the following week, he would be coming to work dressed as a woman and that he wanted to be called Louise. He described this as the start of a process of treatment for his
   a. homosexual desire
   b. gender fetish disorder
   c. gender dysphoria
   d. hermaphroditic disorder

9. Luca has been experiencing high levels of stress because of increased layoffs at work. He and his partner, Bernard, have had a satisfying sexual relationship until recently. Now Luca typically experiences an ejaculation within a minute of initiating sex. He is likely to be suffering from
   a. homosexual disorder
   b. gender dysphoria
   c. primary premature ejaculation
   d. secondary premature ejaculation

10. Susan cannot have sexual intercourse with her boyfriend due to pain in the outer part of her vagina. Susan's gynecologist cannot perform a pelvic exam because she cannot insert a speculum without causing Susan extreme pain from muscle spasms. Which of the following disorders is Susan likely to be suffering from?
    a. dyspareunia
    b. dyspepsia
    c. vaginismus
    d. anorgasmia

11. Which of the following statements best reflects what has been learned about sexual dysfunction from population surveys?
    a. Sexual dysfunctions decrease with age for both sexes.
    b. Sexual dysfunctions are rare among young people but begin to appear in middle age.
    c. Only a small minority of the population ever experiences a sexual dysfunction.
    d. Sexual dysfunctions are fairly common, and many people do not seek help for their problems.

12. The sexual dysfunction most often responsive to pharmacologic treatment is
    a. hormonal insufficiency
    b. erectile dysfunction
    c. female sexual arousal disorder
    d. vaginismus

13. Psychosocial treatments for sexual dysfunctions have been shown to be effective. Among these techniques are
a. sensate focus
b. the stop-squeeze technique
c. nondemand pleasuring
d. all of the above

14. Transvestic disorder is the desire to dress in clothes of the opposite sex for sexual gratification. This disorder is
a. diagnosed almost exclusively in men
b. found in both men and women
c. common in homosexuals
d. diagnosed in transsexuals

15. The most common pedophilic acts are
a. intercourse and rape
b. voyeurism and frotteurism
c. incest and use of pornography
d. fondling and genital exposure

16. The most common age of onset for paraphilic disorders is
a. adolescence to young adulthood
b. adulthood to middle age
c. middle age to later in life
d. childhood

17. The argument that one of the most frequent reasons people abuse children is that they were abused when they were young
a. reflects numerous epidemiological studies of sex offenders
b. fails to consider that the vast majority of abused children do not become pedophiles
c. fails to consider the changing societal and cultural definitions of child abuse
d. explains why child abuse is a self-perpetuating problem

18. The device that measures physical changes in the penis when a man is shown sexually arousing or nonarousing stimuli is called the penile
a. volumetric gauge
b. tumesograph
c. photoplethysmograph
d. plethysmograph

19. Antiandrogen medications are used to treat some forms of paraphilic disorder. Their mechanism of action is to
a. lower the recidivism rate through selective sedation
b. decrease the sexual drive by reducing testosterone levels
c. eliminate recidivism through chemical castration
d. increase normal heterosexual behaviours by decreasing luteinizing hormone levels

20. Treatments for paraphilic disorders that eliminate or decrease inappropriate sexual arousal include
a. rational emotive and cognitive-behavioural therapy
b. social skills training, couples therapy, and sex education
c. satiation, covert sensitization, and olfactory aversion
d. stop-squeeze technique and sensate focus

Answers:
1 c, 2 d, 3 a, 4 a, 5 b, 6 c, 7 d, 8 c, 9 d, 10 c, 11 d, 12 b, 13 d,
14 a, 15 d, 16 a, 17 b, 18 d, 19 b, 20 c.

chapter 9

substance-related and addictive disorders

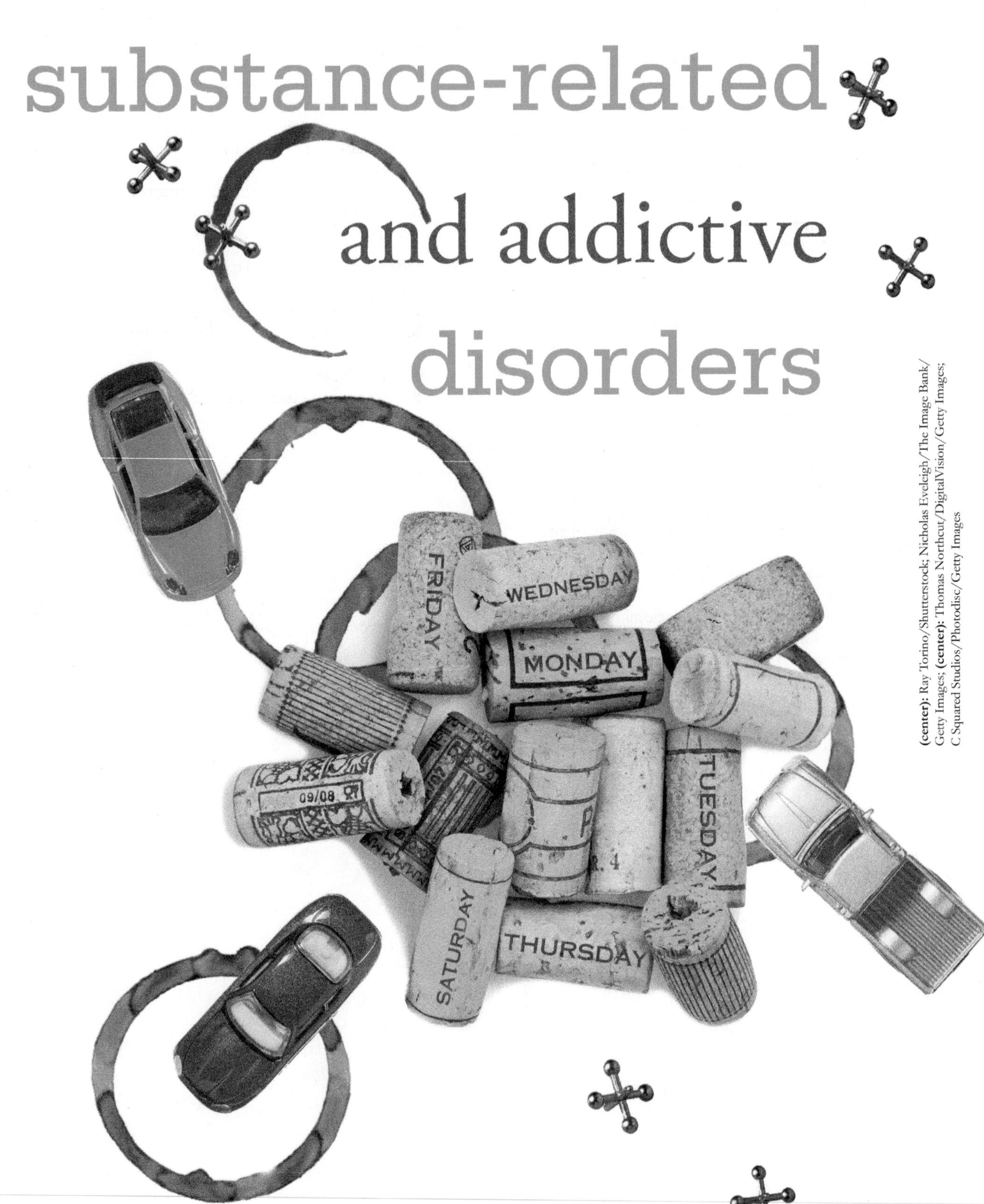

(center): Ray Torino/Shutterstock; Nicholas Eveleigh/The Image Bank/Getty Images; **(center):** Thomas Northcut/DigitalVision/Getty Images; C Squared Studios/Photodisc/Getty Images

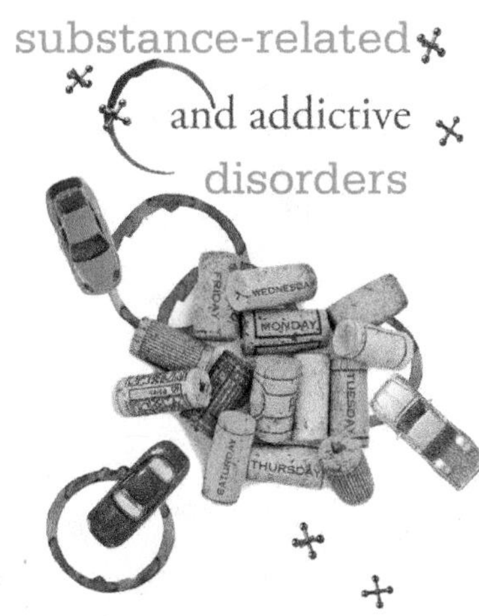

learning objectives

After reading this chapter, you should be able to:

9.1
Define the term "substance use disorder" according to DSM-5 criteria.

9.2
Understand the principles of tolerance and withdrawal and how they differ across various classes of drugs.

9.3
Appreciate how various drugs act in the body to produce their characteristic effects.

9.4
Describe the short- and long-term negative psychological and health consequences of various types of substance use disorders.

9.5
Understand the contributions of biological, genetic, behavioural, cognitive, and sociocultural theories to the etiology of substance use disorders.

9.6
Compare and contrast treatments for various types of substance use disorders.

Karen isn't sure this is the life she wants. Before the kids, she and her husband had a really equal relationship, with both Karen and Scott sharing the household chores—but now they have a traditional sex-role relationship, and she believes there was no way out. She agreed to stay home with Danny, age 2, and Timmy, age 6, until they started school, while Scott pursued a partnership at his law firm. Karen is a good mom, but when her third child, Joey, was born, she felt like she was losing control. Making matters worse, Timmy was becoming jealous of the attention his new brother was getting and was becoming a terror on wheels.

Karen tried to talk with her husband, but he did not understand. Timmy did not talk back to his dad, and when Scott got home from work, Timmy was usually so tired that he would just sit with his dad quietly. When Karen asked for help, Scott agreed, but he continued to work late every night.

Karen tried to talk with her mom and the other moms at the playground, but they rattled off advice that felt very judgmental to her. One day after talking to her mom, she was exasperated. She put the kids up for their nap and decided to have a glass of wine to relax. What started out as an "innocent" drink in the afternoon soon snowballed into a full bottle by the time Scott came home. At first she carefully hid the bottles, but she soon realized that he wasn't paying any attention anyway. At this point, she stopped caring what he thought. Wine became her support system.

She rationalized her drinking and took steps to be safe. She did her errands in the morning and only started drinking around noon. However, she hurt her back, and things got worse. Her doctor prescribed Oxycodone (a narcotic painkiller) and recommended physical therapy. She passed on the therapy, but Oxycodone made her feel as if nothing mattered—and her back stopped hurting! So, still drinking her bottle of wine, she would now also pop a pill or two as needed. Sometimes she would pass out in bed.

One afternoon while she was dozing on the couch, Timmy threw something at his baby brother that cut his forehead. Panic stricken, Karen strapped the kids in their car seats and drove to the emergency room. It was raining, and she lost control of the car. When she woke up, everyone was safe, but she was in the hospital with her arm in a sling. She was okay, but because of her blood alcohol content of 0.12, she was charged with driving under the influence. Scott demanded that she stop drinking immediately. He was surprised to hear her say she didn't think she could stop. He realized that they needed to come together and get Karen professional help.

Substance-Related Disorders

9.1 Define the term "substance use disorder" according to DSM-5 criteria.

9.2 Understand the principles of tolerance and withdrawal and how they differ across various classes of drugs.

In Karen's case, what started out as one "innocent" drink soon progressed to a serious problem that jeopardized her children's safety. Karen found that she needed to drink more and more—one glass of wine no longer allowed her to relax. Known as *tolerance*, this is one property of substances that can propel a person from simple use to a substance use disorder. How does this process occur? Why can some people stop at just one drink while others lack the internal "brakes" that keep them from spiralling into addiction? In this chapter, we discuss how biology, psychology, and culture interact to influence the development of substance use disorders.

Whether the drug is caffeine, nicotine, alcohol, or heroin, most people use substances at some point during their lifetime. **Substance use** refers to low- to moderate-use

Drawing the boundaries between alcohol use and an alcohol use disorder requires the knowledge of the frequency, duration, and severity of the behaviour.

Kzenon/Fotolia

experiences that do not produce problems with social, educational, or occupational functioning (APA, 2000). Drinking caffeinated soft drinks daily, drinking a beer or two at weekend parties, having wine with dinner, or smoking marijuana occasionally all qualify as *substance use*—although some substances are legal and some are illegal. The definition of use makes no claims as to the legality of the substance.

The effect of substance use varies from mild (perking up after morning coffee) to extreme, known as **substance intoxication**, which is categorized in the current DSM as a substance-induced disorder (APA, 2013). The definition of *intoxication* includes several concepts. First, intoxication is reversible (one comes down from the intoxicated state) and substance specific (the features of intoxication vary with the substance ingested). In addition, intoxication results in maladaptive behavioural or psychological changes associated with the central nervous system. Finally, the effects of intoxication emerge during or shortly after drug use. Consider the sports fan who has had too much to drink at a game or someone who is unable to walk a straight line in a sobriety test—these individuals are experiencing intoxication. Intoxication can be an isolated event, or it can be a recurring state in the context of a substance use disorder.

Distinguishing between substance use and problematic use can be complicated. Indeed, cultural norms vary—what is viewed as use in one culture may be regarded as abuse in another. Even legal ramifications differ across cultures. For example, see Table 9.1 for the legal blood alcohol limit across a number of countries showing varying tolerances of alcohol behind the wheel.

The DSM-IV (APA, 2000) categorized substance use disorders as either substance abuse or substance dependence. According to this prior version of the DSM, substance abuse occurs when ingesting the substance leads to disruption in social, occupational, or educational functioning. Substance dependence focused on behavioural

TABLE 9.1

Legal Blood Alcohol Content (BAC) Limits Around the World

Country	BAC Limit (%)
Pakistan, Saudi Arabia	0.00
Norway, Sweden	0.02
China, India, Japan	0.03
Argentina, Australia, Finland, France, Germany, South Africa, Switzerland	0.05
Brazil, Canada, Chile, Fiji, Ireland, New Zealand, Singapore, United Kingdom, United States	0.08

Source: www.drinkdriving.org/worldwide_drink_driving_limits.php. Accessed June 3 14, 2016.

criteria for
Alcohol Use Disorder
DSM-5

A. A problematic pattern of alcohol use leading to clinically significant impairment or distress, as manifested by at least two of the following, occurring within a 12-month period:

1. Alcohol is often taken in larger amounts or over a longer period than was intended.
2. There is a persistent desire or unsuccessful efforts to cut down or control alcohol use.
3. A great deal of time is spent in activities necessary to obtain alcohol, use alcohol, or recover from its effects.
4. Craving, or a strong desire or urge to use alcohol.
5. Recurrent alcohol use resulting in a failure to fulfill major role obligations at work, school, or home.
6. Continued alcohol use despite having persistent or recurrent social or interpersonal problems caused or exacerbated by the effects of alcohol.
7. Important social, occupational, or recreational activities are given up or reduced because of alcohol use.
8. Recurrent alcohol use in situations in which it is physically hazardous.
9. Alcohol use is continued despite knowledge of having a persistent or recurrent physical or psychological problem that is likely to have been caused or exacerbated by alcohol.
10. Tolerance, as defined by either of the following:
    - **a.** A need for markedly increased amounts of alcohol to achieve intoxication or desired effect.
    - **b.** A markedly diminished effect with continued use of the same amount of alcohol.
11. Withdrawal, as manifested by either of the following:
    - **c.** The characteristic withdrawal syndrome for alcohol (refer to Criteria A and B of the criteria set for alcohol withdrawal, pp. 499–500).
    - **d.** Alcohol (or a closely related substance, such as a benzodiazepine) is taken to relieve or avoid withdrawal symptoms.

patterns and pharmacological effects of the substance, including both tolerance (diminished response to a drug after its repeated use) and withdrawal (highly unpleasant physical symptoms when attempting to abstain from use).

In the DSM-5, substance abuse and substance dependence disorders have been combined into a single diagnosis: substance use disorder (see "DSM-5: Alcohol Use Disorder" for an example of the diagnostic criteria for a substance use disorder). The DSM-IV criteria for the two separate disorders have been combined and strengthened. For example, in the DSM-IV, only one symptom was required for a diagnosis of substance abuse. In the DSM-5, two or more symptoms must be present to meet the criteria for a substance use disorder, with severity characterized based on the number of symptoms present with mild = two or three symptoms, moderate = four or five symptoms, and severe = six or more symptoms.

Broadly, a substance use disorder is defined by a cluster of physiological, behavioural, and cognitive symptoms that indicate that the individual continues to use the substance despite significant problems due to use. The substance-related disorders are divided into substance use disorders and substance-induced disorders. Substance-induced disorders include intoxication, withdrawal, and other substance/medication-induced mental disorders (e.g., psychotic disorders, depressive disorders, etc.). The DSM-5 defines **tolerance** as requiring an increased dose of a substance to achieve the desired effect, or having a markedly reduced effect when consuming the usual dose. It defines **withdrawal** as a syndrome that occurs when concentrations of a substance decline in an individual who had maintained prolonged and heavy use of a substance. The physical symptoms of withdrawal vary by the class of substance, but physiological withdrawal symptoms are most apparent with alcohol, opioids, and nicotine, and to a lesser extent sedatives, hypnotics, anxiolytics, and caffeine.

In addition to tolerance and withdrawal, the behavioural features of substance use disorders include using more than the intended amount; desiring or attempting to cut down; spending time trying to acquire the substance; giving up social, occupational, or recreational activities because of substance use; and continuing use despite known physical or psychological problems caused by or exacerbated by the substance use.

Whether a person develops a substance use disorder depends in part on the drug's addictive potential and on the characteristics of the person using the drug. Some drugs such as heroin and alcohol produce more withdrawal symptoms. Some users are more prone to substance problems because of their genetic makeup, ongoing life stress, or immersion in a subculture that involves drug use (Daughters et al., 2007). Therefore, a combination of genetic and environmental factors determines liability to developing a substance use disorder.

CONCEPT check

- A substance use disorder is a cluster of physiological, behavioural, and cognitive symptoms that indicate that the individual continues to use the substance despite significant problems due to use.
- Substance-induced disorders include intoxication, withdrawal, and other substance/medication-induced mental disorders.

critical thinking question What factors do you think contribute to excessive drinking? What are some of the genetic and environmental factors that influence whether drinking becomes a regular event or remains a rare behaviour?

Commonly Used "Licit" Drugs

9.3 Appreciate how various drugs act in the body to produce their characteristic effects.

We focus first on three legal psychoactive drugs that are widely used in our society: caffeine, nicotine, and alcohol. Although the sale of caffeine has no formal restrictions, it is widely considered to be a poor source of energy for young children. Nonetheless, children are introduced to caffeine very early in life through carbonated beverages. In contrast, the purchase and use of nicotine and alcohol have age restrictions with penalties applicable to both the buyer and the seller. We look first at the drug with which millions of people start their day: caffeine.

Caffeine

"One doppio espresso, one grande latte…two shots, one espresso macchiato." Customers place orders like this every morning at countless coffee bars. **Caffeine** is a central nervous system (CNS) stimulant with a kick that boosts energy, mood, awareness, concentration, and wakefulness. Caffeine may be consumed quite safely in moderation to produce these positive effects. Its less desirable side effects include headache, fatigue, depressed mood, inactivity, trouble concentrating, irritability, and feeling "foggy" (Juliano & Griffiths, 2004). Coffee, a robust source of caffeine, has become an important part of our culture and often serves as a backdrop for socializing.

Although less harmful than most other substances, caffeine, like other stimulants, affects multiple organs within the body, and withdrawal after regular use produces short-term effects such as a "crash." It also has long-term effects, including tolerance, dependence, and withdrawal. However, there is no diagnosis for Caffeine Use Disorder in the DSM-5, although there are DSM-5 diagnoses for Caffeine Intoxication and Caffeine Withdrawal; see functional impairment section below). One diet soft drink a day can escalate to 10 during exam time to get the same level of alertness. If you then celebrate the end of exams with a back-to-nature camping trip where getting your coffee fix is not possible, you might find yourself with a blistering caffeine-withdrawal headache. Although caffeine's precise mechanism of action remains unknown, the neurotransmitters adenosine and serotonin may be involved in its effect on the brain (Carrillo & Benitez, 2000). Caffeine has a long half-life (it stays in the bloodstream for a long time), so that some people can experience its effects six hours or more after their last dose.

FUNCTIONAL IMPAIRMENT Because just about everyone consumes caffeine in one form or another—in coffee or soft drinks—it is considered normal, and its potential health effects are often overlooked. However, over time, caffeine may contribute to cardiovascular disorders, reproductive problems, osteoporosis, cancer, and psychiatric disturbances (Barone & Grice, 1994; Carrillo & Benitez, 2000; Garattini, 1993; Massey, 1998). For some people, the equivalent of five to eight cups of coffee per day may lead to anxiety and to respiratory, urinary, gastric, and cardiovascular distress (Carrillo & Benitez, 2000).

While caffeine, at minimum, elicits some physiological effects on healthy individuals, research indicates that caffeine provokes significantly higher anxiety in individuals carrying genes associated with anxiety disorders (e.g., panic disorder) (Alsene et al., 2003). Consuming large amounts of caffeine can produce acute caffeine intoxication, which includes physical symptoms such as restlessness, nervousness, excitement, insomnia, flushed face, diuresis (increased urination), gastrointestinal disturbance, muscle twitching, rambling flow of thought and speech, fast or irregular heartbeat, periods of inexhaustibility, and psychomotor agitation. Although rare and requiring extremely high doses (roughly 50 to 100 240-mL cups of coffee per day), caffeine-associated death can occur. This outcome is increasingly likely with the trend toward high-dose beverages, such as energy drinks like Red Bull or Monster, which contain caffeine far in excess of a regular cup of coffee. Several deaths due to accidental caffeine supplement overdose have been reported (Holmgren et al., 2004; Mrvos et al., 1989).

Caffeine is the most widely used drug in the world. The manner in which it is consumed is often influenced by cultural conditions.

(top): Cathy Melloan Resources/Photoedit; **(bottom):** Evelyn Hockstein/KRT/Newscom

EPIDEMIOLOGY Caffeine is the most widely used drug worldwide. More than 80% of the world's population consumes it daily (James, 1997). Soft drinks typically have between 2 and 5 mg of caffeine per ounce. Tea ranges from about 5 mg per ounce (about 60 total mg in a 12-ounce serving), coffee ranges from about 7 mg per ounce in instant coffee and lattes to more than 20 mg per ounce in stronger brews (ranging from about 80 mg to well over 200 mg in a 12-ounce cup), and espresso has about 50 mg per ounce (about 150 total mg in a double 1.5-ounce serving) (www.energyfiend.com/the-caffeine-database).

An emerging trend, especially among adolescent boys and young men, is the use of highly caffeinated energy drinks. These drinks typically start at around 10 mg per ounce and can exceed 100 mg per ounce at the high end (often referred to as *energy shots*, which are recommended for dilution but often are taken in their packaged form). These drinks have now joined coffee as a legal drug that many use at moderate levels to boost energy, but that also have the potential to produce negative side effects. They may provide a false sense of wakefulness that might replace adequate sleep. In developing adolescents, these effects can lead to especially problematic health consequences.

Nicotine

John looked around the group as the therapist said, "Congratulations. If you are going to quit, you will need to plan for events that trigger your urge to smoke. So I would like everyone to think about an upcoming situation when you will really need a cigarette." John almost laughed. Quitting smoking would be easy. He wouldn't even be here if his wife, Sandra, who was quitting with him, hadn't insisted John come with her. Sheila described how she liked to blow off steam at happy hour, drinking and smoking the stress away. Oscar described trying to drink his morning coffee without a cigarette. Mikey talked about how his work "smoke break" was the only way he managed to calm down and not strangle his boss. Cheryl, a high-powered lawyer, described how, after a big win, she would sit outside on "her bench" and smoke in celebration. When it was Sandra's turn, John was in a cold sweat and could barely concentrate. All this talk about smoking made him think he needed one right now. When the group leader called his name, he blurted out, "Right now, my trigger is right now!"

Especially for people who are genetically susceptible, **nicotine** is a highly addictive drug (Mohammed, 2000). Its most common source is the plant *Nicotiana tabacum*, which has been chewed and smoked for centuries. Cigarettes are the most common method of delivery, but other methods such as cigars, pipes, and smokeless tobacco are widely available.

Nicotine can enter the bloodstream via the lungs (smoking), mucus membranes of the mouth or nose (chewing tobacco, using snuff), and even the skin (using a transdermal nicotine patch). Nicotine is both a stimulant and a sedative; its rapid action (8 to 10 seconds) and rapid effect are part of what makes the drug so rewarding or reinforcing. Many smokers report that nicotine produces temporary tension relief and helps with alertness and concentration. Furthermore, nicotine has strong social determinants. Indeed, subcultures centred on cigars and smokeless tobacco are common, and cigarette smoking provides an instant social affiliation from smokers asking each other for a light at a bar to a few strangers standing outside a restaurant or office building, chatting while they smoke.

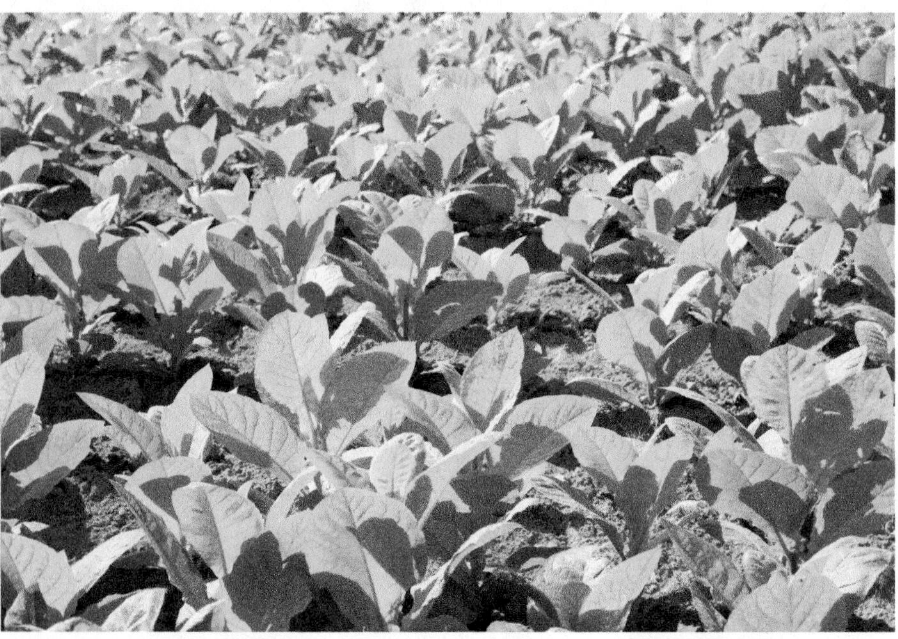

The plant *Nicotiana tabacum* is dried and processed into cigarettes, cigars, pipe tobacco, and smokeless tobacco for consumption.

imagesef/Fotolia

Nicotine also has pervasive physical effects (see Figure 9.1). It stimulates the adrenal glands, causing a discharge of epinephrine (adrenaline), leading to a feeling of a "rush" or a "kick." This stimulation also leads to glucose release and increases blood pressure, respiration, and heart rate. Nicotine affects the pancreas by suppressing insulin secretion, leading to mild hyperglycemia (elevated blood sugar) in smokers. Central to its highly addictive potential, nicotine releases dopamine, directly affecting the brain's pleasure and motivation centres. The release of dopamine is believed to underlie the pleasurable sensations described by many smokers (National Institute on Drug Abuse, 2001).

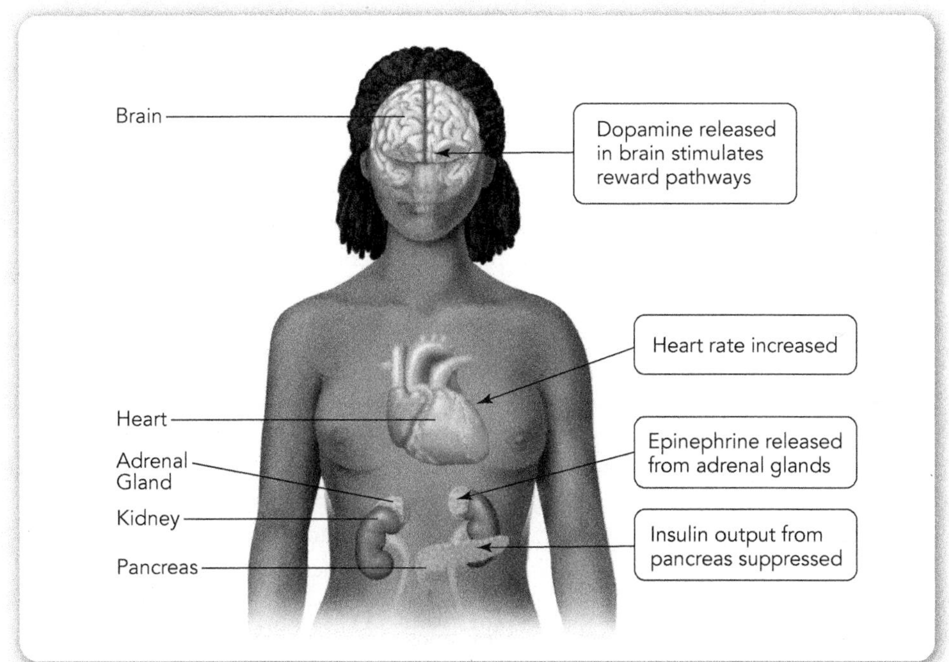

FIGURE 9.1

The Effects of Nicotine on the Body. Nicotine affects many bodily systems, including the brain, the adrenal glands, and the pancreas, influencing the central nervous system, the respiratory system, the cardiovascular system, and the digestive system.

FUNCTIONAL IMPAIRMENT Frequent use of nicotine leads to tolerance and dependence. Highly dependent smokers identify the first cigarette of the day as the hardest one to give up. Overnight, withdrawal has begun, and by morning the "craving" is quite strong. Moreover, giving up smoking leads to withdrawal symptoms that can last up to a month or more, making quitting very difficult. These symptoms may include depressed mood, insomnia, irritability, frustration or anger, anxiety, difficulty concentrating, restlessness, decreased heart rate, increased appetite, and weight gain.

Most smokers are aware of the deleterious health effects. Data from Statistics Canada indicate that about half of Canadian smokers have tried to quit in the past year, mostly unsuccessfully (Leatherdale & Shields, 2009). Tobacco use is the largest preventable cause of death in the world (Fiore, 2000). Smoking increases the risk for many types of cancer, cardiovascular disease, and respiratory illnesses, and other medical problems (Shields, 2005). Most lung cancer patients are current or former smokers, and lung cancer causes more deaths than any other cancer (Janz, 2012). Smoking has a substantial impact on health and life expectancy; Canadian smokers are predicted to lose about nine years of life expectancy because of smoking (Janz, 2012).

EPIDEMIOLOGY In the past few decades, the number of people who smoke has declined dramatically. In 2014, 18% of Canadians aged 12 and older, roughly 5.4 million people, smoked either daily or occasionally. This is a decrease from 2013 (19%) and is the lowest smoking rate reported since 2001. Among the sexes, 21% of males and 15% of females reported that they smoked daily or occasionally in 2014. For males this was a decrease from 2012, and for females it was a decrease from 2013. The rates of smoking have decreased significantly since 2001, when 28% of males and 24% of females smoked daily or occasionally (Janz, 2012).

Alcohol

In the case that opened this chapter, Karen initially used alcohol to relax, but her drinking eventually endangered her own and her children's health. Although many people find a drink stimulating, alcohol is actually a depressant. The active ingredient in any alcoholic drink, *ethyl alcohol,* is quickly absorbed via the stomach and intestines into the bloodstream. Then it is distributed throughout the body and quickly acts to depress the central nervous system. Although alcohol affects many neurotransmitter systems, its effect on receptors in the brain's *gamma aminobutyric acid* (GABA) system are particularly noteworthy. GABA is the brain's primary inhibitory neurotransmitter. So, by increasing GABA firing, alcohol inhibits other brain activity. This explains why alcohol is called a "depressant." Continued drinking leads to a slowing—that is, depression or, more accurately, suppression—of the central nervous system, impairing motor coordination, decreasing reaction times, and leading to impaired memory, poor judgment, and visual and auditory disturbances. Impairment ranges from mild feelings of being "tipsy" to more extreme levels of intoxication, or being drunk.

FUNCTIONAL IMPAIRMENT Although many people drink socially with little or no impairment, others who drink more regularly may experience tolerance. At first, one drink produced relaxation for Karen, but soon, she needed much more, and she eventually added another depressant (pain medicine) to achieve the same effect. Withdrawal symptoms from chronic heavy drinking can range from mild to severe. Signs and symptoms of alcohol withdrawal include tremors, anxiety, irritability, and agitation. Other effects include a craving for alcohol, insomnia, vivid dreams, hypervigilance, vomiting, headache, and sweating. In its most severe form, alcohol withdrawal includes experiencing hallucinations (false sensory perceptions) and seizures. Alcohol hallucinations begin within one to two days of stopping or cutting down and can be auditory, visual, or tactile. They may include a phenomenon known as *formication*, the sensation of having ants or bugs crawling all over the body. Seizures may also occur within one to two days of stopping drinking. Another withdrawal symptom, **delirium tremens (DTs)**, which is characterized by disorientation, severe agitation, high blood pressure, and fever, can last up to three to four days after stopping drinking. This is a severe condition; 5% of individuals die from these metabolic complications (Trevisan et al., 1998).

Depending on its severity, withdrawal can be treated with either careful monitoring (if mild) or the administration of benzodiazepines (see Chapter 4). Benzodiazepines can help decrease neuronal hyperactivity and reduce withdrawal symptoms as well as the risk of seizures and DTs. Alcohol and benzodiazepines have similar mechanisms of action, so individuals become *cross tolerant*—that is, their tolerance to one drug translates to tolerance of the other.

Although alcohol withdrawal can be associated with medical complications, excessive consumption of alcohol can also cause serious long-term health effects. **Alcohol cirrhosis** is a liver disease that occurs in about 10% to 15% of people with alcoholism. Cirrhosis is the slow deterioration and malfunction of the liver due to chronic injury. In the case of alcoholism, the injury is from alcohol exposure. Chronic alcohol consumption can impair the liver's ability to detoxify the blood, leading to the development of scar tissue. In turn, scar tissue obstructs blood flow and impairs the liver's function.

Long-term alcohol abuse also harms the brain. Deficiencies in thiamine secondary to alcohol dependence can cause **Wernicke-Korsakoff syndrome**. The syndrome is

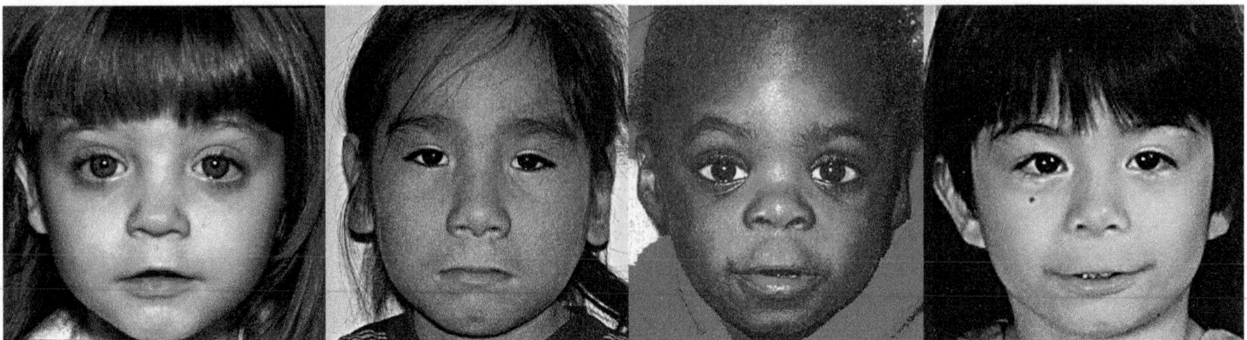

Characteristic features of fetal alcohol syndrome include a short palpebral fissure length (the distance from the inner to outer corner of the eye), a smooth philtrum (area between the nose and upper lip), and a thin upper lip.

Susan Astley

characterized by a cluster of symptoms including confusion, *amnesia* (see Chapter 13), and *confabulation*, an adaptation to memory loss in which the individual "fills in blanks" with made-up information. *Wernicke's encephalopathy* includes short-term memory loss, paralysis of the eyes, and unsteady gait. Because people with Wernicke-Korsakoff syndrome lose the ability to learn from experience, they almost always require custodial care, and 80% of individuals with this condition do not regain full cognitive function.

Fetal alcohol syndrome (FAS) (Jones & Smith, 1973), another severe consequence of alcohol use, occurs when a pregnant woman drinks alcohol and it passes through the placenta and harms the developing fetus. Children with FAS have classic identifiable facial anomalies, including short palpebral fissure lengths (distance from the inner to outer corner of the eye), a smooth philtrum (area between the nose and upper lip), and a thin upper lip. Children with FAS may also have neurodevelopmental abnormalities, including small head size, structural brain abnormalities, and neurological problems such as impaired fine motor skills, hearing loss, poor eye–hand coordination, and abnormal gait. As the child develops, learning difficulties, poor school performance, and impulse control problems may occur. A primary determinant of the severity of FAS is how much and how frequently the mother drinks (Abel & Hannigan, 1995). FAS can be avoided if women abstain from alcohol when pregnant or even if they think they are pregnant.

EPIDEMIOLOGY After caffeine, alcohol is the most commonly used psychoactive substance (APA, 2013). The lifetime prevalence of alcohol use disorder in Canada is 18% (Pearson et al., 2013). The persistence of alcohol problems seems to be best predicted by the frequency of intoxication and the frequency of heavy drinking (more than five drinks a day) (Dawson, 2000).

Considerable differences exist in patterns of alcohol use disorders across sex and racial/ethnic groups. Alcohol use disorders are more than twice as common among males as females (Grant et al., 2004). Although men are at higher risk for alcohol use disorders, women may be more vulnerable to the negative health consequences of heavy drinking (Dawson & Grant, 1993).

CONCEPT check

- Caffeine, a CNS stimulant, is the most widely used drug in the world. Some people develop tolerance and have difficulties with withdrawal; caffeine intoxication is rare but possible.
- Nicotine is highly addictive and is considered to be both a stimulant and a sedative. It produces its effects via the release of dopamine in the brain.
- Alcohol is a CNS depressant that affects GABA receptors in the brain. Extensive alcohol use can lead to serious withdrawal symptoms, such as delirium tremens or DTs, and prolonged abuse can be associated with serious consequences, such as Wernicke-Korsakoff syndrome.

critical thinking question In Western cultures, the use of caffeine, nicotine, and alcohol is common. What do these drugs contribute to our culture, and how would the Western world differ in the absence of these drugs?

Illicit Drugs

Each year, new and often dangerous drugs make their way into the population. Entry points vary from the drug underworld to the doctor's prescription pad—yet the desire for new mind-altering substances continues. Illicit drug use comes with steep emotional, social, legal, and financial costs, but for many individuals, the strong pull of the physiological high or the escape from the real world make long-term abstinence difficult.

The *Cannabis sativa* plant is a major cash crop.

Vitor costa/Shutterstock

We begin this section by focusing on marijuana. We then examine other classes of drugs that have primary effects on the central nervous system: stimulants, depressants, and hallucinogens. Finally, we review inhalants and prescription medicines.

Marijuana

9.4 Describe the short- and long-term negative psychological and health consequences of various types of substance use disorders.

Marijuana comes from the *Cannabis sativa* plant, which also produces the fibre known as *hemp*. Its leaves can be dried and used in food and drink, or—most frequently—smoked. Marijuana is widely used in Canada and in other Western countries. It is legal to possess, consume, or grow marijuana for medicinal purposes under certain circumstances in Canada. It also legal in countries such as the Netherlands, but it is illegal in other countries such as the United States. Although marijuana is regarded as an illicit drug in many countries, most Canadians believe that marijuana should be decriminalized and re-classified as a licit drug (https://en.wikipedia.org/wiki/Legal_history_of_cannabis_in_Canada).

The active ingredient in marijuana is **tetrahydrocannabinol (THC)**. When marijuana is smoked, THC immediately enters the brain and lasts for one to three hours (National Institute on Drug Abuse, 2005b). The user generally experiences a pleasant state of relaxation, intensified colour and sound, and slowed perception of time. Mild effects include dry mouth, and increased hunger ("the munchies") and thirst. The effects of marijuana depend on the dose and the user's characteristics or sensitivity. THC content varies across preparations and methods of delivery. While low doses are commonly associated with relaxation, higher doses are associated with visual and auditory activity and fascination, increased heart rate and blood pressure, bloodshot eyes, and occasionally anxiety, panic, and paranoia.

How does marijuana produce these effects? Its active ingredient, THC, is received by special brain receptors called *cannabinoid receptors*, which influence pleasure, learning and memory, higher cognitive functions, sensory perceptions, and motor coordination (National Institute on Drug Abuse, 2005a). Like most drugs of abuse, THC activates the brain's reward system by stimulating the release of dopamine, leading to the feelings of euphoria associated with being "high."

FUNCTIONAL IMPAIRMENT Heavy marijuana use results in persistent memory loss; impairment of attention, learning skills, and motor movement; addiction; chronic respiratory problems; and an increased risk of head, neck, and lung cancer. However, THC has medicinal effects as well. It is useful in the treatment of nausea in cancer chemotherapy, glaucoma, and appetite stimulation in people with AIDS, and new treatment avenues are currently being investigated (Felder et al., 2006) (see "Research Hot Topic: Medical Uses of Marijuana").

Evidence regarding tolerance to cannabis is unclear. Some studies report tolerance; others do not report a need for increased doses to achieve the same high. Craving for marijuana and withdrawal symptoms can make it difficult to quit (Budney et al., 2003). Withdrawal symptoms include restlessness, loss of appetite, trouble sleeping, weight loss, shaky hands, irritability, and anxiety (Budney et al., 2001; National Institute on Drug Abuse, 2005a).

Normal Behaviour Case Study

Marijuana Use—No Disorder

Meghan was from a conservative family living in a small town in Saskatchewan. She arrived at McGill University for her freshman year. She wanted to fit in so badly. Her roommate was from Toronto and seemed very sophisticated. To Meghan's delight, they really hit it off, despite their vastly different backgrounds. That weekend, they went to their first campus party. Meghan was amazed to find everyone drinking alcohol and smoking marijuana. Her roommate passed her a joint. Meghan held it for a minute while everyone stared at her. Her roommate said, "Meghan's from a small town—we might have to show her how to inhale." So Meghan inhaled just to fit in. She did not want to make a scene. She partied hard that night and felt so cool. This was campus life. Then Meghan joined a track team, and her teammates invited her to a party. Some people were drinking alcohol, but many were just drinking soft drinks. No one pushed her to do drugs. Meghan invited her roommate to the track parties, but she found them dull—not enough "partying." For the rest of the semester, Meghan split her time between partying with her roommate's crowd, where she smoked to "fit in," and hanging out with her track buddies, where she drank soft drinks when she felt like it. At the end of the semester, she moved in with her track buddies, leaving the drugs behind.

Abnormal Behaviour Case Study

Marijuana Use—Disorder

That summer, Josh went to hockey camp while his buddies stayed home. He found his passion, and his buddies found marijuana. At his welcome back party, Ronnie offered him a joint. Josh's coach said that he would kick anyone off the team if he found them using drugs, so Josh refused. The guys teased, but they didn't push too hard. During hockey season, Josh was around less, partly because he was busy and partly because he was afraid the coach would find out about the drugs. Over time, his friends became increasingly angry at Josh's success and his "holier-than-thou" attitude about drugs. They made a big deal each time he refused. One night Josh couldn't take it anymore—he grabbed the joint and inhaled deeply. It didn't taste or feel good, but it was a relief getting everyone off his back. He soon started smoking with his friends and then began using regularly. Soon, he lost his motivation for hockey. He trained with less intensity and began to feel the physical effects of regular marijuana use. Before he knew it, his performance has become so bad that he was kicked off the team.

EPIDEMIOLOGY Marijuana is the most commonly used illicit substance in Canada. The lifetime prevalence of Cannabis abuse or dependence (7%) is more common than that of any other illicit drug in Canada (Pearson et al., 2013).

CNS Stimulants

Tammy was an adult from an early age. Her mother was an alcoholic who brought home different men. When Tammy was 13, one of the men molested her while her mother lay passed out on the sofa. These experiences took a toll on Tammy. She had trouble making friends, and she was incapable of romantic intimacy. At 17, she worked at a clothing store. There she met Margaret, who was fun and easygoing, all the things Tammy wasn't. One night after work, Margaret offered her a ride home and talked her into stopping at a rave. Margaret bought some pills and gave one to Tammy. After about 30 minutes, Tammy felt a wave come over her. The experience was unbelievable. She felt free and wanted to be intimate and close to everyone around her. The next day she slept through her shift at work. She had already missed several shifts because of her mother, and she was fired. She thought about going back to work to beg for her job, but instead she called Margaret to see if she had any more pills.

research **HOT** topic

Medical Uses of Marijuana

Canada is among a handful of countries that lead the world in the medical use of marijuana. Most people agree that illegal substance use is personally and socially hazardous, but over the past decade, many people have been advocating the use of marijuana for medical purposes. Although marijuana has been considered illegal in Canada since 1923, there has been increasing pressure for decriminalization, both in Canada and other countries. In Canada, cannabis is now legal to possess, consume, or grow for medicinal purposes under certain conditions according to Health Canada. In June 2015, the City of Vancouver legalized and regulated the sale of medical marijuana from municipally licensed dispensaries (https://en.wikipedia.org/wiki/Legal_history_of_cannabis_in_Canada, accessed July 23, 2015).

Researchers believe that marijuana has many therapeutic applications, including relief from nausea and appetite loss, reduction of pressure within the eye, reduction of muscle spasms, and relief from some forms of chronic pain. Studies indicate that marijuana can be beneficial for symptoms associated with AIDS, cancer, glaucoma, epilepsy, and multiple sclerosis, and perhaps chronic pain such as migraine headaches, menstrual cramps, and arthritis. In 1997, the National Institute of Health formed a group of eight clinical trials experts. The group concluded that much of the existing evidence for medical marijuana use was anecdotal and that controlled clinical trials were necessary. They noted that there was enough scientific research to suggest that marijuana might have a positive medical role in some areas.

The value and safety of medical marijuana use are severely compromised when it is used in an unregulated manner and administered through smoking. Smoking marijuana is not particularly safe and can be ineffective for medicinal purposes for several reasons. First, medications work best when they are taken in an appropriate dose. Smoking does not provide a precise and controlled dose, and when the drug is obtained through nonregulated sources, purity cannot be guaranteed. A more problematic risk is smoking as a means of drug administration. It is a misconception that only cigarettes impair health; many of the same risks, as well as a few others, are evident when smoking marijuana. Ongoing research must address both the benefits and risks associated with marijuana for medicinal purposes. The scientific process should be allowed to evaluate the potential therapeutic effects of marijuana for certain disorders separately from the societal debate over the potential harmful effects of nonmedical marijuana use.

Having already discussed the effects of two widely used legal stimulants (nicotine and caffeine), we now turn to the illegal stimulants—cocaine and amphetamines. The effects of both drugs include euphoria, increased energy, mental alertness, and rapid speech. Some people also feel a sense of power and courage, the ability to tackle otherwise daunting tasks, and increased feelings of intimacy and sexual arousal. However, the use of cocaine and amphetamines has serious short- and long-term adverse effects, including dangerous elevations in blood pressure and heart rate and cardiovascular abnormalities, potentially leading to heart attack, respiratory arrest, and seizures. These stimulants disrupt the normal communication among brain circuits by increasing dopamine, which leads to elevated mood and increased alertness. In high doses, increased dopamine and norepinephrine can lead to hallucinations, delusions, and paranoia (see Chapter 10).

Amphetamines come in many forms. Legitimate uses include the treatment of asthma, nasal congestion, attention-deficit/hyperactivity disorder (see Chapter 12), and narcolepsy (a sleep disorder). Because these drugs prolong wakefulness, sometimes people who need to stay awake for long periods of time—such as airline pilots, truckers, and students studying for exams—use them. They can also suppress appetite, making them attractive to some dieters. Amphetamines, also known as *uppers*, *bennies*, and *speed*, are produced in laboratories. Three different preparations of amphetamines include *amphetamine* (Benzedrine), *dextroamphetamine* (Dexedrine), and *methamphetamine* (Methedrine). These drugs, swallowed in pill form, inhaled intranasally, or injected for a quicker kick, increase the release of dopamine, norepinephrine, and serotonin in the brain.

Other manufactured amphetamines, sometimes referred to as *designer drugs*, often spread rapidly throughout the community. One example, *methylenedioxymethamphetamine*

(MDMA), interferes with the reuptake of serotonin. Initially used as an appetite suppressant, the pill form of MDMA (**ecstasy**) has become a common "club" drug and a frequent trigger for emergency room visits. Similarly, **crystal methamphetamine** (ice, crank) is a form of methamphetamine that produces longer lasting and more intense physiological reactions than the powdered form. It is smoked in glass pipes or injected. The high is rapid and intense and can last for 12 hours or more.

FUNCTIONAL IMPAIRMENT In addition to increased heart rate and blood pressure, amphetamines can damage blood vessels in the brain, causing stroke. Users can develop paranoid anxiety, confusion, and insomnia—and the psychotic symptoms can persist and recur even months and years after drug use has ended. Over time, users can become violent and aggressive and suffer from emaciation and malnutrition due to appetite suppression. Tolerance develops rapidly, often leading to rapid dose escalation. Withdrawal from extended highs produces "crashes" marked by depression, irritability, and prolonged periods of sleep.

EPIDEMIOLOGY Prescription stimulants can be misused for a variety of reasons (e.g., to get high, to help students remain alert while studying for exams). The misuse of prescription stimulants increases the risk of psychological and physical dependence (Canadian Centre on Substance Abuse [CCSA], 2013d). According to a systematic review of studies, 5% to 35% of adolescents and young adults in North America have used stimulants for nonmedical purposes (CCSA, 2013d). For example, 9% of students in grades 7–12 in Atlantic Canada reported nonmedical stimulant use in 2007 (CCSA, 2013d). Research from Alberta suggests that the most common reason for emergency department visits related to prescription drugs was caused by stimulants other than cocaine (CCSA, 2013d).

With regard to methamphetamine, Manitoba and Ontario have specifically included this drug in their surveys of student drug use. In both provinces, about 3% of students reported using the methamphetamine in the past year (CCSA, 2005). The prevalence of use is considerably higher in homeless youth; in one study, 37% reported using methamphetamine at least once a month (CCSA, 2005).

Regarding ecstasy, the use in the Canadian general population is quite low, with only 0.4% of Canadians over the age of 15 reporting using the drug in the past year (CCSA, 2015). However, the use of ecstasy is higher among specific populations. About 4% of Canadian youth in grades 10–12 reported using ecstasy in the past 12 months (CCSA, 2015). The prevalence of use of the drug in the past year is especially high among homeless youth, with estimates ranging from 28% to 72% (CCSA, 2015).

Cocaine

Namia was an up-and-coming model. At age 16 she travelled all the time. When she wasn't shooting or preparing for a shoot, she was exercising or working with her tutor trying to keep up with her school work. What worried her most, however, was the pressure to stay impossibly thin. Namia was constantly hungry. Before fashion week, an older model saw her struggling, smoking cigarette after cigarette to curb her appetite. She introduced Namia to cocaine, snorting lines in the dressing room saying, "This is the only way to get through the week...and you won't feel hungry at all!" She was right. For the next two days, Namia had a lot more energy. She seemed on top of everything else, including her school work. And then she crashed. Things spiralled out of control. One night right before a big show, she could barely move from exhaustion.

Cocaine, which comes from the leaves of the coca plant, is indigenous to South America. People have chewed coca leaves for centuries to provide relief from fatigue and hunger. Cocaine's introduction to North America in the late 1800s was as a legal additive to cigars and cigarettes and to Coca-Cola. Cocaine was also used as a painkiller because of its anesthetic effects. Once its addictive properties became known, its use declined.

The powdered form of cocaine can be snorted or dissolved in water and injected. Crack cocaine is a smoked form of rock crystal cocaine that is highly addictive, delivers large amounts of drug quickly via the lungs, and produces an immediate euphoric effect. The term *crack* refers to the crackling sound the drug makes when heated (National Institute on Drug Abuse, 2004).

FUNCTIONAL IMPAIRMENT Cocaine is highly addictive. Its powerful stimulant effects are thought to be caused by inhibiting nerve cells' reabsorption of dopamine. When more dopamine is available in the synapses, the stimulation of the brain reward pathways increases and provides more positive feelings. When tolerance develops, use increases in order to get the initial euphoric effects. When users take larger doses, their exposure to the drug is increased, and they are more sensitive to its dangerous effects, such as anesthetic and convulsant effects. This phenomenon may account for reported deaths after relatively low doses (www.nida.nih.gov/researchreports/cocaine/cocaine.html).

EPIDEMIOLOGY In Canada, cocaine is the third most used substance in the general population and among adults, after alcohol and marijuana (CCSA, 2014). The prevalence of past-year cocaine use in the Canadian population in 2012 was 1%, with the prevalence being higher in youths (age 15–24 years) than adults (25+ years) (CCSA, 2014). Cocaine use in Canada—crack cocaine use in particular—is highest in specific groups, such as the homeless and urban youth (CCSA, 2014).

Sedative Drugs

Leila, a nurse, was energetic and loved her work. Another nurse suggested having a poker night. Leila had never gambled, but that first night she cleaned up. After doing it again, she found herself enjoying gambling. As a nurse, she kept unusual hours and came home late at night stressed and looking for a way to relax. Unlike games with her friends, the Internet casino was always available. At first she was so excited about her wins and worried about getting back her losses that she hardly missed the sleep. Soon, however, she was cutting everything and everyone else out of her life. As her losses grew, she opened up new credit cards to get more money to win back her losses. She was convinced that she just needed one good streak to get everything back. When she could no longer open any more credit cards, she followed the advice of another nurse on an Internet gambling site and stole painkillers and Xanax from work to get some quick cash. At first, Leila took just a few pills. After an especially big loss, she felt suicidal. To calm down, she took one Xanax. This helped her walk away from the computer for a while and relax. Over time she needed more and more pills to sell and to take for herself until the hospital found out what she was doing and fired her.

Sedative drugs include two general classes: **barbiturates** and **benzodiazepines**, both of which are central nervous system *depressants*. This means that their mechanism of action is the opposite of the CNS *stimulants* discussed earlier. Initially used to treat anxiety and insomnia, barbiturates are now less commonly prescribed than benzodiazepines due to the high risk of abuse, dependence, and overdose.

Barbiturates or "downers" act on the GABA-ergic system in a manner similar to alcohol. Common barbiturates include amobarbital (Amatol), pentobarbital (Nembutal), and secobarbitol (Seconal). They can be swallowed or injected and are often used to counteract the effect of "uppers" or amphetamines. Initial benefits at low doses include disinhibition and euphoria in an attempt to alleviate feelings of anxiety. In the short term, barbiturate use leads to slurred speech, decreased respiration, fatigue, disorientation, lack of coordination, and dilated pupils. At higher doses, users can experience impaired memory and coordination, irritability, and paranoid and suicidal thoughts.

Benzodiazepines were originally prescribed widely for the treatment of anxiety. They can be used responsibly and effectively for short-term treatment of anxiety and insomnia. However, their prolonged use or use without a prescription can be problematic. At high doses, the drugs produce light-headedness, vertigo, and muscle control problems. Valium would have been a drug that Karen, introduced in the case at the beginning of this chapter, might have been prescribed in the 1960s to deal with the stress of caring for young children. Other benzodiazepines include Xanax and Halcion. Although generally considered to be safer than barbiturates and to have lower potential for abuse and dependence when used as prescribed, they are not completely benign. One powerful benzodiazepine, Rohipnol ("roofies" or "date rape drug"), is available by prescription in many countries but not in Canada or the United States. This drug is 7 to 10 times more potent than Valium and causes partial amnesia—which means that people given the drug often cannot remember certain events when they were intoxicated. It is this feature and its powerful effects that earned it the reputation of being associated with date rape.

FUNCTIONAL IMPAIRMENT If overused, both barbiturates and benzodiazepines can result in oversedation and problems in thinking and interacting with others. Although the drugs are legal if prescribed, their use by those without a prescription or their misuse by people for whom they are medically inappropriate often leads to theft and other dangerous strategies for obtaining the drugs. Tolerance for barbiturates develops rapidly, producing a high risk for overdose. Death results from depression of the brain's respiratory centre. Withdrawal from barbiturates produces tremors, increased blood pressure and heart rate, sweating, and seizures. Tolerance and withdrawal also occur with benzodiazepines. The symptoms mirror alcohol withdrawal and include anxiety, insomnia, tremors, and delirium. Although benzodiazepines can be overused with problematic consequences, they have largely replaced barbiturates due to less potential for dependence and fewer side effects.

EPIDEMIOLOGY The average age of onset of unprescribed benzodiazepine use is around 25 years (Substance Abuse and Mental Health Services Administration, 2005). However, these drugs are also abused in younger populations. A survey of Canadian students in grades 6–12 found that 2% to 3% had used sedative drugs to get high in the past year (CCSA, 2013c). National data are lacking on the prevalence of the use of unprescribed sedatives, although it appears that these drugs are more likely to be abused by women than men (CCSA, 2013c). The abuse of these drugs appears to be higher in certain groups, such as First Nations adults living on reserves or in northern communities (CCSA, 2013c).

Opioids

Dennis had no idea what a panic attack was, but he knew that sometimes his heart would race and he would think he was losing his mind. Dennis mentioned this to his cousin one day at a family BBQ. Dennis's cousin, who playfully referred to himself as a street pharmacist, suggested that he might have something that would help take the edge off. Dennis wasn't crazy about sticking a needle in his arm, but he trusted his cousin. The drug gave him a calm feeling, making him numb to his usual feeling of hyperarousal.

Opium, used primarily to relieve physical pain, has been used in various forms and cultures throughout history. Drugs such as heroin, morphine, and codeine are derived from the opium poppy and are classified as **opioids**. Methadone is an example of synthetic opioid. Thus, this class of drug spans the spectrum from legal and medically prescribed (though carefully controlled) drugs, such as codeine and morphine, to highly illegal and dangerous drugs, such as heroin. Opioids produce pain relief, euphoria, sedation, reduced anxiety, and tranquility. To produce their characteristic high, they mimic the effect of the body's natural opioids, *endorphins* or *enkephalins*, which the body releases in response to pain. Depending on the drug, dose, and method of delivery, opioids produce a broad range of effects. Besides pain relief and sedation, they cause narrowing of the pupils, constipation, flushed skin, itching, lowered blood pressure, slowed heart rate, and lowered body temperature. Opioids can be smoked, snorted, injected beneath the skin ("popped"), or mainlined (injected into the bloodstream).

FUNCTIONAL IMPAIRMENT Tolerance to opioids develops very rapidly, often after only two or three days. Users often increase their dosage, and when taking preparations of unknown strength (as in the case of street drugs), they can unwittingly self-administer lethal doses. Similarly, administering a previously tolerated dose after a period of abstinence can lead to death from overdose (see "Real People, Real Disorders: Amy Winehouse—A Tragic End to a Life of Substance Abuse"). Heroin is dangerous because of its pharmacological effects and its underworld association with drug trafficking. The latter can include tainted preparations (to increase volume and profits), medical risks associated with sharing needles, and violence. All contribute to high mortality. Early withdrawal symptoms, which may appear as soon as four to six hours after stopping the drug, include rapid breathing, yawning, crying, sweating, and a runny nose. Withdrawal symptoms worsen with chronic use and may include hyperactivity, intensified awareness, agitation, increased heart rate, fever, dilated pupils, tremors, hot and cold flashes, aching muscles, loss of appetite, abdominal cramps, and diarrhea (Merck & Co., 1995–2006). Symptoms can continue for one to three days, complicating the addict's task of quitting.

When opiates are popped or mainlined with shared or unsterilized needles, medical complications may include viral hepatitis and liver damage, infections at the injection site, and transmission of the human immunodeficiency virus (HIV), which causes AIDS. Lung and immune system problems can develop, as can neurological problems due to insufficient blood flow to the brain, potentially resulting in coma. Opioid use during pregnancy is particularly dangerous and can result in significant morbidity and mortality for mother and baby (Kaltenbach et al., 1998).

EPIDEMIOLOGY Patterns of opiate use vary by age, socioeconomic status, education, and type of drug used. Many national surveys that target heroin use may underestimate prevalence because of the difficulty of surveying current users due to living situation, failure to disclose, or health status and hospitalizations secondary to the dangers of sharing needles (i.e., HIV, AIDS, and hepatitis).

The lifetime use of heroin in about 1% or less in the Canadian population (CCSA, 2004). However, the prevalence is much higher in particular subgroups of the population, particularly the homeless. For example, one survey found that 36% of a Vancouver homeless sample reported using heroin in the past month (CCSA, 2013a). Opiates other than heroin, such as codeine and morphine, are commonly prescribed for pain relief, particularly for people who are recovering from surgery. However, when not taken as directed, these prescribed drugs can also be abused. About 5% of Canadians aged 15 and older reported nonmedical prescription opioid use (e.g., to get high) in the past year (CCSA, 2013b).

REAL people REAL disorders

Amy Winehouse—A Tragic End to a Life of Substance Abuse

Amy Winehouse (1983–2011) was one of the most successful new artists of the 2000s. Her music, a blend of R&B, pop, and jazz, was incredibly popular in her home country of England, across Europe, and in Canada. Her album *Back to Black* earned her five Grammy awards in 2008, including Best New Artist and Record of the Year. Sadly, Amy became as well known for her struggles with substance use as for her incredible musical talent.

Amy found her first big success in the United Kingdom with her debut album, *Frank*, which was released in 2003. It was during this time that her substance use started to spiral out of control. Amy would regularly show up to performances and interviews under the influence of alcohol and illegal drugs and be unable to perform. Her management team tried to persuade her to get help by entering rehab. Amy refused and instead wrote the hit song "Rehab" in which she repeatedly says that she won't go to rehab. Released as a single off *Back to Black*, "Rehab" would earn Amy a Grammy for Song of the Year.

Adding to Amy's issues with substance use was her relationship with Blake Fielder-Civil. Amy and Blake began dating in 2005, and Blake admits that he was the one to introduce Amy to hard drugs, including heroin. Their sometimes violent, on-and-off relationship was fuelled by addiction. Still, they eloped in 2007. Also in 2007, Amy slipped into a coma after overdosing on what she would later explain was a mix of heroin, cocaine, ecstasy, ketamine, whisky, and vodka. Amy entered rehab briefly in 2008, but her substance issues continued.

Yui Mok/Landov LLC

Throughout 2007 and 2008, Amy was forced to cancel performances and entire tours due to her substance abuse. Amy and Blake separated in late 2008 and eventually divorced in 2009. It seemed as though Amy was gaining more control of her life throughout 2010 and early 2011, but her substance use issues clearly continued and she died of accidental alcohol poisoning on July 23, 2011. Amy was 27 years old.

Source: Amy Winehouse. (2013). *The Biography Channel website.* www.biography.com/people/amy-winehouse-244469. Accessed March 21, 2013.

LSD and Natural Hallucinogens

Hallucinogens produce altered states of bodily perception and sensation, intense emotions, detachment from oneself and from the environment, and, for some users, feelings of insight with mystical or religious significance. The effects are caused by a disruption of the nerve cells that influence the transmission of the neurotransmitter serotonin (National Institute on Drug Abuse, 2005b), resulting in an experience of the world that is very different from reality.

As with marijuana, the perceptual changes are often intensified experiences in which people become fascinated by minute details. Objects can become distorted and appear to shift and change shape. All five senses can be affected. Depending on the situation and the person, such "trips" can be experienced as pleasant and fascinating or deeply disturbing and frightening.

Many naturally occurring and synthetic hallucinogens exist. Naturally occurring hallucinogens include *psilocybin* (magic mushrooms) and *mescaline* (a product of the peyote cactus). The most widely known synthetic hallucinogen, **lysergic acid diethylamide (LSD)**, gained notoriety in the 1960s counterculture movement when the drugs were believed to "expand the consciousness." LSD was first synthesized in the laboratory by Swiss chemist Albert Hoffman in 1938. His self-testing of the compound led to the following observations:

> Last Friday, April 16, 1943, I was forced to stop my work in the laboratory in the middle of the afternoon and to go home, as I was seized by a peculiar restlessness associated with a sensation of mild dizziness. On arriving home, I lay down and sank into a kind of drunkenness which was not unpleasant and which was characterized by

extreme activity of imagination. As I lay in a dazed condition with my eyes closed (I experienced day-light as disagreeably bright) there surged upon me an uninterrupted stream of fantastic images of extraordinary plasticity and vividness and accompanied by an intense, kaleidoscope-like play of colours. This condition gradually passed off after about 2 hours. (www.psychedelic-library.org/hofmann.htm. Accessed April 10, 2013).

FUNCTIONAL IMPAIRMENT Psychological symptoms such as emotional swings, panic, and paranoia can lead to bizarre or dangerous behaviour. Tolerance builds up rapidly but fades after a few days. Hallucinogens do not produce classic withdrawal symptoms and are not physically addictive, but some users may experience perceptual distortions (hallucinations) long after all traces of the drug have left the system. This condition, *hallucinogen persisting perception disorder*, may result from stress or fatigue. The hallucinations and distortions can be persistent or come in periodic short bursts, or "flashbacks."

EPIDEMIOLOGY Information on the epidemiology of hallucinogen use is even more sparse than that for other illicit drugs. According to one survey, 11% of Canadians have used hallucinogens on one or more occasions (CCSA, 2004). Hallucinogen use appears to be somewhat more common in males (18%) than in females (12%) (Substance Abuse and Mental Health Services Administration, 2006).

Inhalants

The drugs most commonly used by teenagers, **inhalants**, include substances such as cleaning fluid, gasoline, paint, and glue that are used as a source of inhalable fumes (Substance Abuse and Mental Health Services Administration, 2003). Inhalants are attractive because their effect is immediate and lasts between a few minutes and a few hours. The reinforcing effects include rapid onset of sedation, euphoria, and disinhibition, as well as the sensation of heat and excitement believed to enhance sexual pleasure. Their immediate adverse effects include dizziness, drowsiness, confusion, slurred speech, and impaired motor skills. Other immediate, and potentially fatal, effects include irregular heartbeat and respiratory failure (Maxwell, 2001). Inhalants act by quickly entering the bloodstream, dispersing throughout the body, and impacting the central nervous system and peripheral nervous system. Many different chemicals can be inhaled, so it is difficult to generalize about their effect. However, the vaporous fumes can change brain chemistry and may permanently damage the brain and central nervous system. Some of the chemicals that are inhaled include toluene (paint thinner, rubber cement), butane and propane gas (lighter fluid, fuel), fluorocarbons (asthma sprays), chlorinated hydrocarbons (dry-cleaning agents, spot removers), and acetone (nail polish remover, permanent markers).

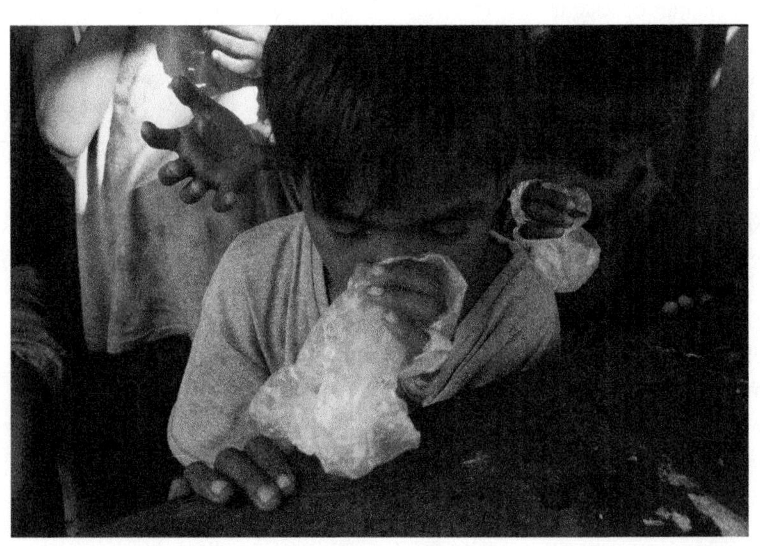

Inhalants are often the drug of choice for youth of poor socioeconomic status around the world.

Yves Gellie/Corbis

FUNCTIONAL IMPAIRMENT Chronic exposure to fumes, regardless of the type, can cause severe damage to all vital organs including the brain and bone marrow, leading to compromised red blood cell production and anemia. Inhalants can also have a profound effect on nerves because they can damage the myelin—the protective fatty tissue that surrounds and protects nerve fibres. Myelin assists with the rapid communication necessary for nerve fibres. Damage can lead to muscle spasms and tremors, causing permanent interference with basic functions such as walking, bending, and talking. Magnetic resonance imaging (MRI) studies of inhalant abusers have found changes in brain structure including shrinkage of the cerebral cortex, cerebellum, and brain stem. These changes lead to permanently impaired motor and cognitive abilities (Sherman, 2005). When people stop using inhalants, withdrawal symptoms include weight loss, muscle weakness, disorientation, inattentiveness, irritability, and depression (National Institute on Drug Abuse, 2004a).

EPIDEMIOLOGY Inhalants are readily available. They are present in most homes, are inexpensive, and can be bought legally, all of which help to explain why they are often one of the first illicit drugs used by young people. Canadian research suggests that about 2% of males and 1% of females aged 15 and older have used inhalants in their lifetime (CCSA, 2006). Most (67%) reported first using inhalants between 12 and 16 years of age (CCSA, 2006). Use decreases with age, and there is little evidence of reliable sex differences in the prevalence of use (CCSA, 2006). Solvent abuse tends to be most prevalent among homeless youth and some First Nations and Inuit youth living in remote areas of Canada (CCSA, 2006).

Non-Substance-Related Disorders

All of the substances that we have reviewed thus far are ingested into the body via one method or another. More recently, other behaviours have been proposed as possible *behavioural addictions* because they produce short-term positive effects that increase the behaviour's frequency even though they also produces negative consequences (Grant et al., 2010). This concept is gaining favour based on similarities in observable behaviours, self-report, and neurobiological research. Considerable controversy remains about whether behaviours such as pathological gambling, kleptomania, compulsive buying, and excessive sexual activity (nonparaphilic hypersexuality; see Chapter 8) should be viewed as addictions. Other behaviours in this category, when repeated excessively, include tanning, Internet use, and computer/video game playing (Holden, 2010). In DSM-5, gambling disorder is included as a type of "Substance-Related and Addictive Disorders" under a subcategory of "Non-Substance-Related Disorders." There was much discussion about whether Internet addiction should be included in DSM-5. However, the workgroup decided that additional research and studies were necessary before a determination on its inclusion is made.

Arguments in favour of the concept of behavioural addictions are based on their many similarities to substance addictions. First, individuals with these behaviours commonly report strong urges or cravings to engage in the behaviour (Grant et al., 2010). Second, these behaviours are commonly comorbid with substance use disorders (Cunningham-Williams et al., 1998). Third, many of the same neurotransmitter systems and brain regions appear to be operative in these behaviours as in substance use disorders (Potenza, 2008). Finally, similar treatment approaches appear to be efficacious in treating both behavioural addictions and substance use disorders (Grant et al., 2010). Although the controversy is far from settled, ongoing neurobiological research may help determine whether these pathological repetitive and all-consuming behaviours are actual addictions.

Sex, Ethnicity, Education, and Illicit Drug Use

We do not yet have enough research to form a clear picture of sex and ethnic differences among individuals with substance use disorders. This is particularly unfortunate because any efforts to prevent or treat substance use disorders need to be tailored to the needs of the population. We do know that the pathway to drug addiction for women differs from that for men. Although women are less likely to be substance abusers and tend to become abusers at later ages, they often become dependent more quickly and experience more severe consequences of drug use over shorter periods of time (e.g., Hser et al., 2004). Substance use in women is also often associated with relationship issues; women

Canadian FOCUS

Alcohol Use Among Canadian Aboriginal Peoples

In Canada, the Aboriginal (First Nations) population consists of three broad groups: North American Indian, Métis, and Inuit people. Each of these broad groups is composed of diverse smaller groups, differing from one another in history, culture, and traditions (Tjepkema, 2002). The abuse of alcohol and drugs in First Nations communities suggests that these problems are linked to poverty (Weir, 2001); that is, Aboriginal communities experiencing greater poverty, such as particular northern or rural communities, tend to have a higher prevalence of drug and alcohol problems. Surveys of people living in First Nations communities reveal that more than 70% of respondents believe that alcohol abuse is an important problem in their community (Rogers & Abas, 1988; Statistics Canada, 1993). Alcohol abuse in Aboriginal communities is often associated with other forms of drug abuse, such as inhalant abuse (Gfellner & Hundelby, 1995).

Aboriginal Canadians, compared to their non-Aboriginal counterparts, are no more likely to drink alcohol. In fact, the Aboriginal population has a *higher* percentage of abstainers compared to the general population (34% vs. 21%) (Anderson, 2007). But those Aboriginal people who do drink are more likely to drink more heavily, even when socioeconomic status is taken into consideration (Anderson, 2007; Haggarty et al., 2000; Tjepkema, 2002). Tjepkema, for example, assessed "heavy drinking" (defined as five or more drinks in a single sitting) in off-reserve Aboriginal and non-Aboriginal Canadians. Fewer Aboriginals than non-Aboriginals were weekly drinkers (27% vs. 38%). The groups did not differ in the proportion of people who were light or abstinent drinkers (both 50%). But Aboriginals had more heavy drinkers (23% vs. 16%). The same pattern was found regardless of whether the respondents lived in urban or rural areas. Similar findings were obtained in a study of women in northern Quebec: Alcohol consumption was less frequent among Aboriginal women, but those who did drink consumed higher quantities of alcohol than non-Aboriginal drinkers (Lavallee & Bourgault, 2000).

Psychosocial factors within cultures may influence the differences in drinking patterns between Aboriginal and non-Aboriginal people. To illustrate, Gfellner and Hundelby (1990) investigated the predictors of drug and alcohol use in a small urban community in Manitoba. The number of one's friends who used alcohol or drugs was the strongest predictor of alcohol or drug use for both Aboriginal and non-Aboriginal students. Peer attitude about drug or alcohol use was also a predictor for Aboriginal students (Gfellner & Hundelby, 1990).

Some writers have argued that prior to the arrival of European settlers in Canada, alcohol problems were far less common among Canadian Aboriginals than they are today, because before the first contact with Europeans, drug and alcohol use was strictly controlled by social customs. The development of problem drinking among Canadian Aboriginals was a learned behaviour modelled by European traders, along with the increased availability of alcohol (Anderson, 2007).

Others have argued that the prevalence of alcohol abuse and dependence among Aboriginals may have been a consequence of the forced attempt by European colonists to eradicate tribal language and culture, leading to a loss of cultural identity that sets the stage for alcoholism, drug abuse, and depression. Kahn (1982) explained the greater incidence of psychopathology among Aboriginals in terms of the disruption in traditional culture caused by the appropriation of their lands by European powers and the attempts to sever them from their cultural traditions while denying them full access to the dominant Western culture. Aboriginals have since lived in severe cultural and social disorganization that has resulted in high rates of psychopathology and substance abuse. Beset by such problems, Aboriginal adults are prone to child abuse and neglect. Abuse and neglect contribute to feelings of hopelessness and depression among adolescents, who then seek to escape their feelings through alcohol and other drugs (Berlin, 1987).

with substance use disorders are more likely to have a partner who also uses illicit drugs (Westermeyer & Boedicker, 2000). Women are more likely than men to turn to alcohol use, binge drinking, and marijuana use when dealing with the breakup of a relationship (Larsen & Sweeten, 2012). Women who use substances also have more psychiatric comorbidity compared with male substance users, with rates approximating 20% more than those in men (Kessler et al., 1997). The disorders include anxiety, depression, borderline personality disorder (see Chapter 11), and post-traumatic stress disorder (Brooner et al., 1997; Cottler et al., 2001).

When attempting to understand the role of ethnicity, two problems arise. First, relatively little research has been conducted explicitly on the topic of ethnicity and drug use. Second, in most of the research, the role of ethnicity is confounded with low socioeconomic status. Thus the relative impact of low socioeconomic status, poverty, and ethnicity must always be kept in mind when considering these data. Studies do indicate unique risks and needs among many minority individuals who misuse drugs (see "Canadian Focus: Alcohol Use Among Canadian Aboriginal Peoples").

Education level is also associated with illicit drug use: It is lower among university graduates (5.9%) than among those who did not graduate from high school (9.2%), high school graduates (8.6%), and those with some university (9.1%) (Substance Abuse and Mental Health Services Administration, 2006).

CONCEPT check

- Marijuana is derived from the *Cannabis sativa* plant. Its active ingredient is THC. Cannabinoid receptors in the brain influence pleasure, learning and memory, higher cognitive functions, sensory perceptions, and motor coordination.
- CNS stimulants, including cocaine and methamphetamine, prolong wakefulness and suppress appetite. They also influence dopamine levels and produce dangerous elevations in blood pressure and heart rate and cardiovascular abnormalities, potentially leading to heart attack, respiratory arrest, and seizures.
- Sedative drugs include barbiturates and benzodiazepines. They are central nervous system depressants that cause sedation and decrease anxiety.
- Hallucinogens include mescaline, LSD, and psilocybin (mushrooms). They produce altered states of bodily perception and sensations, intense emotions, detachment from self and the environment, and, for some users, feelings of insight with mystical or religious significance.
- Inhalants, which are inhalable vapours from a variety of chemicals, yield an immediate effect of euphoria or sedation and can cause permanent damage to all organ systems including the brain.

critical thinking question Because various substances often lead to quite different "highs," what factors might influence drug choice across individuals?

Etiology of Substance-Related Disorders

9.5 Understand the contributions of biological, genetic, behavioural, cognitive, and sociocultural theories to the etiology of substance use disorders.

Friends and family often cannot understand why someone continues to use drugs when so much is at stake. A husband whose marriage is in jeopardy apparently "chooses" to return to drinking knowing divorce will be the consequence. A man who has had one warning at work for a positive urine screen smokes marijuana on a weeknight knowing that another positive test means he will lose his job. A pregnant woman continues to smoke even while reading the warning label on the cigarette pack. What drives people to make these self-destructive choices? Once we blamed personal characteristics such as moral weakness or depravity, but as we have learned more about drug abuse, we have come to acknowledge the contribution of biological, behavioural, and sociocultural factors.

Biological Factors

To understand the biology of substance use, we must appreciate the effects not only of each substance on biology, but also of an individual's biology regarding potential to abuse alcohol or drugs.

FAMILY AND GENETIC STUDIES A substantial body of family, twin, adoption, and molecular genetic research has determined that both genes and environment affect the likelihood of substance abuse. After analyzing more than 17 500 MZ and DZ twin pairs from 14 different studies, researchers concluded that both genetic and environmental factors influence whether a person ever starts smoking, continues smoking, and becomes dependent on nicotine (Sullivan & Kendler, 1999). Environmental factors seem to be particularly important in determining whether a person (especially an adolescent) starts smoking, and genetic factors are more prominent in influencing whether the smoker progresses to nicotine dependence. In addition, studies are underway to identify areas of the genome and specific susceptibility genes that may be important in nicotine dependence (Gelernter et al., 2004). Most genetic association studies have examined the dopaminergic system. These studies have identified associations within this system, including dopamine receptor genes, transporter genes, and others, but not all results have been replicated.

Genetic factors account for about 50% to 60% of the variance in liability for alcohol dependence in both men and women (Prescott, 2001). The search for candidate genes has focused on many systems, including the dopamine, serotonin, and GABA pathways. Studies are underway to further explain how genes influence alcohol dependence. It is perhaps no coincidence that some overlap has been observed in the genes that influence both nicotine and alcohol dependence. Indeed, both disorders often co-occur, and at least some of the same genes may influence the risk of developing each type of dependence (Grucza & Beirut, 2007).

Family, twin, and adoption studies are more difficult to conduct with illicit drug users because people who abuse substances are reluctant to report their use and to participate in research. However, we do know that genetic factors play a substantial role. In a large Norwegian twin study, Kendler et al. (1997) reported heritability estimates for a range of illicit drug use (e.g., cannabis, stimulants, opiates, cocaine, psychedelics) from 58% to 81%. The remaining variance was attributed to individual-specific environmental effects.

We still do not know precisely what is inherited. We have not yet identified specific genes that explain why some people become addicted to substances while others do not. Although the complete picture remains unclear, neurobiology, cognition, personality, and behaviour may all contribute to addiction liability.

NEUROBIOLOGY From a neurobiological perspective, alcohol and drugs act on the part of the brain that is involved with processing pleasurable feelings (the reward system). The reward circuitry includes the ventral tegmental area and the basal forebrain (see Figure 9.2). By using neuroimaging technology, we can observe how this pathway is activated in response to drug administration. Importantly, although dopamine is commonly considered the "pleasure" neurotransmitter, other transmitters are also involved in the development and maintenance of addictive behaviours, including the opioid, serotonergic, and GABA systems.

The endogenous opioid system is clearly involved in the reinforcing effect of opiates as well as that of alcohol and nicotine. This system is directly involved in how pleasurable we perceive the drug to be. As the treatment section of this chapter illustrates, administering an *opiate receptor antagonist*, which blocks the positive effect of the drug, is effective in decreasing alcohol use in humans (Garbutt et al., 1999). Serotonin appears to be associated with alcohol use (LeMarquand et al., 1994) and may also be associated with the reinforcing properties (positive effects) of cocaine (White & Wolf, 1991). Sedative drugs may act primarily through the GABA system.

Thus several neurotransmitters are involved with the experience of reinforcement and reward associated with drug and alcohol use. In addition, genetic and environmental factors may combine to determine who is most vulnerable to the lure of such rewards. One hypothesis is that people at risk for drug and alcohol dependence have deficits in their brain reward pathway. For example, a person whose brain shows "low dopamine or

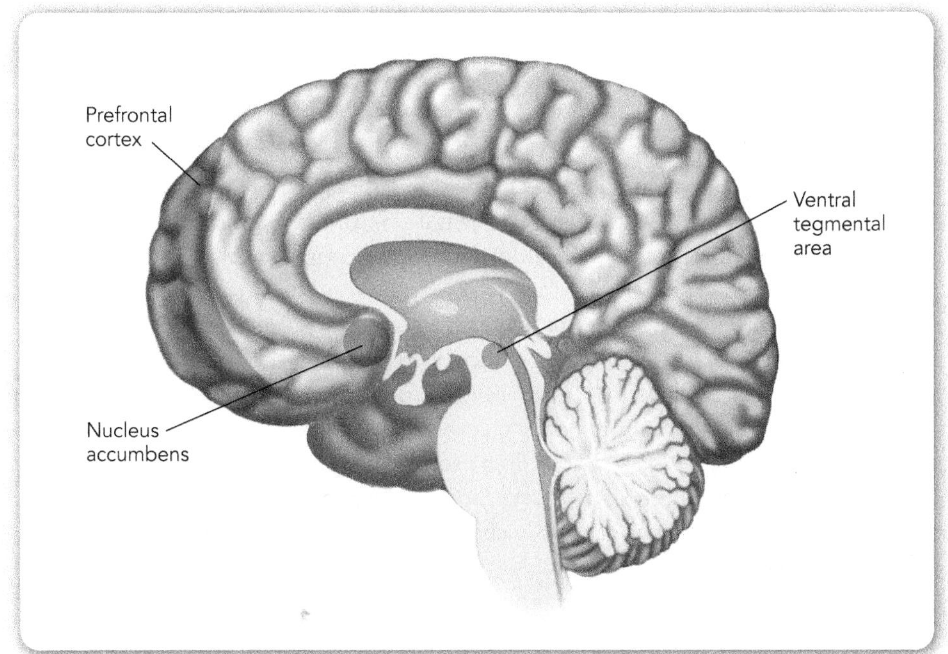

FIGURE 9.2

The Brain's Reward System. The dopaminergic system is the primary reward system in the brain. Major structures in the system including the ventral tegmental area (VTA), the nucleus accumbens, and the prefrontal cortex are highlighted. Information travels from the VTA to the nucleus accumbens and then up to the prefrontal cortex.

hypodopaminergic" traits may need a dopamine "fix" to feel good (Blum et al., 2000). This deficit could lead the person to seek a drug that would provide that good feeling. Maladaptive behaviours that could develop in an attempt to boost dopamine include addictive, impulsive, and compulsive behaviours. Although we need further research to verify this model, recognizing that substance use is the result of a chronically under-rewarded brain system can be a useful way for family and friends to understand the challenges of abstaining from alcohol and drugs that a person faces. This information also may help in developing approaches to treatment for substance dependence that focus on finding alternative rewarding experiences to replace those provided by drugs.

Psychological Factors

Although biology plays a central role, psychological factors also influence critical aspects of drug use, such as the decision to try a drug (initiation), the decision to continue using the drug, the frequency with which a drug is used, and the decision to stop drug use.

Drugs are reinforcers. They produce positive physical feelings, increasing the likelihood that they will be used again.
Life Boat/Getty Images

BEHAVIOURAL FACTORS—DRUGS AS REINFORCERS Drugs are reinforcing in several ways, and operant conditioning helps explain the role of drugs as reinforcers. First, drug-induced euphoria produces positive physical feelings and increases the likelihood that the drug will be used again. This is positive reinforcement. Negative reinforcement also maintains drug use when repeated use removes an unpleasant state. A person feeling tired and lethargic and who grabs a cup of coffee removes that lethargic state and experiences negative reinforcement. Positive reinforcement processes are more directly implicated in the initial stages of addiction, with negative reinforcement mechanisms playing an increasingly important role as addiction progresses.

Conditioning through positive or negative reinforcement involves more than the simple act of using the drug. Environmental aspects such as settings in which the drugs are taken, the people with whom drugs are used, or the paraphernalia used to administer the drugs themselves become cues (signals) to begin drug use (Caprioli et al., 2007). This is why, for example, some people who are trying to quit smoking say, "I do okay till I go into a bar—once I start to drink, I really need a cigarette." This fits well with classical conditioning models of substance use (Domjan, 2005). In these models, external stimuli that have been paired with drug use produce some of the same bodily sensations that previously have been caused by the drug itself (i.e., the conditioned and unconditioned responses are similar). In this way, stimuli that previously had signalled the arrival of a drug (the sight of a person or passing a particular street corner) seem to set off a whole host of feelings and reactions that trigger drug use. In the case of drug-compensatory conditioned responses, regulatory bodily changes occur in the presence of conditioned stimuli (e.g., drug paraphernalia, fellow drug users) to counteract the anticipated effects of drugs or alcohol (Siegel et al., 2000). An individual who does not engage in substance use following these compensatory bodily changes feels considerable pain and discomfort (i.e., withdrawal). As a result, the individual may engage in substance use as a way to escape from or avoid withdrawal symptoms (Domjan, 2005).

Laboratory paradigms can test the reinforcing effects of various drugs from both operant and classical conditioning perspectives. For example, laboratory animals can be given either free access to alcohol or drugs, or they can be trained to work (press a lever) in order to receive a drug. Changing the reinforcement schedule (free versus work) helps the researcher determine how reinforcing the drug is to the animal, allowing comparisons of the relative reinforcing value of two drugs, for example, alcohol versus nicotine. Another approach—*conditioned place preference*—initially exposes the animal to two distinct but neutral environments (Cage A or Cage B). Then a drug is repeatedly paired with one of the environments (Cage A, for example). After the conditioning trials, the amount of time the animal spends in the "drug" environment helps establish its positive effects.

COGNITIVE FACTORS Cognitive theories are based on the premise that how a person interprets a situation influences the decision to use a drug (Beck et al., 1993). A social setting may activate thoughts (e.g., "I am much more relaxed after I have a beer" or "A line of cocaine will make me more sociable") and make the person more likely to use the substance. Cognitions can also affect a person's reaction to physiological symptoms associated with anxiety and craving (Beck et al., 1993). A thought (e.g., "I cannot stand not having a cigarette") will increase awareness of cravings and enhance the reaction when craving occurs.

Based in social learning theory (Bandura, 1977a, 1977b), Bandura's social cognitive approach (1999) explores biased belief systems that maintain substance abuse. Briefly, several factors initiate and maintain substance use disorders: positive drug outcome expectancies (e.g., "this drug will make me feel good"), minimal negative expectancies (e.g., "I have never gotten caught"), and poor self-efficacy beliefs regarding one's ability to cope without drugs (e.g., "I don't think I can survive another day of school without marijuana"). Although empirical studies have demonstrated a relation between positive outcome expectancies and substance use, such approaches rely on self-report of cognition, which is subject to bias.

Behavioural and cognitive theories focus on how expectations of outcome are associated with actual outcomes (i.e., relaxation, pleasure). The associations arise directly from the drug's effects as well as from environmental factors that are paired with those positive feelings. Repeated exposure to the drug and the associated cues bias the information that a person recalls about drug use (i.e., remembering the buzz but not the hangover) (McCusker, 2001). Lapses and relapses occur when the cues for use outweigh the positive features of abstinence (e.g., keeping a relationship).

Sociocultural, Family, and Environmental Factors

Among the factors associated with substance abuse, sociocultural dimensions are critical. Social, family, and environmental variables all combine with genetic predisposition to contribute to substance-related disorders. Many researchers have studied the contribution of family, peer, and socioeconomic factors to the development of substance-related disorders. In studies of both adolescents and adults, family and peer influence (Wang et al., 2007), trauma (Wills et al., 2001), and economic factors (Black & Krishnakumar, 1998; Boles & Miotto, 2003) have all been associated with increased substance use and abuse. Although these relationships highlight the importance of environmental variables, exactly how they interact with genetic predisposition remains unknown.

Cultural, family, and social factors also may buffer or protect against substance abuse. The use of alcohol and nicotine has been found to be strongly and inversely related to strength of religiosity (Kendler et al., 1997). For example, the more strongly people identify themselves as being religious, the less likely they are to smoke or abuse alcohol. Although these relationships—both risk and protective—highlight the role of environmental variables, our understanding demands an integrated perspective on the roles of genes and environment. However, it is also important to consider that substance use may play an important role in some cultures.

Developmental Factors

Many adolescents experiment with drugs, but most do not progress to abuse or dependence (Newcomb & Richardson, 1995). Introduction to substance use at a young age and heavy use during adolescence are two risk factors (Kandel & Davies, 1992). Further, drug-related problems (i.e., experiencing some symptoms without meeting full diagnostic criteria) in adolescence predict future substance use disorders, elevated levels of depression, and antisocial and borderline personality disorder symptoms (see Chapter 11) by age 24 (Rohde et al., 2001).

Drug involvement is typically progressive, beginning with substances that are legal for adults (e.g., alcohol, nicotine), followed by marijuana and then other illicit drugs (Anthony & Petronis, 1995). For this reason, some argue that adolescent marijuana use is a gateway to other drug use, but this statement often is misinterpreted. Marijuana is the initial illicit drug used before that of other more harmful drugs (Daughters et al., 2007). However, "gateway" is usually interpreted to mean that marijuana use somehow precipitates the use of other drugs. Precipitating factors might include environmental factors, such as increased access to other drugs, or pharmacological factors, in which case marijuana use might make one vulnerable to developing dependence on other drugs. It is also important to note that many people never "graduate" past marijuana at all, and others may briefly experiment with other drugs but not progress to regular use (Tarter et al., 2006).

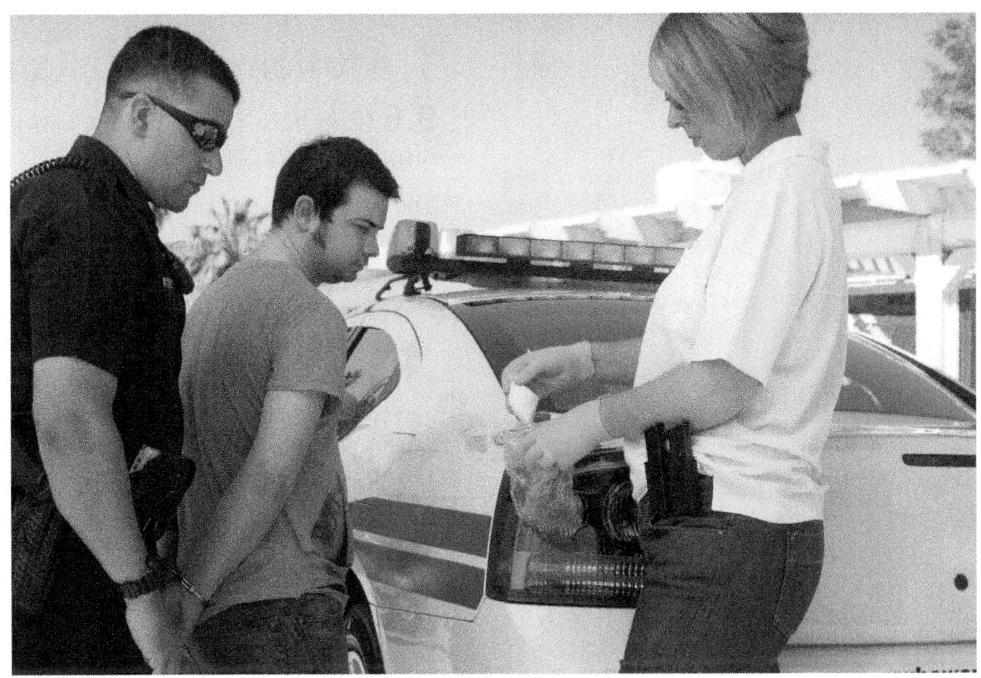

Low socioeconomic conditions and the absence of alternative reinforcers can increase the risk of engaging in substance abuse.

bikeriderlondon/Shutterstock

Regardless of whether marijuana is a gateway drug, more direct developmental consequences are associated with its use. If it is used chronically, any drug can have damaging effects with biological consequences such as compromised brain development. Chronic use also has social consequences such as "arrested development" in which normal developmental experiences and growth opportunities may be missed due to excessive marijuana use. Many individuals who use substances throughout their adolescence simply stop using on their own as they enter adulthood. For individuals who reach the point of developing a substance use disorder, however, recovery is more difficult even with treatment. For this reason prevention efforts are especially relevant for adolescents. The most effective approaches focus on skills-based programs as opposed to providing information or using scare tactics (Nation et al., 2003).

CONCEPT check

- Genetic factors contribute to alcohol and drug use disorders although the specific way in which genes influence substance abuse remains unknown.
- Most drugs of abuse either directly or indirectly stimulate the "reward centre" of the brain, located in the ventral tegmental area.
- Although dopamine is often highlighted as the neurotransmitter involved with pleasure or reward, the serotonergic, GABA, and opioid systems are also involved in the experience of reward associated with drug use.
- Euphoria, excitement, relaxation, and feelings of intimacy are all part of the positive reinforcement that may be experienced when using illicit drugs.
- Cognitive factors including expectancies and self-efficacy influence a person's ability to remain drug free.

critical thinking question Although we discuss how genes and environment interact to influence the risk for drug abuse, can you describe a situation in which someone who is at low genetic risk might develop drug abuse solely due to environmental exposures? Similarly, can you describe a scenario in which someone with very high genetic liability would never develop a drug abuse problem?

Treatment of Substance Use Disorders

9.6 Compare and contrast treatments for various types of substance use disorders.

The choice of treatment is based on several factors, including which drug is being abused and the person's particular characteristics and resources. Treatment should be both multifaceted and individually tailored. Medical treatment both for detoxification and reduction of cravings for a substance may be useful, but the best evidence is for behavioural treatment approaches. For these disorders, treatment should be as intense and long lasting as possible. For severe substance use problems, residential treatment may help people recover away from potential substance use triggers. Less intensive options, such as day hospitalization or outpatient treatment, are also possible. Although treatment is available across all ages and social strata, evidence indicates that minority individuals from low-income settings sometimes have difficulty finding adequate specialized treatments. We cover the treatment of substance abuse broadly here, highlighting evidence-based approaches when they exist.

Judging the effectiveness of an intervention is complex. For some drugs, such as heroin and amphetamines, the goal might be total abstinence and no relapse. For other drugs, such as alcohol, some researchers have argued that drinking moderately, and in a controlled way, may be an acceptable goal (see "Examining the Evidence: Controlled Drinking"). Thus evaluating treatment efficacy can be daunting—especially when comorbid psychopathology, legal, or financial complications may interfere with treatment success.

1. No single treatment is appropriate for all individuals.
2. Treatment needs to be readily available.
3. Effective treatment attends to multiple needs of the individual, not just his or her drug use.
4. An individual's treatment and services plan must be assessed continually and modified as necessary to ensure that the plan meets the person's changing needs.
5. Remaining in treatment for an adequate period of time is critical for treatment effectiveness.
6. Counseling (individual and/or group) and other behavioural therapies are critical components of effective treatment for addiction.
7. Medications are an important element of treatment for many patients, especially when combined with counselling and other behavioural therapies.
8. Addicted or drug-abusing individuals with coexisting mental disorders should have both disorders treated in an integrated way.
9. Medical detoxification is only the first stage of addiction treatment and by itself does little to change long-term drug use.
10. Treatment does not need to be voluntary to be effective.
11. Possible drug use during treatment must be monitored continuously.
12. Treatment programs should provide assessment for HIV/AIDS, hepatitis B and C, tuberculosis, and other infectious diseases, and counselling to help patients modify or change behaviours that place themselves or others at risk of infection.
13. Recovery from drug addiction can be a long-term process and frequently requires multiple episodes of treatment.

References

http://www.nida.nih.gov/PODAT/PODATindex.html, Retrieved June 7, 2013.

FIGURE 9.3

Principles of Effective Treatment for Substance Use Disorders. Because people abuse so many different substances and people who abuse substances have so many different characteristics, treatment for substance use disorders must be multifaceted.

Source: Adapted from the National Institute on Drug Abuse (2000).

Thirteen principles of effective treatment must be considered before deciding on a specific treatment approach. See Figure 9.3 for these guiding principles and a framework for approaching intervention, as well as a glimpse into the complexity of treating these often intractable disorders. With these critical factors in mind, we now explore the various types of interventions.

Therapies Based on Cognitive and Behavioural Principles

Interventions based on cognitive and behavioural principles are efficacious in treating substance use (Dutra et al., 2008). Each strategy targets the function of substance use and uses interventions that focus on the cognitive, behavioural, or environmental factors maintaining substance use.

AVOIDANCE OF THE STIMULUS In some treatments for substance use disorders, people may be instructed to avoid stimuli that are related to past drug use (e.g., fellow drug users, drug paraphernalia) (Read et al., 2001). Evidence for the usefulness of this strategy comes from studies of returning Vietnam veterans who were addicted to heroin while in Vietnam and treated before returning home (Robins & Slobodyan, 2003). The rate of relapse for these soldiers was significantly less than for comparable groups of civilians whose experience with heroin was on their home territory. One reason for the reduced relapse in veterans may have been their removal from the environment in which heroin use occurred. Although avoidance of drug-related stimuli can prevent the occurrence of cravings and relapse, many remain skeptical about the value of this approach. Long-term avoidance of all drug cues is virtually impossible for most people, and complete avoidance of drug-related stimuli fails to teach individuals more adaptive behaviours that are incompatible with taking drugs (Rohsenow et al., 1990).

RELAPSE PREVENTION A widely used cognitive-behavioural intervention is **relapse prevention (RP)** (Marlatt & Gordon, 1985). RP uses *functional analysis* (see Chapter 3) to identify the antecedents and consequences of drug use and then to develop alternative cognitive and behavioural skills to reduce the risk of future drug use. Working together, the therapist and patient identify high-risk situations and the (1) trigger for that situation, (2) thoughts during that situation, (3) feelings experienced in response to the trigger and thoughts, (4) drug use behaviour, and (5) positive and negative consequences of drug use. After analyzing this behaviour chain, the therapist and patient develop strategies for altering thoughts, feelings, and behaviours to help avoid or manage situations that threaten the patient's commitment to abstinence (Marlatt & Gordon, 1985").

In the relapse prevention model, a *lapse* is a single instance of substance use and a *relapse* is a complete return to pretreatment behaviours. A core feature of RP, **abstinence violation effect**, focuses on a person's cognitive and affective responses to engaging in a prohibited behaviour. How a person responds to or interprets the lapse, and not the lapse itself, determines whether the lapse becomes a relapse (Collins & Lapp, 1991; Curry et al., 1987; Larimer et al., 1999; Shiffman et al., 1997). For example, after having one drink, a recovered alcoholic who says, "I'm a failure, I'm an incurable addict, I may as well give up" has a higher chance of progressing to a relapse than someone whose response is "I had one drink, but that doesn't mean I have to have two. I can stop now, pour the rest of this away, and still be successful in my commitment to quit." The abstinence violation effect acknowledges that a person can have positive affective responses to a lapse independent of the cognitions (e.g., "That scotch felt good going down") (Hudson et al., 1992). Attention to these cognitions is essential to successful relapse prevention. In other words, we cannot ignore the fact that drug use simply might be pleasurable. Acknowledging these positives can be explored in functional analysis or problem-solving therapy by focusing on finding both other pleasurable activities and other strategies aside from seeking pleasure to cope with negative events.

STAGES OF CHANGE AND MOTIVATIONAL ENHANCEMENT THERAPY (MET) Despite the severe impairment in social and occupational functioning that substance abuse causes, a drug's reinforcing effect can be so strong that the desire to use it overshadows any negative consequence. Two critical issues related to this situation are how to motivate people to enter treatment and how to tailor treatment to the motivational level of the individual. The **transtheoretical model (TTM)** proposes a five-stage sequential model of behavioural change (Prochaska & DiClemente, 1983). Limited awareness of the problem, few emotional reactions to substance abuse, and resistance to change characterize *precontemplation*. Individuals in the *contemplation* stage are more aware of the problem and weigh the positive and negative aspects of their substance abuse. The *preparation* stage is marked by a decision to take corrective action (within the next month), and the *action* stage is characterized by actual attempts to change environment, behaviour, or experiences. Once entering the *maintenance* stage, individuals are acquiring and engaging in behaviours that are designed to prevent relapse. Evidence strongly supports this model and its relevance for treating substance use disorders (Migneault et al., 2005).

Motivational interviewing begins by identifying each person's place on the TTM model as the entry to motivate people to change. This approach differs greatly from more traditional approaches that are more confrontational and require a patient to be ready to quit for therapy to proceed. Motivational interviewing (Miller, 1983; Miller & Rollnick, 1991) uses principles of motivational psychology to produce rapid, internally motivated change and to mobilize the patient's own resources for change. This may include focusing on patient strengths as opposed to weaknesses and getting the patient to collaborate in the selection of goals and how to achieve them. MET's goal is to help the individual move through the stages of change swiftly and effectively in order to achieve sustained treatment response. MET can be used alone or as preparation for other interventions. It is effective for adults across a wide range of substances (Tait & Hulse, 2003) but may be especially relevant for adolescents whose ambivalence about abstinence may be more common (Grenard et al., 2006; Tevyaw & Monti, 2004).

SKILLS TRAINING Skills training is an important part of cognitive-behavioural therapy. Skills training approaches are based on the idea that substance users may lack some of the basic skills that are necessary for everyday coping. For this reason, these approaches are sometimes called *coping skills interventions.* Approaches targeting coping and social skills training are among the most widely used (O'Leary & Monti, 2002). According to this approach, interpersonal, environmental, and individual skill deficits pose a challenge to sobriety, and the goal is to teach the basic skills that enable substance users to manage problematic aspects of their life. The Community Reinforcement Approach (Hunt & Azrin, 1973; Meyers et al., 2003) is based on the same principles and includes a broad range of skills training, including vocational counselling. It especially targets identifying and building the substance user's social network and other support systems. Data support this approach both as a stand-alone treatment and as an adjunct to medication and other treatment approaches (Read et al., 2001).

Although complete abstinence is a goal of most approaches, treatments for alcohol use disorder such as behavioural self-control training focus on strategies to help the individual control alcohol use. Strategies include goal setting, self-monitoring, efforts to limit use, rewards for achieving goals, functional analysis of drinking situations, learning alternate coping skills, and relapse prevention. Considerable evidence supports the use of this approach (Walters, 2000).

BEHAVIOURAL THERAPIES BASED ON CLASSICAL AND OPERANT CONDITIONING Although many interventions include both behavioural and cognitive components, several are rooted more specifically in behaviour theory. Some behavioural interventions are focused on classical conditioning and centre on the physiological aspects of substance use. One prominent example is **aversion therapy** (also known as *aversive conditioning*). As we have noted, substance use in most cases is associated with positive sensations. Aversion therapy repeatedly pairs drug or alcohol use with an aversive stimulus (e.g., electric shock) or images (e.g., having patients imagine unpleasant images each time they visualize drug use). Although questions remain regarding its efficacy, especially when used alone, it may be an important element of a comprehensive treatment program (Howard et al., 1991; Rimmele et al., 1995; Upadhyaya & Deas, 2008). Similarly, behavioural interventions such as relaxation training and biofeedback can help the individual minimize and overcome physiological urges to use substances, as well as reduce stress and tension for which substance use may be a coping strategy.

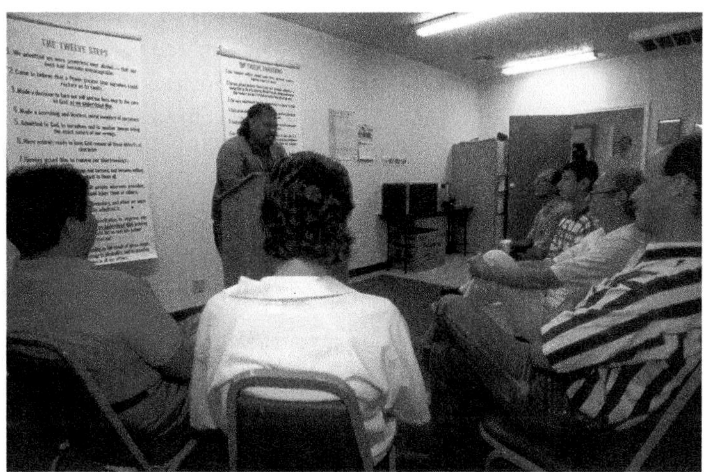

Group meetings help people struggling with substance use disorders find support and accountability.

John Boykin/PhotoEdit

Some behavioural interventions focus more directly on operant conditioning. For example, inpatient and residential treatment programs (and some outpatient programs) may implement **contingency management approaches**

(Prendergast et al., 2006). In these approaches, rewards (either concrete reinforcers such as money or intangible reinforcers such as program privileges) are provided for treatment compliance, such as having negative urine screens for drugs. Compared with 12 weeks of usual treatment alone, adding contingency management for methamphetamine users resulted in less drug use and longer periods of abstinence (Roll et al., 2006). This finding suggests that contingency management holds promise as a component of treatment for methamphetamine use.

TWELVE-STEP APPROACHES If you have ever seen a discreet advertisement for a meeting of "Friends of Bill W," you saw a notice for an Alcoholics Anonymous (AA) meeting. Established in 1935 by "Bill W," Wilson and Robert Hilbrook Smith, AA's 12-step approach (see Figure 9.4) is based on the need for abstinence. It begins with the realization that the individual is powerless over the addiction, and it provides a structured approach to remaining sober. Members attend regular meetings and are assigned a sponsor whom they can call if they feel unable to maintain sobriety or need support. Each year of sobriety is acknowledged, and social support is crucial. Based on the popularity of AA, additional 12-step approaches have been developed, including Narcotics Anonymous (NA) and Overeaters Anonymous (OA).

While behavioural and cognitive-behavioural approaches focus on developing skills to control addiction, the 12-step approach emphasizes an unmanageable life, an inability to control addiction, and participants' belief that only a Higher Power can cure them of their addiction. Although the evidence base is not extensive, some studies suggest that AA is effective. Personal testimonies also attest to its power (Ouimette et al., 1997), as well as other aspects common to more empirically-based treatment reviewed above such as structure, social support, and identification of nonsubstance rewards (Moos, 2008).

Opinions remain divided on 12-step approaches. For people who have found the focus on God inconsistent with their own beliefs, a set of steps that is less focused on

FIGURE 9.4
Twelve Steps of Alcoholics Anonymous.

1. We admitted we were powerless over alcohol—that our lives had become unmanageable.
2. Came to believe that a Power greater than ourselves could restore us to sanity.
3. Made a decision to turn our will and our lives over to the care of God as we understood Him.
4. Made a searching and fearless moral inventory of ourselves.
5. Admitted to God, to ourselves and to another human being the exact nature of our wrongs.
6. Were entirely ready to have God remove all these defects of character.
7. Humbly asked Him to remove our shortcomings.
8. Made a list of all persons we had harmed, and became willing to make amends to them all.
9. Made direct amends to such people wherever possible, except when to do so would injure them or others.
10. Continued to take personal inventory and when we were wrong promptly admitted it.
11. Sought through prayer and meditation to improve our conscious contact with God as we understood Him, praying only for knowledge of His will for us and the power to carry that out.
12. Having had a spiritual awakening as the result of these steps, we tried to carry this message to alcoholics, and to practice these principles in all our affairs.

Source: The Twelve Steps are reprinted with permission of Alcoholics Anonymous World Services, Inc. ("AAWS") Permission to reprint the Twelve Steps does not mean that AAWS has reviewed or approved the contents of this publication, or that AAWS necessarily agrees with the views expressed herein. A.A. is a program of recovery from alcoholism *only*—use of the Twelve Steps in connection with programs and activities which are patterned after A.A., but which address other problems, or in any other non-A.A. context, does not imply otherwise.

religion has been developed (e.g., Rational Recovery). Even without an extensive evidence base, if the 12-step programs are efficacious for only a percentage of addicted individuals, they deserve a place among available treatments.

Ethics and Responsibility

Although psychologists treat substance use disorders, they too can suffer from these disorders, interfering with their ability to practice their profession. The Canadian Psychological Association's *Code of Ethics for Psychologists* states that psychologists should engage in self-care activities if they have activities that could result in impaired judgment and interfere with their ability to benefit and not harm others (Canadian Psychological Association, 2000). When a psychologist is not yet aware or ready to admit that a problem with substance use exists, colleagues are ethically obligated to intervene.

Biological Treatments

Biological interventions play an important role in the treatment of substance use disorders. They can be used as the sole intervention or as an adjunct to psychological or community interventions.

Withdrawal symptoms can be severe and occasionally lethal. **Detoxification**, medically supervised drug withdrawal, is necessary to treat substance use disorders—but it is only the first step. Medications can reduce withdrawal symptoms and decrease the likelihood of adverse effects. For example, benzodiazepines can be administered to reduce the likelihood of an alcoholic developing DTs.

Agonist substitution is a type of therapy that substitutes a chemically similar safe medication for the drug of abuse. *Chemically safe* means several things. First, the substitute drug binds with the same receptors as the target drug, thereby preventing any pharmacological effect ("high") of the target drug. Although the substitute shares many similarities with the target drug, it also differs in several key ways. The substitute works more slowly and has fewer acute pharmacological effects with no resulting high and subsequent crash. Although some potential for developing problems with the substitute drug may exists, these problems are typically far less severe than with the target drug. People taking an agonist substitution drug are still taking a drug regularly, but with few of the social, occupational, and physical impairments associated with the target drug.

The most widely known agonist substitute is **methadone**, used as a replacement for heroin. Distributed under controlled conditions in "methadone clinics," methadone removes the substantial risk associated with obtaining and injecting heroin. Some individuals continue on methadone therapy indefinitely, but considerable evidence suggests that coupling methadone with counselling, individual psychotherapy, or contingency management improves treatment outcome (e.g., Gruber et al., 2008; Hser et al., 2011).

NICOTINE REPLACEMENT THERAPY Whereas methadone replacement substitutes one drug for another, some replacement therapies vary the *method* of drug delivery rather than the drug itself. **Nicotine replacement therapy (NRT)** is safe and effective when used as part of a comprehensive smoking cessation program. NRT is available over the counter as gum or a patch and by prescription as a puffer or inhaler or as sublingual (under the tongue) lozenges. NRT replaces nicotine from cigarettes, reduces withdrawal symptoms, and helps the patient resist the urge to smoke. NRT approaches increase the odds of quitting approximately 1.5- to 2-fold both with and without additional counselling (Silagy et al., 2004).

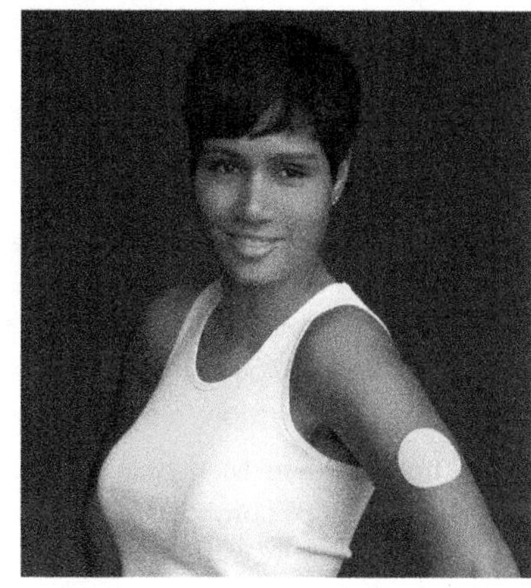

The nicotine patch allows for controlled release of nicotine into the body and helps with smoking cessation.

bikeriderlondon/Shutterstock

ANTAGONIST TREATMENTS Because the positively reinforcing effects of drugs appear to be a major factor in their use, could drug use be discontinued if these sensations were blocked by a drug that *antagonized* (acted against) the action of the drug being abused? Several studies have examined the efficacy of the opioid antagonists *naltrexone* and *nalmefene* to treat alcohol use disorders. Naltrexone reduces the risk of relapse to drink heavily and the frequency of drinking when compared with placebo, but it does not substantially enhance abstinence (Garbutt et al., 1999). More recently, long-acting injectable preparations of naltrexone were found to reduce heavy drinking among alcohol-dependent patients during six months of therapy (Garbutt et al., 2005). Although antagonist drugs do not miraculously reverse drug use, they are a valuable pharmacological tool worth investigating further.

AVERSIVE TREATMENTS Similar to aversion therapy, aversive pharmacological interventions pair ingestion of the substance with a noxious physical reaction. The best known substance is *disulfiram*, or **Antabuse**. Disulfiram prevents the breakdown of *acetaldehyde* (a substance found in alcohol), and the buildup of this substance in the body produces the noxious feelings. While taking Antabuse, people who consume alcohol experience nausea, vomiting, and increased heart rate and respiration. Controlled studies of disulfiram reveal mixed results. Its use reduces drinking frequency, but minimal evidence has been found to support improved continuous abstinence rates (Garbutt et al., 1999). Discontinuing the drug is all that is required to return to drinking without the noxious symptoms.

VACCINES A truly novel approach to treatment is *immunopharmacotherapy*—or vaccination against drug use. A vaccine produces antibodies that bind to the targeted drug before it reaches the brain and therefore blocks its positive, reinforcing effects. Attaching drugs to proteins from the blood can trigger an immune response, and the body generates antibodies against the drugs. As early as 1974, researchers discovered that when rhesus monkeys already addicted to heroin were vaccinated, the monkeys significantly reduced the number of times they pressed a lever for heroin, indicating that the vaccine blocked the heroin high (Bonese et al., 1974). Since then, animal models have been developed for immunization against cocaine, nicotine, hallucinogens, and methamphetamine, suggesting the potential efficacy of these treatments in humans. Human clinical trials are currently under way for vaccines against cocaine and nicotine (Meijler et al., 2004). If effective, this intervention could have intriguing social ramifications. Will parents vaccinate their children against nicotine, alcohol, marijuana, and other drugs just as they do against polio, measles, and mumps? Will the tobacco companies resist the vaccines because they will

examining the EVIDENCE

Controlled Drinking?

- **The Facts** Many conceptualizations (disease model) and treatment approaches (AA, therapeutic communities) for alcohol are based on the idea that complete abstinence is the only acceptable approach to overcoming alcohol dependence. Over the last 50 years, researchers have begun to question this all-or-nothing approach.
- **The Evidence** Mark and Linda Sobell, working at the University of Toronto, conducted the best known study of what is now called *controlled drinking* (Sobell & Sobell, 1973). Results indicated that people receiving behavioural treatment for alcoholism combined with learning skills to engage in nonproblematic drinking had significantly more "days functioning well" during a two year follow-up period than those receiving a treatment aimed at abstinence (Sobell & Sobell, 1973, 1978). Can individuals with alcohol use disorder be taught to control their drinking?
- **Let's Examine the Evidence** Although this research was well received, it also had detractors (Pendery et al., 1982) and inspired spirited criticism in sources such as the *New York Times* and the television news show *60 Minutes*, suggesting that the research was both flawed and potentially fraudulent. However, an independent investigation of the Sobells' research supported the integrity of this work on all counts. Alan Marlatt, a leading researcher in the area of alcohol, suggested that the

media closely covered the critiques of the Sobells' work but paid little attention to the evidence supporting its integrity and validity (Marlatt et al., 1993). The controversy over controlled drinking still continues, but it has taken its toll on the scientific community, and research directly bearing on this question has been pursued less frequently than might be expected (Coldwell & Heather, 2006).

- **What Are Alternative Explanations for This Controversy?** Probably the clearest finding from this research is that controlled drinking approaches may be especially suited to individuals with less severe drinking problems (Sobell & Sobell, 1995), although other researchers question the apparent consensus that it is not a suitable approach for more severe drinkers (Heather, 1995). Today the spirit of controlled drinking lives on, but the name has not widely survived. "Harm reduction" is the most common name now used (Marlatt et al., 1993). Although harm reduction shares many of the same goals of controlled drinking, it has received less critical attack, and initial evidence is encouraging (Witkiewitz & Marlatt, 2006). Furthermore, treatment approaches such as motivational interviewing (Miller, 1983) place the client's preferences and goals at its centre, and allow patients to choose controlled drinking as a strategy for treatment. Yet it is notable that in many cases, even motivational interviewing is conducted within settings favouring an abstinence-only approach (Coldwell & Heather, 2006).
- **Conclusion** Although no one would argue that abstinence is bad, researchers in the tradition of controlled drinking hope to provide alternatives for people who may be able to attain a normal and healthy life without completely avoiding alcohol.

infringe on the free market? Will prisoners who have committed drug-related crimes be vaccinated against their will? Many important ethical and social questions will arise as the efficacy of the immunopharmacotherapy approach becomes clear.

Sex and Racial/Ethnic Differences in Treatment

Women face unique barriers to obtaining treatment for substance use disorders, which may account for findings suggesting that women are less likely to enter treatment than men. For instance, limited access to child care and society's punitive attitude toward mothers who abuse drugs can keep them from admitting that they have a problem and seeking help (Allen, 1995). Women also differ from men in their response to treatment, although the data are inconsistent. Several studies have reported that women are more likely than men to drop out of substance abuse treatment, although this finding is far from conclusive (Bride, 2001; Joe et al., 1999; McCaul et al., 2001; Simpson et al., 1997).

In addition to sex differences, treatment studies also suggest that ethnic and racial minorities are less likely to seek and complete treatment, to receive treatment services, and to achieve recovery (Jerrell & Wilson, 1997; Rebach, 1992). Importantly, however, several studies indicate that minority clients do not differ from nonminority clients in their response to treatment (Pickens & Fletcher, 1991). Clearly, additional research is needed to identify which factors predict poor or favourable treatment outcomes among minority individuals. Lundgren and colleagues (2001) found that different racial and ethnic groups enter different types of drug treatment. Our ability to truly understand how best to prevent and treat substance use disorders will require a solid foundation of research that considers the specific needs and challenges associated with sex, ethnicity and race, and socioeconomic status. Considerable care must be taken not to assume that any particular conclusion applies to all groups.

CONCEPT check

- Substance use disorders are difficult to treat. As part of multifaceted interventions, behaviour therapy procedures such as contingency management therapy and aversion therapy play a prominent role.
- Relapse prevention strategies focus on the cognitive responses to lapses and relapses and help the patient maintain abstinence after successful treatment.

- Twelve-step programs focus on powerlessness over the addictive process and on complete abstinence from the substance.
- Antagonist treatments use one drug to block the reinforcing properties of another drug, thus reducing its pleasurable effects and lessening the risk of relapse.
- Aversive medications such as Antabuse pair the ingestion of a drug with a noxious physical reaction.
- Vaccines are being developed to eliminate the positive and reinforcing physical response to various drugs.

critical thinking question With some psychiatric illnesses, the patient and the therapist are "on the same side." They both want to take the symptoms away (e.g., Doctor, please help me get rid of the phobia that interferes with my life). With substance use disorders, this is often not the case. If you are the therapist, what are the therapeutic challenges of working with a patient whose goals may differ from yours?

real SCIENCE real LIFE

Gloria—Treating Poly-Substance Use

THE PATIENT

The court mandated Gloria, 36 years old, to 30 days of residential treatment at a community centre.

THE PROBLEM

At the time of her arrest, Gloria was living with her boyfriend of three years, their 2-year-old son, and one child from a previous relationship. She had dropped out of high school but did get her GED. She had a series of low-paying jobs and most recently lost her job as a cashier at a diner after she stole money from the cash register. She depended financially on her boyfriend, whose source of income was unknown. When Gloria arrived at the facility, she denied substance use within the prior 24 hours and reported some physical and psychological discomfort due to withdrawal. She was agitated, her speech was pressured, and her thoughts and speech were disorganized. She denied any hallucinations or delusions.

At intake, Gloria met the criteria for current severe crack/cocaine and mild alcohol use disorders. In the past, she had used marijuana, amphetamines, and heroin. A previous HIV test was negative. Her family history was positive for heroin and cocaine use disorders (father), alcoholism (mother), and death by heroin overdose (brother). Her boyfriend was a crack user who was not interested in receiving treatment, and he had interfered with her earlier attempts to get sober. Gloria worried that her daughter was using drugs and engaging in unsafe sexual activity, which concerned her greatly because she hoped her daughter could escape the cycle of high-risk behaviours that characterized her family.

A complete behavioural analysis identified the triggers associated with her cocaine and alcohol use. Her boyfriend, a drug dealer, was a major trigger in her use. Continuing to depend on him financially would seriously increase her risk of relapse.

During her residential treatment, Gloria learned skills for resisting urges to use. She worked through lapse and relapse scenarios and planned strategies for remaining clean. She had several family meetings with her sister and brother-in-law to mobilize family support. The team also helped her mobilize her faith and organized several outings to her church to meet with people who knew her situation and would provide support after treatment. Gloria also attended AA meetings regularly while in treatment and planned to continue attendance after discharge. While in treatment, she was trained in parenting skills. Her daughter, who had indeed started using drugs herself, was referred for treatment. Her social worker helped Gloria to find job placement and low-cost housing.

THE TREATMENT

Gloria's mandated treatment followed her arrest for stealing from the diner, which was her only arrest. She had had three previous contacts with the legal system when neighbours, fearing for her children, called the police in response to loud yelling and throwing objects against the wall. On each occasion, the police left, giving the couple a warning only. Gloria had denied any abuse or imminent danger to herself or her children.

The only hint that Gloria was interested in treatment for her addictions was her concern about her daughter and worry that her baby would be placed in foster care. Although she was clear that her boyfriend was not supporting her treatment, she did mention it to a sister as well as members of her church who she felt would support her.

In addition to her substance use problems, Gloria reported a period lasting for about the past two months when her mood had been consistently low. She reported decreased appetite and poor sleep.

Following the team's review of her initial assessment, they developed a preliminary treatment plan that identified four targets: treat her crack/cocaine use disorder, treat her alcohol use disorder, further evaluate her depression, and mobilize social support for continued abstinence. Her team felt that even though the treatment was court mandated, Gloria was sufficiently concerned about her children that they could enhance her desire to change her behaviours.

THE TREATMENT OUTCOME

At the end of the 30-day treatment, Gloria was afraid to be discharged. She felt as if she had only started to get clean, and she did not know what she would do without the daily support of the centre staff. When she was admitted, she had feared that 30 days was a life sentence, but now she knew that it was really too short a time for true recovery. She was realistic about her chances of staying sober. She knew that the thought of financial security would tempt her to go back to her dealer boyfriend, but each time she considered that, she had to pair that desire with her concern for her children's welfare. She was stepped down to weekly sessions with her social worker to provide ongoing support and early identification of any lapses or relapses. Gloria continued to attend AA meetings at her church. Her sister helped out by providing child care while Gloria worked. In return, Gloria helped her sister with her housekeeping job.

At the one-year anniversary of her discharge, Gloria was still sober. She managed to continue to attend AA, had become a regular member of her church community, and had become a better mother to her daughter, who had also remained drug free since her intervention. She continued to have mood fluctuations and noted honestly that at times she felt poorly equipped to put the required energy into remaining sober. However, her children remained her primary motivator, and her social and family supports helped carry her through the times of highest risk.

summary

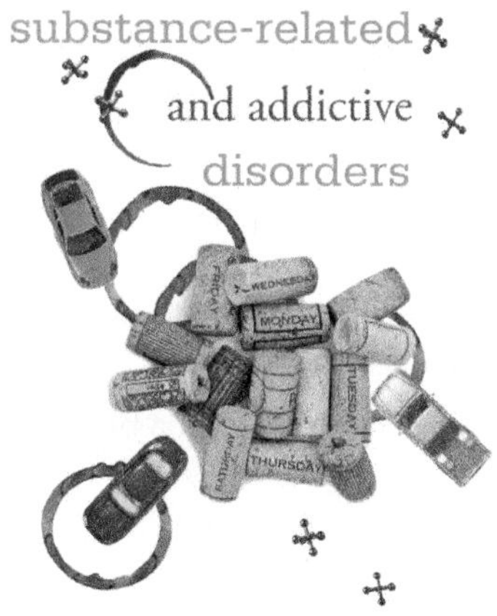

9.1 Define the term "substance use disorder" according to DSM-5 criteria.

A substance use disorder is a cluster of physiological, behavioural, and cognitive symptoms that indicate that the individual continues to use the substance despite significant problems due to use. Symptoms include tolerance; withdrawal; failed attempts to cut down on use; use in larger amounts than intended; spending a lot of time acquiring, using, or under the influence of the substance; continued use despite mental or physical problems due to use; and neglecting other life activities because of use.

9.2 Understand the principles of tolerance and withdrawal and how they differ across various classes of drugs.

Tolerance refers to needing a markedly increased amount of the substance to achieve the same effect. *Withdrawal* symptoms occur when a dependent person attempts to cut down or abstain from regular drug use.

9.3 Appreciate how various drugs act in the body to produce their characteristic effects.

Drugs have specific mechanisms of action to produce their effects. For example, nicotine achieves its rewarding effects through the dopamine system; alcohol modulates receptors in the GABA system; opioids mimic the body's natural opioids; and hallucinogens disrupt serotonergic function and cause the user to experience unusual sensations.

9.4 Describe the short- and long-term negative psychological and health consequences of various types of substance use disorders.

Caffeine produces rapid alertness; nicotine is highly addictive and associated with a rapid pharmacological effect; alcohol creates a sensation of being more relaxed, outgoing, and social; marijuana is associated with an intensified experience of colour and sound and a slowed perception of time; cocaine and methamphetamine are CNS stimulants that can result in dangerous elevations of cardiovascular function; opioids reduce pain; hallucinogens can cause the user to experience unusual sensations; inhalants produce a rapid high and can lead to permanent organ and brain damage.

9.5 Understand the contributions of biological, genetic, behavioural, cognitive, and sociocultural theories to the etiology of substance use disorders.

Drug and alcohol use disorders emerge from a combination of genetic and environmental factors. Environmental factors can serve either to increase risk or to protect an individual from developing a substance use disorder.

9.6 Compare and contrast treatments for various types of substance use disorders.

No single treatment exists for substance use disorders—both pharmacological and behavioural approaches can be combined into a comprehensive treatment program that includes considerable attention to motivation and relapse prevention.

key terms

abstinence violation effect 348
agonist substitution 351
alcohol cirrhosis 328
amphetamines 332
Antabuse 352
aversion therapy 349
barbiturates 334
benzodiazepines 334
caffeine 324
cocaine 334
contingency management approaches 349
crystal methamphetamine 333
delirium tremens (DTs) 328
detoxification 351
ecstasy 333
fetal alcohol syndrome 329
hallucinogens 337
inhalants 338
lysergic acid diethylamide (LSD) 337
marijuana 330
methadone 351
nicotine 326
nicotine replacement therapy (NRT) 351
opioids 336
relapse prevention (RP) 348
sedative drugs 334
substance intoxication 322
substance use 321
tetrahydrocannabinol (THC) 330
tolerance 323
transtheoretical model (TTM) 348
Wernicke-Korsakoff syndrome 328
withdrawal 324

TEST yourself

1. Bob uses illicit drugs "socially." His use does not produce problems with his social, educational, or occupational functioning. Bob's behaviour constitutes
   a. substance withdrawal
   b. substance use
   c. substance intoxication
   d. a substance use disorder
2. Lucy told her therapist that she frequently drinks more than she intended to, and that she has tried to cut down on her drinking several times without being able to do so. She endorsed no other symptoms related to her alcohol use. According to the DSM-5, Lucy meets criteria for
   a. no substance use disorder
   b. a severe alcohol use disorder
   c. a moderate alcohol use disorder
   d. a mild alcohol use disorder
3. The DSM-5 does not include symptoms of withdrawal for the following two categories of substances
   a. hallucinogens and inhalants
   b. stimulants and inhalants
   c. hallucinogens and stimulants
   d. caffeine and hallucinogens
4. The most widely used drug in the world is
   a. nicotine
   b. alcohol
   c. caffeine
   d. marijuana
5. Central to nicotine's highly addictive potential is (are)
   a. its low cost and availability
   b. a supportive "smokers' subculture"
   c. its direct influence on the brain's pleasure centres
   d. its suppression of insulin production, producing hyperglycemia
6. Although alcohol affects many neurotransmitters, its effect is particularly powerful on the neurotransmitter
   a. serotonin
   b. GABA
   c. dopamine
   d. epinephrine
7. In its most severe form, alcohol withdrawal can include which of the following symptoms?
   a. hallucinations and formication
   b. seizures and metabolic complications
   c. delirium tremens
   d. all of the above
8. Dan, now in his mid-50s, has used alcohol heavily since his late 20s. He does not feel well, and his doctors are concerned that his alcohol use may have contributed to a liver disease called
   a. delirium tremens
   b. cirrhosis
   c. FAS
   d. Wernicke-Korsakoff syndrome
9. THC in marijuana produces a sense of euphoria by stimulating
   a. GABA release, which disinhibits various brain systems
   b. epinephrine discharge, leading to heightened pleasure and sensory acuteness
   c. cannabinoid receptors, thereby activating the dopamine reward system
   d. serotonin reuptake, leading to a feeling of contentment
10. Most people who are treated for amphetamine abuse
    a. also report high use of alcohol
    b. never experience tolerance or withdrawal
    c. use depressant drugs to come down from "highs"
    d. do not use another substance
11. Codeine, morphine, and heroin mimic the effects of the body's natural opioids, which include
    a. endorphins and enkephalins
    b. oxycodone and oxycontin
    c. dopamine and ketamine
    d. norepinephrine and epinephrine
12. Alcohol and drugs act on the brain's reward circuitry, which includes the
    a. medial cortex of the prefrontal lobes
    b. ventral tegmental area and the basal forebrain
    c. basal ganglia and hypothalamus
    d. Wernicke-Korsakoff's area

13. Kohana is getting ready for a date. Before he leaves his apartment, he smokes some marijuana, which he believes helps him to be more charming and interesting. Which theoretical perspective best explains his actions?
   a. behavioural
   b. psychodynamic
   c. cognitive
   d. sociocultural

14. Chronic use of illicit drugs during adolescence may result in "arrested development," which is
   a. slowed brain development resulting from metabolic changes
   b. inhibited physical maturation due to a decrease in sex hormones
   c. delays in emotional maturation due to incarceration
   d. missed social experiences and emotional growth opportunities

15. Michelle quit smoking six months ago. She went out drinking with an old friend and had a few cigarettes with her. The next day she bought a pack of cigarettes, saying to herself, "I just won't ever have any willpower." This illustrates the
   a. inescapable cycle of addiction to nicotine
   b. weakness of an unsystematic cessation program
   c. application of controlled smoking
   d. abstinence violation effect

16. What is the fundamental difference between the cognitive-behavioural approach and the 12-step AA approach to the treatment of alcohol abuse?
   a. Cognitive-behavioural approaches emphasize skills to control addiction rather than always requiring complete abstinence.
   b. Twelve-step programs reject the disease or medical model of addiction.
   c. Cognitive-behavioural approaches lack the empirical support that AA programs have established.
   d. No fundamental conflict exists; both approaches are often used successfully in conjunction with one another.

17. In agonist substitution, a chemically similar safe medication is substituted for the drug of abuse. The most common drug used in this manner is
   a. naltrexone
   b. methadone
   c. disulfiram
   d. acetaldehyde

18. As in aversion therapy, aversive pharmacological interventions pair ingestion of the substance with a noxious physical reaction. The best known substance used in this manner is
   a. naltrexone
   b. methadone
   c. disulfiram
   d. acetaldehyde

19. Controlled drinking approaches may be especially suited to individuals who have a
   a. less severe dependence on drinking
   b. severe dependence on drinking
   c. strong religious orientation
   d. history of failure in response to other treatments

Answers:
1 b, 2 d, 3 a, 4 c, 5 c, 6 b, 7 d, 8 b, 9 c, 10 d, 11 a, 12 b, 13 c, 14 d, 15 d, 16 a, 17 b, 18 c, 19 a.

chapter 10

schizophrenia spectrum and other psychotic disorders

(top right): 3dbrained/Getty Images; **(top center):** olgaecat/Getty Images; **(top center):** David Freund/Getty Images; **(bottom):** Koksharov Dmitry/Shutterstock

schizophrenia spectrum and other psychotic disorders

learning objectives

After reading this chapter, you should be able to:

10.1
Distinguish between a psychotic experience and the psychotic disorders.

10.2
Understand that schizophrenia is *not* a condition involving "split personality," nor does it usually involve violent behaviour toward others.

10.3
Identify the positive, negative, and cognitive symptoms of schizophrenia.

10.4
Understand how culture plays a role in the expression and treatment of schizophrenia.

10.5
Discuss the neurodevelopmental model of schizophrenia.

10.6
Understand the interplay of genetic, biological, psychological, and environmental factors in the etiology of schizophrenia.

10.7
Identify efficacious pharmacological and psychological treatments for schizophrenia.

What I remember most is how disoriented and frightened I felt. With little warning, my world had simply shifted under my feet. Over a period of several months, I began to believe that messages were being left for me in graffiti across campus. I also began to believe that my phone was being tapped. My friends insisted I was mistaken. But no one knew enough to realize anything was wrong. And then one day everything changed. One afternoon I realized the people on the radio were talking to me, much the way one has an intuition about a geometry proof, a sudden dawning of clarity or understanding. This clarity was more compelling than reality. It took me several weeks to put the pieces together. What I had known all my life was wrong. My friends were not real friends: at best they were neutral, at worst they were spies for the CIA. Graduate school was a luxury I was no longer allowed. There was a secret history of the world to which I now became attuned. It involved the CIA and the stealth bomber, which flew just out of sight in order to register details regarding my movements. An evil dictator was gathering power to himself, and he meant to perpetuate a holocaust. Only the resistance, of which I was now a part, stood in his way. As time passed I became proficient at reading code. Most of my days were spent reading and responding to the newspaper so that the resistance could gather its military and economic resources to retake territory that had been lost. I learned to communicate by deciphering bits of conversation, reading newspaper articles, and listening to songs on the radio. Everyone could read my mind, so unless I was engaged in conversation, I spoke mostly in my head. I could not read anyone else's mind so I remained dependent on the media for information.

Within six months, I became adept at coordinating different avenues of information. However, I was living a nightmare. When I shut my eyes, I saw neon-coloured cartoon characters that zoomed in and out of my field of vision. They were so bright it hurt. At night I would keep my eyes open until I fell asleep from exhaustion. I also lived in terror of the evil dictator and his minions. I never knew where they might be or how to evade them. I begged my superiors to have me killed. When it became clear that this was not going to happen, I took matters into my own hands. Within the course of a week, I tried to commit suicide four times.

Source: Weiner, S. K. (2003). First person account: Living with the delusions and effects of schizophrenia. *Schizophrenia Bulletin, 29*, 877–879. Copyright © 2007, Oxford University Press and the Maryland Psychiatric Research Center (MPRC).

Psychotic Disorders

10.1 Distinguish between a psychotic experience and the psychotic disorders.

Psychotic disorders are characterized by unusual thinking, distorted perceptions, and odd behaviours. People with a psychotic disorder are considered to be out of touch with reality and to be unable to think in a logical or coherent manner. They sometimes behave oddly, talking or mumbling to themselves or gesturing at someone that no one else can see. Some psychotic disorders are serious and chronic, while others are temporary states of confusion. Before we discuss the different disorders, it is necessary to understand the abnormal cognitive, perceptual, and behavioural features that define these conditions.

What Is Psychosis?

Psychosis is a severe mental condition characterized by a loss of contact with reality. This usually takes the form of a **delusion** (a false belief) or a **hallucination** (a false sensory perception), or both. Both of these phenomena are illustrated in our opening

Delusions and hallucinations are characteristic of schizophrenia. The person who experiences them is in poor touch with reality and often behaves in ways that seem strange or bizarre.

Gideon Mendel/Corbis

case, which involves several false beliefs (being spied on, being part of a resistance movement) and false sensory perceptions (seeing cartoon characters that were not there). Such a dramatic loss of contact with reality can be quite frightening and can affect every aspect of functioning, even leading the affected person to behaviours as extreme as attempting suicide.

Although psychotic symptoms can be quite disturbing, hallucinations or delusions alone do not necessarily mean that a psychotic disorder, such as schizophrenia, is present. Psychotic symptoms may also occur among adults with other psychological disorders including bipolar disorder, major depressive disorder, post-traumatic stress disorder (PTSD), and substance-related disorders.

Nadia is 15 years old. She is sad and very irritable. She cries all the time and refuses to go to school. Her parents brought her to the clinic because of her school refusal, but during the interview, she revealed to the clinician that she has been hearing voices for the past month. One is the voice of Snow White and the other voice sounds like an alien. They whisper "bad things" to her but she would not say what the voices say to her. A month later, when Nadia's mood improved, she said the voices had gone away.

Psychotic experiences such as delusional thinking and hallucinations may also occur in people with physical illnesses such as brain tumours, major or mild neurocognitive disorder due to Alzheimer's disease and Parkinson's disease, and after physical damage to the brain such as brain injuries or exposure to toxic substances. When psychotic experiences occur suddenly, the presence of a serious brain-related medical condition must first be considered.

Finally, psychotic experiences sometimes occur even when no psychological disorder is present. Brief or limited psychotic experiences are common, occurring in 2% to 12% of adults (Hannsen et al., 2005), and may include thoughts of persecution, a feeling that someone is stealing or manipulating one's thoughts, or hearing voices or sounds no one else can hear. One important difference is that individuals without psychotic disorders often report that the voices are positive; they are not upset by the presence of the voices and feel in control of the experience (Honig et al., 1998). In contrast, those suffering from psychosis perceive the voices as negative and do not feel in control of the experience.

Psychotic symptoms may thus occur across many different physical conditions and psychological disorders, and even at times among people with no apparent physical or psychological disorder. However, psychotic symptoms are most often considered as one of the defining characteristics of schizophrenia.

What Is Schizophrenia?

10.2 Understand that schizophrenia is *not* a condition involving "split personality," nor does it usually involve violent behaviour toward others.

Schizophrenia is a severe psychological disorder characterized by disorganization in thought, perception, and behaviour. People with schizophrenia do not think logically, perceive the world accurately, or behave in a way that permits normal everyday life and work. They may worry that the government is spying on them or that voices on the radio are speaking directly to them—giving them instructions about how to behave, or transmitting messages only they can understand. As a result of these delusions or

SIDE by SIDE case studies Dimensions of Behaviour: From Normal to Abnormal

Normal Behaviour Case Study

Comforting Thoughts—No Disorder

→ Daphne had always had a close relationship with her mother. When her mother developed breast cancer, Daphne took care of her, taking a leave of absence from her job and moving in with her mother to make sure that she received the care that she needed. After her mother died, Daphne was devastated. She stayed on to settle her mother's affairs and sell her house. Daphne had mixed feelings when the house was sold. She had grown up there, and knowing that she would never come back was hard. After packing up the last of her belongings, she stood in the kitchen—the place where she and her mother had spent so many happy times. With tears in her eyes, she said, "Well Mom, I guess I have to go." Daphne tells everyone that clear as could be, her mother replied, "Yes, honey. Go live your life." Daphne often relives that moment, feeling comforted by her mother's last words.

Abnormal Behaviour Case Study

Scary Thoughts—Psychotic Disorder

→ Amare had always had a pleasant relationship with his father-in-law, but last week they had some cross words. It was nothing really serious, and Amare planned to apologize when he saw his father-in-law again next week. However, before that could happen, his father-in-law had a heart attack and died. Amare became deeply depressed, regretting that he never had the chance to tell his father-in-law he was sorry. After the funeral, he started hearing voices accusing him of being a bad son-in-law and causing his father-in-law's death by his cross words, and suggesting that perhaps he did not deserve to live. The voices would not let him sleep; they were loud and merciless, calling him "killer." About a week later, his wife found him in the bedroom, arguing with the voices and insisting that his wife had to be hearing them too. Frightened by his behaviour, his wife called the police and had Amare hospitalized.

hallucinations, they behave oddly, appearing to others to be talking to themselves or doing things such as barricading themselves inside their homes to prevent being kidnapped by an unseen enemy. Schizophrenia is a serious psychological disorder because the condition creates severe impairment, and it is often chronic even with the best available treatments.

As discussed in Chapter 1, German psychiatrist Emil Kraepelin and Swiss psychiatrist Eugen Bleuler first defined schizophrenia more than 100 years ago. Kraepelin called this disorder **dementia praecox** to highlight its pervasive disturbances of perceptual and cognitive faculties (*dementia*) and its early life onset (*praecox*), and to distinguish it from the dementia associated with old age. Bleuler focused on four core symptoms of the disorder: ambivalence, disturbances of affect, disturbance of association, and preference for fantasy over reality (Tsuang et al., 2000). Bleuler renamed the condition *schizophrenia*, combining the Greek words for split (*schizo*) and mind (*phrene*), to highlight the splitting of thought, affect, and behaviour that occurs among those with this disorder.

Because almost everyone has felt sad at some time, it is easy for most people to understand that depression is "extreme" sadness. However, it is difficult for people to understand the unusual symptoms of schizophrenia, a disorder that challenges mental health professionals as well. Yet during the last 100 years, our understanding of the clinical presentation, etiology, and treatment of schizophrenia has improved substantially. Before examining its symptoms, it is important to clarify several common misconceptions about schizophrenia.

Perhaps because it is so difficult to understand the experience of schizophrenia, many mistaken ideas exist about this disorder. This lack of understanding has led to many inaccurate media and literary portrayals of schizophrenia. Robert Louis Stevenson's *The Strange Case of Dr. Jekyll and Mr. Hyde* is a classic description of two contradictory personalities that exist within the same individual. Dr. Henry Jekyll is sensitive and kind; Mr. Edward Hyde is a violent murderer. Even today, the term *Jekyll and Hyde* is used to describe behaviours that appear to be polar opposites yet exist within the same person. However, people with schizophrenia do *not* have "split personalities." The Greek word *schizo* describes the split between an individual's thoughts and feelings, not the splitting of the personality.

A similar misconception is that schizophrenia involves multiple personalities. As discussed in Chapter 5, a condition called *dissociative identity disorder* (DID) purportedly does exist. People with DID are considered to have two or more distinct personalities, each with its own thoughts, feelings, and behaviours. As illustrated by books such as *The Three Faces of Eve* and *Sybil*, one personality may be unaware of the other's behaviour. However, each personality perceives, deals with, and interacts with the environment successfully. This ability to successfully negotiate with the environment is what differentiates people with schizophrenia from people with DID. Schizophrenia results in an inability to perceive the environment appropriately or deal with it adequately. In short, people with schizophrenia do *not* have split or multiple personalities.

Schizophrenia in Depth

10.3 Identify the positive, negative, and cognitive symptoms of schizophrenia.

The symptoms of schizophrenia include delusions, hallucinations, disorganized speech, disorganized or catatonic behaviour, and negative symptoms (see "DSM-5: Schizophrenia"). Delusions and hallucinations are sometimes called positive symptoms, but in this case the term *positive* does not mean optimistic or upbeat; it denotes the *presence* of an abnormal behaviour within the individual. **Positive symptoms**, the behaviours that people most often associate with schizophrenia, consist of unusual thoughts, feelings, and behaviours. They vary in intensity, and in many cases are responsive to treatment (Tirupati et al., 2006).

One positive symptom of schizophrenia is the presence of delusions, which are fixed beliefs that are not changeable when presented with conflicting evidence (see Table 10.1).

TABLE 10.1

Types of Delusions and Hallucinations Found in People With Schizophrenia

Symptom	Example
Delusions	
Influence	Beliefs that behaviour or thoughts are controlled by others, including thought withdrawal, broadcasting, or insertion or mind reading by another person
Self-Significance	Thoughts of grandeur, reference (random events, objects, and behaviours of others have a particular and unusual significance to oneself—such as the messages left in graffiti in the introductory case), religion (believing that one is a supreme being), guilt, or sin
Persecution or Paranoid	Thoughts that others are out to harm the person
Somatic	Belief that one's body is rotting away
Hallucinations	
Auditory	Noises or voices, perhaps speaking to or about the person
Visual	Visions of religious figures or dead people
Olfactory	Smells
Gustatory	Tastes
Somatic	Feelings of pain or deterioration of parts of one's body or feeling that things are crawling on, or in, the skin or the body

Sources: Kimhy, D., Goetz, R., Yale, S., Corcoran, C., & Malaspina, D. (2005). Delusions in individuals with schizophrenia: Factor structure, clinical correlates, and putative neurobiology. *Psychopathology, 38*, 338–344; and Mueser, K. T., Bellack, A. S., & Brady, E. U. (1990). Hallucinations in schizophrenia. *Acta Psychiatrica Scandiavica, 82*, 26–29.

Persecutory delusions are the most common. These consist of the belief that someone is harming or attempting to harm the person. Other delusions consist of the belief that the person is a special agent/individual (as in our opening case) (Appelbaum et al., 1999). Although most delusions are distressing in nature, sometimes the delusion is grandiose with negative events occurring when others do not act in accord with the delusional content.

Kim, a university student of Korean descent, was hospitalized after he was found wandering around on the city streets, yelling at strangers because they did not bow when he walked by. Upon questioning, Kim declared that he was the emperor of Korea and that those on the street were not giving him the deference appropriate to his royal status.

People with schizophrenia sometimes believe that their thoughts are being tampered with, for example, being removed from their heads or broadcast on TV. This is a *delusion*, a false belief.

PhotoAlto/Getty Images

Other common delusions are **delusions of influence**, which include beliefs that others control one's behaviour or thoughts. People with schizophrenia often believe that their thoughts are being manipulated by processes known as *thought withdrawal*, *thought broadcasting*, or *thought insertion*. People with delusions of influence believe that the government is inserting thoughts into their head or that evil forces,

criteria for Schizophrenia — DSM-5

A. Two (or more) of the following, each present for a significant portion of time during a 1-month period (or less if successfully treated). At least one of these must be (1), (2), or (3):

1. Delusions.
2. Hallucinations.
3. Disorganized speech (e.g., frequent derailment or incoherence).
4. Grossly disorganized or catatonic behaviour.
5. Negative symptoms (i.e., diminished emotional expression or avolition).

B. For a significant portion of the time since the onset of the disturbance, level of functioning in one or more major areas, such as work, interpersonal relations, or self-care, is markedly below the level achieved prior to the onset (or when the onset is in childhood or adolescence, there is failure to achieve expected level of interpersonal, academic, or occupational functioning).

C. Continuous signs of the disturbance persist for at least 6 months. This 6-month period must include at least 1 month of symptoms (or less if successfully treated) that meet Criterion A (i.e., active-phase symptoms) and may include periods of prodromal or residual symptoms. During these prodromal or residual periods, the signs of the disturbance may be manifested by only negative symptoms or by two or more symptoms listed in Criterion A present in an attenuated form (e.g., odd beliefs, unusual perceptual experiences).

D. Schizoaffective disorder and depressive or bipolar disorder with psychotic features have been ruled out because either 1) no major depressive or manic episodes have occurred concurrently with the active-phase symptoms, or 2) if mood episodes have occurred during active-phase symptoms, they have been present for a minority of the total duration of the active and residual periods of the illness.

E. The disturbance is not attributable to the physiological effects of a substance (e.g., a drug of abuse, a medication) or another medical condition.

F. If there is a history of autism spectrum disorder or a communication disorder of childhood onset, the additional diagnosis of schizophrenia is made only if prominent delusions or hallucinations, in addition to the other required symptoms of schizophrenia, are also present for at least 1 month (or less if successfully treated).

such as alien invaders, are "stealing" thoughts out of their head. In thought broadcasting, the person believes that his or her private thoughts are being revealed to others, usually by being transmitted over the radio or television.

A second positive symptom is hallucinations (which is a perception-like experience without an external stimulus, such as hearing voices when no one is there or seeing visions that no one else sees). Auditory hallucinations are most common (experienced by 71% of one sample; Mueser et al., 1990) and can range from simple noises to one or more voices of either gender. Voices are most commonly negative in quality and content, but on occasion can be comforting or kind (Copolov et al., 2004). Auditory hallucinations that appear to be exclusive to people with schizophrenia are voices that keep a running commentary on the individual's behaviour or several voices that have a conversation. Visual hallucinations are less common (14% in one sample) but do occur, often in those with the most severe form of the disorder (Mueser et al., 1990). Common examples of visual hallucinations include seeing the devil or a dead relative or friend. About 15% of hallucinations are *tactile* (touch). *Olfactory* (smell) and *gustatory* (taste) hallucinations are the least common type (11%).

John was diagnosed with schizophrenia. Despite medication, he continued to have auditory hallucinations consisting of voices that talked to him or directed him to do certain things. John often talked back to the voices or laughed aloud at something that they said. Each day, John came to the local mental health clinic for the free coffee provided to patients waiting for an appointment. He rarely had an appointment, but the staff was sympathetic toward him and would let him sit in the waiting room and drink coffee. He was never violent, but his behaviour often disturbed the clinic patients unfamiliar with schizophrenia. On many occasions, John's behaviour became too upsetting to the other patients, and the staff had to ask him to leave. Even though he was hallucinating, a staff member would approach him and say, "John, it is time to go now." Immediately, John would look up, greet the staff member by name, say, "Sure, see you tomorrow," and calmly leave the clinic.

The catatonic feature of schizophrenia sometimes includes *waxy flexibility*, in which a person's limbs can be "posed" by someone else. The person remains in that position until he or she is moved again.

Grunnitus Studio/Science Source

John's behaviour illustrates a very important point about people suffering with schizophrenia. Hallucinations may persist despite adequate medication dosages, but many patients are able to function at some level and maintain some contact with reality even while hallucinating.

Another positive symptom is disorganized thinking, which is usually assessed by abnormality of speech. When untreated, individuals with schizophrenia usually show strange speech patterns that indicate deterioration in their cognitive functioning. Some examples of this cognitive derailment or deterioration include **loose associations**, or thoughts that have little or no logical connection to the next thought (e.g., "I once worked at an Army base. It is important to soldier on. The Middle East—I like to travel, my favourite pizza place is on Davie Street."). Another symptom is **thought blocking**, exemplified by unusually long pauses in the patient's speech that occur during a conversation. A third symptom is **clang associations** in which speech is governed by words that sound alike, rather than words that have meaning (e.g., "I have bills, summer hills, bummer, drum solo"), rendering communication meaningless.

Another positive symptom is grossly disorganized or abnormal motor behaviour. **Catatonia** is a condition in which a person is awake but is nonresponsive to external stimulation.

The police brought Derek to the psychiatric emergency room. They found him standing naked in an alley downtown. He was mute, he did not make eye contact, and he seemed oblivious to the fact that the outside temperature was subzero. Because he would not speak or move on his own, Derek was hospitalized on the inpatient unit. The next morning, the nurses found him standing in the patient lounge, naked and motionless. They put him in pajamas and sat him in a chair—12 hours later, he was still sitting in the same position.

During a catatonic state, the patient may not move or make eye contact with others. He or she may be *mute* (without speech) or muscularly rigid (like a statue). When **waxy flexibility** is present, parts of the body (usually the arms) remain frozen in a particular posture when positioned that way by another person.

Positive symptoms may be quite dramatic, but they are not the only type of symptom. A second symptom category are the negative symptoms. In this case, the term *negative* does not refer to bad or horrific content, but rather to the *absence* of behaviours that exist in the general population. In schizophrenia, **negative symptoms** are behaviours, emotions, or thought processes (cognitions) that exist in people without a psychiatric disorder but are absent (or are substantially diminished) in people with schizophrenia. Common negative symptoms include *diminished emotional expression*, *anhedonia*, *avolition* or apathy, *alogia*, and *psychomotor retardation.*

Diminished emotional expression describes reduced or immobile facial expressions and a flat, monotonic vocal tone that does not change even when the topic of conversation becomes emotionally laden. This inconsistency between a schizophrenic patient's facial expression and vocal tone and the content of his or her speech is one example of Bleuler's use of the word *split* to describe this disorder—for example, the patient may describe horrific thoughts with very little emotional expression in the face or voice. **Anhedonia** refers to a lack of capacity for pleasure; the person feels no joy or happiness. **Avolition**, or apathy, is an inability to initiate or follow through on plans. Often, relatives of people with schizophrenia interpret this apathy as simple laziness or a deliberate unwillingness to improve their life—an erroneous interpretation that can create distress and discord in the family environment (Mueser & McGurk, 2004). **Alogia** is a term used to describe decreased quality or quantity of speech. **Psychomotor retardation** describes slowed mental or physical activities. When psychomotor retardation affects cognition, for example, speech can be slowed to the point that it is difficult or impossible for others to follow the person's conversation. Unlike positive symptoms, which can be largely controlled by medication, negative symptoms are treatment-resistant; they tend to persist (Fenton & McGlashan, 1991) and restrict the person's ability to hold a job, go to school, or even take care of personal responsibilities such as bathing or dressing. See "DSM-5: Schizophrenia" for the symptoms that are necessary for a diagnosis of schizophrenia.

People with schizophrenia also have **cognitive impairments**. Deficits in cognitive abilities include impairments in visual and verbal learning and memory, inability to pay attention, decreased speed of information processing (how fast information is understood), and impaired abstract reasoning and executive functioning (ability to solve problems and make decisions; Green et al., 2004). To illustrate cognitive impairments, consider the following example of impaired abstract reasoning. People without schizophrenia interpret the phrase "People who live in glass houses should not throw stones" to mean that one should not criticize others when they themselves also may have faults or flaws. However, many individuals with schizophrenia interpret that statement as follows: "It means that you should build a house with bricks because stones cannot break bricks." Cognitive deficits are one of the earliest signs of schizophrenia (Kurtz et al., 2005). Like negative symptoms, cognitive deficits are long-lasting and strongly correlated

REAL people REAL disorders

Marilyn's Paranoid Schizophrenia

For someone who lives in total isolation, Marilyn has a lot of company. She's got the Cabir brothers. All five of them, all abusive, callous, and unrelenting in their verbal insults. Marilyn recalls a beating she suffered at the hands of a Cabir: "He just went crazy and said, 'I hate you.' And he grabbed an ashtray and just—pow!—hit me over the head with it. Put his teeth in my face and was going for the knife..." Marilyn starts to weep. It's a memory so vivid, so real, that the Cabirs' place of residence comes as a shock. "They're all in the wall. They just stand there and keep giving me slurs all the time. They say am I ever ugly, say 'I can't stand the sight of her,'" she explains. "Strange, isn't it?"

Marilyn finds a bi-weekly injection she gets at a downtown Toronto drop-in centre helps quiet the Cabirs. But is doesn't make them go away. They're in the walls every day and every night. They even follow her on the bus. The Cabirs—very real to Marilyn but invisible to a visitor—are only part of the story. The room she lives in is just as surreal—and far more frightening. It is *crawling* with cockroaches.

A swarm of hatchlings has taken over the table—probing every square millimetre of the surface. Marilyn sits, flyswatter in hand, trying to get as many as she can. Her conversation is interrupted frequently by the slap of her weapon. "I wish they'd go away," she says of the Cabirs. (Swat!) "He just stands there in the wall. He just stands there with his hands on his hips. He's there now. The whole family's there." (Swat!) In addition to the cockroaches, Marilyn has caught nine mice in her room. Scattered rodent droppings dot the thick shag carpet, a rug so heavily infested with insects, a visitor is grateful the room is partially dark.

Marilyn was hooked up with a mental health worker, a woman who was astonished at the conditions in which she lived. The worker helped find her a new place; a considerable feat in a city where people like Marilyn languish on waiting lists for up to five years. Marilyn moved to a self-contained subsidized apartment in the Sherbourne-Dundas Streets area. Not exactly prime real estate, but conditions are a world apart from her old place. "It was awful. Unbearable. I left a lot behind because those cockroaches used to get in my clothes." For her new apartment, Marilyn pays $300 a month—$30 less than her old place. And, she says, the surroundings have made a tremendous improvement in her mental health. "Oh, 100 percent better!" she says. But she's still got company. "The Cabirs are here," she says. "There's five of them in the wall."

Source: Simmie, S. (1998). I'd sit in the kitchen and just shake. *Toronto Star*, October 4.

with functional impairment. However, for some people with schizophrenia, many aspects of cognitive functioning can remain in the normal or even the above-normal range.

In addition to general cognitive impairment, people with schizophrenia have a deficit in **social cognition**, which is the ability to perceive, interpret, and understand social information, including other people's beliefs, attitudes, and emotions. People with schizophrenia are often deficient in the basic skills necessary for positive social interactions (Penn et al., 2001), including the ability to perceive social nuances and engage in basic conversation. They show impairment in the ability to identify the emotional states of other people and in the ability to comprehend sarcasm and lies (Sparks et al., 2010). People with schizophrenia also show reduced emotional responses to positive and negative events (Mathews & Barch, 2010). These skills, collectively known as social cognition, are necessary for effective academic, social, and occupational functioning (Green & Horan, 2010; Mathews & Barch, 2010) (see "Treatment of Schizophrenia and Other Psychotic Disorders").

Although a diagnosis of schizophrenia requires the presence of symptoms from each of the three categories, each person has a different set of symptoms. Common features of schizophrenia include delusions and hallucinations. Catatonia, another feature of schizophrenia, includes symptoms such as the following: stupor (i.e., no psychomotor activity), catalepsy (passive induction of a posture), waxy flexibility, mutism (unresponsive to commands or suggestions), agitation, grimacing, and **echolalia** (mimicking another's speech).

People with schizophrenia often have additional psychological disorders as well. Depression affects as many as 45% of people with schizophrenia (Leff et al., 1988). About 40% to 60% attempt suicide, and approximately 10% commit suicide (Health Canada, 2002). Suicide rates are much higher during the initial onset of the disorder (Malla & Payne, 2005) and immediately before or after any inpatient hospitalization (Qin & Nordentoft, 2005). Acts of self-harm do not occur any more frequently for people with schizophrenia than for those with other psychological disorders. Factors that increase the likelihood of self-harm include previous depressed mood or previous suicide attempts, drug abuse, agitation or restlessness, fear of mental deterioration, or delusions or hallucinations that encourage such behaviour (Symonds et al., 2006; Tarrier et al., 2006).

Approximately 47% of people with schizophrenia also have anxiety disorders (Kessler et al., 2005a). Because their disorder leaves people with schizophrenia vulnerable to victimization and violence as a result of poor living conditions or homelessness, PTSD is quite common, occurring in at least 43% of patient samples (Mueser et al., 2002). Up to 80% of individuals with schizophrenia have a lifetime history of substance abuse (Health Canada, 2002). Substance abuse is associated with poor functional recovery, suicidal behaviour, and violence (Health Canada, 2002).

Could the use of alcohol or drugs by people with schizophrenia be a strategy to cope with or escape from negative symptoms, such as the inability to feel pleasure (Khantzian, 1987)? This is known as the *self-medication hypothesis* and has been the subject of much debate and controversy. A recent meta-analysis (i.e., a statistical procedure that analyzes the results of many different research studies) suggests that patients with both schizophrenia and substance use disorders have *fewer* negative symptoms than patients who do not abuse substances (Potvin et al., 2006). However, before concluding that substance abuse decreases symptoms (a cause-and-effect model), remember that all of these data are cross-sectional and correlational in nature (see Chapter 2). Actually, we can interpret the relationship between substance abuse and schizophrenia in two ways. First, substance abuse might relieve negative symptoms such as anhedonia or apathy, providing support for the self-medication hypothesis. Alternatively, those with fewer negative symptoms may simply be less likely to abuse these substances. Experimental and longitudinal designs, rather than correlational studies, are necessary to disentangle this issue.

CONCEPT check

- Schizophrenia is a serious psychological disorder characterized by disorganization in thought, perception, and behaviour. People with schizophrenia do not think logically, perceive the world accurately, or behave in a way that permits normal everyday life and work.
- Schizophrenia includes positive symptoms, such as hallucinations and delusions; negative symptoms, such as diminished emotional expression and anhedonia; and cognitive impairments, such as impaired reasoning.
- Patients with schizophrenia often have other psychological disorders as well. PTSD, substance-related disorder, anxiety, and depression are common. These complicate the patient's long-term adjustment and the likelihood of an optimal treatment outcome.

critical thinking question Your friend is also in your abnormal psychology class. She was robbed at gunpoint the other day, and she confides to you that every time she walks down the street where the robbery occurred, she thinks that she sees the man who robbed her. Then the image disappears. She is afraid that she is developing schizophrenia. What would you tell her?

Functional Impairment

10.4 Understand how culture plays a role in the expression and treatment of schizophrenia.

Dorrie was always shy and did not make friends easily. She was very bright and graduated with good grades from a university in Manitoba. She was admitted to a prestigious master's program in business administration in Ontario. Soon after she arrived, she became very concerned about her safety and worried that others were out to harm her. She began to spend more and more time alone and worried about her personal safety. One day, the school called her parents—Dorrie was walking around campus threatening to shoot "the alien invaders." Although she had no gun, she was dismissed from the program, and her parents took her home. Her symptoms are now partially controlled by medication. She works part-time in the elementary school cafeteria but may never be able to live independently or fulfill her former academic potential.

There is a positive correlation between the severity of the symptoms of schizophrenia and the degree to which those symptoms impair the person's ability to function. Any delay in receiving treatment increases the severity of the functional impairment. Although the long-term outcome is significantly worse when the illness is untreated for a year (Harris et al., 2005), even smaller delays seriously affect the possibility of being able to live and function independently again. This means that treatment should begin as soon as possible to limit the chronic nature of the disorder.

Schizophrenia takes a significant human toll on the person and his or her family. Its social and economic burden makes it one of the 10 most debilitating (medical or psychological) conditions in the world in terms of disability-adjusted life years (Mueser & McGurk, 2004). Among psychological disorders, schizophrenia is one of the most serious conditions and was considered 100 years ago to have a progressively deteriorating course with little to no chance for recovery (Bleuler, 1911; Kraepelin, 1919). As a result of the discovery of effective treatments beginning in the 1960s, positive symptoms such as hallucinations and delusions may lessen and intensify again in severity over an individual's lifetime, resulting in periods of remission followed by relapse. Although the situation has improved somewhat since that time, the long-term outcome of schizophrenia is still quite poor (Jobe & Harrow, 2005).

In one longitudinal study of adults with schizophrenia, only 20% had a good outcome when reassessed after 2 to 12 years (Breier et al., 1991). During this interval, 78% had a relapse requiring hospitalization, 38% had attempted suicide, and 24% had an episode of depression or bipolar disorder. Some people with schizophrenia do have periods of recovery (Harrow et al., 2005). Over a 15-year follow-up period, 41% of patients with schizophrenia had a period of recovery defined as the presence of all of the following for one year: no psychotic symptoms, no negative symptoms, and demonstration of adequate psychosocial functioning (working at least half-time, moderate social activity, and no hospitalizations). This definition of recovery is sometimes described as "recovery from" a serious mental disorder.

Some researchers (e.g., Davidson & Roe, 2007) describe a second type of recovery similar to the conceptualization of recovery among people who were formerly substance dependent; that is, they are considered to be "in recovery." Using this definition, people in recovery from serious mental illnesses such as schizophrenia still may have symptoms of the disorder, but they are able to manage other aspects of their life such as work, education, friendships, and self-determination of life's various challenges. When this definition of recovery is used, perhaps as many as 50% of patients with schizophrenia are considered to be "in recovery."

Like substance-related disorder, coexisting depression increases the chance of a poor overall outcome. Those who have both schizophrenia and depression are likely to be frequently hospitalized and to be unemployed (Sands & Harrow, 1999). Poorer general physical health and excessive medical morbidity (rates of illness) are also common among people with schizophrenia (Brown et al., 2000; Osby et al., 2000), including increased risk of infectious diseases (Rosenberg et al., 2001), physical injury as a result of violent victimization (Walsh et al., 2003), and smoking-related and other illnesses (De Leon et al., 1995).

Cultural factors play a role in the course of schizophrenia; positive outcomes are more often found in developing countries than in developed nations. This may seem contradictory to what one would expect, but it may be the result of fewer social supports for people in more industrialized countries. In industrialized nations, people often leave home and family for better economic opportunities in a distant city and thus have limited family support when illness occurs. Cultural factors that are more prominent in developing countries and appear to be associated with better outcome for patients include differences in social structure, the more central role of the family in caring for psychiatrically ill patients, and differing beliefs about the etiology of the disorder (Tseng, 2003). For example, people in developing nations are more likely to accommodate deviance by a member of the community. In addition, they are more likely to keep a person with mental illness at home rather than seek hospitalization. Such cultures and lifestyles tend to be less complicated, with fewer streets to navigate and more options for employment for those with less education, so it is easier for a patient with cognitive impairments to negotiate the environment. All of these factors have been associated with a more positive patient prognosis (Sartorius et al., 1978), and more recent studies continue to support the role of the family and community in affecting the outcome for people with schizophrenia (Tseng, 2003).

Ethics and Responsibility

A common misconception about schizophrenia is that it is associated with violence. In fact, the rate of violence committed by people with schizophrenia (and other serious mental disorders) is higher than rates of violence for the general population (Hodgins et al., 1996). However, it is not higher (and in some cases, it is lower) than among patients with other serious disorders such as depression and bipolar illness (Monahan et al., 2001a). Among patients with schizophrenia recently discharged from a psychiatric hospital, 8% committed a violent act during the first 20 weeks after hospitalization and 15% committed a violent act after the first year (Monahan et al., 2001a). Definitions of violence include many different behaviours, some of which are considered minor acts (simple assault without injury or weapon use), whereas others represent more serious violence (assault using a lethal weapon, assault resulting in injury, threat with a lethal weapon, or sexual assault; Swanson et al., 2006). When examined by type of violence, the overall rate of violent acts committed by people with schizophrenia during a six month period was 19%, but only 4% were serious acts. An additional factor is that violent acts of any type are more often perpetrated by people with both schizophrenia and substance abuse than by people with schizophrenia alone (Erkiran et al., 2006).

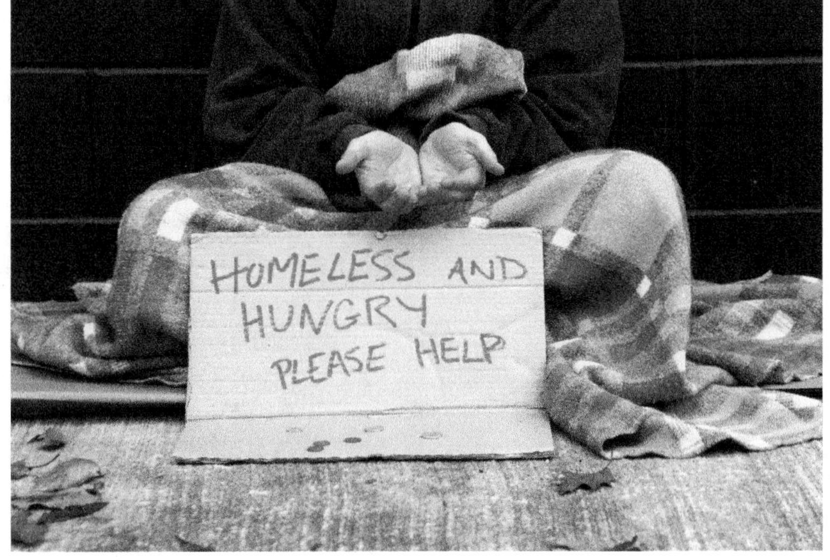

People with schizophrenia are at risk for victimization by others. They often live in unsafe conditions, and their cognitive impairments make them easy targets.
MegWallacePhoto/Fotolia

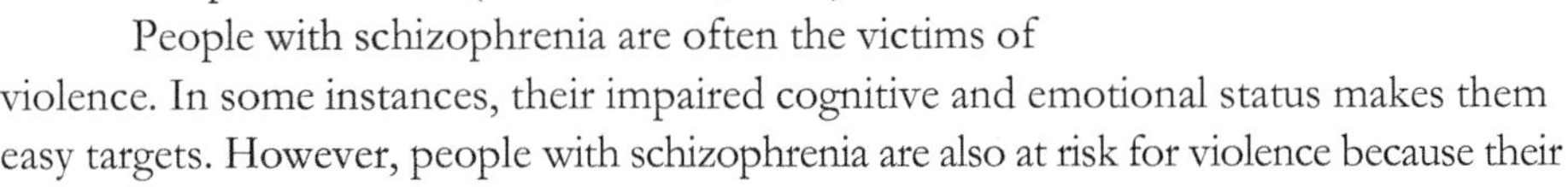

People with schizophrenia are often the victims of violence. In some instances, their impaired cognitive and emotional status makes them easy targets. However, people with schizophrenia are also at risk for violence because their disorder limits their occupational choices and their income. Thus their lower socioeconomic status means that they often live in neighbourhoods where crime is common.

People with schizophrenia are significantly impaired in many aspects of life functioning, including self-care, independent living, interpersonal relationships, work, school, parenting, and leisure time (Mueser & McGurk, 2004). Most people with schizophrenia do not marry (60% to 70%), and most have limited social contacts (Health Canada, 2002). The chronic course of the disorder contributes to ongoing social problems. As a result, individuals with schizophrenia are greatly over-represented in prison and homeless populations (Health Canada, 2002).

The disorder's cognitive deficits are especially important in limiting the ability to function effectively. Even a behaviour as simple as getting dressed requires several different cognitive abilities. *Executive functioning* (the ability to make decisions) is required to initiate the process of getting dressed, *memory* is required to recall where clothing articles are kept (drawers, closets), and *attention* is required in order to complete the process of getting dressed (not being distracted and, therefore, not finishing the process; Velligan et al., 2000).

Delusions and hallucinations distract people with schizophrenia, leaving them with only a limited ability to attend to their environmental surroundings. For example, people with schizophrenia are unable to observe or detect the social cues of other people, leading to awkward social interactions. Finally, deficits in memory and concentration may affect the ability to hold a job (Velligan et al., 2000). Work performance suffers when workers are unable to remember job assignments or follow instructions (e.g., "Mary, sweep the floor once an hour and check every 30 minutes to make sure the hair stylists have clean towels for their stations").

Epidemiology

Schizophrenia is recognized around the world, and the prevalence is approximately the same in all cultures. The lifetime prevalence of schizophrenia averages 1% (Health Canada, 2002). This percentage is consistent across different populations, cultures, and level of industrialization (World Health Organization [WHO], 1973). In any given year, between 16 and 40 of every 100 000 people develop schizophrenia (Jablensky, 2000). A higher incidence is associated with people who live in urban settings (perhaps a more complicated lifestyle), who move to a new area/country (perhaps resulting in social isolation and discrimination), and who are male. Schizophrenia is a very significant public health problem in terms of both its frequency and its disabling effects. Its onset can be either acute or gradual, and in many instances, *premorbid* (before the illness) features exist for many years before the actual psychotic symptoms emerge.

When the onset is gradual, the person often has some deterioration of functioning before the positive symptoms of the disorder emerge. In the *prodromal* phase, social withdrawal or deterioration in personal hygiene, such as not bathing or not changing clothes, may occur. The person may also have difficulty functioning properly at work or school. As the disorder progresses, the person enters the *acute* phase in which he or she exhibits the positive symptoms including hallucinations, delusions, and thought disorder. Negative symptoms are also present, but they are overshadowed by the psychotic behaviours. After the acute episode, some people with schizophrenia have a *residual phase* when the psychotic symptoms are no longer present, but the negative symptoms often remain. The continuing presence of negative symptoms sometimes prevents the person from being successfully employed or having satisfying social relationships.

Sex, Race, and Ethnicity

The sexes differ significantly with regard to the age of onset for schizophrenia as well as its course and prognosis. Women tend to develop schizophrenia at a later age than men do. Perhaps because of this difference, women often have a milder form of the disorder and experience fewer hospital admissions and better social functioning (Mueser & McGurk, 2004). When the disorder develops later, individuals have more opportunity to achieve adolescent and young adult developmental milestones and develop better social functioning (e.g., graduating from high school or college/university or getting married). Of course, simply finding a difference between the sexes does not explain why that difference exists. The sex difference in age of onset may be related to hormonal or sociocultural factors. For example, the female hormone estrogen has a strong protective influence on brain development and is hypothesized to lessen the abnormal brain development commonly seen among those with schizophrenia (Goodman et al., 1996; see also "Etiology of Schizophrenia").

With respect to sociocultural factors, females are often socialized from a very early age to be more socially competent than males, and they usually have more extensive social networks (Combs & Mueser, 2007). As is true for other areas, the answer to why sex differences exist may not be as simple as social competence or more extensive social networks. However, both factors appear to be important influences in lessening the overall impact of schizophrenia among women.

Data from the WHO (1973) reveal that the clinical symptoms of schizophrenia are consistent worldwide. Across all cultures, paranoid schizophrenia is the most common type (39.8%), whereas the catatonic subtype is found least often (6.7%).

11–33
Birth 20 40 60 80

Longitudinal studies that cover 20 or more years have great potential to contribute to our knowledge about the earliest stages of schizophrenia.

Developmental Factors

As children, adults who develop schizophrenia may have situational anxiety, nervous tension, depression, and "psychotic-like" experiences such as perceptual disturbances, magical thinking, and referential ideas (Owens et al., 2005). *Magical thinking* describes the belief that thinking about something can make it happen. For example, after you wish your parents were dead, they are involved in a serious car accident, and you conclude that your thoughts caused the accident. If you have *ideas of reference*, you interpret casual events as being directly related to you. For example, you walk by two people and they start to laugh—you wonder whether they are laughing at you. If you have *delusions of reference*, you would be sure that they were talking about you. These abnormalities in mood and perceptions have been reported consistently in childhood and suggest that some aspects of schizophrenia are present, though often undetected, long before the onset of the more dramatic positive symptoms.

Patients' childhood histories are usually collected retrospectively; that is, once the disorder is diagnosed, patients (or perhaps their parents) are asked to recall "how they were" before the symptoms began. These descriptions are compared with descriptions of people who do not suffer from the disorder. From a scientific perspective, this retrospective design is better than nothing at all, but it has a serious limitation. The cognitive deficits common among people with schizophrenia may limit the ability to accurately recall premorbid functioning. In addition, parents' recall of an adult child's early history may be affected by her or his more recent behaviours. Thus the current illness may bias any recollection of previous events. A prospective research design that would assess premorbid behaviours objectively before an illness developed is the preferable approach.

In one well-designed prospective study (Schiffman et al., 2004), all Danish youth ages 11 to 13 were videotaped under *standardized* (identical) conditions while they were eating lunch at school. Observers rated the children's behaviour for sociability (smiles, laughs, initiates or responds to conversations), involuntary movements (right or left hand, facial movement, other abnormal movements), and general neuromotor signs (raised elbows, eye movements, other abnormal movements). Nineteen years later, when the participants were between the ages of 31 and 33, individuals unaware of the participants' earlier behavioural ratings interviewed them. Twenty-six of the children had developed schizophrenia. Their behaviours at age 11 to 13 were compared with those of adults who had other disorders and to adults who had no disorder. Compared with both groups, adults with schizophrenia were significantly less sociable when they were children. Furthermore, compared with people who had a different psychiatric disorder (such as depression), people who developed schizophrenia had more subtle general neuromotor abnormalities as children. Because this study was prospective in design (not retrospective), included the entire birth registry of all children born in Denmark during a specific time (therefore there was no selection bias that might have influenced the results), used objective measures (rather than subjective report), and included a psychological comparison group, these results provide strong evidence that poor sociability and abnormal motor functioning may be factors uniquely related to the onset of schizophrenia.

Schizophrenia usually begins in late adolescence or early adulthood, but approximately 23% of patients develop the disorder after age 40 (Harris & Jeste, 1988; see also Chapter 13). Canadian investigators recently performed complex statistical analyses (admixture or latent class analyses) of schizophrenia age-of-onset (AOO) data (Liu et al., 2013). This was done in order to objectively determine the mean ages and other data for early-onset and other forms of schizophrenia. The researchers identified the following groups: early onset (mean AOO = 17 years), intermediate onset (mean AOO = 22 years), and late onset (mean AOO = 33 years). The cut-off for classifying **early-onset schizophrenia (EOS)** was age 19. People with EOS, compared to later onset, were more likely to be single, male, have birth complications, and have lower academic achievement.

Biologically, children with EOS lose more cortical grey matter than children without a psychological disorder (Kranzler et al., 2006) over a five year period. This loss occurs on both sides of the brain and progresses from front to back (Vidal et al., 2006), indicating significant biological deterioration in brain functioning. Behaviourally, only between 8% and 20% of those with EOS ever achieve full symptom remission; most have persistent symptoms throughout their lifetimes (Eggers & Bunk, 1997; Röpcke & Eggers, 2005). Even when compared with patients with adult-onset schizophrenia or children with other forms of psychoses, patients with EOS are more impaired; they have additional psychotic episodes, need more continuing psychiatric care, and are more impaired in the area of social functioning and independent living (Hollis, 2000; Kranzler et al., 2006). Perhaps the only positive factor for children with EOS is that their IQ scores remain stable even 13 years after the disorder's onset (Gochman et al., 2005). Clearly, this is one disorder in which the earlier the onset, the more severe the outcome.

Jermaine is 10 years old. When he was little, he played with the children in his preschool and was in the advanced reading class. Now he is behind in reading and gets into fights with his peers. He takes good-natured teasing very seriously and gets angry. He hides when other people come to his home. When he was younger, he was diagnosed with attention deficit hyperactivity disorder, depression, anxiety, and even autism spectrum disorder, but nothing seemed to fit. In all of his school pictures, he has a blank look on his face. His frustrated parents brought him to a new psychologist for an evaluation. After listening to the lack of emotion in Jermaine's voice, the way he would suddenly seem distracted or smile inappropriately, the psychologist asked if he ever heard voices. Almost relieved, Jermaine started talking about the "good voices" and the "bad voices." The good ones, he explained, were trying to help him. The bad ones were trying to trick him into doing "bad things" so he would go to hell. All of the voices commented on his behaviour, telling him he was "good" or "bad."

Even before delusions and hallucinations begin, children and adolescents with EOS are socially withdrawn, have difficulty interacting with peers, and have school adjustment problems (McClellan et al., 2003; Muratori et al., 2005). Because early onset

Canadian FOCUS

Long-Term Course of Schizophrenia: Two Case Examples

Sue and Joe were among a series of patients in a landmark 20- to 30-year follow-up study by Mary Seeman, a psychiatrist at the University of Toronto. They were first treated during the early 1970s at Toronto's Clarke Institute of Psychiatry (now known as CAMH—Centre for Addiction and Mental Health). Nearly two decades later, in 1997, the patients were reassessed (Seeman, 1998). Seeman's study provides a detailed portrait of the long-term outcome of people diagnosed with schizophrenia. The following are two examples, illustrating very different outcomes.

SUE

Sue was born in 1943 in Western Canada but had lived in Toronto since her late teens. In 1997 she was 54 years old. Although Sue did not regularly attend treatment appointments, she was well known to the Clarke staff, especially the staff in the emergency room. Her pattern over the past 10 years was to drop into the Clarke unexpectedly, either to quarrel with staff or to ask for a depot injection of antipsychotic medication (i.e., a slow-release medication given every two to four weeks). Sometimes, when it was cold outside, she visited the emergency room asking for directions to a hostel bed. On other occasions she was brought in by police because of aggressive behaviour. Sue was frequently verbally loud, irritable, and insulting.

Before developing schizophrenia, Sue had superior academic skills and a large network of friends and acquaintances. She left school and began work when she was 16. Sue had various office jobs, and was regularly promoted and received substantial salary increases. Before her first hospital admission, at age 28, she had been married and divorced, and had used hashish and LSD on several occasions. Over the course of the year prior to admission, she developed fears that television personalities were interfering with her life. Despite these fears, she was working regularly until the very day she was admitted to hospital.

During the first decade of her schizophrenia (1971–81), Sue was treated with daily oral doses of chlorpromazine, which managed to keep her symptoms under control. During that period she continued to work steadily. Sue was well-dressed, elegant, well-spoken, and led an active life. She had a job, had intimate relationships, had contact with her family, and was independent. After her first hospital admission, she was rehospitalized only once during 10 years, and for only a short period. Sue changed jobs frequently, but always managed to find employment because of her excellent office skills. Sue's last paid job ended in 1981. She never worked again.

After 1981, when she was 38, Sue's psychotic symptoms progressively worsened. Other problems also worsened, including increasing substance abuse, alienation from her family, fights with boyfriends, and frequent changes in residence. After 1981 she had more and more frequent hospital admissions. From 1971 to 1997 she had 37 psychiatric hospitalizations, some short, and some very long. During this period Sue became increasingly inconsistent in her treatment contacts.

From an elegant, well-groomed, competent woman, Sue devolved into an ill-kempt street person dressed in rags. She became continuously psychotic, difficult to understand, and very delusional, but in a disorganized way, so it was impossible to know what she is delusional about. She was usually homeless, despite efforts to find accommodation for her. She became raucous, disruptive, and verbally abusive, probably due to her addiction to street drugs. On several occasions, while living on the streets, she had been physically and sexually assaulted. Sue was frequently suicidal. She sometimes threatened to harm other people, and so she has become the object of fear.

Looking back over Sue's life, Seeman (1998) observed that Sue's good premorbid skills—that is, her social, financial, and occupational skills—probably shielded her from trouble during the first decade of her illness. The schizophrenia vulnerability, evident in her family history (her father and two of five siblings were diagnosed with schizophrenia), may have then overpowered her compensatory abilities. When assessed in 1997, she had become one of the most seriously ill of all the Clarke's outpatients. Sue's social supports eroded over time; her parents died, and her one healthy sister refused to have any contact with her. As Sue grew less and less attractive, there were fewer boyfriends. Seeman noted that the loss of these social resources may have contributed to Sue's profound deterioration.

JOE

Joe, a Portuguese Canadian, was born in 1949. He was not a good student and left school when he was 14 to work at a manual job. He worked until age 23, when he was abruptly admitted to hospital with psychotic symptoms that had developed over the previous year. Joe believed he was Satan. His delusional symptoms resulted in violent behaviour and did not respond to medication. He received seven sessions of ECT and was subsequently discharged from hospital on depot antipsychotic medication.

Joe was never able to return to work. He lived with his parents and had no friends. During the first decade of his illness he was periodically hospitalized, which seemed to be a result of his nonadherence with depot injections. Whenever he stopped coming in for injections, he was rehospitalized within several months.

(continued)

After his last hospital admission in 1988, Joe's parents refused to allow him to return home because they had become afraid of his violence. Joe went to live in a boarding home, where he met and married the housekeeper. She continued to work and support the household. She looked after Joe, and ensured that he never missed an injection. Despite a family history of schizophrenia (he had a brother diagnosed with the disorder), things turned out reasonably well for him. Joe was neatly groomed, well-dressed, and more sociable than before. He was pleased to do the domestic work in the house, occasionally obtained a paying job to supplement the family income, and appeared to be very happy. Seeman noted that Joe's good outcome was clearly attributable to the influence of his wife, and to his adherence with treatment.

does not allow much opportunity for normal social development, it is not surprising that the long-term outcome for those with EOS is worse than when schizophrenia begins in adulthood. Outcome is extremely poor when the disorder begins before age 14 (Remschmidt & Theisen, 2005).

Other Psychotic Disorders

Schizophrenia is the most common type of psychotic disorder and the one that has been most thoroughly studied. However, psychotic experiences do not always mean that the person is suffering from schizophrenia. We discuss several other types of psychotic disorders next.

Brief psychotic disorder is the sudden onset of any psychotic symptom, such as delusions, hallucinations, disorganized speech, or grossly disorganized or catatonic behaviour. As its name indicates, this disorder may resolve after one day and does not last for more than one month. After the disorder remits (resolves itself), the person returns to a normal level of functioning. Often the disorder's onset is associated with significant psychosocial stressors, such as the death of a loved one or birth of a child (see "Real People, Real Disorders: Andrea Yates and Postpartum Mood Disorder with Psychotic Features").

REAL people REAL disorders

Andrea Yates and Postpartum Mood Disorder with Psychotic Features

Andrea Yates methodically drowned her five children (ages 6 months to 7 years) in the family bathtub on June 20, 2001. She was diagnosed with the DSM-IV-TR disorder known as postpartum psychosis. In DSM-5, her symptoms would meet criteria for recurrent postpartum mood disorders with psychotic features. After drowning her oldest son, she called the police, was arrested, and confessed to the crime. Her defense asserted that this disorder was the reason for the killings. Yates told her prison psychiatrist, "It was the seventh deadly sin. My children weren't righteous. They stumbled because I was evil. The way I was raising them, they could never be saved. They were doomed to perish in the fires of hell." Although all agreed that Mrs. Yates was psychotic, she was found guilty and sentenced to prison. However, her conviction was overturned, and, in her second trial, the jury found her not guilty by reason of insanity. She was committed to a mental institution until she no longer needs treatment.

Richard Carson/Corbis

The birth of a baby is usually a happy and eagerly anticipated event, yet postpartum mood disorder with psychotic features occurs in 1 or 2 women out of every 1000 who give birth (Robertson et al., 2005). Research suggests that both stressful life events and a preexisting psychological disorder (schizoaffective disorder, major depression, bipolar disorder) may be related to its onset (Kumar et al., 1993; Robertson et al., 2005). In some instances, hormonal changes that commonly occur a few days after childbirth also may contribute to the onset of this disorder, particularly in women who had a psychological disorder before they became pregnant (Kumar et al., 1993). As in other disorders, both biological and psychosocial factors appear to play a role.

The symptoms of **schizophreniform disorder** are identical to those of schizophrenia with two exceptions. First, the duration of the illness is shorter, ranging from at least one month to less than six months. In a few instances, the symptoms seem to disappear. In other instances, a person is treated successfully and never has another episode, although why treatment is successful in any particular case is not known.

The second difference between people with schizophrenia and those with schizophreniform disorder is that in the case of schizophreniform disorder, impaired social or occupational functioning is a possibility, but some people can still conduct their daily activities.

Jack was suspicious that his neighbours were listening in on his telephone conversations or were keeping a record of when he entered and left his apartment. However, he did not harbour those same suspicions about co-workers. Therefore although he would not answer his telephone (because his neighbours might be listening) and was reluctant to leave his apartment (because the neighbours would mark down the time), he did leave once a day to go to work.

Individuals with **schizoaffective disorder** might be considered to have both schizophrenia and an affective disorder. That is, in addition to having the symptoms of a psychotic illness, the patient also suffers from a major depressive, manic, or mixed episode disorder at some point during the illness.

Brian admitted himself to the hospital for depression. A talented painter, he had struggled for many years with mood swings, and his paintings reflected his mood. Lately, his friends were worried because his paintings were getting darker in colour and in content. After a few days on the inpatient unit, he came out of his room smiling and joking. He walked up to a nurse and said, "I am making you my director of overseas operations." He passed a research assistant and said, "You are my new head of human resources." He next told a psychiatrist he was being demoted to a shift work position. When the head nurse finally caught up to him and asked how he was feeling, he replied, "Wonderful, honey. I'm Mr. Mellon, the president of Royal Canadian Steel. If you are nice to me, I'll make you my personal assistant." He was sure that he was the owner of a multi-national corporation, and he became angry and belligerent when she tried to remind him that he was Brian the painter.

Schizoaffective disorder is a controversial diagnosis. It has been considered a type of schizophrenia, a type of mood disorder, or an intermediate condition between the two. When patients with schizophrenia, schizoaffective disorder, and mood disorders are compared, positive symptoms are more severe in people with schizophrenia than in people with schizoaffective disorder, but both groups have equally severe cognitive impairments (Evans et al., 1999). In some instances, diagnostic decisions are made on which group of symptoms (psychotic or mood) is considered to be more severe or more impairing.

Delusional disorder consists of the presence of a nonbizarre delusion (defined as an event that might actually happen; see Table 10.2).

Janice does not believe that she needs to see a mental health professional. She is confident that, despite all medical evidence to the contrary, she has cancer. Her belief is based on the fact that she can actually feel the cancer cells eating away at her body. She sits in the psychologist's office, calmly relating the fact that she has consulted at least 20 physicians, all of whom are wrong. Her family physician told her that he would not see her anymore unless she consulted a mental health professional.

TABLE 10.2
Common Delusional Themes Among Individuals With Delusional Disorder

Type	Content
Erotomanic	The person believes that someone of higher status is in love with him/her (sometimes found among "celebrity stalkers").
Grandiose	The person has feelings of inflated worth, power, knowledge, identity, or special relationships to a deity or a famous person.
Jealous	The person's sexual partner is unfaithful.
Persecutory	The person (or someone close to the person) is being badly mistreated.
Somatic	The person has a medical condition or physical defect for which no medical cause can be found.

People with delusional disorder do not have other psychotic symptoms except perhaps hallucinations that are directly related to the delusion (such as Janice's report of feeling the cancer cells eating away inside her). Also, in contrast to schizophrenia, few changes occur in the person's overall functioning other than the behaviours immediately surrounding the delusion (Janice's "doctor-shopping" to find someone who will treat her cancer). Because people with delusional disorder do not believe that they need treatment, it is not clear how many people suffer from this disorder.

When two or more individuals who have a close relationship share the same delusional belief, the disorder is known as **shared psychotic disorder** (folie à deux).

Dorien was a successful businessman. His cognitive faculties began to fade as he approached retirement. He had difficulty with daily activities, and his wife, Alicia, began to have cognitive problems as well (as a result of a car accident in which she sustained head injuries). Concerned about their safety, family members moved them to an assisted living environment where a medical staff monitored their activities. Dorien began complaining that he was being held against his will, that the staff was stealing his belongings, that his food was being poisoned, and that his family was trying to kill him. Initially, Alicia tried to convince him that none of this was real, but after a few weeks, she became convinced that her husband's beliefs were true. Alicia needed surgery and was transferred to a medical centre and then to a rehabilitation centre for physical therapy. As a result of her separation from Dorien, her delusional beliefs quickly disappeared.

Shared psychotic disorder begins when one person (sometimes termed the *inducer* or the *primary case*) develops a psychotic disorder with delusional content. The inducer is the dominant person in the relationship with a second individual (usually related by blood or marriage and living in close physical proximity) and, over time, imposes the delusional system on the second person, who then adopts the belief system and acts accordingly. If the relationship is interrupted (as happened for Dorien and Alicia), the delusional beliefs of the second person quickly disappear. Shared psychotic disorder is equally common among males and females and affects both younger and older patients. Among one sample, 90% of those suffering from this disorder were married couples, siblings, or parent–child dyads (many of whom were socially isolated from others). Dementia, depression, and intellectual disability were common features among those with this disorder (Silveira & Seeman, 1995).

CONCEPT check

- The consequences of schizophrenia are more serious and long-lasting when the disorder begins in childhood, a condition known as early-onset schizophrenia (EOS).
- In contrast to schizophrenia, which is considered to be a chronic disorder, other forms of psychosis may be time limited. Brief psychotic disorder, for example, may last for only one day. Schizophreniform disorder lasts no more than six months.
- Schizoaffective disorder is a condition in which psychotic symptoms and major depression are equal in severity and frequency. In this group of patients, the positive symptoms of psychosis are less severe than in those with schizophrenia alone.

critical thinking question The case of Andrea Yates illustrates how a biological event (the birth of a baby) can result in the onset of a very serious psychological disorder (postpartum mood disorders with psychotic features). Does this mean that childbirth is the reason for this disorder? Why or why not?

Etiology of Schizophrenia

Schizophrenia is a complex disorder. Its symptoms are quite dramatic and not easily understood by the general public. Many different theories about its development have been offered and, in some cases, discarded. Overall, a century of research has been more successful in ruling out than in establishing causes of schizophrenia. For example, it is now clear that this disorder is not caused by "poor" or "bad" parenting—a relief to families who have to cope with someone struggling with this disorder. It is now quite clear that schizophrenia probably involves many different elements. In this section we examine the biological, psychological, and social/environmental factors that may play a role in the onset of schizophrenia.

Biological Factors

10.5 Discuss the neurodevelopmental model of schizophrenia.

Based on research conducted over the past 50 years, the consensus that schizophrenia is a neurodevelopmental disorder is increasing. Research has established that this disorder has a genetic component and that abnormalities exist in both brain structure and brain function. This does not mean that we now thoroughly understand this complex disorder—we still have much to learn. However, we now know that no simplistic explanations and no single biological factor exist. The following describes what we know so far.

NEUROTRANSMITTERS The three different symptom categories that make up schizophrenia might suggest abnormalities in several different neurotransmitter systems. By far the most attention has been paid to neurotransmitters associated with the dramatic positive symptoms. For more than 50 years, schizophrenia has been considered to be a disorder associated with an excess of the neurotransmitter *dopamine*. The **dopamine hypothesis** emerged from clinical observations that chemical compounds such as amphetamines and *levadopa* (also called *L-dopa*, a drug used to treat Parkinson's disease) increase the amount of dopamine available in the neural synapse, which, in turn, can lead to the development or worsening of psychotic symptoms. In contrast, substances that decrease dopamine seem to be associated with the lessening of psychotic symptoms.

We use the term *associated with* because a causal relationship between dopamine and schizophrenia has not been clearly established, and three possibilities must be considered. First, excessive dopamine could lead to the development of schizophrenia. Second, the chronic stress created by a disorder as serious as schizophrenia may create many different brain abnormalities, including excess dopamine. Finally, both excess dopamine and schizophrenia could result from some third, currently unknown, variable.

Although the direction of this relationship remains uncertain, the existence of abnormal dopamine levels in the neural synapses of patients with schizophrenia has been established. The relationship is far from simple, however. It appears that *too much* dopamine in the limbic area of the brain may be responsible for positive symptoms (i.e., overactivity of behaviour and perception), whereas *too little* dopamine in the cortical areas may be responsible for negative symptoms (i.e., impaired cognitive abilities and motivation; Davis et al., 1991; Moore et al., 1999). Therefore, dopamine abnormalities are not simply a matter of too much or too little in the brain; they may take the form of both excesses and deficits within the same individual. This finding may explain why medications that block dopamine levels reduce positive symptoms but do not change negative symptoms (see "Treatment of Schizophrenia and Other Psychotic Disorders").

As you will recall, the second category of symptoms found in people with schizophrenia are the negative symptoms, which are defined as an absence of behaviours that are found in people without the disorder. In many ways, the negative symptoms of schizophrenia (e.g., slowed speech, apathy) are similar to the psychomotor retardation symptoms found in depression. In Chapter 6, we discussed that these symptoms of depression may be related to the limited availability of *serotonin* (a different neurotransmitter) in certain neural synapses. It appears that serotonin deficits may also be present in the same brain areas in people with schizophrenia (Horacek et al., 2006). Finally, evidence exists in both animals and humans that a third set of neurotransmitters, *GABA and glutamate*, play an important role with respect to learning and remembering new material. Therefore, deficits in these neurotransmitters may be associated with some of the cognitive impairments (the third category of symptoms) found among people with schizophrenia (Addington et al., 2005).

GENETICS AND FAMILY STUDIES Determining that too much dopamine exists in the limbic system of patients with schizophrenia may explain some of the disorder's symptomatology, but it does not explain how or why the neurotransmitter abnormalities exist. Genetics may be one explanation. As with some other psychological disorders, schizophrenia seems to "run in families." Again, however, just because a parent has schizophrenia does not mean that the child will also develop the disorder. Genetically, the risk of developing schizophrenia is 15% if one parent has the disorder and 50% if both parents have it (McGuffin et al., 1995). Rates of *concordance*, both twins having the disorder, are higher among monozygotic (MZ, or identical) twin pairs, ranging from 60% to 84%, than dizygotic (DZ, or fraternal) twin pairs (Cardno et al., 1999).

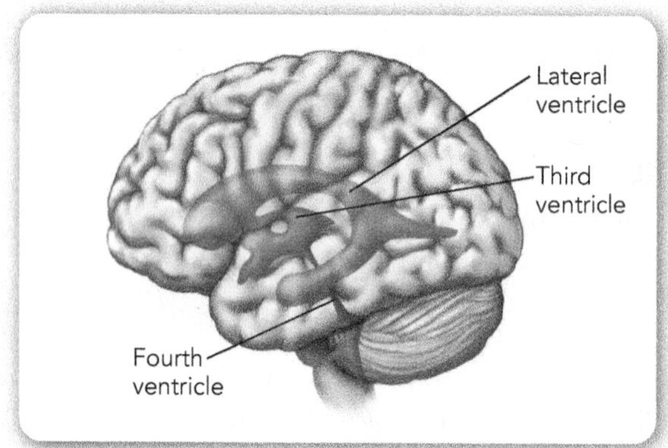

FIGURE 10.1

Ventricles of the Brain. The brain's ventricles contain cerebrospinal fluid, which helps cushion the brain against injury. Compared with people with no disorder, people with schizophrenia have enlarged ventricles. Although the exact meaning of this difference is not clear, it is one bit of evidence suggesting a neurodevelopmental basis for the disorder.

Modern genetic approaches have made significant progress in *mapping* (identifying) specific genes that may be associated with schizophrenia. Nine chromosomes and seven candidate genes have been identified (Harrison & Owen, 2003) as potentially contributing to the development of schizophrenia through at least two possible pathways: direct transmission of the actual disorder from one family member to another, or indirect transmission by affecting the functioning of neurotransmitters such as dopamine (Norton et al., 2006).

Our understanding of the genetics of schizophrenia is advancing rapidly. Scientific breakthroughs have been made secondary to researchers around the world coming together to create very large samples of DNA from people with schizophrenia. In 2011, the Schizophrenia Psychiatric Genome-Wide Association Study (GWAS) Consortium reported a GWAS that included DNA from 21 856 patients with schizophrenia and 33 859 controls. Achieving that large sample allowed them to identify seven loci associated with schizophrenia—five of which were novel findings and two of which replicated previous studies. One of the most intriguing loci that emerged from that study was a variant related to *MIR137*, which is known to be associated with neuronal development. Such discoveries unlock new hints at biological mechanisms that could underlie schizophrenia. Since that time, samples sizes have increased even beyond that impressive number, and scientists associated with the Psychiatric Genomics Consortium are reporting additional genes that are associated with the development of schizophrenia. Expectations are that development of schizophrenia involves the action of hundreds of genes (polygenic influence), and that epigenetic and environmental stressors factors are likely to also play a role (see "Examining the Evidence: Genetics and Environment in the Development of Schizophrenia").

NEUROANATOMY The dramatic abnormalities in perception, thought, and behaviour found among people with schizophrenia led naturally to consideration of brain abnormalities, which may be structural or functional. One consistent neuroanatomical abnormality found among people with schizophrenia is enlargement of the brain *ventricles* (Wright et al., 2000). The ventricles are cavities in the brain that contain cerebrospinal fluid (see Figure 10.1), which acts as a cushion to prevent brain damage if there is a blow to the head. In addition to enlarged ventricles, people with schizophrenia have a reduction in cortical (grey matter) areas of the brain (Andreasen et al., 1994) compared with those with no disorder. Based on MRI data, these structural brain abnormalities clearly are present at the onset of the disorder (Vita et al., 2006). These same abnormalities exist in the non-ill parents of adults with schizophrenia (Ohara et al., 2006), the children of adults with schizophrenia (Diwadkar et al., 2006), and other non-ill relatives (McDonald et al., 2002). The consistency of these abnormalities, coupled with their existence among people who do not show symptoms of the disorder (but who have a relative with the disorder), indicates that these abnormalities are not the result of the illness, but rather are present before the positive symptoms emerge.

Abnormal brain structure exists not only at the macro level of enlarged ventricles and decreased cortical size; differences are also evident at the basic cellular level of the brain. Brain abnormalities that appear specific to people with schizophrenia (compared with those with no psychiatric disorder or a different disorder) include mild structural disorganization at the level of the individual brain cells (evident at autopsy) and altered neuronal connections in multiple brain areas (Opler & Susser, 2005). This type of cellular disorganization cannot happen as a result of brain deterioration or aging; it can occur

Because they have the same genetic makeup, the risk that both monozygotic twins will develop schizophrenia is higher than for dizygotic twins or other non-twin siblings.

Joshua Rainey/Fotolia

examining the EVIDENCE

Genetics and Environment in the Development of Schizophrenia

Because genetically identical (MZ) twins are not 100% concordant for schizophrenia, a strict genetic etiology is unlikely. In fact, 80% of those with psychotic symptoms do not have a parent with the disorder, and in 60% of the cases, no family history can be identified (Gottesman, 2001). Therefore, other factors must contribute to this disorder. One such factor now receiving increased attention is the family environment.

- **The Evidence** In Finland, a national sample of children whose mothers had schizophrenia and were adopted away at birth was compared with children who were also adopted away but whose mothers did not have schizophrenia (Tienari et al., 2004). The family environment in the adoptive family was classified as disordered (high in criticism, conflict, constricted affect, and boundary problems) or healthy (low in criticism, conflict, constricted affect, and boundary problems). The children were interviewed at age 23 and again at age 44. As adults, 36.8% of the biological children of schizophrenic mothers who were raised in a "disordered" family environment developed a "schizophrenic spectrum disorder," whereas only 5.8% of children of schizophrenic mothers who were reared in a "healthy" family environment developed one of these disorders. In contrast, the adoptive family environment was not a factor for those children whose mother did not have schizophrenia; 5.3% of children raised in disordered environments developed a schizophrenic spectrum disorder, as did 4.8% of children raised in healthy family environments.
- **Examining the Evidence** These results suggest that a family environment high in conflict and criticism and low in expressions of emotion may be an important factor in the development of schizophrenia *but only when the child has a parent with schizophrenia*. Whereas overall, about 15% of offspring develop schizophrenia if one parent has the disorder, that percentage doubles when the children are raised in a "disordered" family environment, even when they are not raised by a parent with the disorder.
- **What Do These Data Illustrate About the Role of Genetics?**
  1. Even when a person has a genetic predisposition to develop schizophrenia (mother has the disorder) and is raised in an environment that is not "healthy," 63.2% do *not* develop a schizophrenic spectrum disorder.
  2. Although 36.8% developed a schizophrenic spectrum disorder, only 5.1% developed schizophrenia; many of the others had psychotic disorders or depression with psychosis. This means that what appears to be inherited is a general risk factor for psychosis, not necessarily for schizophrenia.
- **What Do These Data Illustrate About the Role of the Environment?**
  1. A conflictual or disorganized environment appears to increase the risk for a psychotic disorder, but only among those who have relatives with schizophrenia.
  2. Even with no genetic risk and a "healthy family environment," 4.8% of individuals still developed a schizophrenic spectrum disorder.
- **Conclusion** The answer to these questions is not simple because both biological and environmental factors appear to play a role. If you were a psychologist, how would you explain the outcome of this study to your female patient with schizophrenia who wants to have a child?

only early in the process of brain development (before birth). Studies of cerebral development indicate that this phase of cortex development occurs during the second trimester of pregnancy. Therefore, it is clear that these abnormalities develop long before the onset of the observable symptoms of schizophrenia.

VIRAL THEORIES AND OTHER PRENATAL STRESSORS There are now sufficient data, including the neuroanatomical data just discussed, to conclude that structural and functional brain abnormalities exist among people with schizophrenia. Genetics may contribute to this abnormal development but cannot alone account for the onset of schizophrenia. Another aspect that may affect fetal brain development is the prenatal environment. Prenatal factors identified as potentially associated with the later onset of schizophrenia include maternal genital or reproductive infections during the time of conception (Babulas et al., 2006), influenza during the first or second trimester period (Brown et al., 2004), nutritional deprivation during early gestation (Susser et al., 1996), lead exposure during the second trimester (Opler & Susser, 2005), bleeding during pregnancy (Cannon et al., 2002), and severe prenatal maternal stress (King et al., 2005).

Among all of these prenatal risk factors, one of the most thoroughly investigated is maternal exposure to the influenza virus during pregnancy. In an initial report (Mednick et al., 1988), children of mothers who were exposed to an influenza virus during their second trimester (the second three months of pregnancy) were at greater risk of developing schizophrenia when they became adults. Since the publication of this study, the relationship of influenza and schizophrenia has been an area of continuous controversy. About 50% of the research literature confirms this initial relationship, but the other 50% is unable to detect any increased risk for schizophrenia following maternal influenza exposure. One reason for these inconsistent findings is that in many instances, determining whether the mother was exposed to influenza depended on the mother's recall rather than objective medical data. In one of the few studies for which objective evidence exists, exposure to influenza documented by presence of the virus in the mother's blood resulted in a sevenfold increase in the risk of the infant's developing schizophrenia when exposure occurred during the first, but not the second, trimester (Brown et al., 2004).

How could exposure to influenza be related to the development of schizophrenia? Because the influenza virus does not cross the placenta, the virus itself is not responsible for any abnormal brain development. However, when a pregnant woman (or anyone) contracts influenza, her immune system produces antibodies (in this case, IgG antibodies) to fight the infection. These antibodies cross the placental barrier and react with fetal brain *antigens* (a substance that stimulates production of antibodies), producing an immunological response that disrupts fetal brain development. In turn, abnormalities in *structural* brain development may then trigger *functional* abnormalities that in turn result in the onset of schizophrenia (Wright et al., 1999). Think about an automobile engine. If it is not built (structured) correctly, it will not run (function) correctly.

Although no direct studies in humans are available to support this hypothesis, the offspring of pregnant mice that are deliberately exposed to the influenza virus have a reduced number of cells in the cortex and hippocampal areas of the brain. This is a significant finding because these are the same neuroanatomical areas that have been identified as abnormal in patients with schizophrenia (Fatemi et al., 1999). Given the complex nature of schizophrenia, it is far too simplistic to conclude that it is caused simply by exposure to the influenza virus. Its etiology is probably much more complicated. Furthermore, it is important to note that many pregnant women are exposed to influenza each year, and only 1% of adults develop schizophrenia. Therefore, even if influenza is a contributory factor, other factors must play a role.

Many obstetric complications have positive but weak relationships to schizophrenia, but these do not appear to play a major role (Cannon et al., 2002). Overall, the definition of obstetric complications is very broad, and when applied across the general population, 25% to 30% of all pregnancies have some type of complication. So again, we cannot conclude that all children born to women with pregnancy complications will develop schizophrenia (Rapoport et al., 2005). These complications more likely signal the presence of other factors with a more direct role or indicate a general vulnerability to the development of various mental illnesses. In the case of schizophrenia, these factors, when combined with a genetic predisposition, may be the initial triggers leading to the development of the abnormal brain structures we have discussed.

A NEURODEVELOPMENTAL MODEL OF SCHIZOPHRENIA From a biological perspective, schizophrenia is best conceptualized as a neurodevelopmental disorder. Genetic and prenatal or perinatal (occurring at the time of birth) risk factors may set the stage for a disease process that encompasses biological, cognitive, and social changes that occur over time and result in schizophrenia (see Figure 10.2). Longitudinal studies

FIGURE 10.2

Neurodevelopmental Model of Schizophrenia. This general neurodevelopmental model indicates many different biological and environmental factors that probably contribute to the onset of schizophrenia.

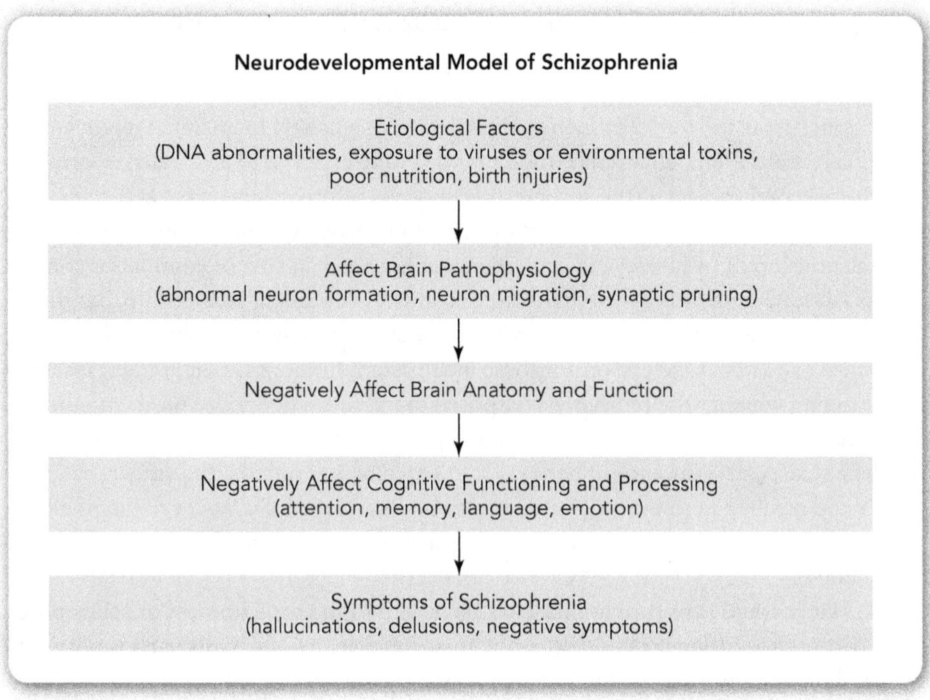

using repeated fMRI neuroimaging (Rapoport et al., 2005) show that people with schizophrenia lose significant grey matter during adolescence through a normal biological process known as **synaptic pruning**. This process eliminates weaker synaptic contacts and enhances the already strong ones. For people with schizophrenia, synaptic pruning occurs at a rate faster than it does in people without schizophrenia, beginning in childhood and accelerating in adolescence. The timing of this acceleration coincides with the emergence of subtle behavioural, motor, and cognitive abnormalities (Jones et al., 1994; Walker et al., 1994). Impaired peer relationships, enhanced social isolation and social anxiety, disruptive behaviours in preadolescent boys, and withdrawal behaviours in preadolescent girls also occur during this time. All of these behaviours are associated with, but not specific to, the onset of schizophrenia in adulthood (Done et al., 1994). However, schizophrenia is not simply a biological process; some of the brain abnormalities seen in people with schizophrenia also occur in their relatives who never develop the disorder. This means that other factors, such as psychological and environmental influences, probably contribute as well.

Neurodevelopmental Model of Schizophrenia
Etiological Factors
(DNA abnormalities, exposure to viruses or environmental toxins, poor nutrition, birth injuries)
Affect Brain Pathophysiology
(abnormal neuron formation, neuron migration, synaptic pruning)
Negatively Affect Brain Anatomy and Function
Negatively Affect Cognitive Functioning and Processing
(attention, memory, language, emotion)
Symptoms of Schizophrenia
(hallucinations, delusions, negative symptoms)

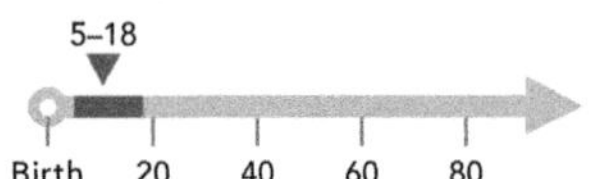

Although the most common age of onset for schizophrenia is young adulthood, the disorder also exists in children and adolescents. The early age of onset is usually associated with a more severe disorder.

Family Influences

10.6 Understand the interplay of genetic, biological, psychological, and environmental factors in the etiology of schizophrenia.

Historically, the "schizophrenogenic mother" was considered as an environmental factor representing either a cause or a response to the presence of schizophrenia in a child (Parker, 1982), even an adult child. This concept emerged from the clinical observations of mental health professionals who worked with families of patients with schizophrenia and who described patients' mothers as dominant, overprotective, and rejecting. However, controlled scientific investigations (including longitudinal designs) did not confirm the existence of such a behaviour pattern (Hartwell, 1996). How do we reconcile the clinical observations with the empirical data? One explanation is that the concept of the "schizophrenogenic mother" was based in part on observations or descriptions of family interactions when the patient already had schizophrenia. However, the presence of a psychological disorder, particularly one that affects cognition and behaviour as seriously as does schizophrenia, also affects family interactions. In many cases, parents must assume substantial responsibility for their children—even their adult children—and this could result in parents acting in a controlling and overprotective fashion, perhaps out of necessity given their child's disorder. However, this does not mean that parents behaved in this way *before* the patient developed the disorder.

Ruling out poor parenting or a "bad" family environment highlights an important point: What science has determined is (or is not) the cause of a disorder is not necessarily the same as what people believe is responsible for their suffering. Earlier we noted that culture may affect the expression and interpretation of the symptoms of schizophrenia. Similarly, culture may also shape explanations of its etiology. Whereas white patients born in the United Kingdom give a biological explanation for their illness (e.g., it is the result of physical illness or substance use) (McCabe & Priebe, 2004), second-generation United Kingdom residents of African Caribbean, Bangladeshi, or West African descent are more likely to provide a social explanation (e.g., interpersonal problems/stress/negative childhood experiences) or a supernatural one (e.g., magic spells/evil forces).

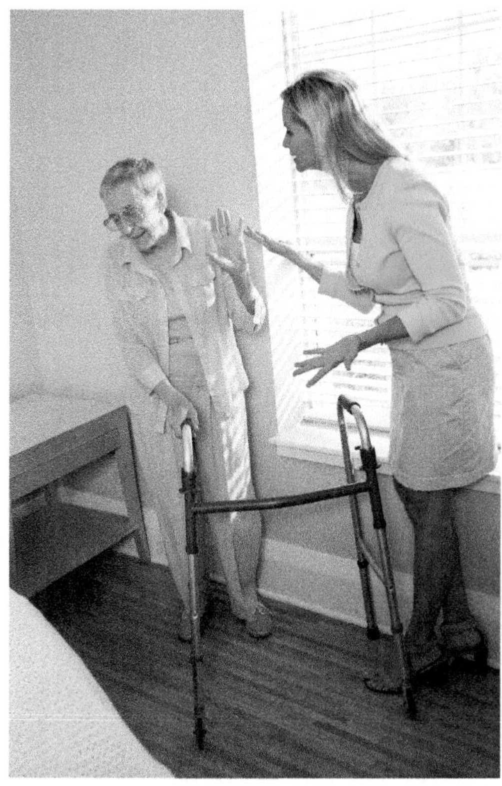

Negative and critical attitudes by family members are correlated with higher rates of relapse among schizophrenic patients.

Kablonk/SuperStock

Returning to our examination of familial factors, even though the notion of a "schizophrenogenic mother" is no longer accepted, environmental factors such as family interaction remain the subject of scientific scrutiny. The concept known as **expressed emotion (EE)** describes a family's emotional involvement and critical attitudes found among people with a psychological disorder, in this case, schizophrenia. Patients with schizophrenia who live in family environments that are high on EE variables (which include high levels of emotional overinvolvement and critical attitudes) are more likely to relapse and have higher rates of rehospitalization (Butzlaff & Hooley, 1998). High EE is an environmental stressor that may increase the likelihood of relapse among those with schizophrenia. However, a treatment designed to increase communication and problem-solving skills among families of a patient with schizophrenia was no more effective than the control condition of monthly family visits to a therapist (Schooler et al., 1997). This means that although high EE may predict relapse, it may not be possible to change these family patterns once they have been established.

Unlike the study presented in "Examining the Evidence: Genetics and Environment in the Development of Schizophrenia" (which was a prospective study), the relationship between high EE and relapse is based mainly on correlational data. Therefore, no conclusions about the role of EE as a *causal* factor are available. It is possible that high levels of emotional involvement and critical family attitudes emerge *after* the onset of the patient's disorder. Coping with someone with schizophrenia can be very stressful, and families worldwide feel its effects (Breitborde et al., 2009; Huang et al., 2009; Zahid & Ohaeri, 2010). Families experience financial and emotional burdens as well as negative health consequences (Dyck et al., 1999). In fact, the family interaction patterns identified as characteristic of EE have been identified with other disorders such as drug and alcohol abuse. High EE may reflect the emotional toll of living with a family member with any type of severely impairing mental disorder.

We noted that schizophrenia "runs in families." In some instances, the relatives of patients with schizophrenia also have schizophrenia; in other instances, they may have some behaviours associated with the disorder, such as exaggerated distrust of strangers, but not at a level that produces impairment. These relatives possess *traits* associated with schizophrenia, such as a deficit in social cognition. Although definitions of this construct differ, it is useful to think of social cognition as the "mental operations underlying social interactions, which include the human ability and capacity to perceive the intentions and dispositions of others" (Brothers, 1990, p. 28). Social cognition, sometimes called *social perception*, includes skills such as the ability to perceive when someone is interested in conversation or to interpret eye contact or a smile from a stranger.

Sigrid, age 20, was diagnosed with paranoid schizophrenia. She was hospitalized after she went to the local police station demanding the surveillance tapes that she believed it had collected regarding her daily activities. When Sigrid's mother, Linda, came to the unit for a consultation with the social worker, the social worker noticed that Linda did not make eye contact and asked the social worker at least 12 times who would have access to her daughter's hospital records.

Although Linda had never been treated for schizophrenia, her behaviour indicated deficits in social cognition. A **gene–environment correlation** means that the same person who provides a patient's genetic makeup also provides the environment in which that person lives. Thus individuals who are at increased genetic risk for schizophrenia may also be exposed to environments that increase the risk of developing symptoms of schizophrenia. Did Linda's mother contribute to her daughter's condition by virtue of shared genes or by fostering an environment limited in appropriate social cognition? In such a case, it is difficult to disentangle genetic and environmental influences on the development of a disorder—they are deeply intertwined.

CONCEPT check

- Advances in neuroscience have allowed for a much better understanding of structural and functional brain abnormalities. Only ventricular enlargement has been a consistently reported structural abnormality in schizophrenia, although many different abnormalities have been hypothesized.
- Evidence indicates a genetic contribution to the development of schizophrenia. Genes may also affect the expression of schizophrenia indirectly by affecting the functioning of neurotransmitters such as dopamine.
- Twin and family studies illustrate the complex roles of genes and the environment in contributing to the development of schizophrenia. Concordance rates (both twins having schizophrenia) are higher among monozygotic (MZ) than dizygotic (DZ) twin pairs. Furthermore, not every child whose parent has schizophrenia develops the disorder, and many people develop schizophrenia even though neither of their parents has ever had the disorder.
- The neurodevelopmental model of schizophrenia suggests that genetics and prenatal or perinatal risk factors may set the stage for a disease process that encompasses biological, social, and cognitive changes. An important concept is synaptic pruning that eliminates weaker synaptic contacts and strengthens the already strong ones. In people with schizophrenia, this process is accelerated and associated with behavioural, motor, and cognitive abnormalities.

critical thinking question A viral model for the development of schizophrenia is illustrated by studies examining exposure to the influenza virus in pregnant women. Given the number of people who catch the flu each year, how strong is the evidence for this theory?

Treatment of Schizophrenia and Other Psychotic Disorders

Much of the historical treatment of mental illnesses discussed in Chapter 1 actually describes treatment of psychotic disorders such as schizophrenia. Until the last 50 years, institutionalization and humane treatments such as those proposed by Pinel, Tuke, Rush, and Dix (see Chapter 1) were among the few courses of action available to treat these disorders or at least separate people suffering from psychological disorders from the rest of society. Surgical treatments in the form of crude lobotomies were performed to decrease a patient's agitated, aggressive, or violent behaviour.

Lobotomies involved first administering anesthesia and then entering the person's brain either through a hole drilled in the skull or by inserting a device similar to an ice pick above the eyeball. The rationale for these procedures was that emotions were seated in the brain and that removing some of the brain matter would alleviate suffering (similar to *trephination* discussed in Chapter 1). The outcomes of lobotomies were generally negative and included cognitive and emotional deficits, and in some cases death.

Until the middle of the twentieth century, no therapies actually reduced symptoms of the disorder. Hydrotherapy (water therapy) was used to calm agitated patients. Hospital staff would give patients prolonged baths (8 to 24 hours in length) or wrap them in wet sheets (either warm or cold), to reduce agitation (Harmon, 2009). During this time, sedative medication was another form of treatment to reduce agitation.

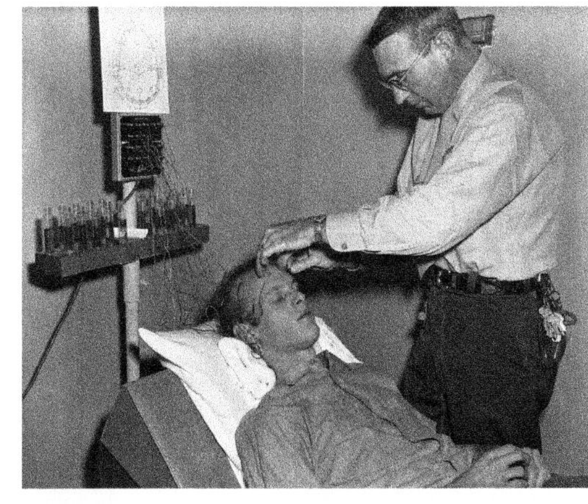

In the 1940s and 1950s, many people who were considered to have uncontrollable behaviour were given a surgical treatment called a *lobotomy.* Although the treatment included different procedures, all were designed to sever some neuronal connections in the brain.

Ted Streshinsky/Corbis

In the 1950s, the discovery of the medication chlorpromazine changed the treatment of schizophrenia. This medication treated the specific symptoms of the disorder, allowing patients to be discharged from the hospital (Drake et al., 2003). The ability of patients to leave the hospital led to the *community mental health movement,* which emphasized treatment, recovery, and reintegration into the community (Drake et al., 2009; see Chapter 15 for more information on this movement). Now, in the twenty-first century, the situation has changed dramatically again; several effective treatments are available for people with schizophrenia. These treatments are far from universally or uniformly effective, but they constitute a great advance over what was available 100 years ago.

Pharmacological Treatment

10.7 Identify efficacious pharmacological and psychological treatments for schizophrenia.

Pharmacotherapy (medication) is the treatment of choice for schizophrenia. The most common medication class is the **antipsychotics**, which block dopamine receptors at four different receptor sites labelled D1, D2, D3, and D4 (Horacek et al., 2006). However, blocking the receptor is not simply an "all-or-nothing" process. Depending on the particular drug, blocking may be temporary, permanent, partial, or complete, and the type of blocking affects how well the drug works. Antipsychotics have only limited effects, however. They do not improve the negative symptoms or the cognitive deficits found among people with schizophrenia. Antipsychotics are efficacious at decreasing positive symptoms and consist of two types, typical and atypical.

TYPICAL ANTIPSYCHOTICS Before the 1990s, the available antipsychotics (now called **conventional or typical antipsychotics**) effectively reduced the positive symptoms of schizophrenia but produced serious side effects. These included muscle stiffness, tremors, and **tardive dyskinesia**, a neurological condition characterized by abnormal and involuntary motor movements of the face, mouth, limbs, and trunk (Gray et al., 2005). The most common symptoms of tardive dyskinesia are movements of the tongue (lip licking, sucking, smacking, and fly-catching movements), jaw (chewing, grinding), face (grimacing, tics), and eyes (blinking, brow arching). Unfortunately, tardive dyskinesia appears to be a fairly common condition; after 15 years of treatment with typical antipsychotics, about 52% of patients will develop this side effect (Tarsy & Baldessarini, 2006). Tardive dyskinesia may begin months or years after the start of the medication (Margolese & Ferreri, 2007). Although it is not clear why this syndrome occurs, one possibility is that the typical antipsychotics create "supersensitivity" of the dopamine receptors, leading them to "overreact" and produce these abnormal movements (Dean, 2006). Unfortunately, discontinuation of the medication does not eliminate tardive dyskinesia, and it is likely that once the receptor sensitivity is altered, it cannot be easily reversed.

ATYPICAL ANTIPSYCHOTICS Since the 1990s, a group of medications called the **atypical antipsychotics** have been preferred for the treatment of schizophrenia in both adults and youth (Kranzler et al., 2005; Mueser & McGurk, 2004). These medications are considered as effective as traditional antipsychotics in treating positive symptoms, and they are much less likely to produce tardive dyskinesia. They also have some effects on negative symptoms and cognitive impairments (Mallinger et al., 2006). The medications do not help everyone, and one study found that over an 18-month period, more than 60% of patients who were prescribed one of these medications discontinued them due to side effects or lack of effectiveness (Lieberman et al., 2005). Still, the atypical antipsychotics may represent an improvement over their predecessors because they help reduce negative symptoms and produce fewer side effects (Fleischhacker & Widschwendter, 2006). Although they are less likely to produce tardive dyskinesia, they have their own significant side effects including producing diabetes and high triglycerides (a type of fat found in the blood). The most dangerous side effect is *agranulocytosis*, which is a lowering of the white blood cell count that could be fatal if not detected in time. Weight gain (sometimes severe) is another side effect that occurs in both children and adults (Kranzler et al., 2006). Therefore, although the atypical antipsychotics are now the most commonly prescribed medication for people with schizophrenia, whether they represent a *significant* improvement remains controversial (Lieberman et al., 2005). Newer biological treatments such as transcranial magnetic stimulation (TMS) attempt to change brain functioning through procedures other than medications (see "Research Hot Topic: Transcranial Magnetic Stimulation").

As illustrated in the sections on symptoms and etiology, cultural factors play a role in the treatment of schizophrenia. White patients more frequently prefer medication and counselling treatments (McCabe & Priebe, 2004). In contrast, patients of Bangladeshi descent prefer a religious activity or no treatment at all, consistent with their beliefs that the cause of their illness is societal or spiritual in nature. Despite their different cultural backgrounds, all patients (white, Bangladeshi, African Caribbean, and West African) are equally likely to comply with their prescribed treatment. Therefore, different cultural preferences do not affect their willingness to accept offered treatments.

One of the greatest challenges to effective pharmacological treatment for people with schizophrenia is medication adherence. Approximately 50% of patients never take their medication or do not take it as prescribed (Fenton et al., 1997). Medication nonadherence is associated with high relapse rates and poor treatment response (Ilott, 2005; Yamada et al., 2006). Nonadherence occurs among chronic patients and those recovering from their first episode (Kamali et al., 2006). The reasons for nonadherence are varied but include distress about side effects and embarrassment or stigma (Perkins et al., 2006; Yamada et al., 2006), more severe positive symptoms, lack of insight regarding symptoms, alcohol and drug abuse (Kamali et al., 2006), and lack of belief in the need for treatment or the benefit of medication (Perkins et al., 2006). Psychoeducation programs aimed at enhancing patients' understanding of medication adherence have produced only moderate results (Ilott, 2005). Interventions may need to tailor the education to each patient's specific concerns rather than only provide general information.

Psychosocial Treatment

Antipsychotic medications are considered the treatment of choice for patients with schizophrenia. However, drugs do not completely eliminate the symptoms of this disorder, and psychosocial strategies are used as *adjunctive* (supplemental) interventions that seek to further reduce primary symptoms and to decrease daily stress on the patient and family, increasing the patient's social skills and helping the patient find and maintain employment when possible.

PSYCHOEDUCATION Schizophrenia is difficult on the patient and the family. Positive symptoms often require hospitalizing the patient, and negative symptoms strain family relationships and cause considerable conflict. For example, a patient who withdraws from family activities and neglects personal hygiene may face hostile criticism from family members. Because family environments characterized by high levels of emotional involvement and critical attitudes toward the patient (high EE) are associated with higher rates of relapse and higher rates of rehospitalization for some patients than others (e.g., Butzlaff & Hooley, 1998), an important treatment component is psychoeducation of the family and significant others. **Psychoeducation** is a process that educates patients and family members about the disorder; it provides the same type of information found in this chapter. The goal of the process is to reduce family members' distress and allow clinicians to increase the effectiveness of their work with the patient and caregiver. These programs reduce relapse rates and shorten length of hospitalization (Motlova et al., 2006; Pitschel-Walz et al., 2001). Although family psychoeducation does not affect the symptoms of the disorder directly, it helps family members understand and deal with the patient and the illness.

COGNITIVE-BEHAVIOURAL TREATMENT Between 20% and 50% of people with schizophrenia continue to have hallucinations despite taking antipsychotic medication (Newton et al., 2005), creating continuing distress and negatively affecting social and occupational adjustment. Psychologists have used behavioural and cognitive-behavioural therapy (CBT) to reduce or eliminate psychotic symptoms, although its use is not common. The literature describing the efficacy of behaviour therapy for schizophrenia dates back 35 years (Glaister, 1985; Nydegger, 1972), and CBT appears effective in reducing psychotic symptoms that remain even with the proper use of medication (Butler et al., 2006; Cather et al., 2005; Gaudiano, 2006). CBT consists of psychoeducation about psychosis and hallucinations, exploration of individual beliefs about hallucinations and delusions, education in using coping strategies to deal with the symptoms, and improving self-esteem (Wykes et al., 2005). Patients take medication while participating in CBT. In one investigation, group CBT significantly reduced the severity of hallucinations (compared with a control group), but only when the therapy was delivered by very experienced group therapists (Wykes et al., 2005). Group CBT for psychotic symptoms appears to be more effective when it is delivered early in the course of the illness (i.e., within the first three years of onset; Newton et al., 2005). Research is now examining why these two factors (very experienced therapists and treatment delivered within the first three years of symptom onset) may be so important.

SOCIAL SKILLS TRAINING Impaired social functioning is a core symptom of schizophrenia, and behaviours such as social isolation and withdrawal often occur before psychotic symptoms appear. The inability to interact with others in a socially acceptable way interferes with social, occupational, and vocational functioning. Effective social skills are needed to interview for a job, maintain employment, establish social support networks, and go to college or university. Social skills training teaches the basics of social interaction, including nonverbal skills such as eye contact, vocal tone, and voice volume, and verbal skills such as initiating and maintaining conversations, expressing feelings, and acting assertively. Although not a comprehensive treatment for schizophrenia, social skills training has a long and successful history improving the social functioning of people with this disorder (Bellack, 2004), even those who are middle aged or older (Granholm et al., 2005) and who have had the disorder for many years.

SUPPORTED EMPLOYMENT The ability to maintain full-time competitive employment is associated with higher rates of symptom improvement, enhanced leisure and

research HOT topic

Transcranial Magnetic Stimulation

Transcranial magnetic stimulation (TMS) is a noninvasive biological approach used to treat several psychological disorders, including depression, obsessive-compulsive disorder, and schizophrenia. The goal of TMS is to provide stimulation to a targeted area of the cerebral cortex to change brain activity. Using a small coil placed over the scalp, a brief but powerful magnetic current passes through the scalp and skull. This induces an electrical current that produces *depolarization* (neuronal discharge) in the area beneath the coil and in functionally related areas (Hoffman et al., 2003). Based on the magnetic frequency used, the stimulation can produce an excitatory or inhibitory effect on the specific neurons (Saba et al., 2006). Although the actual treatment regimen has some variation, one treatment involves 8 minutes of stimulation on Day 1, 12 minutes on Day 2, and 16 minutes on the next 7 days (Hoffman et al., 2003). Side effects appear to be minimal and include brief headaches that are treated with standard over-the-counter medication and concentration and memory difficulties that last no more than 10 minutes after treatment (Hoffman et al., 2003).

The use of TMS in schizophrenia is based on neuroimaging studies that show specific areas of brain activity during auditory hallucinations. For example, areas important for speech perception become activated during periods of hallucinations (Hoffman et al., 2003). These findings have produced several hypotheses regarding the neuroanatomical basis of auditory hallucinations, including (1) the hallucinated voice is the patient's inner speech that is misperceived as coming from outside the brain, and (2) the hallucination is the result of a malfunction of the speech perception system—in effect, the system creates speech without any input from the outside (Lee et al., 2005). TMS changes the activity of these neurons, thereby decreasing (at least temporarily) the frequency of hallucinations.

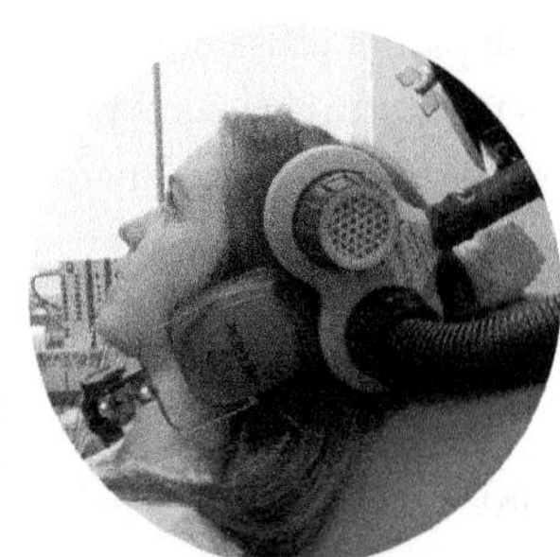

George Ruhe/Redux Pictures

Although this technique has not been intensively studied yet, available data suggest that TMS is more effective than *sham TMS* (using the coil but not delivering the current) in reducing auditory hallucinations that are resistant to medication. Compared with those receiving sham TMS, patients who received actual TMS report reduced frequency of voices, reduced distraction when the voices did occur (Fitzgerald & Daskalakis, 2008; Hoffman et al., 2003), and reduced scores on self-report of positive symptoms (including hallucinations; Lee et al., 2005). However, TMS does not appear to reduce delusions (Saba et al., 2006). Very preliminary evidence suggests that TMS may reduce negative symptoms and enhance cognitive functioning (Fitzgerald & Daskalakis, 2008). Also, its effects are time limited, and it is unclear whether more extended treatment courses could produce more lasting effects.

As discussed in Chapter 2, many differences in available experiments, including sample sizes, strength of an intervention (in this case, strength of the magnetic field), and different outcome variables (in this case, hallucinations versus delusions) make it difficult to determine whether TMS is really effective for schizophrenia. More studies are needed. However, given the impairing nature of residual schizophrenic symptoms, this promising treatment is sure to be the object of much further study. A further question is why TMS should be effective at all. TMS affects brain functioning, but schizophrenia appears to arise from abnormalities in brain structure, which in turn lead to abnormalities in brain function. This suggests that any therapeutic effects of TMS should be transient, unless TMS somehow alters brain structure.

financial satisfaction, and enhanced self-esteem (Bond et al., 2001). However, few patients with schizophrenia (between 10% and 20%; Mueser & McGurk, 2004) are able to work full-time. Schizophrenia begins for many people during the transition from adolescence to adulthood, before they have experience with adult work activities. Supported employment is a psychosocial intervention that provides job skills to people with schizophrenia. The program includes a rapid job search approach; individual job placements that match patient preferences, strengths, and work experience (if any); follow-along support (continued contact with therapists and job counsellors); and integration with the treatment team (Bond et al., 2001). Such programs help people with schizophrenia find and maintain competitive employment, but there are not yet enough programs for all people who could benefit from them.

real SCIENCE real LIFE

Kerry—Treating Schizophrenia

THE PATIENT

Kerry is 19 years old. He has always been a shy, quiet young man. Studious and respectful in high school, he had few friends and never dated. He was accepted at a university 100 kilometres from his home.

THE PROBLEM

During his first semester, he became concerned that those who were living in his dorm were "out to get him." His concerns extended to an instructor who wore a red shirt, which Kerry believed to be a sign of the devil. The archangel Michael began to speak to Kerry, commenting on his behaviour and giving him instructions on how to behave. His roommate became alarmed not only because Kerry accused him of inserting thoughts into his head, but also because Kerry stopped eating (he thought the food might have been poisoned) and bathing (in case the water was contaminated).

Kerry stopped going to classes and was reluctant to leave his room, where he constantly examined light fixtures and electrical outlets for listening devices planted there by government agents. He would call his parents at odd hours of the night, crying and pleading with them to make the voices go away. The next day he would call them and angrily accuse them of being in league with the devil, the government agents, or both. His bizarre behaviour led to an inpatient hospitalization and a diagnosis of paranoid schizophrenia.

THE TREATMENT

Kerry was treated with an atypical antipsychotic, which decreased his auditory hallucinations but did not eliminate them. Kerry was unable to tolerate the medication dosage considered necessary for optimal treatment outcome because of severe side effects, and he continued to express discomfort with auditory hallucinations. He was treated with cognitive-behavioural therapy (CBT) and felt that although he was better able to cope with the hallucinations on a daily basis, they still interfered with his ability to return to school or hold a job. Because he had achieved only a partial treatment response, Kerry had to take a leave of absence from school and returned home to live with his parents. A medical school near his parents' home was offering a research study using TMS, and Kerry enrolled as a participant. TMS decreased the frequency of his symptoms to the extent that he was then able to use the coping skills he acquired through CBT to deal with the remaining hallucinations. His negative symptoms were also somewhat improved. Although he was not able to return to university full-time, he was able to maintain half-time employment as a dishwasher in a restaurant.

THE TREATMENT OUTCOME

One year after treatment was completed, Kerry became depressed at his inability to return to his previous state of functioning. He stopped taking his medication and attempted to commit suicide by choking himself. He passed out before he suffocated and was hospitalized. After rehospitalization and reinstatement of his medication, Kerry was admitted to a partial hospitalization program in which he received group treatments such as social skills training and illness-management skills. Following his discharge, he was rehired at the restaurant and enrolled in one course at a community college. Six months later, he moved out of his parents' house into a supported living facility, allowing him more independence. He continues to struggle with the hallucinations, but has been able to use his coping skills to manage their severity.

CONCEPT check

- Pharmacological treatment is the primary intervention for schizophrenia, particularly the class of medication known as the *atypical antipsychotics*, which appear to help with both the positive and the negative symptoms.
- Use of the typical antipsychotics has declined because they are associated with an irreversible side effect known as *tardive dyskinesia*.
- Some hallucinations are resistant to medication treatment, in which case cognitive-behavioural treatment may have some positive effects.

critical thinking question Given that medications have side effects so severe that a subset of patients discontinues taking medication, why is cognitive-behavioural treatment not used first to treat the positive symptoms of schizophrenia?

summary

schizophrenia spectrum and other psychotic disorders

10.1 Distinguish between a psychotic experience and the psychotic disorders.

A psychotic experience is a single event that involves a loss of contact with reality and usually consists of a delusion or a hallucination. Psychotic experiences occur in people without any psychiatric disorder, people with medical illnesses, and people with many of the different psychological disorders discussed in this text. When psychotic experiences become frequent or continuous and create distress or functional impairment, they are called *psychotic disorders*.

10.2 Understand that schizophrenia is *not* a condition involving "split personality," nor does it usually involve violent behaviour toward others.

Terms such as *multiple personality* and *split personality* are not synonyms for schizophrenia. The term *schizophrenia* describes the "disconnect" among an individual's thoughts, feelings, and behaviour, not the existence of one or more complete personalities within a single person. It is not synonymous with violent behaviour.

10.3 Identify the positive, negative, and cognitive symptoms of schizophrenia.

The positive symptoms of schizophrenia consist of hallucinations, delusions, and bizarre behaviours such as catatonia and waxy flexibility. Negative symptoms consist of diminished emotional expression, anhedonia, alogia, and avolition. Cognitive symptoms consist of deficits in visual and verbal learning and memory, ability to pay attention, speed of information processing, and abstract reasoning and executive functioning.

10.4 Understand how culture plays a role in the expression and treatment of schizophrenia.

Compared with people with schizophrenia who live in developed countries, people with schizophrenia who live in developing nations often have a more positive treatment outcome, possibly because their families are more supportive of, and play a more supportive role in, the patient's care.

10.5 Discuss the neurodevelopmental model of schizophrenia.

The neurodevelopmental model of schizophrenia is based on research indicating that the brain abnormalities commonly associated with schizophrenia occur early in the course of human development, sometimes prenatally. Genetic alterations, prenatal environmental factors, and obstetrical complications may begin an ongoing developmental process that encompasses biological, cognitive, and social changes occurring throughout a lifetime. An accelerated process of synaptic pruning in the brain may also be an important factor in the disorder's etiology.

10.6 Understand the interplay of genetic, biological, psychological, and environmental factors in the etiology of schizophrenia.

Biological factors may combine with environmental influences such as a disordered family environment to result in schizophrenia. Prenatal events associated with the disorder include biological factors such as exposure to influenza and environmental stressors such as maternal malnutrition. Environmental factors that are influential after birth include the family. For example, children of mothers with schizophrenia are more likely to develop the disorder themselves even if they are "adopted away" into a disordered family environment. Psychological factors such as family support may help prevent relapse and rehospitalization.

10.7 Identify efficacious pharmacological and psychological treatments for schizophrenia.

Schizophrenia is a chronic disorder, and full symptom remission is rare. Treatment uses both medication and psychological approaches. The medications of choice are the atypical antipsychotics, which are effective at reducing or eliminating positive symptoms and have some effect on the negative symptoms. Psychological interventions such as social skills training, cognitive-behavioural treatment, and supported employment are effective *adjunctive*, or additional, treatments that may reduce negative symptoms, reduce medication-resistant hallucinations and delusions, and enhance employment skills.

key terms

alogia 365
anhedonia 365
antipsychotics 385
atypical antipsychotics 386
avolition 365
brief psychotic disorder 372
catatonia 364
clang associations 364
cognitive impairment 365
conventional or typical antipsychotics 385
delusion 359
delusional disorder 375
delusions of influence 363
dementia praecox 361
diminished emotional expression 365
dopamine hypothesis 377
early-onset schizophrenia 372
echolalia 366
expressed emotion 383
gene–environment correlation 384
hallucination 359
loose associations 364
negative symptoms 365
persecutory delusions 363
positive symptoms 362
psychoeducation 387
psychomotor retardation 365
psychosis 359
schizoaffective disorder 375
schizophrenia 360
schizophreniform disorder 375
shared psychotic disorder 376
social cognition 366
synaptic pruning 382
tardive dyskinesia 385
thought blocking 364
waxy flexibility 365

TEST yourself

1. Psychotic experiences are characteristic of schizophrenia, but they also occur in people with other disorders. Of the following, they are *least* likely to occur in people with
a. brain tumours
b. mood disorders
c. substance use disorders
d. specific phobias

2. The psychiatrist who introduced the term *dementia praecox* was
a. Emil Kraepelin
b. Benjamin Rush
c. Eugen Bleuler
d. Philippe Pinel

3. Persecutory delusions, auditory hallucinations, and unusual behaviours are examples of
a. positive symptoms
b. cognitive deficits
c. negative symptoms
d. catatonia

4. Frank has a diagnosis of schizophrenia. When his case manager asked what time he went to bed last night, he said, "2 o'clock frick frock tick tock and I won't be wearing a mock." This is an example of
a. loose association
b. thought blocking
c. clang association
d. alogia

5. Blunted affect, anhedonia, avolition, and psychomotor retardation are examples of
a. positive symptoms
b. negative symptoms
c. cognitive deficits
d. catatonia

6. The third category of schizophrenia symptoms is cognitive impairment, which includes
a. delusions and hallucinations
b. personality and affect splits
c. attention and memory deficits
d. anhedonia and avolition deficits

7. Richard has schizophrenia. At times, he maintains a rigid posture and is unresponsive to vocal commands. At other times, he repeats what other people say to him. Which subtype of schizophrenia does Richard most likely have?
a. paranoid
b. undifferentiated
c. catatonic
d. disorganized

8. People with schizophrenia who live in developing countries have a better outcome than do people in developed countries because
a. patients in developed countries do not receive state-of-the-art treatment
b. the chronic nature of schizophrenia is relatively unknown in developing countries
c. alternative folk medicine is as effective as modern medical methods
d. smaller communities and less complex environments offer these people increased social support

9. In one prospective study, Danish youth were videotaped in a school cafeteria when they were 11 to 13 years old. Twenty-nine years later, as adults, some of these individuals had developed schizophrenia. As children, the adults who developed the disorder were
a. less social and exhibited subtle neuromotor abnormalities
b. eccentric or odd, but without delusions or hallucinations
c. showing early signs of split personality
d. not different from the other children

10. Schizophrenia usually begins at what stage of life?
a. early childhood
b. middle childhood
c. early adulthood
d. early middle age

11. Shortly after the police told Lucinda that her 12-year-old daughter had been killed by a hit-and-run driver, she went into a catatonic state. A few hours later she began to hear voices, and her speech became disorganized. She said that an angel had come to visit her. These symptoms stopped after several days. Lucinda was suffering from
    - **a.** catatonic schizophrenia
    - **b.** residual schizophrenia
    - **c.** schizophreniform disorder
    - **d.** brief psychotic disorder
12. Individuals diagnosed with schizoaffective disorder might be considered to have
    - **a.** both schizophrenia and a depressive disorder
    - **b.** only the negative symptoms of schizophrenia plus a mood disorder
    - **c.** a nonpsychotic mood disorder
    - **d.** a brief psychotic disorder
13. The finding that genetically identical twins are not 100% concordant for schizophrenia strongly implies that
    - **a.** a uniquely genetic etiology for schizophrenia is unlikely
    - **b.** environmental factors must be the cause of schizophrenia spectrum disorders
    - **c.** family conflict cannot cause schizophrenia because twins are usually raised in the same family environment
    - **d.** mothers must unconsciously treat twins differently, which leads to vulnerability to schizophrenia
14. Among possible prenatal risk factors for schizophrenia, one of the most thoroughly investigated is
    - **a.** genital or reproductive infections
    - **b.** nutritional deprivation during early gestation
    - **c.** severe prenatal maternal stress
    - **d.** maternal exposure to the influenza virus
15. High levels of emotional involvement, intrusiveness, and critical attitudes among family members of people with schizophrenia may negatively affect treatment outcome. This theory is known as
    - **a.** expressed emotion
    - **b.** emotional scapegoating
    - **c.** family enmeshment
    - **d.** emotional stigmatization
16. Mano has schizophrenia and has developed some unusual movements and tics in his face, mouth, and hands. This condition, called *tardive dyskinesia*, is caused by
    - **a.** exposure to the influenza virus in utero
    - **b.** high expressed emotion (EE) in a patient's family
    - **c.** treatment with typical antipsychotic drugs
    - **d.** a lowering of the white blood cell count
17. One of the greatest challenges to effective pharmacological treatment of schizophrenia is
    - **a.** correct diagnosis of the condition in the first place
    - **b.** medication nonadherence
    - **c.** provision of the correct medication, typically an atypical antipsychotic
    - **d.** all of the above
18. When patients and their families learn about schizophrenia in order to reduce family distress and help the patient cope, the process is known as
    - **a.** psychoeducation
    - **b.** cognitive-behaviour therapy
    - **c.** social skills training
    - **d.** psychotherapy
19. Training that teaches nonverbal skills such as eye contact, vocal tone, voice volume, and verbal skills such as initiating and maintaining conversations, expressing feelings, and acting assertively is called
    - **a.** psychoeducation
    - **b.** cognitive-behaviour therapy
    - **c.** social skills training
    - **d.** psychotherapy

Answers:
1 d, 2 a, 3 a, 4 c, 5 b, 6 c, 7 c, 8 d, 9 a, 10 c, 11 d, 12 a, 13 a, 14 d, 15 a, 16 c, 17 b, 18 a, 19 c.

chapter 11

personality disorders

Siri Stafford/Photodisc/Getty Images

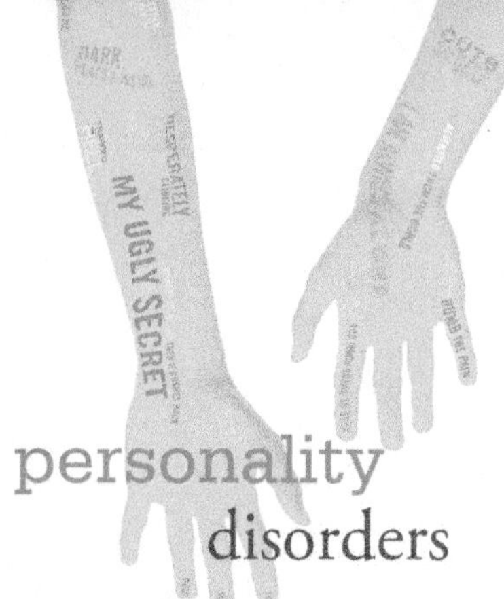

personality disorders

learning objectives

After reading this chapter, you should be able to:

11.1 Discuss how personality disorders differ from other disorders discussed in this text.

11.2 Describe the three clusters of personality disorders and the disorders within each cluster.

11.3 Appreciate the complex nature of personality disorders.

11.4 Understand the role biology may play in the origin of personality pathology.

11.5 Discuss psychodynamic and cognitive-behavioural theories of personality disorders.

11.6 Discuss treatment approaches to personality disorders.

Jacqui was a graduate student in mass communications. She was frankly in danger of getting kicked out of her program. Her explanation was that the professors "just don't f**king get" her creativity. In her first year of grad school, Jacqui had become very close friends with a gay man in her class, and they partied a lot together. At first it was all good, but then she started pushing him to try more drugs and get "really wasted" with her. She got a failing grade on an assignment on a Friday and went to his house to cry on his shoulder. He was very understanding and helped her calm down and figure out how to fix the situation with the professor. She told him he was the kindest friend in the world and she didn't know what she would do without his support. They went out afterward and were drinking and dancing. She drank way too much and accused him of sexually assaulting her. She spread a rumour that he wasn't really gay but that was just a front so he could get closer to women and then rape them. Her classmates seemed to turn on her after she started this rumour; they all came to his defence. She didn't go to class for a week and just stayed in her apartment and smoked. She was sick of everyone, but she felt so alone. She couldn't understand why no one understood her. The only thing that made her feel better was cutting. At first she made cuts where people couldn't see them, such as her thighs and abdomen, but then she wanted to "wear them." So she started cutting her arms and wearing three-quarter sleeves with leather bands on her wrists. She started seeing people looking at her, and she flaunted her cuts. One night she was alone in her apartment drinking and she cut too deep. Blood started pouring from her arm and she got scared. She called her friend who, in an act of extreme kindness after what she had done to him, took her to the ER. The physician tended to her deep cut and talked with her about the cuts all over her body that were in various stages of healing. She called the on-call psychiatrist who evaluated Jacqui on site and with her permission contacted the campus health services and her professors to make sure she received careful follow-up treatment.

We commonly use adjectives to describe someone's typical behaviours, or personality *traits*: Jan is rigid and controlling, Kiara is outgoing and optimistic, Liza is flitty and distractible, Ty is condescending and arrogant, Rolfe is self-interested and untrustworthy. So when does behaviour cross the line from trait to disorder? In some people, characteristic ways of seeing, interpreting, and behaving in the world develop over time in an inflexible and maladaptive way. If someone cannot adapt his or her characteristic approach to the world when necessary and that approach causes significant psychological distress either to the person or to others, then these *traits* may have crystallized into a personality *disorder*. In this chapter, we will discuss personality, personality traits, and personality disorders.

Personality Trait Versus Personality Disorder

11.1 Discuss how personality disorders differ from other disorders discussed in this text.

What is the difference between a personality *trait* and a personality *disorder*? All people can be described in terms of specific patterns of personality, but not all have a disorder. Differentiating between traits and disorders is crucial for both diagnosis and treatment. It is important, though not always easy, to recognize at what point a personality style has become rigid and maladaptive, criteria that we commonly use to decide whether someone has a personality disorder.

A second relevant dimension to consider is that of clinical *state* versus a personality *trait*. A *state* refers to the expression of a personality characteristic that is related to a specific circumstance, clinical condition, or period of time.

Juan, who is usually even-tempered and easygoing, becomes emotionally unstable whenever he is under stress. He lashes out at people and vacillates between being nice and barking at people.

Personality traits are observable from the early years. Many of our perceptions of others are based on our impressions of their personalities. From this picture, whom would you choose as each of these: "Most likely to succeed in business"? "Most likely to graduate from university"? "Most likely to lead a protest march"?

Will Hart/PhotoEdit

Juan's behaviour is a function of his current life events and would be considered a state-dependent change—not his characteristic way of approaching the world. His behaviour would be considered *ego-dystonic*, or distinctly different from the person's self-image.

Conversely, a *trait* refers to the specific and characteristic way someone approaches the world. It is unlikely to change across situations, time, and events. For example, if Juan's behaviour tends to fluctuate unpredictably most of the time, and others describe him as "dramatic" or "Jekyll and Hyde," this behaviour would be considered a personality trait. It is *ego-syntonic*, or consistent with the individual's self-image.

If we observe Juan at any one time and note that his emotions vacillate more often than those of his peers, several explanations are possible. First, his emotional vacillation may not create any significant psychological distress for him or those around him, but may simply reflect a colourful aspect of his unique personality. Alternately, our observation may not have detected important contextual information, namely that Juan is very upset lately because he has been having problems at work. After a comprehensive clinical evaluation, he may receive a diagnosis of major depressive disorder. A third possibility is that Juan's vacillation reflects an ingrained way that he interacts with the world that has caused him to lose relationships, jobs, and ties with his family. In this case, we would say that he has a *personality disorder.*

These three alternative explanations highlight several important aspects of a personality disorder diagnosis. First, it is critical to differentiate between a personality trait and a personality disorder. Second, personality disorders should never be diagnosed after a single brief behavioural observation because they represent enduring ways of dealing with the world. Third, clinicians should not diagnose personality disorders without knowing the surrounding context. So, before deciding whether someone has a personality disorder, a clinician must evaluate the person's problems within the larger diagnostic context: Is the person suffering from a personality disorder, or from another disorder that is influencing his or her personality? For example, many people may seem to have a personality disorder (they are very emotional or abuse substances) when they are in the throes of an acute episode of another disorder (such as bulimia nervosa). It may be necessary to wait until the other disorder remits and then determine whether the troubling behaviours are still present. This example illustrates how difficult it is to diagnose a personality disorder: If Juan seeks treatment, the evaluating clinician must consider that his current state does not necessarily reflect his typical behaviour. So, because we all have distinctive personality traits, how do we know when a personality state constitutes a maladaptive personality disorder? Because no strong evidence supports a clear boundary between personality traits and personality disorders as yet, the best way to think about them is as pathological amplifications of underlying traits.

Determining whether a behaviour is a disorder must consider impairment and distress. This is a particular challenge for diagnosing personality disorders whose clinical features are difficult to quantify. Furthermore, personality disorders have few biological markers. Personality disorders cannot be detected with a blood test, for example, and they must be distinguished from other psychological disorders. You might think of the other psychological disorders in the same manner as an acute medical illness that afflicts a person who functions relatively well in many aspects of life. In contrast, a personality disorder is not an acute illness but a long-term, chronic, pervasive pattern of inflexible and maladaptive functioning. Personality disorders are not so much illnesses as a "way of being." They are typically apparent in late adolescence or early adulthood and may persist throughout life.

One particularly difficult distinction to make diagnostically is between personality disorders and other disorders that have a prolonged course, such as persistent depressive disorder (see Chapter 6). In terms of impairment, what separates the distress caused by disorders described in other chapters from the difficulty created by personality disorders? As we describe the various personality disorder clusters, we will illustrate the ways in which these disorders can impair social and occupational functioning. One interesting characteristic of these disorders is that they often cause more distress to other people than to the person with the disorder. Some people with personality disorders may feel very little distress or even none at all.

One way to understand what distinguishes personality disorders from the other disorders in this book is "the three Ps." These disorders are patterns of behaviour that are *persistent* (over time), *pervasive* (across people and situations), and *pathological* (clearly abnormal). A **personality disorder**, therefore, is "an enduring pattern of inner experience and behaviour that deviates markedly from the expectations of the individual's culture, is pervasive and inflexible, has the onset in adolescence or early adulthood, is stable over time, and leads to distress and impairment" (APA, 2013). Definitions of personality disorders have always highlighted symptom stability: These are not transient moods or temporary quirks of behaviour, but rather are persistent behavioural features.

The DSM divides personality disorders into three clusters: **Cluster A**, "odd or eccentric," **Cluster B**, "dramatic, emotional, or erratic," and **Cluster C**, "anxious or fearful." These labels do not relate directly to the names of the individual disorders within the clusters, but describe an overall style of behaviour that cuts across the individual disorders. However, some researchers and clinicians question the validity of these clusters. Why? Because, as we have seen, personality traits are common to everyone—we all may have enduring tendencies to be somewhat eccentric, emotional, or fearful—and exactly at what point do these traits turn pathological?

According to the DSM, one either has or does not have a particular personality disorder. This is known as the *categorical* model of personality. Many researchers emphasize that a better model would use a *dimensional* approach that captures the full range of a trait.

A dimensional approach would consider personality to be on a continuum; for example, socially outgoing people on one end and extremely shy people on the other. (See Chapter 3 for more discussion of categorical versus dimensional classification.) Indeed, many prominent theories of personality focus more on dimensional than categorical models. The personality disorders work group that deliberated potential revisions for DSM-5 carefully considered a transition to a more dimensional model for personality disorders. In the end, no significant changes were made to the personality disorders section in DSM-5; however, future versions of the DSM may incorporate more dimensional measures.

CONCEPT check

- Distinguishing between personality traits and disorders is critical and must include a careful consideration of interpersonal and environmental contexts.
- Personality disorders represent characteristic but maladaptive and inflexible ways of seeing, interpreting, and behaving that have developed over time.

critical thinking question In an assessment, what kinds of information would a psychologist want to know to determine whether a patient's problem involved a personality disorder?

Normal Case Study

Trait but No Disorder

→ Rasheed's wife calls him a neat freak. He likes his closet in order; everything in his drawers is always neatly folded and tucked away, and he is brilliant at organizing their finances. His wife drives him crazy because she is more of a "piles" person—her clothes are in piles, her work papers ae in piles, everything ends up in a pile. Even though it bugs him and he secretly wishes she were more like him, he learned after he tried to organize her things once early in their marriage, never to touch her piles! Rasheed has a strong tendency to believe the old adage that "if you want something done right, you have to do it yourself," but he has come to learn that doing everything yourself does not really help other people learn how they can help you, and it just ends up causing more and more stress for you. So even though it irks him on some level when something is not done at work or at home as well as he knows he could do it, he can take a deep breath and let it go. His wife can sense his frustration sometimes and occasionally will just tease him about being wound so tight. At least he can laugh at himself . . . and he can always hang out in his closet if he needs to be somewhere tidy!

Abnormal Case Study

Personality Disorder

→ Jeff would be happiest if his life never varied. He is a 52-year-old married statistician with three children, ages 18, 16, and 12. Every day for the past 15 years, he has risen at 5:30, exercised for 30 minutes while reading the paper, drunk two cups of coffee, eaten a bowl of cereal and a piece of fruit, and caught the same train to work. Each time that train is delayed, he anxiously looks at his watch and frets about lost time in the office. The household is run to his specifications. If the kids are asked to fold laundry, they have to do it right. If they do it wrong, he gives them one chance to fix it, and if they still do it wrong, he does it himself. His motto is, "If you want something done right, you have to do it yourself." He reviews his children's homework fastidiously and grills them if their grades slip. Dinner is at 6:30. He plays tennis on Tuesday and Thursday evenings. He has colour-coded sticky notes with lists of things to do. But he is a prisoner of his lists. At times, he would sit at his desk, three different coloured lists in front of him, faced with scores of emails, and simply not know where to begin. As the lists became longer and the inbox fuller, he could become paralyzed by anxiety. One evening he developed chest pains on the tennis court, and his partner drove him to the ER. It was not a heart attack, but his blood pressure was sky high. His doctor had warned him countless times about his lifestyle, pressure, and anxiety, but he had never listened. The doctor called this his wake-up call. She gave him medications for the blood pressure and the name of a psychologist to help him deal with his obsessive-compulsive personality style.

Personality Disorder Clusters

Most mental health professionals follow the DSM categorical approach when characterizing, communicating about, and treating personality disorders. In the following sections, we present both a clinical description and a clinical example of each personality disorder. Keep in mind that impairment is the hallmark of these disorders and that in many instances, impairment is judged from the perspective of others who are affected by the person's personality disorder. Also, remember the three Ps (persistent, pervasive, pathological). In "DSM-5: General Diagnostic Criteria for a Personality Disorder," we present general criteria for a personality disorder to provide the scaffolding around which the specific personality disorder profiles are constructed. Regardless of the specific personality disorder, they all meet the fundamental criteria outlined in the box. Remember, general personality disorder is not a specific personality disorder in DSM-5.

criteria for
General Personality Disorder DSM-5

A. An enduring pattern of inner experience and behaviour that deviates markedly from the expectations of the individual's culture. This pattern is manifested in two (or more) of the following areas:
   1. Cognition (i.e., ways of perceiving and interpreting self, other people, and events).
   2. Affectivity (i.e., the range, intensity, lability, and appropriateness of emotional response).
   3. Interpersonal functioning.
   4. Impulse control.

B. The enduring pattern is inflexible and pervasive across a broad range of personal and social situations.

C. The enduring pattern leads to clinically significant distress or impairment in social, occupational, or other important areas of functioning.

D. The pattern is stable and of long duration, and its onset can be traced back at least to adolescence or early adulthood.

E. The enduring pattern is not better explained as a manifestation or consequence of another mental disorder.

F. The enduring pattern is not attributable to the physiological effects of a substance (e.g., a drug of abuse, a medication) or another medical condition (e.g., head trauma).

The criteria for general personality disorder are based, in part, on the work of W. John Livesley at the University of British Columbia and his colleagues (Livesley & Jackson, 2009; Livesley & Jang, 2005). Livesley's research, particularly his factor analytic studies, suggests that all personality disorders are shaped by a common or general factor. This led to the development of an assessment instrument designed to assess this factor, called the General Assessment of Personality Disorder (Hentschel & Livesley, 2013).

Cluster A: Odd or Eccentric Disorders

11.2 Describe the three clusters of personality disorders and the disorders within each cluster.

The common features of Cluster A (see "DSM-5: Cluster A Personality Disorders") are characteristic behaviours that others would consider odd, quirky, or eccentric (APA, 2013). Disorders in Cluster A include features similar to those seen in psychosis and schizophrenia (see Chapter 10). Indeed, the dividing line between psychosis and Cluster A personality disorders is unclear. Family members of people with schizophrenia have higher rates of Cluster A personality disorders, suggesting possible continuity between psychotic disorders and Cluster A disorders (APA, 2013; Kendler et al., 1993).

Paranoia can include distrust and suspiciousness of family and friends (movie still from the film *Black Swan*).

Everett Collection

PARANOID PERSONALITY DISORDER **Paranoid personality disorder** is a pervasive distrust and suspiciousness of others such that their motives are interpreted as malevolent (APA, 2013). While a little bit of paranoia can be adaptive in some situations (e.g., protecting oneself from dishonest individuals), paranoid personality disorder is characterized by unjustified and pervasive distrust. People with this disorder believe without any evidence that others are out to exploit, harm, or deceive them; bear grudges and are unforgiving of perceived insults; and are hypervigilant for signs of disloyalty or untrustworthiness in friends, family, co-workers, and acquaintances (APA, 2013). Typical beliefs of individuals with paranoid personality disorder may include, "I cannot trust other people"; "Other people have hidden motives"; "If other people find out things about me,

criteria for Cluster A Personality Disorders DSM-5

Paranoid Personality Disorder

A. A pervasive distrust and suspiciousness of others such that their motives are interpreted as malevolent, beginning by early adulthood and present in a variety of contexts, as indicated by four (or more) of the following:

1. Suspects, without sufficient basis, that others are exploiting, harming, or deceiving him or her.
2. Is preoccupied with unjustified doubts about the loyalty or trustworthiness of friends or associates.
3. Is reluctant to confide in others because of unwarranted fear that the information will be used maliciously against him or her.
4. Reads hidden demeaning or threatening meanings into benign remarks or events.
5. Persistently bears grudges (i.e., is unforgiving of insults, injuries, or slights).
6. Perceives attacks on his or her character or reputation that are not apparent to others and is quick to react angrily or to counterattack.
7. Has recurrent suspicions, without justification, regarding fidelity of spouse or sexual partner.

B. Does not occur exclusively during the course of schizophrenia, a bipolar disorder or depressive disorder with psychotic features, or another psychotic disorder and is not attributable to the physiological effects of another medical condition.

Note: If criteria are met prior to the onset of schizophrenia, add "premorbid," i.e., "paranoid personality disorder (premorbid)."

Schizoid Personality Disorder

A. A pervasive pattern of detachment from social relationships and a restricted range of expression of emotions in interpersonal settings, beginning by early adulthood and present in a variety of contexts, as indicated by four (or more) of the following:

1. Neither desires nor enjoys close relationships, including being part of a family.
2. Almost always chooses solitary activities.
3. Has little, if any, interest in having sexual experiences with another person.
4. Takes pleasure in few, if any, activities.
5. Lacks close friends or confidants other than first-degree relatives.
6. Appears indifferent to the praise or criticism of others.
7. Shows emotional coldness, detachment, or flattened affectivity.

B. Does not occur exclusively during the course of schizophrenia, a bipolar disorder or depressive disorder with psychotic features, another psychotic disorder, or autism spectrum disorder and is not attributable to the physiological effects of another medical condition.

Note: If criteria are met prior to the onset of schizophrenia, add "premorbid," i.e., "schizoid personality disorder (premorbid)."

Schizotypal Personality Disorder

A. A pervasive pattern of social and interpersonal deficits marked by acute discomfort with, and reduced capacity for, close relationships as well as by cognitive or perceptual distortions and eccentricities of behaviour, beginning by early adulthood and present in a variety of contexts, as indicated by five (or more) of the following:

1. Ideas of reference (excluding delusions of reference).
2. Odd beliefs or magical thinking that influences behaviour and is inconsistent with subcultural norms (e.g., superstitiousness, belief in clairvoyance, telepathy, or "sixth sense"; in children and adolescents, bizarre fantasies or preoccupations).
3. Unusual perceptual experiences, including bodily illusions.
4. Odd thinking and speech (e.g., vague, circumstantial, metaphorical, overelaborate, or stereotyped).
5. Suspiciousness or paranoid ideation.
6. Inappropriate or constricted affect.
7. Behaviour or appearance that is odd, eccentric, or peculiar.

(continued)

8. Lack of close friends or confidants other than first-degree relatives.
9. Excessive social anxiety that does not diminish with familiarity and tends to be associated with paranoid fears rather than negative judgments about self.

B. Does not occur exclusively during the course of schizophrenia, a bipolar disorder or depressive disorder with psychotic features, another psychotic disorder, or autism spectrum disorder.

Note: If criteria are met prior to the onset of schizophrenia, add "premorbid," e.g., "schizotypal personality disorder (premorbid)."

they will use them against me"; "People often say one thing and mean something else"; and "A person to whom I am close could be disloyal or unfaithful." Unfortunately, this distrust can extend to friends and family members and potentially damage relationships. In paranoid personality disorder, the suspiciousness does not extend to delusional thoughts. If delusions are present, a more serious condition probably exists, such as delusional disorder or schizophrenia.

Arun had done reasonably well as an undergraduate biology major and is now a graduate student in genetics. He is often concerned that fellow students are stealing his ideas or cheating from his papers, but he has never filed any formal complaints. He had gone to a university close to home as an undergraduate and had lived with his parents. Grad school was the first time he was truly away from home. Arun's research focuses on a specific gene associated with a rare form of deafness. He started suspecting that his supervisor had brought him to the university to take credit for his work and claim it as his own. One day, Arun gave his mentor a contract guaranteeing that the supervisor would not steal any of Arun's intellectual property. When the supervisor wouldn't sign, Arun became worried that he was out to get him. Arun wanted to go to the dean, but he knew that the dean and his supervisor were friends and were probably in cahoots anyhow. Arun started locking up his written work and bought extra security for his laptop. He even developed second data sets that were inaccurate so that if his supervisor stole the data and published it, the theft would be evident. When his supervisor confronted him about how he was feeling, Arun interpreted it as yet another attempt to get access to his work. He began writing letters to the chancellor of the university, the provincial premier, and various provincial legislators apprising them of the situation. When the chancellor contacted the dean, who then called Arun's supervisor, it became clear that Arun was disturbed. He was taken to the campus health centre, where he was evaluated and diagnosed with paranoid personality disorder.

Arun's case illustrates several features of paranoid personality disorder. First, his pervasive suspiciousness led him to believe that conspiracies existed all around him. He questioned the loyalty and trustworthiness of fellow students and even departmental faculty. Arun had no evidence that others were trying to steal his data, but he nonetheless persisted in his beliefs. People around him would invariably have perceived him as abrasive, accusing, and suspicious. At first, his faculty adviser and the chancellor may have been willing to listen to and investigate his concerns, perhaps wondering if he had had a bad experience elsewhere that made him protective of his work. However, they soon realized that Arun was suspicious of them as well, and that Arun's reality was very different from their own.

A classic example of the interpersonal difficulties that accompany paranoid personality disorder is the suspicion of infidelity in a partner. At first, it looks like routine jealousy, but then it becomes clear that the suspicion goes far beyond any rational thought, and the partner can do nothing to dispel the fears. Another common feature of paranoid personality disorder is interpreting innocent events as being personally relevant or having personal meaning. For example, getting stuck in the longest line in the grocery store or being singled out for security screening in the airport could be viewed as a personal attack.

SCHIZOID PERSONALITY DISORDER **Schizoid personality disorder** is a pervasive pattern of detachment from social relationships and a restricted range of emotional expression in interpersonal settings (APA, 2013). People with schizoid personality disorder may be introverted, solitary, emotionally unexpressive, and isolated. They derive little enjoyment from or show little interest in belonging to families or social groups. Often absorbed in their own thoughts and feelings, they can be afraid of relationships that require closeness and intimacy. People with this disorder also appear to be indifferent to others' opinions and frequently prefer tasks without human interaction (e.g., laboratory or computer tasks). They seem to experience few emotional extremes such as anger or joy. Instead, they hover indifferently in the middle range of emotion. This disorder is also associated with the absence of enjoyment of sensory, bodily, or interpersonal experiences (APA, 2013). Sometimes the detachment experienced by people with this disorder can lead to impairment in both social and occupational functioning. Often oblivious to normal social cues, these individuals cannot engage in the normal social discourse that maintains relationships and supports occupational success. The lack of social skills can be misinterpreted as aloofness. People with schizoid personality disorder usually do not have the hallucinations, delusions, or the complete disconnection from reality that occurs in untreated (or treatment-resistant) schizophrenia, although they may experience brief psychotic episodes especially in times of stress.

Zack is a 24-year-old stable hand and is most comfortable when alone with the horses and mucking out stalls. He comes in early in the morning, does his work, leaves late at night, and barely speaks to anyone. New people would try to engage him in conversation, but he just wasn't interested. People would sometimes interpret his lack of interest as arrogance and wonder what made him feel so special, but more often they would wonder how anyone could go so long without talking to anyone. A new young rider brought her horse to the stables and took a liking to Zack. Even though he seemed really distant, she thought he was attractive. She asked him out, but he just seemed to have absolutely no interest in her—or anyone else. Zack would visit his parents about once a month. His mother was a seamstress and his father delivered mail. When he went home, he sometimes helped his mother rip out hems of pants she was altering, but the three basically sat in silence or worked while the TV was on.

In lay terms, Zack would be called a loner or a hermit. He is not concerned by his lack of relationships and showed almost no emotional response when the young rider showed interest in him. His work reflects his preference for being alone. The horses place no social demands on him. Yet it does not appear that his job gives him pleasure. In fact, it seems routine and rote. If he was praised, he would accept tips, but he seemed to take no pride in his work and did not express appreciation for others' kind words. The image of Zack and his parents sitting around watching TV and barely talking suggests that a schizoid style might run in the family and reflects the general lack of emotionality and engagement seen in these individuals.

SCHIZOTYPAL PERSONALITY DISORDER **Schizotypal personality disorder** is a pervasive pattern of social and interpersonal deficits marked by acute discomfort, reduced capacity for close relationships, cognitive or perceptual distortions, and behavioural eccentricities (APA, 2013). Features of schizotypal personality disorder are best described as a cluster of idiosyncrasies. People with this disorder may have offbeat, peculiar, or paranoid beliefs and thoughts. Moreover, they have difficulty forming relationships and have extreme social anxiety. During interpersonal interactions, people with this personality disorder may react inappropriately, show no emotion, or inappropriately talk to themselves. Another feature is "magical thinking," an erroneous belief that one can foretell the future or affect events by thinking certain thoughts. People with schizotypal personality disorder may harbour *ideas of reference*. These are incorrect interpretations that events around them have specific and unusual personal meaning. These interpretations are not as severe as *delusions of reference* (see Chapter 10) in which beliefs develop a delusional pattern. People with schizotypal personality disorder also report unusual perceptual experiences or have odd patterns of thinking and speech. Some people with this disorder display suspiciousness or paranoia, and their emotional expressions can be inappropriate and excessive or severely restricted.

The oddities found in people with schizotypal personality disorder are not restricted to thinking and behaviour. Individuals may also have an odd, eccentric, or peculiar physical appearance reflected in their clothing and personal hygiene. These oddities, in addition to their excessive social anxiety and paranoia, may result in limited social relationships.

Everyone on campus knew him as "the pigeon man." When students first saw him, they avoided him by crossing the street. Here was some guy talking to himself (without Bluetooth!). He slept at the local shelter where the workers saw him as harmless. In fact, they told people that the pigeon man was more afraid of them than they should be of him. He rarely washed, had holes in his shoes, and held all of his possessions close to his body in a burlap bag when he slept at night. During the day, he dug scraps out of the trash, sat in the park on a bench surrounded by pigeons, fed them, and carried on extended conversations with the birds. Sometimes he laughed and other times he looked positively angry at the birds. When he finished, he retreated back into his own little world, walking up and down the streets until it was time to go back to the shelter for a meal. His case manager confirmed that he did not have hallucinations or delusions and had never met diagnostic criteria for schizophrenia. Yet this odd pattern of behaviour had been with him since middle school; his caption in its yearbook called him "bird boy."

The pigeon man's history of eccentric involvement with birds existed from childhood. Thus, his unusual behaviours were persistent. Keeping his possessions in his burlap bag close to his body clearly reflected suspiciousness or paranoia about his belongings. Although he was not dangerous, he caused uneasiness in others, probably because of his personal appearance and his erratic behaviours. Clearly, those around him did not share the pigeon man's experience with reality. He saw the world differently although he never had a psychotic episode. Nonetheless, his sustained odd and eccentric behaviour was sufficiently extreme to lead others to avoid him.

Cluster B: Dramatic, Emotional, or Erratic Disorders

The common features of Cluster B are behaviours that are viewed as exaggerated, inflated, dramatic, emotional, or erratic (APA, 2013) (see "DSM-5: Cluster B Personality Disorders"). The four disorders in this cluster are marked by extreme and often colourful patterns of behaviour. Other common features are the fluctuating nature of behaviours—often vacillating between extremes. These patterns can be particularly disrupting interpersonally as the following cases illustrate.

ANTISOCIAL PERSONALITY DISORDER **Antisocial personality disorder (ASPD)** is a pervasive pattern of disregard for and violation of the rights of others (APA, 2013). It is more common in males than in females. This diagnosis is reserved for individuals who are at least 18 years old and who had features of conduct disorder before age 15 (see Chapter 12), illustrating how the pattern of antisocial behaviour begins in childhood and then crystallizes and intensifies over time. Common behaviours in youth include cruelty to animals and people, destruction of property, deceitfulness or theft, or serious violations of rules (APA, 2013).

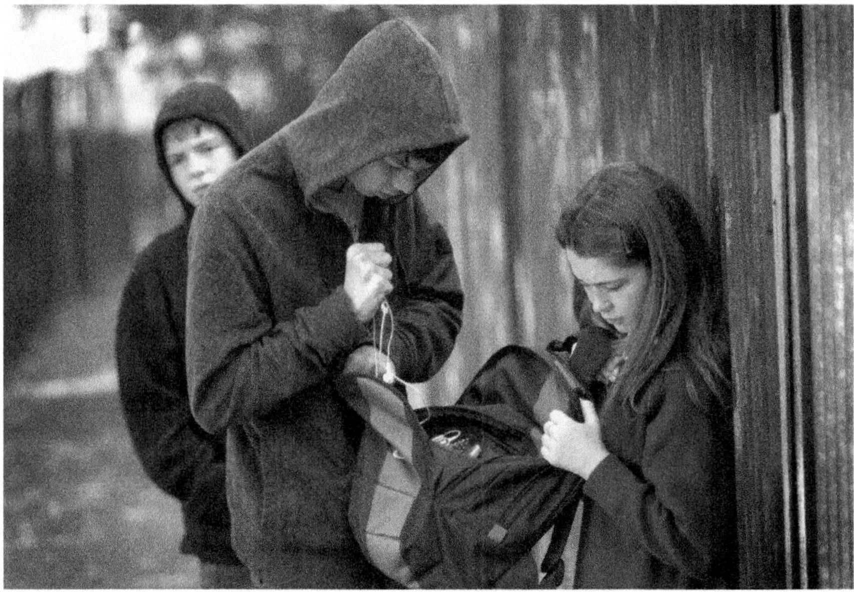

Antisocial personality disorder often has its roots in childhood with antisocial behaviours such as theft and vandalism.

Chris Whitehead/DigitalVision/Getty Images

People with ASPD fail to conform to social norms, which often leads to legal difficulties including arrests. They often lie, use aliases, con others for profit or enjoyment, destroy property, harass others, and engage in behaviours and actions that violate the basic rights, wishes, safety, and feelings of others (APA, 2013). Associated features include being highly impulsive and engaging in problematic activities on the spur of the moment. This can result in physical fights, temper outbursts, physically abusive behaviour, changes in residence, reckless driving, and other impulsive high-risk behaviours that threaten their own safety and well-being (e.g., sexual behaviour, reckless driving or driving while intoxicated causing motor vehicle accidents, drug use). Another common feature is irresponsibility exhibited by unemployment, underemployment, or poor and erratic job performance, and financial irresponsibility including bad debts and failure to support their families or children. In addition, individuals with ASPD fail to take responsibility for their own actions and commonly blame the victims for inciting their behaviour. Examples include saying that a rape victim deserved the assault because of her sexy clothes or blaming physical fights on the other guy (e.g., "He had it coming to him"). Individuals with this personality disorder are also often able to use their charm or persuasiveness to exploit others. Perhaps most disconcerting are the tendencies to minimize the consequences of their actions and to feel no remorse. Indeed, they may be completely indifferent to the consequences of their actions.

Brandon was raised in a family that included his father, mother, and a younger sister, but he did not have a close relationship with anyone. Without parental supervision or involvement, Brandon was often in trouble at school for inappropriate conduct, even at an early age. Despite being very bright, his grades were poor because "he just doesn't care." At 13, he was sent to a youth detention centre for breaking into a neighbour's house while high on marijuana, and soon after being released he began carjacking.

At age 19, he was sent to prison for 18 months for a felony. In prison, Brandon gained a reputation as a "gangsta" for his ability to intimidate other prisoners by physical force, and he had small teardrops tattooed onto his cheek. After he was released, he was arrested as an accomplice to murder in a drive-by shooting in a neighbouring province. He was sent back to jail and then transferred to a federal prison.

In prison, Brandon often bragged about his ability to seduce women, always using fake names, and after gaining their trust, taking a good deal of their money. Brandon had no regrets about his behaviours. If anything, he viewed each incident as another notch in his belt. He could not communicate with others without ultimately resorting to violence. In the beginning, Brandon gained clout with other prisoners with his devil-may-care attitude, but other than a few individuals whom he seemed to have under his cunning influence, most of the other prisoners feared his ruthlessness.

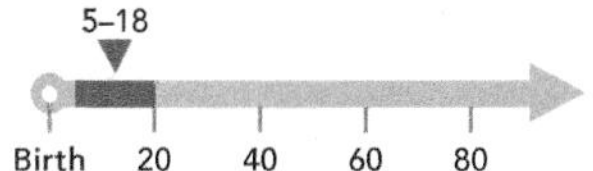

Adults with antisocial personality disorder often show a pattern of callous disregard for others even as children.

criteria for Cluster B Personality Disorders DSM-5

Antisocial Personality Disorder

A. A pervasive pattern of disregard for and violation of the rights of others, occurring since age 15 years, as indicated by three (or more) of the following:
   1. Failure to conform to social norms with respect to lawful behaviours, as indicated by repeatedly performing acts that are grounds for arrest.
   2. Deceitfulness, as indicated by repeated lying, use of aliases, or conning others for personal profit or pleasure.
   3. Impulsivity or failure to plan ahead.
   4. Irritability and aggressiveness, as indicated by repeated physical fights or assaults.
   5. Reckless disregard for safety of self or others.
   6. Consistent irresponsibility, as indicated by repeated failure to sustain consistent work behaviour or honor financial obligations.
   7. Lack of remorse, as indicated by being indifferent to or rationalizing having hurt, mistreated, or stolen from another.

B. The individual is at least age 18 years.

C. There is evidence of conduct disorder with onset before age 15 years.

D. The occurrence of antisocial behaviour is not exclusively during the course of schizophrenia or bipolar disorder.

Narcissistic Personality Disorder

A pervasive pattern of grandiosity (in fantasy or behaviour), need for admiration, and lack of empathy, beginning by early adulthood and present in a variety of contexts, as indicated by five (or more) of the following:
   1. Has a grandiose sense of self-importance (e.g., exaggerates achievements and talents, expects to be recognized as superior without commensurate achievements).
   2. Is preoccupied with fantasies of unlimited success, power, brilliance, beauty, or ideal love.
   3. Believes that he or she is "special" and unique and can only be understood by, or should associate with, other special or high-status people (or institutions).
   4. Requires excessive admiration.
   5. Has a sense of entitlement (i.e., unreasonable expectations of especially favourable treatment or automatic compliance with his or her expectations).
   6. Is interpersonally exploitative (i.e., takes advantage of others to achieve his or her own ends).
   7. Lacks empathy: is unwilling to recognize or identify with the feelings and needs of others.
   8. Is often envious of others or believes that others are envious of him or her.
   9. Shows arrogant, haughty behaviours or attitudes.

Borderline Personality Disorder

A pervasive pattern of instability of interpersonal relationships, self-image, and affects, and marked impulsivity, beginning by early adulthood and present in a variety of contexts, as indicated by five (or more) of the following:
   1. Frantic efforts to avoid real or imagined abandonment. (**Note:** Do not include suicidal or self-mutilating behaviour covered in Criterion 5.)
   2. A pattern of unstable and intense interpersonal relationships characterized by alternating between extremes of idealization and devaluation.
   3. Identity disturbance: markedly and persistently unstable self-image or sense of self.
   4. Impulsivity in at least two areas that are potentially self-damaging (e.g., spending, sex, substance abuse, reckless driving, binge eating). (Note: Do not include suicidal or self-mutilating behaviour covered in Criterion 5.)
   5. Recurrent suicidal behaviour, gestures, or threats, or self-mutilating behaviour.
   6. Affective instability due to a marked reactivity of mood (e.g., intense episodic dysphoria, irritability, or anxiety usually lasting a few hours and only rarely more than a few days).
   7. Chronic feelings of emptiness.

8. Inappropriate, intense anger or difficulty controlling anger (e.g., frequent displays of temper, constant anger, recurrent physical fights).
9. Transient, stress-related paranoid ideation or severe dissociative symptoms.

Histrionic Personality Disorder

A pervasive pattern of excessive emotionality and attention seeking, beginning by early adulthood and present in a variety of contexts, as indicated by five (or more) of the following:

1. Is uncomfortable in situations in which he or she is not the centre of attention.
2. Interaction with others is often characterized by inappropriate sexually seductive or provocative behaviour.
3. Displays rapidly shifting and shallow expression of emotions.
4. Consistently uses physical appearance to draw attention to self.
5. Has a style of speech that is excessively impressionistic and lacking in detail.
6. Shows self-dramatization, theatricality, and exaggerated expression of emotion.
7. Is suggestible (i.e., easily influenced by others or circumstances).
8. Considers relationships to be more intimate than they actually are.

REAL people REAL disorders

Paul Bernardo and Karla Homolka

The crimes of Paul Bernardo and Karla Homolka are among the most sadistic and violent in Canadian history. Paul Bernardo was convicted in 1995 of the rape and murder of two girls, ages 14 and 15, that he and his wife, Karla Homolka, had abducted and used as "sex slaves." The sexual assaults were carefully planned and sadistic. The assaults were recorded by Bernardo on videotape. The jury was shocked and disgusted when the tapes were shown during Bernado's trial (Pron, 1995; Williams, 1996). Homolka "gave" her 15-year-old sister, Tammy, to Bernardo as a Christmas present. Tammy was drugged by Homolka and then raped by Bernado. Tammy died as a result of the drugging.

Bernardo also was the notorious Scarborough rapist, who sexually assaulted as many as 40 women. The rapes were sadistic, involving humiliation and the use of force; during one rape he ripped out a big tuft of the victim's pubic hair, saying, "I want something to remember you by" (Williams, 1996, p. 128). Bernardo's spree of violence lasted about six years, from age 20 to 26. After he was convicted, Bernardo was designated a dangerous offender and is therefore effectively in jail for life. In a plea bargaining agreement, his wife agreed to testify against Bernardo in return for a 12-year prison term. She was released in 2005.

There has been no debate on Paul Bernardo's psychopathology. According to Robert Hare, an expert on psychopathy from the University of British Columbia, Bernardo is a cold-blooded predator lacking in remorse, and the perfect example of a psychopath (Kaihla, 1996). As we will see, psychopathy is similar to antisocial personality disorder, but it also differs in important ways. Other writers have reached similar conclusions about Bernardo (Burnside & Cairns, 1995; Williams, 1996). Paul Bernardo was bright, charming, and popular at high school, but was also sly, manipulative, and grandiose. He got good grades and eventually completed a degree in accounting at the University of Toronto (Burnside & Cairns, 1995). Bernardo had a history of petty theft and various scams, and was involved in cigarette smuggling. He was also violent; he beat his girlfriends and later his wife. After her final beating by Bernardo, Homolka was hospitalized for three days, and finally left him. He showed no remorse or guilt for his crimes, as illustrated by the following examples.

> "One day, when they were driving around . . . Paul [Bernardo] pointed out an attractive, young girl who looked to be about fifteen years old. 'There's the girl I raped,' he said proudly." (Williams, 1996, p. 186)

> "Whether he was talking about smuggling cigarettes, or about how the [chain]saw blade jammed up when he was slicing through Mahaffy's shoulder [one of his victims], Bernardo's voice had a breezy tone to it. Cutting up Mahaffy's body was the most disgusting thing he had ever done, he testified. But he was referring more to the grossness of the act than to its morality." (Pron, 1995, p. 523)

Bernardo is a psychopath who enjoyed sado-masochistic sex: "Paul clearly viewed women as something to be used, dominated, manipulated, and controlled" (Burnside & Cairns, 1995, p. 89).

(*continued*)

Karla Homolka has proved to be a puzzle to psychologists and psychiatrists. Indeed, her inscrutability is a central part of why she seems likely to rank as one of the world's most infamous female criminals (Williams, 1996). How could a person partake in abduction and sexual assault and *not* have something psychologically wrong with them? Experts disagree on her diagnosis (Burnside & Cairns, 1995; Pron, 1985; Williams, 1996, 2003). Some psychologists and psychiatrists regard her as a victim—a battered woman with posttraumatic stress disorder who was caught in Bernardo's web of charm and coercion. Other experts have pointed out that Homolka was a willing accomplice in Bernardo's sexual assaults: she lied and stole to obtain the drugs to render the victims unconscious; she clearly appeared be enjoying herself during some of the videotaped assaults (e.g., when she was performing cunnilingus on an unconscious victim); she showed no remorse over her role in the crimes; she readily testified against Bernardo when it was in her best interests, initiating divorce proceedings, and reporting him for cigarette smuggling; and she quickly began dating again once she left Bernardo, sending her new lover nude photos of herself. The latter behaviours are not what one would expect from a battered woman with posttraumatic stress disorder. These pieces of evidence suggest that she may be a psychopath. But on the other hand, her criminal activities appear to have started and ended with her relationship with Bernardo: "When one considers her character at age 17, prior to her meeting Paul, Karla does not even register a trickle on either the Antisocial Personality Disorder criteria or the Hare's Psychopathy Checklist" (Burnside & Cairns, 1995, p. 559). "If anything, her happy childhood and uneventful teenage development made her subsequent deviant and murderous behaviour even more mysterious" (Williams, 2003, p. 51).

Homolka apparently enjoyed playing a submissive role in some of their sado-masochistic sex play, and seemingly found Bernardo's exploits to be exciting. Williams (1996, 2003) suggests that she suffers from hybristophilia—a phenomena is which a person is sexually aroused by a partner's violent sexual behaviour. The judge who presided over Homolka's trial stated in his sentencing remarks that she was not a danger to society—unless she met another Paul Bernardo (Williams, 2003).

Greig Reekie/Toronto Sun/AP Images

Paul Bernardo is an extreme example of how features of antisocial personality disorder can be associated with criminality. While all individuals who engage in antisocial behaviours are not criminals, 40% of convicted felons do meet the criteria for an antisocial personality disorder. The line between mental illness and criminal behaviour is not clear in this instance, and the distinction between illness and evil will no doubt be debated far into the future in hospitals, jails, and courtrooms.

canadian FOCUS

Psychopathy vs. Antisocial Personality Disorder (ASPD)

Psychopathy and ASPD are two different attempts to define the same disorder. Although related, the two differ in important ways. Critics, such as Robert Hare at the University of British Columbia, have argued that the DSM blurs the distinction between antisocial personality and criminality (Hare et al., 1991, 2012). The DSM emphasizes antisocial behaviours because a history of antisocial acts can be reliably assessed (e.g., by a criminal record check). However, the true meaning of the concept of psychopathy might have been sacrificed in DSM for the sake of improved reliability.

ASPD and psychopathy are similar in that both are characterized by social deviance and behavioural problems (e.g., a history of impulsive and irresponsible behaviour). But ASPD, compared to psychopathy, places a greater emphasis on juvenile delinquency and adult criminal acts. Psychopathy, on the other hand, places greater emphasis on the following personality features: callousness, deceitfulness, egocentricity, failure to form close emotional bonds, low anxiety proneness, superficial charm, lack of remorse, and externalization of blame (Hare & Neumann, 2008; Mokros et al., 2015). When a question such as "Tell me what it is like for you to feel guilt" is posed to a psychopath, the typical reaction is irritation, deflection, or a change of subject. Psychopaths lack insight into what emotions like guilt and remorse actually feel like (Hare et al., 2012; Hare & Neumann, 2008).

ASPD and psychopathy also differ in their prevalence. APSD tends to be the rule rather than the exception in correctional settings, with 50% to 80% of offenders typically meeting diagnostic criteria. In contrast, only about 15% to 30% of correctional offenders are classified as psychopaths (Skeem et al., 2003). Many inmates show the antisocial and aggressive behaviours necessary for a diagnosis of ASPD, but not enough selfish, callous, and exploitative behaviours to qualify for a diagnosis of psychopathy.

A minority of psychopaths—the so-called corporate or white-collar psychopaths—do not meet criteria for ASPD, usually because they have successfully avoided being caught for their criminal acts. Such psychopaths have avoided establishing a record of criminal acts, and therefore are not diagnosed with ASPD. They may operate on the fringes of legality, using charm, deceit, manipulation, and intimidation to satisfy their selfish desires (Babiak & Hare, 2007).

The most widely-used instrument for measuring psychopathy is Robert Hare's Psychopathy Checklist (PCL). The concept of psychopathy, as measured by Hare's PCL, has some advantages over the DSM definition of ASPD. Scores on the PCL are one of the best predictors of which prison inmates are most likely to commit further criminal offences when they are released from prison (Gretton et al., 2004; Hare et al., 2000).

In the corporate world, psychopaths possess the interpersonal qualities that allow them to charm their way up to the top of the corporate ladder (Babiak & Hare, 2007). Screening of corporate leaders for psychopathic traits could prevent some of the massive frauds perpetrated in the business world. Accordingly, Babiak and Hare developed a checklist for identifying corporate psychopaths. According to their measure, corporate psychopaths exhibit traits like the following: They come across as smooth, polished, and charming; they focus most conversations on themselves; they discredit or put down others to build their own image and reputation; they lie to co-workers, customers, and business associates; they are opportunistic, hate to lose, and play ruthlessly to win; they create a power network in the organization to use for personal gain; and they show no regret for making decisions that negatively affect others (e.g., they may take great pleasure in firing someone).

The developmental nature of the disorder can be seen in the early misbehaviour evident in childhood and adolescence. The severity of the misbehaviour intensified as Brandon matured. He lacked empathy for his victims and had no remorse for his behaviour. Although not all individuals with antisocial personality disorder end up in prison, in Brandon's case, his early conduct problems were the first steps on a path to a lifetime of criminal behaviour.

NARCISSISTIC PERSONALITY DISORDER **Narcissistic personality disorder** is a pervasive pattern of grandiosity (in fantasy or behaviour), need for admiration, and lack of empathy (APA, 2013). People with this disorder have an exaggerated sense of self-importance and are often absorbed by fantasies of limitless success. Secondary to this preoccupation with their own superiority, they seek constant attention and may try to win admiration from others by flaunting or boasting about their perceived special abilities. This behaviour often masks fragile self-esteem. Constant external praise or admiration allows them to continue to bolster their own grandiose sense of self.

People with narcissistic personality disorder often express a sense of entitlement—or a belief that they deserve only the best of everything and should associate only with others who are of similarly high calibre. For example, someone with narcissistic personality disorder might be unlikely to visit just any doctor for a minor complaint. She or he is always looking for the best or the most well-known, whether it is a doctor, a lawyer, or a hairstylist; the mundane will not do.

A corollary to this overestimated sense of accomplishment is the converse—namely, a devaluation of what others do or what others have accomplished. Those with narcissistic personality disorder can come off as haughty and arrogant as they constantly flaunt their imagined superiority. Their attitudes toward others can be patronizing and disdainful. People with narcissistic personality disorder are often so self-absorbed that they have a complete lack of empathy for others. They may be so preoccupied with their own need for praise and admiration that they are unable to understand other people's desires, needs, or feelings. People around them often come to feel ignored, devalued, or used.

Nick had always been outwardly confident in his small town high school. He felt that he transcended his prairie environs because he had travelled to Europe as a child. Nick felt that he was unique compared with other students. Generally looking down on what he thought were the "common" tastes of his school, he had few friends and generally kept his high self-opinion to himself. However, during his first year at McGill University, Nick's belief in his own uniqueness became intensified. He sought out friends based on whether he had seen them online or in the society columns of magazines, or knew their parents were significant donors to the university; he was aloof and rude to professors and students in classes that he was "forced" to take due to university standards; and he complained of "wasting time in subjects that have nothing to do with being a CEO of a Fortune 500 company!" While quite charismatic, eloquent, and intelligent in his business courses, he often lied that his knowledge of economics came from his father, a prominent businessman who wrote for the *Wall Street Journal* (in reality his father was a convenience store owner). Although quite successful in his academic pursuits, when faced with group projects, his peers perceived Nick as a nightmare to work with—always blaming them when he made small errors or pitting students against each other and then standing back to watch the arguments. He rarely wrote his own papers, saying, "Why waste my time when I can easily persuade one of the naïve, previous-valedictorian freshmen to do it for me?" While Nick desperately sought and often believed he had the admiration, attention, envy, or even fear of those around him, his classmates often saw him as arrogant and obnoxious.

As illustrated by this case, Nick created a persona that was legendary in his own mind. He considered himself vastly superior to others and grossly overestimated his abilities and prospects for the future. There was a deep disconnect between his beliefs (i.e., that everyone around him admired and respected him) and reality (i.e., that everyone around him found him to be quite insufferable and arrogant).

Although superficially confident, people with narcissistic personality disorder can experience extremes in mood and self-esteem. When their needs for admiration are not met, they may, at least temporarily, feel injured or defeated, resulting in low mood and social withdrawal.

BORDERLINE PERSONALITY DISORDER **Borderline personality disorder** is a pervasive pattern of unstable interpersonal relationships, self-image, affect, and impulsivity (APA, 2013). Its behavioural manifestations can be severe and rapidly fluctuating. Intense bouts of anger, depression, and anxiety may last for hours or as long as a day. As illustrated in Jacqui's case at the beginning of the chapter, other behaviours include impulsive hostility, self-injury, and drug or alcohol abuse. Cognitive distortions and an unstable, conflicted sense of self and self-worth can lead to frequent changes in long-term goals, career plans, jobs, friendships, gender identity, and values. Individuals may feel misunderstood, ill-treated, bored, or empty, and may have an unstable self-identity. At extreme times, the identity disturbance can be so severe that individuals with borderline personality disorder may feel as if they do not exist at all.

People with borderline personality disorder typically have a deep fear of abandonment. Minor separations or endings are misinterpreted as signs that they are being abandoned, left alone, or rejected and can lead to desperate attempts to remain connected and in contact with others. Examples include a therapist going on vacation or a partner having to go out of town for work. To prevent such separations, a person with borderline personality disorder may engage in impulsive and desperate behaviours such as self-mutilation or suicide attempts to keep the person near.

These destructive behaviours and personality style can lead to highly unstable social relationships. Idealization (intense positive feeling) is quickly replaced by devaluation (intense anger and dislike). A person with borderline personality disorder may immediately form an attachment to another person and idealize him or her. Then a minor conflict can lead to a rapid swing to the other extreme, and strong negative emotions toward the person develop. Impulsivity is another hallmark feature and may include binge eating, shoplifting, gambling, irresponsible spending, unsafe sexual behaviours, substance abuse, or reckless driving.

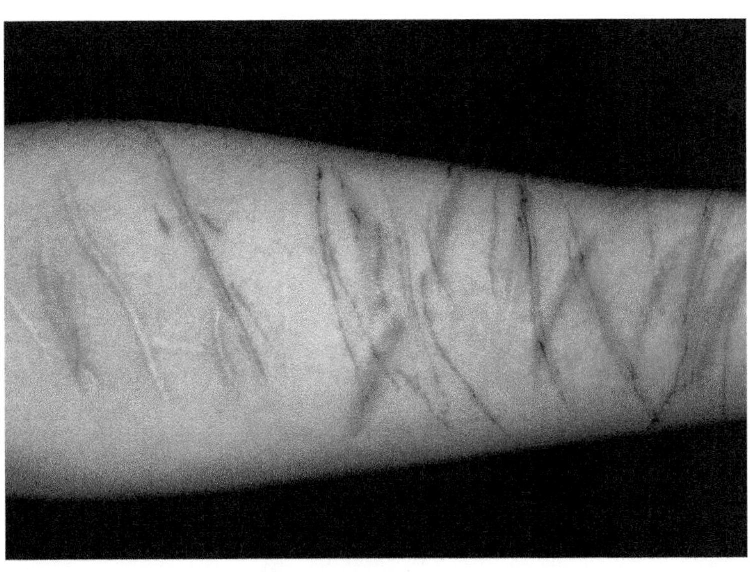

Borderline personality disorder is associated with multiple impulsive behaviours, including self-harm.

Dr. P. Marazzi/Science Source

As noted by McGill University psychiatrist Joel Paris, people with borderline personality disorder are also at high risk for suicide and self-harm because of their tendency to perceive abandonment and to experience feelings of emptiness and nothingness (Paris, 2015). Self-mutilation can include cutting, burning, punching, and a variety of other behaviours that cause bodily injury. These can occur during *dissociative episodes* (in which there is a temporary detachment from reality). Some individuals report that self-harm releases underlying mounting tension. Others say that it helps them know that they can still experience feelings, and still others claim that it helps counteract a belief that they are somehow evil or tarnished.

When people learn about borderline personality disorder, their first question is often "the borderline of what?" Historically, the term refers to the border between neurosis and psychosis, acknowledging that some, but not all, people with this disorder can experience transient psychotic episodes.

Being around or in relationships with people with borderline personality disorder can be extremely challenging. Friends and partners feel like they are on an emotional rollercoaster or that their value rises and falls like the stock market. Jacqui's mother would often say to her husband that she could never predict which Jacqui was going to come home from school or be on the phone, the loving and adoring one or the resentful, hateful one. Those around the person also experience the inconsistent sense of self that the sufferer does. The person is often considered exhausting and "high maintenance." Fostering a sense of stability both in terms of their internal experience and their network of social relationships is critical to levelling out the complex emotions of individuals with borderline personality disorder.

Given the extreme fluctuation in behaviour seen in borderline personality disorder and the highs and lows seen in bipolar disorder (see Chapter 6), how does one best distinguish between these disorders? Recall that people with bipolar disorder have fluctuations in mood with periods of stability in between episodes. In borderline personality disorder, although mood does indeed fluctuate, so do other behaviours and emotions such as feelings about others, feelings about the self, and moving between social approach versus withdrawal. Again, we return to the three Ps: Borderline personality disorder is *persistent*, *pervasive*, and *pathological* rather than episodic like bipolar disorder.

HISTRIONIC PERSONALITY DISORDER **Histrionic personality disorder** is a pattern of excessive emotion and attention-seeking behaviour. *Histrionic* means "dramatic" or "theatrical," and people with this disorder incessantly "perform" and draw attention to themselves (APA, 2013). At first, they are attractive and magnetic as they draw attention by their liveliness, colourful behaviour, and flirtatiousness. Yet when no longer the centre of attention, they engage in behaviours that draw the limelight back to them. Physical appearance or provocative and seductive behaviour are often used to draw people into their circle, causing disruption in a variety of social and occupational settings.

The emotional expressions of people with histrionic personality disorder are pronounced but lack depth and shift rapidly. These changeable, shallow emotions create an impression of not being genuine and of faking their feelings. Histrionic speech also has a dramatic and shallow flair. Someone with this disorder might speak in lavish and colourful terms, express strong opinions, and behave in a dramatic manner, and their actions seem overblown and insincere.

People with histrionic personality disorder consider relationships to be closer or more intimate than they actually are. Coupled with their dramatic flair for language, they may refer to a casual acquaintance as "one of my closest friends in the whole wide world" or describe degrees of closeness in relationships that are in reality quite distant (e.g., seeing a celebrity in a restaurant and subsequently stating that they frequently dine together at their favourite bistro).

When she entered the party with Susan, her partner, Destiny was vibrant, gregarious, and the centre of attention. She was in her element. At first it was very charming: She easily told stories to complete strangers as if she had known them her whole life. But after four hours of Destiny's theatrical socializing and flirtatious behaviour, Susan grew tired and started to feel like an accessory. This was the fourth party this week, and Susan felt disrespected by Destiny's flirting with others. One of Destiny's biggest concerns was what other people thought of her, and, when she felt insecure, she lost her temper. It was often directed at Susan, who had become increasingly tired of bearing the brunt of this behaviour. Because Destiny always needed to be in control and call the shots—fluctuating from enraged to contented based on the circumstances—Susan had thought of leaving her many times. Two weeks ago, Destiny grabbed a glass vase and threw it at the floor, screaming in a fit of rage when Susan suggested that they not go out to dinner because she had a stressful day at work. After the fight, Destiny withdrew from contact and didn't speak for days. When she became less angry, she was extremely sweet and solicitous toward Susan. Destiny's inexorable theatrics and need to be the centre of attention eventually led to the end of the relationship.

Living with someone with histrionic personality disorder can be extremely challenging. Although initially alluring, Destiny, with her constant need to be the centre of attention and her flirtatiousness with others, was unable to engage in a healthy and trusting emotional relationship with Susan. As evidenced by this case, behaviour that is overly dramatic and demanding can be destructive to relationships.

Ethics and Responsibility

The label of borderline personality disorder has been associated with considerable stigmatization in the mental health field. Terms such as "difficult," "treatment resistant," "manipulative," "demanding," and "attention seeking" are commonly associated with borderline personality disorder (Gallop & Wynn, 1987; Nehls, 1998). Such negative perceptions can lead to negative expectations, negative outcomes, and self-fulfilling prophecies. Indeed, negative expectations and perceptions by clinicians are consistent with the core fears of people with borderline personality disorder who are sensitive to rejection and fearful of abandonment. These patients may react to clinicians' negative perceptions in a way that is harmful to themselves by withdrawing from treatment (Aviram et al., 2006). Despite advances in the treatment of borderline personality disorder (see "Treatment of Personality Disorders"), stigmatization persists. Clinicians who use the term "borderline" loosely and inappropriately to label difficult patients can convey negative perceptions and negative expectations to other clinicians as well (Aviram et al., 2006). For all of these reasons, clinicians should give the diagnosis of borderline personality disorder only when the personality traits are consistent with the diagnostic criteria. They should seek supervision or specialized training if they are challenged by their own misperceptions or difficulties dealing with patients with this symptom profile.

Cluster C: Anxious or Fearful Disorders

The common features of Cluster C are characteristic behaviours marked by considerable anxiety or withdrawal (APA, 2013). The three disorders in this cluster share features that reflect some form of anxiety—social anxiety, obsessionality, or fear of independence. As you will see with each disorder, distinctions must be made between the personality disorder and other disorders that share some of the same clinical features. Again, recalling the distinction between "ways of being" vs. illness can guide diagnostic decisions.

AVOIDANT PERSONALITY DISORDER **Avoidant personality disorder** (see "DSM-5: Cluster C Personality Disorders") is a pervasive pattern of social inhibition, feelings of inadequacy, and hypersensitivity to negative evaluation (APA, 2013). People with this disorder avoid social or occupational interactions for fear of rejection, criticism, or disapproval. Common patterns include being excessively shy and uncomfortable in social situations and worrying that what they say will be considered foolish by others. Other fears include blushing or crying in front of others and becoming very hurt by any real or perceived disapproval.

People with avoidant personality disorder may entirely avoid making new friends unless they have complete assurance that they will not be rejected. A common concern is that others will be critical or disapproving unless proved otherwise. This personality disorder can lead individuals to avoid intimate relationships entirely because of worries about being accepted. Avoidant individuals are hypervigilant to signs of rejection or criticism and may over- or misinterpret other peoples' comments about them.

Lou is a 35-year-old mechanic who rarely comes out from under a car. Ever since he could remember, he has been basically terrified of talking to other people. Even though his grades were acceptable throughout high school, he was afraid that people would think he was "simple" because he never knew what to say. He avoided all school social events and group projects and would not attend graduation. He stays in the garage all day working on cars. He quit work in one garage because he had to "cover" the front counter when the clerk went on breaks or lunch. He could not deal with the phones and the customers. Lou would be under the cars, worried that the phone would ring or he would hear the bell on the counter. He did excellent work and was offered several promotions that would require him to supervise others, but he refused because he did not know how to handle teams of people. To this day, Lou has never gone on a date. He eats alone in his house in front of the television every night and avoids all social contacts. When Lou's mother found out he had refused promotions, she decided she had "had it" with his "ridiculous shyness" and brought him in for psychotherapy. Lou has been working for over a year with a therapist trying to develop skills to overcome his pervasive anxiety about the social world.

The core of avoidant personality is shyness and a sense of inadequacy that leads to significant impairment in life both socially and occupationally. People with this disorder may completely avoid talking about themselves or be very withdrawn or restrained due to their fear of potential criticism or disapproval. Others would describe them as quiet, shy, or "wallflowers." People perceive themselves as socially inadequate, inferior, and inept at social interaction. Social self-esteem and self-efficacy tend to be quite low (see "Examining the Evidence: Social Anxiety Disorder vs. Avoidant Personality Disorder").

DEPENDENT PERSONALITY DISORDER **Dependent personality disorder** is a pervasive and excessive need to be taken care of, which leads to submissive and clinging behaviour and fears of separation (APA, 2013). People with dependent personality disorder often have great difficulty making the simplest of everyday decisions, let alone large life choices. This can result in a pattern of relying on others to make decisions and becoming paralyzed if advice and assistance are not available (e.g., not being able to leave the house without advice on which coat to wear). People with this disorder may become passive participants in the world and often allow others to take over responsibility for planning all aspects of their life. The degree of dependency is disproportionate to age-related norms and does not include situations in which depending on others is essential for survival (e.g., medically-related dependence).

People with dependent personality disorder may also have trouble starting projects on their own. Having low confidence in their own ability and a chronic need to check with others for guidance and reassurance, they would rather follow than lead. Because of their exaggerated fears about their incompetence or inability to function or survive independently, a sense of helplessness can develop when they are left alone.

After the break-up of a significant relationship, people with dependent personality disorder quickly rebound into another one. They find it difficult to tolerate periods of independence and desperately embark on another dependent relationship to minimize intense anxiety and fears associated with being alone. These individuals may become so preoccupied with fears of being left alone that they go to extreme measures to arrange situations where they will have assurance of care.

Donna was the younger of two sisters and her mother's favourite "because she was prettier." As a child, Donna was indeed lovely, but she was very shy and clung to her mother's apron strings. She wet the bed until the age of 13 and had sleepovers only at her closest friend's house because she understood the problem and knew why she brought a plastic sheet. Donna's mother was very opinionated and domineering. When she drank alcohol, she would get very loud. Donna was always the one to quietly and gently ask her to be a little quieter. In high school, when Donna's friends began dating, her mother always disapproved of the boys they dated. No one would ever be good enough for her Donna. When it was time to decide about university, despite Donna's good grades, her mother told her that university was a waste of time and suggested she get her realtor's licence—that way she could live at home, save money, and make a good living. Donna agreed and did as her mother suggested. Indeed, she was relieved because she was terrified of having to live alone or in a university dorm. She still went shopping for her mother and did errands for her parents regularly. At 37, she was still living at home. Her sister was married with children and constantly hassled her about "getting a life." Donna loved playing with her little niece because Lily loved her unconditionally. Some of Donna's brief relationships with men had bordered on abusive. She never felt like she had the right to stand up for herself and thought she didn't really have opinions about anything. At least the men were there to care for her if she needed them. Whenever she brought one home to meet her parents, her mother never failed to find fault and interfere in the relationship. Donna could not stand up to her mother or break away and become independent. She spent evenings in her room in tears worrying about her future and what would happen if her mother died and was no longer able to look after her.

Despite the uncomfortable aspects of her life, Donna remained with her mother at home, where she felt someone would look after her and help her make critical decisions. She was preoccupied with worries about her future and fears about being unable to care for herself if her mother was no longer available. Donna's degree of dependence had nothing to do with any physical condition or actual need for dependency on others, and was clearly age inappropriate.

examining the **EVIDENCE**

Social Anxiety Disorder vs. Avoidant Personality Disorder

Since 1987, both the diagnosis of social anxiety disorder and the diagnosis of avoidant personality disorder have been defined by fears of criticism and avoidance of activities that involve many different social interactions, not merely fears of public speaking (see Chapter 4). Both avoidant personality disorder and social anxiety disorder involve restraint in and avoidance of social situations. Because such overlap in the diagnostic criteria exists, are social anxiety disorder and avoidant personality disorder really two separate conditions?

- **The Facts** Only one criterion of avoidant personality disorder—"is reluctant to take personal risks or engage in new activities"—appears to differentiate its diagnostic criteria from social anxiety disorder. In research based on several carefully controlled studies, investigators concluded that avoidant personality disorder and social anxiety disorder were overlapping constructs (Widiger, 1992). Yet the two categories continue to exist, suggesting that some view these conditions as qualitatively distinct. Why?
- **Let's Examine the Evidence** Early studies (Herbert et al., 1992; Holt et al., 1992; Turner et al., 1992) examined a host of variables including the core characteristics of the disorders, the associated symptoms (such as depression), and etiology. Data from all these studies indicated that across all measures, individuals diagnosed with avoidant personality disorder had more severe problems, but the differences were quantitative, not qualitative. In other words, the difference appeared to be one of simple severity, not the qualitative distinction one would hope to find for these separate groups. Studies have continued to search for qualitative distinctions, examining the same variables as the earlier studies but also including variables related to treatment outcome (e.g., Chambless et al., 2008; Huppert et al., 2008; Marques et al., 2012; Rettew, 2000). Although statistical analysis appeared to be able to categorize people as either suffering from social anxiety disorder or avoidant personality disorder, the distinction disappeared when the severity of social anxiety disorder symptoms was statistically controlled. In other words, classification was still based solely on symptom severity. In each case, people with avoidant personality disorder had more severe symptoms and more functional impairment. In many studies, so many people qualified for a diagnosis of both disorders that classification appeared meaningless (Rettew, 2000).
- **Conclusion** Even though several controlled studies have tried to find qualitative differences between social anxiety disorder and avoidant personality disorder, few clear distinctions can be found. The primary difference remains the quantitative distinction of clinical severity, illustrating how early-onset anxiety disorders can become so pervasive that they can affect every aspect of daily functioning.

criteria for
Cluster C Personality Disorders
DSM-5

Avoidant Personality Disorder

A pervasive pattern of social inhibition, feelings of inadequacy, and hypersensitivity to negative evaluation, beginning by early adulthood and present in a variety of contexts, as indicated by four (or more) of the following:

1. Avoids occupational activities that involve significant interpersonal contact because of fears of criticism, disapproval, or rejection.
2. Is unwilling to get involved with people unless certain of being liked.
3. Shows restraint within intimate relationships because of the fear of being shamed or ridiculed.
4. Is preoccupied with being criticized or rejected in social situations.
5. Is inhibited in new interpersonal situations because of feelings of inadequacy.
6. Views self as socially inept, personally unappealing, or inferior to others.
7. Is unusually reluctant to take personal risks or to engage in any new activities because they may prove embarrassing.

(continued)

Dependent Personality Disorder

A pervasive and excessive need to be taken care of that leads to submissive and clinging behaviour and fears of separation, beginning by early adulthood and present in a variety of contexts, as indicated by five (or more) of the following:

1. Has difficulty making everyday decisions without an excessive amount of advice and reassurance from others.
2. Needs others to assume responsibility for most major areas of his or her life.
3. Has difficulty expressing disagreement with others because of fear of loss of support or approval. (**Note:** Do not include realistic fears of retribution.)
4. Has difficulty initiating projects or doing things on his or her own (because of a lack of self-confidence in judgment or abilities rather than a lack of motivation or energy).
5. Goes to excessive lengths to obtain nurturance and support from others, to the point of volunteering to do things that are unpleasant.
6. Feels uncomfortable or helpless when alone because of exaggerated fears of being unable to care for himself or herself.
7. Urgently seeks another relationship as a source of care and support when a close relationship ends.
8. Is unrealistically preoccupied with fears of being left to take care of himself or herself.

Obsessive-Compulsive Personality Disorder

A pervasive pattern of preoccupation with orderliness, perfectionism, and mental and interpersonal control, at the expense of flexibility, openness, and efficiency, beginning by early adulthood and present in a variety of contexts, as indicated by four (or more) of the following:

1. Is preoccupied with details, rules, lists, order, organization, or schedules to the extent that the major point of the activity is lost.
2. Shows perfectionism that interferes with task completion (e.g., is unable to complete a project because his or her own overly strict standards are not met).
3. Is excessively devoted to work and productivity to the exclusion of leisure activities and friendships (not accounted for by obvious economic necessity).
4. Is overconscientious, scrupulous, and inflexible about matters of morality, ethics, or values (not accounted for by cultural or religious identification).
5. Is unable to discard worn-out or worthless objects even when they have no sentimental value.
6. Is reluctant to delegate tasks or to work with others unless they submit to exactly his or her way of doing things.
7. Adopts a miserly spending style toward both self and others; money is viewed as something to be hoarded for future catastrophes.
8. Shows rigidity and stubbornness.

OBSESSIVE-COMPULSIVE PERSONALITY DISORDER **Obsessive-compulsive personality disorder** is a pervasive pattern of preoccupation with orderliness, perfectionism, and mental and interpersonal control at the expense of flexibility, openness, and efficiency (APA, 2013). People with this personality disorder are classic examples of being unable to see the forest for the trees. Being excessively focused on rules, trivial details, lists, or procedures can lead to losing sight of an overarching activity. A common behaviour is checking and rechecking work to ensure complete accuracy. A strong feeling of self-doubt can lead to missing important work or school deadlines. The aspiration for perfection, which sometimes backfires, defines this disorder. For example, an individual may become so preoccupied with the details of perfecting part of a task that he or she never "pulls it all together" and does not complete the entire task. Students may recopy an assignment over and over in search of the "perfect" report, but consequently not finish on time and miss the assignment deadline.

This quest for perfection can often lead to a preoccupation with and devotion to work that leaves little or no time for leisure activities, pleasurable activities, or friendships and relationships. This is quite evident in the abnormal case study earlier in this chapter in which Jeff's entire life is focused on his work schedule. Anxiety increases if activities do not have a goal or a structure, and people with this disorder may even turn to structuring leisure time for themselves or their children. "Chilling" or "kicking back" is not in their vocabulary, and indeed would be highly uncomfortable and even anxiety provoking. Others perceive them as rigid or stubborn.

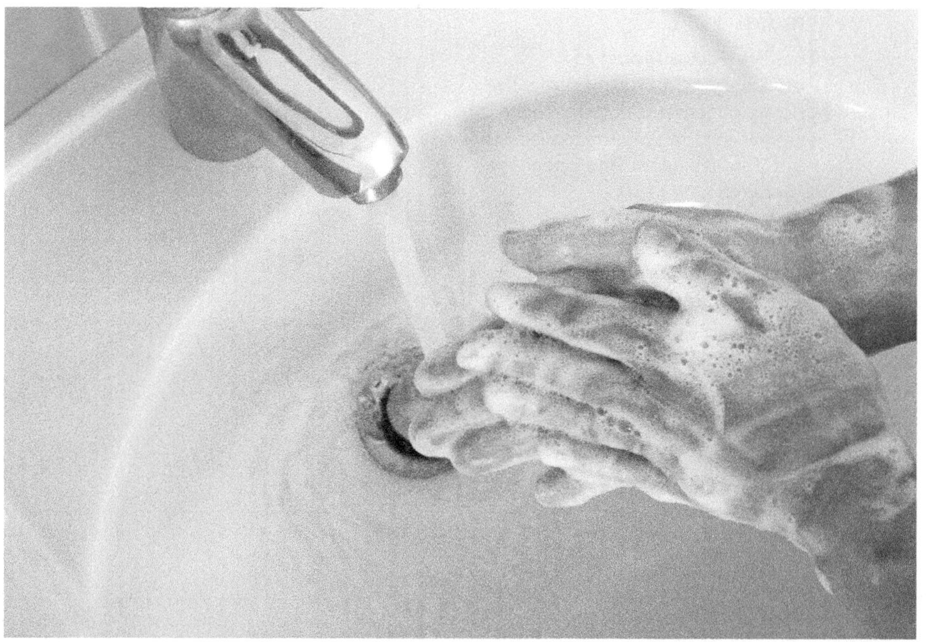

Another common feature of obsessive-compulsive personality disorder is overconscientiousness and strict moral and ethical values that go beyond what is appropriate or normative for the person's cultural background or religious affiliation. This can result in holding oneself (and others) to extraordinarily high standards of moral and ethical conduct and merciless self-punishment if a rule is transgressed.

Other features associated with obsessive-compulsive personality disorder include being "pack rats," unable to discard things that have no use or apparent sentimental value. Hoarded objects may seem completely useless (e.g., old cell phones, old junk mail). Delegation of work to others can also be a challenge, and the belief might be, like Jeff's, "If you want something done right, you have to do it yourself." This leads to feelings of being overwhelmed and unable to accomplish all tasks on the list. Rigidity and control may also extend to the financial area in which people may feel compelled to pinch pennies or save for a rainy day, depriving themselves or their family of various things. The first purchases to be rejected are associated with pleasure or leisure and do not contribute in a direct or meaningful way to the accomplishment of tasks on the list. Like Jeff, the individual with obsessive-compulsive personality disorder is a prisoner of lists and "shoulds."

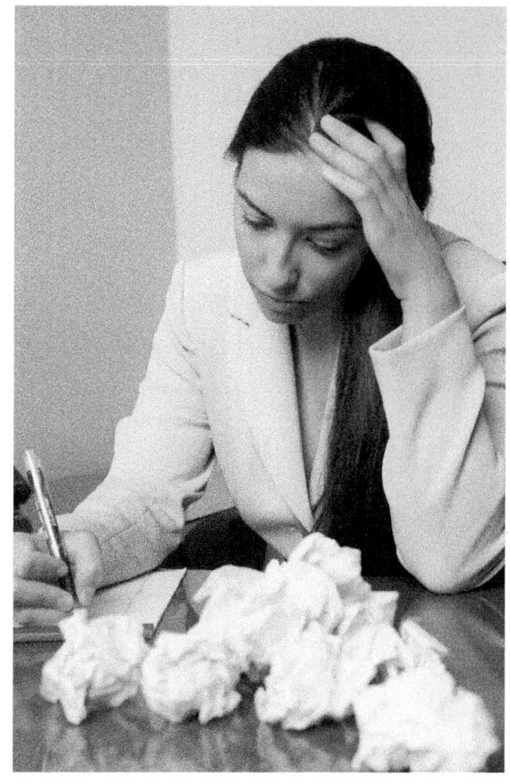

While obsessive-compulsive disorder is marked by obsessions and compulsions (such as excessive hand washing), obsessive-compulsive personality disorder is marked by traits such as orderliness, perfectionism, and rigidity.

(top): Ilya Andriyanov/Shutterstock; **(bottom):** Glow Images

Note that although perfectionism is a defining feature of obsessive-compulsive personality disorder, it is also associated with other disorders such as major depression, eating disorders, social anxiety disorder, and other clinical problems. This has been demonstrated in numerous studies by Paul Hewitt (University of British Columbia), Gordon Flett (York University), and their colleagues (e.g., Flett et al., 2014; Hewitt et al., 2014; Sherry et al., 2014). These researchers have also demonstrated that there are multiple types of perfectionism, such as perfectionism about performing tasks "correctly" and perfectionism about how one presents oneself to others (Casale et al., 2015). Although perfectionism, in its various manifestations, is associated with many different disorders, when perfectionism is one of the person's primary or major problems, a diagnosis of obsessive-compulsive personality disorder is likely.

Other Personality Disorder Models

11.3 Appreciate the complex nature of personality disorders.

Although the three clusters capture a broad range of personality disturbance, they are far from comprehensive. Sometimes people clearly have a personality disturbance (in that the traits are pervasive, persistent, and pathological and are more a "way of being" than

FIGURE 11.1

The Five-Factor Model of Personality. This model posits five primary dimensions of personality: extraversion, neuroticism, conscientiousness, agreeableness, and openness to experience.

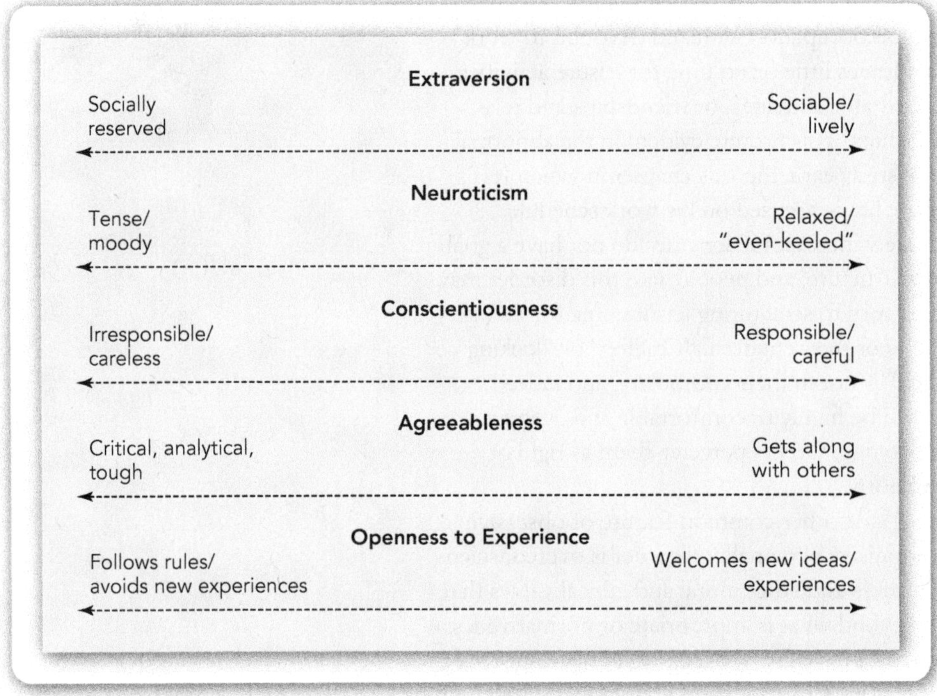

an illness). Yet they do not fit tightly into one of the disorder boxes. These individuals are given a diagnosis of personality disorder—not otherwise specified, which indicates that their clinical problems may represent a mixture of several disorders. Of all of the personality disorders, this is the most frequently used diagnosis in clinical practice (Verheul et al., 2007; Verheul & Widiger, 2004). Some people meet the criteria for more than one personality disorder (e.g., dependent and histrionic or obsessive-compulsive and paranoid).

Although it may be easy and diagnostically convenient to think of mental disorders as clear-cut categories, sometimes they are not. Debate continues within the field about how personality disorders should be understood. Rather than a categorical model, some theorists propose a dimensional model of personality (see Chapter 3). One well-known dimensional model is the five-factor model (FFM). In this model, behaviour is classified along five different dimensions—neuroticism, extraversion, openness, agreeableness, and conscientiousness—and a person would be rated as being maladaptively high or low on each dimension (see Figure 11.1). Integrating these dimensional factors of personality into current DSM-5 diagnoses may make these diagnostic categories more descriptive. For example, a person with schizoid personality disorder would score maladaptively low on extraversion, while someone with borderline personality disorder would score maladaptively high on neuroticism (anxiousness). Proponents of a dimensional model (Widiger & Lowe, 2008) believe that it would provide a more comprehensive picture of personality and would eliminate the need to give several personality disorder diagnoses to describe behaviour adequately. Because this approach highlights personality strengths, it could also reduce the stigma of labelling someone with a personality disorder.

Beyond the debate between categorical vs. dimensional systems, the personality disorders described in DSM-5 may capture only a fraction of the personality-related problems of interest to patients and clinicians (McCrae et al., 2001). In one study (Westen & Arkowitz-Westen, 1998), 60% of patients treated for personality-related problems and distress did not meet criteria for a DSM-5 personality disorder. Yet, personality problems, such as perfectionism and shyness, were among the reasons patients sought treatment. Rarely does someone seeking treatment fit perfectly into one of the personality disorder categories. Typically, people have a varied collection of symptoms that not only cut across disorders within a cluster, but also sometimes across clusters. The psychologist's job is to evaluate and treat the complexity of the personality disturbance as it exists in the person rather than having the person's perspective limited by the published boundaries of any set of diagnostic criteria.

Developmental Factors and Personality Disorders

The DSM helps clinicians make distinctions about the patient's current state in contrast to lifetime patterns of behaviour, but the distinctions are not always entirely clear. For example, how long must a personality disturbance persist to qualify for a personality disorder diagnosis? When significant personality pathology exists in individuals under age 18, is a personality disorder diagnosis appropriate if personality is theoretically still under formation? While a diagnosis may be appropriate if the features are present for at least a year, diagnosing personality disorder in someone under age 18 remains controversial, given the effects of brain maturation on the course of personality maturity (Ceballos et al., 2006).

From a developmental perspective, many manifestations of personality disorders represent typical (although transient) childhood and adolescent behaviours. Dependency, anxiety, hypersensitivity, identity formation problems, conduct problems, histrionics, and testing the limits occur commonly during childhood and adolescence. In general, longitudinal follow-up studies show that such behaviours decrease over time, although high rates of personality disorder-type problems during childhood and adolescence are associated with increased risk for psychological disorders later in life. More flagrant behaviours (such as harming animals or risky sexual behaviour) may be more serious red flags for later personality disturbance. As our understanding of personality formation emerges, evidence has accumulated that personality disorders originate very early in life and may at least in part be programmed at the genetic level. Elements of later personality may even be foreshadowed in the simple behaviours exhibited by babies and toddlers (De Clercq & De Fruyt, 2007). As we watch personality emerge in children, the difference between healthy development of individual personality features and the earliest symptoms of personality pathology remains unclear.

Longitudinal studies such as the Block Project can trace childhood personality features into adulthood to identify early indicators of later psychopathology. Here researchers stand surrounded by years and years of collected data.

R.R. Jones

In community and clinical samples, adolescent personality disorders are associated with emotional distress and psychological impairment. In the Children in the Community study (Johnson et al., 2006b)—a prospective longitudinal investigation of 593 families at four time points from childhood to adulthood—low parental affection or nurturing was associated with elevated risk for antisocial, avoidant, borderline, paranoid, schizoid, and schizotypal personality disorders among adult offspring of these families. Aversive parental behaviour (e.g., harsh punishment) was associated with an elevated risk for borderline, paranoid, and schizotypal personality disorders among adult offspring. Because this study controlled for offspring behavioural and emotional problems and parental psychiatric disorder, these findings suggest that parental rearing styles may affect the development of personality disorders in children. Conduct disorder and antisocial personality disorder represent the clearest case of progression from adolescence through adulthood (Johnson et al., 2006b).

Adolescent personality disorders are also associated with the presence of other psychological disorders. A young woman who shows persistent dependent traits throughout adolescence may find herself at increased risk for developing major depression during adulthood when she experiences loss. Applying dimensional approaches to understanding personality development in children may yield rich information. One longitudinal cohort study, the "Block Project," has followed 100 children since the age of 3 well into adulthood. The Block Project found that characteristic childhood personality and behavioural patterns predicted the later development of problems such as dysthymia. Boys who developed dysthymia by age 18 were observed to be aggressive, self-aggrandizing, and undercontrolled at age 7. Girls with later depressive tendencies were self-critical and overcontrolling as children (Block et al., 1991). Therefore, personality differences that exist in early childhood were associated with the later development of disorders such as depression, but different behaviours were important for boys and girls. However, we need to be careful that we do not immediately assume that every unusual childhood and adolescent behaviour represents a risk factor for the emergence of a later psychological disorder. We do not yet fully appreciate the clinical significance of personality traits during childhood and adolescence.

Comorbidity and Functional Impairment

As each case in this chapter indicates, personality disorders produce substantial functional impairment, most obviously in interpersonal relationships. The person with borderline personality disorder alienates her friends and lovers with her rapidly fluctuating moods of adoration and hatred; the obsessive-compulsive father alienates his family with his rigid approach to the world; the son with schizoid personality disorder abandons his siblings and has few ties to the rest of the world. Perhaps not surprisingly, people with personality disorders create considerable distress for people around them and are often the topic of conversation because of the unusual and extreme aspects of who they are.

Personality disorders also often deeply affect occupational functioning. From the person with avoidant personality disorder who declines promotions to avoid interpersonal contact, to the person with antisocial personality disorder who moves irresponsibly from job to job, to the person with histrionic personality disorder who flirts inappropriately to gain attention from co-workers, personality disorders can lead to occupational problems and failures. Needless to say, managers do not necessarily have the psychological background to understand that these patterns of behaviour are secondary to a personality disorder. These behaviours result in poor or inappropriate performance and potentially loss of employment.

In addition to their problems with social and occupational functioning, in general people with personality disorders are at higher risk for many other psychological disorders. Paranoid and schizoid personality disorders have been most strongly associated with dysthymia and mania (Grant et al., 2004). Avoidant and dependent personality disorders show strong associations with major depression, dysthymia, and mania (Grant et al., 2004). Borderline personality disorder is commonly comorbid with major depression (Sullivan et al., 1994), bulimia nervosa (Rosenvinge et al., 2000), and substance use disorders (Dulit et al., 1993; Skodol et al., 1999). Antisocial personality disorder often occurs within the context of substance abuse and other impulse control disorders (APA, 2013; Dulit et al., 1993; Goldstein et al., 2007). These high rates of comorbidity suggest that the clinical presentation and functional impairment of personality disorders can be compounded by the presence of other disorders. Furthermore, the combination results in significant personal distress and poses considerable treatment challenges. We will see that intervention must address not only the pervasive personality pathology, but also the acute problems associated with comorbid disorders.

Epidemiology

Few epidemiologic data on the prevalence of personality disorders are available. One reason is that personality disorders are difficult to reliably diagnose in a single setting. Most epidemiologic studies rely on a single diagnostic interview (at best) and a series of self-report questionnaires. Capturing the complexity of personality disorder diagnoses in cross-sectional epidemiological studies is a daunting and potentially unreliable task. We need to keep this in mind when considering the data that do exist.

Personality disorders affect an estimated 6% to 15% of Canadians (Langlois et al., 2011). The most common of the personality disorders are obsessive-compulsive (with a prevalence rate of 7.7% according to DSM-IV criteria), avoidant (6.6%), paranoid (5.6%), borderline (5.4%), and schizotypal (5.2%) (Langlois et al., 2011).

Sex, Race, and Ethnicity

Our understanding of sex differences in personality disorders comes from epidemiological studies and studies of clinical populations. However, sex differences reported in clinical studies can be biased and may reflect the likelihood of the different sexes to seek treatment (or be brought in for treatment) rather than true sex differences. When we compare results across epidemiologic studies, two constant patterns emerge. First, antisocial personality disorder is consistently more common in males (Grant et al., 2004). Second, dependent and avoidant personality disorders tend to be more common in females (Grant et al., 2004; Torgersen et al., 2001). Although histrionic personality disorder tends to be diagnosed more often in females and narcissistic personality disorder in males in clinical settings, this pattern is observed in some (Torgersen et al., 2001) but not all (Grant et al., 2004) epidemiologic studies. Beyond those differences, few consistent patterns emerge in terms of sex differences in personality disorders. In addition, little is known about racial and ethnic differences in personality disorders.

CONCEPT check

- Cluster A, the "odd or eccentric" cluster, includes features reminiscent of those seen in psychosis and schizophrenia. This cluster includes paranoid, schizoid, and schizotypal personality disorders.
- Cluster B, the "dramatic, emotional, or erratic" cluster, tends to be marked by dramatic or exaggerated personality features. This cluster includes borderline, narcissistic, histrionic, and antisocial personality disorders.
- Cluster C, the "anxious or fearful" cluster, includes dependent, avoidant, and obsessive-compulsive personality disorders.
- Personality disorders are often associated with substantial functional impairment, especially in the realm of interpersonal relationships.
- Of the personality disorders, antisocial personality disorder has the clearest developmental roots, with origins often clearly traced back to childhood and evidence of conduct disorder before age 15.

critical thinking question Sometimes defining the boundaries between personality disorder and criminal behaviour found in someone like Paul Bernardo can be a daunting task. If you were asked to think about when someone should be considered innocent due to a personality disorder vs. guilty of criminal behaviour, what types of issues would you consider?

The Etiology of Personality Disorders

11.4 Understand the role biology may play in the origin of personality pathology.

What causes a persistent and maladaptive way of dealing with the world? Are there indicators early in life that predict the emergence of personality pathology? Can we use the same tools that we use with other psychological disorders to understand the causes of personality disorders? These are all critical and current questions that are being addressed with active research within the personality disorders field. As with other disorders, neither genetic underpinnings, chemical imbalances, psychological features, nor problematic social environments alone account for the development of personality pathology. Critical to understanding personality pathology is the convergence of both a biopsychosocial perspective and a full understanding of the developmental context. In the remaining sections of this chapter, we outline what is known about biological, psychological, and social factors and how they interact to result in disturbances in personality function.

Temperament, a part of personality that is believed to be biologically based, appears early in life.

Hannamariah/Shutterstock

Biological Perspectives

Ask any mother with more than one child and she will tell you that her babies had distinct and often quite different personalities from birth—and sometimes even from before birth (see "Research Hot Topic: Tracking Temperament from Childhood into Adulthood").

In contrasting her children, Lashanda said, "Ronnie was a holy terror from the day he was born. He would scream and scream and nothing could soothe him. In fact, it went back even further than that. Seems whenever I wanted to sleep when I was pregnant, he wanted to play. I didn't get a minute's rest for 9 months. It's amazing I had another one! Then came Jake. When I was pregnant, he slept when I slept. After he was born, I kept expecting him to be like Ronnie—throwing tantrums in the middle of the night—unable to be consoled. He might yell a little, I would come into his room, rub his back, he would pass a little gas, sigh, smile, roll over and fall back to sleep. Those boys had different wiring!"

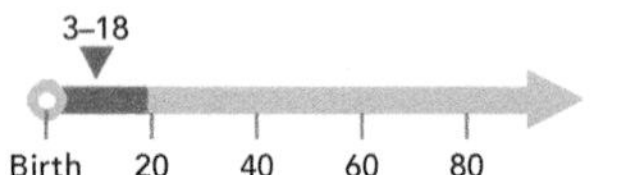

Temperament appears early in life and is relatively stable throughout childhood and adolescence.

Temperament is influenced by genetics and may account for some of the variability in personality traits. Temperament refers to personality components that are biological or genetic in origin, observable from birth (perhaps before), and relatively stable across time and across various situations (Buss, 1999). For example, some children are born fussy and irritable while others are mellow and calm. Even mothers of twins point out fundamental differences in the temperament of babies who developed at the same time in the womb. When these innate biological components interact with the outside world (i.e., experience), personality emerges (Cloninger et al., 1993). Thus, personality traits are a combination of temperament and experience. Personality disorders represent a dysfunctional outcome of this process when certain traits become exaggerated and are applied in maladaptive ways.

The links between various personality dimensions and underlying biological or genetic markers remain theoretical. In 1993, Cloninger proposed that associations between dimensions of temperament and specific neurotransmitter systems exist (Cloninger et al., 1993). As our understanding of temperament and neurobiology has progressed, it is clear that any simplistic theories that link one trait to one neurotransmitter will be replaced by more sophisticated models that account for complex biological underpinnings.

FAMILY AND GENETIC STUDIES Family and twin studies clearly indicate that both personality disorders (Kendler et al., 2007b, 2008) and personality traits (Jang et al., 1996; Rettew et al., 2008) are familial and are influenced primarily by genetic factors. As with all complex traits, a single gene is not responsible for a single temperamental trait; the trait probably results from variations in several genes coupled with environmental influences.

research **HOT** topic

Tracking Temperament from Childhood into Adulthood

Temperament refers to the stable moods and behaviour profiles that appear during infancy and early childhood. Two of the most extensively studied aspects of childhood temperament are the behavioural tendencies to approach or withdraw from unfamiliar stimuli. Some children cower behind their mother when confronted by a stranger (behaviourally inhibited children), while others eagerly engage and approach the stranger (uninhibited children). Jerome Kagan and his colleagues have followed a cohort of children who were categorized as inhibited or uninhibited within the first two years of life. In addition to the observed differences in approach/withdrawal, these researchers also found major differences in the children's underlying biological reactions when they were confronted with unfamiliar individuals. Inhibited children showed faster heart rates and more heart rate variability, pupillary dilation during cognitive tasks, vocal cord tension when speaking under moderate stress, and higher salivary cortisol levels than those who were uninhibited. These differences remained throughout later childhood and adolescence. But what happens when the children become adults? Do they "grow out of" their biology and their tendency to approach or avoid?

Hiroshi Yagi/Getty Images

Schwartz, Wright, and colleagues tracked down 22 adults (mean age 21.8 years) from this study who had been categorized in the second year of life as inhibited (n = 13) or uninhibited (n = 9). Using functional magnetic resonance imaging (fMRI), they measured the response of the amygdala (a brain structure involved in processing the emotional significance of stimuli) to novel vs. familiar faces. The researchers found that the biological footprint of being inhibited or uninhibited was still there. The adults who had been characterized as inhibited as children had more activation in the amygdala to unfamiliar faces than the adults who had been classified as uninhibited. These findings show that some of the basic brain properties relating to temperament are preserved from infancy into early adulthood.

Ongoing studies have explored genetic and environmental factors in personality disorders. Large twin studies indicate that paranoid, schizoid, and schizotypal personality disorders are all moderately heritable (Kendler et al., 2007b, 2008). In a large multivariate twin study, heritability estimates across personality disorders ranged from the lower end (20.5% schizotypal and 23.4% paranoid) to the most heritable (borderline 37.1%, avoidant 37.3%, and antisocial 40.9%).

THE ROLE OF TRAUMATIC EVENTS Although one might consider traumatic events as transient environmental factors (and indeed they are), we now know that especially during critical developmental windows, they can have profound and long-term effects on brain biology (Goodman et al., 2004). People with some personality disorders report increased rates of childhood emotional abuse, physical abuse, and neglect (Battle et al., 2004; Bierer et al., 2003). In addition, childhood history of physical or sexual abuse has been associated with personality disorders (Herman et al., 1989; Ogata et al., 1990; Zanarini et al., 1989). These associations provide an important clue to the biological mechanisms underlying the development of personality disorders. Early maltreatment is associated with problems in basic attachment. Attachment is one of the processes that provides the foundation for our ability later in life to relate to others interpersonally. Poor attachment is believed to interfere with brain structures that underlie development of the ability to think about the mental states of others, called *mentalization* (Fonagy et al., 1991). Early trauma and the subsequent disruption in attachment may lead to neurodevelopmental deficits in interpersonal functioning and create a pathway to the development of severe personality disturbance.

Poor attachment may play a role in the etiology of personality disorders, whereas good attachment may be a protective buffer.

Wong Sze Fei/Fotolia

A person's neurobiological responses to threat stimuli may be changed after traumatic events, including childhood traumatic experiences. Alterations in arousal, fear conditioning, and emotional regulation have been observed in people who have a history of exposure to traumatic events (Arnsten, 1998; Bremner, 2007; Bremner et al., 1999; Mayes, 2000; Shin et al., 2005). These shifts in brain functioning are adaptive in the context of real danger, which requires a rapid automatic response to ensure survival. However, early trauma may permanently impair the biology of arousal regulation and fear conditioning, causing an inappropriate reaction even when danger is not imminent. Thus, trauma might lead to "overperceiving" and "overresponding" to threats. Early childhood trauma may have a permanent effect on brain development, which can set the stage for the emergence of maladaptive personality traits. Because many personality disorders represent maladaptive and, in many cases, exaggerated responses to seemingly innocuous interpersonal events, these fundamental neurobiological disturbances may well underlie the erratic and dysregulated responses to the world commonly seen in people with personality disorders.

BRAIN STRUCTURE AND FUNCTIONING STUDIES Modern assessment tools such as fMRI and PET scans enable us to examine the neurobiology of some personality disorders. Behaviourally, people with schizotypal personality disorder show the same psychotic-like cognitive and perceptual symptoms and cognitive disorganization as people with schizophrenia. Biologically, these two groups show both similarities and differences. Structurally, both schizotypal and schizophrenic individuals show abnormalities in *temporal lobe* volume (Siever et al., 2002), but the decrease in brain volume seen in the *frontal lobe* of people with schizophrenia is not found in people with schizotypal personality disorder. Functionally, there are also subtle biological differences. Whereas both groups show decreased brain activity in the frontal cortex, only people with schizotypal personality disorder appear to be able to activate other regions of their brain as a way to compensate for this deficit (Siever et al., 2002).

With Cluster B disorders, studies examining people with borderline and antisocial personality disorders have focused on brain regions that control rage, fear, and impulsive automatic reactions (the prominent features of the disorders). It appears that the hippocampus and amygdala may be as much as 16% smaller in people with borderline personality disorder than in people with no personality disorder. Traumatic experiences, which are common in people with borderline personality disorder, may create these neuroanatomical changes (Driessen et al., 2000). Neurobiological theories of antisocial personality disorder focus on individual differences in arousal or detection. One theory suggests that people at risk for antisocial personality disorder are in a chronic state of underarousal and that their behaviour represents misguided attempts to seek stimulation (Quay, 1965). Another theory focuses on the apparent fearlessness of people with antisocial personality disorder and hypothesizes that they have a higher fear detection threshold than other people (Lykken, 1982). This difference in detection of fear allows them to enter calmly into situations that others would find overwhelmingly fear inducing.

Psychological and Sociocultural Perspectives

11.5 Discuss psychodynamic and cognitive-behavioural theories of personality disorders.

An entire branch of psychology (personality psychology) deals with the psychological processes underlying healthy and maladaptive personality traits. For decades, various psychological theories dominated our understanding of their etiology. The two most prominent theories, which we review here, are the psychodynamic and the cognitive-behavioural perspectives.

PSYCHODYNAMIC INTERPRETATIONS Most psychodynamic theories focus on early parental interactions that shape behavioural traits that become personality disorders. Theories about the origins of borderline personality disorder, for example, associate a lack of parental acceptance to damaged self-esteem and fears of rejection (Gunderson, 1984). Indeed, this theory is generally consistent with the high rates of abuse and neglect reported by people with borderline personality disorders (Herman et al., 1989; Ogata et al., 1990). According to these theories, people tend to internalize negative parental attitudes, leaving them vulnerable to fears of abandonment and to self-hatred. In addition, they tend to treat themselves as they were treated by their parents. These attitudes prevent the development of mature, consistent, and positive perceptions of themselves and others. They also lead to a severe inability to regulate mood when faced with disappointment, and difficulty in taking another's point of view.

The psychiatrist Otto Kernberg (1975) proposed a continuum of psychopathology from persistent, severe psychosis to severe personality disorders through neurotic to healthy functioning. Kernberg's work focused primarily on the development of borderline personality disorder, but also encompassed other personality disorders. For example, people with narcissistic personality disorder construct a largely inflated view of themselves in order to maintain their self-esteem. On the outside, these individuals appear grandiose, but inside they are often very sensitive to even very minor attacks on the self. They create this enlarged perception of themselves in order to match the grandiose perception of their ideal in their own mind's eye. When events happen that make them feel as if they are not meeting this ideal, they experience shame, sadness, and a sense of failure. Thus, grandiosity protects against these negative emotions.

COGNITIVE-BEHAVIOURAL THEORY Cognitive-behavioural theory proposes that learning is at the basis of personality, which is also substantially moulded by an individual's unique environment. From a cognitive perspective, personality evolves from an interaction between a person's environment and the way he or she processes information. For example, imagine two adolescents—one is fairly outgoing and likes to seek out new experiences, and the other is shy, anxious, and fearful of new experiences. Both are flying as unaccompanied minors when their plane hits turbulence and drops 3050 metres (about 10 000 feet). The first teen treats the experience like a rollercoaster ride and basically says, "Wow, wild ride." The second shakes and cries, thinks he is going to die, and vows never to step into an airplane again. Two temperamentally different boys processed the same environmental event very differently. Experiences like this one—where our temperament and the environment intersect—contribute to the development of our personality.

Cognitive-behavioural theory and therapy have enriched our understanding of personality disorders, contributing concepts such as goals, skills, self-regulation, and schemas, or core beliefs (such as "I am an unlovable person") (Mischel & Shoda, 1995). Considerable focus on how people learn to regulate moods (Linehan et al., 1993) and their development of core beliefs about themselves and their worlds (Beck et al., 2003) has transformed the theory into cognitive-behavioural treatments for personality disorders (see "Treatment of Personality Disorders").

SOCIOCULTURAL THEORIES Sociocultural theories of personality go beyond the study of the individual to include a broader contextual view of personality development, including culture as a critical element in shaping personality (Miller, 1997). Fundamental cultural differences can deeply influence the concept of personality. For example, consider the differences in the concept of "self" in Japanese and Western cultures. In Japanese culture, *self* includes both the personal self and that of the surrounding cultural

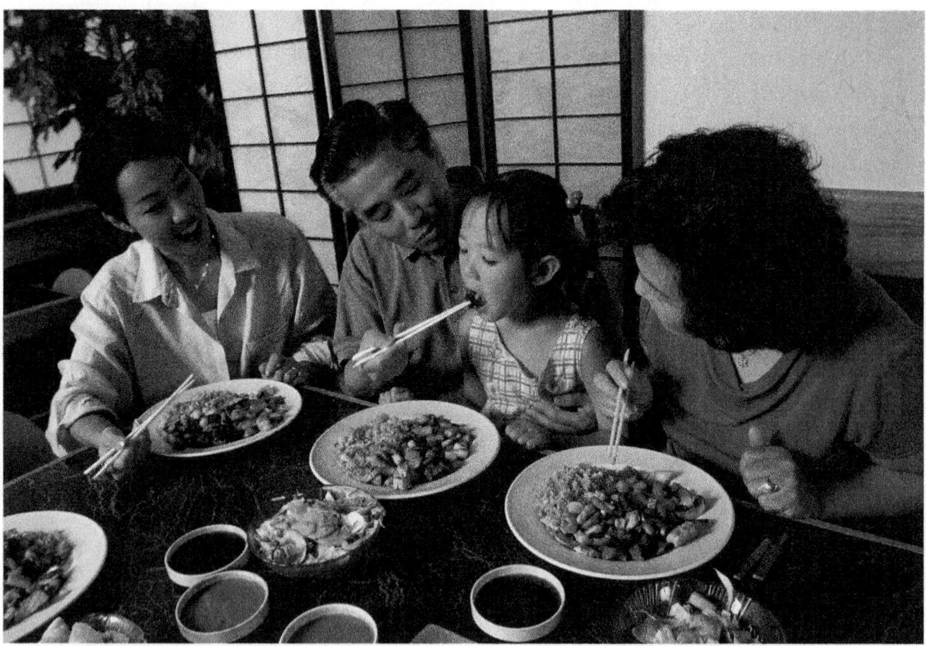

Across cultures, different ideas of basic human concepts such as "self" may lead to very different conceptualizations and treatments of personality disorders. In Japan, the *self* is a broader concept than the individual *self* in Western countries such as Canada.

(top): Guy Cali/Corbis/Glow Images; **(bottom):** SuperStock

community; in dominant Western culture, the *self* is considered independent and not contingent upon others (Markus & Kitayama, 1991). Clearly, this core conceptual difference could influence perceptions of what constitutes abnormal behaviour.

Sociocultural factors concerning the self may play an especially important role in narcissistic personality disorder. According to McGill University psychiatrist Joel Paris, evidence suggests that in Western cultures there has been an increase in narcissism over the past few decades (Paris, 2014). Paris argues that this may be due, at least in part, to modern cultural changes, such as the increasingly greater cultural focus on fame and celebrity. The rise of social media such as Facebook, with its emphasis on the self—and the "selfie"—may be contributing to the apparent increase in narcissism.

Another factor that influences cross-cultural studies of personality is language. Classic Western personality measures may not capture cultural nuances of expression and language, such as the Japanese language term *amae*, meaning the need for dependency (Doi, 1973) or the Hindu language term *anasakti*, meaning nonattachment, a freedom from dependency that is associated with greater peace and mental health (Pande & Naidu, 1992). The similarities in personality disorders that we observe across cultures may simply reflect the imposition of Western language on non-Western cultures. Therefore, although the dimensional aspects of personality appear consistent across cultures, there are also cultural differences that will enrich our understanding of personality disorders (Poortinga & Van Hemert, 2001).

CONCEPT check

- *Temperament* refers to biological features of personality that are present at birth. The interaction between temperament and environmental experience leads to the development of personality.
- Personality traits and personality disorders run in families and have been shown to be moderately heritable.
- Traumatic events, especially during critical periods of development, can have profound and long-term effects on brain biology that influence personality development.
- Psychodynamic theories explored the impact of early interactions with parents on later personality organization.
- Cognitive-behavioural theory holds that personality emerges from learning and an individual's unique environment. The way that the individual processes and interprets information about the self and the world is central to the development of personality.

critical thinking question Imagine a scenario in which two children with very different personalities (one highly neurotic and one highly extraverted) experience a traumatic event (a drive-by shooting in which a stranger is killed). How might their responses differ?

Treatment of Personality Disorders

11.6 Discuss treatment approaches to personality disorders.

Treating long-standing patterns of behaviour is inherently different from treating acute disorders. No magic pill exists to change a person's personality style. Both patient and therapist must make subtle distinctions between healthy and maladaptive behaviour patterns. The patient must understand the perspective of other people whom their disorder affects adversely. In addition, because these behaviour patterns are long standing, one cannot expect rapid improvement—particularly if they reach back to early childhood and involve changes in brain functioning. Other significant challenges include just getting patients with personality disorders into treatment. Often the people around them are more interested in getting them treatment than the patients are themselves. Finally, the treatment can be especially complicated when people have more than one personality disorder and have an acute illness such as major depressive disorder, bipolar disorder, bulimia nervosa, or substance abuse. Such complications can pose treatment challenges for the most dedicated clinician. Patience, consistency, and persistence are valuable therapist characteristics that can facilitate treatment of personality disorders.

Only recently have we witnessed a surge of randomized controlled trials investigating the treatment of personality disorders. Although the overall amount of research remains small, recent studies have explored the efficacy of dynamic therapy and cognitive-behavioural therapy, or their variants. The quality of the research varies because some studies focus on specific personality disorders, others on the personality disorder clusters, and still others on personality disorders in general. This makes the results of the studies difficult to interpret.

Most studies on specific personality disorders have focused on borderline or antisocial personality disorder. Although avoidant personality disorder and Cluster C disorders have received some research attention, there is a dearth of data on the treatment of Cluster A disorders. With this background in mind, we describe various treatments for personality disorders, their empirical basis, and the limitations of the available research. Given the broad and heterogeneous nature of this area, we present treatment approaches and data related to personality disorders generally and borderline personality disorder specifically.

Despite a limited number of treatment studies, recent data support the importance of psychotherapy in the treatment of personality disorders. While pharmacotherapy may help manage associated symptoms such as anxiety or depression, psychosocial treatments and excellent communication among all those delivering care are required for optimal management of personality disorders.

Early treatments for personality disorders were rooted in dynamic psychotherapy and adapted psychoanalytic techniques in long-term therapeutic approaches. Current treatment approaches differ somewhat according to the disorder and often include components to address concurrent comorbid psychological disorders.

Treatment for Cluster A disorders can be challenging. When their core problem is distrust, it can be particularly difficult for people with paranoid personality disorder to trust the motives of a therapist. People with schizoid personality disorders have little desire for social interaction, so it is difficult to convince them that social interactions are often necessary and positively reinforcing (Beck et al., 2003). People with schizotypal personality disorder often benefit from cognitive-behaviour therapy that helps them develop adaptive thoughts and eliminate or modify odd or eccentric cognitions (Beck et al., 2003).

A form of cognitive-behaviour therapy focuses on the challenges inherent in treating people with the rapidly fluctuating behaviours of borderline personality disorder. This approach, *dialectical behaviour therapy* (DBT), has considerable empirical support (Binks et al., 2006; Linehan et al., 2006). DBT is based on a model that focuses on the intersection of biological and environmental causes. DBT hypothesizes that the fundamental biological problem is in the emotion regulation system and may arise from genetics, intrauterine factors, traumatic early events, or some combination of these factors. The environmental component is any set of circumstances that punish, traumatize, or neglect this emotional vulnerability. Borderline personality disorder emerges from ongoing transactions between the individual and the environment, with the individual becoming increasingly unable to regulate emotions and the environment becoming progressively more invalidating (Linehan et al., 2006). The emotional dysregulation in individuals with borderline personality disorder results from emotional vulnerability combined with deficits in the skills needed to regulate emotions. Intriguingly, at the age of 68, Dr. Linehan disclosed that as a youth she was hospitalized for suicidality, self-harm, and emotion dysregulation. At that time she perplexed the mental health system and was inaccurately diagnosed with schizophrenia. In an interview with the *New York Times*, she acknowledged that the treatment she developed, DBT, emerged from her own personal experience and provides the help she needed for so many years and never received.

DBT emphasizes discussion and negotiation between therapist and patient, with a balance between the rational and the emotional and between acceptance and change. The patient and therapist establish a hierarchy of treatment goals, giving the highest priority to eliminating self-harm behaviours. DBT has many principles, but all patients receive skills training in five areas: mindfulness (to improve control of attention and the mind), interpersonal skills and conflict management, emotional regulation, distress tolerance, and self-management. These approaches help the patient to calm down what can feel like a chaotic internal state, to pay attention to emotionally driven behaviour, and to develop skills to manage feelings and impulses more effectively. Medications can also be used to assist with regulating the biological systems.

When compared with treatment as usual (what we call "talk therapy"), DBT and partial hospitalization (a day treatment program) produce superior treatment results (Brazier et al., 2006). Moreover, DBT may be more cost-effective than traditional therapy for borderline personality disorder. Other treatment strategies that are sometimes efficacious for borderline personality disorder include inpatient therapy (Dolan et al., 1997) and step-down programs. These are characterized by short-term inpatient treatment followed by longer-term outpatient and community treatment (Chiesa et al., 2004, 2006).

Dialectical behaviour therapy blends Zen practice with cognitive-behaviour therapy and teaches concepts such as "mindfulness," or being aware of one's experiences and emotional state. Here Dr. Marsha Linehan (the developer of DBT) and her students Trevor Schraufnagel and Andrada Neacsiu illustrate the mindfulness practice of therapists at the start of DBT team meetings.

Dr. Marsha Linehan

Medications including antidepressants, mood stabilizers (drugs that even out the highs and lows seen in mood disorders), and antipsychotics are often prescribed for borderline personality disorder. These drugs target sudden mood swings, impulsivity, and aggression. Although currently few data exist, initial research indicates that the drugs might be helpful (Bellino et al., 2008). The atypical antipsychotics (see Chapter 10) may be helpful for patients with borderline personality disorder who have psychotic-like, impulsive, or suicidal symptoms (Grootens & Verkes, 2005).

It is critical to understand that remission from borderline personality disorder does occur. To illustrate, long-term (15–27 year) studies by Joel Paris and colleagues at McGill University found that people with borderline personality disorder tend to improve over time, to be point that most of them no longer meet full diagnostic criteria for the disorder by the time they reach 40 or 50 years of age (Paris, 2002; Paris et al., 1987; Paris & Zweig-Frank, 2001). In a seven year follow-up study of patients with borderline personality disorder, University of Toronto psychiatrist Paul Links and colleagues found that patients were more likely to improve over time if they did not have another coexisting personality disorder (Links et al., 1998). Paris (2002) proposes that mechanisms behind remission could include maturation and learning to better cope with problems.

CONCEPT check

- Personality disorders are difficult to treat. People who suffer from personality disorders often do not see the effect of their behaviour on others. Treatment is often slow because the maladaptive behaviours have existed for decades. Finally, people with personality disorders often have other psychological disorders as well, complicating treatment.
- Although medications may help manage associated symptoms such as anxiety or depression, psychotherapeutic interventions are the treatment of choice for personality disorders.
- Dialectical behaviour therapy that focuses on the central role of emotion regulation has been shown to be efficacious in the treatment of borderline personality disorder.
- Therapeutic communities that include individual or group psychotherapy are also efficacious in the treatment of personality disorders.

critical thinking question If a patient is suffering from alcohol dependence and a personality disorder, which problem might you consider treating first, and why?

real SCIENCE real LIFE

Robin—Life Transitions and Borderline Personality Disorder

THE PATIENT

Robin was a senior in high school when she began to worry her parents and friends. Her family had moved to a new province in the summer before her senior year. In her previous school, she had been relatively popular, very involved with acting and student government, and, according to her mother, a well-behaved but sensitive and moody girl. She desperately did not want to move. She had a circle of friends and was worried that the new high school would be filled with cliques and she would have trouble making friends.

THE PROBLEM

Soon after they moved, there was a dramatic transformation in Robin. She dyed her hair black, started wearing black eye makeup and black clothing, and rarely spoke at home. She would come home from school, throw her books down, and hide out in her room. She avoided meals with the family and always seemed to be brooding. Whenever anyone showed concern for her well-being, she returned their concern with anger and pushed them away. On the night of her referral, she came running into her mother's bedroom screaming that she was afraid she was going to die. Blood poured from her right arm. Her mother bandaged her up to stop the bleeding and took her directly to the emergency room. There she discovered that this wasn't the first time Robin had cut herself. Under her long black sleeves and skirt, her arms and thighs were covered with cuts. That night she had just gone too deep and was scared.

THE TREATMENT

Robin was admitted to the inpatient unit for evaluation. The psychiatrist diagnosed her with major depression and borderline personality traits and recommended medication and psychotherapy. She also cautioned Robin about drinking and using drugs while taking the medication and warned her of the potential negative interactions. She referred Robin to a therapist who specialized in dialectical behaviour therapy (DBT).

Robin desperately did not want to go into therapy and on the first day adopted a stance that the therapist called "I dare you to care about me," clearly intending to test all the limits. The therapist was no stranger to this personality style and recognized how chaotic and nonconstant the world must seem from Robin's eyes. She knew the key was consistency and firm compassion.

(continued)

As therapy progressed, there were numerous ups and downs. Two trips to the emergency room for cutting returned the focus to the self-destructive behaviours. Gradually, Robin was able to apply the emotion regulation skills she had learned in group at the times when cutting seemed like the only option. She was able to begin to focus on thoughts or behaviours that got in the way of developing a reasonable quality of life, behavioural skills, and, finally, self-validation and self-respect.

All of the "rules" frustrated Robin at first, but after she became accustomed to this type of therapy, she understood that the rules existed because if she were injured or dead, or doing things to interfere with her therapy, there was little point in working on the rest. Moreover, she really wanted to work on other issues, which provided the motivation for her to work on "first things first." After many advances and steps backward over the course of a year and a half of therapy, Robin began to accept herself for who she was while working on changing some of her unhealthy ways of dealing with problems by putting her DBT skills to use.

They established a therapeutic contract that centred around honesty. The DBT approach used a broad array of cognitive and behavioural strategies to help Robin learn to accept herself just as she was within the context of trying to teach her how to change, starting with her self-harming cutting behaviour. The therapist took a firm problem-solving stance, but as is typical with DBT, she recognized that it would be too much to try to get all the skills training accomplished in one individual session per week. She therefore contracted for additional weekly group therapy. The group focused on the development of skills in emotion regulation, distress tolerance, interpersonal effectiveness, self-management, and core mindfulness (a way of learning how best to observe, describe, and participate in the world around you). As she learned these skills in group, Robin's individual therapy could focus on ways to best integrate these skills into daily life. Though reluctant at first to attend a group with "a bunch of 'emos,'" Robin signed a contract with her therapist promising to attend. Robin's therapist agreed to continue working with her in individual therapy only if Robin would also attend weekly groups for the following year, as well as follow some of the basic rules of therapy. After a roller-coaster of emotions about what she was undertaking, Robin signed the contract. The therapist told her that the therapy was very structured and specific in terms of what was considered most important to talk about. If Robin was feeling suicidal or performing any life-threatening or self-damaging behaviours, such as cutting, her therapist wouldn't allow her to address anything else.

The next important issue was focusing on anything that got in the way of therapy. For example, about six months into therapy, Robin brought in a gift for her therapist. It was a button that read, "Your caring about me is starting to piss me off." Sometimes it was really hard for Robin to accept the compassionate side of her therapist's stance. Deep down, she feared she wasn't worth being cared about. With the message inherent in the gesture, the focus of the therapy shifted directly to targeting Robin's feelings about the therapist and her ability to accept being cared for.

THE TREATMENT OUTCOME

Robin graduated from high school and was accepted at the local university. No longer on her parents' insurance, she transferred her care to the campus health services, where she kept up with both individual and group therapy. The therapist occasionally wondered how she fared in the transition to university and after leaving the group. Several years later, an email arrived in the therapist's inbox announcing her university graduation and her plans to become a high school counsellor.

summary

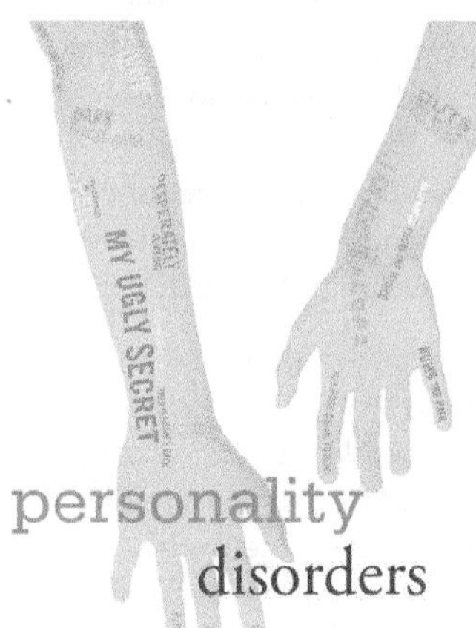

11.1 Discuss how personality disorders differ from other disorders discussed in this text.
Differentiating between a personality trait and a personality disorder is critical. A personality disorder is an enduring pattern of inner experience and behaviour that deviates from the norm; is pervasive, persistent, and pathological; has an onset in adolescence or early adulthood; is stable across time; and leads to distress or impairment.

11.2 Describe the three clusters of personality disorders and the disorders within each cluster.
The personality disorders are grouped into three clusters based on core features: Cluster A, "odd or eccentric," includes paranoid, schizoid, and schizotypal personality disorders; Cluster B, "dramatic, emotional, or erratic," includes antisocial, narcissistic, borderline, and histrionic personality disorders; and Cluster C, "anxious or fearful," includes avoidant, dependent, and obsessive-compulsive personality disorders. Although this is the dominant model, many prefer a more dimensional approach to capturing the essence of personality.

11.3 Appreciate the complex nature of personality disorders.
Personality disorders are complex phenomena with roots in childhood and adolescence. They

are marked by individual experiences that deviate from normative experiences and behaviours that are perceived by others as deviant. Given the nature of personality disorders, they often lead to difficulties with interpersonal functioning.

11.4 Understand the role biology may play in the origin of personality pathology.

Personality traits and disorders are heritable. Some personality disorders may be related to early trauma, which may lead to structural changes in the brain associated with traits such as hypervigilance and impulsivity.

11.5 Discuss psychodynamic and cognitive-behavioural theories of personality disorders.

Psychological theories of personality disorders include the psychodynamic, focusing on the impact of early relationships with the parents on later personality organization, and cognitive-behavioural, focusing on the emergence of personality from learning and the environment and the way in which the individual processes and interprets information about the self and the world.

11.6 Discuss treatment approaches to personality disorders.

Treatment for personality disorders can be particularly challenging because it must address long-standing patterns of behaviour, subtle distinctions between healthy and maladaptive behaviour patterns, and the perspective of other people whom the disorder affects adversely. In general, psychotherapeutic approaches are recommended; medication can be included to manage comorbid disorders or problems.

key terms

avoidant personality disorder 411
antisocial personality disorder 402
borderline personality disorder 408
Cluster A 396
Cluster B 396
Cluster C 396
dependent personality disorder 411
histrionic personality disorder 409
narcissistic personality disorder 407
obsessive-compulsive personality disorder 414
paranoid personality disorder 398
personality disorder 396
schizoid personality disorder 401
schizotypal personality disorder 401
temperament 420

TEST yourself

1. A personality trait is defined as a behaviour pattern that is
   a. inflexible regardless of context within a situation
   b. consistent across situations
   c. emotionally expressive over time within a situation
   d. maladaptive across situations

2. A personality trait may become a personality disorder when
   a. its symptoms can be quantified
   b. it becomes a dramatic, acute illness
   c. it becomes inflexible and maladaptive
   d. it does not reflect a person's typical behaviour

3. According to the DSM-5, personality disorders are usually apparent in
   a. periods of high stress
   b. adolescence or early adulthood
   c. infancy or early childhood
   d. major developmental transitions

4. Cluster A personality disorders are characterized by which of the following?
   a. odd, quirky, or eccentric behaviours
   b. social anxiety, obsessionality, and fear of independence
   c. emotional and erratic behaviours, and the absence of remorse
   d. all of the above

5. Which of the following signs or symptoms differentiate paranoid personality disorder from paranoid schizophrenia?
   a. believing that others intend harm or deception
   b. delusional thinking
   c. reading negative meanings into benign comments
   d. doubting the loyalty or trustworthiness of others

6. Schizoid personality disorder is characterized by which of the following?
   a. social detachment and a general lack of emotionality
   b. clinging to family members
   c. overvaluing the opinions of others
   d. unpredictable emotional lability

7. A characteristic that differentiates schizotypal personality disorder from paranoid or schizoid personality disorder is
   a. social detachment
   b. suspiciousness of others

c. questioning the loyalty of friends
d. eccentric appearance and behaviour as well as magical thinking

8. Mr. C. opened up a financial services company in a small, close-knit retirement community. He promised large returns and little risk using his special investment system. He convinced many retirees to invest their entire savings. After several months, he suddenly disappeared with all of the firm's assets. After an investigation, it was revealed that Mr. C. had done this many times in the past. Mr. C. might have
   a. narcissistic personality disorder
   b. borderline personality disorder
   c. antisocial personality disorder
   d. histrionic personality disorder

9. Persons diagnosed with narcissistic personality disorder need constant praise because
   a. it helps them cope with their fragile self-esteem
   b. they need to have social interaction reinforced or they withdraw
   c. without praise, they lose motivation
   d. praise keeps them from being self-absorbed

10. What feeling is characteristic of persons with borderline personality disorder?
   a. an overinflated sense of self-worth
   b. devaluation of others
   c. lack of empathy for others
   d. fear of abandonment

11. Dawn is a theatre major in university. Her counsellor recently diagnosed her with histrionic personality disorder. What characteristics of this diagnosis make this major a relatively good choice for her?
   a. her boundless energy to devote to her roles and her need for little sleep
   b. her ability to form close relationships with other cast members
   c. her demonstrative and attention-seeking style
   d. her attention to detail and skill at easily memorizing scripts

12. Cluster C personality disorders are characterized by which of the following?
   a. excessive guilt and remorse
   b. lack of emotional expressiveness
   c. distorted thinking and cognition
   d. anxiety and social withdrawal

13. Avoidant personality disorder can be easily confused with which other psychological disorder?
   a. depression
   b. generalized anxiety disorder
   c. generalized social phobia
   d. Alzheimer's disease

14. Although Gisele's boyfriend is physically abusive of her, she worries that he will leave her. This fear leads her to be very submissive to him. She may be suffering from
   a. borderline personality disorder
   b. histrionic personality disorder
   c. narcissistic personality disorder
   d. dependent personality disorder

15. A person with obsessive-compulsive personality disorder may exhibit
   a. mental and interpersonal overcontrol
   b. unrealistic perfectionism
   c. inability to discard things of no use
   d. all of the above

16. Which childhood behaviours are strongly associated with the development of antisocial personality disorder?
   a. identity formation problems and dependency
   b. separation anxiety and hypersensitivity
   c. histrionics and testing the limits
   d. risky sexual behaviour and harming animals

17. Which infant/toddler behaviour is strongly associated with inhibited temperament?
   a. withdrawal from unfamiliar stimuli
   b. intense interest in novel sounds and sights
   c. attention to faces resembling the mother's
   d. attention to sounds resembling human speech

18. Personality disorders may develop as the result of
   a. genetic predisposition
   b. physical and/or sexual abuse
   c. disruption in the attachment phase of development
   d. all of the above

19. To successfully treat patients with personality disorders, therapists need
   a. high intelligence and problem-solving ability
   b. excellent diagnostic skills
   c. patience, consistency, persistence, and dedication
   d. the ability to recognize unconscious conflicts in others

20. The treatment that emphasizes discussion and negotiation between the therapist and patient, balancing the rational and the emotional, and balancing acceptance and change is called
   a. dynamic psychotherapy
   b. cognitive-behaviour therapy
   c. psychoanalytic therapy
   d. dialectical behaviour therapy

Answers:
1 b, 2 c, 3 b, 4 a, 5 b, 6 a, 7 d, 8 c, 9 a, 10 d, 11 c, 12 d, 13 b, 14 d, 15 d, 16 d, 17 a, 18 d, 19 c, 20 d.

chapter 12

neurodevelopmental, disruptive, conduct, and elimination disorders

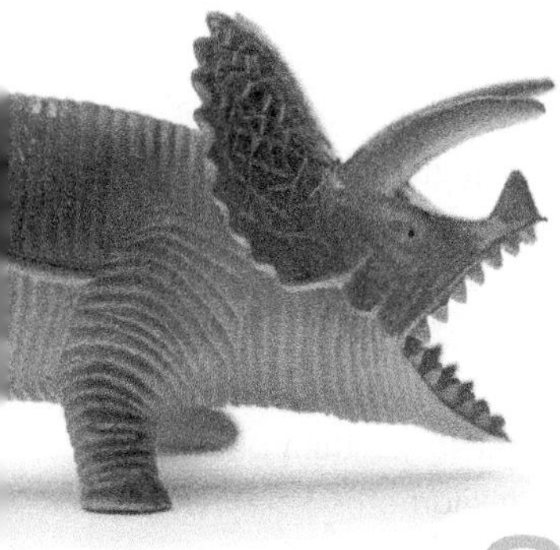

(top left): ballyscanlon/Photodisc/Getty Images; **(middle left):** hocus-focus/Getty Images; sudhirvatsa/Getty Images; **(middle left):** Thomas Northcut/Photodisc/Getty Images; **(bottom centre):** C Squared Studios/Stockbyte/Getty Images; **(bottom right):** 2/Thomas Northcut/Ocean/Corbis

neurodevelopmental, disruptive, conduct, and elimination disorders

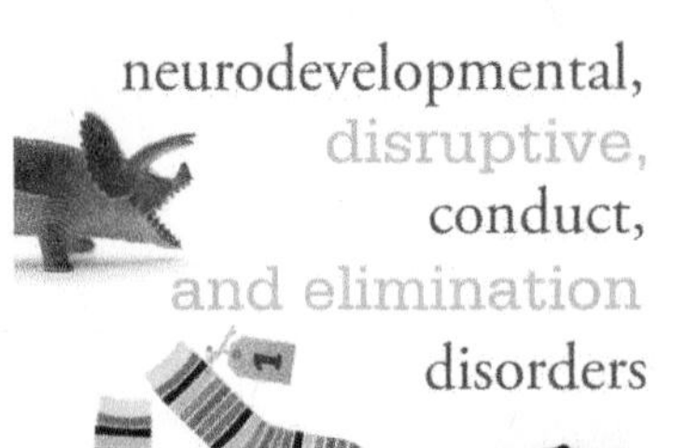

learning objectives

After reading this chapter, you should be able to:

12.1
Describe how basic physical, cognitive, and emotional development during childhood and adolescence affect the expression of psychological disorders.

12.2
Identify psychological disorders that emerge primarily during childhood and adolescence.

12.3
Understand etiological factors that contribute to the development of disorders during childhood and adolescence.

12.4
Identify positive and negative aspects of pharmacological treatments.

12.5
Identify psychosocial treatments for the disorders that emerge during childhood and adolescence.

12.6
Describe the unique role of parents in the treatment of children and adolescents.

Jeremy is 12 years old and in grade 7. He is doing well academically but has significant difficulty with social relationships. He is unaware of social conventions and does not make eye contact with other people. He speaks loudly, often asks inappropriate questions, and makes inappropriate and often irrelevant statements or noises. When conversing, Jeremy engages in lengthy monologues on topics that interest him (dinosaurs, plumbing, and cars) and fails to pick up on others' lack of interest. He has no friends, and peers often ridicule and reject him. He sometimes behaves in ways that are self-injurious, pulling his hair, picking his skin, and hitting himself on the head.

Jeremy first displayed unusual behaviours at 18 months of age. He licked the pavement, chewed on rocks, and put strange things in his mouth. He did not like to be hugged and pushed his parents away if they attempted any physical contact. At age 2, he did not yet speak. He simply grunted or led his mother by the hand to communicate. He began speech therapy shortly thereafter, and by age 3 was talking in complete sentences. As a young child, Jeremy lined up toy cars. He never played with the entire car but would spin the wheels over and over. He did not play with other children but stood alone watching them. Now, at age 12, Jeremy becomes upset by any change in routine, insisting on dressing in a certain order (e.g., socks, then pants, then shirt). He is also hypersensitive to sound; he can hear a siren kilometres away and covers his ears in crowded noisy places such as shopping malls.

12.1 Describe how basic physical, cognitive, and emotional development during childhood and adolescence affect the expression of psychological disorders.

Throughout this book, we have used a developmental perspective to understand abnormal behaviour, and this perspective informs our understanding of psychological disorders in two ways. First, it is important to understand that childhood and adolescence are stages of life characterized by critical physical, cognitive, and emotional development. With respect to physical development, infants first acquire the ability to raise their head, then roll over, sit up, crawl, and finally walk. Physical maturation also includes brain development. The human brain triples in weight during a child's first two years, reaching 90% of its adult weight by the time the child is 5 years of age. Along with brain size, *cognitive abilities* increase throughout infancy and childhood. Children learn to think and solve problems, and their memory improves. During adolescence, they develop the cognitive abilities to understand and use abstract concepts, such as justice and beauty. Adolescents can engage in hypothetical thinking, imagining, for example, the worst thing that could happen to them. Adolescents also begin to use *metacognition*: They can think about thinking, for example, exploring the best way to solve a problem.

Along with physical and cognitive maturity, children also develop *emotionally*. Early in elementary school, children understand basic emotions (happy, sad, mad, scared), but they often attribute facial expression to an external event (e.g., "she is smiling because she is holding a puppy") rather than to an internal emotional state (e.g., "she is smiling because she is happy"). With increasing maturity, adolescents recognize more subtle emotions, such as disgust, worry, and surprise, and associate facial expressions with internal emotional states.

How does understanding this path of human development help us understand psychological disorders in childhood? Quite simply, until children have achieved basic physical, cognitive, and emotional developmental milestones, psychological disorders may express themselves differently in childhood than they do in adulthood. For example, young children cannot *worry* about future events until they have the ability to *think* about future events. Because of these developmental differences, mental health professionals acknowledge that although many psychological disorders may have roots in childhood, they are not often fully manifested until late adolescence or even adulthood.

Using this same developmental perspective, we find that other psychological disorders are more common in children than adults. They are present at birth or emerge during childhood and present significant challenges for those who suffer from them. Some of these disorders, such as intellectual disability or autism, may continue to exist throughout adulthood. In other instances, physical, cognitive, or emotional maturation may function to change the symptoms, lessen their impact, or even make them disappear. This often happens with disorders of elimination, for example. Many different disorders emerge during childhood and adolescence. Some, such as learning disorders, affect specific aspects of functioning such as academic achievement. We begin this chapter by discussing intellectual disability, a common disorder that affects many different aspects of functioning.

Intellectual Disability (Intellectual Developmental Disorder)

12.2 Identify psychological disorders that emerge primarily during childhood and adolescence.

People have different abilities—whether it is the ability to do math problems, to play an instrument, or to read a map. Each person has particular strengths and limitations, which can be affected by a variety of environmental factors. For example, the amount of sleep children get can affect their success in school, and children whose families can afford to pay for tutoring or private lessons may improve a particular skill. Even the extent to which that skill is valued by one's culture can influence how children perform.

Most people understand intellectual disability to mean below-average intellectual functioning (see "DSM-5: Intellectual Disability"). When psychologists measure intelligence, they use a standardized, individualized test. Each person's score is calculated and converted to a standardized scale for which the mean score is 100 and the standard deviation is 15. In the past, a person's test score was called an intelligence quotient (IQ). When psychologists talk about average intelligence, they are referring to the range of intelligence test scores that falls 1 standard deviation above or below the mean score of 100. Therefore, people with IQ scores between 85 and 115 are considered to have average intelligence (as measured by that particular test). In DSM-5, a person's IQ score is not part of the diagnostic criteria, and thus cannot be used alone to determine that a person meets criteria for intellectual disability. Rather, the IQ score or a score from a standardized test of intellectual functioning is used as information to help in estimating the extent of impairment for this diagnosis. (See Chapter 3 for more on intelligence testing.)

criteria for Intellectual Disability (Intellectual Developmental Disorder) DSM-5

Intellectual disability (intellectual developmental disorder) is a disorder with onset during the developmental period that includes both intellectual and adaptive functioning deficits in conceptual, social, and practical domains. The following three criteria must be met:

A. Deficits in intellectual functions, such as reasoning, problem solving, planning, abstract thinking, judgment, academic learning, and learning from experience, confirmed by both clinical assessment and individualized, standardized intelligence testing.

B. Deficits in adaptive functioning that result in failure to meet developmental and sociocultural standards for personal independence and social responsibility. Without ongoing support, the adaptive deficits limit functioning in one or more activities of daily life, such as communication, social participation, and independent living, across multiple environments, such as home, school, work, and community.

C. Onset of intellectual and adaptive deficits during the developmental period.

The new criteria for the diagnosis of **intellectual disability** reflects the approach that no single test of cognitive functioning should be used to determine the diagnosis. Instead, intellectual disability is described as a disorder that includes both intellectual deficits and adaptive functioning deficits in three distinct domains (APA, 2013). Clinicians evaluate potential deficits in three distinct areas/domains, which reflect how well the individual copes with everyday tasks. These three domains are conceptual (language, reading, writing, math, reasoning, knowledge, and memory), social (empathy, social judgment, interpersonal communication, and friendship skills), and practical (personal care, job responsibilities, money management, recreation, and organization skills). The labels that are used to specify the extent of the deficits in intellect and adaptive functioning are mild, moderate, severe, and profound. The DSM-5 includes descriptions of these different levels of impairment to help the clinician make a decision regarding which of the labels is most appropriate. The onset of intellectual disability is always before the age of 18.

Cathy is a pleasant young woman of 24 years with appropriate skills for everyday social interaction. Although she is able to shower independently, someone has to first check the water temperature because otherwise she would burn herself. Although she understands that hamburgers (her favourite food) have to be cooked before eating, her only attempt to cook independently had set the kitchen on fire. As a young woman, she is interested in men but does not understand basic concepts of sexual reproduction.

Clearly, Cathy has great difficulty functioning independently in the areas of self-care, home living, and health and safety, and she had been this way as a child.

In addition to the core diagnostic features, people with intellectual disability are five times more likely than other people to have any of the other psychological disorders discussed in this book (APA, 2013; Bregman, 1991; Rutter et al., 1976), with the possible exception of schizophrenia or substance abuse disorders (Kerker et al., 2004). Other disorders are also common among people with more severe or profound intellectual disability; 15% to 30% have seizure disorders, 20% to 30% have motor handicaps such as cerebral palsy, and 10% to 20% have visual and auditory impairments (APA, 2013; McLaren & Bryson, 1987).

Functional Impairment

As we have noted, adaptive impairment is necessary for a diagnosis of intellectual disability, but the extent and type of impairment are variable. Adults with mild to moderate intellectual disability function in the community with minimal to moderate support. They might be in a group home in which a small number of adults live together under a counsellor's supervision. Some adults are also able to hold traditional jobs in the community, such as working in a grocery store. An intervention known as *supported employment* provides training and a job coach, which can help people succeed in meaningful jobs (Nord et al., 2013; Wehman et al., 2014). Adults with more significant cognitive impairments may work in a *sheltered workshop*, which is usually a free-standing workplace where workers perform tasks for businesses, such as sending out large mailings, packing items for shipment, or assembling certain products. People who work in sheltered workshops are paid wages and learn job skills such as coming to work on time, completing a task assignment, and taking direction from a supervisor.

In schools, *mainstreaming* could be considered supportive education for children with intellectual disability. *Mainstreaming* means that, whenever possible, children with disabilities are included in regular classroom settings, allowing participation in typical childhood experiences. Whereas children with intellectual disability may need separate classroom instruction for mathematics, they may take the same physical education classes as the general student body. Inclusion in regular classroom settings promotes the acceptance of people with intellectual disability and enhances their self-esteem.

About 1% to 3% of the general population has an intellectual disability (APA, 2013). The majority of people with a diagnosis of intellectual disability—about 85%—fall into the mild disability range (APA, 2013; Szymanski & King, 1999). More boys than girls have a diagnosis of intellectual disability, but these sex differences are primarily among those with mild intellectual disability and may result from differences in children's verbal abilities. At younger ages, girls have superior verbal language skills (Harasty et al., 1997; Joseph, 2000), and this may affect their test performance. No sex differences are found among those with the more severe forms of intellectual disability (Richardson et al., 1986).

Mainstreaming children with Down syndrome into regular classroom settings helps develop acceptance and understanding of individual differences.

Bubbles Photolibrary/Alamy Stock Photo

Etiology

12.3 Understand etiological factors that contribute to the development of disorders during childhood and adolescence.

Throughout this text, we have often introduced discussions of etiology with cautionary statements that the cause of a disorder is unknown. However, there are numerous known causes for intellectual disability. Many are biological, and others are environmental. For about 35% of people with intellectual disability, the cause is one of the disorders identified in Table 12.1. Many genetic disorders may produce intellectual disability (Walker & Johnson, 2006). When a genetic cause exists, the disorder is apparent at birth or shortly thereafter. In other cases, intellectual disability may result from environmental

TABLE 12.1

Frequency of Intellectual Disability by Type of Disorder

Types of Disorders	Frequency
Prenatal genetic disorders including Down syndrome, tuberous sclerosis, phenylketonuria, fragile X syndrome, "familial" mental retardation, Williams syndrome, Prader-Willi syndrome	32%
Malformation of unknown causes including neural tube defects and Cornelia deLange Syndrome	8%
External prenatal causes including human immunodeficiency virus (HIV) infection, fetal alcohol syndrome, prematurity	12%
Perinatal (birth) causes including encephalitis, neonatal asphyxia, hyperbilirubinemia	11%
Postnatal causes including encephalitis, lead poisoning, deprivation, trauma, tumour	8%
Unknown causes	25%

Source: Practice parameters for the assessment and treatment of children, adolescents, and adults with mental retardation and comorbid mental disorders (1999, December). *Journal of the American Academy of Child and Adolescent Psychiatry, 38* (Suppl.), 5S–31S. Copyright © 1999 by the American Academy of Child and Adolescent Psychiatry. Reprinted by permission.

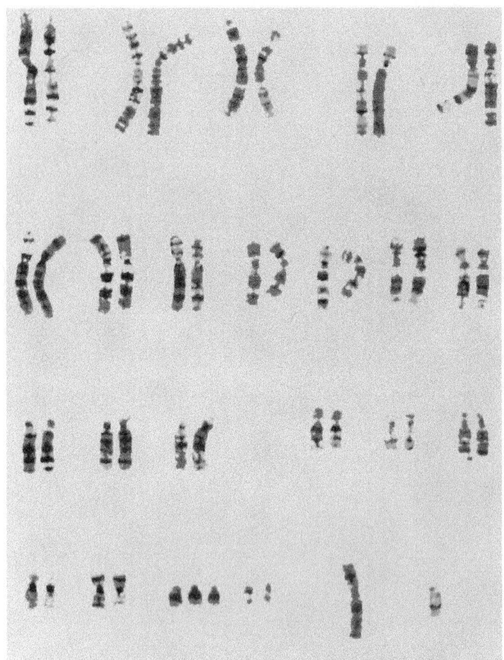

Down syndrome is a chromosomal abnormality that results in three chromosomes on the 21st pair—the third group from the left in the bottom row. The 23rd pair (bottom right) is an XY, so this is a boy.

L. Willatt/East Anglian Regional Genetics Service/ Science Source

factors, a number of which are preventable. We next examine the best-known causes of intellectual disability, beginning with the biological factors. Given the recency of DSM-5 criteria, this discussion of etiology is based on the DSM-IV-TR criteria.

GENETIC FACTORS Named for the British geneticist John Langdon Haydon Down (Czarnetzki et al., 2003), **Down syndrome** (trisomy 21) describes the unusual condition in which a chromosomal set has three chromosomes (i.e., trisomy) rather than the usual set of two. This error occurs during the cell division of a sperm or ovum—the chromosome pair does not divide as it should. Instead, the chromosomes "stick together." Later, when the sperm fertilizes the ovum, rather than each (sperm and ovum) contributing one chromosome to the 21st pair, three are present. People with Down syndrome have three #21 chromosomes in every cell in their body, giving them a total of 47 rather than the usual 46 chromosomes. Other trisomy conditions (trisomy 13, trisomy 18) exist and may also result in intellectual disability, but Down syndrome is by far the most common condition.

Children with Down syndrome have distinctive facial features including oblique eye fissures (slanted eyes), epicanthic eye folds (folds of skin in the corner of the eye), a flat nasal bridge, protruding tongues, short stocky stature, a very short neck, and small ears. Virtually every person with Down syndrome has intellectual disability, most commonly in the mild to moderate range, meaning that they are able to attend school, learn basic living skills, and function in a structured environment. Children with Down syndrome may also have numerous medical problems including heart defects, intestinal abnormalities, visual and hearing impairments, and respiratory ailments (Roubertoux & Kerdelhúe, 2006).

In Canada, the incidence of Down syndrome is approximately 1 in every 800 live births (Public Health Agency of Canada, 2002). Incidence varies with maternal age; much higher rates occur among older mothers (see Table 12.2). Biological factors, such

TABLE 12.2
Relationship of Maternal Age to Incidence of Down Syndrome

Maternal Age	Incidence of Down Syndrome	Maternal Age	Incidence of Down Syndrome
20	1 in 2000	35	1 in 350
21	1 in 1700	36	1 in 300
22	1 in 1500	37	1 in 250
23	1 in 1400	38	1 in 200
24	1 in 1300	39	1 in 150
25	1 in 1200	40	1 in 100
26	1 in 1100	41	1 in 80
27	1 in 1050	42	1 in 70
28	1 in 1000	43	1 in 50
29	1 in 950	44	1 in 40
30	1 in 900	45	1 in 30
31	1 in 800	46	1 in 25
32	1 in 720	47	1 in 20
33	1 in 600	48	1 in 15
34	1 in 450	49	1 in 10

Source: www.ndss.org/Down-Syndrome/What-Is-Down-Syndrome/. Accessed April 13, 2013. Reprinted with permission from the National Down Syndrome Society.

as fewer available ova or decreases in female hormones, are considered to be the reason why older mothers are more likely to have children with Down syndrome, but the specific mechanisms by which these factors might operate are not known (Waburton, 2005). Many environmental factors also have been proposed as causes, including maternal smoking, maternal alcohol use, radiation, and fertility drugs, but none of these factors has been confirmed (Sherman et al., 2007).

In children with Down syndrome, almost all brain structures are smaller than normal (Roubertoux & Kerdelhúe, 2006; Teipel et al., 2004). Another characteristic is the presence of plaques and neurofibrillary tangles, usually found among adults with major or mild neurocognitive disorder due to Alzheimer's disease (see Chapter 13). In people with Down syndrome, this deterioration begins at about age 8 and progresses, accelerating rapidly between the ages of 35 and 45 (Lott & Head, 2005). The result is that almost all people with Down syndrome have some evidence of Alzheimer's disease by age 40.

Phenylketonuria (PKU) is a genetic disorder in which the body cannot break down the amino acid *phenylalanine* because an essential enzyme is absent. Without the enzyme, phenylalanine accumulates in the body, causing mental and physical abnormalities (dos Santos et al., 2006). PKU occurs in about .01% of the population in North America. In Canada, infants are screened for PKU shortly after birth, resulting in few untreated cases of the disorder. Treatment requires daily dietary supplements and a severely restricted low-protein diet. Milk and dairy products, meat, eggs, wheat, beans, corn, peanuts, lentils, and other grains are prohibited (dos Santos et al., 2006), and compliance with these restrictions can be quite poor. This diet must be continued until at least age 8 to prevent intellectual disability; discontinuation of the diet at the time of adolescence is controversial (Hellekson, 2001). Most physicians and researchers advise continuing the diet for life (Pérez-Dueñas et al., 2006).

Fragile X syndrome (FXS) is the most commonly inherited cause of intellectual disability (Sundaram et al., 2005; Valdovinos, 2007). It occurs when a DNA series makes too many copies of itself and "turns off" a gene on the X chromosome. When the gene is turned off, cells do not make a necessary protein, and without the protein, FXS occurs. In addition to intellectual disability, children with FXS have behavioural disorders such as hyperactivity, temper tantrums, irritability, poor eye contact, self-stimulation, and self-injurious behaviours (Crawford et al., 2002; Valdovinos, 2007). Perhaps because girls have two X chromosomes (i.e., they have a "spare" X chromosome), they are only half as likely as boys to have FXS (1 out of 4000 males and 1 out of 8000 females).

Other genetic disorders that can result in intellectual disability include *tuberous sclerosis complex* (*TSC*) and *Lesch-Nyhan syndrome.* Resulting from mutations on at least two different genes (Sundaram et al., 2005), TSC affects 1 in every 30 000 people. In children with TSC, benign tumours affect all body organs, including the brain, and result in developmental delays, seizures, and learning disabilities. About 50% of people with TSC have intellectual disability (Leung & Robson, 2007). Lesch-Nyhan syndrome is a rare genetic disorder that is transmitted on the X chromosome. Because it is a recessive trait, it occurs only in boys. Girls, who have two X chromosomes, are protected from the disorder. Like PKU, this disorder involves a missing enzyme. When the genetic defect is present, excess uric acid accumulates throughout the body. Lesch-Nyhan syndrome causes many different behavioural problems, including cognitive dysfunction, intellectual disability, and aggressive and impulsive behaviours. Intellectual disability is usually moderate but can range from profound to mild (Olson & Houlihan, 2000). Nearly all children with this disorder develop persistent and severe self-injurious behaviour, sometimes with permanent physical damage.

ENVIRONMENTAL FACTORS When genes are not the cause of intellectual disability, factors such as the prenatal or postnatal environment may be responsible. Prenatal influences associated with the presence of intellectual disability include uterine environmental toxins (maternal alcohol use, infections), premature birth, hypoxia (lack of oxygen to the brain, often during birth), and fetal malnutrition. Postnatal factors include malnutrition, bacterial and viral infections, lead exposure, and social factors such as poverty, low environmental stimulation, and poor maternal education (Walker & Johnson, 2006). However, it is important to understand that unlike genetic disorders such as Down syndrome, the presence of these environmental factors does not automatically lead to intellectual disability. For example, many children live in impoverished environments yet have average or above average IQs.

The leading known preventable environmental cause of intellectual disability is drinking alcohol during pregnancy, which can result in **fetal alcohol syndrome (FAS)** (West & Blake, 2005; see Chapter 9). FAS and associated disorders (i.e., fetal alcohol spectrum disorders) are a significant public health problem in Canada and in many other countries (Popova et al., 2015). According to Health Canada (2006), about 9 babies in every 1000 are born with a fetal alcohol spectrum disorder, which includes any of a range of disabilities, including fetal alcohol syndrome, due to drinking alcohol during pregnancy. Women who have an unintended pregnancy, compared to women who have planned pregnancies, are significantly more likely to drink while pregnant and therefore may be at greater risk for FAS in their offspring (Sanders, 2014). Drinking alcohol during pregnancy can affect the physical development of the fetus, including brain development. In addition to intellectual disability, fetal alcohol syndrome is associated with birth defects, abnormal facial features, growth problems, central nervous system abnormalities, memory problems, impaired academic achievement, vision or hearing impairment, and behavioural problems (see Figure 12.1).

Another preventable environmental cause of intellectual disability is exposure to lead, which can enter the bodies of young children in different ways. Many older homes contain lead-based paint, which can peel off and be eaten by young children, who have a tendency to put many things in their mouth. Also, when the paint becomes old and worn, the chips may be ground into tiny particles that mix with dust, which are then inhaled. Ingestion or inhalation leads to a buildup of lead in the body (Brown et al., 2006). Even low levels of exposure to lead in childhood are associated with low intelligence. High levels of exposure are associated with substantially lower IQ scores (Needleman & Gatsonis, 1990).

FIGURE 12.1

Parts of the Brain That Can Be Affected by Maternal Alcohol Consumption. When a woman drinks during pregnancy, many parts of the fetal brain can be damaged.

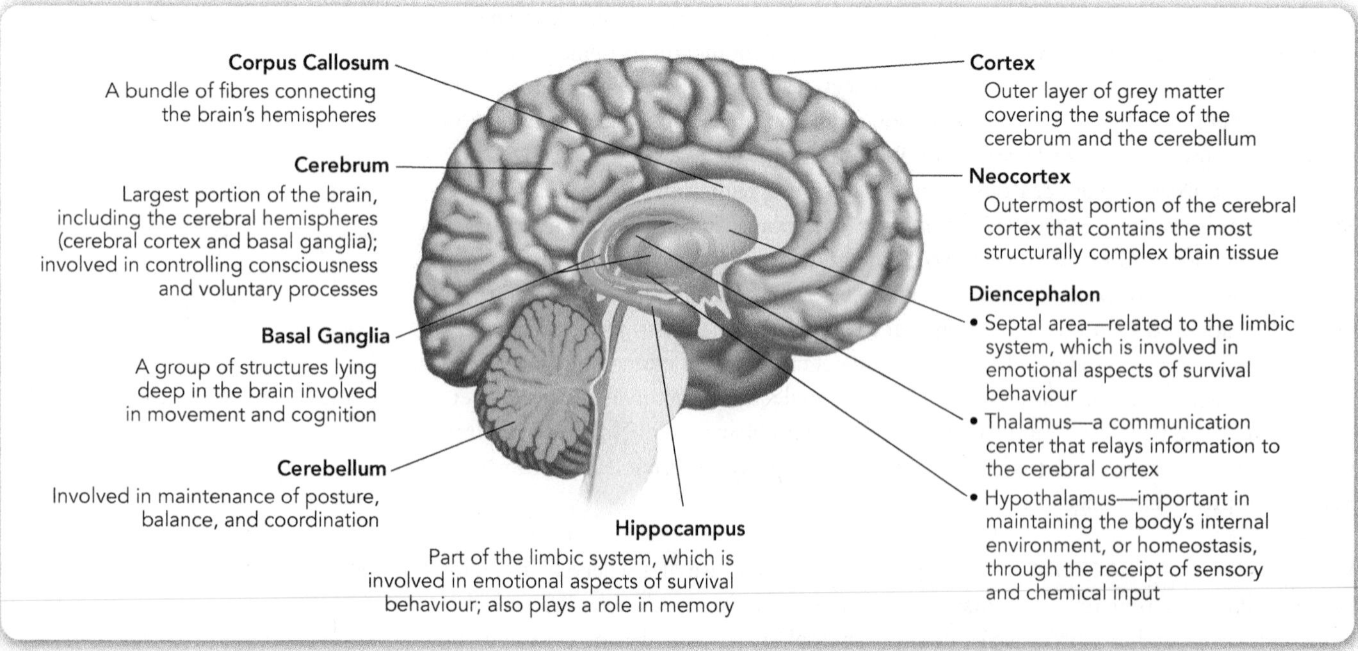
Corpus Callosum
A bundle of fibres connecting the brain's hemispheres
Cerebrum
Largest portion of the brain, including the cerebral hemispheres (cerebral cortex and basal ganglia); involved in controlling consciousness and voluntary processes
Basal Ganglia
A group of structures lying deep in the brain involved in movement and cognition
Cerebellum
Involved in maintenance of posture, balance, and coordination
Hippocampus
Part of the limbic system, which is involved in emotional aspects of survival behaviour; also plays a role in memory
Cortex
Outer layer of grey matter covering the surface of the cerebrum and the cerebellum
Neocortex
Outermost portion of the cerebral cortex that contains the most structurally complex brain tissue
Diencephalon
• Septal area—related to the limbic system, which is involved in emotional aspects of survival behaviour
• Thalamus—a communication center that relays information to the cerebral cortex
• Hypothalamus—important in maintaining the body's internal environment, or homeostasis, through the receipt of sensory and chemical input

Even years later, adults who were exposed to lead in childhood still had academic difficulties and behaviour problems (Needleman et al., 1990).

In many cases of mild intellectual disability, the specific cause is unknown. **Cultural-familial retardation** is defined as "retardation due to psychosocial disadvantage" (Weisz, 1990). Whereas severe intellectual disability exists across all socioeconomic levels, mild intellectual disability is more common among children in the lower socioeconomic classes (Stromme & Magnus, 2000), which include residents of poverty-stricken inner-city areas and poor rural areas, as well as migrant workers.

Among the lowest socioeconomic classes, the prevalence of mild intellectual disability ranges from 10% to 30% of the school-age population (Gillerot et al., 1989; Popper et al., 2004). The reason for the association between lower socioeconomic status and mild intellectual disability is unclear, but both biological and environmental factors may contribute. In the early years of life, the brain is still developing. Environmental factors such as poor nutrition, lack of access to early educational enrichment (e.g., preschool, educational toys), or restricted access to medical care may negatively affect brain development, leading to lower IQ scores.

The importance of environmental factors is further suggested by the work of Elinor Ames and colleagues at Simon Fraser University. They conducted research into the effects of adoption from Romanian orphanages (e.g., Ames & Carter, 1992; Morison et al., 1995). The orphanages were colourless and very quiet, with little visual or auditory stimulation. Children generally spent their days lying or sitting immobile in their cribs. Some of these children were adopted, mostly by families in British Columbia. All of the adopted children were developmentally delayed at the time of the adoption. Once adopted and placed in a more stimulating environment, the majority of children improved in their intellectual and adaptive functioning, although many continued to have academic and behavioural problems at school.

Treatment

Until recently, many people with intellectual disability were housed in institutions. Few community resources were available for them, and parents were encouraged to institutionalize their child when they thought that the necessary extensive care would be available. There was even hope that proper environmental care might reduce deficits, although leaving the institution was not a long-term goal of placement (Brosco et al., 2006). In fact, most people who were institutionalized remained there for the rest of their lives. Today, about 90% of people with intellectual disability live with families or in community placements, such as group homes.

Intellectual disability is not reversible, but many children can learn basic academic and adaptive functioning skills. Psychological treatments focus on teaching skills that facilitate community adjustment, such as self-care, independent living, and job maintenance. Behavioural procedures, such as *shaping* (rewarding successive approximations of desired behaviour) and *chaining* (teaching small, discrete behaviours and then putting them together), allow children with intellectual disability to learn simple tasks such as putting on a pair of pants, or more complicated behaviours such as going to the bank and cashing a check.

Medical treatments to reduce diseases that cause intellectual disability have decreased its general prevalence. The number of children with intellectual disability as a result of measles and whooping cough has decreased since the introduction of successful vaccinations for these diseases (Brosco et al., 2006) (see Figure 12.2). Medication does not treat the core symptoms of intellectual disability but is sometimes used for coexisting psychological disorders such as attentional or aggressive behaviours. Overall, people with intellectual disability respond to medication in the same way as others, but rates of response are poorer and side effects more common (Handen & Gilchrist, 2006).

FIGURE 12.2

Prevalence of Specific Causes of Intellectual Disability Over Time. During the past 50 years, advances in medical science have decreased the prevalence of intellectual disability.

Source: Data from Brosco et al. (2006). *Archives of Pediatrics & Adolescent Medicine, 160*, 302–309.

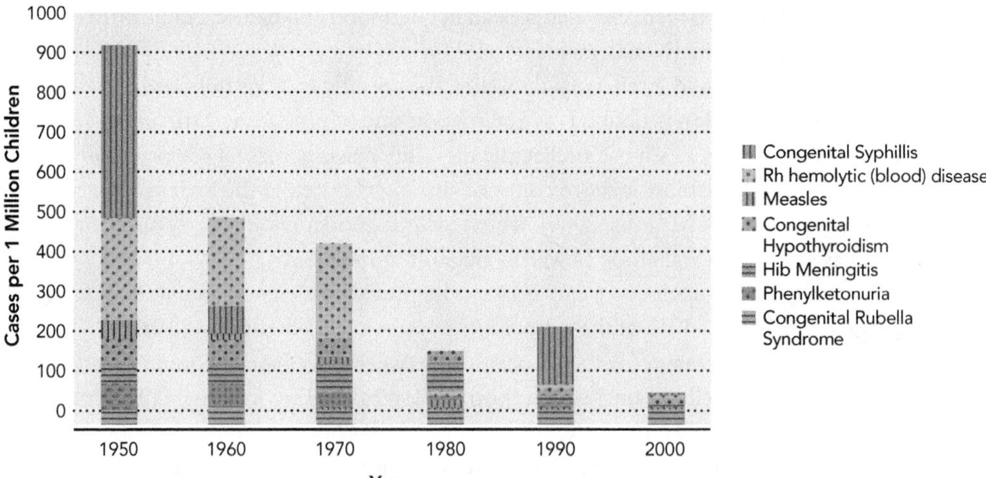

canadian **FOCUS**

Involuntary Sterilization and the Eugenics Movement

George Santayana (1905) once famously observed that "those who cannot remember the past are condemned to repeat it" (p. 284). There have been several dark episodes in the history of mental health treatment. Being aware of the errors of the past may prevent future mistakes.

During the late nineteenth and early twentieth centuries, the eugenics movement gained popularity throughout Canada and the United States. This movement was based on the belief that crimes, sexually transmitted disease, unwanted pregnancies, and other social problems were largely a result of intellectual disability and other forms of psychopathology. It was believed that these disorders were primarily a result of heredity. In hindsight, these ideas are simplistic and flawed. But given the current state of knowledge at the time, the views seemed convincing, both to professionals and the public. Sexual sterilization of people with intellectual disability and other disorders was seen as a way improving the gene pool and reducing crime and other social problems.

In the early 1900s, the United States began to implement legislation to sexually sterilize people considered to be "mentally defective" or suffering from other major mental disorders. The primary focus was on people considered to be "mentally retarded." In 1928, Alberta passed the Sexual Sterilization Act and began sterilizing people deemed to be in danger of transmitting mental deficiency to their children, or incapable of intelligent parenthood. The Act was later strengthened so that it was not necessary to obtain informed consent from the person or from his or her parents. A similar act was introduced in 1933 in British Columbia (Park & Radford, 1998). A leading figure in promoting sterilization was Dr. Clarence Hincks. Writing in *Maclean's* magazine in 1946, he declared that:

> Subnormality and mental unfitness seem to be on the increase in Canada . . . we can expect the percentage to mount unless we act soon to improve the mental quality of our stock. For the mentally unfit are apparently breeding faster than the fit, and will continue to do so until we prevent those with undesirable hereditary traits from passing their disabilities on to their children . . . we have abundant evidence in Canada that the free propagation of mental subnormals is carrying us far in the direction of race deterioration. . . . It is my conviction that highly selective eugenical sterilisation should be part of our expanding health programs. (Cited in Park & Radford, 1998, p. 319)

Dr. Hincks's views, in which breeding humans were seen as no different from breeding cattle, will seem very strange to today's readers, but they were taken seriously at the time. Between 1928 and 1972, more than 4000 Canadians were forcibly sexually sterilized, mostly in Alberta but also in British Columbia (Woodill, 1992). Several surgical methods were used. Males received either a vasectomy (removal of the vas deferens, which is the sperm duct from the testicle to the urethra) or an orchidectomy (removal of the testicles). Orchidectomy served a dual purpose of preventing procreation and supposedly reducing sexually aggressive behaviour. Females received either a salpingectomy (removal of the fallopian tube) or an oophorectomy (removal of ovaries) (Park & Radford, 1998). Some of the victims were misinformed about the operation; for example, told they were having their appendix removed.

The eugenics movement gradually lost favour in Canada and in other Western countries, partly in reaction to the Nazi eugenic policies, and partly because the basic tenets of eugenics were found to be flawed. That is, intellectual disability is not entirely due to genes; eugenic policies do not necessarily improve the gene pool; and social problems are a result of many factors interacting in complex ways, and cannot be blamed on intellectual disabilities. The sterilization acts were repealed in the 1970s. The Canadian Charter of Rights and Freedoms was later revised (e.g., 1992) to firmly establish the rights of people with intellectual disabilities. Effective specialized training programs were also developed to help them with their parenting skills (e.g., Tymchuk et al., 1990).

In a precedent-setting lawsuit, sterilization victim Leilani Muir received a government settlement of $750 000 in 1996. She was sterilized in 1959 at age 14, without her knowledge or consent, after being misdiagnosed as having an intellectual disability. Later IQ testing revealed that her intelligence was, in fact, in the low-normal range (*Edmonton Journal,* September 9, 1995, p. B2). Lawsuits were subsequently filed by other victims of involuntary sterilization. In Alberta, the government agreed to pay $140 million to more than 800 victims (*Edmonton Journal,* February 13, 2000, p. A6). Government officials issued a statement of profound regret for what had happened to these people.

CONCEPT check

- *Intellectual disability* is characterized by both intellectual and adaptive functioning deficits in conceptual, social, and practical domains. Intellect and adaptive functioning exist along a continuum and can range from mild to severe or profound.
- Intellectual disability, both biological and environmental, has many different causes.
- Some causes of intellectual disability are preventable, but once it occurs, available treatments do not reverse the condition. Behavioural and pharmacological treatment may improve functioning and associated conditions.

critical thinking question A significant proportion of mild intellectual disability has a cultural-familial etiology. Can you identify two factors leading to this type of intellectual disability, and if you had unlimited resources, how would you eliminate these causes?

Specific Learning Disorders

A universal task of education is to teach children basic skills such as reading, writing, and mathematics. Yet a number of public school children with at least average intelligence have difficulty mastering these basic academic tasks (APA, 2013). **Specific learning disorder** (see "DSM-5: Specific Learning Disorder") is defined by difficulties learning and using academic skills (reading, writing, arithmetic, or mathematical reasoning) (APA, 2013). Academic skills are below what is expected for chronological age and cause interference in daily functioning, as confirmed by standardized achievement measures and clinical assessment. Affecting both sexes, these disorders can result in demoralization, low self-esteem, and school dropout rates that are higher than those in the general population.

When a clinician makes a diagnosis of specific learning disorder, she or he includes a specifier of one (or more) of the following: with impairment in reading, with impairment in written expression, or with impairment in mathematics. *Impairment in reading* is sometimes known as *dyslexia.* Impairments in reading can include problems with word recognition, reading rate or fluency, or reading comprehension. Children with reading impairments may display oral reading errors such as distortions, substitutions, or omissions of words. Silent reading disabilities include reading very slowly and making comprehension errors. These children often also have difficulty with spelling. Early theories emphasized vision and visual perceptual difficulties such as reversal of letters. However, advances in neurobiology and neuropsychology indicate that reading disorders most likely result from a diminished ability to recognize and produce sounds (*phonemes*) that when put together form words (Shaywitz et al., 2007).

criteria for
Specific Learning Disorder **DSM-5**

A. Difficulties learning and using academic skills, as indicated by the presence of at least one of the following symptoms that have persisted for at least 6 months, despite the provision of interventions that target those difficulties:

1. Inaccurate or slow and effortful word reading (e.g., reads single words aloud incorrectly or slowly and hesitantly, frequently guesses words, has difficulty sounding out words).
2. Difficulty understanding the meaning of what is read (e.g., may read text accurately but not understand the sequence, relationships, inferences, or deeper meanings of what is read).
3. Difficulties with spelling (e.g., may add, omit, or substitute vowels or consonants).
4. Difficulties with written expression (e.g., makes multiple grammatical or punctuation errors within sentences; employs poor paragraph organization; written expression of ideas lacks clarity).
5. Difficulties mastering number sense, number facts, or calculation (e.g., has poor understanding of numbers, their magnitude, and relationships; counts on fingers to add single-digit numbers instead of recalling the math fact as peers do; gets lost in the midst of arithmetic computation and may switch procedures).
6. Difficulties with mathematical reasoning (e.g., has severe difficulty applying mathematical concepts, facts, or procedures to solve quantitative problems).

B. The affected academic skills are substantially and quantifiably below those expected for the individual's chronological age, and cause significant interference with academic or occupational performance, or with activities of daily living, as confirmed by individually administered standardized achievement measures and comprehensive clinical assessment. For individuals age 17 years and older, a documented history of impairing learning difficulties may be substituted for the standardized assessment.

C. The learning difficulties begin during school-age years but may not become fully manifest until the demands for those affected academic skills exceed the individual's limited capacities (e.g., as in timed tests, reading or writing lengthy complex reports for a tight deadline, excessively heavy academic loads).

D. The learning difficulties are not better accounted for by intellectual disabilities, uncorrected visual or auditory acuity, other mental or neurological disorders, psychosocial adversity, lack of proficiency in the language of academic instruction, or inadequate educational instruction.

Note: The four diagnostic criteria are to be met based on a clinical synthesis of the individual's history (developmental, medical, family, educational), school reports, and psychoeducational assessment.

Instruction in reading is based on phonics, the process of "sounding out" a word by converting its visual representation into the appropriate sounds. Difficulty recognizing and articulating sounds leads to a cascade of negative events. "Sounding out" words is slow and required effort; thus, reading is less fluent. Sounding out also requires more concentration to identify and pronounce difficult words, leaving fewer attentional resources for reading comprehension and leading to mental fatigue and behavioural avoidance (Kronenberger & Dunn, 2003). As researchers continue to study reading problems, it is becoming clearer that this is not a single disorder—there may be at least 17 different types of reading impairments (Zoccolotti & Friedmann, 2010).

Children may also have *impairments in mathematics*, sometimes called *dyscalculia.* Mathematics impairments include the diminished ability to understand mathematical terms, operations, or concepts; recognize numerical symbols or arithmetic signs; or copy numbers or figures correctly. Difficulty performing mental calculations may lead affected children to rely on external devices, such as counting on their fingers. They also often have difficulty with the logic of word problems.

The third specific learning disorder specifier, *impairment in written expression*, also called *dysgraphia*, is more than sloppy handwriting. It includes having difficulty composing grammatically correct sentences; making frequent grammatical, punctuation, or spelling errors; and experiencing diminished ability to organize coherent written paragraphs. Effective writing requires different cognitive, visual, and motor skills, including knowledge of vocabulary and grammar, eye–hand coordination and hand movement, and memory (Pratt & Patel, 2007). Deficits in any of these areas can lead to impairment. Children with impairments in writing have no trouble presenting material orally but struggle with putting those same ideas into written form. Their written sentences are short, difficult to understand, and riddled with spelling and grammatical errors.

Between 3% and 10% of school children may suffer from specific learning disorder, most commonly persistent problems in reading (Pratt & Patel, 2007; Shaywitz et al., 2007; Statistics Canada, 2007), which may affect between 2% and 8% of all children. Reading problems that meet diagnostic criteria for specific learning disorder are more common in boys, but the reason is not clear. One hypothesis is that it may not be more common but *more commonly identified* because associated behavioural disorders, such as attention-deficit/hyperactivity disorder (ADHD), lead to a referral to a mental health professional. Difficulty with phonics and reading may lead to the identification of specific learning disorder as early as the preschool years. By contrast, persistent problems written expression is often not apparent until grade 3 or 4 when there are increased demands to present ideas in writing.

Functional Impairment

Children with specific learning disorder are more likely to drop out of school, limiting their opportunities for employment (APA, 2013). They also often feel demoralized by their disabilities and report low self-esteem. Children with specific learning disorder may also have other childhood emotional and behavioural problems such as ADHD, conduct disorder, depression, and anxiety disorders.

Children with mild symptoms may be difficult to identify and may be described by parents or teachers as messy, unfocused, or disorganized (Pratt & Patel, 2007). As adults, children with mild symptoms compensate by developing a working vocabulary in their occupational area that allows them to function effectively. However, they still have difficulty with unfamiliar words. Their reading may be accurate but not fluent or automatic (Shaywitz et al., 2007).

Etiology

The etiology of specific learning disorder is unclear. As we begin to identify many different types of reading and writing difficulties, we must recognize that these impairments probably do not arise from a single neurological abnormality but from different neurocognitive impairments (Zoccolotti & Friedman, 2010) or the inability of several brain areas to work together.

Much more is known about the etiology of reading difficulties than about mathematics or writing difficulties. Structural and functional magnetic imaging studies and positron emission tomography (PET) studies have identified various areas of the brain that appear to be important for reading (Shaywitz et al., 2007). Again, why a child would have abnormal brain functioning is not entirely clear, but genetics appears to play a significant role. Concordance rates for reading impairment are 71% for monozygotic twins and 49% for dizygotic twins (Castles et al., 1999). Although there is some variability, between 23% and 65% of children who have a parent with a reading impairment also have the impairment (Scarborough, 1990). We have much to learn about the biological basis of reading difficulties, but what is clear now is that the impairment does not result from the inheritance of one single gene. It is likely that a number of different genes are involved.

Treatment

Treatment for specific learning disorder usually occurs in the educational setting. Intervention for reading begins early and focuses on developing the skills necessary for phonological processing and fluent reading with later emphasis on reading for comprehension (Kronenberger & Dunn, 2003). Poor readers can make significant progress in their reading skills, but they never achieve the skill level possessed by good readers at the same age. As children mature and gains are consolidated, intervention shifts to disability accommodation (Pratt & Patel, 2007), such as more time for reading and test taking and the use of computers, tape recorders, or recorded books to allow effective functioning in academics and occupational environments.

Treatment for mathematics includes arithmetic drills and memorization. Because writing is considered to result from difficulties in the written expression of ideas, children first engage in simple writing tasks, such as keeping a diary. As their basic writing skills improve, they are given more challenging writing tasks.

Ethics and Responsibility

The lack of efficacious traditional treatments for specific learning disorder with impairment in reading has led some parents to turn to complementary or alternative medicine (Bull, 2009). Among one sample of 148 children with this disorder, 55.4% of their parents reported using nontraditional approaches, including diets and nutritional supplements (42.6%), homeopathic medicines (19.6%), and chiropractic manipulations (19.6%). Other approaches used by these parents included aromatherapy, acupuncture, massage, and reflexology. Although scientists must always be open to new ideas and approaches to a problem to date, none of these interventions has been scientifically verified as an efficacious treatment for this disorder. Mental health professionals who work with parents and children with these disorders are obligated to explain to parents that these procedures, while probably not harmful, have not yet been shown to be helpful.

CONCEPT check

- Specific learning disorder is defined as difficulties learning and using academic skills. Specific learning disorder may be in the area of reading, mathematics, and writing.
- Of the specific learning disorder specifiers, reading is the most common and most likely represents a difficulty in phonological processing resulting from abnormalities in different areas of the brain.
- Genetics appear to play a major role in the etiology of reading problems. The etiology of mathematics or writing problems is unknown.

critical thinking question Treatment for specific learning disorder occurs in educational settings and consists of attempts to teach academic skills. At later ages, treatment takes the form of accommodations to deal with remaining deficits. Based on your knowledge of brain development, why would this radical change in treatment approach occur?

Autism Spectrum Disorder

As in the case of Jeremy at the beginning of this chapter, some childhood behavioural abnormalities are evident very early in life. Most children spontaneously say "mama" or "dada" before age 1. But Jeremy did not speak until age 3 when he had speech therapy. Jeremy also had unusual social behaviours. He refused to make eye contact, spoke too loudly, asked inappropriate questions, and made inappropriate statements or noises. In addition to holding his toy car and spinning the wheels over and over, he showed other stereotyped behaviours. (These are repetitive behaviours that serve no observable social functions, such as hand flapping, spinning, and ritualistic pacing). Such behaviours are characteristic of **autism spectrum disorder** and consist of deficits in social communication and social interaction and the presence of restrictive

criteria for Autism Spectrum Disorder DSM-5

A. Persistent deficits in social communication and social interaction across multiple contexts, as manifested by the following, currently or by history (examples are illustrative, not exhaustive; see text):

1. Deficits in social-emotional reciprocity, ranging, for example, from abnormal social approach and failure of normal back-and-forth conversation; to reduced sharing of interests, emotions, or affect; to failure to initiate or respond to social interactions.
2. Deficits in nonverbal communicative behaviours used for social interaction, ranging, for example, from poorly integrated verbal and nonverbal communication; to abnormalities in eye contact and body language or deficits in understanding and use of gestures; to a total lack of facial expressions and nonverbal communication.
3. Deficits in developing, maintaining, and understanding relationships, ranging, for example, from difficulties adjusting behaviour to suit various social contexts; to difficulties in sharing imaginative play or in making friends; to absence of interest in peers.

Specify current severity:

Severity is based on social communication impairments and restricted, repetitive patterns of behaviour (see Table 2).

B. Restricted, repetitive patterns of behaviour, interests, or activities, as manifested by at least two of the following, currently or by history (examples are illustrative, not exhaustive; see text):

1. Stereotyped or repetitive motor movements, use of objects, or speech (e.g., simple motor stereotypies, lining up toys or flipping objects, echolalia, idiosyncratic phrases).
2. Insistence on sameness, inflexible adherence to routines, or ritualized patterns of verbal or nonverbal behaviour (e.g., extreme distress at small changes, difficulties with transitions, rigid thinking patterns, greeting rituals, need to take same route or eat same food every day).
3. Highly restricted, fixated interests that are abnormal in intensity or focus (e.g., strong attachment to or preoccupation with unusual objects, excessively circumscribed or perseverative interests).
4. Hyper- or hyporeactivity to sensory input or unusual interest in sensory aspects of the environment (e.g., apparent indifference to pain/temperature, adverse response to specific sounds or textures, excessive smelling or touching of objects, visual fascination with lights or movement).

Specify current severity:

Severity is based on social communication impairments and restricted, repetitive patterns of behaviour (see Table 2).

C. Symptoms must be present in the early developmental period (but may not become fully manifest until social demands exceed limited capacities, or may be masked by learned strategies in later life).

D. Symptoms cause clinically significant impairment in social, occupational, or other important areas of current functioning.

E. These disturbances are not better explained by intellectual disability (intellectual developmental disorder) or global developmental delay. Intellectual disability and autism spectrum disorder frequently co-occur; to make comorbid diagnoses of autism spectrum disorder and intellectual disability, social communication should be below that expected for general developmental level.

and repetitive behaviour patterns (APA, 2013) (See "DSM-5: Autism Spectrum Disorder").

In 1943, psychiatrist Leo Kanner described children with *autistic disturbances of affective contact*, highlighting behaviours that are central to this disorder and are apparent before 30 months of age (Rutter, 1978). Key features of autism spectrum disorder include *deficits in social communication and social interaction* (Klin, 2006) across multiple contexts, including delays in acquiring spoken language, the inability to make eye contact and to recognize facial expressions, and a lack of interest in social interaction. Other deficits include the inability to start or continue a conversation, and stereotyped or unusual language, such as *echolalia*, the repetition of the last word, sound, or phrase that was heard.

The second characteristic of autism spectrum disorder is *restricted and repetitive patterns of behaviour, interests, or activities*, which includes intense preoccupation with a particular interest.

Adi has a fascination with pipes and turbines. When he encounters one, he stops and stares, refusing to leave. His parents often find him in the basement staring at the furnace. He knows everything about the mechanics of large machinery and talks incessantly about the advantages and disadvantages of various systems, types of piping, and so on.

Repetitive and stereotyped patterns also include intense adherence to routines (e.g., eating or bedtime rituals) and self-injurious behaviours (e.g., eye gouging, head banging, hand biting). Why children engage in these behaviours is unclear, but some clinicians hypothesize that these behaviours allow the child to stop an aversive environmental stimulus, such as a hug (Matson et al., 1996). For children with limited communication abilities, self-injurious behaviours may be a way to express emotions such as anger or pain (Volkmar & Wiesner, 2009). The diagnostic criteria for autism spectrum disorder include the ability to specify the level of support service that an individual requires. These levels are "requiring support," "requiring substantial support," and "requiring very substantial support."

Infants with autism spectrum disorder are often described as being "too good" and never crying. They lack social interest, do not play interactive or imitative games (such as peek-a-boo), are extremely sensitive to touch and sound, and have abnormal sleep patterns with nighttime awakenings that last for several hours. They also have rigid eating behaviours, refusing to eat certain foods because of the smell, texture, or taste.

Approximately 60% to 75% of children with autism spectrum disorder have IQs below 70 (Barbaresi et al., 2006; Bethea & Sikich, 2007). Behavioural problems such as hyperactivity, impulsivity, social anxiety, general anxiety, irritability, and aggression are common (Bethea & Sikich, 2007), as are depression and phobias (Matson & Nebel-Schwalm, 2007).

Functional Impairment

Autism spectrum disorder is a lifelong impairment that affects the entire family; only about one third of all people with this disorder are ever able to live independently (Klin, 2006). However, deficits in the core areas do improve with age, and there are always exceptions to this generally bleak outlook (see "Real People, Real Disorders: Temple Grandin, Ph.D.").

Children often are socially isolated, desiring social interaction but seeking it inappropriately, including interrupting others, engaging in one-sided conversations about a favourite topic, and speaking too loudly and too rapidly. Some children with autism spectrum disorder require special classroom placement, whereas other children are able to function academically in traditional classroom settings. However, because of their social difficulties, their classmates often bully, tease, or ignore them, resulting in social isolation at school.

The prevalence of autism spectrum disorder has increased dramatically in recent years (see "Examining the Evidence: Vaccines Do Not Produce Autism Spectrum Disorder"). Before 1994, the median prevalence of autism was 0.05% (Fombonne, 2005). The most recent estimate is 0.6% to 1% of the general population may have autism spectrum disorder (APA, 2013; Anagnostou et al., 2014; Waddell, 2014). The increased *prevalence* (proportion of people in the general population who have a disorder) of autism spectrum disorder cannot be attributed to an increase in *incidence* (number of new cases of a disorder during a given time interval). It is likely that changes in diagnostic criteria, diagnostic practices, special education policies, and the availability of diagnostic services are contributing factors (Fombonne, 2005; Klin, 2006).

Overall, autism spectrum disorder is more common among boys than among girls, with 3.5 to 4 boys for every 1 girl diagnosed (Bethea & Sikich, 2007; Nicholas et al., 2008). Little is known about whether the prevalence of autism spectrum disorder differs by race, ethnicity, or social class.

REAL people REAL disorders

Temple Grandin, Ph.D.

Temple Grandin, Ph.D., is a professor of animal science at Colorado State University. She obtained her B.A. at Franklin Pierce College, her M.S. in Animal Science at Arizona State University, and her Ph.D. in Animal Science from the University of Illinois. She has written more than 300 articles and several books. One book, *Animals in Translation*, was a *New York Times* best-seller. Her writings on animal grazing behaviours have helped reduce stress on animals during handling, and in North America, about half of the cattle in livestock yards are handled in a system that she designed.

Dr. Grandin has autism spectrum disorder. She didn't speak until she was 3½ years old, communicating by screaming, peeping, and humming. In 1950, she was labelled "autistic," and professionals recommended that she be institutionalized. The book she eventually wrote, *Emergence: Labeled Autistic*, stunned the world. Until then, most people had assumed that this disorder prevented achievement or productivity in life. She speaks about her disorder because, she says, "I have read enough to know that there are still many parents, and, yes, professionals, too, who believe that 'once autistic, always autistic.' This dictum has meant sad and sorry lives for many children diagnosed, as I was in early life, as autistic. To these people, it is incomprehensible that the characteristics of autism can be modified and controlled. However, I feel strongly that I am living proof that they can."

Newscom

The onset of autism spectrum disorder is always before age 3, and the core features are often clearly present by age 2 or 3 (Lord et al., 2006; Maenner et al., 2013). Parents sometimes recognize that something is wrong at a much earlier age, perhaps as early as 12 to 18 months. However, symptoms may change dramatically between infancy and early childhood (Charman et al., 2005; Lord et al., 2006). Although it is possible that autism spectrum disorder can be reliably detected at 18 to 24 months (Lord et al., 2006), symptoms are more stable beginning at age 3, allowing for a more accurate diagnosis.

The long-term outcome of autism spectrum disorder is variable. In one controlled longitudinal study (Eaves & Ho, 2008), 46% of children who were diagnosed with this disorder had a poor outcome as young adults, 32% had a fair outcome, and 21% had a good to very good outcome. IQ remained stable from childhood to adulthood. Emotional problems were present among 62% of the sample, most commonly obsessive-compulsive disorder or another anxiety disorder. Only 27% had ever been employed for an average of five hours per week and most often in a sheltered workshop. More than half of the adults were living at home (56%) or in a group home or foster care (35%). Despite these figures, some adults with autism spectrum disorder, such as Dr. Temple Grandin, do achieve success.

Etiology

Autism spectrum disorder is a neurodevelopmental disorder associated with the presence of different genetic syndromes and chromosomal abnormalities (Barbaresi et al., 2006). Although its specific genetic mechanism is not yet known, the estimated heritability is higher than 90% (Gupta & State, 2007). Evidence from neuroscience and genetic research indicates that more than 60 genetic and metabolic conditions are associated with autism. This means that it is more likely that autism spectrum disorder represents people with a range of severity and functional impairment (Eichler & Zimmerman, 2008). Contemporary genetic research suggests that large spontaneous deletions or duplications of areas in the genome are among the molecular causes of autism spectrum disorder (Weiss et al., 2008).

examining the EVIDENCE

Vaccines Do Not Cause Autism Spectrum Disorder

- **Fact 1** Forty years ago, 4 of every 10 000 children were diagnosed with autism spectrum disorder. The rate now is 1 of 152 (www.cdc.gov/mmwr/preview/mmwrhtml/ss5810a1.htm. Accessed March 21, 2013).
- **Fact 2** Childhood inoculations (measles-mumps-rubella, or MMR, vaccine) occur between 12 and 18 months of age.
- **Fact 3** Some children with autism spectrum disorder appear to develop normally until around age 2 when developmental regression appears.
- **Possible Conclusion?** Because the incidence of autism spectrum disorder appears to have increased when the MMR vaccine became common, the vaccine caused the rise in rates (Wakefield, 1999). Let's examine the evidence.
- **Let's Examine the Evidence** Wakefield (1999) described a *correlational relationship* between vaccination and autism spectrum disorder, but it was wrongly interpreted as causation. Other studies appeared to confirm this parallel upward trend. However, the studies did not manipulate the variable of interest (MMR vaccine), which would be necessary to conclude causation. When researchers examined variations in the diagnosis of autism spectrum disorder *before* and *after* the termination of a vaccine program (Honda et al., 2005), rates rose when the vaccine was administered. However, *rates continued to rise* after the vaccine was discontinued. If the MMR vaccine were responsible, the rate should have *decreased* once the program was discontinued (but it did not).
- **What are possible alternative explanations for the increased rate of autism spectrum disorder?**
  1. **Change in diagnostic practices.** Until recently, a child with intellectual disability was not given a second diagnosis of autism even if autism spectrum disorder were present. Now both diagnoses can be given, leading to a rise in the total number of autism spectrum disorder diagnoses.
  2. **Changes in diagnostic criteria.** Forty years ago, the term *autism* was restricted to children who would now represent the very extremely impaired end of the spectrum. Now, children with the same behaviours, although milder in severity, are included in the diagnosis of autism spectrum disorder (Rutter, 2005), leading to a rise in the total number of children with one of the disorders.
- **Conclusion** Environmental or biological contributors to autism cannot be discounted, but current data do not support a causal role for MMR vaccinations (Rutter, 2005; Taylor, 2006). After examining all the evidence, the editors of the respected medical journal *BMJ* published an editorial concluding that the article reporting a link between the MMT vaccine and autism spectrum disorder was fraudulent (Godlee & Marcovitch, 2011). Vaccines do not produce autism spectrum disorder.

Whereas advancing maternal age is associated with Down syndrome and intellectual disability, advancing paternal age may be associated with an increased prevalence of autism spectrum disorder (Reichenberg et al., 2006). However, as with Down syndrome and maternal age, it is not clear how a father's advanced age might lead to development of the disorder.

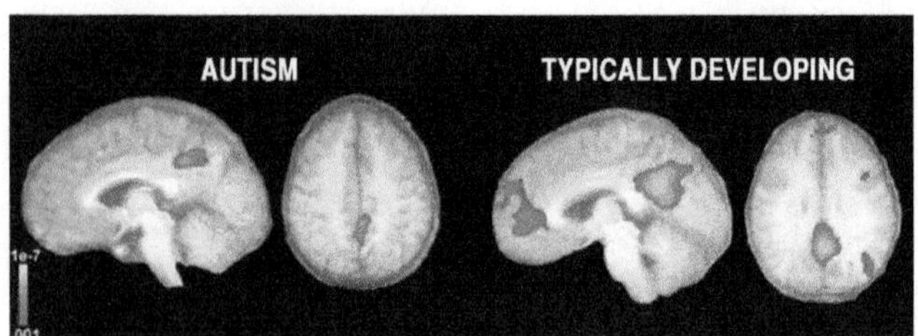

In response to viewing faces of familiar people and strangers, brain activity occurs in both people with autism spectrum disorder and people with no disorder. However, when the two groups are compared, there is stronger activation in people with no disorder and more areas of the brain are activated.

Pierce Karen

One indication of the neurodevelopmental basis of autism spectrum disorder is unusually accelerated head and brain growth during the first few years of life. At birth, children later diagnosed with autism spectrum disorder have a head circumference at the 25th percentile for all infants. Between 6 and 14 months of age, head circumference and brain size reaches the 84th percentile, far exceeding the growth rate for typically developing children (Bethea & Sikich, 2007; Courchesne & Pierce, 2005).

In addition to the abnormal growth rate, diagnostic imaging (MRI, fMRI, and PET scans) provides data that suggest subtle structural and organizational abnormalities in the brains of at least some children with autism spectrum disorder. Particularly affected is the anterior cingulate cortex, an area that integrates verbal information with emotional tone and observation of personally important faces. When shown pictures of familiar and significant faces, children without autism spectrum disorder show activation in the anterior cingulate cortex, while children with autism spectrum disorder do not (Pierce et al., 2004). This would suggest that children with autism spectrum disorder do not have the same neurochemical reaction when they see familiar faces as do typically developing children.

Another area of the brain that appears to be underactivated in children with autism spectrum disorder is the fusiform gyrus (Pierce et al., 2001). This area is important in the recognition of facial expression. Severe underactivation of this area appears to be related to severe social impairment (Schultz et al., 2001). This would suggest that there could be a biological basis for this social impairment. If the part of the children's brain that recognizes faces is not functioning properly, children miss social cues that others "automatically" use to engage in pleasurable social interactions. It is not yet clear whether therapy can change this biological deficit.

There are many avenues of exciting new research about the neurological bases of autism spectrum disorder, but there are many medical misunderstandings about its causes. One theory is that autism spectrum disorder is caused by the measles-mumps-rubella (MMR) vaccine (see "Examining the Evidence: Vaccines Do Not Produce Autism Spectrum Disorder"). Another theory without empirical support is that autism spectrum disorder is caused by thimerosal (a mercury-containing preservative used in vaccines). Why would such theories develop if no evidence supports them? One reason is that in a desperate search for explanations, parents often misinterpret or overinterpret research data in their quest to find a cause for this disorder. Despite the current lack of evidence, some parents refuse to allow their children to be vaccinated for childhood medical disorders, thereby exposing their children to diseases that may result in physical handicaps such as blindness, intellectual disability, or even death. This was illustrated in a recent study conducted at the University of Toronto by Kuwaik and colleagues (2014). They found, as in other studies, that immunization was unrelated to the risk of a child developing autism spectrum disorder. Importantly, the researchers also found that parents who already have one child with autism spectrum disorder may delay or decline immunization for their younger children, potentially placing them at increased risk of preventable infectious diseases.

Ethics and Responsibility

Throughout history, there have also been psychological misunderstandings about the etiology of autism spectrum disorder. In the 1950s and 1960s, psychosocial theories proposed that "refrigerator mothers" (parents who were emotionally unresponsive to their infants) were responsible for its development (Klin, 2006). This concept was discredited in the 1970s when it became clear that the roots of the disorder were neurobiological. Parents do play a critical role in the early detection and treatment for children with this disorder (see "Treatment"), but they do *not* cause autism spectrum disorder.

Currently, scientists have many theories regarding the etiology of autism spectrum disorder and the reasons for the increase in its prevalence over the last 20 years. Researchers point to changing diagnostic criteria, diagnostic substitution, and the decreasing age at which the diagnosis can be assigned (Leonard et al., 2010). Unfortunately, many people in the general population do not accept the current scientific theories but instead adhere to theories of causality that have been discredited, such as vaccines and gluten in the diet (Mulloy et al., 2010, 2011). Other environmental factors considered by some health professionals as valid potential theories to explain increases in autism spectrum disorder include (1) medical technologies such as ultrasound scans and Caesarean sections; (2) drug use/exposure to toxins; (3) changing lifestyles such as working mothers, stress, and indoor air quality; and (4) technology effects such as carbon monoxide exposure, nuclear power stations, and cell phone towers (Russell et al., 2009). Researchers must be sure to be respectful of others' ideas—not discounting every theory outright—but seeking to educate the public about the validity of these hypotheses based on solid science. Failure by scientists to address these theories or pseudotheories in a respectful scientific manner may result in children not getting needed medical services or being subjected to interventions that hold nothing but false promises.

Treatment

Early and intensive behavioural treatment improves the long-term outcome for children with autism spectrum disorder (Barbaresi et al., 2006). Behavioural interventions typically target five groups of problem behaviours: aberrant behaviours, social skills, language, daily living skills, and academic skills (Matson & Smith, 2008; White et al., 2007). For all categories except aberrant behaviours, treatment consists of *positive reinforcement and shaping*, which teaches new and needed behaviours (such as saying a word, putting on clothes, completing homework). Clinicians teach parents to train their children in these skills. *Applied behaviour analysis* (ABA) is a behavioural intervention that uses shaping and positive reinforcement to improve social, communication, and behavioural skills by intensively training (shaping) and rewarding (reinforcing) specific behaviours. Introduced by O. Ivar Lovaas (1987), applied behaviour analysis (conducted for 40 hours per week for more than two years) improved the behaviours in 9 of 19 children with autism spectrum disorder (47%) to the extent that they were indistinguishable from children without the disorder. Although subsequent studies did not replicate this high success rate, empirical data show that ABA is effective, particularly when provided individually for at least 20 hours per week, and started before age 4 (Barbaresi et al., 2006).

In the case of aberrant behaviours, self-injury is an unfortunate part of the clinical syndrome and must be treated quickly or serious and permanent injury or even death may result. Mildly *aversive procedures* (e.g., a short spray of warm water to the face) quickly and painlessly disrupt such behaviours. When such treatments are combined with positive approaches to behaviour change, self-injurious behaviours can be reduced or eliminated (Matson et al., 1996). Aversive procedures are used (1) in very specific instances, (2) when the child's health or welfare is at risk, and (3) under the supervision of a qualified professional. Procedures such as a spray of warm water or placing lemon juice on the tongue are quite effective. Mild electric shocks were used in the past but are now used rarely, if at all, and only when less aversive procedures are not effective and there is danger of severe physical damage (such as brain injury as a result of repeated head banging). Decisions about aversive procedures should never be made by a single person, but only after consultation with other professionals and perhaps an ethics committee.

No medications are efficacious for the social or communication deficits found in children with autism spectrum disorder (Barbaresi et al., 2006). Atypical antipsychotic drugs (see Chapter 10) may manage behaviours such as tantrums, aggression, and self-injurious behaviour (McCracken et al., 2002) and improve restricted, repetitive, and stereotyped patterns of behaviours, interests, and activities (McDougle et al., 2005). Stimulants reduce hyperactivity but are not as effective as they are in children with attention-deficit/hyperactivity disorder (Research Units on Pediatric Psychopharmacology Autism Network, 2005). Selective serotonin reuptake inhibitors (SSRIs) are safe, but it is not clear if they are really effective. They may decrease repetitive behaviours (Hollander et al., 2005) but increase behavioural agitation in a population already prone to this behaviour (Kolevzon et al., 2006).

CONCEPT check

- Autism spectrum disorder is a lifelong condition.
- Autism spectrum disorder is characterized by deficits in social communication and social interaction across multiple contexts, as well as restricted and stereotypical behaviours, interests, and activities.

- Our increasingly sophisticated understanding of genetics now offers more detailed explanations to families of children with autism spectrum disorders. Despite increased understanding, we cannot yet offer treatments that entirely reverse the effects of this disorder. Early and intense interventions can produce symptom improvement and enhance the long-term outcome.

critical thinking question Autism spectrum disorder is neurobiological in nature and appears to have a genetic basis. When looking at faces, certain areas of the brains of children with autism spectrum disorders, such as the fusiform gyrus, do not appear to have the same level of reactivity as the brains of children with no disorder. How does this neurobiological finding relate to the person's ability to interact in a socially appropriate manner with others?

Attention-Deficit/Hyperactivity Disorder

Being active is part of childhood, whether it is playing games at recess, being involved in organized sports, or just wrestling with a sibling. An important developmental process involves the ability to control physical activity and direct it toward the achievement of identified goals. Most children achieve this developmental milestone. However, for a subset of children, physical activity is not goal directed but just excessively overactive, resulting in negative outcomes such as household disruption, academic underachievement, and poor social relationships. These children suffer from *attention-deficit/hyperactivity disorder*, a common behaviour disorder to which we now turn our attention.

Ronnie (see Side-by-Side Case Studies) had a situational problem that was resolved by proper school placement and a challenging curriculum. Jason has **attention-deficit/hyperactivity disorder (ADHD)** (see "DSM-5: Attention-Deficit/Hyperactivity Disorder"), a prevalent, early-onset childhood disorder that affects many aspects of functioning. Early conceptualizations of what is now known as ADHD emphasized hyperactivity. Virginia Douglas and colleagues at McGill University were among the first to establish that attention deficits are also important components of what is now called ADHD (e.g., Douglas, 1972, 1983). Accordingly, the main features of ADHD are now regarded as falling into two categories. First are symptoms of *inattentiveness*, such as daydreaming, distractibility, and an inability to focus on or complete a task. The second component consists of *hyperactivity* (excessive energy, restlessness, excessive talking, and an inability to sit still) (Biederman, 2005) and *impulsivity* (blurting out answers, interrupting others' conversations, and inability to take turns). (Hyperactivity and impulsivity are regarded as a single component because they commonly co-occur.) Some children have predominantly inattentive presentation (showing only inattention symptoms), and others have a predominantly hyperactive/impulsive presentation (showing only hyperactive/impulsive symptoms). Still other children have a combined presentation, with symptoms from both components.

Children with ADHD are impulsive. They cannot inhibit their responses and do not wait to generate a plan before they act. Because they are inattentive, they cannot pay attention in order to store information. Their inability to concentrate keeps them from focusing on one particular idea or activity in order to develop a plan of action or way to behave.

ADHD is associated with a deficit in *executive functioning*, those cognitive abilities needed to formulate a goal, plan a series of actions to achieve the goal, and maintain the plan in memory in order to carry it out (Lesaca, 2001; Sergeant et al., 2002; Willcutt et al., 2005). Jason is an example of a child who has ADHD combined type. Other children, like Allie, have ADHD but are not hyperactive, displaying only attentional problems.

Allie is 12 years old. She has been having problems paying attention since she was in grade 2 and currently she is having problems at home and at school. She has always had difficulty following directions and avoiding careless mistakes, and that affects her schoolwork. Allie's assignments are incomplete, her grades are poor, and her teacher thinks that she just does not care. At home her mom gets frustrated with the length of time that Allie needs to finish her homework. She has difficulty following instructions and organizing tasks and loses things, but she never gets in trouble at home or school for not being able to stay in her seat. During the interview, Allie tapped her foot and played with a pencil.

ADHD is most commonly diagnosed in early elementary school. Establishing the diagnosis early (i.e., during the preschool years) is challenging because many symptoms (short attention span, difficulty sitting still, high activity level) are developmentally appropriate during toddlerhood (Blackman, 1999). When ADHD is diagnosed at the preschool age, the combined type is most common (Lahey et al., 1998; Wilens et al., 2002). When diagnosed at this early age, children continue to have ADHD symptoms during the elementary school years (Lahey et al., 2004).

It was once thought that ADHD typically disappears at or shortly after puberty (Smith et al., 2000). It is now clear that adolescents and adults also suffer from ADHD (Biederman, 2005). Some adults were diagnosed in childhood, but a substantial number are diagnosed for the first time in adulthood. Determining ADHD in adults is a challenge and is controversial. Some of the diagnostic criteria (inability to sit still in class, difficulty playing quietly) are obviously not valid for adults. Also, deciding whether an adult had such symptoms before age 7 is difficult because it is often based solely on retrospective self-report (McGough & Barkley, 2004). In DSM-5, the diagnostic criteria for ADHD are valid for adults as well as children, with the need for five symptoms (rather than six symptoms) for a reliable diagnosis (APA, 2013).

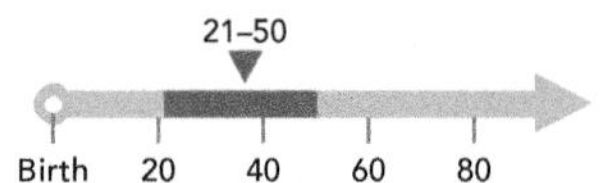

ADHD is considered to have its onset in childhood, but in some cases the disorder is not diagnosed until adulthood.

Children and adults with ADHD often have other disorders, including conduct problems (Wilens et al., 2002), mood disorders, anxiety disorders, and learning disabilities

SIDE by SIDE case studies — Dimensions of Behaviour: From Normal to Abnormal

Normal Behaviour Case Study

Boyish Exuberance

Ronnie is 6 years old. He has older brothers and loves "rough and tumble" play. He has broken a few family possessions but not more than his brothers. He does not like to sit quietly for a long period of time; reading has never been his favourite activity. However, 90% of the time he finishes the activities that he starts. He was eager to start grade 1. He gets good grades and has been sent to the principal only once, for talking out of turn. Sitting still in grade 1 is hard—he says school is boring. Psychological testing revealed a superior IQ score, and when he started the gifted and talented program, his out-of-seat behaviour disappeared and he no longer found school boring.

Abnormal Behaviour Case Study

Attention-Deficit Hyperactivity Disorder

Jason is 7 years old. He has trouble at school academically and complains that he hates school. He has no friends and is constantly picked on by the other children. He wants to socialize, but he always ends up fighting. He is genuinely puzzled about why other children do not like him. Jason is impulsive—he interrupts others, butts in line, and disrupts organized games. He cannot sit still, does not pay attention in class, and will not follow the rules at home. His mother reports that he has been a "wild child" since age 3. During the clinic interview, Jason does not sit in the chair. At times he lies down on the floor, and a few moments later, he is standing on the windowsill.

(Biederman, 2005). Similarly, among adults with ADHD, anxiety disorders are most common, followed by mood disorders, substance abuse, and antisocial personality disorder.

Functional Impairment

Children with ADHD have more accidents and injuries (perhaps as a result of poor motor coordination), poor peer relationships, and academic underachievement, sleep problems, and family stress (Biederman, 2005; Daley, 2006). Among adolescents, school delinquency, failure to graduate from high school, smoking, and substance abuse are common (Biederman & Faraone, 2005; Smith et al., 2000). Perhaps because of inattentiveness and impulsivity, adolescents with ADHD have a higher risk of injury and are more likely to have automobile accidents and to be involved in criminal behaviour than other adolescents (Smith et al., 2000).

The course of ADHD is variable. At mid-adolescence, 20% of boys who had ADHD as children had poor academic, social, and emotional functioning (Biederman et al., 1998). However, 20% were functioning well, and 60% had an intermediate outcome (doing poorly in some areas and well in others).

An estimated 2.5% of Canadian children have ADHD (Waddell et al., 2014). Boys are four to five times more likely than girls to have ADHD (Costello et al., 2003). Boys with ADHD may have more severe symptoms or may suffer more impairment than others, making it more likely that their parents will seek treatment. Compared with boys, girls with ADHD have different impairments. They are more likely to have the predominantly inattentive subtype, less likely to have a learning disability, less likely to have problems in school or in their spare time, and less likely to have comorbid depression, oppositional

criteria for Attention-Deficit/Hyperactivity Disorder — DSM-5

A. A persistent pattern of inattention and/or hyperactivity-impulsivity that interferes with functioning or development, as characterized by (1) and/or (2):

1. **Inattention:** Six (or more) of the following symptoms have persisted for at least 6 months to a degree that is inconsistent with developmental level and that negatively impacts directly on social and academic/occupational activities:

   Note: The symptoms are not solely a manifestation of oppositional behaviour, defiance, hostility, or failure to understand tasks or instructions. For older adolescents and adults (age 17 and older), at least five symptoms are required.

   a. Often fails to give close attention to details or makes careless mistakes in schoolwork, at work, or during other activities (e.g., overlooks or misses details, work is inaccurate).
   b. Often has difficulty sustaining attention in tasks or play activities (e.g., has difficulty remaining focused during lectures, conversations, or lengthy reading).
   c. Often does not seem to listen when spoken to directly (e.g., mind seems elsewhere, even in the absence of any obvious distraction).
   d. Often does not follow through on instructions and fails to finish schoolwork, chores, or duties in the workplace (e.g., starts tasks but quickly loses focus and is easily sidetracked).
   e. Often has difficulty organizing tasks and activities (e.g., difficulty managing sequential tasks; difficulty keeping materials and belongings in order; messy, disorganized work; has poor time management; fails to meet deadlines).
   f. Often avoids, dislikes, or is reluctant to engage in tasks that require sustained mental effort (e.g., schoolwork or homework; for older adolescents and adults, preparing reports, completing forms, reviewing lengthy papers).
   g. Often loses things necessary for tasks or activities (e.g., school materials, pencils, books, tools, wallets, keys, paperwork, eyeglasses, mobile telephones).
   h. Is often easily distracted by extraneous stimuli (for older adolescents and adults, may include unrelated thoughts).
   i. Is often forgetful in daily activities (e.g., doing chores, running errands; for older adolescents and adults, returning calls, paying bills, keeping appointments).

2. **Hyperactivity and impulsivity:** Six (or more) of the following symptoms have persisted for at least 6 months to a degree that is inconsistent with developmental level and that negatively impacts directly on social and academic/occupational activities:

(continued)

Note: The symptoms are not solely a manifestation of oppositional behaviour, defiance, hostility, or a failure to understand tasks or instructions. For older adolescents and adults (age 17 and older), at least five symptoms are required.

a. Often fidgets with or taps hands or feet or squirms in seat.
b. Often leaves seat in situations when remaining seated is expected (e.g., leaves his or her place in the classroom, in the office or other workplace, or in other situations that require remaining in place).
c. Often runs about or climbs in situations where it is inappropriate. (**Note:** In adolescents or adults, may be limited to feeling restless.)
d. Often unable to play or engage in leisure activities quietly.
e. Is often "on the go," acting as if "driven by a motor" (e.g., is unable to be or uncomfortable being still for extended time, as in restaurants, meetings; may be experienced by others as being restless or difficult to keep up with).
f. Often talks excessively.
g. Often blurts out an answer before a question has been completed (e.g., completes people's sentences; cannot wait for turn in conversation).
h. Often has difficulty waiting his or her turn (e.g., while waiting in line).
i. Often interrupts or intrudes on others (e.g., butts into conversations, games, or activities; may start using other people's things without asking or receiving permission; for adolescents and adults, may intrude into or take over what others are doing).

B. Several inattentive or hyperactive-impulsive symptoms were present prior to age 12 years.

C. Several inattentive or hyperactive-impulsive symptoms are present in two or more settings (e.g., at home, school, or work; with friends or relatives; in other activities).

D. There is clear evidence that the symptoms interfere with, or reduce the quality of, social, academic, or occupational functioning.

E. The symptoms do not occur exclusively during the course of schizophrenia or another psychotic disorder and are not better explained by another mental disorder (e.g., mood disorder, anxiety disorder, dissociative disorder, personality disorder, substance intoxication or withdrawal).

defiant disorder, or conduct disorder than other girls (Biederman et al., 2002; Spencer et al., 2007). Teachers rate boys with ADHD as more inattentive and hyperactive/impulsive than girls with this disorder (Greene et al., 2001; Hartung et al., 2002).

Symptoms of ADHD appear to improve at different rates. Symptoms of inattention decline only minimally as children mature, while hyperactivity/impulsivity symptoms show a much higher rate of decline, particularly from elementary school through mid-adolescence (Spencer et al., 2007). About 50% of children diagnosed with ADHD will continue to have the disorder during adolescence (Smith et al., 2000). The outlook is better for adults. Most adults who had ADHD as children will no longer have the disorder by age 30 to 40, but about 50% will still have some functional impairment (Biederman & Faraone, 2005).

Etiology

ADHD is considered to be a neurodevelopmental disorder with genetic, biological, and environmental influences. Like many other disorders, ADHD "runs in families," with between 20% and 25% of family members of someone with ADHD having symptoms. Twin studies also support its heritability. A mean heritability of 77% (Biederman, 2005) suggests a substantial genetic influence. Toronto researchers, including Russell Schachar (at Toronto's Hospital for Sick Children) and colleagues, have conducted a number of studies of the candidate genes for ADHD (e.g., Adams et al., 2004; Couto et al., 2009; Misener et al., 2004; Quist et al., 2003). Their findings suggest that there are probably many genes involved in the disorder, including genes that play a role in regulating the dopamine and serotonin neurotransmitter systems. It appears that different genes may be associated with the inattentive and hyperactivity dimensions (Nikolas & Burt, 2010). Genetics or other prenatal factors may affect fetal or neonatal brain development. Structural brain imaging studies (i.e., MRI) reveal abnormalities in the frontal cortex, cerebellum, and subcortex when children with ADHD are compared with children who do not have the disorder (Castellanos et al., 2002). These structural abnormalities are stable, non-progressive, and unchangeable, even with medication.

Other potential contributory factors include lead contamination, maternal smoking or alcohol use during pregnancy, pregnancy and delivery complications (Biederman, 2005; Biederman & Faraone, 2005), and psychological risk factors such as marital discord, low socioeconomic status, large family size, foster care placement, paternal criminality, and maternal psychological problems (Rutter et al., 1976). It is clear that the etiology of ADHD is complex and is probably influenced by many different factors, each of which makes a single, small contribution (Faraone et al., 2005).

Perhaps because of their inattentiveness, children with ADHD are more likely to have childhood accidents, such as falling off of their bicycles.

Francisco Cruz/Superstock

Treatment

12.4 Identify positive and negative aspects of pharmacological treatments.

Both pharmacological and behavioural interventions have been used effectively to treat ADHD. Stimulant medications, such as Ritalin, have a 40-year record of efficacy for ADHD's core symptoms (Biederman & Faraone, 2005). The drugs work by enhancing the neurotransmission of dopamine and norepinephrine (Spencer et al., 2004), allowing these chemicals to remain in the synapses for a longer period of time, increasing their availability for neurotransmission. These drugs decrease ADHD's core symptoms, but whether they affect other areas of functioning, such as academic achievement, is less clear (Hechtman & Greenfield, 2003; Wells et al., 2000).

The use of stimulants to treat ADHD is controversial. First, up to 30% of children may not respond to stimulant medication (Chronis et al., 2006). Second, side effects include emotional problems, sleep disturbance, appetite decrease, and irritability. The symptoms are more frequent among preschool children (Daley et al., 2009). Stimulant medication may affect physical stature. Children who take stimulants grow more slowly than other children, and recent prescribing practices mean that children are now taking these medications at higher doses, during the summer as well as the school year, and for many more years than in the past. The increase in medication use raises concerns about how these drugs affect height (Lerner & Wigal, 2008). A slower than normal rate of growth is greatest in the first year of use; it continues in the second year, and appears to end in the third year. When considering stimulants as part of treatment for ADHD, parents and mental health professionals must balance the advantages of reducing symptoms against the potential for shorter stature.

For preschool children, parenting programs are recommended as the first treatment for children with ADHD. Medication should be used only when parent training is not efficacious (Daley et al., 2009). Additional psychosocial treatments for school-age children with ADHD include behavioural parent training, classroom behavioural management (daily report cards), social skills training, and an intensive outpatient/summer treatment program (Chronis et al., 2006; Pelham & Fabiano, 2008). *Behavioural parent training* teaches parents how to reward positive behaviours and decrease negative behaviours. In addition to improving core ADHD symptoms and sometimes classroom behaviour (Chronis et al., 2006; Pelham et al., 1998), behavioural parent training improves parenting behaviour and may also decrease stress on parents (Chronis et al., 2004). The *Daily Report Card* is a classroom behavioural management program that targets school-relevant goals such as completing homework and staying in one's seat (Chronis et al., 2004; Smith et al., 2000). Teachers record classroom behaviour on a report card and parents use a reward system to reinforce positive school behaviours. A third behavioural treatment, social skills training, teaches children with ADHD to interact appropriately with others (taking turns, allowing others to decide which game to play). Social skills training appears to be particularly efficacious when combined with behavioural parent training (e.g., Pfiffner & McBurnett, 1997).

Because of the range and severity of their behavioural problems, children with ADHD may require intensive and comprehensive treatment programs. The Summer Treatment Program (Pelham et al., 2000) is an eight week, all-day program that includes a point system, daily report cards, social skills training, academic skills training, problem-solving training, and sports training in a day camp atmosphere. It includes weekly parent management training and has been found to be an efficacious intervention for children with ADHD, decreasing symptoms and increasing associated behavioural functioning (e.g., Pelham et al., 2000, 2004).

The Collaborative Multimodal Treatment (MTA) Study of Children with ADHD is the largest controlled clinical trial comparing behavioural treatment (using the components just described), medication (primarily stimulant medication), a combination of behavioural treatment and medication, and standard community care for preadolescent children with ADHD. At the end of the treatment program, all four treatments improved children's symptoms, but children in the medication only and children in the combined group showed significantly more improvement than children in behavioural treatment alone or community care (MTA Cooperative Group, 1999). Do the results of this study mean that behavioural intervention is not useful for ADHD, or at the least, that it does not add value over medication? When an alternative method of data analysis was used, children who received medication and behaviour therapy had a superior outcome over medication alone, which contradicts the original outcome (Conners et al., 2001). Thus, even though this was the largest child treatment study so far conducted, its results are unclear and subject to various interpretations.

Conduct Disorder and Oppositional Defiant Disorder

12.5 Identify psychosocial treatments for the disorders that emerge during childhood and adolescence.

12.6 Describe the unique role of parents in the treatment of children and adolescents.

All of the disorders discussed this far in this chapter are included in the broad diagnostic category of *neurodevelopmental disorders*. Two other disorders that appear commonly in children are *conduct disorder* and *oppositional defiant disorder*. These disorders are included in a different diagnostic category called *disruptive, impulse control, and conduct disorders*. There are a number of disorders included in this diagnostic category, but here we focus on the two most common and most researched. Although considered separate disorders, conduct disorder and oppositional defiant disorder are characterized by deviant, and sometimes unlawful, behaviours. They are among the most difficult disorders to treat, are the most common reason that a child is brought to a mental health clinic (Loeber et al., 2000), and often lead to incarceration in the juvenile justice system.

Conduct disorder (CD) (see "DSM-5: Conduct Disorder"), by far the more serious disorder, is a repetitive and persistent pattern of behaviour in which the basic rights of others or major age-appropriate societal norms or rules are violated (APA, 2013). Behaviours fall into four different categories: aggression to people or animals, destruction of property, deceitfulness or theft, and serious rule violations.

criteria for Conduct Disorder DSM-5

A. A repetitive and persistent pattern of behaviour in which the basic rights of others or major age-appropriate societal norms or rules are violated, as manifested by the presence of at least three of the following 15 criteria in the past 12 months from any of the categories below, with at least one criterion present in the past 6 months:

Aggression to People and Animals

1. Often bullies, threatens, or intimidates others.
2. Often initiates physical fights.
3. Has used a weapon that can cause serious physical harm to others (e.g., a bat, brick, broken bottle, knife, gun).
4. Has been physically cruel to people.
5. Has been physically cruel to animals.
6. Has stolen while confronting a victim (e.g., mugging, purse snatching, extortion, armed robbery).
7. Has forced someone into sexual activity.

Destruction of Property

8. Has deliberately engaged in fire setting with the intention of causing serious damage.
9. Has deliberately destroyed others' property (other than by fire setting).

Deceitfulness or Theft

10. Has broken into someone else's house, building, or car.
11. Often lies to obtain goods or favours or to avoid obligations (i.e., "cons" others).
12. Has stolen items of nontrivial value without confronting a victim (e.g., shoplifting, but without breaking and entering; forgery).

Serious Violations of Rules

13. Often stays out at night despite parental prohibitions, beginning before age 13 years.
14. Has run away from home overnight at least twice while living in the parental or parental surrogate home, or once without returning for a lengthy period.
15. Is often truant from school, beginning before age 13 years.

B. The disturbance in behaviour causes clinically significant impairment in social, academic, or occupational functioning.

C. If the individual is age 18 years or older, criteria are not met for antisocial personality disorder.

criteria for Oppositional Defiant Disorder DSM-5

A. A pattern of angry/irritable mood, argumentative/defiant behaviour, or vindictiveness lasting at least 6 months as evidenced by at least four symptoms from any of the following categories, and exhibited during interaction with at least one individual who is not a sibling.

Angry/Irritable Mood

1. Often loses temper.
2. Is often touchy or easily annoyed.
3. Is often angry and resentful.

Argumentative/Defiant Behaviour

4. Often argues with authority figures or, for children and adolescents, with adults.
5. Often actively defies or refuses to comply with requests from authority figures or with rules.
6. Often deliberately annoys others.
7. Often blames others for his or her mistakes or misbehaviour.

Vindictiveness

8. Has been spiteful or vindictive at least twice within the past 6 months.

Note: The persistence and frequency of these behaviours should be used to distinguish a behaviour that is within normal limits from a behaviour that is symptomatic. For children younger than 5 years, the behaviour should occur on most days for a period of at least 6 months unless otherwise noted (Criterion A8). For individuals 5 years or older, the behaviour should occur at least once per week for at least 6 months, unless otherwise noted (Criterion A8). While these frequency criteria provide guidance on a minimal level of frequency to define symptoms, other factors should also be considered, such as whether

(*continued*)

the frequency and intensity of the behaviours are outside a range that is normative for the individual's developmental level, gender, and culture.

B. The disturbance in behaviour is associated with distress in the individual or others in his or her immediate social context (e.g., family, peer group, work colleagues), or it impacts negatively on social, educational, occupational, or other important areas of functioning.

C. The behaviours do not occur exclusively during the course of a psychotic, substance use, depressive, or bipolar disorder. Also, the criteria are not met for disruptive mood dysregulation disorder.

The first category, *aggression to people and animals*, includes what is commonly known as *bullying behaviour*—making threats or intimidation directed toward others, such as initiating physical fights, stealing, physical cruelty, or forcing someone to engage in sexual activity. Such children are also physically cruel toward people and animals. The second category is *destruction of property*, such as vandalism or deliberate fire setting. We emphasize that this is a behavioural pattern—not simply an isolated incident of property destruction, as often happens when siblings fight. The third component is *deceitfulness or theft* and includes activities such as breaking into houses or cars, lying, and nonconfrontational theft—shoplifting or forgery. The fourth component includes *serious violations of rules*, such as breaking parental curfews, running away from home overnight, and school truancy.

Cecily is 8 years old. Her mother describes her as a "behaviour problem." Specifically, Cecily often loses her temper and throws tantrums, particularly when she does not get her own way. She is not physically aggressive, but argues with her parents whenever they ask her to do something and is constantly disobedient. She refused to clean up her room unless her parents gave her $10. She deliberately teases her baby brother and then laughs when he cries. Her mother describes her as spiteful. Her older sister received an award for an art project. The day after her sister brought the trophy home, it was discovered broken in half and the art project destroyed. When her mother confronted Cecily about it, Cecily blamed it on her 1-year-old brother.

Cecily's behaviours are characteristic of **oppositional defiant disorder (ODD)**, another disruptive behaviour disorder (see "DSM-5: Oppositional Defiant Disorder"). ODD is a pattern or angry/irritable mood, argumentative/defiant behaviour, or vindictiveness (APA, 2013). It is important to understand that this is a consistent pattern of behaviour and that the behaviour occurs with at least one person who is not a sibling. Whereas the behaviours that are part of conduct disorder (deliberate fire setting, armed robbery, deliberate cruelty to people or animals) are inappropriate at any age, some behaviours that are part of ODD must be considered within a developmental context. For example, temper tantrums are common among 2-year-olds. However, Cecily is not 2 years old, and her temper tantrums are not simply an expression of typical toddler frustration.

The first signs of ODD occur during the preschool years (APA, 2013), and it almost always begins before early adolescence. Unlike ADHD and conduct disorder, characterized by disruptive behaviours in several settings, it is common for children with ODD to behave negatively only at home. At their core, both of these disorders have a pattern of negative behaviours directed against people and society. We examine them together throughout the remainder of this section.

Functional Impairment

These disorders, and particularly conduct disorder, are associated with academic failure, substance abuse, risky sexual behaviour, and criminal activities. Many children with ODD and CD have additional disorders, and the combination negatively affects outcome. Coexisting ADHD is common in boys (Hinshaw, 1994). Commonly co-occurring disorders among girls include anxiety and mood disorders, and girls with both conduct disorder and depression are at increased risk for suicidal behaviours (Keenan et al., 1999). Substance abuse is a common problem among children with CD (Keenan et al., 1999; Loeber et al., 2000). For girls, CD is also associated with early pregnancy (Keenan et al., 1999). As adults, some children with either ODD or CD will have antisocial personality disorder.

In community samples, the prevalence of conduct disorder ranges from about 2% to 16% for boys and 1% to 10% for girls (Loeber et al., 2009). For ODD, prevalence estimates range from about 3% to 16% in community samples (Loeber et al., 2009). Both disorders are more prevalent among children from lower socioeconomic classes and from the worst inner-city neighbourhoods (Loeber et al., 2000). Boys are more likely to have a diagnosis of ODD than girls (13% vs. 9%, respectively, by age 16; Costello et al., 2003). Initially, conduct disorder in girls was relatively understudied because so few girls engage in physical fights. However, it is now clear that girls engage in *relational aggression*, which includes peer alienation, ostracism, manipulating social networks, circulating slanderous rumours, and character defamation (Ehrensaft, 2005; Keenan et al., 1999). When physical aggression does occur, boys target strangers and girls target family or intimate partners (Ehrensaft, 2005). Conduct disorder is stable across time, meaning that children who are diagnosed with this condition usually do not outgrow it. Some children with ODD will develop CD, but others who initially receive a diagnosis of ODD will develop depression or anxiety disorder (Loeber et al., 2000; Rowe et al., 2010).

From a developmental perspective, some mental health clinicians have questioned whether preschool children can be diagnosed with ODD or conduct disorder. For preschoolers, some symptoms of CD are developmentally impossible (forcible sexual activity, truancy), developmentally improbable (fire setting, stealing with confrontation), or developmentally imprecise (often loses temper; Wakschlag et al., 2010). If we think about the core features of CD, there appear to be four elements: temper loss, aggression, noncompliance, and low concern for others. Using a developmental perspective, temper loss in a toddler may be displayed by crying and throwing oneself on the ground; in an adolescent, it may involve the physical assault of another person. Preschoolers do not have access to knives or guns, but they might use sticks or stones for weapons (Keenan & Wakschlag, 2002). Similarly, older children may steal cars, whereas preschool children may steal candy. Behaviours that are part of ODD and CD may change again when adolescents reach adulthood, at which time the diagnosis is antisocial personality disorder (see Chapter 11). Using this developmental perspective, it is clear that disruptive behaviour disorders exist at all ages, even if they are expressed differently at various developmental stages.

Less likely than boys to engage in physical aggression, girls with conduct problems often engage in relational aggression—such as teasing and ostracizing other girls.

Radius Images/Alamy Stock Photo

Etiology

Little is known about the cause of ODD because virtually all of the research on genetics, neuroanatomy, and neurochemistry has been directed at CD. Some evidence for a familial relationship between conduct disorder and adult antisocial personality disorder exists, but to date, genetic studies have not provided specific clues (Burke et al., 2002). Potential environmental causes include prenatal factors such as maternal smoking or substance abuse, pregnancy and birth complications, and postnatal environmental toxins such as lead. Psychological disorders in parents, poor parenting behaviours, child abuse, and socioeconomic status may also play a causal role. Any of these factors may be associated with CD or ODD, but it is highly unlikely that any one factor will be identified as important for all children with disruptive disorders (Burke et al., 2002).

Treatment

Most mental health clinicians agree that psychosocial interventions should be the first line of treatment. Medication, particularly when used alone, has been unsuccessful in treating the core symptoms of ODD and conduct disorder (Bassarath, 2003). There are very few controlled treatment trials for children with ODD or CD, and even fewer with samples in which the children do not also have other disorders. However, given those limitations, atypical antipsychotic drugs such as risperidone reduce symptoms of aggression in children with ODD and conduct disorder (Bassarath, 2003; Pandina et al., 2006).

An effective behavioural treatment for ODD and CD is parent management training (Patterson & Gullion, 1968) (see the discussion of behavioural parent training in the section on ADHD treatment). For ODD and CD, parent management training is more efficacious than treatment as usual or no treatment (Brestan & Eyberg, 1998; Farmer et al., 2002; van den Wiel et al., 2002; Webster-Stratton et al., 1988). Particularly efficacious for preadolescent children, it may reduce criminal arrests, decrease time spent in institutions, and decrease self-reported delinquency compared with usual care or no treatment (Woolfenden et al., 2002).

A community-based intervention for ODD and CD is multisystemic therapy (MST), an intensive case management approach to treatment (Henggeler et al., 1998). MST includes interventions conducted in the clinic, at home, at school—wherever the need exists. The choice of treatment is flexible—individual therapy, family therapy, social work interventions to assist in family functioning, and therapists always "on call" to provide needed services. MST, provided primarily to adolescent populations, is an efficacious intervention that not only decreases symptoms of conduct disorder, but also decreases incarceration in both hospitals and juvenile justice settings (Henggeler et al., 1999).

CONCEPT check

- ADHD has variable symptoms and a complicated and complex etiology. The disorder creates significant functional impairment in many aspects of life.
- ADHD, once considered a disorder that affected only children, is now understood in some cases to continue into adolescence and adulthood. Both pharmacological and behavioural interventions are efficacious for the treatment of this disorder.
- Conduct disorder and ODD might be considered to be disorders of "misbehaviour" and include activities such as disobedience, lying for no apparent reason, truancy, and other delinquent activities. Some children with ODD may develop conduct disorder as adolescents. CD exists in girls but is sometimes overlooked if clinicians do not look for evidence of relational, rather than physical, aggression.
- The causes of ODD and CD are unknown and complex. Treatments must likewise be multifaceted.

critical thinking question A friend in your abnormal psychology class thinks that he has ADHD, but he was never evaluated or diagnosed as a child. How would he go about collecting empirical evidence to demonstrate he had the disorder as a child, which is necessary for a diagnosis?

Elimination Disorders

An important aspect of physical development is controlling bladder and bowel functions, which usually happens in the preschool years. Lack of control after this time may indicate the presence of enuresis or encopresis (see "DSM-5: Elimination Disorders"). **Enuresis** is the repeated voiding of urine into one's clothing or bedding. It may occur during the day (diurnal enuresis), at night (nocturnal enuresis), or both times (diurnal and nocturnal). *Primary* enuresis describes a condition in which a child has never achieved urinary continence (voiding urine is fully under the child's control); *secondary* enuresis occurs if a child who was once fully continent loses that control. Primary nocturnal enuresis, or bed-wetting, is the most common form of the disorder.

Each year, approximately 15% of children with enuresis recover without treatment (Forsythe & Redmond, 1974; Jalkut et al., 2001). Although enuresis may distress children and parents, little actual research has examined which children recover without the need for treatment. Enuresis occurs worldwide, with prevalence estimates ranging from 3.1% to 7.3% depending on age (Costello et al., 1996; Jalkut et al., 2001; Wille, 1994; Yeung et al., 2006). Boys are more likely to have nocturnal enuresis, whereas girls are more likely to have diurnal enuresis (APA, 2013).

Despite many years of study, it is not clear whether children with enuresis have weaker bladders than other children (Jalkut et al., 2001; Wille, 1994). Enuresis does run in families. Between 30% and 40% of children with enuresis have parents who had primary nocturnal enuresis (Jalkut et al., 2001), and monozygotic twins are twice as likely to be concordant for enuresis than dizygotic twins. Multigenerational family studies have implicated areas on four different chromosomes that may hold genes contributing to the cause of enuresis (see Mikkelsen, 2001). However, psychosocial and environmental factors cannot be overlooked (von Gontard et al., 2001).

criteria for Elimination Disorders DSM-5

Enuresis

A. Repeated voiding of urine into bed or clothes, whether involuntary or intentional.

B. The behaviour is clinically significant as manifested by either a frequency of at least twice a week for at least 3 consecutive months or the presence of clinically significant distress or impairment in social, academic (occupational), or other important areas of functioning.

C. Chronological age is at least 5 years (or equivalent developmental level).

D. The behaviour is not attributable to the physiological effects of a substance (e.g., a diuretic, an antipsychotic medication) or another medical condition (e.g., diabetes, spina bifida, a seizure disorder).

Encopresis

A. Repeated passage of feces into inappropriate places (e.g., clothing, floor), whether involuntary or intentional.

B. At least one such event occurs each month for at least 3 months.

C. Chronological age is at least 4 years (or equivalent developmental level).

D. The behaviour is not attributable to the physiological effects of a substance (e.g., laxatives) or another medical condition except through a mechanism involving constipation.

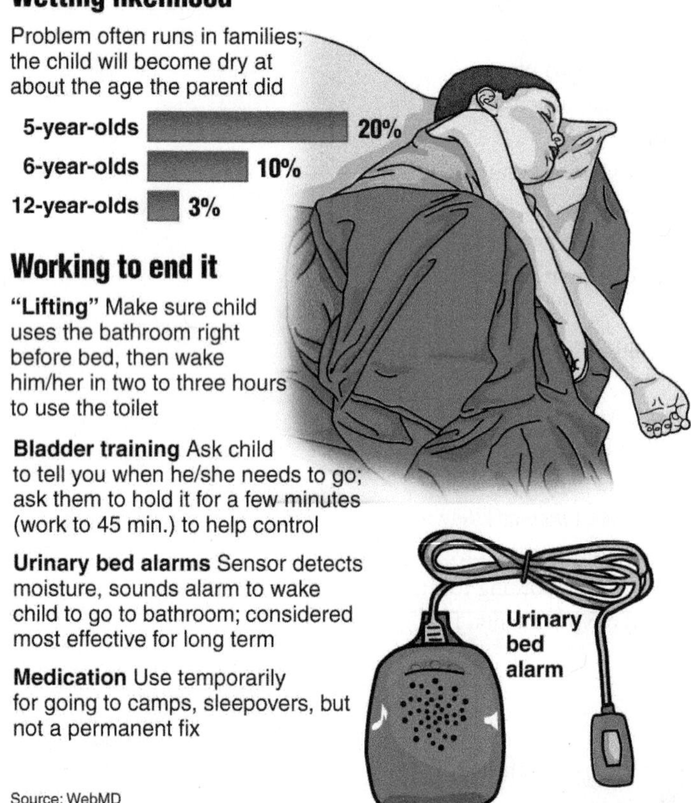

Kids Health Matters
Coping with bedwetting
Pediatricians stress that wetting the bed is not because of laziness or spite; kids simply must mature and grow out of it.
Wetting likelihood
Problem often runs in families; the child will become dry at about the age the parent did
5-year-olds 20%
6-year-olds 10%
12-year-olds 3%
Working to end it
"Lifting" Make sure child uses the bathroom right before bed, then wake him/her in two to three hours to use the toilet
Bladder training Ask child to tell you when he/she needs to go; ask them to hold it for a few minutes (work to 45 min.) to help control
Urinary bed alarms Sensor detects moisture, sounds alarm to wake child to go to bathroom; considered most effective for long term
Medication Use temporarily for going to camps, sleepovers, but not a permanent fix
Urinary bed alarm
Source: WebMD
Graphic: Angela Smith, Garrick Gibson
© 2008 MCT

An alarm device is often used in the treatment of enuresis. A moisture sensor is attached to the child's underwear and detects moisture, triggering an alarm that awakens the child to get up and use the toilet.

Gibson/MCT/Newscom

Environmental and psychological factors that may contribute to the development of secondary enuresis include behavioural disturbances, stressful life events, and delayed achievement of initial bladder control (Eidlitz-Markus et al., 2000; Fergusson et al., 1990; Jalkut et al., 2001), suggesting that both genetic and environmental factors may be the most appropriate model for understanding the development of enuresis.

For enuresis, the most empirically supported treatment is the *enuresis alarm* (Mikkelsen, 2001), initially known as the *bell-and-pad* method when it was introduced in 1902 (Jalkut et al., 2001). The system consists of a battery-operated alarm or vibrator that is connected to a thin wire attached to the child's underwear, sleeping pad, or bedding. When urination begins, the alarm awakens the child, who then goes to the toilet. Over time, the child becomes sensitized to the sensations of a full bladder and awakens before urination. The average success rate for enuresis alarms, defined as 14 consecutive dry nights, is 65% (Butler & Gasson, 2005), but the average relapse rate is 42%. Relapse rates are higher when the intervention is short (less than seven weeks).

Currently, the most common medication for enuresis is desmopressin acetate (DDAVP), which reduces nighttime urinary output and the number of enuretic episodes. However, the reduction in enuretic episodes varies greatly, and only a small percentage continue to "stay dry" once the medication is withdrawn.

Jake is 7 years old. He lives with his parents and a 3-year-old brother. He soils his underwear one or two times per day, always during the daytime. Jake refuses to sit on the toilet, and he shows other oppositional behaviours as well. He interacts well with his peers and is a good student. Jake has been soiling for more than four years. He was never adequately toilet trained and describes defecation as very painful. He does not change his soiled underwear unless he is told to do so. There are no behavioural consequences for soiling; as a matter of fact, his mother leaves a stack of his clean underwear in the bathroom. His father tries to pressure Jake to use the toilet.

Encopresis is the repeated passage of feces on or into inappropriate places, whether voluntary or intentional, by someone over age 4 (see "DSM-5 Elimination Disorders"). Encopresis can be intentional or accidental and, like enuresis, may be primary or secondary.

Children with encopresis often feel ashamed and avoid social interaction. They may be ostracized by peers and be the target of anger, punishment, and rejection by others, including family (APA, 2013). Compared with children with no disorder, children with encopresis had higher parent and teacher ratings of anxiety, depression, and behavioural problems, but only 20% had significant functional impairment or substantial distress (Cox et al., 2002). About 1% of 5-year-old children suffer from encopresis (APA), but they account for 3% of all pediatric appointments and 25% of pediatric gastroenterology appointments (Brooks et al., 2000).

The etiology of encopresis is rarely studied. About 80% of children with encopresis have chronic constipation, and in 90% of all cases of chronic constipation, there is no obvious medical or functional cause (Issenman et al., 1999; van Dijk et al., 2007). Encopresis is often the result of withholding the stool, perhaps as a result of previous painful defecation experiences or extremely hard stools. This leads to chronic constipation and subsequent involuntary leakage of feces as a result of stool impaction (van Dijk et al., 2007).

Medical treatment for encopresis consists of enemas to clear the bowel and laxatives to deal with constipation. However, this intervention is usually considered to be only the first stage and is followed by behavioural interventions to "promote proper toileting behaviour" (daily toilet sitting and use of positive reinforcement). The medical-behavioural intervention is superior to medical treatment alone (Brooks et al., 2000), with improvement rates ranging from 65% to 78% (Borowitz et al., 2002; Cox et al., 1998).

CONCEPT check

- Enuresis appears to have a genetic component, although specific genes have not been identified.
- Encopresis often results from medical problems such as constipation, which may in turn be caused by poor diet.

critical thinking question Enuresis and encopresis are responsive to behavioural interventions, which are considered the treatment of choice. Because these problems appear medical in nature, how would you explain the success of behavioural interventions to the parents of a 9-year-old with enuresis?

real SCIENCE real LIFE

Danny—The Treatment of Social Anxiety Disorder and Autism Spectrum Disorder

THE PATIENT

Danny is 12 years old. He lives with his two older brothers and his parents. From birth, Danny's mother described him as "different." He would not cuddle with her. If someone tried to hold him, he would arch his back and twist away. He is very smart and does well in school, but he has no friends and is often sad. Although he claims that he wants to be left alone, he has tears in his eyes when he says it. At recess, he stands away from the other children but watches them intently.

THE PROBLEM

Danny has a complicated developmental history. He appears to be anxious, has some difficulty paying attention, and is socially awkward. At age 8, he was diagnosed with ADHD and severe depression for which he was treated with medication. The medication for depression seemed to help but the medication for ADHD was ineffective. He has difficulty writing and he sometimes shows a lack of awareness of dangerous situations. He appears incredibly anxious around people. His mother began to worry that Danny was different when he was in grade 1. By the time he was in grade 3, she was convinced that he was different. She brought him at age 12 to the clinic for a thorough evaluation and treatment recommendations.

Danny agrees with his mother's report of his behaviour, but adds that he would really like to have friends but no one wants to be friends with him. On a self-report measure of social anxiety, Danny scored in the "definite social anxiety disorder" range. He describes feeling anxious when someone talks to him or he tries to talk to someone else. The interviewer noted that Danny made little eye contact during the interview and spoke in a very monotonic voice. At the time of the assessment, he was not depressed and he did not display any behaviours consistent with ADHD.

THE TREATMENT PROGRESS

Danny was diagnosed with autism spectrum disorder and social anxiety disorder.

Danny participated in a social skills training group that consisted of four boys, all of whom were diagnosed with autism spectrum disorder. The group met once per week for 12 weeks, and the topics included initiating, maintaining, and ending a

(continued)

conversation; skills for joining groups; giving and receiving compliments; refusing unreasonable requests; asking others to change their behaviour; and using the telephone. In addition to learning this verbal content, the group therapist worked with Danny on making eye contact and varying his vocal tone.

After each group meeting, the boys met for an hour with four peer helpers (boys who were friendly and outgoing) who had agreed to participate in the activities and work with the boys. All of the boys went to an activity (miniature golf, bowling, pizza parlours), and Danny was encouraged to practise that day's social skill with the peers. He was also given a homework assignment each week that was geared to the content of the group activity. For example, if the group had practised introducing oneself to another person, Danny's homework was to introduce himself to one new person every day. At the end of 12 weeks, Danny's social skills were reassessed. He had learned many of the skills necessary to make friends. His mom reported that he still had fewer friends than most boys, but he had made two new friends since joining the group. His score on the self-report measure of social anxiety had decreased from the definite social anxiety disorder range to the possible social anxiety disorder range. Danny told the interviewer that he had learned some skills but was too nervous to try them out.

THE TREATMENT

The clinician administered a structured diagnostic interview that revealed the following. Danny's problems started when he was about 2 years old. He had achieved all of his developmental milestones (walking, talking, bladder, and bowel control) at the typical ages. His difficulties appear to be in the social realm. He is reluctant to make eye contact, rarely smiles at people, has little understanding of jokes or sarcasm, has no friends, and needs constant reminders to "use his manners." He also develops obsessions with certain activities—science and solar systems, steam pipes, and video games. He does not like to be touched, even by his parents, and is extremely sensitive to sound.

Because he was still anxious and avoided social interactions, the therapist decided to conduct exposure therapy with Danny to address his social anxiety. The therapist, Danny, and his mother identified three anxiety-provoking situations: asking others questions, talking on the telephone, and having conversations with peers. In order for Danny to practise asking questions, he was given a survey task. Accompanied by the therapist, he was taken to a crowded environment and instructed to approach people, asking them to complete a short survey (topic depended upon the environment). With respect to the telephone, Danny first practised calling stores and requesting information. Later he called family and classmates to ask questions and carry on a conversation (the last step on the hierarchy). Because exposure therapy is designed to eliminate anxiety, Danny remained in the situation, continuing the task, until he could do it without any distress. Furthermore, he did not move to the next task until he was able to perform the previous task without any initial distress.

THE TREATMENT OUTCOME

After 10 sessions, Danny's mother reported that she observed Danny playing at recess and initiating conversations at the bus stop. In addition, he now maintained conversations with his grandparents and visiting relatives. He had been invited to a friend's house for a sleepover for the first time in his life. She reported that he had hugged her and his friend's mother for the first time. Danny reported that he was not shy anymore, and this was supported by his score on the self-report inventory, which was now in the "no social anxiety disorder" range.

It is important to note that this treatment addressed Danny's social interactions by increasing his social skills and decreasing his anxiety. Danny still met criteria for autism spectrum disorder based on other behaviours—he could still become fixated on unusual activities and topics, had great difficulty writing, had difficulty understanding humour and sarcasm, and did not enjoy physical contact with others.

summary

neurodevelopmental, disruptive, conduct, and elimination disorders

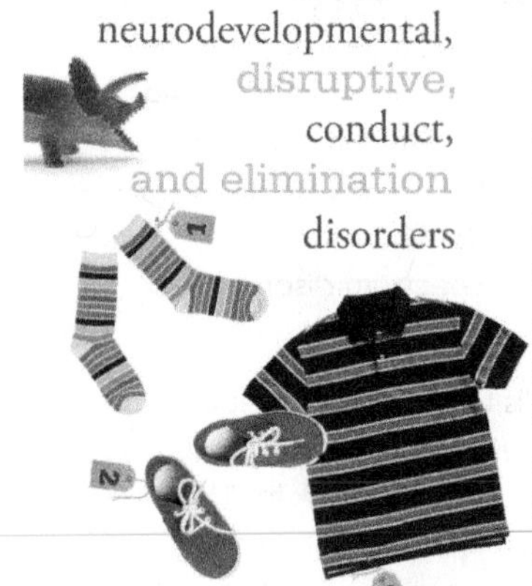

12.1 Describe how basic physical, cognitive, and emotional development during childhood and adolescence affect the expression of psychological disorders.

Physical, cognitive, and emotional growth during childhood and adolescence affect the development and expression of psychological disorders. It is necessary to understand behaviour within the context of normal development rather than immediately assuming that it is abnormal. As children mature and achieve developmental milestones, behaviour once considered appropriate may become symptomatic of a behavioural or an emotional disorder.

12.2 Identify psychological disorders that emerge primarily during childhood and adolescence.

A number of behavioural and emotional disorders emerge during infancy and childhood and are more common among children and adolescents than adults. These include intellectual disability, specific learning disorder, autism spectrum disorder, attention-deficit/hyperactivity disorder, oppositional defiant disorder, conduct disorder, and elimination disorders.

12.3 Understand etiological factors that contribute to the development of disorders during childhood and adolescence.
Both biological and environmental factors may contribute to the etiology of these disorders. A substantial number of biological disorders and conditions contribute to the development of intellectual disability. Similarly, a number of genetic variations appear relevant to the onset of autism spectrum disorders. In the case of other disorders, biological, psychological, and environmental factors are equally important. Furthermore, these factors operate in a complex fashion. Not all children with a particular disorder have the same *type* of disorder, and in many instances, the symptoms are not the same for all children. Therefore, multiple and different factors may eventually lead to the development of the same disorder.

12.4 Identify positive and negative aspects of pharmacological treatments.
Pharmacological interventions appear to be most efficacious for treating the core symptoms of ADHD. For other disorders, medication may control some of the associated features (e.g., aggression), but it is not effective for the core symptoms and is not considered to be useful as a single treatment.

12.5 Identify psychosocial treatments for the disorders that emerge during childhood and adolescence.
For many disorders (e.g., ADHD, CD, ODD), the primary psychological intervention is behavioural in nature and is directed at the parents rather than at the child with the disorder. Although behavioural theories do not necessarily propose that abnormal parent–child interactions are the cause of the psychological distress, they may be a maintaining factor and therefore must be targeted in a comprehensive treatment program. Furthermore, even when the child is the focus of treatment, parents play an important role in helping their child carry out the treatment program.

12.6 Describe the unique role of parents in the treatment of children and adolescents.
Teaching parents the basic skills necessary to effectively manage their children's behaviour is a highly efficacious treatment of choice for many of the disorders in this chapter. In the case of CD or ADHD, comprehensive psychosocial interventions such as summer treatment programs or multisystemic therapy offer great promise, not only in decreasing core symptoms but also in improving overall functioning.

key terms

attention-deficit/hyperactivity disorder (ADHD) 451
autism spectrum disorder 444
conduct disorder (CD) 456
cultural-familial retardation 439
Down syndrome 436
encopresis 462
enuresis 461
fetal alcohol syndrome (FAS) 438
fragile X syndrome (FXS) 437
intellectual disability 434
oppositional defiant disorder (ODD) 458
phenylketonuria (PKU) 437
specific learning disorder 441

TEST yourself

1. Micha is 13 years old. She has a heart defect and very poor eye–hand coordination, and she cannot dress herself. She speaks in simple sentences and can follow only simple instructions, but she is good-natured and friendly. Her IQ is 55. In addition to her intellectual deficit, Micha also has
   a. functional deficits
   b. social deficits
   c. attentional deficits
   d. emotional deficits

2. Down syndrome is caused by
   a. plaques and neurofibrillary tangles
   b. the absence of an essential enzyme
   c. the presence of an extra chromosome
   d. a break in a specific chromosome

3. The rate of Down syndrome as a proportion of live births increases with
   a. alcohol abuse
   b. the mother's age
   c. malnutrition
   d. smoking

4. A form of mild retardation resulting from both biological and environmental factors associated with psychosocial disadvantage is called
   a. Lesch-Nyhan syndrome
   b. environmental deprivation syndrome
   c. FAS
   d. cultural-familial retardation

5. Two behavioural procedures that allow children with intellectual disability to learn simple tasks are
   a. shaping and chaining
   b. affirmation and role-playing
   c. psychoeducation and questioning
   d. covert sensitization and modelling

6. Specific learning disorder is probably the result of
   a. an inability to digest milk products
   b. brain trauma during birth or infancy
   c. biological toxins that affect brain functioning
   d. the inability of several brain areas to work together

7. Which of the following is not a primary characteristic of autism spectrum disorder?
   a. restricted and stereotyped behaviours and activities
   b. difficulties with eye contact
   c. impairments in social interaction
   d. restricted neural synapses

8. The recent increased prevalence of autism spectrum disorders may be due to
   a. increases in the incidence of maternal exposure to toxic chemicals
   b. increases in the number of required childhood vaccines
   c. changes in diagnostic criteria, special education policies, and the availability of diagnostic services
   d. the availability of insurance coverage for expensive treatment, which justifies giving this diagnosis

9. One indication of the neurodevelopmental basis of autism spectrum disorder is
   a. excess activation in several parts of the brain
   b. excessive crying and fussing in infancy
   c. unusually fast head and brain growth in infancy
   d. significant retardation evident shortly after birth

10. The treatment approach that uses shaping and positive reinforcement to improve social, communication, and behavioural skills by intensively shaping and rewarding specific behaviours used to treat autism spectrum disorder is called
   a. applied behaviour analysis
   b. cognitive-behaviour therapy
   c. sensory integration therapy
   d. chelation therapy

11. Ted has been diagnosed with ADHD. Which behaviour is *not* likely to be a problem for him?
   a. inattention
   b. hyperactivity
   c. impulsivity
   d. isolation

12. Which of the following reasons explains why ADHD is most commonly diagnosed in early elementary school?
   a. children develop the disorder around age 7
   b. many symptoms are developmentally appropriate in younger children
   c. children cannot complete the complicated diagnostic assessments until they can read
   d. it is necessary to observe the child's behaviour in a school setting to make a definitive diagnosis

13. Adolescents with ADHD have more car accidents than others. This is most likely due to
   a. inattentiveness and poor motor coordination
   b. co-occurring substance abuse problems
   c. medications used to treat the condition
   d. sleep deprivation

14. Stimulant medications such as Ritalin work to reduce the core symptoms of ADHD by
   a. stimulating the cerebral cortex to create new neural pathways
   b. stimulating the "learning centre" of the brain
   c. enhancing the neurotransmission of dopamine and norepinephrine
   d. enhancing the release of serotonin and GABA

15. Joey has a long history with local law enforcement officers. He has been picked up several times for vandalism. His latest arrest is for deliberately setting fire to his stepfather's storage unit. Joey has also been arrested in the past for putting a cat in a dryer. The most likely diagnosis he would receive for his behaviour is
   a. ADHD
   b. conduct disorder
   c. autism spectrum disorder
   d. oppositional defiant disorder

16. Kaylee is a sweet-tempered 5-year-old who once had such a severe temper tantrum that she broke her finger when she punched a wall. The emergency room physician diagnosed Kaylee with oppositional defiant disorder. This may be an inappropriate diagnosis because
   a. the diagnosis requires a repeated pattern of negative and defiant behaviours
   b. she is older than the typical patient diagnosed with ODD
   c. temper tantrums are a symptom of ADHD
   d. ODD is a diagnosis primarily given to adolescent males

17. Unlike boys with conduct disorder, girls with conduct disorder engage in more
   a. retail theft
   b. hair-pulling fights
   c. relational aggression
   d. cruelty to animals

18. Drew is 9 years old and has recently begun soiling his pants. Drew has
- **a.** primary enuresis
- **b.** primary encopresis
- **c.** secondary enuresis
- **d.** secondary encopresis

19. The most common specific learning disorder is
- **a.** mathematics
- **b.** reading
- **c.** arithmetic
- **d.** writing

20. Kim was toilet trained by the time she was 3 years old. Now, at age 6, she is wetting the bed three nights per week. She has
- **a.** primary enuresis
- **b.** secondary enuresis
- **c.** primary encopresis
- **d.** secondary encopresis

Answers:

1 a, 2 c, 3 b, 4 d, 5 a, 6 d, 7 d, 8 c, 9 c, 10 a, 11 d, 12 b, 13 a, 14 c, 15 b, 16 a, 17 c, 18 d, 19 d, 20 b.

chapter 13

aging and neurocognitive disorders

(bottom right): Gabe Palmer/Alamy Stock Photo; (center): ajt/Shutterstock; (bottom centre): Alfred Gescheidt/The Image Bank/Getty Images

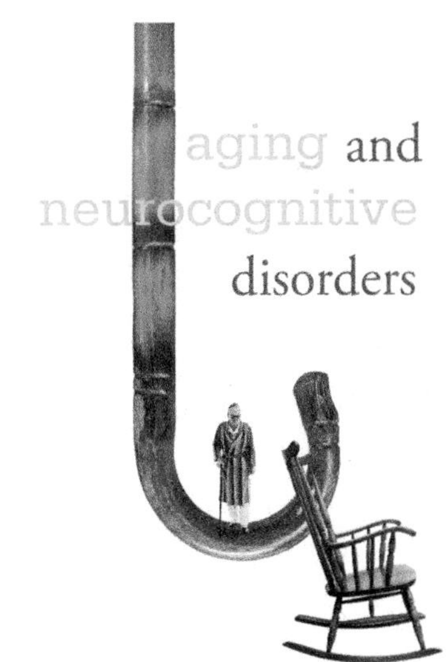

Bernhard was born in 1933. His father died when he was 8, and things became very difficult for Bernhard and his mother. She had to work hard as a seamstress to make ends meet, and as a young teenager, Bernhard had to start taking odd jobs in the neighbourhood to help out with the finances. He felt sad and lonely much of the time, but didn't want to let his mother know because she was working so hard and she did not need another worry. Bernhard thought a lot about his father; he didn't understand why God had taken him away from their family. It just didn't make sense.

As he grew older, Bernhard never really lost his sense of loss or sadness, but he did notice that when he worked hard at school or a job, he didn't notice the sadness so much. So he worked even harder and earned a scholarship to university. His grades there were excellent, and he decided to go to law school. While working as an articling clerk, he met and married a lovely woman named Claire. Bernhard and Claire wanted to start a family, but it took a long time for Claire to conceive. When she finally did, Bernhard thought maybe he would again be able to feel happiness. However, the baby was stillborn, and Claire's next pregnancy ended in a miscarriage. They decided not to try again. It was just too painful. Bernhard threw himself into his work even more. He became a provincial judge, for which he devoted long hours. He and his wife did pleasant things during his off hours, and they had an agreeable relationship, but he just never felt happy. As Bernhard approached 75 years of age, he knew it was time to retire. Mandatory retirement has been recently abolished for most jobs in Canada, but judges are required to retire at age 70 or 75, depending on the court. Bernhard had been a judge for much of his professional career. He had not had a law practice for many decades and felt despondent about the idea of starting a new legal practice, and knew that no one would hire him into a practice because of his age. He saw no option but to retire.

Soon after Bernhard stopped working, he began to feel lost. He didn't have any hobbies, and he had never taken time to make friends outside of work. It had never seemed worthwhile. Claire was busy with her volunteer and church activities, but Bernhard had never been able to join her at church because he no longer believed there was a God. Too many bad things had happened to him, and there was so much suffering in the world. How could there be a God who let things like this happen? As the days passed, Bernhard tried to find things to occupy his time, but nothing was fun. He started having trouble sleeping, and his stomach hurt all the time. He had no appetite and began losing weight. He started spending most days in the house, watching TV and ruminating about his past and all the suffering in the world. Claire tried to get him to go out with her, but he was too despondent. He couldn't concentrate long enough to have a conversation, and couldn't remember details of conversations anymore. He couldn't even remember people's names, and he just didn't have the energy to meet new people. Life was miserable.

learning objectives

After reading this chapter, you should be able to:

13.1 Recognize geropsychology as an emerging area of psychological research and practice.

13.2 Understand the ways in which aging may impact the expression and treatment of psychological symptoms and disorders in older adults.

13.3 Recognize the unique symptoms and issues that affect diagnosis and treatment of bipolar and depressive disorders, anxiety, substance-related disorders, and psychosis in older adults.

13.4 Distinguish between major neurocognitive disorder and delirium, two cognitive disorders that are common among older adults.

13.5 Understand the etiological factors affecting psychological and cognitive disorders of late life.

13.6 Identify empirically supported treatments for psychological and cognitive disorders among older adults.

Despite what many people believe, feeling sad is not a normal part of aging. Many adults do experience psychological symptoms and cognitive decline as they age, but older adults may experience and express psychological symptoms differently from younger adults in part because of the physical, cognitive, and social changes that accompany aging. Understanding the issues that are unique to aging helps clinicians identify and treat the psychological problems associated with old age.

Symptoms and Disorders of Aging

Geropsychology as a Unique Field

13.1 Recognize geropsychology as an emerging area of psychological research and practice.

The population of older adults in Canada and in many other places in the world is increasing rapidly (see Figure 13.1). According to projections from data collected by

FIGURE 13.1

The Aging Population of Canada. The population of older adults in Canada is steadily growing.

Source: Age and sex structure: Canada, provinces and territories, 2010. Ottawa: Statistics Canada.

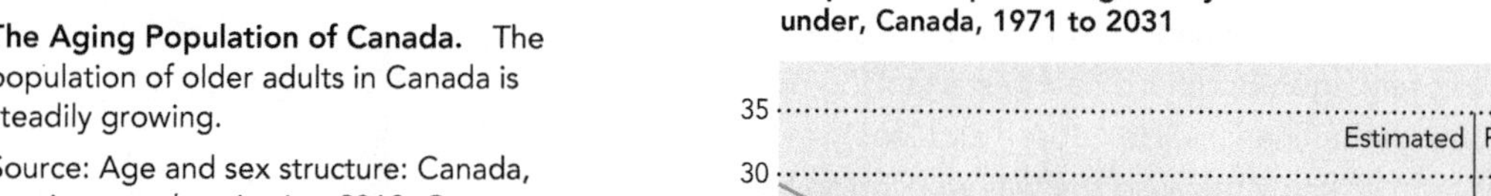

Proportion of persons aged 65 years and over and children aged 14 years and under, Canada, 1971 to 2031

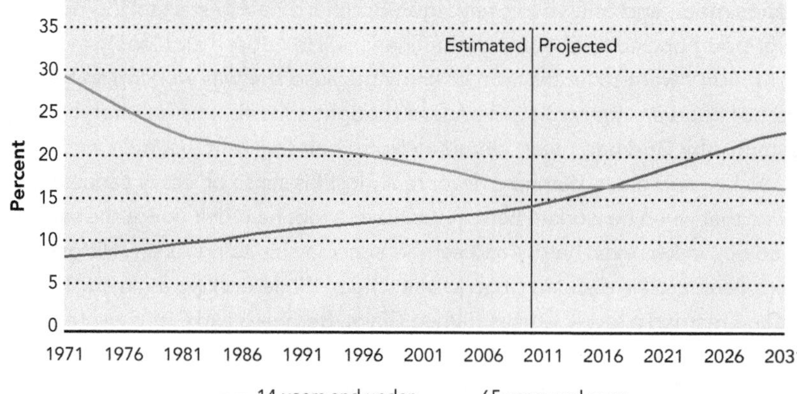

Notes: 1971 to 2005 (final intercensal estimates).
2006 to 2007 (final postcensal estimates).
2008 to 2009 (updated postcensal estimates).
2010 (preliminary postcensal estimates).
2011 to 2031 (population projections, medium-growth - historical trends (1981 to 2008) scenario).

Statistics Canada, older adults (ages 65 and older), could account for more than 20% of the population by 2026, and more than 25% of the population by 2056 (Milan, 2011). With so many older adults in our society, we need to better understand the issues that confront older people. As we age, changes occur in our physical functioning (increased medical problems, decreased sensory capacity), changes occur in our social functioning (retirement because of health or other reasons, reduced social networks as friends and family face health challenges), and we face diminished cognitive abilities (changes in attention, learning, and memory). All of these are important factors that provide a unique sociocultural context by which to understand abnormal behaviour in older adults.

Geropsychology is a subdiscipline of psychology that addresses issues of aging, with particular attention to patterns of normal development, individual differences, and psychological problems that are unique to older persons (usually those ages 65 or older). It has long been recognized that childhood is a developmental stage with particular challenges, and that children have disorders specific to childhood and experience and express psychological symptoms in unique ways. Geropsychology extends this developmental approach to include the challenges and psychological symptoms older adults face, such as physical changes, lifestyle shifts, and role changes.

The field of geropsychology is expanding, with increasing numbers of professional organizations and training programs (Qualls et al., 2005) that focus on providing services to meet the needs of older people. Nevertheless, there remains a worldwide shortage of mental health professionals trained in the provision of mental health services to older adults (Pachana et al., 2010).

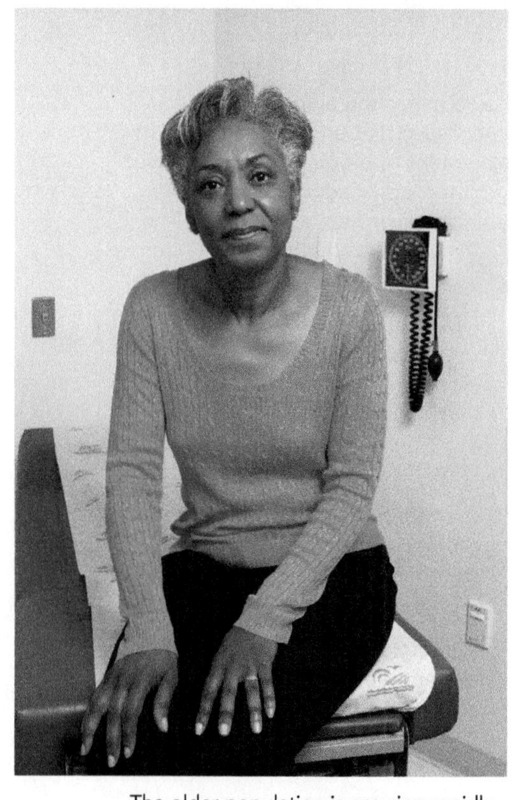

The older population is growing rapidly, but the number of health professionals available who specialize in geriatric care lags far behind.

Blend Images/Alamy Stock Photo

Research efforts are increasing as we strive to understand patterns of typical late-life development, unique problems that older adults experience, and strategies for improving their quality of life. Nevertheless, tremendous gaps still exist in our knowledge of psychological symptoms and disorders among older people and in our ability to identify and treat them. In keeping with the developmental focus of this text, we hope to identify some of the unique ways in which psychological problems affect people in the later decades of life.

ETHICS AND RESPONSIBILITY Most psychologists who provide clinical services see older patients, but many training programs do not provide sufficient education and experience in geropsychology. Psychologists should work within their areas of competence and seek consultation or additional training when needed (Canadian Psychological

Association, 2000). Psychologists working with older adults are encouraged to have knowledge of the aging process, the nature of cognitive and psychological problems among older people, and the assessment tools and treatment procedures specific to working with older adults. The importance of interfacing with other disciplines (e.g., medicine, social work) is also emphasized as a means of providing comprehensive care. Working with older patients requires adequate knowledge and training for ethical practice.

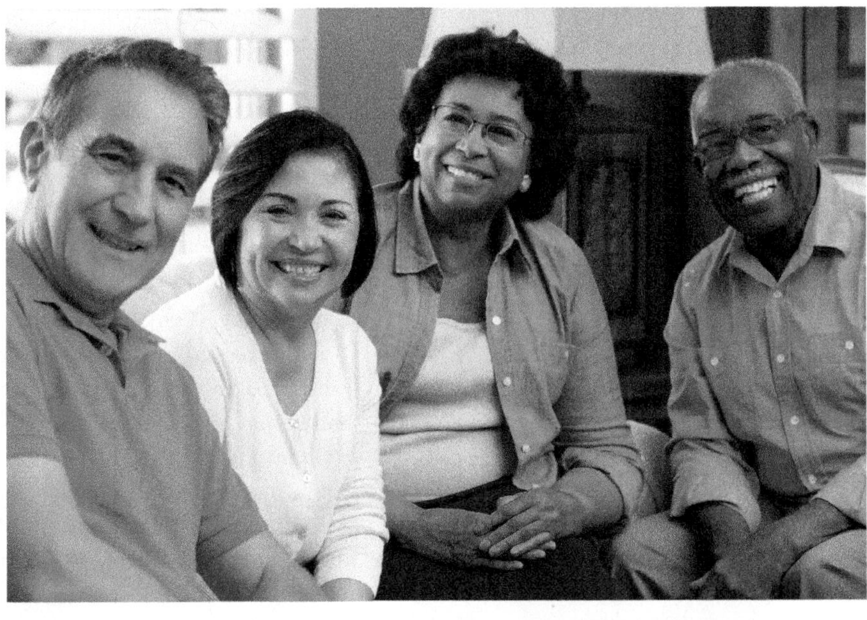

Successful Aging

Leonard is the picture of successful aging. He is 89, lives alone in the house where he has lived for the last 40 years, and periodically drives almost 150 kilometres to visit his son. Leonard retired many years ago, but he continues to spend time in his home office every day. He checks the Internet to keep up with current events, maintains email contact with friends and former classmates, and writes a regular column for his university's alumni magazine. Leonard is also active in a number of civic organizations, takes a nap every day, and enjoys a cocktail before dinner. When his wife died two years ago, Leonard was sad, but he began to spend more time with friends and neighbours, inviting them to his home for afternoon visits. Over time, his home became a centre for neighbourhood socializing. The neighbours listen to his stories about life during World War II, enjoying his sense of humour and positive attitude. Leonard also continues to take a short walk each evening. Although he can't go very far now that his hip hurts, he always has a smile for any neighbour who is passing by. Leonard's optimism about life is infectious; his neighbours often remark that he is more energetic and positive than they are although many are 50 years younger. Leonard has some "rules" for aging well: (1) Use your brain every day, (2) stay active, and (3) socialize with younger people and entertain young ideas.

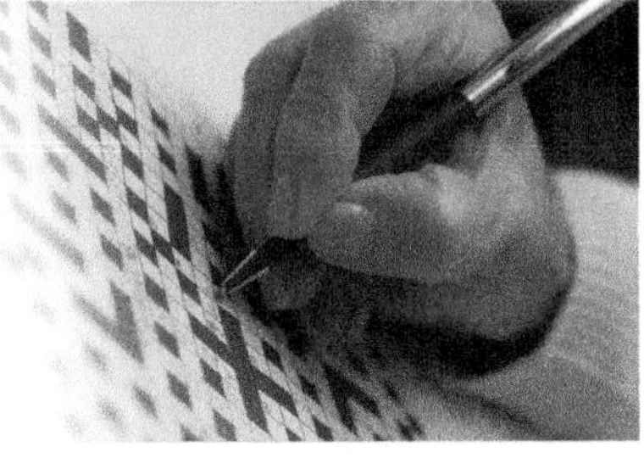

About one third of older adults continue to experience good health and active lives in their later years. Successful aging is encouraged by positive social relationships and continuing mental activity.

(top): Monkey Business Images/Shutterstock; **(bottom):** Tom Foxall/Fotolia

Although Leonard is not a psychologist, his philosophy and lifestyle reflect much of what is known about *successful aging*. Approximately one third of older adults are judged to be aging successfully (Depp & Jeste, 2006), but as yet there is no consistent definition of this term. In fact, Depp and Jeste identified 29 different definitions of successful aging in 28 studies! Common themes across these definitions include perceived good health and an active lifestyle, continued independence in functioning, lack of disability, absence of cognitive impairment (which may be impacted by higher education and increased mental activity), and positive social relationships (Blazer, 2006; Phelan & Larson, 2002). Theories of positive aging also focus on a theoretical model known as *selective optimization and compensation* (Baltes & Baltes, 1990; Grove et al., 2009), meaning that people age more successfully when they modify their goals and choices to make best use of their personal characteristics. These adjustments often require compensating for age-related limitations that reduce one's ability to reach previously valued goals.

Max is an aging fisherman who used to be out on a boat every weekend. He can't fish any longer, but he can spend time reading magazines about fishing, watching television shows about fishing, and trading old fishing stories with his buddies at the local coffee shop.

Leonard also made choices that make the most of his ability to engage in rewarding activities and optimize his social, mental, and physical functioning.

Psychological Symptoms and Disorders Among Older People

13.2 Understand the ways in which aging may impact the expression and treatment of psychological symptoms and disorders in older adults.

In Canada, about 20% of people ages 65 years and older have a psychological disorder (Conn et al., 2006). This figure is broadly consistent with the prevalence of mental illness in other age groups. However, the rates are even higher for seniors living in health-care and social institutions. It has been reported that 80% to 90% of Canadian nursing home residents live with some form of cognitive impairment or other psychological disorder (Conn et al., 2006). The personal and societal costs associated with psychological symptoms in older people are high, and there are simply not enough appropriately trained professionals available to help (Bartels & Smyer, 2002; Pachana et al., 2010).

Only about half of the older adults who report mental health problems receive treatment. Many older people with psychological symptoms do not seek treatment because they fear that others will think they are "crazy," because they lack sufficient resources (money, ability to find a therapist), or because of logistic limitations (inability to drive to the clinician's office, long waiting lists). Those who do seek help typically go to general medical settings, such as their doctor's office, instead of specialized mental health clinics. Unfortunately, many psychological symptoms and disorders go unrecognized in medical settings (Jeste et al., 1999; Heisel et al., 2006; Hogan et al., 2006). Even when problems are identified, treatment is often inadequate (Roundy et al., 2005). One reason for inadequate recognition and treatment is the limited time that physicians now spend with patients during office visits, resulting in insufficient time for assessing and treating mental health problems.

Ageism is an equally serious issue. Many older adults and their doctors consider psychological distress to be a normal part of aging (Gallo et al., 1999) and therefore not something that requires treatment. It is important to remember that psychological distress is usually not a normal consequence of aging (Conn et al., 2006). Cognitive decline is not an inevitable consequence of aging, except for the very old (see "Canadian Focus: The Canadian Study of Health and Aging"). Many emotional disorders experienced by older adults are treatable. Even when the progressive, neurobiological disorders associated with aging cannot be reversed (e.g., Alzheimer's disease or Parkinson's disease), quality of life can be improved.

It is commonly recognized that the symptoms of a disorder may be different for adults and children. Only now are clinicians and researchers beginning to understand how aging may also affect the kinds of psychological symptoms people experience and report. Older adults often report less negative mood and distress than younger adults (Goldberg et al., 2003; Lawton et al., 1993) but it is not entirely clear whether these differences reflect different experiences or simply different ways that people describe or express their moods. In Chapter 4, for example, we noted that boys and girls differ in how much fear they *express*, not how much fear they *experience*. Similarly, older adults often focus more on physical symptoms than on psychological symptoms of distress, and this may be another reason why they seek treatment from primary care physicians rather than mental health clinicians.

Eloise denies feeling anxious, but reports that her back and neck muscles are tight all the time, so much so that they hurt. She isn't able to sit comfortably for long periods anymore, and her stomach "acts up" frequently when stressful events occur. She is hoping for some help to decrease her muscle pain and reduce her acid indigestion and recurrent diarrhea.

Focusing on physical symptoms complicates the identification of psychological disorders in older people, particularly for primary care physicians who are less experienced in this area. The increase in medical problems as people age further complicates the diagnostic challenge. Many medical diseases and treatments create symptoms that mimic psychological disorders. For example, symptoms of diabetes include weight loss and lethargy, which are also symptoms of depression. Even something as seemingly harmless as decongestants can cause nervousness, sleeplessness, and increased blood pressure or heart rate, which are also symptoms of anxiety. When older adults have both medical and psychological difficulties, recognizing psychological problems is a huge challenge.

Although psychological difficulties in older age are often thought to be mainly cognitive (e.g., dementia), many of the disorders that older people face are the same ones that affect younger people, such as depression, anxiety, and substance abuse (Hybels et al., 2009). Within each category of difficulties experienced by older people, understanding normal age-related changes in physical, social, and cognitive functioning enables us to provide a developmental context for evaluating these disorders. As with other age groups, *comorbidity* (multiple disorders occurring together) also occurs.

canadian FOCUS

The Canadian Study of Health and Aging

In 1987, the Canadian federal government assembled an advisory panel to develop a nation-wide research program on **Alzheimer's disease (AD)** and other forms of dementia. This was stimulated by concerns about the anticipated growth in the proportion of the Canadian population aged 60 and older, due to the increase in longevity associated with advances in medical care (McDowell et al., 2004). Given that the risk of dementia increases with age, this means that there would be a dramatic increase in the prevalence of dementia in the coming decades. Accordingly, funding was allocated for a national longitudinal study of dementia, called the Canadian Study of Health and Aging (CSHA), the results of which would help health planners anticipate future health care needs (CSHA, 1994a, b, c; McDowell et al., 2004).

The CSHA had four major objectives, in addition to several other goals addressed in studies added to the main research project. The main objectives were: (1) to estimate the prevalence of dementias among the Canadian elderly; (2) to determine risk factors for dementia; (3) to identify the types of care received by people with dementia and to assess the burden on informal caregivers; and (4) to establish a uniform database for future incidence and longitudinal studies of dementias.

The CSHA was coordinated at the University of Ottawa, with data collected at 18 sites across Canada. The study involved 10 263 people ages 65 or over, sampled representatively from the community and from long-term care institutions. Participants were assessed in 1991, 1996, and 2001 (McDowell et al., 2004). A multi-step assessment procedure was used, beginning with a screening interview for dementia that contained items similar to the Mini-Mental State Examination. A subgroup of participants also completed a series of neuropsychological tests, and received a physical and neurological evaluation by a physician. In cases where one of the study participants was being cared for by an informal caregiver (such as family members or friends), the caregiver was also interviewed. (Informal caregivers differ from formal caregivers in that the latter are paid helpers, such as nurses.)

Over 200 research papers have been published from the CSHA (McDowell et al., 2004). Some of the main findings are as follows. It was found that approximately 8% of Canadians ages 65 and older meet criteria for dementia (CSHA, 1994a). Similar to findings of other studies, the prevalence of dementia increases with age, beginning at 2% percent for those ages 65 to 74 years and rising to 35% for those ages 85 and over (CSHA, 1994a). The prevalence rates increase sharply among the very old; for people ages 100 to 106 years, the prevalence of dementia is 85%. This led some CSHA investigators to conclude that "dementia approaches universality when sufficient aging has taken place" (Ebly et al., 1994, p. 1598).

AD is the most common form of dementia (64% of people with dementia), followed by vascular dementia (19%) and other types of dementia (17%) (Hill et al., 1996). More than half of the people with dementia live in institutions, such as long-term care facilities. The likelihood of living in an institution is influenced by the availability of an informal caregiver, who is typically a spouse, daughter, or son. Half of the informal caregivers are over 60 years of age, and frequently have health problems of their own. Many also have symptoms

(continued)

of depression, possibly because of the burden of caring for someone with dementia. Few informal caregivers make use of paid support services such as home nurses or cleaning/laundry services. This seems to be because informal caregivers view these services as a last resort rather than as a way of alleviating their own stress (CSHA, 1994c). Informal caregivers are likely to feel more burdened and more depressed when the demented person has more disturbing behavioural problems (e.g., aggression) and greater functional limitations, and when the informal caregiver has few other family members or friends to draw on for assistance (Clyburn et al., 2000).

The prospective risk factor analysis from the CSHA (Lindsay et al., 2002) indicated that the following predicts the risk of AD: greater age, lower education, and the *APOE-E4* allele. Use of nonsteroidal anti-inflammatory drugs, wine consumption, coffee consumption, regular physical activity, and past exposure to vaccines are associated with lower risk of AD (Laurin et al., 2001; Verreault et al., 2001). The CSHA was one of the first studies to identify that physical activity is associated with a lower risk of dementia, with the effect seen more clearly for women than for men (Laurin et al., 2001). Further research is needed to verify this and other associations, and to investigate why particular variables have a positive or negative correlation with the risk of dementia (McDowell et al., 2004).

As part of this research effort, McDowell et al. (2007) used the CSHA data to test three hypotheses as to why higher education level is associated with lower risk of dementia. The first hypothesis was that association is a methodological artifact. This could occur, for example, if researchers were able to obtain a representative assessment of the education levels of people with dementia (e.g., by accessing hospital records), but obtained a biased assessment of the education levels of non-demented people (healthy controls). Such a bias would occur, for example, if highly educated controls were more interested in participating in the study, compared to controls with lower education levels. The researchers found no support for this hypothesis.

Their second hypothesis was that higher education may predict better socioeconomic circumstances later on in life, such as working at a more intellectually stimulating job. To test this hypothesis, the researchers examined the relationship between years of education and risk of dementia after statistically controlling a range of socioeconomic indicators, including occupational status. Controlling for these factors reduced the strength of the education–dementia relationship, but did not eliminate it. The findings raised the possibility that there are at least two pathways by which educational attainment influences the risk of dementia: (1) a direct pathway whereby the degree of educational attainment (and its associated level of mental stimulation) reduces the risk of dementia, and (2) an indirect pathway whereby education level improves the person's later socioeconomic circumstances (e.g., whether one has a mentally stimulating job), which in turn reduces the risk of dementia (McDowell et al., 2007).

The third hypothesis was that educational attainment reflects the person's intellectual ability or cognitive capacity ("cognitive reserve"), which may protect against dementia. Put simply, if you start out in life with excellent cognitive abilities (e.g., strong reasoning skills and an excellent memory), then you will able to successfully complete a high level of education and it will also take longer for your cognitive abilities to deteriorate to the extent that the effects of dementia become apparent. McDowell et al. (2007) found that higher intelligence is indeed associated with a lower risk of dementia. However, higher education level is still associated with lower risk of dementia, even after statistically controlling for intelligence level.

Overall, the findings of McDowell et al. (2007) indicate that educational attainment probably does influence risk of dementia, both directly and through a number of intermediate pathways. More research is needed to better understand how education imparts its protective effects. Nevertheless, these findings provide an important example of the research needed to understand why particular variables are positively or negatively correlated with the risk for dementia.

CONCEPT check

- The field of geropsychology addresses normal development, individual differences, and psychological problems unique to aging.
- Psychological problems are usually not a normal part of aging.
- At least 20% of older adults have a psychological disorder.
- Most older adults with psychological problems do not seek help from mental health specialists.
- Psychological problems are sometimes difficult to identify in older adults.

critical thinking question What are some of the factors that influence the experience and expression of psychological problems in older adults?

Depression and Anxiety in Later Life

13.3 Recognize the unique symptoms and issues that affect diagnosis and treatment of bipolar and depressive disorders, anxiety, substance-related disorders, and psychosis in older adults.

Aging is associated with various types of losses (e.g., death of a loved one, changes in job or financial status, deterioration in physical abilities) and uncertainty about the future (e.g., ability to retain independence, future changes in health status, death). It should not be surprising, then, that depression and anxiety disorders are common psychological problems that older adults face. However, depression and anxiety are not a natural consequence of aging. Only recently has research begun to address the nature, etiology, and treatment of these problems in older adults, blending theories and strategies derived from younger adults and emerging ideas that are unique to aging populations.

Bipolar Disorder and Major Depressive Disorder

Jean had devoted her life to being a wife and mother. She raised five children and supported her husband through a very busy career. When Tom retired three years ago, Jean expected to spend the rest of her life travelling with him and visiting her children and grandchildren who lived across the country. However, Tom died suddenly of a heart attack just six months after he retired. Jean feels lost. She has no one with whom to share her thoughts. Her friends, whose husbands were still living, call less often. When she does go out with them, she feels like a "fifth wheel." She travels alone to see her children, and that isn't enjoyable either. Jean finds herself feeling apathetic about life in general, but she doesn't know why. Since Tom died, she has also developed a number of medical problems. Her heart pounds often, she feels full and bloated even when she eats small amounts of food, she is tired most of the time, and she lies awake much of the night thinking about all sorts of things. Her family thinks she ought to get more involved in activities at her local community centre, but she just doesn't have the energy. Her daughter thinks she is depressed, but Jean thinks she is just getting older and adjusting to life as a widow.

Most bipolar and depressive disorders are diagnosed in older and younger adults using the same criteria. However, as Jean's case illustrates, older adults are often reluctant to acknowledge psychological symptoms, not wanting to be viewed as "crazy." Also, they often report symptoms that are different from those in younger adults. As symptoms of depression overlap with symptoms of common medical illnesses, current diagnostic categories may not be the most useful for older adults. In fact, depression among older people often includes cognitive difficulties such as problems with attention, speed of information processing, and **executive dysfunction** (difficulty planning, thinking abstractly, initiating and inhibiting actions, etc.). These symptoms can occur as part of depression even when major neurocognitive disorder is not present (Kindermann et al., 2000; Lockwood et al., 2000). In fact, older adults with depression can sometimes appear to have a neurocognitive disorder that actually resolves after appropriate treatment for depression.

Medical disorders can also produce depressive disorders that are unique to older adults. For example, **vascular depression**, now known as *depressive disorder due to another medical condition*, can be diagnosed in the context of cerebrovascular disease (disease of the arteries that supply blood to the brain). Symptoms of this type of depression include increased difficulties with language (e.g., speaking fluently, naming objects), increased apathy and slowed movements, and less agitation and guilt than patients with other forms of depression (Alexopoulos, 2004). In a person who has major neurocognitive disorder due to Alzheimer's disease, major depressive disorder is diagnosed when the symptoms are present for at least two weeks (Olin et al., 2002).

Suicide is a possible serious consequence of major depressive disorder. Although suicide deaths affect almost all age groups, in Canada, those ages 40 to 59 have the highest suicide rates (Navaneelan, 2012). The rate of suicide is higher in this group than in people younger than 40 and higher than those older than 59 (Navaneelan, 2012). This underscores the point that psychological problems are generally not an inevitable consequence of growing old.

Few adults develop mania or bipolar disorder after the age of 65. Many adults who do show initial signs of bipolar disorder in later life have a history of major depressive disorder. Similarly, older patients who have manic symptoms later in life may have had elements of the disorder earlier in life (Keck et al., 2001). When bipolar disorder occurs in older patients, the intervals between manic and depressive shifts are shorter and the episode duration is longer relative to younger patients (Keck et al., 2001). After the age of 65, medical illnesses, especially stroke, and other medical causes, such as medications, are more likely to be associated with the onset of bipolar disorder than the genetic factors proposed for younger adults (Van Gerpen et al., 1999).

PREVALENCE AND IMPACT In the general population, major depressive disorder and persistent depressive disorder (dysthymia) each affect between 4% and 10% of older adults (Byers et al., 2010; Woodward et al., 2012). These percentages are lower than those found among younger adults, although as many as 25% of older people have depressive symptoms that fail to meet diagnostic criteria but can still create significant distress and impairment (Hybels et al., 2009). According to a recent Canadian community survey, depression symptoms commonly co-occur in various neurological conditions, typically in older individuals, including Alzheimer's disease, multiple sclerosis, Parkinson's disease, and stroke (Bulloch et al., 2015). As many as 23% to 28% of people with these disorders have clinically significant depressive symptoms.

Bipolar and depressive disorders and symptoms can affect daily functioning and even survival in older adults, much as they do in younger adults. Consider two older adults with the same medical condition, one of whom also has major depressive disorder and the other does not. The patient with both a medical disorder and major depressive disorder has an increased risk of death, and not simply because of the increased likelihood of suicide. Depression significantly affects the outcome of medical conditions. People with major depressive disorder and medical illness recover less well, use more health care services, and create higher costs for the health care system (Prina et al., 2012). Late-life depression also decreases quality of life (Unützer et al., 2000), increases physical disability, and reduces the ability of patients to care for themselves (Bruce et al., 1994; Steffens et al., 1999).

As noted earlier, few older adults suffer from bipolar disorder, with prevalence less than 1% (Beyer, 2009; Byers et al., 2010). Mortality rates among older adults with bipolar disorder are elevated, and perhaps even higher than that among older people with major depressive disorder (Beyer, 2009), although the reason for the higher rate is not yet known.

SEX, RACE, AND ETHNICITY As is true of younger adults, depressive disorders among older people occur more often in women than in men (Woodward et al., 2012). Little is known about the relationship between depression and race/ethnicity among the Canadian elderly. In studying race/ethnicity, it is important to tease out confounding factors such as whether or not the person had immigrated to Canada. Immigration is a stressful life event, with possibly long-lasting effects, and might increase the person's chances of becoming depressed. Research based on Canadian census data indicates that immigrants tend to be older than the national average and almost a third of the immigrants from Europe are over 65 years of age (Durst, 2005). Accordingly, in studies investigating the relationship between depression and race/ethnicity in older Canadians, it is important to disentangle any effects due to the stressful experience of immigration. Language is a further confounding effect that needs to be taken into consideration. For example, immigrants to Canada who do not speak English may find themselves isolated, which can lead to depression.

These factors complicate the investigation of the relationship between depression and race/ethnicity among older residents in Canada. To illustrate the problem, consider the findings reported by Lai (2000). He found that the prevalence of depressive symptoms among the Chinese elderly in Canada was twice the estimated prevalence of symptoms in the Canadian general population. Does this mean that being Chinese is a risk factor for depression in the elderly? Not necessarily. The study failed to control for confounding factors such as immigration status and language status; many of the Chinese participants were recent immigrants and most did not speak English. The elevated rate of depression could be entirely due to the stressors of immigrating to a country in which you do not speak the language.

With increasing age come increasing challenges for older adults. Friends pass away and children move to distant cities, potentially creating an environment that can lead to loneliness and depression.

Science Photo Library/Alamy Stock Photo

ETIOLOGY OF DEPRESSION IN LATER LIFE Depressive disorders in late life appear to have causes much like those in younger people. In many cases, late-life depression simply reflects the persistence or recurrence of an earlier episode. However, it is important to identify the original age of onset for depressive disorders (early versus late) because this may have treatment implications (McMahon, 2004). Older adults with *early-onset depression* (typically defined as onset before age 35 or 45) more often have a family history of depression, probably reflecting the genetic contributions discussed in Chapter 6 (Alexopoulos, 2004). In contrast, people with *late-onset depression* are more likely to have coexistent cognitive impairment and more evidence of brain abnormalities, suggesting the presence of brain deterioration (Alexopoulos, 2004). They more often have a family history of dementia as well (van Ojen et al., 1995). Late-onset depression seems to occur more often in the context of vascular, neurological, or other physical diseases that are associated with genetic causes, such as Parkinson's disease, cerebrovascular disease, and Alzheimer's disease. For those with late-onset depression, symptoms of depressive disorders sometimes precede diagnosis of the medical condition by months or years (McMahon, 2004).

Researchers are examining the role of specific genetic factors in the emergence of late-life depression. Some studies have shown a correlation between a gene, the *apo-lipoprotein (APOE) e4 allele*, and late-life depression (Zubenko et al., 1996), although the finding has not always been replicated. We also need to remember that this correlation (between the gene and depression) may merely reflect an underlying and stronger association between *APOE4* and major neurocognitive disorder (Plassman & Steffens, 2004). That is, the gene may be related to the onset of major neurocognitive disorder, and the depressive disorder may result from the cognitive impairment, not the effects of the gene.

Aging is associated with both personal and environmental challenges, and unique environmental stressors may influence the onset of depression among older adults. A number of stressors, for example, often accompany retirement or a loved one's death. These secondary effects include an increased sense of loss, decreased social status, and reduced income. Physical activity is beneficial for mild-to-moderate levels of depression, but older adults may face limitations in physical activity. However, their increased maturity and life experience may better equip them to handle challenging life events.

Biological and environmental factors may interact to contribute to the onset of late-life depression. A **lifespan developmental diathesis-stress model** considers the role of *biological predispositions* (biological variables that carry increased risk for depression such as genetics, medical disease, etc.), stressful life events (typically those that are unique to older people), and personal *protective factors* (e.g., maturity and previous life experiences) that reduce the potential negative impact of biological and environmental risk factors (Gatz, 2000). In this model, the impact of biological and personal protective factors increases with advancing age, while the impact of stressful events remains constant. (See Figure 13.2.)

FIGURE 13.2

Lifespan Diathesis-Stress Model. This model suggests that advanced age increases the influence of biological variables (e.g., genetics, medical diseases) and personal protective factors (e.g., maturity, life experience) on stress. In this model, however, the impact of stressful life events remains constant across the lifespan.

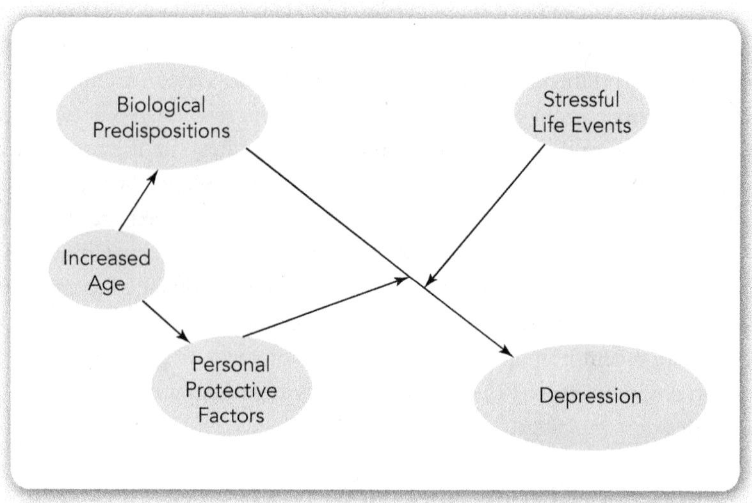

PSYCHOLOGICAL THEORIES Psychological theories of depression etiology also apply to older adults. Recall Max, the aging fisherman who could no longer go out on a boat to fish but found alternative ways to enjoy his hobby. Without such alternatives, loss of pleasant activities and environmental reinforcement could lead to depression-related avoidance and withdrawal behaviours. Older adults also experience learned helplessness; they often feel a loss of control over their environments and suffer from erroneous thinking that is common in depression.

Walter (age 87) and his wife, Caitlin (age 85), recently moved to an assisted living facility. The responsibilities of keeping up their house had become too much for them. Cleaning the house, mowing the lawn, and doing small repairs were no longer easy chores. Running errands had even become difficult given the limitations in Walter's vision that resulted from eye disease. Although Walter and Caitlin hated to move from the house and neighbourhood where they had lived for more than 50 years, their children convinced them that moving into a smaller place where they would have day-to-day help was better. After the move, though, Walter never seemed to regain his strength. He began to feel tired most of the time, and his energy and interest in socializing decreased. He played cards with other residents occasionally, and he went out to lunch when his daughter came to visit. But he missed his old neighbourhood and friends. He felt old and not very useful. His spirits perked up when his grandchildren came to see him, but they never stayed very long, and he had trouble hearing them because they talked too fast. Caitlin became concerned when he started to lose weight and just didn't seem hungry most of the time. Walter also never slept very well anymore except when he took sleeping pills. He often felt that he was just waiting to die.

TREATMENT OF DEPRESSION IN OLDER PATIENTS Because depressive disorders can accompany so many medical diseases, treatment must begin with a physical evaluation to rule out any medical causes, such as thyroid abnormalities, anemia, or diabetes. Once a diagnosis of major depressive disorder is established, treatment options include pharmacological and psychological interventions.

Medications used to treat major depressive disorder in younger adults (see Chapter 6) are also effective with older patients (Alexopoulos, 2004; Blazer et al., 2009; Shanmugham et al., 2005). Approximately 60% of older adults improve with pharmacological treatment, which is significantly higher than the 30% who respond to placebo (Schneider, 1996). Age-related changes in the body's metabolism increase older adults' sensitivity to medication in terms of both positive response and side effects. As a result, doses are typically increased more slowly and the dosage necessary for a positive response is lower than for younger adults (Blazer et al., 2009). Electroconvulsive therapy (ECT) is used infrequently but is valuable for patients who have such severe symptoms that they cannot wait for the medication to have an effect or for those who fail to respond to alternative treatments.

Lithium is used as a treatment for bipolar disorder, but doses for elderly patients are typically one half to two thirds of those used in younger patients (Alexopoulos, 2004). Because lithium can worsen cognitive impairment and create delirium (a syndrome described in more detail later), it must be used carefully (Young, 2005). ECT is also highly effective for mania, with up to 80% improvement reported (Alexopoulos, 2004).

Psychological treatments also are efficacious for late-life depression (Mackin & Areán, 2005). The greatest amount of empirical support exists for behavioural and cognitive-behavioural therapy (CBT). CBT is consistently superior to wait-list or placebo control conditions, and some evidence indicates that it is better for older adults than are alternative psychological approaches. A variation of CBT called *problem-solving therapy* is useful for older adults with persistent depressive disorder or minor depression, common conditions in older age groups (Mackin & Areán, 2005; Kirkham et al., 2015), even when patients are experiencing executive dysfunction (Areán et al., 2010). Other psychological treatments that appear beneficial for late-life depression are interpersonal therapy and brief psychodynamic therapy (see Chapter 6). *Reminiscence therapy*, used more often with older adults, focuses on patients' recall of significant past events and how they manage distress. Reminiscence therapy may reduce late-life depression (Moral et al., 2015), although effects are not as strong as those for CBT and it is not known exactly how this treatment works (Gum et al., 2004).

Several large community studies, conducted in Canada and elsewhere in the Western world, show that older adults, compared to their younger counterparts, are less likely to seek treatment for psychological problems such as mood disorders (and anxiety and substance-use disorders) (Crabb & Hunsley, 2006). Researchers had initially thought that this might be due to negative attitudes about seeking help for psychological problems, such as negative beliefs concerning stigma for seeking help. However, accumulating research suggests that older Canadian adults generally do not differ from younger adults in their attitudes about seeking mental health services. Both age groups tend to be generally positive about the value of such services (Mackenzie et al., 2008). Further research is needed to determine why older adults suffering from mood and other disorders are less likely than younger adults to seek out mental health services. One possibility is that, despite their positive attitudes toward mental health services, older adults perceive (correctly or not) that there are fewer mental health resources available to them, such as clinics and support groups.

Anxiety

As with depression, the diagnostic criteria for anxiety disorders are consistent across the lifespan (see Chapter 4), but important differences exist in the nature of anxiety and worry among older adults. These differences include developmental/life cycle issues, attitudes about mental health problems, *cohort differences* (differences that occur because people are born in different generations), and the presence of medical disorders that can complicate differential diagnosis.

With respect to lifespan issues, worries reported by older people reflect the problems that arise in later stages of life. For example, older people tend to worry more about health and less about work relative to younger and middle-age adults. Older adults often worry about stressful life transitions (e.g., retirement for health or other reasons, widowhood), added caregiving responsibilities (when spouses or aging parents require significant assistance), and economic and legal issues associated with reduced income,

In addition to depressive disorders, anxiety and worry are common psychological symptoms among older people who may have health problems, disabilities, caregiving responsibilities, reduced income, or other sources of concern.

Roy McMahon/Alamy Stock Photo

increased health care costs, and end-of-life planning. Other potentially stressful events include changes in physical health, vision, hearing, sleep, continence, energy levels, memory, and increased disability (Brenes et al., 2005; Lenze et al., 2001). Anxiety can result from these physical changes or may contribute to worsening physical symptoms and lead to poorer physical health, sleep disruption, and memory problems.

Older adults use fewer psychological terms to describe anxiety (e.g., shame, guilt) (Kogan et al., 2000; Lawton et al., 1993) and prefer words such as "fret" or "concern" to describe worry or anxiety (Stanley & Novy, 2000), possibly because they are uncomfortable with more psychologically-oriented terms. Older adults also emphasize physical symptoms (Lenze et al., 2005); this makes recognition of anxiety disorders particularly difficult when medical illnesses are present. Many medical problems have physical symptoms that are common in anxiety (e.g., shortness of breath, chest pain, muscle pain or stiffness, gastrointestinal distress), and many medications produce anxiety-related side effects. For example, some drugs for high blood pressure can create heart rate abnormalities, and bronchodilators that treat breathing disturbance can create nervousness, trembling, and increased heart rate.

Anxiety overlaps significantly with depression among people of all ages, but this overlap is even more common among older adults (Beekman et al., 2000; Lenze et al., 2000; van Balkom et al., 2000). In most cases when an overlap exists, symptoms of anxiety are present before symptoms of depression emerge (Lenze et al., 2000; Schoevers et al., 2005; Wetherell et al., 2001), suggesting that early treatment of anxiety may prevent depression, at least in some cases.

PREVALENCE AND IMPACT Although anxiety disorders receive less attention than depression, they are among the most common and significant mental health problems affecting older adults. As many as 12% of older adults suffer from some kind of anxiety disorder (Byers et al., 2010). Although the prevalence of anxiety disorders is lower among older adults than younger adults (Wolitzky-Taylor et al., 2010), anxiety disorders are more common than major depressive disorder among older adults (Byers et al., 2010; Kessler et al., 2005a). As with depression, anxiety is more common among older patients in medical settings than those in other settings (Kunik et al., 2005; Tolin et al., 2005), and prevalence is high among older adults with cognitive impairment (Seignourel et al., 2008).

Among the anxiety disorders, specific phobias and generalized anxiety disorder (GAD) are most common in late life (Wolitzky-Taylor et al., 2010). Most research has focused on GAD, which occurs in as much as 7% of the general population (Wolitzky-Taylor et al., 2010) and 11% of patients in medical clinics (Tolin et al., 2005). Clinically significant anxiety that does not meet diagnostic criteria is even more common (20% to 40%) (Brenes et al., 2005; Kunik et al., 2003; Mehta et al., 2003; Wittchen et al., 2002). Available figures may underestimate its true prevalence because anxiety can be difficult to recognize, particularly in medical settings (Stanley et al., 2001). GAD may be the most difficult anxiety disorder to diagnose because its physical symptoms (sleep disturbance, fatigue, restlessness, difficulty concentrating) overlap the most with symptoms of normal aging, medical conditions, and medications that are common in later life.

Anxiety in older adults is associated with less physical activity and poorer functioning, more negative perceptions of health, decreased life satisfaction, and more loneliness (Cully et al., 2006; DeBeurs et al., 1999; Kim et al., 2000). Older adults with anxiety have more physical disabilities (Brenes et al., 2005; Lenze et al., 2001) and poorer quality of life (Porensky et al., 2009; Wetherell et al., 2004) than those who do not experience it. They also use more health care services (Porensky et al., 2009; Stanley et al., 2001) and are more dependent on others to function (Naik et al., 2004). Anxiety in later life increases the risk of death (Brenes et al., 2007; van Hout et al., 2004). As in other age groups, anxiety disorders are associated with significant distress and impaired functioning.

SEX, RACE, AND ETHNICITY As with younger adults, anxiety disorders are more common among older women (Wolitzky-Taylor et al., 2010) although women have longer life expectancies. Some studies have not considered this factor when determining prevalence. Furthermore, not all community data indicate that sex is a significant risk factor for anxiety in later life (Ford et al., 2007). Thus, it is unclear whether the differences in the prevalence of anxiety disorders are accurate or merely reflect the higher number of women in the older population. As with depression, little is known about the relationship between anxiety disorders and race/ethnicity in older Canadian adults.

ETIOLOGY OF ANXIETY IN LATER LIFE Most anxiety disorders have their onset in childhood and young adulthood (Chapter 4); very few cases develop in later life (Kessler et al., 2005a). The onset of GAD, however, can be either early or later in life (Beck & Averill, 2004; Stanley, 2003). Many older adults report long-term or lifetime symptoms of anxiety, while others indicate a more recent onset. In the latter cases, stressful life events (financial stress, increased physical disability, loss of social support, etc.) may play a unique role (Ganzini et al., 1990). Some studies suggest no differences in clinical symptoms related to age of onset (Beck et al., 1996), but other data indicate more severe symptoms among patients with earlier onset and more serious functional limitations due to physical problems among those with later onset (Le Roux et al., 2005). PTSD also can begin in later life following traumatic experiences (natural disaster, assault, etc.) (Wolitzky-Taylor et al., 2010).

The biological and psychological theories reviewed in Chapter 4 are relevant particularly for older people who have suffered from anxiety since their younger years. Although little research has specifically addressed the etiology of anxiety in older adults, a recent large twin study demonstrated that approximately 25% of the variance in liability for GAD among older adults (ages 55 to 74) result from genetic factors (Mackintosh et al., 2006). Diathesis-stress hypotheses proposed for late-life depression are also relevant for anxiety for the same reason; biologically inherited vulnerability factors and stressful life experiences probably interact to create these disorders.

Biological factors in late-onset anxiety disorders require serious consideration because anxiety symptoms overlap with those of various medical diseases. Anxiety may also be a psychological response to medical illness (Flint, 2004), a part of the medical picture, or a separate psychological syndrome. Consider chronic obstructive pulmonary disease (COPD), a common lung disease in later life with symptoms including shortness of breath and catastrophic thoughts about physical symptoms. These same symptoms are also characteristic of panic disorder. COPD-related symptoms may precipitate anxiety syndromes in chronically ill people who worry excessively about medical symptoms and associated difficulties.

Curtis has severe COPD that requires oxygen therapy 24 hours a day. He is concerned about his medical condition whenever he goes on an outing with his family. Even mild shortness of breath during an outing causes Curtis to feel panicky—thinking that he might not be able to breathe and that he might die. As he becomes more worried, his breathing worsens and he sometimes experiences dizziness, sweating, and shakiness. Doctors told Curtis and his family that not all of these symptoms would be expected based on his COPD and current treatments, but Curtis worries that the doctors might be missing something. He also begins to feel concerned that he is slowing his family down when they are out, and he chooses to stay home alone more often. As a result, Curtis feels depressed and even more anxious about going out.

TREATMENT OF ANXIETY IN OLDER PATIENTS As with depression, ruling out physical illnesses that may be producing anxiety-like symptoms is necessary. Treatments for anxiety disorders in older adults are similar to those used for younger people, with

Cognitive-behavioural group therapy is effective for older adults with mood or anxiety disorders.

vm/E+/Getty Images

most research examining pharmacological and psychosocial (primarily cognitive-behavioural) treatments.

Because older adults often seek help for mental health problems in a medical setting, most treatment for anxiety involves the use of medication. Among older adults, benzodiazepines are prescribed most frequently; they are given to as many as 43% of patients with persistent anxiety (Schuurmans et al., 2005). Although some data indicate that these medications are superior to placebo (Frattola et al., 1992), benzodiazepines can create serious side effects for older adults, including memory problems and the slowing of motor behaviours. Because these effects can lead to negative consequences, such as decreased ability to drive safely, increased risk of hip fractures due to falls, and significant memory problems, alternative medications are preferred.

Antidepressants, such as selective serotonin reuptake inhibitors (SSRIs), are effective for older adults with anxiety disorders (Katz et al., 2002; Lenze et al., 2009; Schuurmans et al., 2006). These medications have fewer side effects than benzodiazepines and are recommended as the first-line pharmacological treatment. Even antidepressants have side effects, however, and older patients often prefer psychosocial treatment over pharmacotherapy when they have a choice (Gum et al., 2004; van Hout et al., 2004; Wetherell et al., 2004).

Most studies of psychological treatments have examined cognitive-behavioural therapy (CBT), which is considered to be well suited for older patients because it is time limited, directive, and collaborative (Zeiss & Steffens, 1996). CBT is efficacious for patients with GAD (Nordhus & Pallesen, 2003; Stanley et al., 2009), but fewer older adults respond positively to CBT compared with younger patients (Wetherell et al., 2005). Modifying the treatment (slowing the pace, using different learning strategies to teach skills, etc.) may be necessary for older patients, and combining CBT with antidepressant medication produced superior outcome in one pilot investigation (Wetherell et al., 2011). CBT also appears useful for other anxiety disorders (panic disorder, social phobia) (Barrowclough et al., 2001; Schuurmans et al., 2006; Thorp et al., 2009).

CONCEPT check

- Most bipolar and depressive disorders are diagnosed in older and younger adults using the same criteria. However, some medical disorders can produce depressive disorders that are unique to older adults (e.g., vascular depression).
- The suicide rate of older Canadians is not higher than that of younger Canadians.
- Medication and psychological treatments are effective for depression and anxiety in older adults.
- Older adults often describe anxiety differently than younger adults by using fewer psychological terms and putting more emphasis on physical symptoms.
- The most prevalent anxiety disorders in older adults are GAD and specific phobias.

critical thinking question Why do depression and anxiety often remain undiagnosed or untreated in older adults? And why do you think that most older adults prefer therapy over medication for treating anxiety or depression?

Substance-Related Disorders and Psychosis in Later Life

When most people think of older adults with psychological problems, they may not picture an older man who goes to bed drunk at night or a woman who has paranoid delusions. Yet older people suffer from substance abuse problems and psychotic disorders just as some younger people do. As with depression and anxiety, less is known about these disorders among older people than among younger adults. Nevertheless, substance misuse and psychotic symptoms can affect the quality of life and functioning of older people, and research is beginning to address the unique nature, causes, and treatment of these problems.

Substance-Related Disorder

Harold was a 72-year-old divorced man who always enjoyed social events. He could have a few drinks, smoke a few cigarettes, enjoy his friends, and wake up feeling fine the next day. Even as he got older, he could "hold his own" at a party. One night when he was driving home from a gathering, he swerved to miss a car that he thought was too close to the line and ran off the road. His car suffered some damage, and he hurt his back and neck. The doctor gave him some pain medication, which made things much easier. He was already taking a mild tranquilizer for anxiety—but that was from a different doctor. He was sure there would be nothing wrong with adding one pill a day. When he started to have more trouble sleeping because of the pain, he decided to take one extra pill—and sometimes added a beer. That made it even easier to relax. Before long, Harold couldn't get to sleep without the tranquilizer, a double dose of pain medication, and a beer.

Alcohol and other substance-related disorders are underappreciated problems for older adults. Overuse of alcohol, misuse of prescription medications (e.g., benzodiazepines, sedatives, narcotic painkillers), and tobacco use are the most common problems (Atkinson, 2004; Lin et al., 2010). Although the diagnostic criteria are the same as for younger adults (see Chapter 9), the symptoms are not always consistent. Among older people, alcohol abuse is less often associated with antisocial behaviour, legal problems, unemployment, and low socioeconomic status than among younger adults. Instead, problematic substance use in older adults may be recognized only as the individuals increasingly depend on others (who then have more opportunity to observe patterns of use) or as substance use affects medical illnesses and their treatment (Blazer, 2004) or patient safety (car accidents, falls, etc.).

The National Institute on Alcohol Abuse and Alcoholism (NIAAA) recommends that adults ages 65 and over have no more than one drink per day or seven drinks per week (Oslin, 2004), with no more than two drinks on any one occasion (Oslin & Mavandadi, 2009). However, as with younger adults, alcohol use disorder in late life is defined not simply by the number of drinks, but also by use that has adverse consequences (medical, social, or psychological) and that negatively impacts functioning. Determining adverse consequences may be challenging because older adults may have fewer obligations outside home and fewer social contacts.

Bill reports drinking five glasses of wine each evening, but he drinks at home and does not drive. He also no longer has to get up early in the morning to get to work. Therefore, he denies any problems due to alcohol use.

Does Bill have alcohol use disorder?

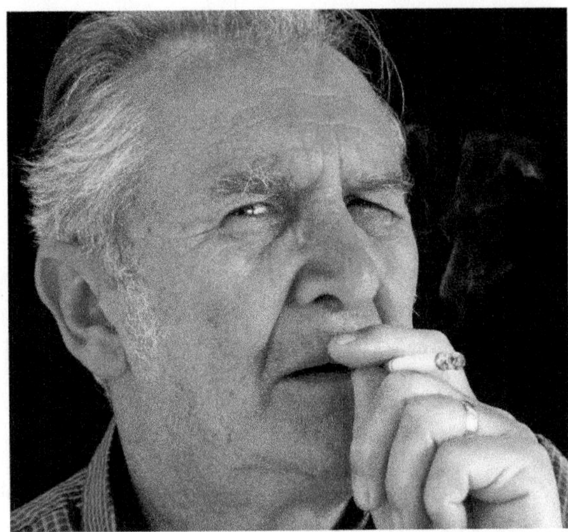

Alcohol, prescription medications, and tobacco are the substances most commonly misused by older adults.

(left): Vinicius Tupinamba/Fotolia; **(centre):** auremar/Fotolia; **(right):** jabiru/Fotolia

Similarly, overuse of prescription drugs may develop gradually and go unrecognized. Patients may be prescribed medications by multiple physicians who are unaware of other medications the patients may be taking. Many older adults tend to take less medication than they are prescribed. However, patients who are more passive and compliant may take multiple medications without questioning their potential overlap (Blazer, 2004). Over-the-counter medications can complicate drug interactions even further. In many cases, prescription abuse among older adults is noticed only when signs of toxicity or withdrawal occur.

PREVALENCE AND IMPACT The most comprehensive picture of the substance use and abuse among Canadian seniors (ages 65 and older) comes from a report by the Public Health Agency of Canada (2010). The findings suggest that in terms of prevalence, substance use and abuse is of less of a problem in Canadian seniors than in other age groups. But in other ways, especially in terms of physical frailty and medication interactions, the use and abuse of substances can be more of a problem for seniors compared to younger people. Specific details are as follows.

Smoking and alcohol problems are less prevalent among Canadian seniors than among younger people. A total of 9% of seniors are current smokers and 6% to 10% have alcohol abuse or dependence, which are lower rates than for other age groups. However, alcohol consumption, regardless of quantity, tends to be more of a problem for seniors compared to younger Canadians. This is because seniors are more vulnerable to the effects of alcohol because they metabolize it more slowly. Alcohol reduces muscle coordination, which may contribute to falls. Falls are of particular concern for seniors suffering from osteoporosis. Alcohol can also exacerbate other health problems, such as dementia, liver disease, diabetes, and hypertension. Also, more than 150 medications commonly prescribed to seniors can result in problems if consumed with alcohol; some may not work as they are meant to, while others may have an increased or dangerous effect (Public Health Agency of Canada, 2010).

SEX, RACE, AND ETHNICITY Older men use alcohol at twice the rate of women, and they are as many as six times more likely to be problem drinkers. These differences are consistent across various ethnic and racial groups (Atkinson, 2004). Women, however, are at higher risk for negative consequences because they do not metabolize alcohol as quickly as men do and need less alcohol to suffer the intoxicating effects (Epstein et al., 2007). Illicit drug use is more common in older men, but women use more prescription medication for nonmedical reasons (National Survey on Drug Use and Health, 2006).

Remarkably little is known about the prevalence of tobacco use and alcohol problems across race and ethnicity in Canada. Tobacco use tends to be more common among Aboriginal seniors not living on a reserve compared to non-Aboriginal seniors (24% vs. 9%; Public Health Agency of Canada, 2010).

ETIOLOGY Theories regarding the development of alcohol and substance-related disorders in younger adults also apply to older patients, particularly when the disorder started early in life. Across the lifespan, some people have a steady use pattern whereas others use alcohol and substances more progressively or variably. When the onset of misuse occurs later in life, there is less evidence that genetic factors are operative, but there is often a personal history of habitual use or risky drinking (Atkinson, 2004; Blazer, 2004). Vulnerability to misuse also increases with medical frailty and the need for multiple medications. Likewise, benzodiazepine overuse increases when patients have a history of alcohol-related disorders.

TREATMENT OF SUBSTANCE-RELATED DISORDERS Most of the research on treating substance-related disorders in older adults focuses on risky or problematic drinking (Oslin, 2004; Oslin & Mavandadi, 2009). Treatment is aimed at both prevention and early intervention. *Brief alcohol counselling* (BAC) may reduce at-risk drinking and prevent more extensive alcohol-related difficulties. BAC typically provides family support and education, including direct feedback about problematic drinking and specific advice on reducing alcohol use. *Behavioural self-control procedures* (e.g., keeping a drinking diary, behavioural contracting) are also sometimes used. In primary care settings, BAC (using either one or four brief patient contacts) has had positive results for at-risk drinking in older adults (Fleming et al., 1999; Moore et al., 2011; Oslin, 2005).

For older adults with diagnosed alcohol or substance-related disorders rather than risky drinking, treatment outcomes are comparable across age groups when older and younger adults are treated together (Atkinson & Misra, 2002). Older patients, however, tend to be more adherent to treatment recommendations (Oslin et al., 2002) and have better outcomes when treatment is age specific (Kashner et al., 1992). Age-specific treatment may foster better peer relationships and longer retention in treatment, which may enhance treatment outcomes (Atkinson, 2004).

Drugs such as naltrexone (see Chapter 9) are safe and beneficial for the treatment of late-life alcohol-related disorder (Oslin et al., 1997). Another drug, disulfiram (Antabuse), is commonly used to prevent drinking in younger adults. However, this drug can be dangerous for older patients if they drink while taking the medication (Atkinson, 2004). Antidepressant medication can be useful for reducing drinking if patients experience depression along with alcohol-related disorders.

Benzodiazepine dependence is usually treated by gradual discontinuation of the drug. However, the outcome is poor if the drug has been used for a long time. When treatment is successful, it improves cognitive functioning and reduces anxiety, depression, and insomnia symptoms. Some symptoms may remain, and older adults are at increased risk for return usage (Atkinson, 2004). Finally, smoking cessation treatments that are efficacious for younger adults (e.g., brief interventions in primary care, transdermal nicotine patch therapy) are also efficacious for older patients (Atkinson, 2004).

Psychosis

Older adults, like younger ones, can experience some of the most severe psychological disorders, the psychoses. In many cases, the diagnostic categories used to describe these disorders are the same for older and younger adults (see Chapter 10). We focus here on different characterizations of schizophrenia that are used to describe subgroups of older patients and on psychotic symptoms that arise in the context of major neurocognitive disorder.

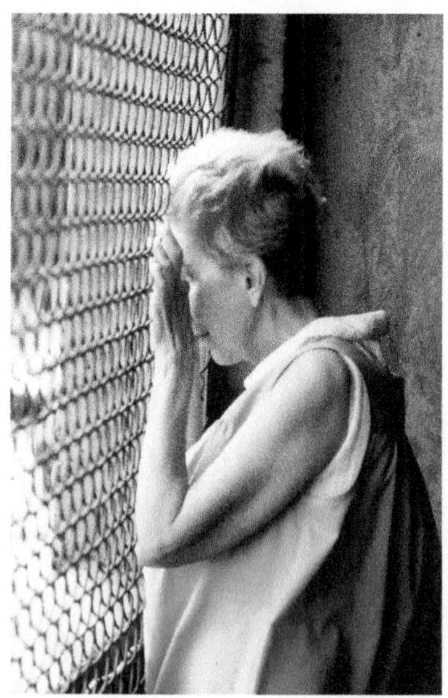

Schizophrenia in older adults is usually a continuation of a disease process that began at an earlier age. It is uncommon for schizophrenia to begin at older ages.
Grunnitus Studio/Science Source

In 80% of older adults with schizophrenia, the onset occurs in young adulthood and continues into older age (Jeste et al., 2004). For 60% of these adults, the disorder is relatively stable over their lifetimes, while another 20% experience worsening of symptoms, and 20% show symptom improvement and even remission in later life. Generally, the symptoms are the same for older and younger adults with one exception: As adults with schizophrenia age, cognitive performance deteriorates, but the rate of decline is no different than among adults without schizophrenia (Eyler Zorrilla et al., 2000).

When the disorder begins late in life, a unique pattern of related symptoms develops (Howard et al., 2000). **Late-onset schizophrenia** is generally thought to first appear after age 40, although Canadian research suggests that it might appear earlier, around age 33 (Liu et al., 2013). Many characteristic risk factors (family history, genetic risk, and childhood maladjustment) are similar to earlier onset (Jeste et al., 2009; Pearman & Batra, 2012), but people with late-life schizophrenia have a higher prevalence of the paranoid subtype and more auditory hallucinations. They also have fewer negative symptoms and less impaired cognitive skills (e.g., learning, ability to abstract, flexibility in thinking). When the disorder begins later in life, patients report higher premorbid functioning (better functioning before the disorder started) and more successful occupational and marital histories (Pearman & Betra, 2012).

Very-late-onset schizophrenia-like psychosis is a heterogeneous category that develops after age 65. In the very-late-onset subgroup, psychotic symptoms result from a stroke, tumour, or other *neurodegenerative* change. Because these symptoms occur after a period of normal neurobiological development, very-late-onset schizophrenia differs from all other forms of schizophrenia, which are considered *neurodevelopmental* (e.g., Jeste et al., 2004; see Chapter 10). Very-late-onset schizophrenia-like psychosis is associated with less genetic susceptibility, less evidence of childhood maladjustment, and fewer negative symptoms (Jeste et al., 2004, 2009).

Approximately 30% to 50% of patients with Alzheimer's disease develop psychotic symptoms (Jeste & Finkel, 2000), usually three to four years after the Alzheimer's diagnosis. The psychotic symptoms are very different from those in late-life schizophrenia (Jeste & Finkel, 2000). In psychosis that occurs with Alzheimer's disease, patients more often report simple and concrete delusions.

Betty repeatedly tells her daughter that the man across the hall in her assisted living community is stealing from her. She is certain that he comes into her room when she is sleeping and takes her things.

Misidentification of a caregiver also is common.

Grace regularly refers to her daughter, with whom she lives, as "that woman who lives here and cleans the house."

Auditory hallucinations are rare, but visual hallucinations are more common.

When she is awake in the middle of the night, Hazel frequently looks out her window and sees fires burning and children dying, but no one comes to help.

A past history of psychosis is rare in patients who develop psychotic symptoms during the course of dementia, and these symptoms often remit during later stages. Compared with dementia patients without psychosis, patients with both disorders show increased aggressive behaviour, wandering, agitation, family problems, and lack of self-care (Jeste et al., 2004).

PREVALENCE AND IMPACT Schizophrenia occurs in 0.6% of people ages 45 to 64 and in 0.1% to 0.5% of people ages 65 and above (Jeste et al., 2004). As many as 29% of patients with schizophrenia report onset after age 40, and up to 12% report onset of symptoms after age 60 (Jeste et al., 2004). Psychotic symptoms are more common among patients who are hospitalized or living in nursing homes. Schizophrenia in later life is tremendously debilitating, significantly impacting functioning, quality of life, health care use and costs, and mortality (Van Citters et al., 2005). Poor functioning is associated with worse cognitive performance, little education, and severe negative symptoms (Evans et al., 2003).

SEX, RACE, AND ETHNICITY Late-onset schizophrenia is more common among women but begins at an earlier age for men (Jeste et al., 2004, 2009). Neuroendocrine changes, increased longevity of women, and differential psychosocial stressors may explain these sex-related differences. Estrogen, for example, may serve as an *endogenous antipsychotic* (a naturally occurring substance that functions in the same way as an antipsychotic medication). In this instance, until menopause, estrogen may prevent psychotic symptoms in women who are biologically at risk for schizophrenia (Seeman, 1996).

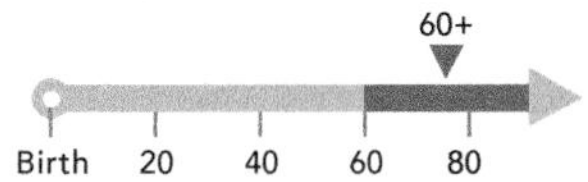

When psychotic symptoms occur for the first time in older adults, the cause is likely to be a stroke or a brain tumour.

As noted in Chapter 10, the symptoms of psychosis are common across racial and ethnic groups of younger adults. Little is known about racial/ethnic differences in late- and very-late onset psychosis in Canadian seniors.

ETIOLOGY Late-onset schizophrenia shares many possible etiological factors with schizophrenia that begins earlier in life. Brain abnormalities are similar to those in patients with earlier onset, including enlarged ventricles, increased density of dopamine receptors, and reduced size of the superior temporal gyrus (see Chapter 10). People with late-onset schizophrenia have better premorbid social functioning than those who develop it earlier, but their social adjustment is poorer and they display more eccentric behaviour than those with earlier onset (Jeste et al., 2004).

As noted earlier, very-late-onset schizophrenia-like psychosis is generally associated with neurological damage, such as a stroke or tumour. In these cases, there is no evidence of a direct genetic role, although both genetic and environmental factors may contribute to medical conditions, such as stroke, that then produce psychotic symptoms. When psychosis occurs in people with Alzheimer's disease, more severe cognitive impairment is present (see "Dementia"). Patients with both disorders have increased degeneration in the brain and increased levels of norepinephrine, decreased levels of serotonin, and other problems, such as tremors, muscle rigidity, and slowed movement, as in Parkinson's disease (Jeste, 2004).

TREATMENT OF PSYCHOSIS As with younger adults, the primary treatments for schizophrenia for older adults include the typical and atypical antipsychotic medications. However, treatment response may differ across age groups. Physical and emotional differences in cognitive and social functioning, age-related changes in metabolism and neurotransmitter receptor sensitivity, medical illnesses, and use of other medications may affect response to antipsychotic medication. Little research has examined the efficacy of antipsychotic medications specifically in older adults, but available data suggest modest improvements in a range of symptoms (Van Critters et al., 2005). The atypical antipsychotics produce better outcome and fewer side effects than do the typical antipsychotics. Because older adults show increased medication sensitivity and much higher rates of movement-related side effects (e.g., tardive dyskinesia; see Chapter 10), medication doses are typically 25% to 50% lower for them than for younger adults (Jeste et al., 2004).

When psychosis occurs in the context of major neurocognitive disorder, antipsychotic medications produce modest effects with atypical variants performing best (Schneider et al., 2006; Weintraub & Katz, 2005). As age increases, medication dosage decreases. Because psychotic symptoms frequently remit in the later stages of dementia, long-term use of medications is often not necessary (Jeste et al., 2004). Patients with major neurocognitive disorder are particularly sensitive to medication side effects, and even the atypical antipsychotic medications can produce sedation, fluctuation in blood pressure, and increased risk of mortality (Schneider et al., 2005).

Only a small number of studies have tested the utility of psychological treatments for schizophrenia in older adults, but skills training and CBT in various combinations have positive effects (e.g., Granholm et al., 2005; Jeste et al., 2009). These interventions help patients challenge their delusional beliefs and change behaviours related to medication noncompliance and health care management. Patients also learn social, communication, and life skills (e.g., organization and planning, financial management) aimed at improving overall functioning. Family support and education are important among patients with psychosis and dementia, along with training to the caregiver on coping skills and behavioural management of problematic behaviours, such as aggression toward caregivers.

CONCEPT check

- Alcohol misuse is less common among seniors compared to younger Canadians, although seniors are more susceptible to the effects of alcohol.
- Brief alcohol counselling includes education about the effects of drinking, direct feedback about problematic drinking, and advice about reducing alcohol intake.
- Compared to patients with an earlier onset of schizophrenia, patients with late-onset schizophrenia have more frequent auditory hallucinations, fewer negative symptoms, less impaired cognitive skills, and better functioning earlier in life.
- Psychosis that occurs with major neurocognitive disorder is uniquely defined by simple and concrete delusions, misidentification of a caregiver, and visual hallucinations.
- Atypical antipsychotic medications are associated with increased risk of mortality in patients with psychosis and major neurocognitive disorder.
- Nonmedication treatment can be helpful for older adults with schizophrenia.

critical thinking question Why are alcohol and substance-related disorders such serious problems for older adults even though prevalence is lower among them than among younger people?

Neurocognitive Disorders

13.4 Distinguish between major neurocognitive disorder and delirium, two cognitive disorders that are common among older adults.

Neurocognitive disorders (disorders of thinking) affect older adults more than the other syndromes discussed in this chapter. As older people live longer and the population of older people continues to increase, more and more people will suffer from these cognitive dysfunctions. Some level of cognitive decline (e.g., in memory, attention, speed of processing information) is associated with normal aging. However, **delirium** and **major neurocognitive disorder** are two disorders that represent deficits in cognitive abilities significantly affecting older people.

Delirium

Elizabeth was an 86-year-old widow with a diagnosis of major neurocognitive disorder. Her children became concerned when she started to lose interest in her usual activities. She was less alert and attentive than usual, cried more often, had little appetite, and wasn't sleeping well. Her children worried that she was depressed. She also had many medical problems, including high blood pressure, chest pain, congestive heart failure, arthritis, cataracts, and "seizures" during which she seemed to go blank and mumbled. Her children believed that these problems were all controlled as well as possible with medications prescribed by her internist and various specialists. When the psychiatrist examined Elizabeth, she was cooperative and pleasant, but she cried occasionally, even when she wasn't talking about anything sad. She was slow to respond, and her voice often trailed off and became inaudible. At these times, her words were jumbled. Her daughter reported that episodes like this were common and usually worse at night. The psychiatrist learned that Elizabeth was taking eight different medications. The psychiatrist reviewed the rationale for each of these medications and made a provisional diagnosis of medication-induced delirium. Over the next two months, the physician discontinued the use of six of the medications, and many of Elizabeth's symptoms improved.

The primary feature of delirium (see "DSM-5: Delirium") is a disturbance in attention or awareness that typically occurs in the context of a medical illness or after ingesting a substance (such as a drug). Altered states of consciousness can range from decreased wakefulness and stupor (*hypoactive type*) to severe insomnia and hyperarousal (*hyperactive type*). The onset of delirium is sudden, typically within hours or days, but it can be slow and progressive among older adults (Raskind et al., 2004). Symptoms of delirium can persist for months in older patients (Levkoff et al., 1992) in contrast to young adults, in whom they typically disappear after only a short time.

PREVALENCE AND IMPACT The prevalence of delirium among older hospitalized patients ranges from 14% to 56%, and delirium is common among older patients seen in the emergency room (30%) and those who have had surgery (15% to 53%; Fearing & Inouye, 2009; Public Health Agency of Canada, 2010). People with major neurocognitive disorder are at a significantly higher risk of experiencing delirium (McCusker et al., 2011; Fearing & Inouye, 2009). Delirium is associated with longer hospital stays for medical patients (Ely et al., 2001; Thomason et al., 2005), more complications following surgery, poorer posthospitalization functioning, and increased risk of institutional placement (Liptzin, 2004). While the number of seniors in the community who experience episodes of delirium is unknown, it is thought that 32% to 67% of seniors with delirium go undiagnosed (Public Health Agency of Canada, 2010).

SEX, RACE, AND ETHNICITY Men are at higher risk for delirium than women (Fearing & Inouye, 2009; Liptzin, 2004). However, incorrectly diagnosed women more often receive a diagnosis of major depressive disorder, and misdiagnosed men are more frequently given no diagnosis (Armstrong et al., 1997).

ETIOLOGY Delirium is associated with a range of biological and environmental factors (Liptzin, 2004; Raskind et al., 2004). However, it is most often brought on by a serious systemic medical illness, such as AIDS, congestive heart failure, infection, or toxic effects of a medication, as the case of Elizabeth illustrates. Medication toxicity occurs more easily among older adults because they metabolize drugs differently and often take multiple medications that could interact to produce adverse drug effects. Other biological causes of delirium include metabolic disorders (e.g., hypothyroidism or hypoglycemia), neurological disorders (e.g., head trauma, stroke, seizure, meningitis), malnutrition or severe dehydration, and alcohol or drug intoxication or withdrawal. The risk of delirium increases with age and cognitive impairment. In some cases, episodes of delirium may be the first symptom of an underlying major neurocognitive disorder (Raskind et al., 2004).

criteria for
Delirium **DSM-5**

A. A disturbance in attention (i.e., reduced ability to direct, focus, sustain, and shift attention) and awareness (reduced orientation to the environment).

B. The disturbance develops over a short period of time (usually hours to a few days), represents a change from baseline attention and awareness, and tends to fluctuate in severity during the course of a day.

C. An additional disturbance in cognition (e.g., memory deficit, disorientation, language, visuospatial ability, or perception).

D. The disturbances in Criteria A and C are not better explained by another preexisting, established, or evolving neurocognitive disorder and do not occur in the context of a severely reduced level of arousal, such as coma.

E. There is evidence from the history, physical examination, or laboratory findings that the disturbance is a direct physiological consequence of another medical condition, substance intoxication or withdrawal (i.e., due to a drug of abuse or to a medication), or exposure to a toxin, or is due to multiple etiologies.

Environmental factors also increase the risk for delirium during hospitalization, including the use of physical restraints, the use of more than three medications, and the use of a bladder catheter (Weber et al., 2004). Risk factors that contribute to dehydration, poor nutrition, and sleep deprivation are also important. How these factors interact is not entirely clear, but delirium is associated with dysfunction in the prefrontal cortex, thalamus, and basal ganglia. Furthermore, a number of neurotransmitters may be involved (e.g., dopamine, serotonin, GABA, acetylcholine) (Liptzin, 2004; Trzepacz et al., 2002). In summary, the onset of delirium is complicated, but determining its origin is necessary because for some older adults, appropriate intervention (rehydration, stopping medication) may reverse its symptoms. Among older patients hospitalized in an acute care unit, daily low-dose melatonin provided protection against the onset of delirium (Al-aama et al., 2011). Although the reason is unclear, melatonin may regulate the sleep–wake cycle. This may be important as sleep deprivation is a risk factor for delirium.

TREATMENT Delirium is often not recognized or is inadequately treated (Weber et al., 2004). As a first step, screening for known risk factors (e.g., major neurocognitive disorder, substance use) is necessary. Precautions to minimize delirium include monitoring medications, ensuring proper nutrition and hydration, and managing the patient's sleep–wake cycle (Liptzin, 2004; Weber et al., 2004). When symptoms occur despite prevention strategies, early detection is important to reduce the episode's duration and impact.

Treatment of delirium begins with manipulating the environment (Fearing & Inouye, 2009). Beneficial environmental manipulations include reducing sensory stimulation (e.g., quiet room, low-level lighting), providing orientation through visual cues such as family pictures and clocks, encouraging the presence of family members, minimizing the use of physical restraints, and maintaining a regular day–night routine with open blinds, limited daytime sleeping, and minimal nighttime wakening for vital signs and other medical procedures (Fearing & Inouye, 2009; Liptzin, 2004). If medication is needed, low-dose antipsychotic medications can help keep the patient safe and reduce symptoms. When delirium is due to withdrawal of alcohol or other sedatives, short-acting benzodiazepines may be used (Liptzin, 2004). Education and supportive care provide information about symptom course, allowing family members to remain with the patient.

Neurocognitive Disorders

Neurocogitive disorders are devastating. They gradually rob patients of their ability to function independently. They also create significant emotional problems for patients and their families, who suffer along with patients through prolonged periods of increasing dysfunction. Treatments are available to slow progression of the disease and improve quality of life, but dementia remains one of the most common and debilitating disorders of older age.

TYPES OF NEUROCOGNITIVE DISORDER The term *neurocognitive disorder* describes different syndromes characterized by cognitive decline from a previous level of performance in cognitive domains (such as attention, executive function, learning and memory, language, perceptual-motor, or social cognition). Major neurocognitive disorder

SIDE by SIDE case studies — Dimensions of Behaviour: From Normal to Abnormal

Normal Case Study

Occasional Forgetfulness

→ Antonia is a 72-year-old woman who worked as an administrative assistant in an elementary school for 35 years before she retired at age 65. She was much loved by her co-workers and the children at her school, but she was looking forward to spending more time with her grandchildren and helping out with various volunteer opportunities. Indeed, Antonia found her retirement years very rewarding. She stayed in contact with co-workers who were also friends, and she enjoyed having more time to spend with her husband. Antonia did notice, however, that as the years went by she didn't think as quickly as she used to. She also began to have trouble recalling people's names, experiences she found really embarrassing, especially when she had known the person for many years. Antonia also misplaced things more often, but her friends said they were having similar experiences, and she always eventually found what she thought she had lost. Her cognitive symptoms did not get in the way of her functioning, so she just chalked the changes up to normal "aging" and continued to enjoy her retirement life by volunteering activities and taking her grandchildren to the park, doing crossword puzzles, and walking her dog.

Abnormal Case Study

Major Neurocognitive Disorder

→ Ernest is a 75-year-old male who was an accountant for 30 years before he retired 10 years ago. He married for the first time when he was 25 and had three children. His wife left their family when the children were 7, 5, and 4 years old. Ernest raised the children on his own with help from his sister, who lived nearby. At age 60, when he was nearing his planned retirement, he married a woman who was 10 years younger. He and his new wife developed an active retirement life filled with travelling, visiting relatives and friends, and playing bridge.

About four years ago, Ernest began to have memory problems. He regularly lost his keys and glasses, and he began to rely more on lists when he went about his daily chores and errands. Over time, he became more confused, and had trouble keeping his lists organized. He began to have difficulty finding the right words to express his thoughts, and his wife noticed that he often repeated himself, telling her the same things several times a day. Ernest had always been very quick with numbers and calculations, but he began to have trouble keeping his mind focused on balancing his cheque book. He made calculation errors and couldn't remember where to record various pieces of financial information. He also got more and more confused during bridge games. As Ernest developed more serious cognitive limitations, he started to feel anxious and depressed. He had always been a cheerful man who was full of life, but as his cognitive difficulties grew, he started to withdraw from social engagements because he was worried that others would notice. He also felt less interested in activities that he used to enjoy. His wife was quite worried about him and how she would be able to continue to care for him if he got more confused.

is different from delirium. In major neurocognitive disorder, cognitive difficulties are not accompanied by changes in consciousness or alertness. The central feature is cognitive impairment (e.g., difficulties with understanding or using words, inability to carry out motor activities, failure to recognize or name objects, or deficits in executive abilities).

Neurocognitive disorders can be classified as either major or mild. *Major neurocognitive disorder* is assigned when there is a significant decline in cognitive performance. *Mild neurocognitive disorder* is diagnosed when there is a modest decline from previous cognitive performance (see "DSM-5 Major and Mild Neurocognitive Disorders"). It is typically diagnosed only after extensive interviews and history taking with the patient and close relatives or friends, cognitive testing and observation, a thorough medical evaluation, and often a neuroimaging test (e.g., CT or MRI; Lyketsos, 2009), although the cost-effectiveness of neuroimaging has been questioned (Raskind et al., 2004). To diagnose mild or major neurocognitive disorder, clinicians compare cognitive difficulties with prior levels of functioning. Understanding the potential etiology is important because reversible causes, although infrequent (9%) (Clarfield, 2003), can include vitamin deficiency (particularly B-12), thyroid dysfunction, drug toxicity, and normal pressure hydrocephalus (an abnormal increase of cerebrospinal fluid in the brain's ventricles, or cavities). In most cases, however, neurocognitive disorder reflects a progressive pattern of cognitive disability and functional impairment.

There are various types of major or mild neurocognitive disorder. *Major or mild neurocognitive disorder due to Alzheimer's disease* (commonly known as Alzheimer's disease)

criteria for

Major or Mild Neurocognitive Disorder Due to Alzheimer's Disease DSM-5

Major Neurocognitive Disorder

A. Evidence of significant cognitive decline from a previous level of performance in one or more cognitive domains (complex attention, executive function, learning and memory, language, perceptual-motor, or social cognition) based on:
   1. Concern of the individual, a knowledgeable informant, or the clinician that there has been a significant decline in cognitive function; and
   2. A substantial impairment in cognitive performance, preferably documented by standardized neuropsychological testing or, in its absence, another quantified clinical assessment.

B. The cognitive deficits interfere with independence in everyday activities (i.e., at a minimum, requiring assistance with complex instrumental activities of daily living such as paying bills or managing medications).

C. The cognitive deficits do not occur exclusively in the context of a delirium.

D. The cognitive deficits are not better explained by another mental disorder (e.g., major depressive disorder, schizophrenia).

Mild Neurocognitive Disorder

A. Evidence of modest cognitive decline from a previous level of performance in one or more cognitive domains (complex attention, executive function, learning and memory, language, perceptual-motor, or social cognition) based on:
   1. Concern of the individual, a knowledgeable informant, or the clinician that there has been a mild decline in cognitive function; and
   2. A modest impairment in cognitive performance, preferably documented by standardized neuropsychological testing or, in its absence, another quantified clinical assessment.

B. The cognitive deficits do not interfere with capacity for independence in everyday activities (i.e., complex instrumental activities of daily living such as paying bills or managing medications are preserved, but greater effort, compensatory strategies, or accommodation may by required).

C. The cognitive deficits do not occur exclusively in the context of a delirium.

D. The cognitive deficits are not better explained by another mental disorder (e.g., major depressive disorder, schizophrenia).

has a gradual onset and continuing cognitive decline. *Major or mild vascular neurocognitive disorder* is diagnosed when cerebrovascular disease, such as stroke, is a potential cause of cognitive dysfunction. *Substance/medication-induced major or mild neurocognitive disorder* reflects cognitive impairment associated with substance use (abuse of a drug or a medication). Major or mild neurocognitive disorders may also be the result of medical conditions such as HIV, head trauma, Parkinson's disease and Huntington's disease, or other medical illness. In many cases, the disorder likely results from multiple etiologies (Lyketsos, 2009).

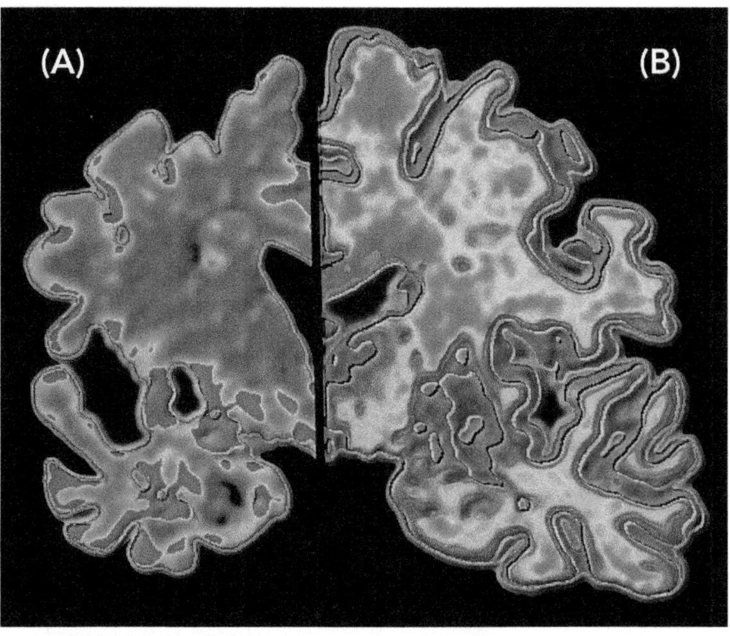

At left, a brain slice from a patient with major neurocognitive disorder due to Alzheimer's disease; at right, the brain of someone without this disorder. The brain on the left is shrunken due to the death of nerve cells.

A. Pakieka/Science Source

Major neurocognitive disorder due to Alzheimer's disease is by far the most common subtype of major neurocognitive disorder, accounting for as much as 75% of all patients (Chapman et al., 2006). It has a slow and progressive course of cognitive decline. Early signs may be subtle and not dramatically different from what is seen in normal aging (Backman et al., 2005). The first noticeable signs include forgetting recent events or names, repeating statements or questions, getting lost while driving in familiar places, and experiencing difficulty with calculations (Chapman et al., 2006; Raskind et al., 2004). A diagnosis of Alzheimer's disease at this early stage does not imply cognitive incompetence, and many people with Alzheimer's disease are able to maintain a positive quality of life for a number of years after diagnosis (see "Treatment"; Morris, 2005b). Over the next 5 to 15 years, Alzheimer's disease results in more severe impairments in the ability to use language, make decisions, and engage in self-care (see "Real People, Real Disorders: Pat Summitt: Decreasing the Stigma of Alzheimer's Disease"). Behavioural problems also occur and include disrupted sleep, wandering, irritability, and aggression. The rate of progressive deterioration in cognitive capabilities and functioning increases as the severity of the disease worsens (Morris, 2005a).

Virginia's difficulties were subtle at first. In fact, only her husband and best friend ever seemed to notice. She was able to hide her memory and language difficulties using jokes about her increasing age and self-imposed memory strategies (e.g., writing notes to herself; sticking to usual routines). However, as time went on, these strategies were less effective, and people began to notice how much trouble she was having. Virginia's husband started to notice that she was becoming less able almost every week.

A long period of gradual deterioration such as Virginia's is typical of this disease and can be devastating to family and friends of the person affected. As one nurse and patient advocate, Norma Wylie, quoted in *Sharing the Final Journey: Walking with the Dying*, 1996, has written: "Alzheimer's can be called the long good-bye. You grieve about the loved one from the moment you begin to observe the gradual loss of memory and the speech and personality changes, because they are incurable. The person you love is gradually changing before your eyes. You say good-bye many times until the final good-bye at death."

We now know that Alzheimer's disease involves the presence of **neurofibrillary tangles** (NFT), twisted protein fibres within neurons, and **cerebral senile plaques (SP)**, deposits of beta-amyloid protein that form between the cells in the hippocampus, cerebral

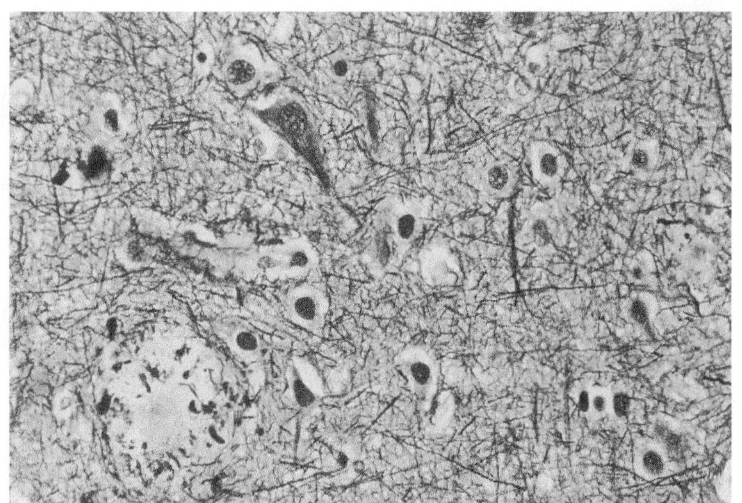

A microscopic examination of brain tissue taken from a patient with Alzheimer's disease reveals the neurofibrillary tangles (dark triangular shapes at left) and cerebral senile (amyloid) plaques (dark round shapes at right) associated with this disorder.

SPL/Science Source

cortex, and other regions of the brain (Chapman et al., 2006; Morris, 2006a). Increased frequency of NFTs and SPs accompanies normal aging, but people with Alzheimer's disease have excessive amounts. Autopsies indicate that current clinical procedures for diagnosing Alzheimer's disease are 90% accurate (Morris, 2005b). Brain changes associated with Alzheimer's probably begin years or even decades before symptoms are evident, and the type of symptoms experienced by patients with Alzheimer's has more to do with the location of the NFTs and SPs and the neurotransmitter systems that are affected (Lyketsos, 2009).

Major or mild vascular neurocognitive disorder is diagnosed when a patient's history, laboratory tests, or brain imaging studies indicate cognitive impairment as a result of cardiovascular disease, such as stroke, transient ischemic attack (TIA, or mini-stroke), coronary artery disease, or untreated high blood pressure. In these conditions, blockages of blood vessels result in tissue death, or *infarction*, in the brain. Damage may be to a single, major vessel or to a number of smaller ones (Morris, 2005b). Vascular neurocognitive disorder has different clinical features than Alzheimer's disease, including more sudden onset, more focal or "patchy" cognitive deficits, and more stepwise progression of cognitive difficulties (Chapman et al., 2006). However, vascular neurocognitive disorder rarely occurs alone and actually may be best considered a heterogeneous category (Lyketsos, 2009). In many cases, symptoms and pathology of Alzheimer's disease are also present (Lyketsos, 2009; Morris, 2005b). Vascular

REAL people REAL disorders

Pat Summitt: Decreasing the Stigma of Alzheimer's Disease

"*Earlier this year the doctors at the Mayo clinic diagnosed me with an early-onset dementia—Alzheimer's type.*"—Pat Summitt, August 23, 2011.

Although Alzheimer's disease typically appears in people who are 65 years or older, it can have particularly devastating effects when it impacts adults who are much younger (called early-onset Alzheimer's disease). Pat Summitt, a well-known women's university basketball coach, received this diagnosis in the summer of 2011 at the age of 59. Summitt initially contacted her doctors at the end of the 2011 basketball season, feeling like she had been having trouble thinking throughout the season. She originally thought her symptoms resulted from medication she was taking for arthritis, but medical evaluation revealed early-onset dementia, Alzheimer's type. Her grandmother also suffered from this same disorder.

Summitt did not plan to retire following her diagnosis, but she would rely more heavily on assistant coaches. She is treating her symptoms by taking medication and staying mentally and physically active. Instead of hiding her diagnosis, Summitt openly disclosed the diagnosis and described the steps she was taking to cope with the disorder. Summitt's actions show that there is nothing to be ashamed about having a neurocognitive disorder. Actions such as hers may help reduce the stigma often associated with Alzheimer's disease.

Jeff Moreland/Cal Sport Media/Newscom

Summitt's work colleagues remind the public that she is not just a coach, but also a mother, daughter, and friend. The road ahead will be difficult, but her courage in speaking out about her diagnosis will help to increase public awareness and decrease the stigma of Alzheimer's disease.

Sources: www.si.com/college-basketball/2011/08/23/pat-summittdementia. Accessed June 1, 2016; espn.go.com/womens-college-basketball/story/_/id/6888321/tennessee-lady-vols-pat-summitt-early-onset-dementia. Accessed May 4, 2013

tissue death may lower the threshold for Alzheimer's disease, although some causes of vascular neurocognitive disorder are modifiable (e.g., untreated hypertension).

Substance use, in particular alcohol-related disorder, can lead to dementia that is difficult to differentiate from Alzheimer's disease. In **substance/medication-induced major or mild neurocognitive disorder**, however, abstinence may stop or even reverse cognitive decline and cortical damage (Atkinson, 2004). Substance use may also increase vulnerability to other forms of dementia and the risk for other contributing factors, such as head trauma, infectious disease, and vitamin deficiency.

A number of medical conditions are also associated with neurocognitive disorders. These syndromes result from damage that occurs primarily in the inner layers of the brain and frequently emerge during the later stages of HIV and in Parkinson's and Huntington's diseases.

PREVALENCE AND IMPACT Major or mild neurocognitive disorder occurs in 5% to 10% of adults age 65 and over (Chapman et al., 2006; Gurland, 2004). Although figures vary across studies, all data suggest that the prevalence of dementia increases dramatically with advancing age (Figure 13.3). As noted earlier, Alzheimer's disease is the most common type, diagnosed in up to 75% of cases. Despite these high prevalence figures, many patients with neurocognitive disorder remain undiagnosed and untreated (Morris, 2005a).

The impact of major neurocognitive disorder on patients, their families, and the health care system is enormous.

Gene finally had to move in with his daughter, Sarah, and her family because he just couldn't function independently anymore. Although Sarah knew this was the right thing to do, it was hard on everyone. Someone had to be with him most of the time, and it was difficult for everyone to observe Gene, who had once been a vibrant man with many interests and skills, gradually deteriorate to a point where he couldn't remember their names.

As cognitive abilities and functional capacity deteriorate, negative emotional, social, and behavioural outcomes occur (Kunik et al., 2003; Lyketsos, 2009). In the early stages, social and emotional withdrawal is common. Remember how Ernest started to withdraw from activities for fear that people would notice his memory problems? Approximately 20% of patients with Alzheimer's disease also have depressive symptoms (Gurland, 1980; Hochang & Lyketsos, 2003), and as many as 70% have anxiety symptoms (Seignourel et al., 2008). These figures are not surprising given the significant distress patients experience when they hear they have this deteriorating, debilitating condition. Anxiety and depression, in addition to Alzheimer's disease, however, result in more behavioural problems and increased limitations in daily activities (Seignourel et al., 2008; Starkstein et al., 2008). The combination also increases social disability, decreases independence (Porter et al., 2003; Schultz et al., 2004), and increases the need for shifting to a nursing home (Gibbons et al., 2002).

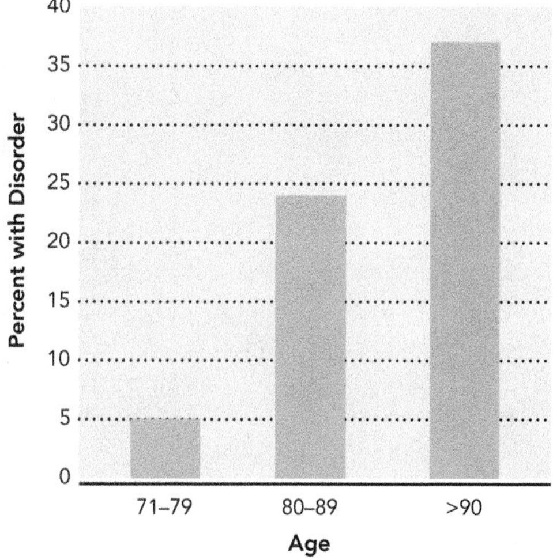

FIGURE 13.3

The Prevalence of Major Neurocognitive Disorder Increases with Age. Although individual studies report different prevalence estimates, all research shows that major neurocognitive disorder becomes more prevalent as people get older.

People with major neurocognitive disorder have more frequent coexisting medical conditions and reduced life expectancy. This disorder may exceed heart disease, stroke, diabetes, and cancer as a predictor of mortality in patients aged 65 and older (Alzheimer's Association, 2009; Tschanz et al., 2004). Major neurocognitive disorder also affects the treatment of medical conditions. Cognitively impaired patients are often unaware of changes in symptoms and treatment needs, and they have limited capacity to participate in health care decision making, self-care, or other health care plans (Boise et al., 2004; Brauner et al., 2000).

As Gene's memory and ability to express himself decreased, Sarah had to accompany him to all doctor appointments and coordinate all of his medical care.

Major neurocognitive disorder also affects family caregivers. Wives, daughters, and daughters-in-law have the heaviest burden of care, including assistance with nutrition and exercise, providing memory aids and activities for daily living, and making behavioural plans to manage associated mood and behaviour problems (Chapman et al., 2006). Caregivers are at increased risk themselves for depression and anxiety (Cooper et al., 2007; Schoenmakers et al., 2010).

For Sarah, taking care of her father was a full-time job. It limited the amount of time she could give to her children, making her feel guilty and sad. It was also difficult to remain patient when she had to answer the same questions over and over.

Family caregiver stress is the most common reason for placing people with major neurocognitive disorder in assisted living facilities (Wright et al., 1993). Use of health services and health care costs are also significantly higher than for patients with similar chronic conditions but no neurocognitive disorder (Bynum et al., 2004; Hill et al., 2002).

SEX, RACE, AND ETHNICITY Alzheimer's disease is more frequent in women than men (Reisberg et al., 2003). There have been inconsistent findings about the relationship between Alzheimer's disease and race/ethnicity, making it difficult to draw any firm conclusions. Even the prevalence of the disorder across countries has been changing (e.g., Western Europe vs. North Africa; Alzheimer's Disease International, 2015), which again makes it impossible to draw any conclusions about the relationship between Alzheimer prevalence and race/ethnicity. Studies of racial differences may shed light on genetic factors in dementia because of racial differences in genetic factors (e.g., *APOE*). However, lifestyle factors may also contribute to racial/ethnic differences in the prevalence of dementia. Among Koreans, Japanese, and Chinese, cases of Alzheimer's disease and vascular neurocognitive disorders have increased over the past 25 years, and the most likely factors are the environmental or dietary changes associated with increased Westernization (Sakauye, 2004).

13.5 Understand the etiological factors affecting psychological and cognitive disorders of late life.

ETIOLOGY OF MAJOR NEUROCOGNITIVE DISORDER As with all complex conditions, neurocognitive disorders most likely result from multiple genetic and environmental factors. Early-onset Alzheimer's disease (before age 55), which accounts for 1% of all Alzheimer's disease cases, is associated with mutations in at least one of three different genes (Morris, 2005b). In most cases, signs and symptoms arise after age 55. Increasing age itself is one of the strongest predictors of major neurocognitive disorder (see "Canadian Focus: The Canadian Study of Health and Aging" earlier in this chapter). Most cases with later onset are associated with multiple genes, but a specific mutation (e4) of the *APOE* gene greatly increases the risk of these disorders, probably through an impact on the age of onset for cognitive problems (Lyketsos, 2009; Morris, 2005b; Tsuang & Bird, 2004). People with a condition known as *mild cognitive impairment* who have the risk variant of the *APOE* gene are at increased risk for developing major neurocognitive disorder (see "Examining the Evidence: What Is Mild Cognitive Impairment (MCI), and Is It a Precursor of Major Neurocognitive Disorder or a Separate Syndrome?"). However, this mutation is neither necessary nor sufficient; only 50% of people with Alzheimer's disease have this gene variant. In addition, many people with

TABLE 13.1

Risk and Protective Factors for Major Neurocognitive Disorder

Risk Factors	Protective Factors
• Increasing age (risk increases dramatically after age 70) • Family history of neurocognitive disorder • Presence of e4 variant of *APOE* gene	• Dietary factors (increased omega-3, decreased fat and cholesterol, vitamins C, D, and E) • Moderate alcohol use (especially red wine) • Mental activities (games, crossword puzzles) • Use of nonsteroidal anti-inflammatory drugs (NSAIDs) • Advanced education • Bilingualism

this variant do not have any cognitive impairment, therefore there is no one-to-one relationship between the presence of the gene form and Alzheimer's disease.

Environmental and other nongenetic factors interact with genetic factors to influence the onset of major neurocognitive disorder. For example, genetic factors appear to be less important after age 85 (Silverman et al., 2003). In addition, certain *protective factors* may reduce the risk of cognitive decline (Table 13.1). Advanced education seems to reduce the risk of dementia (Gurland, 2004) by creating cognitive reserves, such as increased coping skills that minimize the impact of cognitive deterioration. Advanced education may also increase neuronal connections that counterbalance noticeable changes in memory as NFTs and SPs develop (Bourgeois et al., 2003). In addition, older adults with increased education may use more of their frontal lobes; that is, they may have neurobiological reserves that facilitate coping with cognitive deterioration (Springer et al., 2005). Other potential protective factors include diet (e.g., increased intake of omega-3 polyunsaturated fatty acids; decreased fat and cholesterol intake; vitamins C, D, and E), moderate use of alcohol, use of nonsteroidal anti-inflammatory drugs (NSAIDs), and increased engagement in mental activities (e.g., playing games, puzzles, or a musical instrument, using a computer) (Almeida et al., 2012; Chapman et al., 2006; Lyketsos, 2009; Morris, 2005b). Prevention strategies are important as even a one-year delay in the onset of neurocognitive disorder would result in 12 million fewer cases around the world by the year 2050, and this decrease would lower the health care burden (Brodaty et al., 2011).

13.6 Identify empirically supported treatments for psychological and cognitive disorders among older adults.

TREATMENT OF MAJOR NEUROCOGNITIVE DISORDER AND RELATED DIFFICULTIES Most cases of neurocognitive disorder cannot be reversed or cured. Treatment targets delaying disease progression, prolonging independent functioning, improving quality of life, managing associated emotional and behavioural symptoms, and providing support and assistance to caregivers. Treatments include pharmacological and nonpharmacological approaches. Medications known as *cholinesterase inhibitors* (CEIs), such as Aricept, appear to slow cognitive decline and improve global functioning (relative to placebo) for patients with mild-to-moderate Alzheimer's disease (Moore et al., 2014). Alzheimer's disease is associated with the destruction of neurons that release the neurotransmitter acetylcholine. Because it is not yet possible to regenerate these acetylcholine-producing neurons, CEIs block the enzyme that breaks down this neurotransmitter. This process increases the remaining level of acetylcholine in the brain. CEIs do not reverse the damage to the neurons but merely allow whatever neurotransmitter is left to function more effectively. Improvements with these drugs are greatest in the early stages of Alzheimer's disease before extensive neurobiological damage has been done. The use of CEIs may delay placement in a nursing home (Geldmacher et al., 2003), although it is not entirely clear that the medications reduce the costs of caring for patients (Morris, 2005a).

As the severity of Alzheimer's disease increases, another medication (memantine or Ebixa) can be added to block overproduction of the neurotransmitter glutamate (Reisberg et al., 2003; Tariot et al., 2004), which plays a role in learning and memory. High doses of vitamin E also appear to slow the progress of symptoms, but very high doses of vitamin E may increase mortality (Miller et al., 2005). Medications can also control the noncognitive symptoms, including emotional disturbance, aggression, agitation,

examining the EVIDENCE

What Is Mild Cognitive Impairment (MCI), and Is It a Precursor of Major Neurocognitive Disorder or a Separate Syndrome?

- **The Facts:** Mild cognitive impairment (MCI) is a term used to describe cognitive difficulties that are greater than expected for normal aging but that do not meet the criteria for major neurocognitive disorder. Characteristics include the following (Chapman et al., 2006; Petersen et al., 2001):
  1. Subjective cognitive complaints (usually memory but not always), preferably verified by someone who knows the patient well enough to provide meaningful information about his or her condition
  2. Objective evidence of cognitive difficulties as measured by neuropsychological tests
  3. Adequate ability to perform activities of daily living (i.e., no significant impairment in social or work functioning)
  4. Criteria for major neurocognitive disorder not met
- MCI occurs in as many as 18% of people over age 65. **Amnestic MCI** is a subtype in which cognitive complaints focus on memory difficulties (Petersen et al., 2001). There has been great interest lately in the concept of MCI and whether it is a precursor of Alzheimer's disease or other forms of major neurocognitive disorder, or whether it is a variation of normal aging. Determining the nature and predictive value of MCI may be important in establishing prevention strategies or early treatment, although ethical issues arise with the notion of diagnosing a condition about which little is known (Petersen et al., 2001). MCI occurs in 19% of people younger than age 75 and in 29% of people older than age 85 (Lopez et al., 2003).
- **What Data Support MCI as a Precursor of Major Neurocognitive Disorder?**
  1. The majority of people with MCI progress to a diagnosis of major neurocognitive disorder (Lyketsos, 2009).
  2. People with MCI and the *APOE4* allele gene are at increased risk for developing major neurocognitive disorder (Petersen et al., 1995).
  3. Neuroimaging and neuropathology studies suggest that people with MCI share features with Alzheimer's disease, including hippocampal atrophy and neurofibrillary tangles (Petersen et al., 2001).
- **What Data Refute MCI as a Precursor of Major Neurocognitive Disorder?**
  1. Approximately one third of people with MCI improve, and others never progress to any state of significantly worsened cognitive functioning (Lyketsos, 2009; Petersen et al., 2001).
  2. *Conversion rates* (the rates at which people with MCI progress to a diagnosis of major neurocognitive disorder) vary widely across studies, perhaps due to difficulties in diagnosing MCI. It is often difficult to evaluate the extent to which cognitive difficulties interfere with daily functioning.
  3. MCI can result from many different causes, including major depressive disorder, substance-related disorders, and side effects of medications (Morris, 2005).
- **Conclusions.** Like major neurocognitive disorders, there are likely many forms of MCI, and a full evaluation of all possible medical and psychological causes for declining cognitive symptoms is needed. Amnestic MCI is probably a significant risk factor for the development of Alzheimer's disease (Morris, 2005; Petersen et al., 2001; Tabert et al., 2006). All people with suspected MCI should be monitored regularly for any worsening of symptoms.

psychotic symptoms, and sleep disturbance. Antidepressant medications are useful to treat depression and other emotional symptoms (Weintraub & Katz, 2005). Antipsychotic medications can reduce delusions, hallucinations, agitation, and aggression. Because these drugs can have very serious side effects (increased risk of seizures, tardive dyskinesia, cardiovascular adverse events, and mortality), they should be used cautiously (Katz et al., 2002; Schneider et al., 2005; Weintraub & Katz, 2005).

Nonmedication interventions do not affect disease progression directly but may minimize its impact. These strategies include changing the environment to ensure patient safety (e.g., walking aids to prevent falls, driving limitations or discontinuation), structuring daily routines, and facilitating appropriate nutrition, exercise, and social engagement. Caregivers play a major role in helping patients make these changes. Cognitive functioning can also be affected by cognitive training strategies that enhance comprehension, learning, and memory, even among people with major neurocognitive disorder (Bayles & Kim, 2003; Bourgeois et al., 2003; Brush & Camp, 1998; Sitzer et al., 2006). Behavioural interventions may reduce agitation (Teri et al., 2000), anxiety (Paukert et al., 2010), depression (Teri et al., 2003), and behavioural problems (Burgio et al., 2001, 2002). Caregivers may also require cognitive-behavioural interventions to manage stress, increase coping skills, and decrease depression (Cooper et al., 2007; Gallagher-Thompson & Coon, 2007). Using the Internet to deliver these interventions may be a cost-effective and less-burdensome method by which to reach caregivers (Blom et al., 2013).

real SCIENCE real LIFE

Charlotte: The Psychopathology and Treatment of Anxiety Disorder in an Older Adult

THE PATIENT

Charlotte is a 78-year-old widow who was always a worrier and a perfectionist. Her parents were loving but often critical when her school performance or other behaviour wasn't perfect. Charlotte was very successful in her early years. She completed an undergraduate degree and worked as a bank teller and supervisor for eight years before she married and had children. She stopped working when she had her first baby, but remained busy with volunteer work during the years when she raised her three children. Throughout her life, despite outward success, Charlotte was always worried that things might not turn out well enough. She was concerned that her children were not doing well enough in school, that she was not a good enough mother, that her home wasn't clean and orderly enough, and that she and her husband might not have enough money to support themselves as they got older.

THE PROBLEM

Despite this persistent worry over the years, Charlotte functioned well in her roles as a wife, mother, and volunteer. When her husband died five years ago, however, she realized just how much she had relied on him for reassurance. Without him around to remind her that she was doing a good job and that their children were well adjusted, she had more trouble easing her mind of the worries. She began to spend many hours a day worrying about various things—whether people liked her, how well her grandchildren were doing in school, whether she was doing enough to help at the places in which she volunteered, and how she would be able to support herself if she developed serious medical problems.

Charlotte began to experience significant sleep difficulties. She fell asleep easily, but woke up frequently during the night, sometimes to go to the bathroom, but always with many worries on her mind. Her arthritis seemed to be getting worse, possibly because of increased muscle tension, and she developed serious problems such as back and neck pain. Charlotte also found herself more irritable and snappy with her children, and she noticed difficulties with her memory and concentration. She misplaced things regularly and spent a lot of time looking for her keys, purse, and calendar. She had difficulty concentrating when she sat down to read, and her children noticed that she was irritable and preoccupied most of the time.

DIAGNOSIS

Charlotte initially contacted the clinic for an evaluation of her memory. She was worried that she might have Alzheimer's disease. As part of Charlotte's initial evaluation, she also was assessed for the full range of possible psychiatric disorders.

(continued)

Cognitive evaluations showed no excessive deficits in her memory or thinking, but her symptoms met the criteria for generalized anxiety disorder. She also had symptoms of depression but not with sufficient severity for a diagnosis of major depressive disorder.

THE TREATMENT

Initial treatment strategies involved teaching Charlotte how to identify different symptoms of anxiety—for example, physical tension, worry-related thoughts, and behavioural avoidance. Simple self-monitoring forms were created that included spaces for recording various symptoms. As Charlotte became more familiar with her anxiety symptoms, she realized just how often she worried about things. She also learned how to identify physical symptoms of anxiety (e.g., muscle tension) that she had never noticed before.

Next, Charlotte began to learn skills to reduce her anxiety. The goal of this phase of the treatment was to give her a "toolbox" of skills to choose from to manage anxiety. The first skill that she learned was deep breathing. Charlotte used this skill to decrease her anxiety when she noticed her body tensing up. She also learned how to identify and challenge her worry-related thoughts (e.g., "I am a terrible grandmother; my grandchildren don't think I'm any fun.") and substitute them with more realistic thoughts (e.g., "My grandchildren love me. We usually have fun together. It is okay if sometimes they prefer to spend time with someone else."). She also learned how to solve problems instead of just worrying about them.

THE TREATMENT OUTCOME

Over a period of three months, Charlotte learned many skills, and she began to worry less and felt that her life was more fulfilling.

CONCEPT check

- Delirium can arise from serious medical illness or toxic effects of a medication.
- The first step in the treatment of delirium is early detection. The next steps can include environmental changes, support, and medication.
- Neurocognitive disorders, characterized by multiple cognitive impairments, are tremendously debilitating for patients and place great stress on their families.
- The most common form of major neurocognitive disorder is Alzheimer's disease, which is characterized by insidious onset and progressive course.
- Alzheimer's disease is associated with a variant of the *APOE gene (e4)*, but only 50% of people with this disorder have this gene variant.
- Medications used to treat Alzheimer's disease do not reverse damage to neurons, but they may delay disease progression. Nonpharmacological treatments can also reduce the impact of major neurocognitive disorder.

critical thinking question How does the type of major neurocognitive disorder impact the nature and treatment of symptoms?

summary

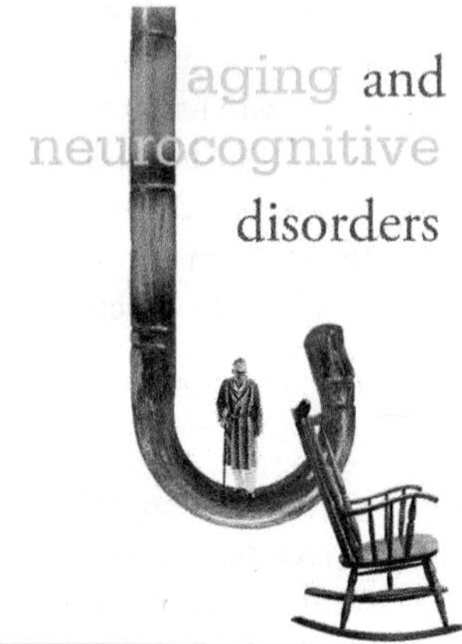

13.1 Recognize geropsychology as an emerging area of psychological research and practice.

Geropsychology is a subdiscipline of psychology that focuses on issues of aging, in particular, patterns of normal development, individual differences, and psychological problems that are unique to older adults.

13.2 Understand the ways in which aging may impact the expression and treatment of psychological symptoms and disorders in older adults.

Psychological symptoms often go unnoticed in older adults, and many people never receive treatment. Older adults with psychological disorders often describe symptoms differently than younger adults do, making recognition difficult. Overlapping medical problems also make the diagnosis of emotional problems difficult among older patients, particularly in medical settings where older adults most often go for help.

13.3 Recognize the unique symptoms and issues that affect diagnosis and treatment of bipolar and depressive disorders, anxiety, substance-related disorders, and psychosis in older adults.

Older adults with depression and anxiety often focus on somatic rather than psychological symptoms. Symptoms of depression and anxiety often overlap with cognitive impairment and medical diseases. The presence of serious medical illness and cognitive impairment puts older adults at increased risk for anxiety and depression. Misuse of alcohol, prescription medications, and tobacco are the most common substance-related problems in older adults. For most older adults with schizophrenia, onset occurred in young adulthood. Late-onset schizophrenia is associated with fewer negative symptoms and less impairment in cognitive skills but higher prevalence of paranoia and more auditory hallucinations. Very-late-onset schizophrenia-like psychosis usually results from a stroke, tumour, or other neurodegenerative change.

13.4 Distinguish between major neurocognitive disorder and delirium, two cognitive disorders that are common among older adults.

Major neurocognitive disorder and delirium are two cognitive disorders that impact older adults. Although both involve difficulties in thinking, delirium is associated with a change in consciousness or alertness, but major neurocognitive disorder is not. Delirium often occurs as a result of serious illness or toxic effects of a medication or multiple medications. Alzheimer's disease, the most common type of neurocognitive disorder, has a slow and progressive course that involves difficulties with memory, language, decision making, and ultimately self-care.

13.5 Understand the etiological factors affecting psychological and cognitive disorders of late life.

Biological and psychological variables often interact in the development of emotional and cognitive disorders in older people. Most often, data point to the possibility of a diathesis-stress model that suggests an integrated impact of biological vulnerabilities (e.g., genetic predispositions) and environmental stressors (e.g., death of a loved one, change in occupational or social status). Psychological disorders with onset in later life are less likely to be associated with a family history of the disorder.

13.6 Identify empirically supported treatments for psychological and cognitive disorders among older adults.

Most of the interventions that are used to treat younger adults with anxiety, depression, substance-related disorders, and psychosis are also efficacious in adults, although medication dosages and the manner in which psychological interventions are conducted may differ. With respect to empirically supported treatments, medication and cognitive-behavioural treatment have the most research support. Medications can slow the progression of major neurocognitive disorder and psychological treatments can improve quality of life, but damage to neurons is not reversed.

key terms

TEST yourself

1. The subdiscipline of psychology that addresses issues of aging, with special attention to psychological problems that are unique to older persons, is
   a. geriatric psychiatry
   b. gerontology
   c. geropsychology
   d. generational psychology

2. Treating older people on the assumption that psychological and medical problems are a normal part of aging is associated with what characteristic in the health care provider?
   a. experience
   b. ageism
   c. acceptance
   d. pessimism

3. Which of the following factors complicates the identification of psychological disorders in older people?
   a. Symptoms of many medical diseases mimic psychological disorders.
   b. Older people are often very tolerant of psychological symptoms.
   c. Older adults express their psychological distress to others very readily.
   d. Psychological disorders are relatively rare in older people and thus are easily missed.

4. Executive dysfunction occurs when a person has difficulty
   a. driving and performing simple self-care activities
   b. remembering past tasks and activities
   c. planning, thinking abstractly, and initiating and inhibiting actions
   d. following instructions from a health care provider

5. Frank was concerned that his mother was suffering from major neurocognitive disorder. She had gotten lost at the shopping centre, misplaced objects, and forgotten names of friends and acquaintances. Her symptoms gradually disappeared after her physician put her on antidepressant medication. Her diagnosis was most likely
   a. Alzheimer's disease
   b. vascular depression
   c. Parkinson's disease
   d. major depressive disorder

6. Harold is a depressed widower who went to a psychologist who specialized in working with older people. The psychologist asked him to talk about significant events in his life and how he managed his loneliness in the past. The type of therapy used by this psychologist is called
   a. reminiscence therapy
   b. cognitive-behavioural therapy
   c. geriatric psychotherapy
   d. problem-solving therapy

7. Anxiety may be difficult to diagnose in older people because
   a. clinicians assume it is rare in older people
   b. worry about life problems is normal in old age
   c. many medical conditions have symptoms that are common in anxiety
   d. older adults are often confused about their symptoms

8. More than 40% of older people who suffer from persistent anxiety are given benzodiazapines, such as Valium. This is remarkable because such medications cause
   a. loss of bowel and bladder control
   b. memory problems and slowing of motor behaviours
   c. manic and hypomanic reactions
   d. elevated heart rate and blood pressure

9. Cognitive-behaviour therapy for anxiety disorders may need to be modified for older patients. The primary adaptation is that
   a. the therapist must speak loudly and use simple language
   b. the pace is slowed, and different learning strategies are used
   c. discussion of certain topics such as sexuality and death is avoided
   d. all of the above

10. Substance-related disorder is often recognized in older people only when
   a. it affects a medical condition or causes accidents
   b. symptoms of withdrawal occur
   c. employment or social life is affected
   d. neurocognitive symptoms are made worse

11. The most commonly misused substance by older adults is
   a. over-the-counter medication
   b. benzodiazapines
   c. tobacco
   d. alcohol

12. As people age, the body's ability to metabolize alcohol, prescribed medication, and illegal drugs decreases. This means that
   a. increased amounts are needed to obtain the same effect
   b. detecting the substance in the blood and urine is more difficult
   c. a very small amount of a substance causes acute illness
   d. toxic levels are reached more rapidly

13. The loss of clarity, attention, and awareness that is often brought on by a serious medical illness, such as AIDS, congestive heart failure, infection, or toxic effects of a medication, is called
   a. delirium
   b. major neurocognitive disorder
   c. stupor
   d. euphoria

14. Jonas had a stroke and no longer recognizes the faces of people he knew or common objects that he encounters. He even has difficulty recognizing his wife and children until he hears their voices. This is termed
   a. aphasia
   b. apraxia
   c. agnosia
   d. amnesia

15. The presence of neurofibrillary tangles and cerebral senile plaques in the hippocampus, cerebral cortex, and other regions of the brain is most often associated with which disorder?
   a. Huntington's disease
   b. Parkinson's disease
   c. HIV
   d. Alzheimer's disease

16. Major or mild vascular neurocognitive disorder can be distinguished from other types of neurocognitive disorder on the basis of the
   a. sudden onset and more stepwise progression of cognitive difficulties
   b. possibility of remission following proper diagnosis and treatment
   c. gradual onset and gradual progression of cognitive difficulties
   d. comorbidity with traumatic brain injuries due to falls and accidents

17. Progressive neurocognitive disorder occurs in what percentage of adults age 65 and over?

a. 5 to 10
b. 15 to 20
c. 10 to 15
d. 20 to 30

18. Late-onset Alzheimer's disease (age 65 or older) is significantly associated with what specific genetic factor?

a. trigene 21
b. mutation of the *APOE* gene
c. a missing *MCI* gene
d. at least seven different genes

19. What protective factor appears to reduce the risk of cognitive decline in Alzheimer's disease and other forms of major neurocognitive disorder?

a. advanced education
b. increased intake of omega-3
c. moderate use of alcohol
d. all of the above

20. The family doctor tells Stacey that she believes that Stacey's mother is showing early signs of Alzheimer's disease. The doctor would like to start Stacey's mother on Aricept, a medication used in the early stages of AD. Aricept is a(n)

a. glutamate blocker
b. cholinesterase inhibitor
c. antidepressant
d. nutritional supplement

Answers:
1 c, 2 b, 3 a, 4 c, 5 d, 6 a, 7 c, 8 b, 9 b, 10 a, 11 c, 12 d, 13 a, 14 c, 15 d, 16 a, 17 a, 18 b, 19 d, 20 c.

chapter 14

health psychology

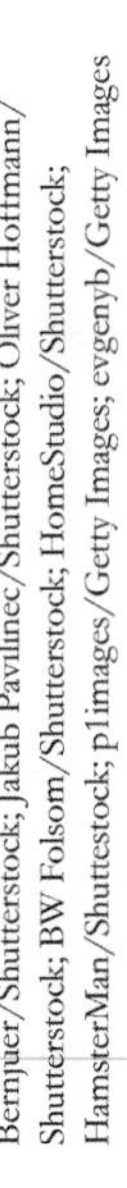
Bernjuer/Shutterstock; Jakub Pavlinec/Shutterstock; Oliver Hoffmann/Shutterstock; BW Folsom/Shutterstock; HomeStudio/Shutterstock; HamsterMan/Shutterstock; p1images/Getty Images; evgenyb/Getty Images

learning objectives

After reading this chapter, you should be able to:

14.1
Define health psychology and the roles of a health psychologist.

14.2
Describe mind–body dualism and its significance for health psychology.

14.3
Define stress, and describe how it is measured.

14.4
Describe the impact of stress on health and the immune system.

14.5
Recognize a range of behaviours that may affect health and how health psychologists help people change behaviours to maintain health.

14.6
Identify factors that affect adjustment to chronic disease and strategies to improve adjustment and quality of life for people with a chronic disease.

Shannon was a 35-year-old woman working in the banking industry. She found a great job after receiving her master's degree in business administration, and she was moving quickly up the corporate ladder. Her job was stressful, but she loved it. Interacting with interesting people, frequent travel, and solving challenging problems kept the work fun and stimulating. As part of her job, especially when she was out of town, Shannon ate at many interesting restaurants, and dinners with customers usually included a glass of wine or two. Often, the dinners were late in the evenings, and sometimes while on the road Shannon smoked a few cigarettes to relax. She wasn't addicted to nicotine—she rarely smoked at home—but it helped her unwind on the road. Being away from home was particularly stressful because the hotel beds weren't always comfortable, and she rarely found the time to exercise. To ease her muscle aches while she was away from home, she often took ibuprofen a few times a day. Sometimes after a heavy meal with a customer, Shannon experienced heartburn. The symptoms were worse if she went back to her room and lay down soon after the meal was over, but she thought the heartburn was manageable and not really a serious problem. Actually, Shannon didn't really give it much thought. One evening, though, after a nice dinner with a customer, she began to experience sharp chest pains that spread up to her throat. She felt that her chest was constricting, and she was having trouble breathing. She worried that something was seriously wrong, and she asked her dinner companion to drive her to an urgent care clinic. The medical staff conducted a thorough workup to test for cardiac difficulties. They found none, but advised Shannon to be evaluated for gastroesophageal reflux disease (GERD). Shannon had heard of this disease, but she hadn't known that the symptoms included chest pains. Nor did she know that stress could make gastrointestinal symptoms worse. After a full evaluation with her physician, Shannon was diagnosed with GERD and learned that she would need to change her eating and drinking habits and work to manage her stress to keep the symptoms under control.

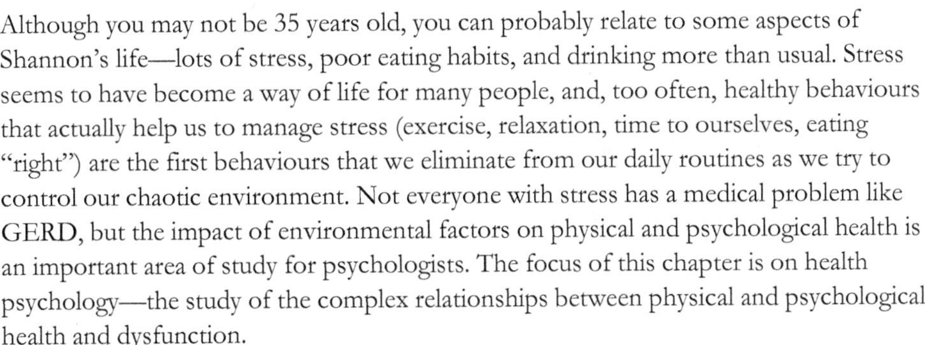

Although you may not be 35 years old, you can probably relate to some aspects of Shannon's life—lots of stress, poor eating habits, and drinking more than usual. Stress seems to have become a way of life for many people, and, too often, healthy behaviours that actually help us to manage stress (exercise, relaxation, time to ourselves, eating "right") are the first behaviours that we eliminate from our daily routines as we try to control our chaotic environment. Not everyone with stress has a medical problem like GERD, but the impact of environmental factors on physical and psychological health is an important area of study for psychologists. The focus of this chapter is on health psychology—the study of the complex relationships between physical and psychological health and dysfunction.

Health Psychology: Defining the Field

14.1 Define health psychology and the roles of a health psychologist.

Good physical health is maintained at least in part by attitudes and behaviours, making health psychology an important subdiscipline of psychology. **Health psychology** uses the principles and methods of psychology to understand how attitudes and behaviours influence health and disease. Health psychologists study how people develop positive and negative health habits (e.g., exercise, eating, smoking), how stress and health are related, and which psychological variables affect the onset and treatment of medical illnesses. *Health* is defined today, as it was in 1948 by the World Health Organization, as a state of mental, social, and physical well-being, not just the absence of illness. In addition to health psychology, related fields of study include **behavioural medicine**, an interdisciplinary field (not just psychology) that studies the relation between behavioural and biomedical science, and **medical psychology**, the study and practice of psychology as it relates to health, disease, and medical treatment. At the heart of health psychology is the **biopsychosocial model**, which suggests that complex interactions among biological, psychological, and social factors determine health. This model is in contrast to a **biomedical model**, which explains diseases solely as biological processes. Over the years, however, and across different disciplines, the relationship between mind and body has not always been well understood.

The Mind–Body Relationship

14.2 Describe mind–body dualism and its significance for health psychology.

Although in some earlier periods of human history there was occasional recognition that mind and body were profoundly linked (see Chapter 1), until very recently our thinking has been dominated by the idea of **mind–body dualism**. This concept, which is associated with the French philosopher René Descartes (1596–1650), holds that the mind and body function independently although they may interact. A philosophy of mind–body dualism has persisted for many centuries with significant efforts to identify biological causes for medical disease and a relative neglect of attention to psychological variables that impact physical health. Only recently has psychology had any role in identifying and treating medical disease. Now psychologists routinely offer services related to the prevention, treatment, or management of physical health problems (such as helping patients with respiratory or cardiac diseases learn to stop smoking or training diabetic children in relaxation techniques that reduce their fear of injections).

In the first half of the twentieth century, the idea of mind–body dualism began to be challenged. Freud linked the mind and body to explain *hysteria* (now known as *conversion disorder*), a condition in which he believed that unconscious psychological conflicts caused unexplained physical complaints, such as physical weakness and paralysis (see Chapter 1, the case of Anna O.). In the 1930s and 1940s, psychiatrists Flanders Dunbar and Franz Alexander proposed associations between certain personality patterns and specific medical diseases (e.g., an *ulcer-prone personality*). At that time, there were new ideas about the relationship between psychological conflicts and physical disease that implicated the autonomic nervous system. In this view, psychological conflicts produce anxiety, which causes the nervous system to create an organic problem (e.g., an ulcer) (Taylor, 2014). From these influences came the development of *biopsychosocial models* of physical disease, which recognize the contributions of body, mind, and the social environment to the development of disease (see Figure 14.1).

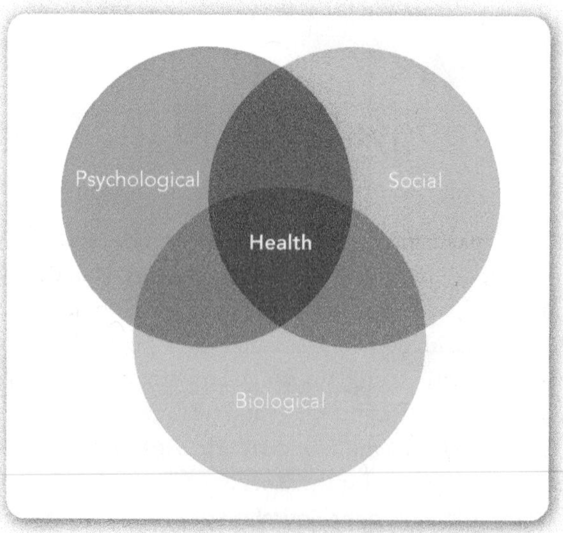

FIGURE 14.1

The Biopsychosocial Model of Health and Disease. Mind, body, and the social environment all contribute to health or to the development of disease.

Mind–body dualism has also been criticized by some philosophers as a model for explaining the relationship between mind and body (Mehta, 2011). Other theories have been proposed, such as theories in which minds, and psychological factors in general, are emergent properties arising from complex networks of interacting neurons activated by internal and external (environmental) stimuli. Although the mind arises from complex physical (neuronal) processes within the body, it has proven useful, at least for understanding health and disease, to distinguish between psychological factors (e.g., thoughts, attitudes, motivations) and physiological factors or reactions (e.g., stomach cramps, heartburn). The biopsychosocial model distinguishes between psychological factors and physical health, while also acknowledging that psychological factors arise, in part, from complex biological processes. This is not biological reductionism because psychological factors are not seen as arising solely from some simple biological process.

Psychological Influences on Health

It is now widely accepted that psychological variables (such as health habits, attitudes, and personality characteristics) and social factors (such as stress and social support) affect physical health. Similarly, diseases can affect psychological health and social functioning. When medical disease and psychological problems coexist, functioning is impaired to an increased extent. Psychological and social variables also influence the treatment of medical disease, especially chronic medical problems (such as diabetes and hypertension, which develop slowly and often persist for a lifetime). These variables include factors such as the doctor–patient relationship, expectations for treatment outcomes, and psychological coping and adjustment. This chapter focuses on three primary topics: the role of stress in physical and mental health, the impact of psychology and behaviour on medical disease and its treatment, and the nature and impact of psychological treatments for health-related conditions.

CONCEPT check

- Health psychology uses the principles and methods of psychology to understand the effects of attitudes and behaviours on health and disease.
- *Health* is defined as a state of mental, social, and physical well-being, not just a lack of disease.
- Mind–body dualism suggests that mind and body function independently. This point of view is not supported by current empirical research.

critical thinking question Although research clearly suggests that psychological and biological variables affect one another, why do you think that a mind–body dualism perspective persists in medical research and health care?

The Role of Stress in Physical and Mental Health

14.3 Define stress, and describe how it is measured.

Marek just couldn't believe how stressful it was to be a university freshman. He had really looked forward to moving away from home and starting this new chapter of his life, but he wasn't at all prepared for how difficult it was to be away from his family and his girlfriend, who was attending university in a different province. He was also shocked at how much work was required for his classes—huge amounts of reading, projects due in different classes every week, tests that covered way too much material. And Marek was having a hard time making new friends. He came from a small town where everyone knew everyone else. Just walking on campus made him feel like he was in a huge city—and he was lost about where and how to meet people. He also wasn't eating well—it was too hard to get to the cafeteria at the right times and much easier to grab fast food between classes. Marek didn't have time to exercise like he used to, and he didn't sleep well in the noisy dormitory. It was getting harder to concentrate in class because he was so tired and he had so much on his mind and his "to do" list. He just wasn't sure if he would make it or not. He had already been to student health services twice, once for a bad cold that wouldn't go away and another time for recurrent headaches.

Defining Stress

Everyone experiences stress—it is part of life. However, the causes of stress and the symptoms that accompany it vary greatly. **Stress** is any negative emotional experience that is accompanied by biochemical, physiological, cognitive, and behavioural responses that attempt to change or adjust to the stressor (Baum, 1990). A **stressor** is any event that produces tension or another negative emotion such as fear (DiMatteo & Martin, 2002) and that prepares the organism for a *fight-or-flight* response (see Chapter 4). Stressors can be physical (a medical disease or physical injury), environmental (natural disaster, high level of noise, change in living situation), interpersonal-social (breakup of a relationship, argument with a family member), or psychological (sudden realization that a final exam is tomorrow instead of the day after).

The characteristics of an event affect the probability that it will produce stress. Perceived stress is more likely if an event has a negative outcome, but positive outcomes also can produce stress. The idea that positive life events or experiences can create stress may seem contradictory, but you can probably recall a positive event that you experienced as stressful (e.g., planning for or going on a big trip, starting a new relationship).

Stress is also more likely when the event is perceived as uncontrollable, unpredictable, or ambiguous (leaving the person uncertain of what action to take), or when it has an impact on a major area of life, such as parenting, personal relationships, or achievement (Taylor, 2014). Because people may react differently to the same event, a stressor can be understood fully only when the interaction between an event and a person is considered. For example, some people are energized and better able to focus on a task when the deadline is near. Others feel so pressured that they lose their ability to concentrate and complete a project. Remember Marek? He had significant stress after leaving home to go to university, while other university freshmen thrive on the changes that occur at this life stage.

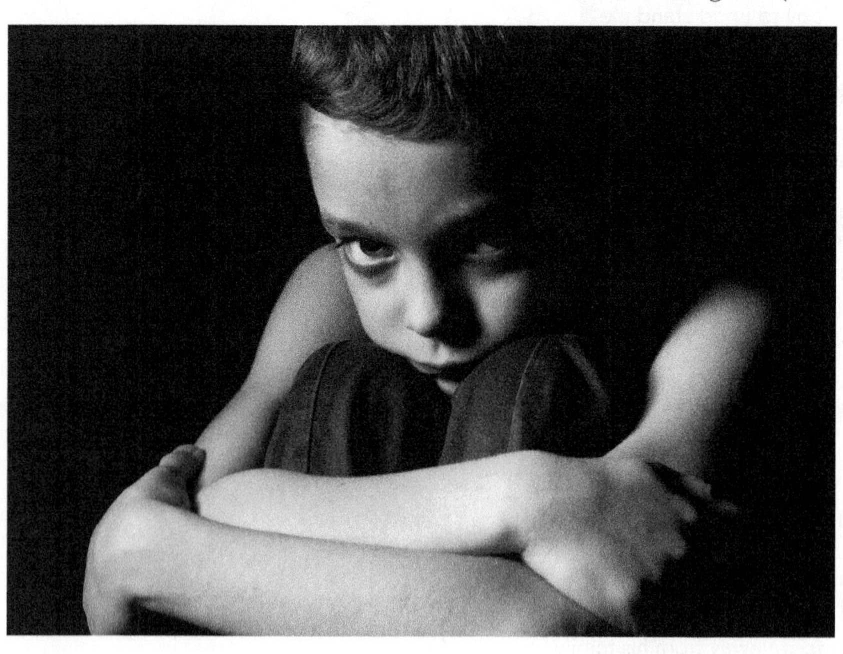

Everyone experiences stress—even young children. Stress can only be understood individually, however, because what is stressful for one person may not be for another.

Tatyana Gladskih/Fotolia

After a stressful event, an interactive **appraisal process** occurs in which a person assesses whether he or she has the resources or coping skills to deal with the event (Lazarus & Folkman, 1984) (see Figure 14.2). First, the person assesses potential harm or threat (*primary appraisal*). Perceptions of threat are heavily influenced by many psychological and social variables, such as a person's beliefs and values that give meaning to the event and its expected outcomes (Lazarus, 1999; Thompson & VanLoon, 2002). For example, losing a job will be perceived as a much greater threat by a middle-aged man who is supporting a family of four than by a university student who is working part-time for extra money.

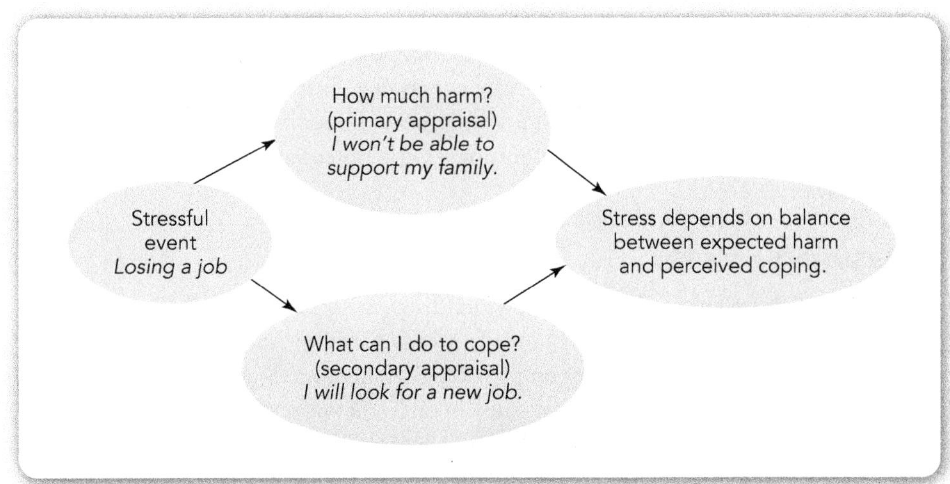

FIGURE 14.2

The Appraisal Process Following a Stressful Event. After a stressful event, the person assesses the potential harm or threat and his or her ability to cope with it. Stress occurs when a person feels unable to cope with the possible threat.

Next, the person identifies available skills to cope with or overcome the possible negative outcomes (*secondary appraisal*). Coping strategies fall into two broad categories: *problem-focused coping* and *emotion-focused coping* (Thompson & VanLoon, 2002). *Problem-focused coping* involves taking action to manage a problem that is creating stress. This type of coping might include gathering information, comparing alternative courses of action, making decisions, and resolving conflicts. Emotion-focused coping occurs when a person focuses on managing emotional distress that results from a stressor rather than trying to change the situation that creates stress. Positive emotion-focused coping might include changing thoughts to decrease distress (e.g., attending to the benefits of a stressful situation) or engaging in behaviours that make one feel better (e.g., getting together with friends, taking a walk). Other emotion-focused strategies may not be as effective (e.g., having a drink, avoiding a difficult situation), and problem-solving coping is generally thought to be a more effective strategy for managing stress. However, in many cases, people use a combination of coping strategies that include both emotion-focused and problem-focused strategies.

When Nancy was diagnosed with asthma, she asked her doctor many questions and read a number of articles about asthma treatment. She quickly realized that she was going to have to change a number of things about her lifestyle (problem-focused coping). This was frustrating to her because she loved the active, outdoor lifestyle she had developed. However, when she shared her feelings with her husband and biking friends (emotion-focused coping), she realized that this was not the end of life as she had known it. She would simply have to adjust to new ways of doing things she enjoyed.

Stress has many forms. *Acute stress* occurs when a potentially threatening event and the associated reaction last for only a brief time—for example, a burglary. *Chronic stress* develops when a threatening event continues over time, such as with a chronic disease, excessive work demands, or long-term poverty, or when a person consistently feels inadequate to deal with ongoing negative outcomes (DiMatteo & Martin, 2002). *Daily hassles*, or minor aversive events that occur day to day (the coffee pot breaks in the morning, the dog has an accident on the rug, a meeting runs overtime and makes you late for class), can accumulate to create stress. Finally, *major life events* that affect the way a person lives, such as starting university, beginning marriage, experiencing divorce, making a job change or home relocation, or being diagnosed with a major disease, can produce stress. Under any of these conditions, the perceived or actual inability to cope

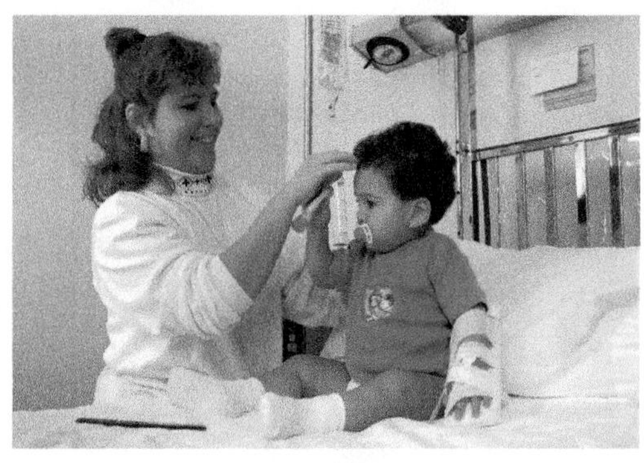

Life events, such as accidents and health problems, can lead to stress responses.

Larry Mulvehill/Corbis/Glow Images

results in a *stress reaction* with symptoms of a *fight-or-flight* response (e.g., increased blood pressure, heart rate, sweating, respiration rate). Adaptive responses help the person react quickly and positively to potentially harmful events (e.g., helping a child who is choking). Detrimental responses disrupt functioning (e.g., stress about a class project leads to poor sleep and missed classes). Detrimental responses also potentially set the stage for poorer health (Taylor, 2014).

Measuring Stress

Various procedures are used to evaluate acute stress, major life events, and daily hassles. Acute stress is often measured with an **acute stress paradigm**. Short-term stress is created in the laboratory, and its effect on physiological, neuroendocrine, and psychological responses is measured. Stress can be created in different ways. A participant may be asked to solve a frustrating math problem or deliver an impromptu speech, or be administered a mild electric shock (Martin & Brantley, 2004; Taylor, 2014). This approach allows researchers to carefully examine biological responses (heart rate, blood pressure, blood chemistry) and psychological variables as measured by interviews and questionnaires (level of chronic stress, personality style) at the same time. When acute stress is measured in the laboratory, researchers must carefully consider the ethical issues involved in placing participants in a stressful situation (e.g., Could participants be harmed in any way?). In addition, laboratory stressors (e.g., mild electric shock) are not usually the same as those commonly experienced in everyday life, and this limits the usefulness of data collected by such procedures.

Measuring the impact of life events is common in stress research. In 1967, researchers studying stress (Holmes & Rahe, 1967) created the *Social Readjustment Rating Scale* (SRRS), which is still used (see Table 14.1). The SRRS lists 43 potentially stressful life events, each of which has a numerical rating that estimates how much life "readjustment" is related to the event. The list includes both positive and negative events, both of which may cause stress and affect health.

The SRRS is a simple way to evaluate the relationship between life events and health, and it generalizes well to "real life" because people rate their real experiences. However, its reliance on people's recall of events may introduce memory bias. Also, measuring the effect of life events with the SRRS does not consider individual differences

TABLE 14.1
Items from the SRRS and Associated Points Assigned to Measure Stress

Event	Number of Points
Death of a spouse	100
Divorce	73
Death of a close family member	63
Marriage	50
Sexual difficulties	39
Taking out a mortgage or loan for a major purchase	31
Beginning or ceasing formal schooling	26
Major change in living conditions	25
Major change in working hours or conditions	20
Major change in sleeping habits	16
Vacation	13

(how various life events affect different people in different ways), nor does it differentiate the impact of positive and negative life events.

The *Hassles Scale* measures the frequency and severity of day-to-day stressors, whereas the *Uplifts Scale* assesses day-to-day events that counteract the negative effects of stress (Kanner et al., 1981). For both measures, people rate the frequency of daily hassles, which include events such as misplacing or losing things or being interrupted. They also rate uplifts, such as completing a task, being complimented, or laughing at a joke. In addition, they rate severity of hassles, and intensity scores are calculated for both hassles and uplifts. Like the SRRS, however, these scales rely on people's ability to recall activities, and people who tend to feel easily stressed and anxious may rate the severity of daily hassles differently than other people, creating problems for studies that examine the relation between stressors and health.

The Impact of Stress on Health

14.4 Describe the impact of stress on health and the immune system.

However we measure it, we know that stress can impact health *indirectly* and *directly*. When people feel stressed, they often stop taking care of themselves and develop poor health habits. Like Marek, people under stress get less sleep, exercise less, change eating habits in unhealthy ways (e.g., eat more fast food, have more irregular meals), and drink more alcohol. These poor health habits can produce negative health consequences that are *indirectly* related to stress (DiMatteo & Martin, 2002). Other indirect pathways between stress and health include injuries, which are more frequent among people who are under stress (e.g., at work, during sports activities, while driving), and the adoption of a "sick role" to avoid obligations and situations when people feel unable to cope. However, stress can have a more *direct* impact on physical functioning and health, causing changes in the nervous and endocrine systems and affecting the immune system.

PHYSIOLOGY OF STRESS In the 1930s, Walter Cannon described the body's well-known flight-or-flight response that occurs during stress (see Chapter 4) (Cannon, 1932). This response prepares any organism to escape or engage in conflict when a potentially dangerous stimulus/event occurs. Physical responses include increased *sympathetic nervous system* activity: increased blood pressure, more rapid heart and respiration rates, increased blood sugar levels, sweaty palms, and muscle tension. Cannon proposed that continual or chronic physical stress responses could impair a person's ability to fight disease. In the 1950s, McGill University physiologist Hans Selye proposed a related theory called the **general adaptation syndrome (GAS)** (Selye, 1956), which has three stages: (1) *alarm*, when the body mobilizes to meet a threat (with increases in activity within the sympathetic nervous system); (2) *resistance*, when the individual attempts to cope with or resist the threat; and (3) *exhaustion*, when continued efforts to overcome the threat deplete physical resources. In this third stage, a person becomes increasingly vulnerable to disease. As you will see throughout the remainder of this chapter, we now know that chronic stress is associated with increased rates of serious medical diseases such as hypertension, cardiovascular disease, diabetes, and arthritis (DiMatteo & Martin, 2002; Taylor, 2014).

When people feel stressed, they may stop taking care of themselves. They may get less sleep, smoke or drink more, or eat irregular or unhealthful meals.

Ken Tannenbaum/Shutterstock

Although both the fight-or-flight and GAS theories propose similar methods by which stress influences physiology and health, they do not address the psychological and social variables that affect the *appraisal process* described earlier. For example, divorce is stressful for most people. However, for people in a very conflictual or abusive marriage, divorce may actually produce less stress than remaining in an abusive relationship.

When stress does occur, the stress responses affect two major systems: the **sympathetic-adrenomedullary system (SAM)** and the **hypothalamic-pituitary-adrenocortical (HPA) axis**. These two systems have different functions. The "revved up" feeling is the *SAM response*: Increased adrenal gland stimulation results in the secretion of epinephrine and norepinephrine. Continuous and long-term SAM activation can suppress immune functioning (see "Stress and the Immune System") and produce changes in resting blood pressure, heart rate, and heart rhythms. The second response, the *HPA response*, involves the hypothalamus. During stress, the hypothalamus increases production of corticotrophin-releasing factor (CRF), which causes increased secretion of adrenocorticotropic hormone (ACTH) and increased cortisol (another hormone). Increased cortisol helps the body store carbohydrates, reduce inflammation, and return the body to a steady state after stress (Taylor, 2014). Repeated HPA stimulation can change daily cortisol patterns, compromising immune functioning and impairing memory and concentration.

STRESS AND THE IMMUNE SYSTEM

Clara was a stellar musician throughout high school. She had dreamed of attending the Royal Conservatory of Music in Toronto, and so was extremely disappointed when her first application was rejected. After two years of university elsewhere, however, she applied again and was granted an audition. Clara was thrilled but also overwhelmed at the prospect of the interview. She prepared intensely and had trouble thinking of anything else during the days before she was to travel. To top it all off, the audition was going to occur right before final exams and right after a major project was due. It was too much all at once, but there was nothing more important in her life. The morning of her flight, Clara woke up with a cough, a terrible sore throat, and a fever. How could she possibly do her best now that she was sick? She just couldn't afford to be ill at this critical moment in her life.

Knowing how the immune system works provides some insights into how Clara's stress contributed to her physical symptoms on the morning of her audition. The immune system protects the body against bacteria, viruses, and carcinogens in both *specific* and *nonspecific* ways (DiMatteo & Martin, 2002; Martin & Brantley, 2004; Taylor, 2014). **Specific immune system** responses protect us against specific infections and diseases, such as chicken pox and tuberculosis. These responses can be the result of natural or artificial processes. Natural immunities are acquired through breast milk or as a result of having a particular disease (once you have had chicken pox, you are no longer susceptible to it). Artificially produced immunities are acquired through vaccinations or inoculations.

Nonspecific immune system responses offer general protection against infections and diseases in four different ways. First, *anatomical barriers*, such as the skin and the mucous membranes in the nose and mouth, prevent microbes from getting into the body. Second, a process called *phagocytosis* leads to the production of more white blood cells that destroy invaders. Certain white blood cells called *T-lymphocytes* (T-cells) are particularly important because they secrete chemicals that attack and kill invading microbes. Some T-cells are *killer cells* (T_c), and others are *helper cells* (T_H). Still other cells known as *natural killer* (NK) cells are also active in this process. Third, other white blood cells known as *B-lymphocytes* secrete antibodies or toxins into the blood to kill invading bacteria and viruses. Last, *inflammation* at the site of an infection, which produces swelling and increased blood flow, allows more white blood cells to move in and attack pathogens.

Psychological and social variables may complicate the functioning of the immune system. **Psychoneuroimmunology** is the study of the relations among social, psychological, and physical responses. We now know that people (like Clara) who are under severe or chronic stress are more likely to catch a cold, develop an upper respiratory infection, or get the flu (Ironson et al., 2002; Pedersen & Fiske, 2010). Stress suppresses the ability of the immune system to function adequately and increases people's susceptibility to bacteria and viruses. When people are under stress, wounds heal more slowly (Gouin & Kiecolt-Glaser, 2011; Walbum et al., 2009), chronic diseases progress more rapidly, and vaccinations are less effective (Ironson et al., 2002; Martin & Brantley, 2004).

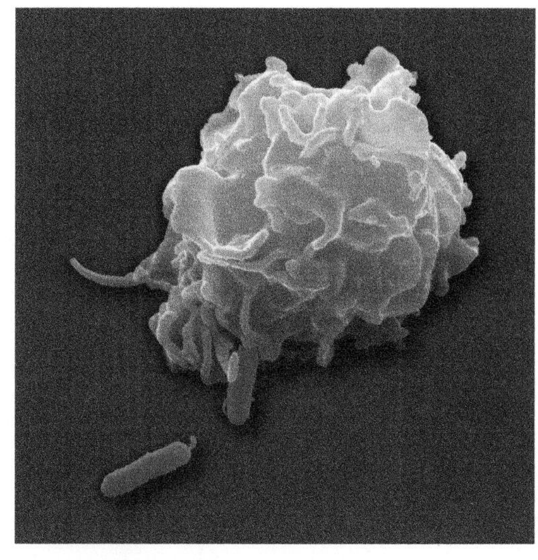

A white blood cell, hugely magnified, engulfing a pathogen. Stress can interfere with the functioning of the immune system, which means that stressed-out people are more likely to become ill.

Juergen Berger/Science Source

Stress increases epinephrine and cortisol levels (the SAM and HPA responses discussed previously), and this decreases the activity of the helper T-cells and lymphocytes that are important for killing bacteria and other toxins. Among medical students, academic stress at exam time was associated with lower T-cell activity and fewer NK cells and activity (Glaser et al., 1985; Workman & LaVia, 1987). People or animals under stress develop fewer antibodies following immunization for flu, hepatitis, and tetanus (Ironson et al., 2002), meaning that these vaccinations are likely to be less effective. However, the relationship between stress and cell activity is not simple. Many variables affect this relationship, including how much time has elapsed since the stressor occurred, how much control people believe they have over the stressor, the person's age, and time of day (Delahanty et al., 2000; Miller et al., 2007; Peters et al., 1998). Interpersonal interactions also affect cell activity and immune functioning. Hostility between spouses, for example, is associated with suppressed (reduced) immune functioning (Kiecolt-Glaser et al., 1998). Loneliness, or perceived social isolation, is also associated with many indicators of poorer immune functioning (Hawkley & Cacioppo, 2003), and positive social support benefits immune functioning (Kiecolt-Glaser et al., 2010; Uchino et al., 1996).

THE PSYCHOLOGICAL IMPACT OF STRESS Stress and poorer immune functioning are associated with increases in negative moods, including depression, anxiety, hostility, and anger. People who are depressed have disrupted immune response, increased inflammation, reduced NK cell activity, a lower lymphocyte response, and more white blood cells (suggesting that the body is trying harder to fight infection) (Herbert & Cohen, 1993; Leonard & Myint, 2009). These associations appear stronger for older people and those who are hospitalized. Other negative moods, including anger, hostility, and anxiety, are also associated with reduced NK cell activity and immune system suppression (DiMatteo & Martin, 2002). On the other hand, positive mood is linked to lower stress, increased resistance to infection, and decreased inflammation (Dockray & Steptoe, 2010; Steptoe et al., 2009).

Several psychological disorders are associated with physical stress responses. Depression, alcoholism, and eating disorders are linked to increased HPA activity (Ehlert et al., 2001). Elevated HPA activity also exists among women who were abused as children, and this relationship is particularly strong when symptoms of depression or anxiety are present (Heim et al., 2000). Of course, one of the most extreme psychological responses is posttraumatic stress disorder (PTSD; see Chapter 4), which consists of vivid and intrusive memories of a trauma, avoidance of people and things that represent the trauma, significant physiological arousal, and emotional numbness. People with PTSD have lower NK cell activity and lower T-cell counts (Pace & Heim, 2011) and more physical health problems (in particular, more frequent cardiovascular, gastrointestinal, and musculoskeletal disorders), and they use medical health services more often than those without the disorder (Jankowsi, 2006).

MODERATORS OF STRESS Variables that affect how stress is experienced and how it affects health and other aspects of functioning are called **stress moderators**. Internal and external variables may moderate the link between stress and health.

We already mentioned the possible role of *personality* in health problems. Characteristic patterns of behaviour, thinking, and feeling can increase or decrease the effect of stress on health. One of the best-known personality styles is the **Type A behaviour pattern**, which has been linked to increased risk of coronary heart disease (CHD). The Type A behaviour pattern (Friedman & Rosenman, 1974) describes behaviours that are associated with consistent strivings for achievement, impatience and time urgency, and aggressiveness toward others.

Mike, a middle-aged father of two boys, aged 12 and 14, works for an Alberta oil company. His job is important to him; he supervises a large group of engineers and he works hard. He gets to work early, completes projects ahead of deadlines, and is always on time for meetings. Mike's co-workers, however, are not as timely or efficient, and this makes him angry when they miss deadlines or ask for extensions. He also becomes irritated with his sons when they don't seem to be doing their best. Sometimes they just seem to be "goofing off," and he doesn't understand why they aren't more competitive. He also can't stand to get behind a slow driver. He can feel his blood pressure rise when he gets stuck behind someone who seems to be out for a "country drive" on the highway. In fact, lately it seems that he is angry all the time. He argues more with his wife, yells too often at his children, and gets into disagreements at work.

Mike's personality could place him at risk for health problems. People with a Type A behaviour pattern, like Mike, tend to feel chronically aroused (always keyed up) and have difficulty relaxing. Other Type A dimensions include a sense of time urgency and competitiveness. However, the feelings of anger and hostility associated with a Type A style are important for predicting increased risk of CHD and heart attack (Gallacher et al., 2003; Moller et al., 1999). In addition, people who are hostile and angry, even if they do not have the full Type A pattern, have an increased risk for cardiovascular problems (Chida & Steptoe, 2009; Taylor, 2014). The role of anger and hostility in cardiovascular health is stronger for men than for women, which may partially explain the increased risk of CHD in men (Chida & Steptoe, 2009; Low et al., 2010).

Social support can reduce the impact of stress when people are confronted with a challenge, such as a natural disaster.
Jeoffrey Maitem/Getty Images

Other personality characteristics (internal moderators), such as *negative affectivity* (the tendency to experience negative mood, including anxiety, depression, and hostility), a *pessimistic explanatory style* (the tendency to blame negative outcomes on some stable characteristic of oneself, for example, "I didn't get that promotion because I am just not very good at my job"), and *optimism* (the tendency to expect positive outcomes) may affect how stress influences health. Negative affectivity and a pessimistic style have been linked to poorer immune functioning (van Eck et al., 1996), poorer response to surgery (Duits et al., 1997), more increased physical complaints even when actual symptoms are not worse (Cohen et al., 2003), and poorer long-term physical health (Maruta et al., 2002). Optimists, on the other hand, are sick less often (Cohen et al., 2003) and have lower blood pressure and less risk of CHD (Kubzansky et al., 2001; Raikkonen et al., 1999). They also function better in the presence of pain (Brenes et al., 2002) and have improved immune function and better health outcomes in many areas, even including cardiovascular health, mortality, and cancer (Rasmussen et al., 2009). Optimists may have better health outcomes because they are better at solving problems, seeking social support, and emphasizing the positive aspects of a situation.

External moderators, such as resources and social support, also influence the impact of stress. People with greater external resources, such as more time and money, a higher level of education, a better job, and a higher standard of living, function better when faced with stress (Taylor, 2014). One of the most important predictors of health is *socioeconomic status* (SES), which is influenced by variables such as education, income, and occupation. People with higher SES have good immune function (Dowd & Aiello, 2009), have fewer medical and psychological disorders, and even have longer lives (Adler et al., 1993). Increased social support from family, significant others, friends, and others in the community also reduces the negative effects of stress. People with more social support are less distressed, have reduced risks of disease or death, and adjust better to chronic diseases (Martin & Brantley, 2004; Taylor, 2014). Even "social" support from animals, particularly dogs, can lower heart rate and blood pressure (Allen et al., 2002) and reduce levels of stress-related hormones (Odendaal & Meintjes, 2003).

There are at least three types of social support. *Tangible support*, such as financial help, goods (food), and services (child care, transportation), can reduce the impact of a stressful event. *Informational support*, which involves the sharing of information to reduce stress, can help solve problems and manage stressful situations. *Emotional support*, such as the provision of caring, can provide reassurance during periods of high stress. Social support may reduce the impact of stress directly (e.g., by improving available coping resources) or indirectly (e.g., by making potentially stressful situations seem less threatening). There is still much to learn about the ways that social support moderates the relationship between stress and health.

Sex, Race/Ethnicity, and Developmental Issues

In comparison to adults, much less is known about children's responses to stress. Many children express distress through physical complaints such as headaches and stomachaches. Recurrent abdominal pain (RAP) is among the most common complaints of childhood. Occurring in approximately 10% of children, RAP consists of at least three bouts of pain that are so severe as to impede daily functioning (Ramchandani et al., 2005). A physical cause is identified only in 10% to 15% of cases. Among children experiencing RAP, those with anxious temperament and anxiety disorders are overrepresented. Because the pain comes and goes, stressful events are assumed to be associated with the pain episodes, but there has been little systematic research on the topic.

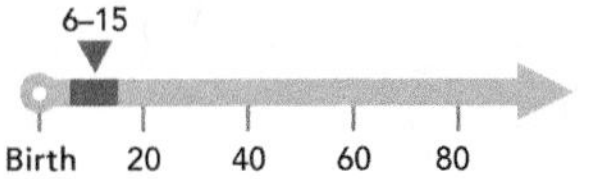

One common response to stress found among children is recurrent abdominal pain.

Although the basic physical response to stress is similar for men and women, men may have greater cortisol and immune system stress responses than women do (Kirschbaum et al., 1999; Rohleder et al., 2001). Recent research also reveals different coping styles. Men are more likely to use *problem-focused coping*, doing something to change stressful conditions. Women more often use *emotion-focused coping*, reducing their emotional distress by expressing feelings and seeking social support to cope with stress (Martin & Brantley, 2004). Women are more likely to use a "tend and befriend" strategy instead of the "fight-or-flight" response (Taylor et al., 2000). Early studies of stress assessed mostly male participants to avoid the need to control for greater cyclical variation in hormone responses (due to the reproductive cycle) among women. Recent animal and human research, however, indicates that women tend to care for and affiliate with others during times of stress (i.e., tending and befriending) (Taylor et al., 2000). This difference may reflect evolutionary influences that dictated different parental roles. Motherhood, for example, requires protecting offspring, getting them out of harm's way,

research HOT topic

Motivational Enhancement Therapy for Developing a Healthy Lifestyle

Motivational Enhancement Therapy (MET) , as described in Chapter 9, uses methods to strengthen a person's motivation for change. MET was originally developed as a method for treating substance-use disorders, but has since been applied to many different clinical conditions. Clinical investigators at the University of British Columbia and University of Regina (Taylor & Asmundson, 2004) have applied MET to the treatment of health anxiety. Researchers at York University in Ontario have also demonstrated that MET may be useful in treating anxiety disorders (Westra, 2012) and binge eating disorder (Vella-Zarb et al., 2015).

MET has been increasingly used by health psychologists and other clinicians as a method for helping people adopt a healthy lifestyle. For example, it has been successfully used to help people increase their intake of fruit and vegetables (Resnicow et al., 2001) and to help people quit smoking (Bock et al., 2014). MET has also proved useful in reducing the prevalence of unprotected sex in HIV-positive youth (Naar-King et al., 2006). A recent meta-analysis of MET studies, based on a variety of targeted behaviours (e.g., substance abuse, health-related behaviours, gambling) further supports the value of MET (Lundahl et al., 2010). For health-related behaviours (e.g., maintaining a healthy diet, exercising, and adhering to medical treatment), the effects of MET are statistically significant but small (Lundahl et al., 2010).

MET might not be more effective than other treatments, but it is still a useful tool for enhancing treatment outcome, and can be easily combined with other interventions. For example, for smoking cessation, MET has been successfully combined with the use of nicotine patches (Bock et al., 2014). Further research is needed to determine which types of people are most likely to benefit from MET when it targets health-related behaviours such as having a healthy diet and exercising.

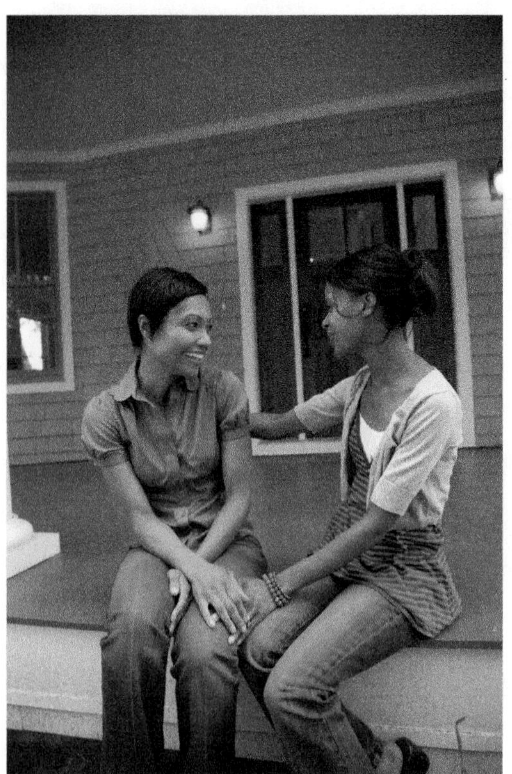

Women may use a "tend and befriend" strategy rather than a "fight-or-flight" response when confronted with stress. This may reflect the influence of evolution—motherhood more often requires protecting offspring than fighting predators directly.

David Sacks/DigitalVision/Getty Images

and calming them down rather than attacking predators and leaving young ones unprotected (Taylor et al., 2000). This different response may reflect different hormones found in males and females.

Little research has examined differences in stress responses among different racial and ethnic groups. Among the few existing studies, factors such as SES or sex have typically not been controlled. As noted earlier, lower SES is associated with higher levels of stress and disease, possibly as a result of discrimination or differential coping and social support (Gallo & Matthews, 2003). Research into the stress-disease relationship across racial/ethnic groups is further complicated because immigration status is not always taken into consideration. Immigration is a stressor most relevant to some ethnic minorities, such as people of Asian descent. A further confounding factor concerns social (i.e., family) support, which may differ across different ethnic groups. Accordingly, very little is known about how race/ethnicity is related to stress among people living in Canada.

CONCEPT check

- The level of stress a person experiences is determined by an interaction between a person and an event. The person first perceives the level of harm associated with an event (primary appraisal) and then assesses his or her ability to cope (secondary appraisal).
- Stress can be acute (short term) or chronic (long term) and can be caused by daily hassles or major life events.
- Stress can be measured in the laboratory, where its impact on physiological, neuroendocrine, and psychological responses can be assessed, or by questionnaires that ask people about major events and daily hassles.
- The impact of stress on health can be indirect (by means of changes in health-related behaviours) or direct (by physical changes in SAM, HPA, and immune functioning).
- *Psychoneuroimmunology* is the study of relations among psychological and social variables, immune system functioning, and disease.

- Moderators of the impact of stress on health include personality style (such as the Type A behaviour pattern), economic resources, and social support.

critical thinking question How would you design a study to test the impact of stress on test performance? How would you measure stress? How would you be able to tell whether a causal link between stress and performance existed?

Psychology and Behaviour in Medical Disease

At age 45, Sharon is married and works as an office manager at a local doctor's office. Although her husband is physically active, she leads a fairly sedentary life and had gained a lot of weight over the past decade. For the past year, she had felt consistently tired and had difficulty sleeping. She scheduled a visit with her internist (whom she hadn't seen in a couple of years) and was diagnosed with type II diabetes. As part of her treatment, Sharon was asked to start an exercise program, lose weight, modify her diet, and manage her stress. Whew! What a tall order—much easier said than done. However, she started walking three times a week and changed her eating habits, counting calories and limiting sweets. Over a couple of months, she saw her glucose levels drop, and she began to feel better in many ways. As time went on, however, she noticed that whenever she had a stressful week at work, her glucose levels were more unstable. During those difficult times, she found it difficult to maintain healthy behaviours. Managing diabetes and sticking to healthy eating and exercise is going to be a lifelong task.

Behaviour and Health

14.5 Recognize a range of behaviours that may affect health and how health psychologists help people change behaviours to maintain health.

Maintaining a healthy diet and weight, getting enough sleep, exercising regularly, limiting alcohol use and smoking, using sunscreen, and wearing seat belts are all ways to prevent disease and accidents. Many of these health behaviours (sometimes called *health habits*) are established early in life when people are not yet worried about their health. However, data clearly link health behaviours and health status (e.g., disease, disability) and even mortality. Given their significant roles in reducing the risk of cardiovascular disease, diabetes, cancer, obesity, and osteoporosis, three important components of healthy behaviour are eating, regular exercise, and not smoking.

HEALTHY EATING Dietary habits play a particularly important role in the development of CHD, hypertension, and some forms of cancer. Less than half (41%) of Canadians consume the daily recommended servings of fruits and vegetables (Statistics Canada, 2013b). Many biological, demographic, psychological, and sociocultural variables affect eating behaviours. Genetic, cultural, and social variables, for example, have a significant effect on taste preferences and food choice. People make food choices based on both innate and learned taste preferences, the foods that are commonly available (e.g., in rural vs. urban settings, in ethnic minority vs. majority families, in settings where financial resources are abundant or limited), and according to their attitudes, knowledge, and beliefs (West et al., 2004). Stress, anxiety, and depression are also associated with less healthy eating patterns (Kiecolt-Glaser, 2010; Taylor, 2014). When stressed, people may have trouble monitoring their food intake and its consequences (Ward & Mann, 2000), and stress can be associated with either increased or decreased eating. People who are anxious or depressed also have difficulty maintaining special diets, such as those implemented to reduce cholesterol (Stilley et al., 2004). In general, recommended dietary

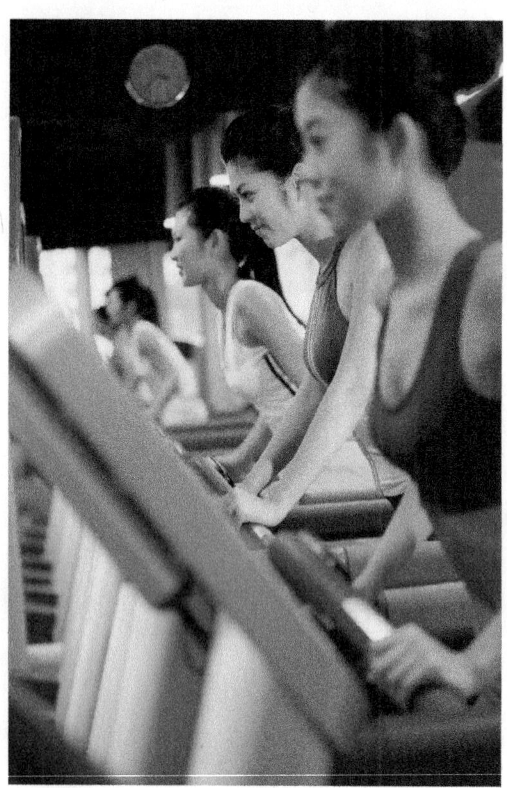

Regular exercise can be an important factor in fighting stress and disease.

Corbis

changes for healthier eating are effective, but they are often difficult to implement due to expense, extra time required for shopping and food preparation, and so forth.

EXERCISE AND PHYSICAL ACTIVITY The benefits of exercise are well known. Increased physical activity is associated with decreased resting heart rate, lower blood pressure, improved sleep, lower rates of obesity and cardiovascular disease, and increased longevity (Taylor, 2014). Regular exercise and increased activity are also associated with improved mood and well-being (Hansen et al., 2001), lower levels of depression (Lindwall et al., 2007), reduced risk of cognitive impairment in older people (Etgen et al., 2010), and reduced perception of pain (Hoffman & Hoffman, 2007). Nevertheless, many people are not active enough to stay healthy. Insufficient physical activity is related to a variety of social, demographic, and psychological variables. People who exercise less have lower incomes and less education and social support (Dubbert et al., 2004).

About 50% of people who start an exercise program continue for up to six months. Psychological variables such as *self-efficacy* (the belief that one is capable of exercising regularly) affect the ability to maintain an exercise program. Most commonly, people report that stress and lack of time are the primary reasons for giving up on exercise (Taylor, 2014). However, people who exercise cope better with stress, and we shall see later that exercise is an important component of stress management treatments.

SMOKING Another major modifiable risk factor for poor health, smoking, is associated with significant increases in rates of lung cancer, cardiovascular disease, emphysema and other respiratory problems, and death. Smoking also increases the risk of accidents and injuries at work and poses health risks for the smoker's family members and coworkers (Taylor, 2014). Although overall rates of smoking are declining in Canada (Janz, 2012), a significant number of Canadians continue to smoke. What do we know about psychological and social variables that lead people to smoke? First, smoking is more common among people who live in poverty and those with less education. Previously more common among males than females, smoking rates are now similar among adult men and women and adolescent boys and girls (Fisher et al., 2004). Most people begin smoking before the age of 18, and starting to smoke is often associated with higher levels of stress and anxiety, increased contact with peers who smoke, and parental modelling (Fisher et al., 2004). Attitudes and knowledge about associated health effects also are important. Adolescents, in particular, are less concerned about the potential health risks associated with smoking and are more susceptible to initiating the behaviour (Chassin et al., 2001). Advertising and marketing campaigns that target adolescents have significant effects on smoking initiation and continued use.

SLEEPING Certainly, you can recall times when you failed to get enough sleep—before a big test or when something stressful was going on in your life. Well, you are not alone. About 13% of Canadians report sleep disruption (Gilmour et al., 2013). This figure rises to 50% of patients in medical clinics (Pegram et al., 2004). Difficulty sleeping can be an acute but short-term problem, such as when better sleep returns after a major exam is over, or it can be a chronic condition lasting anywhere from 30 days to 6 months.

Among children, occasional *sleepwalking* (sitting up in bed, getting out of bed, and walking during sleep), *sleep terrors* (abrupt terror arousals, a panicky scream, intense fear, and autonomic arousal), and *nightmares* (extended, extremely dysphoric, and well-remembered dreams involving efforts to avoid threats to survival or security) are common (APA, 2013). When these behaviours are recurrent, the child may have **non-rapid eye movement sleep arousal disorders (sleepwalking type or sleep terror type) or nightmare disorder**. These conditions are common in children of both genders and across cultures (Agargun et al., 2004; Goodwin et al., 2004; Laberge et al., 2000), but they usually disappear in adolescence (Laberge et al., 2000; Thiedke, 2001).

Typically having its onset in the late teen/young adult years is *narcolepsy*, a sleep disorder defined as irrepressible need to sleep, lapsing into sleep or napping (APA, 2013). Occurring in about 1 out of every 2000 individuals (Jennum et al., 2012), people with narcolepsy have trouble sleeping at night but may fall asleep suddenly during the day, even if they are engaged in an activity such as eating, talking, or driving a car. Narcolepsy also can cause *cataplexy*, which is a condition where a person suddenly loses muscle tone when awake. A person may drop an object or suddenly fall out of a chair. Cataplexy episodes can be triggered by laughing or joking, and loss of muscle tone may last for seconds or minutes. When the sudden sleep attacks occur, the person begins to dream immediately and sometimes experiences hypnopompic or hypogogic hallucinations (see Chapter 4) and sleep paralysis.

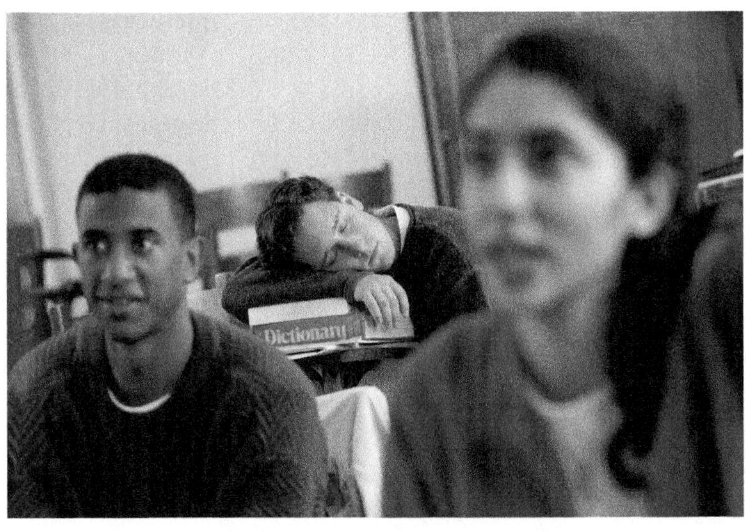

Sleep problems are common, even among young people. Lack of sleep can have a significant impact on daily functioning, including academic achievement.

Doug Menuez/Photodisc/Getty Images

Sleep paralysis is a temporary state of paralysis experienced prior to falling asleep or upon wakening (Paradis & Friedman, 2005). The person can open his or her eyes and is aware of the surroundings, but otherwise cannot move (Cheyne, 2005). Sleep paralysis is often associated with the presence of environmental stressors such as poverty or unemployment.

The most common form of sleep difficulty is **insomnia** (see "DSM-5: Insomnia")—persistent sleep difficulties that are associated with impairment in daily functioning (Morin et al., 2011; Pegram et al., 2004). According to a recent Canadian survey, as many as 40% of the general population have at least one symptom of insomnia (Morin et al., 2011). Symptoms of insomnia include problems falling asleep or staying asleep, waking up too early in the morning, and feeling fatigued upon awakening (often the result of what is called *nonrestorative sleep*) (APA, 2013). Insomnia can lead to daytime sleepiness; impaired work or school performance; difficulties with attention, concentration, and memory; increased risk for medical disease; poorer immune functioning; and increased risk of automobile accidents (Taylor, 2014).

Women have significantly more sleep problems than men (Morin et al., 2011), with differences beginning to emerge after the first menstrual period, known as *menarche*

criteria for Insomnia — DSM-5

A. A predominant complaint of dissatisfaction with sleep quantity or quality, associated with one (or more) of the following symptoms:
1. Difficulty initiating sleep. (In children, this may manifest as difficulty initiating sleep without caregiver intervention.)
2. Difficulty maintaining sleep, characterized by frequent awakenings or problems returning to sleep after awakenings. (In children, this may manifest as difficulty returning to sleep without caregiver intervention.)
3. Early-morning awakening with inability to return to sleep.

B. The sleep disturbance causes clinically significant distress or impairment in social, occupational, educational, academic, behavioural, or other important areas of functioning.

C. The sleep difficulty occurs at least 3 nights per week.

D. The sleep difficulty is present for at least 3 months.

E. The sleep difficulty occurs despite adequate opportunity for sleep.

F. The insomnia is not better explained by and does not occur exclusively during the course of another sleep-wake disorder (e.g., narcolepsy, a breathing-related sleep disorder, a circadian rhythm sleep-wake disorder, a parasomnia).

G. The insomnia is not attributable to the physiological effects of a substance (e.g., a drug of abuse, a medication).

H. Coexisting mental disorders and medical conditions do not adequately explain the predominant complaint of insomnia.

(Johnson et al., 2006b). Older adults have more sleep difficulties than middle-aged adults (Morin et al., 2011). At the other end of the developmental spectrum, adolescents can develop sleep difficulties as they experience increased social pressures and greater demands at school (Pegram et al., 2004). Thus, normal age-related sleep changes occur through the lifespan (Pegram et al., 2004).

Sleep problems can result from stress, anxiety, or depression. In fact, sleep difficulties are part of the diagnostic criteria for depressive disorders and generalized anxiety disorder. Sleep problems also may result from medical problems such as pain, gastrointestinal reflux, and sleep apnea (a condition in which air passages are blocked and sleep is disrupted). Poor sleep habits such as drinking caffeine and exercising too close to bedtime may disrupt sleep. Other poor sleep behaviours include irregular sleep schedules and excessive napping. These kinds of behaviours can occur when patterns of nighttime behaviours do not foster relaxation and sleep. Falling asleep can become difficult for children when the last activity before bedtime involves roughhousing with dad. And, when children are "helped" to fall asleep, they may have trouble falling asleep on their own.

Jacob cannot fall asleep at bedtime or after wakening in the middle of the night unless mom rubs his back.

Understanding how people develop poor sleep habits suggests behavioural interventions to improve sleep. For example, teaching parents how to change bedtime routines and respond to nighttime awakenings can help children learn to comfort themselves and fall asleep on their own. For adults, behavioural treatment involves teaching new sleep habits such as using the bed only for sleep or sex (e.g., getting up out of bed when one can't sleep and reading quietly until feeling tired again), setting a regular bedtime that doesn't vary more than 30 minutes or so even on weekends, limiting naps, and restricting alcohol and nicotine intake (Morin & Espie, 2003; see Table 14.2). Relaxation training and cognitive therapy (changing beliefs about sleep) also can help (Irwin et al., 2006; Morin et al., 2009; Rybarczyk et al., 2005).

TABLE 14.2

Good Sleep Habits

S = Set a regular bedtime and wake time.

- It's helpful to go to bed at the same time and wake up at the same time.

L = Limit the use of the bedroom.

- Limit the use of the bedroom/bed for sleep or sex.

E = Exit the bedroom if you are not asleep in 15 to 20 minutes.

- When you go to bed at your regular time, but don't feel sleepy within 15 to 20 minutes, you should get up and go into another room until you feel sleepy again.
- This rule can be used throughout the night—if you get up in the middle of the night and can't get back to sleep in 15 to 20 minutes, then move to another location until you are sleepy.

E = Eliminate naps.

- Naps can be disruptive to nighttime sleeping. If you are unable to avoid a nap mid-day, limit it to one hour and do not sleep after 3 p.m.

P = Put your feet on the floor at the same time every morning.

- It is important to wake up at about the same time every morning, give or take 30 minutes. Setting an alarm can help this pattern.

Psychological Factors and Medical Diseases

We turn now to the role of psychological, behavioural, and social factors in medical diseases such as HIV/AIDS, cancer, chronic pain, insomnia, and chronic fatigue. Certainly, psychological factors can affect many other physical conditions, but we focus here on this subgroup of diseases.

HIV/AIDS The human immunodeficiency virus (HIV) destroys the body's ability to fight infection and some types of cancer. Early symptoms of HIV infection include fever, headache, and fatigue. These symptoms, however, generally disappear after a short time and may not return in a chronic or severe fashion for as much as 10 years (DiMatteo & Martin, 2002). Yet, the virus continues to grow in the body. Acquired immunodeficiency syndrome (AIDS) is diagnosed when HIV-infected people have a particularly low number of T-cells or when one of 26 clinical conditions appears as a result of *opportunistic infections* (those that do not usually cause disease in healthy persons). In 2011, it was estimated that over 71 000 Canadians were infected with HIV (Public Health Agency of Canada, 2012). At present, more than 33 million people worldwide are living with HIV/AIDS (http://www.niaid.nih.gov/topics/hivaids/Pages/Default.aspx, retrieved June 2, 2016).

HIV is spread through unprotected sex, contact with infected blood, sharing contaminated needles or syringes, and from mother to child. People with other sexually transmitted diseases are more susceptible to HIV infection. High-risk behaviours that facilitate susceptibility to HIV and its transmission are affected by many social and psychological variables including knowledge, attitudes, social support, and self-efficacy (perceived ability) for changing risky behaviour (Taylor, 2014). Even in our current information technology age, many people remain uninformed about HIV and AIDS. Risky behaviours are still common. They are influenced by mood, cultural values, social pressure, and modelling. The stigma of AIDS and potential negative reactions directly affect the willingness to get tested, which then affects early detection and treatment (Herek et al., 2003). Sexual health education about the disease, modes of transmission, and risky/safe behaviours can help to change behaviours that increase the risk of HIV transmission, although actual rates of transmission are not always impacted (Ross, 2010).

People with HIV face many challenges, including gradual deterioration of health and cognitive abilities, potential loss of employment, increased reliance on others, and stigma, fear, and prejudice. Depression, anxiety, and substance abuse are common (Pence et al., 2006) and occur more often among patients with poor social support or severe medical symptoms (Heckman et al., 2004). However, the impact of physical symptoms on negative mood can be reduced when people see some benefit from the disease, as in the case of Magic Johnson, who has taken an active role in the fight to reduce stigma and increase research (Siegel & Schrimshaw, 2007) (see "Real People, Real Disorders: Magic Johnson—Living With HIV"). Social support is particularly important because it helps the patient adjust to the disease and obtain appropriate treatment.

Depression, stress, trauma, and social support also affect disease progression and adjustment (Cruess et al., 2004; Leserman, 2008). Negative beliefs about oneself, the future, and disease course are associated with decreased T-cell counts and more rapid progression from HIV to AIDS (Taylor, 2014). Increased levels of stress reduce immunity to infection and increase the rate of progression from HIV to AIDS (Leserman et al., 2000), although social support can mitigate the effects of stress (Cruess et al., 2000). Depression also increases disease progression and mortality rates in both men and women (Ickovics et al., 2001; Mayne et al., 1996). Bereavement-related depression is a key issue. People with HIV/AIDS frequently live in communities where

REAL people REAL disorders

Magic Johnson—Living With HIV

On November 7, 1991, Magic Johnson shocked the world with an announcement that he was HIV positive and was retiring from an amazing basketball career. He was tested during a routine exam and was suddenly faced with a life-threatening disease and fear for his wife, who was pregnant at the time. Her test came back negative, but his adjustment was difficult. He missed playing basketball and suffered from medication side effects, stress, and mood swings. Nevertheless, Johnson has survived long and well (more than 20 years), probably as a result of his excellent physical condition and his daily "multi-drug cocktail." Magic Johnson also has used his celebrity status and financial advantages to reduce stigma (AIDS isn't just a "gay disease"), educate the public about risks (with particular focus on black men and women among whom prevalence is high), and support AIDS research.

Glenn Weiner/Newscom

Source: www.thedailybeast.com/articles/2011/05/16/magic-johnson-20-years-of-living-with-hiv.html. Accessed March 9, 2013.

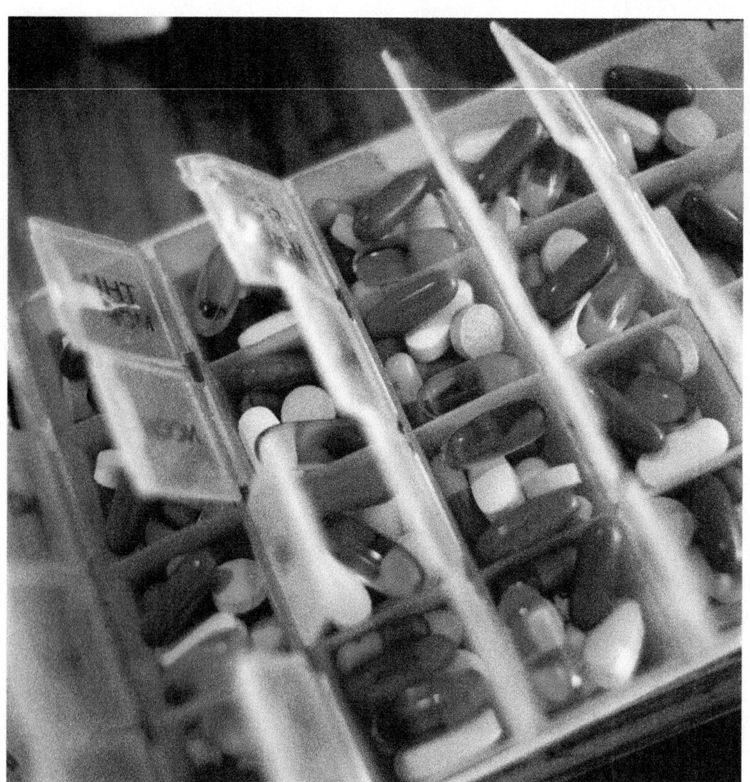

Each row represents one day's dose of HIV medications.

Katja Heinemann/Aurora Photos/Alamy Stock Photo

disease risk is high and where loss of important relationships is frequent.

A number of medicines are now available to slow HIV progression and reduce AIDS-related deaths. These drugs are expensive and have significant side effects, including decrease in red or white blood cells, pancreatic inflammation, nerve damage, and gastrointestinal symptoms. HIV/AIDS is now often a chronic disease (i.e., many people like Magic Johnson live with the disease for a long time), but long-term management requires complicated drug treatment. Adhering to these drug regimens is very difficult, particularly when other stressors are also present. Depression, substance abuse, and reduced social support are associated with poorer treatment adherence in HIV-positive patients (Gonzalez et al., 2004; Malta et al., 2008), whereas education, stress management, and social support may increase adherence and promote improved health.

CANCER Cancer is the second leading cause of death in Canada. About two in five Canadians will develop cancer in their lifetime, and about one in four Canadians will die of cancer (Canadian Cancer Society, 2015). More than half of new cancer cases (51%) will be lung, breast, colorectal, and prostate cancer. Lung cancer is the leading cause of cancer death, causing more cancer deaths among Canadians than the other three major cancer types combined. Despite this large impact, there has been a substantial drop in the lung cancer death rate (especially for men) over the past 25 years (Canadian Cancer Society, 2015). The effects of cancer reach far beyond the patient as family and friends also suffer from the effects of the disease and the grueling nature of the treatment process.

Although genetic factors play a role in the development of many kinds of cancer, some behavioural and lifestyle variables are also important. SES, for example, plays a role in cancer prevalence (Downing et al., 2007), and economic variables influence the use of cancer screening tools such as mammography (McAlearney et al., 2007).

Unhealthy behaviours such as unprotected sun exposure, smoking, alcohol use, and fatty diet without sufficient fruits and vegetables also are linked to increased cancer risk (DiMatteo & Martin, 2002; Taylor, 2014). Early detection through self-examination or medical testing may also improve outcomes and reduce mortality. As discussed previously, many psychological and social factors, including knowledge and beliefs, peer pressure, and stress, in turn influence these behaviours (Henderson & Baum, 2004). Although not all data are consistent, there is some evidence that depression increases the risk of developing cancer (Carney et al., 2003; Henderson & Baum, 2004), possibly by altering cortisol, norepinephrine, and the immune system. Although much has been written about the potential links between cancer and personality style (McKenna et al., 1999), many studies that demonstrate such links have small samples and are not prospective (assessing people over time). A recent study of more than 50 000 people who were assessed over a period of at least 25 years found no relation between personality characteristics (extraversion, neuroticism) and risk of cancer or risk of death after cancer (Nakaya et al., 2010).

Many of the variables that are linked to cancer onset also affect its progression and course as well as patient adjustment to the disease. Depression, pessimism, negative expectations, and an avoidant coping style (one that involves failure to confront the disease or express negative feelings) are associated with more rapid disease progression (Allison et al., 2003; Brown et al., 2003). Similarly, increased stress and reduced social support are associated with more rapid physical deterioration and increased rates of recurrence (Henderson & Baum, 2004; Kerr et al., 2001). Although the effects may vary across different forms of cancer, stress and reduced social support affect natural killer cell activity, which decreases the body's ability to fight virus and tumour growth.

Because many patients diagnosed with cancer survive for many years, adjustment to cancer as a chronic disease is an important issue. Even when a person becomes cancer free, uncertainty about future recurrences can continue to impact adjustment to life (Lee et al., 2009). Patients with cancer deal with many significant challenges, including fatigue, physical limitations and pain, decreased immune function, increased susceptibility to other infections, surgical removal of organs, body image difficulties, and prostheses. Emotional reactions such as depression, anxiety, and hopelessness, as well as changes in interpersonal relationships, are also common. Marital and sexual relationships may change after breast cancer or prostate cancer treatment, for example. Male partners of women with breast cancer have increased risk of depression (Nakaya et al., 2010). When parents are ill, children may have significant fears, and changes in family roles and interaction patterns can be quite stressful (e.g., older children may take on more responsibility at home or have less time with either parent when one parent is ill). Children's adjustment to their parent's cancer is influenced to some degree by family communication and by their mother's depression and level of adjustment (Osborn, 2007).

Predictors of adjustment to cancer overlap with factors that influence its onset and course. Interpersonal support is important, particularly from a spouse or partner. Good marital adjustment predicts less distress from the diagnosis (Banthia et al., 2003), and active conversations about the disease and problem solving between partners are particularly useful (Hagedoorn et al., 2000). Optimism, active coping, feelings of control, and finding meaning in the experience also enhance adjustment, and in some cases improve immune functioning and physical health (Barez et al., 2007; Taylor, 2014). Some evidence indicates that psychosocial treatments, including cognitive-behaviour therapy, supportive treatments, and exercise programs, improve adjustment and coping for patients and their partners (Badger et al., 2007; Mutrie et al., 2007), but generally not survival (Coyne et al., 2007).

CHRONIC PAIN

When Howard woke up, he knew immediately that it was the beginning of another two to three week bout of back pain. He had played golf the day before after a morning of yard work, and it must have been too much strain. Howard was only 50, but he had been dealing with chronic back pain ever since he hurt himself playing hockey when he was 30. He had also had surgery for a ruptured disc three years ago and since that time regularly had episodes of pretty severe pain. As he tried to roll over in bed, he thought about what was ahead. He wouldn't be able to play golf for at least a few weeks, and he would need to increase his daily dose of anti-inflammatory medication. He also wouldn't be able to sit at his desk for very long or play soccer with his kids. Sleep wouldn't be easy either; he knew he would be up walking the floor when the pain got bad. Howard knew he needed to get back on track with the exercises the physical therapist had recommended. When he did those regularly, his back was better, but he has been just too busy lately. He was really tired of dealing with this ongoing problem. It made him tired and grumpy and even a little depressed.

Pain disorder is diagnosed when a patient's primary complaint is persistent pain that occurs without sufficient medical explanation. In Howard's case, persistent back pain has a medical explanation and does not qualify for a DSM diagnosis. Nevertheless, his symptoms produced ongoing distress and dysfunction. Chronic back pain like Howard's is a common cause of disability among Canadians (Ramage-Morin & Gilmour, 2010). According to a Statistics Canada survey, chronic pain affects as many as 22% of Canadian adults (Gilmour, 2015). The lower back is the most common site of chronic pain, and chronic pain is more prevalent in older Canadians (Schopflocher et al., 2011). Chronic back pain is not exclusive to adults; many children and adolescents experience such pain, even though it is not necessarily associated with disease. According to Patrick McGrath and Christine Chambers (Dalhousie University) and their colleagues, 14% to 24% of children and adolescents experience chronic back pain (King et al., 2011).

Pain is useful when it provides feedback about changes that are needed to keep the body healthy or safe (e.g., when to change positions, exercise, or move away from a potential danger such as intense heat). However, there is not always a direct correlation between the location of the pain and its source, making its diagnosis and management a very complex issue.

Pain is generally classified as acute (lasting less than six months) or chronic (lasting six months or longer). Acute pain usually occurs as a result of injury and resolves when the body heals. Chronic pain can be ongoing, as with chronic back pain, or associated with recurrent episodes of acute pain, as with migraines. Some chronic pain gets progressively worse over time, as with rheumatoid arthritis. Biologically, pain involves transmission of information from nerves at the injury site through the spinal cord and to the cerebral cortex. Other messages then go back to the site of the injury and other body parts where physical changes (e.g., muscle contractions, breathing changes) occur to help block the pain (Taylor, 2014).

The experience of pain is not always tied directly to the severity of a medical disease or other biological process. Many environmental, psychological, and socio-cultural factors are involved. For example, the situation in which pain occurs affects its meaning and interpretation, which in turn influences the amount of distress and interference. Psychological variables are also important. Depression and anxiety commonly accompany pain and worsen its experience (Dickens et al., 2003; Vowles et al., 2004). People in pain feel unable to do things they used to enjoy, have decreased feelings of control, and worry about what will happen if the pain gets worse.

Pain is also common among people with depression and predicts poorer response to treatment (Bair et al., 2004). Negative thoughts (e.g., "I'll never get better"; "Things are only going to get worse") and unnecessary withdrawal from pleasurable activities (e.g., "I'd better not go to that basketball game; sitting on those bleachers will be too hard on my back"; "I just can't be around people anymore—it's too hard to concentrate on what they are saying when I am in so much pain all the time") worsen depression and limit the efficacy of treatment (Bishop & Warr, 2003; Severeijns et al., 2004). The experience and expression of pain are sometimes reinforced by people or events. People who express pain through words or behaviour sometimes get more attention, are relieved of responsibility, and receive financial compensation. These environmental reinforcers can be powerful motivators for the continued experience or expression of pain.

There also are individual differences in the frequency with which people report pain, seek help from their doctors, and respond to pain treatments (Turk & Monarch, 2002). These differences are not always related to actual physical conditions, but can be influenced by biological factors, learning history, and sociocultural variables.

Michael Sullivan (McGill University), Gordon Asmundson (University of Regina), and their colleagues have provided evidence that pain catastrophizing (i.e., distorted beliefs about the seriousness and implications of pain) and the fear of pain are important factors in perpetuating pain-related disability (e.g., Niederstrasser et al., 2014; Mankovsky et al., 2012; Thibodeau et al., 2013; Wideman et al., 2013). To illustrate, consider a person with chronic low-back pain. If that person has an intense fear of pain, then he or she is likely to avoid physical activity, leading to muscle wasting (deconditioning), which can worsen chronic pain.

The goals of pain treatment may be to eliminate pain, reduce pain, or improve function in the face of some pain. Treatment includes both medical (medication, surgery, etc.) and nonmedical (acupuncture, psychological) approaches, although medication is used most often. The most popular prescription medication is morphine. However, morphine and other **analgesic medications** in the opioid family (e.g., codeine, hydrocodone, oxycodone) can cause dependence (see Chapter 9), leading to significant controversy over their use (see "Examining the Evidence: Are Opioid Medications Useful or Too Risky in the Treatment of Pain?"). Anti-inflammatory drugs and antidepressants can also reduce pain. Antidepressant drugs reduce anxiety and depression and also act on neural pathways that relay pain information. Anti-inflammatory drugs reduce pain but do not directly alter mood.

Nonmedical treatments for pain include relaxation training, biofeedback, and hypnosis. During **biofeedback**, patients learn to modify physical responses such as heart rate, respiration, and body temperature. During **hypnosis**, patients are taught to relax, a trance-like state is induced, and hypnotic suggestions are used to reduce pain and change pain-related thoughts. All of these interventions show positive effects, although the additional value of biofeedback over relaxation alone is not well established (Taylor, 2014). Cognitive-behavioural treatments that involve relaxation, imagery (imagining a positive scene to induce relaxation or picturing cancer as an enemy to be destroyed), cognitive therapy (changing thoughts about pain), and behavioural changes (becoming more active in managing one's own pain, engaging in positive behaviours despite pain) also can be useful. Typically, both medical and nonmedical strategies are integrated into a pain management program that is individually tailored to meet a patient's needs (Gatchel & Maddrey, 2004).

examining the EVIDENCE

Are Opioid Medications Useful or Too Risky in the Treatment of Pain?

- **The Facts** Opium, derived from the seedpod of poppies, was used to treat pain and other diseases thousands of years ago. Opium-derived drugs became very popular in the nineteenth century, although concerns about misuse and overuse led to serious controls over their legal use by the 1940s (Ballantyne & Mao, 2003). Legal penalties for inappropriate use are severe, and many physicians are reluctant to prescribe these drugs. Are physicians correct to limit their use of opioids for the treatment of pain? Does caution lead to inadequate treatment for many pain sufferers? Can these drugs be used appropriately to manage pain without addiction?
- **What Evidence Suggests That Use of Opioids Is Too Risky?**
  - Opioids are the most commonly abused prescription drug. Rates of its abuse increased significantly from 1994 to 2000 (Atluri et al., 2003).
  - Human and animal studies suggest that long-term use can increase sensitivity to pain (Ballantyne & Mao, 2003).
  - Opioid use is sometimes accompanied by problematic or illegal behaviour, including escalating doses without physician recommendation, requesting multiple prescriptions from different providers, and requesting refills without a physician visit (Webster & Webster, 2005).
  - Rapid dose increases can create life-threatening respiratory depression (although this occurs rarely).
- **What Evidence Supports the Value of Opioid Medications for Pain Treatment?**
  - Studies show that opioid medication is effective for reducing pain in short-term and longer-term (up to 32 weeks) treatment (Ballantyne & Mao, 2003), although mixed results occur with regard to how these medications improve functioning.
  - Approximately 15% of cancer patients and 80% of noncancer patients with chronic pain fail to receive adequate treatment for pain (Chapman & Gavrin, 1999).
  - Addiction occurs infrequently when opioid medications are used to treat pain (Atluri et al., 2003; Taylor, 2014).
  - If one particular medication no longer manages pain, switching to an alternative opioid medication may be of value (rather than increasing the dose of a current drug) because all types of opioids do not act on the same pain receptors (Ballantyne & Mao, 2003).
- **Conclusions** Consensus statements from experts suggest that opioids can be used appropriately to manage pain when guidelines about recommended drugs, doses, and duration of treatment are followed. Generally, a full medical examination is conducted before an initial prescription is given, as well as a careful review of the benefits and risks of opioid use (e.g., the risk of overuse increases if the patient has a personal or family history of substance use or if a psychiatric disorder is diagnosed). Patients appropriate for opioid medication are those whose symptoms have not improved with alternative approaches and who have limited risk factors for abuse. Opioids may even be prescribed, however, when risk factors for abuse are present but the pain is sufficiently severe that treatment of both pain and abuse are necessary. Patients prescribed opioids should work solely with one physician and one pharmacy, and careful follow-up and monitoring are needed to check for signs of overuse or abuse (e.g., requests for early refills, requests for refills without a physician visit).

CONCEPT check

- Many behaviours have a significant impact on health, including eating, sleeping, exercise, use of alcohol and nicotine, level of sun exposure, and risky sexual behaviours.
- Sleep difficulties can include trouble falling asleep, staying asleep, waking too early, or feeling tired upon waking.
- Poorer health habits are typically seen in people with lower education and income as well as in those with increased depression and anxiety.
- Anxiety and depression are common correlates of serious medical diseases such as HIV/AIDS and cancer. Variables such as negative beliefs, poor social support, and increased stress can accelerate the progression of medical symptoms.
- Pain is such a common problem that it is now considered the "fifth vital sign" in medical evaluations.

- The experience of pain is not always directly related to severity of a medical disease or injury. Many psychological, environmental, and cultural factors influence the perception of pain. A diagnosis of pain disorder is not appropriate when chronic pain has a medical explanation.

critical thinking question Your roommate drinks caffeinated soft drinks all the time. After her morning classes, she takes a nap for several hours, and she often stays up all night trying to catch up on schoolwork. Today, she tells you that for the last week she has had trouble falling asleep. What can you tell her to help her understand how some of her behaviours might be affecting her sleep?

Psychological Treatments for Health-Related Conditions

Psychologists and psychological interventions may help in the overall treatment program for many health problems. Treatment may occur in private practice, in a medical setting such as an outpatient clinic or hospital, or within an organization, such as a workplace or school that offers health and wellness programs.

The Role of a Health Psychologist

A health psychologist typically has a doctoral degree (Ph.D. or Psy.D.) in clinical psychology and specialty training in medical/health issues completed during doctoral training (e.g., a specialized Health Psychology track) or during postdoctoral work. Most health psychologists are trained in the scientist-practitioner model with combined expertise in clinical care and research. In clinical settings, health psychologists work with a patient or medical team to change behaviours, attitudes, or beliefs to promote health and improve adjustment to disease. They may work with patients individually or in groups, and they sometimes provide assistance to family members. Health psychologists in research careers typically work in university or medical school settings where they conduct research examining the relations between psychological and physical variables or the effectiveness of interventions to improve health and quality of life.

Ethics and Responsibility

A health psychologist faces unique ethical issues. They typically function within multidisciplinary teams in which different clinical disciplines are represented, each of which has its own set of professional ethical standards. In situations when guidelines of different professionals diverge (e.g., with regard to confidentiality), a psychologist needs to continue to adhere to the standards of practice set out by the Canadian Psychological Association (2000; see Chapter 15). Within medical teams, health psychologists often have the responsibility of determining whether a patient is psychologically well suited for a particular medical procedure such as an organ transplant, bariatric surgery, or an implantable pain device (e.g., spinal cord stimulator, pain pump). In some cases, even though a medical procedure may seem warranted, the psychologist may decide that a patient is not a good candidate because of psychological problems (e.g., depression, substance abuse) or other behavioural issues (e.g., inability to comply with follow-up care). The medical team then may decide not to recommend the procedure or may recommend a more comprehensive treatment plan that includes mental health or other behavioural interventions.

Health Psychology Interventions

14.6 Identify factors that affect adjustment to chronic disease and strategies to improve adjustment and quality of life for people with a chronic disease.

In addition to strategies that health psychologists might use to help patients manage pain and improve sleep, interventions can help people increase healthy behaviours, manage stress, and adjust to chronic disease.

INCREASING HEALTHY BEHAVIOURS It might be interesting to take stock of your own inventory of healthy behaviours. Do you:

- Eat a balanced diet and exercise regularly?
- Sleep at least seven hours a night?
- Smoke? Drink too much alcohol?
- Always wear your seat belt? Use sunscreen?

If you have ever tried to change your behaviour in these areas, you know that it is not always easy. Certainly, it is easier to prevent poor health habits than to change them. Increasing healthy behaviours among people without disease is called **primary prevention** (DiMatteo & Martin, 2002). Developing a program to prevent smoking in teens is an example of this approach.

Secondary prevention includes health-promotion programs for people at increased risk for health problems, such as people with a family history of stroke or heart attack. Initiating a low-cholesterol diet and exercise program for someone whose parent died young from a heart attack is an example of a secondary prevention strategy. The goal is to help people initiate or change behaviours to improve health.

Two of the first areas in which to increase healthy behaviours are education and awareness. Public education campaigns can increase healthy behaviours. For example, in the mid-1960s, there was a mass media campaign to educate the public about the hazards of smoking. This campaign had a significant influence on attitudes and beliefs about smoking (Taylor, 2014). Education also occurs individually when doctors explain the importance of certain health-related behaviours to their patients (e.g., when pediatricians advise parents about a balanced diet and healthy exercise program for their child). Education is sometimes combined with self-monitoring or keeping daily records of health-related behaviours. For example, modifying one's diet might involve first keeping daily records of food intake. Sometimes the simple act of monitoring behaviour can lead to positive changes, although often other strategies are also needed.

Other interventions are based on classical conditioning or operant conditioning. **Stimulus control** is a behaviour change strategy based on classical conditioning. It involves modifying behaviour by changing the stimuli that bring on the behaviour. For example, changing one's diet is much easier if unhealthy stimuli such as cookies and chips that provoke more snacking (the unhealthy behaviour to be changed) are removed from the home. Learning to eat only when sitting down at the table (not when watching television or standing in front of the refrigerator) is another way to control stimuli associated with eating. **Contingency contracting** is a strategy that relies on setting up a reinforcement program to encourage healthier behaviour. For example, a family might set up a program for a child with poor eating habits by offering tokens that can be exchanged for a special (non-food) treat, such as a trip to the zoo.

Increasing healthy behaviour sometimes requires changing attitudes such as *self-efficacy* (how much someone believes he or she can do something). We know that self-efficacy can affect people's ability to maintain exercise programs. Thus, health behaviour plans that involve changing beliefs about abilities can be important for improving health.

STRESS MANAGEMENT Remember that important relationship between stress and health? If stress can negatively affect health, then programs to help people manage stress can help people stay healthy. Stress management skills, such as biofeedback, relaxation, and meditation, can be taught individually or in group or classroom-type settings at the workplace, school, or other community sites. Stress management successfully reduces blood pressure in patients with hypertension (Linden et al., 2001); improves anxiety, depression, and quality of life among patients with HIV (Scott-Sheldon et al., 2008); improves health status for patients with arthritis (Somers et al., 2009); and reduces risk factors in patients with CHD (Daubenmier et al., 2007).

As with increasing healthy behaviours, the first step in stress management is education and awareness. People learn to identify personally stressful situations and how they respond to them. Self-monitoring is one good strategy for increasing awareness. Keeping daily records helps patients understand their personal stressors and the thoughts, feelings, behaviours, and coping patterns that are part of their stress response. Remember Marek? He had difficulty adjusting to the stresses associated with beginning university, such as being away from home, having a much heavier school workload, and making new friends. His typical coping patterns included eating fast food to save time and reducing the amount of time he spent exercising. He also stayed up late trying to keep up with reading and studying.

When Marek went to the infirmary the third time, the nurse suggested that he consider taking a stress-reduction class. He decided to give it a try. When he started paying closer attention, he realized just how tense his body was in many situations and how often he had negative thoughts about himself when he was under stress ("I am just not smart enough to succeed here." "I must be the only one here who is homesick. What a wimp I am."). Marek also began to realize that he actually wasn't very good at managing his study time. School had always been easy for him before, so he never had to spend much time planning his studies. Now things were different.

Once someone is aware of stress-producing situations and responses, the next step is to learn new coping skills such as improving diet and increasing exercise. Exercise training appears to increase resistance to stress (Salmon, 2001). Other coping skills include relaxation training, learning time management skills, and changing thoughts.

For Marek, learning to stop and take a deep breath during stressful situations was very useful.

Well-structured strategies such as progressive deep muscle relaxation can also help reduce stress (see Chapter 4), as can goal setting and changing thoughts.

Marek also benefitted from learning how to plan ahead and set specific goals for studying each day. This helped him feel less overwhelmed by the increased academic load. He also learned how to think differently about himself. Instead of cutting himself down when he was under stress, he learned to say things like: "University is tough, but I am doing ok." "My grades don't have to be as good as they were in high school as long as I am doing my best."

Yoga and meditation are effective stress management techniques.

Corbis

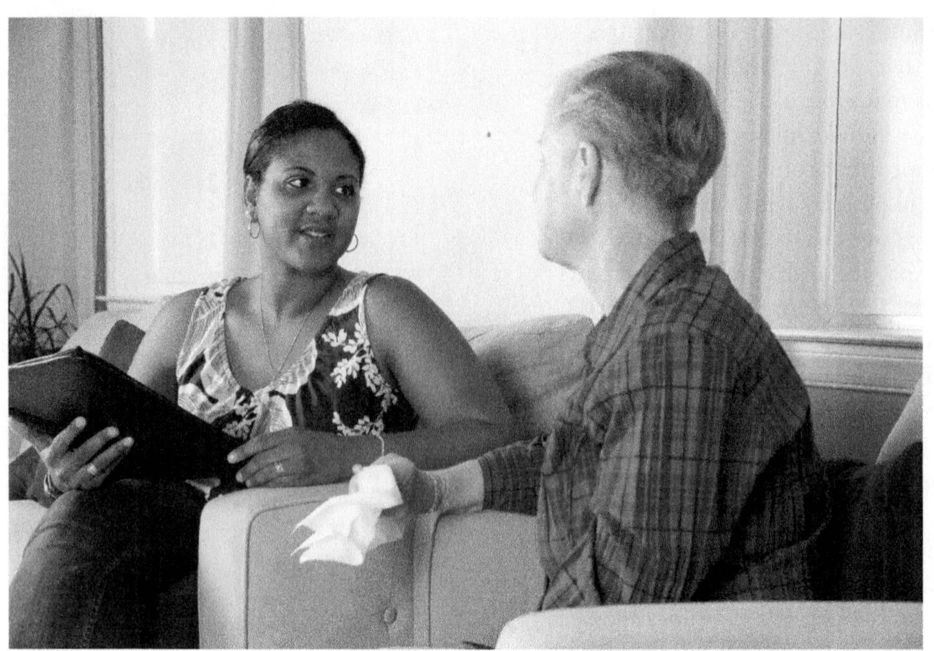

Health psychologists play an important role in helping patients with chronic and life-threatening diseases to feel empowered.

Rob/Fotolia

ADJUSTING TO CHRONIC DISEASE As we have seen, people with chronic disease, such as HIV/AIDS, cancer, chronic pain, diabetes, and CHD, experience many changes including decreased physical capacity, altered relationships with family and friends, financial strain, and high rates of anxiety and depression. How does a health psychologist help people cope with these changes? First, we know that good social support can improve disease outcomes. We also know that stress and negative beliefs about the disease, oneself, and the future predict poor outcomes. Therefore, adjustment to chronic disease might involve continuing social interaction, managing stress, and modifying beliefs. Encouraging patients to seek social support and providing education and support to family members enhance everyone's adjustment. Some patients and families also benefit from formal support groups that provide emotional support and information about ways that others have coped successfully.

In many ways, coping with a medical disease is similar to coping with other stressful experiences, suggesting that stress management can be useful. Learning about the disease (e.g., what to expect in terms of progression, what treatment choices are available) and identifying potential stressors (e.g., trips to the doctor, changing medication) are important first steps. Relaxation and exercise can also improve adjustment, and patients with chronic disease often learn new skills to effectively integrate ongoing medical care into their lives. For example, they may need to learn to eat differently and change their routines to make time for complicated medical treatments (e.g., insulin shots for diabetes before every meal; chemotherapy treatments that affect functioning for days or weeks at a time). Health psychologists help patients integrate long-term medical care into their lives while helping them maintain their identities as parents, spouses, co-workers, and friends (DiMatteo & Martin, 2002).

Behaviours and thoughts that encourage feelings of control over disease can be helpful. Self-efficacy or confidence can affect health behaviours. Increased feelings of self-efficacy and control are associated with good adjustment to diseases such as COPD (Kohler et al., 2002), sickle cell disease (Edwards et al., 2001), and chronic pain (Turner et al., 2007). Therefore, treatments that increase confidence and control can help people adjust to chronic disease. Magic Johnson illustrates the importance of finding benefit or meaning in the experience of disease. Health psychologists can help patients identify positive outcomes associated with their disease and positive ways to use their experiences to help others.

Canadian FOCUS

Innovative Programs in Health Psychology

Throughout this chapter we have seen that health psychology has a lot to offer in terms of improving health and preventing disease. A challenge is that there are relatively few health psychologists compared to the number of patients who could benefit from health psychology. Across Canada, there are an estimated 47 psychologists per 100 000 people (Graff et al., 2012), but only some of these clinicians are trained and experienced in health psychology. According to a recent survey of Canadian psychologists, only 41% provide clinical services (assessment, treatment, or both) to patients with health, injury, or illness problems (Hunsley et al., 2013). This suggests that there are not enough psychologists to provide health psychology services, on a one-to-one, face-to-face basis. There are simply too many patients requiring treatment. A further problem is that Canada is a vast country. Many patients, especially those living in rural areas, must travel great distances in order to receive treatment for health-related problems. Accordingly, there is a great need for innovation in the practice of health psychology in Canada.

Some of the most important new innovations have been developed and implemented by research-practitioners from the Department of Clinical Health Psychology (DCHP) in the Faculty of Medicine at the University of Manitoba. This is the only independent department of psychology in a medical school in Canada and the United States (McIlwraith, 2014). All psychologists in the department also hold appointments as medical staff of the Winnipeg Regional Health Authority. An advantage of being an independent department, as opposed to being a division of some other department, is that it creates visibility that leads to greater understanding among medical colleagues about what psychologists do. In addition, this type of organization supports interprofessional education and promotes clinical and research collaborations with other departments (McIlwraith, 2014). The following are two examples of the health psychology programs—cardiac care and insomnia treatment—developed by Lesley Graff, George Kaoukis, Norah Vincent, and their colleagues at DCHP (Graff et al., 2012).

Cardiac care. It is not uncommon for patients who have suffered a heart attack to become depressed or anxious. These negative emotions are predictive of future medical problems, including non-adherence with medical treatment and future cardiac problems (Graff et al., 2012). The Canadian Association of Cardiac Rehabilitation (2009) recommends that all cardiac patients be screened and, if necessary, treated for clinically significant anxiety or depression. Meta-analytic research by Wolfgang Linden (University of British Columbia) and colleagues indicates that psychological treatments can reduce cardiac mortality, particularly for men (Linden et al., 2007).

The cardiac care program was designed to meet the challenge of providing psychological services for the large numbers of cardiac patients seen at Winnipeg hospitals (Graff et al., 2012). A stepped care screen-and-treat approach was developed, which is implemented in collaboration and coordination with cardiologists (Kaoukis, 2008). Cardiac patients are screened for anxiety and depression, using validated screening questionnaires. Based on their research, 29% of cardiac patients have clinically significant levels of depression or anxiety (Kaoukis, 2004), and of those, about half have suicidal ideation. Patients with clinically elevated scores on questionnaires are interviewed by a psychologist. Patients who are judged, by means of interview, to have significant anxiety or depression are offered empirically supported treatment, with the dose of treatment depending on the severity of the patient's emotional problems. Patients with relatively mild anxiety or depression receive two CBT seminars, conducted in large groups, in which they are educated about relaxation exercises and stress and depression management, particularly as relevant to cardiac rehabilitation. Patients wanting further help are offered a consultation with a psychologist. Those who do not benefit, along with cardiac patients with more severe symptoms of depression or anxiety, are offered three more sessions of CBT. Patients with severe distress receive, in addition to the above-mentioned interventions, further intensive, one-to-one psychological treatment or referral for further treatment.

Insomnia. Over 83% of Canadians have access to the Internet (Statistics Canada, 2012). Accordingly, Internet-based treatment is a promising was of delivering psychological treatment. An advantage is that this type of treatment can reach people from all over Canada, including those living in remote regions. Internet-based assessment and treatment can serve as the first level or entry into a stepped care treatment program (Graff et al., 2012). Norah Vincent and colleagues at DCHP developed the first Canadian CBT online treatment program for chronic insomnia (Vincent & Lewycky, 2009). Such a program was necessary and important because they found that 40% of referrals for chronic insomnia came from rural regions (Graff et al., 2012). The DCHP insomnia clinic, led by a psychologist, works collaboratively with medical sleep specialists. The computerized intervention is a six-week program that can be accessed through the patient's home computer in a series of weekly audiovisual modules, covering areas such as psychoeducation, CBT, sleep restriction, stimulus control, relaxation therapy, mindfulness meditation, and sleep hygiene. This program has the advantage in that it can accommodate thousands of users at a time and has been shown to be efficacious in randomized, controlled treatment studies (Vincent & Lewycky, 2009; Vincent et al., 2013).

Prior to the computerized service, all referrals were assessed individually after spending a lengthy period on a waiting list. Now, once referred, all patients are screened via telephone by an online coordinator, and if psychologically stable (i.e., not currently suicidal or experiencing mania), they are offered the computer-based intervention in which they are provided with the website address, username, and password. Individuals work through the program on the site and submit weekly information about their sleep and adherence to the modules. Following completion of the online service, at the first available opportunity, the patient is offered an in-person consultation with a staff psychologist in the sleep clinic to consider further treatment needs (Graff et al., 2012). Computerization has vastly increased the number of patients who can be assessed and treated.

real SCIENCE real LIFE

Sandy—Victory Over Cancer

THE PATIENT

Sandy is 37 years old. She has a great career and a wonderful family. She exercises three times per week. She does not really watch her diet, but her weight is well within the normal range. People tease Sandy all the time, calling her a "Type A personality without the hostility."

THE PROBLEM

When Sandy was 16 years old, her mother (who was 37) was diagnosed with breast cancer. Despite treatment, her mother died about 10 years after her diagnosis. Because of her mother's history, Sandy's physician insisted that she start having mammograms at a very early age. Sandy just thought of them as routine—surely the same thing would not happen to her. But at age 37, Sandy's mammogram showed a suspicious spot and a biopsy confirmed it—Sandy had breast cancer. She could not believe it—she felt absolutely healthy. How could she have such a life-threatening disease? Sandy cried for two days. Shortly thereafter, she met with a surgeon and had surgery to remove the tumour.

THE TREATMENT

Following her surgery, Sandy had many choices—radiation therapy, chemotherapy, hormonal therapy. Everything was happening fast, and it seemed overwhelming. Sandy was not sure what to do. She felt that her life was out of control. Her family, though emotionally supportive, seemed unable to help her make decisions or chart a course. One member of the comprehensive treatment team at the breast cancer centre was a health psychologist. Sandy was asked to meet with her—to discuss her concerns and fears, and to find a way to cope with the overwhelming nature of the disease.

The health psychologist had several recommendations. First, it was clear that throughout Sandy's life, she had responded to adversity with problem-focused coping strategies. So the psychologist decided to build on these strengths by helping Sandy find more functional ways of coping with her current stress. Sitting around crying, her health psychologist pointed out, was completely natural in the circumstances but would not be very helpful. She assigned Sandy tasks to enhance her coping style. For example, Sandy investigated various forms of breast cancer therapy. Second, because she was such an active person, the health psychologist (after consultation with Sandy's surgeon) asked Sandy to restart her exercise program. Not only did this reduce her stress level, but it also helped restore her energy and hastened her rehabilitation from surgery. Third, to deal with Sandy's feelings of being out of control, the health psychologist encouraged her to return to work—on a part-time basis at first and then full-time. The health psychologist suggested that Sandy consider a breast cancer support group. Sandy attended one session but did not go back. The women in the group, though nice, spent a lot of time talking about breast cancer but did not seem interested in figuring out what to do about it. Instead, Sandy joined more active support groups—participating in a Pink Ribbon running program supported by the Canadian Breast Cancer Foundation and by a local running club. This was much more consistent with her coping style.

THE TREATMENT OUTCOME

Sandy began to realize that although she might not have complete control of the cancer that was in her body, she still had control over other aspects of her life. Finally, the health psychologist helped Sandy break her upcoming course of treatment into a series of smaller steps. By focusing on these short-term goals, Sandy felt more capable of dealing with the long treatment course ahead of her. Sandy's family remained an important source of emotional support, cheering her on as she overcame each hurdle and remained cancer free.

CONCEPT check

- Health psychologists work to help people change behaviours, attitudes, or beliefs in ways that promote health and adjustment to disease.
- The first step toward increasing healthy behaviour involves education about the way behaviours can affect health and gaining awareness of one's own health-related behaviours.
- Stress management can improve the health of patients with medical problems such as cancer, HIV/AIDS, and CHD.
- Strategies for reducing stress and coping with chronic disease include relaxation, changing behaviours, and changing thoughts.

critical thinking question What behaviours could you change to improve your health?

summary

14.1 Define health psychology and the roles of a health psychologist.

Health psychology uses the principles and methods of psychology to understand the effects of attitudes and behaviours on health and disease. Health psychologists study how people develop positive and negative health habits (e.g., exercise, eating, smoking), how stress and health are related, and which psychological variables affect the onset and treatment of medical diseases.

14.2 Describe mind–body dualism and its significance for health psychology.

Mind–body dualism suggests that mind and body function independently. This point of view is not supported by current empirical research, which demonstrates that psychological and social variables have a significant impact on health and physical functioning.

14.3 Define stress, and describe how it is measured.

Stress is determined by an interaction between a person and an event. Stress can be *acute* (short term) or *chronic* (long term) and can be caused by *daily hassles* or *major life events*. Stress can be measured in the laboratory where its impact on physiological, neuroendocrine, and psychological responses can be assessed or by questionnaires that ask people about major events and daily hassles.

14.4 Describe the impact of stress on health and the immune system.

Stress has been linked to an increase in unhealthy behaviours, a higher rate of accidents, increased frequency of anxiety and depression, and poorer immune functioning (e.g., reduced resistance to disease). Variables that affect the role of stress in health include personality style, such as the Type A behaviour pattern, economic resources, and social support.

14.5 Recognize a range of behaviours that may affect health and how health psychologists help people change behaviours to maintain health.

Behaviours that have a significant impact on health include eating, sleeping, exercise, use of alcohol and nicotine, level of sun exposure, and risky sexual behaviours. People with lower education and income, as well as those with depression and anxiety, have poorer health habits. Health psychologists can help people develop healthier patterns of eating and exercising, as well as reduce harmful behaviours such as smoking.

14.6 Identify factors that affect adjustment to chronic disease and strategies to improve adjustment and quality of life for people with a chronic disease.

Anxiety and depression occur commonly in patients with serious medical diseases such as HIV/AIDS and cancer. Variables such as negative beliefs, poor social support, and increased stress can accelerate the progression of medical symptoms. Many psychological, environmental, and cultural factors also influence the perception of pain. Health psychologists work to help people change behaviours, attitudes, or beliefs in ways that promote health and adjustment to disease. Strategies for reducing stress and coping with chronic disease include relaxation, changing behaviours, and changing thoughts.

key terms

TEST yourself

1. The subdiscipline of psychology that studies the interactions among biological, psychological, and social factors is called
   a. developmental psychology
   b. medical psychology
   c. social psychology
   d. health psychology
2. In 1948, the World Health Organization defined health for the first time in terms of
   a. a lack of illness, disease, or suffering
   b. both physical and mental illness
   c. positive lifestyle values
   d. mental, physical, and social well-being
3. The person most associated with the concept of mind–body dualism is
   a. Flanders Dunbar
   b. René Descartes
   c. Franz Alexander
   d. Sigmund Freud
4. Stress is most likely to be present when an event
   a. has an anticipated negative outcome that affects the family
   b. is unpredictable or ambiguous with no clear plan of action
   c. generates an intense emotional reaction
   d. requires a specific set of coping skills
5. Kevin is delayed by road construction on his way to a movie. As he approaches the box office, he notices that the person in front of him is purchasing tickets for a large school group. When he finally gets to the ticket agent, he realizes he does not have cash and the theatre does not take credit or debit cards. These events represent
   a. daily hassles
   b. acute stress
   c. chronic stress
   d. continuous negative outcomes
6. Which of the following is *not* one of Hans Selye's general adaptation syndrome stages?
   a. adaptation
   b. alarm
   c. resistance
   d. exhaustion
7. Bodily responses to stress, such as increased blood pressure, rapid breathing, and sweaty palms, indicate
   a. extreme emotion-focused coping
   b. increased sympathetic nervous system activity
   c. overwhelming daily hassles
   d. detrimental responses to chronic stressors
8. Inflammation in the body is a sign that
   a. a specific immune system response has been triggered by disease
   b. natural immunity has been triggered by stress
   c. the nonspecific immune system is at work
   d. all normal bodily systems have been overwhelmed by stress
9. Depression, alcoholism, and eating disorders have all been linked to elevated
   a. T-cell secretion
   b. phagocytosis
   c. HPA activity
   d. natural killer cell reuptake
10. The Type A characteristic that predicts an increased risk of cardiovascular disease and heart attack is
    a. anger and hostility
    b. time urgency and impatience
    c. sensation and stimulus seeking
    d. competitiveness and achievement orientation
11. Recent research suggests that men and women tend to use different coping styles when under stress. Women more often use
    a. religion and spiritual coping
    b. problem-oriented coping
    c. emotion-focused coping
    d. humour and distraction coping
12. Approximately what percentage of people who start an exercise program continue it for up to six months?
    a. 80
    b. 60
    c. 70
    d. 50
13. The psychological disorder that some evidence has associated with an increased risk for cancer is
    a. depression
    b. anxiety
    c. anorexia nervosa
    d. substance abuse
14. The oncologist described Sarah, a newly diagnosed patient with lung cancer, as having the classic Type C personality. Sarah is likely to be
    a. uncooperative, hostile, and oppositional
    b. assertive, extroverted, and achievement oriented
    c. hostile, angry, and extremely vocal
    d. cooperative, unassertive, and compliant
15. Which of the following statements most accurately characterizes the relationship between pain and psychological disorders?
    a. Psychological problems seldom have much influence on physical pain.
    b. Pain is linked to psychological distress regardless of person or context.
    c. Pain must be treated and reduced before psychological problems are addressed.
    d. Pain may cause psychological distress, and psychological distress may make the experience of pain worse.

16. Physicians are often reluctant to prescribe opiate medications for patients with severe chronic pain because opiates
   a. significantly decrease sexual desire and performance
   b. are more expensive than synthetic alternatives available
   c. quickly lose their effectiveness in relieving chronic pain
   d. are the most commonly abused prescription drugs

17. Which of the following statements about insomnia is true?
   a. Most insomnia is caused by medical disease, not stress.
   b. Insomnia is a chronic problem that affects more than 50% of the population.
   c. Insomnia is more common among women and older adults than other groups in the population.
   d. Sleep difficulties are always a normal part of adolescence.

18. Andre has a desk job and is overweight. Because several members of his family have diabetes, the doctor recommended a program for Andre emphasizing healthy diet and exercise. This program focuses on
   a. primary prevention
   b. secondary prevention
   c. coping skills
   d. psychological medicine

19. Using self-monitoring, biofeedback, coping skills, and relaxation techniques to improve health is known as
   a. restorative health counselling
   b. primary prevention
   c. stress management
   d. psychosomatics

Answers:
1 d, 2 d, 3 c, 4 b, 5 a, 6 a, 7 b, 8 c, 9 c, 10 a, 11 c, 12 d, 13 a, 14 d, 15 d, 16 d, 17 c, 18 b, 19 c.

chapter 15

Sashkin/Shutterstock

abnormal psychology

legal and ethical issues

Therapists Julie Ponder and Connell Watkins were convicted of reckless child abuse and sentenced to 16 years in prison after a young girl died during a "rebirthing" therapy session in April 2000. During the rebirthing session, 10-year-old Candace Newmaker was wrapped tightly in a blanket and pushed on with pillows in an effort to re-create the birth process. Watkins, who was neither licensed nor registered to conduct therapy, held the rebirthing session in her home. At the trial, jurors saw and heard Candace on video begging for her life from under her fabric "womb." Throughout the 70-minute tape, Candace begs the therapists to get off her and let her breathe. At one point, as she cries and pleads for her life, the four adults present pushed even harder on the girl, putting all their adult weight on top of the 32 kg fourth-grader. Here are excerpts from the tape:

CANDACE NEWMAKER: I can't do it. (Screams) I'm gonna die.

JULIE PONDER: Do you want to be reborn or do you want to stay in there and die?

CANDACE NEWMAKER: Quit pushing on me, please. . . . I'm gonna die now.

JULIE PONDER: Do you want to die?

CANDACE NEWMAKER: No, but I'm about to. . . . Please, please I can't breathe. . . .

CANDACE NEWMAKER: Can you let me have some oxygen? You mean, like you want me to die for real?

JULIE PONDER: Uh huh.

CANDACE NEWMAKER: Die right now and go to heaven?

JULIE PONDER: Go ahead and die right now. For real. For real.

CANDACE NEWMAKER: Get off. I'm sick. Get off. Where am I supposed to come out? Where? How can I get there?

CONNELL WATKINS: Just go ahead and die. It's easier. . . . It takes a lot of courage to be born.

CANDACE NEWMAKER: You said you would give me oxygen.

CONNELL WATKINS: You gotta fight for it. . . . (Candace vomits and defecates.)

CONNELL WATKINS: Stay in there with the poop and vomit.

CANDACE NEWMAKER: Help! I can't breathe. I can't breathe. It's hot. I can't breathe. . . .

CONNELL WATKINS: Getting pretty tight in there.

JULIE PONDER: Yep . . . less and less air all the time.

JULIE PONDER: She gets to be stuck in her own puke and poop.

CONNELL WATKINS: Uh huh. It's her own life. She's a quitter.

CANDACE NEWMAKER: No. . . . (This is Candace's last word.)

Radford, B. *Skeptical Inquirer*. Copyright © 2001 by the Committee for the Scientific Investigation of Claims of the Paranormal.

abnormal psychology legal and ethical issues

learning objectives

After reading this chapter, you should be able to:

15.1
Understand legal, ethical, and professional issues related to the practice of psychology.

15.2
Discuss the positive and negative aspects of deinstitutionalization.

15.3
Understand the difference between criminal and civil commitment.

15.4
Identify the reasons for involuntary commitment for psychiatric services.

15.5
Describe documents crucial to the development of rights for research participants.

15.6
Give reasons why some cultural groups may be reluctant to participate in research.

The tragic case of Candace Newmaker illustrates what can happen when untrained (or undertrained) therapists use a treatment for which there is no scientific support. Certainly, this is a very dramatic example, but many therapists use untested or poorly tested treatments every day. Why would these therapists use such a dangerous procedure? There are many reasons, including lack of clinical experience, inability to appropriately evaluate the supporting research, and mistaken beliefs about treatment safety and efficacy (Doust & Del Mar, 2004). Some therapists deny that empirical data alone should be used to determine whether a therapy works. They argue that *clinical expertise* is equally important. However, from the scientist-practitioner perspective that we have used throughout this text, clinical experience alone is no substitute for data that emerge from well-controlled, internally and externally valid, empirical studies.

In this chapter, we examine legal, ethical, and professional issues relevant to understanding abnormal behaviour and its treatment. Why do we include these issues in a book on abnormal psychology? Quite simply, by offering clinical services or conducting research, psychologists assume obligations to patients, to research participants, and to society. To the person seeking treatment, psychologists have the responsibility of practising in their area of expertise, using treatments that are not harmful (and that preferably have a strong scientific basis), and never doing anything that would sacrifice their patient's health and safety. Furthermore, patients have the right to choose whether to participate in treatment, to choose the type of treatment (pharmacological, psychological), and to expect that their participation in therapy will remain confidential. In a research study, participants have the right to be fully informed of all study requirements and the right to refuse to participate. Their participation in a project must clearly involve more benefits than risks, and their rights and dignity must be respected.

As a society, we sometimes decide that protecting the public from potential risk is more important than the rights of an individual in treatment or the needs of a researcher. To protect the public, psychologists might inform appropriate third parties if a patient threatens bodily harm to another person (Canadian Psychological Association, 2000). Sometimes courts decide that people with mental illness who have been arrested for a crime can be forced to take medications to treat their condition. In these instances, basic rights such as the right to confidentiality and the right to refuse treatment are compromised to protect society. In the next section, we examine society's laws and psychologists' ethical obligations when they provide clinical services.

Law, Ethics, and Issues of Treatment

15.1 Understand legal, ethical, and professional issues related to the practice of psychology.

15.2 Discuss the positive and negative aspects of deinstitutionalization.

Many laws regulate common activities such as driving a car, buying and consuming alcohol, voting, and getting married. Other laws strictly prohibit actions such as driving while intoxicated, breaking and entering, and assault. Still other laws regulate the practice of various professions, such as psychology, to protect vulnerable people from unqualified practitioners.

In contrast to laws, **ethics** are accepted values that provide guidance in making sound moral judgments (Bersoff, 2003). Groups including families, religions, universities, and professional organizations develop ethics to guide their members' behaviour. For psychology in Canada, the Canadian Psychological Association's code of ethics guides the behaviour of psychologists (Canadian Psychological Association, 2000). As in many other countries, the Canadian code of ethics contains four principles that should be considered whenever psychologists make decisions concerning ethical issues. Ethical decision making can be complex, and the principles may sometimes come into conflict with one another. The following are the four principles, ordered according to the weight each should generally play whenever they conflict:

1. *Respect for the dignity of persons:* This emphasizes moral rights and the right to privacy and confidentiality, and should be given the highest weight, except when there is a clear and imminent danger to the physical safety of any person, whether they be a patient, research participant, student, or some other individual. One important example of respect for the dignity of persons involves informed consent for research studies or experimental treatments. To obtain informed consent, it is important that the participants understand the nature, risks, and benefits of whatever experiment or treatment that they are participating in, and that they are free to give and withdraw their consent at any time.
2. *Responsible caring:* Responsible caring requires that psychologists be competent in whatever activity that they are conducting (e.g., conducting a diagnostic assessment or implementing a given type of treatment). Ethical psychologists know the

limits of their competence. Responsible caring also requires that psychological services are carried out only in ways that maximize benefit and minimize harm.

3. *Integrity in relationships:* Psychologists are expected to demonstrate the highest integrity in all their relationships. This includes values such as being accurate and honest in their appraisals. For example, a psychologist might be asked to conduct a psychological assessment of a client who was involved in a work-related accident resulting in a possible psychological disorder (e.g., posttraumatic stress disorder). The psychologist might be hired by the client's lawyer, who is clearly invested in seeing that the client receive monetary or other compensation for the accident. In conducting the assessment, the psychologist's report must be accurate and unbiased, and not simply a report supporting the views of the client's lawyer.
4. *Responsibility to society:* Psychologists need to recognize how their actions or inactions affect society at large, while also respecting the dignity of their patients or clients. Responsibility to society also includes educating communities about the nature of psychological problems (e.g., workplace depression) and how such problems can be effectively addressed.

When psychologists join a professional organization such as the Canadian Psychological Association, they agree to behave in a manner consistent with the association's code of ethics. Failure to do so could result in expulsion from the association. Read the following paragraph and identify which ethical principles were violated.

Dr. Smith is conducting research on psychotherapy. He recruits his students to participate in the research project, promising them extra credit in class. He promises that any information they provide will remain confidential. After looking at the videotapes, he realizes that responses illustrate "classic" responses, and he decides to use the tapes in a professional workshop he will do next month.

Dr. Smith violated the aspirational goals of *integrity in relationships* (he was not honest about how he would use the videotapes). He also violated the aspirational goal of *respect for people's dignity* because showing the videos at a workshop without the permission of his students violates their right to confidentiality.

Other guidance on professional practice comes from regional laws. Each region (e.g., each province or territory) has a licensing board that sets the criteria for who can practise as a psychologist. When psychologists apply for a licence, they must agree to adhere to a regional code of ethics (similar to that of many professional organizations) as well as its laws and statutes. If psychologists fail to do so, their licence could be revoked, resulting in an inability to practise. Both licensing laws and codes of ethics promote positive behaviour, and the vast majority of psychologists adhere to both sets of standards.

Even when ethical standards are being carefully upheld, psychologists and society struggle to provide optimal treatment to people with psychological disorders. Throughout history, favoured approaches to treatment have varied. One of the most dramatic changes has been the shift in views regarding the need for institutionalizing patients. Currently, we are in a phase of deinstitutionalization.

Deinstitutionalization

Since the time of Hippocrates, physicians have advocated removing patients from society and housing them in environments where treatment could be provided in a humane setting (see Chapter 1). This idea sparked the nineteenth-century "humane movement," which advocated the *removal* of mentally ill persons from the community to hospital-like or residential settings where they could receive appropriate and adequate care. But many

Until the late 1960s, people with psychological disorders were hospitalized in restrictive settings, and most were simply confined without treatment. Few efficacious psychotherapies or medications existed at that time.

Jerry Cooke/Science Source

such hospitals and residences proved so inadequate—even harmful—that a twentieth-century movement arose to get patients out of institutions and back into the community. At the time, the idea was that needed care would be provided in smaller, more homelike environments where patients could live with fewer restrictions.

Confining patients in hospitals was common mainly because until the 1960s, few treatments controlled aggressive behaviours effectively, making institutionalization the simplest way to protect the public. Institutionalization was also common for people with schizophrenia and mood disorders because effective medications for serious psychological disorders had yet to be discovered. In many Western countries, including Canada, psychiatric hospitals had steadily growing patient populations up until the 1950s to 1960s (Freeman, 1994; Talbott, 1979/2004). By mid-century, however, it was the institutional setting that was considered inhumane. Hospitals were grossly understaffed, treatment was primarily limited to medications, and few, if any, patients were ever discharged. Few psychosocial treatments were available, and most patients spent their days in their beds or watching television. Discharging patients from these institutions so that they could obtain better care in the community was promoted as the humane alternative.

Beginning in the 1960s, effective medications became available, and treatment options expanded dramatically. Many mental health professionals and others outside the profession believed that when properly medicated, people with serious psychological disorders could function outside institutions if appropriate medical and community support were provided. So began the process of **deinstitutionalization**, the release of inpatients from hospitals to community treatment settings. Proponents of deinstitutionalization argued that community care would be better and cheaper than institutional care, particularly when medications constituted at least part of the treatment. Although medications could not cure serious mental illnesses, they could control seriously disordered *behaviour*, allowing some people to leave the locked wards and contribute to society.

In a group home, people with psychological disorders can live in an environment less restricted than institutions and learn skills necessary to stay in the community.

BelayaMedvedica/Fotolia

If we look only at the reductions in numbers of hospitalized patients, the deinstitutionalization movement was very successful. Deinstitutionalization occurred in a dramatic fashion, with many psychiatric hospitals either closing or drastically reducing the number of patients staying there. To illustrate, from 1962 to 1977, the population of Canadian provincial psychiatric hospitals fell by 78%, despite the fact that the number of mentally ill people continued to rise as the Canadian population grew (Freeman, 1994).

Deinstitutionalization clearly reduced the number of people involuntarily housed in mental hospitals, but as early as 1979, signs emerged that the community care solution would fail (Talbott, 1979/2004). While the total number of people hospitalized for reasons of mental illness decreased during this time, the number of people with mental illness who were incarcerated in prisons *increased* dramatically (Lamb & Weinberger, 2005). These data suggest that the movement never achieved its original objective: to allow those with psychological disorders to reintegrate into the community.

Why did the deinstitutionalization movement fail? Perhaps the most important reason was that discharged patients did not receive the outpatient care and supervision they needed. Outpatient clinics, most of which in Canada were government funded, were understaffed and could not provide the treatment needed by patients with severe and chronic disorders. Furthermore, the available staff members were often inadequately trained to deal with people suffering from severe psychological disorders. Patients with schizophrenia, for example, often did not keep clinic appointments and stopped taking their medication, resulting in relapse. Without continued treatment, their mental status deteriorated and many patients became a danger to themselves and society, again necessitating forced removal from the community, sometimes to prisons.

The lack of appropriate follow-up care for deinstitutionalized patients illustrates the basic flaw in the deinstitutionalization process, which involves much more than unlocking the hospital doors and allowing patients to leave. Discharged patients must have appropriate places in the community where they can live, get psychological support, and have easy access to mental health services. Furthermore, most of the patients had been unemployed for many years, so they needed vocational counselling and vocational rehabilitation services to help them re-enter the workforce. Many people with psychological disorders who were released from hospitals quickly became homeless. This additional negative effect of deinstitutionalization became a major social problem in many cities.

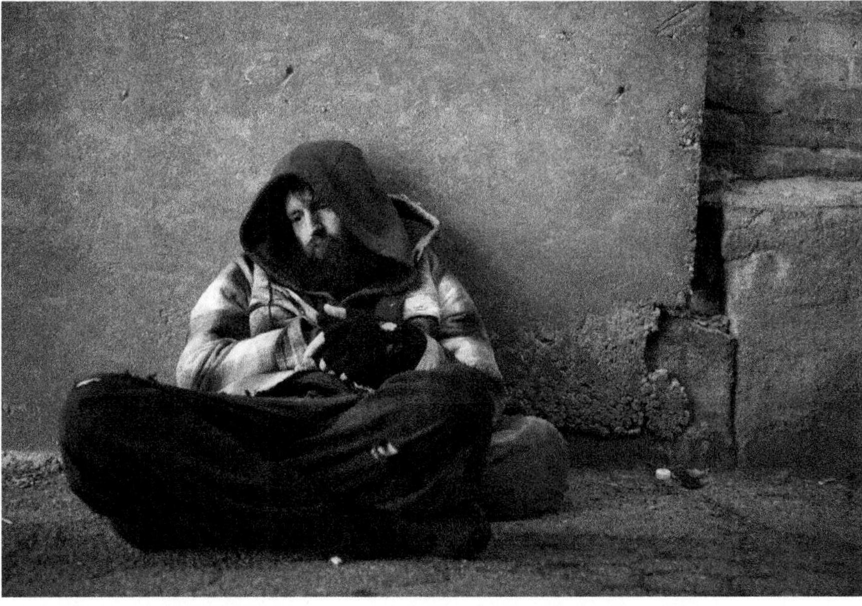

When people with psychological disorders are released from institutions but not given appropriate social supports, they may have difficulty coping with the demands of everyday life. A significant number become homeless.

Rubberball/Brand X Pictures/Getty Images

Ethics and Responsibility

15.3 Understand the difference between criminal and civil commitment.

One of the most negative effects of deinstitutionalization was that many people with psychological disorders ended up living on city streets. Their dishevelled appearance and active psychotic symptoms created concern and sometimes fear among community residents (Talbott, 1979/2004), although people with mental disorders are far more often victims of violence than perpetrators (Brekke et al., 2001; Crocker et al., 2015a). Depending on the particular sample, 33% to 73% of those who are homeless have psychological disorders, which is much higher than that of the general population (Cougnard et al., 2006; Langle et al., 2005; Mojtabai, 2005).

At particularly high risk for homelessness are people with schizophrenia. Once they leave an institutionalized setting, patients with this disorder often stop taking their medication, and their symptoms return (see Chapter 10). Among people with serious mental illnesses (e.g., schizophrenia, bipolar disorder) who were being treated in a large public mental health system, 15% were homeless (Folsom et al., 2005). People who were more likely to be homeless were also more likely to have substance use disorders.

If we consider deinstitutionalization as a process rather than a singular event, it appears that homelessness among people with psychological disorders is not a problem of deinstitutionalization per se but of the implementation of the process. Successful deinstitutionalization requires continued outpatient care as well as the skills and resources for living independently (Lamb & Bachrach, 2001). When this does not occur, recently discharged patients may find themselves returning temporarily to locked or structured institutions (including prison) or requiring rehospitalization (Lamb & Weinberger, 2005). Even when an adequate community treatment plan exists, patients' adjustment is difficult. In one sample, only 33% of recently discharged patients were living stable lives in the community and did not require rehospitalization (Lamb & Weinberger, 2005). Clearly, clinicians working with seriously mentally ill people need to be able to identify which patients need which resources to move successfully from a hospital to a community setting. When patients with psychological disorders cannot care for themselves in the community, or if they become a danger to themselves or others, they may have to be institutionalized against their will, a process known as *civil commitment.*

Civil Commitment

15.4 Identify the reasons for involuntary commitment for psychiatric services.

Michel was brought to the psychiatric emergency room by ambulance. His landlord had called the police because smoke was coming from under Michel's apartment door. When the police finally broke down the door, they found him burning the furniture. He explained that about a month ago, he became suspicious about his co-workers. He feared that they were reading his mind, so he quit his job. Without any other source of income, he was unable to pay his bills and the electric company shut off his heat. To stay warm, he was burning his furniture in the fireplace, creating a significant fire hazard to everyone in the building.

Michel's behaviour (burning furniture in the fireplace) constituted a danger to himself and to others living in the building. **Civil commitment** is a government-initiated procedure that forces involuntary treatment on people who are judged to have a mental illness. It is important to note that that civil commitment does *not* mean the person has committed a crime. Instead, civil commitment is instituted when the person is at risk for harming themselves or others.

Canadian law contains two broad rationales for civil commitment. The first is based on the philosophy that the government has a humanitarian responsibility to care for its weaker members (i.e., the concept of *parens patriae* or "the state as parent"). Under *parens patriae* authority, civil commitment may be justified when a mentally disturbed person is unable to care for themselves. The second rationale for civil commitment is based on the government's *police power*—its duty to protect the public safety, health, and welfare. Here, civil commitment may arise when the person poses a danger to him- or herself or to other people.

Most jurisdictions provide two types of civil commitment procedures: emergency procedures and formal procedures. *Emergency commitment procedures* allow an acutely disturbed individual to be temporarily confined in a psychiatric hospital, typically for no more than a few days. Physicians determine whether an emergency commitment is required. Obviously, such action is taken only when a mental disorder is very serious, and the risk that the patient is dangerous to self or others appears to be very high. Formal procedures for commitment may involve longer durations, which may be mandated by a court.

During the early twentieth century, civil commitment usually meant inpatient hospitalization, and sometimes it still does. However, with the deinstitutionalization movement, there has been a shift to **outpatient commitment**. This involves a court order directing a person suffering from severe mental illness to comply with a specified, individualized treatment plan that has been designed to prevent relapse and deterioration. Persons appropriate for this intervention are those who need ongoing psychiatric care owing to severe illness but who are unable or unwilling to engage in ongoing, voluntary, outpatient care (Lamb & Weinberger, 2005). Outpatient commitment is more coercive than voluntary treatment, but is less coercive than inpatient hospitalization (Swartz & Monahan, 2001) because the person remains in the community with continued access to social supports.

In some instances, outpatient commitment is a condition for being discharged from a hospital. It is also an alternative to hospitalization for people who are currently in the community and whose condition is deteriorating. Outpatient commitment also may be used as a preventive measure for people considered to be at high risk for psychological deterioration and possible hospitalization (Monahan et al., 2001a).

Criminal Commitment

Civil commitment is a response to behaviour that poses a danger to the self or others. **Criminal commitment** occurs when a person with a psychological disorder commits a crime. Within the courtroom, those who are criminally committed may be judged to be not criminally responsible on account of a mental disorder, or incompetent to stand trial.

MENTAL ILLNESS, INSANITY, AND CRIMINAL RESPONSIBILITY Insanity is a *legal* term, not a psychological disorder. Determining whether a person is sane or insane occurs as a result of legal proceedings. How such a determination has changed over time and differs among countries. The idea that insanity should limit criminal responsibility is based on the rationale that the defendant lacked the capacity to distinguish right from wrong. This is known as the mental disorder defence. Committing an illegal act is not the same as committing a crime. To be convicted of committing a crime, a person must possess ***mens rea***, which is Latin for a guilty mind or criminal intent. To be considered guilty of committing a crime, the person must engage in illegal behaviour and have *criminal intent*. In many instances, people with psychological disorders lack the intent to commit the crime with which they are charged. Contemporary laws concerning this defence have their roots in the **M'Naghten Rule**, which was established in England in 1843.

Daniel M'Naghten, possibly as a result of paranoid schizophrenia, believed that the English Tory party was persecuting him. He planned to kill the British prime minister but killed the prime minister's secretary instead.

M'Naghten was tried for the crime, but the court ruled that he was not responsible for his actions if (a) he did not know what he was doing, or (b) he did not know that his actions were wrong.

There have been several revisions to the standard originally established by the M'Naghten Rule. For example, in 1929, the United States introduced the "irresistible impulse" test, allowing consideration of whether the defendant suffered from a "diseased mental condition" that did not allow the resistance of an irresistible impulse, acknowledging the idea of volition (freedom to choose or the ability to control behaviour). In 1985, Canadian Criminal Code allowed a person to be found **not guilty by reason of insanity** (NGRI). People found NGRI were automatically placed in a secure psychiatric facility, indefinitely, "until the pleasure of the Lieutenant Governor is known." That meant that a person was detained until the mental disorder had improved to an extent that would justify release. A person could be detained for a longer period than he or she would have served in prison if convicted for the crime (Gray & O'Reilly, 2005). Some people judged to be NGRI were held in psychiatric hospitals without receiving adequate treatment. Later changes to the criminal code rectified this problem.

Changes came with the case of *R. v. Swain* (1991), which challenged the insanity defence in a number of ways. Owen Swain was charged with aggravated assault after attacking his wife and two children. At the time he was psychotic; he believed his family was being attacked by devils and that he had to perform certain rituals to protect them, including physically assaulting them. Owen was hospitalized, successfully treated with antipsychotic medication, and then released on bail. At his trial, the Crown raised the issue of insanity, despite Owen's objections and those of his lawyer. Owen was judged NGRI, which meant that he would be involuntarily placed in a psychiatric hospital. He appealed the decision, arguing that it violated his rights for the Crown to raise the issue of insanity and to automatically incarcerate people judged to be NGRI. Owen's appeal was successful, which led to important reforms in the Canadian version of the insanity defence.

As a result, the Canadian Criminal Code was amended to give the accused person greater procedural and civil rights. The amendment was an attempt to balance the goals of fair and humane treatment of the offender against the safety of the public (Schneider et al., 2000). Major changes included reductions in how long an accused person could be detained in a psychiatric facility, and changes in the procedures for making appeals. The mental disorder defence was also changed, with NGRI being replaced with **not criminally responsible on account of a mental disorder** (NCRMD). Thus, the Canadian Criminal Code now states that,

> no person is criminally responsible for an act committed or an omission made while suffering from a mental disorder that rendered the person incapable of appreciating the nature and quality of the act or omission or of knowing that it was wrong.
>
> Moreover,
>
> Although personality disorders or psychopathic [antisocial] personalities are capable of constituting a disease of the mind, the defence of insanity is not made out where the accused has the necessary understanding of the nature, character and consequences of the act, but merely lacks appropriate feelings for the victim or lacks feelings of remorse or guilt for what he [or she] has done, even though such lack of feeling stems from a disease of the mind. (Greenspan, 1998, p. 50)

NGRI and NCRMD share many similarities, although there are some important differences. Under NCRMD, for example, the defendant is now considered to be "not criminally responsible" instead of "not guilty." This change more explicitly recognizes that the defendant committed the offence, as opposed to being not guilty (Davis, 1993; Miladinovic & Lukassen, 2014). Under NCRMD, the defendant or his or her legal counsel may raise the insanity defence at any time. The prosecution (i.e., the Crown) can only raise this defence after the accused has been found guilty. The side raising the possibility of NCRMD bears the burden of proving it. Unlike NGRI, under NCRMD an indeterminate confinement in a psychiatric facility is not allowed. There are three possible outcomes under NCRMD, which take into consideration the person's mental condition, his or her needs for treatment, and the protection of society:

- *Absolute discharge.* This is required by law if the person is not a significant threat to the public.
- *Conditional discharge.* For example, discharge in the community on the proviso that the person receives appropriate treatment for his or her mental disorder.
- *Detention in hospital, with periodic assessment to determine whether continued confinement is warranted.* The decision for continued detention is based on several considerations, including the need to protect the public and the mental condition of the person.

Do defendants "walk" or "get away with murder" if they are found NCRMD? Some are incarcerated in psychiatric institutions for much shorter periods of time than if they had been sentenced to prison, while others actually are incarcerated for much longer periods. The duration of incarceration depends on a number of factors, including the seriousness of the offence and the extent to which the defendant is judged to be dangerous to self or others (Crocker et al., 2015b; Davis, 1993; Holley, Arboleda-Flórez, & Crisanti, 1998). Under the current law, a review board decides what will happen to a defendant who is judged to be NCRMD. The board can make its decisions without the need for approval from the Lieutenant Governor. The goal of the review board is to select an option that is appropriate and entails the least amount of restriction on the defendant's rights and freedoms.

In the event of detainment in a psychiatric hospital, government legislation requires that the duration of the stay is set, at least initially, such that the period of detention cannot exceed the maximum sentence that would have been applied if the person had been found guilty of the crime without being NCRMD. However, the duration of hospitalization can be extended for a further period if, for example, the person is judged to be dangerous to self or others. Under these circumstances, the person would be placed under civil commitment (Greenberg & Gratzer, 1994).

Canadian FOCUS

The Insanity Defence in Canada: Three Case Studies

The mental disorder defence is not often used in Canada or in other countries. Even when it is used, few people are judged to be NCRMD. Such cases represent less than 1% of adult criminal court cases in Canada (Miladinovic & Lukassen, 2014). Thus, in any given year there are not many people who are judged to be NCRMD. The burden of proof substantially influences the meaning and likely success of the mental disorder defence. According to Canadian law, the defendant (or his or her legal representative) may raise the issue of NCRMD at any time. In contrast, in order to protect the rights of the defendant, the prosecution may raise the possibility of NCRMD only after the defendant has been found guilty. The side raising the possibility of NCRMD bears the responsibility for proving the person is NCRMD.

The following examples will give you an idea of the sorts of mental health problems required for a person to be deemed (or not deemed) NCRMD and the manner in which cases of NCRMD are handled in the criminal justice system.

André Dallaire. During the early hours of November 5, 1995, 34-year-old André Dallaire, a thin, bespectacled former convenience store worker, broke into the residence of then Prime Minister Jean Chrétien. Armed with a knife, Dallaire climbed the fence surrounding Chrétien's residence, smashed a window, and entered the house with the intention of slitting the prime minister's throat. Outside the bedroom where the prime minister was sleeping, Dallaire encountered Chrétien's wife, Aline. She fled to the bedroom, locked the door, and called the police. While waiting for help to arrive, Prime Minister Chrétien brandished a stone sculpture, just in case Dallaire broke through the door. Shortly afterward, the RCMP arrived and took Dallaire into custody.

A psychiatric assessment revealed that Dallaire was delusional and hallucinating. He heard an inner voice commanding him to kill Chrétien, while another voice told him to stop. Dallaire believed he was a secret agent whose mission was to avenge the "No" side's victory in the Quebec referendum on independence (Fisher, 1996). Dallaire believed he would be glorified for liberating Canada from a "traitorous" prime minister. Thus, he was suffering from delusions of grandeur.

Dallaire had been suffering from paranoid schizophrenia since the age of 16. The judge ruled that Dallaire's intent to kill was the product of a severe mental disorder. Although Dallaire was found guilty of attempted murder, he was not held criminally responsible for his actions because he was suffering from a mental disorder at the time, which prevented him from appreciating the nature and wrongfulness of his actions. As a result, Dallaire was judged to be NCRMD.

After being sent to the Royal Ottawa Hospital and placed on antipsychotic medication, Dallaire was no longer delusional or hearing voices, and expressed remorse for his actions. The court ordered a conditional discharge in which Dallaire was released to an Ottawa-area group home and allowed to come and go as long as he was escorted by a group home staff member (Fisher, 1996). He remained there until August 1996. At that point a review board decided that he was no longer a threat and so was free to move about unsupervised. However, he was not permitted to go within 500 metres of the prime minister or his residence, and was required to continue seeing a psychiatrist and to take antipsychotic medication. In a media interview in 1998, Dallaire publicly apologized for his prior behaviour, reassured the Canadian public that he was now on medication, and that he hoped the Chrétiens were able to forgive his actions (http://www.radio-canada.ca/nouvelles/07/7069.htm. Accessed 25 April, 2008).

Blair Donnelly. In 2006, Blair Donnelly, a 48-eight-year old pulp mill worker in Kitimat, B.C., and former pastor, stabbed his daughter Stephanie, aged 16, to death in the family home. During his trial, the judge ruled that he was in a manic state with psychotic features at the time of the killing and was judged to be NCRMD. A forensic assessment conducted as part of his trial revealed that Blair believed that God had instructed him to kill his daughter.

(continued)

On the morning of the murder, Blair began praying and studying the bible, and claiming that he had been receiving messages from God that he was to kill his wife. He walked around home in the presence of his wife with a knife buried in his jacket. Due to his evidently strange behaviour, Blair's wife asked his pastor to attend their home and they prayed together asking for guidance. Blair did not disclose his intentions or homicidal thoughts during this meeting. After his wife left for work, Donnelly visited with friends and had what has been referred to as unusual conversations. At one point he saw a neighbour's dog carrying a toy skunk, which he interpreted as meaning that "God thinks I'm a skunk" for not following through with killing his wife (Ritchie, 2008).

When Blair returned home that evening, he saw his daughter working on a computer. He took that as a sign from God that he was to kill her. Blair believed that if he didn't kill her, then he would have to kill his entire family. His wife returned home to find Stephanie lying in a pool of blood, dead in the living room. Blair was later found praying in front of a church, with his hands covered in blood (Carrigg, 2008; CBC News, 2008). According to his defence lawyer,

> They were a model Canadian family up to the point of this incident. His [Blair's] conduct that evening can only be explained by aberrant behaviour from a mental disorder. (Carrigg, 2008, p. A3)

But signs of psychological disturbance were apparent years earlier. Several years before the murder, Blair had to leave his position as a pastor at an Ontario church because of fears of being attacked by demons. He believed that he was under constant threat of Satanic attack because he was doing such special work for the Lord. He feared that demons were lurking from the roofs of buildings, peering out from dark alleyways, and following him as he walked down the streets. Finally, he became exhausted and depressed because of the perceived harassment by demons and left the ministry (Carrigg, 2008; CBC News, 2008).

The court ordered that Blair receive an evaluation at a forensic psychiatric unit in Port Coquitlam, B.C. As a result of a psychiatric review, it was decided that Blair would remain in Port Coquitlam's Forensic Psychiatric Institute until his mental condition improved (with the aid of antipsychotic medication). Once he had recovered and was deemed no longer a threat to himself or others, then there was the possibility of escorted access to the community, and possibly a discharge from the institute at some point in the future. It was required that he adhere to any ongoing assessment or treatment deemed necessary, and that he not possess any kind of weapon or any drug unless it was prescribed by a doctor (Heir, 2008). Blair's wife sold the family home shortly after the killing, and she and her surviving daughter moved to Alberta (Carrigg, 2008; CBC News, 2008).

Luca Rocco Magnotta. Luka Magnotta (born Eric Newman), a Canadian former porn actor and sex trade worker, was convicted of first-degree murder along with other crimes including committing an indignity to a human body and criminally harassing the Canadian prime minister and other members of parliament. Magnotta murdered and dismembered Lin Jun, an international student attending Concordia University, and then mailed Jun's body parts to elementary schools in Vancouver and to federal political party offices in Ottawa. A video depicting the murder was posted online in May 2012, after which Magnotta fled Canada and become the subject of an international manhunt. In June 2012, he was apprehended in a café in Berlin while reading news about himself. Extradited to Canada, he was convicted of first-degree murder. His legal defence claimed NCRMD. Psychiatric evaluations found evidence that Magnotta had a history of psychopathology, possibly borderline personality disorder or schizophrenia. However, the Crown prosecutor successfully argued that the murder was premediated and that Magnotta was purposeful, mindful, ultra-organized, and ultimately responsible for his actions. The defence's argument for NCRMD was not accepted by the court. Magnotta was sentenced to serve a mandatory life sentence (25 years) and a concurrent sentence of 19 years for other charges (www.thestar.com/news/canada/2014/12/23/luka_magnotta_is_convicted_of_firstdegree_murder.html#; www.cbc.ca/news/canada/montreal/luka-magnotta-trial-jury-now-sequestered-1.2871549; www.usatoday.com/story/news/world/2014/12/23/canada-killing-dismemberment-life-sentence/20825699/; montrealgazette.com/news/local-news/psychiatrists-report-chronicles-the-making-of-luka-magnotta).

FITNESS TO STAND TRIAL

Elizabeth Ann Smart, aged 14, was kidnapped from her bedroom on June 5, 2002. She was found alive nine months later not far from her home in the company of two homeless adults, Brian David Mitchell and Wanda Ileen Barzee. It was alleged that Mitchell and Barzee had kidnapped Elizabeth to be Mitchell's second wife. After his arrest, a psychological competency evaluation revealed that Mitchell suffered from a delusional disorder. Although he understood the charges against him, he had an impaired capacity to (a) disclose to counsel pertinent facts, events, and states of mind, and engage in reasoned choice of legal strategies and options; (b) manifest appropriate courtroom behaviour; and (c) testify relevantly. During court appearances, Mitchell would begin to sing and had to be forcibly removed from the courtroom. His disorder substantially interfered with his relationship with counsel and his ability to participate in the proceedings against him. On July 26, 2005, he was found incompetent to stand trial and was committed to a psychiatric unit for treatment intended to restore him to competency.

In March 2010, a federal judge ruled that Mitchell was faking mental illness, and on November 1, 2010, his trial began. However, because Mitchell disrupted the court proceedings by singing hymns when he entered the courtroom, he watched his trial on video from his holding cell. In December 2010, Brian David Mitchell was found guilty of the kidnapping of Elizabeth Smart. As the verdict was announced, Mitchell loudly sang, "He died, the Great Redeemer died."

Brian David Mitchell initially was judged by the court to be incompetent to stand trial for the crime of kidnapping and imprisoning Elizabeth Ann Smart. Later a judge ruled he was faking, and he was found guilty of the crimes.

Douglas C Pizac/AP Images

To receive a fair trial, someone accused of a crime must have a rational and factual understanding of court procedures and must be able to consult with his or her lawyer and assist in the defence. An accused person who is considered to be so functionally impaired as to be unable to understand legal proceedings and participate in his or her own defence is considered unfit to stand trial. Under section 2 of the Canadian Criminal Code, a person is considered unfit to stand trial under the following conditions:

> "Unfit to stand trial" means unable on account of mental disorder to conduct a defence at any stage of the proceedings before a verdict is rendered or to instruct counsel to do so, and, in particular, unable on account of a mental disorder to: (a) understand the nature or object of the proceedings, (b) understand the possible consequences of the proceedings, or (c) communicate with counsel.

The question of fitness refers to the defendant's mental state at the time of the trial, not to the mental state at the time of the alleged crime. A person is assumed fit unless there are reasonable grounds to suggest otherwise. A person can be fit to stand trial, yet found to be NCRMD. This would happen, for example, if a person was psychotic when a crime was committed, and then became nonpsychotic (e.g., with the help of medication) by the time he or she went to trial. Note also that the legal definition of "unfitness" is not the same as the psychologist's definition of mental disorder. Even a

REAL people REAL disorders

Kenneth Bianchi, Patty Hearst, and Dr. Martin Orne

In October 1977 and February 1978, 10 women were found tortured, strangled to death, and abandoned in the hills surrounding Los Angeles, thus giving the offender the name The Hillside Strangler. The police finally arrested cousins Kenneth Bianchi and Angelo Buono, both of whom had committed the crimes. After his capture, Bianchi claimed that he had a multiple personality disorder (MPD—now called DID or dissociative identity disorder; see Chapter 5) and that he was insane. Two experts in the disorder examined Bianchi and reported the existence of a second personality, Steve. Both experts agreed that Bianchi was insane, even though people with multiple personality usually have at least three separate personalities and Bianchi did not.

Martin Orne, M.D., Ph.D. (1927–2000), was a preeminent scientist who conducted research in many different areas of psychology including hypnosis, memory, and lie detection. Because of his expertise in basic studies of memory and lie detection, Dr. Orne had developed procedures to determine when people were faking a diagnosis or faking being hypnotized.

Called by the prosecution to conduct an additional examination of Mr. Bianchi, Dr. Orne first discussed MPD with

(continued)

him. Bianchi told Dr. Orne about Steve. Dr. Orne told Bianchi that it was rare for someone with MPD to have only two personalities—most people had at least three. Dr. Orne then hypnotized Bianchi, and suddenly a third personality named Bill appeared. In his court testimony, Dr. Orne pointed out that he was not better than the other clinicians, but he showed that Bianchi faked a third personality because of Dr. Orne's prehypnotic suggestion. Dr. Orne also identified another clue that Bianchi was faking MPD. During his initial examination of Mr. Bianchi, Dr. Orne asked him, under hypnosis, to imagine that his lawyer was sitting in the room; Bianchi actually stood up, walked across the room, shook hands with the imagined attorney, and insisted that Dr. Orne had to be seeing the attorney as well. Dr. Orne testified that people under deep hypnosis do not get out of their seats and attempt to shake somebody's hand unless told by the hypnotist to do so. Dr. Orne did not tell Bianchi to do that. Furthermore, deeply hypnotized subjects do not insist that others also see the image. Later, police discovered that Bianchi had numerous books on psychology, diagnostic testing, hypnosis, and criminal law in his home, suggesting that he could have studied how to present himself in an "insane" manner.

Dr. Orne was not always a witness for the prosecution. In 1976, Patricia Hearst, the heiress who had been abducted by an American radical group known as the Symbionese Liberation Army (SLA), was arrested and tried for participating in a bank robbery. Hearst's lawyers said that her abduction and torture were responsible for her actions, whereas the prosecution suggested that Hearst's appearance during the robbery (she was casually holding a gun) suggested that she was there of her own free will. Although initially concerned that she was faking, Dr. Orne conducted numerous tests, giving her many opportunities to exaggerate or fabricate her story. Unlike Bianchi, Ms. Hearst never picked up on any cues, and according to Dr. Orne, she "really, simply didn't lie" (Woo, 2000). Dr. Orne was a scientist-practitioner who developed scientific methods in a laboratory setting and then applied his research in clinical and legal settings, the embodiment of the scientist-practitioner model of psychology.

AP Images

Bianchi

Emily Carota Orne

Orne

person with untreated schizophrenia may possess enough rational understanding to be deemed fit in the eyes of the law.

THE RIGHT TO REFUSE MEDICATION/TREATMENT When faced with serious, disabling, or terminal illnesses, people often make choices about treatments. They might refuse treatments that produce serious side effects or do not improve their quality of life. With the proclamation of the 1992 *Canadian Charter of Rights and Freedoms*, there has been increasing recognition across the provinces and territories of the right for competent, even involuntarily committed patients to *refuse* treatment (Ambrosini & Crocker, 2007; Gray & O'Reilly, 2005). Today, provincial/territorial mental health legislation generally does not allow for institutionalization and compulsory treatment of people who refuse treatment, unless that person poses a threat to him- or herself or to the general public (Steller, 2003). Fortunately, most people in need of psychiatric treatment do not refuse. In fact, fewer than 10% persistently refuse treatment (Gratzer & Matas, 1994).

CONCEPT check

- As members of society, psychologists are bound to abide by laws and codes of ethics.
- The code of ethics of the Canadian Psychological Association includes the core values of respective for the dignity of persons, responsible caring, integrity of relationships, and responsibility to society.
- The deinstitutionalization movement developed to stop the process of hospitalizing psychiatric patients for the rest of their lives. However, despite the promise of deinstitutionalization,

one unfortunate outcome has been the lack of appropriate living arrangements for those with psychological disorders. The result is that many people with severe psychological disorders are homeless or in jail.

- Outpatient commitment can be used as a condition for release from an inpatient unit, as an alternative to hospitalization, or as a way to provide intensive treatment to prevent inpatient hospitalization.
- *Insanity* is a legal term, not a psychological disorder. Rarely are patients with serious psychological disorders found to be NCRMD.

critical thinking question Patients and mental health professionals alike value the right to refuse treatment. The interesting paradox is that even when patients clearly lack the capacity to understand their actions, their negative behaviour so horrifies the public that there is pressure to restore their mental faculties so that they can be imprisoned for their actions. In such instances, society's need for patients to be accountable for their actions appears to override patients' right to refuse treatment. Is it ethical to treat people who are criminally insane to punish them for committing a horrific crime?

Privacy, Confidentiality, and Privilege in Abnormal Psychology

Fiona has obsessive-compulsive disorder. She has many intrusive thoughts, but the most frightening is that when using a sharp knife, she loses control and stabs her son, severely injuring or perhaps even killing him. Fiona loves her son and is a good mother. She is horrified about these thoughts and does not want to act on them. Yet she is so afraid that she will lose control that she has taken all the knives out of the house (including the butter knives). She has also removed all the scissors. She made an appointment to see a psychologist, but she is worried. What if the psychologist thinks she is crazy?

As we have noted throughout this text, psychological disorders are accompanied by significant emotional distress. Part of this distress relates to patients' concerns that they are "crazy" or that others will think that they are "crazy." To help patients feel comfortable, mental health professionals agree that what is discussed within the therapy session will not be revealed to others. The terms *privacy*, *confidentiality*, and *privilege* describe environments that provide protection against unwilling disclosure of patient information. There are, however, certain conditions in which the therapist must violate these protections, and we address these exceptions later in the chapter when we examine the issue of duty to warn.

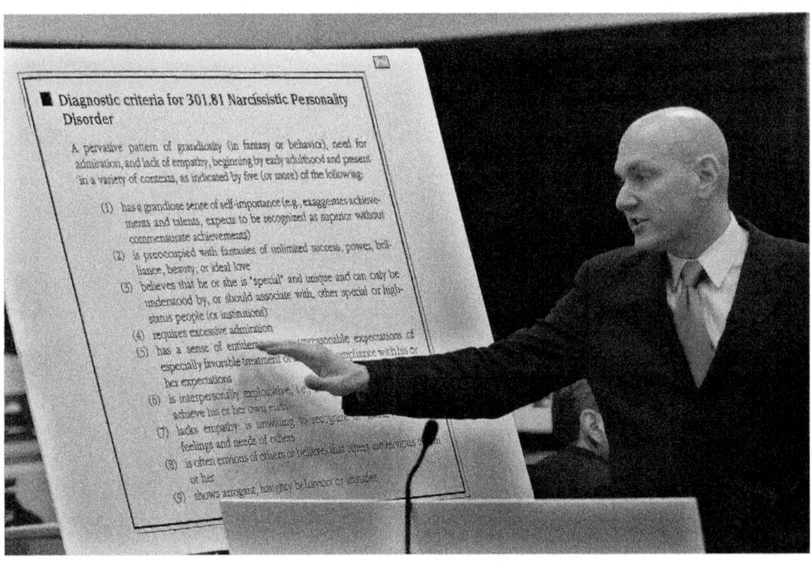

Privileged communications—such as communications between a lawyer and his or her client—are confidential exchanges that legislation explicitly protects from being revealed. Mental health practitioners in Canada generally *do not* have this privilege, and so the practitioner may be required to break confidentiality if this is ordered by the courts.

Ted Fitzgerald/AP Images

Fiona has not told anyone about her intrusive thoughts. At this time, her thoughts are private.

Privacy is a right of the individual who alone can give it away. When a person reveals thoughts, behaviours, and feelings to another person, privacy is lost. In the context of therapy, the private information shared with a therapist is considered confidential.

Confidentiality is an agreement between two parties (in this case, the therapist and patient) that private information revealed during therapy will not be discussed with others except under particular circumstances.

Although it makes her quite uncomfortable, Fiona tells the psychologist, Dr. Jones, about her thoughts. Because she and her therapist have established a therapeutic relationship, the content of her intrusive thoughts is now considered confidential. Dr. Jones may not disclose it to others, within limits.

The psychologist agrees to keep confidential the information that the patient reveals. Even if the patient decides to discuss that information, the psychologist still is bound by confidentiality. There are, however, important limits to confidentiality.

Whereas confidentiality is considered to be an ethical commitment, federal and provincial/territorial law establishes **privilege**. *Privileged communications*—such as communications between a lawyer and his or her client—are confidential exchanges that legislation explicitly protects from being revealed. Mental health practitioners in Canada generally do not have this privilege, and so the practitioner may be required to break confidentiality if this is ordered by the courts (Cram & Dobson, 1993; Mills, 2015). The therapist, for example, might be required to provide the court with details about the client's psychological problems and treatment. The exception is when a psychologist (or other mental health practitioner) is working for a lawyer or during negotiations to mediate a divorce settlement, which is when communication *would* be privileged (Truscott & Crook, 2013), although there may be exceptions, such as when the client reveals information that strongly suggests that he or she is an imminent risk for harming others (Felthous et al., 2007).

Psychologists discuss the limits to confidentiality with the patient at the start of treatment. For example, a graduate student in clinical psychology in training to provide therapy requires supervision by a senior psychologist. In supervisory sessions, the trainee shares patient information with the supervisor to make sure that the treatment is conducted appropriately. In this case, the supervisor is bound by the same confidentiality standard as the therapist. In this situation the patient would be informed that the trainee would be discussing the patient's clinical problems and treatment with the supervisor.

Other situations that require or call for exceptions to confidentiality include instances in which patients make their mental health an aspect of a lawsuit or a criminal defence strategy (such as insanity pleas or malpractice lawsuits). In these cases, confidentiality does not apply because the case cannot be decided without knowledge of the situation. Confidentiality is also limited when health insurance companies require information about diagnosis and aspects of treatment (number of sessions, frequency of sessions) to provide payment for mental health treatment.

Disclosing confidential information is also necessary during civil commitment proceedings when involuntary treatment is necessary because the individual presents a danger to self (such as wanting to commit suicide) or others (a deliberate expression of intent to harm another person).

Fiona denies any thoughts of hurting herself. She vehemently denies that she wants to harm her son and, in fact, has taken steps to make sure that it will not happen (removing the knives and scissors from the house). Therefore, she does not need involuntary commitment, and the psychologist does not have to violate confidentiality.

Finally, confidentiality must also be breached when adults admit that they are physically or sexually abusing children or elders, in which case the therapist must report the abuse to the appropriate authorities.

When the patient is a minor child or an adolescent, other exceptions to confidentiality apply, and, again, therapists discuss these issues at the start of treatment so that the minor and the parent or guardian can make an informed decision about participating in therapy. With respect to children and adolescents, mental health clinicians, including psychologists, are required by law to report physical, sexual, or emotional abuse to the proper authorities, thereby violating confidentiality. Each jurisdiction has its own guidelines, and, in some cases, different clinics in the same region may have different guidelines (Felthous et al., 2007; Gustafson & McNamara, 1987). Exceptions to confidentiality also apply when a child or an adolescent is actively contemplating suicide or homicide, as is the case for adults. Psychologists violate confidentiality to keep their patients and others physically safe. In certain instances, breaking confidentiality is a medical or legal necessity.

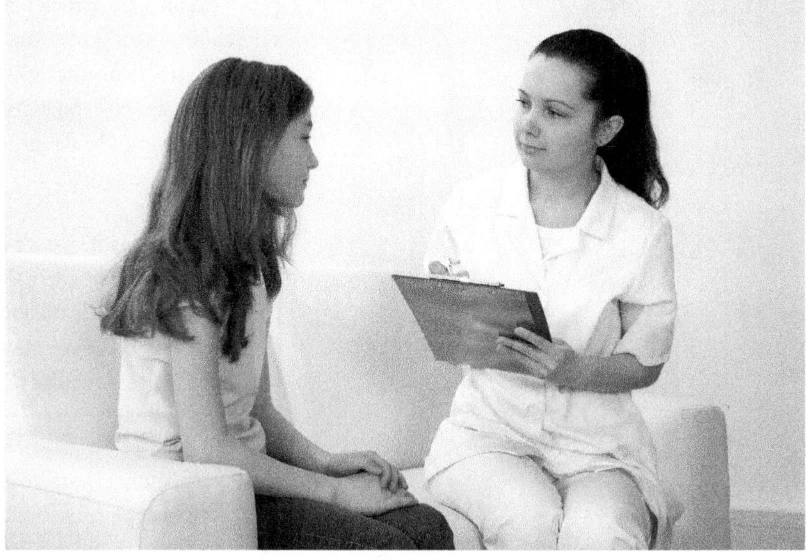

When treating a child, confidentiality issues become more complicated than with most adults. Some information must be shared with parents, whereas other information remains confidential.

Andrey Popov/Fotolia

Duty to Warn

In 1969, University of California student Prosenjit Poddar sought therapy with a psychologist at the university's student health centre because a young woman named Tatiana Tarasoff had spurned his affections. The psychologist believed that Poddar was dangerous because he had a pathological attachment to Tarasoff and he told the psychologist that he had decided to purchase a gun. The therapist notified the police both verbally and in writing. He did not warn Ms. Tarasoff because that would have violated patient–psychologist confidentiality. Poddar was questioned by the police, who found him to be rational. They made him promise to stay away from Tarasoff. Two months later, however, on October 27, 1969, Poddar killed Tarasoff. The Supreme Court of California found that the defendants (the Regents of the University of California) had a **duty to warn** Ms. Tarasoff or her family of the danger. In a second ruling, the court charged therapists with a duty to use reasonable care to protect third parties against dangers posed by patients. In short, the court found that a person has no right to confidentiality when the patient's actions might put the public at risk.

The original Tarasoff decision applied only to the state of California, but since then other U.S. states have adopted a duty to warn, although the specifics of the law vary by state. While both U.S. and Canadian law have their roots in English law, U.S. court decisions do not apply in Canada, and so the legal reasoning that led to the *Tarasoff* decision does not necessarily apply in Canada (Truscott & Crook, 2013). Some civil lawsuits in Canada have raised arguments similar to those in the *Tarasoff* case, although we have yet to see a legal precedent like the *Tarasoff* ruling (Birch, 1992; Schuller & Ogloff, 2000; Truscott & Crook, 2013). Nevertheless, it could be argued that it is ethical for mental health practitioners to warn third parties of impending harm. Indeed, this is present in the code of ethics for the Canadian Psychological Association (2000). The code of ethics for Canadian psychologists is quite similar to the legal requirements imposed by the *Tarasoff* ruling. According to the code, psychologists should do everything reasonably possible to stop or offset the consequences of actions by others when these actions are likely to cause serious physical harm or death. This may include reporting to appropriate authorities (e.g., the police) or an intended victim, and would be done even when a confidential relationship is involved (Canadian Psychological Association, 2000).

The Tarasoff decision (as it is known) has other broad implications for the mental health profession. One is that society does not always hold confidentiality in the same high esteem as do therapists and patients. Society sometimes dictates that safeguarding the public welfare, particularly in the case of potential homicide, is more important than confidentiality. However, duty to warn is a slippery slope. What if the potential threat is not outright death, as was the case for Tatiana Tarasoff, but bodily infection?

Michael is 33 years old. He has been married for eight years and has two children. He had an affair with a neighbour several years ago. His wife never knew about the affair. He recently discovered that the neighbour died of AIDS. Michael had an HIV test, which was positive. He told his therapist that he has no intention of telling his wife about his test results (Chenneville, 2000).

If Michael was your patient, what would you counsel him to do? The laws are not clear in this type of situation. Depending on the particular legal jurisdiction where Michael lives, the therapist may be *permitted* to make a disclosure to the health department or Michael's spouse, *required* to make a disclosure to the health department or Michael's spouse, or *required* to maintain confidentiality at all costs.

PREDICTION OF DANGEROUSNESS The psychologist's duty to warn is based on the belief that mental health clinicians have the ability to predict human behaviour. Psychologists and psychiatrists are often asked to determine how likely it is that a person will become violent when the need for civil commitment is an issue (Skeem et al., 2006). In the past, mental health professionals were unable to predict patient dangerousness at a rate higher than chance alone (Steadman, 1983).

Over the past decade, the ability of mental health clinicians to predict patient violence has significantly improved through the use of *actuarial* (quantitative) prediction measures, particularly when the prediction is based on specific psychological *symptoms* (such as anger or sadness), not psychological *disorders* (major depressive disorder, schizophrenia; Skeem et al., 2006). In particular, anger/hostility is predictive of violence over both short-term (one week) and long-term (six month) follow-up periods (Gardner et al., 1996; Skeem et al., 2006). Other symptoms such as anxiety, depression, or delusional beliefs did not predict acts of violence, at least not in the short term (Skeem et al., 2006).

The accuracy of predicting violence, especially violence in the long term, is improved if clinicians use the Psychopathy Checklist or similar instruments (Bloom et al., 2005; Gray et al., 2007). The Psychopathy Checklist was developed by psychologist Robert Hare at the University of British Columbia and his colleagues (Hare & Neumann, 2006; Hart et al., 1995). People with high scores on the checklist have a higher risk of violence than people with low scores. Another useful assessment instrument is the Historical/Clinical/Risk Management Scheme (HCR-20), developed by Christopher Webster at the University of Toronto and his colleagues (Douglas et al., 2014; Webster et al., 1997). The HCR-20 contains items assessing past history of violence, psychopathy, and current signs and symptoms of psychopathology (e.g., lack of insight that one has a mental disorder in need of treatment).

CONCEPT check

- When a person reveals personal information to a psychologist, the information is considered confidential, within certain limits.
- Sometimes confidentiality must be violated. Such cases include behaviours that are considered dangerous to the patient or others, abuse of children or elders, or substance abuse by children or adolescents.

- If a patient threatens to harm another person and that person can be identified, psychologists have an ethical and sometimes a legal duty to warn the threatened person as well as the police.
- Actuarial predictions allow psychologists to predict violence at levels better than chance alone. One factor that appears to play a role is patients' anger/hostility and level of psychopathy.

critical thinking question Remember Michael, who did not want to tell his wife that he had HIV? What if instead of being married, Michael were single, had gotten HIV as a result of a single encounter with someone he had met in a bar, and now was so angry that he told his therapist that he intended to go out and infect every woman that he could. Does a psychologist have a duty to warn?

Licensing, Malpractice Issues, and Prescription Privileges

Requiring mental health professionals to have a licence serves several functions. It sets minimum standards of training and education, and it protects the public from unskilled or dangerous mental health services or providers. Insurance companies recognize the importance of licensing: They usually will not pay for psychological services unless the professional has a licence.

Licensing

Psychologists who wish to provide professional services in certain settings must be licensed by the jurisdiction (e.g., province or territory) in which they practise. Psychologists who do not provide professional services (such as cognitive psychologists, biological psychologists, or social psychologists who exclusively teach in university settings) are not required to be licensed. The law specifies who can use the terms *psychologist* or *psychology* in their job title or job description, who can provide specific psychological services, and what type of training a person must have to practise psychology. Licensing laws vary by province or territory, and there are many ways that nonqualified individuals can practise what some consider a form of therapy. In some jurisdictions, people who are not psychologists but who wish to provide therapy can do so by avoiding the use of the words *psychology* and *psychologist* and instead using the term *psychotherapy* or *psychotherapist.*

Laws protect the public by setting forth the minimal acceptable level of training and experience necessary for the practice of psychology. Most provinces/territories in Canada and states in the United States have very similar requirements, including a doctorate in psychology and two years of postdoctoral experience (or one year predoctoral internship and one year postdoctoral experience). The psychologist must also pass a national exam and a provincial/territorial exam. Once licensed, psychologists must adhere to the laws and the code of ethics. Failure to do so could result in loss of the licence or claims of malpractice. Furthermore, to maintain their licence, psychologists must engage in *continuing education* by continuing to attend workshops, read articles, and participate in other professional activities to refine and improve their knowledge and skills in psychology.

Malpractice

Psychologists, like all professionals, must meet certain standards when caring for their patients, legally defined as that degree of care which a reasonably prudent person should exercise in same or similar circumstances (Black, 1990). For example, although the law does not require all psychologists to use the same form of therapy, the care they do provide must meet commonly accepted professional standards (Baerger, 2001; Canadian

The most common reason that a psychologist is sued for malpractice is a result of a custody evaluation. It is common for the parent who does not get custody to identify the psychologist as the person responsible for the negative outcome.

Alina Solovyova-Vincent/E+/Getty Images

Psychological Association, 2000). If care is not consistent with standards, the psychologist may be guilty of **malpractice**; that is, professional misconduct or unreasonable lack of skill (Black, 1990). Although psychologists are less likely to be sued for malpractice than are physicians, the number of lawsuits filed against psychologists increases each year.

There have been few studies of malpractice offences committed by mental health clinicians (either psychiatrists or psychologists). In one anonymous survey, 3.5% of psychologists engaged in an inappropriate relationship. The majority of offenders were male psychologists who established a relationship with former female patients (Lamb et al., 2003). Malpractice lawsuits are generally filed against psychologists when there is suspicion of a negligent or improper diagnosis. Malpractice accusations tend to involve child custody evaluation decisions intended to assess how best to meet the child's psychological needs. To arrive at their decisions, psychologists assess parenting abilities, the child's needs, and the resulting parent–child fit. Child custody evaluation is a high-risk task for a psychologist, who must remain neutral in a highly charged situation such as a divorce. Joint physical custody is the most common custody decision today (Bow & Quinnell, 2001). In the second most common decision, the mother is granted custody and the father has visitation rights. Parents who disagree with a custody decision may file a complaint with the regional ethics board or file a malpractice suit. Among psychologists who conducted custody evaluations, ethics complaints were filed against 35%, and 10% were sued for malpractice (Bow & Quinnell, 2001).

In addition to child custody cases, malpractice claims include failure to obtain informed consent for treatment, negligent clinical practice, or negligent release of clinical records (e.g., confidential patient files). For example, grief-stricken family members sometimes blame a mental health professional for not preventing a patient's suicide, although predicting this type of behaviour can be very difficult. Such charges were the sixth most common malpractice complaints in one survey of psychologists who had malpractice insurance (Bongar et al., cited in Baerger, 2001).

In summary, psychologists must adhere to both an ethical code of conduct as well as federal and regional laws and regulations. Licensure ensures that the professional has met minimum educational and training standards, but it does *not* guarantee that the therapist will always behave ethically. When unethical behaviours have occurred, a psychologist may be sued for malpractice.

Prescription Privileges

What is the difference between a psychologist and a psychiatrist? The easy answer used to be the following: A psychiatrist is a physician, trained in abnormal psychology, who can prescribe medication and practise psychotherapy, whereas a psychologist is a doctoral-level health care provider, trained in both normal and abnormal psychology, who cannot prescribe medication but provides psychological assessment and psychotherapy. That distinction is no longer quite so clear. During the past two decades, some psychologists have sought, and received, the legal right to prescribe medication for psychological disorders. Prescription privileges, or the legal right to prescribe medication, is a controversial issue throughout the psychological community (Heiby, 2002; McKay, 2014).

Medications are an important part of the treatment of many psychological disorders, and in some cases, such as schizophrenia, the primary treatment. Although psychiatrists have always been free to use both psychotherapy and medication, psychologists have traditionally provided only psychological treatment. When their patients need medication, most psychologists arrange for treatment by a physician. Some psychologists believe that splitting treatment in this way is not in the best interest of the patient because different therapists may provide the patient different, and sometimes conflicting, viewpoints. With the ability to prescribe medications, these psychologists believe that they would be able to provide both medication and psychotherapy, just as psychiatrists do.

Psychologists propose several reasons for prescription privileges (Bray et al., 2014). First, many psychologists have hospital admitting privileges, enabling them to treat the emotional components related to physical health problems such as stress caused by cancer, serious disabilities, or heart disease. These psychologists view the ability to write prescriptions as a natural extension of their practice (Norfleet, 2002; Welsh, 2003). Second, graduate programs in clinical psychology already offer courses in psychophysiology and psychopharmacology, which are necessary but not sufficient, for prescribing medication. Therefore, psychologists already have some of the training necessary for prescribing medications. Third, because medications are the treatment of choice for some disorders, such as schizophrenia, prescription privileges would allow psychologists to treat patients who might not have access to treatment. Many people lack access to psychiatrists and obtain their medication from general practitioners who are much less knowledgeable about psychological disorders than psychologists. Allowing psychologists to prescribe medications would guarantee treatment by someone with specialized knowledge of abnormal behaviour.

Other psychologists oppose prescription privileges for psychologists (Deacon, 2014; Tumlin & Klepac, 2014). Some (e.g., Albee, 2002) suggest that prescribing medication undermines psychology's unique contributions to understanding behaviour, such as the role of learning and the importance of the environment. From this perspective, seeking prescription privileges suggests that psychologists no longer value psychology's contributions and deemphasizes the efficacy of highly effective psychological treatments.

Psychologists would also need additional training to prescribe medications safely and would require an undergraduate education that would include some of the courses found in a premedicine curriculum (Sechrest & Coan, 2002). Providing appropriate biological training at the graduate level would extend the length of training (Wagner, 2002), which already averages about six years. In the past few years, psychologists have gained the right to prescribe medication in New Mexico, Louisiana, and the island of Guam (Stambor, 2006; van Winkle, 2010) but so far not in Canada.

The Canadian Psychological Association commissioned a taskforce that aims to take a dispassionate look into the issues concerning prescription privileges (RxP) for Canadian psychologists (CPA Task Force on Prescriptive Authority for Psychologists in Canada, 2010). The Task Force concluded that psychological assessment and psychological therapies should continue to be emphasized in the training of Canadian psychologists, although there are also definite advantages for psychologists to have a broader training in psychopharmacology, and such training might eventually evolve into a program for training psychologists to prescribe certain medications:

> Psychosocial assessment and interventions (psychotherapy, cognitive-behaviour therapy, and other approaches) have a proven efficacy and should not in any manner be diminished in training requirements for psychology best practice guidelines. However, there are strong rationales for developing a broader training model that is more inclusive of biological and psychopharmacological knowledge. Brain-behaviour relationships are as intrinsic to psychological science as are psycho-social paradigms, and have not always received adequate emphasis in professional training and continuing education. Clients and patients who seek psychologist consultation frequently use or are considering the use of prescription medications for psychological conditions. Psychologists can only fully serve these clients if they have bio-psychopharmacological as well as psychosocial

knowledge. Thus, it is both consistent with the scientific scope of the discipline and ethically incumbent on practicing psychologists to be sufficiently knowledgeable about psychopharmacology to understand the psychological effects of medications prescribed to their clients, and to provide evidence based consultation to collaborating medical (and other prescribing) practitioners regarding combined pharmacotherapy-psychotherapy interventions. . . . The CPA Prescriptive Authority (RxP) Task Force has taken an evolutionary approach towards the future possibility of Canadian psychologists seeking prescriptive authority and regarded making a specific recommendation on this step as premature. The CPA RxP Task Force recommends evolutionary steps in training standards toward enhanced psychopharmacological training and collaborative roles for psychologist practitioners. At this time in psychology's professional history, prescriptive authority should not be precluded as a future step, but neither should it currently be the primary goal and focus of professional advocacy. (p. 32)

If prescription privileges become part of the treatment arsenal for psychologists, medication providers will face controversial issues that relate to the marketing and funding of pharmacological treatment. Psychiatric drugs are considered a booming business. They are among the industry's most profitable drugs. Their use is increasing among both adults and children, and more recently, there has been an increase in what is known as **polypharmacy**, being prescribed more than one medication for the same disorder. The potential influence of the pharmaceutical industry extends far beyond public media advertisements. In one survey, 60% of published medication trials in psychiatry received funding from a pharmaceutical company (Perlis et al., 2005), although having pharmaceutical company support did not guarantee a positive outcome for the medication. Until recently, pharmaceutical companies provided promotional materials (pens, mouse pads, etc.) to potential medication prescribers. Although such gifts are now prohibited, health professionals must always be careful to guard against marketing influences when deciding on forms of therapy.

CONCEPT check

- Regional jurisdictions (e.g., provinces or territories) regulate the practice of psychology to safeguard the public against those who are not qualified to perform these services.
- Typically, the practice of psychology requires a doctoral degree, at least two years of supervised experience, and a licensing examination.
- Malpractice lawsuits against psychologists are uncommon, but when they occur, the reasons include inappropriate sexual behaviour and dissatisfaction with child custody decisions.
- Some jurisdictions allow psychologists to prescribe medications for psychological disorders, although permitting prescription privileges continues to be controversial.

critical thinking question The ability to prescribe medication leads to potentially vulnerable exposure to pharmaceutical marketing campaigns, all of which seek to have their drug prescribed to patients. Given their extensive background in research training, do you think that psychologists would be able to resist this influence more than physicians can?

Research and Clinical Trials

15.5 Describe documents crucial to the development of rights for research participants.

We have approached the study of abnormal behaviour from a scientist-practitioner perspective, highlighting how designing, conducting, and understanding research in abnormal behaviour contributes to theories of etiology and approaches to treatment. When treatments are not based on science, they may result in harmful consequences. The use of unscientific theories and unsubstantiated treatments can result in the waste of time and money and public mistrust of therapy. But research itself comes with its own ethical issues. Here we focus on four important areas: the rights of research participants, special rights and issues for children and adolescents, the use of placebo controls, and the importance of conducting research that reflects population diversity.

Rights of Participants in Research

On December 9, 1946, the U.S. military initiated a tribunal against 23 German physicians and administrators for war crimes and other crimes against humanity. During World War II, some German physicians conducted a euthanasia program, systematically killing people who they deemed unworthy to live. In a second program, physicians conducted pseudoscientific medical experiments on thousands of concentration camp prisoners (Jews, Poles, Russians, and Gypsies) without their consent (www.ushmm.org/research/doctors, retrieved May 10, 2013). Most participants died or were permanently injured as a result of this inhumane experimentation. Sixteen doctors were found guilty; seven of them were executed.

The horrific and senseless nature of these "experiments" prompted the development of the **Nuremberg Code** (1947), which established directives for experimentation with human subjects. This code specifies that subjects must voluntarily consent to participate in clinical research. Furthermore, participants should know the nature, duration, and purpose of the research, as well as its methods and means and all inconveniences and hazards that could be reasonably expected as a result of participation. The experiment must be conducted by qualified individuals, and the participants must be allowed to withdraw from the research study at any time (Trials of War Criminals before the Nuremberg Military Tribunals, 1949).

A second document developed as a result of Nazi atrocities is the **Declaration of Helsinki**, first adopted by the World Medical Assembly in 1964 and reaffirmed on subsequent occasions (http://history.nih.gov/research/downloads/helsinki.pdf, retrieved May 10, 2013). This document also sets forth basic guidelines for the conduct of research, including the need for clearly formulated experimental procedures, a careful assessment of risks compared with benefits, and the provision of adequate information to the participants including the aims, methods, benefits and risks, and the freedom to withdraw. The Declaration of Helsinki does not specify how these principles are to be implemented; that is left to governments and professional organizations.

A third document relevant to research is the **Belmont Report** (1979). The Belmont Report came to guide research practice in both the United States and Canada. Canada's first attempt to introduce some control of research ethics occurred in 1978. Both the Medical Research Council of Canada (MRC; now known as the Canadian Institutes for Health Research) and the Social Sciences and Humanities Research Council (SSHRC) issued guidelines, which were based on the Belmont Report (Kinsella, 2010). The report identified three basic principles to guide behavioural and biomedical research with human subjects.

The first is *respect for persons*, including the beliefs that (a) individuals should be treated as autonomous agents capable of independent thought and decision-making abilities and (b) persons who have limited or diminished autonomy (such as prisoners or those with limited cognitive ability) are entitled to special protections and should not be coerced or unduly influenced to participate in research activities.

The second principle is *beneficence*, meaning that researchers (a) do no harm (as in the Hippocratic Oath) and (b) maximize potential benefits and minimize possible harm. In short, the study's potential benefits must outweigh the perceived risks (Striefel, 2001), both to the individual and to society at large.

The third and final principle is *justice*: The benefits and burdens of research must be imposed equally. For example, all research on heart disease (much of it funded by the federal government) traditionally was conducted using male participants, so men were primarily benefitting from the results. Only later did researchers begin to study heart disease and its treatment in women. This example illustrates how the *benefits* of research were not being equally distributed; only one sex benefitted from the efforts of scientists. The principle of justice was violated in the Tuskegee experiment, and perhaps also in the Baltimore lead paint study (see "Cultural Perceptions Regarding Research"). In general, the recruitment of research participants must consider whether some classes of participants (welfare recipients, specific racial or ethnic minorities, or persons confined to institutions) are selected simply because they are easily accessible or easily manipulated. In short, no one group should be selected as research participants because of their availability, lack of power, or the possibility of easy manipulation (Striefel, 2001).

Also important to the research process is **informed consent**. Potential participants must understand the aims and methods of the research, what they will be asked to do, and what types of information they will be asked to provide. They must also understand the risks and benefits of research participation. Before starting a research study, the psychologist, or anyone else who wishes to conduct research with human participants, submits the research plan to an **institutional review board (IRB)**. This board is charged by the researcher's institution with reviewing and approving the research using the guidelines just mentioned. An informed consent form, describing all aspects of the study in layperson's language, is included with the research plan. If you participated in research in your introductory psychology class, you probably signed a consent form.

Informed consent is based on the idea that providing enough information will allow cognitively competent people to understand the research process and make a voluntary and rational decision about participation. However, this assumption is not necessarily true. In one study examining the effects of a treatment, 62% of people who read the consent form and agreed to participate in the study failed to understand that treatment would be applied in a standard fashion and not individualized to their needs, or they overestimated the benefit of participating because they did not fully understand the study's methodology (e.g., use of a placebo control group that would provide little to no therapeutic benefit; Appelbaum et al., 2004).

When it came to understanding the disclosed risk, 25% failed to recall any risk listed in the informed consent document, whereas 46% understood the risks of the experimental *treatment* but not the risks of the experimental *design* (Lidz, 2006), such as the possibility of being assigned to the placebo control group. So, despite the profession's efforts to ensure that research participants are fully informed, many people take part in studies lacking full information about the risks and benefits they can expect.

Considerations with Children and Adolescents

Oscar, 14 years old, was extremely anxious in social situations. His parents brought him to the clinic to participate in a research study to treat social anxiety disorder and signed the consent form for Oscar's participation. When Oscar refused to sign the assent form, his father asked the investigator to leave the room, guaranteeing that his son would sign the form "in the next 10 minutes."

Although parental or guardian consent may be necessary for children and adolescents to participate in research, ethical guidelines require that whenever they are able to do so, children and adolescents should be allowed to *assent* to their own participation. Although the ability to give assent varies with the individual child, by age 14 adolescents can understand and make decisions that are similar to the way adults do (Caskey & Rosenthal, 2005). In Oscar's case, the investigator could not enroll him in the study because it was clear that Oscar did not wish to participate, although his parents wanted him to do so.

When a person is under the age of 18, the legal requirements for informed consent vary from jurisdiction to jurisdiction. In some jurisdictions there is an age limit placed on when consent can be given, whereas other jurisdictions use criteria based on the person's capacity for understanding. To illustrate the latter, in British Columbia, the Infants Act (1996) stipulates that a child can give informed consent provided that he or she is able to understand the nature, risks, and benefits of treatment, and if the mental health practitioner believes that the treatment would be in the best interests of the child. If the child does not display this sort of understanding, then consent must be obtained from the next of kin (e.g., parent) or legal guardian.

To honour the principle of *beneficence*, investigators who study children and adolescents must protect the welfare of the participants. Researchers, like clinicians, must violate confidentiality when there is evidence of sexual or physical abuse. In certain instances, researchers must report alcohol or substance abuse to parents (Caskey & Rosenthal, 2005). Finally, *justice* in this case means that adolescents deserve the opportunity to participate in and benefit from research important to the adolescent population. Some adults believe that asking adolescents whether they have thought about committing suicide will instill such thoughts and urges in people who have never considered this behaviour. Psychologists know that this is simply not true, yet many school districts will not allow research that includes questions about suicide. This denies treatment opportunities to adolescents who are seriously depressed and contemplating suicide. In this case, the principle of justice is not fulfilled because adolescents are denied an opportunity to participate in potentially important and helpful research.

Many of the same considerations surrounding the ability of children to consent to participate in research also apply to older adults who have cognitive difficulties and to prisoners who may feel coerced to participate because of their incarcerated status. When the research involves people from racial or ethnic minority groups, additional considerations include making sure that (a) assessments are culturally valid, (b) group differences are not attributed to race or ethnicity when they may be just as likely to result from other demographic variables such as socioeconomic status or level of education, (c) behaviours or developmental patterns of the white majority are not considered the "normal" standard for mental health, (d) research is not coercive, and (e) research teams include someone who is culturally competent (Fisher et al., 2002a).

Ethics and Responsibility

The most rigorous types of scientific research have designs that involve the use of a control group (see Chapter 2). The different types of control groups include a wait list or no-treatment control group, a pill placebo or psychological placebo control group, or another active treatment group. Placebo control groups are used to understand the effects of time (some conditions, such as a cold, resolve with the passage of time) and the effects of clinical attention or education (e.g., people are relieved to know that their response to a traumatic event is typical and not a sign of pathology; see Chapter 4). However, questions often arise as to how and when the use of control groups is ethical (see "Research Hot Topic: The Use of Placebo in Clinical Research").

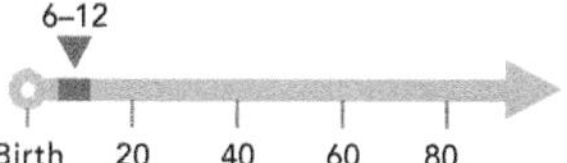

Before children can participate in research, many issues must be considered. Because an adult must consent for a child to participate in research, greater scrutiny of risks and benefits takes place before a study is approved.

Sometimes the use of a placebo control condition is not clinically acceptable. The possibility of denying treatment to a suicidal patient cannot be justified when treatments are available. Among children, the ethical use of a placebo is becoming increasingly complex. Scientifically, we know that placebo effects are more pronounced in children than in adults; specifically, more children than adults have a positive (therapeutic) response to placebo medication (Krummenacher et al., 2014; Waschbusch et al., 2009; Fisher & Fisher, 1996; Malone & Simpson, 1998). One reason for this difference may be that children may not understand the concept of a placebo (i.e., that it is an inactive treatment). Children, who are accustomed to getting medication from a physician for physical illness, may believe that the placebo pill will also make them well. When they take a pill to treat a bacterial infection, a blood test will reveal that the infection

research **HOT** topic

The Use of Placebo in Clinical Research

Placebo-controlled trials are considered rigorous tests used to determine the effectiveness of a new treatment. Deep brain stimulation (DBS), for example, has shown preliminary effectiveness for depression that does not respond to medication. The procedure involves implanting an electrode within the part of the brain that is associated with mood. Electrical impulses are transmitted to and stimulate brain cells in the part of the brain that regulates mood. Although used to treat depression, Health Canada has not yet approved DBS specifically for this purpose, and its effectiveness has not been demonstrated compared with placebo. Imagine that a researcher proposes to conduct a randomized, controlled trial in which one group receives DBS and the second group undergoes the surgical procedure in the brain but the wire is not connected to the stimulator. Is the use of a placebo ethical?

- **Argument in Favour of the Surgical Placebo** Article II.3 of the Declaration of Helsinki states: "In any medical study, every patient—including those of a control group, if any—should be assured of the best proven diagnostic and therapeutic method. This does not exclude the use of inert placebo in studies where no proven diagnostic or therapeutic method exists." The study that the researcher proposes might provide some additional support for the use of DBS, particularly in a group of patients who have not responded to standard medication treatments. However, the researchers must consider the potentially harmful consequences from surgery that has no benefit.
- **Argument Against the Use of the Surgical Placebo** Surgical placebo for DBS involves actual neurosurgery, an invasive procedure. In addition to potential complications of the procedure itself, consequences of the placebo implant include reaction to anesthesia and postoperative infection (La Vaque & Rossiter, 2001). Does the potential for symptom remission in a group with medication-resistant depression outweigh the potential for harm from surgical placebo?
- **Conclusion** When no known standard exists, using a placebo as a control condition to test a new treatment might be appropriate until the efficacy of a new intervention is known and available to the public. In the case of DBS or other invasive medical procedures, the risks associated with neurosurgery are the same whether or not the device is operative. In fact, those in the placebo condition have brain surgery for no therapeutic reason, a very substantial medical risk with no benefit. Of course, if participants in the placebo group are later allowed to have the implant activated, *then* the benefits may outweigh the risks for people whose depressive symptoms have not responded to any currently accepted conventional treatment.

has been cured. However, the outcome of most psychological research is based on the patient's report of changed feelings; there is no "psychological blood test" to independently determine symptom improvement. Therefore, children's reports may be biased based on their belief that they took a pill and so should be feeling better. Adult reports also may be biased by taking a pill, but an adult's cognitive maturity increases the likelihood that the concept of a placebo is understood. To control the assumption (at any age) that taking a pill will make you better, it is clear that placebo controls are necessary, especially for children (March et al., 2004). In summary, placebo controls are necessary for valid scientific research, but ethical issues continue to challenge scientist-practitioners interested in providing effective treatments to children.

Cultural Perceptions Regarding Research

15.6 Give reasons why some cultural groups may be reluctant to participate in research.

A little known fact about the world's mental health database is that the vast majority of research has been conducted in the United States using white university students (Sue, 2003), who represent less than 5% of the world's population. Granting agencies, both in Canada and the United States, and in other countries, have recognized this inequity and now mandate that study samples recruited for federally-funded research be representative of the U.S. population. However, when researchers, particularly white researchers, try to recruit a diverse sample, they often find that historical events have created a climate of cultural mistrust. People familiar with the now infamous **Tuskegee experiment** may worry that they will be mistreated and their rights ignored. In that experiment, each of the three core values of research (respect for persons, beneficence, and justice) was violated.

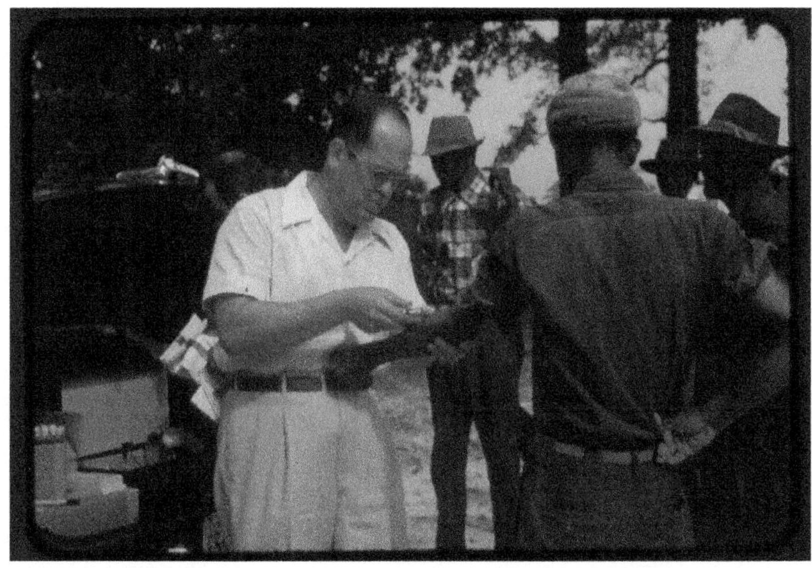

In the Tuskegee experiment, medical treatment was knowingly withheld from patients who suffered from a deadly disease so that the disease could be studied. This unethical experiment on human beings was one factor that led to the development of review boards for institutional research.

National Archives and Records Administration

In 1932, the Public Health Service, working with the Tuskegee Institute, began a study to determine the long-term effects of syphilis. Nearly 400 poor African American men with syphilis from Macon County, Alabama, were enrolled. They were never told that they had syphilis, nor were they ever treated for it. According to the Centers for Disease Control and Prevention, the men were told that they were being treated for "bad blood," a local term that described several illnesses including syphilis, anemia, and fatigue. For participating in the study, the men were given free medical exams, free meals, and free burial insurance. When the study began, no proven treatment for syphilis existed. But even after penicillin became a standard cure in 1947, the medicine was withheld from these men. The Tuskegee scientists wanted to continue to study how the disease spread through the body. Of course, in some cases, the disease killed the patient. The experiment lasted four decades until public health workers leaked the story to the media in 1972. By then, dozens of the men had died, and many wives and children had been infected. After the National Association for the Advancement of Colored People (NAACP) filed a class-action lawsuit in 1973, a $9 million settlement was divided among the study's participants. Free health care was given to the men who were still living and to infected wives, widows, and children.

Not until 1997 did the U.S. government formally apologize for the unethical study. President Clinton delivered the apology, saying that what the government had done was profoundly and morally wrong. "To the survivors, to the wives and family members, the children and the grandchildren, I say what you know: No power on Earth can give you back the lives lost, the pain suffered, the years of internal torment and anguish. What was done cannot be undone. But we can end the silence. We can stop turning our heads away. We can look at you in the eye and finally say on behalf of the American people, what the United States government did was shameful, and I am sorry."

In Canada, the United States, and other countries, the use of IRBs to review research proposals before an investigator can begin a research study guards against many potential abuses of research participants. For example, it is highly unlikely that Watson's experiment with Little Albert could be conducted today. Yet even with all of the current regulations of research activities, some studies still provoke controversy, particularly when the subjects are children. From 1993 to 1995, the Kennedy Krieger Institute (KKI) in Baltimore, Maryland, conducted a study to determine the short- and long-term effects of environmental lead in older homes. Lead is a natural element in the environment, but concentrations of lead in the blood are naturally quite low. At that time in the United States and Canada, higher than acceptable lead levels came primarily from two sources: lead in gasoline and the leaded paint chips and dust associated with deteriorating lead paint. The elimination of lead from gasoline and paint decreased blood level concentrations in children dramatically, although older homes with lead paint remain a source of concern. High lead levels lead to cognitive impairment (low IQ scores), inattention, hyperactivity, aggression, and delinquency (Committee on Environmental Health, American Academy of Pediatrics, 2005).

In Baltimore, attempts to remove lead paint through lead abatement procedures reduced lead dust levels by 80%, and the KKI agreed to conduct a study to examine three different abatement procedures (some representing only partial abatement). In addition to these three experimental groups, there were two control groups, one in which no further abatement occurred and one in which the homes were newer and presumably lead free.

Some of the homes were occupied at the start of the study. In other instances, "inner city families who likely had no choice but to rent non-abated properties elsewhere in Baltimore" were recruited to live in the study houses (Lead-Based Paint Study Fact Sheet, cited in Nelson, 2002). This resulted in two groups of children: those already living in a study home and those recruited to move into these homes. Inducements to move into the houses and participate in the study included T-shirts, food stamps, and $5 to $10 payments. For most of the children in the homes, the additional abatement procedures lowered levels of lead in the children. However, the study had some negative effects: Lead levels increased in some children. In one instance, parental notification was delayed by nine months. Mothers of two study participants later filed lawsuits, stating that they had not been fully informed about the goals of the study and were not promptly notified of the high levels of lead in their children's blood. If they had had this information, they would not have agreed to participate in the study.

This study raises many ethical and moral issues (see "Examining the Evidence: Children and Nontherapeutic Research"). One is the issue of *justice* set forth in the Belmont Report. Was the research unethical if the family's only alternative was to live in other homes that had not undergone any abatement procedures? Should social deprivation be a reason for conducting a "natural experiment," or are researchers taking advantage of the participant's social predicament (Spriggs, 2006)? In other words, is it acceptable to induce low-income children to live in partially lead-abated houses because the alternative might have been worse?

In both the Tuskegee experiment and the Baltimore lead paint study, groups with limited or diminished autonomy were put at risk. Poorly designed experiments such as these have led to grave mistrust among certain minority populations. This cultural mistrust, however, is not the only challenge facing those who wish to conduct sensitive, cross-cultural research. Some members of minority groups are unfamiliar with aspects of the research process, such as telephone interviews about psychological disorders (Okazaki & Sue, 1995). Uncomfortable telephone interviews about personal issues such as anxiety and depression may interfere with valid data collection. Another challenge occurs when survey instruments constructed in English are translated into other languages. For example, English cultural expressions such as "shake off the blues" have no

examining the EVIDENCE

Children and Nontherapeutic Research

Before gaining approval, all proposed research must be reviewed to ensure that the study provides benefit and does not subject participants to undue risk or harm. In the case of the KKI lead-based paint study, concerns were raised that this study did not provide sufficient benefit and exposed children to undue risk. Do parents have the right to enroll their children in "nontherapeutic" research?

LET'S EXAMINE THE EVIDENCE

- **Was There a Direct Benefit for the Children Who Participated in the Study?** The research project offered monitoring of blood levels and notification to the parents if the blood level exceeded a certain standard. But testing is not treatment, and the study did not provide treatment if living in the house resulted in high blood levels of lead in the child (Nelson, 2002).

  Recall that there were two groups of children: those already living in the targeted houses and those who were recruited to live in them. Enticing someone to move into a house that contains lead can hardly be viewed as providing a benefit. For children already living in such homes, the research project offered the benefit of lead abatement. Therefore, the research offered a benefit only to those already living in a house known to contain lead (Spriggs, 2006).

- **Did the Procedure Present More Than Minimal Risk to the Subjects?** Monthly blood testing to determine the level of lead exposure presents only minimal risk. However, living in a home while lead removal occurs involves more than minimal risk because lead levels may increase when the lead is being removed. Parents were not informed that the three different methods might not have equal benefit. Is intentionally recruiting families to move into homes that have had potentially ineffective methods of lead exposure only minimal risk? Do parents deserve the right to know that there was uncertainty about the benefits of these different procedures? Would your answer be different if the researchers told you that it was the best available option for these children?
- **Did the Consent Form Allow Parents to Make a Fully Informed Decision?** The consent document did not inform the parents about (a) the primary aim of the study (to examine the effectiveness of three different methods of lead removal), (b) the different methods used, (c) the importance of blood monitoring and the impact of high lead levels on the development of young children, and (d) the risks of inadequate lead removal (Nelson, 2002). Without this information, did parents have the opportunity to give fully informed consent?
- **Conclusion** The court noted that the institutional review board did not adequately consider the risks to the participants. Would you agree? Because removing lead from homes is an important societal goal, how could you change the study to address the issues raised above?

literal Spanish translation, making the phrase meaningless to Hispanic populations. Without cultural sensitivity, any data collected will be meaningless (Rogler, 1999).

Issues of cultural diversity affect all aspects of the research process, from the initial development of the project to recruitment of participants, to the study design and selection of assessment methods, to how the data are collected and interpreted. All result in scientific data that can be biased and not appropriate to much of the world's population (Turner & Beidel, 2003). Many aspects of human behaviour probably have no differences among racial and ethnic groups. However, until scientists begin to adequately address these issues, our understanding of abnormal behaviour, indeed of all human behaviour, will be limited.

CONCEPT check

- Three universal documents—the Nuremberg Code, the Declaration of Helsinki, and the Belmont Report—set forth important ethical standards for conducting clinical research.
- Respect for persons, beneficence, and justice are important cornerstones of clinical research and of clinical treatment.
- Informed consent implies that the researcher provides a complete explanation of the research project: the aims and methods of the study, what participants will be asked to do, and what type of information participants will be asked to provide.
- When children are research participants, both the child's assent and the parent's consent are needed before the study begins.
- Use of placebo controls is a controversial area of clinical research. They are necessary when no established treatments exist or when there is a suspicion that time or attention alone may change behaviour. Once an effective treatment is established, comparing a new treatment to an established one rather than a placebo may be the most ethical approach.

critical thinking question A medical school that provides treatment to almost exclusively poor populations is concerned about the number of expectant mothers who are addicted to cocaine. The newborns suffer greatly and drain already limited provincial resources. The treatment team institutes a policy of drug testing for all pregnant mothers, but tells patients that it is just "routine blood work." Those who test positive are given the choice of entering a drug abuse program or being reported to the police, resulting in their arrest and going to prison. The program's policy becomes known, and there is public outrage. The treatment team defends the program by calling it a research study to determine whether mothers who are informed of their drug addiction will choose to receive treatment during their pregnancy. How do the principles of respect, beneficence, and justice apply to this situation?

real SCIENCE real LIFE

Edmond Yu—When Psychotic Behaviour Intersects with the Law

As a youngster, Edmond Yu showed he had the drive to achieve great things. He was an excellent student, leaving home early for classes and studying in his room late every night. Yet he balanced his rigorous academic work with a variety of hobbies. After emigrating from Hong Kong to Canada, Edmond spent two years at York University in pre-med classes, and later earned a scholarship to study medicine at the University of Toronto.

In his first term, Edmond's marks were excellent. But during the second term, he started to become reclusive; he began studying from home, avoiding campus except for exams or group projects. The initial signs that all was not well were detected an ocean away by his sister, Katherine Yu, who was living in Hong Kong. She got a phone call saying there had been a serious fight between Edmond and his elder brother. Edmond had been asked to leave the house. There were other calls, too, from Edmond, in which he would ramble about someone stealing his wallet at university. He sounded incoherent, illogical; not himself. "I realized at that point there was something wrong with him," his sister recalls. She flew to Canada.

Things began to quickly spiral downward. Katherine remembers going to his apartment to check up on him. "He said the people in his building, as well as in nearby buildings, were spies," she says. "He believed there were satellites planted in his building—even in his own apartment—watching him." Likely unaware he was suffering from an illness, Edmond rejected Katherine's attempts to get him to seek help.

Katherine went to Edmond, demanding he accept help, see a doctor, take medication. He refused. "I knew there was something wrong with him. He asked me to leave, but I insisted and kept on talking. And then he slapped me in the face." It was painful for Katherine to use the incident against her brother, but she felt his best interests were at stake. The police apprehended Edmond, and he was taken to the Clarke Institute of Psychiatry, where he was diagnosed as having paranoid schizophrenia. He was persuaded that, if he accepted treatment, he might still be able to return to medical school. He consented.

At least initially, Edmond tried to stick with the treatment, which consisted of antipsychotic drugs to quell the delusions. Unfortunately, some people experience severe side effects with psychotropic drugs. Edmond was one of them. "When he was on medication, he seemed to be a totally different person," Katherine says. "All he could do was eat and sleep. He was completely non-communicative. His hands were so shaky he couldn't even hold a bowl of soup properly. The soup would always spill."

It was clear to Edmond he would not be able to attend school while on medication. It was equally clear he would not be able to attend school without it. Edmond requested that a doctor certify him fit for medical school. But because he would not take his medication, the doctor refused.

With no classes to attend and no career as a doctor, Edmond flew back to Hong Kong. Within a month, he was picked up by police on a charge of disturbing the peace. Edmond was sent to a psychiatric hospital. The hospital then decided to impose treatment on Edmond—to force medication. When he returned to Canada, he immediately stopped taking the drugs. His non-compliance marked the start of a long struggle with his family over treatment.

As Edmond's illness deepened, his behaviour worsened. He was overtaken by paranoia and suspicion. He would talk non-stop. He felt he had special influence over world affairs. He feared those around him were conspiring to harm him. On occasion, he would be verbally abusive. And he began burning things—clothes, books, photographs. He would take them out on to the driveway and put a match to them. Edmond also started to meditate in front of the family's Scarborough home, sometimes for hours. On two occasions, he threw a knife at a dartboard he set up outside the garage door. Neighbours called police both times. Other times, they just stared from their windows.

Edmond began to drift, from housing to hostels—where he says he was beaten and robbed—to the street. He made the occasional visit home, his deterioration more evident each time. His clothes were becoming ragged. The family later found him living in a public washroom in Grange Park, behind the Art Gallery of Ontario. His family managed to obtain a court order for him to be assessed by a psychiatrist. As a result he was involuntarily admitted to the Clarke Institute of Psychiatry for more than three months. Doctors declared him incapable of making his own treatment decisions, and his mother was appointed a substitute decision-maker. She had the power to authorize forced medication.

Over the next few years, a pattern set in: arrest, often for some form of assault, incarceration, release. The combination of winter, homelessness, and illness were beginning to wear Edmond down. Late one afternoon, he was at the bus loop at the foot of Spadina Avenue in Toronto. Unaccountably, he struck a woman in the face, then boarded a bus. The police were called. The driver ordered everyone off the bus and left Edmond alone with the doors locked. Three police officers boarded the bus and tried to persuade Edmond to leave with them. At one point, he did agree to leave, but then took a hammer out of his jacket.

"I watched while he waggled his right wrist with the hammer in it," said a witness, who watched from an adjacent streetcar. "Then the movement of his wrist stopped, and seconds passed, when I heard what I thought initially was a cap gun. I could see the red flash of the gun, and the body slumped."

Constable Lou Pasquino fired six shots. One hit Edmond in the throat, his head twisting as the shots continued. A second hit his ear and entered the side of his head. The third hit the back of his skull. Edmond was dead before he hit the floor.

Source: Adapted from Scott Simmie, "Reality is sometimes painful," *Toronto Star*, October 3, 1998.

summary

15.1 Understand legal, ethical, and professional issues related to the practice of psychology.
The work of psychologists is regulated by various entities, including federal and provincial governments, as well as codes of ethics adopted by professional organizations. These codes are developed by professional societies and dictate how members should behave when engaged in their profession. Some of the most important concepts governing the treatment of people with psychological disorders include beneficence, fidelity, integrity, justice, and respect for people's rights and dignity.

15.2 Discuss the positive and negative aspects of deinstitutionalization.
The goal of deinstitutionalization was to allow people with psychological disorders to be treated in the least restrictive environment. Although deinstitutionalization has allowed many individuals with psychological disorders to live in the community, a substantial number have not been successful in achieving community integration, resulting in homelessness or return to other facilities such as prison.

15.3 Understand the difference between criminal and civil commitment.
Civil commitment is a legal process that mandates treatment for people when there is concern that they may be a danger to themselves or others. Patients may be committed to inpatient treatment or outpatient treatment; the latter is far more common. Criminal commitment occurs when someone commits a crime and may result from jury decisions of NCRMD. Criminal commitment involves removal from society; the person is committed to a psychiatric ward within a penal institution.

15.4 Identify the reasons for involuntary commitment for psychiatric services.
Involuntary commitment for treatment is considered appropriate when a person is a danger to her- or himself or to another person. Therefore, a person who threatens to commit suicide or threatens to harm another person may be committed to a psychiatric care facility against her or his will. Similarly, a person may be committed if she or he is so disabled as to be unable to take care of basic needs (does not eat or drink or take care of other activities of daily living).

15.5 Describe documents crucial to the development of rights for research participants.
Participation in research must be a choice; potential participants should never be coerced or misled. The Nuremberg Code, the Declaration of Helsinki, and the Belmont Report are important documents that set standards (rights of participants, beneficence, and justice) that any research project must meet.

15.6 Give reasons why some cultural groups may be reluctant to participate in research.
Lack of attention to these standards is reflected in the maltreatment of research participants in cases such as the Tuskegee experiment and the Baltimore lead paint study. In turn, these experiments, as well as cultural insensitivity, have left many racial and ethnic minority groups mistrustful of research and research participation.

key terms

Belmont Report 557
civil commitment 542
confidentiality 550
criminal commitment 543
Declaration of Helsinki 557
deinstitutionalization 540
duty to warn 551
ethics 538
informed consent 558
institutional review board (IRB) 558
M'Naghten Rule 543
malpractice 554
mens rea 543
not criminally responsible on account of a mental disorder 544
not guilty by reason of insanity 543
Nuremberg Code 557
outpatient commitment 542
polypharmacy 556
privilege 550
Tuskegee experiment 561

TEST yourself

1. Psychologists assume ethical responsibilities for individuals when they
   a. provide clinical services or conduct research
   b. provide services for a fee
   c. represent themselves to the media as psychologists
   d. provide clinical services but not when they conduct research
2. Before the 1960s, severely mentally ill patients were typically confined to hospitals because
   a. large numbers of untreated patients overwhelmed community programs
   b. available psychosocial treatments were best provided in an institutional setting
   c. effective treatments and medications had yet to be discovered
   d. too few psychiatrists provided services in a community setting
3. The effects of deinstitutionalization include
   a. contributions to society by some people who would otherwise not have had the opportunity
   b. fewer psychiatric hospital beds and more community-based care
   c. higher rates of incarceration for mentally disabled individuals
   d. all of the above
4. The deinstitutionalization movement failed because
   a. health insurance never adequately covered the true cost of care
   b. governments gave up on the movement and reopened the hospitals
   c. the new outpatient clinics were underfunded and understaffed
   d. the stigma of mental illness led patients to avoid outpatient clinics
5. Outpatient commitment is most successful when it
   a. is sustained and intensive
   b. alternates with inpatient treatment
   c. is provided by a psychologist
   d. includes pharmacologic treatment
6. A person who is judged to be not criminally responsible on account of a mental disorder
   a. did not commit a crime
   b. is allowed to walk free
   c. is under criminal commitment
   d. is subject to civil commitment
7. The phrase "not criminally responsible on account of a mental disorder"
   a. can be applied to individuals with a variety of psychological disorders
   b. is a legal decision, not a psychiatric diagnosis
   c. implies that the person actually committed the crime
   d. all of the above
8. When a person is found not criminally responsible on account of a mental disorder, the person is
   a. considered criminally guilty and is subject to criminal penalties such as incarceration
   b. considered criminally guilty but is ensured additional mental health treatment
   c. not subject to criminal incarceration
   d. not subject to judgment in a court of law
9. Unlike privacy, confidentiality is held by a therapist and patient and
   a. is legally absolute in all jurisdictions
   b. does not apply in some situations
   c. is an ethical ideal but impractical in reality
   d. also applies to organizations
10. Dr. Amanda Stevens, a clinical child psychologist, shares basic diagnostic and treatment information with a four-year-old child's parents and the health insurance company. Dr. Stevens
    a. violated confidentiality
    b. was legally required to tell the insurance company but not the parents
    c. was ethically required to share information with the parents but not the insurance company
    d. was ethically and legally required to share the information with the parents and the insurance company

11. John sought treatment from a clinical psychologist to deal with his feelings of depression. At his last therapy session, he revealed that he had a serious plan to harm his boss. The psychologist was ethically obligated to
 a. maintain confidentiality despite the risk
 b. simply obtain John's promise not to act on his plan
 c. warn John's boss of the threat and inform appropriate law enforcement personnel
 d. consult with her supervisor or another professional practitioner

12. When psychologists are accused of malpractice, the most common cause is
 a. child custody evaluations
 b. disputes during marital and family counselling
 c. inappropriate relationships with former patients
 d. the involuntary hospitalization of a child

13. Professionals who are licensed to provide mental health services have credentials that
 a. require a uniform and standardized training curriculum
 b. can be different depending on the jurisdiction in question
 c. emphasize training in the scientist-practitioner model
 d. call for a Ph.D. degree and specialized residency

14. Granting prescription privileges to licensed psychologists
 a. will allow any patient who wants medication to get it
 b. will be determined by the laws of each legal jurisdiction
 c. will mean that psychologists will now be granted a medical degree
 d. all of the above

15. Both the Nuremberg Code (1947) and the Declaration of Helsinki (1967) set forth early specific directives for
 a. conducting valid and well-controlled experiments with human subjects
 b. analyzing and reporting the results of placebo research with human subjects
 c. performing involuntary experiments with prisoners and other vulnerable populations
 d. protecting human subjects in all experiments

16. The Belmont Report (1979) identified three basic principles to guide behavioural and biomedical research with human subjects. Which of the following is *not* one of those principles?
 a. respect for persons
 b. justice
 c. beneficence
 d. informed consent

17. Conducting psychological research with children in most circumstances and jurisdictions requires parental or guardian consent and
 a. cooperation from the local school district
 b. each child's assent, when possible
 c. no use of placebos
 d. monitoring by the authorities

18. People who are members of racial and ethnic minority groups are often reluctant to participate in research because
 a. they are not aware of the value of research studies
 b. in the past, researchers mistreated members of these groups
 c. they are more sensitive to privacy issues
 d. research studies take a lot of time

Answers:

1 a, 2 c, 3 d, 4 c, 5 a, 6 c, 7 d, 8 b, 9 b, 10 d, 11 c, 12 a, 13 b, 14 b, 15 d, 16 d, 17 b, 18 b.

glossary

A

Abnormal behaviour. Conduct that is inconsistent with the individual's developmental, cultural, and societal norms, and that creates emotional distress or interferes with daily functioning.

Abstinence violation effect. The core feature of relapse prevention, which focuses on a person's cognitive and affective responses to re-engaging in a prohibited behaviour.

Acute stress paradigm. A procedure in which short-term stress is created in the laboratory and its impact on physiological, neuroendocrine, and psychological responses is measured.

Ageism. The tendency to attribute a multitude of problems to advancing age.

Agonist substitution. A type of therapy that substitutes a chemically similar medication for the drug of abuse.

Agoraphobia. A fear of being in public places or situations where escape might be difficult or help unavailable if a panic attack occurs.

Alcohol cirrhosis. A liver disease that occurs in about 10% to 15% of people with alcoholism.

Alogia. The decreased quality or quantity of speech.

Alzheimer's disease (AD). The most common form of dementia, characterized by a gradual onset and continuing cognitive decline, which includes memory loss, difficulties with language and decision making, and ultimately inability to care for self.

Amenorrhea. The absence of menstruation for at least three consecutive months.

Amnesia. The inability to recall important information; usually occurs after a medical condition or event.

Amnestic MCI. The mild cognitive impairment in which cognitive complaints focus on memory difficulties.

Amphetamines. A group of stimulant drugs that prolong wakefulness and suppress appetite.

Analgesic medications. A group of medications that reduces pain.

Anhedonia. The lack of capacity for pleasure; a condition in which a person does not feel joy or happiness.

Animal magnetism. A force that Mesmer believed flowed within the body and, when impeded, resulted in disease.

Anorexia nervosa. A serious condition marked by a restriction of energy intake relative to needed energy requirements, resulting in significantly low body weight.

Antabuse. An aversive medication that pairs the ingestion of a drug with a noxious physical reaction.

Antidepressants. A group of medications designed to alter mood-regulating chemicals in the brain and body that are highly effective in reducing symptoms of depression.

Antipsychotics. A class of medications that block dopamine receptors at neuron receptor sites.

Antisocial personality disorder. A pervasive pattern of disregard for and violation of the rights of others.

Anxiety. A common emotion characterized by physical symptoms, future-oriented thoughts, and escape or avoidance behaviours.

Anxiety disorders. A group of disorders characterized by heightened physical arousal, cognitive/subjective distress, and behavioural avoidance of feared objects/situations/events.

Appraisal process. An assessment of whether a person has the resources or coping skills to meet the demands of a situation.

Attention-deficit/hyperactivity disorder (ADHD). A common childhood disorder characterized by inattentiveness, hyperactivity, and impulsivity.

Atypical antipsychotic. A group of medication that effectively treats positive symptoms, is much less likely to produce tardive dyskinesia, and has some effect on negative symptoms and cognitive impairments.

Autism spectrum disorder. Consists of deficits in social communication and social interaction and the presence of restrictive and repetitive behaviour patterns.

Aversion therapy. A treatment approach that repeatedly pairs drug or alcohol use with an aversive stimulus or images.

Avoidant personality disorder. A pervasive pattern of social inhibition, feelings of inadequacy, and hypersensitivity to negative evaluation.

Avoidant–Restrictive Food Intake Disorder (AFRID). A disorder that captures the behaviour of those children who exhibit restricted or otherwise inadequate eating.

Avolition. The inability to initiate or follow through on plans.

B

Barbiturates. Sedatives that act on the GABA system in a manner similar to alcohol.

Behavioural avoidance test. The behavioural assessment strategy used to assess avoidance behaviour by asking a patient to approach a feared situation as closely as possible.

Behavioural genetics. The field of study that explores the role of genes and environment in the transmission of behavioural traits.

Behavioural inhibition. A temperamental feature characterized by withdrawal from (or failure to approach) novel people, objects, or situations.

Behavioural medicine. An interdisciplinary field that studies the relation between behavioural and biomedical science.

Behavioural observation. The measurement of behaviour as it occurs by someone other than the person whose behaviour is being observed.

Behaviourism. The theory that the only appropriate objects of scientific study are behaviours that can be observed and measured directly.

Belmont Report. The document that sets forth three basic principles to guide behavioural and biomedical research with human subjects: respect for persons, beneficence, and justice.

Beneficence. The core ethical principle ensuring that researchers do no harm and maximize possible benefits and minimize possible harms.

Benzodiazepines. A group of sedatives that can be used responsibly and effectively for the short term but still have addictive properties.

Binge eating. Consuming a larger amount of food than most people would eat in a discrete period of time and having a sense that eating is out of control.

Binge eating disorder. A condition characterized by regular binge eating behaviour but without the inappropriate compensatory behaviours that are part of bulimia nervosa.

Biofeedback. A process in which patients learn to modify physical responses such as heart rate, respiration, and body temperature.

Biological scarring. The process by which years of living with a disorder cause changes in the brain.

Biomedical model. A perspective that explains illnesses solely by biological processes.

Biopsychosocial model. A theoretical perspective that suggests that health is determined by complex interactions among biological, psychological, and social factors.

Biopsychosocial perspective. The idea that biological, psychological, and social factors probably contribute to the development of abnormal behaviour and that different factors are important for different individuals.

Bipolar disorder. A state of both episodic depressed mood and episodic mania.

Bipolar I. Full-blown mania that alternates with episodes of major depression.

Bipolar II. Hypomania that alternates with episodes of major depression.

Bipolar and depressive disorders. Syndromes whose predominant feature is a disturbance in mood.

Body dysmorphic disorder. An overwhelming concern that some part of the body is ugly or misshapen.

Body mass index (BMI). The formula for weight, in kilograms, divided by height, in metres squared (kg/m^2).

Borderline personality disorder. A pervasive pattern of instability in interpersonal relationships, self-image, and affect with marked impulsive features such as frantic efforts to avoid real or imagined abandonment.

Brain stem. A part of the brain located at its base that controls fundamental biological functions such as breathing.

Brief psychotic disorder. The sudden onset of any psychotic symptom that may resolve after one day and does not last for more than one month.

Bulimia nervosa. A disorder characterized by recurrent episodes of binge eating in combination with inappropriate compensatory behaviour aimed at undoing the effects of the binge or preventing weight gain.

C

Caffeine. A central nervous system stimulant that boosts energy, mood, awareness, concentration, and wakefulness.

Candidate gene association study. A study that compares one or a few genes in a large group of individuals who have a specific trait or disorder with a well-matched group of individuals who do not have the trait or disorder.

Case study. The comprehensive description of an individual (or group of individuals) that focuses on the assessment or description of abnormal behaviour or its treatment.

Catatonia. A condition in which a person is awake but is nonresponsive to external stimulation.

Central nervous system. One part of the human nervous system that includes the brain and the spinal cord.

Cerebral cortex. The largest part of the forebrain; contains structures that contribute to higher cognitive functioning including reasoning, abstract thought, perception of time, and creativity.

Cerebral senile plaque. The deposits of beta-amyloid protein that form between the cells found in the brains of patients with Alzheimer's disease.

Civil commitment. A state-initiated procedure that forces involuntary treatment on people who are judged to have a mental illness and who present a danger to themselves (including the inability to care for themselves) or others.

Clang associations. Conditions in which a person's speech is governed by words that sound alike rather than words that have meaning.

Classical conditioning. A form of learning in which a conditioned stimulus (CS) is paired with an unconditioned stimulus (UCS) to produce a conditioned response (CR).

Clinical assessment. The process of gathering information about a person and his or her environment to make decisions about the nature, status, and treatment of psychological problems.

Clinical interviews. Conversations between an interviewer and a patient whose purpose is to gather information and make judgments related to assessment goals.

Clinical significance. An observed change that is meaningful in terms of clinical functioning.

Cluster A. A group of personality disorders that include characteristic ways of behaving that can be viewed as odd, quirky, or eccentric; includes paranoid, schizoid, and schizotypal personality disorders.

Cluster B. A group of personality disorders that include characteristic ways of behaving that can be viewed as exaggerated, inflated, dramatic, emotional, or erratic; includes antisocial, borderline, narcissistic, and histrionic personality disorders.

Cluster C. A group of personality disorders that include characteristic ways of behaving that are marked by considerable anxiety or withdrawal; includes avoidant, dependent, and obsessive-compulsive personality disorders.

Cocaine. A stimulant that comes from the leaves of the coca plant that is indigenous to South America.

Cognitive impairment. The diminishment in visual and verbal learning and memory, inability to pay attention, decreased speed of information processing, and inability to engage in abstract reasoning, any or all of which may be found in different psychotic disorders.

Cohort. A group of people who share a common characteristic and move forward in time as a unit.

Cohort studies. The study of a group of people who share a common characteristic and move forward in time as a unit.

Comorbidity. The presence of more than one disorder.

Conduct disorder (CD). The continuous and repeated pattern of violating the basic rights of others or breaking societal rules, including aggression toward people or animals, destruction of property, deceitfulness or theft, and serious rule violations.

Confidentiality. An agreement between two parties (in this case, the therapist and patient) that private information revealed during therapy will not be discussed with others.

Consent form. A form agreeing to the terms of a study and indicating that a person understands his or her rights as a participant.

Contingency contracting. A strategy that relies on setting up a reinforcement program to encourage healthier behaviour.

Contingency management approach. A treatment approach in which rewards are provided for treatment compliance.

Contracting. The strategy that relies on setting up a reinforcement program to encourage healthy behaviour.

Control group. The comparison group for an experimental study in which the variable to be studied is absent.

Controlled group design. An experiment in which groups of participants are exposed to different conditions, at least one of which is experimental and one of which is a control.

Conventional or typical antipsychotics. Medications that effectively reduce the positive symptoms of schizophrenia but produce serious side effects.

Conversion disorder. A pseudoneurological complaint, such as motor or sensory dysfunction, that is not fully explained by the presence of a medical condition.

Correlation. The relationship between variables.

Correlation coefficient. A statistical figure that describes the direction and strength of a correlation.

Covert sensitization. A treatment that uses prolonged, imaginal exposure to engagement in a sexually deviant act but that also includes imagining the negative consequences that result from it.

Criminal commitment. A court-ordered procedure that forces involuntary mental health treatment on a person with a psychological disorder who commits a crime.

Cross-sectional design. A research design in which participants are assessed once for the specific variable under investigation.

Crystal methamphetamine. A form of methamphetamine that produces longer lasting and more intense physiological reactions than the powdered form.

Cultural-familial retardation. The mild intellectual disability that is more common among children in the lower socioeconomic classes and is considered retardation due to psychosocial disadvantage.

Culture. The shared behavioural patterns and lifestyles that differentiate one group of people from another.

Culture-bound syndrome. The abnormal behaviours that are specific to a particular location or group.

Cyclothymic disorder. A condition characterized by fluctuations that alternate between hypomanic symptoms and depressive symptoms.

D

Declaration of Helsinki. A document that sets forth basic guidelines for the conduct of research, including the need for clearly formulated experimental procedures, a careful assessment of risks compared with benefits, and the provision of adequate information to the participants.

Deinstitutionalization. The release of inpatients from hospitals to community treatment settings.

Delayed ejaculation. The delay of or inability to achieve orgasm despite adequate sexual stimulation; sometimes known as *retarded ejaculation*.

Delirium. A disturbance in consciousness that typically occurs in the context of a medical illness or after ingesting a substance.

Delirium tremens (DT). A symptom characterized by disorientation, severe agitation, high blood pressure, and fever, which can last up to three to four days after stopping drinking.

Delusion. A false belief.

Delusional disorder. A condition in which a person has a nonbizarre delusion, no other psychotic symptoms, and few changes in overall functioning other than the behaviours immediately surrounding the delusion.

Delusions of influence. The belief that other people are controlling one's thoughts or behaviours.

Dementia due to other general medical conditions. The cognitive impairment related to HIV, head trauma, Parkinson's disease, and Huntington's disease, or other medical illness.

Dementia praecox. Kraepelin's name for a psychological disorder characterized by deterioration of mental faculties (now called *schizophrenia*).

Dementia praecox. The original name for schizophrenia coined by Kraepelin to highlight its pervasive disturbances of perceptual and cognitive faculties (*dementia*) and its early life onset (*praecox*) and to distinguish it from the dementia associated with old age.

Dependent personality disorder. A pervasive and excessive need to be taken care of by others that leads to dependency and fears of being left alone.

Dependent variable. The variable in a controlled experiment that is assessed to determine the effect of the independent variable.

Depersonalization/derealization disorder. Feelings of being detached from one's body or mind; a state of feeling as if one is an external observer of one's own behaviour.

Depression. A mood that is abnormally low.

Detoxification. A medically supervised drug withdrawal.

Developmental trajectory. The idea that common symptoms of a disorder may vary depending on a person's age.

Diagnosis. The identification of an illness.

***Diagnostic and Statistical Manual of Mental Disorders* (DSM).** A classification of mental disorders originally developed in 1952; has been revised over subsequent years and is a standard of care in psychiatry and psychology.

Diathesis-stress model of abnormal behaviour. The idea that psychological disorders may have a biological or psychological predisposition (diathesis) that lies dormant until environmental stress occurs and the combination produces abnormal.

Differential diagnosis. A process in which a clinician weighs how likely it is that a person has one diagnosis instead of another.

Dimensional approach. An approach to understanding behaviour that considers it from a quantitative perspective (a little shy, moderately shy, a lot shy), not a qualitative perspective (shy or not shy).

Diminished emotional expression. Reduced or immobile facial expressions and a flat, monotonic vocal tone that does not change even when the topic of conversation becomes emotionally laden.

Disruptive mood regulation disorder. A disorder for children ages 6 to 18 years old who have severe recurrent temper outbursts that are grossly out of proportion in intensity or duration to the situation.

Dissociative amnesia. An inability to recall important information, usually of a personal nature, that follows a stressful or traumatic event.

Dissociative disorders. A set of disorders characterized by disruption in the usually integrated functions of consciousness, memory, identity, or perception of the environment.

Dissociative fugue. A disorder involving loss of personal identity and memory, often involving a flight from a person's usual place of residence.

Dissociative identity disorder. The presence within a person of two or more distinct personality states, each with its own pattern of perceiving, relating to, and thinking about the environment and self.

Dopamine hypothesis. The theory that a cause of schizophrenia is the presence of too much dopamine in the neural synapses.

Double depression. A combination of episodic major depressions superimposed on chronic low mood.

Down syndrome. The unusual condition in which a chromosomal set has three chromosomes (i.e., trisomy) rather than the usual set of two.

Duty to warn. The duty of therapists to use reasonable care to protect third parties from dangers posed by patients.

E

Early-onset schizophrenia. A form of schizophrenia that develops in childhood or adolescence (usually before age 18).

Eating disorder not otherwise specified. A DSM-IV-TR residual diagnostic category for people who have eating disorders that do not match the classic profile of anorexia nervosa or bulimia nervosa.

Echolalia. The verbatim repetition of what others say.

Ecstasy. The pill form of *methylenedioxymethamphetamine* (MDMA), a common "club" drug and a frequent trigger for emergency room visits.

Ego psychology. A form of psychodynamic theory that focuses on conscious motivations and healthy forms of human functioning.

Electroconvulsive therapy (ECT). The controlled delivery of electrical impulses that cause brief seizures in the brain and reduce depressed mood.

Emotional contagion. The automatic mimicry and synchronization of expressions, vocalizations, postures, and movements of one person by another.

Encopresis. The repeated elimination of feces on or into inappropriate places such as the floor or clothing by someone over age four.

Endocrine system. A system in the body that uses hormones rather than nerve impulses to regulate bodily functions.

Enmeshment. The overinvolvement of all family members in the affairs of any one member.

Enuresis. The voiding of urine into one's clothing or bedding.

Epidemiology. A research approach that focuses on the prevalence and incidence of disorders and the factors that influence those patterns.

Epigenetics. Heritable changes in gene expression.

Erectile disorder. A condition with persistent and recurrent inability to maintain an adequate erection until completion of sexual activity.

Ethics. The accepted values that provide guidance to make sound moral judgments.

Excoriation (skin picking) disorder. Recurrent skin-picking that results in skin lesions.

Executive dysfunction. The condition characterized by difficulty planning, thinking abstractly, initiating, and inhibiting actions.

Exhibitionistic disorder. The recurrent fantasies, urges, or behaviours involving exposing one's genitals to an unsuspecting stranger.

Experimental epidemiology. A research method in which the scientist manipulates exposure to either causal or preventive factors.

Experimental variable. The variable being tested in an experimental study.

Exposure. The crucial ingredient in behaviour therapy in which a person learns to overcome fears by actual or imagined contact with the feared object or event.

Expressed emotion. A concept used to describe the level of emotional involvement and critical attitudes that exist within the family of a patient with schizophrenia.

F

Factitious disorder. The condition in which physical or psychological signs or symptoms of illness are intentionally produced in what appears to be a desire to assume a sick role.

Factitious disorder imposed on another. A condition in which one person induces illness symptoms in someone else.

Factitious disorder imposed on self. A condition in which a person self-engages in deceptive practices to produce signs of illness.

Familial aggregation. The process of examining whether family members of a person with a particular disorder are more likely to have that disorder than family members of people without the disorder.

Female orgasmic disorder. A condition with persistent and recurrent delay or absence of orgasm following the normal excitement phase; sometimes called *anorgasmia.*

Female sexual interest/arousal disorder. A condition with persistent or recurrent inability to maintain adequate vaginal lubrication and swelling response until the completion of sexual activity.

Fetal alcohol syndrome (FAS). A condition in babies that occurs when pregnant mothers drink alcohol and it passes through the placenta and harms the developing fetus; it is the leading known preventable environmental cause of intellectual disability.

Fetishistic disorder. Sexual arousal (fantasies, urges, or behaviours) that involves nonliving objects (not limited to female clothing used in cross-dressing).

Fight or flight. A general discharge of the sympathetic nervous system activated by stress or fear that includes accelerated heart rate, enhanced muscle activity, and increased respiration.

Forebrain. A part of the brain that includes the limbic system, basal ganglia, and cerebral cortex.

Fragile X syndrome (FXS). The most commonly inherited cause of intellectual disability; occurs when a DNA series makes too many copies of itself and "turns off" a gene on the X chromosome, resulting in cells not making a necessary protein.

Frontal lobe. One of the four lobes of the brain; seat of reasoning, impulse control, judgment, language, memory, motor function, problem solving, and sexual and social behaviour that sends messages to the bodily organs via hormones.

Frotteuristic disorder. The consistent and intense sexually arousing fantasies, sexual urges, or behaviours involving touching and rubbing against a nonconsenting person.

Functional analysis. A strategy of behavioural assessment in which a clinician attempts to identify causal links between problem behaviours and environmental variables; also called *behavioural analysis* or *functional assessment.*

G

Gender dysphoria. A strong and persistent cross-sex identification in which a person's biological sex and gender identity do not match.

Gene–environment correlation. The person who contributes to a patient's genetic makeup and provides the environment in which the patient lives.

General adaptation syndrome (GAS). A three-stage process of stress adaptation including alarm, resistance, and exhaustion.

Generalized anxiety disorder (GAS). Excessive worry about future events, past transgressions, financial status, and the health of oneself and loved ones.

Genito-pelvic pain/penetration disorder. Consistent genital pain associated with sexual intercourse.

Genomewide association study. The study of the unbiased search of the human genome comparing cases and controls on genetic variants scattered across the genome for evidence of association.

Genomewide linkage analysis. A technique that uses samples of families with many individuals who are ill with the same disorder or large samples of relatives who have the same disorder to identify genomic regions that may hold genes that influence a trait.

Geropsychology. A subdiscipline of psychology that addresses issues of aging, including normal development, individual differences, and psychological problems unique to older persons.

Goodness of fit. The idea that behaviour is problematic or not problematic depending on the environment in which it occurs.

H

Hallucination. A false sensory perception.

Hallucinogens. Drugs that produce altered states of bodily perception and sensations, intense emotions, detachment from self and environment, and, for some users, feeling of insight with mystical or religious significance.

Health psychology. A subfield of psychology that uses its principles and methods to understand how attitudes and behaviours influence health and illness.

Heritability. The percentage of variance in liability to the disorder accounted for by genetic factors

Hippocampus. The brain region that is part of the limbic system that also has a role in memory formation.

Histrionic personality disorder. A pervasive pattern of excessive emotionality and attention seeking.

Hoarding disorder. A disorder characterized by the persistent difficulty discarding or parting with possessions, regardless of their actual value.

Hormones. Chemical messengers that are released into the bloodstream and act on target organs.

Hypnosis. A procedure for treating pain during which patients relax, a trance-like state is induced, and hypnotic suggestions are used to reduce pain.

Hypomania. A mood elevation that is clearly abnormal yet not as extreme as frank mania.

Hypothalamic-pituitary-adrenocortical (HPA) axis. A system that responds to stress in which the hypothalamus produces increased corticotrophin-releasing factor (CRF), which in turn causes increased secretion of adrenocorticotropic hormone (ACTH) and increased cortisol.

I

Iatrogenic. The term describing a disease that may be inadvertently caused by a physician, by a medical or surgical treatment, or by a diagnostic procedure.

Illness anxiety disorder. The condition of experiencing fears or concerns about having an illness that persists despite medical reassurance.

Inappropriate compensatory behaviour. Any actions that a person uses to counteract a binge or to prevent weight gain.

Incidence. The number of new cases that emerge in a given population during a specified period of time.

Independent variable. The variable in a controlled experiment that the experimenter controls.

Informed consent. The concept that all people who participate in research must understand its aims and methods, what they will be asked to do, what types of information they will be asked to provide, and the risks and benefits of research participation, and based on that information, have the right to agree or refuse to participate in any research project.

Inhalants. The vapours from a variety of chemicals that yield an immediate effect of euphoria or sedation and can cause permanent damage to all organ systems, including the brain.

Insomnia. A condition characterized by difficulty in initiating or maintaining sleep, or nonrestorative sleep, over a period of at least one month and with significant distress or interference with functioning.

Institutional review board (IRB). A committee charged by the researcher's institution with reviewing and approving scientific research.

Intellectual disability. Impairments of general mental abilities that impact functioning in conceptual, social, and practical domains.

Intelligence quotient. A score of cognitive functioning that compares a person's performance to his or her age-matched peers.

Intelligence test. A test that measures intelligence quotient (IQ).

International Classification of Diseases and Related Health Problems (ICD). A classification system for mental disorders developed in Europe that is an international standard diagnostic system for epidemiology and many health management purposes.

Interrater agreement. The amount of agreement between two clinicians who are using the same measure to rate the same symptoms in a single patient.

L

Late-onset schizophrenia. The schizophrenia that first appears after age 40.

Learned helplessness. A term meaning that externally uncontrollable environments and presumably internally uncontrollable environments are inescapable stimuli that can lead to depression.

Left hemisphere. The region of the brain primarily responsible for language and cognitive functions.

Lifespan developmental diathesis-stress model. A model that considers the role of biological predispositions, stressful life events, and personal protective factors in the etiology of depression.

Limbic system. The brain region involved with the experience of emotion, the regulation of emotional expression, and the basic biological drives such as aggression, sex, and appetite.

Lithium. A naturally occurring metallic element used to treat bipolar disorder.

Longitudinal design. A research design in which participants are assessed at least two times and often more over a certain time interval.

Loose association. A thought that has little or no logical connection to the next one.

Lysergic acid diethylamide (LSD). A synthetic hallucinogen, first synthesized in 1938.

M

M'Naghten Rule. A legal principle stating that a person is not responsible for his or her actions if (a) the person did not know what he or she was doing or (b) the person did not know that his or her actions were wrong.

Major depressive disorder. A persistent sad or low mood that is severe enough to impair a person's interest in or ability to engage in normally enjoyable activities.

Major neurocoginitive disorder. A disorder significantly affecting older people that represents deficits in cognitive abilities.

Major or mild vascular neurocognitive disorder. A disorder diagnosed when a patient's history, laboratory tests, or brain imaging studies indicate cognitive impairment as a result of cardiovascular disease, such as stroke, transient ischemic attack (TIA, or mini-stroke), coronary artery disease, or untreated high blood pressure.

Male hypoactive sexual desire disorder. A condition with reduced or absent sexual desires or behaviours, either with a partner or through masturbation.

Malingering. A condition in which physical symptoms are produced intentionally to avoid military service, criminal prosecution, or work, or to obtain financial compensation or drugs.

Malpractice. Professional misconduct or unreasonable lack of skill.

Mania. A mood that is abnormally high.

Marijuana. A drug derived from the *Cannabis sativa* plant that produces mild intoxication.

Mass hysteria. A situation in which a group of people share and sometimes even act upon a belief that is not based in fact (e.g., tarantism and lycanthropy).

Medical psychology. The study and practice of psychology as it relates to health, illness, and medical treatment.

Mens rea. Latin term for guilty mind or criminal intent.

Methadone. The most widely known agonist substitute; used as a replacement for heroin.

Midbrain. A portion of the brain stem that coordinates sensory information and movement; includes the reticular activating system, the thalamus, and the hypothalamus.

Mind–body dualism. A belief that the mind and body function independently; associated with French philosopher René Descartes.

Mixed state. A state characterized by symptoms of mania and depression that occur at the same time.

Molecular genetics. The study of the structure and function of genes at a molecular level.

N

Narcissistic personality disorder. A pervasive pattern of grandiosity, need for admiration from others, and lack of empathy.

Negative symptoms. The behaviours, emotions, or thought processes (cognition) that exist in people without a psychiatric disorder but are absent (or are substantially diminished) in people with schizophrenia.

Neuroanatomy. The brain structure.

Neurofibrillary tangles. The twisted protein fibres within neurons found in the brains of patients with Alzheimer's disease.

Neuroimaging. The technology that takes pictures of the brain.

Neuron. A nerve cell found throughout the body, including the brain.

Neuroscience. The study of the structure and function of the nervous system and the interaction of that system and behaviour.

Neurotransmitter. Chemical substances that are released into the synapse and transmit information from one neuron to another.

Nicotine. A highly addictive component of tobacco that is considered to be both a stimulant and a sedative.

Nicotine replacement therapy. A safe and effective therapy used as part of a comprehensive smoking cessation program.

Non-rapid eye movement sleep arousal disorder or nightmare disorder. When behaviours such as sleepwalking, sleep terrors, and nightmares are recurrent in children.

Nonspecific immune system. General protection against infections and diseases provided by anatomical barriers, phagocytosis, B-lymphocytes, and inflammation.

Normative. A comparison group that is representative of the entire population against which a person's score on a psychological test is compared.

Not criminally responsible on account of a mental disorder. A legal decision in Canada that describes people who commit a crime but who are prevented by a psychological disorder from understanding the seriousness and illegality of their actions.

Not guilty by reason of insanity. A legal decision in the United States that describes people who commit a crime but who are prevented by a psychological disorder from understanding the seriousness and illegality of their actions.

Nuremberg Code. The directives for experimentation with human subjects that specify that voluntary consent is absolutely essential for clinical research.

O

Obsessive-compulsive disorder. A condition involving obsessions (intrusive thoughts), often combined with compulsions (repetitive behaviours) that can be extensive, time consuming, and distressful.

Obsessive-compulsive personality disorder. A pervasive preoccupation with orderliness, perfectionism, and mental and interpersonal control to the point of distress.

Occipital lobe. One of four lobes of the brain, located at the back of the skull; centre of visual processing.

Olfactory aversion. A treatment pairing an extremely noxious but harmless odour (such as ammonia) with either sexual fantasies or sexual behaviours.

Operant conditioning. A form of learning in which behaviour is acquired or changed by the events that happen afterward.

Opioids. A drug group derived from the opium poppy, which includes heroin, morphine, and codeine.

Oppositional defiant disorder (ODD). The negative, hostile, or defiant behaviours that are less severe than those found in conduct disorder.

Osteoporosis. A condition of decreased bone density.

Outpatient commitment. A court order that directs a person to comply with a specified, individualized outpatient mental health treatment plan.

P

Panic attack. A discrete period of intense fear or discomfort (subjective distress) and a cascade of physical symptoms.

Panic disorder. A disorder in which the person has had at least one panic attack and worries about having more attacks.

Paranoid personality disorder. A pervasive distrust and suspiciousness of others such that their motives are interpreted as malevolent.

Parasympathetic nervous system (PNS). The part of the autonomic nervous system that counteracts the effects of system activation by slowing down heart rate and respiration, returning the body to a resting state.

Parietal lobe. One of four lobes of the brain; integrates sensory information from various sources and may be involved with visuospatial processing.

Pedophilic disorder. The consistent and intense sexually arousing fantasies, sexual urges, or behaviours involving sexual activity with a child or children not yet 14 years old; the person involved is at least 16 years old and at least five years older than the child or children.

Peripheral nervous system. One part of the human nervous system that includes the sensory–somatic nervous system (controls sensations and muscle movements) and the autonomic nervous system (controls involuntary movements).

Persecutory delusion. A patient's belief that someone is persecuting her or him or that the person is a special agent/individual.

Persistent depressive disorder. A chronic state of depression in which the symptoms are the same as those of major depression but are less severe.

Personality disorder. An enduring pattern of inner experience and behaviour that deviates from the norm, is pervasive and inflexible, has an onset in adolescence or early adulthood, is stable across time, and leads to distress or impairment.

Personality test. A psychological test that measures personality characteristics.

Phenomenology. A school of thought that holds that one's subjective perception of the world is more important than the world in actuality.

Phenylketonuria (PKU). A genetic disorder in which the body cannot break down the amino acid *phenylalanine*; if untreated, it leads to the development of intellectual disability.

Pica. The recurrent, compulsive consumption of nonnutritive items.

Placebo effect. Effect in which symptoms are diminished or eliminated not because of any specific treatment, but because the patient believes that a treatment is effective.

Plethysmography. A method to measure sexual arousal in men or women.

Polypharmacy. The practice of prescribing more than one medication for a single disorder.

Positive symptoms. A group of schizophrenic symptoms including unusual thoughts, feelings, and behaviours that vary in intensity and in many cases are responsive to treatment.

Posttraumatic stress disorder. The emotional distress that occurs after an event involving actual or threatened death, serious injury, or a threat to physical integrity and that leads to avoidance of stimuli associated with the trauma, feelings of emotional numbness, and persistent symptoms of increased sympathetic nervous system arousal.

Premature (early) ejaculation. The consistent ejaculation with minimal sexual stimulation before, immediately upon, or shortly after penetration and before the person wishes it.

Premenstrual dysphoric disorder (PMDD). A more severe form of premenstrual changes that afflict 3% to 8% of women of reproductive age.

Prevalence. The percentage of people with a disorder in a given population at a designated time.

Primary prevention. An intervention program that focuses on increasing healthy behaviours among people without disease.

Privilege. A legal term that prevents a therapist from revealing confidential information during legal proceedings.

Proband. The person with a particular disorder in a familial aggregation study.

Projective test. A test derived from psychoanalytic theory in which people are asked to respond to ambiguous stimuli.

Psychoanalysis. A theory of abnormal behaviour originated by Sigmund Freud that is based on the belief that many aspects of behaviour are controlled by unconscious innate biological urges that exist from infancy.

Psychoeducation. The teaching of patient and families about the patient's disorder in order to reduce familial distress and equip them to work effectively with the patient.

Psychogenic seizure. A sudden change in behaviour that mimics epileptic seizures but has no organic basis.

Psychological autopsy. An attempt to identify psychological causes of suicide by interviewing family, friends, co-workers, and health care providers.

Psychomotor retardation. A condition in which a person has slowed mental or physical activities.

Psychoneuroimmunology. The study of the relations between social, psychological, and physical responses.

Psychophysiological assessment. The evaluation strategies that measure brain structure, brain function, and nervous system activity.

Psychosis. A severe mental condition characterized by a loss of contact with reality.

Punishment. The application of something painful or the removal of something positive.

Purging. Self-inducing vomiting or using laxatives, diuretics (water pills), or enemas to reverse the effects of a binge or to induce weight loss.

R

Random assignment. The most critical feature of a randomized controlled design in which each participant has an equal probability of being assigned to each experimental or control condition.

Reinforcement. A contingent event that strengthens the response that precedes it.

Relapse prevention (RP). The treatment approach that uses functional analysis to identify the antecedents and consequences of drug use and then develops alternative cognitive and behavioural skills to reduce the risk of future drug use.

Reliability. The extent to which a psychological assessment instrument produces consistent results each time it is given.

Right hemisphere. The region of the brain associated with creativity, imagery, and intuition.

Rumination disorder. The regurgitation of recently eaten food into the mouth followed by either rechewing, reswallowing, or spitting it out.

S

Satiation. A treatment that uses prolonged, imagined exposure to arousing sexual stimuli until it no longer produces positive, erotic feelings.

Schizoaffective disorder. A condition in which, in addition to all of the symptoms of schizophrenia, the patient suffers from a major depressive, manic, or mixed episode disorder at some point during the illness.

Schizoid personality disorder. A pervasive pattern of social detachment and a limited expression of emotion in interpersonal contexts.

Schizophrenia. A severe psychological disorder characterized by disorganization in thought, perception, and behaviour.

Schizophreniform disorder. A condition with symptoms that are identical to those of schizophrenia except that its duration is shorter (less than six months) and it results in less impairment in social or occupational functioning.

Schizotypal personality disorder. A pervasive pattern of social and interpersonal deficits marked by acute discomfort, reduced capacity for close relationships, cognitive or perceptual distortions, and behavioural eccentricities.

Scientist–practitioner model. An approach to psychological disorders based on the concept that when providing treatment to people with psychological disorders, the psychologist relies on the findings of research and in turn, when conducting research, the psychologist investigates topics that help to guide and improve psychological care.

Screening. An assessment process that attempts to identify psychological problems or predict the risk of future problems among people who are not referred for clinical assessment.

Seasonal affective disorder. A subtype of major depression that is characterized by depressive episodes that vary by season.

Secondary prevention. A health-promotion program for people at increased risk for health problems.

Sedative drugs. A substance group, including barbiturates and benzodiazepines, which are central nervous system depressants and cause sedation and decrease anxiety.

Selective serotonin reuptake inhibitor (SSRIs). A group of medications that selectively inhibit the reuptake of serotonin at the presynaptic neuronal membrane, restoring the normal chemical balance; drugs thought to correct serotonin imbalances by increasing the time that the neurotransmitter remains in the synapse.

Self-monitoring. A procedure within behavioural assessment in which the patient observes and records his or her own behaviour as it happens.

Self-referent comparisons. Comparison of responses on a psychological instrument with a person's own prior performance.

Separation anxiety disorder. The severe and unreasonable fear of separation from a parent or a caregiver.

Sex drive. The physical or psychological craving for sexual activity and pleasure.

Sex reassignment surgery. A series of behavioural and medical procedures that matches an individual's physical anatomy to gender identity.

Sexual dysfunction. The absence or impairment of some aspect of sexual response that causes distress or impairment considering age, sex, and culture.

Sexual masochism disorder. A person's consistent intense sexually arousing fantasies, sexual urges, or behaviours involving actual acts of being humiliated, beaten, bound, or otherwise made to suffer.

Shared psychotic disorder. A condition in which two or more persons who have a close relationship share the same delusional belief; also known as *folie à deux*.

Single-case design. An experimental study conducted with a single individual.

Social anxiety disorder. A pervasive pattern of social timidity characterized by fear that the person will behave in a way that will be humiliating or embarrassing.

Social cognition. The ability to perceive, interpret, and understand social information, including other people's beliefs, attitudes, and emotions.

Sociocultural model. The idea that abnormal behaviour must be understood within the context of social and cultural forces.

Somatic symptom disorder. The presence of one or more somatic symptoms plus abnormal/excessive thoughts, feelings, and behaviours regarding the symptoms.

Somatic symptom and related disorders. A condition defined as the presence of one or more somatic symptoms plus abnormal/excessive thoughts, feelings, and behaviours regarding the symptoms

Specific immune system. Protection against specific infections and diseases as a result of natural or artificial processes.

Specific learning disorder. A condition involving persistent difficulty in reading, writing, arithmetic, or mathematics.

Specific phobias. Marked fear or anxiety about a specific object or situation that leads to significant disruption in daily functioning.

Stimulus control. The modification of behaviour by changing the stimuli that bring on the behaviour.

Stress. Any negative emotional experience that is accompanied by biochemical, physiological, cognitive, and behavioural responses that are aimed at changing or adjusting to the stressor.

Stress moderator. A variable that affects how stress is experienced and how it affects health and other aspects of functioning.

Stressor. Any event (or stimulus) that produces tension or other negative emotion, such as fear.

Structured interview. A clinical interview in which the clinician asks a standard set of questions, usually with the goal of establishing a diagnosis.

Substance intoxication. The acute effects of substance use.

Substance use. Low to moderate experience with a substance that does not produce problems with social, educational, or occupational functioning.

Substance/medication-induced major or mild neurocognitive disorder. The cognitive impairment associated with substance use.

Suicidal ideation. A condition characterized by thoughts of death.

Sympathetic nervous system (SNS). The part of the autonomic nervous system that activates the body for the fight-or-flight response; when activated, the sympathetic nervous system increases heart rate and respiration, allowing the body to perform at peak efficiency.

Sympathetic-adrenomedullary system (SAM). A system that responds to stress in which increased adrenal gland stimulation results in the secretion of epinephrine and norepinephrine.

Synapse. A space between neurons.

Synaptic pruning. A process in which weaker synaptic contacts in the brain are eliminated and stronger connections are enhanced.

T

Talking cure. A therapy in the form of discussion of psychological distress with a trained professional, leading to the elimination of distressing symptoms.

Tardive dyskinesia. A neurological condition characterized by abnormal and involuntary motor movements of the face, mouth, limbs, and trunk.

Temperament. Personality components that are biological or genetic in origin, observable from birth (or perhaps before), and relatively stable across time and situations.

Temporal lobe. One of four lobes of the brain; associated with understanding auditory and verbal information, labelling of objects, and verbal memory.

Test-retest reliability. The extent to which a test produces similar scores over time when given to the same individual(s).

Tetrahydrocannabinol (THC). The active ingredient in marijuana.

Thought blocking. An unusually long pause or pauses in a patient's speech that occur during a conversation.

Tolerance. The diminished response to a drug after repeated exposure to it.

Trait anxiety. A personality trait that exists along a dimension; those individuals high on this dimension are more "reactive" to stressful events and therefore more likely, given the right circumstances, to develop a disorder; also called *anxiety proneness*.

Transgender behaviour. The behavioural attempt to pass as the opposite sex through cross-dressing, disguising one's own sexual genitalia, or changing other sexual characteristics.

Translational research. A scientific approach that focuses on communication between basic science and applied clinical research.

Transsexualism. Another term for *gender dysphoria* commonly used to describe the condition when it occurs in adolescents and adults.

Transtheoretical model (TTM). A five-stage sequential model of behavioural change.

Transvestic disorder. The sexual arousal in men that results from wearing women's clothing and is accompanied by significant distress or impairment.

Trephination. The process in which a circular instrument was used to cut away sections of the skull, possibly in an attempt to release demons from the brain.

Trichotillomania. Repetitive hair pulling that results in noticeable hair loss.

Tuskegee experiment. An infamous historical study in which core values of research (respect for persons, beneficence, and justice) were violated.

Type A behaviour pattern. A personality pattern associated with the onset of coronary heart disease, associated with consistent strivings for achievement, impatience and time urgency, and aggressiveness toward others.

U

Unstructured interview. A clinical interview in which the clinician decides what questions to ask and how to ask them.

V

Validity. The degree to which a test measures what it is intended to assess.

Vascular depression. A mood disorder that occurs in the context of cerebrovascular disease.

Vasovagal syncope. A common physiological response consisting of slow heart rate and low blood pressure that sometimes occurs in people with blood/illness/injury phobias.

Very-late-onset schizophrenia-like psychosis. A schizophrenic-like disorder but with symptoms that do not include deterioration in social and personal functioning.

Vicarious conditioning. A distinct type of learning in which the person need not actually do the behaviour in order to acquire it.

Viral infection theory. The theory that during the prenatal period or shortly after birth, viral infections could cause some psychological disorders.

Voyeuristic disorder. Consistent, intense, sexually arousing fantasies, sexual urges, or behaviours centred on observing an unsuspecting person who is naked, disrobing, or engaging in sexual activity.

W

Waxy flexibility. A condition in which parts of the body (usually the arms) remain frozen in a particular posture when positioned that way by another person.

Wernicke-Korsakoff syndrome. A condition caused by deficiencies in thiamine secondary to alcohol dependence.

Withdrawal. A set of symptoms associated with physical dependence on a drug that occur when the drug is no longer taken.

Worry. The apprehensive (negative) expectations or outcomes about the future or the past that are considered to be unreasonable in light of the actual situation.

references

A

Abel, E. L., & Hannigan, J. H. (1995). Maternal risk factors in fetal alcohol syndrome: Provocative and permissive influences. *Neurotoxicology and Teratology, 17,* 445–462.

Abel, G. G., & Osborn, C. (1992). The paraphilias: The extent and nature of sexually deviant and criminal behavior. *Clinical Forensic Psychiatry, 15,* 675–687.

Abel, G. G., Becker, J. V., Cunningham-Rathner, J., Mittelman, M., & Rouleau, J. L. (1988). Multiple paraphilic diagnoses among sex offenders. *Bulletin of the American Academy of Psychiatry and the Law, 16,* 153–168.

Abel, G. G., Huffman, J., Warberg, B., & Holland, C. L. (1998). Visual reaction time and plethysmography as measures of sexual interest in child molesters. *Sexual Abuse: A Journal of Research and Treatment, 10,* 81–95.

Abel, G. G., Jordan, A., Rouleau, J. O. L., Emerick, R., Barboza-Whitehead, S., & Osborn, C. (2004). Use of visual reaction time to assess male adolescents who molest children. *Sexual Abuse: A Journal of Research and Treatment, 16,* 255–265.

Abrahams, P. W., & Parsons, J. A. (1996). Geophagy in the tropics: A literature review. Geographical Journal, 162, 63–72.

Abramowitz, J. S., Fabricant, L. E., Taylor, S., Deacon, B. J., McKay, D., & Storch, E. A. (2014). The relevance of analogue studies for understanding obsessions and compulsions. *Clinical Psychology Review, 34,* 206–217.

Abramson, L., Alloy, L., & Panzarella, C. (2002). Depression. In *Encyclopedia of Cognitive Science.* London: Macmillan.

Acarturk, C., Smit, F., de Graff, R., van Straten, A., Ten Have, M., & Cuijpers, P. (2009). Economic costs of social phobia. *Journal of Affective Disorders, 115,* 421–429.

Acocella, J. (1998, April 6). The politics of hysteria. *New Yorker,* 64–79.

Adams, J., Crosbie, J., Wigg, K., Ickowicz, A., Pathare, T., Roberts, W., . . . Barr, C. L. (2004). Glutamate receptor, ionotropic, N-methyl D-aspartate 2A (GRIN2A) gene as a positional candidate for attention-deficit/hyperactivity disorder in the 16p13 region. *Molecular Psychiatry, 9,* 494–499.

Addington, A. M., Gornick, M., Duckworth, J., Spron, A., Gogtayn N., Bobb, A., Greenstein, D., Lenane, M., Gochman, P., Baker, N., Balissoon, R., Vakkalanka, R. K., Weinberger, D. R., Rapoport, J. L., & Straub R. E. (2005). GAD1 (2q31.1) which encoded glutamic acid decarboxylase (GAD_{67}), is associated with childhood-onset schizophrenia and cortical gray matter volume loss. *Molecular Psychiatry, 10,* 581–588.

Adler, C. M., DelBello, M. P., & Strakowski, S. M. (2006). Brain network dysfunction in bipolar disorder. *CNS Spectrums, 11,* 312–320.

Adler, N. E., Boyce, W. T., Chesney, M. A., Folkman, S., & Syme, S. L. (1993). Socioeconomic inequalities in health. No easy solution. *Journal of the American Medical Association, 269,* 3140–3145.

Agargun, M. Y., Savas Cilli, A., Sener, S., Bilici, M., Ozer, O. A., Selvi, Y., & Karacan, E. (2004). The prevalence of parasomnias in preadolescent school-aged children: A Turkish sample. *Sleep, 47,* 701–705.

Agarwal, S., & Lau, C. T. (2010). Remote health monitoring using mobile phones and Web services. *Telemedicine Journal of E Health, 16,* 603–607.

Aigner, M., Graf, A., Freidl, M., Prause, W., Weiss, M., Kaup-Eder, B., . . . Bach, M. (2003). Sleep disturbances in somatoform pain disorder. *Psychopathology, 36,* 324–328.

Ainsworth, M. (1982). Attachment: Retrospect and prospect. In C. Parkes & J. Stevenson-Hinde (Eds.), *The place of attachment in human behavior* (pp. 3–30). New York, NY: Basic Books.

Al-Aama, T., Brymer, C., Gutmanis, I., . . . Dasqupta, M. (2011). Melatonin decreases delirium in elderly patients: A randomized, placebo-controlled trial. *International Journal of Geriatric Psychiatry, 26,* 687–694.

Albee, G. W. (2002). Just say no to psychotropic drugs! *Journal of Clinical Psychology, 58,* 635–648.

Alexopoulos, G. S. (2004). Late-life mood disorders. In J. Sadavoy, L. F. Jarvik, G. T. Grossberg, & B. S. Meyers (Eds.), *Comprehensive textbook of geriatric psychiatry* (pp. 609–653). New York, NY: W. W. Norton & Co.

Alfano, C. A., Beidel, D. C., & Turner, S. M. (2002). Cognition in childhood anxiety: Conceptual, methodological and developmental issues. *Clinical Psychology Review, 22,* 1029–1038.

Alfano, C. A., Beidel, D. C., & Turner, S. M. (2006). Cognitive correlates of social phobia among children and adolescents. *Journal of Abnormal Child Psychology, 34,* 189–201.

Allen, K. (1995). Barriers to treatment for addicted African-American women. *Journal of the National Medical Association, 87,* 751–756.

Allen, K., Blascovich, J., & Mendes, W. B. (2002). Cardiovascular reactivity and the presence of pets, friends, and spouses: The truth about cats and dogs. *Psychosomatic Medicine, 64,* 727–739.

Allison, P. J., Guichard, C., Fund, K., & Gilain, L. (2003). Dispositional optimism predicts survival status 1 year after diagnosis in head and neck cancer patients. *Journal of Clinical Oncology, 21,* 543–548.

Alloy, L. B., Abramson, L. Y., Whitehouse, W. G., Hogan, M. E., Tashman, N. A., Steinberg, D. L., . . . Donovan, P. (2000). The Temple-Wisconsin Cognitive Vulnerability to Depression Project: Lifetime history of axis I psychopathology in individuals at high and low cognitive risk for depression. *Journal of Abnormal Psychology, 109,* 403–418.

Almeida, O. P., Yeap, B. B., Alfonso, H., Hankey, G. J., Flicker, L. & Norman, P. E. (2012). Older men who use computers have lower risk of dementia. PLoS ONE, *7*(8): e44239. Doi:10.1371/journal.pone.0044239.

Alper, K., Devinsky, O., Perrine, K., Vazquez, B., & Luciano, D. (1993). Nonepileptic seizures and childhood sexual and physical abuse. *Neurology, 43,* 1950–1953.

Alsene, K., Deckert, J., Sand, P., & de Wit, H. (2003). Association between A2a receptor gene polymorphisms and caffeine-induced anxiety. *Neuropsychopharmacology, 28,* 1694–1702.

Althof, S. (2006). The psychology of premature ejaculation: Therapies and consequences. *Journal of Sexual Medicine, 3*(Suppl. 4), 324–331.

Alzheimer's Association. (2009). Alzheimer's disease facts and figures. *Alzheimer's & Dementia, 5,* 234–270.

Alzheimer's Disease International. (2015). *World Alzheimer Report 2015: The global impact of dementia.* London: Author.

Ambrosini, D. L., & Crocker, A. G. (2007). Psychiatric advance directives and the right to refuse treatment in Canada. *Canadian Journal of Psychiatry, 52,* 397–402.

American Academy of Child and Adolescent Psychiatry (2010). Practice parameter for the assessment and treatment of children and adolescents with Posttraumatic Stress disorder. *Journal of the American Academy of Child and Adolescent psychiatry, 49,* 414–430.

American Psychiatric Association. (1952). *Diagnostic and statistical manual of mental disorders* (1st ed.). Washington, DC: American Psychiatric Press.

American Psychiatric Association. (1980). *Diagnostic and statistical manual of mental disorders* (3rd ed.). Washington, DC: American Psychiatric Press.

American Psychiatric Association. (1987). *Diagnostic and statistical manual of mental disorders: Edition III-R* (3rd ed. revised). Washington, DC: American Psychiatric Press.

American Psychiatric Association. (2000a). *Diagnostic and statistical manual of mental disorders* (4th ed., text revision). Washington, DC: American Psychiatric Press.

American Psychiatric Association. (2000b). Practice guidelines for the treatment of patients with major depressive disorder. *American Journal of Psychiatry, 157*(Suppl. 4), 1–45.

American Psychiatric Association. (2006a). *Gay, lesbian, and bisexual issues.* Retrieved June 25, 2007, from http://www.healthyminds.org/glbissues.cfm

American Psychiatric Association. (2006b). Practice Guideline for the Treatment of Patients With Eating Disorders Third Edition, from http://www.psychiatryonline.com/pracGuide/loadGuidelinePdf.aspx?file=EatingDisorders3ePG_04-28-06

American Psychiatric Association. (2013). *Diagnostic and statistical manual of mental disorders* (5th ed.). Washington, DC: American Psychiatric Association Press.

APA Work Group on Eating Disorders (2010). Practice guideline for the treatment of patients with eating disorders (3rd ed.). Washington, DC: Author.

Ames, E. W., & Carter, M. (1992). Development of Romanian orphanage children adopted to Canada. *Canadian Psychology, 33,* 503.

Amsterdam, A., Carter, J., & Krychman, M. (2006). Prevalence of psychiatric illness in women in an oncology sexual health population: A retrospective pilot study. *Journal of Sexual Medicine, 3,* 292–295.

Anagnostou, E., Zwaigenbaum, L., Szatmari, P., Fombonne, E., Fernandez, B. A., Woodbury-Smith, M., . . . Scherer, S. W. (2014). Autism spectrum disorder: Advances in evidence-based practice. *Canadian Medical Association Journal, 186,* 509–519.

Andersch, S., Hanson, L., & Haellstroem, T. (1997). Panic disorder: A five-year follow-up study of 52 patients. *European Journal of Psychiatry, 11,* 145–156.

Anderson, C., & Bulik, C. M. (2003). Gender differences in compensatory behaviors, weight and shape salience, and drive for thinness. *Eating Behaviors, 5,* 1–11.

Anderson, I. M. (2001). Meta-analytical studies on new antidepressants. *British Medical Bulletin, 57,* 161–178.

Anderson, J. F. (2007). Screening and brief intervention for hazardous alcohol use within Indigenous populations. *Addiction Research and Theory, 15,* 439–448.

Andreasen, N. C., Flashman, L., Flaum, M., Arndt, S., Swayze, V., II, O'Leary, D. S., . . . Yuh, W. T. C. (1994). Regional brain abnormalities in schizophrenia measured with magnetic resonance imaging. *Journal of the American Medical Association, 272,* 1763–1769.

Andrews, A. (1999). *Be good, sweet maid: The trials of Dorothy Joudrie.* Ontario: Wilfred Laurier University Press.

Andrews, G., Hobbs, M. J., Borkovec, T. D., Beedsdo, K., Craske, M. G., Heimberg, R. G., . . . Stanley, M. A. (2010). Generalized worry disorder: A review of DSM-IV generalized anxiety disorder and options for DSM-V. *Depression and Anxiety, 27,* 134–147.

Andrews, G., Stewart, G., Allen, R., & Henderson, A. S. (1990). The genetics of six anxiety disorders: A twin study. *Journal of Affective Disorders, 19,* 23–29.

Angold, A., & Costello, E. J. (2006). Puberty and depression. *Child and Adolescent Psychiatric Clinics of North America, 15*(4), 919–937.

Angold, A., Weissman, M. M., John, K., Wickramaratne, P., & Prusoff, B. (1991). The effects of age and sex on depression ratings in children and adolescents. *Journal of the American Academy of Child and Adolescent Psychiatry, 30,* 67–74.

Anthony, J., & Petronis, K. (1995). Early-onset drug use and risk of later drug problems. *Drug and Alcohol Dependence, 407,* 9–15.

Antony, M. M., & Barlow, D. H. (2002). *Handbook of assessment and treatment planning for psychological disorders.* New York, NY: Guilford Press.

Antony, M. M., & Barlow, D. H. (2010). *Handbook of assessment and treatment planning for psychological disorders* (2nd ed.). New York, NY: Guilford.

Antony, M. M., Purdon, C., & Summerfeldt, L. J. (2007). *Psychological treatment of obsessive-compulsive disorder.* Washington, DC: American Psychological Association.

Appelbaum, P. S., Lidz, C., & Grisso, T. (2004). Therapeutic misconception in clinical research: Frequency and risk factors. *IRB: A Review of Human Subjects Research, 26,* 1–8.

Appelbaum, P. S., Robbins, P. C., & Roth, L. H. (1999). Dimensional approach to delusions: Comparison across types and diagnoses. *American Journal of Psychiatry, 156,* 1938–1943.

Applebaum, P. S., & Rumpf, T. (1998). Civil commitment of the anorexia patient. *General Hospital Psychiatry, 20,* 225–230.

Araujo, A., Durante, R., Feldman, H. A., Goldstein, I., & McKinlay, J. B. (1998). The relationship between depressive symptoms and male erectile dysfunction: Cross-sectional results from the Massachusetts Male Aging Study. *Psychosomatic Medicine, 60,* 458–465.

Areán P. A., Raue, P., Mackin, R. S., Kanellopoulos, D., McCulloch, C., & Alexopoulos, G. S. (2010). Problem-solving therapy and supportive therapy in older adults with major depression and executive dysfunction. *American Journal of Psychiatry, 167,* 1391–1398.

Areán, P. A., & Reynolds, C. F., III. (2005). The impact of psychosocial factors on late-life depression. *Biological Psychiatry, 58,* 277–282.

Areán, P. A., Ayalon, L., Hunkeler, E., Lin, E. H., Tang, L., Harpole, L., . . . Unützer, J. (2005). Improving depression care for older, minority patients in primary care. *Medical Care, 43,* 381–390.

Armstrong, S. C., Cozza, K. L., & Watanabe, K. S. (1997). The misdiagnosis of delirium. *Psychosomatics, 38,* 433–439.

Arnold, I. A., de Waal, M. W., Eekhof, J. A., & van Hemert, A. M. (2006). Somatoform disorder in primary care: Course and the need for cognitive-behavioral treatment. *Psychosomatics, 47,* 498–503.

Arnott, R., Finger, S., & Smith, C. (2003). *Trepanation: History, discovery, theory.* Lisse: Swets & Zeitlinger.

Arnsten, A. F. (1998). The biology of being frazzled. *Science, 280,* 1711–1712.

Atkinson, R. M. (2004). Substance abuse. In J. Sadavoy, L. F. Jarvik, G. T. Grossberg, & B. S. Meyers (Eds.), *Comprehensive textbook of geriatric psychiatry* (3rd ed., pp. 723–761). New York, NY: W. W. Norton & Co.

Atkinson, R. M., & Misra, S. (2002). Further strategies in the treatment of aging alcoholics. In A. M. Gurnack, R. M. Atkinson, & N. J. Osgood (Eds.), *Treating alcohol and drug abuse in the elderly* (pp. 50–71). New York, NY: Springer Verlag.

Atluri, S., Boswell, M. V., Hansen, H. C., Trescot, A. M., Singh, V., & Jordan, A. E. (2003). Guidelines for the use of controlled substances in the management of chronic pain. *Pain Physician, 6,* 233–257.

Attie, I., & Brooks-Gunn, J. (1989). Development of eating problems in adolescent girls: A longitudinal study. *Developmental Psychology, 25,* 70–79.

Aviram, R. B., Brodsky, B. S., & Stanley, B. (2006). Borderline personality disorder, stigma, and treatment implications. *Harvard Review of Psychiatry, 14,* 249–256.

Ayoub, C. C. (2006). Munchausen by proxy. In T. G. Plante (Ed.), *Mental disorders of the new millennium: Biology and function* (Vol. 3, pp. 173–193). Westport, CT: Greenwood Publishing Group.

Ayoub, C. C., Alexander, R., Beck, D., Bursch, B., Feldman, K., Libow, J., . . . Yorker, B. (2002). Position paper: Definitional issues in Munchausen by proxy, *Child Maltreatment, 7,* 105–111.

Azevedo, F. A., Carvalho, L. R., Grinberg, L. T., Farfel, J. M., Ferretti, R. E., Leite, R. E., . . . Herculano-Houzel, S. (2009). Equal number of neuronal and nonneuronal cells make the human brain an isometrically scaled-up primate brain. *Journal of Comparative Neurology, 513,* 532–541.

B

Babiak, P., & Hare, R. D. (2007). *Snakes in suits: When psychopaths go to work.* New York, NY: Harper.

Babulas, V., Factor-Litvak, P., Goetz, R., Schaefer, C. A., & Brown, A. S. (2006). Prenatal exposure to maternal genital and reproductive infections and adult schizophrenia. *American Journal of Psychiatry, 163,* 927–929.

Backman, L., Jones, S., Berger, A. K., Laukka, E. J., & Small, B. J. (2005). Cognitive impairment in preclinical Alzheimer's disease: A meta-analysis. *Neuropsychology, 19,* 520–531.

Badger, T., Segrin, C., Dorros, S. M., Meek, P., & Lopez, A. M. (2007). Depression and anxiety in women with breast cancer and their partners. *Nursing Research, 56,* 44–53.

Badman, M., & Flier, J. (2005). The gut and energy balance: Visceral allies in the obesity wars. *Science, 307,* 1909–1914.

Baerger, D. R. (2001). Risk management with the suicidal patient: Lessons from case law. *Professional Psychology: Research and Practice, 32,* 359–366.

Bailer, U. F., & Kaye, W. H. (2011). Serotonin: imaging findings in eating disorders. Current Topics in Behavioral Neurosciences, 6, 59–79.

Bailey, J. M., Kirk, K. M., Zhu, G., Dunne, M. P., & Martin, N. G. (2000). Do individual differences in sociosexuality represent genetic or environmentally contingent strategies? *Journal of Personality and Social Psychology, 78,* 537–545.

Bair, M. J., Robinson, R. L., Eckert, G. J., Stang, P. E., Croghan, T. W., & Kroenke, K. (2004). Impact of pain on depression treatment response in primary care. *Psychosomatic Medicine, 66,* 17–22.

Baker, D., Hunter, E., Lawrence, E., Medford, N., Patel, M., Senior, C., . . . Lambert, M. V. (2003). Depersonalization disorder: Clinical features. *British Journal of Psychiatry, 182,* 428–433.

Baldessarini, R. J., Tondo, L., Davis, P., Pompili, M., Goodwin, F. K., & Hennen, J. (2006). Decreased risk of suicides and attempts during long-term lithium treatment: A meta-analytic review. *Bipolar Disorders, 8,* 625–639.

Ballantyne, J. C., & Mao, J. (2003). Opioid therapy for chronic pain. *New England Journal of Medicine, 349,* 1943–1953.

Baltes, P. B., & Baltes, M. M. (1990). Psychological perspectives on successful aging: The model of selective optimization with compensation. In P. B. Baltes & M. M. Baltes (Eds.), *Successful aging: Perspectives from the behavioral sciences* (pp. 1–34). New York, NY: Cambridge University Press.

Bancroft, J., Loftus, J., & Long, J. S. (2003). Distress about sex: A national survey of women in heterosexual relationships. *Archives of Sexual Behavior, 32,* 193–208.

Bandura, A. (1977a). Self-efficacy theory: Toward a unifying theory of behavioural change. *Psychological Review, 84,* 191–215.

Bandura, A. (1977b). *Social learning theory.* Englewood Cliffs, NJ: Prentice Hall.

Bandura, A. (1999). A sociocognitive analysis of substance abuse: An agentic perspective. *Psychological Science, 10,* 214–217.

Banthia, R., Malcarne, V. L., Varni, J. W., Ko, C. M., Sadler, G. R., & Greenbergs, H. L. (2003). The effects of dyadic strength and coping styles on psychological distress in couples faced with prostate cancer. *Journal of Behavioral Medicine, 26,* 31–52.

Barbaree, H. E., & Marshall, W. L. (1989). Erectile responses among heterosexual child molesters, father-daughter incest offenders, and matched non-offenders: Five distinct age preference profiles. *Canadian Journal of Behavioural Science, 21,* 70–82.

Barbaresi, W. J., Katusic, S. K., & Voigt, R. G. (2006). Autism: A review of the state of the science for pediatric primary health care clinicians. *Archives of Pediatrics & Adolescent Medicine, 160,* 1167–1175.

Barbor, T. F., Higgins-Biddle, J. C., Saunders, J. B., & Montero, M. G. (2001). *AUDIT—The Alcohol Use Disorders Identification Test: Guidelines for use in primary* (Ed. WM 2742001SC, 2nd ed., Doc # WHO/MSD/MSb/01.6a). Geneva: World Health Organization Department of Mental Health and Substance Dependence.

Bardone-Cone, A. M., Wonderlich, S. A., Frost, R. O., Bulik, C. M., Mitchell, J. E., Uppala, S., & Simonich, H. (2007). Perfectionism and eating disorders: current status and future directions. *Clinical Psychology Review, 27,* 384–405.

Barez, M., Blasco, T., Fernandez-Castro, J., & Viladrich, C. (2007). A structural model of the relationships between perceived control and adaptation to illness in women with breast cancer. *Journal of Psychosocial Oncology, 25,* 21–43.

Barlow, D. H. (2002). *Anxiety and its disorders: The nature and treatment of anxiety and panic* (2nd ed.). New York, NY: Guilford Press.

Barnett, J. H., & Smoller, J. W. (2009). The genetics of bipolar disorder. *Neuroscience, 164,* 331–343.

Barone, J., & Grice, H. (1994). Seventh International Caffeine Workshop, Santorini, Greece June 13–17, 1993. *Food Chemistry and Toxicology, 32,* 65–77.

Barrowclough, C., King, P., Colville, J., Russell, E., Burns, A., & Tarrier, N. (2001). A randomized trial of the effectiveness of cognitive-behavioral therapy and supportive counseling for anxiety symptoms in older adults. *Journal of Consulting and Clinical Psychology, 69,* 756–762.

Barsky, A. J., & Klerman, G. L. (1983). Overview: Hypochondriasis, bodily complaints, and somatic styles. *The American Journal of Psychiatry, 140,* 273–283.

Barsky, A. J., Orav, E. J., & Bates, D. W. (2005). Somatization increases medical utilization and costs independent of psychiatric and medical comorbidity. *Archives of General Psychiatry, 62,* 903–910.

Barsky, A. J., Wyshak, G., & Klerman, G. L. (1990). Transient hypochondriasis. *Archives of General Psychiatry, 47,* 746–752.

Bartels, S. J., & Smyer, M. A. (2002). Mental disorders of aging: An emerging public health crisis? *Generations, 26,* 14–20.

Bartholomew, R. E., & Wessely, S. (2007). Canada's "Toxic Bus": the new challenge for law enforcement in the post-911 world—Mass psychogenic illness. *Canadian Journal of Criminology and Criminal Justice, 49,* 657–671.

Bartlett, N. H., & Vasey, P. L. (2006). A retrospective study of childhood gender-atypical behavior in Samoan *fa'afafine*. *Archives of Sexual Behavior, 35,* 659–666.

Bartlett, N. H., Vasey, P. L., & Bukowski, W. M. (2000). Is gender identity disorder in children a mental disorder? *Sex Roles, 43,* 753–785.

Bass, E., & Davis, L. (1988). *The courage to heal.* New York, NY: Harper & Row.

Bassarath, L. (2003). Medication strategies in childhood aggression: A review. *Canadian Journal of Psychiatry, 48,* 367–373.

Bassiony, M. M. (2005). Social anxiety disorder and depression in Saudi Arabia. *Depression and Anxiety, 21,* 90–94.

Basson, R. (2002). Women's sexual desire—disordered or misunderstood? *Journal of Sex and Marital Therapy, 28,* 17–28.

Basson, R., & Brotto, L. A. (2003). Sexual psychophysiology and effects of sildenafil citrate in oestrogenised women with acquired genital arousal disorder and impaired orgasm: A randomised controlled trial. *International Journal of Obstetrics and Gynaecology, 110,* 1014–1024.

Basson, R., Leiblum, S., Brotto, L., Derogatis, L., Fourcroy, J., Fugl-Meyer, K., . . . Weijmar Schultz, W. (2003). Definitions of women's sexual dysfunction reconsidered: Advocating expansion and revision. *Journal of Psychosomatic Obstetrics and Gynecology, 24,* 221–229.

Basson, R., McInnes, R., Smith, M. D., Hodgson, G., & Koppiker, N. (2002). Efficacy and safety of sildenafil citrate in women with sexual dysfunction associated with female sexual arousal disorder. *Journal of Women's Health & Gender-Based Medicine, 11,* 367–377.

Batelaan, N. M., de Graff, R., Spijker, J., Smit, J. H., van Balkom, A. J. L. M., Volleberger, W. A. M., & Beekman, A. T. F. (2010). The course of panic attacks in individuals with panic disorder and subthreshold panic disorder: A population based study. *Journal of Affective Disorders, 121,* 30–38.

Battle, C. L., Shea, M. T., Johnson, D. M., Yen, S., Zlotnick, C., Zanarini, M. C., . . . Morey, L. C. (2004). Childhood maltreatment associated with adult personality disorders: Findings from the Collaborative Longitudinal Personality Disorders Study. *Journal of Personality Disorders, 18,* 193–211.

Baum, A. (1990). Stress, intrusive imagery, and chronic distress. *Health psychology, 9*(6), 653–675.

Baumeister, R. F. (1989). *Masochism and the self.* Hillsdale, NJ: Erlbaum.

Baumeister, R. F., Catanese, K. R., & Vohs, K. D. (2001). Is there a gender difference in strength of sex drive? Theoretical views, conceptual distinctions, and a review of relevant evidence. *Personality and Social Psychology Review, 5,* 242–273.

Baxter, L. R. (1992). Neuroimaging studies of obsessive-compulsive disorder. *Psychiatric Clinics of North America, 15,* 871–884.

Baxter, L. R., Schwartz, J. M., Bergman, K. S., Szuba, M. P., Guze, B. H., Maziotta, J. C., . . . Phelps, M. (1992). Caudate glucose metabolic rate changes with both drug and behavior therapy for obsessive-compulsive disorder. *Archives of General Psychiatry, 49,* 681–689.

Bayles, K. A., & Kim, E. S. (2003). Improving the functioning of individuals with Alzheimer's disease: Emergence of behavioral interventions. *Journal of Communication Disorders, 36,* 327–343.

Beard, C., Miotra, E., Weisberg, R. B., & Keller, M. B. (2010). Characteristics and predictors of social phobia course in a longitudinal study of primary-care patients. *Depression and Anxiety, 27,* 839–845.

Beautrais, A. L., Joyce, P. R., & Mulder, R. T. (1997). Precipitating factors and life events in serious suicide attempts among youths aged 13 through 24 years. *Journal of the American Academy of Child and Adolescent Psychiatry, 36,* 1543–1551.

Beautrais, A. L., Joyce, P. R., & Mulder, R. T. (1998). Psychiatric illness in a New Zealand sample of young people making serious suicide attempts. *New Zealand Medical Journal, 111,* 44–48.

Beck, A. T. (1961). A systematic investigation of depression. *Comprehensive Psychiatry, 2,* 163–170.

Beck, A. T. (1967). *Depression: Clinical, experimental and theoretical aspects.* New York, NY: Hoeber.

Beck, A. T. (1979). *Cognitive therapy for depression.* New York, NY: Guilford Press.

Beck, A. T., Davis, D. D., & Freeman, A. M. (2003). *Cognitive therapy of personality disorders.* New York, NY: Guilford Press.

Beck, A., & Steer, R. (1993). *Beck Anxiety Inventory Manual* (2nd ed.). San Antonio, TX: Psychological Corporation.

Beck, A., Steer, R., & Brown, G. (1996a). *Manual for the Beck Depression Inventory-II.* San Antonio, TX: Psychological Corporation

Beck, A., Wright, F., Neewman, C., & Liese, B. (1993). *Cognitive therapy of substance abuse.* New York, NY: Guilford Press.

Beck, J. G., & Averill, P. M. (2004). Older adults. In R. G. Heimberg, C. L. Turk, & D. S. Mennin (Eds.), *Generalized anxiety disorder: Advances in research and practice* (pp. 409–433). New York, NY: Guilford Press.

Beck, J. G., Stanley, M. A., & Zebb, B. J. (1996b). Characteristics of generalized anxiety disorder in older adults: a descriptive study. *Behaviour Research and Therapy, 34,* 225–234.

Becker, A. E., Burwell, R. A., Gilman, S. E., Herzog, D. B., & Hamburg, P. (2002). Eating behaviours and attitudes following prolonged exposure to television among ethnic Fijian adolescent girls. *British Journal of Psychiatry, 180,* 509–514.

Becker, A. E., Fay, K. E., Agnew-Blais, J., Khan, A. N., Striegel-Moore, R. H., & Gilman, S. E. (2011). Social network media exposure and adolescent eating pathology in Fiji. *British Journal of Psychiatry, 198,* 43–50.

Beekman, A. T., deBeurs, E., van Balkom, A. J., Deeg, D. J., van Dyck, R., & van Tilburg, W. (2000). Anxiety and depression in later life: Co-occurrence and communality of risk factors. *American Journal of Psychiatry, 157,* 89–95.

Beidel, D. C., & Turner, S. M. (1997). At risk for anxiety: I. Psychopathology in the offspring of anxious parents. *Journal of the American Academy of Child and Adolescent Psychiatry, 36,* 918–924.

Beidel, D. C., & Turner, S. M. (1998). *Shy children, phobic adults: The nature and treatment of social phobia.* Washington, DC: American Psychological Association Books.

Beidel, D. C., & Turner, S. M. (2005). *Childhood anxiety disorders: A guide to research and treatment.* New York, NY: Routledge.

Beidel, D. C., Rao, P. A., Scharfstein, L., Wong, N., & Alfano, C. A. (2010). Social skills and social phobia: An investigation of DSM-IV subtypes. *Behaviour Research and Therapy, 48,* 992–1001.

Beidel, D. C., Turner, S. M., & Morris, T. L. (1995). A new inventory to assess childhood social anxiety and phobia: The Social Phobia and Anxiety Inventory of Children. *Psychological Assessment, 7,* 73–79.

Belanger, M.-E., Simard, V., Bernier, A., & Carrier, J. (2014). Investigating the convergence between actigraphy, maternal sleep diaries, and the child behavior checklist as measures of sleep in toddlers. *Frontiers in Psychiatry, 5* (article 158).

Bell, K. (2010). Anorexia nervosa in adolescents: Responding using the Canadian code of ethics for psychologists. *Canadian Psychology, 51,* 249–256.

Bell, R. M. (1985). *Holy anorexia*. Chicago, IL: University of Chicago Press.

Bellack, A. S. (2004). Skills training for people with severe mental illness. *Psychiatric Rehabilitation, 27,* 375–391.

Bellino, S., Paradiso, E., & Bogetto, F. (2008). Efficacy and tolerability of pharmacotherapies for borderline personality disorder. *CNS Drugs, 22,* 671–692.

Bellino, S., Zizza, M., Paradiso, E., Rivarossa, A., Fulcheri, M., & Bogetto, F. (2006). Dysmorphic concern symptoms and personality disorders: A clinical investigation in patients seeking cosmetic surgery. *Psychiatry Research, 144,* 73–78.

Bellis, M. D. (2004). Neurotoxic effects of childhood trauma: Magnetic resonance imaging studies of pediatric maltreatment-related posttraumatic stress disorder versus nontraumatized children with generalized anxiety disorder. In J. M. Gorman (Ed.), *Fear and anxiety: The benefits of translational research* (pp. 151–170). Washington, DC: American Psychiatric Publishing.

Ben-Porath, Y. S. (2012). *Interpreting the MMPI-2-RF.* Minneapolis, MN: University of Minnesota Press.

Bennett, H. A., Einarson, A., Taddio, A., Koren, G., & Einarson, T. R. (2004). Prevalence of depression during pregnancy: Systematic review. *Obstetrics and Gynecology, 103,* 698–709.

Berenbaum, S. A., Duck, S. C., & Bryk, K. (2000). Behavioral effects of prenatal versus postnatal androgen excess in children with 21-hydroxylase-deficient congenital adrenal hyperplasia. *Journal of Clinical Endocrinology and Metabolism, 85,* 727–733.

Bergen, A. W., van den Bree, M. B. M., Yeager, M., Welch, R., Ganjei, J. K., Haque, K., . . . Kaye, W. H. (2003). Candidate genes for anorexia nervosa in the 1p33-36 linkage region: Serotonin 1D and delta opioid receptor loci exhibit significant association to anorexia nervosa. *Molecular Psychiatry, 8,* 397–406.

Berkman, N. D., Lohr, K. N., & Bulik, C. M. (2007). Outcomes of eating disorders: A systematic review of the literature. *International Journal of Eating Disorders, 40,* 293–309.

Berlin, I. N. (1987). Suicide among American Indian adolescents: An overview. *Suicide & Life-Threatening Behavior, 17,* 218–232.

Berman, J. R., Berman, L. A., Toler, S. M., Gill, J., & Haughie, S., & Sildenafil Study Group. (2003). Safety and efficacy of sildenafil citrate for the treatment of female sexual arousal disorder: A double-blind, placebo controlled study. *Journal of Urology, 170,* 2333–2338.

Bersoff, D. N. (2003). Confidentiality, privilege, and privacy. In D. N. Bersoff (Ed.), *Ethical conflicts in psychology* (3rd ed., pp. 155–156). Washington, DC: American Psychological Association.

Bethea, T. C., & Sikich, L. (2007). Early pharmacological treatment of autism: A rationale for developmental treatment. *Biological Psychiatry, 61,* 521–537.

Beyer, J. L. (2009). Bipolar disorder in late life. In D. C. Blazer & D. C. Steffens (Eds.), *Textbook of geriatric psychiatry* (pp. 301–315). Washington, DC: American Psychiatric Publishing, Inc.

Biederman, J., Wilens, T., Mick, E., Faraone, S., & Spencer, T. (1998). Does attention deficit hyperactivity disorder impact the developmental course of drug and alcohol abuse and dependence? *Biological Psychiatry, 44,* 269–273.

Biederman, J. (2005). Attention-deficit/hyperactivity disorder: a selective overview. *Biological Psychiatry, 57,* 1215–1220.

Biederman, J., & Faraone, S. V. (2005). Attention-deficit hyperactivity disorder. *The Lancet, 366,* 237–248.

Biederman, J., Mick, E., Faraone, S. V., Braaten, E., Doyle, A., Spencer, T., . . . Johnson, M. A. (2002). Influence of gender on attention deficit hyperactivity disorder in children referred to a psychiatric clinic. *American Journal of Psychiatry, 159,* 36–42.

Biederman, J., Petty, C. R., Hirshfeld-Becker, D. R., Henin, A., Faraone, S. V., Fraire, M., . . . Rosenbaum, J. F. (2007). Developmental trajectories of anxiety disorders in offspring at high risk for panic disorder and major depression. *Psychiatry Research, 153,* 245–252.

Bierer, L. M., Yehuda, R., Schmeidler, J., Mitropoulou, V., New, A. S., Silverman, J. M., & Siever, L. J. (2003). Abuse and neglect in childhood: Relationship to personality disorder diagnoses. *CNS Spectrums, 8,* 737–754.

Billy, J. O., Tanfer, K., Grady, W. R., & Klepinger, D. H. (1993). The sexual behavior of men in the United States. *Family Planning Perspectives, 25,* 52–60.

Binks, C. A., Fenton, M., McCarthy, L., Lee, T., Adams, C. E., & Duggan, C. (2006). Psychological therapies for people with borderline personality disorder. *Cochrane Database Systematic Reviews, 1,* CD005652.

Binzer, M., & Kullgren, G. (1998). Motor conversion disorder. A prospective 2- to 5-year follow-up study. *Psychosomatics, 39,* 519–527.

Birch, D. E. (1992). Duty to protect: Update and Canadian perspective. *Canadian Psychology, 33,* 94–101.

Birmingham, C., Su, J., Hlynsky, J., Goldner, E., & Gao, M. (2005). The mortality rate from anorexia nervosa. *International Journal of Eating Disorders, 38,* 143–146.

Bishop, S. R., & Warr, D. (2003). Coping, catastrophizing and chronic pain in breast cancer. *Journal of Behavioral Medicine, 26,* 265–281.

Bisson, J. L., Jenkins, P. L., Alexander, J., & Bannister, C. (1997). A randomized controlled trial of psychological debriefing for victims of acute harm. *British Journal of Psychiatry, 171,* 78–81.

Bizzarri, J. V., Sbrana, A., Rucci, P., Ravani, L., Massei, G. J., Gonnelli, C., Spagnolli, S., Doria, M. R., Raimondi, F., Endicott, J., Dell'Osso, L., & Cassano, G. B. (2007). The spectrum of substance abuse in bipolar disorder: reasons for use, sensation seeking and substance sensitivity. *Bipolar Disorders, 9,* 213–220.

Black, H. (1990). *Black's law dictionary.* St. Paul, MN: West.

Black, M. M., & Krishnakumar, A. (1998). Children in low-income, urban settings: Interventions to promote mental health and well-being. *American Psychologist, 53,* 635–646.

Blackman, J. A. (1999). Attention-deficit/hyperactivity disorder in preschoolers: Does it exist and should we treat it? *Pediatric Clinics of North America, 46,* 1011–1025.

Blackwell, R. (2012, September 6). Answering the hiring question with psychological testing. *The Globe and Mail.* Retrieved March 28, 2015 from http://www.theglobeandmail.com/report-on-business/careers/answering-the-hiring-question-with-psychological-testing/article4199936.

Blanchard, R., & Bogaert, A. F. (2004). Proportion of homosexual men who owe their sexual orientation to fraternal birth order. *American Journal of Human Biology, 16,* 151–157.

Blanchard, R., Cantor, J. M., Bogaert, A. F., Breedlove, S. M., & Ellis, L. (2006). Interaction of fraternal birth order and handedness in the development of male homosexuality. *Hormonal Behavior, 49,* 405–414.

Blazer, D. G. (2004). Alcohol and drug problems. In D. G. Blazer, D. C. Steffens, & E. W. Busse (Eds.), *Textbook of geriatric psychiatry* (3rd ed., pp. 351–367). Washington, DC: American Psychiatric Publishing, Inc.

Blazer, D. G. (2006). Successful aging. *American Journal of Geriatric Psychiatry, 14,* 2–5.

Blazer, D. G., Steffens, D. C., & Koenig, H. G. (2009). Mood disorders. In D. C. Blazer & D. C. Steffens (Eds.), *Textbook of geriatric psychiatry* (pp. 275–299). Washington, DC: American Psychiatric Publishing, Inc.

Bleiberg, K. L., & Markowitz, J. C. (2005). A pilot study of interpersonal psychotherapy for posttraumatic stress disorder. *American Journal of Psychiatry, 162,* 181–183.

Bleuler, E. (1911/1950). *Dementia praecox or the group of schizophrenias* (J. Zinkin, Trans.). New York, NY: International Universities Press.

Block, J. H., Gjerde, P. F., & Block, J. H. (1991). Personality antecedents of depressive tendencies in 18-year-olds: A prospective study. *Journal of Personality and Social Psychology, 60,* 726–738.

Blom, M. M., Bosmans, J. E., Cuijpers, P., Zarit, S. H., & Pot, A. M. (2013). Effectiveness and cost-effectiveness of an internet intervention for family caregivers of people with dementia: design of a randomized controlled trial. *BMC Psychiatry, 13,* 17.

Bloom, H., Webster, C., Hucker, S., & De Freitas, K. (2005). The Canadian contribution to violence risk assessment: History and implications for current psychiatric practice. *Canadian Journal of Psychiatry, 50,* 3–11.

Blum, K., Braverman, E., Holder, J., Lubar, J., Monastra, V., Miller, D., . . . Comings, D. E. (2000). Reward deficiency syndrome: A biogenetic model for the diagnosis and treatment of impulsive, addictive, and compulsive behaviors. *Journal of Psychoactive Drugs, 32*(Suppl. i–iv), 1–112.

Bock, B. C., Papandonatos, G. D., de Dios, M. A., Abrams, D. B., Azam, M. M., Fagan, M., . . . Niaura, R. (2014). Tobacco cessation among low-income smokers: Motivational enhancement and nicotine patch treatment. *Nicotine & Tobacco Research, 16,* 413–422.

Boggiano, M. M., Artiga, A. I., Pritchett, C. E., Chandler-Laney, P. C., Smith, M. L., & Eldridge, A. J. (2007). High intake of palatable food predicts binge-eating independent of susceptibility to obesity: An animal model of lean vs obese binge-eating and obesity with and without binge-eating. *International Journal of Obesity* (London)*, 31,* 1357–1367.

Boggiano, M. M., & Chandler, P. C. (2006). Binge eating in rats produced by combining dieting with stress. Ch. 9: Animal Models of Neurologic and Psychiatric Disease, *Current Protocols in Neurosciences,* 9.23A1–9.23A.8.

Boggiano, M. M., Chandler, P. C., Viana, J. B., Oswald, K. D., Maldonado, C. R., & Wauford, P. K. (2005). Combined dieting and stress evoke exaggerated responses to opioids in binge-eating rats. *Behavioral Neuroscience, 119,* 1207–1214.

Boise, L., Neal, M. B., & Kaye, J. (2004). Dementia assessment in primary care: Results from a study in three managed care systems. *The Journals of Gerontology, Series, A. Biological Sciences and Medical Sciences, 59,* M621-M626.

Boles, S., & Miotto, K. (2003). Substance and violence: A review of the literature. *Aggression and Violent Behavior, 8,* 155–174.

Bonanno, G. A. (2004). Loss, trauma, and human resilience. *American Psychologist, 59,* 20–28.

Bonanno, R. A., & Hymel, S. (2013). Cyber bullying and internalizing difficulties: Above and beyond the impact of traditional forms of bullying. *Journal of Youth and Adolescence, 42,* 685–697.

Bond, F. R., Resnick, S. G., Drake, R. E., Xie, H., McHugo, G. J., & Bebout, R. R. (2001). Does competitive employment improve nonvocational outcomes for people with severe mental illness? *Journal of Consulting and Clinical Psychology, 69,* 489–501.

Bonese, K., Wainer, B., Fitch, F., Rothberg, R., & Schuster, C. (1974). Changes in heroin self-administration by a rhesus monkey after morphine immunisation. *Nature, 252,* 708–710.

Bootzin, R. R., & Bailey, E. T. (2005). Understanding placebo, nocebo, and iatrogenic treatment effects. *Journal of Clinical Psychology, 61*(7), 871–880.

Boraska, V., Franklin, C. S., Floyd, J. A. B., Thornton, L. M., Huckins, L. M., Southam, L., . . . Tortorella, A. (2014). A genome-wide association study of anorexia nervosa. *Molecular Psychiatry, 19,* 1085–1094.

Borch-Jacobsen, M., & Spiegel, H. (1997, April 24). Sybil: The making of a disease? An interview with Dr. Herbert Spiegel. *New York Review of Books.* http://www.nybooks.com/articles/1997/04/24/sybil-the-making-of-a-disease/.

Borges, G., Angst, J., Nock, M. K., Ruscio, A. M., Walters, E. E., & Kessler, R. C. (2006). A risk index for 12-month suicide attempts in the National Comorbidity Survey Replication (NCS-R). *Psychological Medicine, 36,* 1747–1757.

Borkovec, (2002). Psychological Aspects and treatment of generalized anxiety disorder, in D. Nutt, K. Rickels, & D. J. Stein (Eds.), *Generalized anxiety disorder: Symptomatology, pathogenesis, & management* (pp. 99–110). UK: Martin Dunitz, Ltd.

Borkovec, T. D., Alcaine, O. M., & Behar, E. (2004). Avoidance theory of worry and generalized anxiety disorder. In R. G. Heimberg, C. L. Turk, & D. S. Mennin (Eds.), *Generalized anxiety disorder: Advances in research and practice* (pp. 22–108). New York, NY: Guilford Press.

Borowitz, S. M., Cox, D. J., Sutphen, J. L., & Kovatchev, B. (2002). Treatment of childhood encopresis: A randomized trial comparing three treatment protocols. *Journal of Pediatric Gastroenterology and Nutrition, 34,* 378–384.

Bouchard, T. J., Jr., Lykken, D. T., McGue, M., Segal, N. L., & Tellegen, A. (1990). Sources of human psychological differences: The Minnesota Study of Twins Reared Apart. *Science, 250,* 223–228.

Boulos, D., & Zamorski, M. A. (2013). Deployment-related mental disorders among Canadian Forces personnel deployed in support of the mission in Afghanistan, 2001–2008. *Canadian Medical Association Journal,* DOI:10.1503/cmaj.122120.

Bourgeois, J. A., Seaman, J. S., & Servis, M. E. (2003). Delirium, dementia, and amnestic disorders. In R. E. Hales & S. C. Yudofsky (Eds.), *Clinical Psychiatry* (4th ed., pp. 259–308). Washington, DC: American Psychiatric Publishing, Inc.

Bourgeois, M. S., Camp, C., Rose, M., White, B., Malone, M., Carr, J., & Rovine, M. (2003). A comparison of training strategies to enhance use of external aids by persons with dementia. *Journal of Communication Disorders, 36,* 361–378.

Bow, J. N., & Quinnell, F. A. (2001). Psychologists' current practices and procedures in child custody evaluations: Five years after American Psychological Association Guidelines. *Professional Psychology: Research and Practice, 32,* 261–268.

Bowman, E. S., & Markand, O. N. (1996). Psychodynamics and psychiatric diagnoses of pseudoseizure subjects. *American Journal of Psychiatry, 153,* 57–63.

Boyle, M. (2000). Emil Kraepelin. In A. Kazdin (Ed.), *Encyclopedia of psychology* (Vol. 4, pp. 458–460). Washington, DC: American Psychological Association.

Bradley, S. J., & Zucker, K. J. (1997). Gender identity disorder: A review of the past 10 years. *Journal of the American Academy of Child and Adolescent Psychiatry, 36,* 872–880.

Braun, D. L., Sunday, S. R., & Halmi, K. A. (1994). Psychiatric comorbidity in patients with eating disorders. *Psychological Medicine, 24,* 859–867.

Brauner, D. J., Muir, J. C., & Sachs, G. A. (2000). Treating nondementia illnesses in patients with dementia. *Journal of the American Medical Association, 283,* 3230–3235.

Braunstein, G. D., Sundwall, D. A., Katz, M., Shifren, J. L., Buster, J. E., Simon, J. A., . . . Watts, N. B. (2005). Safety and efficacy of a testosterone patch for the treatment of hypoactive sexual desire disorder in surgically menopausal women. *Archives of Internal Medicine, 165,* 1582–1589.

Bray, J. H., Tilus, M., Vento, C., Greenspan, M., Wilson, G., & Sammons, M. (2014). Prescriptive authority for psychologists: Current status and future directions. *Behavior Therapist, 37,* 137–143.

Brazier, J., Tumur, I., Holmes, M., Ferriter, M., Parry, G., Dent-Brown, K., & Paisley, S. (2006). Psychological therapies including dialectical behaviour therapy for borderline personality disorder: A systematic review and preliminary economic evaluation. *Health Technology Assessment, 10,* iii, ix–xii, 1–117.

Bregman, J. D. (1991). Current developments in the understanding of mental retardation, Part II: Psychopathology. *Journal of the American Academy of Child and Adolescent Psychiatry, 30,* 861–872.

Breier, A., Schreiber, J. L., Dyer, J., & Pickar, D. (1991). National Institute of Mental Health longitudinal study of chronic schizophrenia. Prognosis and predictors of outcome. *Archives of General Psychiatry, 48,* 239–246.

Breitborde, N. J. K., Lopez, S. R., Chang, C., Kopelowicz, A., & Zarate, R. (2009). Emotional over-involvement can be deleterious for caregivers' health. *Social Psychiatry and Psychiatric Epidemiology, 44,* 716–723.

Brekke, J. S., Prindle, C., Bae, S. W., & Long, J. D. (2001). Risks for individuals with schizophrenia who are living in the community. *Psychiatric Services, 52,* 1358–1366.

Bremner, J. D. (2007). Neuroimaging in posttraumatic stress disorder and other stress-related disorders. *Neuroimaging Clinics of North America, 17,* ix, 523–538.

Bremner, J. D., Krystal, J. H., Charney, D. S., & Southwick, S. M. (1996). Neural mechanisms in dissociative amnesia for childhood abuse: Relevance to the current controversy surrounding the "false memory syndrome." *American Journal of Psychiatry, 153,* 71–82.

Bremner, J. D., Narayan, M., Staib, L. H., Southwick, S. M., McGlashan, T., & Charney, D. S. (1999). Neural correlates of memories of childhood sexual abuse in women with and without posttraumatic stress disorder. *American Journal of Psychiatry, 156,* 1787–1795.

Bremner, J. D., Randall, P., Scott, T. M., Bronen, R. A., Seibyl, J. P, Southwick, S. M., . . . Innis, R. B. (1995). MRI-based measurement of hippocampal volume in patients with combat-related posttraumatic stress disorder. *American Journal of Psychiatry, 152,* 973–981.

Brenes, G. A., Guralnik, J. M., Williamson, J. D., Fried, L. P., Simpson, C., Simonsick, E. M., & Penninx, B. W. (2005). The influence of anxiety on the progression of disability. *Journal of the American Geriatrics Society, 53,* 34–39.

Brenes, G. A., Kritchevsky, S. B., Mehta, K. M., Yaffe, K., Simonsick, E. M., Ayonayon, H. N., . . . Penninx, B. W. (2007). Scared to death: Results from the Health, Aging, and Body Composition Study. *American Journal of Geriatric Psychiatry, 15,* 262–265.

Brenes, G. A., Rapp, S. R., Rejeski, W. J., & Miller, M. E. (2002). Do optimism and pessimism predict physical functioning? *Journal of Behavioral Medicine, 25,* 219–231.

Brent, D. A., & Mann, J. J. (2005). Family genetic studies, suicide, and suicidal behavior. *American Journal of Medical Genetics C Seminars in Medical Genetics, 133,* 13–24.

Brent, D. A., Baugher, M., Bridge, J., Chen, T., & Chiappetta, L. (1999). Age- and sex-related risk factors for adolescent suicide. *Journal of the American Academy of Child and Adolescent Psychiatry, 38,* 1497–1505.

Breslau, J., Aguilar-Gaxiola, S., Kendler, K. S., Su, M., Williams, D., & Kessler, R. C. (2005). Specifying race-ethnic differences in risk for psychiatric disorder in a USA national sample. *Psychological Medicine, 36,* 57–68.

Breslau, N., & Kessler, R. C. (2001). The stressor criterion in DSM-IV posttraumatic stress disorder: An empirical investigation. *Biological Psychiatry, 50,* 699–704.

Brestan, E. V., & Eyberg, S. M. (1998). Effective psychosocial treatments of conduct-disordered children and adolescents: 29 years, 82 studies, and 5,272 kids. *Journal of Clinical Child Psychology, 27,* 180–189.

Breton, J. J., Bergeron, L., Valla, J. P., Bertiaume, C., Gauder, N., Lambert, J., . . . Lépine, S. (1999). Quebec child mental health survey: Prevalence of DSM-III-R mental health disorders. *Journal of Child Psychology and Psychiatry, 40,* 375–384.

Brewerton, T., Lydiard, R., Herzog, D., Brotman, A., O'Neil, P., & Ballenger, J. (1995). Comorbidity of Axis I psychiatric disorders in bulimia nervosa. *Journal of Clinical Psychiatry, 56,* 77–80.

Bride, B. (2001). Single-gender treatment of substance abuse: Effect on treatment retention and completion. *Social Work Research, 25,* 223–232.

Bridge, J. A., Iyengar, S., Salary, C. B., Barbe, R. P., Birmaher, B., Pincus, H. A., . . . Brent, D. A. (2007). Clinical response and risk for reported suicidal ideation and suicide attempts in pediatric antidepressant treatment: A meta-analysis of randomized controlled trials. *Journal of the American Medical Association, 297,* 1683–1696.

Briere, J., Weathers, F. W., & Runtz, M. (2005). Is dissociation a multidimensional construct? Data from the Multiscale Dissociation Inventory. *Journal of Traumatic Stress, 18,* 221–231.

Briggs, K., & Myers, I. (1987). *Myers-Briggs type indicator form G.* Palo Alto. CA: Consulting Psychologist Press.

Brodaty, H., Breteler, M. M. B., DeKosky, S. T., Dorenlot, P., Fratiglioni, L., Hock, C., . . . DeStrooper, B. (2011). The world of dementia beyond 2020. *Journal of the American Geriatrics Society, 59,* 923–927.

Brooks, R. C., Copen, R. M., Cox, D. J., Morris, J., Borowitz, S., & Sutphen, J. (2000). Review of the treatment literature for encopresis, functional constipation, and stool-toileting refusal. *Annals of Behavioral Medicine, 22,* 260–267.

Brooner, R. K., King, V. L., Kidorf, M., Schmidt, C. W., Jr., & Bigelow, G. E. (1997). Psychiatric and substance use comorbidity among treatment-seeking opioid abusers. *Archives of General Psychiatry, 54,* 71–80.

Brosco, J. P., Mattingly, M., & Sanders, L. M. (2006). Impact of specific medical interventions on reducing the prevalence of mental retardation. *Archives of Pediatrics & Adolescent Medicine, 160,* 302–309.

Brothers, L. (1990). The social brain: A project for integrating primate behavior and neurophysiology in a new domain. *Concepts in Neuroscience, 1,* 27–61.

Brotto, L. A., & Klein, C. (2007). Sexual and gender identity disorders. In M. Hersen, S. M. Turner, & D. C. Beidel (Eds.), *Adult psychopathology and diagnosis—fifth edition* (pp. 504–570). New York, NY: John Wiley and Sons.

Brown, A. S., Begg, M. D., Gravenstein, S., Schaefer, C. A., Wyatt, R. J., Brenahan, M., . . . Susser, E. S. (2004). Serological evidence of prenatal influenza in the etiology of schizophrenia. *Archives of General Psychiatry, 61,* 774–780.

Brown, G. W., Harris, T. O., & Eales, M. J. (1996). Social factors and comorbidity of depressive and anxiety disorders. *British Journal of Psychiatry Supplement, 30,* 50–57.

Brown, K. W., Levy, A. R., Rosberger, Z., & Edgar, L. (2003). Psychological distress and cancer survival: A follow-up 10 years after diagnosis. *Psychosomatic Medicine, 65,* 636–643.

Brown, M. J., McLaine, P., Dixon S., & Simon, P. (2006). A randomized, community-based trial of home visiting to reduce blood lead levels in children. *Pediatrics, 117,* 147–153.

Brown, R. J., Schrag, A., & Trimble, M. R. (2005). Dissociation, childhood interpersonal trauma, and family functioning in patients with somatization disorder. *American Journal of Psychiatry, 162,* 899–905.

Brown, S., Inskip, H., & Barraclough, B. (2000). Causes of the excess mortality of schizophrenia. *British Journal of Psychiatry, 177,* 212–217.

Brown, T. A., Campbell, L. A., Lehman, D. L., Grisham, J. R., & Mancill, R. B. (2001). Current and lifetime comorbidity of the DSM-IV anxiety and mood disorders in a large clinical sample. *Journal of Abnormal Psychology, 110,* 585–599.

Brownley, K. A., Berkman, N. D., Sedway, J. A., Lohr, K. N., & Bulik, C. M. (2007). Binge eating disorder treatment: A systematic review of randomized controlled trials. *International Journal of Eating Disorders, 40,* 337–348.

Bruce, M. L., Seeman, T. E., Merrill, S. S., & Blazer, D. G. (1994). The impact of depressive symptomatology on physical disability: MacArthur Studies of Successful Aging. *American Journal of Public Health, 84,* 1796–1799.

Bruce, S. E., Machan, J. T., Byck, I., & Keller, M. B. (2001). Infrequency of "pure" GAD: Impact of psychiatric comorbidity on clinical course. *Depression and Anxiety, 14,* 219–225.

Bruch, H. (1973). *Eating disorders.* New York, NY: Basic Books.

Bruch, H. (1978). *The golden cage.* Cambridge, MA: Harvard University Press.

Brunello, N., Davidson, J. R. T., Deahl, M., Kessler, R. C., Mendloewicz, J., Racagni, G., . . . Zohar, J. (2001). Posttraumatic stress disorder: Diagnosis and epidemiology, comorbidity and social consequences, biology and treatment. *Neuropsychobiology, 43,* 150–162.

Brush, J. A., & Camp, C. J. (1998). *A therapy technique for improving memory: Spaced retrieval.* Paper presented at Menorah Park Center for the Aging, Beachwood, OH.

Bryant, K. (2006). Making gender identity disorder of childhood: Historical lessons for contemporary debates. *Sexuality Research & Social Policy, 3,* 23–38.

Budney, A., Hughes, J., Moore, B., & Novy, P. (2001). Marijuana abstinence effects in marijuana smokers maintained in their home environment. *Archives of General Psychiatry, 58,* 917–924.

Budney, A., Moore, B., Vandrey, R., & Hughes, J. (2003). The time course and significance of cannabis withdrawal. *Journal of Abnormal Psychology, 112,* 393–402.

Buhrich, N., & McConaghy, N. (1985). Preadult feminine behaviors of male transvestites. *Archives of Sexual Behavior, 14,* 413–419.

Bulik, C. M. (2002). Eating disorders in adolescents and young adults. *Child and Adolescent Psychiatric Clinics of North America, 11,* 201–218.

Bulik, C. M., Baucom, D. H., Kirby, J. S., & Pisetsky, E. (2011). Uniting couples (in the treatment of) anorexia nervosa. *International Journal of Eating Disorders, 44,* 19–28.

Bulik, C. M., Berkman, N. D., Brownley, K. A., Sedway, J. A., & Lohr, K. N. (2007). Anorexia nervosa treatment: A systematic review of randomized controlled trials. *International Journal of Eating Disorders, 40,* 310–320.

Bulik, C. M., Devlin, B., Bacanu, S. A., Thornton, L., Klump, K. L., Fichter, M. M., . . . Kaye, W. H. (2003). Significant linkage on chromosome 10p in families with bulimia nervosa. *American Journal of Human Genetics, 72,* 200–207.

Bulik, C. M., Prescott, C. A., & Kendler, K. S. (2001). Features of childhood sexual abuse and the development of psychiatric and substance use disorders. *British Journal of Psychiatry, 179,* 444–449.

Bulik, C. M., Sullivan, P., Carter, F., & Joyce, P. (1995). Temperament, character, and personality disorder in bulimia nervosa. *Journal of Nervous and Mental Disease, 183,* 593–598.

Bulik, C. M., Sullivan, P., Wade, T., & Kendler, K. (2000). Twin studies of eating disorders: A review. *International Journal of Eating Disorders, 27,* 1–20.

Bulik, C., Sullivan, P., Fear, J., & Pickering, A. (1997b). Predictors of the development of bulimia nervosa in women with anorexia nervosa. *Journal of Nervous and Mental Disease, 185,* 704–707.

Bulik, C., Sullivan, P., Tozzi, F., Furberg, H., Lichtenstein, P., & Pedersen, N. (2006). Prevalence, heritability and prospective risk factors for anorexia nervosa. *Archives of General Psychiatry, 63,* 305–312.

Bull, L. (2009). Survey of complementary and alternative therapies used by children with specific learning difficulties (dyslexia). *International Journal of Language & Communication Disorders, 44,* 224–235.

Bulloch, A. G., Fiest, K. M., Williams, J. V., Lavorato, D. H., Berzins, S. A., Jette, N., . . . Patten, S. B. (2015). Depression - a common disorder across a broad spectrum of neurological conditions: A cross-sectional nationally representative survey. *General Hospital Psychiatry, 37*(6), 507–512.

Burgio, L. D., Len-Burge, R., Roth, D. L., Bourgeois, M. S., Dijkstra, K., Gerstle, J., . . . Bankester, L. (2001). Come talk with me: Improving communication between nursing assistants and nursing home residents during care routines. *Gerontologist, 41,* 449–460.

Burgio, L. D., Stevens, A., Burgio, K. L., Roth, D. L., Paul, P., & Gerstle, J. (2002). Teaching and maintaining behavior management skills in the nursing home. *Gerontologist, 42,* 487–496.

Burke, J. D., Loeber, R., & Birmaher, B. (2002). Oppositional defiant disorder and conduct disorder: A review of the past 10 years, Part II. *Journal of the American Academy of Child and Adolescent Psychiatry, 41,* 1275–1293.

Burns, D. D. (1989). *The feeling good handbook.* New York, NY: The Penguin Group.

Burnside, S., & Cairns, A. (1995). *Deadly innocence: The true story of Paul Bernado, Karla Homolka, and the schoolgirl murders.* New York, NY: Warner.

Bushnell, J. A., Wells, E., McKenzie, J. M., Hornblow, A. R., Oakley-Browne, M. A., & Joyce, P. R. (1994). Bulimia comorbidity in the general population and in the clinic. *Psychological Medicine, 24,* 605–611.

Buss, D. M. (1999). Social adaptation and five major factors of personality. In J. S. Wiggins (Ed.), *The five-factor model of personality: Theoretical perspectives* (pp. 180–207). New York, NY: Guilford Press.

Buster, J. E., Kingsberg, S. A., Aguirre, O., Brown, C., Breaux, J. G., Buch, A., . . . Casson, P. (2005). Testosterone patch for low sexual desire in surgically menopausal women: A randomized trial. *Obstetrics and Gynecology, 105,* 944–952.

Butler, A. C., Chapman, J. E., Forman, E. M., & Beck, A. T. (2006). The empirical status of cognitive-behavioral therapy: A review of meta-analyses. *Clinical Psychology Review, 26,* 17–33.

Butler, R. J., & Gasson, S. L. (2005). Enuresis alarm treatment. *Scandinavian Journal of Urology and Nephrology, 39,* 349–357.

Butterfield, M. I., Forneris, C. A., Feldman, M. E., & Beckham, J. C. (2000). Hostility and functional health status in women veterans with and without posttraumatic stress disorders: A preliminary study. *Journal of Traumatic Stress, 13,* 735–741.

Butzlaff, R. L., & Hooley, J. M. (1998). Expressed emotion and psychiatric relapse: A meta-analysis. *Archives of General Psychiatry, 55,* 547–552.

Byers, A. L., Yaffe, K., Covinsky, K. E., Friedman, M. B., & Bruce, B. (2010). High occurrence of mood and anxiety disorders among older adults. *Archives of General Psychiatry, 67,* 489–495.

Byers, E. S., & Grenier, G. (2003). Premature or rapid ejaculation: Heterosexual couples' perceptions of men's ejaculatory behavior. *Archives of Sexual Behavior, 32,* 261–270.

Bynum, J. P., Rabins, P. V., Weller, W., Niefeld, M., Anderson, G. F., & Wu, A. W. (2004). The relationship between a dementia diagnosis, chronic illness, medicare expenditures, and hospital use. *Journal of American Geriatrics Society, 52,* 187–194.

C

Cacioppo, J. T., Hawkley, L. C., & Thisted, R. A. (2010). Perceived social isolation makes me sad: 5-year cross-lagged analyses of loneliness and depressive symptomatology in the Chicago Health, Aging, and Social Relations Study. *Psychology and Aging, 25*(2), 453–463.

Canadian Association of Cardiac Rehabilitation (2009). *Canadian guidelines for cardiac rehabilitation and cardiovascular disease prevention.* Winnipeg, MB: Author.

Canadian Cancer Society (2015). *Canadian cancer statistics, 2015.* Ottawa: Government of Canada.

Canadian Centre on Substance Abuse (2004). *Canadian addiction survey.* Ottawa: Author.

Canadian Centre on Substance Abuse (2005). *Methamphetamine.* Ottawa: Author.

Canadian Centre on Substance Abuse (2006). *Youth volatile solvent abuse.* Ottawa: Author.

Canadian Centre on Substance Abuse (2013a). *Misuse of opioids in Canadian communities.* Ottawa: Author.

Canadian Centre on Substance Abuse (2013b). *Prescription opioids.* Ottawa: Author.

Canadian Centre on Substance Abuse (2013c). *Prescription sedatives and tranquilizers.* Ottawa: Author.

Canadian Centre on Substance Abuse (2013d). *Prescription stimulants.* Ottawa: Author.

Canadian Centre on Substance Abuse (2014). *Cocaine.* Ottawa: Author.

Canadian Centre on Substance Abuse (2015). *MDMA (Ecstasy, Molly).* Ottawa: Author.

Canadian Institute for Health Information (2010). *Depression among seniors in residential care.* Retrieved June 22, 2015 from https://secure.cihi.ca/free_products/ccrs_depression_among_seniors_e.pdf.

Canadian Psychological Association (2000). *Canadian Code of Ethics for Psychologists* (3rd ed.). Ottawa: Author.

Canadian Study of Health and Aging (1994a). Canadian Study of Health and Aging: Study methods and prevalence of dementia. *Canadian Medical Association Journal, 150,* 899–913.

Canadian Study of Health and Aging (1994b). Risk factors for Alzheimer's disease in Canada. *Neurology, 44,* 2073–2080.

Canadian Study of Health and Aging (1994c). Patterns of caring for people with dementia in Canada. *Canadian Journal on Aging, 13,* 470–487.

Cannon, M., Jones, P. B., & Murray, R. M. (2002). Obstetric complications and schizophrenia: Historical and meta-analytic review. *American Journal of Psychiatry, 159,* 1080–1092.

Cannon, W. B. (1929). *Bodily changes in pain, hunger, fear and rage.* New York, NY: Appleton.

Cannon, W. B. (1932). *The wisdom of the body* (2nd ed.) New York, NY: W. W. Norton & Co.

Caprioli, D., Celentano, M., Paolone, G., & Badiani, A. (2007). Modeling the role of environment in addiction. *Progress in Neuro-Psychopharmacology & Biological Psychiatry, 31,* 1639–1653.

Cardno, A., Marshall, E., Coid, B., Macdonald, A. M., Ribchester, T. R., Davies, N. J., . . . Murray, R. M. (1999). Heritability estimates for psychotic disorders: The Maudsley twin psychosis series. *Archives of General Psychiatry, 56,* 162–168.

Carlson, G. A., & Kashani, J. H. (1988). Phenomenology of major depression from childhood through adulthood: Analysis of three studies. *American Journal of Psychiatry, 145,* 1222–1225.

Carnes, P., Delmonico, D. L., & Griffin, E. (2001). *In the shadows of the net: Breaking free of compulsive online sexual behavior.* Center City, MN: Hazelden.

Carney, C. P., Jones, L., Woolson, R. F., Noyes, R., Jr., & Doebbeling, B. N. (2003). Relationship between depression and pancreatic cancer in the general population. *Psychosomatic Medicine, 65,* 884–888.

Carragher, N., Krueger, R. F., Eaton, N. R., & Slade, T. (2015). Disorders without borders: Current and future directions in the meta-structure of mental disorders. *Social Psychiatry and Psychiatric Epidemiology, 50,* 339–350.

Carrigan, M. H., & Randall, C. L. (2003). Self-medication in social phobia: A review of the alcohol literature. *Addictive Behavior, 28,* 269–284.

Carrigg, D. (2008). Father says God told him to kill his daughter. *The Province,* January 25, p. A3.

Carrillo, J., & Benitez, J. (2000). Clinically significant pharmacokinetic interactions between dietary caffeine and medications. *Clinical Pharmacokinetics, 39,* 127–153.

Carter, C. S. (1998): Neuroendocrine perspectives on social attachment and love. *Psychoneuroendocrinology, 23,* 779–818.

Caruso, S., Intelisano, G., Lupo, L., & Agnello, C. (2001). Premenopausal women affected by sexual arousal disorder treated with sildenafil: A double-blind, cross-over, placebo-controlled study. *British Journal of Obstetrics and Gynaecology, 108,* 623–628.

Casale, S., Fioravanti, G., Flett, G. L., & Hewitt, P. L. (2015). Self-presentation styles and problematic use of Internet communicative services: The role of the concerns over behavioral displays of imperfection. *Personality and Individual Differences, 76,* 187–192.

Caskey, J. D., & Rosenthal, S. L. (2005). Conducting research on sensitive topics with adolescents: Ethical and developmental considerations. *Developmental and Behavioral Pediatrics, 26,* 61–67.

Caspi, A., Sugden, K., Moffitt, T., Taylor, A., Craig, I., Harrington, H., . . . Poulton, R. (2003). Influence of life stress on depression: Moderation by a polymorphism in the 5-HTT gene. *Science, 301,* 386–389.

Castellanos, F. X., Lee, P. P., Sharp, W., Jeffries, N. O., Greenstein, D. K., Clasen, L. S., . . . Rapoport, J. L. (2002). Developmental trajectories of brain volume abnormalities in children and adolescents with attention-deficit/hyperactivity disorder. *Journal of the American Medical Association, 288,* 1740–1748.

Castles, A., Datta, H., Gayan, J., & Olson, R. K. (1999). Varieties of developmental reading disorder: Genetic and environmental influences. *Journal of Experimental Child Psychology, 72,* 73–94.

Cather, C., Penn, D., Otto, M. W., Yovel, I., Mueser, K. T., & Goff, D. C. (2005). A pilot study of functional Cognitive Behavioral Therapy (fCBT) for schizophrenia. *Schizophrenia Research, 74,* 201–209.

Cavanagh Johnson, T. (1988) Child perpetrators: children who molest other children: preliminary findings. *Child Abuse and Neglect,* 12: 219–229.

CBC News. (2008). Kitimat father found not responsible for killing daughter. Retrieved April 22, 2008 from http://www.cbc.ca/canada/british-columbia/story/2008/01/24/bc-kitimat-father-not-responsible.html.

CBC News Online. (May 10, 2004). *David Reimer: The boy who lived as a girl.* Retrieved June 30, 2004 from http://www.cbc.ca/news/background/reimer/.

Ceballos, N. A., Houston, R. J., Hesselbrock, V. M., & Bauer, L. O. (2006). Brain maturation in conduct disorder versus borderline personality disorder. *Neuropsychobiology, 53,* 94–100.

Cederlöf, R., Rantasalo, I., Floderus-Myrhed, B., Hammar, N., Kaprio, J., Koskenvuo, M., Langinvainio, H., Sarna, S. (1982). A cross-national epidemiological resource: the Swedish and Finnish cohort studies of like-sexed twins. *International Journal of Epidemiology, 11,* 387–390.

Cerletti, U., & Bini, L. (1938). Un nuovo metodo di shockterapia: "L'elettroshock". *Bollettino ed Atti della Reale Accademia Medica di Roma, 64,* 136–138.

Chalkley, A. J., & Powell, G. E. (1983). The clinical description of forty-eight cases of sexual fetishism. *British Journal of Psychiatry, 142,* 292–295.

Chambless, D. L., Fydrich, T., & Rodebaugh, T. L. (2008). Generalized social phobia and avoidant personality disorder: Meaningful distinction or useless duplication? *Depression and Anxiety, 25,* 8–19.

Chapman, C. R., & Gavrin, J. (1999). Suffering: The contributions of persistent pain. *The Lancet, 353,* 2233–2237.

Chapman, D. P., Williams, S. M., Strine, T. W., Anda, R. F., & Moore, M. J. (2006). Dementia and its implications for public health. *Preventing Chronic Disease, 3,* 1–13.

Chapman, T. R., Mannuzza, S., & Fyer, A. J. (1995). Epidemiology and family studies of social phobia. In R. G. Heimberg, M. R. Liebowitz, D. A. Hope, & F. R. Schneier (Eds.), *Social phobia: Diagnosis, assessment and treatment* (pp. 21–40). New York, NY: Guilford Press.

Charman, T., Taylor, E., Drew, A., Cockerill, H., Brown, J. A., & Baird, G. (2005). Outcome at 7 years of children diagnosed with autism at age 2: Predictive validity of assessments conducted at 2 and 3 years of age and pattern of symptom change over time. *Journal of Child Psychology and Psychiatry, 46,* 500–513.

Chassin, L., Presson, C. C., Rose, J. S., & Sherman, S. J. (2001). From adolescence to adulthood: Age-related changes in beliefs about cigarette smoking in a midwestern community sample. *Health Psychology, 20,* 377–386.

Chen, E. Y., Segal, K., Weissman, J., Zeffiro, T. A., Gallop, R., Linehan, M. M., . . . Lynch, T. R. (2015). Adapting dialectical behavior therapy for outpatient adult anorexia nervosa—A pilot study. *International Journal of Eating Disorders, 48,* 123–132.

Chenneville, T. (2000). HIV, confidentiality, and duty to protect: A decision-making model. *Professional Psychology: Research and Practice, 31,* 661–670.

Chess, S., & Thomas, A. (1991). Temperament and the concept of goodness of fit. In J. Strelau & A. Angleitner (Eds.), *Explorations in temperament: International perspectives on theory and measurement* (pp. 15–28). New York, NY: Plenum Press.

Cheung, A. H., & Dewa, C. S. (2007). Mental health service use among adolescents and young adults with major depressive disorder and suicidality. *Canadian Journal of Psychiatry, 52,* 228–232.

Cheyne, J. (2005). Sleep paralysis episode frequency and number, types, and structure of associated hallucinations. *Journal of Sleep Research, 14,* 319–324.

Chial, H. J., Camilleri, M., Williams, D. E., Litzinger, K., & Perrault, J. (2003). Rumination syndrome in children and adolescents: Diagnosis, treatment, and prognosis. *Pediatrics, 111,* 158–162.

Chida, Y., & Steptoe, A. (2009). The association of anger and hostility with future coronary heart disease: A meta-analytic review of prospective evidence. *Journal of the American College of Cardiology, 53,* 936–946.

Chiesa, M., Fonagy, P., & Holmes, J. (2006). Six-year follow-up of three treatment programs to personality disorder. *Journal of Personality Disorders, 20,* 493–509.

Chodoff, P. (2002). The medicalization of the human condition. *Psychiatric Services, 53,* 627–628.

Chou, K.-L. (2009). Age at onset of generalized anxiety disorder in older adults. *The American Journal of Geriatric Phsychiatry, 17*(6), 455–464.

Chronis, A. M., Chacko, A., Fabiano, G. A., Wymbs, B. T., & Pelham, W. E. Jr. (2004). Enhancements to the behavioral parent training paradigm for families of children with ADHD: Review and future directions. *Clinical Child and Family Psychology Review, 7,* 1–27.

Chronis, A., Jones, H. A., & Raggi, V. L. (2006). Evidence-based psychosocial treatments for children and adolescents with attention-deficit/hyperactivity disorder. *Clinical Psychology Review, 26,* 486–502.

Chung, Y. B., & Harmon, L. W. (1994). The career interests and aspirations of gay men: How sex-role orientation is related. *Journal of Vocational Behavior, 45,* 223–239.

Clarfield, A. M. (2003). The decreasing prevalence of reversible dementias: An updated meta-analysis. *Archives of Internal Medicine, 163,* 2219–2229.

Clark, C. W. (1997). The witch craze in 17th-century Europe. In W. G. Bringman, H. E. Lück, R. Miller, & C. Early (Eds.), *A pictorial history of psychology* (pp. 23–29). Carol Stream, IL: Quintessence Publishing Co.

Clark, D. A., & Beck, A. T. (2011). *Cognitive therapy of anxiety disorders: Science and practice.* New York, NY: Guilford.

Clinical Research News. (2004). Studies of capsulotomy, cingulotomy. *Clinical Research News, 39,* 28.

Cloninger, C. R., Svrakic, D. M., & Przybeck, T. R. (1993). A psychobiological model of temperament and character. *Archives of General Psychiatry, 50,* 975–990.

Clyburn, L. D., Stones, M. J., Hadjistavropoulos, T., & Tuokko, H. (2000). Predicting caregiver burden and depression in Alzheimer's disease. *Journals of Gerontology: Series B: Psychological Sciences and Social Sciences, 55B,* S2-S13.

Cockell, S. J., Hewitt, P. L., Seal, B., Sherry, S., Goldner, E. M., Flett, G. L., . . . Remick, R. A. (2002). Trait and self-presentational dimensions of perfectionism among women with anorexia nervosa. *Cognitive Therapy and Research, 26,* 745–758.

Cohen, S., Doyle, W. J., Turner, R. B., Alper, C. M., & Skoner, D. P. (2003). Emotional style and susceptibility to the common cold. *Psychosomatic Medicine, 65,* 652–657.

Cohen-Bendahan, C. C., van de Beek, C., & Berenbaum, S. A. (2005). Prenatal sex hormone effects on child and adult sex-typed behavior: Methods and findings. *Neuroscience and Biobehavioral Reviews, 29,* 353–384.

Cohen-Kettenis, P. T., Owen, A., Kaijser, V. G., Bradley, S. J., & Zucker, K. J. (2003). Demographic characteristics, social competence, and behavior problems in children with gender identity disorder: A cross-national, cross-clinic comparative analysis. *Journal of Abnormal Child Psychology, 31,* 41–53.

Colapinto, J. (2000). *As nature made him: The boy who was raised as a girl.* New York, NY: HarperCollins.

Colapinto, J. (2004, June 3). Gender Gap. *Slate Magazine.* Retrieved January 1, 2008, from http://www.slate.com.

Coldwell, H., & Heather, N. (2006). Introduction to the special issue. *Addiction Research and Theory, 14,* 1–5.

Combs, D. R., & Mueser, K. T. (2007). Schizophrenia. In M. Hersen, S. M. Turner, and D. C. Beidel (Eds.), *Adult psychopathology and diagnosis.* New York, NY: John Wiley and Sons.

Committee on Environmental Health, American Academy of Pediatrics. (2005). Lead exposure in children: Prevention, detection, and management. *Pediatrics, 116,* 1036–1046.

Compas, B. E., & Gotlib, I. H. (2002). *Introduction to clinical psychology: Science and practice.* New York, NY: McGraw-Hill.

Compton, S. N., March, J. S., Brent, D., Albano, A. M., Weersing, R., & Curry, J. (2004). Cognitive-behavioral psychotherapy for anxiety and depressive disorders in children and adolescents: An evidence-based medicine review. *Journal of the American Academy of Child and Adolescent Psychiatry, 43,* 930–995.

Conn, D. K., Malach, F. M., Wilson, K. J., Buchanan, D., Gibson, M. C., Grek, A., . . . Tourigny-Rivard, M.-F. (2006). National guidelines for senior's mental health: Introduction and project background. *Canadian Journal of Geriatrics, 9 (Suppl. 2),* S36–S41.

Conners, C. K., Epstein, J. N., March, J. S., Angold, A., Wells, K. C., Klaric, J., . . . Wigal, T. . (2001). Multimodal treatment of ADHD in the MTA: An alternative outcome analysis. *Journal of the American Academy of Child and Adolescent Psychiatry, 40,* 159–167.

Cooper, A., Delmonico, D. J., Griffin-Shelley, E., & Mathy, R. M. (2004). Online sexual activity: An examination of potentially problematic behaviors. *Sexual Addiction & Compulsivity, 11,* 120–143.

Cooper, C., Balamurali, T. B., & Livingston, G. (2007). A systematic review of the prevalence and covariates of anxiety in caregivers of people with dementia. *International Psychogeriatrics, 19,* 175–195.

Copolov, D. L., Mackinnon, A., & Trauer, T. (2004). Correlates of the affective impact of auditory hallucinations in psychotic disorders. *Schizophrenia Bulletin, 30,* 163–171.

Coryell, W., & Norten, S. (1981). Briquet's syndrome (somatization disorder) and primary depression: Comparison of background and outcome. *Comprehensive Psychiatry, 22,* 249–255.

Costello, E. J., Angold, A., Burns, B. J., Stangl, D. K., Tweed, D. L., Erkanli, A., & Worthman, C. M. . (1996). The Great Smoky Mountains Study of Youth: Goals, design, methods, and the prevalence of DSM-III-R disorders. *Archives of General Psychiatry, 53,* 1129–1136.

Costello, E. J., Mustillo, A., Erkanli, A., Keeler, G., & Angold, A. (2003). Prevalence and development of psychiatric disorders in childhood and adolescence. *Archives of General Psychiatry, 60,* 837–844.

Cottler, L. B., Nishith, P., & Compton, W. M., III. (2001). Gender differences in risk factors for trauma exposure and post-traumatic stress disorder among inner-city drug abusers in and out of treatment. *Comprehensive Psychiatry, 42,* 111–117.

Cougnard, A., Grolleau, S., Lamarque, F., Beitz, C., Brugère, S., & Verdoux, H. (2006). Psychotic disorders among homeless subjects attending a psychiatric emergency service. *Social Psychiatry and Psychiatric Epidemiology, 41,* 904–910.

Courchesne, E., & Pierce, K. (2005). Brain overgrowth in autism during a critical time in development: Implications for frontal pyramidal neuron and interneuron development and connectivity. *International Journal of Developmental Neuroscience, 23,* 153–170.

Couto, J. M., Gomez, L., Wigg, K., Ickowicz, A., Pathare, T., Malone, M., . . . Barr, C. L. (2009). Association of attention-deficit/hyperactivity disorder with a candidate region for reading disabilities on chromosome 6p. *Biological Psychiatry, 66,* 368–375.

Cox, D. J., & Maletzky, B. M. (1980). Victims of exhibitionism. In D. J. Cox & R. J. Daitzman (Eds.), *Exhibitionism: Description, assessment and treatment* (pp. 289–293). New York, NY: Garland.

Cox, D. J., Morris, J. B. Jr., Borowitz, S. M., & Sutphen, J. L. (2002). Psychological differences between children with and without chronic encopresis. *Journal of Pediatric Psychology, 27,* 585–591.

Cox, D. J., Sutphen, J., Borowitz, S., Kovatchev, B., & Ling, B. (1998). Contribution of behavior therapy and biofeedback to laxative therapy in the treatment of pediatric encopresis. *Annals of Behavioral Medicine, 20,* 70–76.

Coyne, J. C., Stefanek, M., & Palmer, S. C. (2007). Psychotherapy and survival in cancer: The conflict between hope and evidence. *Psychological Bulletin, 133,* 367–394.

CPA Task Force on Prescriptive Authority for Psychologists in Canada (2010). *Report to the Canadian Psychological Association Board of Directors.* Ottawa: Author.

Crabb, R., & Hunsley, J. (2006). Utilization of mental health care services among older adults with depression. *Journal of Clinical Psychology, 62,* 299–312.

Crabtree, F. A. (2000). Mesmer, Franz Anton. In A. Kazdin (Ed.), *Encyclopedia of psychology* (Vol. 4, pp. 200–201). Washington, DC: American Psychological Association.

Craig, T. K., Bialas, I., Hodson, S., & Cox, A. D. (2004). Intergenerational transmission of somatization behaviour: 2. Observations of joint attention and bids for attention. *Psychological Medicine, 34,* 199–209.

Craighead, W. E., & Miklowitz, D. J. (2000). Psychosocial interventions for bipolar disorder. *Journal of Clinical Psychiatry, 61*(13 Suppl.), 58–64.

Cram, S. J., & Dobson, K. S. (1993). Confidentiality: Ethical and legal aspects for Canadian psychologists. *Canadian Psychology, 34*, 347–363.

Craske, M. G., Golinelli, D., Stein, M. B., Roy-Byrne, P., Bystritsky, A., & Grebourne, C. (2005). Does the addition of cognitive-behavioral therapy improve panic disorder treatment outcome relative to medication alone in the primary care setting? *Psychological Medicine, 35,* 1645–1654.

Craske, M. G., Kircanski, K., Epstein, A., Wittchen, H. U., Pine, D. S., Lewis-Fernández, R., . . . DSM-V Anxiety, OC Spectrum, Posttraumatic and Dissociative Disorder Work Group. (2010). Panic disorder: A review of DSM-IV panic disorder and proposals for DSM-V. *Depression and Anxiety 27,* 93–112.

Crawford, D. C., Meadows, K. L., Newman, J. L., Taft, L. F., Scott, E., Leslie, M., . . . Sherman, S. L. (2002). Prevalence of the fragile X syndrome in African-Americans. *American Journal of Medical Genetics, 110,* 226–233.

Creed, F., & Barsky, A. (2004). A systematic review of the epidemiology of somatization disorder and hypochondriasis. *Journal of Psychosomatic Research, 56,* 391–408.

Crider, A., Glaros, A. G., & Gevirtz, R. N. (2005). Efficacy of biofeedback-based treatments for temporomandibular disorders. *Applied Psychophysiology and Biofeedback, 30,* 333–345.

Crimlisk, H. L., Bhatia, K., Cope, H., David, A., Marsden, C. D., & Ron, M. A. (1998). Slater revisited: 6 year follow up study of patients with medically unexplained motor symptoms. *British Medical Journal, 316,* 582–586.

Crocker, A. G., Nicholls, T. L., Seto, M. C., Charette, Y., Cote, G., & Caulet, M. (2015b). The National Trajectory Project of individuals found not criminally responsible on account of mental disorder in Canada. Part 2: The people behind the label. *Canadian Journal of Psychiatry, 60,* 106–116.

Crocker, A. G., Charette, Y., Seto, M. C., Nicholls, T. L., Cote, G., & Caulet, M. (2015a). The National Trajectory Project of individuals found not criminally responsible on account of mental disorder in Canada. Part 3: Trajectories and outcomes through the forensic system. *Canadian Journal of Psychiatry, 60,* 117–126.

Cronbag, H. F. M., Wagenaar, W. A., & van Koppen, P. J. (1996). Crashing memories and the problem of "source monitoring." *Applied Cognitive Psychology, 10,* 95–104.

Cross National Collaborative Panic Study Second Phase Investigation. (1992). Drug treatment of panic disorder: Comparative efficacy of alprazolam, imipramine, and placebo. *British Journal of Psychiatry, 160,* 191–202.

Crow, S. J., Peterson, C. B., Swanson, S. A., Raymond, N. C., Specker, S., Eckert, E. D., & Mitchell, J. E. (2009). Increased mortality in bulimia nervosa and other eating disorders. *American Journal of Psychiatry, 166*, 1342–1346.

Cruess, D. G., Schneiderman, N., Antoni, M. H., & Penedo, F. (2004). Biobehavioral bases of disease processes. In T. J. Boll, R. G. Friedman, A. Baum, & J. L. Wallander (Eds.), *Handbook of clinical health psychology* (pp. 31–79). Washington, DC: American Psychological Association.

Cruess, S., Antoni, M., Cruess, D., Fletcher, M. A., Ironson, G., Kumar, M., . . . Schneiderman, N. (2000). Reductions in herpes simplex virus type 2 antibody titers after cognitive behavioral stress management and relationships with neuroendocrine function, relaxation skills, and social support in HIV-positive men. *Psychosomatic Medicine, 62,* 828–837.

Cuffe, S. P., McKeown, R. E., Addy, C. L., & Garrison, C. Z. (2005). Family and psychosocial risk factors in a longitudinal epidemiological study of adolescents. *Journal of the American Academy of Child and Adolescent Psychiatry, 44,* 121–129.

Cully, J. A., Graham, D. P., Stanley, M. A., Ferguson, C. J., Sharafkhanch, A., Souchek, J., & Kunik, M. E. (2006). Quality of life in patients with chronic obstructive pulmonary disease and comorbid anxiety or depression. *Psychosomatics, 47*, 312–319.

Cunningham-Williams, R. M., Cottler, L. B., Compton, W. M., III, & Spitznagel, E. L. (1998). Taking chances: Problem gamblers and mental health disorders—results from the St. Louis Epidemiologic Catchment Area Study. *American Journal of Public Health, 88,* 1093–1096.

Curry, S., Marlatt, G., & Gordon, J. (1987). Abstinence violation effect: Validation of an attributional construct with smoking cessation. *Journal of Consulting and Clinical Psychology, 55,* 145–149.

Cyranowski, J. M., Bromberger, J., Youk, A., Matthews, K., Kravitz, H. M., & Powell, L. H. (2004). Lifetime depression history and sexual function in women at midlife. *Archives of Sexual Behavior, 33,* 539–548.

Cyranowski, J., Frank, E., Young, E., & Shear, M. (2000). Adolescent onset of the gender difference in lifetime rates of major depression. *Archives of General Psychiatry, 57,* 21–27.

Czarnetzki, A., Blin, N., & Pusch, C. M. (2003). Down's syndrome in ancient Europe. *The Lancet, 362,* 1000.

D

D'Zurilla, T. J., & Nezu, A. M. (1999). *Problem-solving therapy: A social competence approach to clinical intervention.* New York, NY: Springer.

Daley, D. (2006). Attention deficit hyperactivity disorder: A review of the essential facts. *Child Care, Health, and Development, 32,* 193–204.

Daley, D. D., Jones, K. K., Hutchings, J. J., & Thompson, M. M. (2009). Attention deficit hyperactivity disorder in pre-school children: Current findings, recommended interventions and future directions. *Child Care, Health, and Development, 35,* 754–766.

Dallaire, R. (2003). *Shake hands with the devil: The failure of humanity in Rwanda.* Toronto, ON: Random House.

Damon, W., & Simon Rosser, B. R. (2005). Anodyspareunia in men who have sex with men: Prevalence, predictors, consequences and the development of DSM diagnostic criteria. *Journal of Sex & Marital Therapy, 31,* 129–141.

Daneback, K., Cooper, A., & Månsson, S.-A. (2005). An internet study of cybersex participants. *Archives of Sexual Behavior, 14,* 321–328.

Dare, C., le Grange, D., Eisler, I., & Rutherford, J. (1994). Redefining the psychosomatic family: Family process of 26 eating disorder families. *International Journal of Eating Disorders, 16,* 211–226.

Daubenmier, J. J., Weidner, G., Sumner, M. D., Mendell, N., Merritt-Worden, T., Studley, J., & Ornish, D. (2007). The contribution of changes in diet, exercise, and stress management to changes in coronary risk in women and men in the multisite cardiac lifestyle intervention program. *Annals of Behavioral Medicine, 33,* 57–68.

Daughters, S., Bornovalova, M., Correia, C., & Lejuez, C. (2007). Psychoactive substance use disorders: Drugs. In M. Hersen, S. Turner, & D. Beidel (Eds.), *Adult psychopathology and diagnosis* (5th ed., pp. 201–233). Hoboken, NJ: John Wiley & Sons.

Davidson, J. R. T. (1993, March). *Childhood histories of adult social phobics.* Paper presented at the Anxiety Disorders Association of America Annual Convention, Charleston, SC.

Davidson, J. R. T., Foa, E. B., Huppert, J. D., Keefe, F. J., Franklin, M. E., Compton, J. S., . . . Gadde, K. M. (2004). Fluoxetine, comprehensive cognitive behavioral therapy, and placebo in generalized social phobia. *Archives of General Psychiatry, 61,* 1005–1013.

Davidson, L., & Roe, D. (2007). Recovery from recovering in serious mental illness: One strategy for lessening confusion plaguing recovery. *Journal of Mental Health, 16,* 450–470.

Davidson, R. J., Pizzagalli, D., & Nitschke, J. B. (2002). The representation and regulation of emotion in depression: Perspectives from affective neuroscience. In C. L. Hammen & I. H. Gotlib (Eds.), *Handbook of depression* (pp. 219–244). New York, NY: Guilford Press.

Davis, C., Levitan, R. D., Carter, J., Kaplan, A. S., Reid, C., Curtis, C., . . . Kennedy, J. L. (2008). Personality and eating behaviors: a case-control study of binge eating disorder. *International Journal of Eating Disorders, 41,* 243–250.

Davis, K. L., Kahn, R. S., Ko, G., & Davidson, M. (1991). Dopamine in schizophrenia: A review and reconceptualization. *American Journal of Psychiatry, 148,* 1474–1486.

Davis, S. (1993). Changes to the *Criminal Code* provisions for mentally disordered offenders and their implications for Canadian psychiatry. *Canadian Journal of Psychiatry, 38,* 122–126.

Dawson, D. (2000). Drinking patterns among individuals with and without DSM-IV alcohol use disorders. *Journal of Studies on Alcohol, 61,* 111–120.

Dawson, D., & Grant, B. (1993). Gender effects in diagnosing alcohol abuse and dependence. *Journal of Clinical Psychology, 49,* 298–307.

Day, D. O., & Moseley, R. L. (2010). Munchausen by proxy syndrome. *Journal of Forensic Psychology Practice, 10,* 13–36.

De Clercq, B., & De Fruyt, F. (2007). Childhood antecedents of personality disorder. *Current Opinions in Psychiatry, 20,* 57–61.

de Kruiff, M. E., ter Kuile, M. M., Weijenborg, P. T., & van Lankveld, J. J. (2000). Vaginismus and dyspareunia: Is there a difference in clinical presentation? *Journal of Psychosomatic Obstetrics and Gynaecology, 21,* 149–155.

De Leon, J., Dadvanc, M., Canuso, C., White, A. O., Stanilla, J. K., & Simpson, G. M. (1995). Schizophrenia and smoking: An epidemiological survey at a state hospital. *American Journal of Psychiatry, 152,* 453–455.

Deacon, B. (2014). Introduction: Prescriptive authority for psychologists. *Behavior Therapist, 37,* 136.

Dean, C. E. (2006). Antipsychotic-associated neuronal changes in the brain: Toxic, therapeutic, or irrelevant to the long-term outcome schizophrenia? *Progress in Neuro-Psychopharmacology and Biological Psychiatry, 30,* 174–189.

DeBeurs, E., Beekman, A. T., van Balkom, A. J., Deeg, D. J., van Dyck, R., & van Tilburg, W. (1999). Consequences of anxiety in older persons: Its effect on disability, well-being and use of health services. *Psychological Medicine, 29,* 583–593.

DeBuono, B. A., Zinner, S. H., Daamen, M., & McCormack, W. M. (1990). Sexual Behavior of College Women in 1975, 1986, and 1989. *New England Journal of Medicine, 322,* 821–825.

Decker, H. S. (2004). The psychiatric works of Emil Kraeplein: A many faceted story of modern medicine. *Journal of the History of the Neurosciences, 13,* 248–276.

Delahanty, D. L., Wang, T., Maravich, C., Forlenza, M., & Baum, A. (2000). Time-of-day effects on response of natural killer cells to acute stress in men and women. *Health Psychology, 19,* 39–45.

Delemarre-van de Waal, H. A., & Cohen-Kettenis, P. T. (2006). Clinical management of gender identity disorder in adolescents: A protocol on psychological and paediatric endocrinology aspects. *European Journal of Endocrinology, 155,* S131–S137.

Dell, P. F., & Eisenhower, J. W. (1990). Adolescent multiple personality disorder: A preliminary study of eleven cases. *Journal of the American Academy of Child and Adolescent Psychiatry, 29,* 359–366.

Delvenne, V., Goldman, S., De Maertelaer, V., & Lotstra, F. (1999). Brain-glucose metabolism in eating disorders assessed by positron emission tomography. *International Journal of Eating Disorders, 25,* 29–37.

Depp, C. A., & Jeste, D. V. (2006). Definitions and predictors of successful aging: A comprehensive review of larger quantitative studies. *American Journal of Geriatric Psychiatry, 14,* 6–20.

Derogatis, L. R., & Lynn, L. L. (1999). Psychological tests in screening for psychiatric disorders. In M. E. Maruish (Ed.), *The use of psychological testing for treatment planning and outcomes assessment* (2nd ed., pp. 41–79). Mahwah, NJ: Lawrence Erlbaum Associates.

Devlin, B., Bacanu, S., Klump, K., Bulik, C. M., Fichter, M., Halmi, K., . . . Kaye, W. H. (2002). Linkage analysis of anorexia nervosa incorporating behavioral covariates. *Human Molecular Genetics, 11,* 689–696.

Diamond, L. M. (2003). What does sexual orientation orient? A biobehavioral model distinguishing romantic love and sexual desire. *Psychological Review, 110,* 173–192.

Diamond, L. M. (2008). Female bisexuality from adolescence to adulthood: Results from a 10-year longitudinal study. *Developmental Psychology, 44,* 5–14.

Diamond, M. (1982). Sexual identity, monozygotic twins reared in discordant sex roles and a BBC follow-up. *Archives of Sexual Behavior, 11,* 181–186.

Diamond, M. (1993). Homosexuality and bisexuality in different populations. *Archives of Sexual Behavior, 22,* 291–310.

Diamond, M., & Sigmundson, H. K. (1997). Sex reassignment at birth. Long-term review and clinical implications. *Archives of Pediatrics & Adolescent Medicine. 151,* 298–304.

Dickens, C., McGowan, L., & Dale, S. (2003). Impact of depression on experimental pain perception: A systematic review of the literature with meta-analysis. *Psychosomatic Medicine, 65,* 369–375.

Didie, E. R., Tortolani, C., Walters, M., Menard, W., Fay, C., & Phillips, K. A. (2006). Social functioning in body dysmorphic disorder: Assessment considerations. *Psychiatric Quarterly, 77,* 223–229.

Digdon, N., Powell, R. A., & Harris, B. (2014). Little Albert's alleged neurological impairment: Watson, Rayner, and historical revision. *History of Psychology, 17,* 312–324.

DiMatteo, M. R., & Martin, L. R. (2002). *Health Psychology.* Boston, MA: Allyn and Bacon.

Diwadkar, V. A., Montrose, D. M., Dworakowski, D., Sweeney, J. A., & Keshavan, M. S. (2006). Genetically predisposed offspring with schizotypal features: An ultra high-risk group for schizophrenia. *Progress in Neuro-Psychopharmacology & Biological Psychiatry, 30,* 230–238.

Dobbs, D. (2012) The New Temper Tantrum Disorder. Retrieved December 31, 2012 from http://www.slate.com/articles/double_x/doublex/2012/12/disruptive_mood_dysregula-tion_disorder_in_dsm_5_criticism_of_a_new_diagnosis.html.

Dockray, S., & Steptoe, A. (2010). Positive affect and psychobiological processes. *Neuroscience and Biobehavioral Review, 35,* 69–75.

Docter, R. F., & Prince, V. (1997). Transvestism: A survey of 1032 cross-dressers. *Archives of Sexual Behavior, 26,* 589–605.

Doi, T. (1973). *The anatomy of dependence.* Tokyo: Kodansha International.

Dolan, B. M., Warren, F., & Norton, K. (1997). Change in borderline symptoms one year after therapeutic community treatment for severe personality disorders. *British Journal of Psychiatry, 171,* 274–279.

Dolan, R., Mitchell, J., & Wakeling, A. (1988). Structural brain changes in patients with anorexia nervosa. *Psychological Medicine, 18,* 349–353.

Domes, G., Heinrichs, M., Michel, A., Berger, C., & Herpertz, S. C. (2007). Oxytocin improves "mind-reading" in humans. *Biological Psychiatry, 61,* 731–733.

Domjan, M. (2005). Pavlovian conditioning: A functional perspective. *Annual Review of Psychology, 56,* 179–206.

Done, D. J., Crow, T. J., Johnestone, E. C., & Sacker, A. (1994). Childhood antecedents of schizophrenia and affective illness: Social adjustment at ages 7 and 11. *British Medical Journal, 309,* 699–703.

Donohue, B., Thevenin, D. M., & Runyon, M. K. (1997). Behavioral treatment of conversion disorder in adolescence. *Behavior Modification, 21,* 231–251.

dos Santos, L. L., de Castro Magalhãs, M., Januário, J. N., Burle de Agular, M. J., & Santos Carvalho, M. R. (2006). The time has come: A new scene for PKU treatment. *Genetics and Molecular Research, 5,* 33–44.

Dougherty, D. D., Baer, L., Cosgrove, G. R., Cassem, E. H., Price, B. H., Nierenberg, A. A., . . . Rauch, S. L. (2002). Prospective long-term follow-up of 44 patients who received cingulotomy for treatment-refractory obsessive-compulsive disorder. *American Journal of Psychiatry, 159,* 269–275.

Douglas, K. S., Hart, S. D., Webster, C. D., Belfrage, H., Guy, L. S., & Wilson, C. M. (2014). Historical-Clinical-Risk Management-20, Version 3 (HCR-20^{V3}): Development and overview. *International Journal of Forensic Mental Health, 13,* 93–108.

Douglas, V. I. (1972). Stop, look, and listen: The problem of sustained attention and impulse control in hyperactive and normal children. *Canadian Journal of Behavioural Science, 4,* 259–282.

Douglas, V. I. (1983). Attention and cognitive problems. In M. Rutter (Ed.), *Developmental Neuropsychiatry* (pp. 280–329). New York, NY: Guilford.

Doust, J., & Del Mar, C. (2004). Why do doctors use treatments that do not work? *British Medical Journal* (Clinical research ed.), *328,* 474–475.

Dowd, J. B., & Aiello, A. E. (2009). Socioeconomic differentials in immune response. *Epidemiology, 20,* 902–908.

Downing, A., Prakash, K., Gilthorpe, M. S., Mikeljevic, J. S., & Forman, D. (2007). Socioeconomic background in relation to stage at diagnosis, treatment and survival in women with breast cancer. *British Journal of Cancer, 96,* 836–840.

Drake, R. E., Essock, S. M., & Bond, G. R. (2009). Implementing evidence-based practices for people with schizophrenia. *Schizophrenia Bulletin, 35,* 704–713.

Drake, R. E., Green, A. I., Mueser, K. T., & Goldman, H. H. (2003). The history of community mental health treatment and rehabilitation for persons with severe mental illness. *Community Mental Health Journal, 39,* 427–440.

Dreger, A., Feder, E. K., & Tamar-Mattis, A. (2010, June 29). Preventing homosexuality (and uppity women) in the womb? *The Bioethics Forum.* Retrieved January 16, 2011 from http://thehastingscenter.org/Bioethicsforum/Post.

Driessen, M., Herrmann, J., Stahl, K., Zwaan, M., Meier, S., Hill, A., . . . Petersen, D. (2000). Magnetic resonance imaging volumes of the hippocampus and the amygdala in women with borderline personality disorder and early traumatization. *Archives of General Psychiatry, 57,* 1115–1122.

Driscoll, J. W. (2006). Postpartum depression: The state of the science. *Journal of Perinatal and Neonatal Nursing, 20,* 40–42.

Drummond, K. D., Bradley, S. J., Peterson-Badall, M., & Zucker, K. J. (2008). A follow-up study of girls with gender identity disorder. *Developmental Psychology, 44,* 34–45.

Dubbert, P. A. M., King, A. C., Marcus, B. H., & Sallis, J. F. (2004). Promotion of physical activity through the life span. In T. J. Boll, J. M. Raczynski, & L. C. Leviton (Eds.), *Handbook of clinical health psychology* (pp. 147–181). Washington, DC: American Psychological Association.

Duits, A. A., Boeke, S., Taams, M. A., Passchier, J., & Erdman, R. A. (1997). Prediction of quality of life after coronary artery bypass graft surgery: A review and evaluation of multiple, recent studies. *Psychosomatic Medicine, 59,* 257–268.

Dulit, R. A., Fye, R. M. R., Miller, F. T., Sacks, M. H., & Frances, A. J. (1993). Gender differences in sexual preference and substance abuse of inpatients with borderline personality disorder. *Journal of Personality Disorders, 7,* 182–185.

Durst, D. (2005). Aging amongst immigrants in Canada: Population drift. *Canadian Studies in Population, 32,* 257–270.

Dutra, L., Stathopoulou, G., Basden, S., Leyro, T., Powers, M., & Otto, M. (2008). A meta-analytic review of psychosocial interventions for substance use disorders. *American Journal of Psychiatry, 165,* 179–187.

Dyck, D. G., Short, R., & Vitaliano, P. P. (1999). Predictors of burden and infectious illness in schizophrenia caregivers. *Psychosomatic Medicine, 61,* 411–419.

E

Eaves, L. C., & Ho, H. H. (2008). Young adult outcome of autism spectrum disorders. *Journal of Autism and Developmental Disabilities, 38,* 739–747.

Ebbeling, C. B., & Ludwig, D. D. (2010). Pediatric obesity prevention initiatives: More questions than answers. *Archives of Pediatric and Adolescent Medicine, 164,* 1067–1069.

Ebersole, J. S. (2002). *Current practice of clinical electroencephalography.* Philadelphia, PA: Lippincott Williams & Wilkins.

Ebly, E. M., Parhad, I. M., Hogan, D. B., & Fung, T. S. (1994). Prevalence and types of dementia in the very old: Results from the Canadian Study of Health and Aging. *Neurology, 44,* 1593–1600.

Ebmeier, K. P., Donaghey, C., & Steele, J. D. (2006). Recent developments and current controversies in depression. *Lancet, 367*(9505), 153–167.

Edginton, B. (1997). Moral architecture: The influence of the York Retreat on asylum design. *Health & Place, 3,* 91–99.

Edwards, R., Telfair, J., Cecil, H., & Lenoci, J. (2001). Self-efficacy as a predictor of adult adjustment to sickle cell disease: One-year outcomes. *Psychosomatic Medicine, 63,* 850–858.

Eggers, C., & Bunk, D. (1997). The long-term course of childhood-onset schizophrenia: A 42 year follow-up. *Schizophrenia Bulletin, 23,* 105–117.

Eggert, L. L., Thompson, E. A., Herting, J. R., & Nicholas, L. J. (1995). Reducing suicide potential among high-risk youth: Tests of a school-based prevention program. *Suicide Life Threatening Behaviors, 25,* 276–296.

Ehlers, C. L., Frank, E., & Kupfer, D. J. (1988). Social zeitgebers and biological rhythms: A unified approach to understanding the etiology of depression. *Archives of General Psychiatry, 45,* 948–952.

Ehlert, U., Gaab, J., & Heinrichs, M. (2001). Psychoneuroendocrinological contributions to the etiology of depression, posttraumatic stress disorder, and stress-related bodily disorders: The role of the hypothalamus-pituitary-adrenal axis. *Biological Psychology, 57,* 141–152.

Ehrensaft, M. K. (2005). Interpersonal relationships and sex differences in the development of conduct problems. *Clinical Child and Family Psychology Review, 8,* 39–63.

Eichler, E. E., & Zimmerman, A. W. (2008). A hot spot of genetic instability in autism. *New England Journal of Medicine, 358,* 737–739.

Eidlitz-Markus, T. Shuper, K., & Amir, A. (2000). Secondary enuresis: post-traumatic stress disorder in children after car accidents. *Israeli Medical Association Journal, 2,* 135–137.

Einat, H., Yuan, P., & Manji, H. K. (2005). Increased anxiety-like behaviors and mitochondrial dysfunction in mice with targeted mutation of the Bel-2 gene: Further support for the involvement of mitochondrial function in anxiety disorders. *Behavior and Brain Research, 165,* 172–180.

Eisen, A. (1999). *Recommendations for the practice of clinical neurophysiology.* Amsterdam: Elsevier.

Eisendrath, S. J., & Young, J. Q. (2005). Factitious physical disorders: A review. In M. Maj, H. S. Akiskal, J. E. Mezzich, & A. Okasha (Eds.), *Somatoform disorders* (pp. 325–351). Hoboken, NJ: John Wiley & Sons.

Eldh, J., Berg, A., & Gustafsson, M. (1997). Long-term follow up after sex reassignment surgery. *Scandinavian Journal of Plastic and Reconstructive Surgery and Hand Surgery, 31,* 39–45.

Ely, E. W., Gautam, S., Margolin, R., Francis, J., May, L., Speroff, T., . . . Inouye, S. K. (2001). The impact of delirium in the intensive care unit on hospital length of stay. *Intensive Care Medicine, 27,* 1892–1900.

Elzinga, B. M., van Dyck, R., & Spinhoven, P. (1998). Three controversies about dissociative identity disorder. *Clinical Psychology and Psychotherapy, 3,* 13–23.

Epstein, E. E., Fischer-Elber, K., & Al-Otaiba, Z. (2007). Women, aging, and alcohol use disorders. *Journal of Women and Aging, 19,* 31–48.

Erkiran, M., Özünalan, H., Evren, C., Aytaçlar, S., Kirisci, L., & Tarter, R. (2006). Substance abuse amplifies the risk for violence in schizophrenia spectrum disorder. *Addictive Behaviors, 31,* 1797–1805.

Ernst, C., Földényi, M., & Angst, J. (1993). The Zurich Study: XXI. Sexual dysfunctions and disturbances in young adults. *European Archives of Psychiatry and Clinical Neuroscience, 243,* 179–188.

ESEMeD/MHEDEA 2000 Investigators, 2004. Prevalence of mental disorders in Europe: results from the European Study of the Epidemiology of Mental Disorders (ESEMeD) project. *Acta Psychiatrica Scandinavica, 109*(1), 21–27.

Essau, C. A., Conradt, J., & Peterman, F. (1999). Frequency of panic attacks and panic disorder in adolescents. *Depression and Anxiety, 9,* 10–26.

Essau, C. A., Conradt, J., & Peterman, F. (2000). Frequency, comorbidity and psychosocial impairment of specific phobia in adolescents. *Journal of Clinical Child Psychology, 29,* 221–231.

Etgen, T., Sander, D., Huntgeburth, U., Poppert, H., Förstl, H., & Bickel, H. (2010). Physical activity and incident cognitive impairment in elderly persons: The INVADE study. *Archives of Internal Medicine, 170,* 186–193.

Evans, J. D., Heaton, R. K., Paulsen, J. S., McAdams, L. A., Heaton, S. C., & Jeste, D. V. (1999). Schizoaffective disorder: A form of schizophrenia or affective disorder. *Journal of Clinical Psychiatry, 60,* 874–882.

Evans, J. D., Heaton, R. K., Paulsen, J. S., Palmer, B. W., Patterson, T., & Jeste, D. V. (2003). The relationship of neuropsychological abilities to specific domains of functional capacity in older schizophrenia patients. *Biological Psychiatry, 53,* 422–430.

Exner, J. (2005). *A Rorschach Workbook for the Comprehensive System* (5th ed.) Asheville, NC: Rorschach Workshops.

Eyler Zorrilla, L. T., Heaton, R. K., McAdams, L. A., Zisook, S., Harris, M. J., & Jeste, D. V. (2000). Cross-sectional study of older outpatients with schizophrenia and healthy comparison subjects: no differences in age-related cognitive decline. *American Journal of Psychiatry, 157,* 1324–1326.

F

Fagan, P. J., Wise, T. N., Schmidt, C. W., Jr., & Berlin, F. S. (2002). Pedophilia. *Journal of the American Medical Association, 288,* 2458–2465.

Fairbrother, N. (2002). The treatment of social phobia—100 years ago. *Behaviour Research and Therapy, 40,* 1291–1305.

Fairburn, C. G. (1981). A cognitive-behavioural approach to the treatment of bulimia. *Psychological Medicine, 11,* 707–711.

Fairburn, C. G. (1993). Interpersonal psychotherapy for bulimia nervosa. In G. Klerman & M. Weissman (Eds.), *New applications of interpersonal psychotherapy* (pp. 355–378). Washington, DC: American Psychiatric Press.

Fairburn, C. G., Cooper, Z., Doll, H. A., Norman, P., & O'Connor, M. (2000). The natural course of bulimia nervosa and binge eating disorder in young women. *Archives of General Psychiatry, 57,* 659–665.

Fairburn, C. G., Jones, R., Peveler, R. C., Carr, S. J., Solomon, R. A., O'Connor, M. E., Burton, J., & Hope, R. A. . (1991). Three psychological treatments for bulimia nervosa: A comparative trial. *Archives of General Psychiatry, 48,* 463–469.

Fairburn, C. G., & Walsh, B. (2002). Atypical eating disorders (eating disorders not otherwise specified). In C. Fairburn & K. Brownell (Eds.), *Eating disorders and obesity: A comprehensive handbook* (2nd ed., pp. 171–177). New York, NY: Guilford Press.

Fairburn, C. G., Welch, S. L., Doll, H. A., Davies, B. A., & O'Connor, M. E. (1997). Risk factors for bulimia nervosa: A community-based case-control study. *Archives of General Psychiatry, 54,* 509–517.

Fairburn, C., Jones, R., Peveler, R., Hope, R., & O'Connor, M. (1993). Psychotherapy and bulimia nervosa: Longer-term effects of interpersonal psychotherapy, behavior therapy, and cognitive-behavioral therapy. *Archives of General Psychiatry, 50,* 419–428.

Faraone, S. V., Perlis, R. H., Doyle, A. E., Smoller, J. W., Goralnick, J. J., Holmgren, M. A., & Sklar, P. (2005). Molecular genetics of attention-deficit/hyperactivity disorder. *Biological Psychiatry, 57,* 1313–1323.

Faravelli, C., Salvatori, S., Galassi, F., Aiazzi, L., Drei, C., & Cabras, P. (1997). Epidemiology of somatoform disorders: A community survey in Florence. *Social Psychiatry and Psychiatric Epidemiology, 32,* 24–29.

Farley, M., Lynne, J., & Cotton, A. J. (2005). Prostitution in Vancouver: Violence and the colonization of First Nations women. *Transcultural Psychiatry, 42,* 242–271.

Farmer, E. M., Compton, S. N., Burns, B. J., & Robertson, E. (2002). Review of the evidence base for treatment of childhood psychopathology: Externalizing disorders. *Journal of Consulting and Clinical Psychology, 70,* 1267–1302.

Farr, C. B. (1994). Benjamin Rush and American psychiatry. *American Journal of Psychiatry, 151,* 65–73.

Fassino, S., Amianto, F., Gramaglia, C., Facchini, F., & Abbate, G. (2004). Temperament and character in eating disorders: Ten years of studies. *Eating and Weight Disorders, 9,* 81–90.

Fatemi, S. H., Emamian, E. S., Kist, D., Sidwell, R. W., Nakajima, K., Akhter, P., . . . Bailey, K. (1999). Defective corticogenesis and reduction in immunoreactivity in cortex and hippocampus of prenatally infected neonatal mice. *Molecular Psychiatry, 4,* 145–154.

Fava, G. A., Bartolucci, G., Rafanelli, C., & Mangelli, L. (2001). Cognitive-behavioral management of patients with bipolar disorder who relapsed while on lithium prophylaxis. *Journal of Clinical Psychiatry, 62,* 556–559.

Fearing, M. A., & Inouye, S. K. (2009). Delirium. In D. C. Blazer & D. C. Steffens (Eds.), *Textbook of geriatric psychiatry* (pp. 229–241). Washington, DC: American Psychiatric Publishing, Inc.

Federoff, J. P., Fishell, A., & Federoff, B. (1999). A case series of women evaluated for paraphilic sexual disorders. *Canadian Journal of Human Sexuality, 8,* 127–140.

Felder, C., Dickason-Chesterfield, A., & Moore, S. (2006). Cannabinoids biology: The search for new therapeutic targets. *Molecular Interventions, 6,* 149–161.

Feldman, H. A., Goldstein, I., Hatzichristou, D. G., Krane, R. J., & McKinlay, J. B. (1994). Impotence and its medical and psychosocial correlates: Results of the Massachusetts Male Aging Study. *Journal of Urology, 151,* 54–61.

Felthous, A. R., O'Shaughnessy, R., Kuten, J., François-Pursell, I., & Medrano, J. (2007). The clinician's duty to warn or protect: In the United States, England, Canada, New Zealand, France and Spain. In A. R. Felthous & H. Saß (Eds.), *International handbook on psychopathic disorders and the law* (vol. 2, pp. 75–94). New York, NY: Wiley.

Fenton, W. S., Blyler, C. R., & Heinssen, R. K. (1997). Determinants of medication compliance in schizophrenia: Empirical and clinical findings. *Schizophrenia Bulletin, 23,* 637–651.

Fenton, W. S., & McGlashan, T. H. (1991). Natural history of schizophrenia subtypes: II. Positive and negative symptoms and long term course. *Archives of General Psychiatry, 48,* 978–986.

Ferguson, J. M. (2001). The effects of antidepressants on sexual functioning in depressed patients: A review. *Journal of Clinical Psychiatry, 62*(Suppl. 3), 22–34.

Fergusson, D. M., Horwood, L. J., & Shannon, F. T. (1990). Secondary enuresis in a birth cohort of New Zealand children. *Pediatrics and Perinatal Epidemiology, 4*, 53–63.

Fernandez-Aranda, F., Pinheiro, A. P., Tozzi, F., Thornton, L. M., Fichter, M. M., Halmi, K. A., . . . Bulik, C. M. (2007) Symptom profile of major depressive disorder in women with eating disorders. *Australian and New Zealand Journal of Psychiatry, 41*, 24–31.

Fichter, M., & Quadflieg, N. (1997). Six-year course of bulimia nervosa. *International Journal of Eating Disorders, 22,* 361–384.

Fichter, M. M., Quadflieg, N., & Gnutzmann, A. (1998). Binge eating disorder: Treatment outcome over a 6-year course. *Journal of Psychosomatic Research, 44*, 385–405.

Findlay, L. C., & Sunderland, A. (2014). Professional and informal mental health support reported by Canadians aged 15 to 24. *Health Reports, 25,* 3–11.

Finkenbine, R., & Miele, V. J. (2004). Globus hystericus: A brief review. *General Hospital Psychiatry, 26,* 78–82.

Fiore, M. C. (2000). A clinical practice guideline for treating tobacco use and dependence: A US Public Health Service report. *The Journal of the American Medical Association, 283,* 3244–3254.

Fischer, S., & Peterson, C. (2015). Dialectical behavior therapy for adolescent binge eating, purging, suicidal behavior, and non-suicidal self-injury: A pilot study. *Cognitive-Behavioral Psychotherapy, 52,* 78–92.

Fisher, C. B., Hoagwood, K., Boyce, C., Duster, T., Frank, D. A., Grisso, T., . . . Zayas, L. H. (2002a). Research ethics for mental health science involving ethnic minority children and youths. *American Psychologist, 57,* 1024–1040.

Fisher, E. B., Brownson, R. C., Heath, A. C., Luke, D. A., & Sumner, W., II. (2004). Cigarette smoking. In T. J. Boll, J. M. Raczynski, & L. C. Leviton (Eds.), *Handbook of clinical health psychology* (pp. 75–120). Washington, DC: American Psychological Association.

Fisher, H. E., Aron, A., Mashek, D., Li, H., & Brown, L. L. (2002b). Defining the brain systems of lust, romantic attraction, and attachment. *Archives of Sexual Behavior, 16,* 413–419.

Fisher, L. (1996). Bizarre right from Day 1. *MacLean's, 109*(28), 14.

Fisher, R. A. (1936). Has Mendel's work been rediscovered? *Annals of Science 1,* 115–137.

Fisher, R. L., & Fisher, S. (1996). Antidepresssants for children. Is scientific support necessary? *Journal of Nervous and Mental Disease, 184,* 99–102.

Fitzgerald, P. B., & Daskalakis, Z. J. (2008). A review of repetitive transcranial magnetic stimulation use in the treatment of schizophrenia. *The Canadian Journal of Psychiatry, 53,* 567–576.

Flament, M. F., Henderson, K., Buchholz, A., Obeid, N., Nguyen, H. N., Birmingham, M., . . . Goldfield, G. (2015). Weight status and DSM-5 diagnoses of eating disorders in adolescents from the community. *Journal of the American Academy of Child and Adolescent Psychiatry, 54,* 403–411.

Flavell, J. H., Flavell, E. R., & Green, F. L. (2001). Development of children's understanding of connections between thinking and feeling. *Psychological Science, 12,* 430–432.

Fleischhacker, W. W., Cetkovich-Bakmas, M., De Hert, M., Hennekens, C. H., Lambert, M., Leucht, S., . . . Lieberman, J. A. (2008). Comorbid somatic illnesses in patients with severe mental disorders: clinical, policy, and research challenges. *Journal of Clinical Psychiatry, 18,* e1–e6.

Fleischhacker, W. W., & Widschwendter, C. G. (2006). Treatment of schizophrenia patients: Comparing new-generation antipsychotics to each other. *Current Opinions in Psychiatry, 19,* 128–134.

Fleming, M. F., Manwell, L. B., Barry, K. L., Adams, W., & Stauffacher, E. A. (1999). Brief physician advice for alcohol problems in older adults: A randomized community-based trial. *The Journal of Family Practice, 48,* 378–384.

Flett, G. L., Besser, A., & Hewitt, P. L. (2014). Perfectionism and interpersonal orientations in depression: An analysis of validation seeking and rejection sensitivity in a community sample of young adults. *Psychiatry, 77,* 67–85.

Flint, A. J. (2004). Anxiety disorders. In J. Sadavoy, L. F. Jarvik, G. T. Grossberg, & B. S. Meyers (Eds.), *Comprehensive textbook of geriatric psychiatry* (3rd ed., pp. 687–699). New York, NY: W. W. Norton & Co.

Foley, D. L., Pickles, A., Maes, H. M., Silberg, J. L., & Eaves, L. J. (2004). Course and short-term outcomes of separation anxiety disorder in a community sample of twins. *Journal of the American Academy of Child and Adolescent Psychiatry, 43,* 452–460.

Folkman, S., & Lazarus, R. S. (1986). Stress-processes and depressive symptomatology. *Journal of Abnormal Psychology, 95*(2), 107–113.

Folsom, D. P., Hawthorne, W., Lindamer, L., Filmer, T., Bailey, A., Golshan, S., . . . Jeste, D. V. (2005). Prevalence and risk factors for homelessness and utilization of mental health services among 10,340 patients with serious mental illness in a large public mental health system. *American Journal of Psychiatry, 162,* 370–376.

Folstein, S. E., & Rosen-Sheidley, B. (2001) Genetics of autism: complex aetiology for a heterogeneous disorder. *Nature Reviews Genetics, 2,* 943–955.

Fombonne, E. (2005). The changing epidemiology of autism. *Journal of Applied Research in Intellectual Disabilities, 18,* 281–294.

Fonagy, P., Steele, M., & Moran, G. (1991). The capacity for understanding mental states: The reflective self in parent and child and its significance for security of attachment. *Infant Mental Health Journal, 12,* 200–217.

Foote, B., Smolin, Y., Kaplan, M., Legatt, M. E., & Lipschitz, D. (2006). Prevalence of dissociative disorders in psychiatric outpatients. *American Journal of Psychiatry, 163,* 623–629.

Ford, B. C., Bullard, K. M., Taylor, R. J., Toler, A. K., Neighbors, H. W., & Jackson, J. S. (2007). Lifetime and 12-month prevalence of *Diagnostic and Statistical Manual of Mental Disorders*, Fourth Edition, disorders among older African Americans: Findings from the National Survey of American Life. *American Journal of Geriatric Psychiatry, 15,* 652–659.

Ford, C. V. (2005). Deception syndrome: Factitious disorders and malingering. In J. L. Levenson (Ed.), *The American psychiatric publishing textbook of psychosomatic medicine* (pp. 297–309). Washington, DC: American Psychiatric Press.

Forsythe, W. I., & Redmond, A. (1974). Enuresis and spontaneous cure rate: Study of 1129 enuretics. *Archives of Disorders in Childhood, 49,* 259.

Foxx, R. M., & Martin, E. D. (1975). Treatment of scavenging behavior (coprophagy and pica) by overcorrection. *Behaviour Research and Therapy, 13,* 153–162.

Frances, A. (2012). DSM-5 is a guide not a bible: Simply ignore its 10 worst changes. Retrieved December 31, 2012 from http://www.huffingtonpost.com/allen-frances/dsm-5_b_2227626.html.

Frank, E., Hlastala, S., Ritenour, A., Houck, P., Tu, X. M., Monk, T. H., . . . Kupfer, D. J. (1997). Inducing lifestyle regularity in recovering bipolar disorder patients: Results from the maintenance therapies in bipolar disorder protocol. *Biological Psychiatry, 41,* 1165–1173.

Frank, E., Kupfer, D. J., Thase, M. E., Mallinger, A. G., Swartz, H. A., Fagiolini, A. M., . . . Monk, T. (2005a). Two-year outcomes for interpersonal and social rhythm therapy in individuals with bipolar I disorder. *Archives of General Psychiatry, 62,* 996–1004.

Frank, E., Kupfer, D. J., Wagner, E. F., McEachran, A. B., & Corner, C. (1991). Efficacy of interpersonal psychotherapy as a maintenance treatment of recurrent depression: Contributing factors. *Archives of General Psychiatry, 48*, 1053–1059.

Frank, E., Swartz, H. A., Mallinger, A. G., Thase, M. E., Weaver, E. V., & Kupfer, D. J. (1999). Adjunctive psychotherapy for bipolar disorder: Effects of changing treatment modality. *Journal of Abnormal Psychology, 108*, 579–587.

Fraser, S. L., Geoffroy, D., Chachamovich, E., & Kirmayer, L. J. (2015). Changing rates of suicide ideation and attempts among Inuit youth: A gender-based analysis of risk and protective factors. *Suicide and Life-Threatening Behavior, 45*, 141–156.

Frattola, L., Piolti, R., Bassi, S., Albizzati, M. G., Cesana, B. M., Bottani, M. S., . . . Morselli, P. L. (1992). Effects of alpidem in anxious elderly outpatients: a double-blind, placebo-controlled trial. *Clinical Neuropharmacology, 15*, 477–487.

Freeman, S. J. J. (1994). An overview of Canada's mental health system. In L. L. Bachrach, P. Goering, & D. Wasylenki (Eds.), *Mental health care in Canada* (pp. 11–20). San Francisco, CA: Jossey-Bass.

Fremont, W. P. (2004). Childhood reactions to terrorism-induced trauma: A review of the past 10 years. *Journal of the American Academy of Child and Adolescent Psychiatry, 43*, 381–392.

Freud, S. (1917). Mourning and melancholia. In J. Strachey & A. Freud (Eds.), *The standard edition of the complete psychological works of Sigmund Freud, 1953–1974* (Vol. 14, p. 248). London: Hogarth Press.

Friedman, M., & Rosenman, R. H. (1974). *Type A behavior and your heart.* New York, NY: Alfred A. Knopf.

Froguel, P. (1998). The genetics of complex traits: From diabetes mellitus to obesity. *Pathologie Biologie* (Paris), *46*, 713–714.

Frohlich, P. F., & Meston, C. M. (2002). Sexual functioning and self-reported depressive symptoms among college women. *Journal of Sex Research, 39*, 321–325.

Fugl-Meyer, A. R., & Sjögren Fugl-Meyer, K. (1999). Sexual disabilities, problems and satisfaction in 18–74 year old Swedes. *Scandinavian Journal of Sexology, 2*, 79–105.

G

Gadalla, T., & Piran, N. (2008). Psychiatric comorbidity in women with disordered eating behavior: A national study. *Women & Health, 48*, 467–484.

Gallacher, J. E., Sweetnam, P. M., Yarnell, J. W., Elwood, P. C., & Stansfeld, S. A. (2003). Is type A behavior really a trigger for coronary heart disease events? *Psychosomatic Medicine, 65*, 339–346.

Gallagher-Thompson, D., & Coon, D. W. (2007). Evidence-based psychological treatments for distress in family caregivers of older adults. *Psychology and Aging, 22*, 37–51.

Gallo, J. J., Ryan, S. D., & Ford, D. E. (1999). Attitudes, knowledge, and behavior of family physicians regarding depression in late life. *Archives of Family Medicine, 8*, 249–256.

Gallo, L. C., & Matthews, K. A. (2003). Understanding the association between socioeconomic status and physical health: Do negative emotions play a role? *Psychological Bulletin, 129*, 10–51.

Gallop, R., & Wynn, F. (1987). The difficult inpatient: Identification and response by staff. *Canadian Journal of Psychiatry, 32*, 211–215.

Ganzini, L., McFarland, B. H., & Cutler, D. (1990). Prevalence of mental disorders after catastrophic financial loss. *The Journal of Nervous and Mental Disease, 178*, 680–685.

Garattini, S. (1993). *Caffeine, coffee, and health.* New York, NY: Raven Press.

Garb, H. N., Wood, J. M., Lilienfeld, S. O., & Nezworski, M. T. (2005). Roots of the Rorschach controversy. *Clinical Psychology Review, 25*, 97–118.

Garber, B. G., & Zamorski, M. A. (2012). Evaluation of a third-location decompression program for Canadian Forces members returning from Afghanistan. *Military Medicine, 177*, 397–403.

Garbutt, J., Kranzler, H., O'Malley, S., Gastfriend, D., Pettinati, H., Silverman, B., . . . the Vivitrex Study Group. (2005). Efficacy and tolerability of long-acting injectable naltrexone for alcohol dependence: A randomized controlled trial. *Journal of the American Medical Association, 293*, 1617–1625.

Garbutt, J., West, S., Carey, T., Lohr, K., & Crews, F. (1999). Pharmacological treatment of alcohol dependence: A review of the evidence. *Journal of the American Medical Association, 281*, 1318–1325.

Garcia, A. M., Freeman, J. B. Himle, M. B., Berman, N. C., Ogata, A. K., Ng, J., . . . Leonard, J. (2009). Phenomenology of early childhood onset obsessive compulsive disorder. *Journal of Psychopathology and Behavioral Assessment, 31*, 104–111.

Gardner, W., Lidz, C. W., Mulvey, E. P., & Shaw, E. C. (1996). Clinical versus actuarial predictions of violence in patients with mental illness. *Journal of Consulting and Clinical Psychology, 64*, 602–609.

Garfinkel, P. E., Moldofsky, H., & Garner, D. M. (1980). The heterogeneity of anorexia nervosa. *Archives of General Psychiatry, 37*, 1036–1040.

Garner, D. M., Garfinkel, P. E., Rockert, W., & Olmsted, M. P. (1987). A prospective study of eating disturbances in the ballet. *Psychotherapy and Psychosomatics, 48*, 170–175.

Gartlehner, G., Hansen, R. A., Carey, T. S., Lohr, K. N., Gaynes, B. N., & Randolph, L. C. (2005). Discontinuation rates for selective serotonin reuptake inhibitors and other second-generation antidepressants in outpatients with major depressive disorder: A systematic review and meta-analysis. *International Clinical Psychopharmacology, 20*, 59–69.

Gatchel, R. J., & Maddrey, A. M. (2004). The biopsychosocial perspective of pain. In T. J. Boll, J. M. Raczynski, & L. C. Leviton (Eds.), *Handbook of clinical health psychology* (pp. 357–403). Washington, DC: American Psychological Association.

Gatz, M. (2000). Variations on depression in later life. In S. H. Qualls & N. Abeles (Eds.), *Psychology and the aging revolution: How we adapt to longer life.* Washington, DC: American Psychological Association.

Gaudiano, B. A. (2006). Is symptomatic improvement in clinical trials of cognitive-behavioral therapy for psychosis clinically significant? *Journal of Psychiatric Practice, 12*, 11–23.

Gavin, N. I., Gaynes, B. N., Lohr, K. N., Meltzer-Brody, S., Gartlehner, G., & Swinson, T. (2005). Perinatal depression: a systematic review of prevalence and incidence. *Obstetrics and Gynecology, 106*, 1071–1083.

Geldmacher, D. S., Provenzano, G., McRae, T., Mastey, V., & Ieni, J. R. (2003). Donepezil is associated with delayed nursing home placement in patients with Alzheimer's disease. *Journal of the American Geriatrics Society, 51*, 937–944.

Gelernter, J., Liu, X., Hesselbrock, V., Page, G., Goddard, A., & Zhang, H. (2004). Results of a genomewide linkage scan: Support for chromosomes 9 and 11 loci increasing risk for cigarette smoking. *American Journal of Medical Genetics B, Neuropsychiatric Genetics, 128*, 94–101.

Geller, B., & Luby, J. (1997). Child and adolescent bipolar disorder: A review of the past 10 years. *Journal of the American Academy of Child and Adolescent Psychiatry, 36*, 1168–1176.

Geller, D., Biederman, J., Jones, J., Park, K., Schwartz, S., Shapiro, S., & Coffey, B. (1998). Is juvenile obsessive-compulsive disorder a developmental subtype of the disorder? *Journal of the American Academy of Child and Adolescent Psychiatry, 40*, 773–779.

Geller, J. L., & Morrissey, J. P. (2004). Asylum within and without asylums. *Psychiatry Services, 55*, 1128–1130.

Gendall, K., Joyce, P., Carter, F., McIntosh, V. V., Jordan, J., & Bulik, C. (2006). The psychobiology and diagnostic significance of amenorrhea in patients with anorexia nervosa. *Fertility and Sterility, 85*, 1531–1535.

Gerard, D. L. (1998). Chiarugi and Pinel considered: Soul's brain/person's mind. *Journal of the History of the Behavioral Sciences, 33*, 381–403.

Gfellner, B. M., & Hundelby, J. D. (1990). Family and peer predictors of substance use among Aboriginal and non-Aboriginal adolescents. *Canadian Journal of Native Studies, 10*, 267–294.

Gfellner, B. M., & Hundelby, J. D. (1995). Patterns of drug use among native and white adolescents: 1990–1993. *Canadian Journal of Public Health, 86*, 95–97.

Gibbons, L. E., Teri, L., Logsdon, R., McCurry, S. M., Kukull, W. A., Bowen, J. D., . . . Larson, E. (2002). Anxiety symptoms as predictors of nursing home placement in patients with Alzheimer's disease. *Journal of Clinical Geropsychology, 8*, 335–342.

Gijs, L., & Gooren, L. (1996). Hormonal and psychopharmacological interventions in the treatment of paraphilias: An update. *Journal of Sex Research, 33*, 273–290.

Gilleland, J., Soveg, C., Jacob, J. L., & Thomassin, K. (2009). Understanding the medically unexplained: Emotional and familial influences on children's somatic functioning. *Child: Care, Health and Development, 35*, 383–390.

Gillerot, Y., Koulischer, L., Yasse, B., & Wetzburger, C. (1989). The geneticist and the so-called "socio-cultural" familial mental retardation. *Journal de Génétique Humaine, 37*, 103–112.

Gilmour, H. (2015). Chronic pain, activity restriction and flourishing mental health. *Health Reports, 26*, 15–22.

Gilmour, H., Stranges, S., Kaplan, M., Feeny, D., McFarland, B., Huguet, N., . . . Bernier, J. (2013). Longitudinal trajectories of sleep duration in the general population. *Health Reports, 24*, 14–20.

Gitlin, M. (2006). Treatment-resistant bipolar disorder. *Molecular Psychiatry, 11*, 227–240.

Gladstone, G., Parker, G., Mitchell, P., Wilhelm, K., & Malhi, G. (2005). Relationship between self-reported childhood behavioral inhibition and lifetime anxiety disorders in a clinical sample. *Depression & Anxiety, 22,* 103–113.

Glaister, B. (1985). A case of auditory hallucination treated by satiation. *Behaviour Research and Therapy, 23,* 213–215.

Glaser, R., Kiecolt-Glaser, J. K., Speicher, C. E., & Holliday, J. E. (1985). Stress, loneliness, and changes in herpesvirus latency. *Journal of Behavioral Medicine, 8,* 249–260.

Gleaves, D. H., May, M. C., & Cardeña, E. (2001). An examination of the diagnostic validity of dissociative identity disorder. *Clinical Psychology Review, 21,* 577–608.

Glick, I. D., Clarkin, J. F., Haas, G. L., & Spencer, J. H. Jr. (1993). Clinical significance of inpatient family intervention: Conclusions from a clinical trial. *Hospital and Community Psychiatry, 44,* 869–873.

Goar, C. (2005). Tackling the issue of teen suicide. *Toronto Star,* February 11. Retrieved February 6, 2008, from www.thestar.com/NASApp/cs/ContentServer?pagen.c=Article&cid=1108075812063&call_pageid=971358637177.

Gochman, P. A., Greenstein, D., Sporn, A., Gogtay, N., Keller, B., Shaw, P., & Rapoport, L. (2005). IQ stabilization in childhood-onset schizophrenia. *Schizophrenia Research, 77,* 271–277.

Godlee, F., Smith, J., & Marcovitch, J. (2011). Wakefield's article linking MMR vaccine and autism was fraudulent. *British Medical Journal, 342,* c7452.

Goisman, R. M., Warshaw, M. G., Peterson, L. G., Rogers, M. P., Cuneo, P., Hunt, M. E., . . . Epstein-Kaye, T. (1994). Panic, agoraphobia, and panic disorder with agoraphobia: Data from a multicenter anxiety disorders study. *Journal of Nervous and Mental Disease, 182,* 72–79.

Gokalp, P. G., Turkel, R., Solmaz, D., Demir, T., Kizillan, E., Demir, D., & Baboolu, A. N. (2001). Clinical factors and comorbidity of social phobics in Turkey. *European Psychiatry, 16,* 115–121.

Gold, L. (2005). American Psychiatric Association honors Dorothea Dix with first posthumous fellowship. *Psychiatric Services, 56,* 502.

Goldberg, D. P., & Hillier, V. F. (1979) A scaled version of the General Health Questionnaire. *Psychological Medicine, 9,* 139–145.

Goldberg, J. H., Breckenridge, J. N., & Sheikh, J. I. (2003). Age differences in symptoms of depression and anxiety: Examining behavioral medicine outpatients. *Journal of Behavioral Medicine, 26,* 119–132.

Goldberg, P. D., Peterson, B. D., Rosen, K. H., & Sara, M. L. (2008). Cybersex: The impact of a contemporary problem on the practices of marriage and family therapists. *Journal of Marital and Family Therapy, 34,* 469–480.

Golden, C. J., Purisch, A. D., & Hammeke, T. A. (1980). *The Luria-Nebraska Neuropsychological Battery: Manual* (Revised ed.). Los Angeles, CA: Western Psychological Services.

Goldfield, G. S., Adamo, K. B., Rutherford, J., Legg, C. (2008). Stress and the relative reinforcing value of food in female binge eaters. *Physiological Behavior, 93,* 579–587.

Goldstein, A. J., & Chambless, D. L. (1978). A reanalysis of agoraphobia. *Behavior Therapy, 9,* 47–59.

Goldstein, R. B., Dawson, D. A., Saha, T. D., Ruan, W. J., Compton, W. M., & Grant, B. F. (2007). Antisocial behavioral syndromes and DSM-IV alcohol use disorders: Results from the National Epidemiologic Survey on Alcohol and Related Conditions. *Alcoholism Clinical and Experimental Research, 31,* 814–828.

Gonzalez, J. S., Penedo, F. J., Antoni, M. H., Duran, R. E., Pherson-Baker, S., Ironson, G., . . . Schneiderman N. (2004). Social support, positive states of mind, and HIV treatment adherence in men and women living with HIV/AIDS. *Health Psychology, 23,* 413–418.

Goodman, M., New, A. S., & Siever, L. J. (2004). Trauma, genes, and the neurobiology of personality disorders. *Annals of the New York Academy of Sciences, 1032,* 104–116.

Goodman, Y., Bruce, A. J., Cheng, B., & Mattson, M. P. (1996). Estrogens attenuate and corticosterone exacerbates excitotoxicity, oxidative injury and amyloid beat-peptide toxicity in hippocampal neurons. *Journal of Neurochemistry, 5,* 1836–1844.

Goodwin, J. L., Kaemingk, K. L., Fregosi, R. F., Rosen, G. M., Morgan, W. J., Smith, T., & Quan, S. F. (2004). Parasomnias and sleep disordered breathing in Caucasian and Hispanic children—The Tucson children's assessment of sleep apnea study. *Biomedcentral (BMC) Medicine, 2,* 14.

Gooren, L. (2006). The biology of human psychosexual differentiation. *Hormonal Behavior, 50,* 589–601.

Gordis, L. (2013). *Epidemiology.* New York, NY: Saunders.

Gottesman, I. I. (2001). Psychopathology through a life span-genetic prism. *American Psychologist, 56,* 867–878.

Gottfredson, L. S. (1997). Why g Matters: The Complexity of Everyday Life. *Intelligence, 24,* 79–132.

Gouin, J. P., & Kiecolt-Glaser, J. K. (2011). The impact of psychological stress on wound healing: Methods and mechanisms. *Immunology and Allergy Clinics of North America, 31,* 81–93.

Gould, M. S. (1990). Teenage suicide clusters. *Journal of the American Medical Association, 263,* 2051–2052.

Gould, R., Buckminster, S., Pollack, M., Otto, M., & Yap, L. (1997). Cognitive-behavioral and pharmacological treatment for social phobia: A meta-analysis. *Clinical Psychology: Science and Practice, 4,* 291–306.

Grabe, H. J., Meyer, C., Hapke, U., Rumpf, H. J., Freyberger, H. J., Dilling, H., & John, U. (2003). Specific somatoform disorder in the general population. *Psychosomatics, 44,* 304–311.

Graff, L. A., Kaoukis, G., Vincent, N., Piotrowski, A., & Ediger, J. (2012). New models of care for psychology in Canada's health services. *Canadian Psychology, 53,* 165–177.

Graham, J. R. (2000). *MMPI-2: Assessing Personality and Psychopathology* (Third ed.). New York, NY: Oxford University Press.

Grandin, L. D., Alloy, L. B., & Abramson, L. Y. (2006). The social zeitgeber theory, circadian rhythms, and mood disorders: Review and evaluation. *Clinical Psychology Review, 26,* 679–694.

Granholm, E., McQuaid, J. R., McClure, F. S., Auslander, L. A., Perivoliatis, D., Pedrelli, P., . . . Jeste, D. V. (2005). A randomized, controlled trial of cognitive-behavioral social skills training for middle-aged and older outpatients with chronic schizophrenia. *American Journal of Psychiatry, 162,* 520–529.

Grant, B. F., Hasin, D. S., Stinson, F. S., Dawson, D. A., Chou, S. P., Ruan, W. J., & Pickering, R. P. (2004). Prevalence, correlates, and disability of personality disorders in the United States: results from the national epidemiologic survey on alcohol and related conditions. *Journal of Clinical Psychiatry, 65*(7), 948–958.

Grant, J. E., Potenza, M. N., Weinstein, A., & Gorelick, D. A. (2010). Introduction to behavioral addictions. *American Journal of Drug and Alcohol Abuse, 36,* 233–241.

Gratzer, T. G., & Matas, M. (1994). The right to refuse treatment: Recent Canadian developments. *Bulletin of the American Academy of Psychiatry and Law, 22,* 249–256.

Gray, J. E., & O'Reilly, R. L. (2005). Canadian compulsory community treatment laws: Recent reforms. *International Journal of Law and Psychiatry, 28,* 13–22.

Gray, N. S., Fitzgerald, S., Taylor, J., MacCulloch, M. J., & Snowden, R. J. (2007). Predicting future reconviction in offenders with intellectual disabilities: The predictive efficacy of the VRAG, PCL-SV, and the HCR-20. *Psychological Assessment, 19,* 474–479.

Gray, R., Parr, A. M., & Robson, D. (2005). Has tardive dyskinesia disappeared? *Mental Health Practice, 8,* 20–22.

Green, M. F., Nuechterlein, K. H., Gold, J. M., Barch, D. M., Coehen, J., Essock, S., . . . Marder, S. R. (2004). Approaching a consensus battery for clinical trials in schizophrenia: The NIMH-MATRICS conference to select cognitive domains and test criteria. *Biological Psychiatry, 56,* 30–307.

Green, M., & Horan, W. P. (2010). Social cognition in schizophrenia. *Current Directions in Psychological Science, 19,* 243–248.

Greenberg, B., Malone, D., Friehs, G., Rezai, A., Kubu, C., Malloy, P., . . . Rasmussen, S. A. (2006). Three-year outcomes in deep brain stimulation for highly resistant obsessive-compulsive disorder. *Neuropsychopharmacology, 31,* 2384–2393.

Greenberg, D. M., & Gratzer, T. G. (1994). The impact of the Charter of Rights and Freedoms on the mental disorder provisions of the Criminal Code. *Canada's Mental Health,* Spring, 6–9.

Greene, R. W., Biederman, J., Faraone, S. V., Monuteaux, M. C., Mick, E., Fine, C. S., & Goring, J. C. (2001). Social impairment in girls with ADHD: Patterns, gender comparisons, and correlates. *Journal of the American Academy of Child and Adolescent Psychiatry, 40,* 704–710.

Greenspan, E. L. (Ed.) (1998). *Annotations at Section 16 of Martin's Criminal Code.* Ontario: Canada Law Book Inc.

Gren-Landell, M., Tillfors, M., Furmark, T., Bohlin, G., Andersson, G., & Svendin, C. G. (2009). Social phobia in Swedish adolescents. *Social Psychiatry and Psychiatric Epidemiology, 44,* 1–7.

Grenard, J., Ames, S., Pentz, M., & Sussman, S. (2006). Motivational interviewing with adolescents and young adults for drug-related problems. *International Journal of Adolescent Medical Health, 18,* 53–67.

Grenier, G., & Byers, E. S. (2001). Operationalizing premature or rapid ejaculation. *Journal of Sex Research, 38,* 369–378.

Gretton, H., Hare, R. D., & Catchpole, R. (2004). Psychopathy and offending from adolescence to adulthood: A ten-year follow-up. *Journal of Consulting and Clinical Psychology, 72,* 636–645.

Grice, D. E., Halmi, K. A., Fichter, M. M., Strober, M., Woodside, D. B., Treasure, J. T., . . . Berrettini, W. H. (2002). Evidence for a susceptibility gene for anorexia nervosa on chromosome 1. *American Journal of Human Genetics, 70,* 787–792.

Grilo, C. M., & Masheb, R. M. (2000). Onset of dieting vs binge eating in outpatients with binge eating disorder. *International Journal of Obesity and Related Metabolic Disorders, 24,* 404–409.

Grilo, C. M., White, M. A., Masheb, R. M. (2009) DSM-IV psychiatric disorder comorbidity and its correlates in binge eating disorder. *International Journal of Eating Disorders, 42(3),* 228–234.

Grob, G. N. (1994). *The mad man among us: A history of the care of America's mentally ill.* Cambridge, MA: Harvard University Press.

Grootens, K. P., & Verkes, R. J. (2005). Emerging evidence for the use of atypical antipsychotics in borderline personality disorder. *Pharmacopsychiatry, 38,* 20–23.

Groth-Marnat, G. (2009). Handbook of Psychological Assessment (5th ed.). Hoboken, NJ: John Wiley & Sons.

Grove, L. J., Loeb, S. J., & Penrod, J. (2009) Selective optimization with compensation: A model for older health programming. *Clinical Nurse Specialist, 23,* 25–32.

Grove, W. M. (2005). Clinical versus statistical prediction: The contribution of Paul E. Meehl. *Journal of Clinical Psychology, 61,* 1233–1243.

Grove, W. M., Zald, D. H., Lebow, B. S., Snitz, B. E., & Nelson, C. (2000). Clinical versus mechanical prediction: A meta-analysis. *Psychological Assessment, 12,* 19–30.

Growe, S. J. (2000). PTSD. *Toronto Star,* September 24, 2000.

Gruber, V. A., Delucchi, K. L., Kielstein, A., & Batki, S. L. (2008). A randomized trial of 6-month methadone maintenance with standard or minimal counseling versus 21-day methadone detoxification. *Drug and Alcohol Dependence, 94,* 199–206.

Grucza, R., & Beirut, L. (2007). Co-occurring risk factors for alcohol dependence and habitual smoking: Update on findings from the Collaborative Study on the Genetics of Alcoholism. *Alcohol Research & Health, 29,* 172–177.

Grunhaus, L., Schreiber, S., Dolberg, O. T., Polak, D., & Dannon, P. N. (2003). A randomized controlled comparison of electroconvulsive therapy and repetitive transcranial magnetic stimulation in severe and resistant nonpsychotic major depression. *Biological Psychiatry, 53,* 324–331.

Guarnaccia, P. J., De La Canela, V., & Carrillo, E. (1989). The multiple meanings of ataques de nervios in the Latino community. *Medical Anthropology, 11,* 47–62.

Gull, W. W. (1874). Anorexia nervosa (apepsia hysterica, anorexia hysterica). *Transactions of the Clinical Society of London, 7,* 22–28.

Gum, A. M., Areán, P. A., Hunkeler, E., Tang, L., Katon, W., & Hitchcock, P., . . . Unützer, J. (2004). Depression treatment preferences in older primary care patients. *The Gerontologist, 46,* 14–22.

Gunderson, J. (1984). *The borderline patient.* Washington, DC: American Psychiatric Press.

Gupta, A. R., & State, M. W. (2007). Recent advances in the genetics of autism. *Biological Psychiatry, 61,* 429–437.

Gureje, O., Simon, G. E., Ustun, T. B., & Goldberg, D. P. (1997). Somatization in cross-cultural perspective: A World Health Organization study in primary care. *American Journal of Psychiatry, 154,* 989–995.

Gurland, B. J. (1980). *Handbook of mental health and aging.* Englewood Cliffs, NJ: Prentice Hall.

Gurland, B. J. (2004). Epidemiology of psychiatric disorders. In J. Sadavoy, L. F. Jarvik, G. T. Grossberg, & B. S. Meyers (Eds.), *Comprehensive textbook of geriatric psychiatry* (3rd ed., pp. 3–37). New York, NY: W. W. Norton & Co.

Gurvits, T. V., Shenton, M. E., Hokama, H., Hirokazu, O., Lasko, N. B., Gilbertson, M. W., . . . Pitman, R. K. (1996). Magnetic resonance imaging study of hippocampal volume in chronic, combat-related posttraumatic stress disorder. *Biological Psychiatry, 40,* 1091–1099.

Gurwitch, R. J., Kees, M., & Becker, S. M. (2002). In the face of tragedy: Placing children's reactions to trauma in a new context. *Cognitive and Behavioral Practice, 9,* 286–295.

Gustafson, K. E., & McNamara, J. R. (1987). Confidentiality with minor clients: Issues and guidelines for therapists. *Professional Psychology: Research and Practice, 18,* 503–508.

H

Haas, L. F. (1993). Benjamin Rush (1745–1813). *Journal of Neurology Neurosurgery and Psychiatry, 56,* 741.

Haas, L. F. (2001). Jean Martin Charcot (1825–93) and Jean Baptiste Charcot (1867–1936). *Journal of Neurology Neurosurgery and Psychiatry, 71,* 524.

Hagedoorn, M., Kuijer, R. G., Buunk, B. P., DeJong, G. M., Wobbes, T., & Sanderman, R. (2000). Marital satisfaction in patients with cancer: Does support from intimate partners benefit those who need it the most? *Health Psychology, 19,* 274–282.

Haggarty, J., Cernovsky, Z., Kermeen, P., & Merskey, H. (2000). Psychiatric disorders in an Arctic community. *Canadian Journal of Psychiatry, 45,* 357–362.

Halbreich, U., Borenstein, J., Pearlstein, T., Kahn, LS. (2003) The prevalence, impairment, impact, and burden of premenstrual dysphoric disorder (PMS/PMDD). *Psychoneuroendocrinology, 28*(Supplement 3), 1–23.

Hall, W. D. (2006). How have the SSRI antidepressants affected suicide risk? *Lancet, 367,* 1959–1962.

Haltigan, J. D., & Vaillancourt, T. (2014). Joint trajectories of bullying and peer victimization across elementary and middle school and association with symptoms of psychopathology. *Developmental Psychology, 50,* 2426–2436.

Hamm, M. P., Newton, A. S., Chisholm, A., Shulhan, J., Milne, A., Sundar, P., . . . Hartling, L. (2015). Prevalence and effect of cyberbullying on children and young people. *JAMA Pediatrics, 169*(8), 770–777.

Handen, B. L., & Gilchrist, R. (2006). Practitioner review: Psychopharmacology in children and adolescents with mental retardation. *Journal of Child Psychology and Psychiatry, 47,* 871–882.

Hanna, G. H. (2000). Clinical and family-genetic studies of childhood obsessive-compulsive disorder. In W. K. Goodman, M. V. Rudofer, & J. D. Maser (Eds.), *Obsessive-compulsive disorder: Contemporary issues in treatment* (pp. 87–103). Mahwah, NJ: Lawrence Erlbaum Associates.

Hansen, C. J., Stevens, L. C., & Coast, J. R. (2001). Exercise duration and mood state: How much is enough to feel better? *Health Psychology, 20,* 267–275.

Hanson, R. K., & Slater, S. (1988). Sexual victimization in the history of sexual abuses: A review. *Annals of Sex Research, 1,* 485–499.

Hanssen, M., Bak, M., Bijl, R., Vollebergh, W., & van Os, J. (2005). The incidence and outcome of subclinical psychotic experiences in the general population. *British Journal of Clinical Psychology, 44,* 181–191.

Harasty, J., Couble, K. L., Hallliday, G. M., Kril, J. J., & McRitchie, D. A. (1997). Language-associated cortical regions are proportionally larger in the female brain. *Archives of Neurology, 54,* 171–176.

Hare, R. D., Clark, D., Grann, M., & Thornton, D. (2000). Psychopathy and the predictive utility of the PCL-R: An international perspective. *Behavioral Sciences and the Law, 18,* 623–645.

Hare, R. D., Hart, S. D., & Harpur, T. J. (1991). Psychopathy and the DSM-IV criteria for antisocial personality disorder. *Journal of Abnormal Psychology, 100,* 391–398.

Hare, R. D., & Neumann, C. S. (2006). The PCL-R assessment of psychopathy: Development, structural properties, and new directions. In C. J. Patrick (Ed.), *Handbook of psychopathy* (pp. 58–88). New York, NY: Guilford.

Hare, R. D., & Neumann, C. S. (2008). Psychopathy as a clinical and empirical construct. *Annual Review of Clinical Psychology, 4,* 217–246.

Hare, R. D., Neumann, C. S., & Widiger, T. A. (2012). Psychopathy. In T. A. Widiger (Ed.), *The Oxford handbook of personality disorders* (pp. 478–504). New York, NY: Oxford University Press.

Harmon, R. B. (2009). Hydrotherapy in state mental hospitals in the mid-twentieth century. *Issues in Mental Health Nursing, 30,* 491–494.

Harris, E. C., & Barraclough, B. (1997). Suicide as an outcome for mental disorders. A meta-analysis. *British Journal of Psychiatry, 170,* 205–228.

Harris, M. G., Henry, L. P., Harrigan, S. M., Purcell, R., Schwartz, O. S., Farrelly, S. E., . . . McGorry, P. D. (2005). The relationship between duration of untreated psychosis and outcome: An eight-year prospective study. *Schizophrenia Research, 70,* 85–93.

Harris, M. J., & Jeste, D. V. (1988). Late-onset schizophrenia: An overview. *Schizophrenia Bulletin, 14,* 39–45.

Harrison, P. J., & Owen, M. J. (2003). Genes for schizophrenia: Recent findings and their pathophysiological implications. *The Lancet, 361,* 417–419.

Harrow, M., Grossman, L. S., Jobe, T. H., & Herbener, E. S. (2005). Do patients with schizophrenia ever show periods of recovery? *Schizophrenia Bulletin, 31,* 723–734.

Harsh, V., Meltzer-Brody, S., Rubinow, D. R., & Schmidt, P. J. (2009). Reproductive aging, sex steroids, and mood disorders. *Harvard Review of Psychiatry, 17,* 87–102.

Hart, S. D., Cox, D. N., & Hare, R. D. (1995). *Manual for the Hare Psychopathy Checklist: Screening Version.* Toronto, ON: Multi-Health Systems.

Hartung, C. M., Willcutt, E. G., Lahey, B. B., Pelham, W. E., Loney, J., Stein, M. A., & Keenan, K. (2002). Sex differences in young children who meet criteria for attention deficit hyperactivity disorder. *Journal of Clinical Child and Adolescent Psychology, 31,* 453–464.

Hartwell, C. E. (1996). The schizophrenogenic mother concept in American psychiatry. *Psychiatry, 59,* 274–297.

Hatfield, E., Cacioppo, J. T., & Rapson, R. L. (1993). Emotional contagion. *Psychological Science, 2,* 96–99.

Hawkley, L. C., & Cacioppo, J. T. (2003). Loneliness and pathways to disease. *Brain Behavior, Immunity, 17*(Suppl. 1), S98–S105.

Hawton, K. (1995). Treatment of sexual dysfunctions by sex therapy and other approaches. *The British Journal of Psychiatry, 167,* 307–314.

Hay, P. (1998). The epidemiology of eating disorder behaviors: An Australian community-based survey. *International Journal of Eating Disorders, 23,* 371–382.

Hay, P. J., Mond, J., Buttner, P., & Darby, A. (2008). Eating disorder behaviors are increasing: findings from two sequential community surveys in South Australia. *PloS one, 3*(2), e1541.

Hayden, E. P., & Nurnberger, J. I. Jr. (2006). Molecular genetics of bipolar disorder. *Genes Brain and Behavior, 5,* 85–95.

Haynes, S. N., Keuthen, N. J., Wagener, P. D., & Stanley, M. A. (2006). *Principles and practice of behavioral assessment.* New York, NY: Kluwer Academic/Plemum Press.

Hayward, C., Killen, J. D., Kraemer, H. C., & Taylor, C. B. (1998). Linking self-reported childhood behavioral inhibition to adolescent social phobia. *Journal of the American Academy of Child and Adolescent Psychiatry, 37,* 1308–1316.

Hayward, C., Killen J. D., Kraemer, H. C., & Taylor, C. B. (2000). Predictors of panic attacks in adolescents, *Journal of the American Academy of Child and Adolescent Psychiatry, 39,* 1–8.

Health Canada (2002). *A report on mental illnesses in Canada.* Ottawa: Author.

Health Canada (2006). *Fetal alcohol spectrum disorder.* Ottawa: Author.

Heather, J. (1995). The great controlled drinking consensus: It is premature? *Addiction, 90,* 1160–1163.

Hebb, D. O. (1949). *The organization of behavior.* New York, NY: Wiley.

Hechtman, L., & Greenfield, B. (2003). Long-term use of stimulants in children with attention deficit hyperactivity disorder. *Paediatric Drugs, 5,* 787–794.

Heckman, T. G., Anderson, E. S., Sikkema, K. J., Kochman, A., Kalichman, S. C., & Anderson, T. (2004). Emotional distress in nonmetropolitan persons living with HIV disease enrolled in a telephone-delivered, coping improvement group intervention. *Health Psychology, 23,* 94–100.

Hegel, M. T., Ravaris, C. L., & Ahles, T. A. (1994). Combined cognitive-behavioral and time-limited alprazolam treatment of panic disorder. *Behavior Therapy, 25,* 183–195.

Heiby, E. M. (2002). Concluding remarks on the debate about prescription privileges for psychologists. *Journal of Clinical Psychology, 58,* 709–722.

Heim, C., Ehlert, U., & Hellhammer, D. H. (2000). The potential role of hypocortisolism in the pathophysiology of stress-related bodily disorders. *Psychoneuroendocrinology, 25,* 1–35.

Heim, C., & Nemeroff, C. (1999). The impact of early adverse experiences on brain systems involved in the pathophysiology of anxiety and affective disorders. *Biological Psychiatry, 46,* 1509–1522.

Heiman, J. R. (2002). Sexual dysfunction: Overview of prevalence, etiological factors, and treatments. *Journal of Sexual Research, 39,* 73–78.

Heiman, J. R., & LoPiccolo, J. (1987). *Become orgasmic: A sexual and personal growth program for women.* New York, NY: Simon & Schuster.

Heir, N. (2008). The father of slain teenager Stephanie Joy Donnelly will remain in a Forensic Psychiatric Institute until he is integrated back into society. Retrieved April 22, 2008 from http://www.princerupert.themixbc.com/node/678572.

Heisel, M. J., Grek, A., Moore, S. L., Jackson, F., Vincent, G., Malach, F. M., . . . Mokry, J. (2006). National guidelines for seniors' mental health: The assessment and treatment of mental health issues in long-term care homes (focus on mood and behaviour symptoms). *Canadian Journal of Geriatrics, 9*(Suppl. 2), S65–S70.

Hellekson, K. L. (2001). NIH consensus statement on phenylketonuria. *American Family Physician, 63,* 1430–1432.

Henderson, B. N., & Baum, A. (2004). Neoplasms. In T. J. Boll, S. Bennett Johnson, N. W. Perry, & R. H. Rozensky (Eds.), *Handbook of clinical health psychology* (pp. 37–64). Washington, DC: American Psychological Association.

Henggeler, S. W., Rowland, M. D., Randall, J., Ward, D. M., Pickrel, S. G., Cunningham, P. B., . . . Santos, A. B. (1999). Home-based multisystemic therapy as an alternative to the hospitalization of youths in psychiatric crisis: Clinical outcomes. *Journal of Clinical Child Psychology, 38,* 1381–1389.

Henggeler, S. W., Schoenwald, S. K., Borduin, C. M., Rowland, M. D., & Cunningham, P. B. (1998). *Multisystemic treatment of antisocial behavior in children and adolescents.* New York, NY: Guilford Press.

Henshaw, C. (2003). Mood disturbance in the early puerperium: A review. *Archives of Womens' Mental Health, 6,* S33–S42.

Hentschel, A. G., & Livesley, W. J. (2013). The general assessment of personality disorder (GAPD): Factor structure, incremental validity of self-pathology, and relations to DSM-IV personality disorder. *Journal of Personality Assessment, 95,* 479–485.

Hepp, U., Kraemer, B., Schnyder, U., & Delsignore, A. (2005). Psychiatric comorbidity in gender identity disorder. *Journal of Psychosomatic Research, 58,* 259–261.

Hepp, U., Wittmann, L., Schnyder, U., & Michel, K. (2004). Psychological and psychosocial interventions after attempted suicide: An overview of treatment studies. *Crisis, 25,* 108–117.

Herbert, J. D., Hope, D. A., & Bellack, A. S. (1992). Validity of the distinction between generalized social phobia and avoidant personality disorder. *Journal of Abnormal Psychology, 101,* 332–339.

Herbert, T. B., & Cohen, S. (1993). Depression and immunity: A meta-analytic review. *Psychological Bulletin, 113,* 472–486.

Herd, D., & Grube, J. (1996). Black identity and drinking in the US: A national study. *Addiction, 91,* 845–857.

Herek, G. M., Capitanio, J. P., & Widaman, K. F. (2003). Stigma, social risk, and health policy: Public attitudes toward HIV surveillance policies and the social construction of illness. *Health Psychology, 22,* 533–540.

Herman, J. L., Perry, J. C., & van der Kolk, B. A. (1989). Childhood trauma in borderline personality disorder. *American Journal of Psychiatry, 146,* 490–495.

Herzog, D., Dorer, D., Keel, P. K., Selwyn, S., Ekeblad, E., Flores, A., . . . Keller, M. B. (1999). Recovery and relapse in anorexia and bulimia nervosa: A 7.5-year follow-up study. *Journal of the American Academy of Child and Adolescent Psychiatry, 38,* 829–837.

Hettema, J. M., Prescott, C. A., & Kendler, K. S. (2001). A population-based twin study of generalized anxiety disorder in men and women. *Journal of Nervous and Mental Disease, 189,* 413–420.

Hettema, J. M., Prescott, C. A., Myers, J. M., Neale, M. C., & Kendler, K. S. (2005). The structure of genetic and environmental risk factors for anxiety disorders in men and women. *Archives of General Psychiatry, 62,* 182–189.

Hewitt, P. L., Caelian, C. F., Chen, C., & Flett, G. L. (2014). Perfectionism, stress, daily hassles, hopelessness, and suicide potential in depressed psychiatric adolescents. *Journal of Psychopathology and Behavioral Assessment, 36,* 663–674.

Hibbard, S. (2003). A critique of Lilienfeld et al.'s (2000) "The scientific status of projective techniques." *Journal of Personality Assessment, 80,* 260–271.

Hill, G., Forbes, W., Berthelot, J.-M., Lindsay, J., & McDowell, I. (1996). Dementia among seniors. *Health Reports, 8,* 7–10.

Hill, J. W., Futterman, R., Duttagupta, S., Mastey, V., Lloyd, J. R., & Fillit, H. (2002). Alzheimer's disease and related dementias increase costs of comorbidities in managed Medicare. *Neurology, 58,* 62–70.

Hillebrand, J. J., Koeners, M. P., de Rijke, C. E., Kas, M. J., & Adan, R. A. (2005). Leptin treatment in activity-based anorexia. *Biological Psychiatry, 58,* 165–171.

Hines, M., Brook, C., & Conway, G. S. (2004). Androgen and psychosexual development: Core gender identity, sexual orientation and recalled childhood gender role behavior in women and men with congenital adrenal hyperplasia (CAH). *Journal of Sex Research, 41,* 75–81.

Hinshaw, S. P. (1994). Conduct disorder in childhood: Conceptualization, diagnosis, comorbidity, and risk status for antisocial functioning in adulthood. *Progress in Experimental Personality & Psychopathology Research, 15,* 3–44.

Hirshfeld, D. R., Rosenbaum, J. F., Biederman, J., Bolduc, E. A., Faraone, S. V, Snidman, N., . . . Kagan, J. (1992). Stable behavioral inhibition and its association with anxiety disorder. *Journal of the American Academy of Child and Adolescent Psychiatry, 31,* 301–311.

Hochang, B. L., & Lyketsos, C. G. (2003). Depression in Alzheimer's disease: Heterogeneity and related issues. *Biological Psychiatry, 54,* 353–362.

Hodgins, S., Mednick, S. A., Brennan, P. A., Schulsinger, F., & Engberg, M. (1996). Mental disorder and crime: Evidence from a Danish birth cohort. *Archives of General Psychiatry, 53,* 489–496.

Hoek, H., Bartelds, A., Bosveld, J., van der Graaf, Y., Limpens, V., Maiwald, M., & Spaaij, C. J. (1995). Impact of urbanization on detection rates of eating disorders. *American Journal of Psychiatry, 152,* 1272–1278.

Hoek, H., & van Hoeken, D. (2003). Review of the prevalence and incidence of eating disorders. *International Journal of Eating Disorders, 34,* 383–396.

Hoffman, G. W., Ellinwood, E. H. Jr., Rockwell, W. J., Herfkens, R. J., Nishita, J. K., & Guthrie, L. F. (1989). Cerebral atrophy in bulimia. *Biological Psychiatry, 25,* 894–902.

Hoffman, M. D., & Hoffman, D. R. (2007). Does aerobic exercise improve pain perception and mood? A review of the evidence related to healthy and chronic pain subjects. *Current Pain and Headache Reports, 11,* 93–97.

Hoffman, R. E., Hawkins, K. A., Gueorguieva, R., Boutros, N. N., Rachid, F., Carroll, K., & Krystal, J. H. (2003). Transcranial magnetic stimulation of left temporoparietal cortex and medication-resistant auditory hallucinations. *Archives of General Psychiatry, 60,* 49–56.

Hofmann, S. G., Asnaani, A., & Hinton, D. E. (2010). Cultural aspects in social anxiety and social anxiety disorder. *Depression and Anxiety, 27,* 1117–1127.

Hogan, D. B., Gage, L., Bruto, V., Burne, D., Chan, P., Wiens, C., . . . Mokry, J. (2006). National guidelines for seniors' mental health: The assessment and treatment of delirium. *Canadian Journal of Geriatrics, 9*(Suppl. 2), S42–S49.

Holden, C. (2010). Behavioral addictions debut in proposed DSM-V. *Science, 327,* 935.

Hollander, E., Friedberg, J. P., Wasserman, S., Yeh, C. C., & Iyengar, S. (2005). The case for the OCD Spectrum. In J. Abramowitz & A. C. Houts (Eds.), *Concepts and controversies in obsessive compulsive disorder* (pp. 95–118). New York, NY: Springer Publishing.

Holley, H., Arboleda-Flórez, J, & Crisanti, A. (1998). Do forensic offenders receive harsher sentences? *International Journal of Law and Psychiatry, 21,* 43–57.

Hollis, C. (2000). Adult outcomes of child- and adolescent-onset schizophrenia: Diagnostic stability and predictive validity. *American Journal of Psychiatry, 157,* 1652–1659.

Hollon, S. D., DeRubeis, R. J., Evans, M. D., Wiemer, M. J., Garvey, M. J., Grove, W. M., & Tuason, V. B. (1992). Cognitive therapy and pharmacotherapy for depression: Singly and in combination. *Archives of General Psychiatry, 49,* 774–781.

Holmes, A. J., MacDonald, A., Career, C. S., Barch, D. M., Stenger, V. A., & Cohen, J. D. (2005). Prefrontal functioning during context processing in schizophrenia and major depression: An event-related fMRI study. *Schizophrenia Research, 76,* 199–206.

Holmes, E. A., Brown, R. J., Mansell, W., Fearon, R. P., Hunter, E. C., Frasquilho, F., & Oakley, D. A. (2005b). Are there two qualitatively distinct forms of dissociation? A review and some clinical implications. *Clinical Psychology Review, 25,* 1–23.

Holmes, T. H., & Rahe, R. H. (1967). The Social Readjustment Rating Scale. *Journal of Psychosomatic Research, 11,* 213–218.

Holmgren, P., Norden-Pettersson, L., & Ahlner, J. (2004). Caffeine fatalities—Four case reports. *Forensic Science International, 139,* 71–73.

Holt, C. S., Heimberg, R. G., & Hope, D. A. (1992). Avoidant personality disorder and the generalized subtype of social phobia. *Journal of Abnormal Psychology, 101,* 318–325.

Honda, H., Shimizu, Y., & Rutter, M. (2005). No effect of MMR withdrawal on the incidence of autism: A total population study. *Journal of Child Psychiatry and Psychology, 46,* 572–579.

Honig, A., Romme, M., Ensink, B., Escher, S. D., Pennings, M. H. A., & Devries, M. W. (1998). Auditory hallucinations: A comparison between patients and nonpatients. *Journal of Nervous and Mental Disease, 186,* 646–651.

Honigman, R. J., Phillips, K. A., & Castle, D. J. (2004). A review of psychosocial outcomes for patients seeking cosmetic surgery. *Plastic and Reconstructive Surgery, 113,* 1229–1237.

Hope, D. A., Heimberg, R. G., & Bruch, M. A. (1995). Dismantling cognitive-behavioral therapy for social phobia. *Behaviour Research and Therapy, 33,* 637–650.

Hopko, D. R., Lejuez, C. W., Ruggiero, K. J., & Eifert, G. H. (2003). Contemporary behavioral activation treatments for depression: Procedures, principles, and progress. *Clinical Psychology Review, 23,* 699–717.

Horacek, J., Cubenikova-Balesova, V., Kopecek, M., Palenicek, T., Dockery, C., Mohr, P., & Höschl, C. (2006). Mechanism of action of atypical antipsychotic drugs and the neurobiology of schizophrenia. *CNS Drugs, 20,* 389–409.

Horner, A. (1974). Early object relations and the concept of depression. *International Journal of Psychoanalysis, 1,* 337–340.

Hornstein, N. L., & Putnam, F. W. (1992). Clinical phenomenology of child and adolescent dissociative disorders. *Journal of the American Academy of Child and Adolescent Psychiatry, 31,* 1077–1085.

Hoshiai, M., Matsumoto, Y., Sato, T., Ohnishi, M., Okabe, N., Kishimoto, Y., . . . Kuroda, S. (2010). Psychiatric comorbidity among patients with gender identity disorder. *Psychiatry and Clinical Neuroscience, 64,* 514–519.

Houy, E., Debono, B., Dechelotte, P., & Thibaut, F. (2007). Anorexia nervosa associated with right frontal brain lesion. *International Journal of Eating Disorders, 40,* 758–761.

Howard, M., Elkins, R., & Rimmele, C. (1991). Chemical aversion treatment of alcohol dependence. *Drug and Alcohol Dependence, 29,* 107–143.

Howard, R., Rabins, P. V., Seeman, M. V., & Jeste, D. V. (2000). Late-onset schizophrenia and very-late-onset schizophrenia-like psychosis: An international consensus. The International Late-Onset Schizophrenia Group. *American Journal of Psychiatry, 157,* 172–178.

Hser, Y., Huang, Y., Teruga, C., & Anglin, M. (2004). Gender differences in treatment outcomes over a three-year period: A path model analysis. *Journal of Drug Issues, 34,* 419–440.

Hser, Y.-I., Li, J., Haifeng, J., Zhang, R., Du, J., Zhang, C., Zhang, B., Evans, E., Wu, F., Chang, Y.-J., Peng, C., Huamng, D., Stitzer, M. L., Roll, J., & Zhao, M. (2011). Effects of a randomized contingency management intervention on opiate abstinence and retention in methadone maintenance treatment in China. *Addiction, 106,* 1801–1809.

Hsu, L. K., Rand, W., Sullivan, S., Liu, D. W., Mulliken, B., McDonagh, B., & Kaye, W. H. (2001). Cognitive therapy, nutritional therapy and their combination in the treatment of bulimia nervosa. *Psychological Medicine, 31,* 871–879.

Huang, X. Y., Jung, B. J., Sun, F. K., Lin, J. D., & Chen, C. C. (2009). The experiences of careers in Taiwanese culture who have long-term schizophrenia in their families. *Journal of Psychiatric and Mental Health Nursing, 16,* 874–883.

Hucker, S. J., Langevin, R., Wortzman, G., Dickey, R., Bain, J., Handy, L., Chambers, J., & Wright, P. (1988). Cerebral damage and dysfunction in sexually aggressive men. Annals of Sex Research, 1, 33–47.

Hudson, J., Lalonde, J., Pindyck, L., Bulik, C. M., Crow, S., McElroy, S., . . . Pope, H. (2006). Familial aggregation of binge-eating disorder. *Archives of General Psychiatry, 63,* 313–319.

Hudson, J. I., Hiripi, E., Pope, H. G., & Kessler, R. C. (2007). The prevalence and correlates of eating disorders in the National Comorbidity Survey Replication. *Biological Psychiatry, 61,* 348–358.

Hudson, J. I., Pope, H. G., Jonas, J. M., Yurgelun-Todd, D., & Frankenburg, F. R. (1987). A controlled family history study of bulimia. *Psychological Medicine, 17,* 883–890.

Hudson, S., Ward, T., & Marshall, W. (1992). The abstinence violation effect in sexual offenders: A reformulation. *Behavior Research and Therapy, 30,* 435–441.

Hughes, I. (2006). Prenatal treatment of congenital adrenal hyperplasia: Do we have enough evidence? *Treatments in Endocrinology, 5,* 1–6.

Hunsley, J., Lee, C. M., Wood, J. M., & Taylor, W. (2015). Controversial and questionable assessment techniques. In S. O. Lilienfeld, S. J. Lynn, & J. M. Lohr (Eds.), *Science and pseudoscience in clinical psychology* (2nd ed., pp. 42–82). New York, NY: Guilford.

Hunsley, J., & Mash, E. J. (2007). Evidence-based assessment. *Annual Review of Clinical Psychology, 3,* 29–51.

Hunsley, J., Ronson, A., & Cohen, K. R. (2013). Professional psychology in Canada: A survey of demographic and practice characteristics. *Professional Psychology: Research and Practice, 44,* 118–126.

Hunt, G., & Azrin, N. (1973). A community-reinforcement approach to alcoholism. *Behaviour Research and Therapy, 11,* 91–104.

Hunter, E. C., Baker, D., Phillips, M. L., Sierra, M., & David, A. S. (2005). Cognitive-behaviour therapy for depersonalization disorder: An open study. *Behaviour Research and Therapy, 43,* 1121–1130.

Huppert, J. D., Strunk, D. R., Ledley, D. R., Davidson, J. R., & Foa, E. B. (2008). Generalized social anxiety disorder and avoidant personality disorder: Structural analysis and treatment outcome. *Depression and Anxiety, 25,* 441–448.

Hurd, H. M., Drewry, W. F., Dewey, R., Pilgrim, C. W., Blumer, G. A., & Burgess, T. J. W. (1916). *The institutional care of the insane in the United States and Canada.* Baltimore, MD: Johns Hopkins University Press.

Hurwitz, T. A., & Prichard, J. W. (2006). Conversion disorder and fMRI. *Neurology, 67,* 1914–1915.

Husain, M. M., Rush, A. J., Fink, M., Knapp, R., Petrides, G., Rummans, T., . . . Kellner, C. H. (2004). Speed of response and remission in major depressive disorder with acute electroconvulsive therapy (ECT): A Consortium for Research in ECT (CORE) report. *Journal of Clinical Psychiatry, 65,* 485–491.

Hybels, C. F., Blazer, D. C., & Hays, J. C. (2009). Demography and epidemiology of psychiatric disorders in late life. In D. C. Blazer & D. C. Steffens (Eds.), *Textbook of geriatric psychiatry* (pp. 19–43). Washington, DC: American Psychiatric Publishing, Inc.

I

Ickovics, J. R., Hamburger, M. E., Vlahov, D., Schoenbaum, E. E., Schuman, P., Boland, R. J., . . . HIV Epidemiology Research Study Group. (2001). Mortality, CD4 cell count decline, and depressive symptoms among HIV-seropositive women: Longitudinal analysis from the HIV Epidemiology Research Study. *Journal of the American Medical Association, 285*(11), 1466–1474.

Ilott, R. (2005). Does compliance therapy improve use of antipsychotic medication? *British Journal of Community Nursing, 10,* 514–519.

Insel, T. R., & Winslow, J. T. (1992). Neurobiology of obsessive-compulsive disorder. *Psychiatric Clinics of North America, 15,* 813–824.

International Society for the Study of Dissociation. (2005). Guidelines for treating dissociative identity disorder in adults. *Journal of Trauma & Dissociation, 6,* 69–149.

Ironson, G., Balbin, E., & Schneiderman, N. (2002). Health psychology and infectious diseases. In T. J. Boll, S. Bennett Johnson, & N. W. Perry (Eds.), *Handbook of clinical health psychology* (pp. 5–36). Washington, DC: American Psychological Association.

Irving, L. M. (1990). Mirror images: Effects of the standard of beauty on the self- and body-esteem of women exhibiting varying levels of bulimic symptoms. *Journal of Social and Clinical Psychology, 9,* 230–242.

Irwin, M. R., Cole, J. C., & Nicassio, P. M. (2006). Comparative meta-analysis of behavioral interventions for insomnia and their efficacy in middle-aged adults and in older adults 55+ years of age. *Health Psychology, 25,* 3–14.

Isidori, A. M., Giannetta, E., Gianfrilli, D., Greco, E. A., Bonifacio, V., Aversa, A., . . . Lenzi, A. (2005). Effects of testosterone on sexual function in men: Results of a meta-analysis. *Clinical Endocrinology, 63,* 381–394.

Issenman, R. M., Filmer, R. B., & Gorski, P. A. (1999). A review of bowel and bladder control development in children: How gastrointestinal and urological conditions relate to problems in toilet training. *Pediatrics, 103,* 1346–1352.

J

Jablensky, A. (2000). Epidemiology of schizophrenia: The global burden of disease and disability. *European Archives of Psychiatry & Clinical Neuroscience, 250,* 274–285.

Jacobson, N. S., & Truax, P. (1991). Clinical significance: A statistical approach to defining meaningful change in psychotherapy research. *Journal of Consulting and Clinical Psychology, 59,* 12–19.

Jalkut, M. W., Lerman, S. E., & Churchill, B. M. (2001). Enuresis. *Pediatric Urology, 48,* 1461–1488.

James, K. (1997). *Understanding caffeine: A biobehavioral analysis.* Thousand Oaks, CA: Sage Publications.

Jamison, K. (1993). *Touched with fire: Manic-depressive illness and the artistic temperament.* New York, NY: Free Press/Macmillan.

Jamison, K. R., & Baldessarini, R. J. (1999). Effects of medical interventions on suicidal behavior. *Journal of Clinical Psychiatry, 60*(Suppl. 2), 4–6.

Jang, K. L. (2005). *The behavioral genetics of psychopathology.* Mahwah, NJ: Erlbaum.

Jang, K. L., Livesley, W. J., Taylor, S., Stein, M. B., & Moon, E. C. (2004). Heritability of individual depressive symptoms. *Journal of Affective Disorders, 80,* 125–133.

Jang, K. L., Livesley, W. J., & Vernon, P. A. (1996). Heritability of the big five personality dimensions and their facets: A twin study. *Journal of Personality, 64,* 577–591.

Jang, K. L., Taylor, S., & Livesley, W. J. (2006). The University of British Columbia Twin Project: Personality is something and personality does something. *Twin Research and Human Genetics, 9,* 739–742.

Janicak, P. G., Dowd, S. M., Martis, B., Alam, D., Beedle, D., Krasuski, J., . . . Viana, M. (2002). Repetitive transcranial magnetic stimulation versus electroconvulsive therapy for major depression: Preliminary results of a randomized trial. *Biological Psychiatry, 51,* 659–667.

Jankowski, K. (2006). *PTSD and physical health.* U. S. Department of Veterans Affairs, National Center for Post-Traumatic Stress Disorder. Retrieved January 15, 2007 from http://www.ncptsd.va.gov/facts/specific/fs_physical_health.html

Janoff-Bulman, R. (1992). *Shattered assumptions: Towards a new psychology of trauma.* New York, NY: Free Press.

Janz, T. (2012). *Current smoking trends.* Ottawa: Statistics Canada, catalogue no. 82-624-X.

Jenkins, E. J., & Bell, C. C. (1994). Violence among inner city high school students and posttraumatic stress disorder. In S. Friedman (Ed.), *Anxiety disorders in African Americans* (pp. 76–88). New York, NY: Springer.

Jennum, P., Ibsen, R., Petersen, E. R., Knudsen, S., & Kjellberg, K. (2012). Health, social, and economic consequences of narcolepsy. *Sleep Medicine, 13,* 1086–1093.

Jerrell, J., & Wilson, J. (1997). Ethnic differences in the treatment of dual mental and substance disorders. *Journal of Substance Abuse Treatment, 14,* 133–140.

Jeste, D. V., Alexopoulos, G. S., Bartels, S. J., Cummings, J. L., Gallo, J. J., Gottlieb, G. L., . . . Lebowitz, B. D. (1999). Consensus statement on the upcoming crisis in geriatric mental health: Research agenda for the next 2 decades. *Archives of General Psychiatry, 56,* 848–853.

Jeste, D. V., & Finkel, S. I. (2000). Psychosis of Alzheimer's disease and related dementias: Diagnostic criteria for a distinct syndrome. *American Journal of Geriatric Psychiatry, 8,* 29–34.

Jeste, D. V., Lanouette, N. M., & Vahia, I. V. (2009). Schizophrenia and paranoid disorders. In D. C. Blazer & D. C. Steffens (Eds.), *Textbook of geriatric psychiatry* (pp. 317–332). Washington, DC: American Psychiatric Publishing, Inc.

Jeste, D. V., Wetherell, J. L., & Dolder, C. R. (2004). Schizophrenia and paranoid disorders. In D. G. Blazer, D. C. Steffens, & E. W. Busse (Eds.), *Textbook of geriatric psychiatry* (3rd ed., pp. 269–281). Washington, DC: American Psychiatric Publishing, Inc.

Jimerson, D. C., Wolfe, B. E., Metzger, E. D., Finkelstein, D. M., Cooper, T. B., & Levine, J. M. (1997). Decreased serotonin function in bulimia nervosa. *Archives of General Psychiatry, 54,* 529–534.

Jobe, T. H, & Harrow, M. (2005). Long-term outcome of patients with schizophrenia: A review. *Canadian Journal of Psychiatry, 50,* 892–900.

Joe, G., Simpson, D., & Broome, K. (1999). Retention and patient engagement models for different treatment modalities in DATOS. *Drug and Alcohol Dependence, 57,* 113–125.

Johansen, H., Sanmartin, C., & the LHAD Research Team. (2011). *Mental comorbidity and its contribution to increased use of acute care hospital services.* Ottawa: Statistics Canada, catalogue no. 82-622-X – no. 006.

Johnson, E. O., Roth, T., Schultz, L., & Breslau, N. (2006a). Epidemiology of DSM-IV insomnia in adolescence: Lifetime prevalence, chronicity, and an emergent gender difference. *Pediatrics, 117,* e247–e256.

Johnson, J. G., Cohen, P., Kasen, S., & Brook, J. S. (2006b). Dissociative disorders among adults in the community, impaired functioning, and axis I and II comorbidity. *Journal of Psychiatric Research, 40,* 131–140.

Jones, K., & Smith, D. (1973). Recognition of the fetal alcohol syndrome in early infancy. *The Lancet, 2,* 999–1001.

Jones, P., Rodgers, B., Murray, R., & Mormot, M. (1994). Child development risk factors for adult schizophrenia in the British 1946 birth cohort. *The Lancet, 344,* 1398–1402.

Joseph, R. (2000). The evolution of sex differences in language, sexuality, and visual-spatial skills. *Archives of Sexual Behavior, 29,* 35–66.

Judd, L. L., Akiskal, H. S., Schettler, P. J., Endicott, J., Maser, J., Solomon, D. A., Leon, A. C., Rice, J. A., & Keller, M. B. (2002). The long-term natural history of the weekly symptomatic status of bipolar I disorder. *Archives of General Psychiatry, 59,* 530–537.

Juliano, L. M., & Griffiths, R. R. (2004). A critical review of caffeine withdrawal: Empirical validation of symptoms and signs, incidence, severity, and associated features. *Psychopharmacology, 176,* 1–29.

K

Kabakçi, E., & Batur, S. (2003). Who benefits from cognitive behavioral therapy for vaginismus? *Journal of Sex & Marital Therapy, 29,* 277–288.

Kafka, M. (2010). Hypersexual disorder: A proposed diagnosis for DSM-V. *Archives of Sexual Behavior, 39,* 377–400.

Kagan, J. (1982). Heart rate and heart rate variability as signs of a temperamental dimension in infants. In E. D. Izard (Ed.), *Measuring emotions in infants and children* (pp. 38–66). Cambridge, England: Cambridge University Press.

Kahn, M. W. (1982). Cultural clash and psychopathology in three aboriginal cultures. *Academic Psychology Bulletin, 4,* 553–561.

Kaltenbach, K., Berghella, V., & Finnegan, L. (1998). Opioid dependence during pregnancy: Effects and management. *Obstetric and Gynecological Clinics of North America, 25,* 139–151.

Kamali, M., Kelly, B. D., Clarke, M., Browne, S., Gervin, M., Kinsella, A., . . . O'Callaghan, E. (2006). A prospective evaluation of adherence to medication in first episode schizophrenia. *European Psychiatry, 21,* 29–33.

Kanayama, G., Barry, S., Hudson, J. I., & Pope, H. G., Jr. (2006). Body image and attitudes toward male roles in anabolic-androgenic steroid users. *American Journal of Psychiatry, 163,* 697–703.

Kandel, D., & Davies, M. (1992). Progression to regular marijuana involvement: Phenomenology and risk factors for near-daily use. In M. Glantz & R. Pickens (Eds.), *Vulnerability to drug abuse* (pp. 211–253). Washington, DC: American Psychological Association.

Kanner, A. D., Coyne, J. C., Schaefer, C., & Lazarus, R. S. (1981). Comparison of two modes of stress measurement: Daily hassles and uplifts versus major life events. *Journal of Behavioral Medicine, 4,* 1–39.

Kaoukis, G. (2004, October). *A regional psychological screening program for cardiac rehabilitation patients.* Paper presented at the annual meeting of the Canadian Association of Cardiac Rehabilitation, Calgary, AB.

Kaoukis, G. (2008). A regional psychology service for cardiac patients enrolled in cardiac rehabilitation. *Current Issues in Cardiac Rehabilitation and Prevention, 16,* 7–10.

Kaplan, H. S. (1974). *The new sex therapy.* New York, NY: Brunner Mazel.

Kaplan, H. S. (1979). *Disorders of sexual desire.* New York, NY: Brunner Mazel.

Kaplan, R. M., & Saccuzzo, D. P. (2012). *Psychological testing: Principles, applications, and issues.* New York, NY: Wiley.

Kaplan, S. A., Reis, R. B., Kohn, I. J., Ikeguchi, E. F., Laor, E., Te, A. E., . . . Martins, A. C. (1999). Safety and efficacy of sildenafil in postmenopausal women with sexual dysfunction. *Urology, 53,* 481–486.

Kara, H., Aydin, S., Yücel, M., Agargün, M. Y., Odabaş, O., & Yilmaz, Y. (1996). The efficacy of fluoxetine in the treatment of premature ejaculation: A double-blind placebo controlled study. *The Journal of Urology, 156,* 1631–1632.

Karavidas, M. K., Tsai, P. S., Yucha, C., McGrady, A., & Lehrer, P. M. (2006). Thermal biofeedback for primary Raynaud's phenomenon: a review of the literature. *Applied Psychophysiology and Biofeedback, 31*(3), 203–216.

Kas, M. J., Van Elburg, A. A., Van Engeland, H., & Adan, R. A. (2003). Refinement of behavioural traits in animals for the genetic dissection of eating disorders. *European Journal of Pharmacology, 480,* 13–20.

Kashner, T. M., Rodell, D. E., Ogden, S. R., Guggenheim, F. G., & Karson, C. N. (1992). Outcomes and costs of two VA inpatient treatment programs for older alcoholic patients. *Hospital and Community Psychiatry, 43,* 985–989.

Katon, W. J., & Walker, E. A. (1998). Medically unexplained symptoms in primary care. *Journal of Clinical Psychiatry, 59*(Suppl. 20), 15–21.

Katz, I. R., Reynolds, C. F. III, Alexopoulos, G. S., & Hackett, D. (2002). Venlafaxine ER as a treatment for generalized anxiety disorder in older adults: Pooled analysis of five randomized placebo-controlled clinical trials. *Journal of the American Geriatrics Society, 50,* 18–25.

Katzman, M. A., Bleau, P., Chokka, P., Kjernisted, K., van Ameringen, M., . . . Walker, J. R. (2014). Canadian clinical practice guidelines for the management of anxiety, posttraumatic stress and obsessive-compulsive disorders. *BMC Psychiatry, 14*(Suppl 1), article 51.

Kaufman, J., & Charney, D. (2001). Effects of early stress on brain structure and function: Implications for understanding the relationship between child maltreatment and depression. *Development and Psychopathology, 13,* 451–471.

Kauth, M. R. (2005). Revealing assumptions: Explicating sexual orientation and promoting conceptual integrity. *Journal of Bisexuality, 5,* 81–105.

Kaufman, M. R., & Heiman, M. (1964). *Evolution of psychosomatic concepts: Anorexia nervosa: A paradigm.* New York, NY: International Universities Press.

Kawakami, N., Takeskima, T., Ono, Y., Uda, H., Hata, Y., Nakane, Y., . . . Kikkawa, T. (2005). Twelve-month prevalence, severity, and treatment of common mental disorders in communities of Japan: Preliminary finding from the World Mental Health Survey 2002–2003. *Psychiatry and Clinical Neuroscience, 59,* 441–452.

Kaye, W. (1997). Anorexia nervosa, obsessional behavior, and serotonin. *Psychopharmacology Bulletin, 33,* 335–344.

Kaye, W. H., Bulik, C. M., Thornton, L., Barbarich, B. S., Masters, K., & The Price Foundation Collaborative Group. (2004). Comorbidity of anxiety disorders with anorexia and bulimia nervosa. *American Journal of Psychiatry, 161,* 2215–2221.

Kaye, W. H., Gwirtsman, H. E., George, D. T., & Ebert, M. H. (1991). Altered serotonin activity in anorexia nervosa after long-term weight restoration. Does elevated cerebrospinal fluid 5-hydroxyindoleacetic acid level correlate with rigid and obsessive behavior? *Archives of General Psychiatry, 48,* 556–562.

Kaye, W. H., Klump, K. L., Frank, G. K., & Strober, M. (2000). Anorexia and bulimia nervosa. *Annual Review of Medicine, 51,* 299–313.

Kayiran, S., Dursun, E., Dursun, N., Ermutlu, N., & Karamürsel, S. (2010). Neurofeedback intervention in fibromyalgia syndrome; a randomized, controlled, rater blind clinical trial. *Applied Psychophysiology and Biofeedback, 35,* 293–302.

Kazdin, A. (2003). *Research design in clinical psychology.* 4th ed. Boston, MA: A Pearson Education Company.

Keck, P. E., Jr., McElroy, S. L., & Arnold, L. M. (2001). Bipolar disorder. *Medical Clinics of North America, 85,* ix, 645–661.

Keel, P. K., Haedt, A., & Edler, C. (2005). Purging disorder: An ominous variant of bulimia nervosa? *International Journal of Eating Disorders, 38,* 191–199.

Keel, P. K., & Klump, K. (2003). Are eating disorders culture-bound syndromes? Implications for conceptualizing their etiology. *Psychological Bulletin, 129,* 747–769.

Keenan, K., Loeber, R., & Green, S. (1999). Conduct disorder in girls: A review of the literature. *Clinical Child and Family Psychology Review, 2,* 3–19.

Keenan, K., & Wakschlag, L. S. (2002). Can a valid diagnosis of disruptive behavior disorder be made in preschool children? *American Journal of Psychiatry, 159,* 351–358.

Keller, M. B. (2003). The lifelong course of social anxiety disorder: A clinical perspective. *Acta Psychiatrica Scandinavia, 108,* 85–95.

Kendler, K. (1996). Major depression and generalized anxiety disorder: Same genes, (partly) different environments: Revisited. *British Journal of Psychiatry, 168,* 68–75.

Kendler, K. S. (2005). Toward a philosophical structure for psychiatry. *American Journal of Psychiatry, 162,* 433–440.

Kendler, K. S., Aggen, S. H., Czajkowski, N., Roysamb, E., Tambs, K., Torgersen, S., . . . Reichborn-Kjennerud, T. (2008). The structure of genetic and environmental risk factors for DSM-IV personality disorders: A multivariate twin study. *Archives of General Psychiatry, 65,* 1438–1446.

Kendler, K. S., Hettema, J. M., Butera, F., Gardner, C. O., & Prescott, C. A. (2003). Life event dimensions of loss, humiliation, entrapment, and danger in the prediction of onsets of major depression and generalized anxiety. *Archives of General Psychiatry, 60,* 789–796.

Kendler, K. S., Karkowski, L. M., & Prescott, C. A. (1998). Stressful life events and major depression: Risk period, long-term contextual threat, and diagnostic specificity. *Journal of Nervous and Mental Disease, 186,* 661–669.

Kendler, K. S., MacLean, C., Neale, M. C., Kessler, R. C., Heath, A. C., & Eaves, L. J. (1991). The genetic epidemiology of bulimia nervosa. *American Journal of Psychiatry, 148,* 1627–1637.

Kendler, K. S., McGuire, M., Gruenberg, A. M., O'Hare, A., Spellman, M., & Walsh, D. (1993). The Roscommon family study III: Schizophrenia-related personality disorders in relatives. *Archives of General Psychiatry, 50,* 781–788.

Kendler, K. S., Myers, J., Prescott, C. A., & Neale, M. C. (2001). The genetic epidemiology of irrational fears and phobias in men. *Archives of General Psychiatry, 58,* 257–265.

Kendler, K. S., Myers, J., Torgersen, S., Neale, M. C., & Reichborn-Kjennerud, T. (2007b). The heritability of cluster A personality disorders assessed by both personal interview and questionnaire. *Psychological Medicine, 37,* 655–665.

Kendler, K. S., Neale, M. C., Kessler, R. C., Heath, A. C., & Eaves, L. J. (1992). Major depression and generalized anxiety disorder: Same genes, (partly) different environments? *Archives of General Psychiatry, 49,* 716–722.

Kendler, K. S., Thornton, L. M., & Gardner, C. O. (2000a). Stressful life events and previous episodes in the etiology of major depression in women: An evaluation of the "kindling" hypothesis. *American Journal of Psychiatry, 157,* 1243–1251.

Kendler, K. S., Thornton, L. M., Gilman, S. E., & Kessler, R. C. (2000b). Sexual orientation in a US national sample of twin and non-twin sibling pairs. *American Journal of Psychiatry, 157,* 1843–1846.

Kendler, K., Gardner, C., Gatz, M., & Pedersen, N. (2007a). The sources of co-morbidity between major depression and generalized anxiety disorder in a Swedish national twin sample. *Psychological Medicine, 37,* 453–462.

Kendler, K., Gardner, C., & Prescott, C. (1997). Religion, psychopathology, and substance use and abuse: A multimeasure, genetic-epidemiologic study. *American Journal of Psychiatry, 154,* 322–329.

Kendler, K., & Karkowski-Shuman, L. (1997). Stressful life events and genetic liability to major depression: Genetic control of exposure to the environment? *Psychological Medicine, 27,* 539–547.

Kendler, K., Kessler, R. C., Walters, E. E., MacLean, C., Neale, M. C., Heath, A. C., & Eaves, L. J. (1995). Stressful life events, genetic liability, and onset of an episode of major depression in women. *American Journal of Psychiatry, 152,* 833–842.

Kendler, K., & Prescott, C. (1999). A population-based twin study of lifetime major depression in men and women. *Archives of General Psychiatry, 56,* 39–44.

Kennedy, S. H., Giacobbe, P., Rizvi, S. J., Placenza, F. M., Nishikawa, Y., Mayberg, H. S., & Lozano, A. M. (2011). Deep brain stimulation for treatment-resistant depression: follow-up after 3 to 6 years. *American Journal of Psychiatry, 168,* 502–510.

Kennedy, S. H., Milev, R., Giacobbe, P., Ramasubbu, R., Lam, R. W., Parikh, S. V. . . . Ravindran, A. V. (2009). Canadian Network for Mood and Anxiety Treatments (CANMAT) clinical guidelines for the management of major depressive disorder in adults. IV. Neurostimulation therapies. *Journal of Affective Disorders, 117,* S44–S53.

Kent, D. A., Tomasson, K., & Coryell, W. (1995). Course and outcome of conversion and somatization disorders. A four-year follow-up. *Psychosomatics, 36,* 138–144.

Keppel-Benson, J. M., Ollendick, T. H., & Benson, M. J, (2002). Post-traumatic stress in children following motor vehicle accidents. *Journal of Child Psychology & Psychiatry, 43,* 203–212.

Kerker, B. D., Owens, P. L., Zigler, E., & Horwitz, S. M. (2004). Mental health disorders among individuals with mental retardation: challenges to accurate prevalence estimates. *Public Health Reports, 119,* 409–417.

Kernberg, O. (1975). *Borderline conditions and pathological narcissism.* New York, NY: Jason Aronson.

Kerr, L. R., Hundal, R., Silva, W. A., Emerman, J. T., & Weinberg, J. (2001). Effects of social housing condition on chemotherapeutic efficacy in a Shionogi carcinoma (SC115) mouse tumor model: Influences of temporal factors, tumor size, and tumor growth rate. *Psychosomatic Medicine, 63,* 973–984.

Kessler, R. C. (2003). The impairments caused by social phobia in the general population: Implications for intervention. *Acta Psychiatricia Scandinavica, 108*(Suppl. 417), 19–27.

Kessler, R. C., Berglund, P., Demler, O., Jin, R., Koretz, D., Merikangas, K. R., . . . Wang P. S. (2003). The epidemiology of major depressive disorder: Results from the National Comorbidity Survey Replication (NCS-R). *Journal of the American Medical Association, 289,* 3095–3105.

Kessler, R. C., Berglund, P., Demler, O., Jin, R., Merikangas, K. R., & Walter, E. E. (2005a). Lifetime prevalence and age-of-onset distributions of DSM-IV disorders in the National Comorbidity Survey Replication. *Archives of General Psychiatry, 62,* 593–602.

Kessler, R. C., Birnbaum, H., Demler, O., Falloon, I. R. H., Gagnon, E., Guyer, M., . . . Wu, E. Q. (2005). The prevalence and correlates of nonaffective psychosis in the National Comorbidity Survey Replication (NCS-R). *Biological Psychiatry, 58,* 668–676.

Kessler, R. C., Chiu, W. T., Jin, R., Ruscio, A. M., Shear, K., & Walters, E. F. (2006). The epidemiology of panic attacks, panic disorder, and agoraphobia in the National Comorbidity Survey Replication. *Archives of General Psychiatry, 63,* 415–424.

Kessler, R. C., Crum, R. M., Warner, L. A., Nelson, C. B., Schulenberg, J., & Anthony, J. C. (1997). Lifetime co-occurrence of DSM-III-R alcohol abuse and dependence with other psychiatric disorders in the National Comorbidity Survey. *Archives of General Psychiatry, 54,* 313–321.

Kessler, R. C., Foster, C. L., Saunders, W. B., & Stang, P. E. (1995). Social consequences of psychiatric disorders, I: Education attainment. *The American Journal of Psychiatry, 152,* 1026–1032.

Kessler, R. C., & Frank, R. G. (1997). The impact of psychiatric disorders on work loss days. *Psychological Medicine, 27,* 861–873.

Kessler, R. C., Walters, E. E., & Wittchen, H. U. (2004). Epidemiology. In R. G. Heimberg, C. L. Turk, & D. S. Mennin, (Eds.), *Generalized anxiety disorder: Advances in research and practice* (pp. 29–50). New York, NY: Guilford Press.

Khan, A., Leventhal, R. M., Kahn, S., & Brown, W. A. (2002). Suicide risk in patients with anxiety disorders: a meta-analysis of the FDA database. *Journal of Affective Disorders, 63,* 183–191.

Khantzian, E. D. (1987). The self-medication hypothesis of addictive disorders: Focus on heroin and cocaine dependence. In D. Allen (Ed.), *The cocaine crisis* (pp. 65–74). New York, NY: Plenum Press.

Kiecolt-Glaser, J. K., Glaser, R., Cacioppo, J. T., & Malarkey, W. B. (1998). Marital stress: Immunologic, neuroendocrine, and autonomic correlates. *Annals of the New York Academy of Sciences, 840,* 656–663.

Kiecolt-Glaser, J. K., Gouin, J. P., & Hantsoo, L. (2010). Close relationships, inflammation, and health. *Neuroscience and Biobehavioral Reviews, 35,* 33–38.

Kihlstrom, J. F. (2001). Dissociative disorders. In H. E. Adams & P. B. Sutker (Eds.), *Comprehensive handbook of psychopathology* (pp. 259–276). New York, NY: Academic/Plenum Publishers.

Killen, J., Hayward, C., Hammer, L., Wilson, D., Miner, B., Taylor, C., , Varady, A., & Shisslak, C. (1992). Is puberty a risk factor for eating disorders? *American Journal of Diseases of Children, 146,* 323–325.

Killen, J., Taylor, C., Hayward, C., Wilson, D., Haydel, K., Hammer, L., . . . Kraemer, H. (1994). Pursuit of thinness and onset of eating disorder symptoms in a community sample of adolescent girls: A three-year prospective analysis. *International Journal of Eating Disorders, 16,* 227–238.

Kim, H. F., Kunik, M. E., Molinari, V. A., Hillman, S. L., Lalani, S., Orengo, C. A., . . . Goodnight-White, S. (2000). Functional impairment in COPD patients: The impact of anxiety and depression. *Psychosomatics, 41,* 465–471.

Kim, S. J., Lee, H. S., & Kim, C. H. (2005). Obsessive-compulsive disorder, factor-analyzed symptom dimensions and serotonin transporter polymorphism. *Neuropsychobiology, 52,* 176–182.

Kindermann, S. S., Kalayam, B., Brown, G. G., Burdick, K. E., & Alexopoulos, G. S. (2000). Executive functions and P300 latency in elderly depressed patients and control subjects. *American Journal of Geriatric Psychiatry, 8,* 57–65.

King, S., Chambers, C. T., Huguet, A., MacNevin, R. C., McGrath, P. J., Parker, L., . . . MacDonald, A. J. (2011). The epidemiology of chronic pain in children and adolescents revisited: A systematic review. *Pain, 152,* 2729–2738.

King, S., Laplante, D., & Joober, R. (2005). Understanding putative risk factors or schizophrenia: Retrospective and prospective studies. *Journal of Psychiatry and Neuroscience, 30,* 342–348.

Kingsberg, S. (2007). Testosterone treatment for hypoactive sexual desire disorder in postmenopausal women. *Journal of Sexual Medicine, 4*(Suppl. 3), 227–234.

Kinsella, D. (2010). Research ethics boards: A historical background. Retrieved October 7, 2015, from: http://www.chrcrm.org/en/conference-proceedings/research-ethics-boards-historical-background

Kirby, M. J. L., & Keon, W. J. (2006). *Out of the shadows at last: Transforming mental health, mental illness and addiction services in Canada.* Retrieved February 6, 2008, from http://www.parl.gc.ca/39/1/parlbus/commbus/senate/com-e/soci-e/rep-e/rep-02may06-e.htm

Kirk, K. M., Bailey, J. M., Dunne, M. P., & Martin, N. G. (2000). Measurement models for sexual orientation in a community twin sample. *Behavior Genetics, 30,* 345–356.

Kirkham, J. G., Choi, N., & Seitz, D. P. (2015). Meta-analysis of problem solving therapy for the treatment of major depressive disorder in older adults. *International Journal of Geriatric Psychiatry, 31*(5), 526–535.

Kirmayer, L. (2001). Cultural variations in the clinical presentation of depression and anxiety: Implications for diagnosis and treatment. *Journal of Clinical Psychiatry, 62,* 22–28.

Kirmayer, L., Young, A., & Hayton, B. (1995). The cultural context of anxiety disorders. *Psychiatric Clinics of North America, 18,* 503–521.

Kirmayer, L. J., Groleau, D., Looper, K. J., & Dao, M. D. (2004). Explaining medically unexplained symptoms. *Canadian Journal of Psychiatry, 49,* 663–672.

Kirmayer, L. J., & Looper, K. J. (2007). Somatoform disorders. In M. Hersen, S. M. Turner, & D. C. Beidel (Eds.), *Adult psychopathology and diagnosis* (5th ed., pp. 410–472). Hoboken, NJ: John Wiley & Sons.

Kirschbaum, C., Kudielka, B. M., Gaab, J., Schommer, N. C., & Hellhammer, D. H. (1999). Impact of gender, menstrual cycle phase, and oral contraceptives on the activity of the hypothalamus-pituitary-adrenal axis. *Psychosomatic Medicine, 61,* 154–162.

Klatzkin, R. R., Gaffney, S., Cyrus, K., Bigus, E., Brownley, K. A. (2015). Binge eating disorder and obesity: Preliminary evidence for distinct cardiovascular and psychological phenotypes. *Physiology & Behavior, 142,* 20–27.

Klein, R. G. (1995). Is panic disorder associated with childhood separation anxiety disorder? *Clinical Neuropharmacology, 18*(Suppl. 2), S7–S14.

Klerman, G. L., Weissman, M. M., Rounsaville, B. J., & Chevron, E. S. (1984). *Interpersonal psychotherapy for depression.* New York, NY: Basic Books.

Klesges, R. C., Obarzanek, E., Kumanyka, S., Murray, D. M., Klesges, L. M., . . . Slawson, D. L. (2010). The Memphis Girls' health Enrichment Multi-site Studies (GEMS): An evaluation of the efficacy of a 2-year obesity prevention in African American girls. *Archives of Pediatric and Adolescent Medicine, 164,* 1007–1014.

Klin, A. (2006). Autism and Asperger syndrome: An overview. *Revista Brasileira de Psiquiatria, 28*(1 Suppl.), S3–S11.

Kluft, R. P. (1993). Multiple personality disorder. In D. Spiegel (Ed.), *Dissociative disorders: A clinical review* (pp. 17–44). Lutherville, MD: Sidran Press.

Klump, K. L., Gobrogge, K. L., Perkins, P. S., Thorne, D., Sisk, C. L., & Breedlove, S. (2006). Preliminary evidence that gonadal hormones organize and activate disordered eating. *Psychological Medicine, 36,* 539–546.

Koenigs, M., & Grafman, J. (2009). The functional neuroanatomy of depression: Distinct roles for ventromedial and dorsolateral prefrontal cortex. *Behavioural Brain Research, 201,* 239–243.

Koessler, L., Maillard, L., Benhadid, A., Vignal, J. P., Braun, M., & Vespignani, H. (2007). Spatial localization of EEG electrodes. *Neurophysiology Clinics, 37,* 97–102.

Kogan, J. N., Edelstein, B. A., & McKee, D. R. (2000). Assessment of anxiety in older adults: Current status. *Journal of Anxiety Disorders, 14,* 109–132.

Kohler, C. L., Fish, L., & Greene, P. G. (2002). The relationship of perceived self-efficacy to quality of life in chronic obstructive pulmonary disease. *Health Psychology, 21,* 610–614.

Kolb, B., & Whishaw, I. (2008). *Fundamentals of Human Neuropsychology,* 4th ed. New York, NY: Worth Publishers.

Kolevzon, A., Mathewson, K. A., & Hollander, E. (2006). Selective serotonin reuptake inhibitors in autism: A review of efficacy and tolerability. *Journal of Clinical Psychiatry, 67,* 407–414.

Kosfeld, M., Heinrichs, M., Zak, P. J., Fischbacher, U., & Fehr, E. (2005). Oxytocin increases trust in humans. *Nature, 435,* 673–676.

Kovacs, M. (2011). *Children's Depression Inventory-2.* Ontario: Multi-Health Systems.

Kozloff, N., Cheung, A. H., Schaffer, A., Cairney, J., Dewa, C. S., Veldhuizen, S., . . . Levitt, A. J. (2010). Bipolar disorder among adolescents and young adults: Results from an epidemiological sample. *Journal of Affective Disorders, 125,* 350–354.

Kozlowska, K., Nunn, K. P., Rose, D., Morris, A., Ouvrier, R. A., & Varghese, J. (2007). Conversion disorder in Australian pediatric practice. *Journal of the American Academy of Child and Adolescent Psychiatry, 46,* 68–75.

Kraepelin, E. (1919/1971). *Dementia praecox and paraphrenia* (R. M. Barclay, Trans.). New York, NY: Robert E. Krieger Publishing Co.

Krahn, L. E., Li, H., & O'Connor, M. K. (2003). Patients who strive to be ill: Factitious disorder with physical symptoms. *American Journal of Psychiatry, 160,* 1163–1168.

Kranzler, H. N., Kester, H. M., Gerbino-Rosen, G., Henderson, I. N., Youngerman, J., Beauzile, G., . . . Kumra, S. (2006). Treatment-refractory schizophrenia in children and adolescents: An update on clozapine and other pharmacological interventions. *Child and Adolescent Psychiatric Clinics of North America, 15,* 135–159.

Kranzler, H. N., Roofeh, D., Gerbino-Rosen, G., Dombrowski, C., McMeniman, M., DeThomas, C., . . . Kumra, S. (2005). Clozapine: Its impact on aggressive behavior among children and adolescents with schizophrenia. *Journal of the American Academy of Child and Adolescent Psychiatry, 44,* 53–63.

Krem, M. M. (2004). Motor conversion disorders reviewed from a neuropsychiatric perspective. *Journal of Clinical Psychiatry, 65,* 783–790.

Krieg, J. C., Lauer, C., & Pirke, K. M. (1989). Structural brain abnormalities in patients with bulimia nervosa. *Psychiatry Research, 27,* 39–48.

Krishnan KR. (2005) Psychiatric and medical comorbidities of bipolar disorder. *Psychosomatic Medicine, 67,* 1–8.

Kroenke, K., & Spitzer, R. L. (1998). Gender differences in the reporting of physical and somatoform symptoms. *Psychosomatic Medicine, 60,* 150–155.

Kronenberger, W. G., & Dunn, D. W. (2003). Learning disorders. *Neurological Clinics of North America, 21,* 91–952.

Krueger, R. B., & Kaplan, M. S. (1997). Frotteurism: Assessment and treatment. In D. R. Laws & W. O'Donohue (Eds.), *Sexual Deviance. Theory, Assessment, and Treatment* (pp. 131–151). New York, NY: Guilford Press.

Krueger, R. B., & Kaplan, M. S. (2001). The paraphilic and hypersexual disorders: An overview. *Journal of Psychiatric Practice, 7,* 391–403.

Krueger, R. B., & Kaplan, M. S. (2002). Behavioral and psychopharmacological treatment of the paraphilic and hypersexual disorders. *Journal of Psychiatric Practice, 8,* 21–32.

Krueger, R. F., Watson, D., & Barlow, D. H. (2005). Introduction to the special section: toward a dimensionally based taxonomy of psychopathology. *J Abnorm Psychol, 114*(4), 491–493.

Krummenacher, P., Kossowsky, J., Schwarz, C., Brugger, P., Kelley, J. M., Meyer, A., . . . Gaab, J. (2014). Expectancy-induced placebo analgesia in children and the role of magical thinking. *Journal of Pain, 15,* 1282–1293.

Kubzansky, L. D., Sparrow, D., Vokonas, P., & Kawachi, I. (2001). Is the glass half empty or half full? A prospective study of optimism and coronary heart disease in the normative aging study. *Psychosomatic Medicine, 63,* 910–916.

Kuhn, T. S. (1962). *The structure of scientific revolutions.* Chicago, IL: University of Chicago Press.

Kumar, R., Marks, M., Wieck, A., Hirst, D., Campbell, I., & Checkley, S. (1993). Neuroendocrine and psychosocial mechanisms in post-partum psychosis. *Progress in Neuropsychopharmacology and Biological Psychiatry, 17,* 571–579.

Kunik, M. E., Roundy, K., Veazey, C., Souchek, J., Richardson, P., Wray, N. P., . . . Stanley, M. A. (2005). Surprisingly high prevalence of anxiety and depression in chronic breathing disorders. *Chest, 127,* 1205–1211.

Kunik, M. E., Snow, A. L., Molinari, V. A., Menke, T. J., Souchek, J., Sullivan, G., Ashton, C. M. (2003). Health care utilization in dementia patients with psychiatric comorbidity. *Gerontologist, 43,* 86–91.

Kunik, M. E., Veazey, C., Cully, J. A., Souchek, J., Graham, D. P., Hopko, D., . . . Stanley, M. A. (2008). COPD education and cognitive behavioral therapy group treatment for clinically significant symptoms of depression and anxiety in COPD patients: A randomized controlled trial. *Psychological Medicine, 38,* 385–396.

Kupfer, D. J. (2005) The increasing medical burden in bipolar disorder. *Journal of the American Medical Association, 293,* 2528–2530.

Kurtz, M. M., Seltzer, J. C., Ferrand, J. L., & Wexler, B. E. (2005). Neurocognitive function in schizophrenia at a 10-year follow-up: A preliminary investigation. *CNS Spectrums, 10,* 277–280.

Kushner, M. G., Sher, K. J., & Beitman, B. D. (1990). The relationship between alcohol problems and the anxiety disorders. *American Journal of Psychiatry, 147,* 685–695.

Kuwabara, H., Shioiri, T., Nishimura, A., Abe, R., Nushida, H., Ueno, Y., . . . Someya, T. (2006). Differences in characteristics between suicide victims who left notes or not. *Journal of Affective Disorders, 94,* 145–149.

Kuwaik, G. A., Roberts, W., Zwaigenbaum, L., Bryson, S., Smith, I. M., Szatmari, P., . . . Brian, J. (2014). Immunization uptake in younger siblings of children with autism spectrum disorder. *Autism, 18,* 148–155.

L

La Vaque, T. J., & Rossiter, T. (2001). The ethical use of placebo controls in clinical research: The Declaration of Helsinki. *Applied Psychophysiology and Biofeedback, 26,* 23–37.

Laberge, L., Tremblay, R. E., Vitaro, F., & Montplaisir, J. (2000). Development of parasomnias from childhood to early adolescence. *Pediatrics, 106,* 67–74.

Lackner, J. M., Gudleski, G. D., & Blanchard, E. B. (2004). Beyond abuse: The association among parenting style, abdominal pain, and somatization in IBS patients. *Behaviour Research and Therapy, 42,* 41–56.

Ladouceur, R., Gosselin, P., & Dugas, M. J. (2000). Experimental manipulation of uncertainty. *Behaviour Research and Therapy, 38,* 933–941.

Lahey, B. B., Pelham, W. E., Loney, J., Kipp, H., Ehrhardt, A., Lee, S. S., Willcutt, E. G., Hartung, C. M., Chronis, A., & Massetti, G. (2004). Three-year predictive validity of DSM-IV attention deficit hyperactivity disorder in children diagnosed at 4-6 years of age. *American Journal of Psychiatry, 161,* 2014–2020.

Lahey, B. B., Pelham, W. E., Stein, M. A., Loney, J., Trapani, C., Nugent, K., Kipp, H., Schmidt, E., Lee, S., Cale, M., Gold, E., Hartung, C. M., Willcutt, E., & Baumann, B. (1998). Validity of DSM-IV attention-deficit/hyperactivity disorder for younger children. *Journal of the American Academy of Child and Adolescent Psychiatry, 37,* 695–702.

Lai, D. W. (2000). Prevalence of depression among the elderly Chinese in Canada. *Canadian Journal of Public Health, 91,* 64–66.

Lake, J. (2007, September-October). Emerging paradigms in medicine: Implications for the future of psychiatry. *Explore (NY), 3,* 467–477.

Lalonde, J. K., Hudson, J. I., Gigante, R. A., & Pope, H. G., Jr. (2001). Canadian and American psychiatrists' attitudes toward dissociative disorders diagnoses. *Canadian Journal of Psychiatry, 46,* 407–412.

Lalumière, M. L., & Quinsey, V. L. (1994). The discriminability of rapists from non-sex offenders using phallometric measures. A meta-analysis. *Criminal Justice and Behavior, 21,* 150–157.

Lam, R., & Levitt, A. (1999). *Canadian consensus guidelines for the treatment of seasonal affective disorder.* Vancouver, Canada: Clinical & Academic Publishing.

Lam, R. W., Kennedy, S. H., Grigoriadis, S., McIntyre, R. S., Milev, R., Parikh, S. V., . . . Ravindran, A. V. (2009). Canadian Network for Mood and Anxiety Treatments (CANMAT) clinical guidelines for the management of major depressive disorder in adults. III. Pharmacotherapy. *Journal of Affective Disorders, 117,* S26–S43.

Lamb, D. H., Catanzaro, S. J., & Moorman, A. S. (2003). Psychologists reflect on their sexual relationships with clients, supervisees, and students: Occurrence, impact, rationales and collegial intervention. *Professional Psychology: Research and Practice, 34,* 102–107.

Lamb, H. R., & Bachrach, L. I. (2001). Some perspectives on deinstitutionalization. *Psychiatric Services, 52,* 1039–1045.

Lamb, H. R., & Weinberger, L. E. (2005). The shift of psychiatric inpatient care from hospitals to jails and prisons. *Journal of the American Academy of Psychiatry and the Law, 33,* 529–534.

Lambert, M. V., Sierra, M., Phillips, M. L., & David, A. S. (2002). The spectrum of organic depersonalization: A review plus four new cases. *Journal of Neuropsychiatry and Clinical Neurosciences, 14,* 141–154.

Landén, M., Eriksson, E., Agren, H., & Fahlen, T. (1999). Effect of buspirone on sexual dysfunction in depressed patients treated with selective serotonin reuptake inhibitors. *Journal of Clinical Psychopharmacology, 19,* 268–271.

Landén, M., Wålinder, J., Hambert, G., & Lundsström, B. (1998). Factors predictive of regret in sex reassignment. *Acta Psychaitrica Scandinavia, 97,* 284–289.

Laney, C., & Loftus, E. F. (2005). Traumatic memories are not necessarily accurate memories. *Canadian Journal of Psychiatry, 50,* 823–828.

Langer, L., Warheit, G., & Zimmerman, R. (1992). Epidemiological study of problem eating behaviors and related attitudes in the general population. *Addictive Behaviors, 16,* 167–173.

Langle, G., Egerter, B., Albrecht, F., Petrasch, M., & Buchkremer, G. (2005). Prevalence of mental illness among homeless men in the community—Approach to a full census in a southern German university town. *Social Psychiatry and Psychiatric Epidemiology, 40,* 382–390.

Langlois, K. A., Samokhvalov, A. V., Rehm, J., Spence, S. T., & Connor-Gorber, S. K. (2011). *Health state descriptions for Canadians: Mental illnesses.* Ottawa: Statistics Canada.

Larimer, M., Palmer, R., & Marlatt, G. (1999). Relapse prevention: An overview of Marlatt's cognitive-behavioral model. *Alcohol Research & Health, 23,* 151–160.

Larsen, M., & Sweeten, G. (2012). Breaking up is hard to do: Romantic dissolution, offending, and substance use during the transition to adulthood. *Criminology: An Interdisciplinary Journal, 50,* 605–636.

Lasègue, E.-C. (1873). On hysterical anorexia. *Medical Times and Gazette,* 265–266, 367–369.

Lask, B., & Bryant-Waugh. (2000). *Anorexia nervosa and related eating disorders in children and adolescence.* Hove, East Sussex, United Kingdom: Psychology Press.

Lau, E. (2001). More and more. In L. Crozier & P. Lane (Eds.), *Addicted: Notes from the belly of the beast* (pp. 73–84). Vancouver, BC: Greystone.

Laumann, E. O., Gagnon, J. H., Michale, R. T., & Michales, S. (1994). *The social organization of sexuality: Sexual practices in the United States.* Chicago, IL: University of Chicago Press.

Laumann, E. O., Nicolosi, A., Glasser, D. B., Paik, A., Gingell, C., Moreira, E., . . . GSSAB Investigators' Group. (2005). Sexual problems among women and men aged 40–80 years: Prevalence and correlates identified in the Global Study of Sexual Attitudes and Behaviors. *International Journal of Impotence Research, 17,* 39–57.

Laumann, E. O., Paik, A., & Rosen, R. C. (1999). Sexual dysfunction in the United States. *The Journal of the American Medical Association, 281,* 537–544.

Laurin, D., Verreault, R., Lindsay, J., MacPherson, K., & Rockwood, K. (2001). Physical activity and risk of cognitive impairment and dementia in elderly persons. *Archives of Neurology, 58,* 498–504.

Lavallee, C., & Bourgault, C. (2000). The health of Cree, Inuit and southern Quebec women: Similarities and differences. *Canadian Journal of Public Health, 91,* 212–216.

Lawrence, A. A. (2003). Factors associated with satisfaction or regret following male-to-female sex reassignment surgery. *Archives of Sexual Behavior, 32,* 299–315.

Lawrence, A. A., & Zucker, K. J. (2012). Gender identity disorders. In D. C. Beidel & M. Hersen (Eds.), *Adult psychopathology and diagnosis* (6th ed.). New York, NY: Wiley.

Laws, D. R. (2001). Olfactory aversion: Notes on procedure, with speculations on its mechanism of effect. *Sexual Abuse: A Journal of Research and Treatment, 13,* 275–287.

Lawton, M. P., Kleban, M. H., & Dean, J. (1993). Affect and age: Cross-sectional comparisons of structure and prevalence. *Psychology and Aging, 8,* 165–175.

Lazarus, R. S. (1999). *Stress and emotion: A new synthesis.* New York, NY: Springer.

Lazarus, R. S., & Folkman, S. (1984). Coping and adaptation. In W. D. Gentry (Ed.), *The handbook of behavioral medicine* (pp. 282–325). New York, NY: Guilford Press.

le Grange, D., Crosby, R. D., Rathouz, P. J., & Leventhal, B. L. (2007). A randomized controlled comparison of family-based treatment and supportive psychotherapy for adolescent bulimia nervosa. *Archives of General Psychiatry, 64,* 1049–1056.

Le Roux, H., Gatz, M., & Wetherell, J. L. (2005). Age at onset of generalized anxiety disorder in older adults. *American Journal of Geriatric Psychiatry, 13,* 23–30.

Leatherdale, S. T., & Shields, M. (2009). Smoking cessation: Intentions, attempts and techniques. *Health Reports, 20,* 31–39.

LeBeau, R. T., Glenn, D., Liao, B., Wittchen, H. U., Beesdo-Baum, K., Ollendick, T., & Craske, M. G. (2010). Specific phobia: A review of DSM-IV specific phobia and preliminary recommendations for DSM-V. *Depression and Anxiety, 27,* 148–167.

LeBlanc, H. (2014). *Eating disorders among girls and women in Canada.* Ottawa: House of Commons, Parliament of Canada.

Lecrubier, Y., Wittchen, H. U., Faravelli, C., Bobes, J., Patel, A., & Knapp, M. (2000). A European perspective on social anxiety disorder. *European Psychiatry, 15,* 5–16.

Lee, B., & Newberg, A. (2005). Religion and health: A review and critical analysis. *Journal of Religion and Science, 40,* 443–468.

Lee, S. H., Kim, W., Chung, Y. C., Jung, K. H., Bahk, W. M., Jun, T. Y., . . . Chae, J. H. (2005). A double blind study showing that two weeks of daily repetitive TMS over the left or right temporoparietal cortex reduces symptoms in patients with schizophrenia who are having treatment-refractory auditory hallucinations. *Neuroscience Newsletters, 376,* 177–181.

Lee, Y. L., Gau, B. S., Hsu, W. M., & Chang, H. H. (2009). A model linking uncertainty, post-traumatic stress, and health behaviors in childhood cancer survivors. *Oncology Nursing Forum, 36,* E20–E30.

Leff, J., Tress, K., & Edwards, B. (1988). The clinical course of depressive symptoms in schizophrenia. *Schizophrenia Research, 1,* 25–30.

Leiblum, S. R. (2000). Vaginismus: A most perplexing problem. In S. R. Leiblum & R. C. Rosen (Eds.), *Principles and practice of sex therapy* (3rd ed., pp. 181–202). New York, NY: Guilford Press.

Leichsenring, F. (2005). Are psychodynamic and psychoanalytic therapies effective? *International Journal of Psychoanalysis, 86,* 841–868.

Leit, R. A., Gray, J. J., & Pope, H. G., Jr. (2002). The media's representation of the ideal male body: a cause for muscle dysmorphia? *International Journal of Eating Disorders, 31,* 334–338.

Lejuez, C. W., Hopko, D. R., & Hopko, S. D. (2001). A brief behavioral activation treatment for depression: Treatment manual. *Behavior Modification, 25,* 255–286.

LeMarquand, D., Pihl, R., & Benkelfat, C. (1994). Serotonin and alcohol intake, abuse, and dependence: Clinical evidence. *Biological Psychiatry, 36,* 326–337.

Lenz, A. S., Taylor, R., Fleming, M., & Serman, N. (2014). Effectiveness of dialectical behavior therapy for treating eating disorders. *Journal of Counseling and Development, 92,* 26–35.

Lenze, E. J., Karp, J. F., Mulsant, B. H., Blank, S., Shear, M. K., Houck, P. R., & Reynolds, C. F. (2005). Somatic symptoms in late-life anxiety: treatment issues. *Journal of Geriatric Psychiatry and Neurology, 18,* 89–96.

Lenze, E. J., Rogers, J. C., Martire, L. M., Mulsant, B. H., Rollman, B. L., Dew, M. A., . . . Reynolds, C. F. (2001). The association of late-life depression and anxiety with physical disability: A review of the literature and prospectus for future research. *American Journal of Geriatric Psychiatry, 9,* 113–135.

Lenze, E. J., Rollman, B. L., Shear, M. K., Dew, M. A., Pollock, B. G., Ciliberti, C., . . . Reynolds, C. F. (2009). Escitalopram for older adults with generalized anxiety disorder: A randomized controlled trial. *Journal of the American Medical Association, 301,* 295–303.

Leon, G., Fulkerson, J., Perry, C., & Cudeck, R. (1993). Personality and behavioral vulnerabilities associated with risk status for eating disorders in adolescent girls. *Journal of Abnormal Psychology, 102,* 438–444.

Leonard, B. E., & Myint, A. (2009). The psychoneuroimmunology of depression. *Human Psychopharmacology, 24,* 165–175.

Leonard, H., Gixon. G., Whitehouse, A. J. O., Bourke, J., Aiberti, K., Nassar, N., . . . Glasson, E. J. . (2010). Unpacking the complex nature of the autism epidemic. *Research in Autism Spectrum Disorders, 4,* 548–554.

Lerner, M., & Wigal, T. (2008). Long-term safety of stimulant medications used to treat children with ADHD. *Journal of Psychosocial Nursing and Mental Health Services, 46,* 39–48.

Lesaca, T. (2001). Executive functions in parents with ADHD. *Psychiatric Times, XVIII,* Issue 11.

Leserman, J. (2008). Role of depression, stress, and trauma in HIV disease progression. *Psychosomatic Medicine, 70,* 539–545.

Leserman, J., Petitto, J. M., Golden, R. N., Gaynes, B. N., Gu, H., Perkins, D. O., . . . Evans, D. L. (2000). Impact of stressful life events, depression, social support, coping, and cortisol on progression to AIDS. *American Journal of Psychiatry, 157,* 1221–1228.

Leung, A. K. C., & Robson, W. L. M. (2007). Tuberous sclerosis complex: A review. *Journal of Pediatric Health Care, 21,* 108–114.

Levine, S. B. (2010). What is sexual addiction? *Journal of Sex and Marital Therapy, 36,* 261–275.

Levinson, D. F. (2005). Meta-analysis in psychiatric genetics. *Current Psychiatry Reports, 7,* 143–151.

Levkoff, S. E., Evans, D. A., Liptzin, B., Cleary, P. D., Lipsitz, L. A., Wetle, T. T., Rowe, J. (1992). Delirium: The occurrence and persistence of symptoms among elderly hospitalized patients. *Archives of Internal Medicine, 152,* 334–340.

Lewinsohn, P., Seeley, J., Moerk, K., & Striegel-Moore, R. H. (2002). Gender differences in eating disorder symptoms in young adults. *International Journal of Eating Disorders, 32,* 426–440.

Lewinsohn, P. M. (1974). A behavioral approach to depression. In R. J. Friedman & M. M. Katz (Eds.), *Psychology of depression: Contemporary theory and research* (pp. 157–178). Oxford, UK: Wiley.

Lewinsohn, P. M., & Graf, M. (1973). Pleasant activities and depression. *Journal of Consulting and Clinical Psychology, 41,* 261–268.

Lewis, D. O., Yeager, C. A., Swica, Y., Pincus, J. H., & Lewis, M. (1997). Objective documentation of child abuse and dissociation in 12 murderers with dissociative identity disorder. *American Journal of Psychiatry, 143,* 1703–1710.

Lewis, R. W., Sadovsky, R., Eardley, I., O'Leary, M., Seftel, A., Wang, W. C., . . . Ahuja, S. (2005). The efficacy of tadalafil in clinical populations. *Journal of Sexual Medicine, 2,* 517–531.

Lewis-Fernandez, R. (1998). A cultural critique of the DSM-IV dissociative disorders section. *Transcultural Psychiatry, 35,* 387–400.

Li, Q. (2010). Cyberbullying in high schools: A study of students' behaviors and beliefs about this new phenomenon. *Journal of Aggression, Maltreatment & Trauma, 19,* 372–392.

Li, Y., Chen, F., Lu, F., & Wang, Y. (2015). Effect of cyber victimization on deviant behavior in adolescents: The moderating effects of self-control. *Chinese Journal of Clinical Psychology, 23,* 896–900.

Libbey, J. E., Sweeten, T. L., McMahon, W. M., & Fujinami, R. S. (2005). Autistic disorder and viral infections. *Journal of Neurovirology, 11,* 1–10.

Libow, J. A. (2000). Child and adolescent illness falsification. *Pediatrics, 105,* 336–342.

Lidz, C. W. (2006). The therapeutic misconception and our models of competency and informed consent. *Behavioral Sciences and the Law, 24,* 535–540.

Lieb, R., Wittchen, H., Höfler, M., Fuetsch, M., Stein, M., & Merikangas, K. (2000). Parental psychopathology, parenting styles, and the risk of social phobia in offspring: A prospective-longitudinal community study. *Archives of General Psychiatry, 57,* 859–866.

Lieberman, J. A., Stroup, T. S., McEvoy, J. P., Swartz, M. S., Rosenheck, R. A., Perkins, D. O., . . . Clinical Antipsychotic Trials of Intervention Effectiveness (CATIE) Investigators. (2005). Effectiveness of antipsychotic drugs in patients with chronic schizophrenia. *New England Journal of Medicine, 353,* 1209–1223.

Lightner, D. L. (1999). *Asylum, prison, and poorhouse.* Illinois: Southern Illinois University Press.

Lilienfeld, S. O. (2007). Psychological treatments than cause harm. *Perspectives on Psychological Science, 2,* 53–70.

Lilienfeld, S. O., Lynn, S. J., Kirsch, I., Chaves, J. F., Sarbin, T. R., & Ganaway, G. K. (1999). Dissociative identity disorder and the sociocognitive model: Recalling the lessons of the past. *Psychological Bulletin, 125,* 507–523.

Lilienfeld, S. O., Wood, J. M., & Garb, H. N. (2000). The scientific status of projective techniques. *Psychological Science in the Public Interest, 1,* 27–66.

Lin, J. C., Karno, M. P., Grella, C. E., Warda, U., Liao, D. H., Hu, P., & Moore, A. A. (2010). Alcohol, tobacco, and nonmedical drug use disorders in U. S. adults aged 65 years and older: Data from the 2001–2002 National Epidemiologic Survey of Alcohol Related Conditions. *American Journal of Geriatric Psychiatry, 25,* 292–299.

Linden, W., Lenz, J. W., & Con, A. H. (2001). Individualized stress management for primary hypertension: A randomized trial. *Archives of International Medicine, 161,* 1071–1080.

Linden, W., Phillips, M. J., & Leclerc, J. (2007). Psychological treatment of cardiac patients: A meta-analysis. *European Heart Journal, 28,* 2972–2984.

Lindsay, J., Laurin, D., Verreault, R., Hébert, R., Helliwell, B., Hill, G. B., & McDowell, I. (2002). Risk factors for Alzheimer's disease: A prospective analysis from the Canadian Study of Health and Aging. *American Journal of Epidemiology, 156,* 445–453.

Lindwall, M., Rennemark, M., Halling, A., Berglund, J., & Hassmen, P. (2007). Depression and exercise in elderly men and women: Findings from the Swedish national study on aging and care. *Journal of Aging and Physical Activity, 15,* 41–55.

Linehan, M. M., Comtois, K. A., Murray, A. M., Brown, M. Z., Gallop, R. J., Heard, H. L., . . . Lindenboim, N. (2006). Two-year randomized controlled trial and follow-up of dialectical behavior therapy vs therapy by experts for suicidal behaviors and borderline personality disorder. *Archives of General Psychiatry, 63,* 757–766.

Linehan, M. M., Heard, H., & Armstrong, H. (1993). Naturalistic follow-up of a behavioral treatment for chronically parasuicidal borderline patients. *Archives of General Psychiatry, 50,* 971–974.

Linet, O. I., & Ogrinc, F. G. (1996). Efficacy and safety of intracavernosal alprostadil in men with erectile dysfunction. The Alprostadil Study Group. *New England Journal of Medicine, 334,* 873–877.

Links, P. S., Heslegrave, R., & van Reekum, R. (1998). Prospective follow-up study of borderline personality disorder: Prognosis, prediction of outcome, and Axis II comorbidity. *Canadian Journal of Psychiatry, 43,* 265–270.

Linton, S. J. (2002). A prospective study of the effects of sexual or physical abuse on back pain. *Pain, 96,* 347–351.

Lipsitz, J. D., Gur, M., Miller, N. L., Forand, N., Vermes, D., & Fyer, A. J. (2006). An open pilot study of interpersonal psychotherapy for panic disorder (IPT-PD). *Journal of Nervous and Mental Disease, 194,* 440–445.

Lipsitz, J. D., Markowitz, J. C., Cherry, S., & Fyer, A. J. (1999). Open trial of interpersonal psychotherapy for the treatment of social phobia. *American Journal of Psychiatry, 156,* 1814–1816.

Liptzin, B. (2004). Delirium. In J. Sadavoy, L. F. Jarvik, G. T. Grossberg, & B. S. Meyers (Eds.), *Comprehensive textbook of geriatric psychiatry* (3rd ed., pp. 525–544). New York, NY: W. W. Norton & Co.

Litz, B. T., Gray, M. J., Bryant, R. A., & Adler, A. B. (2002). Early intervention for trauma: Current status and future directions. *Clinical Psychology: Science and Practice, 9,* 112–134.

Liu, J. J., Norman, R. M., Manchanda, R., & De Luca, V. (2013). Admixture analysis of age at onset in schizophrenia: Evidence of three subgroups in a first-episode sample. *General Hospital Psychiatry, 35,* 664–667.

Livesley, W. J., & Jackson, D. (2009). *Manual for the Dimensional Assessment of Personality Pathology.* Port Huron, MI: Sigma Assessment Systems.

Livesley, W. J., & Jang, K. L. (2005). Differentiating normal, abnormal, and disordered personality. *European Journal of Personality, 19,* 257–268.

Lochner, C., du Toit, P. L., Zungu-Dirwayi, N., Marais, A., van Kradenburg, J., Seedat, S., . . . Stein, D. J. (2002). Childhood trauma in obsessive-compulsive disorder, trichotillomania, and controls. *Depression and Anxiety, 15,* 66–78.

Lock, J., le Grange, D., Agras, W. S., & Dare, C. (2002). *Treatment manual for anorexia nervosa: A family based approach.* New York, NY: Guilford Press.

Lock, J., le Grange, D., Agras, W. S., Moye, A., Bryson, S. W., & Jo, B. (2010). Randomized clinical trial comparing family-based treatment with adolescent-focused individual therapy for adolescents with anorexia nervosa. *Archives of General Psychiatry, 67,* 1025–1032.

Lockwood, K. A., Alexopoulos, G. S., Kakuma, T., & van Gorp, W. G. (2000). Subtypes of cognitive impairment in depressed older adults. *American Journal of Geriatric Psychiatry, 8,* 201–208.

Loeber, R., Burke, J. D., Lahey, B. B., Winters, A., & Zera, M. (2000). Oppositional defiant and conduct disorder: A review of the past 10 years, Part I. *Journal of the American Academy of Child and Adolescent Psychiatry, 39,* 1468–1484.

Loeber, R., Burke, J., & Pardini, D. A. (2009). Perspectives on oppositional defiant disorder, conduct disorder, and psychopathic features. *Journal of Child Psychology and Psychiatry, 50,* 133–142.

Loewenstein, R. J. (2005). Psychopharmacologic treatments for dissociative identity disorder. *Psychiatric Annals, 35,* 666–673.

Loftus, E. F. (1993). The reality of repressed memories. *American Psychologist, 48,* 518–537.

Loftus, E. F., & Pickrell, J. E. (1995). The formation of false memories. *Psychiatric Annals, 25,* 720–725.

Lohr, J. M., Hooke, W., Gist, R., & Tolin, D. F. (2003). Novel and controversial treatments for trauma-related stress disorders. In S. O. Lilienfeld, S. J. Lynn, & J. M. Lohr (Eds.), *Science and pseudoscience in clinical psychology* (pp. 243–272). New York, NY: Guilford.

Long, D. N., Wisniewski, A. B., & Migeon, C. J. (2004). Gender role across development in adult women with congenital adrenal hyperplasia due to 21-hydroxylase deficiency. *Journal of Pediatric Endocrinology & Metabolism, 17,* 1367–1373.

Lopez, O. L., Jagust, W. J., DeKosky, S. T., Becker, J. T., Fitzpatrick, A., Dulberg, C., . . . Kuller, L. H. (2003). Prevalence and classification of mild cognitive impairment in the Cardiovascular Health Study Cognition Study: part 1. *Arch. Neurol, 60,* 1385–1389.

Lopez, S. R., & Guarnaccia, P. J. (2000). Cultural psychopathology: Uncovering the social world of mental illness. *Annual Review of Psychology, 51,* 571–598.

Lopez, S. R., & Guarnaccia, P. J. (2007). Cultural dimensions of psychopathology: The social world's impact on mental illness. In J. E. Maddux & B. A. Winstead (Eds.), *Psychopathology: Foundations for a contemporary understanding* (pp. 19–38). New York, NY: Routledge.

Lord, C., Risi, S., DiLavore, P. S., Shulman, C., Thurn, A., & Pickles, A. (2006). Autism from 2 to 9 years of age. *Archives of General Psychiatry, 63,* 694–701.

Lott, I. T., & Head, E. (2005). Alzheimer disease and Down syndrome: Factors in pathogenesis. *Neurobiology of Aging, 26,* 383–389.

Lovaas, O. I. (1987). Behavioral treatment and normal educational and intellectual functioning in young children. *Journal of Consulting and Clinical Psychology, 55,* 3–9.

Lovato, C., Watts, A., Brown, K. S., Lee, D., Sabiston, C., Nykiforuk, C., . . . Thompson, M. (2013). School and community predictors of smoking: A longitudinal study of Canadian high schools. *American Journal of Public Health, 103,* 362–368.

Low, C. A., Thurston, R. C., & Matthews, K. A. (2010). Psychosocial factors in the development of heart disease in women: Current research and future directions. *Psychosomatic Medicine, 72,* 842–854.

Lozano, A. M., Mayberg, H. S., Giacobbe, P., Hamani, C., Craddock, C., & Kennedy, S. H. (2008). Subcallosal cingulate gyrus deep brain stimulation for treatment-resistant depression. *Biological Psychiatry, 64,* 461–467.

Luchins, A. S. (2001). Moral treatment in asylums and general hospitals in 19th-century America. *American Journal of Psychiatry, 123,* 585–607.

Lundahl, B. W., Kunz, C., Brownell, C., Tollefson, D., & Burke, B. L. (2010). A meta-analysis of motivational interviewing: Twenty-five years of empirical studies. *Research on Social Work Practice, 20,* 137–160.

Lyketsos, C. G. (2009). Dementia and milder cognitive syndromes. In D. C. Blazer & D. C. Steffens (Eds.), *Textbook of geriatric psychiatry* (pp. 243–260). Washington, DC: American Psychiatric Publishing, Inc.

Lykken, D. (1982). Fearlessness: Its carefree charms and deadly risks. *Psychology Today, 16,* 20–28.

Lynn, K. S. (1987). *Hemingway.* New York, NY: Simon & Schuster.

Lyons, A. P., & Lyons, H. D. (2006). The new anthropology of sexuality. *Anthropologica, 48,* 153–157.

M

Mackenzie, C. S., Scott, T. S., Mather, A., & Sareen, J. (2008). Older adults' help-seeking attitudes and treatment beliefs concerning mental health problems. *American Journal of Geriatric Psychiatry, 16,* 1010–1019.

Mackin, R. S., & Arean, P. A. (2005). Evidence-based psychotherapeutic interventions for geriatric depression. *Psychiatric Clinics of North America, 28,* 805–820.

Mackintosh, M. A., Gatz, M., Wetherell, J. L., & Pedersen, N. L. (2006). A twin study of lifetime Generalized Anxiety Disorder (GAD) in older adults: Genetic and environmental influences shared by neuroticism and GAD. *Twin Research and Human Genetics, 9,* 30–37.

Macy, R. D., Behar, L., Paulson, R., Delman, J., Schmid, L., & Smith, S. F. (2004). Community-based, acute posttraumatic stress management: A description and evaluation of a psychosocial-intervention continuum. *Harvard Review of Psychiatry, 12,* 217–228.

Maenner, M. J., Schieve, L. A., Rice, C. E., Cunniff, C. Giarell, E., Kirby, R. S., Lee, L. C., Nicholas, J. S., Wingate, M. S., & Durkin, M. S. (2013). Frequency and pattern of documented diagnostic features and the age of autism identification. *Journal of the American Academy of Child and Adolescent Psychiatry, 52,* 401–413.

Magee, W. J., Eaton, W. W., Wittchen, H. U., McGonagle, K. A., & Kessler, R. C. (1996). Agoraphobia, social phobia and simple phobia in the National Comorbidity Survey. *Archives of General Psychiatry, 53,* 159–168.

Magill, F. (1983). Ernest Hemingway. In F. Magill (Ed.), *The critical survey of long fiction* (pp. 953–967). New York, NY: Salem Press.

Maher, W. B., & Maher, B. A. (1985). Psychopathology: I. From ancient times to the 18th century. In G. A. Kimble & K. Schlesinger (Eds.), *Topics in the history of psychology* (Vol. 2, pp. 251–294). Hillsdale, NJ: Erlbaum.

Maier, W., Gansicke, M., Freyberger, H. J., Linz, M., Heun, R., & Lecrubier, Y. (2000). Generalized anxiety disorder (ICD-10) in primary care from a cross-cultural perspective: A valid diagnostic entity? *Acta Psychiatrica Scandinavica, 101,* 29–36.

Maj, M. (2005). "Psychiatric comorbidity": An artifact of the current diagnostic system? *British Journal of Psychiatry, 186,* 182–184.

Malhotra, A., Murphy, G., & Kennedy, J. (2004). Pharmacogenetics of psychotropic drug response. *American Journal of Psychiatry, 161,* 780–796.

Malla, A. K., & Payne, J. (2005). First-episode psychosis: Psychopathology, quality of life, and functional outcome. *Schizophrenia Bulletin, 31,* 650–671.

Mallinger, J. B., Fisher, S. G., Brown, T., & Lamberti, J. S. (2006). Racial disparities in the use of second-generation antipsychotics for the treatment of schizophrenia. *Psychiatric Services, 57,* 133–136.

Malone, R. P., & Simpson, G. M. (1998). Use of placebos in clinical trials involving children and adolescents. *Psychiatric Services, 49,* 1413–1414, 1417.

Malta, M., Strathdee, S. A., Magnanini, M. M., & Bastos, F. I. (2008). Adherence to antiretroviral therapy for human immunodeficiency virus/acquired immune deficiency syndrome among drug users: A systematic review. *Addiction, 103,* 1242–57.

Mankovsky, T., Lynch, M. E., Clark, A. J., Sawynok, J., & Sullivan, M. J. (2012). Pain catastrophizing predicts poor response to topical analgesics in patients with neuropathic pain. *Pain Research & Management, 17,* 10–14.

Mann, J. J., Brent, D. A., & Arango, V. (2001). The neurobiology and genetics of suicide and attempted suicide: A focus on the serotonergic system. *Neuropsychopharmacology, 24,* 467–477.

Marazatti, D. (1999). Obsessive-compulsive disorders: experimental pharmacology. *CNS Spectrums, 6*(5 Suppl), 41–46.

March, J., Kratochvil, C., Clarke, G., Beardslee, W., Derivan, A., Emslie, G., Green, E. P., . . . Wells, K. (2004). AACAP 2002 research forum: placebo and alternatives to placebo in randomized controlled trials in pediatric psychopharmacology. *Journal of the American Academy of Child and Adolescent Psychiatry. 43*(8), 1046–1056.

March, J. S., Parker, J. D., Sullivan, K., Stallings, P., & Conners, K. (1997). The Multidimensional Anxiety Scale for Children (MASC): Factor structure, reliability and validity. *Journal of the American Academy of Child and Adolescent Psychiatry, 36,* 554–565.

Marcus, M. D., Moulton, M. M., & Greeno, C. G. (1995). Binge eating onset in obese patients with binge eating disorder. *Addictive Behaviors, 20,* 747–755.

Margolese, H. W., & Ferreri, F. (2007). Management of conventional antipsychotic-induced tardive dyskineisa. *Journal of Psychiatry & Neuroscience, 32,* 72.

Markus, H. R., & Kitayama, S. (1991). Culture and the self: Implications for cognition, emotion and motivation. *Psychological Review, 98,* 244–253.

Marlatt, G. A., & Gordon, J. R. (1985). *Relapse prevention: Maintenance strategies in the treatment of addictive behaviors.* New York, NY: Guilford Press.

Marlatt, G. A., Larimer, M., Baer, J., & Quigley, L. (1993). Harm reduction for alcohol problems: Moving beyond the controlled drinking controversy. *Behavior Therapy, 24,* 461–504.

Marques, L., Alegria, M., Becker, A. E., Chen, C. N., Fang, A., Chosak, A., Diniz, J. B. (2011). Comparative prevalence, correlates of impairment, and service utilization for eating disorders across U. S. ethnic groups: Implications for reducing ethnic disparities in health care access for eating disorders. *International Journal of Eating Disorders, 44,* 412–420.

Marques, L., Porter, E., Keshaviah, A., Pollack, M. H., van Ameringen, M., Stein, M. B., . . . Simon, N. M. (2012). Avoidant personality disorder in individuals with generalized social anxiety disorder: What does it add? *Journal of Anxiety Disorders, 26,* 665–672.

Marshall, W. L., & Eccles, A. (1991). Issues in clinical practice with sex offenders. *Journal of Interpersonal Violence, 6,* 68–93

Marshall, W. L., Marshall, L. E., & Serran, G. A. (2006). Strategies in the treatment of paraphilias: A critical review. *Annual Review of Sex Research, 17,* 162–182.

Martin, L. R., & Brantley, P. J. (2004). *Stress, coping, and social support in health and behavior* (Vol. 2). Washington, DC: American Psychological Association.

Martin, N., Boomsma, D., & Machin, G. (1997). A twin-pronged attack on complex traits. *Nature Genetics, 17,* 387–392.

Martin, S. (December 1, 2006). Shot 6 times by his wife, tycoon pleaded with her to call 911 and he'd say nothing. *Globe and Mail.* Retrieved June 4, 2015 from http://www.theglobeandmail.com/news/national/shot-6-times-by-his-wife-tycoon-pleaded-with-her-to-call-911-and-hed-say-nothing/article4113116/

Martinez-Barrondo, S., Saiz, P. A., Morales, B., Garcia-Portilla, M. P., Coto, E., Alvarez, Y., & Bobes, J. (2005). Serotonin gene polymorphisms in patients with panic disorder. *Actas España Psiquiatrica, 33,* 210–215.

Maruish, M. E. (2004). *The use of psychological testing for treatment planning and outcomes assessment (vol 1.).* Mahwah, NJ: Erlbaum.

Maruta, T., Colligan, R. C., Malinchoc, M., & Offord, K. P. (2002). Optimism-pessimism assessed in the 1960s and self-reported health status 30 years later. *Mayo Clinic Proceedings, 77,* 748–753.

Marzuk, P., Leon, A., Tardiff, K., Morgan, E., Stajic, M., & Mann, J. (1992). The effect of access to lethal methods of injury on suicide rates. *Archives of General Psychiatry, 49,* 451–458.

Mashour, G. A., Walker, E. E., & Martuza, R. L. (2005). Psychosurgery: Past, present, and future. *Brain Research Reviews, 48,* 409–419.

Masi, G., Millipiedi, S., Mucci, M., Poli, P., Bertini, N., & Milantoni, L. (2004). Generalized anxiety disorder in referred children and adolescents. *Journal of the American Academy of Child and Adolescent Psychiatry, 38,* 916–922.

Massey, L. (1998). Caffeine and the elderly. *Drugs and Aging, 13,* 43–50.

Masters, W. H., & Johnson, V. E. (1966). *Human sexual response.* Boston, MA: Little, Brown.

Masters, W. H., & Johnson, V. E. (1970). *Human sexual inadequacy.* Boston, MA: Little, Brown.

Mathews, J. R., & Barch, D. M. (2010). Emotion responsivity, social cognition, and functional outcome in schizophrenia. *Journal of Abnormal Psychology, 119,* 50–59.

Matson, J. L., Benavidez, D. A., Compton, L. S., Paclawskyj, T., & Baglio, C. (1996). Behavioral treatment of autistic persons: A review of research from 1980 to the present. *Research in Developmental Disabilities, 17,* 433–465.

Matson, J. L., Hattier, M. A., Belva, B., & Matson, M. L. (2013). Pica in persons with developmental disabilities: Approaches to treatment. *Research in Developmental Disabilities, 34,* 2564–2571.

Matson, J. L., & Nebel-Schwalm, M. S. (2007). Comorbid psychopathology with autism spectrum disorder in children: An overview. *Research in Developmental Disabilities, 28,* 341–352.

Matson, J. L., & Smith, K. R. M. (2008). Current status of intensive behavioral interventions for young children with autism and PDD-NOS. *Research in Autism Spectrum Disorders, 2,* 60–74.

Mattis, S. (2001). *Dementia rating scale-2*: Professional Manual. Odessa.

Maurice, W. L. (2005). Male hypoactive sexual desire disorder. In R. Balon & R. T. Segraves (Eds.). *Handbook of sexual dysfunction* (pp. 76–109). Boca Raton, FL: Taylor & Francis.

Maxwell, J. (2001). Deaths related to the inhalation of volatile substances in Texas: 1988–1998. *American Journal of Drug and Alcohol Abuse, 27,* 689–697.

Mayberg, H. S., Keightley, M., Mahurin, R. K., & Brannan, S. K. (2004). Neuropsychiatric aspects of mood and affective disorders. In R. E. Hales & S. C. Yudofsky (Eds.), *Essentials of neuropsychiatry and clinical neurosciences* (pp. 489–517). Washington, DC: American Psychiatric Publishing.

Mayes, L. C. (2000). A developmental perspective on the regulation of arousal states. *Seminars in Perinatology, 24,* 267–279.

Mayes, R., & Horwitz, A. V. (2005). DSM-III and the revolution in the classification of mental illness. *Journal of the History of the Behavioral Sciences, 41,* 249–267.

Mayne, T. J., Vittinghoff, E., Chesney, M. A., Barrett, D. C., & Coates, T. J. (1996). Depressive affect and survival among gay and bisexual men infected with HIV. *Archives of Internal Medicine, 156,* 2233–2238.

Mayou, R. A., Ehlers, A., & Hobbs, M. (2000). Psychological debriefing for road traffic accident victims. Three-year follow-up of a randomised controlled trial. *British Journal of Psychiatry, 176,* 589–593.

Mazzeo, S. E., Trace, S. E., Mitchell, K. S., & Gow, R. W. (2007). Effects of a reality TV cosmetic surgery makeover program on eating disordered attitudes and behaviors. *Eating Behaviors, 8,* 390–397.

McAlearney, A. S., Reeves, K. W., Tatum, C., & Paskett, E. D. (2007). Cost as a barrier to screening mammography among underserved women. *Ethnicity and Health, 12,* 189–203.

McCabe, R., & Priebe, S. (2004). Explanatory models of illness in schizophrenia: Comparison of four ethnic groups. *British Journal of Psychiatry, 185,* 25–30.

McCaul, M., Svikis, D., & Moore, R. (2001). Predictors of outpatient treatment retention: Patient versus substance use characteristics. *Drug and Alcohol Dependence, 62,* 9–17.

McClellan, J., Breiger, D., McCurry, C., & Hlastala, S. A. (2003). Premorbid functioning in early-onset psychotic disorders. *Journal of the American Academy of Child and Adolescent Psychiatry, 42,* 666–673.

McClure, E. R., Davis, P. M., Meadow, S. R., & Sibert, J. R. (1996). Epidemiology of Munchausen Syndrome by Proxy, non-accidental poisoning, and non-accidental suffocation. *Archives of Diseases of Childhood, 75,* 57–61.

McCracken, J. T., McGough, J., Shah, B., Cronin, P., Hong, D., Aman, M. G., Research Units on Pediatric Psychopharmacology Autism Network. (2002). Risperidone in children with autism and serious behavioral problems. *New England Journal of Medicine, 347,* 314–321.

McCrae, R. R., Yang, J., Costa, P. T., Dai, X., Yao, S., Cai, T., & Gao, B. (2001). Personality profiles and the prediction of categorical personality disorders. *Journal of Personality, 69,* 155–174.

McCusker, C. (2001). Cognitive biases and addiction: An evolution in theory and method. *Addiction, 96,* 47–56.

McCusker, J., Cole, M. G., Voyer, P., Monette, J., Champoux, N., Ciampi, A., Bu, M., & Belzile, E. (2011). Prevalence and incidence of delirium in long-term care. *International Journal of Geriatric Psychiatry, 26,* 1152–1161.

McDonald, C., Grech, A., Toulopoulou, T., Schulze, K., Chapple, B., Sham, P., . . . Murray, R. M. (2002). Brain volumes in familial and non-familial schizophrenic probands and their unaffected relatives. *American Journal of Medical Genetics and Neuropsychiatric Genetics, 114,* 616–625.

McDonald, K. C., Bulloch, A. G., Duffy, A., Bresee, L., Williams, J. V., Lavorato, D. H., . . . Patten, S. B. (2015). Prevalence of bipolar I and II disorder in Canada. *Canadian Journal of Psychiatry, 60,* 151–156.

McDougle, C. J., Scahill, L., Aman, M. G., McCracken, J. T., Tierney, E., Davies, M., . . . Vitiello, B. (2005). Risperidone for the core symptom domains of autism: Results from the study by the Autism Network of the Research Units on Pediatric Psychopharmacology. *American Journal of Psychiatry, 162,* 1142–1148.

McDowell, I., Xi, G., Lindsay, J., & Tierney, M. (2007). Mapping the connections between education and dementia. *Journal of Clinical and Experimental Neuropsychology, 29,* 127–141.

McDowell, I., Xi, G., Lindsay, J., & Tuokko, H. (2004). Canadian study of health and aging: Study description and patterns of early cognitive decline. *Aging Neuropsychology and Cognition, 11,* 149–168.

McElroy, S. L., Soutullo, C. A., Taylor, P., Jr., Nelson, E. B., Beckman, D. A., Brusman, L. A., . . . Keck, P. E., Jr. (1999). Psychiatric features of 36 men convicted of sexual offenses. *Journal of Clinical Psychiatry, 60,* 414–420.

McGee, B. L., Hewitt, P. L., Sherry, S. B., Parkin, M., & Flett, G. L. (2005). Perfectionistic self-presentation, body image, and eating disorder symptoms. *Body Image, 2,* 29–40.

McGough, J. J., & Barkley, R. A. (2004). Diagnostic controversies in adult attention deficit hyperactivity disorder. *American Journal of Psychiatry, 161,* 1948–1956.

McGrath, E., Keita, G. P., Stickland, B. R., & Russo, N. F. (1990). *Women and depression: Risk factors and treatment issues.* Washington, DC: American Psychological Association.

McGuffin, P., Owen, M. J., & Farmer, A. E. (1995). Genetic basis of schizophrenia. *The Lancet, 346,* 678–682.

McGuffin, P., Rijsdijk, F., Andrew, M., Sham, P., Katz, R., & Cardno, A. (2003). The heritability of bipolar affective disorder and the genetic relationship to unipolar depression. *Archives of General Psychiatry, 60,* 497–502.

McIlwraith, R. D. (2014). Psychology departments in medical schools: There's one in Canada, eh? *American Psychologist, 69,* 934.

McIntosh, V. V., Bulik, C. M., McKenzie, J. M., Luty, S. E., & Jordan, J. (2000). Interpersonal psychotherapy for anorexia nervosa. *International Journal of Eating Disorders, 27,* 125–139.

McIntosh, V. V., Jordan, J., Carter, F., Luty, S., McKenzie, J., Bulik, C. M., Frampton, C. M., & Joyce, P. R. . (2005). Three psychotherapies for anorexia nervosa: A randomized controlled trial. *American Journal of Psychiatry, 162,* 741–747.

McKay, D. (2014). Prescription privileges and cognitive-behavior therapy. *Behavior Therapist, 37,* 133–136.

McKenna, M. C., Zevon, M. A., Corn, B., & Rounds, J. (1999). Psychosocial factors and the development of breast cancer: A meta-analysis. *Health Psychology, 18,* 520–531.

McLaren, J., & Bryson, S. E. (1987). Review of recent epidemiological studies of mental retardation: Prevalence, associated disorder, and etiology. *American Journal of Mental Retardation, 92,* 243–254.

McMahon, C. G., Althof, S., Waldinger, M. D., Porst, H., Dean, J., Sharlip, I., . . . International Society for Sexual Medicine Ad Hoc Committee for Definition of Premature Ejaculation. (2008). An evidence-based definition of lifelong premature ejaculation. *BJU International, 102,* 338–350.

McMahon, F. J. (2004). Genetics of mood disorders and associated psychopathology. In J. Sadavoy, L. F. Jarvik, G. T. Grossberg, & B. S. Meyers (Eds.), *Comprehensive textbook of geriatric psychiatry* (3rd ed., pp. 85–104). New York, NY: W. W. Norton & Co.

McNally, R. J. (1995). Automaticity and the anxiety disorders. *Behaviour Research and Therapy, 33,* 747–754.

McNally, R. J. (1999). EMDR and Mesmerism: A comparative historical analysis. *Journal of Anxiety Disorders, 13,* 225–236.

McNally, R. J. (2001). Vulnerability to anxiety disorders in adulthood. In R. E. Ingram & J. M. Price (Eds.), *Vulnerability to psychopathology: Risk across the lifespan* (pp. 304–321). New York, NY: Guilford Press.

McNally, R. J. (2005). Debunking myths about trauma and memory. *Canadian Journal of Psychiatry, 50,* 817–822.

McNally, R. J. (2009). Can we fix PTSD in DSM-V? *Depression and Anxiety, 26,* 597–600.

McSherry, B. (1998). Getting away with murder? Dissociative states and criminal responsibility. *International Journal of Law and Psychiatry, 21,* 163–176.

Medina-Moira, M. E., Borges, G., Lara, C., Benjet, C., Blanco, J., Fleiz, C., . . . Zambrano, J. (2005). Prevalence, service use, and demographic correlates of 12-month DSM-IV psychiatric disorders in Mexico: Results from the Mexican National Comorbidity Survey. *Psychological Medicine, 35,* 1773–1783.

Mednick, S. A., Machon, R. A., Huttunen, M. O., & Bonett, D. (1988). Adult schizophrenia following prenatal exposure to an influenza epidemic. *Archives of General Psychiatry, 45,* 189–192.

Mehta, K. M., Simonsick, E. M., Penninx, B. W., Schulz, R., Rubin, S. M., Satterfield, S., & Yaffe, K. (2003). Prevalence and correlates of anxiety symptoms in well-functioning older adults: Findings from the health aging and body composition study. *Journal of the American Geriatrics Society, 51,* 499–504.

Mehta, N. (2011). Mind-body dualism: A critique from a health perspective. *Mens Sana Monographs, 9,* 202–209.

Meijler, M., Matsushita, M., Wirsching, P., & Janda, K. (2004). Development of immunopharmacotherapy against drugs of abuse. *Current Drug Discovery Technology, 1,* 77–89.

Meilman, P. W., & Hall, T. M. (2006). Aftermath of tragic events: The development and use of community support meetings on a university campus. *Journal of American College Health, 54,* 382–384.

Mendlowicz, M. V., & Stein, M. B. (2000). Quality of life in individuals with anxiety disorders. *American Journal of Psychiatry, 157,* 669–682.

Merck & Co. (1995–2006). *Drug use and dependence.* Retrieved June 12, 2011, from http://www.merck.com/mmpe/sec15/ch198/ch198a.html?qt=drug%20use%20and%20dependence&alt=sh

Merikangas, K. R., Akiskal, H. S., Angst, J., Greenberg, P. E., Hirschfeld, R. M., Petukhova, M., & Kessler, R. C. (2007). Lifetime and 12-month prevalence of bipolar spectrum disorder in the National Comorbidity Survey replication. *Archives of General Psychiatry, 64,* 543–552.

Metz, M. E., Pryor, J. L., Nesvacil, L. J., Abuzzahab, F., Sr., & Koznar, J. (1997). Premature ejaculation: A psychophysiological review. *Journal of Sex & Marital Therapy, 23,* 3–23.

Meyer, G. J., Finn, S. E., Eyde, L. D., Kay, G. G., Moreland, K. L., Dies, R. R., . . . Reed, G. M. (2001b). Psychological testing and psychological assessment: A review of evidence and issues. *American Psychologist, 56,* 128–165.

Meyer, W. J., III. (2004). Comorbidity of gender identity issues. *American Journal of Psychiatry, 161,* 934–935.

Meyer, W. J., III, Bockting, W. O., Cohen-Kettenis, P., Coleman, E., DiCeglie, D., Devor, H., . . . Wheeler, C. C. (2001a). The Harry Benjamin International Gender Dysphoria Association's Standards of Care for Gender Identity Disorders, Sixth version. *Journal of Psychology & Human Sexuality, 13,* 1–30.

Meyer-Bahlburg, H. F. L., Dolezal, C., Baker, S., & New, M. I. (2008). Sexual orientation in women with classical or non-classical congenital adrenal hyperplasia as a function of degree of prenatal androgen excess. *Archives of Sexual Behavior, 37,* 85–99.

Meyers, R., Smith, J., & Lash, D. (2003). The community reinforcement approach. In M. Galanter (Ed.), *Recent developments in alcoholism: Vol. 16: Research on alcoholism treatment* (pp. 183–195). New York, NY: Kluwer Academic/Plenum Publishers.

Michel, A., Mormont, C., & Legros, J. J. (2001). A psycho-endocrinological overview of transsexualism. *European Journal of Endocrinology, 145,* 365–376.

Migneault, J., Adams, T., & Read, J. (2005). Application of the transtheoretical model to substance abuse: Historical development and future directions. *Drug and Alcohol Review, 24,* 437–438.

Mikkelsen, E. J. (2001). Enuresis and encopresis: Ten years of progress. *Journal of the American Academy of Child and Adolescent Psychiatry, 40,* 1146–1158.

Miklowitz, D. J., Otto, M. W., Frank, E., Reilly-Harrington, N. A., Wisniewski, S. R., Kogan, J. N., . . . Sachs, G. S. (2007). Psychosocial treatments for bipolar depression: a 1-year randomized trial from the Systematic Treatment Enhancement Program. *Archives of General Psychiatry, 64,* 419–427.

Miklowitz, D. J., & Scott, J. (2009). Psychosocial treatments for bipolar disorder: Cost-effectiveness, mediating mechanisms, and future directions. *Bipolar Disorders, 11,* 110–122.

Miladinovic, Z., & Lukassen, J. (2014). *Verdicts of not criminally responsible on account of mental disorder in adult criminal courts, 2005/2006–2011/2012.* Ottawa: Statistics Canada. Retrieved January 15, 2016 from http://www.statcan.gc.ca/pub/85-002-x/2014001/article/14085-eng.htm

Milak, M. S., Parsey, R. V., Keilp, J., Oquendo, M. A., Malone, K. M., & Mann, J. J. (2005). Neuroanatomic correlates of psychopathologic components of major depressive disorder. *Archives of General Psychiatry, 62,* 397–408.

Milan, A. (2011). *Age and sex structure: Canada, provinces and territories, 2010.* Ottawa: Statistics Canada.

Miller, E. R. III, Pastor-Barriuso, R., Dalal, D., Riemersma, R. A., Appel, L. J., & Guallar, E. (2005). Meta-analysis: High-dosage vitamin E supplementation may increase all-cause mortality. *Annals of Internal Medicine, 142,* 37–46.

Miller, G. E., Chen, E., & Zhou, E. S. (2007). If it goes up, must it come down? Chronic stress and the hypothalamic-pituitary-adrenocortical axis in humans. *Psychological Bulletin, 133,* 25–45.

Miller, J. G. (1997). Theoretical issues in cultural psychology. In J. W. Berry, Y. H. Poortinga, & J. Pandey (Eds.), *Handbook of cross-cultural psychology* (2nd ed.). Boston, MA: Allyn and Bacon.

Miller, W. (1983). Motivational interviewing with problem drinkers. *Behavioural Psychotherapy, 11,* 147–172.

Miller, W., & Rollnick, S. (1991). *Motivational interviewing: Preparing people to change addictive behavior.* New York, NY: Guilford Press.

Millon, T., Millon, C., Davis, R., & Grossman, S. (2006). *MCMI-III Manual* (3rd ed.). Minneapolis, MN: Pearson Education.

Mills, J. (2015). Psychotherapist-patient privilege, recordkeeping, and maintaining psychotherapy case notes in professional practice: The need for ethical and policy reform. *Canadian Journal of Counseling and Psychotherapy, 49,* 96–113.

Mineka, S., & Cook, M. (1986). Immunization against the observational conditioning of snake fear in rhesus monkeys. *Journal of Abnormal Psychology, 95,* 307–318.

Mineka, S., & Zinbarg, R. (2006). A contemporary learning theory perspective on the etiology of anxiety disorders: It's not what you thought it was. *American Psychologist, 61,* 10–26.

Minuchin, S., Rosman, B. L., & Baker, L. (1978). *Psychosomatic families: Anorexia nervosa in context.* Cambridge, MA: Harvard University Press.

Miranda, A. O., & Fraser, L. D. (2002). Culture-bound syndromes: Initial perspectives from individual psychology. *Journal of Individual Psychology, 58,* 422–433.

Mischel, W., & Shoda, Y. (1995). A cognitive-affective system of personality: Reconceptualizing situations, dispositions, dynamics and invariance in personality structure. *Psychology Review, 102,* 246–268.

Misener, V. L., Luca, P., Azeke, O., Crosbie, J., Waldman, I., Tannock, R., . . . Barr, C. L. (2004). Linkage of the dopamine receptor D1 gene to attention deficit/hyperactivity disorder. *Molecular Psychiatry, 9,* 500–509.

Mitchell, J., Specker, S., & De Zwaan, M. (1991). Comorbidity and medical complications of bulimia nervosa. *Journal of Clinical Psychiatry, 52,* 13–20.

Mitchell, J. E. (1990). *Bulimia nervosa.* Minneapolis, MN: University of Minnesota Press.

Mohammed, A. H. (2000). Genetic dissection of nicotine-related behaviour: A review of animal studies. *Behavioural Brain Research, 113,* 35–41.

Mojtabai, R. (2005). Perceived reasons for loss of housing and continued homelessness among homeless persons with mental illness. *Psychiatric Services, 56,* 172–178.

Mokros, A., Hare, R. D., Neumann, C. S., Santtila, P., Habermeyer, E., & Nitschke, J. (2015). Variants of psychopathy in adult male offenders: A latent profile analysis. *Journal of Abnormal Psychology, 124,* 372–386.

Molgat, C. V., & Patten, S. B. (2005). Comorbidity of major depression and migraine—A Canadian population-based study. *Canadian Journal of Psychiatry, 50,* 832–837.

Moller, J., Hallqvist, J., Diderichsen, F., Theorell, T., Reuterwall, C., & Ahlbom, A. (1999). Do episodes of anger trigger myocardial infarction? A case-crossover analysis in the Stockholm Heart Epidemiology Program (SHEEP). *Psychosomatic Medicine, 61,* 842–849.

Monahan, J., Bonnie, R. J., Appelbaum, P. S., Hyde, P. S., Steadman, H. J., & Swartz, M. S. (2001b). Mandated community treatment: Beyond outpatient commitment. *Psychiatric Services, 52,* 1198–1205.

Monahan, J., Steadman, H. J., Silver, E., Appelbaum, P. S., Robbins, P. C., Mulvey, E. P., . . . Banks, S. (2001a). *Rethinking risk assessment: The MacArthur study of mental disorder and violence.* New York, NY: Oxford University Press.

Monroe, S. M., Harkness, K., Simons, A. D., & Thase, M. E. (2001). Life stress and the symptoms of major depression. *Journal of Nervous and Mental Disease, 189,* 168–175.

Moore, A. A., Blow, F. C., Hoffing, M., Welgreen, S., Davis, J. W., Lin, J. C., . . . Barry, K. L. (2011). Primary care-based intervention to reduce at-risk drinking in older adults: A randomized controlled trial. *Addiction, 106,* 111–120.

Moore, A., Patterson, C., Lee, L., Vedel, I., & Bergman, H. (2014). Fourth Canadian consensus conference on the diagnosis and treatment of dementia. *Canadian Family Physician, 60,* 433–438.

Moore, H., West, A. R., & Grace, A. A. (1999). The regulation of forebrain dopamine transmission: Relevance to the pathophysiology and psychopathology of schizophrenia. *Biological Psychiatry, 46,* 40–55.

Moore, K., & McLaughlin, D. (2003). Depression: The challenge for all healthcare professionals. *Nursing Standard, 17,* 45–52.

Moos, R. (2008). Active ingredients of substance use-focused self-help groups. *Addiction, 103,* 387–396.

Moradi, B., Dirks, D., & Matteson, A. V. (2005). Roles of sexual objectification experiences and internalization of standards of beauty in eating disorder symptomatology: A test and extension of objectification theory. *Journal of Counseling Psychology, 51,* 420–428.

Moral, J. C., Terrero, F. B., Galan, A. S., Rodriguez, T. M. (2015). Effect of integrative reminiscence therapy on depression, well-being, integrity, self-esteem, and life satisfaction in older adults. *Journal of Positive Psychology, 10,* 240–247.

Moreira, E. D., Brock, G., Glasser, D. B., Nicolosi, A., Laumann, E. O., Paik, A., . . . GSSAB Investigators' Group. (2005). Help-seeking behavior for sexual problems. The global study of sexual attitudes and behaviors. *International Journal of Clinical Practice, 59,* 6–16.

Moreno, M. A. (2014). Cyberbullying. *Journal of the American Medical Association Pediatrics, 168,* 500.

Morey, L. C. (2007). *Personality Assessment Inventory professional manual* (2nd ed.). Lutz, FL: Psychological Assessment Resources.

Morgan, D., & Morgan, R. (2001). Single-participant research design: Bringing science to managed care. *American Psychologist, 56,* 119–127.

Morin, C. M., & Espie, C. A. (2003). *Insomnia: A clinical guide to assessment and treatment.* New York, NY: Kluwer Academic/Plenum.

Morin, C. M., LeBlanc. M., Belanger, L., Ivers, H., Merette, C., & Savard, J. (2011). Prevalence of insomnia and its treatment in Canada. *Canadian Journal of Psychiatry, 56,* 540–548.

Morin, C. M., Vallieres, A., Guay, B., Ivers, H., Savard, J., Merette, C., . . . Baillargeon, L. (2009). Cognitive behavioral therapy, singly and combined with medication, for persistent insomnia: A randomized controlled trial. *Journal of the American Medical Association, 301,* 2005–2015.

Morison, S. J., Ames, E. W., & Chisholm, K. (1995). The development of children adopted from Romanian orphanages. *Merrill-Palmer Quarterly, 41,* 411–430.

Morris, J. C. (2005a). Dementia update 2005. *Alzheimer Disease and Associated Disorders, 19,* 100–117.

Morris, J. C. (2005b). Early-stage and preclinical Alzheimer disease. *Alzheimer Disease and Associated Disorders, 19,* 163–165.

Mossakowski, K. N. (2003). Coping with perceived discrimination: Does ethnic identity protect mental health? *Journal of Health and Social Behavior, 44,* 318–331.

Motlova, L., Dragomirecka, E., Spaniel, F., Goppoldova, E., Zalesky, R., Selepova, P., . . . Höschl, C. (2006). Relapse prevention in schizophrenia: Does group family psychoeducation matter? One year prospective follow-up field study. *International Journal of Psychiatry in Clinical Practice, 10,* 38–44.

Mouton-Odum, S., Keuthen, N. J., Wagener, P., & Stanley, M. A. (2006). StopPulling.com: An interactive, self-help program for trichotillomania. *Cognitive and Behavioral Practice, 13*(3), 215–226.

Moynihan, R. (2006). Scientists find new disease: Motivational deficiency disorder. *British Medical Journal, 332,* 745.

Mrvos, R., Reilly, P., Dean, B., & Krenzelok, E. (1989). Massive caffeine ingestion resulting in death. *Veterinary and Human Toxicology, 31,* 571–572.

MTA Cooperative Group. (1999). A 14-month randomized clinical trial of treatment strategies for attention-deficit/hyperactivity disorder. *Archives of General Psychiatry, 56,* 1073–1086.

Mueser, K. T., Bellack, A. S., & Brady, E. U. (1990). Hallucinations in schizophrenia. *Acta Psychiatrica Scandiavica, 82,* 26–29.

Mueser, K. T., & McGurk, S. R. (2004). Schizophrenia. *The Lancet, 363,* 2063–2072.

Mueser, K. T., Rosenberg, S. D., Goodman, L. A., & Trumbetta, S. L. (2002). Trauma, PTSD, and the course of schizophrenia: An interactive model. *Schizophrenia Research, 53,* 123–143.

Mufson, L., Moreau, D., Weissman, M., Wickramaratne, P., Martin, J., & Samoilov, A. (1994). Modification of interpersonal psychotherapy with depressed adolescents (IPTA-A): Phase I and II studies. *Journal of the American Academy of Child and Adolescent Psychiatry, 33,* 695–705.

Muhlau, M., Gaser, C., Ilg, R., Conrad, B., Leibl, C., Cebulla, M. H., . . . Nunne, S. (2007). Gray matter decrease of the anterior cingulate cortex in anorexia nervosa. *American Journal of Psychiatry, 164,* 1850–1857.

Mulloy, A., Lang, R., O'Reilly, M., Sigafoos, J., Lancioni, G., & Rispoli, M. (2010). Gluten-free and casein-free diets in treatment of autism spectrum disorders: A systematic review. *Research in Autism Spectrum Disorders, 4,* 328–339.

Mulloy, A., Lang, R., O'Reilly, M., Sigafoos, J., Lancioni, G., & Rispoli, M. (2011). Addendum to "gluten-free and casein-free diets in treatment of autism spectrum disorders: A systematic review." *Research in Autism Spectrum Disorders, 5,* 86–88.

Muratori, F., Salvadori, F., D'Arcangelo, G., Viglione, V., & Picchi, L. (2005). Childhood psychopathological antecedents in early onset schizophrenia. *European Psychiatry, 20,* 309–314.

Muris, P., Schmidt, H., & Merckelbach, H. (1999). The structure of specific phobia symptoms among children and adolescents. *Behaviour Research and Therapy, 37,* 863–868.

Murphy, D., & Peters, J. M. (1992). Profiling child sexual abusers. Psychological considerations. *Criminal Justice and Behavior, 19,* 24–37.

Muse, L., Harris, S., & Field, H. (2003). Has the inverted-u theory of stress and job performance had a fair test? *Human Performance, 16,* 349–364.

Mutrie, N., Campbell, A. M., Whyte, F., McConnachie, A., Emslie, C., Lee, L., . . . Ritchie, D. (2007). Benefits of supervised group exercise programme for women being treated for early stage breast cancer: Pragmatic randomised controlled trial. *British Medical Journal, 334,* 517.

N

Naar-King, S., Wright, K., Parsons, J. T., Frey, M., Templin, T., Lam, . . . Murphy, D. (2006). Healthy choices: Motivational enhancement therapy for health risk behaviors in HIV-positive youth. *AIDS Education and Prevention, 18,* 1–11.

Naik, A. D., Concato, J., & Gill, T. M. (2004). Bathing disability in community-living older persons: Common, consequential, and complex. *Journal of the American Geriatrics Society, 52,* 1805–1810.

Nakabayashi, K., Komaki, G., Tajima, A., Ando, T., Ishikawa, M., Nomoto, J., . . . Shirasawa, S. (2009). Identification of novel candidate loci for anorexia nervosa at 1q41 and 11q22 in Japanese by a genome-wide association analysis with microsatellite markers. *Journal of human genetics, 54(9),* 531–537.

Nakaya, N., Bidstrup, P. E., Saito-Nakaya, K., Frederiksen, K., Koskenvuo, M., Pukkala, E., . . . Johansen C. (2010). Personality traits and cancer risk and survival based on Finnish and Swedish registry data. *American Journal of Epidemiology, 172,* 377–385.

Namanzi, M. R. (2001). Avicenna, 980–1037. *American Journal of Psychiatry, 158,* 1796.

Nanda, S. (1985). The hijras of India: Cultural and individual dimensions of an institutionalized third gender role. *Journal of Homosexuality, 11,* 35–54.

Nathan, D. (2011). *Sybil exposed: The extraordinary story behind the famous multiple personality case.* New York, NY: Free Press.

Nation, M., Crusto, C., Wandersman, A., Kumpfer, K., Seybolt, D., Morrisey-Kane, E., & Katrina, D. (2003). What works in prevention: Principles of effective prevention programs. *American Psychologist, 58,* 449–456.

National Institute of Clinical and Health Excellence. (2004). Retrieved June 11, 2011, from http://www.nice.org.uk/page.aspx?o=101239.

National Institute of Mental Health. (2005). *Antidepressant medications for children and adolescents: Information for parents and caregivers.* Retrieved from http://www.nimh.nih.gov/healthinformation/antidepressant_child.cfm

National Institute on Drug Abuse. (2001). *Nicotine addiction.* Bethesda, MD: National Institutes of Health.

National Institute on Drug Abuse. (2004). *Inhalant abuse.* Bethesda, MD: National Institutes of Health.

National Institute on Drug Abuse. (2005a). *Hallucinogens and Dissociative Drugs.* Bethesda, MD: National Institutes of Health.

National Institute on Drug Abuse. (2005b). *Marijuana.* Bethesda, MD: National Institutes of Health.

National Survey on Drug Use and Health: *Substance use among older adults: 2002 & 2003 update.* (2006). Retrieved from http://www.oas.samhsa.gov

Navaneelan, T. (2012). *Suicide rates: An overview.* Ottawa: Statistics Canada. (Catalogue no. 82-624-X).

Nay, M. (1994, September). Beliefs and practices about food during pregnancy. *Economic and Political Weekly,* 2427–2438.

Neaton, J. D., & Wentworth, D. (1992). Serum cholesterol, blood pressure, cigarette smoking, and death from coronary heart disease. Overall findings and differences by age for 316,099 white men. Multiple Risk Factor Intervention Trial Research Group. *Archives of Internal Medicine, 152,* 56–64.

Needleman, H. L., & Gatsonis, C. A. (1990). Low-level lead exposure and the IQ of children: A meta-analysis of modern studies. *Journal of the American Medical Association, 263,* 673–678.

Needleman, H. L., Schell, A., Bellinger, D., Leviton, A., & Allred, E. N. (1990). The long-term effects of exposure to low doses of lead in childhood: An 11-year follow-up report. *New England Journal of Medicine, 322,* 83–88.

Nehls, N. (1998). Borderline personality disorder: Gender stereotypes, stigma, and limited system of care. *Issues in Mental Health Nursing, 19,* 97–112.

Neisser, U., & Harsch, N. (1992). Phantom flashbulbs: False recollections of hearing the news about Challenger. In E. Winograd & U. Neisser (Eds.), *Affect and accuracy in recall: Studies of flashbulb memories* (pp. 9–31). Cambridge, MA: Cambridge University Press.

Nelson, E. C., Grant, J. D., Bucholz, K. K., Glowinski, A., Madden, P. A. F., Reich, W., & Heath, A. C. (2000). Social phobia in a population-based female adolescent twin sample: Comorbidity and associated suicide-related symptoms. *Psychological Medicine, 30,* 797–804.

Nelson, E. C., Heath, A. C., Madden, P. A., Cooper, M. L., Dinwiddie, S. H., Bucholz, K. K., . . . Martin, N. G. (2002). Association between self-reported childhood sexual abuse and adverse psychosocial outcomes. *Archives of General Psychiatry, 59,* 139–145.

Nelson, R. M. (2002). Appropriate risk exposure in environmental health research. The Kennedy-Krieger lead abatement study. *Neurotoxicology and Teratology, 24,* 445–449.

Nestoriuc, Y., & Martin, A. (2007). Efficacy of biofeedback for migraine: a meta-analysis. *Pain, 128* (1-2), 111–127.

Newcomb, M., & Richardson, M. A. (1995). Substance use disorders. In M. Hersen & R. Ammerman (Eds.), *Advanced abnormal child psychology* (pp. 411–431). Hillsdale, NJ: Lawrence Erlbaum Associates.

Newton, E., Landau, S., Smith, P., Monks, P. N., Sherrill, S., & Wykes, T. (2005). Early psychological intervention for auditory hallucinations. *Journal of Nervous and Mental Disease, 193,* 58–61.

NICE. (2004). Depression: Management of depression in primary and secondary care. *Clinical Guideline 23.* London: National Institute for Clinical Excellence.

Nicholas, J. S., Charles, J. M., Carpenter, J. A., King, L. B., Jenner, W., & Spratt, E. G. (2008). Prevalence and characteristics of children with autism spectrum disorders. *Annals of Epidemiology, 18,* 130–136.

Nichols, D. S., Padilla, J. & Gomez-Maqueo, E. L. (2000). Issues in the cross-cultural adaptation and use of the MMPI-2. In R. H. Dana (Ed.), *Handbook of cross-cultural and multicultural assessment* (pp. 247–292). Mahwah, NJ: Erlbaum.

Nicolosi, A., Laumann, E. O., Glasser, D. B., Brock, G., King, R., & Gingell, C. (2006). Sexual activity, sexual disorders and associated help-seeking behavior among mature adults in five Anglophone countries from the Global Survey of Sexual Attitudes and Behaviors (GSSAB). *Journal of Sex & Marital Therapy, 32,* 331–342.

Nicolosi, A., Laumann, E. O., Glasser, D. B., Moreira, E. D., Jr., Paik, A., Gingell, C., & Global Study of Sexual Attitudes and Behaviors Investigators' Group. (2004). Sexual behavior and sexual dysfunctions after age 40: The Global Study of Sexual Attitudes and Behaviors. *Urology, 64,* 991–997.

Niedermeyer, E. (1999). Historical aspects. In *Electroencephalography: Basic Principles, Clinical Applications and Related Fields* (pp. 1–13). Philadelphia, PA: Lippincott Williams & Wilkins.

Niederstrasser, N. G., Slepian, P. M., Mankovsky-Arnold, T., Lariviere, C., Vlaeyen, J. W., & Sullivan, M. J. (2014). An experimental approach to examining psychological contributions to multisite musculoskeletal pain. *The Journal of Pain, 15,* 1156–1165.

Nieto, J. A. (2004). Children and adolescents as sexual beings: Cross-cultural perspectives. *Child and Adolescent Psychiatric Clinics of North America, 13,* 461–477.

Nikolas, M. A., & Burt, S. (2010). Genetic and environmental influences on ADHD symptom dimensions of inattention and hyperactivity: A meta-analysis. *Journal of Abnormal Psychology, 119,* 1–17.

Nimkarm, S., & New, M. I. (2010). Congenital adrenal hyperplasia due to 21-hydroxylase deficiency : A paradigm for prenatal diagnosis and treatment. *Annals of the New York Academy of Science, 1192,* 5–11.

Nolen-Hoeksema, S. (2001). Gender differences in depression. *Current Directions in Psychological Science, 10,* 173–176.

Nord, D., Luecking, R., Mank, D., Kieman, W., & Wray, C. (2013). The state of the science of employment and economic self-sufficiency for people with intellectual and developmental disabilities. *Intellectual and Developmental Disabilities, 51,* 376–384.

Nordhus, I. H., & Pallesen, S. (2003). Psychological treatment of late-life anxiety: An empirical review. *Journal of Consulting and Clinical Psychology, 71,* 643–652.

Norfleet, M. A. (2002). Responding to society's needs: Prescription privileges for psychologists. *Journal of Clinical Psychology, 58,* 599–610.

North, C. S., Ryall, J. E. M., Ricci, D. A., & Wetzel, R. D. (1993). *Multiple personalities, multiple disorders.* New York, NY: Oxford University Press.

Norton, N., Williams, H. J., & Owen, M. J. (2006). An update on the genetics of schizophrenia. *Current Opinion in Psychiatry, 19,* 158–164.

Novy, D. M., Stanley, M. A., Averill, P., & Daza, P. (2001). Psychometric comparability of English- and Spanish-language measures of anxiety and related affective symptoms. *Psychological Assessment, 13,* 347–355.

Nusbaum, M. R., Gamble, G., Skinner, B., & Heiman, J. (2000). The high prevalence of sexual concerns among women seeking routine gynecological care. *Journal of Family Practice, 49,* 229–232.

Nydegger, R. V. (1972). The elimination of hallucinatory and delusional behavior by verbal conditioning and assertive training: A case study. *Journal of Behavior Therapy and Experimental Psychiatry, 3,* 225.

O

O'Brien, M. D., Bruce, B. K., & Camilleri, M. (1995). The rumination syndrome: Clinical features rather than manometric diagnosis. *Gastroenterology, 108,* 1024–1029.

O'Carroll, R. (1989). A neuropsychological study of sexual deviation. *Sexual and Marital Therapy, 4,* 59–63.

O'Connor, K., & Roth, B. (2005). Finding new tricks for old drugs: An efficient route for public-sector drug discovery. *Nature Reviews Drug Discovery, 4,* 1005–1014.

O'Leary, T., & Monti, P. (2002). Cognitive-behavioral therapy for alcohol addiction. In S. Hofmann & M. Tompson (Eds.), *Treating chronic and severe mental disorders: A handbook of empirically supported interventions* (pp. 234–257). New York, NY: Guilford Press.

Odendaal, J. S., & Meintjes, R. A. (2003). Neurophysiological correlates of affiliative behaviour between humans and dogs. *Veterinary Journal, 165,* 296–301.

Ogata, S. N., Silk, K. R., Goodrich, S., Lohr, N. E., Westen, D., & Hill, E. M. (1990). Childhood sexual and physical abuse in adult patients with borderline personality disorder. *American Journal of Psychiatry, 147,* 1008–1013.

Ohara, K., Sato, Y., Tanabu, S., Yoshida, K., & Shibuya, H. (2006). Magnetic resonance imaging study of the ventricle-brain ratio in parents of schizophrenia subjects. *Progress in Neuro-Psychopharmacology & Biological Psychiatry, 30,* 89–92.

Okazaki, S., & Sue, S. (1995). Methodological issues in assessment research with ethnic minorities. *Psychological Assessment, 7,* 367–375.

olde Hartman, T. C., Borghuis, M. S., Lucassen, P. L. B. J., van de Laar, F. A., Speckens, A. E., & van Weel, C. (2009). Medically unexplained symptoms, somatization disorder and hypochondriasis: Course and prognosis. A systematic review. *Journal of Psychosomatic Research, 66,* 363–377.

Oleseon, O. F., Bennike, B., Hansen, E. S., Koefoed, P., Woldbye, D. P., Bolwig, T. G., & Erling, M. (2005). The short/long polymorphism in the serotonin transporter gene promoter is not associated with panic disorder in a Scandinavian sample. *Psychiatric Genetics, 15,* 159.

Olin, J. T., Schneider, L. S., Katz, I. R., Meyers, B. S., Alexopoulos, G. S., Breitner, J. C., . . . Lebowitz, B. D. (2002). Provisional diagnostic criteria for depression of Alzheimer disease. *American Journal of Geriatric Psychiatry, 10,* 125–128.

Ollendick, T. H., & King, N. J. (1991). Origins of childhood fears: An evaluation of Rachman's theory of fear acquisition. *Behaviour Research and Therapy, 29,* 117–125.

Ollendick, T. H., King, N. J., & Muris, P. (2004). Phobias in children and adolescents. In M. Maj, H. S. Akiskal, J. J. Lopez-Ibor, & A. Okasha (Eds.), *Phobias* (pp. 245–279). London, UK: John Wiley & Sons.

Ollendick, T. H., Raishevich, N., Davis, T. E., Sirbu, C., & Öst, L. G. (2010). Specific phobia in youth: Phenomenology and psychological characteristics. *Behavior Therapy, 41,* 133–141.

Olson, L., & Houlihan, D. (2000). A review of behavioral treatments used for Lesch-Nyhan syndrome. *Behavior Modification, 24,* 202–222.

Opler, M. G. A., & Susser, E. S. (2005). Fetal environment and schizophrenia. *Environmental Health Perspectives, 113,* 1239–1242.

Osborn, T. (2007). The psychosocial impact of parental cancer on children and adolescents: A systematic review. *Psycho-oncology, 16,* 101–126.

Osby, U., Correia, N., Brandt, L., Ekbom, A., & Sparen, P. (2000). Mortality and causes of death in schizophrenia in Stockholm County, Sweden. *Schizophrenia Research, 45,* 21–28.

Oslin, D. (2005). Brief interventions in the treatment of at-risk drinking in older adults. *Psychiatric Clinics of North America, 28,* 897–911.

Oslin, D. W. (2004). Late-life alcoholism: Issues relevant to the geriatric psychiatrist. *American Journal of Geriatric Psychiatry, 12,* 571–583.

Oslin, D. W., Liberto, J. G., O'Brien, J., Krois, S., & Norbeck, J. (1997). Naltrexone as an adjunctive treatment for older patients with alcohol dependence. *The American Journal of Geriatric Psychiatry, 5,* 324–331.

Oslin, D. W., & Mavandadi, S. (2009). Alcohol and drug problems. In D. C. Blazer & D. C. Steffens (Eds.), *Textbook of geriatric psychiatry* (pp. 409–428). Washington, DC: American Psychiatric Publishing, Inc.

Oslin, D. W., Pettinati, H., & Volpicelli, J. R. (2002). Alcoholism treatment adherence: Older age predicts better adherence and drinking outcomes. *American Journal of Geriatric Psychiatry, 10,* 740–747.

Ost, L. G. (1996). Long-term effects of behavior therapy for specific phobia. In M. Mavissakalian & R. R. Prien (Eds.), *Long-term treatments of anxiety disorders* (pp. 121–170). New York, NY: Plenum.

Osterloh, I. H., & Riley, A. (2002). Clinical update on sildenafil citrate. *British Journal of Clinical Pharmacology, 53,* 219–223.

Otto, M. W., Pollack, M. H., Maki, K. M., Gould, R. A., Worthington, J. J., III, Smoller, J. W., & Rosenbaum, J. F. (2001). Childhood history of anxiety disorders among adults with social phobia. *Depression and Anxiety, 14,* 209–213.

Otto, M. W., Pollack, M. H., Sachs, G. S., Reiter, S. R., Meltzer-Brody, S., & Rosenbaum, J. R. (1993). Discontinuation of benzodiazepine treatment: Efficacy of cognitive-behavioral therapy for patients with panic disorder. *American Journal of Psychiatry, 150,* 1485–1490.

Ouimette, P. C., Finney, J. W., & Moos, R. H. (1997). Twelve-step and cognitive-behavioral treatment for substance abuse: A comparison of treatment effectiveness. *Journal of Consulting and Clinical Psychology, 65,* 230–240.

Overall, J., & Gorham, D. (1988). The Brief Psychiatric Rating Scale (BPRS): recent developments in ascertainment and scaling. *Psychopharmacology Bulletin, 24,* 97–99.

Owens, D. G., Miler, P., Lawrie, S. M., & Johnstone, E. C. (2005). Pathogenesis of schizophrenia: A psychopathological perspective. *British Journal of Psychiatry, 186,* 386–393.

P

Pace, T. W., & Heim, M. (2011). A short review on the psychoneuroimmunology of posttraumatic stress disorder: From risk factors to medical comorbidities. *Brain, Behavior and Immunology, 25,* 6–13.

Pachana, N. A., Emery, E., Konnert, C. A., Woodhead, E., & Edelstein, B. A. (2010). Geropsychology content in clinical training programs: A comparison of Australian, Canadian and U. S. data. *International Psychogeriatrics, 22,* 909–918.

Padma-Nathan, H., Brown, C., Fendl, J., Salem, S., Yeager, J., & Harning, R. (2003). Efficacy and safety of topical alprostadil cream for the treatment of female sexual arousal disorder (FSAD): A double-blind, multicenter, randomized, and placebo-controlled clinical trial. *Journal of Sex & Marital Therapy, 29,* 329–344.

Padma-Nathan, H., Hellstrom, W. J., Kaiser, F. E., Labasky, R. F., Lue, T. F., Nolten, W. E., . . . Gesundheit, N. (1997). Treatment of men with erectile dysfunction with transurethral alprostadil. Medicated Urethral System for Erection (MUSE) Study Group. *New England Journal of Medicine, 336,* 1–7.

Palazzoli, M. (1978). *Self-starvation: From individual to family in the treatment of anorexia nervosa.* New York, NY: Jason Aronson.

Pande, N., & Naidu, R. K. (1992). Anasaki and health: A study of non-attachment. *Psychology and Developing Societies, 4,* 91–104.

Pandina, G. J., Aman, M. G., & Findling, R. L. (2006). Risperidone in the management of disruptive behavior disorders. *Journal of Child and Adolescent Psychopharmacology, 16,* 379–392.

Paradis, C. M., & Friedman, S. (2005). Sleep paralysis in African-Americans with panic disorder. *Transcultural Psychiatry, 42,* 123–134.

Pare, J.-R. (2011). *Post-traumatic stress disorder and the mental health of military personnel and veterans.* Ottawa: Library of Parliament.

Parikh, S. V., Segal, Z. V., Grigoriadis, S., Ravindran, A. V., Kennedy, S. H., Lam, R. W., . . . Patten, S. B. (2009). Canadian Network for Mood and Anxiety Treatments (CANMAT) clinical guidelines for the management of major depressive disorder in adults. II. Psychotherapy alone or in combination with antidepressant medication. *Journal of Affective Disorders, 117,* S15–S25.

Paris, J. (2002). Implications of long-term outcomes research for the management of patients with borderline personality disorder. *Harvard Review of Psychiatry, 10,* 315–323.

Paris, J. (2014). Modernity and narcissistic personality disorder. *Personality Disorders: Theory, Research, and Treatment, 5,* 220–226.

Paris, J. (2015). *A concise guide to personality disorders.* Washington, DC: American Psychological Association.

Paris, J., Brown, R., & Nowlis, D. (1987). Long-term follow-up of borderline patients in a general hospital. *Comprehensive Psychiatry, 28,* 530–535.

Paris, J., & Zweig-Frank, H. (2001). A 27-year follow-up of patients with borderline personality disorder. *Comprehensive Psychiatry, 42,* 482–487.

Park, D. C., & Radford, J. P. (1998). From the case files: Reconstructing a history of involuntary sterilisation. *Disability & Society, 13,* 317–342.

Park, J., & Knudson, S. (2007). Medically unexplained physical symptoms. *Health Reports, 18,* 43–47.

Parker, G. (1982). Researching the schizophrenogenic mother. *Journal of Nervous and Mental Disease, 170,* 452–462.

Parker, G. B., & Brotchie, H. L. (2004). From diathesis to dimorphism: The biology of gender differences in depression. *Journal of Nervous and Mental Disease, 192,* 210–216.

Patel, V. (2001). Cultural factors and international epidemiology. *British Medical Bulletin, 57,* 33–45.

Patten, S. B., Williams, J. V., Lavorato, D. H., & Bulloch, A. G. (2010). Reciprocal effects of social support in major depression epidemiology. *Clinical Practice & Epidemiology in Mental Health, 6,* 126–131.

Patterson, G. R., & Gullion, M. E. (1968). *Living with children: New methods for parents and teachers.* Champaign, IL: Research Press.

Paukert, A. L., Calleo, J., Kraus-Schuman, C., Snow, L., Wilson, N., Petersen, N. J., . . . Stanley, M. A. (2010). Peaceful mind: An open trial of cognitive-behavioral therapy for anxiety in persons with dementia. *International Psychogeriatrics, 22,* 1012–1021.

Pauls, D. L., Alsobrook, J. P., Goodman, W., Rasmussen, S., & Leckman, J. F. (1995). A family study of obsessive-compulsive disorder. *American Journal of Psychiatry, 152,* 76–84.

Pearlstein, T., Howard, M., Salisbury, A., & Zlotnick, C. (2009). Postpartum depression. *American Journal of Obstetrics and Gynecology, 200,* 357–364.

Pearman, A., & Batra, A. (2012). Late-onset schizophrenia: A review for clinicians. *Clinical Gerontologist, 35,* 126–147.

Pearson, C., Janz, T., & Ali, J. (2013). *Mental and substance use disorders in Canada.* Ottawa: Statistics Canada.

Pearson, C., Zamorski, M., & Janz, T. (2014). *Mental health of the Canadian Armed Forces.* Ottawa: Statistics Canada.

Pedersen, N. L., & Fiske, A. (2010). Genetic influences on suicide and nonfatal suicidal behavior: Twin study findings. *European Psychiatry, 25,* 264–267.

Pedersen, N. L., McClearn, G. E., Plomin, R., & Friberg, L. (1985) Separated fraternal twins: resemblance for cognitive abilities. *Behavior Genetics, 15,* 407–419.

Pegram, G. V., McBurney, J., Harding, S. M., & Makris, C. M. (2004). Normal sleep and sleep disorders in adults and children. In T. J. Boll, J. M. Raczynski, & L. C. Leviton (Eds.), *Handbook of clinical health psychology* (pp. 183–230). Washington, DC: American Psychological Association.

Pelham, W. E., & Fabiano, G. A. (2008). Evidence-based psychosocial treatments for attention-deficit/hyperactivity disorder. *Journal of Clinical Child and Adolescent Psychology, 37,* 184–214.

Pelham, W. E., Fabiano, G. A., Gnagy, E. M., Greiner, A. R., & Hoza, B. (2004). Intensive treatment: Summer treatment program for children with ADHD. In E. D. Hibbs & P. S. Jensen (Eds.), *Psychosocial treatment for child and adolescent disorders: Empirically based strategies for clinical practice* (2nd ed.). Washington, DC: American Psychological Association Press.

Pelham, W. E. Gnagy, E. M., Greiner, A. R., Hoza, B., Hinshaw, S. P., Swanson, J. M., . . . McBurnett, K. (2000). Behavioral versus behavioral and pharmacological treatment in ADHD children attending a summer treatment program. *Journal of Abnormal Child Psychology, 28,* 507–525.

Pence, B. W., Miller, W. C., Whetten, K., Eron, J. J., & Gaynes, B. N. (2006). Prevalence of DSM-IV-defined mood, anxiety, and substance use disorders in an HIV clinic in the Southeastern United States. *Journal of Acquired Immune Deficiency Syndrome, 42,* 298–306.

Pendery, M., Maltzman, I., & West, L. (1982). Controlled drinking by alcoholics? New findings and a reevaluation of a major affirmative study. *Science, 217,* 169–175.

Penn, D. L., Combs, D. R., & Mohamed, S. (2001). Social cognition and social functioning in schizophrenia. In P. W. Corrigan & D. L. Penn (Eds.), *Social cognition and schizophrenia* (pp. 97–122). Washington, DC: APA Press.

Peplau, L. A. (2003). Human sexuality: How do men and women differ? *Current Directions in Psychological Science, 12,* 37–40.

Pérez-Dueñas, B., Pujol, J., Soriano-Mas, C., Ortiz, H., Artuch, R., Vilaseca, M. A., & Campistol, J. (2006). Global and regional volume changes in the brains of patients with phenylketonuria. *Neurology, 66,* 1074–1078.

Perkins, D. O., Johnson, J. L., Hamer, R. M., Zipursky, R. B., Keefe, R. S., Centorrhino, F., . . . HGDH Research Group. (2006). Predictors of antipsychotic medication adherence in patients recovering from a first psychotic episode. *Schizophrenia Research, 83,* 53–63.

Perkonigg, A., Kessler, R. C., Storz, S., & Wittchen, H. U. (2000). Traumatic events and post-traumatic stress disorder in the community: Prevalence, risk factors and comorbidity. *Acta Psychiatric Scandinavia, 101,* 46–59.

Perlis, R. H., Brown, E., Baker, R. W., & Nierenberg, A. A. (2006). Clinical features of bipolar depression versus major depressive disorder in large multicenter trials. *American Journal of Psychiatry, 163,* 225–231.

Perlis, R. H., Perlis, C. S., Wu, Y., Hwang, C., Joseph, M., & Nierenberg, A. A. (2005). Industry sponsorship and financial conflict of interest in the reporting of clinical trials in psychiatry. *American Journal of Psychiatry, 162,* 1957–1960.

Perreault, S. (2011). *Self-reported internet victimization in Canada, 2009.* Ottawa: Statistics Canada. (Catalogue no. 85-002-X).

Peters, M. L., Godaert, G. L., Ballieux, R. E., van, V. M., Willemsen, J. J., Sweep, F. C., & Heijnen, C. J. (1998). Cardiovascular and endocrine responses to experimental stress: Effects of mental effort and controllability. *Psychoneuroendocrinology, 23,* 1–17.

Petersen, R. C., Doody, R., Kurz, A., Mohs, R. C., Morris, J. C., Rabins, P. V., . . . Winblad, B. (2001). Current concepts in mild cognitive impairment. *Archives of Neurology, 58,* 1985–1992.

Petersen, R. C., Smith, G. E., Ivnik, R. J., Tangalos, E. G., Schaid, D. J., Thibodeau, S. N., . . . Kurland, L. T. (1995). Apolipoprotein E status as a predictor of the development of Alzheimer's disease in memory-impaired individuals. *Journal of the American Medical Association, 273,* 1274–1278.

Peterson, C. B., Thuras, P., Ackard, D. M., Mitchell, J. E., Berg, K., Sandager, N., Wonderlich, S. A., Pederson, M. W., Crow, S. J. (2010) Personality dimensions in bulimia nervosa, binge eating disorder, and obesity. *Compr Psychiatry, 51(1),* 31–36.

Petronis, A. (2010). Epigenetics as a unifying principle in the aetiology of complex traits and diseases. *Nature, 465,* 721–727.

Pfiffner, L. J., & McBurnett, K. (1997). Social skills training with parent generalization: Treatment effects for children with attention deficit disorder. *Journal of Consulting and Clinical Psychology, 65,* 749–757.

Phelan, E. A., & Larson, E. B. (2002). Successful aging: Where next? *Journal of the American Geriatrics Society, 50,* 1306–1308.

Phillips, K. A., Coles, M. E., Menard, W., Yen, S., Fay, C., & Weisberg, R. B. (2005). Suicidal ideation and suicide attempts in body dysmorphic disorder. *Journal of Clinical Psychiatry, 66,* 717–725.

Phillips, K. A., Didie, E. R., Menard, W., Pagano, M. E., Fay, C., & Weisberg, R. B. (2006b). Clinical features of body dysmorphic disorder in adolescents and adults. *Psychiatry Research, 141,* 305–314.

Phillips, K. A., & Dufresne, R. G. (2002). Body dysmorphic disorder: A guide for primary care physicians. *Primary Care, 29,* 99–110.

Phillips, K. A., & Menard, W. (2006). Suicidality in body dysmorphic disorder: A prospective study. *American Journal of Psychiatry, 163,* 1280–1282.

Philips, K. A., Menard, W., Pagano, M. E., Fay, C., & Stout, R. L. (2006a). Delusional versus nondelusional body dysmorphic disorder: Clinical features and course of illness. *Journal of Psychiatric Research, 40,* 95–104.

Phillips, K. A., & Taub, S. L. (1995). Skin picking as a symptom of body dysmorphic disorder. *Psychopharmacology Bulletin, 31,* 279–288.

Phillips, K. A., Wilhelm, S., Koran, L. M., Didie, E. R., Fallon, B. A., Feusner, J., & Stein, D. J. (2010). Body dysmorphic disorder: Some key issues for DSM-V. *Depression and Anxiety, 27,* 573–591.

Pickens, R., & Fletcher, B. (1991). Overview of treatment issues. In R. Pickens, C. Leukefeld, & C. Schuster (Eds.), *Improving drug abuse treatment. National Institute on Drug Abuse (NIDA) Research Monograph No. 106* (pp. 1–19). Rockville, MD: NIDA.

Pierce, K., Haist, R., Sedaghat, F., & Courchesne, E. (2004). The brain response to personally familiar faces in autism: Findings of fusiform activity and beyond. *Brain, 12,* 2703–2716.

Pierce, K., Muller, R. A., Ambrose, J., Allen, G., & Courchesne, E. (2001). Face processing occurs outside the fusiform "face area" in autism: Evidence for functional MRI. *Brain, 124,* 2059–2073.

Pike, K., Loeb, K., & Vitousek, K. (1996). Cognitive-behavioral therapy for anroexia nervosa and bulimia nervosa. In J. Thompson (Ed.), *Eating disorders, obesity, and body image: A practical guide to assessment and treatment.* Washington, DC: APA Books.

Piotrowski, C. (1995). A review of the clinical and research use of the Bender-Gestalt Test. *Perceptual and Motor Skills, 81,* 1272–1274.

Piper, A., & Merskey, H. (2004a). The persistence of folly: A critical examination of dissociative identity disorder. Part I. The excesses of an improbable concept. *Canadian Journal of Psychiatry, 49,* 592–600.

Piper, A., & Merskey, H. (2004b). The persistence of folly: A critical examination of dissociative identity disorder. Part II. The defence and decline of multiple personality or dissociative identity disorder. *Canadian Journal of Psychiatry, 49,* 678–683.

Pitschel-Walz, G., Leucht, S., Bauml, J., Kissling, W., & Engel, R. R. (2001). The effect of family interventions on relapse and rehospitalization in schizophrenia—a meta-analysis. *Schizophrenia Bulletin, 27,* 73–92.

Pittenger, D. J. (2005). Cautionary comments regarding the Myers-Briggs Type Indicator. *Consulting Psychology Journal: Practice and Research, 57,* 210–221.

Plassman, B. L., & Steffens, D. C. (2004). Genetics. In D. G. Blazer, D. C. Steffens, & E. W. Busse (Eds.), *Textbook of geriatric psychiatry* (3rd ed., pp. 109–120). Washington, DC: American Psychiatric Publishing, Inc.

Plomin, R., DeFries, J. C., McClearn, G. E., & Rutter, M. (1994). *Behavioral genetics* (3rd ed.). New York, NY: W. H. Freeman & Co.

Politi, P., Minoretti, P., Falcone, C., Martinelli, V., & Emanuele, E. (2006). Association analysis of the functional Ala111Glu polymorphism of the glyoxalase I gene in panic disorder. *Neuroscience Letter, 396,* 163–166.

Pollack, M. H., & Marzol, P. C. (2000). Panic: Course, complications, and treatment of panic disorder. *Journal of Psychopharmacology, 14*(1 Suppl), S25–S30.

Poortinga, Y. H., & Van Hemert, D. A. (2001). Personality and culture: Demarcating between the common and the unique. *Journal of Personality Disorders, 69,* 1033–1060.

Pope, H. G., Lalonde, J. K., Pindyck, L. J., Walsh, T., Bulik, C. M., Crow, S. J., . . . Hudson, J. I. . (2006). Binge eating disorder: A stable syndrome. *American Journal of Psychiatry, 163,* 2181–2183.

Popova, S., Lange, S., Burd, L., & Rehm, J. (2015). The economic burden of fetal alcohol spectrum disorder in Canada in 2013. *Alcohol and Alcoholism,* in press.

Popper, C. W., Gammon, G. D., West, S. A., & Bailey, C. E. (2004). Disorders usually first diagnosed in infancy, childhood, or adolescence. In R. E. Hales and S. G. Yudofsky (Eds.), *Essentials of clinical psychiatry* (2nd ed., pp. 591–735). Washington, DC: American Psychiatric Publishing.

Porensky, E. K., Dew, M. A., Karp, J. F., Skidmore, E., Rollman, B. L., Shear, M. K., . . . Lenze, E. J. (2009). The burden of late-life generalized anxiety disorder: Effects on disability, health-related quality of life, and healthcare utilization. *American Journal of Geriatric Psychiatry, 17,* 473–482.

Porst, H., Rosen, R., Padma-Nathan, H., Goldstein, I., Giuliano, F., Ulbrich, E., . . . Bandel, T. (2001). The efficacy and tolerability of vardenafil, a new, oral, selective phosphodiesterase type 5 inhibitor, in patients with erectile dysfunction: The first at-home clinical trial. *International Journal of Impotence Research, 13,* 192–199.

Porter, V. R., Buxton, W. G., Fairbanks, L. A., Strickland, T., O'Connor, S. M., Rosenberg-Thompson, S., . . . Cummings, J. L. (2003). Frequency and characteristics of anxiety among patients with Alzheimer's disease and related dementias. *The Journal of Neuropsychiatry and Clinical Neuroscience, 15,* 180–186.

Post, R. M., Denicoff, K. D., Leverich, G. S., Altshuler, L. L., Frye, M. A., Suppes, T. M., . . . Nolen, W. A. (2003). Morbidity in 258 bipolar outpatients followed for 1 year with daily prospective ratings on the NIMH life chart method. *Journal of Clinical Psychiatry, 64,* 680–690.

Post, R. M., Speer, A. M., Weiss, S. R., & Li, H. (2000). Seizure models: Anticonvulsant effects of ECT and rTMS. *Progress in Neuro-psychopharmacology and Biological Psychiatry, 24,* 1251–1273.

Potenza, M. N. (2008). The neurobiology of pathological gambling and drug addiction: An overview and new findings. *Philosophical Transactions of the Royal Society of London. Series B, Biological Sciences, 363,* 3181–3189.

Potvin, S., Sepehry, A. A., & Stip, E. (2006). A meta-analysis of negative symptoms in dual diagnosis schizophrenia. *Psychological Medicine, 36,* 431–440.

Powell, R. A., Digdon, N., Hiss, B., & Smithson, C. (2014). Correcting the record on Watson, Rayner, and Little Albert: Albert Barger as "Psychology's lost boy." *American Psychologist, 69,* 600–611.

Pratt, H. D., & Patel, D. R. (2007). Learning disorders in children and adolescents. *Primary Care: Clinics in Office Practice, 34,* 361–374.

Prendergast, M., Podus, D., & Finney, J. (2006). Contingency management for treatment of substance use disorders: A meta-analysis. *Addiction, 101,* 1546–1560.

Prescott, C. (2001). The genetic epidemiology of alcoholism: Sex differences and future directions. In D. Agarwal & H. Seitz (Eds.), *Alcohol in health and disease* (pp. 125–149). New York, NY: Marcel Dekker.

Prien, R. F., & Kupfer, D. J. (1986). Continuation drug therapy for major depressive episodes: How long should it be maintained? *American Journal of Psychiatry, 143,* 18–23.

Prina, A. M., Deeg, D., Brayne, C., Beekman, A., & Huisman, M. (2012). The association between depressive symptoms and non-psychiatric hospitalization in older adults. *PlosOne, 7,* e34821. Doi:10.1371/journal.pone.0034821.

Prochaska, J., & DiClemente, C. (1983). Stages and processes of self-change of smoking: Toward an integrative model of change. *Journal of Consulting and Clinical Psychology, 51,* 390–395.

Pron, N. (1995). *Lethal marriage: The unspeakable crimes of Paul Bernado and Karla Homolka.* Toronto, ON: Seal Books.

Psychiatric GWAS Consortium Bipolar Disorder Working Group. (2011). Large-scale genome-wide association analysis of bipolar disorder identifies a new susceptibility locus near ODZ4. *Nature Genetics, 43,* 977–983.

Psychological Assessment Resources. (2003). *Computerised Wisconsin Card Sort Task Version 4 (WCST).* Lutz, FL: Psychological Assessment Resources.

Public Health Agency of Canada (2002). *Congenital anomalies in Canada: A perinatal health report.* Ottawa: Author.

Public Health Agency of Canada (2010). *The Chief Public Health Officer's report on the state of public health in Canada, 2010: Growing older – adding life to years.* Ottawa: Author.

Public Health Agency of Canada (2011). *Report on the state of public health in Canada.* Ottawa: Author.

Public Health Agency of Canada (2012). *Estimates of HIV prevalence and incidence in Canada, 2011.* Ottawa: Author.

Pulay, A. J., Dawson, D. A., Hasin, D. S., & Grant, B. F. (2008). Violent behavior and DSM-IV psychiatric disorders: Results from the National Epidemiologic Survey on Alcohol and Related Conditions. *Journal of Clinical Psychiatry,* 69, 12–22.

Putnam, F. W. (1989). *Diagnosis and treatment of multiple personality disorder.* New York, NY: Guilford Press.

Putnam, F. W. (1993). Dissociative disorders in children: Behavioral profiles and problems. *Child Abuse & Neglect, 17,* 39–45.

Putnam, F. W., Guroff, J. J., Silberman, E. K., Barban, L., & Post, R. M. (1986). The clinical phenomenology of multiple personality disorder: Review of 100 recent cases. *Journal of Clinical Psychiatry, 47,* 285–293.

Q

Qin, P., Agerbo, E., & Mortensen, P. B. (2002). Suicide risk in relation to family history of completed suicide and psychiatric disorders: A nested case-control study based on longitudinal registers. *Lancet, 360,* 1126–1130.

Qin, P., & Nordentoft, M. (2005). Suicide risk in relation to psychiatric hospitalization: Evidence based on longitudinal registers. *Archives of General Psychiatry, 62,* 427–432.

Qualls, S. H., Segal, D. L., Benight, C. C., & Kenny, M. P. (2005). Geropsychology training in a specialist geropsychology doctoral program. *Gerontology and Geriatrics Education, 25,* 21–40.

Quan, D. (2015, March 26). Suicide by plane extremely rare but "suck it up" culture exists among pilots over mental health. *National Post.* Retrieved March 31, 2015 from http://news.nationalpost.com/2015/03/26/suicide-by-plane-extremely-rare-but-suck-it-up-culture-exists-among-pilots-over-mental-health/.

Quay, H. C. (1965). Psychopathic personality as pathological stimulation-seeking. *American Journal of Psychiatry, 122,* 180–183.

Quist, J. F., Barr, C. L., Schachar, R., Roberts, W., Malone, M., Tannock, R., . . . Kennedy, J. L. (2003). The serotonin 5-HT1B receptor gene and attention deficit hyperactivity disorder. *Molecular Psychiatry, 8,* 98–102.

R

Radloff, L. S. (1977). The CES-D Scale: A self-report depression acale for research in the general population. *Applied Psychological Measurement, 1,* 385–401.

Rahman, Q., & Wilson, G. D. (2003). Born gay? The psychobiology of human sexual orientation. *Personality and Individual Differences, 34,* 1337–1382.

Raikkonen, K., Matthews, K. A., Flory, J. D., Owens, J. F., & Gump, B. B. (1999). Effects of optimism, pessimism, and trait anxiety on ambulatory blood pressure and mood during everyday life. *Journal of Personality and Social Psychology, 76,* 104–113.

Ramage-Morin, P. L., & Gilmour, H. (2010). Chronic pain at ages 12 to 44. *Health Reports, 21,* 53–61.

Ramchandani, P. G., Hotopf, M., Sandhu, B., Stein, A., & the ALSPAC Study Team. (2005). The epidemiology of recurrent abdominal pain from 2 to 6 years of age: Results of a large, population-based study. *Pediatrics, 116,* 46–50.

Ranta, K., Kaltiala-Heino, R., Rantanen, P., & Marttunen, M. (2009). Social phobia in Finnish general adolescent population: Prevalence, comorbidity, individual and family correlates, and service use. *Depression and Anxiety, 26,* 528–536.

Raphael, K. G., Widom, C. S., & Lange, G. (2001). Childhood victimization and pain in adulthood: A prospective investigation. *Pain, 92,* 283–293.

Rapoport, J. L., Addington, A. M., Frangou, S., & Psych, M. R. (2005). The neurodevelopmental model of schizophrenia: Update 2005. *Molecular Psychiatry, 10,* 434–449.

Raskind, M., Bonner, L. T., & Reskind, E. R. (2004). Cognitive disorders. In D. G. Blazer, D. C. Steffens, & E. W. Busse (Eds.), *Textbook of geriatric psychiatry* (3rd ed., pp. 207–229). Washington, DC: American Psychiatric Publishing, Inc.

Rasmussen, H. N., Scheier, M. F., & Greenhouse, J. B. (2009). Optimism and physical health: A meta-analytic review. *Annals of Behavior Medicine, 37,* 239–256.

Read, J., Kahler, C., & Stevenson, J. (2001). Bridging the gap between alcoholism treatment research and practice: Identifying what works and why. *Professional Psychology: Research and Practice, 32,* 227–238.

Reagan, P., & Hersch, J. (2005). Influence of race, gender, and socioeconomic status on binge eating frequency in a population-based sample. *International Journal of Eating Disorders, 38,* 252–256.

Rebach, H. (1992). Alcohol and drug use among ethnic minorities. In J. Trimble, C. Bolek, & S. Niemcryk (Eds.), *Ethnic and multicultural drug abuse: Perspective on current research* (pp. 23–57). New York, NY: Haworth Press.

Reck, C., Stehle, E., Reinig, & Mundt, K. C. (2009). Maternity blues as a predictor of DSM-IV depression and anxiety disorders in the first three months postpartum. *Journal of Affective Disorders, 113,* 77–87.

Reichborn-Kjennerud, T., Bulik, C. M., Tambs, K., & Harris, J. (2004). Genetic and environmental influences on binge eating in the absence of compensatory behaviours: A population-based twin study. *International Journal of Eating Disorders, 36,* 307–314.

Reichenberg, A., Gross, R., Weiser, M., Bresnahan, M., Silverman, J., Harlap, S., & Centers for Disease Control and Prevention. (2006). Advance paternal age and autism. *Archives of General Psychiatry, 63,* 1026–1032.

Reisberg, B., Doody, R., Stoffler, A., Schmitt, F., Ferris, S., & Mobius, H. J. (2003). Memantine in moderate-to-severe Alzheimer's disease. *New England Journal of Medicine, 348,* 1333–1341.

Reissing, E. D., Binik, Y. M., Khalifé, S., Cohen, D., & Amsel, R. (2004). Vaginal spasm, pain and behavior: An empirical investigation of the diagnosis of vaginismus. *Archives of Sexual Behavior, 33,* 5–17.

Reitan, R. L., & Davidson. (1974). *Halstead-Reitan Neuropsychological Battery.* Reitan Neuropsychology Laboratories, University of Arizona.

Rekers, G. A., & Lovaas, O. I. (1974). Behavioral treatment of deviant sex-role behaviors in a male child. *Journal of Applied Behavior Analysis, 7,* 173–190.

Rekers, G. A., Lovaas, O. I., & Low, B. (1974). The behavioral treatment of a "transsexual" preadolescent boy. *Journal of Abnormal Child Psychology, 2,* 99–116.

Rekers, G. A., & Mead, S. (1979). Early intervention for female sexual identity disturbance: Self-monitoring of play behavior. *Journal of Abnormal Child Psychology, 7,* 405–423.

Remschmidt, H., & Theisen, F. M. (2005). Schizophrenia and related disorders in children and adolescents. *Journal of Neural Transmission Supplement, 69,* 121–141.

Repetti, R. L., Taylor, S. E., & Seeman, T. E. (2002). Risky families: Family social environments and the mental and physical health of offspring. *Psychological Bulletin, 128,* 230–266.

Research Units on Pediatric Psychopharmacology (RUPP) Autism Network. (2005). Randomized, controlled, crossover trial of methylphenidate in pervasive developmental disorders with hyperactivity. *Archives of General Psychiatry, 62,* 1266–1274.

Resnicow, K., Jackson, A., Wang, T., de Anindya, K., McCarty, F., Dudley, W. N., . . . Baranowski, T. (2001). A motivational interviewing intervention to increase fruit and vegetable intake through black churches: Results of the Eat for Life trial. *American Journal of Public Health, 91,* 1686–1693.

Rettew, D. C. (2000). Avoidant personality disorder, generalized social phobia, and shyness: Putting the personality back into personality disorders. *Harvard Review of Psychiatry, 8,* 283–297.

Rettew, D. C., Rebollo-Mesa, I., Hudziak, J. J., Willemsen, G., & Boomsma, D. I. (2008). Non-additive and additive genetic effects on extraversion in 3314 Dutch adolescent twins and their parents. *Behavior Genetics, 38,* 223–233.

Rice, M. E., & Harris, G. T. (2002). Men who molest their sexually immature daughters: Is a special explanation required? *Journal of Abnormal Psychology, 111,* 329–339.

Richardson, S. A., Katz, M., & Koller, H. (1986). Sex differences in number of children administratively classified as mildly mentally retarded: An epidemiological review. *American Journal of Mental Deficiency, 91,* 250–256.

Rickels, K., Downing, R., Schweizer, E., & Hassman, H. (1993). Antidepressants for the treatment of generalized anxiety disorder: A placebo-controlled comparison of imipramine, trazodone, and diazepam. *Archives of General Psychiatry, 50,* 884–895.

Rickels, K., Pollack, M. H., Sheehan, D. V., & Haskins, J. T. (2000). Efficacy of extended-release venlafaxine in nondepressed outpatients with generalized anxiety disorder. *American Journal of Psychiatry, 157,* 968–974.

Rieber, R. W. (1999). Hypnosis, false memory and multiple personality: A trinity of affinity. *History of Psychiatry, 10,* 3–11.

Rimmele, C., Howard, M., & Hilfrink, M. (1995). Aversion therapies. In R. Hester & W. R. Miller (Eds.), *Handbook of alcoholism treatment approaches: Effective alternatives* (2nd ed., pp. 134–147). Needham Heights, MA: Allyn & Bacon.

Ritchie, M. (2008). Stephanie Donnelly was wrong target. *Kitimat Daily.* Retrieved April 22, 2008 from http://www.kitimatdaily.ca/go683a/STEPHANIE_DONNELLY_WAS_WRONG_TARGET.

Robbins, J. M., & Kirmayer, L. J. (1996). Transient and persistent hypochondriacal worry in primary care. *Psychological Medicine, 26,* 575–589.

Robertson, E., Jones, I., Haque, S., Holer, R., & Craddock, N. (2005). Risk of puerperal and non-puerperal recurrence of illness following bipolar affective puerperal (post-partum) psychosis. *British Journal of Psychiatry, 186,* 258–259.

Robertson, I., & Cairns, A. (2000). Horror on the subway: Toronto doctor throws herself and six-month-old son in front of moving train. *Toronto Sun,* August 12.

Robins, L., & Slobodyan, S. (2003). Post-Vietnam heroin use and injection by returning US veterans: Clues to preventing injection today. *Addiction, 98,* 1053–1060.

Robinson, T. N., Matheson, D. M., Kraemer, H. C., Wilson, D. M., . . . Killen, J. D. (2010). A randomized controlled trial of culturally tailored dance and reducing screen time to prevent weight gain in low-income African American girls: Stanford GEMS. *Archives of Pediatric and Adolescent Medicine, 164,* 995–1004.

Roccatagliata, G. (1997). Classical psychopathology. In W. G. Bringman, H. E. Lück, R. Miller, & C. Early (Eds.), *A pictorial history of psychology* (pp. 383–390). Carol Stream, IL: Quintessence Publishing Co.

Rode, S., Salkovskis, P. M., & Jack, T. (2001). An experimental study of attention, labeling and memory in people suffering from chronic pain. *Pain, 94,* 193–203.

Rodebaugh, T. L., Holaway, R. M., & Heimberg, R. G. (2004). The treatment of social anxiety disorder. *Clinical Psychology Review, 24,* 883–908.

Rogers, D. D., & Abas, N. (1988). A survey of native mental health needs in Manitoba. *Arctic Medical Research, 47 (Suppl. 1),* 576–580.

Rogler, L. H. (1999). Methodological sources of cultural insensitivity in mental health research. *American Psychologist, 54,* 424–433.

Rohan, K. J., Lindsey, K. T., Roecklein, K. A., & Lacy, T. J. (2004). Cognitive-behavioral therapy, light therapy, and their combination in treating seasonal affective disorder. *Journal of Affective Disorders, 80,* 273–283.

Rohde, P., Lewinsohn, P., Kahler, C., Seeley, J., & Brown, R. (2001). Natural course of alcohol use disorders from adolescence to young adulthood. *Journal of the American Academy of Child and Adolescent Psychiatry, 40,* 83–90.

Rohleder, N., Schommer, N. C., Hellhammer, D. H., Engel, R., & Kirschbaum, C. (2001). Sex differences in glucocorticoid sensitivity of proinflammatory cytokine production after psychosocial stress. *Psychosomatic Medicine, 63,* 966–972.

Rohsenow, D., Niaura, R., Childress, A., Abrams, D., & Monti, P. (1990). Cue reactivity in addictive behaviors: Theoretical and treatment implications. *International Journal of the Addictions, 25,* 957–993.

Roid, G. H., & Miller, L. J. (2013). *Leiter International Performance Scale* (3rd ed.). Torrance, CA: Western Psychological Services.

Roll, J., Petry, N., Stitzer, M., Brecht, M., Peirce, J., McCann, M., . . . Kellogg, S. (2006). Contingency management for the treatment of methamphetamine use disorders. *American Journal of Psychiatry, 163,* 1993–1999.

Röpcke, B., & Eggers, C. (2005). Early-onset schizophrenia. *European Child & Adolescent Psychiatry, 14,* 341–350.

Rosario-Campos, M. C., Leckman, J. F., Mercadante, M. R., Shavitt, R. G., Prado, H. D., Sada, P., . . . Miguel, E. C. (2001). Adults with early-onset obsessive-compulsive disorder. *American Journal of Psychiatry, 158,* 1899–1903.

Rose, E. A., Porcecelli, J. H., & Neale, A. V. (2000). Pica: Common but commonly missed. *Journal of the American Board of Family Practice, 13,* 353–358.

Rosenberg, S. D., Goodman, L. A., Osher, F. G., Swartz, M. S., Essock, S. M., Butterfield, M. I., . . . Salyers, M. P. (2001). Prevalence of HIV, hepatitis B and hepatitis C in people with severe mental illness. *American Journal of Public Health, 91,* 31–37.

Rosenvinge, J. H., Martinussen, M., & Ostensen, E. (2000). The comorbidity of eating disorders and personality disorders: A meta-analytic review of studies published between 1983 and 1998. *Eating and Weight Disorders, 5,* 52–61.

Rösler, A., & Witztum, E. (2000). Pharmacotherapy of paraphilias in the next millennium. *Behavioral Sciences and the Law, 18,* 43–56.

Ross, C. A. (1997). *Dissociative identity disorder: Diagnosis, clinical features and treatment of multiple personality.* New York, NY: John Wiley & Sons.

Ross, D. A. (2010). Behavioural interventions to reduce HIV risk: What works? *AIDS, 24,* S4–S14.

Roth, B., & Shapiro, D. (2001). Insights into the structure and function of 5-HT2 family serotonin receptors reveal novel strategies for therapeutic target development. *Expert Opinion on Therapeutic Targets, 5,* 685–695.

Rothbaum, B. O., Hodges, L., Anderson, P. L., Price, L., & Smith, S. (2002). Twelve-month follow-up of virtual reality and standard exposure therapies for the fear of flying. *Journal of Consulting and Clinical Psychology, 70,* 428–432.

Roubertoux, P. L., & Kerdelhúe, B. (2006). Trisomy 21: From chromosomes to mental retardation. *Behavior Genetics, 36,* 346–354.

Roundy, K., Cully, J. A., Stanley, M. A., Veazey, C., Souchek, J., Wray, N. P., & Kunik, M. E. (2005). Are anxiety and depression addressed in primary care patients with chronic obstructive pulmonary disease? A chart review. *Primary Care Companion to the Journal of Clinical Psychiatry, 7,* 213–218.

Rowe, R., Costello, E. J., Angold, A., Copeland, W. E., & Maughan, B. (2010). Developmental pathways in oppositional defiant disorder and conduct disorder. *Journal of Abnormal Psychology, 119,* 726–738.

Rowland, D., Perelman, M., Althof, S., Barada, J., McCullough, A., Bull, S., . . . Ho, K. F. (2004). Self-reported premature ejaculation and aspects of sexual functioning and satisfaction. *Journal of Sexual Medicine, 1,* 225–232.

Roy-Byrne, P. P., Craske, M. G., Stein, M. B., Sullivan, G., Bystritsky, A., Katon, W., Golinelli, D., & Sherbourne, C. D. (2005). A randomized effectiveness trial of cognitive-behavioral therapy and medication for primary care panic disorder. *Archives of General Psychiatry, 62,* 290–298.

Roy-Byrne, P. P., Sherbourne, C. D., Craske, M. G., Stein, M. B., Katon, W., Sullivan, G., Means-Christensen, A., & Bystritsky, A. (2003). Moving treatment research from clinical trials to the real world. *Psychiatric Services, 54,* 327–332.

Ruitenberg, A., van Swieten, J. C., Witteman, J. C., Mehta, K. M., van Duijn, C. M., Hofman, A., & Breteler, M. M. (2002). Alcohol consumption and risk of -dementia: The Rotterdam Study. *Lancet, 359,* 281–286.

Russell, G. F. M. (1979). Bulimia nervosa: An ominous variant of anorexia nervosa. *Psychological Medicine, 9,* 429–448.

Russell, G. F. M., Szmukler, G. I., Dare, C., & Eisler, I. (1987). An evaluation of family therapy in anorexia and bulimia nervosa. *Archives of General Psychiatry, 44,* 1047–1056.

Russell, G., Kelly, S., & Golding, J. (2009). A qualitative analysis of lay beliefs about the aetiology and prevalence of autistic spectrum disorders. *Child Care, Health, and Development, 36,* 431–436.

Rutter, M. (1978). Diagnosis and definitions of childhood autism. *Journal of Autism and Developmental Disorders, 8,* 139–161.

Rutter, M. (2005). Incidence of autism spectrum disorders: Changes over time and their meaning. *Acta Pediatrica, 94,* 2–15.

Rutter, M., Tizard, J., Yule, W., Graham, P., & Whitmore, K. (1976). Research report: Isle of Wight Studies, 1964–1974. *Psychological Medicine, 6,* 313–332.

Rybarczyk, B., Stepanski, E., Fogg, L., Lopez, M., Barry, P., & Davis, A. (2005). A placebo-controlled test of cognitive-behavioral therapy for comorbid insomnia in older adults. *Journal of Consulting and Clinical Psychology, 73,* 1164–1174.

S

Saba, G., Verdon, C. M., Kalalou, K., Rocamora, J. F., Dumortier, G., Benadhira, R., . . . Januel, D. (2006). Transcranial magnetic stimulation in the treatment of schizophrenic symptoms: A double blind sham controlled study. *Journal of Psychiatric Research, 4,* 147–152.

Sagan, C. (1996). *The demon-haunted world: Science as a candle in the dark.* New York, NY: Ballantine Books.

Sakauye, K. (2004). Ethnocultural aspects of aging in mental health. In J. Sadavoy, L. F. Jarvik, G. T. Grossberg, & B. S. Meyers (Eds.), *Comprehensive textbook of geriatric psychiatry* (pp. 225–250). New York, NY: W. W. Norton & Co.

Salaberria, K., & Echeburua, E. (1998). Long-term outcome of cognitive therapy's contribution to self-exposure in vivo to the treatment of generalized social phobia. *Behavior Modification, 22,* 262–284.

Salkovskis, P. M. (1989). Somatic problems. In K. Hawton, P. M. Salkovskis, J. Kirk, & D. M. Clark (Eds.), *Cognitive-behavior therapy for psychiatric problems* (pp. 235–276). Oxford,UK: Oxford University Press.

Salmon, P. (2001). Effects of physical exercise on anxiety, depression, and sensitivity to stress: A unifying theory. *Clinical Psychology Review, 21,* 33–61.

Sanchez, J., Ladd, C., & Plotsky, P. (2001). Early adverse experiences as developmental risk factor for later psychopathology: Evidence from rodent and primate models. *Development and Psychopathology, 13,* 419–449.

Sandberg, D. E., Meyer-Bahlburg, H. F., Ehrhardt, A. A., & Yager, T. J. (1993). The prevalence of gender-atypical behavior in elementary school children. *Journal of the American Academy of Child and Adolescent Psychiatry, 32,* 306–314.

Sanders, J. (2014). Looking further upstream to prevent fetal alcohol spectrum disorder in Canada. *Canadian Journal of Public Health, 105,* e450–e452.

Sands, J. R., & Harrow, M. (1999). Depression during the longitudinal course of schizophrenia. *Schizophrenia Bulletin, 25,* 157–171.

Santayana, G. (1905). *The life of reason* (vol. 1). New York, NY: Scribner's.

Şar, V., Unal, S. N., Kiziltan, E., Kundakci, T., & Ozturk, E. (2001). HMPAO SPECT study of regional cerebral blood flow in dissociative identity disorder. *Journal of Trauma & Dissociation, 2,* 5–25.

Sartorius, N., Jablensky, A., & Shapiro, R. (1978). Cross-cultural differences in the short-term prognosis of schizophrenic psychosis. *Schizophrenia Bulletin, 4,* 102–113.

Saunders, J., & Procuta, E. (2009). Coroner probing subway suicide. *Globe and Mail.* Retrieved June 30, 2015 from http://www.theglobeandmail.com/news/national/coroner-probing-subway-suicide/article1041839/.

Scammell, T., & Saper, C. B. (2005). Orexin, drugs and motivated behaviors. *Nature Neuroscience, 8,* 1286–1288.

Scarborough, H. S. (1990). Very early language deficits in dyslexic children. *Child Development, 61,* 1728–1743.

Schienle, A., Schafer, A., Hermann, A., Vaitl, D. (2009). Binge-eating disorder: reward sensitivity and brain activation to images of food. *Biological Psychiatry, 65,* 654–661.

Schiffman, J., Walker, E., Ekstrom, M., Schulsinger, F., Sorensen, H., & Mednick, S. (2004). Childhood videotaped social and neuromotor precursors of schizophrenia: A prospective investigation. *American Journal of Psychiatry, 161,* 2021–2027.

Schizophrenia Psychiatric Genome-Wide Association Study (GWAS) Consortium (2011). Genome-wide association study identifies five new schizophrenia loci. *Nature Genetics, 43,* 969–976.

Schneider, J. P. (2003). The impact of compulsive cybersex behaviours on the family. *Sexual and Relationship Therapy, 18,* 329–354.

Schneider, L. S. (1996). Pharmacologic considerations in the treatment of late-life depression. *American Journal of Geriatric Psychiatry, 4,* S51–S65.

Schneider, L. S., Dagerman, K. S., & Insel, P. (2005). Risk of death with atypical antipsychotic drug treatment for dementia: Meta-analysis of randomized placebo-controlled trials. *Journal of the American Medical Association, 294,* 1934–1943.

Schneider, L. S., Dagerman, K., & Insel, P. S. (2006). Efficacy and adverse effects of atypical antipsychotics for dementia: Meta-analysis of randomized, placebo-controlled trials. *American Journal of Geriatric Psychiatry, 14,* 191–210.

Schneider, R. D., Glancy, G. D., Bradford, J. M., & Seibenmorgen, E. (2000). Canadian landmark case, Winko v. British Columbia: Revisiting the conundrum of the mentally disordered accused. *Journal of the American Academy of Psychiatry and Law, 28,* 206–212.

Schoenmakers, B., Buntinx, F., & Delepeleire, J. (2010). Factors determining the impact of care-giving on caregivers of elderly patients with dementia. *A systematic literature review, 66,* 191–200.

Schoevers, R. A., Deeg, D. J., van Tilburg, . W., & Beekman, A. T. (2005). Depression and generalized anxiety disorder: Co-occurrence and longitudinal patterns in elderly patients. *American Journal of Geriatric Psychiatry, 13,* 31–39.

Schooler, N. R., Keith, S. J., Severe, J. B., Matthews, S. M., Bellack, A. S., Glick, I. D., . . . Woerner, M. G. (1997). Relapse and rehospitalization during maintenance treatment of schizophrenia: The effects of dose reduction and family treatment. *Archives of General Psychiatry, 54,* 453–463.

Schopflocher, D., Taenzer, P., & Jovey, R. (2011). The prevalence of chronic pain in Canada. *Pain Research and Management, 16,* 445–450.

Schuller, R. A., & Ogloff, J. R. P. (2000). *Introduction to psychology and law: Canadian perspectives.* Toronto: University of Toronto Press.

Schultz, R. T., Grelotti, D. J., Klin, A., Levitan, E., Cantey, T., Gore, J. C., . . . Cohen, D. J. . (2001). *An fMRI study of face recognition, facial expression detection, and social judgment in autism spectrum disorders.* International Meeting for Autism Research, San Diego, CA.

Schultz, S. K., Hoth, A., & Buckwalter, K. (2004). Anxiety and impaired social function in the elderly. *Annals of Clinical Psychiatry, 16,* 47–51.

Schuurmans, J., Comijs, H. C., Beekman, A. T., de Beurs, E., Deeg, D. J., Emmelkamp, P. M., & van Dyck, R. (2005). The outcome of anxiety disorders in older people at 6-year follow-up: Results from the Longitudinal Aging Study Amsterdam. *Acta Psychiatrica Scandinavia, 111,* 420–428.

Schuurmans, J., Comijs, H., Emmelkamp, P. M., Gundy, C. M., Weijnen, I., van denHout, M., & van Dyck, R. (2006). A randomized, controlled trial of the effectiveness of cognitive-behavioral therapy and sertraline versus a waitlist control group for anxiety disorders in older adults. *American Journal of Geriatric Psychiatry, 14,* 255–263.

Scott-Sheldon, L. A., Kalichman, S. C., Carey, M. P., & Fielder, R. L. (2008). Stress management interventions for HIV+ adults: A meta-analysis of randomized controlled trials, 1989 to 2006. *Health Psychology, 27,* 129–139.

Scoville, W. B., & Milner, B. (1957). Loss of recent memory after bilateral hippocampal lesions. *Journal of Neurology, Neurosurgery & Psychiatry, 20,* 11–21.

Scull, A. (2004). The insanity of place. *History of Psychiatry, 15,* 417–436.

Sechrest, L., & Coan, J. (2002). Preparing psychologists to prescribe. *Journal of Clinical Psychology, 58,* 649–658.

Sedlak, A. J., & Broadhurst, D. D. (1996). *Executive summary for the Third National Incidence Study of Child Abuse and Neglect.* Washington, DC: U.S. Department of Health and Human Services: Administration for Children and Families; Administration on Children, Youth and Families; National Center on Child Abuse and Neglect.

Seeman, M. V. (1996). The role of estrogen in schizophrenia. *Journal of Psychiatry and Neuroscience, 21,* 123–127.

Seeman, M. V. (1998). Narratives of twenty- to thirty-year outcomes in schizophrenia. *Psychiatry, 61,* 249–261.

Seftel, A. D., & Althof, S. E (2000). Rapid ejaculation. *Current Urological Reports, 1,* 302–306.

Seignourel, P. J., Kunik, M. E., Snow, L., Wilson, N., & Stanley, M. A. (2008). Anxiety in dementia: A critical review. *Clinical Psychology Review, 28,* 1071–1082.

Seles, M. (2009). *Getting a grip: On my body, my mind, my self.* New York, NY: Penguin.

Seligman, M. (1975). *Helplessness: On depression, development, and death.* San Francisco, CA: W. H. Freeman.

Selye, H. (1956). *General adaptation syndrome (GAS).* New York, NY: McGraw-Hill.

Semans, J. H. (1956). Premature ejaculation: A new approach. *Southern Medical Journal, 49,* 353–358.

Sergeant, J. A., Geurts, H., & Oosterlaan, J. (2002). How specific is a deficit of executive functioning for attention-deficit/hyperactivity disorder? *Behavioural Brain Research, 130,* 3–28.

Seto, M. C. (2001). The value of phallometry in the assessment of male sex offenders. *Journal of Forensic Psychology Practice, 1,* 65–75.

Severeijns, R., Vlaeyen, J. W., van den Hout, M. A., & Picavet, H. S. (2004). Pain catastrophizing is associated with health indices in musculoskeletal pain: A cross-sectional study in the Dutch community. *Health Psychology, 23,* 49–57.

Shaffer, D., Gould, M. S., Fisher, P., Trautman, P., Moreau, D., Kleinman, M., & Flory, M. (1996). Psychiatric diagnosis in child and adolescent suicide. *Archives of General Psychiatry, 53,* 339–348.

Shah, S. G., Klumpp, H., Angstadt, M., Nathan, P. J., & Phan, K. L. (2009). Amygdala and insula response to emotional images in patients with generalized social anxiety disorder. *Journal of Psychiatry and Neuroscience, 34,* 296–302.

Shanmugham, B., Karp, J., Drayer, R., Reynolds, C. F. III, & Alexopoulos, G. (2005). Evidence-based pharmacologic interventions for geriatric depression. *Psychiatric Clinics of North America, 28,* 821–835.

Shapiro, J. R., Berkman, N. D., Brownley, K. A., Sedway, J. A., Lohr, K. N., & Bulik, C. M. (2007). Bulimia nervosa treatment: A systematic review of randomized controlled trials. *International Journal of Eating Disorders,* 321–336.

Sharma, B. R. (2007). Gender identity disorder and its medico-legal considerations. *Medicine, Science, and the Law, 47,* 31–40.

Shavers, V., Lynch, D., & Burmeister, L. (2002). Racial differences in factors that influence the willingness to participate in medical research. *Annals of Epidemiology, 12,* 248–256.

Shaywitz, S. E., Gruen, J. R., & Shaywitz, B. A. (2007). Management of dyslexia, its rationale, and underlying neurobiology. *Pediatric Clinics of North America, 54,* 609–623.

Sheikh, A. (2006). Why are ethnic minorities under-represented in US research studies? *PLOS Medicine, 3,* e49.

Sheikh, J. I., & Yesavage, J. A. (1986). Geriatric depression scal (GDS): recent evidence and development of a shorter version. *Clinical Gerontologist, 5,* 165–173.

Sheridan, M. S. (2003). The deceit continues: An updated literature review of Munchausen syndrome by proxy. *Child Abuse & Neglect, 27,* 431–451.

Sherman, C. (2005). Dopamine enhancement underlies a toluene behavioral effect. *NIDA Notes, 19,* 4–5.

Sherman, S. L., Allen, E. G., Bean, L. H., & Freeman, S. B. (2007). Epidemiology of Down syndrome. *Mental Retardation and Developmental Disabilities, 13,* 221–227.

Sherry, S. B., Sabourin, B. C., Hall, P. A., Hewitt, P. L., Flett, G. L., & Gralnick, T. M. (2014). The perfectionism model of binge eating: Testing unique contributions, mediating mechanisms, and cross-cultural similarities using a daily diary methodology. *Psychology of Addictive Behaviors, 28,* 1230–1239.

Shiffman, S., Hickcox, M., Paty, J., Gnys, M., Kassel, J., & Richards, T. (1997). The abstinence violation effect following smoking lapses and temptations. *Cognitive Therapy and Research, 21,* 497–523.

Shin, L. M., Wright, C. I., Cannistraro, P. A., Wedig, M. M., McMullin, K., Martis, B., . . . Rauch, S. L. (2005). A functional magnetic resonance imaging study of amygdala and medial prefrontal cortex responses to overtly presented fearful faces in posttraumatic stress disorder. *Archives of General Psychiatry, 62,* 273–281.

Shiren, J. L., Braunstein, G. D., Simon, J. A., Casson, P. R., Buster, J. E., Redmond, G. P., . . . Mazer, N. A. (2000). Transdermal testosterone treatment in women with impaired sexual function after oophorectomy. *New England Journal of Medicine, 343,* 682–688.

Shuttleworth-Edwards, A. B., Kemp, R. D., Rust, A. L., Muirhead, J. G., Hartman, N. P., & Radloff, S. E. (2004). Cross-cultural effects on IQ test performance: A review and preliminary normative indications on WAIS-III test performance. *Journal of Clinical and Experimental Neuropsychology, 26,* 903–920.

Siegel, K., & Schrimshaw, E. W. (2007). The stress moderating role of benefit finding on psychological distress and well-being among women living with HIV/AIDS. *AIDS and Behavior, 11,* 421–433.

Siegel, S., Baptista, M. A., Kim, J. A., McDonald, R. V., & Weise-Kelly, L. (2000). Pavlovian psychopharmacology: The associative basis of tolerance. *Experimental and Clinical Psychopharmacology, 8,* 276–293.

Siever, L. J., Koenigsberg, H. W., Harvey, P., Mitropoulou, V., Laruelle, M., Abi-Dargham, A., . . . Buchsbaum, M. (2002). Cognitive and brain function in schizotypal personality disorder. *Schizophrenia Research, 54,* 157–167.

Sigerist, H. E. (1943). *Civilization and disease.* Ithaca, NY: Cornell University Press.

Sijbrandij, M., Olff, M., Reitsma, J. B., Carlier, I. V. E., & Gersons, B. P. R. (2006). Emotional or educational debriefing after psychological trauma. *British Journal of Psychiatry, 189,* 150–155.

Silagy, C., Lancaster, T., Stead, L., Mant, D., & Fowler, G. (2004). Nicotine replacement therapy for smoking cessation. *Cochrane Database of Systematic Reviews, 3,* CD000146.

Silber, M. H., Ancoli-Israel, S., Bonnet, M. H., Chokroverty, S., Grigg-Damberger, M. M., Hirshkowitz, M., . . . Iber, C. (2007). The visual scoring of sleep in adults. *Journal of Clinical Sleep Medicine, 3,* 121–131.

Silveira, J. M., & Seeman, M. V. (1995). Shared psychotic disorder: A critical review of the literature. *Canadian Journal of Psychiatry, 40,* 389–395.

Silverman, J. M., Smith, C. J., Marin, D. B., Mohs, R. C., & Propper, C. B. (2003). Familial patterns of risk in very late-onset Alzheimer disease. *Archives of General Psychiatry, 60,* 190–197.

Silverman, W. K., & Dick-Niederhauser, A. (2004). Separation anxiety disorder. In T. L. Morris & J. S. March (Eds.), Anxiety disorders in children and adolescents (pp. 164–188). New York, NY: Guilford.

Simansky, K. J. (2005). NIH symposium series: Ingestive mechanisms in obesity, substance abuse and mental disorders. *Physiology and Behavior, 86,* 1–4.

Simeon, D., Guralnik, O., Knutelska, M., Hollander, E., & Schmeidler, J. (2001a). Hypothalamic-pituitary-adrenal axis dysregulation in depersonalization disorder. *Neuropsychopharmacology, 25,* 793–795.

Simeon, D., Guralnik, O., Schmeidler, J., Sirof, B., & Knutelska, M. (2001b). The role of childhood interpersonal trauma in depersonalization disorder. *American Journal of Psychiatry, 158,* 1027–1033.

Simeon, D., Knutelska, M., Nelson, D., & Guralnik, O. (2003). Feeling unreal: A depersonalization disorder update of 117 cases. *Journal of Clinical Psychiatry, 64,* 990–997.

Simon, G. E., VonKorff, M., Piccinelli, M., Fullerton, C., & Ormel, J. (1999). An international study of the relation between somatic symptoms and depression. *New England Journal of Medicine, 341,* 1329–1335.

Simpson, D., Joe, G., Rowan-Szal, G., & Greener, J. (1997). Drug abuse treatment process components that improve retention. *Journal of Substance Abuse Treatment, 14,* 565–572.

Sinadinovic, K., Berman, A. H., Hasson, D., & Wennberg, P. (2010). Internet-based assessment and self-monitoring of problematic alcohol and drug use. *Addictive Behaviors, 35,* 464–470.

Singh, S. P., & Lee, A. S. (1997). Conversion disorders in Nottingham: Alive, but not kicking. *Journal of Psychosomatic Research, 43,* 425–430.

Sinyor, M., & Levitt, A. J. (2010). Effect of a barrier at Bloor Street Viaduct on suicide rates in Toronto: Natural experiment. *BMJ online, 341,* c2884.

Sitzer, D. I., Twamley, E. W., & Jeste, D. V. (2006). Cognitive training in Alzheimer's disease: A meta-analysis of the literature. *Acta Psychiatrica Scandinavia, 114,* 75–90.

Sivec, H. J., & Lynn, S. J. (1995). Dissociative and neuropsychological symptoms: The question of differential diagnosis. *Clinical Psychology Review, 15,* 297–316.

Sjögren Fugl-Meyer, K., & Fugl-Meyer, A. R. (2002). Sexual disabilities are not singularities. *International Journal of Impotence Research, 14,* 487–493.

Skeem, J. L., Poythress, N., Edens, J. F., Lilienfeld, S. O., & Cale, E. M. (2003). Psychopathic personality or personalities? Exploring potential variants of psychopathy and their implications for risk assessment. *Aggression and Violent Behavior, 8,* 513–546.

Skeem, J. L., Schubert, C., Odgers, C., Mulvey, E. P., Gardner, W., & Lidz, C. (2006). Psychiatric symptoms and community violence among high-risk patients: A test of the relationship at the weekly level. *Journal of Consulting and Clinical Psychology, 74,* 967–979.

Skinner, B. (1953). *Science and human behavior.* New York, NY: Free Press.

Skodol, A. E., Oldham, J. M., & Gallaher, P. E. (1999). Axis II comorbidity of substance use disorders among patients referred for treatment of personality disorders. *American Journal of Psychiatry, 156,* 733–738.

Slagboom, P., & Meulenbelt, I. (2002). Organisation of the human genome and our tools for identifying disease genes. *Biological Psychology, 61,* 11–31.

Smith, B. H., Waschbusch, D. A., Willoughby, M. T., & Evans, S. (2000). The efficacy, safety, and practicality of treatments for adolescents with attention-deficit/hyperactivity disorder (ADHD). *Clinical Child and Family Psychology Review, 3,* 243–267.

Smith, D. E., Marcus, M. D., Lewis, C. E., Fitzgibbon, M., & Schreiner, P. (1998). Prevalence of binge eating disorder, obesity, and depression in a biracial cohort of young adults. *Annals of Behavioral Medicine, 20,* 227–232.

Smith, Y. L., van Goozen, S. H., & Cohen-Kettenis, P. T. (2001). Adolescents with gender identity disorder who were accepted or rejected for sex reassignment surgery: A prospective follow-up study. *Journal of the American Academy of Child and Adolescent Psychiatry, 40,* 472–481.

Smith, Y. L., van Goozen, S. H., Kuiper, A. J., & Cohen-Kettenis, P. T. (2005). Sex reassignment: Outcomes and predictors of treatment for adolescent and adult transsexuals. *Psychological Medicine, 35,* 89–99.

Smolak, L., Levine, M. P., & Thompson, J. K. (2001). The use of the sociocultural attitudes towards appearance questionnaire with middle school boys and girls. *International Journal of Eating Disorders, 29,* 216–223.

Sobell, M., & Sobell, L. (1973). Alcoholics treated by individualized behavior therapy: One year treatment outcomes. *Behavior Research and Therapy, 11,* 599–618.

Sobell, M., & Sobell, L. (1978). *Behavioral treatment of alcohol problems: Individualized therapy and controlled drinking.* New York, NY: Plenum Press.

Sobell, M. B., & Sobell, L. C. (1995). Controlled drinking after 25 years: How important was the great debate? *Addiction, 90,* 1149–1153.

Sobin, C., Blundell, M. L., & Karayiorgou, M. (2000). Phenotypic differences in early- and late-onset obsessive-compulsive disorder. *Comprehensive Psychiatry, 41,* 373–379.

Sochting, I. (2004). Painful pasts: Post-traumatic stress in women survivors of Canada's Indian residential schools. *Visions Journal, 2(4),* 13–14.

Sollman, M. J., Ranseen, J. D., & Berry, D. T. R. (2010). Detection of feigned ADHD in college students. *Psychological Assessment, 22,* 325–335.

Somers, T. J., Keefe, F. J., Godiwala, N., & Hoyler, G. H. (2009). Psychosocial factors and the pain experience of osteoarthritis patients: New findings and new directions. *Current Opinion in Rheumatology, 21,* 501–506.

Song, Y., Shiraishi, Y., & Nakamura, J. (2001). Digitalis intoxication misdiagnosed as depression-revisited [letter]. *Psychosomatics, 42,* 369–370.

Southern, S. (2008). Treatment of compulsive cybersex behavior. *Psychiatric Clinics of North America, 31,* 697–712.

Soykan, I., Chen, J., Kendall, B., & McCallum, R. W. (1997). The rumination syndrome: Clinical and manometric profile, therapy, and long-term outcome. *Digestive Diseases and Sciences, 42,* 1866–1872.

Spanos, N. P. (1994). Multiple identity enactments and multiple personality disorder: A sociocognitive perspective. *Psychological Bulletin, 116,* 143–165.

Spanos, N. P., Weekes, J. R., & Bertrand (1985). Multiple personality: A social psychological perspective. *Journal of Abnormal Psychology, 94,* 362–376.

Sparks, A., McDonald, S., Lino, B., O'Donnell, M., & Green, M. J. (2010). Social cognition, empathy, and functional outcome in schizophrenia. *Schizophrenia Research, 122,* 172–178.

Spencer, T. J., Biederman, J., & Mick, E. (2007). Attention-deficit/hyperactivity disorder: Diagnosis, lifespan, comorbidities, and neurobiology. *Ambulatory Pediatrics, 7,* 73–81.

Spencer, T. J., Biederman, J., & Wilens, T. (2004). Stimulant treatment of adult attention-deficit/hyperactivity disorder. *Psychiatric Clinics of North America, 27,* 361–372.

Spitzer, R. L., Williams, J. B. W., Kroenke, K., Linzer, M., deGruy, F. V., Hahn, S. R., . . . Johnson, J. G. (1994, December). Utility of a new procedure for diagnosing mental disorders in primary care: The PRIME-MD 1000 study. *Journal of the American Medical Association, 272*(22), 1749–1756.

Spriggs, M. (2006). Canaries in the mines: Children, risk, non-therapeutic research, and justice. *Journal of Medical Ethics, 30,* 176–181.

Springer, M. V., McIntosh, A. R., Winocur, G., & Grady, C. L. (2005). The relation between brain activity during memory tasks and years of education in young and older adults. *Neuropsychology, 19,* 181–192.

Stafford, J., & Lynn, S. J. (2002). Cultural scripts, memories of childhood abuse, and multiple identities: A study of role-played enactments. *International Journal of Clinical and Experimental Hypnosis, 50,* 67–85.

Stambor, Z. (2006). Psychology's prescribing pioneers. *APA Monitor on Psychology, 37,* 30.

Stanford, J. L., Feng, Z., Hamilton, A. S., Gilliland, F. D., Stephenson, R. A., Eley, J. W., . . . Potosky, A. L. (2000). Urinary and sexual function after radical prostatectomy for clinically localized prostate cancer: The Prostate Cancer Outcomes Study. *Journal of the American Medical Association, 283,* 354–360.

Stanley, M. A. (2003). Generalized anxiety disorder in late life. In D. J. Nutt, K. Rickels, & D. J. Stein (Eds.), *Generalized anxiety disorder: Symptomatology, pathogenesis, and management.* London, UK: Martin Dunitz Limited.

Stanley, M. A., & Novy, D. M. (2000). Cognitive-behavior therapy for generalized anxiety in late life: An evaluative overview. *Journal of Anxiety Disorders, 14,* 191–207.

Stanley, M. A., Roberts, R. E., Bourland, S. L., & Novy, D. M. (2001). Anxiety disorders among older primary care patients. *Journal of Clinical Geropsychology,* 7(2), 105–116.

Stanley, M. A., Wilson, N., Novy, D. M., Rhoades, H., Wagener, P., Greisinger, A. J., . . . Kunik, M. E. (2009). Cognitive behavior therapy for older adults with generalized anxiety disorder in primary care: A randomized clinical trial. *Journal of the American Medical Association, 301,* 1460–1467.

Stanley, M., Veazey, C., & Hopko, D. (2005). Anxiety and depression in chronic obstructive pulmonary disease: A new intervention and case report. *Cognitive and Behavioral Practice, 12,* 424–436.

Starkstein, S. E., Mizrahi, R., & Power, B. D. (2008). Depression in Alzheimer's disease: Phenomenology, clinical correlates and treatment. *International Review of Psychiatry, 20,* 382–388.

Statistics Canada. (1993). *Language, health and lifestyle issues: 1991 Aboriginal Peoples Survey* (Catalogue no. 89-533*).* Ottawa: Statistics Canada.

Statistics Canada (2004). *Canadian community health survey: Mental health and well-being.* Ottawa: Author.

Statistics Canada. (2007). *Participation and activity limitation survey.* Ottawa: Author.

Statistics Canada. (2012a). *Canadian community health survey: Mental health and well-being.* Ottawa: Author.

Statistics Canada. (2012b). *Canadian Internet use survey, 2012.* Retrieved from http://www.statcan.gc.ca/daily-quotidien/131126/dq131126d-eng.htm

Statistics Canada (2013a). *Hospital mental health database, 2012–2013.* Retrieved July 12, 2015 from http://www.google.ca/url?sa=t&rct=j&q=&esrc=s&source=web&cd=1&ved=0CB4QFjAA&url=http%3A%2F%2Fwww.cihi.ca%2Fweb%2Fresource%2Fen%2Featingdisord_2014_infosheet_en.pdf&ei=xPmiVZj0PMas-AHdhp6oBw&usg=AFQjCNHaviOcomqyLKUBW-F1owFYw3_DMw&sig2=mV2Wy9H3i4It5-YD1l0Vvw&bvm=bv.97653015,dcWw.

Statistics Canada (2013b). *Fruit and vegetable consumption, 2013.* Retrieved September 1, 2015 from http://www.statcan.gc.ca/pub/82-625-x/2014001/article/14018-eng.htm.

Steadman, H. J. (1983). Predicting dangerousness among the mentally ill: Art, magic, and science. *International Journal of Law and Psychiatry, 6,* 381–390.

Steckler, T., & Risbrough, V. (2012). Pharmacological treatment of PTSD – Established and new approaches. *Neuropharmacology, 62,* 617–627.

Steffens, B. A., & Rennie, R. L. (2006). The traumatic nature of disclosure for wives of sexual addicts. *Sexual Addiction and Compulsivity, 13,* 247–267.

Steffens, D. C., Hays, J. C., & Krishnan, K. R. (1999). Disability in geriatric depression. *American Journal of Geriatric Psychiatry, 7,* 34–40.

Steiger, H., Gauvin, L., Israel, M., Kin, N., Young, S., & Roussin, J. (2004). Serotonin function, personality-trait variations, and childhood abuse in women with bulimia-spectrum eating disorders. *Journal of Clinical Psychiatry, 65,* 830–837.

Steiger, H., Joober, R., Israël, M., Young, S., Ng Ying Kin, N., Gauvin, L., . . . Torkaman-Zehi, A. (2005). The 5HTTLPR polymorphism, psychopathological symptoms, and platelet paroxetine binding in bulimic syndromes. *International Journal of Eating Disorders, 37,* 57–60.

Stein, D. J. (2002). Obsessive-compulsive disorder. *Lancet, 360,* 397–405.

Stein, D. J., & Hugo, F. J. (2004). Neuropsychiatric aspects of anxiety disorders. In S. C. Yudofsky & R. E. Hales (Eds.), *Essentials of neuropsychiatry and clinical neurosciences* (pp. 1049–1068). Washington, DC: American Psychiatric Association.

Stein, D. J., Fineberg, N. A., Bienvenu, O. J., Denys, D., Lochner, C., Nesdtadt, G., . . . Phillips, K. A. (2010). Should OCD be classified as an anxiety disorder in DSM-V? *Depression and Anxiety, 27,* 495–506.

Stein, D. J., Westenberg, H. G. M., Yang, H., Li, D., & Barbato, L. M. (2003). Fluvoxamine CR in the long-term treatment of social anxiety disorder: The 12- to 24-week extension phase of a multicentre, randomized, placebo-controlled trial. *International Journal of Neuropsychopharmacology, 6,* 317–325.

Stein, M. B., Koverola, C., Hanna, C., Torchia, M. G., & McClarty, B. (1997). Hippocampal volume in women victimized by childhood sexual abuse. *Psychological Medicine, 27,* 951–960.

Stein, M. B., Roy-Byrne, P. P., Craske, M. G., Bystritsky, A., Sullivan, G., Pyne, J. M., . . . Sherbourne, C. D. (2005). Functional impact and health utility of anxiety disorders in primary care outpatients. *Medical Care, 43,* 1164–1170.

Stein, S., Chalhoub, N., & Hodes, M. (1998). Very early-onset bulimia nervosa: Report of two cases. *International Journal of Eating Disorders, 24,* 323–327.

Steinberg, M., Cicchetti, D., Buchanan, J., Hall, P., & Rounsaville, B. (1993). Clinical assessment of dissociative symptoms and disorders: The Structured Clinical Interview for DSM-IV Dissociative Disorders (SCID-D). *Dissociation, 6,* 3–15.

Steketee, G., & Barlow, D. H. (2002). Obsessive compulsive disorder. In D. H. Barlow (Ed.), *Anxiety and its disorders: The nature and treatment of anxiety and panic* (2nd ed., pp. 516–550). New York, NY: Guilford Press.

Steller, S. (2003). *Special study on mentally disordered accused in the criminal justice system.* Ottawa, ON: Statistics Canada.

Stemberger, R. L., Turner, S. M., Beidel, D. C., & Calhoun, K. (1995). Social phobia: An analysis of possible developmental factors. *Journal of Abnormal Psychology, 104,* 526–531.

Steptoe, A., Dockray, S., & Wardle, J. (2009). Positive affect and psychobiological processes relevant to health. *Journal of Personality, 77,* 1747–1776.

Stice, E., Agras, W., & Hammer, L. (1999). Risk factors for the emergence of childhood eating disturbances: A five-year prospective study. *International Journal of Eating Disorders, 25,* 375–387.

Stice, E., & Shaw, H. (2002). Role of body dissatisfaction in the onset and maintenance of eating pathology: a synthesis of research findings. *Journal of Psychosomatic Research*, 3, 985–993.

Stiegler, L. N. (2005). Understanding pica behavior: A review for clinical and education professionals. *Focus on Autism and Other Developmental Disabilities, 20,* 27–38.

Stilley, C. S., Sereika, S., Muldoon, M. F., Ryan, C. M., & Dunbar-Jacob, J. (2004). Psychological and cognitive function: Predictors of adherence with cholesterol lowering treatment. *Annals of Behavioral Medicine, 27,* 117–124.

Stinson, F. S., Dawson, D. A., Chou, S. P., Smith, S., Goldstein, R. B., Ruan, W. J., & Grant, B. F. (2007). The epidemiology of DSM-IV specific phobia in the USA: Results from the National Epidemiological Survey on Alcohol and Related Conditions. *Psychological Medicine, 37,* 1047–1059.

Storch, E. A., Larson, M. J., Merlo, L. J., Keeley, M. L., Jacob, M. L., Geffken, G. R., . . . Goodman, W. K. (2008). Comorbidity of pediatric obsessive-compulsive disorder and anxiety disorders: Impact on symptom severity and impairment. *Journal of Psychopathology and Behavioral Assessment, 30,* 111–120.

Strassberg, D. S., de Gouveia Brazao, C. A., Rowland, D. L., Tan, P., & Slob, K. (1999). Clomipramine in the treatment of rapid (premature) ejaculation. *Journal of Sex & Marital Therapy, 25,* 89–101.

Striefel, S. (2001). Ethical research issues: Going beyond the Declaration of Helsinki. *Applied Psychophysiology and Biofeedback, 26,* 39–59.

Striegel-Moore, R. H., & Bulik, C. M. (2007). Risk factors for eating disorders. *American Psychologist, 62,* 181–198.

Striegel-Moore, R. H., Cachelin, F. M., Dohm, F. A., Pike, K. M., Wilfley, D. E., & Fairburn, C. G. (2001). Comparison of binge eating disorder and bulimia nervosa in a community sample. *International Journal of Eating Disorders, 29*(2), 157–165.

Striegel-Moore, R. H., Rosselli, F., Holtzman, N., Dierker, L., Becker, A. E., & Swaney, G. (2011). Behavioral symptoms of eating disorders in Native Americans: Results from the Add Health Survey Wave III. *International Journal of Eating Disorders, 44*(4), 10.

Striegel-Moore, R. H., Silberstein, L., & Rodin, J. (1986). Toward an understanding of risk factors for bulimia. *American Psychologist, 41,* 246–263.

Strober, M., Freeman, R., Lampert, C., Diamond, J., & Kaye, W. (2000). Controlled family study of anorexia nervosa and bulimia nervosa: Evidence of shared liability and transmission of partial syndromes. *American Journal of Psychiatry, 157,* 393–401.

Stromme, P., & Magnus, P. (2000). Correlations between socioeconomic status, IQ and aetiology in mental retardation: A population-based study of Norwegian children. *Social Psychiatry and Psychiatric Epidemiology, 35,* 12–18.

Stuart, S. (1995). Treatment of postpartum depression with interpersonal psychotherapy. *Archives of General Psychiatry, 52,* 75–76.

Studer, L. H., & Aylwin, A. S. (2006). Pedophilia: The problem with diagnosis and limitations of CBT in treatment. *Medical Hypotheses, 67,* 774–781.

Substance Abuse and Mental Health Services Administration. (2003). *Results from the 2002 National Survey on Drug Use and Health: National findings* (No. NHSDA Series H-22: DHHS Publication No. SMA 03-3836). Rockville, MD: Substance Abuse and Mental Health Services Administration, Office of Applied Studies.

Substance Abuse and Mental Health Services Administration. (2005). *Results from the 2004 National Survey on Drug Use and Health: National findings* (No. Office of Applied Studies, NSDUH Series H–28, DHHS Publication No. SMA 05-4062). Rockville, MD: Author.

Substance Abuse and Mental Health Services Administration. (2006). *Results from the 2006 National Survey on Drug Use and Health: National findings*. Rockville, MD: Author.

Sue, S. (2003). Science, ethnicity and bias. In A. E. Kazdin (Ed.), *Methodological issues and strategies in clinical research* (3rd ed, pp. 173–188). Washington, DC: American Psychological Association.

Suhr, J. A., Hammers, D., Dobbins-Buckland, K., Zimak, E., & Hughes, C. (2008). The relationship of malingering test failure to self-reported symptoms and neuropsychological findings in adults referred for ADHD evaluation. *Archives of Clinical Neuropsychology, 23,* 512–530.

Sullivan, P. F. (2008). Schizophrenia genetics: The search for a hard lead. *Current Opinions in Psychiatry, 21,* 157–160.

Sullivan, P. F., Bulik, C. M., Fear, J. L., & Pickering, A. (1998). Outcome of anorexia nervosa. *American Journal of Psychiatry, 155,* 939–946.

Sullivan, P. F., & Kendler, K. S. (1999). The genetic epidemiology of smoking. *Nicotine and Tobacco Research, 1*(Suppl. 2), S51–S57, discussion S69–S70.

Sullivan, P. F., Neale, M. C., & Kendler, K. S. (2000). Genetic epidemiology of major depression: Review and meta-analysis. *American Journal of Psychiatry, 157,* 1552–1562.

Sumter, S. R., Bokhorst, C. L., & Westenberg, P. M. (2009). Social fears during adolescence: Is there an increase in distress and avoidance. *Journal of anxiety Disorders, 23,* 897–903.

Sundaram, S. K., Chugani, H. T., & Chugani, D. C. (2005). Positron emission tomography methods with potential for increased understanding of mental retardation and developmental disabilities. *Mental Retardation and Developmental Disabilities Research Reviews, 11,* 325–330.

Susser, E. S., Naugebauer, R., Hoek, H. W., Brown, A. S., Lin, S., Labovitz, D., & Gorman, J. M. (1996). Schizophrenia after prenatal famine: Further evidence. *Archives of General Psychiatry, 53,* 25–31.

Sussman, S. (1998). The first asylums in Canada: A response to neglectful community care and current trends. *Canadian Journal of Psychiatry, 43,* 260–264.

Sutherland, A. J., & Rodin, G. M. (1990). Factitious disorders in a general hospital setting: Clinical features and a review of the literature. *Psychosomatics, 31,* 392–399.

Suzuki, L. A., Ponterotto, J. G., & Meller, P. J. (2001). *Handbook of multicultural assessment (Clinical, Psychological, and Educational Applications)* (2nd ed.). San Francisco, CA: Jossey-Bass.

Swanson, J. W., Swartz, M. S., Van Dorn, R. A., Elbogen, E. B., Wagner, R., Rosenheck, R. A., . . . Lieberman, J. A. (2006). A national study of violent behavior in persons with schizophrenia. *Archives of General Psychiatry, 63,* 490–499.

Swanson, S. A., & Colman, I. (2013). Association between exposure to suicide and suicidality outcomes in youth. *Canadian Medical Association Journal, 185,* 870–877.

Swartz, M. S., & Monahan, J. (2001). Special section on involuntary outpatient commitment: Introduction. *Psychiatric Services, 52,* 323–324.

Swartz, M., Landerman, R., George, L. K., Blazer, D. G., & Escobar, J. (1991). Somatization disorder. In L. N. Robins & D. A. Fegier (Eds.), *Psychiatric disorders in America: The Epidemiological Catchment Area Study* (pp. 220–257). New York, NY: Free Press.

Swerdlow, N. (2001). Obsessive-compulsive disorder and tic syndromes. *Medical Clinics of North America, 85,* 735–755.

Switzer, W. M., Jia, H., Hohn, O., Zheng, H. Q., Tange, S., Shankar, A., . . . Heneine, W. (2010). Absence of evidence of xenotropic murine leukemia virus-related viral infection on persons with chronic fatigue syndrome and healthy controls in the United States. *Retrovirology, 7,* 57. doi:10.1186/1742-4690-7-57

Symonds, C. S., Taylor, S., Tippens, V., & Turkington, D. (2006). Violent self-harm in schizophrenia. *Suicide and Life-Threatening Behavior, 36,* 44–49.

Symonds, T., Roblin, D., Hart, K., & Althof, S. (2003). How does premature ejaculation impact a man's life? *Journal of Sex & Marital Therapy, 29,* 361–370.

Szeto, A. C., & Dobson, K. S. (2013). Mental disorders and their association with perceived work stress: An investigation of the 2010 Canadian Community Health Survey. *Journal of Occupational Health Psychology, 18,* 191–197.

Szymanski, L., & King, B. H. (1999). Summary of the practice parameters for the assessment and treatment of children, adolescents, and adults with mental retardation and comorbid mental disorders. *Journal of the American Academy of Child and Adolescent Psychiatry, 38,* 1606–1610.

T

Tabert, M. H., Manly, J. J., Liu, X., Pelton, G. H., Rosenblum, S., Jacobs, M., . . . Devanand, D. P. (2006). Neuropsychological prediction of conversion to Alzheimer disease in patients with mild cognitive impairment. *Archives of General Psychiatry, 63,* 916–924.

Taher, N. S. (2007). Self-concept and masculinity/femininity among normal male individuals and males with gender identity disorder. *Social Behavior and Personality, 35,* 469–478.

Tait, R., & Hulse, G. (2003). A systematic review of the effectiveness of brief interventions with substance using adolescents by type of drug. *Drug and Alcohol Review, 22,* 337–346.

Talbott, J. A. (1979/2004). Care of the chronically mentally ill—still a national disgrace. Psychiatric Services, 55, 1116–1117.

Tan, S. Y., & Yeow, M. E. (2003). Paracelsus (1493–1541): The man who dared. *Singapore Medical Journal, 44,* 5–7.

Tan, S. Y., & Yeow, M. E. (2004). Philippe Pinel (1745–1826): Liberator of the insane. *Singapore Medical Journal, 45,* 410–412.

Tanofsky-Kraff, M., Bulik, C. M., Marcus, M. D., Striegel, R. H., Wilfley, D. E., Wonderlich, S. A., . . . Hudson, J. I. (2013). Binge Eating eating disorder: The next generation of research. *International Journal of Eating Disorders, 46,* 193–207.

Tanofsky-Kraff, M., Cohen, M. L., Yanovski, S. Z., Cox, C., Theim, K. R., Keil, M., & Yanovski, J. A. (2006). A prospective study of psychological predictors of body fat gain among children at high risk for adult obesity. *Pediatrics, 117,* 1203–1209.

Tanofsky-Kraff, M., Goossens, L., Eddy, K. T., Ringham, R., Goldschmidt, A., Yanovski, S. Z., . . . Yanovski, J. A. (2007) A multisite investigation of binge eating behaviors in children and adolescents. *Journal of Consulting and Clinical Psychology, 75,* 901–913.

Tariot, P. N., Farlow, M. R., Grossberg, G. T., Graham, S. M., McDonald, S., & Gergel, I. (2004). Memantine treatment in patients with moderate to severe Alzheimer disease already receiving donepezil: A randomized controlled trial. *Journal of the American Medical Association, 291,* 317–324.

Tarrier, N., Haddock, G., Lewis, S., Drake, R., & Gregg, L. (2006). Suicide behavior over 18 months in recent onset schizophrenic patients: The effects of CBT. *Schizophrenia Research, 83,* 15–27.

Tarsy, D., & Baldessarini, R. J. (2006). Epidemiology of tardive dyskinesia: Is risk declining with modern antipsychotics? *Movement Disorders, 21,* 589–598.

Tarter, R. E., Hegadus, A. M., Alterman, A. I., & Katz-Garris, L. (1983). Cognitive capacities of juvenile, violent, nonviolent, and sexual offenders. *Journal of Nervous and Mental Disease, 171,* 564–567.

Tarter, R., Vanyukov, M., & Kirisci, L. (2006). Predictors of marijuana use in adolescents before and after licit drug use: Examination of the gateway hypothesis. *American Journal of Psychiatry, 163,* 2134–2140.

Tatum, W. (2014). *Handbook of EEG interpretation* (2nd ed.). New York, NY: Demos Medical.

Taylor, B. (2006). Vaccines and the changing epidemiology of autism. *Child Care, Health, and Development, 32,* S11–S19.

Taylor, M. J., Freemantle, N., Geddes, J. R., & Bhagwagar, Z. (2006). Early onset of selective serotonin reuptake inhibitor antidepressant action: Systematic review and meta-analysis. *Archives of General Psychiatry, 63,* 1217–1223.

Taylor, S. (1995). Anxiety sensitivity: Theoretical perspectives and recent findings. *Behaviour Research and Therapy, 33,* 243–258.

Taylor, S. (1996). Meta-analysis of cognitive-behavioral treatments for social phobia. *Journal of Behavior Therapy and Experimental Psychiatry, 27,* 1–9.

Taylor, S. (2006). *Clinician's guide to PTSD.* New York, NY: Guilford.

Taylor, S. (2011a). Early versus late onset obsessive-compulsive disorder: Evidence for distinct subtypes. *Clinical Psychology Review, 31,* 1083–1100.

Taylor, S. (2011b). Etiology of obsessions and compulsions: A meta-analysis and narrative review of twin studies. *Clinical Psychology Review, 31,* 1361–1372.

Taylor, S. (2013). Molecular genetics of obsessive-compulsive disorder: A comprehensive meta-analysis of genetic association studies. *Molecular Psychiatry, 18,* 799–805.

Taylor, S., & Asmundson, G. J. G. (2004). *Treating health anxiety.* New York, NY: Guilford Press.

Taylor, S., Asmundson, G. J. G., & Jang, K. L. (2011). Etiology of obsessive-compulsive symptoms and obsessive-compulsive personality traits: Common genes, mostly different environments. *Depression and Anxiety, 28,* 863–869.

Taylor, S., & Jang, K. L. (2011). Biopsychosocial etiology of obsessions and compulsions: An integrated behavioral-genetic and cognitive-behavioral analysis. *Journal of Abnormal Psychology, 120,* 174–186.

Taylor, S., Jang, K. L., Stein, M. B., & Asmundson, G. J. G. (2008). A behavioral-genetic analysis of health anxiety: Implications for the cognitive-behavioral model of hypochondriasis. *Journal of Cognitive Psychotherapy, 22,* 143–153.

Taylor, S. E. (2014). *Health Psychology.* New York, NY: McGraw-Hill.

Taylor, S. E., Klein, L. C., Lewis, B. P., Gruenewald, T. L., Gurung, R. A., & Updegraff, J. A. (2000). Biobehavioral responses to stress in females: Tend-and-befriend, not fight-or-flight. *Psychological Review, 107,* 411–429.

Teipel, S. J., Alexander, G. E., Schapiro, M. B., Moller, H. J., Rapoport, S. I., & Hampel, H. (2004). Age-related cortical grey matter reductions in non-demented Down's syndrome adults determined by MRI with voxel-based morphometry. *Brain, 127,* 811–824.

Tempelman, T. L., & Stinnett, R. D. (1991). Patterns of sexual arousal and history in a "normal" sample of young men. *Archives of Sexual Behavior, 20,* 137–150.

ter Kuile, M. M., van Lankveld, J. J., de Groot, E., Melles, R., Neffs, J., & Zandbergen, M. (2007). Cognitive-behavioral therapy for women with lifelong vaginismus: Process and prognostic factors. *Behaviour Research and Therapy, 45,* 359–373.

Teri, L., Gibbons, L. E., McCurry, S. M., Logsdon, R. G., Buchner, D. M., Barlow, W. E., . . . Larson, E. B. (2003). Exercise plus behavioral management in patients with Alzheimer disease: A randomized controlled trial. *Journal of the American Medical Association, 290,* 2015–2022.

Teri, L., Logsdon, R. G., Peskind, E., Raskind, M., Weiner, M. F., Tractenberg, R. E., . . . Thal, L. J. (2000). Treatment of agitation in AD: A randomized, placebo-controlled clinical trial. *Neurology, 55,* 1271–1278.

Tevyaw, T., & Monti, P. (2004). Motivational enhancement and other brief interventions for adolescent substance abuse: Foundations, applications and evaluations. *Addiction, 99,* 63–75.

Thase, M. E., & Kupfer, D. J. (1996). Recent developments in the pharmacotherapy of mood disorders. *Journal of Consulting and Clinical Psychology, 64,* 646–659.

Thibodeau, M. A., Fetzner, M. G., Carleton, R. N., Kachur, S. S., & Asmundson, G. J. (2013). Fear of injury predicts self-reported and behavioral impairment in patients with chronic low back pain. *The Journal of Pain, 14,* 172–181.

Thiedke, C. C. (2001). Sleep disorders and sleep problems in childhood. *American Family Physician, 63,* 277–284.

Thomason, J. W., Shintani, A., Peterson, J. F., Pun, B. T., Jackson, J. C., & Ely, E. W. (2005). Intensive care unit delirium is an independent predictor of longer hospital stay: A prospective analysis of 261 non-ventilated patients. *Critical Care, 9,* R375–R381.

Thompson, C. M., & Durrani, A. J. (2007). An increasing need for early detection of body dysmorphic disorder by all specialties. *Journal of the Royal Society of Medicine, 100,* 61–62.

Thompson, E. A., & Eggert, L. L. (1999). Using the suicide risk screen to identify suicidal adolescents among potential high school dropouts. *Journal of the American Academy of Child and Adolescent Psychiatry, 38,* 1506–1514.

Thompson, E. A., Eggert, L. L., & Herting, J. R. (2000). Mediating effects of an indicated prevention program for reducing youth depression and suicide risk behaviors. *Suicide and Life Threatening Behaviors, 30,* 252–271.

Thompson, R. J., & VanLoon, K. J. (2002). Mental disorders. In T. J. Boll, S. Bennett Johnson, N. W. Perry, & R. H. Rozensky (Eds.), *Handbook of clinical health psychology* (pp. 143–172). Washington, DC: American Psychological Association.

Thorp, S. R., Ayers, C. R., Nuevo, R., Stoddard, J. A., Sorrell, J. T., & Wetherell, J. L. (2009). Meta-analysis comparing different behavioral treatments for late-life anxiety. *American Journal of Geriatric Psychiatry, 17,* 105–115.

Tiefer, L. (2001). A new view of women's sexual problems. Why new? *Journal of Sex Research, 38,* 89–96.

Tienari, P., Wynne, L. C., Sorri, A., Lahti, I., Laksy, K., Morning, J., . . . Wahlberg, K.-E. (2004). Genotype-environment interaction in schizophrenia-spectrum disorder. *British Journal of Psychiatry, 184,* 216–222.

Tjepkema, M. (2002). The health of the off-reserve Aboriginal population. *Health Reports, 13*(Suppl.), 73–86.

Tolin, D. F., Robison, J. T., Gaztambide, S., & Blank, K. (2005). Anxiety disorders in older Puerto Rican primary care patients. *American Journal of Geriatric Psychiatry, 13,* 150–156.

Tolman, D. L., & Diamond, L. M. (2001). Desegregating sexuality research: Cultural and biological perspectives on gender and desire. *Annual Review of Sex Research, 12,* 33–74.

Torgersen, S. (1983). Genetic factors in anxiety disorders. *Archives of General Psychiatry, 40,* 1085–1089.

Torgersen, S., Kringlen, E., & Cramer, V. (2001). The prevalence of personality disorders in a community sample. *Archives of General Psychiatry, 58,* 590–596.

Tozzi, F., Thornton, L., Klump, K., Bulik, C. M., Fichter, M., Halmi, K., . . . Kaye, W. H. (2005). Symptom fluctuation in eating disorders: Correlates of diagnostic crossover. *American Journal of Psychiatry, 162,* 732–740.

Tracey, S. A., Chorpita, B. F., Doubn J., & Barlow, D. H. (1997). Empirical evaluation of DSM-IV generalized anxiety disorder criteria in children and adolescents. *Journal of Child Clinical Psychology, 26,* 404–414.

Trevisan, L., Boutros, N., Petrakis, I., & Krystal, J. (1998). Complications of alcohol withdrawal: Pathophysiological insights. *Alcohol Health & Research World, 22,* 61–66.

Trials of war criminals before the Nuremberg Military Tribunals under Control Council law no. 10, Nuremberg, October 1946–April 1949. Washington, DC: U. S. Government Printing Office, 1949–1953.

Trivedi, M. (1996). Functional neuroanatomy of obsessive-compulsive disorder. *Journal of Clinical Psychiatry, 57,* 26–36.

Troxel, W. M., Buysse, D. J., Monk, T. H., Begley, A., & Hall, M. (2010). Does social support differentially affect sleep in older adults with versus without insomnia? *Journal of Psychosomatic Research, 69,* 459–466.

Trudel, G., Marchand, A., Ravart, M., Aubin, S., Turgeon, L., & Fortier, P. (2001). The effect of a cognitive-behavioral group treatment program on hypoactive sexual desire in women. *Sexual and Relationship Therapy, 61,* 145–164.

Truscott, D., & Crook, K. H. (2013). *Ethics for the practice of psychology in Canada.* Edmonton, AB: University of Alberta Press.

Trzepacz, P. T., Meagher, D. J., & Wise, M. G. (2002). Neuropsychiatric aspects of delirium. In R. E. Hales & S. C. Yudofsky (Eds.), *The American psychiatric publishing textbook of neuropsychiatry and clinical neurosciences* (4th ed., pp. 525–564). Washington, DC: American Psychiatric Publishing, Inc.

Tsai, J. L., Butcher, J. N., Muñoz, R. F., & Vitousek, K. (2001). Culture, ethnicity, and psychopathology. In P. B. Sutker & H. E. Adams (Eds.), *Comprehensive handbook of psychopathology* (3rd ed., pp. 105–127). New York, NY: Kluwer Academic/ Plenum Publishers.

Tschanz, J. T., Corcoran, C., Skoog, I., Khachaturian, A. S., Herrick, J., Hayden, K. M., . . . Breitner, J. C. (2004). Dementia: The leading predictor of death in a defined elderly population: The Cache County Study. *Neurology, 62,* 1156–1162.

Tseng, W. S. (2003). *Clinician's guide to cultural psychiatry.* San Diego, CA: Academic Press.

Tsoi, Y. F., & Kok, L. P. (1995). Mental disorders in Singapore. In T. Y. Lin, W. S. Tseng, & E. K. Yeh (Eds.), *Chinese societies and mental health* (pp. 266–278). Hong Kong: Oxford University Press.

Tsuang, D. W., & Bird, T. D. (2004). Genetics of dementia. In J. Sadavoy, L. F. Jarvik, G. T. Grossberg, & B. S. Meyers (Eds.), *Comprehensive textbook of geriatric psychiatry* (3rd ed., pp. 39–84). New York, NY: W. W. Norton & Co.

Tsuang, M. T., Stone, W. S., & Faraone, S. V. (2000). Toward reformulating the diagnosis of schizophrenia. *American Journal of Psychiatry, 157,* 1041–1050.

Tumlin, T. R., & Klepac, R. K. (2014). The long-running failure of the American Psychological Association's campaign for prescription privileges: When is enough enough? *Behavior Therapist, 37,* 144–152.

Turk, D. C., & Monarch, E. S. (2002). Biopsychosocial perspective on chronic pain. In D. C. Turk & R. J. Gatchel (Eds.), *Psychological approaches to pain management* (pp. 3–29). New York, NY: Guilford Press.

Turner, H., & Bryant-Waugh, R. (2003). Eating disorders not otherwise specified (EDNOS): Profiles of clients presenting at a community eating disorders service. *European Eating Disorders Review, 12,* 18–26.

Turner, J. A., Holtzman, S., & Mancl, L. (2007). Mediators, moderators, and predictors of therapeutic change in cognitive-behavioral therapy for chronic pain. *Pain, 127,* 276–286.

Turner, S. M., & Beidel, D. C. (2003). The enriching experience. In J. D. Robinson & L. C. James (Eds.), *Diversity in human interactions* (pp. 195–205). New York, NY: Oxford University Press.

Turner, S. M., Beidel, D. C., & Frueh, B. C. (2005). Multicomponent behavioral treatment for chronic combat-related posttraumatic stress disorder: Trauma management therapy. *Behavior Modification, 29,* 39–69.

Turner, S. M., Beidel, D. C., & Townsley, R. M. (1992). Social phobia: A comparison of specific and generalized subtypes and avoidant personality disorder. *Journal of Abnormal Psychology, 101,* 326–331.

Tymchuk, A., Andron, I., & Tymchuk, M. (1990). Training mothers with mental handicaps to understand behavioral and developmental principles. *Mental Handicap Research, 3,* 51–59.

Tyron, W. W. (1998). Behavioral observation. In A. S. Bellack & M. Herson (Eds.), *Behavioral assessment: A practical handbook* (pp. 79–103). Boston, MA: Allyn & Bacon.

U

Uchino, B. N., Cacioppo, J. T., & Kiecolt-Glaser, J. K. (1996). The relationship between social support and physiological processes: A review with emphasis on underlying mechanisms and implications for health. *Psychological Bulletin, 119,* 488–531.

Uebel, H., Albrecht, B., Kirov, R., Heise, A., Döpfner, M., Freisleder, F. J., . . . Rothenberger, A. (2010). What can actigraphy add to the concept of labschool design in clinical trials? *Current Pharmaceutical Design, 16,* 2434–2442.

Uhde, T. W., & Singareddy, R. (2002). Biological research in anxiety disorders. *Psychiatry as a neuroscience* (pp. 237–285). New York, NY: John Wiley and Sons.

Unützer, J., Katon, W., Callahan, C. M., Williams, J. W. Jr., Hunkeler, E., Harpole, L., . . . Langston, C. (2002). Collaborative care management of late-life depression in the primary care setting: A randomized controlled trial. *Journal of the American Medical Association, 288,* 2836–2845.

Unützer, J., Patrick, D. L., Diehr, P., Simon, G., Grembowski, D., & Katon, W. (2000). Quality adjusted life years in older adults with depressive symptoms and chronic medical disorders. *International Psychogeriatrics, 12,* 15–33.

Upadhyaya, H., & Deas, D. (2008). Pharmacological interventions for adolescent substance use disorders. In Y. Kaminer & O. Bukstein (Eds.), *Adolescent substance abuse: Psychiatric comorbidity and high-risk behaviors* (pp. 145–161). New York, NY: Routledge/Taylor & Francis Group.

V

Valdovinos, M. G. (2007). Brief review of current research in FXS: Implications for treatment with psychotropic medication. *Research in Developmental Disabilities, 28,* 539–545.

Valleni-Basile, L. A., Garrison, C. Z., Jackson, K. L., Waller, J. L., McKeown, R. E., Addy, C. L., & Cuffe, S. P. (1994). Frequency of obsessive-compulsive disorder in a community sample of young adolescents. *Journal of the American Academy of Child and Adolescent Psychiatry, 33,* 782–791.

van Ameringen, M., Mancini, C., Patterson, B., & Boyle, M. H. (2008). Post-traumatic stress disorder in Canada. *CNS Neuroscience & Therapeutics, 14,* 171–181.

van Balkom, A. J., Beekman, A. T., de, Beurs, E., Deeg, D. J., van Dyck, R., & van Tilburg, W. (2000). Comorbidity of the anxiety disorders in a community-based older population in The Netherlands. *Acta Psychiatrica Scandinavia, 101,* 37–45.

Van Citters, A. D., Pratt, S. I., Bartels, S. J., & Jeste, D. V. (2005). Evidence-based review of pharmacologic and nonpharmacologic treatments for older adults with schizophrenia. *Psychiatric Clinics of North America, 28,* 913–39, ix.

van den Wiel, N., Matthys, W., Cohen-Kettenis, P. C., & van Engeland, H. (2002). Effective treatments of school-aged conduct disordered children: Recommendations for changing clinical and research practices. *European Child and Adolescent Psychiatry, 11,* 79–84.

van Dijk, M., Benninga, M. A., Grootenhuis, M., Nieuwenhuizen, A. M., & Last, B. F. (2007). Chronic childhood constipation: A review of the literature and the introduction of a protocolized behavioral intervention program. *Patient Education and Counseling, 67,* 63–77.

van Eck, E. M., Berkhof, H., Nicolson, N., & Sulon, J. (1996). The effects of perceived stress, traits, mood states, and stressful daily events on salivary cortisol. *Psychosomatic Medicine, 58,* 447–458.

van Geel, M., Vedder, P., & Tanilon, J. (2014). Relationship between peer victimization, cyberbullying, and suicide in children and adolescents: A meta-analysis. *JAMA Pediatrics, 168,* 435–442.

Van Gerpen, M. W., Johnson, J. E., & Winstead, D. K. (1999). Mania in the geriatric patient population: A review of the literature. *American Journal of Geriatric Psychiatry, 7,* 188–202.

van Hout, H. P., Beekman, A. T., de Beurs, E., Comijs, H., van Marwijk, H., de Haan, M., . . . Deeg, D. J. (2004). Anxiety and the risk of death in older men and women. *British Journal of Psychiatry: The Journal of Mental Science, 185,* 399–404.

Van Kuyck K., Gerard N., Van Laere K., Casteels C., Pieters G., Gabriels L., & Nuttin, B. (2009). Towards a neurocircuitry in anorexia nervosa: Evidence from functional neuroimaging studies. *Journal of Psychiatric Research, 43,* 1133–1145.

van Melle, J. P., de Jonge, P., Spijkerman, T. A., Tijssen, J. G., Ormel, J., van Veldhuisen, D. J., . . . van den Berg, M. P. (2004). Prognostic association of depression following myocardial infarction with mortality and cardiovascular events: A meta-analysis. *Psychosomatic Medicine, 66,* 814–822.

van Ojen, R., Hooijer, C., Bezemer, D., Jonker, C., Lindeboom, J., & van Tilburg, W. (1995). Late-life depressive disorder in the community. II. The relationship between psychiatric history, MMSE and family history. *British Journal of Psychiatry: The Journal of Mental Science, 166,* 316–319.

Van Winkle, K. A. (2010). Prescription privileges for non-MDs: A retrospective look at the Department of Defense Psychopharmacology Demonstration Project and its influence on the profession of psychology. *Annals of the American Psychotherapy Association, 13,* 62–64.

Vandenberg, B. (1993). Fears of normal and retarded children. *Psychological Reports, 72,* 473–474.

Varon, S. R., & Riley, A. W. (1999). Relationship between maternal church attendance and adolescent mental health and social functioning. *Psychiatric Services, 50,* 799–805.

Vasey, P. L., & Bartlett, N. H. (2007). What can the Samoan *Fa'afafine* teach us about the Western concept of gender identity disorder in childhood? *Perspectives in Biology and Medicine, 50,* 481–490.

Vella-Zarb, R. A., Mills, J. S., Westra, H. A., Carter, J. C., & Keating, L. (2015). A randomized controlled trial of motivational interviewing + self-help versus psychoeducation + self-help for binge eating. *International Journal of Eating Disorders, 48,* 328–332.

Velligan, D., Bow-Thomas, C. C., Mahurin, R. D., Miller, A. L., & Halgunseth, L. C. (2000). Do specific neurocognitive deficits predict specific domains of community function in schizophrenia? *Journal of Nervous and Mental Disease, 188,* 518–524.

Verheul, R., Bartak, A., & Widiger, T. (2007). Prevalence and construct validity of personality disorder not otherwise specified (PDNOS). *Journal of Personality Disorders, 21,* 359–370.

Verheul, R., & Widiger, T. A. (2004). A meta-analysis of the prevalence and usage of the personality disorder not otherwise specified (PDNOS)-diagnosis. *Journal of Personality Disorders, 18,* 309–319.

Vermetten, E., Schmahl, C., Lindner, S., Loewenstein, R. J., & Bremner, J. D. (2006). Hippocampal and amygdala volumes in dissociative identity disorder. *American Journal of Psychiatry, 163,* 630–636.

Verplanken, B., Friborg, O., Wang, C. E., Trafimow, D., & Woolf, K. (2007). Mental habits: Metacognitive reflection on negative self-thinking. *Journal of Personality and Social Psychology, 92*(3), 526–554.

Verreault, R., Laurin, D., Lindsay, J., & De Serres, G. (2001). Past exposure to vaccines and subsequent risk of Alzheimer's disease. *Canadian Medical Association Journal, 165,* 1495–1498.

Vidal, C. N., Rapoport, J. L., Hayashi, K. M., Geafa, J. A., Sui, Y., McLemore, L. E., . . . Thompson, P. M. (2006). Dynamically spreading frontal and cingulated deficits mapped in adolescents with schizophrenia. *Archives of General Psychiatry, 63,* 25–34.

Vincent, M., & Pickering, M. R. (1988). Multiple personality disorder in childhood. *Canadian Journal of Psychiatry, 33,* 524–529.

Vincent, N., & Lewycky, S. (2009). Logging on for better sleep: RCT of the effectiveness of online treatment for insomnia. *Sleep, 32,* 807–815.

Vincent, N., Walsh, K., & Lewycky, S. (2013). Determinants of success for computerized CBT: Examination of an insomnia program. *Behavioral Sleep Medicine, 11,* 328–342.

Vita, A., De Peri, L., Silenzi, C., & Dieci, M. (2006). Brain morphology in first-episode schizophrenia: A meta-analysis of quantitative magnetic resonance imaging studies. *Schizophrenia Research, 82,* 75–88.

Volkmar, F. R., & Wiesner, L. A. (2009). *A practical guide to autism.* Hoboken, NJ: John Wiley and Sons.

von Gontard, A., Schaumburg, H., Hollmann, E., Eiberg, H., & Rittig, S. (2001). The genetics of enuresis: A review. *Journal of Urology, 166,* 2438–2443.

Vowles, K. E., Zvolensky, M. J., Gross, R. T., & Sperry, J. A. (2004). Pain-related anxiety in the prediction of chronic low-back pain distress. *Journal of Behavioral Medicine, 27,* 77–89.

W

Waddell, C., Shepherd, C., Schwartz, C., Barican, J. (2014). *Child and youth mental disorders: Prevalence and evidence-based interventions.* Vancouver, BC: Children's Health Policy Centre, Simon Fraser University.

Wade, A., & Beran, T. (2011). Cyberbullying: The new era of bullying. *Canadian Journal of School Psychology, 26,* 44–61.

Wadsworth, M. E., & Achenbach, T. M. (2005). Exploring the link between low socioeconomic status and psychopathology: Testing two mechanisms of the social causation hypothesis. *Journal of Consulting and Clinical Psychology, 73,* 1146–1153.

Wagner, A., Greer, P., Bailer, U., Frank, G., Henry, S., Putnam, K., . . . Kaye, W. H. (2006). Normal brain tissue volumes after long-term recovery in anorexia and bulimia nervosa. *Biological Psychiatry, 59,* 291–293.

Wagner, M. K. (2002). The high cost of prescription privileges. *Journal of Clinical Psychology, 58,* 677–680.

Wakefield, A. J. (1999). MMR vaccinations and autism. *The Lancet, 354,* 949–950.

Wakschlag, L. S., Tolan, P. H., & Levanthal, B. L. (2010). Research review: "Ain't misbehavin": Towards a developmentally-specified nosology for preschool disruptive behavior. *Journal of Child Psychology and Psychiatry, 51,* 3–22.

Walbum, J., Vedhara, K., Handkins, M., Rixon, L., & Weinman, J. (2009). Psychological stress and wound healing in humans: A systematic review and meta-analysis. *Journal of Psychosomatic Research, 67,* 253–271.

Waldinger, M. D. (2002). The neurobiological approach to premature ejaculation. *Journal of Urology, 168,* 2359–2367.

Walker, E. F., Savoie, T., & Davis, D. (1994). Neuromotor precursors of schizophrenia. *Schizophrenia Bulletin, 20,* 441–451.

Walker, W. O. Jr., & Johnson, C. P. (2006). Mental retardation: Overview and diagnosis. *Pediatrics in Review, 27,* 204–212.

Wallace, J. M. Jr., & Forman, T. A. (1998). Religion's role in promoting health and reducing risk among American youth. *Health Education & Behavior, 25,* 721–741.

Waller, J., Kaufman, M., & Deutsch, F. (1940). Anorexia nervosa: A psychosomatic entity. *Psychosomatic Medicine, 11,* 3–16.

Wallien, M. S. C., & Cohen-Kettenis, P. T. (2008). Psychosexual outcome of gender-dysphoric children. *Journal of the American Academy of Child and Adolescent Psychiatry, 47,* 1413–1423.

Walsh, E., Moran, P., Scott, C., McKenzie, K., Burns, T., Creed, F., . . . Fahy, T. (2003). Prevalence of violent victimization in severe mental illness. *British Journal of Psychiatry, 183,* 233–238.

Walters, G. D. (2000). Behavioral self-control training for problem drinkers: A meta-analysis of randomized control studies. *Behavior Therapy, 31,* 135–149.

Walton, D. (2010). *Appeal to expert opinion: Arguments from authority.* PA: Penn State Press.

Wang, A., Peterson, G., & Morphey, L. (2007). Who is more important for early adolescents' developmental choices? Peers or parents? *Marriage & Family Review, 42,* 95–122.

Wang, G. J., Geliebter, A., Volkow, N. D., Telang, F. W., Logan, J., Jayne, M. C., . . . Fowler, J. S. (2011). Enhanced striatal dopamine release during food stimulation in binge eating disorder. *Obesity, 19,* 1601–1608.

Wang, P. S., Berglund, P., Olfson, M., Pincus, H. A., Wells, K. B., & Kessler, R. C. (2005). Failure and delay in initial treatment contact after first onset of mental disorders in the National Comorbidity Survey Replication. *Archives of General Psychiatry, 62,* 603–613.

Warburton, D. 2005. Biological aging and the etiology of aneuploidy. *Cytogenet Genome Research, 111,* 266–272.

Ward, A., & Mann, T. (2000). Don't mind if I do: Disinhibited eating under cognitive load. *Journal of Personality and Social Psychology, 78,* 753–763.

Warheit, G., Langer, L., Zimmerman, R., & Biafora, F. (1993). Prevalence of bulimic behaviors and bulimia among a sample of the general population. *American Journal of Epidemiology, 137,* 569–576.

Warsh, C. L. (1989). *Moments of unreason: The practice of Canadian psychiatry and the Homewood Retreat, 1883–1923.* Montreal, QC: McGill-Queen's University Press.

Warshaw, M. G., Dolan, R. T., & Keller, M. B. (2000). Suicidal behavior in patients with current or past panic disorder: Five years of prospective data from the Harvard/Brown Anxiety Research Program. *American Journal of Psychiatry, 157,* 1876–1879.

Waschbusch, D. A., Pelham, W. E., Waxmonsky, J., & Johnston, C. (2009). Are there placebo effects in the medication treatment of children with attention-deficit hyperactivity disorder? *Journal of Developmental and Behavioral Pediatrics, 30,* 158–168.

Watson, D. (2005). Rethinking the mood and anxiety disorders: A quantitative hierarchical model for DSM-V. *Journal of Abnormal Psychology, 114,* 522–536.

Watson, H. J., & Bulik, C. M. (2013). Update on the treatment of anorexia nervosa: review of clinical trials, practice guidelines and emerging interventions. *Psychological Medicine, 43,* 2477–2500.

Watson, J. B., & Rayner, R. (1920). Conditioned emotional reactions. *Journal of Experimental Psychology, 3,* 1–14.

Watson, T. L., Bowers, W. A., & Andersen, A. E. (2000). Involuntary treatment of eating disorders. *American Journal of Psychiatry, 157,* 1806–1810.

Weber, J. B., Coverdale, J. H., & Kunik, M. E. (2004). Delirium: Current trends in prevention and treatment. *Internal Medicine Journal, 34,* 115–121.

Webster, C. D., Douglas, K. S., Eaves, D., & Hart, S. D. (1997). Assessing risk of violence to others. In C. D. Webster & M. A. Jackson (Eds.), *Impulsivity: Theory, assessment, and treatment* (pp. 251–276). New York, NY: Guilford.

Webster, L. R., & Webster, R. M. (2005). Predicting aberrant behaviors in opioid-treated patients: Preliminary validation of the Opioid Risk Tool. *Pain Medicine, 6,* 432–442.

Webster-Stratton, C., Kolpacoff, M., & Hollinsworth, T. (1988). Self-administered videotape therapy for families with conduct-problem children: Comparison with two cost-effective treatments and a control group. *Journal of Consulting and Clinical Psychology 56,* 558–566.

Wechsler, D. (1939). *The measurement of adult intelligence* (1st ed.). Baltimore, MD: Waverly Press.

Wechsler, D. (2008). *Wechsler adult intelligence scale—fourth edition, Canadian.* Toronto, ON: Pearson.

Wehman, P., Chan, F., Ditchman, N., & Kang, H. J. (2014). Effect of supported disability on vocational rehabilitation outcomes of transition-age youth with intellectual and developmental disabilities: A case control study. *Intellectual and Developmental Disabilities, 52,* 296–310.

Weijmar Schultz, W. C. M., & Van de Wiel, H. B. M. (2005). Vaginismus. In R. Balon & R. T. Segraves (Eds.), *Handbook of sexual dysfunction* (pp. 43–65). Boca Raton, FL: Taylor and Francis.

Weintraub, D., & Katz, I. R. (2005). Pharmacologic interventions for psychosis and agitation in neurodegenerative diseases: Evidence about efficacy and safety. *Psychiatric Clinics of North America, 28,* 941–983.

Weir, E. (2001). Inhalant use and addiction in Canada. *Canadian Medical Association Journal, 164,* 397.

Weiss, L. A., Shen, Y., Korn, J. M., Arking, D. E., Miller, D. T., Fossdal, R., . . . Autism Consortium. (2008). Association between microdeletion and microduplication at 16p11.2 and autism. *New England Journal of Medicine, 358,* 667–675.

Weissman, M. M., Bland, R. C., Ganino, G. J., Greenwald, S., Hwo, H. G., Lee, C. K., . . . Yeh, E.-K. (1994). The cross national epidemiology of obsessive compulsive disorder. *The Journal of Clinical Psychiatry, 55,* 5–10.

Weissman, M. M., Bland, R., Joyce, P. R., Newman, S., Wells, J. E., & Wittchen, H. U. (1993). Sex differences in rates of depression: cross-national perspectives. *Journal of Affective Disorders, 29,* 77–84.

Weissman, M. M., Wolk, S., Goldstein, R. B., Moreau, D., Adams, P., Greenwald, S., . . . Wickramaratne, P. (1999). Depressed adolescents grown up. *Journal of the American Medical Association, 281,* 1707–1713.

Weisz, J. R. (1990). Cultural-familial mental retardation: A developmental perspective on cognitive performance and "helpless" behavior. In R. M. Hodapp, J. A. Burack, & E. Zigler (Eds.), *Issues in the developmental approach to mental retardation* (pp. 137–168). New York, NY: Cambridge University Press.

Weller, E. B., Weller, R. A., & Fristad, M. A. (1995). Bipolar disorder in children: Misdiagnosis, underdiagnosis, and future directions. *Journal of the American Academy of Child and Adolescent Psychiatry, 34,* 709–714.

Wellings, K., Field, J., Johnson, A. M., & Wadsworth, J. (1994). *Sexual behavior in Britain: The National Survey of sexual attitudes and lifestyles.* Harmondsworth, England: Penguin.

Wells, K. C., Pelham, W. E., Kotkin, R. A., Hoza, B., Abikoff, H. B., Abramowitz, A., . . . Schiller, E. (2000). Psychosocial treatment strategies in the MTA study: rationale, methods, and critical issues in design and implementation. *Journal of Abnormal Child Psychology, 28,* 483–505.

Welsh, R. S. (2003). Prescription privileges: Pro or con. *Clinical Psychology: Science and Practice, 10,* 371–372.

Wentzel, A., Statler-Cowen, T., Patton, G. K., & Holt, C. S. (1998). *A comprehensive meta-analysis of psychosocial and pharmacological interventions for social phobia and social anxiety.* Poster presented at the 19th Annual Conference of the Anxiety Disorders Association of America, San Diego, CA.

West, D. S., Harvey-Berino, J., & Raczynski, J. M. (2004). Behavioral aspects of obesity, dietary intake, and chronic disease. In T. J. Boll, J. M. Raczynski, & L. C. Leviton (Eds.), *Handbook of clinical health psychology* (pp. 9–41). Washington, DC: American Psychological Association.

West, J. R., & Blake, C. A. (2005). Fetal alcohol syndrome: An assessment of the field. *Experimental Biology and Medicine, 230,* 354–356.

Westen, D. (1998). The scientific legacy of Sigmund Freud. *Psychological Bulletin, 124,* 333–371.

Westen, D., & Arkowitz-Westen, L. (1998). Limitations of axis II in diagnosing personality pathology in clinical practice. *American Journal of Psychiatry, 155,* 1767–1771.

Westermeyer, J., & Boedicker, A. (2000). Course, severity, and treatment of substance abuse among women versus men. *American Journal of Drug Alcohol Abuse, 26,* 523–535.

Westermeyer, J., Khawaja, I. S., Freerks, M., Sutherland, R. J., Engle, K., Johnson, D., . . . Hurwitz, T. (2010). Quality of sleep in patients with posttraumatic stress disorder. *Psychiatry, 7,* 21–27.

Westra, H. A. (2012). *Motivational interviewing in the treatment of anxiety.* New York, NY: Guilford.

Wetherell, J. L., Gatz, M., & Pedersen, N. L. (2001). A longitudinal analysis of anxiety and depressive symptoms. *Psychology of Aging, 16,* 187–195.

Wetherell, J. L., Kaplan, R. M., Kallenberg, G., Dresselhaus, T. R., Sieber, W. J., & Lang, A. J. (2004). Mental health treatment preferences of older and younger primary care patients. *International Journal of Psychiatry in Medicine, 34,* 219–233.

Wetherell, J. L., Lenze, E. J., & Stanley, M. A. (2005). Evidence-based treatment of geriatric anxiety disorders. *Psychiatric Clinics of North America, 28,* 896.

Wetherell, J. L., Stoddard, J. A., While, K. S., Kornblith, S., Nguyen, H., Andreescu, C., Zisook, S., & Lenze, E. J. (2011). Augmenting antidepressant medication with modular CBT for geriatric generalized anxiety disorder: a pilot study. *International Journal of Geriatric Psychiatry, 26,* 869–875.

Wetterneck, C. T., Teng, E. T., & Stanley, M. E., (2010). Currents issues in treatment of obsessive compulsive spectrum conditions. *Bulletin of the Menninger Clinic.*

Weyers, S., Elaut, E., De Sutter, P., Gerris, J., T'sjoen, G., Heylens, G., . . . Verstraelen, H. (2008, November 17). Long-term assessment of the physical, mental, and sexual health among transsexual women. *Journal of Sexual Medicine* [Epub ahead of print].

Whaley, A. L. (1998). Cross-cultural perspective on paranoia: A focus on the Black American experience. *Psychiatric Quarterly, 69,* 325–343.

White, F., & Wolf, M. (1991). Psychomotor stimulants. In J. Pratt (Ed.), *The biological bases of drug tolerance and dependence* (pp. 153–197). London: Academic Press.

White, S. W., Koenig, K., & Scahill, L. (2007). Social skills development intervention in children with autism spectrum disorders: A review of the intervention research. *Journal of Autism and Developmental Disorders, 37,* 1858–1868. doi:10.1007/s10803-006-0320-x.

Whitehead, W. E., Crowell, M. D., Heller, B. R., Robinson, J. C., Schuster, M. M., & Horn, S. (1994). Modeling and reinforcement of the sick role during childhood predicts adult illness behavior. *Psychosomatic Medicine, 56,* 541–550.

Wideman, T. H., Asmundson, G. J., Smeets, R. J., Zautra, A. J., Simmonds, M. J., Sullivan, M. J., . . . Edwards, R. R. (2013). Rethinking the fear avoidance model: Toward a multidimensional framework of pain-related disability. *Pain, 154,* 2262–2265.

Widiger, T. A. (1992). Generalized social phobia versus avoidant personality disorder: A commentary on three studies. *Journal of Abnormal Psychology, 101,* 340–343.

Widiger, T. A., & Lowe, J. R. (2008). A dimensional model of personality disorder: Proposal for DSM-V. *Psychiatric Clinics of North America, 31,* v, 363–378.

Widiger, T. A., & Samuel, D. B. (2005). Diagnostic categories or dimensions? A question for the *Diagnostic And Statistical Manual Of Mental Disorders*—fifth edition. *Journal of Abnormal Psychology, 114*, 494–504.

Wilens, T. E., Biederman, J., Brown, S., Tanguay, S., Monuteaux, M. C., Blake, C., & Spencer, T. J. (2002). Psychiatric comorbidity and functioning in clinically referred preschool children and school-age youths with ADHD. *Journal of the American Academy of Child and Adolescent Psychiatry, 41,* 262–268.

Wilfley, D., Agras, W., Telch, C., Rossiter, E., Schneider, J., Cole, A., Sifford, L. A., & Raeburn, S. D. (1993). Group cognitive-behavioral therapy and group interpersonal psychotherapy for the nonpurging bulimic individual: A controlled comparison. *Journal of Consulting and Clinical Psychology, 61,* 296–305.

Wilkinson, K. (2013, July 11). Companies turn to psych tests to screen out workplace weirdos. *Canadian Business.* Retrieved March 28, 2015 from http://www.canadianbusiness.com/business-strategy/psychological-testing-job-search.

Willcutt, E. G., Doyle, A. E., Nigg, J. T., Faraone, S. V., & Pennington, B. F. (2005). Validity of the executive function theory of attention-deficit/hyperactivity disorder: A meta-analytic review. *Biological Psychiatry, 57,* 1336–1346.

Wille, S. (1994). Functional bladder capacity and calcium creatinine quota in enuretic patients, former enuretic and nonenuretic controls. *Scandinavian Journal of Urology and Nephrology, 28,* 353–357.

Williams, S. (1996). *Invisible darkness: The horrifying case of Paul Bernado and Karla Homolka.* Toronto, ON: McArthur & Co.

Williams, S. (2003). *Karla: A pact with the devil.* Toronto, ON: Cantos.

Wills, T., Sandy, J., & Yaeger, A. (2001). Coping dimensions, life stress, and adolescent substance use: A latent growth analysis. *Journal of Abnormal Psychology, 110,* 309–323.

Wilson, M. (1993). DSM-III and the transformation of American psychiatry: A history. *American Journal of Psychiatry, 150,* 399–410.

Wines, D. (1997). Exploring the applicability of criteria for substance dependence to sexual addiction. *Sexual Addiction & Compulsivity, 4,* 195–220.

Wisner, K. L., Peindl, K. S., Gigliotti, T., & Hanusa, B. H. (1999). Obsessions and compulsions in women with postpartum depression. *Journal of Clinical Psychiatry, 60,* 176–189.

Witkiewitz, K., & Marlatt, G. (2006). Overview of harm reduction treatments for alcohol problems. *International Journal of Drug Policy, 17,* 285–294.

Wittchen, H. U., & Hoyer, J. (2001). Generalized anxiety disorder: Nature and course. *Journal of Clinical Psychiatry, 62,* 15–19.

Wittchen, H. U., Kessler, R. C., Beesdo, K., Krause, P., Hofler, M., & Hoyer, J. (2002). Generalized anxiety and depression in primary care: Prevalence, recognition, and management. *Journal of Clinical Psychiatry, 63*(8 Suppl), 24–34.

Wittchen, H. U., Stein, M. B., & Kessler, R. C. (1999). Social fears and social phobia in a community sample of adolescents and young adults: Prevalence, risk factors and comorbidity. *Psychological Medicine, 29,* 309–323.

Wittchen, H. U., Zhao, S., Kessler, R. C., & Eaton, W. W. (1994). DSM-III-R generalized anxiety disorder in the National Comorbidity Survey. *Archives of General Psychiatry, 51,* 355–364.

Wolitzky-Taylor, K. B., Castriotta, N., Lenze, E. J., Stanley, M. A., & Craske, M. G. (2010). Anxiety disorders in older adults: A comprehensive review. *Depression and Anxiety, 27,* 190–211.

Wolpe, J. (1958). *Psychotherapy by reciprocal inhibition.* Stanford, CA: Stanford University Press.

Wonderlich, S., Lilenfeld, L., Riso, L., Engel, S., & Mitchell, J. (2005). Personality and anorexia nervosa. *International Journal of Eating Disorders, 37,* S68–S71.

Woo, E. (2000, February 18). Dr. Martin Orne: Hypnosis expert detected Hillside Strangler ruse. *Los Angeles Times,* p. A28.

Wood, J. M., Nezworski, M. T., Garb, H. N., & Lilienfeld, S. O. (2006). The controversy over Exner's Comprehensive System for the Rorschach: The critics speak. *The Independent Practitioner.* Retrieved from http://www.division42.org/MembersArea/IPfiles/Spring06/practitioner/rorschach.php

Woodill, G. (1992). Controlling the sexuality of developmentally disabled persons: Historical perspectives. *Journal of Developmental Disabilities, 1,* 1–14.

Woodman, C. L., Noyes, R., Black, D. W., Schlosser, S., & Yagla, S. J. (1999). A 5-year follow-up study of generalized anxiety disorder and panic disorder. *Journal of Nervous and Mental Disease, 187,* 3–10.

Woodside, D. B., Garfinkel, P. E., Lin, E., Goering, P., Kaplan, A. S., Goldbloom, D. S., & Kennedy, S. H. (2001). Comparisons of men with full or partial eating disorders, men without eating disorders, and women with eating disorders in the community. *American Journal of Psychiatry, 158,* 570–574.

Woodward A. T., Taylor, R. J., Bullard, K. M., Aranda, M. P., Lincoln, K. D., & Chatters, L. M. (2012). Prevalence of lifetime DSM-IV affective disorders among older African Americans, Black, Caribbeans, Latinos, Asians, and Nin-Hispanic White people. *International Journal of Geriatric Psychiatry, 27,* 816–827.

Woolfenden, S. R., Williams, K., & Peat, J. K. (2002). Family and parenting interventions for conduct disorder and delinquency: A meta-analysis of randomised controlled trials. *Archives of Disease in Childhood, 86,* 251–256.

Workman, E. A., & La Via, M. F. (1987). T-lymphocyte polyclonal proliferation: Effects of stress and stress response style on medical students taking national board examinations. *Clinical Immunology and Immunopathology. 43,* 308–313.

World Health Organization (WHO). (1973). *The international study of schizophrenia.* Geneva: Author.

World Health Organization. (2007). International classification of disease. Retrieved from http://www.who.int/classifications/icd/en/.

World Health Organization (WHO). (2011). *Depression.* Retrieved from http://www.who.int/mental_health/management/depression/definition/en/.

Wright, J. C., Rabe-Hesketh, S., Woodruff, P. W., David, A. S., Murray, R. M., & Bullmore, E. T. (2000). Meta-analysis of regional brain volumes in schizophrenia. *American Journal of Psychiatry, 157,* 16–25.

Wright, L., Clipp, E., & George, L. (1993). Health consequences of caregiver stress. *Medicine, Exercise, Nutrition and Health, 2,* 181–195.

Wright, P., Takei, N., Murray, R. M., & Sham, P. C. (1999). Seasonality, prenatal influenza exposure, and schizophrenia. In E. S. Susser, A. S. Brown, & J. M. Gorman (Eds.), *Prenatal exposures in schizophrenia* (pp. 89–112). Washington, DC: American Psychiatric Press.

Wykes, T., Hayward, P., Thomas, N., Green, N., Surguladze, S., Fannon, D., & Landau, S. (2005). What are the effects of group cognitive behaviour therapy for voices? A randomized trial. *Schizophrenia Research, 77,* 201–210.

Y

Yamada, K., Watanabe, K., Nemoto, N., Fujita, H., Chikaraishi, C., Yamauchi, K., . . . Kanba, S. (2006). Prediction of medication noncompliance in outpatients with schizophrenia: 2-year follow-up study. *Psychiatry Research, 141,* 61–69.

Yap, P. M. (1967). Classification of the culture-bound reactive syndromes. *Australia and New Zealand Journal of Psychiatry, 1,* 172–179.

Yatham, L. N., Kennedy, S. H., Parikh, S. V., Schaffer, A., Beaulieu, S., Alda, M., . . . Berk, M. (2013). Canadian Network for Mood and Anxiety Treatments (CANMAT) and International Society for Bipolar Disorders (ISBD) collaborative update of CANMAT guidelines for the management of patients with bipolar disorder: Update 2013. *Bipolar Disorders, 15,* 1–44.

Yehuda, R. (2002). Current concepts: Posttraumatic stress disorder. *New England Journal of Medicine, 346,* 108–114.

Yeung, C. K., Sreedhar, B., Sihoe, J. D., Sit, F. K., & Lau, J. (2006). Differences in characteristics of nocturnal enuresis between children and adolescents: A critical appraisal from a large epidemiological study. *British Journal of Urology International, 97,* 1069–1073.

Yorbik, O., Birmaher, B., Axelson, D., Williamson, D. E., & Ryan, N. D. (2004). Clinical characteristics of depressive symptoms in children and adolescents with major depressive disorder. *Journal of Clinical Psychiatry, 65,* 1654–1659.

Young, L. J., & Wang, Z. (2004). The neurobiology of pair bonding. *Nature Neuroscience, 7,* 1048–1054.

Young, R. C. (2005). Evidence-based pharmacological treatment of geriatric bipolar disorder. *The Psychiatric Clinics of North America, 28,* 837–869.

Yule, W., Bolton, D., Udwin, O., Boyle, S., O'Ryan, D., & Nurrish, J. (2000). The long-term psychological effects of a disaster experienced in adolescence: I: The incidence and course of PTSD. *Journal of Child Psychology and Psychiatry, 41,* 503–511.

Yurgelun-Todd, D. A., & Ross, A. J. (2006). Functional magnetic resonance imaging studies in bipolar disorder. *CNS Spectrums, 11,* 287–297.

Z

Zahid, M. A., & Ohaeri, J. U. (2010). Relationship of family caregiver burden with quality of care and psychopathology in a sample of Arab subjects with schizophrenia. *BMC Psychiatry, 10,* 71.doi:10.1186/1471-244X-10-71

Zahl, D. L., & Hawton, K. (2004). Repetition of deliberate self-harm and subsequent suicide risk: Long-term follow-up study of 11,583 patients. *British Journal of Psychiatry, 185,* 70–75.

Zaider, T. I., & Heimberg, R. G. (2003). Non-pharmacologic treatments for social anxiety disorder. *Acta Psychiatrica Scandinavica, 108*(Suppl. 417), 72–85.

Zamorski, M. A., Guest, K., Bailey, S., & Garber, B. G. (2012). Beyond Battlemind: Evaluation of a new mental health training program for Canadian Forces personnel participating in third-location decompression. *Military Medicine, 177,* 1245–1253.

Zamorski, M. A., Rusu, C., & Garber, B. G. (2014). Prevalence and correlates of mental health problems in Canadian Forces personnel who deployed in support of the mission in Afghanistan: Findings from postdeployment screenings, 2009–2012. *Canadian Journal of Psychiatry, 59,* 319–326.

Zanarini, M. C., Gunderson, J. G., Marino, M. F., Schwartz, E. O., & Frankenburg, F. R. (1989). Childhood experiences of borderline patients. *Comprehensive Psychiatry, 30,* 18–25.

Zeiss, A. M., & Steffens, A. (1996). *A guide to psychotherapy and aging: Effective clinical interventions in a late-stage context.* Washington, DC: American Psychological Association.

Zhang, W., Ross, J., & Davidson, J. R. (2004). Social anxiety disorder in callers to the Anxiety Disorders Association of America. *Depression and Anxiety, 20,* 101–107.

Zhou, J. N., Hofman, M. A., Gooren, L. J., & Swaab, D. F. (1995). A sex difference in the human brain and its relation to transsexuality. *Nature, 378,* 68–70.

Zirpolo, K. (as told to Debbie Nathan) (2005, October 30). A long delayed apology from one of the accusers in the notorious McMartin Pre-school molestation case. *Los Angeles Times.* Retrieved from http://articles.latimes.com/2005/oct/30/magazine/tm-mcmartin44

Zoccolotti, P., & Friedmann, N. (2010). From dyslexia to dyslexias, from dysgraphia to dysgraphias, from a cause to causes: A look at current research on developmental and dysgraphia. *Cortex: A Journal Devoted to the Study of the Nervous System and Behavior, 46,* 1211–1215.

Zohar, A. H., & Felz, L. (2001). Ritualistic behavior in young children. *Journal of Abnormal Child Psychology, 29,* 121–128.

Zubenko, G. S., Henderson, R., Stiffler, J. S., Stabler, S., Rosen, J., & Kaplan, B. B. (1996). Association of the APOE epsilon 4 allele with clinical subtypes of late life depression. *Biological Psychiatry, 40,* 1008–1016.

Zucker, K. J. (2004). Gender identity development and issues. *Child and Adolescent Psychiatric Clinics of North America, 13,* 551–568.

Zucker, K. J. (2008). On the "natural history" of gender identity disorder in children. *Journal of the American Academy of Child and Adolescent Psychiatry, 47,* 1361–1363.

Zucker, N., Ferriter, C., Best, S., & Brantley, A. (2005). Group parent training: A novel approach for the treatment of eating disorders. *Eating Disorders: The Journal of Treatment & Prevention, 13,* 391–405.

name index

A

B

C

H

I

J

K

T

U

V

W

Y

Z

subject index

A

B

C

E

F

G

H

M

N

R

S

T

U

V

W

X

Y

Z